Jerzy Linderski

Roman Questions

Heidelberger
Althistorische
Beiträge und
Epigraphische
Studien

herausgegeben
von
Géza Alföldy

Band 20

Jerzy Linderski

Roman Questions

Selected Papers

Franz Steiner Verlag Stuttgart
1995

Die Deutsche Bibliothek - CIP-Einheitsaufnahme

Linderski, Jerzy:
Roman questions : selected papers 1958 - 1993 / Jerzy Linderski.
- Stuttgart : Steiner, 1995
      (Heidelberger althistorische Beiträge und epigraphische Studien ; Bd.
      20)
      ISBN 3-515-06677-2
NE: GT

ISO 9706

For
D.

CONTENTS

Contents

VORWORT DES HERAUSGEBERS

Es ist für mich eine besondere Freude, einen Wunsch Jerzy Linderskis, des langjährigen Freundes des Seminars für Alte Geschichte in Heidelberg, zu erfüllen und seine „Kleinen Schriften" in der Reihe „Heidelberger Althistorische Beiträge und Epigraphische Studien" zu veröffentlichen. Erfaßt sind in diesem Band 64 an sehr weit verstreuten Stellen publizierte Arbeiten des Verfassers, darunter 10 Buchbesprechungen und ein Review-Article, veröffentlicht in englischer und deutscher Sprache, dazu noch ein kurzer Artikel in lateinischer Sprache. Die Beiträge umfassen eine 35jährige Zeitspanne, die mit „Notes on CIL I² 364" aus dem Jahre 1958 beginnt (S. 362–365) und mit einem Aufsatz über „Roman Religion in Livy" aus dem Jahre 1993 (S. 608–625) endet.

Es ist ein beredtes Zeugnis für die Internationalität unserer Wissenschaft, daß ein Gelehrter, der aus Polen stammt und der später in den Vereinigten Staaten von Amerika eine neue Heimat fand, den Ertrag seiner Forschungsarbeit in einem in Deutschland erscheinenden Sammelband vorlegt. Die „Kleinen Schriften" Linderskis gestatten zugleich einen Einblick in seine wissenschaftliche Entwicklung und verraten auch etwas von seinem Lebensweg. Die vom Verfasser selbst bestimmte Reihenfolge seiner abgedruckten Beiträge, die sich nicht nach zeitlichen, sondern nach sachlichen Gesichtspunkten richtet, läßt kaum erkennen, daß seine Schriften in chronologischer Hinsicht zwei Gruppen bilden. Die ersten zehn Artikel wurden im Zeitraum von 1958 bis 1966 veröffentlicht. Abgesehen von einem im Jahre 1968 in der damaligen DDR mit mehrjähriger Verspätung erschienenen Aufsatz gehört alles weitere in den Zeitraum von 1971 bis 1993. Was dazwischen lag, kann der mit dem Schicksal des Verfassers nicht vertraute Leser höchstens durch die Hinweise auf seinen Dienstort erahnen, die am Ende mancher Beiträge erscheinen: in der ersten Phase Krakau, in der zweiten zuerst Eugene/Oregon, dann Chapel Hill/North Carolina. Die Ursache für die fünfjährige Unterbrechung – nicht der Forschungsarbeit, wohl aber der schriftstellerischen Aktivität – heißt: Emigration.

Die Emigration erweist sich im Leben eines jeden, der sich dazu gezwungen sah, als tiefer Einschnitt. Sie bedeutet eine neue Umgebung, zumeist eine neue Sprache, ungewohnte Denk- und Verhaltensweisen, ein neues Arbeitsfeld, neue Kollegen, neue Perspektiven, neue Möglichkeiten, neue Probleme. Wissenschaftlern, die in ihrem Fach eine Stelle finden, fällt es zwar häufig nicht allzu schwer, in einem ihnen zunächst fremden Land allmählich eine neue Heimat zu erkennen. Dank der Kontinuität ihrer Forschungsarbeit, die

den wichtigsten Lebensinhalt bildet, wiegen manche Schwierigkeiten oftmals
nicht so schwer, wie dies sonst der Fall wäre; und der Drang, sich – ohne im
neuen Milieu verwurzelt zu sein und oft auch unter höheren Anforderungen
als in der früheren Heimat gewohnt – durchzusetzen, kann höchst stimulie-
rend wirken. Dennoch ist es keineswegs selbstverständlich, daß ein Emigrant
es schafft, alle neuen Herausforderungen zu meistern, ganz zu schweigen
davon, daß er nicht überall mit offenen Armen empfangen wird. Bei den
meisten Gelehrten kommt hinzu, daß sie eine Fremdsprache (oder mehrere
Sprachen) auf einem Niveau erlernen müssen, das sie befähigt, in dieser
Sprache zu publizieren, zu unterrichten und in leitender Position Verwal-
tungsarbeit zu leisten. Um mit allen genannten - und mit vielen ungenannten -
Herausforderungen fertig zu werden, braucht man einerseits nicht wenig
Glück, andererseits entsprechende persönliche Fähigkeiten, vor allem Bega-
bung, Begeisterung für die Wissenschaft, zielstrebigen Arbeitsfleiß und Durch-
setzungsvermögen. „La fortune ne favorise que les âmes préparées."
   Für den Werdegang eines Historikers kann die Emigration von besonderer Bedeutung sein. Sir Ronald Syme, der mehrmals zum Ausdruck brachte,
was er für „the making of the historian" für nötig hielt, sah eine der wichtigsten Voraussetzungen hierfür in der Vertrautheit mit der Politik und der
menschlichen Natur, und sein Zauberrezept dafür, wie diese Vertrautheit am
ehesten zu erwerben sei, lautete: „exile" (wobei er den Historikern, deren
Lebensweg, wie sein eigener, dieses „Privileg" missen läßt, als Ersatz hierfür
„foreign travel" empfahl). Für die Historiker, deren Sichtweise von den
Erfahrungen der Emigration in besonderem Maße geprägt wurde, seien hier
nicht nur die von Syme so oft genannten Beispiele, Thukydides und Edward
Gibbon, genannt, sondern auch so unterschiedliche Historiker Roms in unserem Jahrhundert wie Michael Rostovtzeff, Andreas Alföldi, Arnaldo Momigliano, Hans-Georg Pflaum.
   Auch Jerzy Linderski ist durch diese „Schule der Geschichte" gegangen.
Er hatte jedoch auch noch das zusätzliche „Privileg", daß er – ganz zu
schweigen von der Kindheit in den Jahren der Zerstörung und Verwüstung
seiner polnischen Heimat – während der zwei besonders wichtigen Jahrzehnte
seines Lebens, in denen ein Wissenschaftler die entscheidenden Impulse
erhält, nämlich im Studium und zu Beginn seiner beruflichen Tätigkeit, unter
dem Druck eines totalitären Regimes zu leiden hatte. „The making of the
historian" kann auch von der langjährigen, bewußten inneren Opposition zu
einer Gewaltherrschaft geprägt sein, wobei dann das Erlebnis der Befreiung
durch die Emigration erst recht einem Neubeginn gleichkommt. Nicht zufällig verraten die Arbeiten Linderskis auch eine überdurchschnittliche Vertrautheit mit der Geschichte unserer eigenen Zeit.
   Seine Schriften zeigen darüber hinaus zum einen, daß seine bestimmen-
den wissenschaftlichen Hauptinteressen bereits in seinen jungen Jahren aus-
geprägt waren. Im Mittelpunkt seiner frühen Beiträge steht, ebenso wie in

seinen späteren Schriften, die römische Republik - ein Staatswesen, in dem die beiden wichtigsten konstituierenden Elemente der römischen Geschichte und auch ihrer Erforschung, „law and power" (S. 43), in einer so einzigartigen Weise miteinander verbunden waren. Diese Problematik macht sich schon in den Schriften des jungen Gelehrten in einer beachtlichen Vielfalt bemerkbar, die sich insbesondere mit den Stichworten Wahlen, Vereinswesen, Prosopographie kennzeichnen läßt. Zugleich bringt aber der vorliegende Sammelband zum Ausdruck, wie sich die Perspektive des reifen Forschers in seiner neuen Heimat ausweitete. Dies gilt nicht nur im chronologischen Sinne, insofern er in seine Forschungsarbeit auch Probleme der römischen Kaiserzeit einbezog. Entscheidend ist die Vielfalt der Fragestellung: Die Themen sind über die bereits oben genannten hinaus nunmehr auch Forschungsgeschichte, philologische, sprachwissenschaftliche und epigraphische Probleme, die Persönlichkeit antiker Autoren, herausragende historische Figuren, Verfassung, Ämterwesen, Recht, Strafprozesse, Politik, Sozialgeschichte, Religion – insbesondere Sakralrecht sowie Orakelwesen – und vieles andere mehr.

Die Vielfalt der Thematik bedeutet nicht, daß wir es mit disparaten Beiträgen zu tun haben. Sie sind nicht nur durch den gleichen zeitlichen Rahmen, sondern auch durch eine Reihe weiterer Gemeinsamkeiten miteinander verbunden. Der Ausgangspunkt ist immer eine konkrete Frage. Die meisten Artikel Linderskis beginnen entweder mit einer antiken Autorenstelle, in der ein Problem liegt, oder mit der Wiedergabe unzureichender Lösungsvorschläge und Meinungen moderner Forscher. „Prüfen wir nun die Quellen!" (S. 165), „Let us, however, look more closely into the passage in question" (S. 232): Die häufigen Aufforderungen dieser Art, die der Autor an sich selbst richtet, werden konsequent befolgt. Er ist ein Forscher, der sich bei jedem Gedanken, bei jeder Aussage unmittelbar auf die Quellen stützt. Zugleich ist er ehrlich und bescheiden genug, dort, wo die Quellen nicht ausreichen, den hypothetischen Charakter seiner Thesen einzugestehen: „We should not convert possibilities into facts and pretend to know more than we do" (S. 250). Diejenigen, die Fakten durch Theorien zu ersetzen pflegen, werden von diesem Band enttäuscht sein. Auch die Grenzen verschiedener Forschungsmethoden werden klar gezogen. Die Prosopographie z. B. „can open some doors that had hitherto been firmly locked, but it is not a master key and still less a picklock" (S. 142).

Dies alles bedeutet jedoch keineswegs Konzeptlosigkeit oder einen Mangel an Ideen. Linderskis Beiträge strotzen von originellen Gedanken. Welchem Althistoriker fällt es schon ein, sich nicht nur über die Menschen und Institutionen Roms, sondern auch über seine Vögel Gedanken zu machen (S. 44-66), nicht etwa aus antiquarischen oder ornithologischen Interessen, sondern um die Subtilität der römischen Adelskultur besser zu begreifen? Die intellektuellen Ansprüche des Verfassers sind sehr hoch, nicht zuletzt in der so gerne geführten Diskussion mit anderen Forschern. Mit seinen Kollegen geht er nicht immer sonderlich nett um, so etwa, wenn er den „delphischen" Charakter ihrer unverständlichen Äußerungen mit Worten wie „oracular pronouncement" geißelt (S. 38) oder ein Gegenargument als „secret weapon" der Lächerlichkeit preisgibt (S. 103) oder wenn er einer Autorin empfiehlt, dem Titel ihres Buches den Untertitel „Or, the Pitfalls of Evidence" hinzuzufügen (S. 600). Doch ist das nichts anderes als ein Ausdruck der Liebe zur Wahrheit und zu ihrer klaren Formulierung. „Amicus Palmerus, magis amica veritas", lesen wir zu Beginn einer Auseinandersetzung mit R. E. A. Palmer (S. 289). Es überrascht nicht, daß diese bis zur Begeisterung gesteigerte Liebe der Wahrheitssuche auch auf den Gegenstand der Arbeit übertragen wird. „A charming set!", lesen wir über die Orte, in denen sich Ciceros Dialogszenen abspielen (S. 47). „A fascinating list!", vernehmen wir über die Gesprächspartner dieser Dialoge (S. 48). „A marvellous statement!", heißt es zu einer Aussage Ciceros über seine Unkenntnis des ius pontificium (S. 498). „A charming, fascinating and marvellous attitude of a scholar", möchte man hinzufügen.

Mit dem vorliegenden Band werden der althistorischen Forschung die zusammengefaßten Ergebnisse der langjährigen, präzisen und weiterführenden Forschungsarbeit eines höchst kompetenten Fachmannes zur Verfügung gestellt. Der aufmerksame Leser wird aber in diesem Band mehr als nur stupende Gelehrsamkeit entdecken können. Wer die Wissenschaft nicht nur als trockene Präzisionsarbeit versteht, sondern auch Witz und Ironie zuläßt und temperamentvolle Diskussion begrüßt, wird an diesem Band ebenso seine Freude haben wie auch jener, der weiß, daß man in einem wissenschaftlichen Werk nicht nur das Produkt der Gehirnzellen eines Autors erblicken sollte, sondern auch vom Schlag seines Herzens etwas verspüren darf.

Géza Alföldy

PREFACE

This collection contains sixty four papers written over a period of thirty five years on two continents, in various places but mainly at three universities of which I will mention *animo grato* two, The University of Oregon and its Department of History, and my present home, The University of North Carolina at Chapel Hill and its Department of Classics.

It is a source of particular joy, and an honor, that this collection appears in the series *Heidelberger Althistorische Beiträge und Epigraphische Studien*, and that the Editor of the series, Professor Géza Alföldy was kind enough to contribute a generous *Vorwort*. "Laetus sum laudari me ... a laudato viro". The *Addenda* and *Corrigenda* show that much was in need of improvement, and that scholarship did not stand still. The title of the collection I borrowed from Plutarch as encouragement and warning: only those scholars do not fail who do not ask questions.

My thanks also go to the Steiner Verlag for their unstinting cooperation, and to Ms. Diane Smith for her help in the composition of the volume.

Sixty four pieces remind us of the sixty four fields in the game of chess. Scholarship is a game conducted according to certain rules. The goal of that game is to best the opponent and to gain knowledge. On a deeper level texts are evanescent, facts illusions, and interpretations mere *doxai*. But the planets are also ultimately composed of atoms and quarks, yet the astronomers have charted their course, and although physical objects *sensu alto* do not exist, knowledge about them is not impossible. So is also knowledge achievable about *verba* and *gesta*. It is in this spirit of ultimate scepticism and practical positivism that these pieces of philology, history, and of polemic are offered.

Of the long procession of names I remember with gratitude or loathing I will omit the latter, and of the former I shall mention only three. Of the long passed, my first Teacher and Master, Ludwik Piotrowicz. He taught me to read the sources first. Without him I would not have come to know Mommsen and Syme, Taylor and Broughton. Of the ancients, Marcus Terentius Varro. He was possessed of erudition, curiosity, and wit. Of the present, always D.

Chapel Hill, April 1995

1

SI VIS PACEM, PARA BELLUM:
CONCEPTS OF DEFENSIVE IMPERIALISM

Theodor Mommsen is the originator, and to many the holy patron, of the idea of defensive imperialism. In a footnote in a recent book from the pen of a most knowledgeable author he appears in the company of two lesser stars, Maurice Holleaux and Tenney Frank.[1] But in fact there is little similarity between the members of this trinity; philosophy separates them. Mommsen's *Römische Geschichte* and Holleaux's studies on Roman expansion are products of different epochs, different spirits. They were nourished by different political experiences, and they belong to different literary genres. Mommsen's is a sweeping course of destiny that came to an abrupt halt with the person of Caesar;[2] Holleaux held forth ostensibly no philosophy; the impartial study of facts was his professed goal.[3]

When Mommsen set out to compose his *Roman History* he was only thirty-two years old; more than fifty years of scholarly greatness and academic power lay ahead of him. But in 1854, when the first volume appeared,[4] he was only a professor in Breslau; four years separated him from his appointment in Berlin, and he had only just returned to Germany from his exile in Swiss Zürich. And he had always been a professor of law, not history. He himself stood on the threshold between these two disciplines which were in a state of turmoil and upheaval. Friedrich von Savigny and his historicism now dominated the study of law.[5] A war was being waged against the abstract tenets of the natural law school. The comprehension of history was turned upside down by Hegel, the court philosopher of the Prussian monarchy.[6]

But above all the *Römische Geschichte* was a product of the painful and sobering experiences of the revolution of 1848. Benedetto Croce called it a poetic history;[7] and he was right. It was the fruit of romanticism. In a grand and curious way it combines the principles of historicism and of the romantic vision of the past.[8] Mommsen believed

133

1

in historical development, leading necessarily, though through toil and trial, from lower to higher stages of human existence. The nation is the supreme subject of history and its ultimate goal the national state. The greatness of Rome resided in her unification of Italy.[9]

Who can fail to recognize in this glowing admiration for Rome's role in Italy a reflection, patriotic and idealized, of Germany and Prussia? Rome was imagined to have achieved in Italy what Prussia was fervently expected to accomplish in Germany; and at the same time the Prussians were exhorted to follow in the footsteps of the Romans and live up to their historical destiny.[10] When these thoughts poured down from Mommsen's pen, his dreams lay shattered; what he had hoped for and what he had fought for, a peaceful unification of Germany as a liberal and lawful state, proved a lost cause; he himself, accused of treason, was chased away from his chair in Leipzig. United Germany remained his goal, but liberalism had to be tossed aside. Liberal Prussia was a phantom, but not the Prussia of *Blut und Eisen*. Mommsen opposed Bismarck and once called his policy a swindle,[11] but Mommsen's unification of Italy parallels Bismarck's unification of Germany. The unification of Latium corresponds to the Prussian-led North German Federation (*Nord-Deutscher Bund*); and the unification of Italy after the war against Pyrrhus to the unification of Germany after the war against the France of Napoleon III. The theme of blood hovered in the air; such was the *Zeitgeist*, the contemporaries would explain. It settled on the lips of the Iron Chancellor and on the pen of Mommsen, who used it to paint the laurels of Sulla. He praises Sulla as the creator of the final and complete unity of Italy; the price was endless misery and streams of blood – for such an achievement not too high a price.[12]

A history this is not; as a grandiose political pamphlet it has few equals. But how could it have escaped the *sguardo linceo* of Mommsen that the unification of Italy, even of Latium, was a forced unification, most often an outright conquest? It did not. The answer lies in Mommsen's understanding of conquest and unification. Conquest is the forceful combination of things that do not organically belong together; when they do belong together the combination bears the name of unification, not conquest. And then it does not really matter whether it was achieved through peace or through iron. Italy was for Mommsen a geographic, cultural and ethnic unit, it was like a beautiful vase shattered into hundreds of pieces. Inertia compelled them to lie in dust and oblivion; but when one sherd developed the

134

2

strength and will to pull the pieces together, even against their selfish resistance, can we call this an act of conquest? It was a process of restoration.[13]

But where can we find that lost paradise of original unity? In the grey morning of history when the Indo-European tribes poured down into the peninsula. A fairy tale but also pure Hegel. Unity is the thesis. As an antithesis the Italian tree splits up into a plethora of branches and twigs. In the third stage the process of synthesis sets in: Rome and Italy become gradually one and the same organism; the Italian nation finds at last its form and its soul.[14] For Mommsen it was the most perfect and most natural development to be found in history – a prototype and paradigm for Prussia and Germany.[15]

Disquiet persists. Even if we grant that Rome's conquest of Latium, of Samnium, of Umbria, and of other Italic tribes was a process of unification ordained by history, still this does not produce a perfect union of all Italy. Non-italic tribes, Greeks and Etruscans remain. No problem. They were a foreign body on Italian soil.[16] In principle they were entitled to a separate and independent existence, but this is not an absolute principle. They had to bend before the necessity of history, before that highest Good, the national state. If they had had their chance, they lost it. Once the creation of the Italian nation began, this was the supreme right; all other rights that stood in its way had to retreat.[17]

Mommsen's sentiment is paralleled by his attitude to the problem of national minorities in Prussia-Germany and Austria. In 1848 he was still able to muster some cool understanding for the rebellion in the Polish provinces of Prussia, mixed, however, with antipathy for its leaders;[18] half a century later he grossly intervened in the strife between languages in Austria. In an open letter " To the Germans in Austria " which appeared in October 1897 in the Viennese daily *Neue Freie Presse* he preached:

" The skulls of the Czechs are closed to reason; to the stick they are open. Untimely surrender is sinful and damaging; and this is what has been happening in Austria. Everything is at stake; to lose means to cease to exist. The Austrian Germans cannot emigrate, like the Jews from Russia, from the frontier provinces which they have brought to full economic and cultural bloom. If you give in you must know that either your children or certainly your grandchildren will become Czechs ".[19]

The unification of Italy was thus the highest point of ancient

135

history, but the Romans did not stop at the straits that separate the peninsula from Sicily. Strictly speaking this must mean that at the moment of their crossing to Messana the Romans began their long descent, although, on the other hand, they were still ascending as the transformation of Italy into one nation was still two centuries away.

At the aftermath of Pydna, directing his gaze back on the road Rome had traversed, Mommsen wrote his two famous pages, the cradle of the defensive theory of Roman imperialism.[20] In the end, he mused, it might appear that all the states and nations of antiquity existed solely for the purpose of helping to build the greatness of Italy. Alas this greatness was also her fall and collapse.

Grand words and obscure. But once we return to Germany Mommsen's idea will stand out lucid and in high relief. In 1858, not a full two years after the appearance of the third volume of the *Römische Geschichte*, Mommsen published a remarkable essay in the first volume of the liberal and nationalist *Preussische Jahrbücher*: a long review of Adolphe Thiers' *Histoire du Consulat et de l'Empire*.[21] What Mommsen thought of Thiers is of interest, but not of importance; Mommsen's view of Napoleon sheds light on Rome and Caesar. Napoleon was the embodiment of France's longing after glory, but he was an Italian. His policy was antinational: had he succeeded France would have been absorbed in his world empire just as Macedonia perished in Alexander's empire. The Napoleonic empire was a denationalized state: this was the source of its precipitous collapse, its greatness being only glitter. When a nation transgresses its natural frontiers it finds itself on the way to self-annihilation.[22] It is of course in this sense that we have to take Mommsen's words about Italy's greatness being also her destruction.

The *ipsissima origo* of Mommsen's theory of defensive expansion lies in his wish to free the Romans from responsibility for destroying their own work in Italy. Mommsen does not explain Roman expansion; he explains it away by shifting the blame from Rome to her neighbors. Roman conquest did not flow from a master plan of world dominion. It was foisted upon Rome by circumstances.

Roman foreign policy was run by the senate and the senate was an assembly of honest but limited men; not for them the conquering flair of a Caesar or a Napoleon; instead of showing any desire for conquest they were rather seized by fear of conquests. Rule over Italy was the sole desire of the Romans; but they perceived correctly that neighbors who were too powerful could suffocate them. This could not be

4

tolerated. The ring surrounding Italy was broken in Africa, in Greece, in Asia; step by step the Romans were forced to broaden the circle of their involvement and defend the *status quo*.[23]

As the two features of a true expansionist policy Mommsen posits extensive annexations and dreams of world domination. He finds both of them wanting in Rome and concludes that the senate was not bent on expansion. He points his finger to the senate's reluctance to annex foreign territories but forgets that this vaunted reluctance was applied rather very selectively and that expansion need not proceed by way of indiscriminate annexations.[24] Results matter, not style.

Nor does Mommsen ask whether the neighboring states had any reason to be distrustful of Rome and concerned with their own security. He tacitly assumes the moral superiority of Rome and of his own idea of Italy over any rights of other states. Wars which the Romans undertook in the belief, even a mistaken belief, of defending the security of Italy thus become wars if not just, then at least justified.

And then there is the concept of *status quo*, soothing and reassuring. It belongs to the language of diplomacy rather than history, for it always conceals something. What is concealed in Mommsen's *status quo* which the Romans so assiduously observed? The war against Perseus for one was fought in its defense. The *status quo* thus reveals itself as any regulation the Romans imposed upon the vanquished. It is a very Roman conception of *foedus* and a very broad understanding of security indeed. *Praeteritio* and *dissimulatio* are effective figures, but they hardly prove what Mommsen set out to prove, the restraint of Rome.

Yet Mommsen had to concede that in victory the Romans did not show the required moderation. The clinging to Spain, the protectorate over Africa, the lasting immersion in Greek affairs were three sins against Rome's Italian mission. But it soon turns out that however mortal it was, the error of expansion was unavoidable: the ancient world did not know the idea of balance of power.[25]

As a chance happening, what a lamentable and unbearable spectacle it would have been, the subjugation by Rome of so many talented nations. Unlike Polybius, Mommsen and his age feared and detested chance, and wished to relegate it from history. And so it was not chance that brought Rome to the pinnacle; it was destiny, necessary, inexorable, acceptable.[26] Acceptable because it was not the force of arms that decided the struggle, the mere superiority of the legion over the phalanx. The superiority of the legion was only an

137

5

outward manifestation of Rome's inner excellence. And this excellence all flowed from one source: the national unity of Italy. One nation, one state: this nobody achieved in antiquity but Rome and Italy.[27]

It was a blind belief in these two idols, the nation and the national state – to Mommsen " the sacred shrine of our times " [28] – that led him to accept and praise the consequences of expansion. For necessity is the goddess of history, of victors and vanquished alike. Mommsen admired courage; in ringing and moving words he described the struggle of Hamilcar and Hannibal against Rome, and his portrait of Vercingetorix is a call to the fight for liberty. But they were heroes in a subjective sense only; objectively they tried to stem the progress of history, they fought against fate.[29] Mommsen and Marx drank from the same murky Hegelian source.

Recent biographers and interpreters of Mommsen often characterize him as an anti-imperialist, whether he dwelled in ancient Rome or in modern Germany.[30] But labels tell us little; to affix them does not mean to understand them.

Mommsen was a political realist and he believed, and for good reasons, that the policy of balance of power in Europe was advantageous not only to England, but to Germany as well. After all it was only at the Berlin conference of 1878 that the new German Empire was accepted for good into the concert of great powers. He looked with anger and foreboding at those who were seducing the German nation with fantastic plans of conquest.[31] But at the same time he also believed that in history a general law operated which in a gripping metaphor he compared to the law of gravity. This law decreed that " a nation which has constituted itself as a state will absorb those neighbors who are not of age politically; and a civilized nation will absorb those neighbors who spiritually are not of age ".[32]

With Mommsen's law itself one can have no quarrel: the course of history has borne it out often enough; yet in each case its validity is apparent only *ex eventu*. It worked at Rome: politically Rome absorbed the Greek world and imposed *Romanitas* on the culturally inferior West. But as a slogan and justification of current practices Mommsen's law could have come straight from the mouth of a Cecil Rhodes or Jules Ferry.[33] Expansion by verdict of God and Fate and the *mission civilisatrice* were the twin *paroles* of nineteenth century imperialists. Mommsen himself did not hesitate to extend the application of this law to his own times. Enraged by Czech efforts to preserve their language and culture, he lashed out in the letter of 1897 to the Germans in Austria against " the apostles of barbarism who strive to bury the five hundred years of German work in the abyss of their non-culture ".[34]

In Mommsen's love for Italy, in his deep appreciation of French culture and French language some detect an anti-imperialist nature.[35] But Mommsen was only akin to Flamininus. The symbiosis of Rome and Hellas he saw reflected in the cultural union of Romance and Germanic nations, with the former playing the role of the Greeks, the latter that of the Romans.[36] For others he hardly saw a place in this community; the Czechs and other lesser nations were for him as much a pebble of history as the Samnites or Celts. In his divided mind lived side by side the revolutionary of 1848, the enemy of Bismarck, junkers and clericals, and the nationalist who applauded the results of Bismarck's and Caesar's policies.

Mommsen has Roman history move in two opposite directions: one wheel rolls in the direction of the national state in Italy; the other rolls in the direction of the empire thus imperilling the formation and survival of the Italian nation. The senate, and Rome's enemies, tried to slow its course. In vain: both wheels were the wheels of necessity. In fact the second wheel was driven by the success of the first: it was the Roman unification of Italy that engendered the empire. For the Italian wheel the lasting involvement in Spain and Greece was an aberration; but for the imperial wheel it was a natural development. This allowed the Romans to conquer the world without being responsible for it.

If the Empire was a negation of Italy, a synthesis required the negation of negation. Mommsen fortunately does not dress his thoughts in Hegelian garb; substance speaks. The idea of an Italo-Hellenic state hung in the air; but the corrupt aristocracy was not able to solve the contradiction between Italy and Empire. A genius was necessary, and Caesar appeared. Italy had been home to the Roman Italic nation: now the whole of the Mediterranean was to become a vast new home to the rejuvenated Italo-Hellenic nation. With Caesar the circle of development reached a new height and promise.[37]

Mommsen's idea of defensive conquest flows from his concept of national state; it evokes a vision of Aristotelian celestial mechanics. It is as grounded in Roman history as Aristotle's theory was in astronomy. But it provided soothing music to those who for whatever reason wanted to hear it. Hence its lasting popularity.[38]

After this long sojourn in Berlin, and in the realm of philosophy, with glimpses on Rome, it is high time to move on to Paris. We descend to the bare facts, or so Maurice Holleaux promises us.[39] Polemic is the heart of scholarship, and the ideas and methods of Holleaux will shine most conspicuously in his defensive attack on Monsieur Tadeusz Walek, a " young and learned professor at the University of Warsaw ", as Holleaux described him half-ironically.[40] One year previously, in 1925, in an article in *Revue de Philologie*,[41] Walek had criticized Holleaux' understanding of Roman policy towards the Hellenistic World; the Romans, he wrote, were the imperialists, and nothing but imperialists. This of course meant that Holleaux comprehended nothing. But Walek's was a demonstration neither elegant nor erudite, and Holleaux was able to overwhelm it with his tone of polite superiority and an avalanche of facts.

Here we observe a positivist historian in action. The facts are there to be picked up; the same facts for Holleaux and for his opponent. Of course Holleaux leaves no doubt as to who does it better; he parades his erudition; and yet a tone of resignation resounds in his voice: he and his opponent are impregnable to each other; the quarrel in which Holleaux engages is a frivolous affair for it has every chance of perpetuating itself. Prophetic words! Generations of students of Roman expansion would walk into the trap of matching their facts with the facts of Holleaux and his disciples. The most recent and most resolute adversary of Holleaux, William Harris, has attempted to show, successfully, most of his readers will agree, that the real outlook of the Romans was belligerent, not defensive. Yet I do not doubt for a moment that the glove he has thrown at the feet of the defensive school of Roman expansion will soon be thrown back at him.[42] For Roman facts are not waiting there to be collected; the act of picking them up is the act of choice and interpretation. No fact exists without an interpretation imposed upon it. For facts are like words in a dictionary; they are dead. In the real language words come to life only in enunciations; in the real world facts come to life only in the flow of history. And the flow of history, as we know it, flows from the ordering mind of the historian, ancient or modern. The tools of order are unexpressed philosophy and assumed terminology. Hence even the most extensive erudition and deepest knowledge of the quisquilia of epigraphy may still result in specious history. In order to understand or refute what a historian says, we must investigate his frame of mind. This appears to us a natural postulate with respect to our ancient forefathers, but the dissecting of the minds of our contemporary colleagues many would feel is a different matter: a task unbecoming a

140

scholar and gentleman. Yet we are not questioning honesty; we are questioning philosophy. We are seeking premises unexpressed, unrealized, unsuspected.

Take for example the First Illyrian War. The Romans, says Holleaux at the very outset of his investigations, did not do anything that was not " absolutely legitimate ".[43] But " legitimate " is a word loaded with bias; a cautious historian, and one not burdened with a preconceived *parti pris*, would rather say: " the Romans did not do anything they did not regard as legitimate ". Holleaux betrays himself as a cultural imperialist (*sit venia verbo*); he slavishly follows Polybius and faithfully reproduces his anti-Illyrian bias; he makes no attempt to use the Polybian facts for a reconstruction of the Illyrian side of the story. Illyrian piracy is the magic word; but as Ernst Badian has shown, a magic word engenders fairy-tale, not history.[44] The Illyrian land invasion of Epirus and the naval attacks against Phoinike, Epidamnos and Korkyra will appear in a different light once we take them not as random acts of piracy and robbery, but rather as a co-ordinated and strategically sound plan aimed at extending south-wards the possessions and influence of the Illyrian kingdom. This was the first stage of the Illyrian empire-building; an act neither more nor less legitimate than the expansion of Macedonia or Rome, only less successful. Whether Queen Teuta behaved insolently towards the Roman envoys is of little importance; important is that her reply, as Polybius presents it,[45] contained an element of compromise: while refusing to constrain private piracy by her subjects she promised that the Illyrian state would take no action hostile to Rome. In other words, and in the terms of politics, she guaranteed the security of Italy, but attempted to stake out her claim to her newly acquired possessions and dependencies and to control over the Adriatic. The menacing response of one of the envoys shows that the senate expected complete compliance with their demands and that the envoys had in fact delivered an ultimatum.

That the murder of the younger of the Coruncanii was the cause of the war hardly needs refutation; no state goes to war over the death of an ambassador unless it wishes war. Few people will see in the assassination of Archduke Ferdinand (which Holleaux mentions in this context) [46] *the* cause of the First World War; if the Austrian government were not bent on destroying Serbia, which they thought was necessary for the protection of the Austrian possession of Bosnia, they would not have produced an unacceptable ultimatum. Or have we

141

forgotten the picturesque story of the German ambassador to France who on instructions from his government shortly before the declaration of war in 1914 promenaded publicly in Paris in the hope that somebody would shoot him and provide a clean *casus belli*? The assassination of L. Coruncanius provided the senate with a clean *casus belli*, but we have to remember that in the language of diplomacy *casus* means pretext, not cause.

Reprisals were in order, says Holleaux; it was a course of action right and just. But the Roman military response, the large concentration of warships and legionaries, was rather excessive if the senate intended merely to curb Illyrian piracy or punish Teuta; it is fully understandable if the Roman goal was to break the Illyrian kingdom. The campaign over, the Romans proceeded to what Holleaux calls regulation of Illyrian affairs.[47] One need not be reminded that regulation, *réglement*, is not a neutral word; it presupposes the moral superiority of the regulator who creates order where chaos had prevailed. In this case order meant the Roman protectorate over part of the Illyrian and Epirotan coast.[48] This was a natural result of the Roman victory, so Holleaux proclaims. The Roman presence on the Illyrian side of the Adriatic was of course defensive in character. First of all the Romans attempted to secure toward the East their natural frontiers; here Holleaux quotes Täubler, but the whole idea comes straight from Mommsen, who discussed the Illyrian War in the chapter dealing with the natural frontiers of Italy.[49] In other words the natural political frontiers of Rome are here identified with the geographical frontiers of Italy. A remarkable assumption for it amounts to a tacit identification of the security of Rome with the security of Roman domination in Italy.[50] The study of terminology in instructive: it was Rome that proved dangerous to Illyria, and not vice versa; and yet if the Illyrians had attempted to establish strongholds on the coast of Italy Holleaux would probably have hesitated to call it a prudent and defensive precaution.

B t the Romans took precautions not only against Illyria but also against Macedonia; this idea of Holleaux strangely runs counter to his own thesis of Roman lack of interest in Greek affairs. He concedes that Macedonia, her navy weak and unprepared, could not at that time pose any real danger to Rome; but he immediately retorts that one can feel threatened even if there is no visible danger present.[51] Ernst Badian, not a defensive imperialist himself, produced a simplified version of Holleaux' explanation: it was Illyria not Macedon the Romans were

142

afraid of, and it was this Roman misapprehension that was responsible for the Illyrian wars.[52] But people who fear every roaring mouse do not conquer empires.

We tend to use terms denoting emotions loosely and imprecisely. This is unfortunate for it distorts history. If we are afraid of potential enemies it means we assume, correctly or not, that they are able to defeat us; but in such a situation few governments, rulers or nations would willingly start a war – unless miscalculation, fanaticism or hysteria intervened. The Romans intervened in Illyria and in scores of other places because they had nothing to fear; Illyria presented a nuisance, not danger. The *metus hostilis* as a popular feeling seems to have been associated primarily with enemies who in the past had inflicted disasters on Rome, with the Gauls and Carthaginians. After 216 the senate may have viewed with some apprehension the successors and shadows of Alexander, the Macedonian and Seleucid monarchies, but in all Roman enterprises in the East the initial war effort was moderate. A telling story. Does it not show that the senate did not anticipate any immediate danger to Italy and still less to the security of Rome herself? In fact it does show that the senate did not consider any outright failure possible. Most Roman wars, if not all, were undertaken from a position of strength when Rome was secure in its military superiority. Hence no fear of the enemy; rather underestimation, most glaringly visible at the beginning of the Hannibalic War. Apprehensions concerning some distant future are a different matter. They may have played some role as a stimulus for expansion, and some will say that the tragedy of Roman imperialism, and its undoing, was that the Romans stopped before the end of the horizon.[53]

Holleaux cherished facts and this admiration of his derives from an important current in French historical writing.[54] Ernest Renan declared in 1862 that for a historian only facts exist, causes and laws;[55] and Fustel de Coulanges, in a bitter fruit of the war of 1870, the essay on the manner of writing history in France and in Germany, asserted his commitment to history as a science pure and disinterested, grounded in an erudition calm, simple and elevated.[56] These are all features of Holleaux' writing; and this is understandable for early in his life he came under the influence of Fustel de Coulanges.[57] Yet program and reality are not one and the same thing. Renan's *Life of Jesus* and *The Ancient City* by Fustel de Coulanges are not simple assemblages of facts; they are powerful visions governed by laws,

143

premises and causes peculiar to them. The same is true of Holleaux; his conviction that the Romans never practised an imperialist policy in Greece acquired a life and a momentum of its own.

In devoting his talents to the study of Roman expansion in Greece Holleaux followed in the footsteps of Fustel de Coulanges who composed in 1858 as his French thesis a long essay entitled *Polybius or Greece conquered by the Romans*; [58] his Latin thesis dealt with the cult of Vesta. A few years later, in 1864, Fustel incorporated substantial portions of *Vesta* and *Polybius* into his *Ancient City* as its prologue and conclusion. The main proposition of his essay on Polybius is this: from the Peloponnesian War onwards the Greek World was divided into two warring parties, rich and poor, aristocracy and democracy. Democracy tended to accept willingly any imperial domination; of Athens and then of Aetolia. Aristocracy was more concerned with liberty. But in the age of Polybius the aristocracy looked to Rome for salvation and security. Its battle cry was property, not liberty. The state of Greece, and indeed of the entire world, made the Empire of Rome a necessity. This fits perfectly into Fustel's scheme of development from family to clan to tribe to city. But the city-state had run its course; the souls of men now longed after the broad horizons of a world empire; they desired security from incessant revolutions. Rome merited her empire; but the legions and the senate accomplished part of the work only. For the Greeks could perhaps stop the advance of Rome; but they wished not. Through her willing submission to Rome Greece saved herself from her own destructive forces.

The affinity of this vision to Mommsen's idea of Rome's being involuntarily drawn into Greece is apparent; it extends even to the figurative use of the legion by Mommsen and Fustel.[59] This is the more striking as we are here in the presence of a veritable and fortuitous congruity, not influence: explaining the origin of his *Ancient City* Fustel confessed that in order to keep his mind fresh for his own appreciation of ancient evidence he refrained from reading modern authorities, Mommsen in particular.[60]

The task of Holleaux was to turn this inspired vision into history, where facts will march and speak, not ideas. But Fustel de Coulanges commented on two sides of Roman policy: he saw moderation and a desire to conquer; when facts crystallized on the pen of Holleaux the figure of moderation emerged, and no other side remained.

Fustel de Coulanges appreciated the value of doubt; the historian begins his work by dubitation.[61] Holleaux echoed this sentiment. He

144

exhorted his students to protect the spirit of critical reflection.[62] But he also echoed another sentiment of Fustel. Man, wrote de Coulanges, can never completely forget the past. It lives in him. If he descends down into his soul he will discover relics of each of the epochs of the past.[63] Now Holleaux in his inaugural lecture in Lyons in 1888 proclaimed the existence of " magnificent hours in the life of a historian. Then a grand vision fills his mind. The men of the past move towards him; no more inert shadows, but people of flesh and life. The historian communicates with them not through long reflection and patient induction, but through an immediate contact. In a mysterious way the soul of old had replaced in him the soul of to-day; the moment of divination has come. The historian can now entrust himself to his inspiration; it will not deceive him ".[64]

Holleaux was not only a collector of facts; he felt he penetrated the thoughts of the Romans, their fears and their desires. If not for the schemes and machinations of Philip and Antiochus, of Attalus and Eumenes, and of Rhodes, Rome would never have crossed the Adriatic. Rome and Greece, and the Greek East, would have forever remained two worlds apart. Then the Romans would have concentrated their efforts on the barbarians to the west of Italy. This reason dictated, and profit.[65] In the West, Mommsen, and Holleaux, and Tenney Frank allowed the Romans to conquer, to exploit, to be imperialists; but not in Greece. This Mommsen and Frank called the sentimental policy; [66] it was a policy born of German nationalism, of French admiration for Rome, and of American pacifism.

And so we are on our way from Berlin and Paris to Bryn Mawr, where on the eve of the First World War Tenney Frank composed his *Roman Imperialism*. The date and the place are significant: [67] in Europe history was being made and written in grand capitals, in America in small cities and small colleges. This entailed a new shape of history: civil, optimistic and moderately dull.

Any book on Roman imperialism is a Polybian venture; Polybius tried to explain the rise of Rome for the Greeks, Tenney Frank explained it for the Americans, as an example and a warning. Polybius looked for his answer to the marvellous constitution of Rome, and Frank looked for his to the constitution of the United States. His book is a monument to the conviction that there is an American way to Roman historical truth.

In books purporting to deal with History and not merely with isolated happenings it is well to read the preface; for in the preface the

145

13

author reveals his motives and confesses his dreams. " Old-world political traditions ", Tenney Frank wrote in his preface,[68] " have taught historians to accept territorial expansion as a matter of course ". " For hundreds of years ", he continued, " the church, claiming universal dominion, proclaimed the doctrine of world-empire; the monarchs of the Holy Roman Empire and of France reached out for the inheritance of ancient Rome ". The nations on the continent of Europe, overcrowded and with scant means of subsistence, have been forced to fight to make for themselves " a place in the sunlight ". This phrase enjoyed current topicality. " We wish to overshadow nobody, but we demand our place under the sun ". In this sentence Chancellor Bernhard von Bülow [69] encapsuled in December 1897 before the Reichstag the goals of German foreign policy and charted its course to catastrophe. Tenney Frank extended the application of the maxim to all continental nations. Hence his argument: it is European history, past and present, that has led continental writers to assume that " the desire to possess must somehow have been the mainspring of action whether in the Spanish-American war or the Punic wars of Rome ". Rome and America make a perfect pair; this juxtaposition tells its story: both republics pursued the same policy.[70] Hence a consideration of the American-Spanish war may prove instructive – even if this was not a Punic, but merely an Illyrian war.

In his message to the Congress of 11 April 1898 President William McKinley listed four reasons that justified American intervention in the hostilities between (as he termed it) the Government of Spain and the people of Cuba. First, humanity, justice, and an American sense of duty. Next, the protection of American citizens in Cuba. Third, the very serious injury to the commerce, trade and business of America. Fourth, the menace to peace presented by the condition of affairs in Cuba. Under this heading the President mentioned in particular the seizures of American trading vessels " at our very door by war ships of a foreign nation ", although he admitted that some of those vessels may have been engaged in " expeditions of filibustering that we are powerless to prevent altogether ".[71]

The Roman envoys to the Queen of Illyria spoke of the Roman sense of justice, of outrages and wrongs committed against Roman citizens, of injury to Italian commerce and maritime trade, and they threatened war to enforce their demands.[72] The murder of L. Coruncanius created great indignation in Rome; in February 1898 the American battleship *Maine* was destroyed in the harbor of Havana,

146

while being there " on a mission of peace ". " The destruction of that noble vessel has filled the national heart with inexpressible horror " – these are the words of President McKinley. The American goal, as the President defined it, was now " the enforced pacification of Cuba ".[73]

The war was expected to be an easy affair and it was an easy affair; [74] and yet pamphlets and books circulated in America exalting the Spanish danger. Few historians, if any, picked up this claim and adopted it as a serious explanation; unlike some modern students of Roman expansion they concentrated on the assessment of the balance of power, on deeds not words. Politicians behaved differently. The theme of the Spanish danger to peace was taken up by President McKinley a few months later, in September 1898, in his instructions to the American Peace Commissioners. The conduct of the United States, he wrote, is " an example of moderation, restraint, and reason in victory ". " The abandonment of the Western Hemisphere by Spain was an imperative necessity. In presenting this requirement, we only fulfilled a duty universally acknowledged ". It was a necessary precondition for a lasting peace. The United States when it entered upon war " had no design of aggrandizement and no ambition of conquest ". Yet " the march of events rules and overrules human action "; it created a new situation in the Philippines: " the presence and success of our arms at Manila imposes upon us obligations which we cannot disregard ... without any design or desire on our part the war has brought us new duties and responsibilities which we must meet and discharge as becomes a great nation on whose growth and career from the beginning the Ruler of Nations has plainly written the high command and pledge of civilization ".[75] In plain language this meant the annexation of the Philippines.

Tenney Frank's Rome was a mirror image of the America of McKinley and Theodore Roosevelt; of the America of manifest destiny.[76] This concept was everywhere: in the writings of the ideologues, and in the actions of politicians. It proclaimed the superiority of American civilization and its ultimate spread over the whole world. The tools and means of this ascent were to be America's industrial might and its trade. Some demanded annexations; but annexations did not figure prominently in the original or in the developed program; they proved to be a passing stage. The goal remained the hegemonial position in the Western Hemisphere – and beyond. The professed course was the open door policy, and doors were to be opened – if need be – by the application of force.

147

15

Frank had mixed feelings about annexations. " Rome was now a democracy ", he says describing the beginning of the First Punic War, " and so when the senate refused to give a favorable answer to the Mamertines the jingoes took the matter to the plebeian assembly ".[77] The footnote explains that the jingoes were primarily the urban plebeians. When Rome secured Sicily as a province it " set out on the devious road of imperialism ".[78] Not a very auspicious beginning for the policy of restraint. For according to what Frank writes in his preface such a thing was not supposed to happen because in a peasant republic in which the final decision on war rests with the people there are " enough ... cross currents to neutralize ... the blind instinct to acquire ".[79]

The conquest of Spain during the Hannibalic War was " a political necessity ", yet in the subsequent years " nowhere did Roman warfare and diplomacy descend to such devious ways as in Spain ". Nevertheless the retention of Spain was " of course, the only conceivable course ". Why this should be so Frank does not explain – or perhaps this is the explanation: " The Spanish tribes ", he asserts, " were far from ripe for political responsibilities and they had no love for an orderly regime ".[80] Hence the need for " the policing of Spain " by Rome. For a parallel and inspiration we do not have far to seek. In his message to the Congress in December 1904 President Theodore Roosevelt proclaimed a new interpretation of the Monroe doctrine: the United States does not harbor plans of conquest and annexation; but it is interested in the stability, peace and prosperity of the neighboring countries. In order to protect these values and prevent injuries to the interests of the United States and other countries of the Western Hemisphere it is the duty of the United States to assume the role of an " international police force ".[81]

Times and nations change; words remain. Instead of Roman wars of aggression we are served the *topos* of generous Rome, unruly tribesmen and thankless Greeks.

Tenney Frank attempts to explain " the apparent paradox that Rome became mistress of the whole world while adhering with a fair degree of fidelity to a sacred rule which forbade wars of aggression ".[82] As his prime authority he quotes Emperor Augustus: a source not beyond suspicion. The paradox does not exist. Roman history makes better sense when it is stood on its feet. In 264 the senate was opposed to war, the popular assembly was for it; in 200 the popular assembly was opposed to war, and the senate was for it: in both cases the war party prevailed. Whether cloaked in fetial formulas or not such was the pattern of Roman expansion: *volentem fata ducunt*.

Gaetano De Sanctis would agree.[83] In Italy, for various reasons, the doctrine of defensive imperialism has never taken root. This does not mean, however, that there are no points of contact between the three protagonists of defensive conquest and the *princeps* of Italian historians. The comparison imposes itself for two reasons: *Storia dei Romani* is a grand counterpart to Mommsen's *Römische Geschichte*, and the concept of imperialism stood at the center of De Sanctis' thought. We turn to the fourth volume of the *Storia*, the *Fondazione dell'Impero*, the first part of which traces the establishment of Rome's domination from Zama to Pydna. It matured during the convulsions of the World War, and appeared in 1923, almost simultaneously with Holleaux' studies, but how different was its tone! De Sanctis looked at the past – as every great historian must – with the eyes of the present. The only novelty, he wrote, which he tried to introduce into his work was the rethinking of the ancient happenings in the light of those most variegated experiences that have enriched humanity in its laborious way toward the better future.[84] If the last phrase sounds sentimental, it also contains a message: whatever the price Rome and the peoples of the Mediterranean paid for the Roman conquest, whatever the cost of the World War, however thorny the way, mankind continued to advance toward an " avvenire migliore ".

In this wish the teleological concept of history stands revealed: and in fact the tension between history as providence and history as the fight for liberty permeates the thought of De Sanctis. But words are only masks; if we strip this historiosophical doctrine of its catholic coating it will appear close to the vision of the romantics, the religious Schelling and the atheist Mommsen. For the *storia provvidenziale* versus *storia come lotta per la libertà* [85] is nothing other than the fight of *Notwendigkeit* and *Freiheit* in history, a problem every historian worthy of that name must face, if not answer. The practical results in Mommsen's *Geschichte* and De Sanctis' *Storia* were not dissimilar – with one exception, however. Both of them believed not only in the superiority of unity over particularism but also in the march of History toward that unity. Mommsen spoke of the unification of Italy, De Sanctis of *la conquista del primato in Italia*,[86] but the essence was the same. As the reader of the *Storia* finds out, when De Sanctis wrote

149

Sentino he thought of Solferino; the march toward unity began for him with Camillus' conquest of Veii and ended at Porta Pia.[87] And when the Romans embarked on the second round of their expansion, Mommsen, Holleaux, Frank and De Sanctis, all of them, had ready two sets of glasses, one for scrutinizing the progress of the legions in the West, and the other in the East.

In the West the *caliga* was the symbol of culture, in Greece they would have preferred not to see the Romans at all. In his famous essay of 1920, *Dopoguerra antico*,[88] in which De Sanctis paints the developments after the Hannibalic War, but thinks of Europe after Versailles, he comes to speak of the conquest of Gaul: should the historian adopt the point of view of the Gauls, he is entitled to bewail the conquest and romanization; but if he overcomes this particular point of view, whether Gaulish or Roman, and considers the interests of humanity and culture, he must acknowledge that Roman victory in Gaul signalled a remarkable event in the history of progress. Thus De Sanctis arrived at his most arresting distinction between imperialism and colonialism: imperialism was calamity for all concerned, colonization and colonialism sound and wholesome – as the etymology informs. This distinction led him ultimately to support and praise the colonial ventures of the new *Impero Romano* of his times. But De Sanctis was also a humanist, and he knew how to appreciate courage. He dedicated his *Fondazione dell'Impero*, the story of Roman imperialism triumphant, " a quei pochissimi che hanno parimente a sdegno d'essere oppressi e di farsi oppressori ", " to those few who feel equal contempt for being oppressed and for becoming oppressors ". A noble dedication, and justly famous, and yet it reverberates with a hollow sound. De Sanctis admired the courage and patriotism of Viriathus and Vercingetorix no less than Mommsen.[89] Both of them dolefully laid the heroes in their useless graves lest they block the " avvenire migliore ". " Nell'Europa barbara " opportunities not realized did not count.

Imperialists and oppressors and disruptors of progress the Romans were in Greece. Here De Sanctis parted company with Mommsen and Holleaux. Roman intervention was unprovoked and unjustified for in view of the impotence of the Hellenistic monarchies demonstrated during the second Punic War Rome had nothing to fear from the East.[90] Quite possibly the Romans interrupted in Greece a movement toward unity; the result was confusion and the progressive decadence

150

of the Greek world. In this assessment of Greek affairs De Sanctis followed in the footsteps of his esteemed and beloved *maestro* Julius Beloch who some twenty years previously accused the Romans of putting an end to the renaissance of Greek culture in the third century and thus plunging classical culture into a downward spiral from which it never recovered.[91] Fustel de Coulanges saw in the Romans the saviours of Greece, but he did not think of culture but rather of class struggle. De Sanctis saw this problem as well, but he saw Roman conquest not as a cure for class struggle, but rather as its fuel and cause. It exacerbated or created social conflicts in Rome itself, prevented necessary reforms and spelt ruin to the Republic and liberty. At the end, stood, it is true, the *pax Romana*, security from foreign invasions and internal wars, but it was a peace ill-gained and ill-used, with the fruits of prosperity going to few, and the islands of Greco-Roman culture not able to tame the ocean of provincial barbarity.[92]

It is in the nature of grand visions to be full of contradictions; for Plinio Fraccaro these " moralistic theories " were devoid of any value. Thus the stage was set for a clash between the two *lumina* of Italian historiography, Gaetano De Sanctis and Plinio Fraccaro. As Piero Treves compellingly put it, De Sanctis interpreted " la realtà del presente nella ricostruzione del passato e la realtà del passato nel travaglio del presente ", and suppressed " ogni distinzione o distanza di tempi ".[93] In his celebrated review of the first part of the fourth volume of the *Storia* Fraccaro urged historians to keep the past and the present separate, and keep to the facts.[94] But in the House of History there are many mirrors and the sober historian clinging to his facts may be a reflection of any of them. Fraccaro embraced Holleaux and Frank and proclaimed that around 200 B.C. the social, economic and demographic conditions in Rome precluded any possibility of imperialism. Aversion to conceptual history can thus produce curious results. The *umbrae rerum*, the words, are in our power; are the *res ipsae*?

Two precepts of politics are often ascribed to the Romans. *Divide et impera* is one; *si vis pacem, para bellum*, is the other. In this form neither is Roman in origin. The former betrays its late provenance by its faulty grammar. It probably originated at the court of Louis XI of France.[95] The latter appears in various shapes in many Roman authors. *Ostendite modo bellum; pacem habebitis*, says Livy, and Cicero instructs us: *si pace frui volumus, bellum gerendum est*.[96] When he

151

19

thought of peace, he thought of war. And indeed republican Latin is rich in words pertaining to war, poor in praises of peace.[97] Its equivalent of peaceful is *pacatus*, subdued. In Rome even peace was aggressive.[98] *

NOTES

[1] W. V. Harris, *War and Imperialism in Republican Rome 327-70 B.C.* (Oxford, 1979) 169, n. 1. For a lucid appraisal of Roman imperialism, see also P. A. Brunt, " Laus imperii ", *Imperialism in the Ancient World*, ed. by P.D.A. Garnsey and C. R. Whittaker (Cambridge, 1978) 159-191 and C. Nicolet, *Rome et la conquête du monde méditerranéen* 2 (Paris, 1978) 883-920. As to Mommsen's and Holleaux' followers, their name is legion. Imperialism is an imprecise term: this observation was made sixty years ago by O. Spann in *Handwörterbuch der Staatswissenschaft* 5 (4th ed., Jena, 1923) 383-385; it was repeated by M. Hammond, " Ancient Imperialism ", *HSCP* 58-59 (1948) 125, n. 3, and again by D. Flach, " Der sogenannte römische Imperialismus. Sein Verständnis im Wandel der neuzeitlichen Erfahrungswelt ", *Historische Zeitschrift* 222 (1976) 37-42, who would prefer to abandon this term altogether. But imprecise are many other expressions pertaining to human affairs; those who wish to purge imperialism from the language have no greater chance of success than those who wish to purge it from history.

[2] Three monographs (hereafter referred to by the name of the author alone) are indispensable to any student of Mommsen: L. Wickert, *Theodor Mommsen. Eine Biographie*, vols. 1-4 (Frankfurt a.M., 1959, 1964, 1969, 1980); A. Heuss, *Theodor Mommsen und das 19. Jahrhundert* (Kiel, 1956); A. Wucher, *Theodor Mommsen. Geschichtsschreibung und Politik* (Göttingen, 1956, 2nd ed. 1968). Wickert provides a chronicle of Mommsen's life and work; detailed and reasoned, occasionally chaotic but always fascinating. Heuss and Wucher attempt to interpret Mommsen's *Geschichtsauffassung* against the background of contemporary history and culture. Wucher is a modern historian dealing with Mommsen as a nineteenth century figure (cf. the interesting analysis of Wucher's book by F. Sartori, *Paideia* 16 [1961] 3-11); Heuss and Wickert are eminent historians of Rome; this imparts Roman color to their presentation. Heuss is more inclined to philosophical theory; Wickert favors enumeration. Wickert's views on Roman history are probably best gleaned from his article " Princeps " in *RE* 22 (1954) 1998-2296; of Heuss one should read not only his *Römische Geschichte* (2nd ed. Braunschweig, 1964), with its sensible remarks on Roman imperialism (cf. Harris, *War and Imperialism* 162, n. 1), but also and above all his many studies on the concept of revolution (see below, nn. 6, 12). Very useful are the introductions by T.R.S. Broughton to the new English edition of the fifth volume of Mommsen's history, *The Provinces of the Roman Empire* (Chicago, 1968) IX-XXV and by K.

153

Christ to the new edition of *Römische Geschichte* (in vol. 8 [München, 1976] 7-66). Christ treats of Mommsen also in his *Von Gibbon zu Rostovtzeff. Leben und Werk führender Althistoriker der Neuzeit* (Darmstadt, 1972) 84-118, and above all one has now to consult his *Römische Geschichte und deutsche Geschichtswissenschaft* (München, 1982).

[3] See below, n. 39.

[4] For the publication history of the *Römische Geschichte*, see Wickert 3.399-422, 619-675. In February 1854 the printing of vol. 1 was almost concluded, and it was out by the end of May or the beginning of June at the latest (Wickert 3.400, 623-624, nn. 36-38), almost simultaneously with Mommsen's *Ruf* to Breslau (Wickert 3.298-304, 545-548, nn. 22-28). Vol. 2 appeared in 1855, vol. 3 in 1856. The second edition appeared in 1856-1857; and the third in 1861. It differed from the second, to quote Mommsen, " nicht beträchtlich ". In subsequent editions Mommsen introduced practically no changes.

[5] On Mommsen and von Savigny, see Wickert 1.161, 170-171, 454-456, nn. 217-222. Mommsen regarded himself as a successor of both B. G. Niebuhr and von Savigny, and he expressed it forcefully in his famous *Antrittsrede* of 1858 as a member of the Berlin Academy (*Reden und Aufsätze* [Berlin, 1905] 36). Cf. A. Heuss, " Niebuhr und Mommsen ", *Antike und Abendland* 14 (1968) 1-18, and on the natural law school versus the historical school of law, see now P. Stein, *Legal Evolution* (Cambridge, 1980) 1ff., 51ff.

[6] There are no direct quotes of Hegel by Mommsen, but the philosopher's unseen presence nobody could escape, even Mommsen. See Wickert 1.117-118; Wucher 91, n. 17; Heuss 131ff., 259ff., and idem, " Theodor Mommsen und die revolutionäre Struktur des römischen Kaisertums ", *ANRW* II 1 (1974) 88-90.

[7] B. Croce, *Teoria e storia della storiografia³* (Bari, 1927) 26-27 and 255: " il romanticismo ... creò ... il tipo del filologo-pensatore (e talvolta altresì poeta), dal Niebuhr al Mommsen, dal Thierry al Fustel de Coulanges ". Mommsen's *Geschichte* was for Croce one of the *pseudostorie*, as also were the histories of Droysen and Grote (p. 27). For an excellent short appraisal of Croce's thought, see A. Momigliano, " Reconsidering B. Croce ", *Quarto Contributo alla storia degli studi classici e del mondo antico* (Roma, 1969) 95-115.

[8] Romanticism and historicism were in fact in many respects close to each other. Both idolized the *Volk* (the pedigree goes back to Herder) and both treated it as a living and developing organism (this they shared with Burke). Compare, for instance, Adam Müller, *Die Elemente der Staatskunst* (Berlin, 1809, new ed. Jena, 1922) 1.145: " Ein Volk ist die erhabene Gemeinschaft einer langen Reihe von vergangenen, jetzt lebenden und noch kommenden Geschlechtern, die alle in einem grossen innigen Verband zu Leben und Tod zusammenhängen ", and F. von Savigny, *Vermischte Schriften* 5 (Berlin, 1850) 141-142: " Das wahrhaft historische Verfahren strebt ... darnach, das Gegebene aufwärts durch alle seine Verwandlungen hindurch bis zu seiner Entstehung aus des Volkes Natur,

154

21

Schicksal und Bedürfnis zu verfolgen ... Die allgemeine Voraussetzung bei diesem Verfahren ist die, dass jedes Volk ... eine nicht bloss zufällige, sondern wesentliche und nothwendige ... Individualität habe ". For Schlegel and Schelling, see below, nn. 26, 27 and for a discussion of the concepts *Volk, Nation* and *Staat*, see P. Catalano, *Populus Romanus Quirites* (Torino, 1974) 21-49 (with ample literature).

[9] Cf. Wucher 63-85. The history of Italy is not " was man die Bezwingung Italiens durch die Römer zu nennen gewohnt ist ", but rather " die Einigung zu einem Staate des gesammten Stammes der Italiker " (*Römische Geschichte*[8] 1.6). The national unification is " die Vollendung des menschlichen Daseins " (*Reden u. Aufsätze* 316) – this thought quite appropriately appears at the head of a lecture delivered in March 1871. It dealt with the German policy of Augustus, but above and beyond this it celebrated the victory of Prussia over France. Mommsen concluded his lecture with praise of the " Schlachtruf der Deutschen ... in der Varusschlacht und zuletzt bei Mars-la-Tours und Sedan " (pp. 342-343).

[10] Cf. Z. Yavetz, " Why Rome? Zeitgeist and Ancient Historians in Early 19th Century Germany ", *AJP* 97 (1976) 276-296.

[11] This accusation (made in 1881) concerned Bismarck's protectionist economic policy. See Wickert 4.94-121.

[12] *Römische Geschichte*[8] 2.373. At the same time " Sulla hat die italische Revolution (which began with the Gracchi) endgültig geschlossen ". On Mommsen's concept of revolution, see A. Heuss, " Der Untergang der römischen Republik und das Problem der Revolution ", *Historische Zeitschrift* 182 (1956) 4ff.; E. Tornow, *Der Revolutionsbegriff und die späte römische Republik – eine Studie zur deutschen Geschichtsschreibung im 19. und 20.Jh.* (Frankfurt a.M., 1978) 9-34.

[13] See above, n. 9. Mommsen speaks further of the progress " von dem cantonalen Particularismus, mit dem jede Volksgeschichte anhebt und anheben muss, zu der nationalen Einigung, mit der jede Volksgeschichte endigt oder doch endigen sollte " (*Römische Geschichte*[8] 1.41, cf. 14) – observe the remarkable juxtaposition of the supposedly general truth (*endigt*) and the modal wishfulness (*endigen sollte*). But Mommsen was well aware of the fact that in Italy " Das Einigungswerk nicht mit dem schonenden Messer des Arztes durchgeführt worden war ". The unification of Italy by Rome was a " Zwangsehe ", but " was die Völker anlangt, so fragt die Geschichte wenig nach dem Einigungsgrund, wenn nur das Ziel erreicht, ... das Volk zum Staat zusammengefasst wird " (*Reden u. Aufsätze* 316-317).

[14] *Römische Geschichte*[8] 1.6ff.

[15] *Ibid.* 1.176.

[16] Mommsen strives constantly to diminish Etruscan and Greek influences

155

on Rome and Latium; the Etruscans produced a barren civilization, and from the Greeks the Latins received only "Anregungen" and some practical skills (*Römische Geschichte*[8] 1.116ff., 237-239).

[17] *Römische Geschichte*[8] 1.320ff., esp. 338, 380: " das unerbittliche Schicksal fragt nicht nach Schwüren und verzweifeltem Flehen " (referring to the debacle of the Samnites and their *iurati milites*).

[18] Cf. Wickert 2.212-213.

[19] Wickert 4.74-75. *Ad rem*, see the excellent studies by B. Sutter, *Die Badenischen Sprachenverordnungen von 1897* (Wien, 1960-1965) 1.128ff., 2.41ff., and especially " Theodor Mommsens Brief ' An die Deutschen in Oesterreich ' ", *Ostdeutsche Wissenschaft* 10 (1963) 152-225. According to the *Verordnung* of 5 April 1897 Czech was recognized as the official administrative language (on a par with German) in the Kingdom of Bohemia.

[20] *Römische Geschichte*[8] 1.781-782.

[21] *Preussische Jahrbücher* 1 (1858) 225-244, esp. 240, 242. It was published anonymously, cf. Wickert 3.371-376, 570-577.

[22] *Reden und Aufsätze* 318.

[23] The *spiritus movens* of Roman expansion was not " die Eroberungslust " but rather " die Philisterfurcht ". But at the same time Mommsen maintains that the Romans were prompted to go to war only " durch eine unerhörte Störung der bestehenden politischen Verhältnisse " (*Römische Geschichte*[8] 1.781-782).

[24] On the policy of annexation and non-annexation, see Harris, *War and Imperialism* 131ff. Cf. also A. Lintott, " What was the ' Imperium Romanum '? ", *Greece and Rome* 27 (1981) 53-67, esp. 54.

[25] *Römische Geschichte*[8] 1.782. Mommsen was quite preoccupied with this idea. In his article about Thiers and Napoleon (above, n. 21) he postulated as a program for Prussia in international politics " das Gleichgewicht der grossen Nationen " (p. 244). But in 1858 Prussia could hardly aspire to any more ambitious role.

[26] *Römische Geschichte*[8] 1.782: " die nothwendige Entwickelung der Völkerverhältnisse des Altertums ". On chance and destiny compare F. Schelling, *Die Vorlesungen über die Methode des akademischen Studiums* (Berlin, 1803, reprint in *Ausgewählte Werke* 8, Darmstadt, 1976) 545: " (Historie) wird ... jene Identität der Freiheit und Notwendigkeit in dem Sinne darstellen müssen, wie sie vom Gesichtspunkt der Wirklichkeit aus erscheint ... Von diesem aus ist sie aber nur als unbegriffene und ganz objektive Identität erkennbar, als Schicksal " and Mommsen, *Römische Geschichte*[8] 2.454: " Die Geschichte, der Kampf der Nothwendigkeit und der Freiheit, ist ein sittliches Problem; Polybios behandelt

156

sie als wäre sie ein mechanisches ". *Schicksal* and *Notwendigkeit* were the trademarks of romantic parlance. On Polybius' concept of Tyche, see F. W. Walbank, *A Historical Commentary on Polybius* (Oxford, 1957) 1.16-28.

[27] *Römische Geschichte*[8] 1.30: Italy " errang allein unter allen Kulturvölkern des Altertums ... die nationale Einheit ". Cf. F. Schlegel according to whom the Romans were " die einzige Nation, die ganz Nation war " (*Athenaeum* 3 [Berlin, 1800] 14). But in 1880 we read a surprising statement: " Die alte Welt kennt das nicht, was wir heute den nationalen Staat nennen " (*Reden u. Aufsätze* 413).

[28] Quoted by Christ, *Von Gibbon zu Rostovtzeff* (above, n. 2) 108.

[29] *Römische Geschichte*[8] 1.531ff., esp. 536, 561ff., esp. 565 (Hamilcar's " Kampf ... gegen das Schicksal "), 570ff. (Hannibal); 3.291-292 (synkrisis of Hannibal and Vercingetorix).

[30] Wucher 67. But cf. Wickert 4.81-82.

[31] Wucher 194ff. In a letter of 30 October 1870 Mommsen so characterized the results of the war against France: " Der grauenvolle Ruin Frankreichs ... ist ein Ärmerwerden auch für uns, da wir nun allein bleiben; und unsere innere Entwickelung wird es auch merken, dass die Nation sich durch die philisterhafte Furcht vor dem unbequemen Nachbarn ins Erobern hineinhetzen lässt " (Wickert 4.67). About Roman expansion in Greece Mommsen spoke in almost exactly the same words, in 1854 (*Römische Geschichte*[8] 1.781-782), and again in 1871 (*Reden u. Aufsätzee 318*).

[32] *Römische Geschichte*[8] 3.220. Mommsen formulated his " law " as a prelude to his description of the conquest and romanization of the West.

[33] For the pronouncements of Rhodes and Ferry (French prime minister 1880-81, 1883-85), see the excellent source collection by W. Mommsen, *Imperialismus. Seine geistigen, politischen und wirtschaftlichen Grundlagen* (Hamburg, 1977) 48-49, 61, 63-64, 83-85, 88-91.

[34] Wickert 4.75. See above, n. 19.

[35] Wucher 196-197. Cf. *Reden u. Aufsätze* 113-114 (1881), 142-143 (1885), 410ff. (1888), 430-431 (1895). On Mommsen and France, see Wickert 4.137-170. But it is instructive to read also the openly nationalist lines, *Reden u. Aufsätze* 18-19, 27, 31 (1875), 55-56 (1875).

[36] In fact Prussia surpassed Rome: Germany was not only militarily but also culturally superior to contemporary France and Italy, cf. Mommsen's comments in a letter written shortly after the battle of Sedan (Wickert 4.66), and above all *Reden u. Aufsätze* 7: " Lange bevor die deutschen Waffen auf dem Schlachtfeld den Sieg gewannen, hat die deutsche Forschung auf ihrem Gebiet die gleiche Anerkennung sich erobert und die Nachbarn gezwungen unsere strenge, aber

157

unentbehrlich gewordene Sprache widerwillig zu lernen" (*Rektoratsrede* of 1874). Cf. *ibid.* 130.

[37] *Römische Geschichte*[8] 3.547-549. This was " das Werk des dritten und grössten der demokratischen Staatsmänner Roms ". On the myth of democracy in Rome, see J. Linderski, *CJ* 77 (1982) 275-277.

[38] This does not mean that it enjoyed a monopoly. At the turn of the century it was largely supplanted in Germany by an " aggressive " interpretation of Roman expansion. No wonder: in the last decennia of the nineteenth century the ideal and the goal was no longer national unification – of Germany by Prussia or Italy by Rome – but rather world-wide expansion and colonization. The writings of Heinrich v. Treitschke and Max Weber and the political proclamations of the time provide eloquent testimony. In its proclamation of 1897 *Allgemeiner Deutscher Verband* exhorted the *Volk* to vie with the Romans in building up their own *Weltreich*, and Max Weber wrote in the same year that foreign markets can be controlled by no other means than *die Macht* and *die nackte Gewalt* (quoted by W. Mommsen [above, n. 33] 127, 130). The content of J. Kromayer's *Roms Kampf um die Weltherrschaft* (Leipzig, 1912) matches its title. But Kromayer was not an admirer of Roman expansion: Roman conquest bears out the old truth that the domination of one nation over another leads inevitably to the degeneration of both the conqueror and the conquered (p. 74).

[39] " La politique romaine en Grèce et dans l'Orient hellénistique au IIIe siècle ", *Études d'épigraphie et d'histoire grecques* 4.1 (Paris, 1952) 26-75 at 27 (originally published in *Revue de Philologie* 50 [1926] 46-66, 194-218).

[40] *Ibid.* 26.

[41] " La politique romaine en Grèce et dans l'Orient hellénistique au IIIe siècle ", *Revue de Philologie* 49 (1925) 28-54, 118-142. The object of Walek's criticism was Holleaux' book *Rome, la Grèce et les monarchies hellénistiques au IIIe siècle avant J.C.* (Paris, 1921, reprinted 1935 and 1969). Walek, who received his doctorate from the University of Berlin in 1911 (his *Referenten* were Eduard Meyer and Otto Hirschfeld), expressed similar views also in his book *Dzieje upadku monarchii macedońskiej* (with French summary: *Les derniers rois de Macédoine* [Cracow, 1924]). This was not a novel stance in Polish historical writing. In the same year K. Morawski, professor of classics at Cracow University, published a collection of essays *Rzym i narody* (*Rome and the Nations* [Warsaw 1924]) in which he pictured Rome, to use Mommsen's famous phrase (*Reden u. Aufsätze* 319), as " den grossen Völkerzwinger ". The historical vicissitudes of Poland nourished this attitude. The eastward expansion of Poland in the XIV-XVII centuries was never perceived, in history or historiography, as a conquest, but rather presented strictly legalistically as an act (or acts) of union. Hence no political need to admire Roman conquests; admiration was reserved for the constitution of the Roman republic, which many Polish writers of the XVI-XVIII centuries and still Rousseau in his *Considerations sur le gouvernement de Pologne* fancied to have rediscovered in the constitution of Poland-Lithuania.

With the collapse of the Polish commonwealth toward the end of the eighteenth century the perspective changed: now Prussia, Russia and Rome all appeared as " die grossen Völkerzwinger ".

[42] J. A. North, " The Development of Roman Imperialism ", *JRS* 81 (1981) 1-9, accords Harris cautious acknowledgement (or is it endorsement?). But the title – and the content – of the review by A. N. Sherwin-White (*JRS* 80 [1980] 177-181) exude bewilderment at the sight of this marvellous and strange beast, Rome the Aggressor. Apparently West Europe (and America too) have lost not only the spirit but also the understanding of Empire. To taste conquest, and find out what the obligations are, and delights, of domination, we have to travel eastwards. Or backwards: to London, Paris, Berlin – and Rome.

[43] *Op. cit.* (above, n. 39) 28ff. Cf. Polybius 2. 2-12.

[44] " Notes on Roman Policy in Illyria ", *Studies in Greek and Roman History* (Oxford, 1964) 1ff. (originally published in 1952).

[45] 2. 8. 8-9.

[46] *Op. cit.* (above, n. 39) 28. Cf. Walek, *op. cit.* (above, n. 41) 33.

[47] *Op. cit.* 36.

[48] For the territorial details of the Roman settlement, see Badian, *op. cit.* (above, n. 44) 6-7, 23-25.

[49] Holleaux, *op. cit.* (above, n. 39) 36; E. Täubler, *Die Vorgeschichte des zweiten punischen Krieges* (Berlin, 1921) 17, 23; Mommsen, *Römische Geschichte*[8] 1.550ff.

[50] So also Sherwin-White, *op. cit.* (above, n. 42) 178: during the invasions of Pyrrhus, Hannibal and the Celts " Rome was undoubtedly defending Italy against foreign assault ". Let us ask the Samnites.

[51] *Rome, la Grèce* (above, n. 41) 109-112; " La politique romaine " (above, n. 39) 36-39.

[52] Badian, *op. cit.* (above, n. 44) 3-5. Familiarity with Badian's *Roman Imperialism* (Ithaca, 1968) is of course assumed throughout this paper. He rightly stresses – following in the footsteps of Rostovtzeff – the importance of the " hegemonial imperialism " (p. 9).

[53] Cf. J. Linderski, *CP* 77 (1982) 175-177.

[54] An excellent introduction to historical writing in nineteenth century France is provided by P. Stadler, *Geschichtschreibung und historisches Denken*

159

in Frankreich 1789-1871 (Zürich, 1958) esp. 303-324 (Renan and Fustel de Coulanges).

[55] Renan expressed this idea in the programmatic pamphlet " La Chaire d'Hébreu au Collège de France ", *Oeuvres complètes* 1 (Paris, 1947) 165.

[56] " De la manière d'écrire l'histoire en France et en Allemagne depuis cinquante ans ", *Questions historiques* (Paris, 1893) 3-16 at 15-16 (originally published in 1872). For an appraisal of Fustel's thought, see J. Herrick, *The Historical Thought of Fustel de Coulanges* (Washington, 1954) and A. Momigliano, " La città antica di Fustel de Coulanges ", *Rivista Storia Italiana* 82 (1970), 81-98.

[57] L. Robert in Holleaux, *Études* 6 (Paris, 1968) 59. In this volume L. Robert assembled a number of obituaries and commemorations of Holleaux.

[58] *Polybe ou la Grèce conquise par les Romains* reprinted in *Questions historiques* 119-211.

[59] Mommsen, *Römische Geschichte*[8] 1.782; Fustel de Coulanges, *Polybe* 121.

[60] Momigliano, *op. cit.* (above, n. 56) 94.

[61] " Fragments sur la méthode historique ", quoted by Stadler, *op. cit.* (above, n. 54) 318.

[62] In his inaugural lecture of 1888 quoted by M. Roques, " Notice sur la vie et les travaux de Maurice Holleaux ", *CRAI* (1943) 70.

[63] *La Cité antique*[10] (Paris, 1883) 4-5.

[64] Quoted by M. Roques, *op. cit.* (above, n. 62) 66-67. Roques discovers here " le souffle de Michelet ".

[65] *Cambridge Ancient History* 8 (1930) 239 = *Etudes* 5.2 (Paris, 1957) 431-432.

[66] Mommsen, *Römische Geschichte*[8] 1.720-721; T. Frank, *Roman Imperialism* (New York, 1914) 138ff., esp. 157-159. For a masterly analysis of the concept of " sentimental politics ", see E. Badian, *Titus Quinctius Flamininus* (Lectures in Memory of Louise Taft Semple, Cincinnati, 1970) 18-21. Badian characterizes Frank's book as " divided between the obviously wrong-headed and the flash of insight illuminating the obviously true " (pp. 18-19). It was " written ... with little contact with the mainstream of international scholarly discussion, especially as written in foreign languages ". And " among much else that Frank did not know " Badian accuses him of not knowing " the immense tome " by G. Colin, *Rome et la Grèce de 200 a 146 av. J.C.* (Paris, 1905). But Frank mentions Colin as one of his

160

authorities in note 1 to chapter VIII (p. 159), and on p. IX he lists the names of eighteen scholars (Colin included) who " would fill pages of additional notes if I could have recorded all my obligations ". On p. 149 (perhaps not the page to which one would normally go to find this information) he speaks of various theories of Roman expansion, and in footnotes 22-25 (p. 161) records in addition to Mommsen the names of Peter, Ihne, Meyer, Wilamowitz and Duruy, the last one despite Badian's remark: " the translation of Duruy ... should have been available in this country " (p. 19). But Frank does not need any defense in the matter of footnotes. This is a wrong measure for a work of intellectual vision. We do not miss references to modern literature in Mommsen's *Geschichte* or Fustel's *La Cité*. These works belong to the realm of ideology, and their success, failure or greatness has nothing to do with the *minutiae* of pedantic scholarship.

[67] Significant was also the title: *Roman Imperialism*. Before Frank only one book in English on Roman history displayed the word " imperialism " on its title-page: W. T. Arnold's *Studies of Roman Imperialism* (Manchester, 1906); however, it was published posthumously, its title was due to the editor, and it did not deal with Roman expansion but rather with the administration of the Roman empire. Mommsen in his *Roman History* did not use the term " imperialism " at all; the first modern author to apply it extensively to characterize Roman policy in the third and second centuries seems to have been Guglielmo Ferrero in his once famous *Grandezza e decadenza di Roma* 1 (Milano, 1902). On the semantic development of the term " imperialism ", see R. Koebner and H. D. Schmidt, *Imperialism. The Story and Significance of a Political Word, 1840-1960* (Cambridge, 1964), and, for Roman history, D. Flach, " Der sogenannte römische Imperialismus ", *Historische Zeitschrift* 222 (1976) 1-42. Cf. also D. Musti, *Polibio e l'imperialismo romano* (Napoli, 1978) 13ff., esp. n. 4 on pp. 35-36, who, however, did not consider the works by Koebner-Schmidt and Flach. For various theories of imperialism in modern times, see the surveys by W. Mommsen, *Theories of Imperialism* (New York, 1980) and N. Etherington, " Reconsidering Theories of Imperialism ", *History and Theory* 21 (1982) 1-36.

[68] P. VII. All subsequent quotes of Frank in this paragraph are taken from his preface, pp. VII-IX.

[69] See W. Mommsen, *op. cit.* (above, n. 33) 130.

[70] History and vogue dictated the comparison of the two great republics: in the same year in which Frank's *Roman Imperialism* appeared Guglielmo Ferrero published his *Ancient Rome and Modern America* (New York, 1914). Cf. M. Hammond, " Ancient Rome and Modern America Reconsidered ", *Proceedings of the Massachusetts Historical Society* 73 (1961 [1963]) 3-17.

[71] *Papers Relating to the Foreign Relations of the United States 1898* (Washington, 1901) 757-759.

[72] Polybius 2.8.

161

[73] *Op. cit.* (above, n. 71) 758-759.

[74] A " splendid little war ", as John Milton Hay, Secretary of State under McKinley and Theodore Roosevelt, called it. Cf. G. F. Linderman, *The Mirror of War. American Society and the Spanish-American War* (Ann Arbor 1974) 175, and passim for the war propaganda.

[75] *Op. cit.* (above, n. 71) 907. A. March in his book *The History and Conquest of the Philippines* (1899) p. X, found better words, the words of Kipling, to describe America's mission: " Take up the white man's burden - / Ye dare not stoop to less – ". But the president spoke not only of civilization. " Incidental to our tenure in the Philippines is the commercial opportunity to which American statesmanship can not be indifferent " (p. 907).

[76] See A. K. Weinberg, *Manifest Destiny: A Study of Nationalist Expansion in American History* (Baltimore, 1935).

[77] *Roman Imperialism* 89 and 107 n. 5.

[78] *Ibid.* 93.

[79] *Ibid.* VIII.

[80] *Ibid.* 129.

[81] *Papers Relating to the Foreign Relations of the United States 1904* (Washington, 1905) IX.

[82] *Roman Imperialism* VIII; 8-9 and 12 n. 20.

[83] For Gaetano De Sanctis' philosophy of history, see E. Gabba, " Riconsiderando l'opera storica di Gaetano De Sanctis ", *RFIC* 99 (1971) 5 25, L. Polverini, " Gaetano De Sanctis recensore ", *Annali della Scuola Normale Superiore di Pisa*, serie 3, 3 (1973) 1047-1094; G. Bandelli, " Imperialismo, colonialismo e questione sociale in Gaetano De Sanctis ", *Quaderni di Storia* 12 (1980) 88ff.; M. Pani, " Gaetano De Sanctis e l'imperialismo antico ", *Studi in onore di Fulvio Grosso* (Roma, 1982) 475-492. For a lucid introduction to Italian historiography from the turn of the century until World War II, see A. Momigliano, *Contributo alla storia degli studi classici* (Roma, 1955) 275-297 (originally published in 1950). For Ettore Pais, see R. T. Ridley, " Ettore Pais ", *Helikon* 15-16 (1975-76) 500-533, and for Guglielmo Ferrero: P. Treves, *L'idea di Roma e la cultura italiana del secolo XIX* (Milano-Napoli, 1962) 261-293, and the collection of articles *Guglielmo Ferrero. Histoire et politique au XXᵉ siècle* (Genève, 1966).

[84] *Storia dei Romani*² 4.1 (Firenze, 1969) VII.

[85] I borrow this expression from Gabba, *op. cit.* (above, n. 83) 18. See

also idem, " L'ultimo volume della Storia dei Romani di G. De Sanctis ", *Rivista Storica Italiana* 76 (1964) 1050-1057 at 1053-1054.

[86] This was the title of the first two volumes of the *Storia* (published in 1907).

[87] *Storia dei Romani*[2] 2 (Firenze, 1960) 339-340 (= 1st ed. 357-358). Cf. P. Treves, *Lo studio dell'antichità classica nell'ottocento* (Milano-Napoli, 1962) XXXIX; E. Gabba, *op. cit.* (above, n. 83) 17.

[88] *Atene e Roma* 1 (1920) 3-14, 73-89, reprinted in *Scritti Minori* 4 (Roma, 1976) 9-38, but which ought to be read in the edition with commentary by P. Treves, *Lo studio* (above, n. 87) 1247-1282 at 1264.

[89] Cf. on Viriathus, Mommsen, *Römische Geschichte*[8] 2.12-13 and De Sanctis, *Storia* 4.3 (Firenze, 1964) 222-223, 232.

[90] *Storia dei Romani* 4.1. 23ff.

[91] J. Beloch, " Der Verfall der antiken kultur ", *Historische Zeitschrift* 84 (1900) 1-38. See the stimulating remarks by Gabba, *op. cit.* (above, n. 83) 14-16. On De Sanctis and Beloch, see De Sanctis' commemoration of his old teacher edited with commentary by P. Treves, *Lo studio* (above, n. 87) 1231-1246.

[92] This picture emerges above all from De Sanctis' review of M. Rostovtzeff, *The Social and Economic History of the Roman Empire* (*RFIC* 54 [1926] 537-554 = *Scritti Minori* 6.1 [Roma, 1972] 295-313), from his article " Rivoluzione e reazione nell'età dei Gracchi ". (*Atene e Roma* 2 [1921] 209-237 = *Scritti Minori* 4 [Roma, 1976] 39-69), and his *prolusione* of 1929, " Essenza e caratteri della storia greca " (*ibid.* 4.419-459). Cf. Gabba, *op. cit.* (above, n. 83) 21-23; Pani, *op. cit.* (above, n. 83) 480-483.

[93] *Lo studio* (above, n. 87) XL, and, for Fraccaro versus De Sanctis, 1248.

[94] *Rivista Storica Italiana* 2 (1924) 12-26 = *Opuscula* 2 (Pavia, 1957) 5-18, esp. 15-16.

[95] J. Vogt, " Divide et impera – die angebliche Maxime des römischen Imperialismus ", in: *Das Staatsdenken der Römer*, ed. by R. Klein (Darmstadt, 1966) 15-38 (originally published in 1940).

[96] Liv. 6.18.7; Cic. *Phil.* 7.19. Cf. Vegetius, *r. mil.* 3 praef.: *qui desiderat pacem, praeparet bellum*.

[97] E. Wölfflin, " Krieg und Frieden im Sprichworte der Römer ", *Sitzungsberichte der Bayerischen Akad. d. Wiss. zu München, Phil.-Hist. Classe* (1888) 1.197-215.

163

[98] These remarks are not to be construed as condemnation of Roman expansion but rather as an attempt to call a spade a spade. Nor are they to be construed as censure of great scholars whose names appear on the preceding pages but rather as an attempt to understand their views.

Mommsen and Syme:
Law and Power in the Principate
of Augustus

Two scholars and two works of genius have defined for all time the battleground for our understanding of Rome and Augustus: Theodor Mommsen and Ronald Syme, *Römisches Staatsrecht* and *The Roman Revolution*. "Men and dynasties pass, but style abides,"[1] and these two works are as dissimilar in style as they are in content. Are they also mutually exclusive, one wrong and the other right? Is there a middle ground between them, or do Mommsen and Syme perhaps illuminate two different aspects of the same phenomenon? Depending upon the method and the instrument of observation light comes out as a corpuscle or as a wave. But the new physics did not simply prove Newton wrong; it also showed that the world reveals itself to observers in guises that mechanistic physics was not capable of conjuring up or understanding. Depending upon whether we look through the prism of prosopography or the prism of law we arrive at one of two appearances of the principate, the vision of Syme or the vision of Mommsen, neither true or false in itself, and neither complete. It is otiose to ask what the

1. R. Syme, *Tacitus*, vol. 2 (Oxford 1958) 624.

42

principate was; in doing so we continue the tradition of Aristotle and the Scholastics, the pernicious preoccupation with definitions and the "essence" of things. It was the liberation from that tradition that gave us the achievements of modern science: we do not define things but ask how they behave.[2] Nature does not answer inane questions, nor does history. But neither scientist nor scholar lives in a void; the world in which we live impinges upon us, suggests questions, and colors perceptions.

"The menace of despotic power hung over Rome like a heavy cloud";[3] it also hung over the world of Syme. *The Roman Revolution* was published in the fatal year of 1939, in the month of September. Although conceived in tranquil Oxford, it was born amid the rising tide of Fascist charismatic dictatorships in Europe; and the scholarly environment was one of adulation of Augustus, which oozed from the sugar-coated commentaries on the Augustan poets, and from new and disquieting arrivals, books like *Princeps* by Wilhelm Weber (Stuttgart 1936), a murky harangue (stuffed with antiquarian footnotes) on the greatness of Augustus, his *Mut, Wut,* and *Kraft.* In 1937–38 the world beheld the extravagant celebrations of the *bimillenario augusteo,* of the old *impero* and the new.[4] Syme's book was a Tacitean reaction to his times,[5] and to cheerful credulity.

Weber's *Princeps* duly appears in Syme's bibliography, but when we arrive at the letter *M,* of all Mommsen's works we find only three listed: one volume of his *Gesammelte Schriften,* the edition of the *Res Gestae Divi Augusti,* and two volumes of his *Römische Forschungen.* The two *Meisterwerke, Römisches Staatsrecht* and *Römisches Strafrecht* are

---

2. Cf. K. Popper, *The Open Society and Its Enemies* (London, 1945), vol. 1, chap. 3, sect. 6; vol. 2, chap. 11, sect. 2 (= 5th ed., rev. [Princeton 1966] 1: 31–34; 2: 9–26); id., *Conjectures and Refutations* (London and New York 1962) 20–21, 103.

3. R. Syme, *The Roman Revolution* (Oxford 1939) 8.

4. "A memorable and alarming anniversary looms heavily upon us. The poet of the Italian nation was paid his due honours seven years ago, and now all Italy will conspire to acclaim the Princeps who was also Dux," so wrote R. Syme in a review published in *CR* 51 (1937) 194. On the celebrations of the *bimillenario augusteo* and on Mussolini's identification with Augustus, see the informative article (although written from a Marxist perspective) by M. Cagnetta, "Il mito di Augusto e la 'rivoluzione' fascista," *QS* 2 (1976) 139–81.

5. Cf. esp. A. Momigliano, *Terzo contributo alla storia degli studi classici e del mondo antico* (Rome 1966) 729–32 (originally published as the introduction to the Italian translation of *The Roman Revolution* [Turin 1962]); F. Millar, *JRS* 71 (1981) 146 (review of Syme's *Roman Papers,* vols. 1–2); W. Schmitthenner, "Caesar Augustus—Erfolg in der Geschichte," *Saeculum* 36 (1985) 286–91.

missing. No accident here. In his preface Syme professes his debt to five scholars:[6] to the "prosopographical studies of Münzer, Groag and Stein"[7] and in particular to Münzer's "supreme example and guidance";[8] further he acknowledges that his "opinions about the oath of allegiance of 32 B.C. and about the position of the Princeps as a party-leader naturally owe much" to Anton von Premerstein's "illuminating work" (*Vom Werden und Wesen des Prinzipats* [Munich 1937]);[9] finally, gracious mention is made of W. W. Tarn's "writings about Antonius and Cleopatra"—the only author writing in English so honored. Among the German, Swiss, and Austrian *lumina* Mommsen's name is again missing; but even more striking is the absence of Matthias Gelzer.

This fact did not escape the keen eye of Géza Alföldy. In *Sir Ronald Syme, "Die römische Revolution" und die deutsche Althistorie,*[10] Alföldy presents an excellent panorama of Syme's "reception" in Ger-

6. Syme (supra n. 3) VIII.

7. On Münzer (1868–1942, in a concentration camp), see now A. Kneppe and J. Wiesehöffer, *Friedrich Münzer: ein Althistoriker zwischen Kaiserreich und Nationalsozialismus* (Bonn 1983). Edmund Groag (1873–1945) and Arthur Stein (1871–1950) were, *inter alia*, the editors of the second edition of the *Prosopographia Imperii Romani* (1933–1952, vols. 1–4, fasc. 2), but to render *suum cuique* one should not forget that the impulse to elaborate the prosopography of the Roman Empire came from Theodor Mommsen (see his *praemonitum* to the first edition of vol. 1 of the *Prosopographia* [Berlin 1897]).

8. This guidance will have presumably emanated above all from Münzer's numerous prosopographical contributions to *RE* rather than from his *Römische Adelsparteien und Adelsfamilien* (Stuttgart 1920; reprint Darmstadt 1963)—a grand work but one in which there are already present the germs of the sickness that rendered hollow so many prosopographical constructs of the epigones, showing a tendency to infer the behavior of individuals from the behavior of groups. Such inferences have only statistical validity, not factual (cf. C. Nicolet, "Prosopographie et histoire sociale: Rome et l'Italie à l'époque républicaine," *Annales ESC* 25 [1970] 1209–28, esp. 1226; J. Linderski, *CP* 72 [1977] 55–56). On Münzer and Syme, see Millar (supra n. 5) 146 (he evaluates the *Adelsparteien* much more positively); Alföldy (infra n. 10) 18. Alföldy gives an engrossing assessment of Syme's prosopographical method in his review of Syme's *Roman Papers*, vols. 1–2, in *AJAH* 4 (1979 [1981]) 167–85.

9. AbhMünch N.F. no. 15 (1937). After the death of von Premerstein (1869–1935) the work was edited by Hans Volkmann. For an evaluation of von Premerstein's scholarly career, see K. Christ, *Römische Geschichte und Wissenschaftsgeschichte*, vol. 3 (Darmstadt 1983) 115–27.

10. SBHeid 1983, no. 1. Cf. Inez Stahlmann, *Imperator Caesar Augustus: Studien zur Geschichte des Principatsverständnisses in der deutschen Altertumswissenschaft* (Darmstadt 1988). For the enduring fascination with the Roman revolution and *The Roman Revolution*, both in the West and in the East, see the collection *La Rivoluzione Romana: Inchiesta tra gli antichisti*, Biblioteca di Labeo 6 (Naples 1982). On the concept of revolution in Mommsen (and Syme), see also A. Heuss, "Der Untergang der römischen Republik und das Problem der Revolution," *HZ* 182 (1956) 1–28; id., "Theodor Mommsen und die revolutionäre Struktur des römischen Kaisertums," *ANRW* 2.1 (1974) 77–90; E. Tornow, *Der Revolutionsbegriff und die späte römische Republik—eine Studie zur deutschen Geschichtsschreibung im 19. und 20. Jh.* (Frankfurt 1978) 9–34; J. F. McGlew, "Revolution and Freedom in Theodor Mommsen's *Römische Geschichte*," *Phoenix* 40 (1986 [1987]) 424–45.

many. Gelzer's monograph *Die Nobilität der römischen Republik* (Leipzig and Berlin 1912) has rightly been described as "a turning-point" in the study of Roman republican politics.[11] Whence this lack of acknowledgment? The acknowledgment comes, but it comes not in the preface but in a footnote. This is not as surprising as it might seem. Gelzer's express aim was to overcome Mommsen's legacy of a legal (or legalistic) approach to Roman society, but (as Alföldy points out) in contrast to the works of Münzer, *Die Nobilität* is not a prosopographical, but rather a structural, investigation of Roman oligarchy.[12] Syme explicitly accepts Gelzer's definition of the term *nobilis,* and writes, "Gelzer's lucid explanation of the character of Roman society and Roman politics, namely a nexus of personal obligations, is here followed closely."[13] Still, *The Roman Revolution* would have been possible without Gelzer; without Münzer, however, "it could hardly have existed."[14]

The implicit condemnation of *Staatsrecht* spells out the program: a plea for narrative history. Many years later, in a splendid essay, entitled "Three English Historians," Syme made plain that his sympathies lay "with the narrative historians Gibbon and Macauley, not with the saints and thinkers who are eager to use history for our amendment or punishment."[15] This is what Syme may think he wrote but it is not what he did, for *The Roman Revolution* is no more a work composed *sine ira et studio* (Tac. *Ann.* 1.1.6) than are the *Annals* of Tacitus or the *Decline and Fall* of Gibbon. To appreciate the winner,[16] it was written from the graves of the vanquished: it certainly "amended" both the writing of history and the history of Augustus. It punished credulity and moralistic obfuscation, rewarded clear thought and scepticism. This was achieved not by the impartial assemblage of facts but by selection and comment. The standard modern book on Caesar is Matthias Gelzer's renowned monograph.[17] Syme offers unqualified and instructive praise: "The au-

11. R. T. Ridley, "The Genesis of a Turning-Point: Gelzer's *Nobilität,*" *Historia* 35 (1986) 474–502. Cf. also C. Simon, "Gelzer's *Nobilität der römischen Republik* als 'Wendepunkt,'" *Historia* 37 (1988) 222–40; and the contributions of J. Bleicken, C. Meier, and H. Strasburger in J. Bleicken, ed., *Matthias Gelzer und die römische Geschichte,* Frankfurter Althistorische Studien 9 (Kallmünz 1977).
12. Alföldy (supra n. 10) 14.
13. Syme (supra n. 3) 10, n. 3.
14. Ibid., VIII.
15. "Three English Historians: Gibbon, Macauley, Toynbee," *The Emory University Quarterly* 18 (1962) 140. On Gibbon and Syme, cf. G. Bowersock, "The Emperor of Roman History," *The New York Review of Books,* 6 March 1980, 10.
16. For a composite picture of Syme's Augustus, see Alföldy (supra n. 10) 21–22.
17. *Caesar, der Politiker und Staatsmann,* originally published in Stuttgart and Berlin in 1921. The last edition, the sixth, appeared in Wiesbaden in 1960 (trans. P. Needham [Oxford 1968]).

thor is not arguing a thesis; and remembering that history is narrative, not research, disputation, and the passing of judgments, he lets facts speak for themselves." [18] But "facts" never speak for themselves; it is the historian who weaves happenings into history. [19]

Eadem magistratuum vocabula (Tac. *Ann.* 1.3.7); "Names persist everywhere while substance changes." [20] In procedures and institutions the new Tacitus shows as little interest as the old. It is "the real and ultimate power" that "needs to be discovered." [21]

People, not institutions, are the natural subject of narrative history, and, for Syme, not all people but (almost solely) the governing class. Slaves and other lower classes may be boring indeed (unless they cause trouble), [22] but the soldiers? In the civil wars they were a ubiquitous and decisive fact of life—and death; in *The Roman Revolution*, however, they take a back seat to even those nobles who barely escaped their swords. We are offered no analysis of military institutions or of the *milites* as a social group—a surprising omission in a work devoted to the discovery of "the real and ultimate power" behind the veil of the principate. [23]

Syme's attitude toward institutions is perhaps best illustrated in his chapters 26 and 27, "The Government" and "The Cabinet" (the latter in its modernistic outlook reminiscent of the young Mommsen's linguistic innovations in his *Roman History*). Syme refers to the government and the cabinet as "they," not "it." He does not talk of the senate and its organization or of the *consilium principis,* but of the men who ruled and administered the empire, of the *principes* of the dying Republic, of Agrippa, Maecenas, and Livia (no less a man than they), of Marcellus, of Livia's sons, Drusus and Tiberius, and of that splendid and evanescent constellation of generals and administrators who helped Augustus to become a success in history, in all a procession of some forty names or so. Syme talks of men who led the armies of conquest and governed the provinces (whether in the name of the *princeps* or the senate) or who

18. *JRS* 32 (1944) 92 (= *Roman Papers,* vol. 1 [Oxford 1979] 149). Syme reviewed the enlarged and thoroughly revised second edition of 1941.
19. For a critique of the "positivist" understanding of "facts," see J. Linderski, "*Si vis pacem, para bellum:* Concepts of Defensive Imperialism," *PAAR* 29 (1984) 140–41.
20. Syme (supra n. 3) 406.
21. Ibid.
22. See the delightful pronouncement of Syme quoted by Alföldy (supra n. 10) 17.
23. Cf. now H. Botermann, *Die Soldaten und die römische Politik in der Zeit von Caesars Tod bis zur Begründung des zweiten Triumvirats* (Munich 1968); K. Raaflaub, "Die Militärreformen des Augustus und die politische Problematik des frühen Prinzipats," in G. Binder, ed., *Saeculum Augustum,* vol. 1 (Darmstadt 1987) 246–307.

supervised the treasury and took care of the aqueducts. He does not talk of the duties of provincial governors, of the voting arrangements in the senate, or of the *aerarium* or the *cura aquarum*.

In the Republic it is the consulars who are "the government"; in the new state of Augustus, "the Princeps, the members of his family and his personal adherents." The description of the working of the "Cabinet" ends thus quite appropriately on the theme of "a crisis . . . at the very core of the party," the scheme of Augustus to promote his adoptive grandsons, and Tiberius' morose retirement to Rhodes. That is not to say that after 6 B.C. the government ceased to function. Far from it. The "New State" endured, as it had after the death of Agrippa, for "it was well equipped with the ministers of the government," except that "the enemies of Tiberius . . . now had their turn" in "the syndicate of government." "The Succession" now becomes the prevailing aspect of the *arcanum imperii*, and it is to this murderous subject that Syme directs his pen. *Primum facinus novi imperii* (Tac. *Ann.* 1.6), the execution of Agrippa Postumus at the accession of Tiberius, prompts the author to a remark that may stand as an emblem of his perception of the political and the legal: "The arbitrary removal of a rival was no less essential to the Principate than the public conferment of legal and constitutional power."[24]

At the very outset of *The Roman Revolution* a phrase catches the eye: Augustus' "constitutional reign as acknowledged head of the Roman State." Augustus' title was, however, "specious"; the revival of republican institutions "convenient"; but "all that made no difference to the source and facts of power." To the source perhaps; but if it made no difference to the facts of power, why did Augustus promote the myth? At the same time, " 'the Restoration of the Republic' was not merely a solemn comedy, staged by a hypocrite." There is discrepancy here, and uneasiness. The letter of the law did not matter: "The Princeps stood pre-eminent . . . and not to be defined."[25] The same chapter and verse is repeated again and again, and rightly so, for there were, and are, students of the past who from willful blindness or good nature remove all unpleasantness from history and lose sight of that new, permanent, and overwhelming alien body, the *dux*, the *princeps*, the *imperator*.[26]

24. Syme (supra n. 3) 387, 414, 413, 401, 425, 439.
25. Ibid., 1, 2, 3.
26. Cf. ibid., 324, n.5 and the names of the scholars mentioned there; and see now, for example, H. Castritius, *Der römische Prinzipat als Republik* (Husum 1982), who maintains: "[Es] erweist sich als nötig der von Augustus restituierten römischen Republik eine juristische und politische Wirklichkeit—und dies für einen längeren Zeitraum—zuzuer-

When a contemporary ancient historian professes to be writing history, it is likely that what he really is engaged in is prosopography. This is in keeping with "Syme's law," according to which "in all ages, whatever the form and name of government, be it monarchy, republic or democracy, an oligarchy lurks behind the façade."[27] But the strange peculiarity of an authoritarian regime is that there is also a despot, cruel or benign. To find him one need not look behind the façade: he lurks everywhere.

The story of the young adventurer seizing power with the help of his acolytes and the army, and maintaining it through repression and intimidation, is banal enough; however, the story of the same adventurer creating in a great empire a new and enduring form of government is a theme of world history; for "power" cannot be separated from the form in which it is ensconced. Searching after a tangible "substance,"[28] we often forget that forms too are real and can be brushed aside only with great peril to the actors (they risk their lives, as Caesar the dictator can testify), and to the historians (they risk being drowned in "facts" and rhetoric).

An oracular pronouncement by Christian Meier in his Delphic *Res Publica Amissa* captures exquisitely the reality of the formal transition from the Republic to the principate: the crisis of the Republic was a crisis without a solution ("Krise ohne Alternative"), and as a result "die bestehende Ordnung [wurde] allmählich vernichtet, ohne dass sie verneint worden wäre" ("The existing order was destroyed without being negated"). No power existed that was able either to defend the whole of the old system or to create an entirely new one.[29] The "collective monarchy of the nobles" was abolished,[30] but the husk of the Republic endured, and it endured because it mattered: the shadow of the past provided legitimacy for the victor in the Roman Revolution, and for that reason the elusive form of the principate was also its substance.

---

kennen" (21). Castritius concludes that Cicero's declaration (*Leg. agr.* 2.17) that *omnes potestates, imperia, curationes ab universo populo Romano proficisci convenit* "galt . . . kaum weniger für die sog. Prinzipatszeit" (111).

27. Syme (supra n. 3) 7.

28. Ibid., VII: "The composition of the oligarchy of the government . . . emerges . . . as the binding link between the Republic and the Principate: it is something real and tangible, whatever may be the name or theory of the constitution."

29. C. Meier, *Res Publica Amissa* (Wiesbaden 1966) 201–5, and L, LIV, LVII in the new introduction to the reprint edition (Frankfurt 1980).

30. To borrow the phrase from Andreas Alföldi, *Caesariana* (Bonn 1984) 316 (=id., Review of *Die Vergottung Caesars*, by H. Gesche [Kallmünz 1968], *Phoenix* 24 [1970] 166).

It is reported that the notorious constitution of the Soviet Union of 1936, "the Stalin Constitution," as it was called in adulation, made a profound impression on Syme as a supreme sham.[31] To the citizens it guaranteed all sorts of civil liberties, and to the constituent republics the right to free and unconditional secession from the union. In the eyes of the West, and in plain fact, Stalin was a dictator, but the form of his constitutional rule as the acknowledged head of the Soviet state continued to baffle observers no less than the "constitutional reign" of Caesar Augustus. Like the Caesars, Stalin was the master of death; but to live and rule he had to remain a comrade within the party, as his Roman counterparts had to remain the *principes* within the *res publica*.

In his review of *The Roman Revolution* Arnaldo Momigliano remarks concisely and cogently that Syme considers "spiritual interests of the people . . . much less than their marriages." And he continues: "But if L. Caesar, cos. 64 B.C., wrote a book *de auspiciis,* Ap. Claudius Pulcher, cos. 54 B.C., a work on augural discipline . . . and if C. Scribonius Curio gave the name to the *logistoricus* of Varro *de deorum cultu* . . . , then the way to the religious policy of Augustus is clearer."[32] And as *religio* and *res publica* were in Rome intertwined, a consideration of the juristic and antiquarian preoccupations of the defeated, but not annihilated, republican aristocracy might have thrown light on the constitutional sensitivities of the principate. It will not do simply to discard Appius Claudius Pulcher as "superstitious" or Varro as "the old scholar" who "lacked style, intensity, a guiding idea,"[33] memorable as these phrases may be, and unjust; Varro was possessed of a quick wit and a robust sense of humor, and Appius Claudius was the guiding light for Cicero the augur.[34]

Men (and princes) sought enlightenment from the astrologers and believed in "the inexorable stars";[35] politically the *quattuor amplissima sacerdotia* were more important, and we should not treat the priests solely as quarries for the prosopographical hunt.[36] They were the ex-

31. Millar (supra n. 5) 146.
32. *JRS* 30 (1940) 76 (= *Secondo contributo alla storia degli studi classici e del mondo antico* [Rome 1960] 409).
33. Syme (supra n. 3) 45, 247.
34. Cf. J. Linderski, "Cicero and Roman Divination," *PP* 37 (1982 [1983]) 31–32; id., "The *Libri Reconditi*," *HSCP* 89 (1985) 226–27.
35. Syme (supra n. 3) 9, 418.
36. Characteristically enough, in two recent books on the *fratres Arvales,* John Scheid's *Les Frères Arvales* (Paris 1975) and Ronald Syme's *Some Arval Brethren* (Oxford 1980), there are hundreds of names and (again to quote Momigliano) "marriages," but only scant word about doctrine and ritual.

pounders of a doctrine. And both Caesar the dictator and Augustus the *princeps* paid a great deal of attention to priestly doctrines.[37]

If *The Roman Revolution* is "a modern version of the book on Augustus that Tacitus failed to write,"[38] should we say that Mommsen's *Staatsrecht* is the modern version of a lost republican treatise *De magistratibus?*[39]

First of all we have to dispel the persistent and noxious myth that the Romans were not interested in public or "constitutional" law. They were; and if all the writings in this field had survived, they would have filled many Oxford or Teubner volumes.[40] But Sempronius Tuditanus, Valerius Messala, or Varro would feel much more at home in the *Römische Alterthümer* of Ludwig Lange (1825–85) than in Mommsen's *Staatsrecht.*[41] To judge from the extant fragments, Roman writings on sacral and public law were explanatory and antiquarian; and Lange was the last true antiquarian, and a resolute critic of Mommsen. Indeed, Mommsen's *Staatsrecht* was directed against this antiquarianism. It was an offspring of the *Pandektistik,* and it brilliantly applied the *begriffslogische Methode,* triumphant in civil law, to the description of the Roman state and its public law. As Mommsen put it himself, in the preface to the first edition of the first volume (p. ix); his was "die begrifflich geschlossene und auf consequent durchgeführten Grundgedanken wie auf festen Pfeilern ruhende Darlegung" ("the conceptually complete presentation, resting, as if on firm pillars, on notions that are basic and are consequently carried out").[42] The guiding notions of the *Staatsrecht*

37. Cf. J. Linderski, "The Augural Law," *ANRW* 2.16.3 (1986) 2181–84.

38. "Es ist die neuzeitliche Version des Buches über Augustus, das Tacitus nie geschrieben hat": A. Momigliano in his review of Syme's *Tacitus, Gnomon* 33 (1961) 55 (= id. [supra n. 5] 740).

39. I give here a synopsis of the editions of Mommsen's *Römisches Staatsrecht,* all published in Leipzig: vol. 1 (1871), 1² (1876), 1³ (1877); vol. 2, parts 1 and 2 (1874–1875), 2² (1877), 2³ (1887); vol. 3, parts 1 and 2 (1887–1888).

40. See the fragments of various "constitutional" writers in the collections of F. P. Bremer, *Iurisprudentiae Antehadrianae quae supersunt,* vols. 1 and 2, parts 1–2 (Leipzig 1896–1901); and H. Funaioli, *Grammaticae Romanae Fragmenta* (Leipzig 1907); and for Varro, B. Riposati, *Varro: De vita populi Romani fragmenta* (Milan 1939); and B. Cardauns, *M. Terentius Varro: Antiquitates Rerum Divinarum,* 2 vols. (Wiesbaden 1976). For a summary discussion of this literature, see E. Rawson, *Intellectual Life in the Late Roman Republic* (Baltimore 1985) esp. 201–14, 233–49, 298–316.

41. The editions of Lange's work: vol. 1³ (Berlin 1876; 1st ed., 1856); vol. 2³ (1879; 1st ed., 1862); vol. 3² (1876; 1st ed., 1871). For Lange's critique of Mommsen, see his review of vol. 1 of the *Staatsrecht,* in his *Kleine Schriften,* vol. 2 (Göttingen 1887) 154–65 (originally published in 1872). Against Mommsen's "dogmatisch-juristische Formulierung des römischen Staatsrechts" Lange upholds the validity of "historisch-antiquarische Forschung" (155). Even a cursory comparison of *Römische Alterthümer* and *Römisches Staatsrecht* demonstrates the enormous conceptual difference between these works—and the greatness of Mommsen's achievement.

42. Mommsen (supra n. 39) 1¹:IX.

were not (as Jochen Bleicken reminds us)[43] simply excogitated by Mommsen, but derived directly from Roman sources. The pivots of the *Staatsrecht*, the concepts of *magistratus* and *privatus*, of *imperium* and *auspicium*, of *potestas* and *coercitio*, are all Roman notions familiar to every reader of Latin literature.

But legal notions are often a poor guide to history, and nowhere is this more glaringly obvious than in Mommsen's treatment of the institution of the principate. The second volume of the *Staatsrecht* treats of "die einzelnen Magistraturen" ("the individual magistracies"). It begins with the kingdom and ends with the principate. That *princeps qua princeps* was a magistrate is dubious,[44] but a special fury of criticism today greets Mommsen's theory of dyarchy, the co-rule of the princeps and the senate.[45] This criticism is based on a grievous misunderstanding. The accusers depict Mommsen as oblivious to the historical and social realities of the empire, a picture neither likely nor reasonable. Where the source of power lay Mommsen was well aware, but he was not writing of the *arcana imperii*.[46] The "formal and official theory of the Principate as the government of the Senate and the People" was for him "hollow"—as hollow as the presentation of the senatorial government in the Republic as the "Selbstregierung der freien Bürgerschaft" ("the self-government of the free citizenry").[47] An essential feature of a republican magistracy was the strict delimitation of its sphere of competence; in the principate the notion of magisterial competence is so broad that it comes close to license: "der Competenzbegriff . . . ist in dem Principat so weit ausgedehnt, dass diese Schranken factisch der Schrankenlosigkeit nahe kommen."[48] It is only at this point, after all these caveats, that Mommsen formulates his idea of dyarchy. From the point of view of public law—*staatsrechtlich*—the principate cannot be described as monarchy; hence "the description as dyarchy . . . will express more cor-

---

43. J. Bleicken, *Lex Publica: Gesetz und Recht in der römischen Republik* (Berlin 1975) 16–51, esp. 23–24, 36–38, 41, 49. For a recent appraisal and critique of the *Staatsrecht*, see also Y. Thomas, *Mommsen et l'"Isolierung" du Droit (Rome, l'Allemagne et l'État)*, published separately (Paris 1982) and as the introduction to the reprint of the French translation of the *Staatsrecht*. Thomas' study will be read with profit in conjunction with the remarks of G. Crifò, review of Thomas' *Mommsen*, SDHI 52 (1986) 485–91; and E. Gabba, review of Thomas' *Mommsen*, Athenaeum 64 (1986) 245–47.

44. Mommsen himself admits ([supra n. 39] 2³: 749, n. 2) that he does not know of any source in which the emperor is described as *magistratus*.

45. Cf., for instance, Z. Yavetz, "The *Res Gestae* and Augustus' Public Image," in F. Millar and E. Segal, eds., *Caesar Augustus: Seven Aspects* (Oxford 1984) 24.

46. Mommsen (supra n. 39) 2³ VII.

47. Ibid., 747.

48. Ibid., 747–48.

rectly the essence of this remarkable institution." [49] The essence, *das Wesen*, of which Mommsen writes is—in contraposition to von Premerstein and Syme—not the historical and social essence of the principate but solely legal. The principate was a social institution of which Mommsen intended to give, and gave, a legal description.[50] Or as Wolfgang Kunkel expressed it, Mommsen largely excluded from his discussion the political and social aspects not because he failed to see them or was not interested in them ("das Gegenteil beweist jede Seite seiner Römischen Geschichte," "each page of his *Roman History* proves the opposite"), but because he wished to present the Roman state "as a pure legal system" ("als reine Rechtsordnung").[51]

"Das reale" is buried in a footnote.[52] Commenting on the claim of Augustus in the *Res Gestae* (6.12) *in consulatu sexto et septimo . . . rem publicam ex mea potestate in senat[us populique Romani a]rbitrium transtuli,* Mommsen writes that this testimony and other contemporary texts are "decisive for the formal interpretation of the act," and he adds that among the contemporaries only the Greek Strabo gives "the real interpretation." And Strabo (13.3.25 = p. 840) stresses that Augustus, far from restoring the Republic, remained *kyrios* of war and peace for life. Mommsen expressed the same thought even more clearly in his commentary on the *Res Gestae: Vides aetatis Augustae auctores Romanos plane ut facit ipse Augustus rem ita narrare, quasi vere tum rem publicam reddiderit; solus Strabo . . . liberius sic enuntiat non rerum speciem, sed ipsam rem.*[53] Mommsen was well aware that the *Staatsrecht* dealt with the *species rerum*, but unlike many recent interpreters he also knew that no *res* exists *sine specie.*

If Mommsen had ever written a fourth volume of his *Römische Geschichte,*[54] he probably would have preempted Syme—not in his proso-

49. Ibid., 748: "Die Bezeichnung als Dyarchie, das heisst als eine zwischen dem Senat einer- und dem Princeps als dem Vertrauensmann der Gemeinde andrerseits ein für allemal getheilte Herrschaft, würde das Wesen dieser merkwürdigen Institution zutreffender ausdrücken."

50. Alan Watson's definition comes to mind: "A legal institution is a social institution looked at from the legal point of view" (*The Evolution of Law* [Baltimore 1985] 111).

51. W. Kunkel, "Theodor Mommsen als Jurist," *Chiron* 14 (1984) 371.

52. Mommsen (supra n. 39) 2³: 746, n. 2.

53. T. Mommsen, *Res Gestae Divi Augusti²* (Berlin 1883) 146.

54. The third volume ends with the battle of Thapsus. Why Mommsen failed to produce the history of the empire has been the subject of much speculation; see Demandt (infra n. 55) 497–506 (a full catalogue of various opinions); G. Bowersock, "Gibbon's Historical Imagination," *The American Scholar* 57 (1988) 46–47. For the history of the composition of the *Römische Geschichte* and for its evaluation and appreciation, see L. Wickert, *Theodor Mommsen*, vol. 3 (Frankfurt 1969) 399–422, 618–75, and vol. 4

pographical analyses, but as a Tacitean judgment of Augustus. His university lectures on the empire are fairly well documented, and in these lectures he spoke with the voice and style of *Römische Geschichte*, not that of the *Staatsrecht*. He shares with Syme an admiration for Gibbon and Tacitus, and Asinius Pollio; he shares with Syme the conviction that in the empire "die Geschichte in dem Kabinett liegt," and, like Syme, he detests Augustus but appreciates his achievement.[55]

In July 1858, in his *Antrittsrede* as a member of the Berlin Academy, Mommsen forcefully pleaded for "die Verschmelzung von Geschichte und Jurisprudenz" as "die erste Bedingung organischer Behandlung der römischen Dinge" ("the amalgamation of history and jurisprudence" as "the first premise for an organic treatment of Roman matters").[56] This is still our goal; for the *Staatsrecht*, in its grand fallacy that it is possible to describe and understand a social organism by studying only its formal law, has (against the wish of its creator) largely eliminated history,[57] and *The Roman Revolution*, in its contempt for fiction, is oblivious to the fact that fictions abide too.

The reconciliation of Mommsen and Syme, of law and power, is a Vergilian and Augustan theme, ambiguous like the principate itself:

Remo cum fratre Quirinus . . . / iura dabunt.[58]

(1980) 332–48; and the introduction of K. Christ to the new edition of Mommsen's *Römische Geschichte*, vol. 8 (Munich 1976) 7–66 (= Christ [supra n. 9] 26–73).

55. Cf. V. Ehrenberg, "Theodor Mommsens Kolleg über römische Kaisergeschichte," *Heidelberger Jahrbb.* 4 (1960) 94–107 (= K. F. Stroheker and A. J. Graham, eds., *Polis und Imperium: Beiträge zur Alten Geschichte* [Zurich and Stuttgart 1965] 613–30, esp. 618–21); and, above all, A. Demandt, "Die Hensel-Nachschriften zu Mommsens Kaiserzeit-Vorlesung," *Gymnasium* 93 (1986) 497–519, esp. 512–15. On the striking similarities between Mommsen's and Syme's art of writing and understanding history, see Alföldy (supra n. 10) 33–40.

56. T. Mommsen, *Reden und Aufsätze*² (Berlin 1905) 36.

57. But it is important to remember that in his *Abriss des römischen Staatsrechts* (Leipzig 1893), before proceeding to a systematic presentation, Mommsen devoted the whole first book to a historical outline of constitutional developments. Cf. Gabba (supra n. 43) 246. Crifò (supra n. 43) 487, rightly observes that "Lo stesso Mommsen . . . la cui intera attività era rivolta al superamento della frattura [tra 'storia' e 'diritto'] paradossalmente . . . aveva contribuito con la sua 'scientificizzazione' dell'esperienza pubblicistica romana a costruire un sistema di diritto pubblico che con la storia sembrava aver poco a che fare."

58. Verg. *Aen.* 1.292–93.

3

Garden Parlors: Nobles and Birds

Birds in a garden, dancing, jumping, feeding, perched or caught in flight, are a frequent motif in Roman landscape painting. The frescoes in the house of Livia on the Palatine come to mind and the garden pictures in Pompeii which the happy conjunction of Wilhelmina and Stanley Jashemski's archaeological scholarship and artistic camera brought so brilliantly to life.[1] These paintings reflect the genteel mode of leisurely existence which in the last century of the Republic became a norm for a Roman of culture, and of means.

The third book of Varro's *De Re Rustica* is a treatise *de villaticis fructibus*: here the birds and their masters received a literary monument. The sober interlocutors in Varro's dialogue were passionately interested in *fructus*, the profits to be derived from a villa, but they were also devoted to the pleasures of the palate and of the eyes. There are two kinds of aviaries, explains one of the characters in the dialogue, one for profit in which birds are kept in enclosures and fattened for the market. The other is *delectationis causa*, for pleasure, *ut Varro hic fecit noster sub Casino*.[2] Having thus skilfully introduced his estate near Casinum Varro proceeds to describe its fabulous aviary. It was a maze in which his guests may have been as easily lost as modern commentators are today.[3] Walking alongside the bank of a stream, and meandering through the aviary where water fowl floated in ponds and all kind of singing birds were enclosed with nets between the rows of columns, the visitor would finally arrive at the *Museum*, where Varro worked and where he kept his library.

Varro's *Museum* reminds one of the *Academia* and *Lyceum* in Cicero's Tusculan estate and of Atticus' *Amaltheum* which Cicero was so eager to imitate in his villa at Arpinum.[4] These are the hallmarks of the cultural parvenus who in their vast domains strove to recreate the philosophical gardens of Athens and emulate the erudition of Alexandria. These country-side pavilions with fancy names replaced the agoras, palaestras and gymnasia of the Greeks.[5]

For of all the ridiculous things, the uncountable *ineptiae*, what is more ridiculous than the Greek custom of engaging in disputes with any person in any place about matters either defying solution or frivolous? Cicero puts this sentiment into the mouth of the orator Crassus;[6] he himself certainly did not share Crassus' dislike for the matters discussed by the Greeks, but could not agree more with him that both the *locus* of the Greek dialogues and the choice of interlocutors were most unsuitable for the Romans. And indeed the first Roman dialogue on record strikes an unmistakably Roman tone: the father instructs his son and not the master his pupils, as in Greece; and the subject of the dialogue is not philosophy but law. Its author was M. Iunius Brutus, praetor ca. 140 B.C., one of the founders of the *ius civile*.[7] If the form of this dialogue was Roman, the familiar series of legal *responsa*,[8] its scenery was not less so: its three books are located in succession *in Privernati*, *in Albano* and *in Tiburti*, the three country estates of Brutus. Thus the Romans found the *aptus locus* for their literary dialogue, the *villa*; and the proper interlocutors, the *principes civitatis*, their sons, friends and relatives, the future *principes*.

Cicero became the acknowledged master of this genre. Four consulars appear in his dialogue *De Oratore* (composed in 55): the two protagonists, the supreme orators L. Licinius Crassus (cos. 95) and M. Antonius (cos. 99); the victor of the Cimbri, Q. Lutatius Catulus (cos. 102); and the elder statesman, Crassus' father-in-law, the famous lawyer and augur, Q. Mucius Scaevola (cos. 117). In the colloquy also participate three younger men, C. Aurelius Cotta, the future consul of 75, at the dramatic date of the dialogue, September 91, a candidate for the tribunate of the plebs; P. Sulpicius Rufus who three years later as a tribune of the plebs was to impress an indelible stamp on the history of the Republic; and C. Iulius Caesar Strabo, Catulus' half-brother, the curule aedile in 90 and unsuccessful candidate for the consulship in 88, the author of tragedies and perhaps incongruously enough renowned as an orator for his *facetiae*.

The company met in the villa of Crassus in Tusculum. Its portico and palaestra evoked memories of the gymnasia and disputes of the Greeks (*De Orat.* 2. 20, Crassus speaking). The plane tree in the garden reminded Scaevola of the plane tree in Plato's *Phaedrus*; but while Socrates threw himself down on the grass, the Roman party reposed on benches; the servants brought cushions.[9] The concluding discussion took place *in media silva*, a shady grove in the center of the estate.[10]

A similar cast of characters inhabits the *De Re Publica* (composed in 54-51): the towering figure of Scipio Aemilianus; his trusted friend the sage C. Laelius (cos. 140); the great jurist M' Manilius (cos. 149); the follower of Carneades C. Furius Philus (cos. 136); Scipio's nephew (*sororis filius*), the stern Stoic Q. Aelius Tubero; the two sons-in-law of Laelius, at the time of the dialogue in 129 of quaestorian age, C. Fannius and Q. Mucius Scaevola, both destined to become consuls (in 122 and in 117) and to gain fame, Fannius as a historian and Scaevola as a *iuris peritus*; Sp. Mummius, the refined brother of the brutish conqueror of Corinth; and the young P. Rutilius Rufus (cos. 105).

This time the dialogue is not staged in a country estate but in the Roman villa and *horti* of Scipio.[11] In fact all dialogues of Cicero (with the exception of the fifth book of the *De Finibus* and *Timaeus*, which are located in Athens and in Ephesus) take place in urban houses and country-side villas of the *principes*. Here is a synopsis of the *dialogorum loca*:[12]

De Oratore and *De Re Publica*: see above.

De Legibus: Cicero's villa in Arpinum, but on a metaphorical level an imitation of Plato's scenery in *The Laws*.[13] Cicero and his companions admire the oak of Marius (1.1) and stroll along the shady bank of Liris (1.14); they repose on an island in the Fibrenus (Cicero calls it his *palaestra*, 2.6) and in the afternoon return to the shade of the alders on the Liris (Macrob. *Sat.* 6.4.8).

De Partitione Oratoria: a villa of Cicero outside Rome.[14]

Brutus: Cicero's Roman house, *in pratulo propter Platonis statuam*.[15]

Hortensius: Lucullus' villa in Tusculum, *omni adparatu venustatis ornata*.[16]

Academica Priora: Catulus' (cos. 78) villa at Cumae; on the second day the scene is set in a colonnade (*in xysto*) in the villa of Hortensius at Bauli (*Acad.* 2.9).

De Finibus: the first dialogue is staged in Cicero's *Cumanum* (1.14; cf. 2.119: *finem fecimus et ambulandi et disputandi*); the second in the famed library in Lucullus' *Tusculanum* (3.7); the third disputation takes place in Athens during an *ambulatio postmeridiana* in the Academy (5.1).

Academica Posteriora: Varro's villa at Cumae (1.1; cf. 1.14: *consedimus omnes*). The scene of the second dialogue seems to have been laid out at the *Lacus Lucrinus*, not far from Varro's villa.[17]

Tusculanae Disputationes: Cicero's Tusculan villa (1.8–9, *aut sedens aut ambulans disputabam*). Before noon the discussion apparently took place in the upper gymnasium, the Lyceum; it was devoted to rhetoric. To discuss philosophy *post meridiem in Academiam descendimus* (2.9).

De Natura Deorum: the house of C. Aurelius Cotta (cos. 75), probably in Rome; the participants sit in an *exedra*.[18]

De Divinatione: the *Lyceum* in Cicero's *Tusculanum*. In the first book Cicero and his brother walk about (1.8: *cum ambulandi causa in Lyceum venissemus*), in the second book they are seated *in bibliotheca quae in Lyceo est* (2.8, cf. 2.150).[19]

De Fato: Cicero's *Puteolanum* (1.1).
Timaeus: the scene is laid out in Ephesus (fr. 1).
De Senectute: apparently Cato the Elder's house in Rome (1.3).
De Amicitia: the house of Laelius in Rome (1.5).

A charming set! It tells us something about literary conventions, and still more about Cicero himself. To own a villa, and especially a villa on the Campanian shore, was a symbol of status. But for a moralist only a thin line separated pleasing *amoenitas* from slothful *luxuria*:[20] "I scorn villas richly appointed, marble floors and panelled ceilings," exclaims Cicero.[21] His avowed ideal was the simplicity of the ancients,*nihil splendidum, nihil ornatum*.[22] He heaped scorn and contempt upon the heads of the *piscinarii*,[23] and yet it was deeply gratifying to him to have Lucullus and Hortensius for his neighbors.[24] He did not keep this sentiment merely to himself or to Atticus, he left a literary monument to testify to it: three of his dialogues were placed amidst "marble floors and panelled ceilings," amidst the *magnificentia* of Hortensius and Lucullus, and in two dialogues these two great *piscinarii* were honored with the leading roles: they dissected philosophy, not mullets. Deep in his heart Cicero the philosopher remained a *homo novus*.

The villas are arresting, but nothing is more revealing than the *dramatis personae*. Of Cicero's dialogues the two earliest ones, *D e Oratore* and *De Republica*, display the most numerous and the most elaborately interconnected cast of aristocratic characters. But his other dialogues also have a social message to impart. It will be useful to provide a full list of participants. I present it, for illustration and instruction, in Roman fashion, according to the *gradus dignitatis*:[25]

I. The consulars at the time of the dialogue or the future consuls:
1. Cicero himself, cos. 63 (*Leg., Part. Orat., Brut., Hort., Acad. Pr.* and *Post., Fin., Fat., Nat.D., Div., Tim.*)
2. Marcus Porcius Cato the Elder, cos. 195 (*Sen.*)
3. M' Manilius, cos. 149 (*Rep.*)
4. P. Cornelius Scipio Aemilianus, cos. 147, 134 (*Rep., Sen.*)
5. C. Laelius, cos. 140 (*Rep., Sen., Amic.*)
6. C. Furius Philus, cos. 136 (*Rep.*)
7. C. Fannius, cos. 122 (*Rep., Amic.*)
8. Q. Mucius Scaevola, cos. 117 (*De Or., Rep.*)
9. P. Rutilius Rufus, cos. 105 (*Rep.*)
10. Q. Lutatius Catulus, cos. 102 (*De Or.*)
11. M. Antonius, cos. 99 (*De Or.*)
12. L. Licinius Crassus, cos. 95 (*De Or.*)
13. Q. Lutatius Catulus, cos. 78 (*Hort., Acad. Pr.*)
14. C. Aurelius Cotta, cos. 75 (*Nat.D., De Or.*)

15. L. Licinius Lucullus, cos. 74 (*Hort., Acad. Pr.*)
16. Q. Hortensius, cos. 69 (*Hort., Acad. Pr.*)
17. M. Pupius Piso, cos. 61 (*Fin.*)
18. A. Hirtius, cos. 43 (*Fat.*)
19. Cicero's son Marcus, cos. suff. 30 (*Part. Or.*)

II. The praetorii at the time of the dialogue or the future praetors:
20. Cicero's brother Quintus, pr. 62 (*Leg., Fin., Div.*)
21. M. Terentius Varro, pr. probably soon after 76 (*Acad. Post.*)
22. P. Nigidius Figulus, pr. 58 (*Tim.*)
23. M. Porcius Cato, pr. 54 (*Fin.*)
24. L. Manlius Torquatus. pr. 49 (*Fin.*)
25. M. Iunius Brutus, pr. 44 (*Brut.*)

III. Other senators:
26. C. Iulius Caesar Strabo, aed. 90 (*De. Or.*)
27. Q. Aelius Tubero, tr. pl. before 129 (*Rep.*)
28. P. Sulpicius Rufus, tr. pl. 88 (*De Or.*)
29. C. Velleius, senator, perhaps tr. pl. before 90 (*Nat.D.*)
30. Sp. Mummius, as a member of a senatorial commission in 140–39 no doubt a senator[26] (*Rep.*)

IV. Others:
31. Q. Lucilius Balbus, no information available (*Nat. D.*)
32. C. Valerius Triarius, *praef. classis* under Pompey 49–48 (*Fin.*)
33. L. Tullius Cicero, Cicero's *frater patruelis*, no information available (*Fin.*)
34. T. Pomponius Atticus (*Leg., Brut., Fin., Acad. Post.*)
35. Cratippus, from (probably) 46 the head of the Peripatetic school in Athens (*Tim.*)

A fascinating list! The consuls, past or future, occupy more than half of its slots. Among the relatively few speakers who reached only the praetorship we have the *lumina* of Roman history and Latin letters: this was their entry ticket. Of the lower magistrates Caesar Strabo was patrician and a most colorful person, and the tribunes Aelius Tubero and Sulpicius Rufus were each remarkable in disparate ways; the latter would have certainly reached the highest magistracies had he not perished in the vortex of the civil war. Also Valerius Triarius fell as a young man, at the battle of Pharsalus, it would appear. Wealth, scholarship, political influence, and Cicero's *amicitia* procured a spot for the knight Atticus. The figures in Cicero's dialogues enter the stage ostensibly as men of letters, as friends and relatives of Scipio, of Laelius, of Cicero himself, but it is remarkable how few of them failed to combine their literary culture with political significance. In this context the *De Natura Deorum* stands out as a social anomaly: out of the three principal speakers (not counting Cicero) two appear to have been men of no consequence, politically speaking. Velleius is introduced as a simple senator, and Balbus' fame rested on philosophy, not magistracy.[27]

But the oddest is the last name on the list. No Greek philosopher appears as a participant in a Roman dialogue. A demonstration of Roman tact, says Hirzel;[28] arrogance is a better word. Greek rhetors and philosophers may have been teachers and confidants of the Romans; social chasm separated them. Cicero's dialogues did not treat only of oratory and philosophy; they were social statements. To have Greek characters associating in full view and on an equal level with the *principes civitatis* would be false and inappropriate. But if no Panaetius, no Posidonius, not even Polybius *noster* made a dialogue, then why should have obscure Cratippus? That Cicero wished to honor the man who presided over the Peripatos when Cicero's son studied in Athens[29] is a lame explanation. Cratippus is to be struck from the list of *dialogorum personae*; the discussion in the *Timeaus*, if it really was a dialogue, will have been sustained, *comme il faut*, by the Roman senators alone, Cicero and Nigidius.

Ambulating in their gardens and amateurishly talking of philosophy the Roman aristocrats had every reason to feel superior to their Greek tutors: the Greeks were the masters of argument, but they were the masters of the world. They realized the dream of Plato, and improved upon it. To demonstrate the ideal state, the *optimus status civitatis*, Scipio Aemilianus needed only to point to the growth of Rome, whereas Plato was forced to excogitate a fictitious construct.[30]

But not only the place and the participants in the dialogue had to be *apti* but also the time. The dispute in the *De Oratore* takes place during the Roman games,[31] when the statesmen were able to spare a few days of *otium* from their pressing obligations, and it is the Latin holidays that provide leisure for the discussion in *The Republic* and in *On the Nature of Gods*.[32] The philosophical *ambulatio* in the *De Legibus* is set on the longest day of the year, the Midsummer Day, a time for merry festivities.[33]

When Cicero stood at the helm of the state he was able to spare for his literary endeavours—so he intimates—only *subsiciva tempora*, odds and ends of time, only a few days *ad rusticandum*.[34] The enforced retirement from politics under the dictatorship of Caesar provided him with *otium* unbounded and unwelcome,[35] but how fortunate for European culture. Philosophical compilations poured from his pen, and there was no urgent need to justify to many of his colleagues so frivolous an activity befitting a Greek client rather than a Roman statesman.[36] Indications of the dramatic time of a dialogue become sparser and less detailed; *cum inambularem in xysto et essem otiosus domi* is all we get in *Brutus*.[37] It is hardly by chance that the three dialogues set in a time when the republic was still run by the *principes*, *On the Orator*, *On the Republic*, and *On the Nature of the Gods*, were all placed on the holidays.

If the color of Cicero's dialogues was Roman, the *principes* in their urban mansions and country retreats, their topics became more and more Greek: not only oratory or the constitution of the state, the subjects of eminent practical importance and which Roman statesmen discussed in Cicero's dialogues with an air of supreme authority,[38] but increasingly abstruse philosophy. It was a bold move to introduce Roman nobles into this domain of the Greeks. Why did they not talk of law? Out of thirty-four Roman characters in Cicero's dialogues only five, none of them Cicero's contemporary, are mentioned as outstanding jurists in the *liber singularis enchiridii* of Sex. Pomponius, a legal scholar who flourished under Hadrian and Antoninus Pius.[39] These five persons are:

1. M. Cato, but in the *De Senectute* the Censor speaks about old age not law, and indeed he was an orator skilled in law rather than a jurist *sensu stricto* as, for instance, his son Cato Licinianus.

2. M' Manilius, the author of *venalium vendendorum leges*, but in the *De Republica* he is introduced as a jurist only in an oblique manner: at 1.20 Laelius jocularly suggests that Manilius issue an *interdictum* concerning the appearance of the two suns; at 3.17 Furius Philus in his discourse on the arbitrariness of the law styles him *iuris interpres* who after the enactment of each new statute *alia iura dicat*.

3. and 4. Two further characters from the *De Republica*, Q. Aelius Tubero and P. Rutilius Rufus. Tubero does not say anything about law, and Rutilius was at the time of the dialogue too young to say anything.

5. L. Licinius Crassus, whom Pomponius confused with P. Licinius Crassus Mucianus (cos. 131).

Another character should be added to this list, Q. Mucius Scaevola the Augur. In *Brutus* Cicero does not reckon him among the orators, but praises him as being supreme in civil law.[40] In the *De Republica* he speaks but once (1.33), in the *De Amicitia* he and Fannius form merely a passive background for Laelius' monologue. In the *De Oratore*, overshadowed by Crassus and Antonius, he exits at the end of Book I.[41]

Even if matters of law loomed large in this book, Antonius and Crassus were not engaged in a systematic exposition of legal principles; they merely debated, with passion and erudition, the place of *ius civile* in the education and practice of the orator, a very different proposition. For Antonius the knowledge of law was of secondary importance: his own ignorance of the matter had never hampered him in cases he argued in court. To be effective an orator need not be a *iuris prudens*, an expert in abstruse and technical parts of the *ius civile*.[42]

Crassus argued that the orator must master the civil law very well: *perdiscendum ius civile*, and he went on to illustrate this point with a plethora of examples.[43] Cicero has him sing a most extravagant praise of *ius civile*: the small *libellus* of the XII Tables surpasses all the libraries of all philosophers both in the weight of its authority and the wealth of its usefulness; the study of *ius civile* is wondrously charming and delightful; the *domus* of the *iuris consultus* is like an *oraculum civitatis*.[44]

In view of all these *laudes iuris* Cicero felt he may well have been expected by his friends to compose a special dialogue on this most Roman subject of all, the *ius civile*. At the outset of the dialogue *On the Laws* various topics for discussion are brought up. Atticus suggests the *ius civile*: Cicero will surely be able to expound this matter in a more refined way than had been done previously.[45] When we read in the *Brutus* Cicero's praise of Servius Sulpicius—for his predecessors the *ius civile* had merely been a useful tool, Servius alone made an art of it[46]—we may indeed wonder why he had never proceeded to write a dialogue named, for instance, *Sulpicius sive de iure civili*. Cicero's reply to Atticus is very characteristic. The *ius civile* as handled by the *iuris consulti* is useful and necessary, but it is also extremely trivial. Surely you do not want me to compose a treatise *de stillicidiorum ac de parietarum iure*, on the law of eaves and house-walls?[47] Cicero's attitude was that of an orator; he shared with Crassus his appreciation of the civil law, but at the same time was repelled by its pettiness which made the jurist appear as "a pettifogger, a crier of legal actions, a chanter of formulas, a catcher of syllables."[48] The subject for Cicero the statesman and philosopher who fancied himself a Roman Plato was the *leges*, the constitution of an ideal state.[49] The *ius civile*, petty and practical, made Rome great; the quest after an ideal made Greek philosophy great, Greek states pitiful. Cicero the legislator did not fare much better.

If not law, then perhaps a dialogue about another hallowed subject, agriculture? No, Cicero was definitely not in the mood to provide a literary version of the Carthaginian Mago's famous handbook. There is no reason to learn the *libri* of Mago by heart.[50] Again, like the law, the subject was not elevated enough. This task was reserved for Varro.

Varro was the only character in Cicero's dialogues who himself was engaged in writing dialogues. This makes his literary contacts with Cicero doubly interesting. As early as 54 when Cicero was working on the *De Republica* Varro coveted a place in a dialogue of Cicero;[51] it took him nine years to break through the Ciceronian wall of literary nobles. In 45 Varro renewed his efforts: he again communicated his wish to Atticus, Atticus exerted pressure and persuasion on Cicero, and Cicero finally decided to transfer his *Academica* from Catulus, Lucullus and Hortensius, the *homines nobiles*, but hardly scholars, *nullo modo philologi*,[52] to Varro, the *vir Romanorum eruditissimus*, as Quintilian calls him.[53] In June 45 Cicero sent Varro a copy of the *Academica* together with an elaborately polite dedicatory letter.[54] "I placed our discussion in my *Cumanum*, in the presence of Atticus," Cicero wrote. "You might wonder," he continued, "when you read it, that we were talking about matters which we in fact had never discussed together, but you are well conversant with the dialogue convention." This convention applied of course also to other dialogues of Cicero, and to Varro's dialogues as well.[55] Though Varro employed some form of dialogue in at least some of his *Menippean Satires* and in the *Logostorici* they present today a morass of fragments and conjectures.[56] If we seek *terra firma* it is to the *Res Rusticae* that we have to turn.

First, the subject. For Cato the Elder the *vir bonus* was *bonus agricola*[57] or, as he put it in his instructions for his son: *Vir bonus, Marce fili, colendi peritus, cuius ferramenta splendent.*[58] The Roman senate as an institution was interested in books mostly in a negative way: are they pernicious to the morals and established cult? Hence the burning of suspicious books.[59] But books on agriculture were always wholesome, even if they came from the land of a bitter foe. After the destruction of Carthage the senate set up a committee to procure an official translation from the Punic of Mago's erudite manual.[60]

Thus at the beginning of Latin prose stand historical annals, legal *responsa* and textbooks of agriculture, Cato's *De Re Rustica* being the oldest preserved prose work. If we exclude *De Consulatu Suo* and *D e Iure Civili In Artem Redigendo*, lost and of little literary consequence, Cicero did not write on any of these subjects, a very unRoman attitude indeed. Cato included a section on agriculture in his *libri ad filium*; Varro twisting this very Roman concept of instruction wrote his *D e Re Rustica* as a manual for his wife: in this way he will be able to give her advice even after his death (1.1.1–4). But it was for him also a sort of literary testament: "my eightieth year admonishes me to collect my pack (*sarcinas colligere*) before I depart from life."[61]

There were many agricultural authors before Varro and many after him; none of them wrote a dialogue. The originality of Varro stands out in full relief: on the one hand a strict and schematic manual—in Book one, for instance, he presents in turn eighty-one technical points—but on the other the author of the *Menippean Satires* imparts to this dry topic charm and laughter. His style catches one's eye and ear and exercises the linguistic abilities of the modern reader to the utmost: as J. Heurgon felicitously observed, the style of Varro is a strange amalgam of colloquial negligence and rhetorical artifice.[62] It is simultaneously a textbook, a comedy and a satire: the characters receive their roles, *partes*,[63] they come and go, they speak and listen, they move from one topic or *actus*[64] to another.[65] The dialogue is a festival of puns and jokes. In serious Peripatetic garb the old Cynic frolics.

It was a time-honored convention—which Cicero confesses to have violated in the *Academica Priora*[66]—not to let the characters speak over their heads. Varro embraced wholeheartedly this rule, and gave it a comical turn. Not only are the real interests of his interlocutors consistent with their *partes*, also hilariously congruous are their names. Varro's wife Fundania bought a farm, *fundus*. The avowed purpose of the *De Re Rustica* was to instruct Fundania how to manage her *fundus*. This triggered a chain reaction of name puns. In Book I, devoted to agriculture proper, the land and its fruits, six persons appear (in addition to Varro who figures in all three books): Varro's father-in-law C. Fundanius and his linguistic twin L. Fundilius; two further agricultural mutants, C. Agrius and P. Agrasius; C. Licinius Stolo, a nice etymological and antiquarian touch for one ancestor of this "sucker" (*stolo*) sponsored a famous agrarian law, and another "was the first to lead the people, for the voting on the laws, from the *comitium* into the seven *iugera* of the forum" (admittedly a rather recherché joke);[67] finally Cn. Tremelius Scrofa ("Sow"), a great authority on agriculture. He speaks wisely and profusely, but acquires his own comical part only in Book II.

This book has as its subject the *res pecuaria*, and Scrofa naturally enough lectures, *inter alia*, about swine (2.4.1). The second *actus* comes, on the larger animals, and one of the interlocutors, Vaccius by name, exclaims "Since there are cows in it, that is where my part comes in" (2.5.2–3). When the party broke up Scrofa and Varro departed *in hortos ad Vitulum* (2.11.12). Varro dedicated this dialogue to Turranius Niger (2. *praef.* 6), who was a dedicated cattleman and whose name was probably connected with the Umbrian word for "bull" (*toru*).[68] The recipient of Book III, on the birds, was, however, entirely on the comical mark: he was called Pinnius, "Mr. Feathery" (3.1.1; 17.10). Among the *dialogi personae* five *aves* appear: L. Cornelius Merula ("Blackbird"), Fircellius Pavo ("Peacock"),

Minucius Pica ("Magpie"), M. Petronius Passer ("Sparrow"), and Pantuleius Parra ("Owl"). They are mostly mute; only the Blackbird Merula was very talkative and he lectured about bird-houses, pigeons, doves, hens, geese and ducks; and when Fircellius Pavo departed he was encouraged to speak freely about peacocks for "if you should say anything out of the way about them, he would perhaps have a bone to pick with you for the credit of the family" (3.6.1). Merula may indeed have been an authority on this subject, but I suspect there is more to his perorations than meets the ear: the blackbird was believed to be capable of human speech.[69]

In Cicero's dialogues birds do not speak: they make noise. When at Cicero's bidding the Epicurean Atticus admitted that the gods govern the universe, he observed with a sigh of relief: "The singing of the birds and the rushing of the streams," *concentus avium* and *strepitus fluminum*, "relieve me from all fear that I may be overheard by my fellow disciples."[70] But birds were above all the winged messengers of gods, the carriers of omens. *Nuntia fulva Iovis miranda visa figura*, "Jove's golden messenger of wondrous form," the eagle which Jupiter sent to Marius as a presage of good tidings, soars prominently at the outset of the *De Legibus* (1.2). Varro in his *Antiquitates Rerum Divinarum* devoted one learned book to the augurs;[71] he was intimately conversant with the birds of augury and omen. The comical dimension of this avian lore was too exquisite to be allowed to slip by. Of course Varro's augural birds are scaled down from the heroic flight (literal and figurative) of Cicero's *Marius* to the more mundane interests of his interlocutors. Of eagles he does not speak, rather of chickens. Eagles were reserved for momentous occasions and for the poets; the everyday communication with the gods was conducted through the intermediary of the *pulli*. Chickens were the first birds to be raised in a villa: first by the Roman augurs for their auspices, next by the *patres familias* in the country (3.3.5). The *mise en scene* in the third book is deservedly famous for its wit and inventiveness. On a hot day, during the election of the aediles, Varro and his fellow *tribulis* the senator Q. Axius seek shade in the *Villa Publica* in the Campus Martius—we need not be reminded that seeking shade is a standard Ciceronian device of introducing a conversation.[72] There the augur Appius Claudius Pulcher sat on a bench flanked by Cornelius Merula and Fircellius Pavo on his left, and Minucius Pica and M. Petronius Passer on his right. "Will you accept us into your aviary?",[73] Axius asked with a smile, and so a dispute about the villas and their *aves* was off to an auspicious start.

The priestly bird-watcher sitting among the "birds" is a sight comical enough especially if we realize that the augural birds often come in pairs, two on the left and two on the right. The standard formula for the auspices from the flight of birds ran as follows (Plaut. *Asin.* 260–61):

picus et cornix ab laeva, corvos parra ab dextera consuadent

[Woodpecker and crow on the left, raven and barn-owl on the right]

"Go ahead," they counsel.

Appius sat among the birds all right, but they were the wrong birds![74] Soon a fifth bird appeared, Pantuleius Parra, a bird of evil omen,[75] and he brought bad news indeed: the *custos*[76] of the candidate whom Pavo supported was apprehended while stuffing the box with false ballots (3.5.18).

Many a reader of Varro would now wonder: are these people with funny names for real or are they merely fictitious? But jokes about figments would fall flat. All the names which Varro employs are independently attested, in literature and inscriptions. Varro himself points out that Roman names, both *nomina* and *cognomina*, were often derived from various animals.[77] And indeed one has only to think of the heroic Decii Mures, named after that most easily freightened of all animals, to realize the comical potential of Roman nomenclature. Varro's dialogue is an exquisite pun on Roman name system. He knew his audience: the Romans thoroughly enjoyed this type of humor.[78]

But at the same time Varro's dialogue is also a paean to the Italy of agricultural entrepreneurs, sturdy and robust in their *mores* and their language. As C. Nicolet perceptively observed, the *De Legibus* of Cicero is in many respects "un véritable manifeste municipal,"[79] the praise of great Romans who came from small *municipia*, like Cato, Marius, Cicero himself, the praise of their way of life and their (in the past) modest farms. But how much closer to the pulse of Italy is Varro's dialogue! Surely the people in small towns of Italy much oftener talked of hogs than of natural law. Philosophically Arpinum was for Cicero his *germana patria* but practically a summer retreat; for Varro's townsmen from Reate who populate the pages of the *De Re Rustica* this Sabine town was their true home and not only a distant cradle.

Out of twenty interlocutors[80] in Varro's dialogue (two of them only potential speakers) only one was a true noble: Appius Claudius Pulcher, consul in 54 and censor in 50, Cicero's colleague on the augural college and the elder brother of the notorious P. Clodius. Several reasons account for his appearance. First his fame as augur.[81] If an augur was to figure in a dialogue devoted to birds, Appius was the person. His *praenomen* offered an additional bonus: in a nice display of popular etymology Appius claims to know everything about

bees, *apes* (3.16). Next, the Sabine origin of his family and his personal contacts with Reate: he was involved in some capacity in the dispute between Interamna and Reate concerning the *Lacus Velinus*;[82]
when on this occasion he recently visited Reate he was lavishly entertained by Q. Axius: the sumptuous fare was the birds of course (3.2.3).
This Reatine legal and gastronomical connection provided for a marvellously smooth opening of the dialogue in Book III: Appius and
Axius meet in Rome at the aedilician elections and start
talking—about what else?—birds!

Two senators of praetorian rank follow, Varro himself and Cn.
Tremelius Scrofa,[83] the seventh man in his family to reach the praetorship (2.4.2). Their immediate contact with agriculture is underscored by the fact that they were colleagues on the board of twenty *a d
agros dividendos Campanos* (1.2.10) under Caesar's agrarian laws. C.
Fundanius, Varro's father-in-law (1.2.1) was quaestor ca. 100;[84] Q.
Axius of Reate, explicitly introduced as senator (3.2.1), was probably
also of quaestorian rank. Q. Lucienus *senator*, a land-owner in Epirus
(2.5.1), about whom nothing is known beyond this notice, closes this
short and undistinguished list of certain senators.[85] But L. Cornelius
Merula, *consulari familia ortus* (3.2.2) and C. Licinius Stolo, who also
had distinguished ancestors (1.2.9), may have been senators as well.[86]

Next, the equestrians. Surprisingly enough, the list comprises
only three names: T. Pomponius Atticus, the mutual friend of Cicero
and Varro; Cossinius (his *praenomen* is lost in a gap at the beginning of
Book II), no doubt identical with L. Cossinius, *eques Romanus* and a
friend of Atticus.[87] He is introduced as one of the rich cattle-owners
in Epirus (2. *praef.* 6; 2.1.1), which explains his close contacts with
Atticus, another Epirotan *latifondista*. The third equestrian is C.
Agrius, *eques Romanus Socraticus* (1.2.1).

P. Agrasius, *publicanus* (1.2.1), may well have been an *eques*.[88] This
is true also of other characters, but it is perhaps more likely that they
belonged to the stratum just below the senators and equestrians, the
municipal aristocracy. They were the *domi nobiles*, as Cicero calls
them, the backbone of Italy. These were the people who voted in the
centuriate assembly in the first class and decided the consular and
praetorian contests, and who through their network of *vicinitates* controlled the elections in the tribal assembly. To cultivate them was the
first commandment of every politician, and in Varro's dialogue we see
the patrician Appius Claudius doing just that. His friends named after
birds were undoubtedly *domi nobiles*: we can certainly surmise this as
regards Pantuleius Parra, Minucius Pica, M. Petronius Passer, and we
know it for certain with respect to Fircellius Pavo of Reate (3.2.2):
Varro's maternal aunt, a rich lady, seems to have been a Fircellia

(3.2.15 in conjunction with 3.4.1). Then there are two rich land-owners in Epirus, who join the senator Lucienus and the *equites* Cossinius and Atticus: they are Murrius of Reate[89] (2.6.1), who speaks of that famous Sabine specialty, asses and mules, and our old acquaintance Vaccius. And finally we have L. Fundilius, the overseer, *aedituus*, of the temple of Tellus (2.1.2), and a certain Menates (2.1.1; 8.1; 11.12), probably also an *aedituus*, in Rome or rather in Epirus.[90] These two men, for quite disparate reasons, never come to speak.

The contrast between the characters in Cicero's dialogues and in Varro's *De Re Rustica* could hardly be more profound. Excluding few exceptions, names, station, culture and language separated them. But it would be premature to conclude that Varro manifested anti-noble feelings. It was the subject-matter that dictated the choice of characters, and the choice of style. To rectify the balance we should consider another work of Varro, the *Logistorici*. The *Logistorici* appears to have been dialogues (in seventy-six books) similar in form to Cicero's *Cato De Senectute* or *Laelius De Amicitia*.[91] Double titles of this type, for instance *Pius De Pace*, are the prosopographer's treasure trove. We know sixteen (or perhaps seventeen) names that figured in the title of a *logistoricus*; fourteen can be assigned with certainty or a great degree of probability to known historical persons.[92] Of the men thus honored we have:

I. Nine consuls: C. Marius, Q. Mucius Scaevola (cos. 95), Q. Caecilius Metellus Pius (cos. 80), C. Scribonius Curio (cos. 76), Cn. Aurelius Orestes (cos. 71), Q. Caecilius Metellus Nepos[93] (cos. 57), M. Valerius Messala (cos. 53), M. Claudius Marcellus (cos. 51), Q. Fufius Calenus (cos. 47).

II. Three praetors: the famous historian, L. Cornelius Sisenna (pr. 78), M. Aemilius Scaurus (pr. 56), M. Iuventius Lateranensis (pr. 51).

III. One senator of quaestorian rank: Varro's father-in-law C. Fundanius.

IV. One eques: T. Pomponius Atticus.

The social paradigm stands out in all clarity: in a literary dialogue history and philosophy were a preserve of the highest senatorial aristocracy. Only people attached to the author of a dialogue by close ties of family or friendship could break through the ranks of the nobles which both Cicero and Varro were laboriously instructing. Agriculture was, however, a very different proposition: no obstacle of *urbanitas* or *genus* barred entry. Varro strictly followed *to prepon*: in the *Res Rusticae* it is Scrofa who speaks of swine, in the *Logistorici* the topic of the *Marius* is *fortuna*.

The dialogues of Cicero find their congenial surrounding in the *amoenitas* of private villas. Villas figure prominently in the *Res*

Rusticae but only as a subject for discussion. The first dialogue, about *fundi* and *agri*, is placed, very characteristically, in the temple of Tellus[94] on the *feriae sementivae*,[95] the Sowing Festival (1.2.1). This location is a program and a proclamation: agriculture is a hallowed occupation and not merely a private pastime of the urbanites, like philosophy. The religious aura is further bestowed on the subject by Varro's invocation at the outset of the first book of the twelve deities of agriculture, the Father Jupiter and Tellus, the Mother Earth, Sol and Luna, Ceres and Liber, Robigus and Flora, Minerva and Venus, Lympha and Bonus Eventus. But this serious and holy subject receives a jocular form. The dialogue thus faithfully reproduces the solemnity and merriment of rustic festivals.

The setting is ingenious. Varro, his father-in-law, Scrofa and Stolo, Agrius and Agrasius come to dinner at the temple of Tellus at the invitation of L. Fundilius, the keeper of the temple.[96] Waiting for his return the company engages in a learned and merry discussion. Finally the freedman of Fundilius comes running with tears in his eyes. He invites the gentlemen to a funeral the next day. Whose funeral?—they cry. Why, his patron's funeral; he had just been stabbed in the crowd with a knife by someone, apparently by mistake. The company dispersed; "and we departed," writes Varro, "rather lamenting the mischances of human life than wondering that such thing had happened in Rome" (1.69.2–3). For the dramatic date of the dialogue is January 57 or 56,[97] the period of street fights between the gangs of Clodius and Milo.

Cicero was much more careful than the poor Fundilius. When in February 56 there again came to blows between the *nostri*, that is the thugs of Milo and the bandits of Clodius, Cicero hastily escaped from the scene of the *mêlée*, *ne quid in turba*, lest something untoward happen in the crowd.[98]

The conversation in Book II also takes place on a *dies festus* (2.11.12), and as the subject is the *res pecuaria* Ursinus concluded that the feast in question was the Palilia or Parilia (21 April), and that the participants met in Rome in the temple of Pales.[99] From 2.8.1 we learn that they were invited to offer the sacred cakes;[100] this suits the feast of Parilia very well indeed.[101] But the place of the dialogue will hardly be Rome; rather Epirus.[102] After all, the dialogue purports to recount the conversations which Varro had with cattle-owners of Epirus when during the war with the pirates (67 B.C.) he was in command of the fleets *inter Delum et Siciliam* (2. *praef.* 6).

But Varro's originality in choosing a startling setting for his dialogues shines especially in Book III. The place is the *Villa Publica*[103] in the Campus Martius, and the occasion the elections of the aediles

(3.2.1).[104] This gave Varro a marvellous opportunity to play on the various meanings of the term *villa*. His characters sit in a villa, but it is neither a farmstead nor a luxurious country-side retreat. It is not mares and asses, but the citizens who come to this villa from the field (*campus*); here the cohorts assemble when summoned by the consul for a levy; here the censors carry out the census of the people (3.2.3–7). But in Varro's dialogue, in a faint echo of Aristophanes' *Birds*, the *Villa* is occupied by the citizens with bird names who had just cast their ballots, and talking about birds, wait for the outcome of the voting. Finally the herald announces the results (3.17.1). Appius hurriedly rises and accompanied by Merula leaves the *Villa*. But the candidate supported by Varro and Axius was also victorious; a noise is heard on the propitious right, and the aedile-designate enters the *Villa*. Varro and Axius accompany him to the Capitol to render thanksgivings to Jupiter (3.17.10).

Thus agriculture blends with religion and politics, with all its frauds and joys. The bird-citizens symbolize the electorate very well, but it is the nobles who get elected to high offices and earn the right to stroll in literary gardens next to the statues of Plato and Aristotle.

NOTES

1. W. F. Jashemski, *The Gardens of Pompeii* (New Rochelle 1979), pp. 80 and 368 (Index, s.v. birds).

2. *Rust.* 3.4.2–3; 5.1–8.

3. *Rust.* 3.5.9–17. Cf. B. Tilly, *Varro the Farmer* (London 1973), pp. 112–16, 283–89, who summarizes major modern reconstructions of the aviary and provides a sensible short commentary.

4. O. E. Schmidt, *Ciceros Villen* (Darmstadt 1972; reprint with bibliographical additions of the article originally published in 1899 in *Neue Jahrbücher für das klassische Altertum*), pp. 15–19, 34–35.

5. See P. Grimal, *Les jardins romains* (Paris 1943), pp. 75–76, 262–65, 384–85.

6. *De Or.* 2.18.

7. Cic. *De Or.* 2.224; *Clu.* 141; Pompon. *Dig.* 1.2.2.39. On Brutus' dialogue, see R. Hirzel, *Der Dialog*, 2 vols. (Leipzig 1895), 1: 428–31. On the date of his praetorship, see Broughton, *MRR*, 1: 480.

8. Cf. Cic. *De Or.* 2.142.

9. *De Or.* 1.28–29. At *Leg.* 2.7, Cicero observes that the finest plane trees grow in Atticus' Epirotan *Amaltheum*.

10. *De Or.* 3.18.

11. *Rep.* 1.14, 17–18. On the *horti* of Scipio, see Grimal *Jardins* (supra n.5), pp. 128–29; F. Coarelli, "La doppia tradizione sulla morte di Romolo e gli *auguracula* dell'Arx e del Quirinale," in *Gli Etruschi a Roma: Atti dell'incontro di studi in onore di Massimo Pallotino* (Rome 1981), pp. 186–87.

12. As a general guide to Cicero's villas, Schmidt, *Ciceros Villen* (supra n. 4), still remains unsurpassed. For the Campanian villas of Cicero, Catulus, Hortensius and Varro, see J. H. D'Arms, *Romans on the Bay of Naples* (Cambridge, Mass. 1970), pp. 39 ff., 181, 188–89, 197–200. For a discussion of the setting of Cicero's dialogues, see also E. Becker, "Technik und Szenerie des ciceronischen Dialogs" (Diss. Münster 1938), pp. 11 ff.

13. *Leg.* 1.15; cf. Hirzel, *Der Dialog* (supra n. 7), 1: 475, n. 2; E. Rawson, "The Interpretation of Cicero's *De Legibus*," *ANRW* I,4 (Berlin 1973), pp. 338–40.

14. *Part. Or.* 1.1, cf. *QFr.* 3.3.4 and M. Schanz-C. Hosius, *Geschichte der römischen Literatur*, 4 vols. (Munich 1927), 1: 463.

15. *Brut.* 10, 24. Cf. A. E. Douglas, *M. Tulli Ciceronis Brutus* (Oxford 1966), ad locc., pp. 7, 16–17, and Cic. *Att.* 12.16.2 with D. R. Shackleton Bailey's commentary, *Cicero's Letters to Atticus*, 7 vols. (Cambridge 1965–1970), 5: 353–54.

16. *Hort.* fr. 17–19 Müller (Leipzig 1893–1923); *Acad.* 2.148. Cf. Hirzel, *Der Dialog* (supra n. 7), 1: 499, n. 3; M. Ruch, *L'Hortensius de Cicéron* (Paris 1958), pp. 69–70; J. van Ooteghem, *Lucius Licinius Lucullus* (Brussels 1959), pp. 180–86.

17. Nonius p. 65 = p. 91 Lindsay = fr. 13 Müller = Plasberg p. 90 *in app.*; cf. 2.125.

18. *Nat. D.* 1.15, and cf. ad loc. A. S. Pease, *M. Tulli Ciceronis De Natura Deorum* (Cambridge, Mass. 1955), pp. 163–64.

19. Cf. A. S. Pease, *M. Tulli Ciceronis De Divinatione Libri Duo* (Urbana 1920–23; reprint Darmstadt 1963), pp. 16–17, 65–66, 587.

20. On the villa as a subject of moralistic diatribes, see the excellent remarks by D'Arms, *Romans* (supra n. 12), pp. 40 ff.

21. *Leg.* 2.1: *magnificasque villas et pavimenta marmorea et laqueata tecta contemno*; 2.30: the *magnificentia* of Lucullus' villa at Tusculum affords an example that *cupiditatibus principum et vitiis infici solet tota civitas.*

22. *Parad. Stoic.* 38.

23. *Att.* 1.18.6, 19.6, 20.3; 2.1.7. Cf. Macrob. *Sat.* 3.15.6: *illi nobilissimi principes, Lucullus Philippus et Hortensius, quos Cicero piscinarios appellat*; Varro, *Rust.* 3.3.10: *quis enim propter nobilitates ignorat piscinas Philippi, Hortensii, Lucullorum?*

24. *Att.* 5.2.1; *Acad.* 2.9.

25. In no publication is such a list available at a glance. Detailed information on the careers of the persons listed can easily be gleaned from *RE* or *MRR*; see also the very conscientious but unfortunately unpublished study by L. E. Austin, "A Study of the Characters in Cicero's Dialogues" (Ph.D. Diss. University of North Carolina, Chapel Hill 1932). After each name are indicated the dialogue or dialogues in which the person in question appears.

26. But on his status in 146, cf. Broughton, *MRR*, 1: 468.

27. *Nat. D.*. 1.15. P. Levine, "Cicero and the Literary Dialogue," *CJ* 53 (1958): 147, clearly exaggerates the *auctoritas* of Balbus and Velleius. The father of Balbus may have been a senator: he seems to have been present at the debate in the senate in 162, but the words *ut e patre audiebam* (*Nat. D.* 2.11) may merely be a rhetorical device containing no historical information.

28. Hirzel, *Der Dialog* (supra n. 7), 1: 542, n. 1.

29. So *Ibid.*, p. 542.

30. *Rep.* 2.3.

31. *De Or.* 1.24. Cf. H. H. Scullard, *Festivals and Ceremonies of the Roman Republic* (Ithaca 1981), pp. 183–86.

32. *Rep.* 1.14; *Nat. D.* 1.15 and cf. Pease, *De Natura Deorum* (supra n. 18), p. 163. On the *feriae Latinae*, see Scullard, *Festivals* (supra n. 31), pp. 111–15. Originally Cicero intended to place the dialogue in the *De Republica* on the *novendiales feriae* (of 129), *QFr.* 3.5.1.

33. *Leg.* 3.30. Cf. Hirzel, *Der Dialog* (supra n. 7), 1: 475, n. 3; H. Stern, *Le Calendrier de 354* (Paris 1953), pp. 107–08.

34. *Leg.* 1.9. On *otium* as a prerequisite for literary activity, see M. Kretschmar, "Otium, studia litterarum, Philosophie und bios theōrētikos im Leben und Denken Ciceros" (Diss. Leipzig 1937), esp. pp. 50–61; J.-M. André, *L'otium dans la vie morale et intellectuelle romaine* (Paris 1966), pp. 310 ff.

35. Cf. esp. *Div.* 2.6; *Nat. D.* 1.7; *Off.* 2.2; 3.1–2.

36. See esp. *Arch.* 13.

37. *Brut.* 10.

38. *Rep.* 1.33; cf. *QFr.* 3.5.1.

39. *Dig.* 1.2.2.35 ff. For a list of republican jurists, see W. Kunkel, *Herkunft und soziale Stellung der römischen Juristen* (Graz 1967), pp. 7 ff.; F. Schulz, *Geschichte der römischen Rechtswissenschaft* (Weimar 1961), pp. 54–57 and 203–05 (on Pomponius' *Enchiridium*).

40. *Brut.* 102.

41. *De Or.* 1.265; cf. *Att.* 4.16.3.

42. *De Or.* 1.234–50.

43. *De Or.* 1.159, 166–200.

44. *De Or.* 1.193, 200.

45. *Leg.* 1.13.

46. *Brut.* 152.

47. *Leg.* 1.14.

48. *De Or.* 1.236 (Antonius speaking).

49. In fact Cicero did compose a treatise—not a dialogue—*De iure civili in artem redigendo* (for the fragments, see F. P. Bremer, *Iurisprudentiae antehadrianae quae supersunt*, 2 vols. [Lipsiae 1906], 1: 129–30), thus fulfilling the plan he had put into the mouth of Crassus (*De Or.* 2.142). But as Cicero's *ars* is lost the monument he left for us is above all his merciless ridicule of the pettifoggery of the *iuris consulti*—of Servius Sulpicius himself—in the *Pro Murena* 25–29; cf. the excellent exposition by A. Bürge, "Die Juristenkomik in Ciceros Rede Pro Murena" (Diss. Zürich 1974).

50. *De Or.* 1.249.

51. *Att.* 4.16.2.

52. *Att.* 13.12.3; 13.13.1: *totam Academiam ab hominibus nobilissimis abstuli, transtuli ad nostrum sodalem* (as Shackleton Bailey perceptively notes, this demonstrates that Varro was not considered a *nobilis, Cicero's Letters to Atticus* [supra n. 15], 5: 367, 369); 13.14.1; 13.16.1: Cicero admits that it was *para to prepon* to entrust the dialogue in the *Academica* to Catulus, Hortensius, and Lucullus; their lack of expertise in these matters was notorious. Cicero cogitated to transfer *illos sermones* to Cato and Brutus but *ecce tuae litterae de Varrone*; 13.18.1, 19.3–5, 22.1–3, 23.2, 24.1, 25.3. Cf. R. E. Jones, "Cicero's Accuracy of Characterization in his Dialogues," *AJP* 60 (1939): 307ff., esp. 324–25.

53. *Inst.* 10.1.95.

54. *Fam.* 9.8, cf. *Att.* 13.25.3.

55. But Cicero's remarks at *QFr.* 3.5.1 seem to imply, as D. R. Shackleton Bailey observes (*Cicero. Epistulae Ad Quintum Fratrem* [Cambridge 1980], p. 218), that "readers of *De Oratore* were expected to believe that the dialogue was at least in part based on real conversations."

56. For orientation and introduction, see H. Dahlmann, s.v. M. Terentius Varro, *RE, Suppl.* 6 (1935), cols. 1261–76; Hirzel, *Der Dialog* (supra n. 7), 1: 436–54, 552–65; for the Menippean Satires, the great commented edition by J.-P. Cèbe, *Varron, Satires Ménippées* (Paris 1972–), now in the course of publication; for the *Logistorici*, B. Zucchelli, *Varro Logistoricus. Studio letterario e prosopografico* (Parma 1980).

57. *Agr., praef.* 2.

58. H. Jordan, *M. Catonis praeter librum De re rustica quae extant* (Lipsiae 1860), p. 78.

59. Cf. W. Speyer, *Bücherfunde in der Glaubeswerbung der Antike* (Göttingen 1970), pp. 51ff.

60. Colum. *Rust.* 1.1.13; Plin. *HN.* 18.22. Cf. R. Reitzenstein, "De scriptorum rei rusticae qui intercedunt inter Catonem et Columellam libris deperditis" (Diss. Berlin 1884), pp. 47 ff.

61. Thus the date of the publication of the *De Re Rustica* was 37 B.C., but it is eminently possible that Varro composed drafts of individual books much earlier, cf. in this sense R. Martin, *Recherches sur les agronomes latins et leurs conceptions économiques et sociales* (Paris 1971), pp. 213–35; J. Heurgon, *Varron, Économie rurale*, (Paris 1978), 1: XXI–XXVI.

62. Heurgon, *Varron* (supra n. 61), p. L; E. Laughton, "Observations on the Style of Varro," *CQ* 10 (1960): 1–28.

63. Cf. e.g. 2.5.2, 10.1.

64. Cf. Hirzel, *Der Dialog* (supra n. 7), 1: 554, n. 3.

65. See the marvellous appreciation of the *De Re Rustica* as a literary work by Dahlmann, "M. Terentius Varro" (supra n. 56), cols. 1186–94. Hirzel is too much under the spell of Cicero to perceive the greatness of Varro; the peculiarities of Varro's dialogue are for him symptoms of literary decline (*Der Dialog* [supra n. 7], 1: 559). For Varro's dialogue as a scholarly treatise, see J.

E. Skydsgaard, *Varro the Scholar. Studies in the First Book of Varro's De Re Rustica* (Hafniae 1968).

66. *Att.* 13.16.1. Cf. supra n. 52.

67. Cf. G. Niccolini, *I fasti dei tribuni della plebe* (Milan 1934), pp. 60–61, 133–35; L. R. Taylor, *Roman Voting Assemblies* (Ann Arbor 1966), pp. 23–24.

68. Cf. Tilly, *Varro* (supra n. 3), p. 230; J. W. Poultney, *The Bronze Tables of Iguvium* (Baltimore 1959), p. 328; A. Ernout, *Le dialecte Ombrien* (Paris 1961), p. 99.

69. Philostr. *VA* 6.36, adduced by J. M. C. Toynbee, *Animals in Roman Life and Art* (Ithaca 1973), pp. 277, 399, n. 298. But the magpie, *pica*, was also famous for uttering intelligible sounds (*Ibid.*, pp. 275–76), and yet Minucius Pica opens his mouth only once (3.7.11).

70. *Leg.* 1.21.

71. August. *De civ. D.* 6.3.

72. Cf. *De Or.* 3.18; *Leg.* 1.14; Macrob. *Sat.* 6.4.8.

73. Varro's description of Appius' *ornithon* is so vivid that a diligent scholar mistook it in his otherwise very useful book for a real bird-house, cf. I. Shatzman, *Senatorial Wealth and Roman Politics* (Brussels 1975), p. 323: Appius "had gardens in Rome...in which there were aviaries."

74. Cf. Pease, *De Divinatione* (supra n. 19), pp. 74–77; J. André, *Les noms d'oiseaux en Latin* (Paris 1967), pp. 61–63, 118–22, 127–30.

75. Cf. Horace, *Carm.* 3.27.1. This applied to the *parra* as an unsolicited omen, the *auspicium oblativum*; in the *auspicia impetrativa*, the solicited auspices, the *parra*, if it appeared *ab dextera*, was a propitious sign.

76. Each candidate was entitled to appoint one or more *custodes* whose official task was to see to it that no false ballots were cast, see T. Mommsen, *Römisches Staatsrecht*, 3 vols. (Leipzig 1887–88), 3: 406–07. See now the excellent studies by C. Nicolet, "Le livre III des *res rusticae* de Varron et les allusions au déroulement des comices tributes," *REA* 72 (1970): 113–37; and *Idem*, "Tessères frumentaires et tessères de vote," in *L'Italie préromaine et la Rome républicaine. Mélanges offerts à Jacques Heurgon*, 2 vols. (Rome 1976), : pp. 695–716, esp. 709–10.

77. *Rust.* 2.1.10; 3.3.10. Cf. I. Kajanto, *The Latin Cognomina* (Helsinki 1965), pp. 84–88, 325–34; A. Alföldi, "Les *cognomina* des magistrats de la République romaine," in *Mélanges d'Archeologie et d'Histoire offerts à André Piganiol*, ed. R. Chevallier, 3 vols. (Paris 1966), 2: 709–22.

78. In the inscription *CIL* XI. 1777 three brothers appear named Ursus, Aper, Lupus. We also meet M. Porcius Aper (*CIL* II. 4238) and P. Vaccius Vitulus (*CIL* IX. 2827), the latter name reminding us of Varro's Vaccius and Vitulus (I owe these examples to W. Schulze, *Zur Geschichte lateinischer Eigennamen* [Berlin 1904], pp. 115, n. 2; 234, n. 1). Here also belongs Fircellius Pavo. The name Fircellius is apparently derived from *fircus* which in the Sabine dialect, as Varro notes in the *De Lingua Latina* (5.97), corresponded to Latin *hircus*. This Fircellius Pavo was really "Mr. Buck Peacock." Varro must have relished this etymological joke, but it is rather doubtful whether his non-Sabine audience was able to appreciate it. Cf. M. G. Bruno, "I Sabini e la loro lingua," *RendIstLomb* 95 (1961): 539; 96 (1962): 571–72. In

another field of onomastic fun the family composed of Eroticus (*pater*), Eroticus (*filius*) and Erotica (*filia*) stands out (*AÉpigr.* [1966], no. 199).

79. C. Nicolet, "Arpinum, Aemilius Scaurus et les Tullii Cicerones," *REL* 45 (1967): 276. Cf. Rawson, "Interpretation" (supra n. 13), pp. 339–40.

80. Again detailed information can easily be obtained from *RE, MRR,* and C. Nicolet, *L'ordre équestre à l'époque républicaine,* vol. 2: *Prosopographie des chevaliers Romains* (Paris 1974), ad loc.

81. See Cic. *Div.* 1.29, 132; 2.75 and Pease, *De Divinatione* (supra n. 19), ad locc. He composed a learned treatise, *Auguralis disciplinae libri,* in which he discussed various kinds of augural birds. For an (incomplete) collection of fragments, see H. Funaioli, *Grammaticae Romanae fragmenta* (Lipsiae 1907), pp. 426–27.

82. For this dispute, see also Cic. *Att.* 4.15.5, and Shackleton Bailey, *Cicero's Letters to Atticus* (supra n. 15), 2: 209.

83. On Scrofa, see the erudite article by G. Perl, "Cn. Tremelius Scrofa in Gallia Transalpina," *AJAH* 5 (1980): 97–105.

84. F. Münzer, s.v. Fundanius, *RE* 7 (1912): 291–92, identified him also with the tribune of the plebs of (probably) 68, but this is highly unlikely; the tribune will be his son, and hence Varro's brother-in-law, see R. Syme, "Ten Tribunes," *JRS* 53 (1963): 58 = *Roman Papers,* 5 vols. (Oxford 1979-88), 2: 563; M. H. Crawford, *Roman Republican Coinage,* 2 vols. (Cambridge 1974), 1: 328.

85. On Axius (and Lucienus), see L. R. Taylor, *The Voting Districts of the Roman Republic* (Rome 1960), p. 197; T. P. Wiseman, *New Men in the Roman Senate 139 B.C.–14 A.D.* (Oxford 1971), pp. 216, 234.

86. Neither of them is mentioned in Broughton's supplementary list of senators, *MRR,* 2: 486ff. Stolo was probably the father of C. Licinius Calvus Stolo, *quindecimvir sacris faciundis* (and a *praetorius*) in 17 B.C. (*Acta ludorum saeculariorum, ILS* 5050, lines 150, 167). See *PIR²,* vol. 5, 1 (Berlin 1970), p. 32, L 179.

87. Cf. Nicolet, *L'ordre équestre* (supra n. 80), 2: 856–57.

88. Both names, Agrius and Agrasius, are well attested epigraphically, Agrius, *inter alia,* also in Casinum (*CIL* I². 1541) where Varro had one of his estates.

89. Cf. *ILS* 3484, a dedication by Q. *Murrius Cn. f.* to the Sabine deity *Vacuna.*

90. On the various categories of the *aeditui* and their social standing, see J. Marquardt, *Römisches Staatsverwaltung²,* 3 vols. (Leipzig 1881-85), 3: 214–18.

91. See ucchelli, *Varro Logistoricus* (supra n. 56), pp. 23 n. 16 and 32 ff.

92. See *Ibid.,* pp. 37ff. (with further literature). I doubt if it is possible to identify with any reasonable degree of probability the persons named in the titles of Catus, *De Liberis Educandis* and Tubero, *De Origine Humana.*

93. Unless the *logistoricus Nepos* was named after the historian Cornelius Nepos.

94. On the temple of Tellus, see A. Aust, "De aedibus sacris populi Romani" (Diss. Marburg 1889), p. 14; S. B. Platner and T. Ashby, *A*

Topographical Dictionary of Ancient Rome (Oxford 1929), p. 511.

95. On this festival, see W. W. Fowler, *The Roman Festivals of the Period of the Republic* (London 1889), pp. 294–96; Scullard, *Festivals* (supra n. 31), p. 68; G. Wissowa, *Religion und Kultus der Römer*[2] (Munich 1912), pp. 193–95; P. Ovidius Naso. *Die Fasten* ed. F. Bömer, 2 vols. (Heidelberg 1958), 2: 73 (ad v. 658), 74 (ad v. 669).

96. On the *aedilician aedium sacrarum procuratio*, Mommsen, *Römisches Staatsrecht* (supra n. 76), 1[3]: 507. The *aedituus* L. Fundilius again appears to have been a historical person, and not a literary figment. The famous inscription *CIL* 1[2].709 = *ILLRP* 515 (dated to 17 Nov. 89) contains a list of the members of the *consilium* of the consul Cn. Pompeius Strabo. In this list as the twenty-first name (line 7) appears a *C. Fundilius C. f.*, most probably a military tribune, belonging (as it seems) to the tribe Quirina. Now Quirina was the tribe of Reate, and the Fundilii are known from inscriptions (*CIL* IX. 4673, 4691) as an important Reatine family. Thus it is very likely that also our L. Fundilius came from this Sabine town; this would explain very well his acquaintance with Varro. See, above all, C. Cichorius, *Römische Studien* (Leipzig 1922), pp. 153–54, 191. Cf. also Taylor, *Voting Districts* (supra n. 85), pp. 216, 274; N. Criniti, *L'epigrafe di Cn. Pompeo Strabone* (Milan 1970), pp. 19 n. 24, 120–21.

97. Cf. Perl, "Cn. Tremelius Scrofa" (supra n. 83), p. 97.

98. Cic. *QFr.* 2.3.2.

99. See Dahlmann, "M Terentius Varro" (supra n. 56), col. 1190, with further literature.

100. *Cum haec loquerentur, venit a Menate* (cf. 2.1.1: *cum Menates discessisset.* He did not reappear, cf. 2.11.12: *Itaque discedimus...illi partim domum, partim ad Menatem) libertus, qui dicat liba absoluta esse* (the translation in the Loeb Classical Library edition is erroneous: *liba absoluta esse* does not mean "the cakes had been offered" but "the cakes are ready") *et rem divinam paratam; si vellent, venirent illuc et ipsi pro se sacrificarentur.*

101. Cf. Ovid. *Fast.* 4.721ff., esp. 743–44: *libaque de milio milii fiscella sequatur: rustica praecipue est hoc dea laeta cibo.* See A. Schleicher, *Meletematon Varronianorum specimen I* (Diss. Bonn 1846), pp. 2–3; Bömer, *Die Fasten* (supra n. 95), pp. 271ff.; Scullard, *Festivals* (supra n. 31), pp. 103–05.

102. Cf. Tilly, *Varro* (supra n. 3), p. 231.

103. On the *Villa Publica*, see G. Tossi, "La Villa Publica di Roma nelle fonti letterarie e numismatiche," *Atti dell'Istituto Veneto, Classe di Scienze Morali, Lettere ed Arti* 135 (1976–77): 413–26.

104. Since Schleicher, *Meletematon Varronianorum specimen* (supra n. 101), p. 10, it had until recently been assumed that the dramatic date of Book III was 54 B.C. But a number of scholars, especially D. R. Shackleton Bailey, *Cicero's Letters to Atticus* (supra n. 15), 2: 208–10 and C. Nicolet, *"Le livre III des res rusticae"* (supra n. 76), pp. 113, n. 2; 116, n. 1, have called this date in question, and E. Badian, "Additional Notes on Roman Magistrates," *Athenaeum* n.s. 48 (1970): 4–6, disproved it decisively. His own dramatic date is 50 B.C. Now J. S. Richardson, "The Triumph of Metellus Scipio and the Dramatic Date of Varro, *RR* 3," *CQ* 33 (1983): 456–63, apparently unaware of Badian's article, attempts to revive the traditional date. His argument is eru-

dite and sophisticated, but I doubt if it is going to carry the day. See now my "The Dramatic Date of Varro, *de re rustica*, Book III and the Elections in 54," *Historia* 34 (1985): 248–54.

4

The Roman Republic. By MICHAEL CRAWFORD. Fontana History of the Ancient World. Hassocks, Nr. Brighton, Sussex: The Harvester Press, Ltd.; Atlantic Highlands, N.J.: Humanities Press, Inc. (in association with Fontana), 1978. Pp. 224 + 8 pls.; 4 maps + 12 figs. in text. $18.50.

This is not a book from which one can learn what traditionally passes for the facts of Roman history. In Crawford's presentation there are few heroes or villains; he does not write of dates and names, of noble and base deeds, but of social groups and historical processes; he dissects and analyzes. Ample quotations of ancient sources enliven the narrative and lend credence to the argument, although at times one may doubt whether it is really the modern author who speaks the idiom of the sources or the ancient authors who are made to conform to the views of their modern colleague. Yet such shrewd observers of the Roman scene as Polybius or that splendid historian who shines through the text of Appian would find much to agree with and to admire in C.'s dispassionate vision of Republican history. The present reviewer finds that he and C. are often of one mind; whether this makes C. right is another question.

First, the credibility and uses of the sources. The patricians "had been defined already under the monarchy by a process which is now unknowable" (p. 32). C.'s cheerful epistemological agnosticism is reassuring, although the ambitious scholar or the dreamer will not be deterred.[1] That Roman accounts of the early

1. Cf. recently P.-Ch. Ranouil, *Recherches sur le patriciat* (Paris, 1975); J.-C. Richard, *Les origines de la plèbe romaine: Essai sur la formation du dualisme patricio-plébéien* (Paris, 1978).

Republic and of the regal period constitute a fanciful fiction is not exactly a discovery. C. stresses, however, an important point which has not received all the attention it deserves, namely, that the Romans did believe in that fiction (p. 20). Historical fictions throw an interesting light on the society that maintains them. They perform an important social and political function; one might be tempted to describe Roman tales of the *origines* as a Roman version of the "magnificent myth"—"facilius autem quod est propositum [i.e., to illustrate the *optimus status civitatis*] consequar, si nostram rem publicam vobis . . . ostendero, quam si mihi aliquam, ut apud Platonem Socrates, ipse finxero" (Cic. *Rep.* 2. 3).

Next, Rome, Italy, and the Empire. This leads us to the problems of Roman "character" and Roman imperialism. It is a much trodden ground, first by Roman legionaries, then by modern scholars, the latter often no less formidable in their naiveté than the former in their seriousness. That Roman authors, Cicero and Virgil in the forefront, were taken in by the idea of Rome's imperial destiny, is understandable and excusable: they were Romans, they had a personal interest in Rome's success, and they did a good job as national propagandists. That so many modern authors followed in their footsteps is to be understood as well, but hardly pardoned. The writing of history is only partially a *Wissenschaft;* in part it is self-serving propaganda. Here lies the clue to the modern fascination with the idea of Rome. C., as was to be expected of a British author living in an age when the notion of the *pax Britannica* is merely an antiquarian term and when no Kipling exhorts the progeny of Boudicca to rule over high seas and wide lands, is remarkably free from any such preconceived misconception. He utters a salutary warning: the history of the Roman Republic is the history of Italy as well as of Rome (p. 124). This is just and right, but it is a difficult task to write Roman history from that perspective. Difficult, for as seen from the *Arx*, Italy and the World appear as objects, not subjects of history:[2]

> These small peoples are thick as flies, to the point of irritation,
> satiation and nausea.

Yet on occasion even C. would be admitted to the distinguished company of the men around Scipio Aemilianus, who in Cicero's dialogue have just concluded that Romulus was a cultured gentleman, in no respect inferior to the Greeks (Cic. *Rep.* 1. 58). C. tells us that for the Greek cities of southern Italy the choice lay between "the barbarian tribes and Rome" (p. 27). If one recalls the splendor and the prosperity of southern Italy before the Hannibalic War and the many *lumina* of Latin literature who came from that part of the peninsula, doubt may be entertained as to the alleged cultural superiority of Rome. In fact C. wishes to have it both ways; stating that "in some respects . . . Italy was in advance of Rome," he observes that "the tenth-rate Samnite town of Pompeii possessed a stone theatre from the late second century B.C." (p. 130; the first permanent stone theater in Rome was built by Pompey in 52 B.C.). This is not relevant: political and ideological reasons, not economic or cultural, prevented Rome from erecting a stone theater at an earlier date. When in 154 "censores theatrum lapideum in

2. W. Szymborska, "Voices," trans. M. J. Krynski and R. A. Maguire, *The Polish Review* 24. 3 (1979): 18–19.

urbe constitui censuerunt, quod ne tunc fieret, Scipio Nasica [cos. 162, 155, cens. 159, pont. max. 150–41] gravissima oratione obstitit, dicens, inimicissimum hoc fore bellatori populo ad nutriendam desidiam lasciviamque commentum, adeoque movit senatum, ut non solum vendi omnia theatro comparata iusserit, sed etiam subsellia ludis poni prohibuerit" (Oros. 4. 21. 4). Cicero (referring to the Greek practice) concurs: "cum in theatro imperiti homines rerum omnium rudes ignarique consederant, tum bella inutilia suscipiebant, tum seditiosos homines rei publicae praeficiebant, tum optime meritos civis e civitate eiciebant" (*Flac.* 16). These and other texts, "buried in a footnote ... of Mommsen's *Römisches Staatsrecht*" (3:396, n. 3), have been resurrected by L. R. Taylor, who devoted a lucid and penetrating analysis to this question.[3] Rome was spared for some time the enormity of a permanent theater, but she was not able to combat all the dangers of Hellenism (cf. pp. 85–87). When the Byzantine Greeks started calling themselves οἱ 'Ρωμαῖοι, this meant the ultimate triumph of Rome and the ultimate subversion of *Romanitas*.

C. is perplexed that as late as in 149 "a desire for security, understandable in any community, amounted in Rome almost to a neurosis over her supposed vulnerability" (p. 53). Again, let the poet speak; two fictitious Roman statesmen exchange their thoughts:[4]

> I feel threatened by every new horizon.
> That's how I see the problem, O Hostius Melius.
>
> To that I, Hostius Melius, reply to you,
> O Appius Papius: Forward. Somewhere out there the world must have an end.

The poet and the scholar, those two dissimilar worlds, share the same lack of understanding of a true imperial mentality. What the Romans of the second century were concerned with was not only the security, the mere existence of the City of Rome, but the security of the Empire of Rome. This is not one and the same thing. When a state passes from the stage of the struggle for survival to the stage of a balance of power in international politics and ultimately to the position of a superpower, its notion and perception of security dramatically changes. Small states cannot worry too much about their security, for they are never secure; their security depends on the goodwill of the others, on diplomacy and not on their own strength. To the imperial power a sign of independence on the part of a dependent ally or subject is an alarming signal not to be taken lightly, for it may be the first step leading to the dissolution of the Empire, to the retreat into the dismal world of *Kleinstaatlichkeit*. Carthage showed some faint signs of independence, and the world was taught the lesson. Britain, for one, was never in this position, for in Europe she had to accept the policy of the concert of powers. On the other hand, this is exactly the position of the Soviet Union today.

C. praises the innovativeness of the Roman oligarchy in the East and castigates its stubbornness in Spain (p. 94). In fact, I would contend, we here have to do

---

3. *Roman Voting Assemblies* (Ann Arbor, 1966), pp. 29–32, 123–125. Mommsen does not appear in C.'s bibliography; Taylor does, but obviously her book was not read very carefully. It does not pay to disregard either of them.
4. Szymborska, "Voices."

with two sides of the same coin. An imperial power can afford withdrawing troops from a foreign country only after an unequivocal victory, never after a stalemate or defeat, for this would amount to the loss of international credibility. When Augustus adopted the policy of containment, Rome chose the sure though comfortable way to the ultimate disaster. Through their stubborn engagement in Spain the republican statesmen strengthened the Empire and weakened, possibly lost, the Republic.

Thus the rise of the Empire and the dissolution of the Republic are inextricably connected with each other. "A part-time peasant army conquered the Mediterranean; that conquest then facilitated its destitution" (p. 107). Tiberius Gracchus would agree. But it was not only the peasants who were adversely affected by the imperial aggrandizement. Individual nobles prospered, but their rule as a class was undermined. It was the empire, C. points out, that made possible various *largitiones* and the *popularis ratio* (p. 113); the fortunes robbed or extorted in the East "fed through competition in display of wealth, and through bribery in elections and trials, the internal conflict within the Roman oligarchy" (p. 134; cf. p. 172). Numerous laws destined to curb extortion, bribery, and *sumptus* were enacted in quick succession; the *leges annales* were erected as a barrier against the ambition of powerful individuals. The ruling group tried hard to preserve its own cohesion (pp. 75-83, esp. p. 88). All in vain; it would not be unfair to apply to the nobles of the second and first centuries the *bon mot* of Tacitus referring to Pompeius: "suarum . . . logum idem auctor ac subversor" (*Ann.* 3. 28; on the close connection between provincial extortion and electoral bribery, see Asc. 19 Clark).

The dissolution of the traditional concept and essence of the Roman citizenship was an important factor in the transition from the Republic to the Principate or, more exactly, from the social system of a city-state to that of an empire. C.'s analysis of that process coincides in a large measure with the views expressed some time ago by the present writer,[5] but it is worth pondering not only for that reason. The Roman citizenship articulated itself in three ways: the Roman citizen appeared as a voter, as a soldier, and as a member of a property class (pp. 168–69). No account of the Roman expansion can fail to stress the spectacular success of the Republican citizenship policy, which, as Philip V was so well aware, was unlike anything known in Greece (pp. 38–48, esp. p. 45). The greatest success of Rome came when the *socii* rose in arms because they were denied the Roman citizenship (and with it the spoils of the empire). But when ultimately the citizenship of Rome spread all over the peninsula it "had become detached from *de facto* possibility of voting" (p. 112); thus once again the very success of Rome subverted the traditional structure of *civitas Romana*. But the real blow had been dealt by the Marian reform: the dissociation of military service from the property qualification altered the very essence of the Republican citizenship (p. 126). The "homines honesti atque in suis vicinitatibus et municipiis gratiosi" (Cic. *Mur.* 47) retained their (progressively useless) votes and (happily) lost their swords. As history instructs us, in times of crisis swords or bullets carry more weight than

---

5. J. Linderski, *Roman Electoral Assemblies from Sulla to Caesar* (Wrocław, 1966), pp. 156–66.

votes. The center of political power moved from the Senate and the (centuriate) Assembly to the army and its leaders. This spelled ruin to the Republic.[6]

6. Of course, there are in C.'s book a number of points of detail or interpretation which are open to criticism. I append a selection of *controversiae*. P. 35: C. speaks of the continuity of the institution of *clientela* in Rome. But the archaic *clientela* was defined legally and not only socially; we can surmise that it stood in approximately the same relationship to the late Republican *clientela* as the patriciate (which was both a legal and a social category) to the nobility (which was only a social category). P. 52: Rome was more militaristic than Sparta. The comparison misses the point. Sparta was a petrified relic from the tribal past, a community of warriors, which Rome was not. Rome was militaristic in a manner not unlike the Prussian state of the eighteenth and nineteenth centuries with its junker officer class and peasant army. P. 97: App. Claudius Pulcher triumphed in 143 "evading a threatened tribunician veto . . . by taking his daughter with him in the triumphal chariot." His daughter *qua* daughter would be of no help to him; she was a Vestal (for sources, see Broughton, *MRR*, 1:471). Pp. 109–10: Commenting on the deposition of Octavius ("unprecedented, but . . . hardly illegal") C. writes: ". . . if one accepted the principle of popular sovereignty, it was undoubtedly the right of the people to take away what it had given." This is fallacious logic. The Roman public law did not know the principle of popular sovereignty. It was a Greek and a very un-Roman concept. Although the individual tribunes of the plebs were selected through a process of popular election, it is important to realize that their prerogatives did not derive from the people but from the original *lex sacrata*, a sworn, divinely protected, and unalterable law which could not be abridged or modified by any *plebiscitum* or *lex publica*. P. 127: C. Marius was forced "to bow to public opinion" and act against Saturninus and Glaucia. This is a superficial explanation. E. Badian has long ago brilliantly shown the real reason for Marius' action: "Saturninus, having won the attachment of Marius' soldiers, proceeded to use them for his own schemes. . . . With his ally apparently stealing his clients from him . . . Marius could not hesitate" ("Marius and the Nobles," *Durham University Journal* [1964]: 148).

5

CONSTITUTIONAL ASPECTS OF THE CONSULAR ELECTIONS IN 59 B.C.

It had been generally held since Mommsen that the order of the consuls' names in the official lists had no significance and that it was determined purely by chance.[1] In 1949, however, L. R. Taylor and T. R. S. Broughton in a paper that deserves much more attention than has been paid to it, proved that the order of the consuls' names was based on a strict system.[2] They established that 1) the men named first in the lists usually held the fasces in January and in the odd-numbered months of the year 2) the men mentioned first in the Fasti are, in a number of cases, known to have been elected first. There is no case, at least in the late republic, of the man elected after his colleague appearing first in the yearly list. Thus the term consul prior received a new explanation and new significance: the priority in the Fasti and in holding the fasces did not depend, as many scholars believed, on greater age,[3] nor was it determined by lot, but was based on priority of election. The consul holding the fasces in the odd months had some important advantages over his colleague;[4] Taylor and Broughton observed further that, as the elections in the post-sullan period took place normally in the odd month of July, they were apparently presided over by the first consul. It is to be noted that Mommsen was of the opinion that the decision regarding the conducting of the elections was made by lot or by agreement (comparatio) between the consuls.[5]

The events connected with the consular elections in 59 B.C. are highly interesting both from the political and the constitutional point of view, and I propose to re-examine them taking full account of the rules established by Taylor and Broughton[6].

There is a widespread opinion that the comitia consularia in that year were presided over by Caesar;[7] as his name appears first in all the lists and consular

---

[1] Th. Mommsen, Römisches Staatsrecht I³, Leipzig 1887, 37–41; II³, Leipzig 1887, 90. Cf. B. Kübler, RE IV (1900), 1118 s. v. consul.

[2] The Order of the Two Consuls' Names in the Yearly Lists, Memoirs of the American Academy in Rome 19, 1949, 3–14 (hereafter cited as Taylor-Broughton).

[3] Cf. e. g. L. Lange, Römische Alterthümer I³, Berlin 1876, 731.

[4] See esp. Taylor-Broughton 4–5.   [5] Staatsrecht I³ 41–42.

[6] The article of W. C. Grummel, The Consular Elections of 59 B.C., CJ 49, 1953–1954, 351–355 is concerned only with some political questions and does not present any new point of view.

[7] Cf. e. g. J. Carcopino, César (Histoire Générale: Histoire Romaine, vol. II), Paris 1936, 689.

datings[8] the accepted facts seem to correspond perfectly with the theory of Taylor and Broughton.

However, there is preserved in a letter to Atticus a curious statement that, although of great importance for the proper understanding of the constitutional aspects of the consular elections in 59, has until now been either ignored or misinterpreted. We read Cicero, ad Att. 2. 20. 6: Comitia Bibulus Archilochio edicto in ante diem XV. Kal. Novembr. distulit. A few days later[9] Cicero informs Atticus (2. 21. 5): Bibuli qui sit exitus futurus nescio. Ut nunc res se habet, admirabili gloria est. Qui cum comitia in mensem Octobrem distulisset, quod solet ea res populi voluntatem offendere, putarat Caesar oratione sua posse impelli contionem ut iret ad Bibulum; multa cum seditiosissime diceret, vocem exprimere non potuit.

We have a very curious situation: Bibulus postpones the election and what is Caesar doing? On July 25 he addresses a meeting, with Pompey present and also speaking (ad Att. 2. 21. 3), criticizes the edicts of Bibulus and in order to compell Bibulus to withdraw his edict delaying the comitia tries to induce the crowd to march against the latter's house; after his efforts fail he finally gives up. The elections eventually did not take place in July. What is especially strange about this situation is the fact that Caesar did not contest the validity of Bibulus' action. Now any attempt at interpretation must be concerned with two principal questions: 1) why did Caesar acknowledge the validity of Bibulus' act? 2) what was the legal basis of Bibulus' edict?

Let us now see how the scholars tried to answer the above questions.

According to Lange[10] Caesar had issued an edict announcing the date of the elections, but Bibulus encouraged by signs of the diminishing popularity of the triumvirs decided to put off the comitia. Lange cites no evidence concerning the edict of Caesar and in fact there is no such evidence. His reconstruction is based exclusively on the belief that it was Caesar who was to conduct elections. This, however, is not the weakest poin tof his thesis. Throughout the republic we find only one of the consuls in charge of elections:[11] the Lange's thesis implies that the orders issued by the presiding consul could have been revoked or vetoed by his colleague. Again, one can adduce no evidence to prove that. Mommsen has rightly pointed out that, as far as elections were concerned, collegial veto was forbidden.[12]

Bibulus did not, however, simply recall or veto the presumed edict of Caesar: he ordered the assembly to convene on October 18. To announce the date of elections was a prerogative of the presiding officer; consequently, it would follow that either there were two presidents of the assembly at one

---

[8] See below p. 433 and note 42.
[9] The letter 2. 21 was written immediately after July 25 and 2. 20 about July 20.
[10] RA III[2], Berlin 1876, 293.   [11] Mommsen, Staatsrecht I[3] 41.
[12] Staatsrecht I[3] 285–286.

time, or that Bibulus had usurped that post, which, as the attitude of Caesar proves, clearly was not the fact.

Professor Lily Ross Taylor in her article on the Vettius affair holds that Bibulus proclaimed he would watch the heavens till October 18 and that in this way he made it impossible for Caesar to gather the assembly earlier.[13] She also believes that Caesar was in charge of elections but seeking explanation for the action of Bibulus in his right of obnuntiatio she is on much firmer ground than Lange. Although this is a really ingenious solution I would contend that 1) it is inconsistent with theory and practice of obnuntiatio 2) the wording of Cicero is against it.

Considering the problem of obnuntiatio the following points are to be taken into account: 1) in order to hinder the presiding magistrate from summoning the comitia (or, if he chose not to obey, to make the acts of the assembly legally null and void) the notice of observation of lightning had to be served personally early in the morning before the assembly gathered. Only this notice (dico: fulmen vidisse) can technically be termed as obnuntiatio. Though the announcement se de caelo servare meant the threat of obnuntiatio it did not legally bind the presiding officer. This basic rule of magisterial obnuntiatio is illustrated by Cicero's vivid description of Milo's efforts to stop the election of Clodius to the curule aedilship in 57. The consul Metellus Nepos in spite of Milo's announcement that he would be watching the heavens on all comitial days attempted to convene the electoral assembly and only the actual obnuntiatio by Milo stopped him at the last moment from doing so.[14] 2) It is true that Bibulus posted edicts containing the formula se de caelo servare probably separately for every comitial day,[15] however, as he had shut himself up in his house he failed to serve the notice in person. His "obnuntiationes" (so normally though incorrectly called) were therefore invalid from the standpoint of augural discipline and this point of view was of course shared as well by Caesar. It has been common opinion among scholars that in practice it was sufficient for a magistrate who wanted to call off an assembly to declare that he was watching the heavens. It was sufficient as long as the presiding officer could not hinder a magistrate watching for bad omens from serving him the notice and it was then reasonable to resign at once from summoning the comitia after a magistrate announced he would watch the heavens. The situation that developped in 59 does not, however, fit in with this pattern. Caesar was able not to allow anybody watching for bad signs to approach him: he once

---

[13] The Date and Meaning of the Vettius Affair, Historia 1, 1950, 46.

[14] Cic., Att. 4. 3. 3–4. Cf. I. M. J. Valeton, De iure obnuntiandi comitiis et conciliis, Mnemosyne N. S. 19, 1891, 82–83, 101–102.

[15] Suet., Caes. 20. Cf. Cass. Dio 38. 6. 5, who, however, confused the obnuntiationes of Bibulus with indictiones feriarum. Valeton, op. cit. 106–107 has shown convincingly that it was against the spirit of augural law to announce in one edict the intention of heaven watching during a period of time.

chased Bibulus from the Forum[16] and he was ready to repeat this action. It was a violation of the other consul's rights, but it was not a violation of augural law. Bibulus did not succeed in conveying Caesar the will of the gods, i. e. he did not recite the ritual formula on the prescribed spot and at the prescribed time. And the enunciation of a formula was the only thing that really counted in augural discipline. This point, I think, has been completely missed in all modern studies dealing with obnuntiatio. The entire problem of heaven watching and especially the question of the validity of Caesar's legislation thus calls for a renewed discussion.

The "obnuntiationes" of Bibulus did not hinder Caesar and Vatinius from carrying through their laws; why then should Caesar have accepted so easily the authority of Bibulus' edict aimed at delaying the elections?

The last point I should like to make is that it is by no means clear if obnuntiatio was allowed at all before the lex Clodia at electoral assemblies. Professor Taylor and many other scholars believe that it was; unfortunately this extremely complicated question cannot be gone into here. It is, however, to be noted that Lange and Valeton, the authors of to date by far best treatments of the whole subject, are against this view[17] and, in my opinion, the studies of McDonald, Weinstock and Sumner[18] did not weaken them on that point.

The analysis of the technicalities of obnuntiatio thus lends heavy support to our thesis that the edict of Bibulus cannot be interpreted as an announcement of heaven watching.

Let us now pass to the terminology used by Cicero. There is no explicit allusion to obnuntiatio in the text of Cicero. Cicero speaks only of an edict. The assumption it contained the announcement se de caelo servare is based merely on the fact that Bibulus did issue such edicts, but this is hardly a proof.

Cicero writes Bibulus edicto comitia distulit. What is the precise meaning of "edictum" and "comitia differre"?

To begin with, the term comitia differre is a technical expression to denote the postponement of an assembly.[19] The term has been discussed by Mommsen;[20]

---

[16] Suet., Caes. 20: obnuntiantem collegam (against the first agrarian law) armis foro expulit.

[17] L. Lange, De legibus Aelia et Fufia commentatio, Gissae 1861 = Kleine Schriften I, Göttingen 1887, 329 ff.; Valeton, op. cit. 94, 261.

[18] W. F. McDonald, Clodius and the Lex Aelia Fufia, JRS 19, 1929, 164 ff.; S. Weinstock, Clodius and the Lex Aelia Fufia, JRS 27, 1937, 215 ff.; G. V. Sumner, Lex Aelia, Lex Fufia, AJPh 74, 1962, 343–344. But Sumner succeeded – and this is his great achievement especially in view of fruitless efforts of many students – in establishing a valid distinction between the Fufian and Aelian law.

[19] It is to be noted that the term comitia (without a more particular specification) normally denotes the electoral assembly. For this usage see esp. G. W. Botsford, The Roman Assemblies, New York 1909, 133–134.

[20] Staatsrecht III, Berlin 1887, 415–416.

some instances may be added from the Thesaurus Linguae Latinae.[21] Theoretically two basic types of postponements are to be discerned, both of them covered by the term comitia differre: 1) the dilatio comitiorum could be ordered after the date of meeting had already been announced. Here two further variants were possible: either in the announcement of the dilatio a new date was given or not. In the latter case a new announcement was needed. 2) the dilatio could occur after the assembly convened. It amounted then to dissolving of the comitia. Two further variants were possible as above under (1).

The most important fact is that in none of the cases adduced by Mommsen and the Thesaurus Linguae Latinae the term comitia differre can be understood as corresponding to "comitia obnuntiando differre"; on the contrary, in all cases the action of the presiding officer is implied. If the senate voted that the comitia should be postponed, the execution of the senate's decree was undoubtedly the obligation of the president of the assembly. If a magistrate in person served the notice of a bad sign, the presiding officer could not legally convene the assembly, if an augur, the president was bound to dissolve the comitia; also any further action as to whether or when, to summon the assembly again rested with the presiding officer.[22]

---

[21] S. vv. differo p. 1074 and comitium p. 1803.

[22] The most important instances are: Cic., Att. 1. 16. 13: ita comitia in a. d. VI Kal. Sext. dilata sunt (in order to pass before the election a bribery law); Att. 4. 17. 3: comitia dilata ex s. c., dum lex de tacito iudicio ferretur; pro Mur. 51: meministis fieri senatus consultum referente me, ne postero die comitia haberentur; Liv. 6. 37. 12: omniumque earum rogationum comitia in adventum eius exercitus differunt qui Velitras obsidebat (cf. 6. 36. 9); 8. 23. 14: tamen ad interregnum res redit, dilatisque alia atque alia de causa comitiis; 9. 34. 20: nisi duo (sc. censores) confecerint legitima suffragia, non renuntiato altero comitia differantur; 7. 17. 13: cum intercedendo tribuni nihil aliud quam ut differrent comitia valuissent, duo patricii consules creati sunt. Of these texts only Liv. 7. 17. 13 presents difficulty. It is, however, to be observed that the dilatio is here only a consequence of intercessio. To put it in other words, the tribunes having interposed veto prohibited the assembly from convening; the presiding officer was able to hold the consular election only after they gave up. (On the veto as stopping an action and not annulling it see esp. A. Eigenbrodt, De magistratuum Romanorum iure intercedendi, Lipsiae 1875). In a much discussed passage, crucial for the reconstruction of the Roman theory of obnuntiatio (Phil. 2. 81), in which Cicero uses the most exact terminology he speaks of Antonius: multis ante mensibus in senatu dixit se Dolabellae comitia aut prohibiturum aut id facturum esse, quod fecit. Antonius tried to dissolve the assembly as augur after it had convened (the technical expression for this is comitia dimittere, see Mommsen, Staatsrecht III 415 note 6), although he had previously made it known that he would watch the heavens in his capacity as consul (that is before the beginning of the comitia). For interpretation of this passage see Valeton, op. cit. 95–96. For the usage of the expression comitia prohibere see also Liv. 4. 25. 1. The rule that the magisterial obnuntiatio prevents the comitia from being convened and not postpones them (although the postponement is really brought about by the obnuntiatio, technically it results from the action of the presiding officer and, moreover, only in the case of his trying to gather the assembly for the same purpose at a later date; if he had dropped his original plan of gathering the comitia we cannot speak

According to the Roman system any official communication by the magistrate having the ius edicendi was called edictum; it had to be announced orally by a herold and exhibited in the written from in a public place. Any matter could be dealt with; as it is well known, the consul or any other magistrate who was to preside over an assembly announced the date and the subject of the comitia by a special edict.[23] Now, if he decided or was compelled to postpone the assembly, there was no other way of informing the citizens that the comitia would not take place on the previously fixed day, than to issue a new edict calling off the gathering. And this is precisely what Cicero says of Bibulus' action.

As far as the juridical base is concerned, there is no difference between the announcement and the postponement of an assembly: the magistrate who had the right to convene the comitia had also the right to dissolve or to postpone them. For our purpose, however, it is more convenient to express this in reverse order: the magistrate who had the right to postpone the comitia must have had also the right to gather them. Now, Bibulus' right to postpone the elections was not questioned; if our argumentation that he did not and could not, bring about the postponement by means of obnuntiatio, be granted, there is no other alternative, but to accept that in 59 not Caesar, but Bibulus was in charge of elections.

As one can see this is a solution that answers perfectly the questions put forward at the beginning of the present paper and I think that this point has been proved beyond any reasonable doubt.

The results reached above pose new problems, but at the same time open up new perspectives for solving them. The solutions I am going to present in most cases bear the character of tentative propositions; many of them will be, no doubt, modified in the course of further research.

Let us return at first to the theory of Taylor and Broughton. According to it the consul elected first held the fasces in the odd months and it fell therefore to his lot to conduct the elections. From the fact that Bibulus presided over the elections it is consequently to be inferred that he and not Caesar was elected first, that Bibulus and not Caesar was consul prior.

But there is something more. The right to preside over elections depended,

at all of a postponement) is illustratend by the use of obnuntiatio in 54 B.C. (cf. Cic., Att. 4. 17. 4; Q. fr. 3. 3. 2) and by a testimony of Appian concerning the consular election in 84 B.C. (B. C. I. 78. 358–359): ἀπειλησάντων δὲ ἰδιώτην ἀποφανεῖν, ἐπανῆλθε μὲν καὶ χειροτονίαν προύθηκεν ὑπάτου· ἀπαισίου δὲ τῆς ἡμέρας γενομένης ἑτέραν προύγραφεν· κἂν ταύτῃ κεραυνοῦ πεσόντος .. οἱ μάντεις ὑπὲρ τὰς θερινὰς τροπὰς ἀνετίθεντο τὰς χειροτονίας. The consul because of an adverse omen postponed the election; after a new portent occurred the augurs declared the period until after the summer solstice unfit for holding the election. The right to fix a new date rested with the presiding consul who, however, was obliged not to trespass the provision of the augural decree.

[23] Mommsen, Staatsrecht I³ 205–207; III 370.

according to Taylor and Broughton, on holding the fasces. What, however, would have happened if the comitia were postponed and took place eventually in an even month? Was in that case the prerogative to conduct the elections transferred together with the fasces from the first consul to his colleague?[24]

Happily we are in a position to give at once a definite answer. Comitia Bibulus ... in ante diem XV. Kal. Novembr. distulit – writes Cicero (ad Att. 2. 20. 6) and elsewhere (ad Att. 2. 21. 5): qui cum comitia in mensem Octobrem distulisset ... Note that October is an even month; if Bibulus had the fasces in July, in October they had to be handed over to Caesar. If we accept the thesis that the presidency was based on holding the fasces, it would mean that Bibulus delaying the elections until October deliberately resigned the post of presiding officer and put Caesar in charge of the electoral assembly, This is an evident absurdity and I see no other alternative but to abandon the thesis cited above and to admit that the privilege of holding the elections was not connected with actual possession of the fasces.

The theory of Taylor and Broughton in the part concerning the post of the president of elections has thus proved to be untenable, but there is still a possibility not to damage it, but to give it a new shape. It seems that the presidency over elections was a special prerogative of the consul prior. It was probably based directly on priority of election and was not connected with holding the fasces.

I have had the privilege of discussing some of the questions involved with Professors T. R. S. Broughton and L. R. Taylor. They are now inclined to think that the arrangements for presiding over elections were independent of either priority of election or the month in which the consul held the fasces and that the decision regarding the holding of elections was made by lot or by agreement between the consuls. In assigning the first consul the exclusive right to direct elections I may be of course wrong, but there are some arguments that tend to corroborate my thesis and I consider them worth stating.

[24] Professor Taylor made an attempt to interpret in view of her thesis the postponement ordered by Bibulus. She writes (On the Chronology of Caesar's First Consulship, AJPh 72, 1951, 262 note 29; hereafter cited as Chronology) as follows: "In an edict issued in July ... Bibulus postponed the consular comitia from July to October 18, that is, according to my view, from a month when Caesar held the fasces to a month when Bibulus, as the holder of the fasces, would have conducted the election. In the end Bibulus was apparently intimidated and the election was conducted by Caesar, who may have postponed it to his month, November". This interpretation resembles that of Lange and is open to the same objections. First of all it does not answer the question regarding the legal basis of Bibulus' edict. If Caesar held the fasces in July and if the prerogative to conduct the elections belonged to the holder of the fasces, only Caesar had the right to issue in July edicts concerning elections. But, this being the case, the edict of Bibulus becomes mysterious. (It is to be noted that the article cited is subsequent to Professor Taylor's paper on the Vettius affair and that the interpretation according to which Bibulus brought about the postponement by means of obnuntiatio is here dropped).

It will be a reasonable procedure to keep apart facts from the periods before and after Sulla; actually I know no cases of sortitio or comparatio in the post-Sullan period. Professor Broughton himself remarks that instances one can adduce go rather far back. In any case an agreement between Caesar and Bibulus seems to be out of the question; sortitio is still a theoretical possibility, though cases of presidency over elections in the period between 78 and 49 argue strongly against it. The evidence has been partially collected by Taylor and Broughton;[25] they cite the presidents of the electoral assembly in the years 67, 63 and 55. To this list the names of presidents in the years 78, 66, 58, 57, 56 may be added. Of those years, in 78, 67, 63, 58, 56 and 55 the elections were conducted (or, if they did not actually take place, were to be conducted) by the consuls whose names appear first in the yearly lists, respectively by M. Aemilius Lepidus[26] in 78, C. Calpurnius Piso[27] in 67, M. Tullius

[25] Taylor-Broughton 12 note 24.

[26] Appian B. C. 1. 107. 502 informs us that the consul M. Aemilius Lepidus did not return to Rome ἐπὶ τὰ ἀρχαιρέσια. If we combine this with the fact that the elections were adjourned and finally took place early in 77 under the presidency of an interrex (Sall., Hist. 1. 77. 22 M; cf. T. R. S. Broughton, The Magistrates of the Roman Republic II, New York 1952, 89, 92 note 4) it seems reasonable to infer that the electoral comitia were originally to be presided over by Lepidus. E. Gabba (Appiani Bellorum civilium liber primus, Firenze 1958, 294 ad loc.) refers the Appian statement to Lepidus' bid for re-election to the consulship (cf. Sall., Hist. 1. 77. 15M; Plut., Pomp. 16), on p. 423, however, he translates (or, rather interprets) the text under discussion as follows: Lepido ... non ritornò per presiedere i comizi consolari. The senate until the end of the year sought reconciliation with Lepidus; here seems to lie the explanation of why Lepidus had not been deprived of his post of president of the elections at once after he revolted against the senate. For full references to ancient sources and elucidating discussion on Lepidus' consulship see esp. T. Rice Holmes, The Roman Republic I, Oxford 1923, 365–369.

Lepidus' name comes first in the Fasti Capitolini and the consular datings, see A. Degrassi, Inscriptiones Italiae 13. 1, pp. 57, 484–485 (hereafter cited as Degrassi). On CIL I² 588 (SC de Asclepiade) where Lucius Caesar's rule seems to apply (Lepidus being probably absent from Rome) see Taylor-Broughton 8.

[27] The professions of the candidates were accepted by Piso (Val. Max. 3. 8. 3) and he subsequently conducted the elections. The elections because of the strife concerning a bribery law (cf. Cass. Dio 36. 38–39; Asconius p. 57–59 Clark) were postponed in that year and held at the end of August or at the beginning of September. The August date since Piso's colleague M'. Acilius Glabrio left Rome for his province of Bithynia and Pontus already in July (see Lange RA III² 213; Klebs, RE I 256–257 s. v. Acilius no 38; Broughton, MRR II 142–143, 154) does not involve the question concerning the presumable right of the holder of the fasces to direct elections. At the same time I should stress that the elections were originally scheduled for July and the prerogative to conduct them belonged undoubtedly to Piso who had already accepted professiones and spoke of his right to refuse the renuntiatio to M. Lollius Palicanus even if the latter were elected by the people (Val. Max. 3. 8. 3.).

The FC for this year are not preserved. In six out of eight instances collected by Degrassi (pp. 488–489) Piso is listed first. The exceptions are CIL I² 957 (where sole Acilius Glabrio appears) and Cass. Dio 36. 12. 1. In another place of Cass. Dio (36. 24. 3; omitted

Cicero[28] in 63, L. Calpurnius Piso[29] in 58, Cn. Cornelius Lentulus Marcellinus[30] in 56 and Cn. Pompeius[31] in 55. Of these, Lepidus, Cicero and Pompey (together with Crassus) were elected without doubt and L. Piso probably, at the head of the poll.[32] Only two years, 66 and 57, seem to show irregularity; however, as we shall see, this is not true of 57. In fact, we do not know which of the consuls conducted the consular and praetorian elections in that year; the elections of the curule aediles were to be presided over (in November) by Q. Caecilius Metellus Nepos.[33] Metellus Nepos is listed second in the Fasti and consular datings.[34] Trying to explain the fact of his presidency over elections

by Degrassi) Piso appears first. Cf. P. Stein, Die Senatssitzungen der Ciceronischen Zeit, Münster 1930, 5 (cited hereafter as Senatssitzungen); Taylor-Broughton 4 and 11 note 10.

[28] There are numerous references to Cicero's presidency over elections (Cic., Mur. 1–2, 51–52; Sull. 51; Cat. 1. 11; Sallust, Cat. 26. 5). He is first in the Fasti Amiternini (Degrassi 171; the FC are not preserved) and in all but one (CIL I² 750) consular datings (Degrassi 490–491). The elections were postponed in that year (the question of the date at which the comitia consularia eventually took place cannot be gone into here), but it was Cicero who presented a motion to that effect in the senate (Cic., Mur. 51). It is clear that he was prepared to conduct the election in July and the decision to adjourn it was made at the last moment.

[29] The praetorian elections were conducted in July by Piso (Cic., de domo 112; for the date see Cic., Att. 3. 13. 1; 14. 1); it is to be noted that the consular and praetorian comitia were performed under the same auspices. Piso is listed first by the FC (Degrassi 57); he is also first in all consular datings (Degrassi 492–493). Only in CIL I² 2500 (lex Gabinia de Delo) Gabinius is put ahead of him. Cf. Stein, Senatssitzungen 27f.; Taylor-Broughton 4 and 11 note 13.

[30] Although the elections did not take place in that year there is good reason to assume that they were to be presided over by Marcellinus: in the senate he asked Pompey and Crassus (after the election had already been announced) if they considered running for the consulship (Cass. Dio 39. 30. 1–2, cf. 39. 27. 3; Plut., Crass. 15; Pomp. 51 – Plutarch places the event at a contio). Marcellinus appears first in the Fasti and in all consular datings (Degrassi 492–493). Cf. Stein, Senatssitzungen 37ff.; Taylor-Broughton 4 and 11 note 15.

[31] The comitia praetorum (for 55) were directed by Pompey (Plut., Pomp. 52; cf. Taylor-Broughton 12 note 24); he also presided over the election of the curule aediles for 55. According to unanimous opinion of scholars the aedilician elections were conducted by Crassus; L. R. Taylor has proved, however, by an ingenious argument (auctor legis is by Cicero not the lator, but the man who uses his authority to support the law) that Cicero's words quae comitia primum habere coepit consul cum omnibus in rebus summa auctoritate, tum harum ipsarum legum ambitus auctor (pro Planc. 49) are to be referred to Pompey. See her article Magistrates of 55 B.C. in Cicero's Pro Plancio and Catullus 52, Athenaeum N. S. 42, 1964, 12ff. – Pompey's name is listed first in all datings (Degrassi 494–495). The FC are not preserved for that year. Cf. Stein, Senatssitzungen 45; Taylor-Broughton 4 and 11 note 19.

[32] For evidence see Drumann-Groebe, Geschichte Roms II 53; IV 524; Taylor-Broughton 4, 6, 8 and 12 notes 29, 31.

[33] Cic., Att. 4. 3. Because of the obstruction of Milo the comitia aedilicia did not take place until January 56. See above p. 425 and note 14; Broughton, MRR II 208.

[34] Degrassi 492–493.

of the curule aediles one can adduce two possible solutions: 1) perhaps the rule of the first consul holding elections applied only to consular and praetorian elections which were performed under the same auspices in the centuriate assembly, while the presidency over elections of minor magistrates (comitia leviora as Cicero pro Plancio 7 characterizes them) was a prerogative of the other consul. Theoretically this is possible, but taking into account the aedilician elections of 55 (for 55) presided over by Pompey, I do not think this explanation to be probable. 2) It is much more likely to suppose that the consul prior P. Cornelius Lentulus Spinther was at that time absent from the city. In fact, he left Rome before his term of office expired.[35] The date of his departure cannot be determined exactly, but it is to be noted that while in October the decree of the senate concerning Cicero's house had been brought about consulibus referentibus, at the meeting of the senate on November 14 only Metellus Nepos seems to have been acting.[36] This is especially striking since November is an odd month and the fasces should have been held by Lentulus Spinther.

On the contrary the situation in 66 is indeed confusing and to propose an explanation which would meet general acceptation seems to be extremely difficult. The consul L. Volcatius Tullus refused to accept the professio of Catiline;[37] as this was a prerogative of the presiding officer, he had apparently the right to conduct elections. Professor Broughton remarks (in a letter) that Volcatius is usually listed second.[38] It is true that in all consular datings preserved for the year Volcatius' name comes after that of his colleague. It is, however, to be noted that the Fasti Capitolini are not preserved for this year and the indications of the literary sources are contradictory.[39] Under these circumstances complete certainty regarding the position of Volcatius Tullus cannot be reached. Of course this may be used as an argument against my thesis, but certainly need not be and, in any case, it is not a damaging argument. A comparison may be helpful: in January 49 L. Cornelius Lentulus Crus, named second in the yearly list, held the fasces.[40] No one would see in this fact a proof against the rule established by Taylor and Broughton giving the first consul priority in holding the fasces. The evidence collected by Taylor and Broughton clearly does not allow of such an interpretation; accordingly the case of the second consul holding the fasces in January is to be viewed as an exception to the rule.

Of eight cases in which the names of presiding consuls are known, six exhibit perfect agreement with the theory giving the first consul the prerogative

---

[35] See Münzer, RE IV 1395 s. v. Cornelius no 238.

[36] Cic., Att. 4. 2. 4–5; de har. resp. 13. Cf. Stein, Senatssitzungen 35–36.

[37] Ascon. p. 89 Clark.   [38] The evidence is collected by Degrassi 488–489.

[39] The Fasti Hydatiani, Chronicon Paschale, Cassius Dio and Sallust give priority to Volcatius.   [40] See Taylor-Broughton 4 and 11 note 20.

to direct elections and none is against it. In one case the presidency of the consul listed second finds easy explanation in the absence of the consul prior which, in fact, lends further support to our thesis. In one case the evidence is confused allowing for divergent interpretations. This is hardly likely to be the result of chance and, consequently, there is no reason for returning to Mommsenian conception of sortitio and comparatio.[41]

This conclusion will of course have its bearing on reconstruction and evaluation of many events of 59 B.C. and it is now to be discussed what particular implications it entails.

As we have seen the consul elected first gained three important privileges: 1) the right of having his name inscribed in the first place in the Fasti 2) holding the fasces in the odd months and calling the senate for the first meeting of the year 3) presiding over elections.

The theory of Taylor and Broughton as developped above, when consequently applied to the facts reconstructed in the preceding section, leads to some important conclusions: 1) Bibulus' right to hold the elections at whatever date they occurred was based on his position of consul prior 2) from this, in turn, it is to be inferred that he was elected first and that 3) he held the fasces in January and in the odd-numbered months of the year. These conclusions, if granted, entail a thorough revision of many accepted facts concerning the history of Caesar's consulship; in particular they are inconsistent with the view propounded by Professor L. R. Taylor that Caesar carried through his first agrarian law not in April or March, as had been believed until recently, but already in January.

Caesar's name in the Fasti. Against the argumentation presented in the preceding section one serious objection may be raised: the fact that Caesar's name comes first in the yearly lists and consular datings preserved for the year.[42] As things would appear we have then two indisputable facts: Bibulus having the right to preside over elections and Caesar appearing first in the Fasti. As we know from the study of L. R. Taylor and T. R. S. Broughton first position in the Fasti depended on priority of election and indicated priority in holding the fasces. Now, we have shown that the right to direct elections depended also on priority of election. Positing the correctness of both my and

[41] Professor Taylor pointed out to me an interesting passage of Livy that may give some additional support to my thesis. It reads as follows (32. 28. 4): neque ulla alia res maius bello impedimentum ad eam diem fuisset, quam quod ... in ipso conatu gerendi belli prior consul revocaretur. L. R. Taylor remarks rightly that at that time (197 B.C.) either accomodation or sortitio prevailed. I am therefore inclined to think that here Livy projected the late republican usage into the second century. The case of M. Aemilius Lepidus in 78 (see above, note 26) offers a striking parallel to his report. Professor Taylor notes further that in the lex Malacitana 52 the duumvir maior natu is directed to hold comitia; this reflects, however, rather Augustan than republican arrangements.

[42] See Degrassi 492–493.

Taylor-Broughton's theory there is only one way of escape from this seemingly unsolvable contradiction: to assume that in 59 the Fasti are out of order. This is not so hazardous a solution as it might seem at first sight. Professor Taylor herself has shown that the Augustan editors of the consular list reconstructed it so as to make it fitting for the political goals of the new regime. It is especially conspicuous and most important for our argument that in many cases in which the order of the consuls' names, as given by the Fasti, is divergent from that transmitted by Livy and other writers, the names of predecessors of Augustus' family and of the pontifices who made up the commission editing the list, are put in the Fasti in the first place.[43] It had a priori to be expected that by the re-edition of the yearly list Caesar's name would be placed first. The name of divus Iulius, the father of Augustus, could not have appeared after that of M. Bibulus, his political and personal enemy. So the order was reversed.

The consular datings are perhaps more intriguing. We may, however, suppose that in those datings the rule of L. Caesar was applied, according to which the term consul maior designated vel eum penes quem fasces sint vel eum qui prior factus sit.[44] So in the datings the name of the consul actually holding the fasces, though elected after his colleague, could have been placed first. This is the more probable as since the time Bibulus had shut himself up in his house only Caesar could have been considered as acting consul (i. e. consul maior according to the first definition of L. Caesar). This situation is excellently depicted by a popular witticism circulating in Rome that it was the year of the consulship of Iulius and Caesar.[45]

Caesar's election to the consulship. Is there any indication in the sources that Caesar was elected to the consulship after Bibulus? A pendant question would be: is there any indication that he was elected first? The answer to either query is: no. The sources say simply nothing definite. Plutarch states in a rhetorical fashion that Caesar was elected brilliantly,[46] Cassius Dio informs that his election was unanimous,[47] but he is speaking here only of the attitude adopted by the followers of Pompey and Crassus. One gets an impression that Caesar's election is referred to in view of his further accomplishments. Besides, a possibility cannot be excluded that Caesar and Bibulus got all the votes; in that case the decision regarding the priority was probably made by lot. At any rate Bibulus emerged as consul prior and the evidence concerning Caesar's election is not against this view.

The date of Caesar's first agrarian law. The belief that Caesar held the fasces in January and that only the consul being in actual possession of the fasces

---

[43] L. R. Taylor, New Indications of Augustan Editing in the Capitoline Fasti, CPh 46, 1951, 73 ff.   [44] Festus p. 154 L. Cf. Taylor-Broughton 6.

[45] Suet., Caes. 20.   [46] Caes. 14, Crass. 14.

[47] 37. 54. 3. Full references to ancient sources will be found in Drumann-Groebe III 177.

could preside in the senate is essential for L. R. Taylor's theory putting the passage of Caesar's first agrarian law on one of the last days of January.[48] The point concerning the presidency in the senate seems to me to be proved beyond any doubt,[49] but if our argumentation that Bibulus was the first consul and that he held the fasces in January is accepted, one of the pillars of L. R. Taylor's theory will be damaged. It is to be noted that the question of whether only the consul holding the fasces could exercise the ius cum populo agendi (which seems very doubtful) has no bearing on dating of Caesar's legislation: before submitting the project of his bill to the vote of the tribes Caesar presented it to the senate and did not turn directly to the assembly until after his plans had been disapproved by the senate.

A letter of Cicero written in December 60 is claimed by Taylor and Broughton[50] to produce unmistakable evidence that Caesar did have the fasces in January. Because of importance attached to that text by the scholars named above I reproduce it below. Cicero, ad Att. 2. 3. 3: Venio nunc ad mensem Ianuarium et ad ὑπόστασιν nostram ac πολιτείαν, in qua Σωκρατικῶς εἰς ἑκάτερον sed tamen ad extremum, ut illi solebant, τὴν ἀρέσκουσαν. Est res sane magni consilii; nam aut fortiter resistendum est legi agrariae, in quo est quaedam dimicatio sed plena laudis, aut quiescendum, quod non est dissimile atque ire in Solonium aut Antium, aut etiam adiuvandum, quod a me aiunt Caesarem sic expectare ut non dubitet.

It is to be stressed that the letter does not contain any direct information concerning the fasces of Caesar, nor does it say anything definite about the date of Caesar's agrarian law. This being the case, any conclusion we infer from the words of Cicero is a matter of interpretation and it is not impossible to imagine an interpretation divergent from that put forward by Taylor and Broughton. Should we not, for instance, take the expression venio nunc ad mensem Ianuarium to mean the year 59 in general, January 1 marking the beginning of Caesar's consulship?

It seems that there are only two certain facts we know about the date of Caesar's law: that the terminus ante quem for it is the beginning of April and that it was passed on a comitial day preceding the senatorial meeting at which Bibulus tried in vain to find some one who would bring forward the question of the validity of Caesar's law.[52] If this meeting was held under the presidency

[48] On the Chronology of Caesar's First Consulship, AJPh 72, 1951, 254–268. In that paper Professor Taylor dates the passage of the law on January 28; in the notes for an unwritten paper on chronology of 59 (which she had kindly put at my disposition) she argues, however, that the law was passed on the 29th.

[49] Ch. Meier (Zur Chronologie und Politik in Caesars erstem Konsulat, Historia 10, 1961, 69 note 2) denies this; however, he adduces no arguments. The circumstances of Cic., Phil. 8. 33 (cited by O'Brien Moore, RE Suppl. VI 701) are quite exceptional.

[50] Taylor, Chronology 258; Broughton, MRR II 187.

[51] Taylor, Chronology 257.   [52] Suet., Caes. 20.

of Bibulus[53] the law was passed either in a month in which Bibulus had the fasces (i. e. according to our thesis in an odd month) or on the last day of the preceding month (the senatorial meeting in that latter case is to be placed on the first day of an odd month). Only March and February 28 fit in with this scheme, January being excluded since Caesar could not convene the senate until February. Under a lex Gabinia February was reserved for hearings of the foreign embassies: these hearings could, however, have been postponed (as was the case in 56 and probably in 60[54]) and it is possible that Caesar presented his bill to the senate in February (when he had the fasces). When reconstructing the chronology of Caesar's consulship one should remember that Caesar was pontifex maximus and therefore it is tempting to assume an intercalary month.[55] There is no indication in the sources as to whom the fasces belonged in that month: did they rest with the consul holding them in February or pass over to the other one? When, however, we consider that the intercalary month was inserted after Terminalia and lasted until Regifugium, i. e. that after it followed still five days of February, it will appear rather improbable that there should have been any change in holding the fasces. It seems therefore possible to assume that the lex agraria was voted on in March or on February 28, the discussion in the senate taking place in the intercalary month.

Cicero, ad Atticum 2. 15. 2 and the dilatio comitiorum. It is a striking fact about the postponement of elections in 59 that the letter Cic., ad Att. 2. 20. 6 which we have discussed above, was not the first to mention a dilatio comitiorum. In ad Att. 2. 15. 2 we read as follows: Bibuli autem ista magnitudo animi in comitiorum dilatione quid habet nisi ipsius iudicium sine ulla correctione rei p. ? The letter is dated between April 24 and 29[56] and since in that month normally no elections took place Cicero's information becomes enigmatic. Most scholars who have commented on the text under discussion have interpreted it as a reference to the regular elections for 60.[57] Bibulus could indeed have announced in April that he would not convene the electoral assembly on its normal July term. This solution, however, seems somewhat strange, because in that case the edict of Bibulus would have amounted to the postponing of an assembly that had not been previously ordered to convene. On

---

[53] The questions concerning the senatorial procedure cannot be discussed here. L. R. Taylor in her paper on the chronology of Caesar's consulship (p. 260) thought that the meeting referred to by Suetonius (Caes. 20) was presided over by Caesar, however, subsequently, she changed her view (in the "Notes" cited above, note 48) and returned to the opinion held by E. Meyer, Caesars Monarchie und das Principat des Pompeius[3], Stuttgart u. Berlin 1922, 71 that Bibulus was presiding.

[54] Cic., Q. fr. 2. 3. 1; Att. 1. 18. 7.

[55] A possibility of an intercalary month is assumed also by L. R. Taylor in her "Notes" (see above, note 48).

[56] See L. A. Constans, Cicéron, Correspondance I, Paris 1950, 189, 239.

[57] E. Meyer, Caesars Monarchie 81 note 4; Ch. Meier, op. cit. 93.

the other hand, however, since July was, in the post-Sullan period, the normal term for elections, any announcement to the effect that they would not take place at that time might easily have been looked upon as a dilatio. If this were the case, why then, did Bibulus issue a new edict in July? An explanation can be afforded of this query as well: it is possible that the April edict either did not fix a definite date for the elections, or if it did, perhaps Bibulus wanted to change it and announce a still later one. The other problem is, does the above reconstruction fit the political situation in April and July? One may ask why Caesar did not react immediately in April, when his political position was strong, but waited until July. Moreover, from Cicero's description one gains a strong impression that Caesar was completely baffled by Bibulus' July maneuver. However, let it be remarked that the impressions of different scholars are normally also different and any such argumentation is bound to remain inconclusive.

None the less there is still a possibility that has escaped the scholars. Bibulus' edict could have been concerned with an election called to fill a vacancy and not with regular elections for 58. Unfortunately we know of no magistrate who died in office early in 59; we only happen to know that an augur, Q. Caecilius Metellus Celer (cos. 60), died before leaving the city. His death occurred probably before April and not later than the middle of that month.[58] A candidate for the augurate was P. Vatinius,[59] archenemy of the optimate faction. It would be tempting to suppose that Bibulus delayed just these augural elections; this idea is, however, unacceptable: since the lex of T. Labienus in 63 the elections of the priests had occurred only at a set time between the consular and praetorian ones.[60] The only remaining possibility is to consider the election for a vacant magistracy which is possible, but cannot be positively proved.

The lex Campana and the professio of candidates. The second agrarian law concerning the ager Campanus and the campus Stellas passed by the end of May[61] contained a clause requiring the candidates to take an oath of allegiance to the leges Iuliae before a contio. Cicero informs us of this provision reporting as follows (ad Att. 2. 18. 2): Habet etiam Campana lex execrationem in contione candidatorum, si mentionem fecerint quo aliter ager possideatur atque ut ex legibus Iuliis. Non dubitant iurare ceteri; Laterensis existimatur laute fecisse quod tribunatum pl. petere destitit ne iuraret.

[58] T. R. S. Broughton, Metellus Celer's Gallic Province, TAPhA 79, 1948, 73–76; MRR II 183.

[59] Cic., Att. 2. 5. 2; 9. 2; 7. 3. Vatinius was not elected, see Cic., Vat. 19; cf. Cael. 59, Sest. 130, Sch. Bob. p. 147 Stangl.

[60] Mommsen, Staatsrecht II³ 31–32; L. R. Taylor, The Election of the Pontifex Maximus in the Late Republic, CPh 37, 1942, 422.

[61] On the date see Taylor, Chronology 256.

According to L. R. Taylor the letter cited above belongs to the time of the
professio of tribunicial candidates;[62] she seems thus to assume that the professio was performed at the contio referred to by Cicero. Ch. Meier objects to
that interpretation that in fact we do not know whether the contio took place
at or after, the time of the professio.[63]

It is surprizing that the scholars who discussed our text have spoken only
of the professio of the tribunicial candidates. To be sure, Cicero does not say
that the oath was taken exclusively by the candidates for the tribunate; he
reports that of all candidates only Iuventius Laterensis refused to take the
prescribed oath and therefore resigned from running for the tribunate. His
information regarding the clause from the lex Campana bears a general character and it is clear that the law did not single out the tribunicial candidates.
If Cicero refers to a tribunicial candidate it is only for that reason that the
only candidate who refused to take the oath happened to be standing for the
tribunate of the plebs.

By the time the letter under discussion was written[64] the contio of the candidates had already taken place – according to our interpretation it was a
contio of all candidates and not exclusively of tribunicial ones. Could this
mean that by that time the professio of all candidates, including those standing for the curule magistracies, was over as well?

First of all it is to be stressed that there is no explicit mention of the professio in Cicero's letter. Any view that identifies the contio candidatorum with
the act of professio or tries to establish the sequence of these events must be
carefully argued. L. R. Taylor holds that the contio and professio were simultaneous, Ch. Meier that the professio preceded the contio.[65] There is only one
possibility left and I am going to show that the professio could have taken
place only after the contio candidatorum.

The first problem to be solved is which magistrate had the duty of convening the contio. There must have been a special point in the lex dealing
with the president of the contio. The legislator had only two possibilities to
choose from: he could assign the duty of summoning the contio either to the
presidents of the electoral assemblies or to another magistrate, probably a
consul. In the first case two separate meetings would have been required, respectively for the candidates running for the curule offices and those standing
for the plebeian ones. The language of Cicero (as we have argued above) who
speaks only of one contio and of candidates in general is not in favour of this
possibility (with which, however, both the interpretation proposed by Taylor
and that of Meier correspond). Moreover it seems hardly likely that Caesar

---

[62] The Vettius Affair, Historia 1, 1950, 47.   [63] Op. cit. 93 note 10.

[64] It was written at any rate before the ludi Apollinares were over (that is before July
12) and since in ad Att. 2. 19. 3 an incident in the theater is referred to, probably before
the beginning of the ludi.   [65] See above, notes 62 and 63.

should have entrusted the president of the electoral comitia – that is Bibulus – with a prerogative so important for the sake of his legislation. Probably Caesar in his law directed one of the consuls to convene the meeting of the candidates (with an unexpressed but clear intention that he himself would see that the contio be summoned before the elections).

The consideration of the technicalities of professio lends further support to our thesis. The act of professio never took place before the people (i. e. the contio) but before a magistrate (the president of the electoral assembly) and there is no evidence that it was performed by all candidates at one time.[66] To be sure, what we know of Caesar's professio in 60 shows clearly that it could have been performed on any day within the legally prescribed period.[67] If all legal requirements were not complied with by a candidate the presiding magistrate was obliged to refuse to accept the professio (unless a dispensation had been decreed by the senate). These requirements were set up mostly by special statutes such as the Sullan law de magistratibus or the lex annalis; new provisions were subsequently added by other bills, as did also the lex Campana. The presiding officer having accepted the professio of a candidate stated officially that the latter was legally entitled to stand for a magistracy. Probably by the act of rationem accipere the president bound himself not to refuse to announce officially (renuntiare) the election of any of the accepted candidates. This precludes the possibility of professio preceding the contio candidatorum: it is clear that until the necessary legal requirement in 59 – the oath taking, had not been complied with by the candidates, they could not present themselves before the presidents of the electoral assemblies.[68]

The conclusion we have reached above implies that by the time of Cic., ad Att. 2. 18 the elections both of the curule and the plebeian magistrates had not yet been announced. According to Mommsen's view which like so many others became an article of faith, the act of professio in the post-Sullan epoch had to be performed in a period of time preceding the announcement of elections. The edict would then not only fix the date of the elections, but contain

---

[66] Mommsen, Staatsrecht I³ 471 note 1, 501 ff.

[67] Cf. App., B. C. 2. 8; Plut., Caes. 13; Suet., Caes. 18.

[68] A striking analogy to the clause of Caesar's law is to be found in the provision of the lex Latina Tabulae Bantinae (on this law which is to be dated in the post-Gracchan period see G. Barbieri, Dizionario Epigrafico IV 716–717 s. v. lex; the edition cited is that by S. Riccobono, Fontes Iuris Romani Anteiustiniani I, Florentiae 1941, 82–84). We read linn. 19–20: Qu]ei ex h(ace) l(ege) non iourauerit, is magistratum inperiumue nei petito neiue gerito neiue habeto, neiue in senatu [sententiam deicito deicereue eum] ni quis sinito, neiue eum censor in senatum legito. It is interesting that the law barred those who had not sworn not only from habere and gerere a magistracy, but also from petere. A similar provision must have been inserted in the law of Caesar: Laterensis tribunatum pl. petere destitit, we read in Cicero's letter. On the oath taking by the senators see E.Meyer, Caesars Monarchie 67–68 and L. R. Taylor, Party Politics in the Age of Caesar, Berkeley and Los Angeles 1949, 134.

also a list of candidates[69] (becoming thus formally comparable to the promulgatio of a law). It has never been clear when, in the view of Mommsen and his followers, the period of presenting of the candidatures began. If we place it with Mommsen before the announcement of elections it will appear that in 59 the professio should already have taken place in April. If Bibulus' edict set a date for elections (according to Ch. Meier an August date[70]) the electioneering period would have already begun in April and by that time the professions must have been over. No one will readily subscribe to this reconstruction which is, however, clearly implied by the common view of the time of professio. But perhaps Bibulus did not set a definite date in April. Then the electioneering period began in July and lasted till October 18. The terminus ante quem for professio of candidates running for curule offices would in that case have been the date of Bibulus' edict. Here, however, a new difficulty arises. There is no doubt that to accept professions was an exclusive right of the president of elections. But Bibulus remained shut up in his house and consequently he was not able to accept the professions of the candidates (it is almost certain that the act of professio had to be performed in a public place, probably in the Forum). Who then did accept them? Unless there was a strictly limited period for the candidates to present themselves during which the consul acting in the capacity of the president of elections must have been uninterruptedly on hand, I see no possibility of solving this difficulty. If the consul who was to accept candidacies had, because of a prolonged illness or some other reason, been prevented from fulfilling his duty, it is most probable to assume that his colleague automatically took over his task. At any rate it is clear that the period of professions must not have stretched over many months. I would suggest that this period is to be placed not before but after the announcement of elections.[71] It was probably the period of 24 days counting back from the day for which the comitia were scheduled. This proposition has, at any rate, one advantage: a clause of the lex Fufia is believed to have provided that no law could be promulgated or passed in the period between the announcement and the holding of the elections.[72] This period is usually thought to have lasted 24 days (trinum nundinum); what, however, would be the solution if the elections were postponed or announced long in advance (as in 59)? Is it conceivable that in that case the clause prohibiting legislation before elections was valid during the two, three or more months that had elapsed since the original announcement? It seems therefore reasonable to assume that the Fufian law forbade proposing and voting on laws only in the period of 24 consecutive days immediately preceding the election day.

---

[69] Staatsrecht I³ 471–472, 502–504. Cf. A. E. Astin, "Professio" in the Abortive Election of 184 B.C., Historia 11, 1962, 252 ff.

[70] Op. cit. 94 note 14.   [71] I shall discuss this question in detail elsewhere.

[72] On the whole problem see now esp. G. V. Sumner, op. cit., 340 ff.

Bibulus, Caesar and the consular elections. Let us now present a tentative reconstruction of Bibulus' and Caesar's maneuvres concerning the elections. About the end of April Caesar posted his project of the lex Campana; Bibulus on hearing that it included a clause to the effect that all candidates had to take an oath to adhere to the leges Iuliae decided to counteract and announced that he would not convene the electoral comitia in July.[73] About the end of June Caesar acting according to the provision of his law summoned the contio and the candidates (except Iuventius Laterensis) took the oath. Not long before July 25 Bibulus postponed the comitia to October 18. While doing so he evidently hoped that something favourable to the optimates would happen. The political situation did not, however, change and in October Bibulus had not enough courage to leave his house and resume his duties as consul and president of elections.[74] Caesar then appeared on the stage and took over (as he was probably required to do by a constitutional rule) the task of accepting professiones and conducting elections. The henchmen of the triumvirs Piso and Gabinius were elected to the consulship.

Further remarks are needed here. No source explicitly states that Caesar conducted the elections personally; it is, however, very probable that they really did take place on October 18 since in a letter written after October 25 a praetor designatus is referred to.[75] Cicero speaks of Piso (in Pis. 3): tu consul es renuntiatus ... impeditis rei publicae temporibus, dissidentibus consulibus. Professor Broughton notes (in a letter) that, if Bibulus held the election, he had to announce as consuls strongly opposed to him Piso and Gabinius. The expression dissidentibus consulibus seems to be in that case an unusually mild statement. I have nothing to add to these just remarks. In fact, it is highly improbable that Bibulus directed the elections and performed the solemn act of renuntiatio of Piso and Gabinius – had he done so, it would have amounted to his having surrendered to the triumvirs. On the contrary, Cicero took active part in the election serving as custos on behalf of Piso.[76]

There is still one question. One may ask why Bibulus did not delay the election until the end of the year. The answer may be that either the president

---

[73] Bibulus' edict is mentioned in ad Att. 2. 15; the first reference to the lex Campana is in ad Att. 2. 16 which was written on April 29 or May 1. The only date mentioned in 2. 15 is the 5th of May: Cicero informs Atticus that he will wait for him in Formiae usque ad III Nonas Maias. This letter may have been written on May 2 or 3 and it seems therefore quite possible that 2. 16 preceded 2. 15.

[74] I do not propose to discuss here the Vettius affair which is rather a political and not a constitutional problem. It seems to me still likely, in spite of Ch. Meier's criticism, to date it with L. R. Taylor in mid-July. One might object to this that our thesis of professio following the contio candidatorum is inconsistent with L. R. Taylor's dating of the Vettius affair. This is not so. The tribunicial elections may have been announced immediately after the contio candidatorum.

[75] Cic., Q. fr. 1. 2. 10.   [76] Cic., post red. in sen. 17; Pis. 11.

of elections was legally bound (unless prevented by a hindrance) to announce and convene the electoral assembly before his term of office expired, or that Bibulus fearing that Caesar might resort to violence simply gave up.

I hope that the theory of the order of the consuls' names in the yearly lists built up more than a decade ago by eminent Bryn Mawr scholars and developped in the present paper as the theory of presidency over elections may prove to be a useful tool in further investigations of Rome's complicated political and constitutional history in the post-Sullan period. It should be given priority over any even ingenious but isolated conjecture and interpretation and it ought not to be abandoned unless refuted by clear and unmistakable facts.

6

WERE POMPEY AND CRASSUS ELECTED IN ABSENCE TO THEIR FIRST CONSULSHIP?

In summer 71 two victorious generals Cn. Pompeius Magnus and M. Licinius Crassus, having crushed respectively Sertorius in Spain and the uprising of Spartacus in Italy, stood at the head of their armies outside the gates of Rome demanding consulship and triumph[1]. This, at any rate in respect to Pompey, was a totally unconstitutional demand, for Pompey had not yet reached the age prescribed for consulship by the annal law and had not previously held any other regular magistracy. In view of a coalition between the generals and the popular leader the tribune M. Lollius Palicanus the senate was, however, compelled to yield and to exempt Pompey from observing the *lex annalis*[2], to vote a triumph for him and an ovation for Crassus. And so Pompey, an *eques Romanus*, and Crassus were elected to the highest magistracy of the Roman state.

Now, there are scholars who assert that the senate granted Pompey and Crassus two further dispensations from the provisions of the Sullan law *de magistratibus*: 1) from the provision forbidding the election of absent candidates, 2) from the provision requiring the candidates to perform in person the act of *professio*[3], that is the act of the official announcement of candidature to the presiding officer of the electoral assembly[4].

[1] For detailed description and analysis of Pompey's, Crassus' and the senate's manoeuvres in 71 see T. RICE HOLMES, The Roman Republic and the Founder of the Empire, I, Oxford 1923, 161 ff.; M. GELZER, Das erste Consulat des Pompeius und die Übertragung der grossen Imperien, Kleine Schriften II, Wiesbaden 1963, 158 ff. (published originally in Abh. d. Preuss. Akad. d. Wiss., Phil-Hist. Kl. 1943 no 1); J. VAN OOTEGHEM, Pompée le Grand, Bruxelles 1954, 138 ff.

[2] The question whether Crassus also needed a dispensation from the *lex annalis* depends upon whether he held his praetorship in 72 (so LAST in Cambridge Ancient History 9,333; HOLMES, op. cit. 159; OOTEGHEM, op. cit. 138) or in 73, which seems more plausible (see GELZER, RE s. v. Licinius no 68, col. 302; T. R. S. BROUGHTON, The Magistrates of the Roman Republic II, New York 1952, 110, 118, 121 note 2). In that latter case there would have been the normal interval of two years between his praetorship and consulship, so that he could seek the consulship in 71 (for 70) in full accordance with the existing laws.

[3] On *professio* in general see esp. Th. MOMMSEN, Römisches Staatsrecht I³, Leipzig 1887, 501–504. On the announcements of candidature in the post-Sullan period see the chapter on *professio* in J. LINDERSKI, Rzymskie zgromadzenie wyborcze od Sulli do Cezara (The Roman Electoral Assembly from Sulla to Caesar), Kraków 1966.

[4] The problems concerning the presidency over the electoral assembly after Sulla are discussed in my article: Constitutional Aspects of the Consular Elections in 59 B. C., Historia 14, 1965, 392 ff.

That assertion has recently been restated by J. P. V. D. Balsdon in his study on *absentis ratio*[5]. He registers Pompey and Crassus as elected in 71 in absence to their first joint consulship. Balsdon tries to prove this thesis by subtle reasoning; he is, however, not the first to propound it. The same opinion was expressed in 1954 by J. Van Ooteghem[6], in 1952 by F. Miltner[7] and still earlier, in 19th century by W. Drumann[8].

The thesis of Pompey and Crassus being elected in absence to the consulship of 70 rests on three laboriously erected pillars — but I would contend that all of them are fragile or — I even dare to say — non-existent.

I. The first one may conveniently be characterized as tacit identification of *professio* and *electio*. The scholars cited above are, of course, well aware that profession and election were two different acts — but nevertheless they are ignoring the basic fact that *professio* and *electio* did not take place either on the same day or on the same spot. This is especially characteristic of Balsdon's arguing based on the following premise: if a candidate was required by law to be present at election, he was also required to make his *professio* in person. In this way *professio* and *electio* become, in respect to the presence or absence of a candidate, interchangeable terms and they are used as such in Balsdon's argumentation. A few examples will illustrate this method. P.141 Balsdon writes: "From earlier than the time of Marius the law forbade the election to curule office of anyone who was not present at the *professio*". The source for this contention is Plutarch, Marius 12; in fact, Plutarch's passage contains no word about *professio*[9]. He says only that the law forbade the election of absent candidates; whether it also forbade professions in absence we are not told.

According to Mommsen[10] the obligation of *professio* in person was introduced between January 63 and July 60. In any case it existed in 60 when Caesar canvassed for the consulship. Balsdon alleges that Caesar addressed the application to the senate "to be allowed to stand in absence for the consulship of 59" (p. 141). The relative sources[11] leave, however, no doubt that what Caesar really wanted to get was not the general permission "to stand in absence for the consulship" (that is permission to be elected in absence), but only exemption from the provision requiring personal *professio*. As Caesar had still in prospect his triumph from Spain and without forfeiting the right to it he could not cross the pomerium, it has rightly been reasoned that the

---

[5] Roman History, 65–50 B. C.: Five Problems. V. *Absentis Ratio*, JRS 52, 1962, 140–141. In spite of the article by Balsdon (with whom I disagree on most points) the problem of *absentis ratio* and elections in absence (which is not at all the same thing, as Balsdon seems to admit) still calls for a special and detailed discussion. Here I shall confine myself only to problems having immediate bearing on the query expressed in the title of the present paper.

[6] Op. cit., 139–140.

[7] RE s. v. Cn. Pompeius Magnus, col. 2087–2088.

[8] W. Drumann–P. Groebe, Geschichte Roms, IV, Leipzig 1908, 395 (going back to Drumann's original edition). Drumann assumes that the war against Spartacus lasted until winter (an error corrected by Groebe: the revolt of Spartacus was already crushed in spring) and that for that reason Crassus was far away from Rome at the moment of election. In respect to Pompey he writes: "Es ist ungewiss, ob er sich zu rechter Zeit meldete; in jedem Falle aber war auch er als Abwesender zu betrachten". However, Pompey and Crassus do not appear on Groebe's list of men elected in absence (ibid., IV, 138, n. 7).

[9] The text reads as follows: Καὶ τὸ δεύτερον ὕπατος ἀπεδείχθη, τοῦ μὲν νόμου κωλύοντος ἀπόντα καὶ μὴ διαλιπόντα χρόνον ὡρισμένον αὖθις αἱρεῖσθαι, τοῦ δὲ δήμου τοὺς ἀντιλέγοντας ἐκβαλόντος.

[10] Op. cit., I³, 503, n. 3.

[11] Appian B. c. II 8; Plutarch, Caes. 13; Suetonius, Caes. 18.

act of *professio* had to be performed inside the pomerium, probably on the Comitium[12]. It was therefore essential to him to be exempted from the obligation of *professio* in person; to which end, however, would he (as he waited before the gates of Rome) have needed the general permission "to stand in absence for the consulship" is not comprehensible to the present writer (see below the remarks in section III).

On the other hand the *professio* in person was not obligatory still in January 63. The information to that effect is contained in Cicero's speech *de lege agraria* 2.24. Criticizing the Rullus' plan to elect a special land commission the orator says: "Presentem enim profiteri iubet, quod nulla allia in lege umquam fuit ne in iis quidem magistratibus, quorum certus ordo est". Balsdon interprets this that according to Rullus' project "no candidate's name could be accepted unless he was present in Rome at the election" (p. 141). Let us, however, observe that there is in Cicero's text no mention of election: Cicero speaks only of *professio*. Also Mommsen's and Lange's discussion of the problem lacks sharp distinction between *professio* and *electio*. Like Balsdon, they see a contradiction between information supplied by Plutarch and Cicero, but, unlike him, dismiss the former one. Mommsen seems to interpret both texts as concerning *professio*[13] which, as we have seen, is true only in the case of Cicero's words. Lange is of the opinion that before 63 both elections and professions were allowed in absence[14]. Balsdon, on the contrary, holds that from the end of the second century elections and professions in absence were forbidden. He asserts that "what Rullus must have proposed was that in no circumstances whatever should either the people or the Senate be allowed to give special exemption to any single individual to stand in absence for a place on the commission" (p. 141).

But the explanation is much simpler. There is no contradiction between Plutarch and Cicero. The law forbidding elections in absence was already in force at the time of Marius and remained so to the end of the republic. That law is referred to in Plutarch, Marius 12. The idea of *professio* in person was first conceived by Rullus (in 63) in respect to election of land-commissioners. A provision to that effect concerning all regular magistracies was laid down in a law enacted shortly afterwards.

II. An essential factor in the misinterpretation of the circumstances of Pompey's and Crassus' election in 71 is the belief that their case was wholly parallel to that of Caesar in 60. F. Miltner's article on Pompey in RE (21 col. 2087) is the most representative for that belief: "Solange er an der Spitze der Truppen stand... konnte er sich nicht zur Konsulatswahl präsentieren. Es was das gleiche Dilemma, das rund ein Jahrzehnt später Caesar durch den überraschenden Verzicht auf den Triumph in seiner Weise löste... (col. 2088): Der Senat musste sich beugen... und so gewährte er dem Feldherrn die Dispens von den Gesetzen".

The analogy is indeed attractive. Caesar waited for his triumph and so did Pompey; at the same time both canvassed for the consulship. Caesar, however, was not given dispensation from the provision requiring the candidates to profess in person and, seeking his main goal — the consulship, gave up the triumph. Pompey, on the other hand, broke through the senate's opposition, gained the consulship and on 29th December, the last day of the year (in the pre-

---

[12] MOMMSEN, op. cit. I³ 503.

[13] Op. cit., I³, 503, n. 3.

[14] L. LANGE, Römische Alterthümer I³, Berlin 1876, 718; III² (1876), 263. Cf. also NEUMANN, RE I s. v. *absentia*, col. 116–117.

Julian calendar) celebrated his second triumph. Is it legitimate to infer from this that he was granted by the senate that exemption that eleven years later was refused to Caesar? Such a conclusion is suggested by Miltner, Balsdon and Drumann.

So we have here a fine piece of syllogistic thinking, but this is hardly a method for historical research. The truth is that Pompey's and Crassus' situation in 71 resembled that of Caesar in 60 only to some extent; it is not to be forgotten that the differences between the electoral law in force in 71 and 60 are equally, if not even more important, than the similarities. As we have seen, the provision forbidding elections in absence dates from before 104 (the second consulship of Marius). On the contrary, the law requiring *professio* in person was enacted at earliest in 63. So, from the constitutional point of view, in any case as far as the presence or absence of a candidate at the act of *professio* is concerned, no analogy can be detected between Pompey's and Caesar's situation. Pompey and Crassus simply could not have been exempted from a provision that did not yet exist at that time.

III. But personal attendance of candidates at election was required by law in 71. Perhaps Pompey and Crassus were granted dispensation from that provision? This is the view of Ooteghem: "Un sénatus-consulte affranchit Pompée des dispositions de la lex Villia annalis et de la lex Cornelia de magistratibus et lui permit d'accéder au consulat, bien qu'il... fût absent de Rome au moment du vote" (pp. 139–140). One may, however, ask: where did Ooteghem find the information to that effect? In the sources there is no such evidence. Obviously he reached this conclusion in the same way as Balsdon who contends that Pompey and Crassus were elected in absence "for Pompey's triumph on 29th December and Crassus' ovation were considerably later than the consular elections" (p. 140).

This contention constitutes the main and, at the same time, most fallacious pillar of the theory under criticism. Balsdon obviously thinks that as Caesar having crossed the pomerium forfeited his right to the triumph, Pompey and Crassus would have done the same. Caesar did not, however, cross the pomerium in order to participate at his election, but only because of the fact that on the last day reserved for the professions to be made at that time in person he was not yet ready with the preparations for his triumph. In 71 Pompey and Crassus could announce their candidature through the intermediary of their friends.

The elections of consuls and praetors were performed by the *comitia centuriata*. In this connection it is to be borne in mind that the centuriate assembly as originally, and, at least in theory until its ultimate disparition under the empire, a military assembly could not gather within the pomerium, the sacred boundary of Rome. And indeed the meeting-place of the *comitia centuriata*, the Campus Martius lay outside the pomerium. These facts are easily to be found in any handbook of Roman antiquities or Roman topography.

Pompey and Crassus did not need any exemption from the law forbidding elections in absence: the *comitia centuriata* gathering outside the pomerium, they could take part at the electoral meeting that returned them as consuls and, at the same time, retain their right to celebrate triumph resp. ovation.

Balsdon writes that Pompey's "other disqualifications were so numerous that his 'absence' is not stressed at all in our sources" (p. 140 n. 50). The "absence" of Pompey and Crassus at their election is not mentioned in our sources for one reason: because they were present.

7

A. GABINIUS A. F. CAPITO

AND THE FIRST VOTER IN THE LEGISLATIVE COMITIA TRIBUTA

E. S. Staveley in his interesting article on the role of the first voter in Roman legislative assemblies has convincingly argued that the first voter in the legislative tribal assembly was selected by the presiding magistrate. [1] As evidence he adduces Cicero, pro Plancio 35 and de domo 79–80. An inscription from Delos omitted by Staveley (lex Gabinia Calpurnia de Delo of 58)[2] offers additional support for his theory. Line 4 reads as follows: A. Gabinius A.f. Capito pr [. The letters pr [have been interpreted as the beginning of the phrase pr [o tribu primus scivit. [3] The consuls who presented the law were A. Gabinius A.f. and L. Calpurnius L.f. Piso. The upper part of the stone where the names of the rogators were engraved is broken off, but they are partially preserved in the Greek text in lines 37–38: [Αὖλος Γ]αβείνιος Αὖλου [υἱὸς –] υ [| ...υἱὸ]ς Πείσων ὕπατ[. The restoration of a blank space between Αὖλου and the next legible υ presents a difficulty. After Αὖλου must follow υἱὸς[4] but the effaced space is larger and υἱὸς does not fill it. According to E. Cuq, the first editor of the whole inscription, the cognomen Καπείτων should be inserted after υἱὸς; he also believed that the next

---

1) E. S. Staveley, The Role of the First Voter in Roman Legislative Assemblies, Historia 18, 1969, 513–520. Cf. also his recent book, Greek and Roman Voting and Elections, London 1972, 165–168, 254.

2) Fragments of this inscription (found in 1907 on Mykonos) were published by P. Roussel in his book, Délos, colonie Athénienne, Paris 1916, 334 notes 3 and 4. Editio princeps of the whole text and an important commentary by E. Cuq, BCH 46, 1922, 198–215; afterwards reprinted or republished in: F. Durrbach, Choix d'inscriptions de Délos, Paris 1923, no 163; AÉp. 1923, 19; SEG 1.335; CIL 1^2 2500; F. F. Abbott and A. C. Johnson, Municipal Administration in the Roman Empire, Princeton 1926, p. 284–285; Inscriptions de Délos, Paris 1937, no 1511.

3) For the reading pr [and not pro [or pro [, and for a discussion of the formula pro tribu primus scivit, see below, p. 251.

4) With the exception of Roussel and Launey (Insc. Délos 1511) all the editors have read after Αὖλου an υ, i.e. the beginning of υἱὸς. On the photograph of the squeeze there is no trace of an υ in this place.

legible υ was the beginning of ὕ[πατος.[5] Cuq's text was reprinted by R. Cagnat and M. Besnier (AÉp. 1923,19); his restoration Καπείτων has also been accepted by F. Durrbach. Hondius in SEG 1.335 introduced a correction in the Greek spelling of the cognomen Capito printing it as Καπίτων.[6] This reading also appears in the collection of Abbott-Johnson, and above all, in the most recent and the best edition of the inscription by Roussel and Launey (Insc. Délos 1511).[7]

The insertion of Καπείτων or Καπίτων entails two important consequences:
a) we woluld have to accept that A. Gabinius, the consul of 58, had the cognomen Capito, a fact not attested anywhere else,[8] although there are numerous references to him;[9] b) we would have to equate the consul A. Gabinius A. f. , the rogator of the law, with A. Gabinius A. f. Capito (mentioned in line 4) who cast the first vote for the law.[10]

---

5) SEG, Durrbach, Abbott-Johnson read ὕπ[ατος, Roussel-Launey more cautiously υπ[ατος. This is doubtful. The trace visible on the photograph does not look like the upper bar of a π; it is rather a scratch on the stone.

6) This is undoubtedly the correct form, attested many times in the Greek inscriptions. As the i in Capito is short, Καπείτων would be highly unusual.

7) They propose the following restoration of lines 37–38:
[Αὖλος Γ]αβείνιος Αὖλου [υἱὸς Καπίτων] ὕπ[ατος καὶ Λεύκιος Καλπόρνιος Λευκί-]
[ου υἱὸ]ς ̇ Πείσων ὕπατ[ος] –

8) Unless we would like to see an allusion to it in Cicero's scornful remarks about Gabinius' curled hair (p.red. in sen. 12-13,16; Sest.18; Pis.25). But Capito does not mean "curlyheaded" but "having too large a head". Cf. I.Kajanto, The Latin Cognomina, Helsinki 1965, 118-119,235.

9) There appears, however, among the Catilinarian conspirators a Roman knight P. Gabinius Capito; see on him Münzer, RE 7,1912,431 s.v. Gabinius 15, and esp. E. Badian, The Early Career of A. Gabinius (cos. 58 B.C.), Philologus 103, 1959,97-99. Badian discusses the possibility of his having been a son of P. Gabinius A. f. , praetor (probably) in 88, and thus according to his reconstruction of the stemma of the Gabinii a relative of the consul. But it is difficult to fit A. Gabinius A. f. into the stemma of the Gabinii, and therefore Badian concludes that for the time being the Gabinii Capitones must be left unattached. Distant relationship seems to be the most likely solution.

10) According to Badian (op. cit.98) this would have been a constitutional anomaly, but Gabinius "was no stickler for constitutional propriety". At the same time, however, he concedes that it is impossible to establish whether or not law and custom gave the presiding officer the right to cast the first vote for his own law. This raises an important question: when did the presiding officer cast his vote? As the last voter in his tribe? Or perhaps he did not vote at all? As the presiding magistrate had the right to select the first voter, there does not seem to have been any constitutional obstacles to his voting at the head of his tribe.

The cognomen Capito for A. Gabinius (cos. 58) has been accepted by most editors and commentators of the text; it has also found its way as a firmly established fact to standard works of reference as Dizionario Epigrafico or Ancient Roman Statutes.[11] Some historians and prosopographers remained sceptical. T. R. S. Broughton firmly rejected the identification of the two Gabinii, and R. Syme never attributes the cognomen Capito to the consul.[12] E. Badian in his article on the early career of A. Gabinius came to the conclusion (p.98) that "we have no right to restore the unattested name, unless the inscription demands it." Among the editors of the inscription only E. Lommatzsch has seen no epigraphical reason for assigning to A. Gabinius the consul the cognomen Capito. He has proposed the following restoration of line 37 (CIL 1.^{2} 2500): Αὖλος Γ]αβείνιος Αὔλου υ[ἰὸς ὕπατος καὶ Λε]ύ[κιος Καλπούρνιος. The CIL editor asserts that there is no space for the cognomen. This makes one wonder since in the blank space where other editors have proposed to read υ[ἰὸς (or [υἰὸς) Καπίτων (or Καπείτων)] i.e. 10 or 11 letters,[13] Lommatzsch found enough room to insert 14 or rather (see note 13) 15 letters. E. Badian (op.cit. p.99 and n.1) was rightly not satisfied with the alternative reading suggested by the CIL editor; on the one hand, he remarked, "it is not by any means certain that the insertion of the name is even possible", but on the other "the Latin text can easily be restored so as to permit it, and the beginning of the Greek text (11. 37 f.) has almost certainly been wrongly restored". He concluded that "if, ... (as seems likely) the line[i.e. 1.37]should be shortened, there would be no room for the name "Capito"." In fact the possibility of the restoration of the name Capito depends above all upon the length of the blank space between Αὔλου and υ. Badian reports that he had tried in vain "to get information from Delos, where the stone is said to be".[14]

11) See G. Tibiletti, DE 4,1957, s.v. lex, p.722; A.C. Johnson, P.R. Coleman-Norton, F.C. Bourne, Ancient Roman Statutes, Austin 1961, no 87, p.78. See also E.M. Sanford, The Career of Aulus Gabinius, TAPA 70,1939,66 : "an inscription recently discovered at Delos gives (sic) the name of the consul in 58 B.C. as A.Gabinius A.f. Capito".

12) T.R.S. Broughton, The Magistrates of the Roman Republic 2, New York 1952,199; R. Syme, The Roman Revolution, Oxford 1939, passim (according to index).

13) In fact 11 or 12 letters: the correct reading is [υἰὸς and not υ[ἰὸς; see above n.4.

14) Op.cit. 99 n.2. Apparently also A. Degrassi was not able to get any information: there is no photograph of this important document in his Inscriptiones Latinae liberae rei publicae. Imagines, Berolini 1965.

Although it seems a more arduous task to reach a stone in a museum than a rock on the moon,
the situation is not quite desperate. E. Cuq provides in BCH 46, 1922, plate XIV, a
serviceable photograph of a squeeze of the inscription. This allows the reader to verify
different restorations. Exactly nine letters are required to fill the effaced space in line 37.
Consequently both the restoration of those scholars who proposed to read υἱὸς (or [υἱὸς
Καπίτων (or Καπείτων)] and of course also that of Lommatzsch who read υἱὸς ὕπατος
καὶ Λε] are too long for the space and ought to be abandoned. We propose the following
reading of line 37: [Αὖλος Γ]αβείνιος Αὔλου [υἱὸς καὶ Λε]ύ[κιος Καλπούρνιος Λευκ].
If we accept this restoration we have to introduce a small correction in line 38. We read:
Λευκ[ίου υἱὸ]ς Πείσων ὕπατ[οι. Instead of the hitherto accepted reading ὕπατος after
the name of each of the consuls we must restore in line 38 the plural ὕπατοι. For ὕπατοι
following the names of the consuls some parallels may be adduced, see e.g. R.K. Sherk,
Roman Documents from the Greek East, Baltimore 1969, nos 12, line 9, p.64; 20, col. II E,
lines 4-5, p.117; 22, lines 24, 28, p.127; 23, lines 1-2, 63-64, pp.134-135; 31, lines
84-85, p.176.

In this way the alleged cognomen of A. Gabinius (cos. 58) definitely disappears, but
the theory of Staveley gains a strong support. The coincidence of the names of the consul
who presented the law and the first voter is striking and it cannot be explained away as
due merely to chance. It is a reasonable supposition that A. Gabinius A.f. Capito was
a close associate, probably a distant relative of the consul, who had especially selected
him to cast the first vote. This clearly disproves the interpretation of the selection of
the first voter put forward by U. Hall. Commenting upon the fact that Plancius senior
was the first man to vote on the lex Iulia de publicanis she wrote: "Presumably all that
Caesar could have done to ensure this was, knowing Plancius' importance in his own tribe
and expecting him to vote first in it, to see that his tribe was the first to vote".[15] Now,
whereas it is possible to argue that Plancius, a prominent publicanus, was a likely man to
vote first in his tribe on a law concerning the publicans, this certainly cannot have been
true with respect to A. Gabinius Capito, probably a young, and in any case an obscure
person. But this raises the question why it was precisely he who received the honour of
casting the first vote. Staveley observes that the first voter invariably supported the measure

---

15) U. Hall, Voting Procedure in Roman Assemblies, Historia 13, 1964, 277 n.37.

before the assembly and that the support of a prominent individual could exert considerable
influence upon the voters. It is difficult to imagine that Gabinius was not able to find
anyone of a more elevated status to act as the first voter. Let us, however, observe that
the lex de Delo was sponsored, at least formally, [16] by both consuls and was undoubtedly
carried de senatus sententia. Only a contested law was in need of a special support and
the lex Gabinia Calpurnia does not seem to have been a controversial measure. The vote
cast by Gabinius Capito was certainly not meant to influence the wavering or uncommitted
voters.

We read in the text of the law (lines 14-16) that the praedones quei orbem te[r]rarum
conplureis [annos vexarint - -] [. . . fan] a delubra simu[la]cra deorum immor[t]alium
loca religio[sissuma - -]| [devast]arint, lege Ga[b]linia (obviously the lex Gabinia of
67 that gave Pompey command in the war against the pirates) superatei ac deletei s[u]nt.
It was then to the law of Gabinius carried by him as tribune that Delos owed its
preservation (of Pompey no word: should we attach any significance to this fact ?). The
law of 58 implies that since the time of the bellum piraticum there had existed a special
bond between Gabinius and the island. Now as consul Gabinius was again appearing
as a benefactor of Delos, and a Gabinius was casting the first vote on the law. This
may have been intended as an additional demonstration of the personal ties between the
consul and the island of Apollo. But we should not forget that the tribe acting as
principium was selected by lot, and Gabinius could not have known that the lot would
fall upon the tribe of Capito. He profited by the occasion, but it is difficult to see here
any preconceived or far-reaching plan.

The person of the first voter has been duly recorded in our inscription, but the
received restoration of lines 3 and 4 is open to doubt. All editors and commentators have
accepted in line 4 the ingenious interpretation of Cuq: A. Gabinius A.f. Capito
pro[tribu primus scivit. [17] All of them have read on the stone after Capito the letters
pro (or pro). However, Roussel and Launey could see only pr[. This reading is clearly
corroborated by the photograph. The stone is broken off in such a way that only a part
of R remained. It is important to realize what is visible on the stone (or rather squeeze)

---

16) L. Piso played only a secondary role as it was clearly Gabinius who presided over
the comitia.

17) P. Roussel read in 1916 pro[cos., (Délos, colonie Athénienne, p.333 n.5).

since the formula that has hitherto been accepted in line 4 is unusual. No parallel can be found for a formula in which the name of the first voter was followed by the phrase pro tribu primus scivit. In the praescriptiones of the Roman laws a slightly different formula was used: pro tribu (the name of the first voter) primus scivit. This usage is born out by examples ranging from the late second century to 9 B.C.:

1. Lex agraria of 111 B.C. (CIL 1.^{2} 585 = FIRA 1^2 no 8; cf. Degrassi, Imagines 385 b): Tribus . . . princi]pium fuit, pro tribu Q. Fabius Q.f. primus scivit.

2. Lex Cornelia de XX quaestoribus, 81 B.C. (CIL 1.^{2} 587 = FIRA 1^2 no 10; cf. Degrassi, Imagines 387): tribus . . .] principium fuit, pro tribu [. . . primus scivit.

3. Lex Quinctia de aquaeductibus, 9 B.C. (Frontinus, De aquaeductu urbis Romae 129. 2-3, ed. P. Grimal, Paris 1961 = FIRA 1^2 no 14): Tribus Sergia principium fuit, pro tribu Sex. [. . .] L.f. Virro [primus scivit].

In view of these examples it seems virtually certain that lines 3 and 4 of the lex Gabinia Calpurnia should be restored as follows (we also print the end of line 2 and the beginning of line 5): pro | aede Clastor(is) a(nte) d(iem) VI kall(endas) ..., tribus ... principium fuit, pro | tribu] A. Gabinius A.f. Capito pr[imus scivit. ... Veli |tis, iu]beatis.$^{18)}$

---

18) For the sake of comparison we reproduce lines 3-4 as given by Roussel-Launey (Inscr. Délos 1511): pro | aede Clastor(is) a(nte) d(iem) VI kallendas - - - , tribus - - - - - principum | fuit,] A. Gabinius A.f. Capito pr[o tribu primus scivit - - - - - - - Veli | tis, iu]beatis.

8

THE DRAMATIC DATE OF VARRO, *DE RE RUSTICA*, BOOK III
AND THE ELECTIONS IN 54

I. Puzzles are irresistible: the dramatic date of the third book of Varro's *de re rustica* continues to stir excitement. Who will snatch the top prize? The most recent entrant is J. S. Richardson: with new guns he defends the traditional date, 54 B. C.[1] But his erudite salvos carry blank cartridges, and his own armour is not impenetrable. In fact he has left both flanks entirely unprotected.

II. But first let us consider the traditional argument for 54. In its most ample form it was presented by August Schleicher in his Bonn dissertation of 1846.[2] The place of the dialogue is the

---

[1] 'The Triumph of Metellus Scipio and the Dramatic Date of Varro, *RR* 3', *CQ* 33 (1983), 456-63.

[2] *Meletematon Varronianorum specimen I* (Diss. Bonn, 1846), 10. After his dissertation Schleicher went on to become one of the founders of modern comparative Indo-European studies.

villa publica in the Campus Martius,[3] and the time the elections to the curule[4] aedileship
(3. 2. 2–3). Varro and his *tribulis*, the senator Q. Axius, meet in the *villa* Appius Claudius, sitting
on a bench and flanked hilariously by four companions named after birds (Merula, Pavo, Pica,
Passer). Appius is explicitly introduced as an augur, the priestly bird-watcher.[5] As it turns out, a
few days previously Appius went to Reate in the matter of the dispute between the Reatines and
the people of Interamna; on this occasion he stayed with Axius in his villa.[6] Schleicher combines
this information with the news transmitted by Cicero to Atticus on 27 July 54: Cicero also went
to Reate to plead the case of the Reatini (concerning *lacus Velinus*) against the Interamnates before
the consuls and ten assessors; he stayed with Axius and returned to Rome on 9 July.[7] Schleicher's
conclusion: Varro and Cicero speak of one and the same episode; the consul[8] before whose
consilium Cicero defended the Reatini was none other than Appius; the conversation in Book III
and the aedilician elections took place on the first or second day after Cicero's return to Rome, on
July 10 or 11.[9] This is a 'juxtapositional' argument of classical simplicity; no wonder Schleicher's
date became an article of faith, often adduced as a fact, never scrutinized afresh.

---

[3] On the *villa publica*, see G. Tossi, 'La Villa Publica di Roma nelle fonti letterarie e
numismatiche', *Atti dell'Istituto Veneto, Classe di Scienze Morali, Lettere ed Arti* 135 (1976–77),
413–26.

[4] This follows from the fact that the presiding consul is mentioned, 3. 2. 2, 7. 1. Cf. Mommsen,
StR II[3]. 483.

[5] *RR* 3. 2. 2: 'ibi Appium Claudium augurem sedentem invenimus in subselliis, ut consuli,
siquid usus poposcisset, esset praesto'. On the augural assistance at the elections, see J. Linderski,
'The Augural Law', *ANRW* II. 16. 3 (forthcoming).

[6] *RR* 3. 2. 3, Appius jestingly remarks to Axius: I shall readily admit you to my 'ornithon',
you 'quoius aves hospitales etiam nunc ructor, quas mihi apposuisti paucis ante diebus in villa
Reatina ad lacum Velini eunti de controversiis Interamnatium et Reatinorum'.

[7] *Att.* 4. 15. 5–6: 'His rebus actis Reatini me ad sua Τέμπη duxerunt ut agerem causam contra
Interamnatis apud consules (so Shackleton Bailey on the basis of Cic. *Scaur. 27*; *consulem* Mss.) et
decem legatos, qua lacus Velinus a M'. Curio emissus interciso monte in Nar⟨em⟩ defluit; . . . vixi
cum Axio; . . . redii Romam Fontei causa a. d. VII Id. Quint. veni spectatum'. *Ad rem*, see
D. R. Shackleton Bailey, *Cicero's Letters to Atticus* II (Cambridge, 1965), 208–10. He is of the
opinion that the phrase *ut agerem* 'does not necessarily imply that the case was heard locally'. He
may well be right, but the curious term *decem legati* impels caution. This would be the only
known instance in which the councillors of the consuls sitting in Rome would have been so called.
Mommsen, of course, did not miss the passage; buried in a footnote is his observation that in this
case Cicero calls the councillors *legati* because the hearing took place locally, *an Ort und Stelle*,
StR II[3]. 693–4 n. 4; cf. 109. So also B. Schleussner, *Die Legaten der römischen Republik* (Munich,
1978), 73.   [8] He follows the manuscript reading *apud consulem*. See the preceding note.

[9] We may note that Schleicher takes Varro's 'quoius aves hospitales etiam nunc ructor' quite
literally. Now a careful reading of Cicero's letter should have been sufficient to overturn
Schleicher's construction. After his return to Rome Cicero went to the theatre (*veni spectatum*);
between July 6 and 13 the *ludi Apollinares* were celebrated (cf. A. Degrassi, *Inscr. It.* XIII. 2.
477–82) and although July 10–13 were the comitial days it is not very likely that the elections
would be held on any of these days. But above all at 4. 15. 7 Cicero complains of the bribery of the
consular candidates and describes the arrangement between the tribunician candidates and Cato as
umpire to prevent bribery at the election of the tribunes. These elections were scheduled for
28 July. Of the aedilician elections not a word; I do not wish to introduce an *argumentum e
silentio*, but in the course of this article Cicero's silence will become louder and louder.

III. Now the classical counter-argument: it took more than one hundred years to develop it. With their customary acumen D. R. Shackleton Bailey,[10] L. R. Taylor[11] and C. Nicolet[12] saw clearly that Schleicher's proof was a mere house of cards: in 54 no elections for regular magistracies took place. Furthermore the dispute between Interamna and Reate was a long-drawn affair: the visits of Appius and Cicero to Reate need not have belonged to one and the same year.

In fact we know for certain that no consuls and praetors were elected in 54;[13] that no curule aediles were elected is an inference based on Mommsen's (incontestable, it would seem) finding that the elections of regular magistrates were always held in a strict descending order.[14]

IV. This leads us to the neo-arguments for 54. Enthusiastic assumption of Schleicher's juxtaposition and an open attack on Mommsen's rule are their twin characteristics. Priority goes to I. Shatzman.[15] He advanced three points, uneven in value. That Appius appears as augur and not as consul is due solely to the comical exigencies of the dialogue, Varro's conceit of having an augur talk of birds (quite right and quite inconclusive, either way). That no consuls and praetors were elected in 54 need not militate against placing the dialogue in that year for 'it is still possible that the curule aediles were elected'. How can we prove this? No problem: Varro's mention (3. 2. 16) of the triumph of Metellus Scipio offers the key. Shatzman places Scipio's praetorship in 56, his provincial command in 55, and his triumph in 54, which will thus be also the dramatic date of Book III. Consequently the elections of the curule aediles did take place in 54, and Mommsen's rule is overturned.

It does not require any perspicacity to detect that Shatzman's argument is an embryonic Richardson's scheme, or, should we rather say, Richardson's argument is a developed Shatzman's scheme. Developed independently, for he does not quote his predecessor's effort. Again we have the three familiar points: Appius as an augur, the aedilician elections in 54, and the triumph of Metellus Scipio. We can proceed straight to the elections.

Richardson admits that under normal circumstances the customary order of elections was followed and Mommsen's rule fully obtained. However, if a year ended in an interregnum this rule need not have applied. For 'abnormal' years Richardson postulates two distinct sets of *comitia*: a) the consular and praetorian; if the consuls were not elected, the praetors were not elected either b) the aedilician and quaestorian; we know from Cass. Dio (39. 7. 4) that if the aediles had not been chosen the quaestorian election could not take place.

Proof for two such distinct sets of elections is hard to come by. In particular there is no shred of evidence that in 56, 54, and 53, the years in which no higher magistrates were elected, the consuls ever attempted to convene the aedilician *comitia*: the successful obstruction of the consular elections, by sheer violence or by the tribunes, is all we hear of.[16] In 56 with the help of friendly tribunes Pompey and Crassus engineered an interregnum; they were elected to the consulship for 55 some time before 11 February of that year, and subsequently they held the elections of praetors and aediles.[17] To an unprejudiced eye this is a perfect example of the working of Mommsen's rule.

---

[10] Op. cit. (above, n. 7), 208–10. He particularly stresses that 'nothing in the dialogue indicates that Appius was consul at the time'.

[11] *Roman Voting Assemblies* (Ann Arbor, 1966), 135 n. 58. Her own dramatic date is rather indefinite, 'probably within the two decades before 50 when Appius Claudius Pulcher, *cos.* 54, was an augur'.

[12] *REA* 72 (1970), 113 n. 2 and esp. 116 n. 1. As the dramatic date of the dialogue he excludes 54, 53–51 (when Appius was in Cilicia), and also 59, when Varro was a *vigintivir ad agros dividendos Campanos* (*RR* 1. 2. 10; cf. Broughton, *MRR* II. 191–2); it is, however, not clear why this function should have prevented Varro from coming to the aedilician elections.

[13] Cass. Dio 40. 45. 1–4.   [14] *StR* I³. 580–2.   [15] *Athenaeum* 46 (1968), 350–1.

[16] Cic. *Att.* 4. 16. 5–6; 4. 15. 4, 7–8; 4. 17. 4; *Q. fr.* 3. 3. 2; Cass. Dio 39. 27–31; 40. 45–6; Livy, *Per.* 105; *Sch. Bob.* 172 St.   [17] Cass. Dio 39. 32.

But it is high time to face Richardson's secret weapon, the triumph of Metellus Scipio. Richardson acutely observes that in fragment XXXIX of the *Fasti Triumphales Capitolini* the triumph of the *Ignotus* in 54 follows immediately upon Pompey's triumph in 61.[18] Consequently the triumph of Metellus Scipio must fall between January 54 and June 53, when a *tessera* attests him as *interrex*.[19] But beware: here we enter the opening curve of a *circulus vitiosus*: because Richardson believes the dramatic date of Book III to be 54 (see below), he excludes 53 as the year of Scipio's triumph.

Now Degrassi identified the *Ignotus* with C. Pomptinus, who celebrated his triumph in November 54, but observed that the stone leaves space for a *cognomen*. His conclusion was that Pomptinus must have had a *cognomen* of which we are not informed.[20] But with Metellus Scipio on the stage, the possessor of a number of *cognomina* to choose from,[21] it would appear that at last we have an ideal candidate to fill the gap. But this is not so: Degrassi too hastily assumed a lacuna.[22] In the garb of *Ignotus* hides either Scipio or Pomptinus.[23]

---

[18] A. Degrassi, *Inscr. It.* XIII. 1. 84–5, 566. But Richardson was not the first to make this observation; see below, n. 34.

[19] *CIL* I². 2663c. Cf. Broughton, *MRR* II. 229.   [20] Op. cit. 566.

[21] His full name was Q. Caecilius Metellus Pius Scipio Nasica, but unfortunately as the *Fasti Consulares* for 52 are lost we do not know his official style. Perhaps Q. Caecilius Metellus Pius Scipio. In the *tesserae CIL* I². 2663c (June 53) and 933 (Sept. 52) we read Q. *Met(ello)*, and on the coins he minted as *proconsul* and *imperator* in Africa in 47 and 46 he styles himself either Q. *Metell(us) Pius Scipio Imp.* (four issues) or Q. *Metell(us) Scipio Imp.* (one issue). See M. H. Crawford, *Roman Republican Coinage* 1 (Cambridge, 1974), 471–2, nos. 459–61.

[22] Degrassi (p. 85) reconstructed the entry for 54 as follows:

[C. *Pomptinus* – f. – n. – – – pro pr(aetore)] a. DCXCIX
[de Allobrogibus IV? non. Nov.]

(in his commentary, p. 566, he mistakenly placed the number in line 2).

It has been my good luck to be able to discuss this matter with Professor T. R. S. Broughton. With his unerring prosopographical *sguardo linceo* he immediately pointed out that a parallel case is offered by the triumph of M'. Aquillius in 126. This entry is fully preserved and it reads as follows (Degrassi, p. 83, frg. XXXIII and XXXIV):

M'. Aquillius M'. f. M'. n. pro co(n)s(ule) an. DCXXVII
ex A[si]a III idus Novembr.

There are twenty-two letters in line 1; in the Pomptinus entry, as reconstructed by Degrassi but without the hypothetical cognomen, we have twenty or possibly twenty-one letters (it seems that at the end of line one before the number we should read *a]n* and not *]a*; cf. Tab. LI). In other words there is no need to assume a lacuna. Degrassi was apparently misled by the fact that the triumphator's cognomen was normally accommodated in line 1 of each entry. However, if the triumphator lacked the cognomen line 1 could be filled in a variety of ways; see e. g. the following years: 223, where *anno* is spelt in full and a blank space is left between cos. and *anno*; 93, where the *provincia* in which the victory was achieved is recorded; 172, where the phrase *qui s]crib(a) [fuera]t* is added.

[23] In fact it is preferable to date Scipio's triumph to 53: if the dramatic date of Book III was 50 (see below), then *nuper* used with respect to Scipio's triumph may well be taken to indicate that it was the last triumph before the dramatic date of the dialogue. Unfortunately this consideration is not conclusive, for *nuper* may have been used very loosely; Scipio may have triumphed in November or December 54; and finally Pomptinus' triumph certainly was not so lavish as Scipio's. But 53 is the only slot that can accommodate Scipio's triumph without disturbing his aedileship in 57 (see *MRR* II. 201 and 207 n. 1), and one should not lightly introduce disturbances into *MRR*.

After this preliminary barrage Richardson is ready to mount a frontal assault on the dramatic date of Book III. His opening moves are deftly executed: a) Varro's mention of the triumph of Metellus Scipio precludes a dramatic date for Book III earlier than January 54 b) ingeniously utilizing the *cistophori* of Apamea he has established that Appius must have left Rome in May 53 at the latest; consequently he could not have been present at the aedilician elections of 53 for 53 since the consuls were not elected before July of that year c) Appius was still in Cilicia in August 51, and hence could not have attended the aedilician election in that year[24] d) in 49 Varro was away from Rome as Pompey's legate in Spain.

The conclusion: the dramatic date of Book III must be either 54 or 50. Richardson opts for 54, on a flimsy basis. At 3. 2. 17 we read: 'M. Cato nuper . . . Luculli accepit tutelam.' Now Cato assumed the guardianship of the young Lucullus in 57 or 56. Richardson opines that as this occurred *nuper*, 54 is much more likely as the dramatic date of the dialogue than 50. But *nuper* is treacherous. The following examples, from two contemporaries of Varro, should dampen the faith of those who would use *nuper* as a peg upon which to hang a precise chronological computation:

Cic. *Planc.* 41: 'An vero nuper clarissimi cives nomen editicii iudicis non tulerunt' ('Recently our most distinguished citizens rejected the very notion of a nominated jury'). The speech was delivered in 54, and *nuper* most probably refers to the measures proposed by Servius Sulpicius in 63.[25]

[Q. Cic.] *Comm. Pet.* 11: 'Quanto melior tibi fortuna petitionis data est quam nuper homini novo C. Coelio' ('How much more advantageous are to you the circumstances of your candidacy than they had recently been to the new man C. Coelius'). C. Coelius Caldus was consul in 94; *nuper* covers the span of thirty years.

The pride of place goes to Cic. *N. D.* 2. 126: 'nuper, id est paucis ante saeclis'.[26]

But in fact no assistance is needed from Cicero and his brother: Varro's own use of *nuper* in the *RR* is vague enough. Out of five other instances only once does *nuper* refer to the immediate past, a remark just made in the conversation;[27] once it alludes to a business transaction the precise time of which we are not able to establish;[28] two times the reference is to 'recent' discoveries or improvements, one concerning the grafting of trees, and the other the fattening of hares. In the former case, as in this chapter Varro quotes and paraphrases Theophrastus, the new method of grafting will be 'recent' in the sense that it had been unknown to Theophrastus (and probably Cato);[29] as to the fattening of hares, this is a 'recent' development, for Archelaos (floruit ca. 300), whom Varro adduced in the preceding sentence as an authority on hares, apparently did not

---

[24] The curule aediles were elected before July 19; Cic. *Fam.* 8. 4. 3.

[25] See T. Mommsen, *De collegiis et sodaliciis Romanorum* (Kiliae, 1843), 63ff. J. L. Strachan-Davidson, *Problems of the Roman Criminal Law* II (Oxford, 1912), 103–4 and H. B. Mattingly, *CQ* 25 (1975), 260–1, refer Cicero's remark to the abrogation of the *lex Servilia Glaucia*; in this case *nuper* would be stretched even further.

[26] Cf. A. S. Pease, *M. Tulli Ciceronis De Natura Deorum* (Cambridge, Mass., 1958), 872–3 (with further examples).

[27] *RR* 2. 2. 1: 'Nos te non dimittemus . . . antequam illa tria explicaris, quae coeperas *nuper* dicere, ⟨cum⟩ sumus interpellati'.

[28] *RR* 3. 7. 10: 'Quas (i. e. the pigeons) *nuper* cum mercator tanti emere vellet a L. Axio, equite Romano, minoris quadringentis denariis daturum negavit'. On L. Axius, see C. Nicolet, *L'ordre équestre* II (Paris, 1974), 800–1.

[29] *RR* 1. 40. 6: 'Est altera species ex arbore in arborem inserendi *nuper* animadversa in arboribus propinquis'. *Ad rem*, see J. Heurgon, *Varron, Économie rurale* I (Paris, 1978), 164ff., esp. 168 n. 16; J. E. Skydsgaard, *Varro the Scholar* (Hafniae, 1968), 68ff.; K. D. White, *Roman Farming* (London, 1970) 248ff.

mention it.[30] Particularly telling is the passage in which Varro promises his wife to write down for her instruction the conversations which he 'recently' had about agriculture.[31] Now Varro composed the *RR* in his eightieth year, in 37 B. C.,[32] and the dramatic date of Book I is January 57 or 56;[33] Book II is placed in 67, when Varro was Pompey's legate in the war against the pirates (2. *praef.* 6).

V. But ultimately it is not *nuper* that settles the dramatic date of Book III but another adverb, *tunc*, and, yes indeed, the triumph of Metellus Scipio. To have resuscitated this triumph from long oblivion has been Shatzman's great merit, but it is neither he nor Richardson who has won the prize, a ride in Scipio's triumphal chariot to the dramatic date of Book III. Long before Richardson entered the race this prize had already been successfully claimed by another contestant. In a brilliant article Ernst Badian demolished Shatzman's construct and established 50 B. C. as the date of action in Book III.[34] Had Richardson consulted Badian's paper he would probably have abandoned his project, and then there would have been no need either (*horribile dictu*) for this rebuttal.

The way in which Varro presents the triumph of Metellus Scipio precludes 54 as the dramatic date of Book III. Once pointed out, this conclusion springs to the reader's eyes. We read (3. 2. 15–16):

> Atque in hac villa (i. e. in the villa of Varro's maternal aunt) qui est ornithon, ex eo uno quinque milia scio venisse turdorum denariis ternis, ut sexaginta milia ea pars reddiderit *eo anno* villae . . . Sed ad hunc bolum ⟨ut⟩ pervenias, opus erit tibi aut epulum aut triumphus alicuius, ut *tunc* fuit Scipionis Metelli, aut collegiorum cenae, quae *nunc*[35] innumerabiles excandefaciunt annonam macelli. Reliquis annis omnibus si ⟨non⟩ hanc expectabis summam, spero, non tibi decoquet ornithon.
>
> (Well, I happen to know that from the aviary alone which is in that villa there were sold five thousand fieldfares, for three denarii apiece, so that that division of the villa in that year brought in sixty thousand sesterces . . . But to achieve such a haul as that you will need a public banquet or somebody's triumph, such as that of Metellus Scipio at that time, or the dinners of the *collegia*, which are so countless just now as to send soaring the price of the produce in the market. Even if you can't look for this sum in all other years, your aviary, I hope, will not go bankrupt on you').

Richardson gives the following interpretation (p. 456): 'The unemphatic use of *tunc* and *nunc* serves to contrast the occasional nature of a triumphal celebration (especially such a one as Scipio's) with the current frequency of collegiate banquets 'quae *nunc* innumerabiles', rather than

---

[30] *RR* 3. 12. 5: 'Hos (i. e. *lepores*) quoque *nuper* institutum ut saginarent plerumque, cum exceptos e leporario condant in caveis et loco clauso faciant pingues'. On Archelaos, see R. Reitzenstein, *RE* 2 (1896), 453–4, and on the breeding of hares, cf. D. W. Rathbone, *ZPE* 47 (1982), 281–4.

[31] *RR* 1. 1. 7: 'ego referam sermones eos quos de agri cultura habuimus *nuper*, ex quibus quid te facere oporteat animadvertere poteris'.

[32] *RR* 1. 1. 1. R. Martin, *Recherches sur les agronomes latins et leurs conceptions économiques et sociales* (Paris, 1971), 213–35, 282–6, argues that 37 is the date only of the final composition of the whole work; single books Varro would have composed much earlier, Book I around 55, Book II at some time which we are not able exactly to determine, and Book III close to the publication date. Martin's argument has been accepted by Heurgon, op. cit. (above, n. 29), XXI–XXVI, but in any case as far as Book I is concerned it is based on a deceitful and circular premise, the word *nuper* at 1. 1. 7.

[33] See the excellent study by G. Perl, *AJAH* 5 (1980), 97.

[34] *Athenaeum* 48 (1970), 4–6.

[35] Here *nunc* is an emendation by H. Keil, but it is undoubtedly correct; cf. Richardson 456 n. 5.

to emphasise how long ago the former took place'. But this begs the question. How do we know that *tunc* and *nunc* are used unemphatically in this passage? Apparently because we have already decided, on different grounds, that 54 is the dramatic date of the book. However, in the only other occurrence of this locution in the *RR tunc* and *nunc* are used quite emphatically (2. 2. 2): 'Atticus, qui tunc (i. e. in 67, the dramatic date of Book II) Titus Pomponius, nunc (i. e. 37 when Varro composed or published the *RR*[36]) Quintus Caecilius cognomine eodem'. It is a good methodological principle to explain obscure passages with the help of passages in which the sense of a disputed phrase is not in doubt. If as regards Atticus the use of *tunc-nunc* is emphatic, there is no reason to suppose that it should be unemphatic with respect to Metellus Scipio.

Richardson considered only the middle of the three passages reproduced above. In the first of them *eo anno* stares at the reader. It is the year to which *tunc* refers. *Reliquis annis* also points to two different years: *tunc*, the year of Scipio's triumph, and *nunc*, the year of the *collegiorum cenae*.[37] No interlocutor would use simultaneously *eo anno* and *tunc* to refer to the very year of the conversation. The earliest date for Scipio's triumph is 54, and the latest 53; and with Appius away from Rome between 53 and 51 the only year left for *nunc*, the dramatic date of the dialogue, is 50 B. C.[38]

54 as the dramatic date of Book III has exerted an alluring appeal; it is sad to part with it. It can still be rescued, but at a very high price – for Varro: if we ascribe sloppiness and inaccuracy[39] to this *vir accuratissime doctus*.[40]

[36] *RR* 2. *praef.* 6, and above, n. 32.

[37] On the feasts of the *collegia*, see J.-P. Waltzing, *Étude historique sur les corporations professionnelles chez les Romains* I (Louvain, 1895), 322ff., esp. 325.

[38] In 50 Appius was censor (Broughton, *MRR* II. 247–8) and it is quite likely that his visit to Reate and his intervention in the controversy between the Reatini and the Interamnates was in some way connected with the operations of the census.

[39] L. R. Taylor (above, n. 11), 135 n. 58, has come very close to this conclusion: 'In the writing of his dialogues Varro was less careful than Cicero'. I doubt this very much.

[40] Apul. *Apol.* 42.

9

Buying the Vote:
Electoral Corruption in the Late Republic[1]

In a speech delivered in the senate in the year 376, the tenth year of the emperor Gratian, and the second year of his independent reign, an eminent defender of Roman traditions, Q. Aurelius Symmachus, painted the horrors of the republican dispensation and the humiliations to which the senators were then subjected (*Or.* 4.7):

To challenge the present let antiquity produce the tribes smeared with freedmen and the plebeian scum; we call upon the patricians. Let it conjure up the distributors (*divisores*)[2] of electoral bribes; we call upon the emperors. We understand very well the blessings of our age: the hideous voting tablet (*cera turpis*), the crooked distribution of the seating places in the theater among the clients,[3] the venal urn,[4] all of these are no more! The elections are transacted between the senate and the emperors: equals elect equals, and the final decision rests with the superiors.

In his fulsome praise of the present age and his condemnation of corrupt *vetustas* Symmachus was, however, easily outtoadied by the poet Ausonius. Expressing his gratitude to the emperor Gratian for the bestowal of the consulship, Ausonius wrote (*Grat. actio* 3.13):

I became consul, O most august Emperor, solely by your favor; I did not undergo the ordeal of the voting enclosure and the Campus Martius; the ordeal of the balloting, the counting of votes, the depositing of the tablets in a box.[5] I was not obliged to shake

---

1. A comprehensive study of electoral malpractices in Rome is a desideratum. T. Mommsen, *Römisches Strafrecht* (Leipzig, 1899) 865-875 and E. Gruen, *The Last Generation of the Roman Republic* (Berkeley, 1974), esp. 212-239, 271-276, offer a succinct introduction, legal and political. But the most detailed discussion is still to be found in two monographs, very antiquarian in character (they were composed in response to the question concerning *ambitus* in Rome put forth in 1853 by the *Ordo Iurisconsultorum in Academia Rheno-Traiectina*): S.H. Rinkes, *Disputatio de crimine ambitus et de sodaliciis apud Romanos tempore liberae reipublicae* (Lugduni Batavorum, 1854) and I. Telting, *Disputatio Juridica de crimine ambitus et de sodaliciis apud Romanos* (Groningae, 1854).
2. The manuscript reading is *fauisores; diuisores* is the conjecture of O. Seeck in his edition of Symmachus in the *Monumenta Germaniae Historica* (Berlin, 1883). For a defense of the reading *fauisores*, see now F. Del Chicca, "*Favisores* o *Divisores?* (Per Symm. *or.* 4,7)," *Sandalion* 4 (1981) 165-176. On *divisores*, see below, nn. 5 and 29.
3. *diribitio corrupta clientelarum cuneis.* Cf. Cic. *pro Mur.* 67, 72, 73; *CIL* VI 32098f = *ILS* 5654f: *client (ibus)*, on a *gradus* in the Flavian Amphitheatre. Cf. A. Chastagnol, *Le sénat romain sous le règne d'Odoacre. Recherches sur l'épigraphie du Colisée au Ve siècle* (Bonn, 1966) 24-27.
4. *sitella venalis.* The term *sitella* is not quite appropriate: *sitella* was a pitcher used for the *sortitiones* at the *comitia;* the voters deposited their ballots in the *cistae,* see L.R. Taylor, *Roman Voting Assemblies* (Ann Arbor, 1966) 25, 29, 43, 70-74. For the tampering with the ballots, cf. Plut *Cat. Min.* 46; Varro, *de re rust.* 3.15.18, and, on Varro's passage, see C. Nicolet, "Tessères frumentaires et tessères de vote," *L'Italie préromaine et la Rome républicaine. Mélanges offerts à Jacques Heurgon* (Rome, 1976) 709-710.
5. *consul ego ... munere tuo non passus saepta neque campum, non suffragia, non puncta, non loculos.* For *puncta,* see below n. 18; for *loculi,* see Varro, *de re rust.* 3.15.8; Mamert. *grat. act.* 19.1: *nota diuisorum flagitia, notae loculorum prestigiae;* and the article of C. Nicolet quoted in the preceding note; for *sequestres* see below, nn. 7 and 29.

hands nor was I so overwhelmed by crowds of well-wishers as to forget the names of my friends or to address them by names which were not theirs. I did not canvass the tribes, I did not flatter the centuries, I did not tremble when the classes were called upon to vote. I deposited no money for bribes with a trustee (cum sequestre) nor did I have any dealings with distributors of bribes. The Roman People, the Campus Martius, the Equestrian Order, the Rostra, the voting enclosure, the Senate and the Senate house — Gratian alone was all of these for me.

Under an authoritarian regime, ancient or modern, official documents tend to depict the present times as the golden age, breathing contentment, felicity and prosperity. Thus Symmachus and Ausonius merely conformed to the rule, but they did it con amore. They genuinely shivered at the thought of shaking the hands of commoners. Before their eyes may have hovered examples of disgraceful humiliations like that of P. Sulpicius Galba, who in his bid for the consulship of 63 started "shaking the hands" more than one year in advance, and all he got for his effort was an immediate and plain rejection, without white-wash or excuse, as Cicero gleefully reports (Att. 1.1). Or still worse the case of another patrician, P. Scipio Nasica, consul in 111, the togatae potentiae clarissimum lumen (Val. Max. 7.5.2) who as a candidate for the aedileship eagerly embraced the dextra of a rustic, so hardened by work that Nasica jestingly inquired whether he employed his hands for walking. The joke was picked up by the bystanders, made the rounds in the assembly, and as a result all the rural tribes, enraged by Nasica's contumeliosa urbanitas, turned him down. Can anyone imagine Symmachus in that role?

The speeches of Cicero could provide dreadful reading as well. "It is the privilege of free peoples," he wrote (Planc. 9, 11-12), "and especially of the Roman people, to be able by its votes to bestow offices on anyone or take them away as it likes. We, the senators, tossed as we are upon the stormy waves of popular favor, must modestly bear the fluctuations of the people's will, win it over, retain or assuage it when it is angered. If the honores, which the people alone dispenses, are important to us, we must never grow weary in courting the people's favor. For the populus always desires to be asked, always desires that the candidates appear in the guise of suppliants. The populus promotes to the offices those candidates by whom it is canvassed most assiduously, a quibus est maxime ambitus." This verb, ambeo, innocuous at the start, spawned two notorious nouns, ambitio and ambitus,[6] repositories at once of all corrupt longings for the honores and all corrupt electoral practices, and at the same time the catalysts of pious outrages against these practices.

In the eyes of Symmachus and his friends, the comitia, in which ideally the will of the people manifested itself, became not only the scene of the humiliations visited upon the patricians, but also, and above all, an arena of disgusting bribery.

Their opinion echoes the sentiment expressed by another imperial grandee, of an earlier, though not necessarily more fortunate or secure age. In a letter to Lucilius (118.3) the advice of Seneca the sage is nihil petere: to disdain all the comitia fortunae. This phrase triggered in his mind a picture of republican elections: the tribes had been called upon to vote, and the candidates, visible on the platform, wait in anxious suspense. They are engaged in frantic last minute efforts: one candidate publicly proclaims the amount of money he is prepared to pay; another conducts his dealings through the agency of a trustee;[7] still another assiduously rubs his kisses onto the hands of people to whom, once

---

6. Cf. F. Teichmüller, Ambire, -tio, -tiosus, -tiose, -tus (Prog. Wittstock, 1901); J. Helleguarc'h, Le vocabulaire latin des relations et des partis politiques sous la république (Paris, 1963) 208-211.

7. Quam putas esse iucundum tribubus vocatis, cum candidati in templis suis pendeant et alius nummos pronuntiet, alius per sequestrem agat. Templum here is the inaugurated spot, the tribunal on which both the presiding magistrate and the candidates were seated. Cf. Varro, de ling. Lat. 6.91; Val. Max. 4.5.3; I.M. J. Valeton, "De templis romanis," Mnemosyne 23 (1895) 28-35. The translation of R.M. Gummere in the Loeb Classical Library ("the candidates are making offerings in their favourite temples") is a disaster. For an interpretation of Seneca's passage, see also R. Frei-Stolba, Untersuchungen zu den Wahlen in der römischen Kaizerzeit (Zürich 1967) 173-174.

appointed to office, he would refuse even the touch of his hand. All this suits the *nundinae*, the vanity fair, full of buyers and sellers. *Nihil rogo:* I ask for nothing. Not quite. It was obviously proper and in good taste to court one's equals and entreat one's superiors.

Velleius Paterculus is an eloquent and eager witness to the dawn of this golden age: among other magnificent things that came to pass under Tiberius, riotous behavior was chased away from the *forum*, and unseemly canvassing from the *campus* (2.126.2)[8]. The *forum* was the meeting place of the *comitia tributa* (and the *concilium plebis*), which elected the lower magistrates; in the late republic this assembly was dominated by the easily excitable city mob; the *campus* stands for the *comitia centuriata*, which elected the higher magistrates, praetors and consuls, and was the scene of unbounded *ambitus*.

Now, painting the gloomy decline of republican liberty, Tacitus reports *(Ann.* 1.14.4) that upon Tiberius' accession to power the elections were for the first time transferred from the people to the senate, *tum primum e campo comitia ad patres translata sunt.* This famous passage incited a torrent of modern literature;[9] among conflicting interpretations one thing stands firm: the popular assemblies continued to meet at least until the beginning of the third century, but their sole function was to approve, probably by acclamation, the list of candidates presented by the senate and the *princeps.* Idle talk was the only reaction of the people to that loss of their republican birthright; and the senators, Tacitus writes, gladly accepted the change; it freed them from *largitio,* the bribery expenditures, and from *preces sordidae,* undignified canvassing. This revulsion, understandable no doubt, against humbling oneself before the imperious mob of impecunious voters, goes a long way toward explaining why, despite occasional grumblings, the senatorial aristocracy resoundingly accepted the principate.

Sallust was of one mind with Symmachus, Ausonius and Velleius. The age in which he was born was one of corruption and decline. *Pudor, abstinentia, virtus* were forgotten, *audacia, largitio, avaritia* flourished *(BCat.* 3.4).[10] Unaware of the future splendors of the authoritarian dispensation, Sallust, like so many dreamers and pamphleteers of all times, sought the golden age in an imaginary past. He was not alone in dating the turning point to the middle of the second century, when Carthage, the *aemula imperii Romani,* was razed to the ground. Now *ambitio* and the desire for riches invaded Rome. The first victim was internal concord. But before we are completely inundated by these moralizing accusations, let us turn to the cool and sober mind of a pragmatic historian. Polybius saw the beginnings of the process against which Sallust fulminates; when a state has achieved uncontested supremacy and prosperity, he wrote (6.57.5-9), life will become more profligate, with the love of office and display of wealth in the forefront. But the engine of this change for the worse will be the populace itself: it will favor those candidates for office who flatter it. The people will no longer simply obey the ruling class, but will demand the lion's share for themselves. The end result of this development will inevitably be ochlocracy, mob-rule. Now this is a rather schematic analysis of the decay of the mixed constitution,[11] but not all of it is abstraction, pure and simple. *Largitio* and *ambitus* was indeed in Rome a symptom of the change, not the cause of it.

For why was it necessary to buy the vote? The answer is simple. If you do not immediately control the voters, you must pay for their support. This can be done in two ways: by means of legislation appealing to special interest groups or directly by handing

---

8. Cf. ad loc. A.J. Woodman, *Velleius Paterculus. The Tiberian Narrative* (Cambrige, 1977) 237-238.
9. Cf. Frei-Stolba, *Untersuchungen* (above, n. 7) 130 ff.; M. Pani, *Comitia e senato. Sulla trasformazione della procedura elettorale a Roma nell'eta di Tiberio* (Bari, 1974) passim (both with further literature).
10. On these code-words, and Sallust's idelology, see Helleguarc'h, *Le vocabulaire* (above, n. 6) 27, 116, 196, 203, 219-221, 242-245, 260-261, 274-277, 476-483; D.C. Earl, *The Political Thought of Sallust* (Cambridge, 1961) esp. 5-17.
11. Cf. F.W. Walbank, *A Historical Commentary on Polybius* 1 (Oxford, 1957) 743-746.

out money and gifts. The appearance of such legislation and of direct bribery unmistakably points to grave social shifts, and there is never a dearth of reckless politicians
ready to exploit the new situation for their personal aggrandizement, however ultimately
pernicious their conduct might prove for their class as a whole.

If this model holds any substance *ambitus* should make its debut as a social and
political problem some time in the second century; it should have grown to prominence
in the last century of the republic and reached its peak in the age of Pompey and Caesar.
One test we can apply to check the validity of this hypothesis is the occurence of legislation against electoral abuse.

The first law *de ambitu* on record Livy dates to 358 BC (7.5.12). The *lex Poetelia*[12] was
sponsored by a tribune of the plebs *auctoribus patribus* and was intended, we are told, to
curb the *ambitio* of the *homines novi* who used to canvass at the *nundinae* and *conciliabula*.
Ambitus is here clearly to be taken in its original meaning of "canvassing by going
around";[13] it contains no intimation of outright bribery. But as any case of tribunician
legislation before the *lex Hortensia* is suspect,[14] the law in question may well be a figment
of the annalists. But if this is so, it is a deft figment; the goal of the *lex Poetelia* was to protect the interests of the established *patres* and to insulate their *clientelae* from the wooing
of the *homines novi*. How this was to be achieved we are not informed, but the general
perception given by the annalist is remarkably unclouded by moral posturing. *Cui bono*
is the question which not only the stern judge L. Cassius asked,[15] but which also every
historian should constantly repeat. Electoral *largitio* was always an instrument of
wresting electoral *clientelae* from their inherited allegiances. It required huge sums of
ready cash not only for direct bribery, but above all for lavish games and gladiatorial
shows. Both Sallust and Polybius stress *divitiae* as a prerequisite of *largitio*. One obvious
source of money for bribes was extortion in the provinces; this link between *ambitus* and
repetundae did not escape the keen eye of Asconius.

In 54 M. Aemilius Scaurus, the son of the famous *princeps senatus* at the turn of the
century, was indicted before the *quaestio de repetundis* for extortions he had committed
as governor of Sardinia and Corsica. The accusation coincided with Scaurus' campaign
for the consulship. Asconius relates (19 C.) that the prosecutors did not utilize the thirty
days they received for the inquiries in Sardina, and insisted upon immediate trial: they
were afraid that Scaurus would buy the consulship with the money he had extorted in
the province and would enter upon office before the conclusion of the trial, thus securing for himself immunity from further prosecution. Scaurus mustered for his defense the
unprecedented number of six patrons, among them a most unlikely pair of collaborators,
Cicero and P. Clodius. Cicero should have known from his own experience the painful
plausibility of the accusers' fears. Fourteen years earlier as a candidate for the aedileship
and at the same time the accuser of Verres, he himself had to fend off the torrent of
Sicilian money (*Verr.* 1.22-23). The consuls of this year M. Hortensius and Q. Metellus
were elected *pecunia Siciliensi*, and Verres used to boast *Metellum non fato, sed opera sua
consulem factum*. At the time of Naevius the consulship was a birthright of the Metelli;[16]
now times had changed: even a Metellus had to practice electoral *largitio*.

12. The *lex Poetelia* attracted some attention. See M. Isler, "Ueber das Poetelische Gesetz de ambitu," *RhM*
28 (1873) 473-478; L. Lange, "Ueber das Poetelische Gesetz de ambitu," *RhM* 29 (1874) 500-505 [reprinted in
L. Lange, *Kleine Schriften* 2 [Göttingen, 1887] 195-202); and recently L. Fascione, "Alle origini della legislazione de ambitu," in: F. Serrao (ed.), *Legge e società nella repubblica romana* 1 (Napoli, 1981) 269-279. All three
authors display a very credulous attitude toward the annalistic source of Livy's information, an attitude
characteristic of old antiquarianism and, alas, also of contemporary Italian legal *dottrina*.
13. Varro, *de ling. Lat.* 5.28; Festus (Paulus) s.v. *ambitus*, 20 L.
14. Cf. E.S. Staveley, "Tribal legislation before the *lex Hortensia*," *Athenaeum* 33 (1955) 3-31; J. Bleicken, *Das
Volkstribunat der klassischen Republik²* (München, 1968) 11 ff.
15. Asc. *in Mil.* 45 C.
16. Cf. H.B. Mattingly, "Naevius and the Metelli," *Historia* 9 (1960) 414-439, esp. 417-418.

Extortion leads us back to the second century: this is the earliest date money from this source would be freely forthcoming. But money in the pockets of the candidates is only one part of the equation. The other are the recipients of the bribes. The economic upheavals of the second century, the rise of the *latifundia*, the impoverishment of the farmers, the migration to Rome created a large group of voters who were ready to sell their votes to the highest bidder. Since the Gracchi a long series of agrarian and grain laws appealed to this group; as they owed no direct allegiance to the nobility as a class, they could easily be swayed by promises of grain or land or by the outright distribution of money. But perhaps the most important event in the spread of *ambitus* was the one that was hailed as the dawn of popular liberty: the introduction of written and hence secret ballot - *tabella vindex libertatis* was the *parole* of the reformers (Cic. *de leg.* 3.39; *Planc.* 16). Four tribunician laws in quick succession established written ballots: in 139 in electoral assemblies (*lex Gabinia*); in 137 in judicial, with the exception of *perduellio*, (*lex Cassia*); in 131 in legislative (*lex Papiria*); and finally in 107 also in the comitial trials for treason (*lex Caelia*).[17] In the era of oral voting the voters indicated their preference to the *rogatores*, selected from prominent men in the state. The *rogatores* recorded the votes by placing dots, *puncta*, one dot for one vote, on special tablets.[18] Now, with the written *tabella*, a client could vote as he pleased, without his patron being able to control or intimidate him. No wonder the nobility was adamantly opposed to this form of voting; for them as for Symmachus five hundred years later the waxed voting tablet was the harbinger of all evil: *cera turpis*. Cicero in his ideal Roman state would curiously enough retain the written ballot, but stipulates that before being deposited in the urn the ballots be shown to the leading men of the state: the *suffragia* should be *populo libera*, but *optimatibus nota* (*de leg.* 3. 10, 33, 38).[19]

Thus it should come as no surprise that the first historically attested *leges de ambitu* date to the second century. Two laws are on the books (Livy 40.19.11, *Per.* 47), the *lex Cornelia Baebia* of 181, and a law of 159, normally attributed to the consuls of that year Cn. Cornelius Dolabella and M. Fulvius Nobilior. About their content and generally about *ambitus* in the second century we know unfortunately little; as one probably should have expected Cato the Elder delivered a speech *de ambitu*,[20] and we have occasional references to illegal *ambitio* in the Livian tradition (Obs. 12) and Plautus (*Trin.* 1033). In the prologue to *Amphitryo* 60ff. (which may or may not have been written by Plautus himself) the corrupt solicitation by the actors for applause, and particularly the distribution of the bands of claqueurs is compared to the illegal soliciting for votes at the elections. The author of the prologue proposes that any actor found guilty of having hired the *favitores* or having engineered the failure of a rival should have his actor's costume, his *ornamenta*, cut to pieces. It is perhaps not too adventurous to detect here a comical allusion to the punishment meted out to the candidates convicted of bribery: the loss of their rank, the civic *ornamenta*.

If we are to trust Polybius they stood to lose something even more precious: whereas at Carthage candidates for office used to practice bribery openly, in Rome *thanatos* is the penalty (6.56.4). But this information is to be taken *cum grano salis*. We probably have to

17. For the references, see G. Rotondi, *Leges Publicae Populi Romani* (Milano, 1912, repr. Hildesheim, 1962) 297, 302, 324-325.
18. See T. Mommsen, *Römisches Staatsrecht* 3 (Leipzig, 1887) 404, 407 n. 5.
19. For an interpretation of this law of Cicero, see the excellent article of C. Nicolet, "Cicéron, Platon et le vote secret," *Historia* 19 (1970) 39-66. According to L. Troiani, "Sulla lex de suffragiis in Cicerone, de legibus III, 10," *Athenaeum* 59 (1981) 180-184, Cicero proposes "il voto palese" for the optimates and "il voto libero" for the plebs. But the passage *de leg.* 3.39: "habeat sane populus tabellam quasi vindicem libertatis, dummodo haec optimo cuique et gravissimo civi ostendatur ultroque offeratur" shows clearly that it was the *suffragia* of the *populus* that were to be *nota* to the *optimates*.
20. H. Malcovati, *Oratorum Romanorum Fragmenta*[2] (Turin, 1955) fr. 136, p. 54. See also his *ne lex Baebia derogaretur*, ibid., frgs. 137, 138, p. 54. Cf. A. Astin, *Cato the Censor* (Oxford, 1978) 120-121, 329-331.

admit that for some forms of bribery the *caput* of the offender was the penalty, but at the same time Polybius himself (6.14.7) tells us that the people fearing conviction on capital charges would habitually remove themselves from Rome and live peacefully in exile in one of the allied communities of Italy.[21] They would lose their *caput* in the civil but not in the physical sense of the word.

But Polybius' account causes trouble. A Ciceronian scholiast (Schol. Bob. p. 78 St.) reports that before the *lex Calpurnia* of 67 the candidates convicted of *ambitus* on the basis of a *lex Cornelia* were merely prohibited for ten years from standing for office. This *lex Cornelia* will certainly be a law of Sulla; but if so, a remarkable lowering of the penalty will have occurred between the age of Polybius and the beginning of the first century. This evolution we should connect with the introduction of the standing court *de ambitu;* no source remarks on this event and no constituent law stands on record. Yet the trial of Marius for bribery, arising from his campaign for the praetorship of 115, clearly took place before the jurors of a *quaestio* and not before the judicial *comitia* of the people (Plut. *Mar.* 5).[22] Thus the *quaestio de ambitu* must have been introduced sometime before 116[23] - it is difficult not to see here a connection with the *leges tabellariae*. On the one hand its establishment corresponds to the general legal trend of transferring the handling of delicts from the *comitia* to the standing courts, but on the other it is also an indirect testimony to the increase in *ambitus* accusations which the judicial assembly of the people was apparently unable to handle.

We pick up again the thread of the legal development only in the age of Sulla; from his time a special praetor was in charge of the *quaestio de ambitu*. In the post-Sullan legislation three trends are discernible: first, the gradual sharpening of the penalties for candidates convicted of bribery; second, the introduction of penalties for the associates and helpers in bribery; and third, a more precise definition of the crime of *ambitus*, and the progressive inclusion in it of a number of previously allowed practices, as for instance the limitation of the number of *sectatores* who accompanied the candidates on their daily peregrinations around the city (introduced by a *lex Fabia*, perhaps in 65)[24] or the ban on *nomenclatores* disregarded by everybody but religiously observed by Cato as a candidate for the military tribunate (Plut. *Cat. Min.* 8).[25]

The *lex Calpurnia* of 67 threatened expulsion from the senate and perpetual exclusion from the *honores* (Sch. Bob. 78-79 St.); four years later the law sponsored by Cicero stipulated the penalty of exile (*Mur.* 45, 47, 89; *Planc.* 8, 83), limited however to ten years, according to Cassius Dio (37.29).[26] The law of Pompey of 52 contained a *poena gravior*, no doubt exile for life.[27] A pecuniary penalty was included in the *lex Calpurnia* and was probably increased substantially by the Pompeian law.[28].

But perhaps the most telling facet of *ambitus* legislation are the provisions concerning the distributors of bribes, the notorious *divisores*.[29] Originally their trade seems to

21. Cf. G. Crifò, *Ricerche sull'exilium nel periodo repubblicano* (Milano, 1961) 44 ff.
22. Cf. T. Carney, "Two Notes on Republican Roman Law," *Acta Iuridica* (1959) 232-234.
23. Cf. E. Gruen, *Roman Politics and the Criminal Courts* (Cambridge, Mass., 1968) 124.
24. On this law, see T.E. Kinsey, "Cicero, Pro Murena 71," *Revue Belge de Philologie et d'Histoire* 43 (1965) 57-59.
25. Cf. Bernert, "Nomenclator," *RE* 18 (1936) 817-820; J. Vogt, "Nomenclator," *Gymnasium* 85 (1978) 327-338.
26. Cf. E. Levy, *Die römische Kapitalstrafe (Sitzungsberichte d. Heidelberger Akad. d. Wiss., Phil. -hist. Kl. 1930/1931, 5 Abh.)* 31-32; E. Grassmück, *Exilium. Untersuchungen zur Verbannung in der Antike* (Padeborn, 1978) 102-103, who, however, omits to discuss the *exilium* of the *lex Pompeia* (see below, n. 27).
27. Asc. *in Mil.* 36 C.; Plut. *Cat. Min.* 48; Cic. *ad Att.* 9.14.2; Mommsen, *Strafrecht* 874 n. 7.
28. Sch. Bob. 78 St.; according to the *lex Pompeia* the victorious accuser was to receive a pecuniary *praemium* (Asc. *in Mil.* 54 C.), no doubt from the property of the *condemnatus*.
29. W. Liebenam, "Divisor," *RE* 5 (1905) 1237-1238. Still very useful is F.H. Weismann, *De divisoribus et sequestribus ambitus apud Romanos instrumentis* (Diss. Heidelberg, 1831).

have been an honest one; their task was to distribute various gratuities among the *tribules,* the members of the same tribe. But in the later republic they offered a ready conduit for the flow of bribes. Cicero speaks in one breath of thieves and *divisores (Verr.* 3.161), and in another passage he jestingly remarks that a certain *divisor* Nummius acquired his name on the Campus Martius (*de Or.* 2.63). When Cicero thundered against Verres he was, no doubt, describing a familiar scene (*Verr.* 1.22-23): "Some ten baskets of Sicilian money were left at the house of a certain senator for the purpose connected with my candidacy (i.e. this senator was to act as the go-between, *sequester* or *interpres*); a meeting of *divisores* of all tribes was convened one night at Verres' house ... Verres reminded them how generously he had treated them, both when he himself was a candidate for the praetorship some time ago, and at the recent elections of consuls and praetors; and he then at once promised them as much money as they might wish if only they succeeded in turning down my bid for the aedileship ... Some of them replied they did not believe it could be managed; however, a friend and kinsman of Verres, Q. Verres of the Romilian tribe, a fine specimen of the bribery-agent, declared he would undertake this task for the sum of five hundred thousand sesterces paid down." This sum attracts attention: it was a larger amount than that needed for the equestrain census; Roman elections were definitely not for the poor. To distribute bribes evidently was a lucrative occupation. When the consul in 67 C. Calpurnius Piso included in his law penalties against bribery agents, the crowd of *divisores* chased him from the forum; but the consul returned with a stronger bodyguard, and pushed his law through.[30]

But the clubs and stones were as effective a means of persuasion as gold. In 55 the *lex Licinia de sodaliciis,* sponsored by the triumvir M. Crassus, attacked associations organized for the purpose of bribery and intimidation. Their members could now be prosecuted and punished both for violence and bribery, *vis* and *ambitus.*[31] In 61 the proposal of a curious law was ventilated: those who merely promised cash for the tribes but failed to pay would go unpunished; those who were convicted of living up to their promise would be obliged to pay annually to each tribe three thousand sesterces for life (Cic. *Att.* 1.16.13).

All these numerous measures, some seven laws and a dozen senatorial decrees, whether serious or ridiculous, were ultimately utterly ineffective, for they approached *ambitus* as a moral or at best political issue, but failed to address its social roots and causes. The stakes were too high and rewards too enticing to contend for office merely *virtute,* and not *favitoribus,* as Plautus had exhorted. The breakdown of old *clientelae,* and the rise of the new ones, of Pompey, Caesar, or Catiline, were facts of life that could not be exorcised by the letter of the law. The conservative senators and the "dynasts," as they were called, competed with each other on two curiously incompatible levels. They posed as the saviours of the Republic, bent upon eradicating corruption. The legislation against the *divisores* was initiated by the tribune C. Cornelius, a former quaestor of Pompey, but was carried to fruition, after prolonged bickering and tortuous compromises, by Pompey's foe, the consul Calpurnius Piso. On the other hand it was Hortensius who sponsored in 56 a senatorial decree directed against the electoral *sodalitates.* The comitial legislation to this effect was stalled by the machinations of the triumvirs but ironically enough it was Crassus who as consul in the next year claimed

30. Asc. *in Corn.* 75-76 C.; Cass. Dio 36.38-39. Cf. W. McDonald, "The Tribunate of Cornelius," *CQ* 23 (1929) 196-208, esp. 200-205; C. Nicolet, "Le sénat et les amendements aux lois à la fin de la république," *Revue Hist. de droit francais et étranger* 36 (1958) 262-266; M. Griffin, "The Tribune C. Cornelius," *JRS* 63 (1973) 196-203.
31. See J. Linderski, "Ciceros Rede *Pro Caelio* und die Ambitus- und Vereinsgesetzgebung der ausgehenden Republik," *Hermes* 89 (1961) 106-119, with sources and further literature. The loose divagations of P. Grimal, "La lex Licinia de sodaliciis," in: *Ciceroniana. Hommages à K. Kumaniecki* (Leiden, 1975) 107-115, contain little of use.

the credit for a tough law *de sodaliciis.*[32] But behind this screen of moral probity, electoral life flourished untainted by Utopian sentiments. Two patterns emerge. One is the traditional competition in bribery between members of the senatorial class dictated by personal ambition and the instinct for survival. The ensuing accusations and trials provided interesting divertissment for high society, but were devoid of any immediate political consequence. The other pattern was much more ominous: the contest between the "dynasts" and their senatorial opponents. It was an ominous pattern for it demonstrated *ad nauseam* the puny role the *comitia* of the people now played. Whenever the triumvirs wished to occupy the consulship or to give it to one of their partisans, they were always able to crush the opposition through the force of their gold and their veterans. The people bestowed offices but no power. Soon they were to lose their liberty, and with it its *vindex*, the *tabella. Largitio* remained: a bribe for torpid docility, not *fasces* and *imperia.*

---

32. J. Linderski, "Two Speeches of Q. Hortensius," *PP* 16 (1961) 304-311. Cf. E. Gruen, *The Last Generation* (above, n. 1) 229-230.

10

THREE TRIALS IN 54 B. C.:
SUFENAS, CATO, PROCILIUS AND CICERO,
'AD ATTICUM', 4. 15. 4

The passage on which I propose to present a commentary reads as follows, Cicero, *ad Att.*, 4. 15. 4:

> *Nunc Romanas res accipe. A. d. IIII Nonas Quintiles Sufenas et Cato absoluti, Procilius condemnatus. ex quo intellectum est* τρισαρεοπαγίτας *ambitum, comitia, interregnum, maiestatem, totam denique rem p. flocci non facere, patrem familias domi suae occidi nolle, neque tamen id ipsum abunde; nam absolverunt XXII, condemnarunt XXVIII. Publius sane diserto epilogo criminans mentes iudicum moverat. Hortalus in ea causa fuit cuiusmodi solet. nos verbum nullum; veritast enim pusilla, quae nunc laborat, ne animum Publi offenderem* (¹).

The most important and intricate question that faces any scholar trying to interpret the text reproduced above is to reconstruct the political setting of the trials mentioned by Cicero and to find out what specific charges were brought in against Sufenas, Cato and Procilius. The knowledge of the *curriculum vitae* of those men and especially of Cato may here be helpful.

C. Porcius Cato (²) made his political debut in 59 B. C. with an

---

(¹) L. A. Constans, *Cicéron, Correspondance*, III, Paris, 1950.

(²) See Drumann-Groebe, *Geschichte Roms*, V, Leipzig, 1919, 215-217; Fr. Miltner, s.v. *Porcius* (n° 6), in *RE*, XXII. 1, Stuttgart, 1953, 105-107; G. Niccolini,

assault upon the consul designate C. Gabinius against whom he attempted to bring a law-suit *de ambitu*; the praetors, however, fearing that Pompeius might be infuriated by the indictment of his henchman, did not accept the accusation. Cato assailed then publicly the *triumvir* labelling him *privatus dictator*, an audacious step, that drew Cicero's scorn upon him ([3]) and justifies Fenestella's opinion of Cato: *turbulentus adulescens* ([4]). In 57 he was elected to the tribunate of the plebs (for 56) and about the same time he became Clodius' ally and Milo's enemy. As tribune he supported Clodius (who was then a candidate for the curule aedilship) and agitated for the immediate holding of the aedilician elections ([5]) which were delayed until January 56 because of Milo's obstruction and the hostility of the consul Cn. Cornelius Lentulus Marcellinus and the tribune L. Racilius to Clodius ([6]). He also took an active part in the strife concerning the restitution of the king Ptolemy Auletes ([7]) and opposed in this connection both Pompeius and P. Cornelius Lentulus Spinther (cos. 57 and governor of Cilicia), the senate's candidate for carrying through the restoring of the king. In February he promulgated two laws, one *de imperio P. Cornelio Lentulo abrogando* ([8]), and the other concerning Milo, probably proposing to establish a special court to prosecute him ([9]). In the senate he vehemently attacked Pompeius ([10]). The proposals of Cato were strongly opposed by the consul Lentulus Marcellinus who having proclaimed *feriae* and *supplicationes* on the comitial days made it impossible for Cato to put his motions to the vote of the tribes ([11]). The tribune, angry at this, declared he would in revenge impede the holding of the regular elections ([12]).

I Fasti dei tribuni della plebe, Milano, 1934, 303-308; T. R. S. BROUGHTON, *The Magistrates of the Roman Republic*, II, New York, 1952, 209.

([3]) *Ad. Q. fr.*, I. 2. 15.

([4]) Nonius Marcellus, *de comp. doctr.*, 385 (MÜLLER) (= Fenestella, frg. 21 [PETER]).

([5]) Cicero, *ad fam.*, I. 4. 1; *ad. Q. fr.*, 2. 1. 2-3.

([6]) Cicero, *ad Att.*, 4. 3. 3-5; *ad Q. fr.*, 2. 1. 2-3; cf. *ad Q. fr.*, 2. 2. 2.

([7]) Cf. T. R. HOLMES, *The Roman Republic*, II, Oxford, 1923, 66 ff.; E. MEYER, *Caesars Monarchie und das Principat des Pompejus*[3], Stuttgart-Berlin, 1922, 126 ff.

([8]) Cicero, *ad Q. fr.*, 2. 3. 1. 4; *ad fam.*, I. 5. 2; cf. I. 5a. 2.

([9]) Cicero, *ad Q. fr.*, 2. 3. 4.

([10]) Cicero, *ad Q. fr.*, 2. 3. 4.

([11]) Cicero, *ad Q. fr.*, 2. 4. 4-6.

([12]) Cicero, *ad Q. fr.*, 2. 4. 6: *C. Cato contionatus est comitia haberi non siturum si sibi cum populo dies agendi essent exempti* (March 56).

The political sympathies of Cato are thus clearly delineated: he was neither a supporter of Pompeius nor of the optimates; on the whole the view of the scholars who consider him a partisan of Crassus seems most plausible ([13]). After the conference at Luca he was reconciled with Pompeius, probably through Crassus' mediation; his co-operation proved very effective to the triumvirs.

According to the decision reached at the conference of Luca Pompeius and Crassus were to stand for the consulship for 55. The realisation of this plan was, however, seriously endangered by the resistance of the consul Cn. Cornelius Marcellinus, a staunch optimate, though once a quaestor of Pompeius, who declared he would not accept Pompeius and Crassus as candidates ([14]). According to the Roman electoral system there was no legal means of inducing the consul presiding over the electoral assembly to accept against his will a candidature or to announce officially (*renuntiare*) the results of the voting. In order to overcome the consul's opposition the dynasts decided to impede the holding of the elections and to delay them until the end of the year. The *interregnum* would then result and they hoped that finally one of the *interreges* would admit their *professio*. In fact they succeeded in bringing about the *interregnum* and eventually Pompeius and Crassus were elected to the consulship early in 55 under the presidency of an *interrex*.

And it is in this connection that the name of Cato reappears. Cassius Dio, *hist.*, 39. 27. 3, states that the triumvirs διεπράσσοντο τὰς ἀρχαιρεσίας ἐν τῷ ἐνιαυτῷ ἐκείνῳ μὴ γενέσθαι, ἄλλους τε καὶ τὸν Κάτωνα τὸν Γάιον ἐνιέντες, ἵνα μεσοβασιλέως αἱρεθέντος καὶ αἰτήσωσι κατὰ τοὺς νόμους τὴν ἀρχὴν καὶ λάβωσι, and the same information is to be found in Livy's *Periochae*, 105: *cum C. Catonis tribuni plebis intercessionibus comitia tollerentur, senatus vestem mutavit.*

There is no doubt that Cicero while mentioning in *ad Att.*, 4. 15. 4, *comitia* and *interregnum* in relation to the trial of Cato makes an allusion to the latter's activity in 56 as the principal agent of the triumvirs in delaying the elections and bringing about the interregnum. But in the same context Sufenas also is referred to and it is

---

([13]) L. LANGE, *Römische Alterthümer*, III², Berlin, 1876, 320-321, 333; MEYER, *Caesars Monarchie*, 132-133. This view is based on Cicero, *ad Q. fr.*, 2. 3. 4: *Nam Pompeius haec intellegit nobiscumque communicat, insidias vitae suae fieri, C. Catonem a Crasso sustentari.*

([14]) Cassius Dio, *hist.*, 39. 27-31.

a plausible suggestion to identify him with one of those ἄλλοι mentioned by Cassius Dio who co-operated with Cato in 56. One important fact should be stressed: it is exclusively on the basis of Cicero's letter to Atticus here under discussion that M. Nonius Sufenas is normally listed among the tribunes of the plebs of 56 ([15]).

In an article on *Magistrates of 55 B.C. in Cicero's Pro Plancio and Catullus 52* ([16]) to be viewed as one of the most important contributions to the late republican prosopography published in recent years, L. R. Taylor has presented powerful arguments for the identification of Nonius Sufenas with Catullus' *struma* Nonius ([17]). At first she proved by a really ingenious argument that the curule aedilship of Cn. Plancius and A. Plotius, since Wunder ([18]) dated beyond question in 54, belongs in fact to 55. As a starting point she took the observation that in the Ciceronian (and even more general, the republican) usage the term *auctor legis* did not denote the lator of a law but the man who used his authority to support the proposal. Consequently in the phrase of Cicero: *quasi non comitiis iam superioribus sit Plancius designatus aedilis; quae comitia primum habere coepit consul cum omnibus in rebus summa auctoritate, tum harum ipsarum legum ambitus auctor (pro Planc.*, 49), the consul referred to is not Crassus (who passed the *lex de sodaliciis*) but Pompeius. The *comitia superiora* at which Plancius had already been designated were apparently dissolved before the final *renuntiatio*; thus they are easily to be identified with the violent elections of the curule aediles for 55 at which Pompeius' garments were bespattered with blood ([19]).

Broughton registers as curule aediles in 55 L. Aemilius Paullus and Nonius Struma ([20]), but there is no certainty and for Aemilius

---

([15]) See Münzer, s.v. *Nonius* (n° 52), in *RE*, XVIII. 1, Stuttgart, 1936, 900-901; Niccolini, *Fasti*, 303-304; Broughton, *Magistrates*, II, 209.

([16]) In *Athenaeum*, N.S., 42, 1964, 12-28.

([17]) Catullus, *carm.*, 52:
  Sella in curuli struma Nonius sedet,
  per consulatum perierat Vatinius.

([18]) E. Wunder, *Pro Cn. Plancio oratio*, Lipsiae, 1830, LXVIII ff.; Münzer, s.v. *Plancius* (n° 4), in *RE*, XX. 2, Stuttgart, 1950, 2014-2015; Broughton, *Magistrates*, II, 223.

([19]) Cassius Dio, *hist.*, 39. 32. 2-3; Valerius Maximus, *mem.*, 4. 6. 4; Plutarch, *Pomp.*, 53. Cf. Appian, *bell. civ.*, 2. 17.

([20]) *Magistrates*, II, 216.

Paullus another date has also been proposed ([21]): he may equally well have held his aedilship in 56. The only basis for assigning Nonius the curule aedilship in 55 is Catullus, *carm.*, 52, where he is depicted as sitting in a curule chair, but this may also be interpreted as a reference to his praetorship. Now there is a question whether *struma* is to be taken as a nickname or cognomen: both interpretations are possible and both were adhered to, but on the whole the first one seems to be more plausible ([22]).

Two Nonii are a possibility for the identification with Catullus' *struma Nonius*: M. Nonius Sufenas and L. Nonius Asprenas, *consul suffectus* in 36 and praetor before 46 ([23]). Sufenas, who appears at any rate as early as 54 and whose tribunate in 56 seems to be certain is, no doubt, a better choice than Asprenas, of whom, as L. R. Taylor has pointed out, nothing is known before 46 ([24]).

It may be further observed that M. Nonius Sufenas was governor of an eastern province in 51-50 ([25]); if the regulations of the senatorial decree of 53 which provided for the interval of five years between consulship or praetorship and provincial command ([26]) were here applied, Nonius' praetorship would have to be dated precisely in 55 ([27]).

Of course there is still the question to which year Catullus' poem belongs, but, on various counts, 55 is more likely than 54, probably the year of the poet's death. In any case it must have been the year in which Vatinius' chances for the consulship were especially promising and in 55 when he won the election to the praetorship they were uncontestably better than in 54 when he was accused *de sodaliciis*.

([21]) See M. I. Henderson, in *JRS*, 49, 1959, 167 (review of A. E. Astin's book, *The Lex Annalis before Sulla*, Bruxelles, 1958); L. R. Taylor, *op. cit.*, 17-18. Cf., however, E. Badian, *Caesar's cursus and the intervals between offices*, in *JRS*, 49, 1959, 82-83.

([22]) See L. R. Taylor, *op. cit.*, 19 with nt. 18, where also the views of other scholars are quoted. To the literature cited we may add C. J. Fordyce, *Catullus. A Commentary*, Oxford, 1961, 221-222, who also interprets *struma* as a nickname.

([23]) See on him Münzer, s. v. *Nonius* (nr. 14), in *RE*, XVIII, 1, 865-866; Broughton, *Magistrates*, II, 287, 399.

([24]) *Op. cit.*, 20. This is also the opinion of M. Gelzer, s.v. *Tullius* (n° 29), in *RE*, VII A. 1, Stuttgart, 1939, 859, and Fordyce, *op. cit.*, 222 (who, however, holds him curule aedile in 54).

([25]) Cicero, *ad Att.*, 6. 1. 13; 8. 15. 3.

([26]) Cassius Dio, *hist.*, 40. 30; 40. 46. 2.

([27]) L. R. Taylor, *op. cit.*, 19-20.

Fordyce ([28]) suggests that his name may have appeared on the *paginulae futurorum consulum* ([29]) composed by the triumvirs at their meeting at Luca.

Plancius, Plotius and Sufenas were the tribunes of the plebs in 56; the first two would thus have been curule aediles and the third praetor immediately afterwards in 55. Is this conciliable with the provisions of the *leges annales*? Such immediate successions between plebeian and regular magistracies were frequent before 196, but according to Mommsen's generally accepted opinion, at that time a regulation was enforced that forbade the magistrates to present themselves as candidates for any other magistracy before the expiration of their term of office ([30]). Under normal circumstances this provision had to bring about an interval of at least one year between a plebeian and a regular office ([31]).

But, as L. R. Taylor pointed out, the year in question was not a normal year: in 56 the electoral *comitia* did not take place. The elections of praetors, curule aediles and quaestors were held in 55 under the presidency of Pompeius and the candidates for those offices could present themselves only after the consular elections were over ([32]).

([28])   *Op. cit.*, 222.

([29])   Cicero, *ad Att.*, 4. 8. 2.

([30])   *Römisches Staatsrecht*, I³, Leipzig, 1887, 531-535. Cf. A. E. Astin, *The Lex Annalis*, 27; G. Rögler, *Die Lex Villia Annalis*, in *Klio*, 40, 1962, 103.

([31])   It should be remembered that the *biennium* was compulsory only between regular magistracies, but not between plebeian and regular.

([32])   On the date of the consular elections cf. P. Stein, *Die Senatssitzungen der Ciceronischen Zeit*, Münster, 1930, 44 nt. 22. Pompeius and Crassus were elected in any case before February 11 and probably at the end of January. L. R. Taylor, *op. cit.*, 21 writes that in 56 the « candidates declared themselves late » and further (p. 22) that many of the triumvirs' henchmen « must have been late in declaring their candidacy ». This, as far as the chronology of events is concerned, is uncontestably true, but at the same time not very accurate from the constitutional point of view. The *professiones* of the candidates were acepted by the president of the electoral assembly, i.e. in 56 by the consul Marcellinus. But the elections were delayed and eventually took place under the presidency of an *interrex* (the *comitia consularia*) and the newly elected consul Pompeius (the elections of praetors, aediles and quaestors). Neither the successive *interreges*, nor Pompeius were constitutionally bound to respect the decisions of Marcellinus. All the candidates who still wanted to stand for an office had to present themselves before the new president of elections, also those whose *professio* had already been accepted by Marcellinus. For details see the chapter on *professio* in my book *Rzymskie zgromadzenie wyborcze od Sulli do Cezara* (*The Roman Electoral Assembly from Sulla to Caesar*), Kraków, 1966, 52 ff.

The tribunes of 56 after having laid down their office on December 9 became private citizens and as such could begin canvassing for regular magistracies in full accordance with the annal laws. At the elections the optimate candidates were eliminated and almost all posts were filled by the triumvirs with their henchmen. Among praetors we find the Caesarian Vatinius, the Pompeians Milo and (probably) P. Plautius Hypsaeus, probably also Q. Caecilius Metellus Pius Scipio Nasica (who was later to become Pompeius' father-in-law) ([33]). To this list a further Pompeian, M. Nonius Sufenas, is now to be added. The triumvirs' henchmen were also Cn. Plancius and A. Plotius, whose curule aedilship in 55 has been proved by L. R. Taylor beyond any reasonable doubt, the plebeian aedile C. Messius and all but two the tribunes of the plebs ([34]).

One name is conspicuously missing on this list, that of C. Cato. This is especially striking now, after it has been established that at least three tribunes of the plebs of 56 gained higher magistracies in 55. Nonius Sufenas was rewarded with a praetorship for his part in delaying the elections in 55; would Cato, who is in this respect credited by the sources with the greatest merits for the dynasts, have been refused a reward?

In 54 Cato was at any rate an important person, so that Cicero and even Milo managed to be on good terms with him ([35]). A curious testimony of Cicero's should here be taken into account. Cicero informing his brother of Gabinius' acquittal on the charge de maiestate characterizes the jury in the following words (ad Q. fr., 3. 4. 1).

> Quid plura de iudicibus? duo praetorii sederunt, Domitius Calvinus (is aperte absolvit ut omnes viderent) et Cato (is diribitis tabellis de circulo se subduxit et Pompeio primus nuntiavit) ([36]).

([33]) L. R. Taylor, op. cit., 23 nt. 30, suggests that Caesar's sympathiser and Livia's father M. Livius Drusus also held his praetorship in 55.

([34]) See Niccolini, Fasti, 309-310; Broughton, Magistrates, II, 215-217; L. R. Taylor, op. cit., 22-24.

([35]) Cicero, ad Att., 4. 16. 5.

([36]) Miltner refers this notice erroneuosly to the trial of M. Aemilius Scaurus; he writes about Cato (s. v. Porcius [nº 7], in RE, XXII. 1, 107): « Nachher setze er sich für seinen Verteidiger (see below) M. Aemilius Scaurus ..., als dieser selbst angeklagt war, ein, ohne dass die Annahme, Cato hätte als einer der Richter in diesem Prozess fungiert, angesichts der unklaren Überlieferung (Cicero, ad Q. fr., 3. 4. 1; bes. 3. 8. 6) berechtigt wäre ». To be sure, Cicero, ad Q. fr., 3. 4. 1

Who was this Cato? Of course it could not have been M. Cato: not speaking even of the utmost improbability of Cato Uticensis having jubilantly informed Pompeius of Gabinius' acquittal, he was in 54 actually praetor and not *praetorius* (and as such not eligible for jury duty). One may consider him — as Drumann-Groebe ([37]) are inclined to do — an unknown son of M. Cato ([38]), praetor about 92, but this is a slight possibility. Another explanation proposed is to emend the text and read Cotta ([39]) instead of Cato — in that case M. Aurelius Cotta who commanded in Sardinia in 49 and was probably praetor by 54 might have been referred to ([40]). But the emendation of a text is the last escape to which one should resort; why should we not admit the most natural explanation and identify the juror mentioned by Cicero with C. Cato, the tribune in 56? The principal objection that has, so far, been raised against this identification is that in 54 C. Cato was *tribunicius* and not *praetorius* ([41]). This objection is based exclusively on the belief that C. Cato as tribune in 56 could not have been praetor in the following year. But, as we have seen, the career of M. Nonius Sufenas affords an example that under specific conditions, such as those in 55, the immediate succession from tribunate to praetorship was possible. In this way any obstacle for the identification of Cato the *praetorius* in 54 with Cato the tribune in 56 seems to be removed. I would contend that now as we know that he could have been praetor in 55, the information supplied by Cicero is to be taken as a proof that in fact he was. This conclusion fits in so excellently with the general picture of the triumvirs' policy in 56 and 55 emerging from recent studies that it corroborates in turn the solutions advanced by L. R. Taylor ([42]).

---

leaves no doubt that Cato functioned as a juror, and in 3. 8. 6 the reading of manuscripts is Gutta and not Cato. This reading has been often emended into Cotta, but it has been retained by BROUGHTON, *Magistrates*, II, 215-216. Nothing is known about that person save the information supplied by Cicero in the passage quoted above. Gutta appears there as a candidate for the consulship of 52, supported by Pompeius.

([37]) *Op. cit.*, V, 217 nt. 2.
([38]) Cf. BROUGHTON, *Magistrates*, II, 13, 14 nt. 2.
([39]) See DRUMANN-GROEBE, *loco cit.*
([40]) BROUGHTON, *Magistrates*, II, 222, 227 nt. 2, lists him as praetor in 54.
([41]) See DRUMANN-GROEBE, *loco cit.*; CONSTANS, *Cicéron, Correspondance*, III, 255.
([42]) One should not, however, forget that in our case, as far as the *leges annales* are concerned, it is not sufficient to prove only the possibility of the im-

The political evolution of C. Cato is significant: in 59 he accused Gabinius and attacked Pompeius, in 54 he acquitted Gabinius and tried to gain Pompeius' favour.

The optimate faction defeated in 56 and 55 scored some important victories in the elections for 54: L. Domitius Ahenobarbus was elected to the consulship and M. Cato became praetor. Under Cato's leadership the optimates strove to take revenge upon the triumvirs' henchmen. Many of them were indicted on various charges, but at the courts the Catonians were not very fortunate. P. Vatinius whose contest for the praetorship with M. Cato in 55 focused the attention of both ancient and modern authors was accused de sodaliciis. Cn. Plancius and C. Messius, respectively the curule and the plebeian aediles of 55, were treated under the same charge. The trials of Vatinius and Plancius and probably that of Messius too resulted in acquittals. A. Gabinius, consul of 58, was acquitted of the charge de maiestate, but condemned for extortion ([43]). Among the partisans of the dynasts unsuccessfully prosecuted in 54 we also find C. Cato and M. Sufenas, the tribunes of the plebs of 56 and praetors in 55; on Procilius see the remarks below.

------

mediate succession from plebeian to regular offices: the interval between quaestorship and praetorship and the minimum age laid down for that latter office must also be taken into account. BROUGHTON, Magistrates, II, 175, assignes the quaestorship of Sufenas to 62, but the date is queried. H. II. Mattingly (in an article cited by BROUGHTON, Magistrates, Suppl. 43) dates his quaestorship in 62 or 63. Thus we obtain an interval of six or seven years which is in perfect accordance with other known careers in the post-Sullan period (cf. A. E. ASTIN, The Lex Annalis, 39). With Cato the question is more complicated. As the evidence concerning the date of his quaestorship seems to be lacking, his tenure of that office is not even mentioned by Broughton, and Miltner also made no attempt to attribute it to a definite year. One may of course suppose that he held his quaestorship at about the same time as Sufenas. The difficulty is that he must have reached before entering upon praetorship (in February or March 55) the statutory age of 39 (finished) years. Now in 59, when according to the above computation he would have been already in his 36th year, Cicero (ad Q. fr., 2. 1. 15) calls him still adulescens. This need not, however, be used as an argument against Cato's praetorship in 59: Fenestella, frg. 21 (PETER), still terms Cato adulescens in 57/56, when he was already the tribune of the plebs. For the similar usage of adulescens cf. Cicero, de rep., 1. 18: doctos adulescentes iam aetate quaestorios and esp. Valerius Maximus, mem., 7. 5. 2: cum aedilitatem curulem adulescens peteret.

([43]) Cf. H. GUNDEL, s.v. Vatinius (n° 3), in RE, VIII A. 1, Stuttgart, 1955, 508; MÜNZER, s.v. Messius (n° 2), in RE, XV. 1, Stuttgart, 1931, 1243; VONDER MÜHLL, s.v. Gabinius (n° 11), in RE, VII. 1, Stuttgart, 1910, 429-430.

Let us now return to the question of charges brought by the prosecution against Cato, Sufenas and Procilius.

The scholars are unanimous, in any case as far as Cato and Sufenas are concerned, that it was the conduct of their tribunate with which they were charged. But in details opinions are divergent. Broughton ([44]) writes that Cato, Sufenas and Procilius were prosecuted for their « part in delaying the elections » in 56; Miltner states that Cato was accused « wegen seines Verhaltens als Volkstribun » ([45]) and Zwicker writes in similar words about Procilius: « zugleich mit Sufenas and Cato wegen seiner Amtsführung angeklagt » ([46]). L. R. Taylor thinks that « it is not unlikely that the trials of C. Cato and Sufenas had to do with interference with elections » ([47]).

In this connection two facts must not be lost of sight: 1) no one is likely to question that the role played by Cato and Sufenas in impeding the elections in 56 aroused the optimates' hatred against them and that it was the principal cause of their having been accused; but while being in full agreement with the opinions of the scholars cited above we must not forget that they are expressing themselves in political and not in legal terms. Cato and Sufenas could not have technically been charged « with their part in delaying elections » or « with the manner of conducting their tribunate ». These offences (or alleged offences) must have been entered under some more general headings, e. g. *maiestas minuta*, and treated as a breach of the law under which the trials were to take place; 2) the verdicts were returned in each case on the same day (July 4); it follows that Cato, Sufenas ad Procilius were treated in three separate courts and on different charges. This observation had already been made by Zumpt and recently restated by L. R. Taylor ([48]). Zumpt conjectured that Sufenas was accused of electoral bribery, Procilius of *crimen laesae maiestatis* and that Cato's trial was in connection with the *comitia*.

Let us now see if there is a possibility of saying something more definite. Cicero after having informed Atticus of Sufenas' and Cato's acquittal and the condemnation of Procilius continues that from these

---

([44])   *Magistrates*, II, 209.

([45])   S. v. *Porcius* (n° 6), in *RE*, XXII. 1, 107.

([46])   S. v. *Procilius* (n° 1), in *RE*, XXIII. 1, Stuttgart, 1957, 68.

([47])   *Op. cit.*, 19 nt. 19.

([48])   A. W. Zumpt, *Der Criminalprocess der römischen Republik*, Leipzig, 1871, 509, 532; L. R. Taylor, *op. cit.*, 19 nt. 19.

verdicts the conclusion might be drawn that the τρισαρεοπαγίται ([49]) had not bothered themselves with *ambitus, comitia, interregnum, maiestas,* but that on the other hand they did not approve the killing of a *pater familias* in his own house, though even in this respect they were not unanimous. Thus the acquittal of Sufenas and Cato is linked with the jurors' lack of interest in public affairs and the condemnation of Procilius with their attitude towards the crime of murdering the *pater familias.* If we do not have to do here with a merely rhetorical figure this might mean that the charge against Procilius was murder and that his trial took place under the law *de vi* ([50]).

In any case it seems to be the best solution we are now able to afford. It entails one important conclusion: if Procilius was found

---

([49]) The word τρισαρε(ι)οπαγίτης is a *hapax*, coined by Cicero. ZUMPT, *Der Criminalprocess der römischen Republik*, 509, interprets it, apparently erroneuosly, as an allusion to « drei damaligen Machthaber des Staates ». The context shows clearly that this expression is employed with regard to the jurors. LIDDELL-SCOTT-JONES, *A Greek-English Lexicon*, II⁹, Oxford, 1948, 822, *s. h. v.*, give as the meaning « an Aeropagite thrice over, i.e. a stern and rigid judge ». Cf. W. PAPE, *Griechisch-Deutsches Handwörterbuch³*, Braunschweig, 1902, 1147, *s. h. v.*: « ein dreifacher Aeropagit, d.i. sehr streng, ernsthaft ». Cf. also H. Stephanus: « ter areopagita ». Constans translates it as « nos aréopagites renforcés » and E. O. WINSTEDT, *Cicero, Letters to Atticus*, I, Cambridge (Mass.)-London, 1953, 307, paraphrases the expression as « our lights of the law ». R. B. STEELE, *The Greek in Cicero's Epistles*, in *Am. Journ. Philol.*, 21, 1900, 405, lists the word τρισαρειοπαγίτης among new expressions coined by Cicero, but does not discuss its precise meaning (the study of R. LOEW, *Quaestiones de Graecorum verborum, quae in epistulis Ciceronis extant, fontibus, usu, condicionibus*, Basileae, 1889, has been inaccessible to me; the books of O. WEISE, *Die griechischen Wörter im Latein*, Leipzig, 1882, and P. OKSALA, *Die Griechischen Lehnwörter in den Prosaschriften Ciceros*, Helsinki, 1953, are concerned only with Greek loan-words in Latin and not with Greek citations). All these translations and paraphrases miss the pointed meaning of Cicero's expression being a biting allusion to the composition of juries of representatives of the three orders (i.e. senators, knights and *tribuni aerarii*) and stressing at the same time the notorious corruption and lack of competence of this threefold body, a « threefold Areopagus ».

([50]) This is also the opinion of TYRREL-PURSER, *The Correspondence of M. Tullius Cicero*, II², Dublin, 1906, 149, *ad h.l.*, recently restated by L. R. TAYLOR, *op. cit.*, 19 nt. 19. Cf. also W. STERNKOPF, *Die Blätterversetzung im 4. Buche der Briefe ad Atticum*, in *Hermes*, 40, 1905, 26-27; MEYER, *Caesars Monarchie*, 201. According to TYRREL-PURSER, *loco cit.*, a remark of Cicero, *ad Att.*, 4. 18. 3 (written at the end of October), lends support to this thesis: *sed omnes absolventur, nec posthac quisquam damnabitur, nisi qui hominem occiderit.* Procilius is not, however, mentioned here and the reference may equally be to M. Fulvius Nobilior of whose condemnation Cicero speaks in the next sentence (cf. on him MÜNZER, s. v. *Fulvius* (nº 94), in *RE*, VII. 1, Stuttgart, 1910, 268).

guilty of murder the crime with which he was charged had nothing
in common with delaying the elections. In any case — and independently of whether the charge against him was murder or not — it is
evident that Sufenas and Cato were linked with the *comitia* and
interregnum and Procilius was not. It should be recalled that the
only basis for assigning to Sufenas the tribunate of the plebs in 56 is
the fact that he appears together with C. Cato as prosecuted for offences concerning in some way the elections in 56. It has been thought
that Procilius was alluded to in the same context, but this belief, as
we have seen, proves to have been based on a rather superficial analysis
of Cicero's passage. One cannot but agree with Zumpt ([51]) and
Taylor ([52]) that this passage affords no evidence for a tribunate of
Procilius.

An important contribution concerning the trial of Procilius has
recently been presented by D. R. Shackleton Bailey in his stimulating
researches on the text of the *ad Atticum* ([53]). *Publius sane diserto
epilogo criminans mentes iudicium moverat* — so reads the text as
printed in most editions and nobody before Shackleton Bailey had
questioned its genuineness ([54]). But was Clodius really the accuser?
Shackleton Bailey proposes to emend *criminans* in *lacrimans* (tears
were often resorted to in Roman courts) and to assign Clodius to the
defence.

This question having been put forward by Shackleton Bailey
must not be avoided in a paper concerned precisely with the same passage of Cicero, but it ought to be examined in view of the results
achieved above. Shackleton Bailey points out that for Clodius to
summon Procilius before the court would make no political sense.
Of course not if Procilius were the tribune in 56 and a colleague of
Cato and Sufenas, as Shackleton Bailey thinks him to have been. But

---

([51]) *Criminalprocess*, 509 nt. 3.

([52]) *Op. cit.*, 20 nt. 10. To be sure, she formulates this opinion in a more
positive manner, that there is no evidence at all for his tribunate. She may be right,
but see the remarks below.

([53]) *Towards a text of Cicero: Ad Atticum*, Cambridge, 1960, 19 ff. Cf. now
also D. R. SHACKLETON BAILEY, *Cicero's Letters to Atticus*, II, Cambridge, 1965, 116-
119, 201-202, 207-208. Unfortunately this important edition and commentary became
available only after this article was already sent to the Editol. The emendation
proposed by Shackleton Bailey has recently been accepted by L. R. TAYLOR, in *Class.
Phil.*, 62, 1967, 197.

([54]) J. N. MADVIG, *Adversaria critica*, III, Hauniae, 1884, 173, read ⟨*me*⟩ *criminans*. Cf. STERNKOPF's criticism of this reading: *op. cit.*, 26-27.

as we have seen, the tribunate of Procilius is lacking solid foundations.
Shackleton Bailey. has, however, one strong argument for his thesis:
Cicero's evident dislike of Procilius.

Of Procilius' previous career we know only a few facts [55].   In
ad Q. fr., 2.6. (7 or 8) 1, Cicero writes of him (in May 56):

> *Sed cetera, ut scribis, praesenti sermoni reserventur; hoc*
> *tamen non queo differre: Idibus Maiis senatus frequens di-*
> *vinus fuit in supplicatione Gabinio deneganda. adiurat Pro-*
> *cilius hoc nemini accidisse. foris valde plauditur. mihi cum*
> *sua sponte iucundum tum iucundius, quod me absente; est*
> *enim* εἰλικρινές *iudicium, sine oppugnatione, sine gratia no-*
> *stra.*

It is perhaps legitimate to conclude from this, as Shackleton Bailey
does, that Procilius protested against the feelings of the majority, but
it is also possible to conceive him as stressing triumphantly the degree
of Gabinius' humiliation. And that latter explanation is perhaps even
preferable: see below. Shackleton Bailey opines, however, that in view
of Cicero's sarcasm expressed in *ad Att.*, 4. 15. 4, the first interpretation
must be given priority. He takes Cicero's remark (*ad Att.*, 4. 16. 6) *de*
Procilio rumores non boni, sed iudicia nosti to be only « mock
concern ».

All this is of course possible. But there is something more. From
the text cited above important conclusions may be inferred. If Procilius spoke in the senate and did not express his view in private (this
is a very important reservation), he could do this only either asked
for his opinion by the presiding magistrate (this implies that he was
a member of the senate and at least *quaestorius* at that time), or beyond
the set order of « Umfrage » as a magistrate, presumably as tribune.
Thus there is a possibility (a very slight one: it must be conceded) to
recover from this text the tribunate of Procilius.

Let it, however, be observed that according to Cicero the intervention of Procilius came after the motion to decree the *supplicationes*
in honour of Gabinius' military efforts in Syria had already been
refuted: this means that he did not make his observation while
participating in discussion preceding the voting on the proposal.   If

---

[55] Zwicker, s. v. *Prociliuss* (n° 1), in *RE*, XXIII. 1, 68, holds that he was
quaestor in 59. Again no proof. CIL I², 918 (a *tessera nummularia* of 59 B.C.)
demonstrates only the existence in 59 B.C. of a Procilius and nothing more.   On
tesserae nummulariae cf. the basic study of R. Herzog, *Aus der Geschichte des*
Bankwesens im Altertum, Giessen, 1919, *passim*.

this was a formal speech the only possibility that seems to be left is to assume that it was delivered after the meeting had been reconvened by a tribune, possibly by Procilius himself.

The above reconstruction is theoretically possible, but on the whole it seems too artificial to be true. Further it is not easy to conceive why anyone speaking in favour of Gabinius should have noticed that nobody had met with such an affront until that time: should it have induced the opponents to change their minds and vote for Gabinius? It is therefore, no doubt, preferable to interpret Procilius' words adduced by Cicero as a private comment on the result of the voting.

Shackleton Bailey holds that Procilius' comment « would hardly have been worth repeating unless it was in oppositon to the general sentiment, i. e. a protest against Gabinius' treatment » [56]. An excellent suggestion by Halkin [57] helps here: he identifies our Procilius with Procilius, the historian and antiquarian [58]. The remark of such an authority *hoc nemini accidisse* [which, in fact, was not true [59]] pointing to the extent of Gabinius' defeat and stressing its uniqueness seemed to Cicero so important and gave him such great pleasure that he could not resist the temptation of transmitting it immediately to Quintus (*hoc tamen non queo differre*) and even many years later he repeated this allegation in his Philippics [60].

Thus on this interpretation it can safely be admitted that in May 56 Procilius sympathized with the optimates [61]. A query is, however,

---

(56) *Op. cit.*, 20.

(57) L. HALKIN, *La supplication d'action de graces chez les Romains*, Paris, 1953, 93-94.

(58) On Procilius the historian see K. ZIEGLER, s. v. *Procilius* (n° 2), in *RE*, XXIII. 1, 68-69. According to Ziegler's opinion to identify this Procilius with the tribune is « eine nahelicgende, aber nicht beweisbare Vermutung » (speaking of Procilius the tribune Ziegler thinks, of course, of Procilius condemned in 54). For fragments of his works (quoted by Varro and Plinius) cf. PETER, *Historicorum romanorum reliquiae*, I, Lipsiae, 1883, 316-317. Also Cicero read Procilius' works and his judgement was not so unfavourable to Procilius as Ziegler holds it to have been: no wonder that when comparing Procilius with Dicaearchus Cicero exclaims: *O magnum hominem et unde multo plura didiceris quam de Procilio* (*ad Att.*, 2. 2. 1, December 60).

(59) HALKIN, *op. cit.*, 94 ff.

(60) 14. 24: ... *quod praeter Gabinium contigit nemini.*

(61) To generalize this conclusion might be, however, deceptive. The exemple of C. Cato who in February 56 *Pompeium tamquam reum accusavit* (Cicero, *ad Q. fr.*, 2. 3. 3) and a few months later co-operated with him must be borne in mind.

here in place: is Procilius the historian (and possibly senator) mentioned by Cicero in 56 and Procilius condemned in 54 one and the same
person? Nothing compels us to identify them. It is only a possibility,
not a fact.

Procilius was defended by Q. Hortensius Hortalus. The remark:
Hortalus in ea causa fuit cuiusmodi solet is not very definite, but
taking into account that no instance of Hortensius acting as prosecutor
can be adduced, there does not seem to be even the slightest doubt
that in this trial also he appeared as advocate [62]. As his part was
evidently not a very significant one, this does not contradict the thesis
assigning to Clodius the principal role in the defence.

What Cicero has to say of himself is more interesting: *nos verbum nullum; veritast enim pusilla, quae nunc laborat, ne animum
Publi offenderem* [63]. It follows that had he spoken he would have
taken a stand against Clodius; now in the period of time that had
elapsed between the trial of Verres and that of T. Munatius Plancus
Bursa in December 52 Cicero never supported a prosecution and there
is no reason to assume that he would have done so in this case [64]. This
conclusion is clearly incompatible with the thesis that Clodius spoke
for the defence. But there is still another possibility. One may also
admit that Cicero does not allude to the possibility of his appearing
in the court in the capacity of accuser or advocate, but only as a witness
in order to give evidence. To give evidence for or against Procilius:
for — if Clodius was prosecuting, and against — if he was defending.
The passage may be interpreted either way, but the odds seem to be
against Shackleton Bailey's ingenious emendation.

The queries concerning the trials of Sufenas and Cato are perhaps even more numerous. In connection with them *ambitus, comitia, interregnum* and *maiestas* are referred to; of these only the
first and the last item could have constituted a formal charge. Solely
on the basis of internal analysis of the text we are not able to establish
for certain with which of these offences Sufenas and Cato were charged. If the order in which the charges are listed corresponds to that
in which the defendants are named, it might follow that Sufenas
was prosecuted *de ambitu* and Cato *de maiestate*.

---

[62] Cfr. Drumann-Groebe, *Geschichte*, III, 94; H. Malcovati, *Oratorum Romanorum Fragmenta²*, Aug. Taurinorum-Mediolani, 1955, 310 ff., esp. 327.

[63] *Offenderet* Mss; *offenderem* Manutius.

[64] Cf. Drumann-Groebe, *Geschichte*, VI, 27.

In a letter of Cicero's we find a remark that throws light on the legal circumstances of Cato's trial. We read *ad Att.*, 4. 16. 5:

> *Nunc ad ea quae quaeris de C. Catone. lege Iunia et Licinia scis absolutum; Fufia ego tibi nuntio absolutum iri, neque patronis suis tam libentibus quam accusatoribus* [65].

Thus C. Cato was twice prosecuted in 54: under the *lex Iunia Licinia* and afterwards under the *lex Fufia.*

Who Sufenas' accuser was does not stand on record. We are, however, fortunate to know the names both of Cato's prosecutor and his advocates.

Seneca and Tacitus [66] inform us that a suit against Cato was brought in by C. Asinius Pollio, then 21 years old. In the future Pollio was to become consul (in 40 B.C.) and, above all, a renowned historian and man of letters [67]. In 56 he supported P. Lentulus Spinther in the strife concerning the restoring of the king Ptolemy Auletes [68]; Pollio and Cato thus belonged to the opposite factions.

C. Licinius Calvus [69] spoke for the defence [70]. Seneca records that the quarrel reached a point at which Asinius Pollio was about to be killed by the clients of Cato and only the resolute intervention of Licinius Calvus saved him life [71].

---

[65] This letter was written before 4. 15. 4, between June 29 and July 3. See STERNKOPF, *op. cit.*, 13-17.

[66] Seneca, *contr.*, 7. 4. 7; Tacitus, *dial. de or.*, 34. 7.

[67] See the monograph of J. ANDRÉ, *La vie et l'oeuvre d'Asinius Pollion*, Paris, 1949.

[68] Cicero, *ad fam.*, 1. 6. 1.

[69] On Calvus as orator see MÜNZER, s. v. *Licinius* (n° 113), in *RE*, XII. 1, Stuttgart, 1926, 428 ff.; MALCOVATI, *Orator. rom. fragm.*², 492 ff.; E. CASTORINA, *Licinio Calvo*, Catania, 1946.

[70] Seneca, *contr.*, 7. 4. 7. This is the common opinion of scholars cf. e.g. MALCOVATI, *Orator. rom. fragm.*², 948 f.; ANDRÉ, *op. cit.*, 12. Münzer, however, had once expressed the view that Calvus was the accuser (s. v. *Licinius* (n° 113), in *RE*, XIII. 1, 432). Cato is termed by Seneca in respect to Calvus *reus suus*. But this expression is rather to be understood as « the accused whose case is pleaded by Calvus » and not as « the one who is accused by Calvus ». The context is in any case in favour of the first interpretation.

[71] Seneca, *contr.*, 7. 4. 7: *idem (Calvus) postea cum videret a clientibus Catonis rei sui Pollionem Asinium circumventum in foro caedi, inponi se supra cippum iussit... et iuravit, si quam iniuriam Cato Pollioni Asinio accusatori suo fecisset, se in eum iuraturum calumniam; nec umquam postea Pollio a Catone advocatisque eius aut re aut verbo violatus est.* ANDRÉ, *op. cit.*, 12, states mistakenly that he was rescued by Aemilius Scaurus.

Asconius supplies the information that M. Aemilius Scaurus ([72]) after having returned to Rome (on June 29) from his province *dixerat pro C. Catone isque erat absolutus a.d. IIII Non. Quint* ([73]). Here the reference is to Cato's second trial, that referred to by Cicero in *ad Att.*, 4. 15. 4.

Thus two trials, one accuser, two advocates. How to assign the roles? André seems to assume the possibility that Asinius Pollio acted on both occasions as prosecutor, Licinius Calvus and Aemilius Scaurus being his adversaries ([74]). This thesis cannot be accepted. Cicero asserts that on his second trial, that under the *lex Fufia*, Cato was going to be acquitted *neque patronis suis tam libentibus quam accusatoribus*. On the other hand we have the information of Seneca regarding the assault of Cato's clients upon Asinius Pollio. Such an attack would have been inexplicable if the prosecutor acted in collusion with the defendant. The testimonies of Cicero and Seneca are to

---

([72]) Cf. Klebs, s. v. *Aemilius* (nº 141), in *RE*, I. 1, Stuttgart, 1893, 589.

([73]) Asconius, *in Scaur.*, p. 18 (Clark). The date supplied by Asconius is the basis for emendation in *ad Att.*, 4. 15. 4, where the Mss reading is *a.d. III Nonas Quintiles*.

([74]) He writes (*op. cit.*, 12): «... après leur sortie de charge, deux procès furent intentés aux tribuns en vertu des lois Iunia Licinia et Fufia. Pollion se porta accusateur de C. Caton qui fut défendu par un familier de Crassus, C. Licinius Calvus, et un familier de Pompée, M. Aemilius Scaurus». Cf., however, p. 68: « on ne sait si Pollion intervint dans les deux causes ». Malcovati, *Orator. rom. fragm.?*, 498, is even more positive: «C. Cato... ab Asinio Pollione accusatus est lege Licinia Iunia et lege Fufia ». P. Groebe, in Drumann-Groebe, *Geschichte*, V, 216 nt. 10, accepts the thesis of Lange, *Röm. Alterthümer*, III², 347, that « es sei hier nicht von einem, sondern von zwei Prozessen die Rede, dessen erster sich nur gegen Cato richtete und im Juni mit der Freisprechung endete, während der zweite Cato und Sufenas betraf ». Cf. Lange, *loco cit.*: « Gleich darauf wurde (Cato), und mit ihm M. Nonius Sufenas, wegen Hinderung der Wahlcomitien nach der *lex Fufia* angeklagt ». Cf. also Sternkopf, *op. cit.*, 26: « Sufenas und Cato waren wegen eines politischen Vergehens angeklagt, wahrscheinlich beide wegen desselben und zwar nach der *lex Fufia*. Ihr Ankläger ist uns nicht bekannt » (p. 26 nt. 2, he writes: « C. Cato wurde im 54 zweimal belangt; in welchem dieser Prozesse C. Asinius Pollio sein Ankläger war, steht dahin »). Miltner, s. v. *Porcius* (nº 5), in *RE*, XXII. 1, 107, records only one trial of Cato in 54; he does not mention his prosecution by Asinius Pollio and his defence by Licinius Calvus. But to admit, as Lange, Groebe, Sternkopf and André do, that other tribunes (that is, in fact, Sufenas) were either also twice prosecuted in 54 or, in any case, under the same laws as Cato runs clearly counter both the contents of the analysed texts and the rules of Roman court procedure. It is to be repeated that, as the verdicts were returned on the same day, Cato and Sufenas must have been treated on different charges.

be referred to two different trials and, no doubt, that of Seneca to the first one.

To sum up: the suit brought in by C. Asinius Pollio was based on the *lex Iunia Licinia*; Pollio's adversary was C. Licinius Calvus. Shortly afterwards Cato stood trial under the *lex Fufia*; this time he was defended by M. Aemilius Scaurus and acquitted with the connivance of the prosecution.

The *lex Iunia Licinia* (passed in 62 by the consuls M. Iunius Silanus and L. Licinius Murena) was concerned with some technicalities of the legislation; according to its provision the copies of (promulgated) laws had to be deposited in the *aerarium* [75]. The accuser must have asserted that Cato while proposing his legislation as tribune in 54 had in some way violated the prescriptions of this law [76].

The trial of C. Cato under the *lex Fufia* has aroused considerable interest among modern scholars, above all because of its relation to the problem of *obnuntiatio* and its bearing on the recontruction of the provisions of the *leges Aelia* and *Fufia* [77]. There is no doubt that the *lex Fufia* referred to is to be identified with the *lex Fufia* which was concerned with *obnuntiatio* and which is normally mentioned together with the *lex Aelia*. McDonald has, however, pointed to the existence of a *lex Fufia iudiciaria* and expressed the opinion that « it is not inconceivable that it was under this law .... that C. Cato was indicted » [78]. Theoretically this is possibile, but one must not forget Cicero's remark about *comitia* and *interregnum* that unmistakably point in the right direction: would it have not been

---

[75] MOMMSEN, *Röm. Staatsrecht*, II³, 546; III, 371. F. VON SCHWIND, *Zur Frage der Publikation im römischen Recht*, München, 1940, 28 ff., argues, however, that the Iunian and Licinian law was not concerned with the projects of laws, but rather with depositing the final texts of laws after they had already been voted on by the popular assembly. But the fact that Cato only promulgated his laws and did not pass them is against this thesis.

[76] Cato's accuser under the *lex Iunia Licinia* was Pollio: note that in 56 Pollio supported P. Cornelius Lentulus Spinther and Cato promulgated a law *de imperio P. Lentulo abrogando*.

[77] The entire problem of the *lex Fufia* and *obnuntiatio* cannot be gone into here. It needs a detailed discussion that can be undertaken only in a larger context. Accordingly I shall concentrate myself only on those points that are of special importance in the proper understanding of the analysed texts.

[78] W. F. McDONALD, *Clodius and the Lex Aelia Fufia*, in *JRS*, 19, 1929, 179 nt. 3. On the *lex Fufia iudiciaria* see Broughton, *Magistrates*, II, 188-189; C. MACDONALD, *The Lex Fufia of 59 B. C.*, in *Class. Rev.*, N. S., 7, 1957, 198.

extremely odd, if this were to be understood as a comment on the prosecution under a judiciary law ([79])? If this conclusion needs further support, attention should be called to a passage of Cicero to be found in the same letter in which he speaks of Cato's trials: *ad Att.,* 4. 16. 6: *putant fore aliquem qui comitia in adventum Caesaris detrudat, Catone praesertim absoluto.* The reference is here, as Sumner ([80]) rightly argues, not to Cato's acquittal under the *lex Iunia Licinia,* but to his future acquittal under the Fufian law; as Cicero had already said that the prosecutors did not in fact wish Cato to be condemned, he treated his acquittal as a foregone conclusion. Besides that it is not easy to imagin what connection there could have been between the Iunian and Licinian law concerning legislation and the question of delaying the elections.

But there is still one point that, as it seems, has been missed in recent discussion. Two passages of Cicero inform us how the electoral comitia were impeded in 54: *ad Att.,* 4. 17. 4 (dated October 1): *... obnuntiationibus per Scaevolam* ([81]) *interpositis singulis diebus usque ad pr. Kal. Octob.,* and *ad Q. fr.,* 3. 3. 2 (dated October 21): *comitiorum cotidie singuli dies tolluntur obnuntiationibus magna voluntate bonorum omnium.*

Two statements may be inferred from the texts reproduced above: 1) the acquittal of Cato under the *lex Fufia* was understood by Cicero as encouragement to impeding the elections; 2) the elections in 54 were prevented from being held by means of *obnuntiatio* (and not *intercessio*).

It follows that: 1) Cato's trial under the *lex Fufia* was connected with his obstruction of elections in 56; 2) the elections were impeded in that year (as in 54) by announcements of bad signs ([82]); 3) the *lex Fufia* contained prescriptions concerning *obnuntiatio,* or, at any rate, the application of *obnuntiatio* at elections.

([79]) Cf. also the criticism of S. WEINSTOCK, *Clodius and the Lex Aelia Fufia,* in *JRS,* 27, 1937, 220 nt. 20.

([80]) G. V. SUMNER, *Lex Aelia, Lex Fufia,* in *Am. Journ. Philol.,* 84, 1963, 339.

([81]) Q. Mucius Scaevola, *tr. plebis,* in 54.

([82]) Livy's *periochae,* 105, state, however, that the elections were prohibited in 56 by the tribunician *intercessio.* This information has been generally accepted, cf. e.g. E. MEYER, *Caesars Monarchie,* 150. But it is to my knowledge the only instance of *intercessio* against elections after Sulla and there are strong reasons to doubt the credibility of this information. In any case the question of *intercessio* in the post-Sullan period urgently calls for a detailed analysis.

Let us now compare these conclusions with the results achieved by Sumner in his analysis of the contents of the Fufian law ([83]). Discussing the trial of Cato he comes to the conclusion that « the *lex Fufia* contained a provision concernéd with preventing the obstruction of elections » — note that he speaks of obstruction in general with no word of qualification. This is in harmony with his theory according to which the *lex Aelia* was concerned with *obnuntiatio* and *intercessio* (exclusively) at the legislative assemblies, while the Fufian law contained provisions with regard to *ius et tempus legum rogandarum* (prescribing that the legislative *comitia* could meet only on *dies comitiales*) and to obstruction of elections (enabling the prosecution for impeding the elections and forbidding in particular the summoning of the legislative assembly in the period between the announcement and the holding of elections).

Summer's discussion, especially as compared with solutions proposed by his predecessors, is a great advance; of special importance are his efforts to differentiate between the two laws. But there are some points that need further investigation. We have tried above to show that the *lex Fufia* must also have contained certain provisions concerning the practice of *obnuntiatio* with regard to electoral assemblies. I think that this does not contradict Summer's thesis, but rather supplements it.

The *lex Fufia* is said by Cicero to have been totally repealed by Clodius ([84]); among modern scholars this opinion is shared also by Valeton ([85]). In spite, however, of Cicero's rhetorics and Valeton's arguing, the fact that Cato could have been accused under the Fufian law seems to afford an irrefutable proof that at least some provisions of this law remained in force after 58 as well ([86]).

The question of whether the holding of elections could have legally been impeded before 58 by means of *obnuntiatio* is open to discussion ([87]); on the other hand the numerous examples of heaven

---

([83]) *Op. cit.*, 338 ff. The important article of A. E. ASTIN, *Leges Aelia et Fufia*, in *Latomus*, 23, 1964, 421 ff., reached me only after this paper was already in the press.

([84]) *De prov. cons.*, 46; *pro Sest.*, 33; *post red. in sen.*, 11; *har resp.*, 58; *pro Pis.*, 9, 10; *pro Vat.*, 18.

([85]) I. M. J. VALETON, *De iure obnuntiandi comitiis et conciliis*, in *Mnemosyne*, N. S., 19, 1891, 268-270.

([86]) Cf. SUMNER, *op. cit.*, 351.

([87]) Cf. L. LANGE, *De legibus Aelia and Fufia commentatio*, in *Kleine Schriften*, I, Göttingen, 1887, 329 ff.; VALETON, *op. cit.*, 94, 261.

watching after the *lex Clodia* in order to prohibit the convening of the electoral assembly leave no doubt that at that time the *obnuntiatio* was legally allowed at elections ([88]).

Now, if *obnuntiatio* was allowed at elections after 58 and if Cato was prosecuted for having impeded the *comitia consularia* by the device of heaven watching, it follows that it could not have been the prosecution for practicing of *obnuntiatio* as such, but only for trespassing the rules of its application. According to Cicero, *ad Att.*, 4. 15. 4, Cato was charged either with *maiestas* or *ambitus*; as, however, the electoral malpractices have clearly no immediate connection with the question of *obnuntiatio*, only the first possibility holds good ([89]). Thus the prosecution under the *lex Fufia* technically took place as a charge *de maiestate minuta.* However, a difficulty arises here. As the *lex Fufia*, according to different datings, was passed between 154 and 132 B.C. ([90]), it could not have contained the notion of *maiestas minuta.* The explanation may be that the offences punished originally by the Fufian law were subsequently entered by one of the *leges maiestatis* under the heading *maiestas minuta.* In our case a provision to this effect must have been enforced by the *lex Cornelia* of Sulla. That this not only a theoretical possibility is clearly shown by a Ciceronian passage (*in Pis.*, 50) where we read that certain deeds such as *exire de provincia, educere exercitum, bellum sua sponte gerere, in regnum iniussu populi Romani aut senatus accedere* were forbidden by *plurimae leges veteres tum lex maiestatis Cornelia.* And that illegal obstruction of proceedings of an assembly was in fact considered as *crimen maiestatis* is testified by the *Auctor ad Herennium*, 2. 17: *maiestatem is minuit, qui ea tollit, ex quibus rebus civitatis amplitudo constat. quae sunt ea, Q. Caepio? suffragia, magistratus. nempe igitur tu et populum suffragio et magistratum consilio privasti, cum pontes disturbasti.*

To obnuntiate against the holding of the electoral assembly was in itself a legal act, but the way in which C. Cato announced and applied his obnuntiations must have been viewed by the prosecution

---

([88]) See the chapter on *obnuntiatio* in my book *Rzymskie zgromadzenie wyborcze*, 74 ss.; SUMMER, *op. cit.*, 353 ff.

([89]) Cf. LANGE, *op. cit.*, 334 nt. 3.

([90]) 154 or 153 is the traditional date. According to L. R. TAYLOR, *Forerunners of the Gracchi*, in *JRS*, 52, 1962, 22, the law was passed at about 150. SUMMER, *op. cit.*, 349-350, has proposed 132 B. C.

as illegal. The accusers must have argued that by having acted in this manner he — to borrow the expression from the *Auctor ad Herennium* — *populum suffragio privavit.*

Which provision was allegedly violated by Cato in 56 while obnuntiating against the consular elections is not easy to detect. But one may try. The announcement *se de caelo servare* had according to the augural discipline to be made separately for each comitial day and not in one act for a period of time ([91]). It is possible that Cato failed to observe this rule (as did Milo before him in 57) — note that after Cato's trial this principle was strictly adhered to by tribunes announcing the watching of heavens ([92]). But there is still another possibility. According to augural law the magistrate observed the sky for purposes of his own. Now, C. Cato had as early as in March 56 made it plain that he would not allow the regular elections to be held. In consequence he might have been accused of having forged the *auspicia (ementiri auspicia).*

C. Cato being prosecuted under the charge of *maiestas*, the accusation of *ambitus* mentioned in Cicero's letter is to be referred to Sufenas. It is most probable that he was accused of electoral malpractices committed by him while canvassing for praetorship in 55 (for 55). Thus he is to be added to the list of triumvirs' henchmen prosecuted for ambitus in 54.

([91]) VALETON, *op. cit.*, 106-107. Cf. also J. LINDERSKI, *Constitutional Aspects of the Consular Elections in 59 B. C.*, in *Historia*, 14, 1965, 394.

([92]) See Cicero, *ad Att.*, 4. 17. 4: ... *obnuntiationibus per Scaevolam interpositis singulis diebus usque ad pr. Kal. Octob., quo ego haec die scripsi; ad Q. fr.,* 3. 3. 2: *comitiorum cotidie singuli dies tolluntur obnuntiationibus.* On Milo's obnuntiatio in 57 see Cicero, *ad Att.*, 4. 3. 3: *proscripsit se per omnes dies comitiales de caelo servaturum.*

11

L'ordre équestre à l'époque républicaine (312–43 av. J.-C.), vol. 2: *Prosopographie des chevaliers romains*. By CLAUDE NICOLET. Bibliothèque des Écoles Françaises d'Athènes et de Rome, fasc. 207. Paris: Éditions E. de Boccard, 1974. Pp. xvii + 755–1150 + 3 folding maps.

The first volume of C. Nicolet's magnum opus, *L'ordre équestre à l'époque républicaine*, appeared in 1966. It bore the subtitle, *Définitions juridiques et structures sociales*. Now we also have the long-awaited volume 2: *Prosopographie des chevaliers romains*. Together they constitute an inseparable whole (not only because of continuous pagination): volume 2 contains a list and a detailed discussion of all known *equites*, and thus it forms the basis and foundation on which N. has erected his imposing edifice of the *ordo equester*. Hence, when volume 2 is discussed, it is necessary to refer frequently to volume 1, especially as pages 147–60 have been intended by the author as an introduction to his method and his prosopographical lists.

The subtitles are telling. N.'s *thèse* is a study in social phenomenology; its subject is the equestrian order in its two *Erscheinungsformen* as a legal institution and as a social structure. And his method is prosopographical. Three questions can be addressed to the author: what was the *ordo equester*, who were the *equites*, and what is the prosopographical method? To none of these questions, including the last, is the answer self-evident.

The importance of method is obvious. Fortunately we can here have recourse to N.'s own reflections on the subject in his article, "Prosopographie et histoire sociale: Rome et l'Italie à l'époque républicaine" (*Annales ESC* 25 [1970]: 1209–28), the mature fruit of his "equestrian" studies. Prosopography is of course collection and description of πρόσωπα, and hence it begins with the compilation of different kinds of *indices nominum* and *onomastica*, embracing finally all known persons in a given period of time. But, as N. rightly points out, this is only a preliminary stage, at least for a social historian. The next step is the establishment of *fasti* or, more generally, of lists of people having a common distinguishing feature, be it that they hold a magistracy (or magistracies), that they are members of a specific *gens*, *ordo*, or association, or that they belong to a certain social stratum or occupational group (e.g., as *publicani*, *negotiatores*, *mercatores*, *liberti*, or *milites*). Such groups ought to be analyzed from various points of view: chronology and geography, family connections, property, political and economic activities, and terminology, especially honorific titles and set expressions, are all important criteria. N.'s definition of prosopography is as follows ("Prosopographie et histoire sociale," p. 1226): "la prosopographie suppose la mise en série, elle ne met en évidence l'individuel et l'exceptionnel que pour dégager, par contraste, le collectif et le normal." As this definition runs counter to the habitual practice of most Roman prosopographers, a few words of comment are in place.

Even if the known members of a group form only a small fraction of the total, it is often possible to establish social, political, and economic patterns. However, a historian can succeed only rarely in reducing such inductively established patterns to individual cases. In other words, there is no secure method of inferring from a general pattern the likely behavior or situation of an individual. This is a basic rule of statistical patterns and one of which both physicists and sociologists are well aware, but which apparently is unknown to classicists, for they so often indulge in this kind of upside-down prosopography. Moreover, as we normally know only a chance fraction of the total, it is impossible to establish a margin of error for such inferences. The situation is different with respect to legal definitions, legal rules, and set patterns (as opposed to statistical patterns). In this case it is often (but by no means always) possible and legitimate to make inferences concerning individual instances. Three sets of examples will illustrate our point.

Legal rules: (1) The *lex Acilia* (*lex tabulae Bembinae*) excluded the senators and their relatives from service on juries. Hence, if a person is attested as a *iudex* between 122 and 106 (the date of the *lex Servilia Caepionis*), he obviously was an *eques ex definitione legis Aciliae*. Conversely, a juror attested between the *lex Cornelia* and the *lex Aurelia* was undoubtedly a senator. After the *lex Aurelia*, no such automatic inferences are possible. (2) The *lex Roscia* of 67 reserved for the *equites* the first fourteen rows in the theater. Hence a man attested to have sat in the *quattuordecim ordines* can safely be regarded as an *eques*—whatever the exact meaning of the term.

Set patterns: As set patterns we can define those patterns in which one element appears in all known instances in a constant correlation with another element, as, for example, if A either entails or excludes B. This is often the case with set expressions. N. was able to establish (*a*) that there is a relatively high percentage of *negotiatores* and *argentarii* among the *equites* (46 examples, 12.8% of the total); and (*b*) that on the other hand "aucun chevalier n'est jamais appelé *mercator*" (*L'ordre équestre*, 1:364, 367). As (*a*) represents only a statistical pattern, it does not allow any particular inferences; but if a person was (in the Republican period) a *mercator*, he certainly was not an *eques*.

Statistical patterns: Owing to the particular structure of Roman politics and society, Broughton's *MRR* is bound to remain the most significant study in Roman social history. In the *fasti magistratuum* we can see year-by-year tangible results of the politics of *Adelsparteien* and *Adelsfamilien*, not yet distorted by unfounded conclusions. *Adelsparteien* and *Adelsfamilien* constituted the essence of Roman political and social life. This essence was, however, formed of constantly and unpredictably shifting elements. There are no set political patterns: in politics we have only statistical patterns, and it is therefore impossible, on the basis of the known general pattern, to reconstruct individual elements, that is, to divine the actual course of political events. As an illustration we may cite the famous example (produced by A. Heuss) of Caesar's being a dear friend of Bibulus because they held together all the magistracies from the aedileship to the consulate. It is also well known that the consul often exerted decisive influence upon the election of his successor, and it might therefore be tempting to suppose that C. Calpurnius Piso owed his election to the friendly support of C. Calpurnius Bibulus. Unfortunately, despite all prosopographical appearances, there was no Julio-Calpurnian faction rolling down the highway of Roman politics in 59–58. This reasoning seems absurd only because we happen to know that the conclusions are false, but the works of Münzer's *epigoni* (although the Master himself is not completely innocent either) are littered with similar inferences which pass for historical scholarship. N.'s book is a prosopographical study, for it proceeds from the individual to the general. Scholars who prefer a different direction ought to be aware that they are engaged in creating a prosopographical fantasy.

Now to our next question: who were the *equites?* The Roman knights had been of great interest to students of Roman antiquities since the time of Pantagathus,

Panvinius, and Manutius, but, strangely enough, it was not until 1912 that an attempt was made to collect all persons attested as *equites*. P. Schmidt, a pupil of Cichorius, adopted in his Breslau dissertation (*Die römischen Ritter von den Gracchen bis zum Tode Ciceros*) a severe criterion, but the only reasonable one: he included in his *fasti equitum* only those men who were explicitly termed *equites* or for whom the holding of the public horse was attested. However, he did not offer any historical or sociological analysis, and so his bare list of 196 names failed to exert any significant influence. The study of the *equites* continued to follow a devious course. The field was dominated by the preconceived idea, most forcefully expressed by E. J. Belot (*Histoire des chevaliers romains*, 2 vols. [Paris, 1866–73]), that all "rich" men who were not senators were *equites*. The culmination of this line was achieved—25 years after A. Stein's *Der römische Ritterstand* (Munich, 1927) had put the study of the knights in the imperial period on firm ground!—by H. Hill (*The Roman Middle Class in the Republican Period* [Oxford, 1952]), who imagined the republican *equites* as a kind of "middle class," thus unduly modernizing and misinterpreting Pliny's characterization of the knights as the *tertium corpus* (*NH* 33. 34, cf. 33. 29). Hill's theory has been deservedly criticized, most notably by Gelzer (*Gnomon* 25 [1953]: 319–23) and Gabba (*Athenaeum* n.s. 32 [1954]: 336–45), but it is not an easy task to lay a myth to rest. One myth was that the *equites* were primarily rich businessmen and bankers (*argentarii, negotiatores, foeneratores*). P. A. Brunt ("The Equites in the Late Republic," *The Crisis of the Roman Republic*, ed. R. Seager [Cambridge, 1969], p. 88) has clearly, albeit rather intuitively, seen the fallacy of this contention, but it was only thanks to the prosopographical approach that N. has been able to show the statistical and economic importance of landed proprietors among the *equites* (*L'ordre équestre*, 1:285–315).

N.'s *Prosopographie* contains 400 alphabetically arranged entries (nos. 95–99 are missing—through oversight?—and there is one double entry). His criterion of inclusion is twofold. The core of his list consists of the *equites certi:* persons explicitly called *equites*, or described as being *ex equestri ordine*, or mentioned in connection with the *anulus aureus, equus publicus*, or the *centuriae* and *recognitio equitum* (223 entries according to my count). The other category is made up of *equites probabiles* (177 entries). This is by the nature of things a tenuous category, for it is often rather difficult to estimate the degree of probability. N. lists here (among others) some *praefecti* and *tribuni militum* (see below), some *homines novi*, some *scribae*, *publicani*, and officials of the *societates*, some relatives of senators and *equites*, and finally some men who are included on the basis of their honorific titles (e.g., *splendidus, ornatissimus*).

Prosopography was the basis of N.'s admirable treatment of *structures sociales*, but unfortunately prosopography does not tell who were the *equites* as legally defined. We learn only who were the *equites* on the list. N.'s contention that only the *equites equo publico* formed the *ordo equester* (*L'ordre équestre*, 1:162–76) was discussed with his usual acumen by T. P. Wiseman ("The Definition of 'Eques Romanus' in the Late Republic and Early Empire," *Historia* 19 [1970]: 67–83), and recently E. Badian has offered penetrating remarks (*Publicans and Sinners* [Ithaca, 1972], pp. 82–87, 144–46). N. takes up the question again in volume 2, especially in connection with his discussion of T. Catienus ("homo levis ac sordidus, sed tamen equestri censu," Cic. *QFr.* 1. 2. 6), C. Cluvius ("si ex censu spectas, eques Romanus," Cic. *QRosc*. 42), the squanderer Gellius ("nomen ordinis equestris retinet, ornamenta confecit," Cic. *Sest.* 111), D. Laberius, and the *scribae* C. Cicereius and Maevius. The three distinguished authors do not seem, however, to have paid enough attention to the importance of the *lex Roscia* for the legal definition of the *ordo*. The *lex Roscia* of 67 reserved for the *equites* the first fourteen rows in the theater. Was this right limited only to the holders of the *equus publicus* (so essentially N.; cf. Mommsen, *Staatsrecht*, 3:521, and Wiseman, "Definition of 'Eques,'" p. 72) or was it extended (as Badian thinks, *Publicans*, p. 84; cf. Stein, *Ritterstand*, p. 26) to all those who possessed the *census equester* of 400,000 HS? Badian points out that if the fourteen rows had been provided exclusively for the *equites* proper, it is hardly conceivable that Cicero (*Mur.* 40) would have so extravagantly praised the *lex Roscia* before a jury one-third of which was composed of the *tribuni aerarii*, who not only did not gain any additional *dignitas* through the law, but were clearly the losers. Hence the law must have benefited both the *equites* and the *tribuni aerarii*: it reserved the fourteen rows for all men with the equestrian census (it is virtually certain, as N. accepts hesitatingly, and Wiseman and Badian, following Mommsen, state quite decisively, that the census of the *tribuni aerarii* was the same as the *census equester*, and not an inferior one, viz. 300,000 HS).

Badian has obviously made a point, but his conclusion is as fallacious as his argument is persuasive. He seems to overlook the close connection between the *ornamenta equestria*, symbolized especially by the gold ring, and the *ius in XIV ordinibus sedere*. The examples of Roscius, Laberius, and Maevius, the *scriba* of Verres, show that the *census equester* was a necessary but not a sufficient prerequisite: not every *homo equestri censu* had the *ornamenta equestria*. N. (*L'ordre équestre*, 1: 92 ff.) is inclined to think that the *anulus aureus* automatically assured a man of a place in the *centuriae equitum*. But the scene staged by Pompey in 70 (Plut. *Pomp.* 22; cf. *L'ordre équestre*, 2:986–87) demonstrates that it was still the duty of the censors to review the membership of the eighteen centuries, although there is little doubt that the censors would normally enroll all the men who had received from the *imperatores* the grant of the *anulus aureus*. The *lustrum* of 70 was to be the last one performed before Augustan times. The result was a severe and constantly increasing disorder in the membership of the *centuriae*, and a baffling lack of clarity in the legal concept and colloquial usage of the term *eques*. In 67 the *lex Roscia* intervened, and in the absence of the censorship the fourteen rows replaced the eighteen centuries as the basic framework for the legal definition and delimitation of the *ordo equester*. In fact all those who could claim a seat in the *quattuordecim ordines* were now regarded as *equites*. There were several categories of persons who qualified, including (1) the actual holders of the *equus publicus*, (2) the sons of senators, and (3) the sons of *equites* (i.e., *equites equo publico*), often referred to as *equestri loco nati* or *orti* (cf. on this expression N.'s brilliant article "Les *finitores ex equestri loco* de la loi Servilia de 63 av. J.C.," *Latomus* 29 [1970]: 72–103). The sons of *equites* had a hereditary claim to the *equus publicus*, and perhaps could even be placed on the roll of the *centuriae* by the clerks. Privileged seats could also be claimed by (4) all those who were in possession of the *census equester* and had received the *ornamenta equestria* (without a censorial action, however, they could hardly have been enrolled in the equestrian voting centuries). In addition to these groups, the *lex Roscia* provided the first two rows for (5) the military tribunes and the *tribunicii*. The military tribunes of nonequestrian origin were thus automatically receiving the grant of the *anulus aureus* and promotion to the equestrian order (cf. the cases of L. Petronius, T. Marius, and Horace). It is therefore a pity that N. has (and for no compelling reason) excluded the military tribunes from his prosopography. (He now concedes this point; cf. his article "Armée et société à Rome sous la république: À propos de l'ordre équestre," *Problèmes de guerre à Rome*, ed. J.-P. Brisson [Paris, 1969], p. 140.) Furthermore, it follows from Ovid *Fast.* 4. 383 (cf. Mommsen, *Staatsrecht*, 3:521) that also (6) the *decemviri stlitibus iudicandis* (and no doubt other minor magistrates) acquired the right to sit in the first two rows. Finally, Badian is undoubtedly right in contending that Cicero would not have praised the *lex Roscia* in front of (7) the *tribuni aerarii* if they had been excluded from the fourteen rows, though this need not mean, and, as we have seen, it did not mean, that all *homines equestri censu* sat in the fourteen rows. If we turn Badian's conclusion around we may arrive at the right answer: the *lex Roscia* gave the *ius in XIV ordinibus sedere* only to those *tribuni aerarii* who served as *iudices*. From the point of view of the *lex Roscia*, the jurors from the *decuria tribunorum aerariorum* formed an integral part of the equestrian order (cf. *Schol. Bob.* on Cic. *Flac.* 4, p. 94 Stangl = p. 34 Hildebrandt, where *tribuni aerarii* and *equites* are glossed as *eiusdem scilicet ordinis viri*), but from the point of view of the older classification based upon membership in the *centuriae equitum* (a classification not formally abolished), they had no claim to the title of *eques Romanus*.

The utter confusion in the equestrian terminology thus finds a reasonable explanation in the lapsing of the censorship and in the substitution of other criteria, principally the *ius XIV ordinum*, for defining the *ordo equester*. This interpretation seems to be confirmed by Pliny *NH* 33. 29–32 (I am not convinced by E. S. Staveley's explanation of this passage in *RhM* 96 [1953]: 201–213). Pliny there discusses the connection between the *anulus aureus*, the *iudices*, and the *equites:*

> divo Augusto decurias ordinante maior pars iudicum in ferreo anulo fuit iique non equites, sed iudices vocabantur. equitum nomen subsistebat in turmis equorum publicorum. . . . decuriae quoque ipsae pluribus discretae nominibus fuere, tribunorum aeris et selectorum et iudicum. praeter hos etiamnum nongenti vocabantur ex omnibus electi ad custodiendas suffragiorum cistas in comitiis. et divisus hic quoque ordo erat superba usurpatione nominum, cum alius se nongentum, alius selectum, alius tribunum appellaret. Tiberii demum principatu nono anno in unitatem venit equester ordo, anulorumque auctoritati forma constituta est . . . constitutum, ne cui ius esset nisi qui ingenuus ipse, patre, avo paterno, HS CCCC census fuisset et lege Iulia theatrali in quattuordecim ordinibus sedisset.

Pliny's train of thought is tortuous, but nevertheless the following observations can be made: (*a*) the nonequestrian jurors "in anulo ferreo fuerunt": the jury service did not lead to the *anulus aureus;* (*b*) Augustus apparently restored the preRoscian definition of *equites* based on the holding of the *equus publicus;* (*c*) Pliny nevertheless regards the nonequestrian *iudices* as members of the *ordo equester;* (*d*) the *unitas* of the *ordo* (i.e., of the members of the *turmae* and the nonequestrian jurors) was achieved on the basis of the *census equester* and the *lex Iulia theatralis* (which undoubtedly incorporated most provisions of the *lex Roscia*); (*e*) it follows from this provision that not all *homines equestri censu* had the *ius XIV ordinum* (otherwise the mention of the *lex theatralis* would be redundant); (*f*) it also follows that the nonequestrian jurors had the right of the fourteen rows, for otherwise they could not have been "united" on this basis with the *equites* proper. In the case of *définitions juridiques* Mommsen obviously beats Münzer.

Lawrence Stone once composed the following grandiloquent encomium of prosopography: "Prosopography . . . contains within it the potentiality to help in the re-creation of a unified field out of the loose confederation of jealously independent topics and techniques which at present constitutes the historian's empire. It could be a means to bind together constitutional and institutional history on the one hand and personal biography on the other . . . " (*Historical Studies Today*, ed. F. Gilbert and S. R. Graubard [New York, 1972], p. 134). Nicolet's opus comes as close as possible to this lofty ideal, and it is very far. Prosopography can open some doors that had hitherto been firmly locked, but it is not a master key and still less a picklock.

LEGIBUS PRAEFECTI MITTEBANTUR
(Mommsen and Festus 262. 5, 13 L)

The present note is not intended to provide a detailed discussion of the vexed question of Roman prefectures in Italy. Its aim is a very limited one: to attempt to clear up current misconceptions concerning Mommsen's interpretation of Festus' phrase *legibus praefecti mittebantur*. In order to understand the nature of the controversy, it is necessary to adduce the text of Festus *in extenso*. It reads as follows (p. 262. 2–16 L):

> Praefecturae eae appellabantur in Italia, in quibus et
> ius dicebatur, et nundinae agebantur; et erat
> quaedam earum R. P., neque tamen magistratus suos
> 5   habebant. in quas[1] legibus praefecti mittebantur
> quotannis qui ius dicerent. Quarum genera fuerunt
> duo: alterum, in quas solebant ire praefecti quat-
> tuor, ⟨qui⟩ viginti sex virum numero[2] populi suffragio
> creati erant, in haec oppida: Capuam, Cumas,
> 10   Casilinum, Volturnum, Liternum, Puteolos, Acer-
> ras, Suessulam, Atellam, Calatium: alterum, in quas
> ibant, quos praetor urbanus quotannis in quaeque lo-
> ca miserat legibus, ut Fundos, Formias, Caere,
> Venafrum, Allifas, Privernum, Anagniam, Frusi-
> 15   nonem, Reate, Saturniam, Nursiam, Arpinum,
> aliaque conplura.

The point to which we would like to address ourselves is the meaning of 'legibus'. Brunt[3] has the following comment: "According to Festus they [*i.e.* the prefects] were appointed 'legibus'; the plural may be noted; the *concession* was made first to one, then to another" (*sc. municipium*; cf. Brunt's remark a couple of lines above: "it was a concession to the convenience of the *municipes*"). This statement is not completely explicit, but it is clear that Brunt understands 'legibus' as referring to Roman *leges comitiales*. It is undoubtedly a sound interpretation, but unfortunately Brunt has coupled it with the following critique of Mommsen (p. 531 n. 2): "Mommsen's assumption (*StR* iii. 582 n. 2) that the *leges* were the charters of the municipalities need not be right".

Brunt was, however, not the first to attribute this interpretation of 'legibus' to Mommsen. A. N. Sherwin-White wrote in the first edition[4] of his *Roman Citizenship* (Oxford 1939, 42): "Festus ... says that the second type [*i.e.* the prefects appointed by the praetor] were sent out by the praetor *legibus*, that is, as Mommsen saw, in accordance with the charters of the municipalities" (p. 42 n. 5[=2nd ed. p. 45 n. 2]. He gives the same reference as Brunt, but in a somewhat developed form: "*St. R.* III, 582, n. 2, quoting the *lex* of Acerrae").

It is important to note that Sherwin-White (and, as he thinks, also Mommsen) is of the opinion that only the prefects appointed by the praetor were sent out in accordance with the municipal charters; the *praefecti Capuam Cumas* elected by the people were sent out on the basis of the Roman *leges*. Hence the first 'legibus' in Festus (line 5), as far as it

---

[1] Lindsay prints *in †qua his†*, but Ursinus' reading *in quas* is quite certain.

[2] Lindsay's text is *†viginti sex virum nū pro†*; the corrections go back to Ursinus and Mommsen.

[3] P. A. Brunt, Italian Manpower (Oxford 1971) 531.

[4] Repeated verbatim in the second edition Oxford 1973, 45.

concerns the elective *praefecti*, would denote the Roman *leges comitiales*; it is only the second 'legibus' (line 13), referring exclusively to the appointed prefects, which would signify the municipal charters, *i.e.* the *leges datae* by the Roman authorities[5].

But enough for the time being of ἐπίγονοι. Let us now consult the *ipsissima verba* of the 'Altmeister'. First, the incriminated passage, *Staatsrecht* III 582, n. 2: "... *legibus* (d. h. nach dem constituirenden Gesetz, wie das papirische für Acerrae war ...) *praefecti mittebantur quotannis qui ius dicerent*. Nach Erörterung der comitialen *praefecti Capuam Cumas* fügt er hinzu: *alterum* (*genus fuerat*) *in quas ibant quos praetor quotannis in quaeque loca miserat legibus*". Two observations: this passage does not tell us explicitly anything about how Mommsen interpreted the second 'legibus' in Festus, but there is in any case nothing to show that he understood under the *leges* the municipal charters[6]. On the other hand Mommsen explained the first 'legibus' as referring to the *constituirendes Gesetz*, adducing as an example the *lex Papiria*, which was a *lex rogata* voted by the Roman *comitia*[7]. He defines the *constituirendes Gesetz* (III 576 quoting again the *lex Papiria*) as "ein die Stellung derselben [*i.e.* of a 'Halbbürgergemeinde'] regulirender Beschluss der römischen Bürgerschaft". The *lex Papiria* was a Roman law, but from the point of view of the Acerrani it could be regarded as a *lex data*. It is, however, important to realize that the prefect was not sent out on the basis of the municipal charter (contained in the *lex*

[5] In this context Sherwin-White (p. 41; 2nd ed. p. 43) also discusses Liv. 9. 20. 5: "primum praefecti Capuam creari coepti legibus a L. Furio praetore datis, cum utrumque ipsi pro remedio aegris rebus discordia intestina petissent" (we are not interested here in the veracity of Livy's information; Sherwin-White accepts it, but most other scholars reject it). His translation of the passage is as follows (p. 41 n. 3): "Prefects for Capua first began to be created with plenipotentiary powers legally derived from the praetor, L. Furius, when in a time of civil discord they themselves had asked for both as a cure for their political disease" (in the second edition, p. 43 n. 4, the phrase "with plenipotentiary powers" is replaced by "with rules of law"). This interpretative translation is certainly incorrect; it reads into the text of Livy notions that are not present there. Sherwin-White combines *praefecti ... creari coepti* with *legibus a ... praetore datis*, and consequently imagines the prefects as appointed by L. Furius on the basis of his *leges*. But *legibus datis* and *creari coepti* ought to be kept apart; one should not disregard the following *cum utrumque ipsi ... petissent*. The Capuans asked the Romans to provide them with the *leges* (cf. Liv. 9. 20. 10: "nec arma modo sed etiam iura Romana late pollebant"), and to send prefects for the administration of justice. If *legibus datis* should refer only to *creari coepti*, then the *leges* as the charter of Capua must simply disappear, as they do in Sherwin-White's translation (thus leaving incomprehensible the meaning of *utrumque*). In spite of, and contrary to, his translation, Sherwin-White manages, however, somehow to believe that "the *leges a praetore datae* should have provided a permanent solution of the troubles of the time". It is obvious that a praetor could not give *leges* to anyone or send out the prefects without being authorized to do so by the senate or the people; the ultimate basis both for the dispatching of the prefects and for the *leges datae* must have been either a *senatus consultum* or a *lex comitialis* (cf. Mommsen, *Staatsrecht* II[3] 594 n. 5). For further criticism of Sherwin-White's interpretation of Livy, see my note "*Primum creati* and *primum creari coepti*" (forthcoming).

[6] Sherwin-White, *op. cit.* 43 n. 5 (2nd ed. 45 n. 2) mistranslates Mommsen's "für Acerrae" as "of Acerrae".

[7] See G. Rotondi, *Leges Publicae Populi Romani* (Milano 1912, repr. Hildesheim 1962) 228–229, and esp. T. R. S. Broughton, *The Magistrates of the Roman Republic* I (New York 1951) 142 n. 2, with a discussion of the *lator* of the *lex*.

comitialis or drawn up according to the instructions spelt out by it), but rather on the basis of the 'constituirendes Gesetz' itself, *i.e.* the Roman *lex lata*[8].

At this juncture Sherwin-White and Brunt could well retort that our arguments are valid only with respect to the first set of Festus' *leges*, and that they do not apply in the least to the *leges* mentioned in connection with the appointed prefects. They could also point out that Festus places Acerrae in the sphere of jurisdiction of an elective prefect. Sherwin-White and Brunt overlook, however, a crucial point for the proper interpretation of Mommsen's *Lehre*: according to the latter the introduction of the popular election of the prefects was a later development; originally all of the prefects were appointed by the praetor on the basis of an 'Einzelgesetz', *i.e.* a Roman, and not a municipal law (*Staatsrecht* II[3] 608–609). The fact is that Mommsen does not make any distinction between the two sets of *leges* in Festus. In the *Staatsrecht* II[3] 608 he writes: "*praefecti iure dicundo* ... sind, durchaus auf Grund von Einzelgesetzen, von dem römischen Stadtprätor an verschiedenen Punkten Italiens bestellt worden". Mommsen illustrates the 'Einzelgesetze' by a reference to Festus (II[3] 608 n. 4): "*legibus praefecti mittebantur* und nachher: *miserat legibus*"[9]. If the *leges* mentioned in the first instance are the *leges comitiales* (as Sherwin-White agrees), the same must also hold with respect to Festus' second mention of *leges*. And finally, we have *Staatsrecht* III 583 (commenting upon Liv. 9. 20. 5, reproduced and discussed above, n. 5): "Für Capua ist dies [*i.e.* the bestowal of the *leges*] nachweislich bei der Einrichtung selbst geschehen ... in der Weise, daß, ohne Zweifel auf Grund eines römischen Volksschlusses, der römische Prätor, der den ersten *praefectus* für Capua ernannte, zugleich das Stadtrecht feststellte". Mommsen regards the praetor as empowered by a *lex comitialis* to establish the municipal charter (the *lex data*) and to send a prefect.

No municipal charter could on its own authority lay down in a binding way that the praetor send out a prefect[10]. This could have been done only by a *lex, senatus consultum*

---

[8] On the concept of the *lex data*, see the illuminating studies by G. Tibiletti, "Leges datae", estratto from *Novissimo Digesto Italiano* (Torino, n.d.); "Lex", *DE* 4 (1957) 706–708; and above all "Sulle 'Leges' romane", *Studi in onore di P. de Francisci* 4 (Milano 1956) 595ff., esp. 602–625. On p. 612 he gives the following definition: "le leggi *datae* sono norme provenienti dall'esterno, alla formazione delle quali non hanno partecipato gli interessati". Cf. also p. 608: "Le *leges datae* ... potevano essere leggi o decreti" (this last statement does not seem to be completely satisfactory; we should rather say that the *leges datae* could be established by laws or decrees – the *leges datae* themselves in their capacity as local charters certainly were neither laws nor decrees).

[9] Cf. also II[3] 609 n. 1, and 608 n. 5, where Mommsen lists Festus' prefectures Fundos Formias etc. as the cities to which prefects were sent on the basis of the 'Einzelgesetze'.

[10] The same misunderstanding as in Sherwin-White also in H. Siber, *Römisches Verfassungsrecht* (Lahr 1952) 202: the four *praefecti Capuam Cumas* "werden zuerst 318 auf Grund einer prätorischen *lex data* ... bestellt", and further: "andere Präfekten ... werden auf Grund von *leges rogatae* oder *datae* ohne Volkswahl durch den Stadtprätor ernannt". Also Toynbee's treatment of the question is open to criticism. He translates the Festus passage in the following way (*Hannibal's Legacy* I, Oxford 1965, 241 n. 4): "Praefecti, instructed [by the praetor urbanus], were sent to these praefecturae annually to administer justice there". The word 'instructed' renders here Festus' 'legibus', the result being that any notion of a *lex*, comitial or municipal, completely evaporates from the text; *mittebantur* is dissociated from *legibus* and combined immediately with *praefecti*, and finally *legibus* receives as a complement the phrase "by the praetor urbanus" imported here with the change of the grammatical construction (and without any compelling justifi-

(or *constitutio principis*). On the other hand it is to be expected that the local statutes had to take account of the existence of the *praefecti* appointed by the central government, and had to contain provisions concerning them; a good example, unfortunately dating from a later period, is provided by the *lex Salpensana* (*cap.* 24)[11].

It is perhaps not a vain hope that it should by now be clear to everyone that the interpretation advanced by Sherwin-White and Brunt lacks any factual foundation. Mommsen would undoubtedly have been perplexed and astonished to see the peculiar idea that the prefects were sent out to the Italian communities on the basis of municipal charters not only ascribed to him, but also paraded as an example of his perspicacity ("as Mommsen saw").

cation) from line 12. In word this is not Festus' text, but Toynbee's. Toynbee's translation obscures and eludes the very pertinent question of the legal basis of the activity of the *praefecti* in Italy. There is no discussion of the meaning of 'legibus' in the two books, which, one would expect, ought to have addressed themselves to the problem: E. Manni, *Per la storia dei municipii fino alla guerra sociale* (Roma 1947) 69ff., and W. Simshäuser, *Iuridici und Munizipalgerichtsbarkeit in Italien* (München 1973) 85–109. On the other hand, correct interpretation is given by L. Lange, *Römische Alterthümer* I[3] (Berlin 1876) 907: the urban praetor sent out the prefects "ermächtigt durch Volksbeschlüsse", and by F. de Martino, *Storia della costituzione romana* II (ristampa riveduta, Napoli 1960) 118: "I prefetti erano ... nominati dal pretore Romano, in virtù di leggi". So also J. Heurgon, *Recherches sur l'histoire ... de Capoue préromaine* (Paris 1942) 239 n. 4: the annual prefectures were established successively, and "chaque fois en vertu d'une loi particulière ... d'où le pluriel *legibus* dans Festus". Cf. also W. Ensslin, "Praefectus", *RE* 22A (1954) 1309; E. Sachers, "Praefectus iure dicundo", *ibid.* 2382–3.

11 *ILS* 6088; S. Riccobono, *Fontes iuris Romani antejustiniani* I[2] (Firenze 1941) 205; A. D'Ors, *Epigrafía jurídica de la España Romana* (Madrid 1953) 290–291 (with a commentary).

Addendum

Since this note was submitted, two works dealing with Roman prefectures in Italy have appeared: E. Ratti, "I praefecti iure dicundo e la praefectura come distinzione gromatica", *CSDIR Atti* 6, 1974-75, 251-264, and H. Galsterer, *Herrschaft u. Verwaltung im republikanischen Italien,* München 1976, 27-33. Neither of them discusses the meaning of 'legibus' in Festus.

13

ROME, APHRODISIAS AND THE *RES GESTAE*:
THE *GENERA MILITIAE* AND THE STATUS OF OCTAVIAN

When in the autumn of 44 Octavian embarked on his perilous journey as heir to Caesar's mantle he and his soldiers were branded as brigands or extolled as saviours of their country. What was their legal status ? Most modern historians, fascinated with naked power, tacitly dismiss this question as utterly frivolous. They are fully satisfied with Ciceronian epithets. Octavian and Cicero were not. The Roman doctrine of the *genera militiae* afforded Octavian a comfortable legal niche at each stage of his career. It allows us to comprehend the intricate manoeuvres in the senate at the turn of 44 and 43 B.C.; it also sheds light on the crowning *coup* of Octavian when he led Italy as a *dux* against Antonius and the Queen. But this antiquarian doctrine, attested only in late authors, could easily be dismissed as an artificial construct far removed from real life. Historical puzzles lie dormant and insoluble until a spark of insight creates an instant enlightenment. And the spark comes from Aphrodisias, from the new documents published in an exemplary way by Joyce Reynolds, *Aphrodisias and Rome* (1982). It comes in the shape of a new puzzle.

Document 9 (pp. 92–3) contains excerpts from various Roman acts granting privileges to Plarasa/Aphrodisias. Lines 2–4 read as follows:

μήτε μὴν ἄρχοντά τινα ἢ ἀντάρχοντα δήμου ʽΡωμαίων ἕτερόν τέ τινα εἰς τὴν πόλιν ἢ
καὶ τὴν χώ-

ραν ἢ καὶ τοὺς ὅρους τοὺς Πλαρασέων καὶ ʼΑφροδεισιέων στρατιώτην καὶ ἀντιστρατιώτην, ἱππέα,

ἕτερόν τινα εἰς παραχειμασίαν πρὸς αὐτοὺς δίδοσθαι μηδὲ καταθέσθαι κελεύειν.

This clause comes from the *S.C. de Aphrodisiensibus* (39 B.C.); it recurs in the new fragment of this decree, Doc. 8, lines 32–4, where the supplements are assured by Doc. 9.

The expression στρατιώτην καὶ ἀντιστρατιώτην is baffling. Reynolds translates it (p. 62) ' a soldier or a substitute soldier ' or (p. 93) ' an infantry man or one substituting for such ', and she comments (p. 78): ' The most satisfying explanation that I can propose is that of Lawrence Keppie, who compares it with *vicarii* (*milites*) in Pliny, *Ep.* 10. 30 '.

Ingenious but hardly correct, as a glance at Pliny's text will show. In *Ep.* 10. 29 Pliny informs Trajan that two slaves were discovered among *tirones*; should they be executed ? They had already taken the military oath (' iam dixerant sacramento '), but had not yet been posted to a unit (' nondum distributi in numeros erant ').[1] Trajan replies (*Ep.* 10. 30) that the latter point is of no consequence for they were obliged to reveal their status (*origo*) at their enlistment, on the very day ' quo primum probati sunt '. What does matter is whether ' they were volunteers (*voluntarii*) or conscripts (*lecti*), or possibly offered as substitutes (*vicarii*). If they are conscripts, the recruiting officer was at fault; if substitutes, then those who offered them as such are guilty; but if they volunteered for service, well aware of their status, then they will have to be executed '.

According to A. N. Sherwin-White,[2] followed by Reynolds, this is the earliest evidence for *vicarii milites*. In fact the earliest mention is in Livy. He reports (29. 1) that in 205 Scipio conscripted (*legit*) in Sicily out of all younger men (*iuniores*) three hundred horsemen, men of high rank and wealth. But when they proved reluctant to go with him to Africa he released them all from their military oath, on condition, however, that they provide horses, armament and military training to three hundred *vicarii*. But it was not the conscripted Sicilian *equites* who were to furnish these substitutes: the *imperator* himself

[1] G. R. Watson, *The Roman Soldier* (1969), 43, and R. W. Davies, ' Joining the Roman Army ', *BJ* 169 (1969), 214, take this phrase to refer to rolls or records. But in a fundamental article J. F. Gilliam, ' Enrolment in the Roman Imperial Army ', *Eos* 48, 2 (1956), 212, perspicaciously observed that *in numeros distribuere* (or *per numeros distribuere* in Trajan's reply) ' is not equivalent to *in numeros referre* '. In the latter phrase *numeri* means rolls, but in the former probably units. The *tirones*, Gilliam suggests, ' were still at some recruiting center and had not yet been divided among or at any rate dispatched to units '.

[2] *The Letters of Pliny. A Historical and Social Commentary* (1966), 601.

supplied them. They were the young Roman volunteers: ' thus three hundred Sicilians were replaced by Roman horsemen without expense to the state '. A curious story, very embellished, and hardly reliable.[3] It belongs to the genre of *strategemata*. But it is instructive: it presents the institution of *vicarii* as something exotic, alien to normal Roman practice.[4] Thus it does not lend any support to Reynolds's interpretation.

Nor does the letter of Trajan. Trajan speaks of the three categories of recruits *voluntarii, lecti, vicarii*. There is no reason to suppose that the *vicarii* should have served in special units; occasionally we hear of the *cohortes voluntariorum*,[5] but the *cohortes vicariorum* are not on record. Once he swore the military oath the *vicarius* was a regular soldier, *miles*; his legal status did not differ from that of his companions, conscripts or volunteers.

Vicarii discarded, where are we to turn? ''Αντιστρατιώτης is unique', writes Reynolds, ' and the implied *pro milite* is also unknown ' (p. 78).[6] But ' the implied *pro milite* ' is in fact quite well known, though not fully understood. Sallust, *Hist. frg. inc.* 8 M. (p. 202), reads: ' Neu quis miles neve pro milite ', which forms a striking parallel to μήτε μήν . . . στρατιώτην καὶ ἀντιστρατιώτην. This fragment of Sallust did not, of course, escape Mommsen's attention. His comments in *StR* II³, 577 are worth quoting. He argues that as military service ' has in principle no time limits ', so also ' the prorogation generally did not apply to the soldier and officer rank '. And he continues (n. 4): ' When Sallust . . . distinguishes between *miles* and *pro milite* he does not have in mind those who serve beyond the space of one year but rather those who strictly speaking are not authorized to serve '. In other words the expression *pro milite* cannot be explained by analogy with *pro consule, pro praetore* or *pro quaestore*. Hence *pro milite* must describe somebody ' who strictly speaking is not authorized to serve ', ' der eigentlich zu dienen nicht befugt ist '. This sounds mysterious, but fortunately Mommsen directs us for further information to Cicero, *de off.* 1. 36:

> Popilius imperator tenebat provinciam in cuius exercitu Catonis filius tiro militabat. Cum autem Popilio videretur unam dimittere legionem, Catonis quoque filium, qui in eadem legione militabat, dimisit. Sed cum amore pugnandi in exercitu remansisset, Cato ad Popilium scripsit, ut, si eum patitur in exercitu remanere, secundo eum obliget militiae sacramento, quia priore amisso iure cum hostibus pugnare non poterat.

Most editors bracket this passage as either an interpolation or Cicero's own earlier version which his posthumous and *pius editor* could not bring himself to excise.[7] This passage is followed by another one of similar content, less detailed but stylistically much superior (1. 37):

> Marci quidem Catonis senis est epistula ad Marcum filium, in qua scribit se audisse eum missum factum esse a consule cum in Macedonia bello Persico miles esset. Monet igitur ut caveat ne proelium ineat; negat enim ius esse, qui miles non sit cum hoste pugnare.

There are some discrepancies between these two versions,[8] but their legal message is identical: only the person who had sworn the *sacramentum* is a *miles*. When the legion is dismissed the soldiers are automatically released from their military oath. A person who in

---

[3] As H. H. Scullard writes, Scipio's preparations for his expedition to Africa are ' shrouded in doubt ' (*Scipio Africanus* (1970), 111). For the story itself, see A. Passerini, *Le coorti pretorie* (1939), 6 ff.

[4] The custom of providing *vicarii* may have come into being during the civil wars, but it is doubtful if any conclusions can be drawn from the story in Macrobius 2. 4. 27 (brilliantly elucidated by C. Cichorius, *Römische Studien* (1922), 282–5): ' exclamavit ingenti voce veteranus: at non ego, Caesar, periclitante te Actiaco bello vicarium quaesivi sed pro te ipse pugnavi '.

[5] On the *cohortes voluntariorum*, see K. Kraft, *Zur Rekrutierung der Alen und Kohorten an Rhein und Donau* (1951), 82–95, who criticizes the idea of G. L. Cheesman, *The Auxilia of the Roman Imperial Army* (1914), 65–7, 186–7, that the majority of these units

were the *cohortes libertinorum*. The inscription of the ' captor of Decebalus ' clearly supports Kraft's view; cf. M. Speidel, *JRS* 60 (1970), 151.

[6] The Greek sense of ἀντιστρατιώτης is not in dispute: ' soldier of the enemy ', as *LSJ* duly records. The Roman development thus parallels that of ἀντιστράτηγος from ' enemy's general ' to ' acting commander ' or ' governor '. But ' acting soldier ' does not take us very far: see below in the text.

[7] cf. C. Atzert in his Teubner edition, pp. xxviii–xxix.

[8] In any case Cato will not have written two identical letters, one in 173 when his son served as a *tiro* in Liguria under the consul M. Popillius Laenas, and the other in 168 when Licinianus was in the army of Aemilius Paullus and took part in the battle of Pydna. Cf. Drumann-Groebe, *Geschichte Roms* v, 160–1.

this sense ceased to be a *miles* cannot *iure* engage in combat, for the killing of a *hostis* would then amount to murder and would not be a legitimate act of war (cf. Plut., *Quaest. Rom.* 39). Combining Sallust and Cicero, Mommsen deduced the status of the person who stayed with the army without valid *sacramentum*: he acted *pro milite*. Mommsen's explanation is brilliant at first sight, but lame on closer scrutiny. Cicero does not use the expression *pro milite*, and for a very good reason: the person who was not under oath was not a soldier at all, neither *miles* nor *pro milite*. He was a civilian.

It is surprising that Mommsen did not feel in this place any need to consider the context in which Sallust's fragment was recorded. And the context is this: in his commentary *ad Aen.* 2. 157 Servius attempts to explain the *militiae tria genera*. About one of them he writes:

> plerumque enim 'evocati' dicuntur, et non sunt milites, sed pro milite: unde Sallustius 'neu quis miles neve pro milite', item ipse 'ab his omnes evocatos et centuriones' (*Cat.* 59. 3).

Should we conclude hastily that ἀντιστρατιώτης — *evocatus*? *Festina lente*! For what does Servius understand by the term *evocatus*? To answer this question we have to investigate the doctrine of the *genera militiae*. Servius' comments on *Aen.* 7. 614 and 8. 1 also belong here. The former passage corresponds almost verbatim to Isidorus, *Etym.* 9. 3. 53–5; part of the same tradition is extant in Donatus' *Commentum Terenti, Eun.* 772 (vol. I, p. 434 Wessner). Here is the synopsis of this antiquarian theory of the *tria genera militiae*:

(a) the *militia legitima* (8. 1). It was the *plena militia*: it lasted twenty-five years (2. 157; Isid.).[9] The soldiers were *sacramento rogati* (2. 157, cf. 8. 1); they took their oath individually (8. 1 'singuli iurabant'; 7. 614 and Isid., 'iurat unusquisque miles'). They swore 'pro republica se esse facturos' (8. 1, cf. 2. 157) and 'non recedere, nisi praecepto consulis post completa stipendia' (7. 614 and Isid., who omits 'praecepto consulis'). The individual oath appears as the most characteristic feature of the *militia legitima*: 'sacramentum vocabatur' (8. 1). In two other passages (7. 614 and Isid.) the term *sacramentum* is used *tout court* to denote this *genus* of service.[10]

(b) the *coniuratio* (8. 1; 7. 614 and Isid.). It occurs *in tumultu*, i.e. 'Italico bello et Gallico (7. 614; 8. 1) quando vicinum urbis periculum singulos iurare non patitur (7. 614 and Isid.; cf. 8. 1), sed repente colligitur multitudo' (Isid.). The person who was to lead the army (8. 1: 'qui fuerat ducturus exercitum', hence not necessarily a magistrate) 'pedites evocabat' (and equites) saying ' " qui rem publicam salvam esse vult, me sequatur ", et qui convenissent simul iurabant: et dicebatur ista militia coniuratio' (8. 1). The soldiers so assembled were called ' " tumultuarii ", hoc est qui ad unum militabant bellum' (2. 157).

(c) the *evocatio* (8. 1; 7. 614 and Isid.; Donat.). It occurs *in tumultu* (8. 1; Donat.) or in the case of a *subitum bellum* (7. 614 and Isid.). The consul (7. 614 and Isid.) or *dux* (Donat.; hence again not necessarily a magistrate) 'alloquitur cives (Donat.) " qui rem publicam salvam esse vult me sequatur " ' (7. 614 and Isid.; cf. Donat.). The *evocati* were not *milites* but only *pro milite* (2. 157); on the other hand Isid. reports that 'non solum miles sed et ceteri evocantur'. To achieve this 'ad diversa loca diversi propter cogendos mittebantur exercitus' (8. 1: a clear allusion to the *conquisitores*). Quite characteristically no oath is mentioned.

It does not require any perspicacity to see that our antiquarians distinguished rather successfully between the *militia legitima* and the two other *genera*, but failed miserably to make clear what really differentiated *coniuratio* from *evocatio*.

Their modern colleagues did not fare much better: Mommsen thrice reshuffled the ingredients of this antiquarian puzzle without really solving it;[11] and three more permut-

---

[9] Clearly a later addition reflecting imperial practice. R. E. Smith, *Service in the Post-Marian Roman Army* (1958), 29–33, rightly observes that until Augustus the length of service was not explicitly specified and the *sacramentum* contained no reference to it.

[10] cf. *Bell. Alex.* 56. 4; Tac., *Ann.* 16. 13. 3; *Hist.* I. 5. 1; Flor., I. 22. 23; Iuv., 16. 35–6.
[11] *Römische Forschungen* II (1879), 247–57; *Eph. Ep.* 5 (1885), 142–5 = *Ges. Schr.* VIII, 446–9; *StR* I³ (1887), 695–6.

ations were offered by Johann Schmidt,[12] Salvatore Tondo[13] and Jochen Bleicken.[14] Bleicken perspicaciously recognized two and only two forms of the levy: the regular *militia* based on *dilectus* and the individual oath, *sacramentum*; and the irregular *coniuratio*, the voluntary and joint oath of those who banded together to follow the call ' to save the republic '. But his treatment of *evocatio* was not entirely satisfactory: the scraps (' Fetzen ') of Sallust in Servius, *ad Aen*. 2. 157 would refer to the late republican *evocatio*, ' the recalling of veterans to active service '.

This is true of *Cat*. 59. 2–3, but in this passage Sallust does not characterize the *evocati* as *pro milite*, and in the fragment from the *Histories*, while juxtaposing *miles* and *pro milite*, he does not mention the *evocati* at all. It is the antiquarians who arbitrarily connected these two separate enunciations. It is apparent that they confused the late republican *evocatio* of veterans with the old institution of *coniuratio*. But how did this confusion arise?

Now *sacramentum* is a form of oath, and *coniuratio*, strictly speaking, is another form of oath, and not a form of levy. The *sacramentum* follows upon *dilectus*,[15] and the *coniuratio* upon the call to arms ' Qui rem publicam salvam . . .'. The *dux* (whether a *privatus* or a magistrate) *vocat* or *evocat* the citizens to defend the republic. What was the name of this call? *Evocatio*, certainly. The most characteristic element of *evocatio*, and one that constituted it as a *militia*, was the joint oath, the *coniuratio*. The *evocati* assemble, and *iurant* or *coniurant*. What did they swear? They swore to follow their leader *ad bellum unum*, the war at hand. At the end of the war they had to be automatically dismissed. On the other hand, in the formula of *sacramentum* the length of service was not specified; the dismissal of the soldiers was in the free *arbitrium* of the senate and the commander.[16] The *sacramentum* could be sworn only in the *verba* of the legitimate *imperium*-holder;[17] the oath of *evocatio* also in the *verba* of a *dux privatus*. Those who ' sacramento dixerunt ' were regular soldiers, *milites*; those who joined in a military *coniuratio* served *pro milite*.

Now, just as *sacramentum* was occasionally used as the code-word for the regular service, so also *evocatio* received from the form of the oath its own code-word, *coniuratio*. In fact in its original sense the *evocatio* lived on in the antiquarian tradition only, but the antiquarians split the *evocatio/coniuratio* into two separate (but hardly distinguishable) forms of tumultuary levy. The oath they assigned, quite naturally, to the *coniuratio*. Thus when the *coniuratio* gained its antiquarian independence and ascendancy, the *evocatio* was consigned to a shadowy and uncertain existence. Next the antiquarians confounded this denuded, oathless *evocatio* with the *evocatio* of veterans. Their modern successors took this false coin for solid gold and concluded that the *evocati*, the picked soldiers of the triumviral armies, were bound by no military oath.[18] But an oathless *miles* is an impossibility. A gloss (*CGL* v, 195, 15) explains the *evocati* as ' qui militant sine sacramento '. The lack of *sacramentum* presupposes the existence of another oath, the oath of *coniuratio*.

The Italy of the civil wars from Marius to Actium was filled with irregular armies raised without express authorization by the senate or the assembly, and thus enjoying at best the ambiguous status of *evocati/coniurati*. It was also filled with the *evocati*, the veterans

---

[12] ' Die Evocati ', *Hermes* 14 (1879), 322–31.

[13] ' Il *sacramentum militiae* nell'ambiente culturale romano-italico ', *SDHI* 29 (1963), 1–25.

[14] ' Coniuratio ', *Jahrb. f. Numismatik u. Geldgeschichte* 13 (1963), 51–70.

[15] On *dilectus*, see the brilliant exposition by P. A. Brunt, *Italian Manpower* (1971), 625–44. But cf. also the objections by E. Rawson, *PBSR* 39 (1971), 15 ff.

[16] It is important to keep apart the length of the legal obligation to serve and the length of the actual service. Only the soldiers whose *stipendia* were *emerita* or *confecta* had a legal claim to a *missio*; cf. Livy 34. 56. 9; 39. 19. 4; 39. 38. 12; 40. 35. 11; 43. 14. 9, and the passages adduced by Smith, *Service*, 35 n. 3, whose illuminating discussion (27 ff.) dispersed many common misconceptions. See also Brunt, *JRS* 52 (1962), 80–2; *Manpower*, 399 ff.; J. Harmand, *L'armée et le soldat à Rome de 107 à 50 avant notre ère* (1967), 245 ff. The idea of the twenty *legitima stipendia* in the late Republic has no source authority.

[17] And moreover this *imperium*-holder had to be authorized by the senate (or the people) to hold the levy. Mommsen believed (*StR* I³, 119) that the magistrate *cum imperio* did not need any permission from the senate for *dilectus*, but see the convincing critique of this theory by Brunt, *ZPE* 13 (1974), 162 ff. The antiquarians connect *coniuratio* with *tumultus*, but in the annalistic tradition tumultuary levies are as a rule ordered by the senate, and the *milites tumultuarii* are often *sacramento rogati*, cf. esp. Livy 32. 26. 10–12; 40. 26. 7; 41. 5. 11 (in conjunction with 41. 5. 4). We can put forth the following scheme: the regular *dilectus* was always accompanied by *sacramentum*; the tumultuary *dilectus* was accompanied by a *sacramentum* when it was conducted on express orders from the senate by a magistrate *cum imperio*. The *coniuratio* comes into the picture when a magistrate acted on his own initiative or when the *dux* was a *privatus*.

[18] cf. O. Fiebiger, *RE* 6 (1909), 1146; A. Neumann, *Der Kleine Pauly* 2 (1975), 471.

recalled to the ranks. These two categories, more often than not, coincided with each other, for it was the *veterani* to whom the call to save the republic (and promote a leader) was most frequently addressed. This is the *fons* and *origo* of ancient and modern confusion.

But verbal and legal puzzles remain barren unless implanted in the soil of history. And there is no richer or darker soil than that from which Octavian sprang. But while the statement of the *Res Gestae*, ' exercitum privato consilio et privata impensa comparavi ', has enjoyed all scholarly attention, few questions have been asked about the status of Octavian's followers. In October 44 Octavian visited the colonies of veterans at Calatia and Casilinum and won them over by promising five hundred denarii apiece to those who would join him.[19] Early in November he stepped forward as *dux privatus* and raised the standard of *evocatio*.[20] He assembled at Capua his followers from Casilinum, Calatia, and other places in Campania. He divided them into centuries,[21] and they undoubtedly swore by centuries [22] a joint oath. And he paid out the promised money. Not counting the money, these are all the traditional acts of *evocatio/coniuratio*, the assembling ' in formam iusti exercitus ' (cf. Vell. 2. 61. 1–2). Cassius Dio (45. 12. 3) describes the veterans who in 44 answered Octavian's call as τὸ τῶν ἠουοκάτων σύστημα. He also avers (55. 24. 8) that under the empire the *evocati* formed a separate corps (this is correct), and that this institution goes back to the time when Augustus summoned to arms the former soldiers of Caesar. Here Cassius Dio is guilty of a grave but venial inaccuracy. He confused the imperial *evocati* [23] with the republican emergency soldiers. The followers of Octavian were the *evocati* in both senses of the word: the veterans who rejoined the ranks and the *coniurati* who banded together to defend the republic.

The army led by a *dux privatus* could not be bound by *sacramentum*. When the ' milites veterani qui . . . pro republica arma ceperant volebant sibi ab illo imperari ', and when the ' legio Martia et legio quarta ita se contulerant ad auctoritatem senatus . . . ut deposcerent imperatorem et ducem C. Caesarem ' (Cic., *Phil.* 11. 20), they must have sworn some sort of oath of allegiance to the republic and Octavian, but whatever they called it, formally it was a private compact only. They formed a *coniuratio*. Depending on their success they would be branded as brigands or praised as courageous citizens. Of course they acted ' optimo in rem publicam consensu ' (Cic., *Phil.* 5. 46; cf. 3. 7, 31, 38); a deft phrase, for *consensus* has a noble ring and avoids the hallowed but sinister implications of *coniuratio*.[24] To legalize their position, on 1 January Cicero moved a decree *de exercitu Caesaris* (*Phil.* 5. 53). In his motion he distinguished carefully between the *milites veterani*, who followed the *auctoritas* of (the young) Caesar (observe that they were civilians when they joined Octavian) and the Legio Martia, Legio quarta and the soldiers ' of the second and thirty-fifth legions who joined the consuls C. Pansa and A. Hirtius and gave in their names '. In Cicero's decree there is a remarkable provision: ' easque legiones bello confecto missas fieri placere '; a similar provision with respect to the *milites veterani* is conspicuously absent. Apparently they did not need any formal *missio*. This is correct: there was no formal release for *coniurati*; the presumption was that they would automatically be dismissed *bello confecto*.[25] Thus Cicero draws a line between those soldiers who were

---

[19] For sources and discussion, see H. Botermann, *Die Soldaten und die römische Politik in der Zeit von Caesars Tod bis zur Begründung des zweiten Triumvirats* (1968), 36 ff.

[20] Appian (*BC* 3. 40) reports that the veterans collected by Octavian in Campania marched ὑφ' ἑνὶ σημείῳ, under one *vexillum*: a fair description of a *manus tumultuaria*.

[21] On 4 November 44 Cicero wrote (*Att.* 16. 9): Octavian ' rem gerit palam, centuriat Capuae, dinumerat '. A. Alföldi, *Oktavians Aufstieg zur Macht* (1976), 108 n. 401, maintains that ' centuriat Capuae ' does not refer to the formation of military units at all: ' Centuriare und dinumerare sind Ausdrücke der stadtrömischen Wahlbestechung '. This is true of *decuriatio* (cf. J. Linderski, *Hermes* 89 (1961), 106 ff.), but *centuriare* is not attested in this sense. The explanation in *OLD* (s.v. ' dinumero '): he ' is giving the soldiers their pay ' is marred by ' pay ', which introduces a wrong emphasis. D. R. Shackleton

Bailey's rendering is exemplary (*Cicero's Letters to Atticus* VI, 189): ' he's . . . forming companies at Capua and paying out bounties '.

[22] cf. Livy 22. 28. 1: ' inter sese decuriati equites, centuriati pedites coniurabant '; Caes., *BC* 1. 76. 3: ' centuriatim producti milites idem iurant '.

[23] On the *evocati* under the empire, in addition to the works of Mommsen, Schmidt and Fiebiger quoted in notes 11, 12, and 18, see A. v. Domaszewski, *Die Rangordnung des römischen Heeres* (1908; 2nd ed. by B. Dobson, 1967), 75–8; M. Durry, *Les cohortes prétoriennes* (1938), 117–26; E. Birley, *ZPE* 43 (1981), 25–9.

[24] cf. R. Syme, *Roman Revolution*, 160–1; J. Helleguarc'h, *Le vocabulaire latin des relations et des partis politiques sous la république* (1963), 95–7, 123–5.

[25] Brunt, *JRS* 52 (1962), 81, reads (through a *lapsus calami*) ' bello confectae ' (sc. *legiones*), which of course affected his argument.

sub sacramento and those who were not. The former soldiers of Antonius Cicero apparently regarded as bound by their *sacramentum* to the republic, and thus their oath as still valid. In fact the formula of *sacramentum* seems to have contained the phrase 'pro republica se esse facturos' (Serv., *ad Aen.* 8. 1). But it also contained the sacred words 'se iussu consulum conventuros neque iniussu abituros' (Livy 3. 20. 3; 22. 38. 3), which is what they did when they left Antonius and embraced Octavian. No problem: they did not abandon a consul; they abandoned an enemy of the state. 'Iure laudantur' (Cic., *Phil.* 5. 3–4; cf. 4. 3–6; 12. 8).

When the fateful year of the two consuls who fell in battle began, the *evocati* of Octavian ceased to be a private army, but did not automatically become a regular one: they were now the emergency soldiers, the *coniurati* in the service of the republic. On 2 January 43 their *dux* received from the senate the command *pro praetore*; [26] and his *dies imperii* was 7 January, when he assumed the *fasces*. It is logical to suppose that on this day the soldiers who remained under Octavian's command (the Fourth and the Martian legions were probably taken over by Hirtius [27]) swore the *sacramentum* in his *verba*; and it is not implausible that the veterans and the new recruits were organized as the now formally reconstituted seventh and eighth legions. [28] The veterans obviously retained their quality of *evocati*, but were now regular soldiers: they began a new round of *militia legitima*.

Repetition justifies and perfects illegality. Not for nothing did Cicero hold up for the senate and Octavian the example of Pompey, the original *adulescentulus carnifex*: 'great honours were paid to Cn. Pompeius though he was a young man, and indeed rightly; for he came to the assistance of the state' (*Phil.* 5. 43). He assembled an army of volunteers; [29] technically they were the *coniurati* and he a *dux privatus*.

In 32 B.C. Octavian repeated his early steps on a grand scale. It was now not merely the soldiers of the Fourth and the Martian legions who 'deposcerent imperatorem et ducem C. Caesarem', but 'tota Italia'. Which student of the *Res Gestae* has not pondered over these two chapters:

Milia civium Roma[no]rum [sub] sacramento meo fuerunt circiter [quingen]ta. (3. 3).

Iuravit in mea verba tota Italia sponte sua, et me be[lli] quo vici ad Actium ducem depoposcit; iuraverunt in eadem ver[ba provin]ciae Galliae, Hispaniae, Africa, Sicilia, Sardinia. Qui [sub signis meis tum] militaverint, fuerunt senatores plures quam DCC, in ii[s qui vel antea vel pos]tea consules facti sunt ad eum diem, quo scripta su[nt haec, LXXXIII, sacerdo]tes ci[rc]iter CLXX (25. 2–3).

This is not the place for dissecting the opinions and interpretations of Kromayer, v. Premerstein, Syme, Herrmann and of scores of other scholars; [30] I wish merely to point out that these passages make perfect sense and find a coherent explanation within the doctrine of the *genera militiae*.

In the first passage we deal with the regular military oath, the *sacramentum*. As there is no mention of *sacramentum* in the other passage, and the context is unmistakably military, we are there in the presence of a military oath of a different sort. We know of only one such other oath, the oath of *coniuratio*. Now *iurare in verba* appears in Livy as a virtual synonym of *sacramentum*, but it is important to note that this very meaning can in each instance be ascertained only from the context. [31] In the phrase itself there is nothing that

[26] P. A. Brunt and J. M. Moore, *Res Gestae Divi Augusti* (1967), 38–9, opt for 1 January, but see the discussion by P. Stein, *Die Senatssitzungen der ciceronischen Zeit* (Diss. Münster, 1930), 80–3.
[27] App., *BC* 3. 65; cf. Cic., *Phil.* 14. 26–7; *Fam.* 10. 30. 1; 11. 19. 1.
[28] Botermann, *Die Soldaten*, 42, 202–3; Brunt, *Manpower*, 481–2.
[29] Livy, *Per.* 85; Plut., *Pomp.* 6. 3–4.
[30] J. Kromayer, *Die rechtliche Begründung des Prinzipats* (1888), 16 ff.; Syme, *Rom. Rev.*, 284 ff.; A. v. Premerstein, *Vom Werden und Wesen des Prinzipats* (Abh. Münch., 1937), 36 ff.; P. Herrmann, *Der römische Kaisereid* (1969), 78 ff. (cf. J. Briscoe, *CR* 21 (1971), 260–3); Brunt–Moore (above, n. 26),

67–8; V. Fadinger, *Die Begründung des Prinzipats* (1969), 18 ff.; H. Benario, *Chiron* 5 (1975), 301–9.
[31] Livy 2. 32. 1; 3. 20. 3–5. See also 28. 29. 12, where the phrase *in verba iurare* refers (as follows from 28. 27. 4 and 12) to the renewal of *sacramentum*. The *iurare in verba* and *dilectus*: 6. 2. 6; 22. 11. 9. Cf. also 7. 16. 8; 45. 2. 10. At 22. 53. 12 the phrase does not refer to *sacramentum*, but to an oath of the type 'ut victor revertar', and in four other passages it appears in a non-military context (6. 22. 7; 7. 5. 5; 32. 5. 4; 41. 15. 11). Cf. Herrmann, (above, n. 30), 42 n. 75; 81 n. 89. On Tac., *Ann.* 1. 7. 2 (the oath *in verba Tiberii Caesaris*), see the judicious remarks by F. R. D. Goodyear, *The Annals of Tacitus* 1 (1972), 138–9.

would connect it exclusively with *sacramentum*. The person who is *sacramento rogatus* and the person who joins in a military *coniuratio* both swear to follow their commanders. But the *sacramentum* presupposes a general obligation to military service; it is connected with the *dilectus*. Its function was to transform this general obligation to serve into concrete military service. Although it could be taken voluntarily, it was not a voluntary oath. The conscript could not refuse to swear it; if he did he was severely punished (cf. Livy 4. 53. 9). In their capacity as *milites* the citizens had no influence upon the choice of their commanders; this choice was reserved for them only indirectly, in their earlier hypostasis as citizen voters, when they cast their votes at the consular or praetorian elections (cf. Livy 24. 8. 19). In a word the *sacramentum* presupposes an *imperium*-holder in whose *verba* it was sworn, but in this chapter Augustus is conspicuously reticent about his official position. The *imperium*, so prominently displayed at the outset of the *Res Gestae*, here receives no mention.

On the other hand, the oath of *evocatio/coniuratio* was formally a voluntary and, in the case of a *dux privatus*, legally constitutive oath: it established the leader and his followers as the bona fide saviours of the republic. A *coniuratio* need not have been an illegal or—to use a more ambiguous and hence a more appropriate word—extra-legal affair; it could be initiated by a competent magistrate or the senate. In 52 B.C., after the death of P. Clodius, the senate decreed, lest the urban riots spread throughout Italy, ' ut omnes iuniores Italiae coniurarent ' (Caes., *BG* 7. 1). How this was accomplished we do not know, but two decades later, as we gather from Suetonius (*Aug.* 17. 2), the *coniurationes* (this time of *tota Italia*, and hence, militarily speaking, of all *iuniores* and *seniores*) were organized locally in each community of Italy: Augustus ' Bononiensibus quoque publice, quod in Antoniorum clientela antiquitus erant, gratiam fecit coniurandi cum tota Italia pro partibus suis '.

The controversy whether the oath of 32 was a *Treueid* or a military oath appears barren: every military oath was an oath of allegiance as well. One thing, however, is clear: the oath of 32 was not an oath of allegiance in the sense of the later *Kaisereide*. The imperial oaths of allegiance expressed the perpetual allegiance of the population to the princeps and imperator. On the other hand, the men of Italy and the western provinces swore in 32 their allegiance to Octavian solely in his capacity as *dux* in the war at hand; *ad bellum unum*, as a Roman constitutional expert would have described it. The end of the war would mark the end of their obligation. As they did not swear the *sacramentum*, but only the *ius iurandum* of a *coniuratio*, technically they were not *milites*; to use the idiom of Sallust, the antiquarians and the *senatus consultum de Aphrodisiensibus*, those who then actually served with the standards did it *pro milite*.

The documents from Aphrodisias restore to life the antiquarian distinction between the *militia legitima* and *coniuratio*, between *milites* and *pro milite*. They illuminate the quality of mind that made the Romans pay attention to these legal distinctions, even in time of war. They illuminate the young Octavian's *arcana imperii*.

14

Usu, farre, coemptione.

Bemerkungen zur Überlieferung eines Rechtsatzes

Die XII Tafeln haben sich bekanntlich mit der Ehe als solcher nicht beschäftigt, sondern vielmehr mit den verschiedenen Rechtsmitteln, durch welche die *manus*-Gewalt über die Frau erworben werden konnte, In den vorhandenen Testimonien wird jedoch nur eines dieser Mittel, der *usus*, erwähnt[1]); die *confarreatio* und die *coemptio* fehlen. Nun hat Alan Watson in seinem sehr verdienstvollen Buch Rome of the XII Tables (Princeton 1975) 9—12 erneut die These aufgestellt[2]), daß die uns in einigen späteren Schriftstellern begegnende Reihe *usu, farreo (farre), coemptione* einundderselben Quelle entstamme; er behauptet, diese Quelle könne keine andere sein als das Zwölftafelgesetz.

Größerer Anschaulichkeit halber gebe ich die von Watson angeführten Stellen wieder:

Gaius I 110 (ed. David-Nelson): Olim itaque tribus modis in manum conueniebant: usu, farreo, coemptione.
Servius auctus ad Verg. Georg. I 31 (ed. Thilo): tribus enim modis apud veteres nuptiae fiebant: usu, ... farre, ... coemptione.
Arnobius, Adv. nat. IV 20 (ed. Marchesi): Uxores enim dii habent. Usu, farre, coemptione genialis lectuli sacramenta condicunt?
Boethius ad Cic. Top. III 14 (FIRA II 307): Tribus enim modis uxor habebatur: usu farreo coemptione.

Die merkwürdige Reihenfolge — immer dieselbe — *usu, farre(o), coemptione* fällt auf (über die Diskrepanz zwischen *farre* und *farreo*, s. unten); man notiere auch den Gebrauch des instrumentalen Ablativs. Es unterliegt wohl keinem Zweifel, daß alle vier Berichte auf eine gemeinsame Vorlage zurückzuführen sind; es folgt aber nicht, daß diese gemeinsame Quelle die XII Tafeln sind oder sein müssen. In den erhaltenen Bruchstücken des Zwölftafelgesetzes ist der Gebrauch des *ablativus instrumentalis* nicht nachweisbar; und natürlich glaubt niemand daran, daß Boethius, Arnobius oder Servius die XII Tafeln mit ihren eigenen Augen gelesen haben. Wir müssen also nach einem Vermittler suchen. War es Gaius?

---

[1]) Gaius I 111 = Tab. VI 5 (FIRA I 44). Zur *manus* und Ehe siehe die bahnbrechenden Studien von E. Volterra, besonders La conception du mariage d'après les juristes romains (Padova 1940), bes. 10ff.; Nuove ricerche sulla „conventio in manum", Memorie della Accad. dei Lincei ser. VIII, vol. XII, fasc. 4, 1966; La „conventio in manum" e il matrimonio romano, Temis 22, 1967, 11—28; Precisazioni in tema di matrimonio classico, BIDR 78, 1975, 245—270. Siehe auch J. Gaudemet, Observations sur la manus, AHDO-RIDA 2, 1953, 323—353; M. Kaser, Das altrömische ius (Göttingen 1949), 316ff., 343ff.; Ehe und „conventio in manum", Iura 1, 1950, 64—101 und zusammenfassend ders., Das römische Privatrecht I² (München 1971), 71ff.; F. Benedek, Die *conventio in manum* und die Förmlichkeiten der Eheschließung im römischen Recht (Pécs 1978), bes. 3—23.
[2]) Er hat dies schon in SDHI 29, 1963, 337—338 vorgeschlagen; dazu zweifelnd Kaser, Privatrecht 76 Anm. 1. Vgl. Volterra, Nuove ricerche 283 Anm. 64: « L'ipotesi è verosimile, ma gli argomenti addotti per dimostrarla mi sembrano alquanto deboli ».

Nun hat Watson selbst bemerkt[3]), daß Boethius in seinem Kommentar zu Ciceros Topica III 14 von der *coemptio* spricht und als seine Quelle Ulpians Institutionen anführt. Es ist also recht wahrscheinlich, daß er auch die Reihenfolge *usu, farreo, coemptione* in derselben Schrift vorfand. Da die Institutionen nicht erhalten sind, können wir nicht mit Sicherheit entscheiden, woher der Kompilator sein Material geschöpft hat; noch ist in den sogenannten Tituli ex corpore Ulpiani der Abschnitt *de his qui in manu sunt* erhalten. Wir besitzen davon nur ein kleines Bruchstück (cap. IX, FIRA II 272), das jedoch für unsere Beweisführung von Interesse ist: *Farreo conuenitur in manum certis uerbis et testibus X praesentibus et sollemni sacrificio facto, in quo panis quoque farreus adhibetur.* Dieser Text erweist sich sofort als eine gekürzte Fassung von Gaius I 112; man vergleiche nur die folgenden von Gaius gebrauchten Wendungen: *farreo in manum conueniunt: (sacrificium) in quo farreus panis adhibetur; cum certis et sollemnibus uerbis praesentibus decem testibus.* Ob auch die Institutiones Ulpiani auf Gaius zurückgehen, ist schwer zu sagen; Boethius' Bericht über die *coemptio* zeigt fast keine Berührungspunkte, stilistisch oder sachlich, mit dem des Gaius. Als ein unabhängiger Zeuge für die Reihe *usu, farreo, coemptione* scheidet Boethius jedenfalls aus. Denn das einzige, für uns gerade wichtigste Wort, das für Vergleichszwecke in Frage kommt, ist die Form *farreo*, die auch in Ulpians Tituli und Gaius vorkommt, während Arnobius und Servius auctus die Form *farre* aufweisen. Es scheint also, daß wir es mit zwei Überlieferungen zu tun haben, einer juristischer und einer antiquarischer. Es soll jetzt untersucht werden, wann und auf welche Weise diese Spaltung aufgekommen ist, und wohin uns diese beiden Überlieferungsfäden führen werden.

Der Text von Arnobius erlaubt seiner Kürze wegen keine sicheren Schlüsse; es empfiehlt sich dagegen, die Berichte von Gaius und Servius auctus einer vergleichenden Analyse zu unterziehen. In der folgenden Zusammenstellung werden in gesperrter Schrift die wörtlichen Entsprechungen bezeichnet, in Kursivschrift dagegen die Aussagen, die auf verschiedene Weise denselben Gedanken ausdrücken:

Gaius I 109—113:	Servius auctus ad Verg. Georg. I 31:
109 In manum autem feminae tantum conueniunt.	
110 *Olim* itaque tribus modis in manum conueniebant[4]): usu, farreo, coemptione.	Tribus enim modis *apud veteres* nuptiae fiebant:
111 Usu in manum conueniebat,	usu, si verbi gratia
quae anno *continuo* nupta	*mulier* anno *uno* cum viro, licet sine legibus,
perseuerabat.	*fuisset.*

[3]) The Law of Persons in the Later Roman Republic (Oxford 1967), 19 Anm. 1; Rome of the XII Tables, 9 Anm. 4.

[4]) Den Vorschlag von R. G. Böhm, Gaiusstudien X (Freiburg im Breisgau 1972), 63—66, *Olim namque ueteres tribus modis in manum uiri sui perueniebant* zu widerlegen, erübrigt sich. Seine Lesungen in I 111—113 (S. 69—105) produzieren ein nicht minder gefoltertes Latein; I 112: *in quo noster farreus panis adhibetur, unde etiam de nuptiis pane dicitur,* ist ein musterhaftes Beispiel.

In Gaius folgt eine detaillierte Diskussion von *usus* und *trinoctium* (mit dem Verweis auf die XII Tafeln), die in Servius auctus keine Entsprechung findet.

112 *Farreo* in manum conueniunt per quoddam genus sacrificii, quod Ioui Farreo fit; in quo *farreus panis adhibetur,* unde etiam confarreatio *dicitur.*	*farre,* cum per pontificem maximum et Dialem flaminem *per* fruges et *molam salsam* coniugebantur, unde confarreatio *appellabatur,* ex quibus nuptiis patrimi et matrimi nascebantur;

Im Folgenden erwähnt Gaius die *decem testes* und die Sakralregel, nach der die *flamines maiores* und der *rex sacrorum nisi ex farreatis nati non leguntur; ac ne ipsi quidem sine confarreatione sacerdotium habere possunt.* In Servius auctus' Kommentar zu Georg. I 31 finden diese Nachrichten keine Entsprechung; von der Priesterehe spricht Servius auctus aber an manchen anderen Stellen, ad Aen. IV 339, 374 und besonders 103: *quae res ad farreatas nuptias pertinet, quibus flaminem et flaminicam iure pontificio in matrimonium necesse est convenire.*

103 Coemptione uero *in manum conueniunt* per mancipationem, id est quandam imaginariam uenditionem: nam adhibitis non minus quam V testibus ciuibus Romanis puberibus, item libripende, emit eum ⟨mulier et is⟩ mulierem, cuius in manum conuenit.	coemptione vero atque *in manum conventione* cum illa in filiae locum[5]), maritus in patris veniebat, ut siquis prior fuisset defunctus, locum hereditatis iustum alteri faceret.

Auf den ersten Blick haben diese Beschreibungen der *coemptio* nur sehr wenig miteinander zu tun; an anderer Stelle schreibt aber Servius auctus (ad Aen. IV 103): *coemptio enim est ubi libra atque aes adhibetur, et mulier atque vir inter se quasi emptionem faciunt.* So auch Servius ad Georg. I 31, unmittelbar vor den oben wiedergegebenen Stellen des Servius auctus: *quod autem ait ‚emat'* *ad antiquum pertinet ritum, quo se maritus et uxor invicem coemebant, sicut habemus in iure* (vgl. Isid. Etym. V 26: *nam antiquus nuptiarum erat ritus quo se maritus et uxor invicem coemebant*). Dies dürfte nur ein Stück falschen Etymologiesierens sein, indem ein Antiquar das *co-emere* als das gegenseitige *emere* auffaßte; dieser Antiquar wird aber keineswegs Varro sein, da sich seine Etymologie für diesmal mit der modernen Auslegung deckt. Er interpretiert *co-emere* im Sinne von

---

5) Diese Wendung kehrt bei Gaius sehr oft wieder, siehe besonders I 111 (bei der Besprechung des *usus*): *filiaeque locum optinebat;* I 114: *quae enim cum marito suo facit coemptionem,* ⟨*ut*⟩ *apud eum filiae loco sit, dicitur matrimonii causa fecisse coemptionem.* Vgl. Boethius ad Cic. Top. III 14 (FIRA II 307): *Itaque mulier uiri conueniebat in manum, et uocabantur hae nuptiae per coemptionem, et erat mulier, materfamilias uiro loco filiae.* Für eine eingehende Interpretation des Ausdruckes und der Rechtslage siehe Gaudemet, Observations, 335 f.; Volterra, Nuove ricerche, 329 ff.

in unum cogere (Ling. Lat VI 43), womit A. Ernout und A. Meillet[6]) zu vergleichen sind: in *co-emo* « le préverbe marque l'aspect 'déterminé'». Aus diesen
Gründen ist die Ergänzung in Gaius I 113 *emit eum ⟨mulier et is⟩ mulierem* nicht
nur zweifelhaft, wie sie David und Nelson in ihrem Kommentar zu der Stelle
bezeichnen[7]), osndern ganz und gar unmöglich. Es ist schwer vorstellbar, daß
ein Antiquar oder ein Jurist der besseren Zeit für eine solche Fehlauslegung
der *coemptio* verantwortlich sein sollte.

In Boethius ad Cic. Top. III 14 lesen wir: *coemptio uero certis sollemnitatibus
peragebatur, et sese in coemendo inuicem interrogabant* (sc. *uir* und *mulier*). Die
Fragen und Antworten, die er anführt, beziehen sich aber offensichtlich nicht
auf den Libralakt der *coemptio*, sondern drücken den gegenseitigen Ehekonsens
aus, der sicherlich der eigentlichen *coemptio* unmittelbar voranging[8]). Auf diese
Weise wird bei Boethius die *coemptio* mit dem Ehekonsens verwechselt und
verschmolzen; diese Verwechslung ist in Servius und Isidor noch weiter fort-
geschritten, indem sie die Gegenseitigkeit des Ehekonsenses auf die *coemptio*
erstreckten.

In der Sache der „Kaufehe" gibt es noch einen anderen Berührungspunkt
zwischen Servius und Boethius. Letzterer bemühte sich, die Bedeutung des
Ausdruckes *materfamilias* bei Cicero, Top. III 14 zu illustrieren. Ciceros Text
lautet wie folgt: *genus est, uxor; eius duae formae: una matrum familias, eae
sunt, quae in manum conuenerunt, altera earum quae tantummodo uxores habentur.*
Cicero erwähnt nur generell die *conuentio in manum*; es war ja für seinen Zweck
nicht notwendig, die Rechtswege, auf denen die *manus* übertragen werden
konnte, einzeln zu nennen. Wenn also Boethius schreibt: *quae autem in manum
per coemptionem conuenerant, eae matresfamilias uocabantur, quae uero usu uel
farreo, minime,* so hat er Cicero und vielleicht auch seine unmittelbare Vorlage,
die dem Ulpian zugeschriebenen Institutionen, arg mißverstanden.

Was uns zum Bedenken mahnt, ist die enge Verwandtschaft zwischen diesem
Satz und zwei Stellen des Servius und Servius auctus. Wir lesen bei Serv. auct.
ad Aen. XI 470. *multem uero familias eam esse, quae in mariti manu mancipioque*[9]),
aut in cuius maritus manu mancipioque (dies scheint ein Zusatz eines späteren
Antiquars zu sein) *esset, quoniam in familiam quoque mariti et sui heredis locum
uenisset. Alii matronas uirgines nobiles dicunt, matresfamilias uero illas quae in
matrimonium per coemptionem conuenerunt: nam per quandam iuris sollemnitatem
in familiam migrant mariti;* Serv. ad Aen. XI 581: *materfamilias uero illa dicitur
quae in matrimonium conuenit per coemptionem: nam per quandam iuris sollemnitatem in familiam migrat mariti.*

In Boethius erscheint die *coemptio* als die wichtigste, ja fast die einzige Form
der *conuentio in manum.* Dasselbe gilt für die beiden oben wiedergegebenen
Stellen, und in Servius auctus, ad Georg. I 31, lesen wir den merkwürdigen
Satz *coemptione uero atque in manum conuentione,* wo *atque* störend wirkt und

---

[6]) Dictionnaire étymologique de la langue latine[3] (Paris 1951), 347.
[7]) Gai Institutionum Commentarii IV. Kommentar, 1 Lieferung (Leiden 1954),
134—138.
[8]) Vgl. Volterra, La conception 20ff.
[9]) Für eine Diskussion dieses Ausdruckes siehe Gaudemet, Observations,
332f.; Volterra, Nuove ricerche, 274ff.

wo die *coemptio* mit der *conventio in manum* tatsächlich identifiziert wird[10]).
Nur bei der Darstellung der *coemptio* spricht Servius von den Rechtsfolgen,
die die *conventio in manum* nach sich zieht. In der Tat erwähnt er die *conventio
in manum* nur bei dieser Gelegenheit[11]).

Es ist nicht unmöglich, daß alle drei Autoren, Boethius, Servius und Servius
auctus, ihre übereinstimmende Interpretation der *coemptio* und ihre ebenfalls
übereinstimmende Auslegung des Terminus *materfamilias* in Ulpians Institutionen vorfanden. Wir sollten aber einen groben juristischen Fehler nicht
voreilig einer juritischen Quelle zur Last legen, besonders, wenn wir eine viel
wahrscheinlichere Lösung zur Hand haben. Die gleiche Auslegung der *coemptio*
findet sich nämlich in Aelius Donatus' Terenzkommentar, Andria 297: *confir-
matae sunt legitimae nuptiae per in manum conventionem.* Was nun die Quellen
des sogenannten Servius auctus oder Servius Danielis anlangt, wird jetzt allgemein angenommen, daß in seinem Kommentar die Trümmer der großen
Vergilauslegung des Aelius Donatus verborgen sind. Es scheint, daß dem Servius-
Kommentar das Werk des Donatus als Vorlage diente und daß später, wahrscheinlich im siebenten oder achten Jahrhundert, ein anderer Kommentator,
den wir Servius auctus oder Danielis nennen, diesem meistens grammatisch
angelegten Schulauslegung eine prächtige Reihe antiquarischer Notizen bei-
steuerte, die er ebenfalls aus dem Donatus-Kommentar herausgelesen hat[12]).
Der Donatus-Kommentar wurde auch von Macrobius benutzt, und wie wir
jetzt sehen, es verwendete ihn auch Boethius (neben den Institutiones Ulpiani)
bei seiner Auslegung von Ciceros Topica. Es darf uns also nicht wunder nehmen,
daß dieselbe Fehlinterpretation der *coemptio* bei allen Autoren wiederkehrt,
die von Donatus abhängen.

Die Darstellung des Gaius ist klar und präzis; die des Servius konfus und
entstellt. Die Ursache dieser Korruptel liegt auf der Hand. Gaius und die anderen
Rechtsgelehrten beschäftigten sich mit der juristischen Frage des *manus-*

---

[10]) Vgl. Gaudemet, Observations, 328 Anm. 30, 330 Anm. 41. Nach Volterra, Nuove ricerche, 299—300 Anm. 97, « Servio ... giunge a considerare come
forme diverse di matrimonio la *coemptio* e la *conventio in manum* ». Servius
auctus spricht aber von den *tres modi nuptiarum*; er interpretiert also die *conventio in manum* eher als eine andere Benennung der *coemptio.*

[11]) Siehe auch Serv. auct. ad Aen. IV 103: *quoniam coemptione facta mulier in
potestatem viri cedit atque ita sustinet conditionem liberae servitutis ... quoque
omnis iste mos coemptionis et citra nominis nuncupationem dotis datae taxatione
expediretur, quae res in manum conventio dicitur, subiunxit* (sc. Vergilius) *,dotales-
que tuae Tyrios permittere dextrae'. quid est enim aliud ,permittere dextrae', quam in
manum convenire?* So weit, so gut; lesen wir aber, was folgt: *quae conventio eo
ritu perficitur, ut aqua et igni adhibitis, duobus maximis elementis, natura coniuncta
habeatur: quae res ad farreatas nuptias pertinet, quibus flaminem et flaminicam
iure pontificio in matrimonium necesse est convenire.* Die *coemptio* wird also mit der
confarreatio verwechselt und die *conventio in manum* als ein Heiratsbrauch aufgefaßt (vgl. Volterra, La conception, 20—21).

[12]) Siehe dazu die ausgezeichneten Untersuchungen von A. Santoro, Il
Servio Danielino e Donato, SIFC 20, 1946, 79ff.; R. B. Lloyd, Republican
Authors in Servius and the Scholia Danielis, HSCP 65, 1961, 291ff., bes. 234—237;
R. Kaster, Macrobius and Servius: Verecundia and the Grammarian's Function,
HSCP 84, 1980, 219ff., bes. 224ff., 255ff.

Erwerbes; Donatus, Servius und die anderen späteren literarischen Kommentatoren bemühen sich dagegen, die *nuptiae* zu erklären; sie verkennen aber dabei die Tatsache, daß die römische Ehe eine sozial-religiöse, nicht aber eine juristische Erscheinung war, und gehen infolgedessen fehl, weil sie die *nuptiae* mit Hilfe rechtlicher Kategorien zu erfassen versuchen. Schon in seiner Einleitung zum Thema hebt Gaius (I 110) die *manus*-Übertragung hervor, während Servius auctus sofort in die Irre geht, indem er die drei *modi* des *manus*-Erwerbes als die drei *modi* der Eheschließung interpretiert. Sein Vorgehen wird immer klarer bei seiner Darstellung des *usus*, wo Gaius ganz korrekt die Frau, die auf diese Weise *in manum conueniebat*, als *nupta* schon am Anfang der Einjahresperiode bezeichnet, während Servius die *nuptiae* nur am Ende dieser Frist eintreten läßt und von der *mulier*, die *cum viro* nur *verbi gratia, sine legibus* zusammenlebte, etwas abschätzig spricht, wodurch er den juristischen Bezug des *usus* und die außerrechtliche Natur der römischen Ehe mißdeutet.

Es sieht also so aus, als ob Gaius und Servius auctus (d. h. sein Gewährsmann Donatus) eine Quelle von juristisch-antiquarischem Charakter benutzten, bei derer Wiedergabe aber Donatus die juristischen Einzelheiten entweder beseitigte oder umdeutete. Daß es aber ein und dieselbe Quelle war, wird zur Genüge durch die Redewendungen gezeigt, die bei beiden Autoren wiederkehren, wie besonders *tribus modis, unde confarreatio dicitur* bzw. *appellabatur, coemptione vero*. Dies wird kaum auf einem Zufall beruhen. Daß Servius Gaius benutzte, ist wohl auszuschließen, da sein Text Zusätze enthält die sich in Gaius nicht befinden.

Um die Identität dieser gemeinsamen Vorlage feststellen zu können, müssen wir uns den lateinischen Glossen zuwenden. Im Jahre 1878 veröffentlichte G. Löwe[13]) eine Glosse aus dem Codex Montecassinensis 439; sie wurde später von G. Goetz in das Corpus Glossariorum Latinorum aufgenommen[14]) und dann von W. M. Lindsay in die Glossaria Latina[15]), wo sie als Abolita CO 102 erscheint. In Lindsays Wiedergabe lautet sie folgendermaßen:

Confarreatis nuptiis: multis modis nuptiae fiunt; usu, si anno verbi gratia cum viro, licet sine legitimis sollemnitatibus, fieret[16]); vel manuum (in manum?) conventione[m][17]), cum in filiae locum, maritus in patris venit, ut si quis prior fuerit defunctus, locum hereditatis iustum alteri faciat; fratre (farre), cum per pontificem maximum e⟨t⟩ Diale⟨m⟩ flaminem per fruges et molam salsam coniunguntur, ex quibus nuptiis patrimi et matrimi nascuntur.

Nach *fieret* lesen Löwe und Goetz *coemptione[m];* diese, offenbar korrekte, Lesung wurde auch von Lindsay angenommen, als er unsere Glosse 1930 in seiner Pariser Edition des Festus abdruckte[18]) *(coemptione vel in manum conventione).*

---

13) RhM 33, 1878, 631—633.
14) Bd. 4 (Lipsiae 1889), 41, Anm. z. Zeile 2; Bd. 6 (1899), 253.
15) Bd. 3 (Paris 1926), 113; siehe auch seine *praefatio*, S. 93—95.
16) Nach Löwes Emendation *fuerit*; cf. Goetz CGL 6, 253 *(fuerit?).*|
17) Diese Wendung ist interessant, weil der Glossator die *conventio in manum* mit der *dextrarum iunctio* verwechselt zu haben scheint; vgl. die oben (Anm. 11) angeführten Stellen des Serv. auct.
18) Glossaria Latina 4, 175.

Dieser Text stimmt mit dem Servius-auctus-Bericht fast wörtlich überein; die folgenden Divergenzen sind jedoch von Interesse: die ungewöhnliche Reihenfolge *usu, coemptione, farre*; und zweitens der Gebrauch des Präsens und nicht des Imperfekts, wie in Servius auctus.

In Paulus' Excerpta aus Festus erscheint das folgende Stichwort (65 L.): *Diffareatio genus est sacrificii, quo inter virum et mulierem fiebat dissolutio. Dicta diffareatio, quia fiebat farreo libo*[19]) *adhibito.* Es ist klar, daß der Festustext einst eine parallele Notiz über die *confarreatio* enthalten haben muß. Diese verschollene Festusangabe hat Lindsay in der Glosse des Codex Montecassinensis erkannt[20]) und sie seiner zweiten Edition des Festus einverleibt[21]). Damit ist aber die Sage der Glossa Montecassinensis noch nicht zu Ende. In seinen berühmten Verrianischen Forschungen[22]) hat R. Reitzenstein den Nachweis erbracht, daß eine größere Anzahl von Lemmata in Festus aus Ateius Capitos Büchern *de iure pontificio* geschöpft ist. Er hat auch eine andere Quelle des Verrius-Festus nachgewiesen, den Anonymus *de nuptiis*. Auf Reitzensteins Forschungen fußend, hat W. Strzelecki[23]) mit zwingenden Gründen dargetan, daß Reitzensteins Anonymus *de nuptiis* kein anderer gewesen ist als Ateius Capito: wir wissen, daß er, vermutlich in seinen *libri de iure pontificio,* von den *nuptiae* schrieb, besonders denen der *flamines.* Unter diesen Umständen lag es gewiß sehr nahe, hierher auch die Glosse von Monte Cassino heranzuziehen, und sie dem Anonymus *de nuptiis* oder Ateius Capito zuzuschreiben. Dies ist aber erst 1963 geschehen, als W. Strzelecki in einem Festschrift-Aufsatz sie in der Tat als eine Ateianische zu erweisen unternommen hat[24]).

Unter den wenigen Buchbesprechungen, die dauernden Ruhm erlangt haben, nimmt E. Fränkels Besprechung der Editio Harvardiana des Servius einen hervorragenden Platz ein[25]). Er warf den Editores Harvardiani vor, daß sie in ihrem Testimonien-Apparatus das größte Buch, das die römische Zivilisation hervorbrachte, vernachlässigten, und dadurch die korrekte Deutung von unzähligen Stellen sehr erschwerten. Fränkel dachte an die Digesten; einen ähnlichen Vorwurf können wir auch Strzelecki machen. Hätte er Gaius herangezogen, so würde er sicherlich die Textgeschichte des Ateius anders rekonstruiert und das Fragment des Ateius über die *confarreatio* anders gestaltet haben.

Wir haben die folgende Überlieferungskette vor uns: Gaius und Servius auctus weisen Übereinstimmungen solcher Art auf, daß sie letzten Endes von ein- und derselben Quelle abstammen müssen; eine gewisse stilistische Verwandtschaft besteht auch zwischen Paulus' Stichwort *diffareatio* und Gaius I 112; Servius stimmt mit der Glosse von Monte Cassino fast völlig überein; diese

---

[19]) *farre oliuo* E. Vgl. Gaius I 112 *farreus panis.*
[20]) Glossaria Latina 3, 113 in app.
[21]) Glossaria Latina 4, 175; siehe jedoch seine Anmerkung in app.: *si Festina sint.*
[22]) Breslau 1887, 41ff. (Breslauer Philol. Abh. I 4).
[23]) De Ateio Capitone nuptialium caerimoniarum interprete (Wrocław 1947), passim.
[24]) De glossarii ‚Abolita' quadam glossa, Lanx Satura N. Terzaghi oblata (Genova 1963), 321—324.
[25]) JRS 38, 1948, 131—143, bes. 142; 39, 1949, 145—154.

Glosse stammt, wie es scheint; aus der Epitome des Festus; Verrius Flaccus benutzte Ateius Capito, besonders für seine Darstellung des *ius pontificium* und der *caerimoniae nuptiales*. Die Folgerung: Als die gemeinsame Quelle mancher späteren Darstellungen der *nuptiae* und der *conventio in manum*, des *usus*, der *confarreatio* und der *coemptio* ist Ateius Capito anzusehen. Unsere Aufgabe ist, nun den Weg zu zeigen, der von Ateius Capito zu Gaius und Servius auctus führt.

Zuerst ein paar Bemerkungen über die Natur des Werkes Ateius Capitos. W. Strzelecki hat in seiner Sammlung der Fragmente des Ateius Capito die Glossa Montecassinensis als ein *fragmentum Ateianum* ohne Weiteres abgedruckt[26]). Dies ist irreführend und für den *morbus philogorum*, Texte juristischen Inhalts ohne hinreichende juristische Kenntnisse beurteilen zu wagen, sehr bezeichnend. Für einen Juristen ist es sofort klar, daß wir hier keinen echten Wortlaut des Ateius haben, sondern nur ein sehr verkürztes und entstelltes Exzerpt. Der wirkliche Charakter des Ateianischen Urtextes ergibt sich aus dem Vergleich zwischen Gaius und Servius auctus. Wie wir schon betont haben: Die Quelle, die sie benutzten, wies juristische und antiquarische Eigenschaften auf. Dies paßt aufs Beste zu den *libri de iure pontificio* des Ateius, der ja ein Rechtsgelehrter und zugleich ein Antiquar gewesen ist.

Wie gesagt, hat Verrius Flaccus eine große Anzahl seiner Angaben aus Ateius Capitos *libri de iure pontificio, de iure sacrificiorum* und *de iure augurali* geschöpft. Den Büchern *de iure pontificio* wird jedoch in Festus expressis verbis nur das Stichwort *mundus* zugeschrieben[27]). Über diese Frage schrieb Capito *in lib. VI Pontificali*; Verrius (Festus) zitiert auch einen Satz aus den *commentarii iuris civilis* des Cato (d. h. Cato *filius*), den er jedoch wahrscheinlich nur durch Capitos Vermittlung kannte. Die Excerpta Pauli geben dieses Stichwort im Großen und Ganzen recht genau wieder, beseitigen aber den Verweis auf Capito und Cato. Ob wir dasselbe auch für das oben wiedergegebene Stichwort *diffareatio* annehmen dürfen, ist ungewiß, da diese Notiz nur als eine Art Verweis auf das Grundstichwort *confarreatio* dienen konnte. Daß aber Ateius Capito die *confarreatio* speziell behandelte, wissen wir aus Plutarchs Quaestiones Romanae 50, wo er von der Ehe der *flamines* spricht und Ateius Capito ausdrücklich zitiert. Plutarch hat Ateius Capito sicherlich selbst nicht gelesen; das Ateianische Gut (dem er auch seine übrigen Angaben über den *flamen Dialis* und die *caerimoniae nuptiales* zu verdanken scheint) ist an ihn durch Juba[28]) oder Verrius Flaccus[29]) gekommen (es ist durchaus möglich, daß auch Juba Ateius Capito nur aus Verrius kannte[30])).

Die Epitome des Festus enthält reiche Angaben über die *caerimoniae*, berührt aber das *ius civile* nur selten. Dies sind gerade die Eigenschaften, die Servius auctus charakterisieren. Daß Donatus Verrius Flaccus (oder Festus) ausschrieb,

---

[26]) C. Atei Capitonis Fragmenta (Lipsiae 1967), 30 (Suppl. 6a).
[27]) 144—146 L. = Strzelecki Frg. 11.
[28]) R. Peter, Quaestionum pontificalium specimen (Diss. Argentorati 1886), 20ff.; Strzelecki, De Ateio Capitone 23ff.; ders., C. Atei Capitonis Fragmenta (Wrocław 1960), 17f. (mit weiterer Literatur).
[29]) H. J. Rose, The Roman Questions of Plutarch (Oxford 1924), 35ff.
[30]) Rose 38—40.

scheint gesichert zu sein[31]), obwohl die Identität seiner Anmerkung zu Georg. I 31 mit der Glossa Montecassinensis keinen sicheren Beweis dafür bildet, da der Glossator seine Notiz nicht nur direkt dem Festus, sondern auch dem Donatus entnehmen konnte.

Aulus Gellius war ein Zeitgenosse des Gaius. In seinen Noctes Atticae führt er Ateius Capito manchmal an; für uns ist aber die Stelle X 15, 1—18 besonders wichtig, weil Gellius dort von den *caerimoniae impositae flamini Diali* spricht und auf die *libri, qui de sacerdotibus publicis compositi sunt,* und auf Fabius Pictor verweist. Am Ende seiner Darstellung zitiert er aber eine Angabe von Masurius Sabinus; es unterliegt keinem Zweifel, daß er in der Tat den ganzen Abschnitt aus den *Memorialium libri* des Sabinus (vgl. VII 7, 8) geschöpft hat[32]). In demselben Werk schrieb Sabinus auch über den *ritus nuptiarum*; wenn wir uns nun den Umstand gegenwärtig halten, daß Ateius Capito von dem *flamen Dialis* und den *nuptiae* ausführlich handelte und daß Sabinus der Tradition gemäß Capitos Schüler und Nachfolger war[33]), liegt die Annahme sehr nahe, daß die Bücher des Sabinus De flamine Diali und De ritu nuptiarum von den *libri* Capitos De iure pontificio abhängig sind.

Dieser Schluß ist wichtig, weil er die Brücke zu Gaius schlägt. Gaius verweist auf Sabinus manchmal[34]), auf Ateius Capito nie. Es wäre also sehr verwunderlich, wenn er seine Darstellung der *conventio in manum* unmittelbar aus Ateius Capito herausgelesen hätte; als seinen Gewährsmann sollten wir eher Masurius Sabinus annehmen. Betrachten wir also die Quellenlage: Gaius weist eine große Ähnlichkeit mit dem Text des Servius auctus, d. h. Donatus, auf; Donatus benutzte Festus oder Verrius, welch letzterer Ateius Capito ausgeschrieben hat. Der Schluß ist unausweichlich: nämlich, um die trefflichen Worte Strzeleckis zu zitieren, *Masurium Sabinum alacri animo ex Ateianis lignatum esse silvis*[35]). Dies gilt natürlich für seine Memorialium libri; ich glaube aber, daß Gaius eher die berühmten Libri iuris civilis als seine Vorlage benutzte. Sabinus

---

[31]) G. Rowoldt, Librorum pontificiorum Romanorum de caerimoniis sacrificiorum reliquiae (Diss. Halis Saxonum 1906), 33, 43 (Frg. 6: Festus 292 L. *pura vestimenta,* vgl. Serv. auct. ad Aen. IV 683, Serv. und Serv. auct. XII 169), 44f. (Frg. 9: Paulus 82 L. *flaminius camillus,* von Strzelecki, Suppl. 55, Ateius Capito zugeschrieben; vgl. Serv. auct. XI 543), 46 (Frg. 15: Paulus 101 L. *inarculum,* vgl. Serv. auct. IV 137).

[32]) Vgl. Peter, Quaest. pontif. 15f., 20f.; Rowoldt, Libr. pontif. 27f.

[33]) Ich sehe keinen Grund, mit F. Schulz, Geschichte der römischen Rechtswissenschaft (Weimar 1961), 141f., diese Tradition als „eine verfehlte geschichtliche Kombination des Pomponius oder seiner Quelle" zu bezeichnen. Diesen Schluß begründet er durch folgende Beweisführung: „Capito hat auf dem Gebiete des Privatrechts nur Unbedeutendes geleistet, die Rechtsschulen des 1. Jahrhunderts beschränkten sich aber auf das Zivilrecht." Der erste Satz trifft zu (vgl. aber Gellius X 20, 2, der Capito *publici privatique iuris peritissimum* nennt), der andere viel weniger. Masurius Sabinus hat sich auf dem Gebiete des Staats- und Sakralrechtes eifrig betätigt, und mindestens in dieser Hinsicht ist er als ein Nachfolger des Capito anzusehen.

[34]) F. P. Bremer, Iurisprudentiae antehadrianae quae supersunt II 1 (Lipsiae 1901), 331f.; A. M. Honoré, Gaius (Oxford 1962), 22.

[35]) C. Atei Capitonis Fragmenta (Lipsiae 1967), XIX f.

behandelte dort das Personenrecht und die Gewaltverhältnisse[36]); er muß
von dem *manus*-Erwerb gesprochen haben. Dies war aber nicht nur ein Teil
des *ius civile*, sondern auch, besonders was die *confarreatio* und die Flaminenehe
anbelangt, ein Teil des *ius pontificium*; also steht nichts der Annahme im Wege,
daß Sabinus seine Darstellung dieses Sachverhalts aus den Büchern des Ateius
Capito über das Pontifikalrecht entlehnt hat.

So sind wir imstande, die Überlieferungstradition und die Bedeutung der
einzelnen Schlüsselphrasen zu beleuchten: Zuerst noch einmal die Reihenfolge
usu, farre(o), coemptione. Da uns diese Reihenfolge sowohl in der juristischen
(Gaius) wie auch der antiquarischen (Servius auctus) Tradition begegnet, muß
sie auf den gemeinsamen Nenner, d. h. Ateius Capito, zurückgeführt werden.
Die Gründe für diese überraschende Sequenz sind nicht schwer zu erahnen:
Es ist eine streng juristische, nicht eine religiöse Klassifikation. Durch *usus*
wird die *manus* ganz unmerkbar, nur tatsächlich, ohne irgendeinen rechtlichen
Akt erworben. Die *confarreatio* ist eine religiöse Zeremonie, aber rechtlich ist sie
eine Anomalie; sie ist nach Kaser[37]) „das einzige Rechtsinstitut, das die privat-
rechtlichen Wirkungen ausschließlich aus der rein sakralen Form schöpft".
Sie war auch, jedenfalls in der frühen Republik, ein patrizisches Rechtsinstitut;
es scheint, daß sogar in der ciceronischen Zeit Plebeier untereinander die kon-
farreierte Ehe nicht eingehen konnten[38]). Unter diesen Umständen erscheint
die *coemptio*, der feierliche Akt *per aes et libram*, als, juristisch gesehen, der
Hauptmodus des *manus*-Erwerbes. Für einen Kompilator lag es also sehr nahe,
die *coemptio* und die *conventio in manum* zu verschmelzen.

Auf welche Weise ist aber die abweichende Reihenfolge in der Glossa Montecassinensis — *usu, coemptione, farre* — zu erklären? Vielleicht sollten wir die
Antwort in der Lemmaüberschrift *confarreatis nuptiis* suchen: der Haupt-
gegenstand dieses Stichwortes, die *confarreatio*, wurde von dem zweiten an den
letzten, mehr hervorgehobenen Platz gerückt. Übrigens sieht diese Überschrift
wie ein später Zusatz oder ein Fall der Mißlemmatisierung aus. In Festus und
Paulus sind die Überschriften keine gesonderten Titel (wie *confarreatis nuptiis*
in dieser Glosse); sie bilden vielmehr den Satzanfang. Es ist also vielleicht
nicht allzu abenteuerlich vorzuschlagen, daß der Text Servius auctus ad Georg.
I 31 (= Glossa Montecassinensis) ursprünglich zu einem anderen Lemma gehörte.
Verrius Flaccus und Festus haben von den *tres modi* der *conventio in manum*
(bzw. der *nuptiae*) sicherlich an mehreren Stellen gehandelt; es ist durchaus
möglich, daß ihre Werke die Stichwörter *coemptio* (oder *coemptione*) und *conventio in manum* (oder desgleichen[39])) enthielten. In der Tat hat Lindsay
dem Festus das Lemma *comtionalis (coemptionalis) senex* revindiziert[40]). Das
Stichwort *coemptio* würde in der Reihe *conciliatrix, conventae condicio, caelibari*

---

[36]) Schulz, Geschichte, 186ff.
[37]) Das altrömische ius, 343.
[38]) Watson, The Law of Persons, 23f.
[39]) Vielleicht *in manum conventio*, vgl. Festus 242 L.: *Remancipatam Gallus
Aelius esse ait, quae mancipata sit ab eo, cui in manum convenerit.*
[40]) Glossaria Latina 3, 175.

hasta, cingillo, camelis virginibus, cinxiae Iunonis und *cumerum*[41]) seinen Platz leicht finden. Für dieses Stichwort können wir die traditionelle Reihenfolge der Modi der *manus*-Übertragung ohne Weiteres annehmen.

Es bleibt noch die Divergenz zwischen *farre* und *farreo* zu erklären. Das Substantiv *farreum* hat sich aus dem Adj. *farreum* (sc. *libum*) entwickelt; *farre* erscheint also als eine ältere Form. Sie begegnet uns in den XII Tafeln[42]), Dionysios von Halikarnassos II 25 spricht sehr charakteristisch von der κοινωνία τοῦ φαρρός, und das Wort erscheint bei den Dichtern im Zusammenhang mit den Opferhandlungen[43]). Ich möchte also *farre* als die ursprüngliche Lesung annehmen; bei Gaius wurde sie in Anlehnung an die folgenden Worte *genus sacrificii, quod Ioui Farreo fit, in quo farreus panis adhibetur*, durch *farreum* verdrängt. Die Lesung *farreum* in der gaianischen Tradition beruht also wohl nur auf einem Abschreibfehler.

E. Volterra[44]) hat in seinen gelehrten Nuove ricerche sulla ,conventio in manum' die Vermutung ausgesprochen: „non sembra assurdo congetturare che Servio aveva attinto talune notizie (d. h. seine Angaben über die *coemptio* und *confarreatio*) da un testo giuridico". Der vorliegende Aufsatz ist ein Versuch, diese Vermutung zu belegen. Wir haben die Quellen des Servius und des Gaius bis auf Ateius Capito zurückverfolgt; können wir nun, über Capito hinauf, unseren Blick auf die republikanischen Gelehrten lenken? Es ist mehrfach beobachtet worden, daß das System des Masurius Sabinus von dem des Q. Mucius Scaevola hergeleitet war; ob aber Scaevola die drei Modi des *manus*-Erwerbes gerade auf eine ähnliche Weise wie Gaius (und vermutlich Sabinus und Capito) behandelte, vermögen wir nicht sagen. Ein Anhaltspunkt wird allerdings durch die schon oben besprochene Stelle des Gellius (X 15, 1—18) gegeben. Gellius führt Masurius Sabinus und Fabius Pictor namentlich an, d. h. seine unmittelbare Vorlage sowie den ältesten von Sabinus erwähnten Schriftsteller. Sabinus hat sehr wahrscheinlich außer Fabius auch die Verfasser der übrigen *libri, qui de sacerdotibus publicis compositi sunt*, genannt, vor allem Ateius Capito, dessen Bücher er ausgeschrieben hat und dem er auch seine Nachricht über Fabius Pictor verdankt haben wird. Auf diese Weise reicht unsere Quellenkette bis zu Fabius Pictor und dessen Iuris pontificii libri. Dies betrifft nur den Sachverhalt, die *caerimoniae* des *flamen Dialis* und die damit zusammenhängende *confarreatio*, nicht aber die Formulierungen. Daß also die XII Tafeln sich mit allen drei Modi des *manus*-Erwerbes beschäftigt haben, bleibt eine anziehende Idee; die Reihenfolge *usu, farre, coemptione* läßt sich jedoch über Ateius Capito hinaus nicht zurückverfolgen[45]).

---

[41]) Paulus 54—55 L. Alle diese Stichwörter sind von Strzelecki (Suppl. Frg. 1—2, 9—11, 19) Ateius Capito revindiziert worden.

[42]) FIRA I 33 (Tab. III 4).

[43]) Vgl. Thes. Ling. Lat. und Oxford Latin Dictionary s. v.

[44]) Nuove ricerche 300 in Anm.

[45]) Für stilistische Verbesserung meines Textes bin ich Herrn Christoph Konrad sehr dankbar.

15

Der Senat und die Vereine

Das Problem des Übergangs von dem Vereinsrecht, das zur Zeit
der Republik gegolten hatte, zur kaiserzeitlichen Vereinsordnung
wurde zum Gegenstand der Untersuchungen mancher hervorragenden
Gelehrten[1]; viele Grundfragen sind aber bisher ungeklärt geblieben. Nicht anders verhält sich die Sache mit dem Senatsbeschluß
vom J. 64, der als der Anfangspunkt der Entwicklung des spätrepublikanischen Vereinsrechts allgemein anerkannt ist. Nach der Lehre
Mommsens[2] wurde das Senatsconsult gegen die, meistens aus Sklaven
und Freigelassenen zusammengesetzten Vereine gerichtet, die sogenannten collegia compitalicia, die für den Larenkultus sorgten und
alljährlich zu Ehren dieser Gottheiten auf Kreuzwegen Spiele veranstalteten. Cohn und Waltzing[3] haben diese These Mommsens einer
scharfen Kritik unterzogen; der Senatsbeschluß bezog sich ihrer
Ansicht nach nicht auf die collegia compitalicia, deren Existenz
sie bestritten, sondern auf die Berufsvereine, von denen nur die
wenigen ausdrücklich genannten verschont werden sollten. Es ist zu
betonen, daß die Grundlage für diese, der Mommsenschen so entgegengesetzte Auffassung derselbe Text bildet, auf welchen sich die
These Mommsens stützt: der Bericht von Asconius in seinem Kommentar zu Ciceros Reden Pro Cornello und In Pisonem. In den letzten
Jahren hat man versucht, mit Hilfe des neuen epigraphischen Materials die Schwierigkeiten der Interpretation des Asconiustextes zu
überwinden. Die Beschäftigung mit den inschriftlichen Quellen hat
zur Wiederaufnahme der Lehre Mommsens geführt[4], aber wie wir sehen
werden, erwecken auch Konstruktionen neuerer Forscher Bedenken.
Unter diesen Umständen scheint eine neue Untersuchung auf diesem
Gebiet notwendig: sie kann nicht nur ein neues Licht auf die uns
hier interessierende Frage werden, sondern dadurch auch unsere
Kenntnis der Sozialgeschichte der Spätrepublik bereichern.

Prüfen wir nun die Quellen!

Cicero, In L. Pisonem (ed. R. Klotz) 8:

Cuius fuit initium ludi compitalicii, tum primum facti post
L. Iulium et Q. Marcium consules, contra auctoritatem huius ordi-

nis: quos Q. Metellus - facio iniuriam fortissimo viro mortuo, qui illum, cuius paucos pares haec civitas tulit, cum hac importuna belua conferam - sed ille designatus consul, quum quidam tribunus plebis suo auxilio magistros ludos contra senatus consultum facere iussisset, privatus fieri vetuit, atque id, quod nondum potestate poterat, obtinuit auctoritate. Tu, quum in Kalendas Ianuarias compitaliorum dies incidisset, Sex. Clodium, qui numquam antea praetextatus fuisset, ludos facere et praetextatum volitare passus es, hominem impurum ac non modo facie, sed etiam oculo tuo dignissimum.

Asconius (ed. Clark, 6-7) ad loc.:

L. Iulio C. Marcio consulibus quos et ipse Cicero supra memoravit senatus consulto collegia sublata sunt quae adversus rem publicam videbantur esse constituta[5]. Solebant autem magistri collegiorum ludos facere, sicut magistri vicorum[6] faciebant Compitalicios praetextati, qui ludi sublatis collegiis discussi sunt. Post VI deinde annos quam sublata erant P. Clodius tr. pl. lege·lata restituit collegia. Invidiam ergo et crimen restitutorum confert in Pisonem, quod, cum consul esset, passus sit ante quam lex ferretur facere Kal. Ianuar. praetextatum ludos Sex. Clodium. Is fuit familiarissimus Clodii et operarum Clodianarum dux, quo auctore postea illato ab eis corpore Clodii curia cum eo incensa est. Quos ludos tunc quoque fieri prohibere temptavit L. Ninnius tr. pl. Ante biennium autem quam restituerentur collegia, Q. Metellus Celer consul designatus magistros vicorum[6] ludos Compitalicios facere prohibuerat, ut Cicero tradit, quamvis auctore tribuno plebis fierent ludi; cuius tribuni nomen adhuc non inveni.

Cicero, Pro Cornelio (ed. Clark) 75:

Quid ego nunc tibi argumentis respondeam posse fieri ut alius aliquis Cornelius sit qui habeat Philerotem servum; volgare nomen esse Philerotis, Cornelios[7] vero ita multos ut iam etiam collegium constitutum sit?

Asconius (ed. Clark, 75) ad loc.:

Frequenter tum etiam coetus factiosorum hominum sine publica auctoritate malo publico fiebant: propter quod postea collegia et S. C. et pluribus legibus sunt sublata praeter pauca atque certa quae utilitas civitatis desiderasset, sicut fabrorum lictorumque[8].

Es besteht jetzt wohl kein Zweifel darüber, daß der von Asconius in In. Pis. erwähnte Senatsbeschluß aus dem J. 64 stammte;
auf dieses Jahr weisen sowohl sachliche wie paläographische Gründe[9]. Man kann sich fragen, ob Asconius auch im Kommentar zu der
Rede Pro Cornelio von demselben Senatsconsult spricht. An dieser
letzteren Stelle steht die Abkürzung S.C.; je nach der angenommenen
Lösung s(enatus) c(onsulto) oder s(enatus) c(onsultis)[10] hat man
diese Frage bejaht[11] oder negiert[12]. Dies kann aber nicht den Anfangspunkt der Analyse des Asconiustextes bilden; es scheint, daß
die Frage, wie diese Abkürzung zu lesen ist, die Aufmerksamkeit
der Forscher von einer anderen, viel wichtigeren Sache abgelenkt
hat. Man muß zuerst untersuchen, in welchem Zusammenhang die beiden Berichte Asconius' miteinander stehen. Unserer Ansicht nach
bildet die Antwort auf diese Frage nicht nur den Kernpunkt der
Diskussion über das Senatsconsult vom J. 64, sondern ist auch überhaupt für die Beurteilung der Entwicklung des Vereinsrechts in den
letzten Jahren der Republik von entscheidender Bedeutung. Der besseren Anschaulichkeit halber geben wir unten die beiden uns hier
interessierenden Stellen des Asconius nebeneinander wieder:

In Pis. S. 6:
L. Iulio C. Marcio consulibus...
senatus consulto collegia sublata sunt quae adversus rem
publicam videbantur esse constituta.

In Corn. S. 75:
Frequenter tum etiam coetus factiosorum hominum sine publica
auctoritate malo publico fiebant:
propter quod postea collegia et
S. C. et pluribus legibus sunt
sublata praeter pauca atque certa quae utilitas civitatis desiderasset, sicut fabrorum lictorumque.

Es ist vor allem zu bemerken, daß wir, gleichgültig ob wir
die von Asconius in In Pis. und in In Corn. erwähnten Senatsbeschlüsse für ein und dasselbe Senatsconsult halten oder nicht,
nicht ohne weiteres berechtigt sind, den ganzen Inhalt der Stelle
aus dem Kommentar zur Corneliana dem Senatsbeschluß vom J. 64 zuzuschreiben. Dies würde bedeuten, daß die von Asconius angedeuteten weiteren leges nichts Neues eingeführt, sondern nur die Vorschriften des Senatsbeschlusses vom J. 64 wiederholt haben. Diese
unwahrscheinliche These wurde aber erstaunlicherweise zur herrschenden Meinung von drei Generationen von Gelehrten, wie aus den

unten angeführten Worten Mommsens, Waltzings und De Robertis' klar
hervorgeht:

Mommsen, De collegiis 74: Ne tamen hoc SCto (d.h. aus dem
J. 64) omnia collegia peraeque dissoluta putes, excepta sunt certa
quaedam quae publicam utilitatem haberent.

Waltzing, Étude I 106: C'était (d. h. das Senatsconsult aus
dem J. 64) une mesure générale: les collèges épargnés formaient
une si minime exception que le Sénat les désigna nominativement.

De Robertis, Dir. ass. 93: (das Senatsconsult vom J. 64 war)
un provvedimento generale ... che... soppresse tutti le associa-
zioni, eccetto alcune poche specificamente indicate.

Die obengenannten Gelehrten haben aber gewiß nicht daran ge-
dacht, welche weitreichende Folgerungen sich aus ihren Worten ergeben: wörtlich genommen haben sie anstatt der lex Iuliä das Senatsconsult vom J. 64 zum Grundstein der kaiserlichen Vereinsordnung
gemacht.

Unsere Theorie, die sich von der bisher herrschenden Meinung
grundsätzlich unterscheidet, können wir folgendermaßen formulieren:
1) auf das senatus consultum de collegiis vom J. 64 beziehen sich
unmittelbar nur die Bemerkungen des Asconius im Kommentar zu der
Rede In Pisonem; 2) der Kommentar zu der Rede Pro Cornelio enthält
dagegen einen kurzen Abriß der Entwicklung des Vereinsrechts von
dem Senatsbeschluß vom J. 64 bis zur Gesetzgebung des Augustus
einschließlich.

Dieser Leitfaden unserer Erörterungen muß jetzt etwas ausführ-
licher begründet werden.

Schon auf den ersten Blick sieht man klar, daß Asconius an den
beiden Stellen sich der verschiedenen Terminologie bedient, daß sie
verschiedenartig stilisiert sind.

Im Kommentar zur Pisoniana lesen wir, daß nur diese Vereine
aufgelöst worden sind, die für das Staatswohl gefährlich waren
(quae adversus rem publicam videbantur esse constituta). Man erin-
nere sich in diesem Zusammenhang an die von Gaius überlieferte Bestimmung des Zwölftafelgesetzes: his (sodalibus) potestatem facit
lex (XII Tab.) pactionem quam velint sibi ferre, dum ne quid ex
publica lege corrumpant[13]; der Senat hat im J. 64 augenscheinlich
dieselben rechtlichen Möglichkeiten ausgenutzt, wie im J. 186 während der Bacchanalien-Affäre[14]. Der Senatsbeschluß änderte gar
nichts an der bestehenden Vereinsgesetzgebung, er schuf keine neuen

Regeln der Staatspolitik bezüglich der Vereine. Der Senat wirkte
nur auf Grund seiner Befugnis, für die Sicherheit der Republik
zu sorgen, und in seinem Beschlusse stellte er fest, daß eine Anzahl der Kollegien adversus rem publicam gegründet worden waren.
Er empfahl der Magistratur, diese staatsgefährliche Kategorie der
Kollegien aufzulösen.

Im Kommentar zu der Rede für Cornelius legt Asconius das
Schwergewicht nicht auf die aufgehobenen Vereine, sondern auf
jene, die verschont wurden. Bei dem Tatbestand, der im Kommentar
zur Pisoniana geschildert wird, sollte ein Verein, um verschont
zu werden, nur nicht adversus rem publicam sein; in In Pis. betont
Asconius dagegen, daß dies zur Verschonung nicht genügte: um weiterbestehen zu können mußte jeder Verein seine Nützlichkeit für
den Staat nachweisen. Es ist wohl verständlich, daß Asconius Beispiele solcher Kollegien gibt und daß dieselben verhältnismäßig
nicht zahlreich waren.

Der Ausdruck utilitas civitatis war in dem oben angedeuteten
Sinn der republikanischen Staatstheorie fremd. Es ist zwar offensichtlich, daß die ideologische Terminologie des Prinzipats vieles aus der politischen Sprache der ausgehenden Republik übernommen hat[15], es ist aber ebenso klar, daß die alten termini sehr
oft neue Bedeutung erhielten. Offizielle Dokumente und literari-
sche Texte aus der Zeit der Republik sprechen zwar von der utilitas publica, aber der Ausdruck wird in der Regel nur als allgemeiner Begriff verwendet und nicht als eine streng präzisierte
juristische Regel[16].

Man kann zwar behaupten, daß wir an der hier in Rede stehenden Stelle mit einer gewissen Modernisierung zu tun haben, indem
Asconius Anschauungen seiner Epoche in die Zeiten der Republik
verlegt hat[17]. Diese These ist zwar möglich, aber unbeweisbar;
sie würde sonst unsere Ansicht bestätigen, daß der Senatsbeschluß
vom J. 64 den Gedanken der utilitas civitatis nicht enthalten hat.
Es ist aber viel wahrscheinlicher, daß Asconius den Begriff der
utilitas civitatis aus einer der von ihm erwähnten leges geschöpft
hat. Es wird von ihm im Kommentar zur Corneliana eine lange legislative Tätigkeit geschildert: den Ausgangspunkt bildet die Ver-
mehrung von coetus factiosorum hominum, d. h. von Vereinen, die
adversus rem publicam videbantur esse constituta; gegen diese
Organisationen richteten sich aufeinanderfolgende Senatsbeschlüsse

und Gesetze, die die Vereinsfreiheit immer mehr beschränkten, bis schließlich nur diese Vereine geblieben sind, quae utilitas civitatis desiderasset.

Aus den obigen Ausführungen ergibt sich zugleich die Antwort auf die Frage, wie die Abkürzung S.C. in In Corn. zu lesen ist: als einzige, durch sachliche Gründe berechtigte Lösung wird man s(enatus) c(onsultis) und nicht s(enatus) c(onsulto) anerkennen müssen.

Was für Senatsbeschlüsse und Gesetze hatte Asconius im Sinn? Man kann an folgende Akte denken: 1) senatus consultum de collegiis vom J. 64; 2) senatus consultum vom J. 56 (ut sodalitates decuriatique discederent); 3) lex Licinia de sodaliciis vom J. 55; 4) lex Iulia (von Caesar oder Augustus)[18].

Das Senatsconsult vom J. 64 war unserer Interpretation gemäß ausschließlich gegen die Vereine gerichtet, die adversus rem publicam videbantur esse constituta. Der Senatsbeschluß vom J. 56 und die lex Licinia bezogen sich auf die von Clodius gestifteten Vereine, bzw. auf die Vereinigungen, die die Wahlbestechungen organisierten. In keinem von diesen Akten finden wir - soweit wir auf Grund der uns überlieferten Quellen darüber urteilen können - irgendeine Berufung auf utilitas civitatis oder utilitas publica. Dieser Begriff als Grundgedanke für Umgestaltung des Vereinsrechts ist erst durch die lex Iulia eingeführt worden. Dieser Schluß ergibt sich zwingend aus der bekannten Inschrift des collegium symphoniacorum[19]: Dis Manibus collegio symphoniacorum. Qui sacris publicis praestu sunt, quibus senatus c(oire) c(ollegium) c(onstituere)[20] permisit e lege Iulia ex auctoritate Augusti ludorum causa.

Das Kollegium der symphoniaci ist also ludorum causa autorisiert worden; seine Nützlichkeit beruhte offenbar auf der Tätigkeit der symphoniaci während der Spiele. Nicht anders wird sich die Sache mit den von Asconius erwähnten fabri und lictores verhalten. Was die lictores anbetrifft, ist ihre Nützlichkeit für den Staat ganz augenscheinlich[21], aber auch die collegia fabrum erhielten die staatliche Autorisation wegen der von ihnen ausgeübten Funktionen der Feuerlöschmannschaft[22].

Die oben vorgeschlagene These wird noch deutlicher durch einige Äußerungen der späteren Juristen bestätigt, die in der Stilisierung und Terminologie eine überraschende Ähnlichkeit mit der hier analysierten Stelle des Asconius aufweisen:

Caius, Dig.3,4,1: _Paucis_... _in causis_ concessa sunt huiusmodi corpora und weiter: item Romae _collegia certa_ sunt, quorum corpus senatus consultis atque constitutionibus principalibus confirmatum est, veluti pistorum et quorundum aliorum, et naviculariorum, qui et in provinciis sunst. (Asconius: _collegia_... _pauca atque certa_).

Callistratus, Dig.27,1,17,2: Eos, qui in corporibus sunt, veluti _fabrorum_, immunitatem habere dicimus... (Asconius: collegia ... sicut _fabrorum_ lictorumque).

Callistratus, Dig.50,6,6,12: Quibusdam collegiis vel corporibus, quibus ius coeundi lege permissum est, immunitas tribuitur: scilicet eis collegiis vel corporibus, in quibus artificii sui causa unusquisque adsumitur, ut _fabrorum_ corpus est et sie quae eandem rationem originiis habent, id est idcirco instituta sunt, ut necessariam operam _publicis utilitatibus_ exhiberent. (Asconius: collegia... quae _utilitas civitatis_ desiderasset).

Die juristische und terminologische Übereinstimmung zwischen Asconius, Gaius und Callistratus kann am besten durch die Annahme einer gemeinsamen Quelle erklärt werden. Als solche gemeinsame Quelle kann nur die lex Iulia, das Grundgesetz des kaiserzeitlichen Vereinssystems, angesehen werden.

Dieses Gesetz enthielt wahrscheinlich nicht das Verzeichnis der autorisierten Vereine, sondern vielmehr die Aufzählung der causae, auf Grund deren die staatliche Genehmigung erteilt werden konnte[23]. Beispielsweise wurden aber wohl einige Kategorien der Kollegien angeführt, jedenfalls sicher die fabri. Die Tatsache, daß die fabri bei Asconius und an zwei verschiedenen Stellen des Callistratus in einem ähnlichen Kontext erscheinen, wird schwerlich auf einem Zufall beruhen[24]. Asconius betont nur den Grundgedanken der lex Iulia: Rücksicht auf die utilitas civitatis[25]; das geltende Vereinsrecht wurde aber dann durch die sich an das Iulische Gesetz anknüpfenden Senatsbeschlüsse und Kaisererlässe weiterentwickelt, und dieser Tatbestand wird von Gaius und Callistratus geschildert. Es ist also wohl möglich und sogar wahrscheinlich, daß sie nicht unmittelbar aus der lex Iulia geschöpft haben, sondern durch Vermittlung der von Gaius erwähnten senatus consulta und constitutiones; diese aber enthielten einige aus diesem Gesetz stammende Formeln und Ausdrücke, wie die Berufung auf die utilitas civitatis bzw. utilitas publica, oder die Erwähnung der collegia fabrorum.

Die bisherigen Erwägungen haben zur Rekonstruktion der Entwicklung des Vereinsrechts in den letzten Jahren der Republik geführt; es ist nun notwendig, das senatus consultum vom J. 64 einer weiteren Analyse zu unterziehen.

Welches war also im einzelnen der Inhalt dieses Senatsbeschlusses? Eine Antwort auf diese Frage kann uns nur eine kritische Erörterung der uns von Asconius in In Pis. 6-7 C überlieferten Nachrichten geben.

Zunächst ist zu bemerken, daß die übliche Bezeichnung senatus consultum de collegiis den wesentlichen Inhalt des Beschlusses nicht adäquat wiedergibt. Der Senatsbeschluß - wie ihn Cicero darstellt und Asconius erläutert - betraf nämlich wenigstens zwei Probleme: erstens verfügte er die Auflösung der Kollegien, quae adversus rem publicam videbantur esse constituta, zweitens verbot er die Veranstaltung und Abhaltung der alljährlichen Spiele auf Kreuzwegen, der ludi compitalicii. Aus den Worten Asconius' "qui ludi sublatis collegiis discussi sunt" könnte man zwar schließen, daß die Aufhebung der ludi lediglich eine Folge der Auflösung der Kollegien war, aber die Worte Ciceros selbst (ludi compitalicii tum primum facti... contra auctoritatem huius ordinis und weiter ...tribunus plebis suo auxilio magistros ludos contra senatus consultum facere iussisset), lassen keinen Zweifel über den wahren Sachverhalt bestehen[26].

Jedenfalls standen diese beiden Faktoren - Kollegien und ludi - miteinander in einem gewissen Zusammenhang. Der wichtigste Punkt ist hier die Interpretation des Satzes: solebant autem magistri collegiorum ludos facere sicut magistri vicorum faciebant Compitalicios praetextati, qui ludi sublatis collegiis discussi sunt, den man je nach der angenommenen Interpunktion verschieden verstehen kann. Bei rein theoretischer Prüfung der Texte Ciceros und des Asconius ergeben sich nämlich mehrere Interpretationsmöglichkeiten: 1) wenn wir, wie die Mehrzahl der Herausgeber, in dem oben angeführten Satz zwei Beistriche, nach facere und nach faciebant, setzen, so bekommen wir, daß in die toga praetexta gekleidete magistri collegiorum die ludi compitalicii zusammen mit magistri vicorum veranstalteten. Hier sind zwei weitere Varianten möglich: diese magistri collegiorum konnten sein: a) magistri spezieller, zur Pflege des Larenkultus und zur Veranstaltung von Spielen berufener Vereinigungen, der sogenannten collegia compita-

licia; b) magistri verschiedener, bei der Veranstaltung der ludi
compitalicii mitwirkender Handwerkergenossenschaften. Die erste
Variante lag der Theorie Mommsens zugrunde[27], für die zweite Möglichkeit hat sich dagegen Waltzing ausgesprochen[28]; 2) setzen wir
jedoch nur einen Beistrich, und zwar nach facere, so ist anzunehm-
men, daß die magistri der Kollegien irgendwelche nicht näher
bezeichnete Spiele organisierten, hingegen die compitalicia nur
von den magistri vicorum veranstaltet wurden[29].

An dieser Stelle ist zu bemerken, daß der Text die Möglichkeit der Veranstaltung von ludi compitalicii allein von den magistri collegiorum nicht zuläßt. Cicero berichtet nämlich, daß
schon nach dem J. 64, also nach Auflösung der Kollegien und dem
Verbot der Abhaltung von kompitalischen Spielen, magistri existierten, die sich bemühten, die ludi wieder einzuführen. Dies konnten
natürlich keine magistri der Kollegien sein; Asconius identifiziert
sie denn auch ausdrücklich mit den magistri vicorum[30].

Man muß es klar heraussagen, daß der Text des Asconius keine
Grundlage für eine eindeutige Lösung dieses Problems bietet. Besonders viele Mißverständnisse entstanden im Zusammenhang mit der
Frage der sogenannten collegia compitalicia. Da gerieten die zwei
großen Autoritäten Mommsen und Waltzing aneinander, und es entbrannte sodann unter späteren Forschern eine heiße Polemik.

Man muß bedenken, daß die Antwort auf die Frage, ob Kollegien
dieser Art tatsächlich existierten, für die Darstellung des ganzen
Problems der Lage der römischen Kollegien in der Mitte des ersten
Jahrhunderts keineswegs ohne Bedeutung ist. Denn wenn wir uns der
These Mommsens anschließen, so müssen wir annehmen, daß der Senats-
beschluß vor allem gegen jene collegia compitalicia lediglich von
Mommsen ersonnen sind, so sind die aufgelösten Vereine insbesondere
unter den verschiedenartigen Handwerkervereinigungen zu suchen.
Und eine solche Lösung wirft natürlich ein anderes Licht auf das
Verhalten der römischen Handwerker und ihrer Organisationen in den
heißen Jahren der Verschwörung Catilinas und der Tätigkeit des
Clodius. Unter diesen Umständen erscheint eine möglichst allseiti-
ge Erörterung dieser Frage unerläßlich. Es ist vor allem - auch
zum Zweck der Verifikation der schon durchgeführten Analyse des
Textes des Asconius - unbedingt notwendig, nach anderen Quellen zu
suchen. Besonders große Bedeutung haben epigraphische Denkmäler,
die, wie z. B. die neuen Inschriften aus Minturnae, Mommsen und

Waltzing noch nicht bekannt waren.

Aufklärung erfordern vor allem der Charakter der ludi compitalicii und der Zusammenhang, der zwischen ihnen und der Organisation der einzelnen vici bestand. Erst auf diesem Grund wird man etwas Konkreteres über den wichtigsten Gegenstand der gegenwärtigen Erwägungen, die collegia compitalicia, sagen können.

Ludi compitalicii. Alljährlich veranstaltete man auf Kreuzungen von Wegen und Rainen öffentliche Spiele zu Ehren der Laren als Schutzgötter der Arbeit des Landmannes. Auf einer solchen Kreuzung, die die Bezeichnung compitum trug, befand sich gewöhnlich eine Kapelle – sacellum –, ein Mittelpunkt des Larenkultus. Daher stammt die Bezeichnung der dort verehrten Laren: Lares compitales, des Feiertages: Compitalia und der Spiele: Ludi compitalicii. Es war dies also, wenigstens ursprünglich, ein ausgesprochen bäuerlicher Feiertag; auf dem Gebiet der Stadt Rom nahm er jedoch mit der Zeit einen anderen Charakter an, indem er speziell die Handwerk betreibende Bevölkerung der Hauptstadt heranzog. Varro bezeichnet die Compitalia als feriae conceptivae[32], beweglicher Feiertag. Dieser fiel in der Regel in die ersten Tage des Januar und wurde jedesmal nach den Saturnalien vom Prätor bestimmt. Der Kult der Lares compitales war hauptsächlich in den niedrigeren Schichten der Bevölkerung verbreitet. Auf dem Land war es vor allem ein Feiertag des unfreien Gesindes[33].

Dieser Kult hatte naturgemäß zugleich einen territorialen Charakter. Von diesem Gesichtspunkt gesehen bezeichnete der Terminus compitum nicht nur eine Straßenkreuzung, sondern auch das Gebiet, dessen Einwohner gemeinsam die Laren verehrten und gemeinsam an den Spielen zu ihren Ehren teilnahmen. Was für ein Gebiet ein solches compitum umfaßte, ist nicht ganz klar; die Frage der Einteilung des republikanischen Italiens in pagi, vici, fora, conciliabula und compita, ihres Verhältnisses zueinander, ihrer inneren Organisation und ihres rechtlichen Status, gehört übrigens zu den schwierigsten Problemen bei der Erforschung der Verfassungsgeschichte der Republik. Dieses Thema kann an dieser Stelle nur flüchtig berührt werden; aber auch hier muß man trachten, sich ein möglichst klares Bild zu verschaffen; ohne Erörterung der Frage des Zusammenhanges von compitum, vicus und pagus ist das Rätsel der collegia compitalicia nicht zu lösen.

Compitum. Man hat bemerkt, daß die innere Organisation der
pagi und vici in einem gewissen Sinn der Organisation der römischen
Kollegien der Handwerker und Kaufleute und den religiösen Kollegien
entspricht[34]. An der Spitze der pagi und vici standen - ebenso wie
in den Kollegien - magistri (einer oder mehrere), sie besaßen oft
eigene Statuten (pactiones und leges paganae), die ihre inneren
Angelegenheiten regelten, erließen für die Einwohner des gegebenen
pagus oder vicus verbindliche Dekrete, hatten endlich die Fähig-
keit, Rechtshandlungen vorzunehmen; sie besaßen Vermögen, unter-
nahmen verschiedene Bauarbeiten, speziell die Renovierung von Tem-
peln, der Zentren ihres Kultes. Die Gesamtheit der Einwohner eines
pagus oder vicus entspricht damit der Gesamtheit der Mitglieder
eines Kollegiums. Die Stellung der magistri des pagus bekleideten
in der Regel ingenui; die magistri vicorum waren hingegen vorwiegend Freigelassene, ihnen halfen ministri, in der Regel Sklaven.
Es gab jedoch ziemlich oft Abweichungen von dem oben angegebenen
Schema. Der Wirkungskreis der einzelnen pagi und vici war übrigens
keineswegs gleich. Die Lage der pagi und vici war anders dort, wo
es keine städtische Organisation gab, wo sie - das ist verständlich - am intensivsten lebten und einen Teil der anderwo von
Städten erfüllten Aufgaben auf sich nahmen (ein klassisches Beispiel sind die pagi Campani), anders auf Territorien, die zu Städten gehörten, anders endlich in Rom selbst. Man nimmt gewöhnlich
an, daß der pagus eine größere territoriale Einheit bildete als
der vicus, d. h., daß der pagus mehrere vici umfaßte. Das war aber
keine allgemein bindende Regel. Es sind Fälle bekannt, in denen
ein pagus nur einen vicus enthielt oder einzelne vici überhaupt
außerhalb der pagi lagen, ohne zu irgendeinem von ihnen zu gehören[35].

Mommsen meinte, daß jedes compitum, mit dem Zentrum um das
sacellum der Laren, mehrere vici umfaßte. Über die Organisation
des Lareskultus schreibt er wie folgt: Cultores autem Larum compitalium constituere solebant collegium compitalicium[36]. Die Mitglieder eines solchen Kollegiums wählten eigene magistri, die
nicht mit den magistri der entsprechenden vici zu verwechseln sind.
Diese magistri sollten zusammen die ludi compitalicii veranstaltet haben.

In der Konstruktion Mommsens ist es jedoch nicht klar, ob zu
einem solchen Kollegium alle Einwohner der gegebenen vici oder nur

einige (cultores Larum) gehörten. Mommsen scheint zu dieser zweiten Möglichkeit zu neigen. Dann bleibt jedoch die rechtliche Lage
dieser Vereine weiterhin unklar.

Erwähnungen der collegia compitalicia befinden sich nach
Mommsen nicht nur bei Asconius; auch Cicero soll bei der Beschreibung der Bildung der Kollegien durch Clodius auf Grund seines den
Senatsbeschluß über die Kollegien vom J. 64 aufhebenden Gesetzes
vom J. 58 davon sprechen. Cicero schreibt nämlich u. a.: servorum
dilectus habebatur pro tribunali Aurelio nomine collegiorum cum
vicatim homines conscriberentur, decuriarentur[37], und an anderer
Stelle: cum in tribunali Aurelio conscribebas palam non modo liberos, sed etiam servos ex omnibus vicis concitatos[38]. Diese Vereine
bildeten sich also in den einzelnen vici, und es gehörten ihnen
vorwiegend Sklaven an, was tatsächlich dem Charakter des Kompitalkults gut entspricht. Cicero erwähnt zwar nirgends die Bezeichnung
"collegium compitalicium", es sieht aber tatsächlich nicht so aus,
als hätte Cicero hier gewöhnliche Handwerkerkollegien im Sinn gehabt. Die Kritik Waltzings ist hier also nicht gut begründet[39].
Einen entscheidenden Beweis des Bestehens dieser Kollegien und dessen, daß ihre Bezeichnung tatsächlich "collegium compitalicium"
lautete, hoffte aber Mommsen in der Inschrift CIL XI 1550 aus Faesulae zu finden, die jedoch schon aus der Kaiserzeit stammt: D.M.L.
Terentio Fido et Noviciae contubernali eius collegius compitalicius. Diese Inschrift bietet tatsächlich einen unwiderlegbaren Beweis, daß es in der Periode des Kaisertums (wahrscheinlich im
3. Jh.) in Faesulae eine Vereinigung gab, die collegius compitalicius genannt wurde. Wir wissen jedoch nicht, ob das Kollegium aus
Faesulae und die in Frage stehenden collegia compitalicia aus der
Zeit der Republik miteinander das Wesen oder nur den Namen gemeinsam hatten. Die zitierte Inschrift trennt vom Ende der Republik
ein genügend langer Zeitraum, um ähnliche Vorbehalte zu machen.
Das Kollegium aus Faesulae war, wie dies schon die Stilisierung
der Inschrift andeutet, wahrscheinlich ein Verein privater cultores oder ein Begräbnisverein[40]. Wie wir sehen werden, entspricht
das nicht ganz dem Wesen der collegia compitalicia, wenigstens in
der Auffassung Mommsens.

Wie wir gesehen haben, läßt sich der Text des Asconius auch
abweichend von der Theorie Mommsens, welche das Bestehen der collegia compitalicia annimmt, sinnvoll interpretieren; gegen diese

Theorie wurden jedoch auch gewisse sachliche Einwürfe erhoben.

So stellte Waltzing schon den ersten Punkt der Beweisführung Mommsens in Abrede, die Behauptung, daß compitum aus mehreren vici bestehe. Nach seiner Ansicht verhielt sich die Sache anders: der Terminus "compitum" war nur ein Synonym der Bezeichnung vicus, vicinitas[41]. Im J. 7 v. u. Z. führte Kaiser Augustus eine Reform der administrativen Einteilung Roms durch[42]: die Stadt wurde in 14 regiones (es verschwanden damals die alten montes und pagi urbani) eingeteilt, die wieder in kleinere territoriale Einheiten zerfielen. Suetonius nennt sie vici[43], Plinius bezeichnet sie ausdrücklich als compita Larum[44]. So ist also vicus hier gleich compitum. Tatsächlich erhielt damals jeder vicus ein eigenes sacellum, das Zentrum zugleich des Lareskults und des Kultus des Kaiserhauses. Augustus ließ auch das alte Amt der magistri vicorum bestehen; es wurden seit dieser Zeit e plebe cuiusque viciniae je vier gewählt[45]; ministri halfen ihnen, Sklaven. Zu ihren Obliegenheiten gehörte u. a. die Veranstaltung der von Augustus nach langer Unterbrechung erneuerten ludi compitalicii[46].

Die Tatsache, daß vicus und compitum fortan identisch waren, konnte vielleicht nur eine Neueinführung des Augustus sein, eine Möglichkeit, die Waltzing nicht wahrgenommen hat. Er war wahrscheinlich der Ansicht, daß die (zwar aus Pompeji und nicht aus Rom stammende) Inschrift CIL I^2 777=IV 66, welche eine Liste der magistri aus den Jahren 47 und 46 v.u.Z. enthält, die als mag(istri) vici et compiti bezeichnet sind, alle Zweifel zerstreuen muß. Es ist daher - so schloß er - unmöglich, daß auf dem Gebiet desselben vicus = compitum gleichzeitig voneinander unabhängige magistri vici und magistri eines collegium compitalicium tätig waren[47]. So existierten also nach Ansicht dieses Forschers diese Kollegien überhaupt nicht; die ludi compitalicii organisierten ganz einfach die magistri vicorum zusammen mit dem magistri verschiedener Handwerkergenossenschaften.

Die Wahl zwischen den Theorien Mommsens und Waltzings ist schwer: beide sind Beispiele eindringlicher Quelleninterpretation und entwickeln logisch die im Text des Asconius gegebenen Interpretationsmöglichkeiten. Unter diesen Umständen erscheint es notwendig, noch gewisse terminologische und insbesondere juristische Präzisierungen durchzuführen.

1) Waltzing behauptet, daß vicus dasselbe war wie compitum, Mommsen hingegen, daß compitum mehrere vici umfaßte. Es sind aber beide angeführten Behauptungen berechtigt. Es hängt davon ab, was wir unter compitum verstehen. Wenn es das Gebiet ist, dessen Einwohner zusammen die Lares anbeteten und ihre auf der Wegkreuzung stehende Kapelle betreuten, so folgt aus dieser Bezeichnung nicht, daß compitum dem vicus gleich sein mußte. Dies war nur in dem Fall, wenn, sofern man so sagen kann, der vicus die territoriale Basis des Kultes war; auf solche Beispiele beruft sich Waltzing, und so war es wahrscheinlich im republikanischen Rom und ganz bestimmt im kaiserlichen. Wenn jedoch nicht die Einwohner eines vicus, sondern die eines pagus gemeinsam die Laren anbeteten, dann war compitum in der oben angegebenen Bedeutung identisch mit pagus[48]. Es ist nicht ausgeschlossen, daß es sich in Kampanien so verhielt. Es ist ferner klar, daß der Begriff compitum im Gegensatz zu pagus oder vicus juristisch nichts besagt; compitum ist überhaupt keine administrative Einheit.

2) Keiner der bisherigen Forscher hat im Zusammenhang mit der Frage der collegia compitalicia über die rechtliche Stellung jener Beamten und Kollegien nachgedacht, die sich mit dem Larenkultus und speziell mit den Kompitalspielen befaßten. Man muß bedenken, daß die Compitalia kein Fest rein privaten Charakters waren. Ihr Termin wurde vom Prätor festgesetzt, und schon das allein machte sie zu einem der staatlich anerkannten Festtage und öffentlichen Spiele. Sie hatten also offiziellen, öffentlichen Charakter; die während dieser Feste den Laren dargebrachten Opfer waren nicht nur sacra privata[49]. Es war dies jedoch ein offizieller Charakter besonderer Art: im Gegensatz zu anderen Festen und Spielen, wie ludi magni oder capitolini, waren die ludi compitalicii eigentlich ein Ständefest, und zwar ein Fest des niedrigstens Volkes, vor allem der Freigelassenen und Sklaven. Die magistri, die diese Spiele veranstalteten, waren jedoch nichtsdestoweniger offizielle Persönlichkeiten, selbstverständlich nicht Repräsentanten des Staates, sondern nur des vicus oder pagus. Ein sichtbares Zeichen ihrer offiziellen Stellung war das Recht, die toga praetexta zu tragen. Asconius bezeichnet die magistri, welche den Spielen vorstanden, ausdrücklich als praetextati. In diesem Zusammenhang verdient eine Stelle des Livius Beachtung, die für die dort gegebene Schilderung der Rechte und Privilegien der niedrigsten Schichten und Stände

der römischen Gesellschaft sehr charakteristisch ist. Livius bei der Erzählung der Ereignisse des Jahres 195 schreibt: purpura viri utemur, praetextati in magistratibus, in sacerdotiis; liberi nostri praetextis purpura togis utentur; magistratibus in coloniis municipiisque, hic Romae infimo generi, m a g i s t r i s v i c o r u m , togae praetextae habendae ius permittemus[50]. Die Worte des Livius schildern zwar eher die Stimmung der Augusteischen Epoche, geben ein ideales Bild der realisierten concordia ordinum nicht nur von den Spitzen der Gesellschaft, sondern auch von ihrer untersten Schicht. Jeder Stand, selbst der niedrigste hat einen Platz im Staat und seinen Wirkungskreis. Was aber die Befugnisse der magistri vicorum betrifft, war dies bestimmt keine Innovation des Augustus; Augustus hat dieses Amt nur erneuert[51].

Hier liegt m. E. der schwächste Punkt der Hypothese Mommsens: die collegia compitalicia müßten, damit ihre magistri den Spielen vorstehen und vor allem die toga praetexta tragen könnten, Organisationen offiziellen Charakters gewesen sein. Und das hat Mommsen keinesfalls bewiesen. Das Kollegium aus Faesulae, auf das er sich beruft, war bestimmt keine offizielle Organisation.

Um ein mögliches Mißverständnis zu vermeiden, muß man sich dagegen verwahren, daß die obigen Bemerkungen lediglich das rechtliche Wesen der collegia compitalicia und ihren Zusammenhang mit den ludi betreffen; es erscheint hingegen nicht richtig, mit Waltzing ihre Existenz überhaupt in Abrede zu stellen.

3) Diese Befugnisse der magistri vicorum schließen jedoch die Möglichkeit nicht aus, daß in einzelnen Fällen der Kompitalkultus speziellen Organisationen übertragen wurde. Ohne auf den Streit um den Namen einzugehen - es waren nicht Kollegien jener Art, für die Mommsen sie hielt. Den Terminus "collegium" kann man nämlich verstehen a) als Versammlung einer gewissen Anzahl Personen mit den von ihnen gewählten Beamten, den magistri, an der Spitze. Die collegia compitalicia betrachtete Mommsen eben als solche Organisationen, als "wirkliche" Vereine; b) als ein Kollegium der Beamten, erwählten oder durch die Organisationen designierten, die nicht die technische Bezeichnung collegium trugen. Anders gesagt, es handelt sich um Unterscheidung zwischen m a g i s t r i   c o l l e g i o r u m   und   c o l l e g i a   m a g i s t r o r u m .

Obige Bemerkungen im Gedächtnis behaltend, können wir an die Erörterung der epigraphischen Quellen herantreten.

I. Unter den zahlreichen Inschriften, die sich auf die sogenannten magistri Campani beziehen[52], befindet sich u. a. folgende Inschrift[53]:

Pagus Herculaneus scivit a.d.X Termina[lia]. Conlegium, seive magistrei Iovei Compagei [sunt], utei in porticum paganam reficiendam pequniam consumerent ex lege pagana, arbitratu Cn. Laetori Cn. f. magistrei pagei; uteique ei conlegio, seive magistri sunt Iovei Compagei, locus in teatro esset tam quasei ludos fecissent (weiter folgen die Namen von 12 Freigelassenen – magistri und das Datum: die Namen der Konsuln des Jahres 94).

Diese Inschrift gestattet einige wichtige Beobachtungen zu machen:

1) Auf dem Gebiet des pagus Herculaneus[54] gab es neben dem Amt des magister (oder der magistri) des pagus noch andere magistri; zu den Obliegenheiten dieser letzteren gehörte die Betreuung des Heiligtums und des Kults der obersten Gottheit des pagus – des Juppiter Compages[55] sowie die Veranstaltung der Spiele, wahrscheinlich der paganalia.

2) Die Wendung conlegium seive magistrei Iovei Compagei beweist deutlich, daß dies nicht magistri irgendeiner Vereinigung von cultores waren, sondern daß eben sie selbst ein Kollegium von 12 Beamten bildeten[56].

3) Aus der Inschrift ergibt sich hingegen keinesfalls, daß diese magistri im Verhältnis zum magister pagi eine übergeordnete Stellung einnahmen (wie dies Hatzfeld[57] wollte), oder umgekehrt, daß sie diesem unmittelbar untergeordnet waren (wie Mommsen und Schulten behaupteten[58]).

4) Höchstwahrscheinlich war dieses Kollegium seive magistrei Iovei Compagei von der Pagusversammlung und ihren Beschlüssen (pagi scita[59]) abhängig. Diese magistri wurden wahrscheinlich alljährlich von der Gesamtheit der Einwohner des pagus gewählt und waren selbstverständlich vor dem pagus verantwortlich.

Heurgon hat also auch nicht recht, wenn er beweisen will, daß ursprünglich zwischen den Kollegien der magistri und der Organisation der pagi kein Zusammenhang bestand und daß diese magistri erst allmählich von den einzelnen pagi abhängig gemacht wurden[60]. Zwischen den Jahren 112/111, aus denen die ersten Inschriften der magistri Campani datieren, und dem Jahr 94, aus welchem die in Rede stehende Inschrift stammt, sind in der Lage der pagi Campani

keinerlei Veränderungen eingetreten, die eine solche Abhängigma-
chung bedingt hätten. Überdies verwechselt Heurgon ganz deutlich
die Abhängigkeit von Beamten, den magistri pagi, mit der Abhängigkeit vom ganzen pagus (d. h. seiner Versammlung), die zweifellos
vom Anfang des Erscheinens der Inschriften der magistri an bestand. Die Tatsache, daß wir in anderen von magistri Campani stammenden Inschriften einer Intervention des pagus nicht begegnen[61],
findet eine ganz einfache Erklärung darin, daß sich die magistri
in allen diesen Fällen ausschließlich mit dem Wiederaufbau von
Heiligtümern und mit Kultusangelegenheiten, also damit befassen,
was gewissermaßen von vornherein zu ihren Pflichten gehörte. In
unserer Inschrift erweitern sie ihren Wirkungskreis; da die Be-
dürfnisse des Heiligtum offenbar schon befriedigt waren, restau-
rieren sie eine zum pagus gehörende porticus. Aber die Genehmigung
eines solchen Verbrauchs von Geldern, die grundsätzlich für einen
anderen Zweck bestimmt waren, erforderte einen speziellen Beschluß
des pagus[62]: Pagus Herculaneus scivit...

So war also der Wirkungskreis des Kollegiums der 12 magistri
durch die lex pagana und die pagiscita begrenzt. Wohl begründet
erscheint die Behauptung, daß ähnliche Verhältnisse auch in den
übrigen, leider (wahrscheinlich mit Ausnahme des pagus Dianae Tifa-
tinae) dem Namen nach nicht bekannten pagi Campani bestanden[63].

Die vorstehenden Erwägungen werfen ein gewisses Licht auf
eine andere Inschrift aus dem ager Campanus, die sich schon unmittelbar auf den Lareskultus bezieht[64]:

Hisce ministris Laribus faciendum coe[raverunt]...

Weiter folgen die Namen von ministri (ein Freigelassener und
einige Sklaven).

Wir wissen leider nicht, auf welchen pagus sich diese Inschrift bezieht. Nichtsdestoweniger ist die Stellung dieser ministri ziemlich deutlich sichtbar:

1) Mit dem Hauptkult des pagus befaßten sich die Kollegien
der magistri, die aus ingenui und Freigelassenen bestanden. Eine
solche Organisation war das uns schon bekannte conlegium seive
magistrei Iovei Compagei; hierzu sind auch andere magistri Campani
zu zählen, wie z. B. magistreis Venerus Ioviae, magistreis Cererus,
magistreis Castori et Polluci[66].

2) Der im Verhältnis zu diesem Hauptkult untergeordnete Larenkult war vom pagus einem aus Sklaven bestehenden Kollegium von

ministri (in unserem Fall mit einem Freigelassenen an der Spitze) anvertraut. Diese ministri standen also keinem religiösen Verein, keiner privaten Vereinigung von cultores Larum vor, sondern bildeten selbst ein offiziell mit dem Kult dieser Gottheiten betrautes Beamtenkollegium. Es wäre also vergeblich, hier das Mommsensche collegium compitalicium zu suchen. So wie die Kollegien der kampanischen magistri für die Heiligtümer Juppiters, der Diana, Ceres, des Kastor und des Pollux sorgten, so betreuten diese ministri die Kapellen der Laren; in der zitierten Inschrift der ministri sind pondera und pavimentum erwähnt – wahrscheinlich Blöcke zum Bau einer Kapelle und ihr Fußboden. So wie die magistri öffentliche Spiele (paganalia) und Bühnenvorstellungen organisierten, so veranstalteten auch die ministri Larum für den betreffenden pagus ludi compitalicii.

Die aus Tibur bekannten ministri Laribus[67] nahmen wahrscheinlich eine ähnliche Stellung ein, allerdings nur für die Stadt und nicht für den pagus.

II. Bei den in den Jahren 1932/33 auf dem Gebiet von Minturnae durchgeführten Ausgrabungen wurden 29 steinerne Stelen und Bruchstücke von zwei weiteren ans Tageslicht gebracht[68]. Jede von ihnen war von einem besonderen aus 12 (in einem Fall 9) magistri, Freigelassenen und Sklaven, bestehenden Kollegium errichtet; fünf von diesen Kollegien setzten sich ausschließlich aus Frauen zusammen. Diese Stelen stammen aus dem ersten Jahrhundert v.u.Z.; im ersten Jahrhundert u.Z. verwendete man sie als Baumaterial für das Ortsheiligtum, infolgedessen sind die Inschriften teilweise beschädigt. Man nimmt fast allgemein an, daß sie sursprünglich als die einfachste Form von arae oder sacella Larum dienten[69]. Es ist zwar nirgends deutlich gesagt, daß sie den Laren gewidmet sind, wohl aber sind sie nach einigen auf den Inschriften erhaltenen Dedikationen den in den ländlichen Kreisen zusammen mit den Laren verehrten Gottheiten gewidmet[70].

In Minturnae pflegten also den Kompitalkult die collegia von magistri und magistrae; um dieses Problem entstand jedoch eine ernste Kontroverse. Vor allem ist die Datierung dieser Inschriften stritt. Der erste Herausgeber, J. Johnson, datierte sie sukzessiv von den ersten Jahren des 1. Jh. v.u.Z. bis zum Jahr 64, so daß jedes Kollegium seiner Ansicht nach auf ein anderes Jahr entfallen sollte. Im Jahr 64 sollen die minturnaeischen collegia magistrorum

auf Grund des eben in Rede stehenden Senatsbeschlusses aufgelöst
worden sein; hingegen wurden nach der lex Clodia noch zwei weitere
Altäre errichtet[71].

Die Hypothese Johnsons unterzog E. Staedler[72] einer scharfen
Kritik; er sprach sich für eine Verbindung der Ausstellung der Inschriften und der Bildung der Kollegien der magistri mit der Augusteischen assignatio nova aus, die im Jahre 28 zustande gekommen
sein soll. Die colonia Minturnae erhielt damals ein bedeutendes
Gebiet jenseits des Liris-Flusses; dieses Gebiet sollte in 30 länd-
liche pagi geteilt werden, jeder pagus aus 4 vici bestehend. Zum
Zwecke der sakralen Konsekration dieses Territoriums und seiner
Übergabe in die Obhut der Feldgottheiten wurden ebenjene 30 Kollegien von magistri und magistrae, je eins für jeden pagus, gebildet.
Alle Stelen mit den Inschriften wurden gleichzeitig und im voraus
hergestellt; das sumpfige Terrain hinter dem Liris wurde jedoch
niemals wirklich in Benutzung genommen und die Stelen-sacella wurden dort niemals aufgestellt. Die auf ihnen angeführten magistri
verrichteten auch niemals ihren Dienst.

Die im vorstehenden in allgemeinen Umrissen dargestellte Konstruktion Staedlers ist zweifelsohne geistreich, aber zugleich in
hohem Maße künstlich. Eins scheint nämlich sicher zu sein: die
Inschrift Nr.6 (=CIL I^2 2683) stammt, entgegen den Einwürfen Staedlers und übereinstimmend mit der ursprünglichen Datierung Johnsons,
bestimmt aus dem Jahr 65. Am Ende der Inschrift lesen wir das Datum: L. Manlio L. Aurelio. Staedler behauptet, daß in den Fasti
Capitolini die Namen der beiden Konsuln in umgekehrter Reihenfolge
auftreten, er betont ferner, daß hier das gewöhnlich bei den Konsulnnamen sorgsam angeführte Patronymikon fehlt; auf Grund dieser
Argumentation hält er genannte Persönlichkeiten für lokale Beamte,
duoviri, und nicht für römische Konsuln[73].

Die Fasti Capitolini sind aber für das Jahr 65 bekanntlich
nicht erhalten[74], und was Staedler über die Regeln der Reihenfolge
der Konsulnnamen auf den Fasti sagt, ist ganz verfehlt[75]. Staedler
vergißt auch, daß die praenomina patrum sorgsam nur auf den Fasti
angeführt wurden, aber nicht in den Inschriften, wo die Namen der
Konsuln nur zum Zweck der Datierung stehen[76].

In der Inschrift Nr. 28 (=CIL I^2 2705) tritt Philemo Mari
C(ai) s(ervus)[77] auf. Wie bekannt, hat die Stadt Minturnae im Leben
des Marius eine dramatische Rolle gespielt; es ist nicht ausge-

schlossen, daß er in ihrer Umgebung eine Besitzung hatte und eben
deshalb seine Schritte dorthin lenkte, als er im Jahre 88 vor Sulla
floh. Der in der Inschrift erwähnte Sklave konnte also tatsächlich
ein Sklave des historischen Gajus Marius sein. Der Terminus ante
quem für diese Inschrift wäre dann Januar 86[78]. Diese Vermutung
bestätigen drei weitere Inschriften, in denen wir den Namen C. Titinius lesen. Es war dies möglicherweise derselbe C. Titinius, den
wir aus dem von Marius entschiedenen Scheidungsprozeß der Fannia
kennen[80].

Gegen die These Staedlers spricht noch ein bisher nicht wahr-
genommener Umstand. In der Inschrift Nr. 10 (=CIL I^2 2687) lesen
wir nach dem Namen magistri: isdemque lu [dum] fecer. scaen.
Es erscheint höchst unwahrscheinlich, daß man bei der gleichzeiti-
gen und, wie Staedler behauptet, in großer Eile erfolgten Herstel-
lung aller Stelen an die Erwähnung von ludi scaenici dachte, die
erst stattfinden sollten. Dasselbe kan man von der Inschrift Nr. 28
(=CIL I^2 2705) sagen, in der Chillus Arri C(ai) s(ervus) mag (ister)
lud(i) oder lud(orum) erscheint.

Alle im vorstehenden angeführten Beweise sprechen deutlich
für die ursprüngliche Datierung Johnsons[81]. Das bedeutet aber nicht,
daß die von Johnson vorgeschlagene Deutung der Inschriften aus Minturnae mit allen Einzelheiten angenommen werden kann. Und so ist
es nicht wahrscheinlich, daß jedes der erwähnten Kollegien, wie
Johnson meint, auf ein anderes Jahr entfiel. Es ist schwer anzunehmen, daß man den Kult der Laren und mit ihnen verwandter Gottheiten in irgendeinem Jahr einem Kollegium anvertraute, daß ausschließlich aus Frauen bestand, welches überdies nur für Vesta
(oder Venus) eine Widmung ausstellte[82]. Wahrscheinlicher und im
Einklang mit dem, was wir aus dem ager Campanus und der lex Coloniae Iuliae Genetivae wissen, ist anzunehmen, daß in Minturnae in
jedem Jahr mehrere solche Kollegien von magistri und magistrae
tätig waren.

Wir wissen leider nichts Gewisses von der Art und Weise der
Berufung dieser Organisationen. Die Ansicht Johnsons, wonach Minturnae in 4 vici zerfiel und jeder vicus drei magistri delegierte,
stützt sich auf eine ganz unbewiesene Annahme. Es ist nicht ausgeschlossen, daß diese Kollegien vom Rat der Dekurionen bestimmt
wurden; man kann sich hier auf die Analogie mit den allerdings
späteren Bestimmungen der schon zitierten lex Coloniae Iuliae

Genetivae berufen[84].

Von unserem Standpunkt aus ist besonders wichtig, daß die collegia magistrorum und magistrarum aus Minturnae auf keinen Fall mit den collegia compitalicia in der Mommsenschen Auffassung dieses Terminus identifiziert werden können, wie dies Johnson tut[85]. In Minturnae haben wir es mit den collegia magistrorum und nicht mit Vereinen von cultores mit magistri an der Spitze zu tun. Ganz verfehlt ist auch die These Johnsons, daß die Mitteilung des Asconius bezüglich der Auflösung der Kollegien durch den Senat sich auch auf die Kollegien der magistri aus Minturnae beziehe; Asconius hat Kollegien eines ganz anderen Typus im Sinn. Die Tatsache, daß nach dem Jahr 64 die collegia magistrorum in Minturnae, wie es scheint, verschwunden sind, konnte lediglich eine Folge der Verordnung des Senats sein, welche die Abhaltung der ludi compitalicii verbot. Dadurch verloren diese Kollegien ihren eigentlichen Wirkungskreis und wurden nicht mehr einberufen[86].

III. Viele Inschriften, die eine deutliche Ähnlichkeit mit den Inschriften aus dem ager Campanus und mit den epigraphischen Denkmälern aus Minturnae verraten, wurden auf Delos entdeckt, dem Hauptzentrum der Italiker im Osten seit der zweiten Hälfte des 2. Jh. Einige dieser Inschriften hängen unmittelbar mit dem Problem der collegia compitalicia und dem Larenkult zusammen[87]. Die älteste von ihnen stammt aus dem Jahre 99/98, die übrigen beziehen sich gleichfalls auf die ersten Jahre des 1. Jh. v.u.Z., keine von ihnen stammt aus einem späteren Zeitpunkt als dem Jahr 88, dem Datum der Zerstörung von Delos durch die Truppen des Mithridates.

In formeller Hinsicht haben alle erwähnten Inschriften den gleichen Charakter:

a) Sie bringen die Namen einiger Freigelassenen und Sklaven (in den einzelnen Inschriften schwankt ihre Zahl von 5 bis 12; diese letztere Zahl finden wir auch in den uns schon bekannten Inschriften aus Kampanien und Minturnae).

b) Sie enthalten eine Formel, welche die genannten Persönlichkeiten als κομπεταλιασταὶ γενόμενοι bezeichnet.

c) Sie enthalten eine Formulierung, welche Aufschluß gibt, welcher Gottheit das Opfer dargebracht oder ein Denkmal errichtet wurde.

Es entsteht die Frage, was die Formel κομπεταλιασταί γενόμενοι bedeutet. Man sieht jedenfalls, daß der griechische Terminus
κομπεταλιαστής mit dem lateinischen compitum, compitalicius im
Zusammenhang steht. Überdies fand man die besprochenen Inschriften
auf den Kreuzungen einiger Straßen, die eine Art compitum bildeten, auf dem "Agora der Kompetaliasten" genannten Terrain[88]. Die
Beurteilung der erwähnten Inschriften wird leichter sein, wenn wir
zu unseren Erwägungen einige andere Inschriften aus Delos heran-
ziehen, die ähnlichen Charakter besitzen.

So lesen wir also u. a.:
Οἱ ῾Ερμαϊσταί ῾Ερμεῖ καὶ Μαίαι τὸν ναὸν ἀνέθηκαν.
Magistreis   Mercurio et Maiae   fecerunt[89].
Ποσειδωνιασταί Ποσειδῶνι.
Mag. Neptunales   Neptuno[90].
Οἱ ῾Ερμαϊσταί καὶ ᾽Απολλωνιασταί καὶ Ποσειδωνιασταί ῾Ηρακλεῖ.
Magistreis Mirquri   Apollonis   Neptuni   Hercoli[91].
Wie wir sehen, entspricht den griechischen Termini ῾Ερμαϊσταί
Ποσειδωνιασταί, ᾽Απολλωνιασταί der lateinische Ausdruck magistreis
mit hinzugefügtem Adjektiv oder Substantiv, manchmal aber ohne
irgendeine nähere Bezeichnung (῾Ερμαϊσταί. =magistreis oder magistreis Mirquri, Ποσειδωνιασταί . = magistreis, magistreis Neptunales oder magistreis Neptuni, ᾽Απολλωνιασταί= magistreis Apollonis). Wie schon darauf aufmerksam gemacht wurde, besaß die griechische Sprache keinen entsprechenden Fachausdruck, um den ganzen
im lateinischen Wort "magister" steckenden Begriff wiederzugeben,
und mußte sich jedesmal anderer, je nach dem Charakter der gegebenen Verbindung gebildeter Formulierungen bedienen[92].

Die uns überlieferten, sich auf die κομπεταλιαστα beziehenden
Texte sind leider ausschließlich in der griechischen Sprache ver-
faßt; es unterliegt jedoch keinem Zweifel, daß der Terminus κομπεταλιασταί ebenso zu verstehen ist wie die Termini ῾Ερμαϊσταί,
Ποσειδωνιασταί, ᾽Απολλωνιασταί So erhalten wir also als Äquivalent
der Bezeichnung κομπεταλιασταί magistreis compiti oder magistreis
compitales. Die lateinische Bezeichnung wird zwar als magistri
Larum oder cultores Larum compitalium rekonstruiert[93], die oben
angegebene Übersetzung entspricht jedoch zweifellos besser dem
griechischen Original (das übrigens eine wörtliche Übersetzung aus
dem Lateinischen war[94]).

So befaßten sich also unter den auf Delos angesiedelten Ita-
likern mit dem Kult der höchsten Gottheiten (Mercurius, Neptunus,
Apollo) aus ingenui und liberti zusammengesetzte Organisationen,
mit dem untergeordneten, obwohl ebenso offiziellen Lareskultus hingegen κομπεταλιασται, vor allem Sklaven. Man sieht da eine auffal-
lende Ähnlichkeit mit dem, was wir auf dem ager Campanus beobach-
ten; es wäre daher der Terminus κομπεταλιασται analog zu den kapua-
nischen ministri Laribus noch besser als ministreis compitales zu
rekonstruieren.

Aber so wie bei den epigraphischen Denkmälern aus Kampanien
und Minturnae kann man auch hier die Frage stellen: bildeten die
in den hier besprochenen delischen Inschriften erwähnten Persönlichkeiten selbst ein Kollegium der magistri, oder waren sie ein
ausübendes Organ irgendeines "wirklichen" sakralen Vereins? Zur
Beantwortung dieser Frage und der damit zusammenhängenden allge-
meineren Frage der Organisation der italischen Kolonie auf Delos
wurden verschiedene Hypothesen aufgestellt[95], auf deren Besprechung wir an dieser Stelle nicht eingehen können. Eines aber ist
sicher: der Termin γενόμενοι, welcher in den Inschriften aller
vier erwähnten Organisationen auftritt, besagt deutlich, daß das
Amt der magistri zeitlich begrenzt war (die Dauer ihrer Amtsführung betrug wahrscheinlich, wie gewöhnlich, ein Jahr), er belehrt
aber nicht über die Art und Weise der Berufung dieser magistri
und über den Charakter ihres Kollegiums. Es ist jedoch wahrscheinlich, daß, wenn wir es hier mit wirklichen Kollegien und nicht
nur mit collegia magistrorum zu tun hätten, der lateinische Text
dies durch die Wendung z. B. magistreis collegii Neptuni oder
collegii neptunalium andeuten und nicht das bloße magistreis Neptuni oder Neptunales anwenden würde. Für die Diskussion über die
collegia compitalicia ist die Tatsache von besonderer Wichtigkeit,
daß man auch in den delischen κομπεταλιασταί nur ein collegium der
ministri und nicht ein privates collegium cultorum Larum sehen
soll. Wichtig ist weiter der Umstand, daß auf Delos die ludi compitalicii stattfanden[96], von deren offiziellem Charakter schon
zuvor die Rede war. Die Veranstalter dieser Spiele bekleideten
also im Verhältnis zur Bevölkerung der Insel eine offizielle Stellung; auch aus diesem Grund ist es schwer, in den delischen κομπεταλιασταί nur eine private Vereinigung von Anbetern der Laren zu
sehen.

Die oben erörterten Quellen widersprechen ganz deutlich der Behauptung, daß die ludi compitalicii der Fürsorge der collegia compitalicia anvertraut waren: gerade umgekehrt begegnen wir sowohl auf Delos wie in Kampanien und in Minturnae offiziellen und halboffiziellen collegia magistrorum und ministrorum[97] und nicht den Vereinigungen von cultores Larum. Das bedeutet zwar nicht, daß solche Vereine von cultores überhaupt nicht existierten; in den ludi compitalicii nahmen sie jedenfalls einen untergeordneten Platz nach dem magistri vicorum bzw. den offiziellen collegia magistrorum ein.

Man hat versucht, die in dem Problem der collegia compitalicia liegenden Schwierigkeiten noch auf einem anderen Wege zu lösen. Es sollten die magistri vicorum während der ludi compitalicii als magistri collegiorum compitaliciorum auftreten[98]. Diese Theorie ist absolut unannehmbar: sie steht in krassem Widerspruch mit dem Text des Asconius, der die erste Grundlage aller Erwägungen dieser Frage bilden muß. Asconius identifiziert die magistri vicorum nicht mit den magistri der Kollegien, sondern unterscheidet sie genau. Und sonderbarerweise hat gerade diese am wenigsten wahrscheinliche Hypothese die weiteste Verbreitung gefunden, besonders in neueren Arbeiten[99]. Zu ihrer Unterstützung kann man jedoch nicht eine einzige Quelle anführen, und das weder aus der Zeit der Republik noch aus der Kaiserzeit. Die Deutung dieser Quellen, auf die sich die Verteidiger dieser Anschauung berufen, beruht auf einem offenbaren Mißverständnis[100].

Im Vorstehenden war schon die Rede von den Reformen des Augustus auf diesem Gebiet. Die bedeutendste Neuerung bestand in der Verbindung des Larenkultus mit dem Kultus des Kaiserhauses und der Person des Kaisers. Fortan sollte man nicht die Lares im allgemeinen, sondern die Lares domus Augustae zusammen mit dem Genius des Kaisers verehren[101]. Auf dem stadtrömischen Gebiet befaßten sich mit diesem Kult aus vier magistri und vier ministri bestehende Kollegien[102]. Nach dem Beispiel der Hauptstadt verbreitete sich der offizielle Kult der kaiserlichen Laren auf dem Gebiet des ganzen Reiches. Es befaßten sich mit ihm jedoch nicht nur magistri vicorum, sondern auch, besonders auf dem Gebiet einiger Munizipien, spezielle collegia magistrorum und ministrorum. Sie trugen den Titel magistri (ministri) Larum (Augustorum)[103]. Diese Verfügung des Augustus trug außerordentlich zur Verbreitung des Kultes dieser

Gottheiten bei; es entstanden auch zahlreiche Vereinigungen von cultores Larum[104]. Im Gegensatz jedoch zu den offiziellen magistri Larum waren dies Vereine ausschließlich privaten Charakters. Eine solche private Vereinigung von cultores bildete auch wahrscheinlich das bereits erwähnte Kollegium aus Faesulae.

Der Irrtum vieler neuerer Forscher bestand also in der Verwechslung der offiziellen magistri Larum (Augustorum) mit den Vorstehern privater Kultusverbände, mit magistri collegiorum Larum (Augustorum). Der Unterschied in der Terminologie ist scheinbar nicht groß, aber sehr prinzipiell. Die ersten dieser Organisationen (magistri Larum) waren keine wirklichen Kollegien, hatten aber einen offiziellen Charakter, die zweiten (collegia Larum mit magistri an der Spitze) waren wirkliche Kollegien, aber ohne offiziellen Charakter.

Ganz ähnlich waren die Verhältnisse auf diesem Gebiet auch zur Zeit der Republik. Daß es schon damals offizielle magistri und ministri gab, kann im Lichte der bisherigen Beweisführung keinem Zweifel unterliegen. Es ist auch wahrscheinlich, daß zu derselben Zeit die ersten privaten Verbände von Verehrern der Laren entstanden[105]; leider ist ein Kollegium dieser Art für die Zeit der Republik nirgends ausdrücklich bezeugt. Suchen kann man sie - worauf schon Mommsen hinwies - nur unter den im J. 58 von Clodius gebildeten Vereinen. Wenn also De Robertis die Existenz solcher Vereinigungen von cultores Larum zur Zeit der Republik annimmt, so kann man ihm zustimmen, besonders wenn er behauptet, es sei nicht wesentlich, ob sie die Benennung collegium compitalicium oder eine andere Bezeichnung trugen. Wenn er aber weiter schreibt: certo si è che esse organizzavano i giuochi compitalici[106], so widerspricht dieser Anschauung unsere ganze bisherige Beweisführung.

Schließlich ist noch eine sich aus dem Text des Asconius ergebende Möglichkeit in Erwägung zu ziehen. Wie wir gesehen haben, kann man diesen Text bei entsprechender Interpunktion auch so verstehen, daß die ludi compitalicii ausschließlich die magistri vicorum, die magistri collegiorum hingegen andere von Asconius nicht näher bezeichnete Spiele veranstalteten[107]. Zur Unterstützung dieser These sammelte man auch gewisse sachliche Beweise. Es ist bekannt, das einige Kollegien eigene Spiele hatten; solche Spiele konnte Asconius gemeint haben. In diesem Zusammenhang führt

man gewöhnlich die von den tibicines veranstalteten Spiele und die
ludi piscatorii an. Im ersten Fall handelt es sich jedoch um ein
spezielles Privilegium der tibicines, deren Kollegium überhaupt
zur Kategorie der apparitores, also zu den halboffiziellen Verbän-
den gezählt werden muß[108]. Was die ludi piscatorii anbetrifft[109],
so ist nirgends ausdrücklich bezeugt, daß sich an ihrer Organisation ein collegium von piscatores beteiligt hat. Das corpus pisca-
torum et urinatorum totius alvei Tiberis, dem man die Organisierung
dieser Spiele zuschreibt, ist spät, nämlich erst im J. 205 bezeugt[110]. Auf dieser Grundlage ist es schwer, irgendwelche Schlüsse
für die Periode der Republik zu ziehen. Spiele dieser Art mußten
jedenfalls eine ganz ausnahmsweise Erscheinung gewesen sein. Unter
vielen hundert Inschriften, die sich auf Kollegien beziehen, kennen
wir nicht eine einzige, die über die ludi irgendeines anderen Kollegiums informiert. Übrigens können Spiele dieser Art hier noch
aus einem anderen und entscheidenden Grund nicht in Betracht kommen: Asconius schreibt nämlich ausdrücklich über die Worte Ciceros:
dicit de ludis compitaliciis[111].

Nach Ansicht Waltzings organisierten zwar die magistri vicorum
die ludi compitalicii, sie spielten aber dabei nicht die entscheidende Rolle. Diese Rolle sollen die magistri der verschiedenen
Handwerkerkollegien gehabt haben, die an den ludi teilnahmen[112].
Es ist in der Tat durchaus verständlich, daß sich an den Kompitalfeierlichkeiten sowohl einzelne Personen wie auch ganze Organisationen beteiligen konnten. Nichts steht dem im Wege, daß wir annehmen, daß z. B. Mitglieder des collegium hortolanorum[113] in Kapua
zusammen an den Feierlichkeiten zu Ehren der Laren, der Schutzgott-
heiten ihrer Arbeit, teilnahmen. In Rom, dem Zentrum des Handwerks,
wurden die Laren natürlicherweise zu Schutzgöttern der Arbeit des
Handwerkers. Überdies muß man bedenken, daß sich in Rom, ähnlich
wie in vielen mittelalterlichen Städten, die Handwerker einer Spe-
zialität häufig in einem Bezirk gruppierten[114]. Man kann sich also
sehr gut vorstellen, daß die magistri der in einem Bezirk tätigen
Handwerkerkollegien bei der Organisierung von Spielen mit den magistri vicorum mitwirkten. Die Behauptung aber, daß sie bei den
ludi compitalicii den Vorsitz führten, ist absolut unannehmbar.
Nur die magistri vicorum waren offizielle Persönlichkeiten, nur sie
hatten das Recht, die toga praetexta zu tragen. Unsere Ansicht wird
bestätigt nicht nur durch die oben angeführte Stelle des Livius

bezüglich der magistri vicorum, sondern vor allem durch die Tatsache, daß die magistri vicorum nach Auflösung der Kollegien im J. 61 selbst Spiele zu organisieren versuchten. Asconius schreibt: solebant autem magistri collegiorum ludos facere; wenn es sich hier um Kollegien handeln würde, die offiziell zur Pflege des Kompitalkults berufen sind, so wäre die Verwendung des Wortes solere ausgeschlossen. Asconius hätte dann eher ganz einfach gesagt: magistri collegiorum ludos faciebant, ähnlich, wie er weiter von den magistri vicorum schreibt: magistri vicorum faciebant Compitalicios praetextati.

Die ludi compitalicii veranstalteten also die magistri vicorum; bei den Kompitalfeierlichkeiten traten jedoch, wenn auch in zweiter Linie, Handwerkerkollegien und religiöse Organisationen, collegia opificum und cultores Larum auf. Nur eine solche Lösung stimmt mit dem Text des Asconius überein und entspricht zugleich allen anderen Quellen.

Die Ergebnisse unserer Erörterungen bezüglich des Problems der collegia compitalicia können wir wie folgt zusammenfassen:

1) Die Pflege des offiziellen Larenkults und die Organisierung der ludi compitalicii war anvertraut: a) den magistri vicorum (in Rom und wahrscheinlich in Pompeji), b) den aus höchstens 12 Personen bestehenden collegia magistrorum und ministrorum.

Zur Bezeichnung dieser letzteren Organisationen kann man den Terminus "collegium" nicht im Sinne von "Verein" anwenden; es ist auch klar, daß die Bezeichnung collegium compitalicium (wenn man dieses collegium für einen wirklichen Verein hält) weder auf die magistri vicorum, noch auf die collegia magistrorum bezogen werden kann.

2) Asconius berichtet, daß in den ludi compitalicii neben den magistri vicorum auch die magistri von Kollegien tätig waren; es konnten dies nur Handwerkerkollegien oder religiöse Vereine (insbes. cultores Larum) sein. Diese letzteren konnten faktisch die Benennung collegium compitalicium tragen; beim gegenwärtigen Stand der Quellen läßt sich das jedoch nicht beweisen. Eins ist aber nach unseren Ausführungen sicher: es waren dies jedenfalls Vereine privaten Charakters, die mit den offiziellen Vorstehern des Kompitalkults rechtlich nichts gemein hatten.

3) Damit ergibt sich auch die Antwort auf die Frage, gegen welche Kategorien der Kollegien der Senatsbeschluß vom J. 64 gerich-

tet war. Entgegen der verbreiteten Meinung wurden von dieser Maßnahme die offiziellen Vorsteher des Kompitalkults nicht betroffen:
das Senatsconsult bezog sich weder auf die magistri vicorum, noch
auf die verschiedenen collegia magistrorum. Der Sentat hat nur
durch das Verbot der Abhaltung der ludi compitalicii diesen Organisationen den wichtigsten Gegenstand ihrer Tätigkeit weggenommen.
Es folgt aber aus dem Text des Asconius, daß die aufgelösten Vereine in einem Zusammenhang mit den ludi compitalicii gestanden
haben; da aber an diesen Spielen sowohl Berufsvereine, wie religiöse Vereinigungen teilnahmen, sind die verbotenen Vereine unter
diesen beiden Kategorien zu suchen. Der Senat hat alle Kollegien
aufgelöst, die adversus rem publicam videbantur esse constituta:
es konnten demnach sowohl Handwerkergenossenschaften wie auch
collegia cultorum Larum gewesen sein.

Anmerkungen

1 Siehe dazu von der neueren Literatur L. Schnorr von Carolsfeld,
  Geschichte der juristischen Person, 1, München 1933, 258.262;
  F.M. De Robertis, Il diritto associativo romano, Bari 1934,
  65-162; derselbe, Il fenomeno associativo nel mondo romano,
  Napoli 1955, 33-36; S. Accame, La legislazione romana intorno
  ai collegi nel I secolo a. C., Bulletino del Museo dell'Impero
  Romano 13, 1942, 13-49.
2 Th. Mommsen, De collegiis et sodaliciis Romanorum, Kiliae 1843,
  73-76.
3 M. Cohn, Zum römischen Vereinsrecht, Berlin 1873, 39-55;
  J. P. Waltzing, Étude historique sur les corporations professio-
  nelles chez les Romains, 1, Louvain 1895, 90-11.
4 Siehe J. Johnson, Excavations at Minturnae, 2: Inscriptions, 1:
  Republican Magistri, Philadelphia 1933, 8, 122-125; derselbe,
  Minturnae, RE Suppl. 7, 1940, 474; Accame 27-29; L.R. Taylor,
  Party Politics in the Age of Caesar, Berkeley and Los Angeles
  1949, 43-44; E. Bickel, Pagani, Kaiseranbeter in den Laren-
  Kapellen der pagi urbani im Rom Neros und des Apostels Petrus,
  Rh. Mus. 97, 1954, 29; G. Niebling, Laribus Augustis Magistri
  Primi, Historia 5, 1956, 307-309; F. Bömer, Untersuchungen über
  die Religion der Sklaven in Griechenland und Rom, 1, Wiesbaden
  1958, 35-38 (Abh. Mainz 1957 Nr. 7).
5 Th. Stangl in seiner Ausgabe von Asconius (Ciceronis Orationum
  Scholiastae), 2, Vindobonae-Lipsiae 1912, 15 nimmt die Lesart
  admissa an. Nach dieser Stelle befindet sich eine Lücke, die in
  den verschiedenen Handschriften 6 bis 10 Buchstaben beträgt.
6 An der ersten Stelle steht in zwei maßgebenden Handschriften
  vicorum, in einer dagegen ludorum; an der zweiten Stelle weisen
  alle Handschriften die Lesart ludorum auf. Siehe dazu Clark und
  Stangl in apparatu critico und unten Anm. 30.
7 Über dieses collegium Corneliorum siehe jetzt J. Ceska, Deset
  tisic Corneliu, Listy Filologicke 78, 1955, 177-181.
8 Die (von Stangl 59 angenommene) Lesart lictorum befindet sich in
  allen Handschriften. Clark hat nach Manutius in den Text die Konjektur fictorum eingeführt; die Lesart der Handschriften muß
  aber, wie wir sehen werden, aus den sachlichen Gründen bevorzugt
  werden.

9 Mommsen, De coll., 73-74; W. Liebenam, Zur Geschichte und Organisation des römischen Vereinswesens, Leipzig 1890, 21; O. Karlowa, Römische Rechtsgeschichte, 2, Leipzig 1892, 66-67; Waltzing, 1, 92-93; E. Kornemann, Collegium, RE 4, 1900, 406; De
Robertis, Dir. ass. 77-79; Accame, 13-16. Auf das J. 68 datierten das Senatsconsult A. Pernice, M. Antistius Labeo. Das römische Privatrecht 1, Halle 1873, 301; Cohn, 39-41; V. Bandini,
Appunti sulle corporazioni romane, Milano 1937, 51.

10 Paläographisch genommen sollte die Mehrzahl durch die Schreibweise S.CC. angedeutet werden (vgl. De Robertis, Dir. ass., 77);
es ist aber zu bemerken, daß in In Corn. 58 Z. 6 und 10 (Clark)
die Abkürzung S.C. steht, obwohl Asconius an diesen Stellen
nicht von einem, sondern von mehreren Senatsbeschlüssen spricht.

11 Mommsen, De coll., 73; Liebenam, 23; Waltzing, 1,91; G.M. Monti,
Le corporazioni nell'evo antico e nell'alto medio evo, Bari
1934, 23-24. Vgl. De Robertis, Dirr. ass., 76-77.

12 P. Kayser, Abhandlungen aus dem Process- und Strafrecht, 2:
Die Strafgesetzgebung der Römer gegen Vereine, Berlin 1873, 160;
Cohn, Römisches Vereinsrecht, 53-54.

13 D.47,22,4.

14 J. Linderski, Państwo a kolegia (Staat und Vereine), Kraków
1961, 55-65.

15 J. Béranger, Remarques sur la langue politique du Principat,
REL 30, 1952, 42.

16 J. Gaudemet, Utilitas publica, Revue hist. de droit franc. et
étr. 29, 1951, 467-470.

17 Vgl. De Robertis, Dir. ass., 87.

18 Siehe dazu meine Arbeiten Państwo a kolegia, 66-114; Ciceros
Rede pro Caelio und die Ambitus- und Vereinsgesetzgebung der
ausgehenden Republik, Hermes 89, 1961, 106-119; Suetons Bericht
über die Vereinsgesetzgebung unter Caesar und Augustus, SZ 79,
1962, 322-328, wo die Quellen und weitere Literatur angegeben
werden.

19 CIL VI 4416.

20 Für die Rechtfertigung dieser Neulesung verweise ich auf meine
Arbeit Państwo a kolegia, 107-108.

21 De Robertis, Dir. ass., 75.

22 J. Linderski, Collegia centonariorum , Przeglad historyczny 48,
1957, 28-37 mit weiterer Literatur.

23 De Robertis, Dir. ass., 239-240.

24 Es ist zu betonen, daß in den Inschriften die normale Form collegium fabrum lautet und nicht fabrorum, wie bei Asconius und Callistratus. Die erste dieser Formen gehörte wahrscheinlich der Umgangssprache, die zweite dagegen der literarischen und juristischen Sprache an.

25 Gaudemt, Utilitas, 476, vermutet, daß an der Stelle von Callistratus D.50,6,6,12 die Worte ...id est idcirco instituta sunt, ut necessariam operam publicis utilitatibus exhiberent interpoliert worden sind. Im Lichte unserer Beweisführung muß diese Vermutung abgelehnt werden.

26 Waltzing, 1, 92-93.

27 Mommsen, De coll., 74-75.

28 Waltzing, 1, 98-99; nach ihm Kornemann, 406; B. Eliachevitch, La personnalité juridique en droit privé romain, Paris 1942, 213-218.

29 Cohn, Römisches Vereinsrecht, 40 Anm. 62; De Robertis, Dir. ass. 84 Anm. 45.

30 Die Schwierigkeiten der Interpretation vergrößert noch die Tatsache, daß in den Handschriften des Asconius an einigen für das richtige Verständnis des Textes entscheidenden Stellen verschiedene Lesarten vorkommen. So lesen wir in dem von Asconius kommentierten Satz Ciceros ...cum quidam tr. pl. suo auxilio magistros ludos contra senatus consultum facere iussisset (In Pis. 8) in zwei von drei grundlegenden codices magnos ludos und in einem magis ludos. Diese letztere Lesart ist offensichtlich ein gewöhnlicher Fehler; was die erste anbelangt, so konnte der Kopist sehr leicht magistros in magnos umändern, dies um so leichter, als magnos ludos auch richtigen Sinn hatte. Cicero spricht jedoch an dieser Stelle ausdrücklich von ludi compitalicii und nicht von ludi magni. Wir sind hier überdies in der glücklichen Lage, daß man die keinen Zweifel erweckende Konjektur magistros auch in Anlehnung an die Handschriften Ciceros einführen konnte. Ferner schwanken im Kommentar selbst die Kodices des Asconius zwischen den Lesarten magistri vicorum und magistri ludorum (siehe oben Anm. 6). Die Mehrzahl der Herausgeber nimmt die erste Lesung an (mit größter Vorsicht Stangl), aber auch die Lesart magistri ludorum ist aus sachlichen Gründen nicht ausgeschlossen. Für die Zeit der Republik können wir

eine der Inschriften aus Minturnae anführen (CIL I^2 2705) in
der Chillus Arri C.s. mag(ister) lud(orum) oder lud(i) auftritt. Vgl. aus der Kaiserzeit magister ludi (CIL IX 4226 Amin-
ternum) und magister ludorum (AÈ 1914 Nr. 6 Scarbantia). In
unserem Fall ist aber die Lesart magistri vicorum wahrscheinlicher; siehe aber dagegen Accame, 27-28.

31 Mommsen, De coll., 74: Collegia quae dicto SCto sublata sunt
erant urbana tantummodo, maxime compitalicia.

32 De lingua lat. VI 25. 29.

33 G. Wissowa, Compitalia, RE 4, 1900, 791-792; derselbe, Religion
und Kultus der Römer, 2. Aufl., München 1912, 168-172; Boehm,
Lares, RE 12, 1925, 807-809; A. Piganiol, Recherches sur les
jeux romains, Strasbourg 1923, 127-134; L.A. Holland, The Shrine of the Lares Compitales, Trans. Am. Philol. Ass. 68, 1937,
428-441; L. Delatte, Recherches sur quelques fêtes mobiles du
calendrier romain, L'Ant. Class. 6, 1937, 111-114; Niebling
307-309; Bömer, Untersuchungen, 35-37; K. Latte, Römische Religionsgeschichte, München 1960, 90-94. Vgl. auch Thes. 1.1.
s. vv. compitalia, compitum.

34 H. Rudolph, Stadt und Staat im römischen Italien, Leipzig 1935,
50-53. Es ist aber zu bemerken, daß die pagi und vici offizielle Organisationen waren; die entschiedene Mehrzahl der Kollegien bilden dagegen Genossenschaften mit ausschließlich priva-
tem Charakter. Diesen prinzipiellen rechtlichen Unterschied
scheint Rudolph überhaupt nicht wahrgenommen zu haben. Über die
Organisation der italischen pagi und vici siehe auch E. Kornemann, Pagus, RE 18, 1942, 2322-2324; A.W. van Buren, Vicus,
RE 8 A, 1958, 2090-2094.

35 Vgl. CIL I^2 1002 mag(istri) de duobus pageis et vicei Sulpicei
(vgl. aber auch Accame 19 Anm. 58); CIL IX 3521: die magistri
pagi handeln de vici sententia.

36 De coll. 75-76.

37 Pro Sest. 34.

38 De domo 54.

39 1, 99-104.

40 Für Verbindungen dieser Art findet sich am häufigsten der Terminus collegius anstatt collegium. Vgl. z. B. CIL IX 1505,
1688, 3447, 4129, 6154; XI 2720. Siehe auch zu dieser Inschrift
Bömer, Untersuchungen 28.

41 Waltzing, 1, 98-102. Die Beweisführung Waltzings hat zuletzt
Eliachevitch, Personnalité, 215-218 erneuert.

42 Siehe dazu Niebling, 303-307. 321-331.

43 Aug.30.

44 Nat. hist. III 66.

45 Suet. Aug. 30.

46 Cass. Dio LV 8,6; Suet. Aug. 31.

47 Aber gerade in Pompeji waren die Verhältnisse besonders ver-
wickelt.Es fungierten dort außer den oben erwähnten magistri
vici et compiti noch die untereinander unabhängigen ministri
Fortunae, ministri Mercurii Maiae, magistri und ministri pagi
Augusti Felicis suburbani. Siehe dazu G. Grether, Pompeian
"ministri", Class. Phil. 27, 1932, 59-65 und besonders Börner,
Untersuchungen, 105-109 (mit weiterer Literatur).

48 Siehe Verg. Georg. II 382 pagos et compita circum (vgl. Hor.
Epist. I,1,49) und Philargyrius ad loc. (Servii Grammatici
Commentarii, III P. 252, Lipsiae 1887, ed. Thilo-Hagen): compita... ubi pagani agrestes bucina convocati solent certa inire consilia: hinc et Lares compitales et feriae compitalicae. CIL IX 1618
(Beneventum): zwei Spender schenken paganis communib(us) pagi Lucul...,
porticum cum apparitorio et compitum (compitum bedeutet hier offensichtlich das sacellum der Laren; es war aber im Besitz des pagus
und nicht des vicus). CIL XIV 2121 begegnen uns municipes compiten-
ses veicorum quinque. In diesem Fall gruppierten sich, wie es
scheint, die Einwohner von fünf vici um ein compitum = sacellum.

49 Festus p. 284 (ed. Lindsay): publica sacra, quae publico sumptu
pro populo fiunt, quaeque pro montibus, pagis, curiis, sacellis. Die sacra pro sacellis waren, wie Wissowa, Religion und
Kultus 398-399 eindringlich bemerkte, - Compitalia, so wie die
sacra pro pagis - Paganalia. Compitalia waren jedoch nicht nur
die sacra publica, sondern zugleich die sacra popularia, an
denen die gesamte Bevölkerung und nicht nur spezielle Repräsentanten (Beamte, Priester und hierzu bestimmte Familien) teilnahmen. Siehe Festus p. 298 (ed. Lindsay): popularia sacra
sunt, ut ait Labeo, quae omnes cives faciunt, nec certis fami-
liis adtributa sunt: Fornacalia, Parilia, Laralia (d. h. Compitalia). Vgl. diesbezüglich auch Eliachevitch, 213-214.

50 34,7,2. Über bildliche Darstellungen der magistri in toga praetexta siehe Niebling, 310-322; K. Meuli, Altrömischer Masken-

brauch, Mus. Helv. 12, 1955, 219 Anm. 51. 230-231 mit Abb. 1
und 2; Bömer, Untersuchungen, 40-41.

51 Vgl. Accame, 19-20.

52 CIL I^2 672-691. 2506. Die Zusammenstellung aller bisher ent-
deckten Inschriften der magistri Campani gibt M.W. Frederiksen,
Republican Capua, Papers of the British School at Rome 27,
1959, 121-130. Die älteste von diesen 28 Inschriften stammt
aus dem J. 112 oder 111, die letzte aus dem J. 71 v.u.Z.

53 CIL I^2 682 = Dessau, ILS 6302.

54 Pagus Herculaneus befand sich auf dem Gebiete, das vor 211 zu
Kapua gehörte. E. Staedler, Zu den 29 neu aufgefundenen Inschriftstelen von Minturno, Hermes 77, 1942, 177 Anm. 6 bringt
ihn irrtümlich mit der Stadt Herculaneum in Verbindung.

55 Die Form Iovei Compagei ist nicht klar. Iovei ist jedenfalls
bei dem Nom. Iuppiter ein Dativ (conlegium Iovei Compagei =
conlegium für Iuppiter). Man weiß aber nicht, ob compagei als
Adj. (vom*compax,-agis oder*compages,-is) zu behandeln ist,
oder als Subst. vom compagus. J. Heurgon, Les magistri des
collèges et le relèvement de Capoue de 111 à 71 avant J.C.,
Mélanges d'archéologie et d'histoire 56, 1939, 16 Anm. 1 erklärt sich für diese zweite Möglichkeit, zu deren Unterstützung
er die Worte des Ps.-Fulgentius, Serm. 11 (Migne, Series Latina 65, 872) zitiert: unius compagi tegmine retentae. Compagei
wäre dann Gen. und die Form compagus das substantivische Gegenstück zum Adj. compaganus. Vgl. CIL XI 5375 Iuppiter paganicus;
Liv. 24,44,8 Iuppiter vicilinus. Heurgon erklärt compagus als
l'ensemble des habitants d'un pagus. Der Name der Gottheit würde also Iuppiter compagi lauten (die Form Iuppiter Compagus,
wo compagus Adj. ist, scheint schwer annehmbar zu sein). Möglich ist aber auch die Rekonstruktion Iovius Compages; Iovei
wäre dann Gen. (E.H. Warmington, Remains of Old Latin, 4: Archaic Inscriptions, London 1953, 109 Anm. 7). Ich nehme die
Form Iuppiter Compages an: in diesem Fall sind Iovei und Compagei Dative.

56 Es ist ein entschiedenes Mißverständnis, wenn man (wie dies
Heurgon, 12-17, tut) auf Grund der Tatsache, daß es in Kampanien und in den italischen Städten wirkliche Berufs- und Kult-
vereine gab, denselben Charakter automatisch auch unseren magistri = conlegium Iovei Compagei und anderen Kollegien von

magistri Campani zuschreibt. Ähnlich wie Heurgon auch Accame,
18. Mommsen hat zweifellos recht (CIL X S. 366-368), wenn er
die magistri Campani mit den in der lex Ursonensis auftretenden
mag(istri) ad fana templa delubra (CIL I^2 594 cap. 128) ver-
gleicht, bezüglich deren kein Zweifel besteht, daß sie nur
collegia magistrorum bildeten und nicht die magistri der Kult-
vereine gewesen sind. Vgl. auch die Ausführungen von A.E.R.
Boak, The Magistri of Campania and Delos, Class. Phil. 11, 1916,
25-34.

57 J. Hatzfeld, Les Italiens résidant à Délos, Bull. Corr. Hell.
   36, 1912, 186-188; derselbe, Les trafiquants Italiens dans
   l'Orient hellénique, Paris 1919, 257-260.

58 Mommsen, CIL X, 367-368; A. Schulten, De conventibus civium
   Romanorum, Berolini 1892, 44-45. 71-77; derselbe, Die Landge-
   meinde im römischen Reiche, Philologus 53, 1894, 632-634. Ähnlich wie Mommsen und Schulten Frederiksen, 89-90 (für den Titel
   s. Anm. 52). Vgl. auch R.M. Peterson, The Cults of Campania,
   Rome 1919, 348.

59 Vgl. CIL I^2 686 =Dessau ILS 6303: Heisc. magistr. ex pagei
   scitu in servom Iunonis Gaurae [ee]ntule(runt); vgl. auch
   CIL X 829 = Dessau ILS 5706 (s. zu dieser Inschrift Frederiksen, 89). Über leges paganae s. auch G. Tibiletti, Lex, Dizionario Epigrafico 4, 1957, 81.

60 Heurgon, 18 (für den Titel s. Anm. 55).

61 Die Ausnahme bilden CIL I^2 686 und 684 (diese letztere Inschrift
   ist aber stark beschädigt).

62 Anders Frederiksen, 89.

63 Die Behauptung Schultens, De conventibus, 44-45, 57-59, daß es
   nur dan pagus Herculaneus gab, halte ich für unwahrscheinlich.
   Ebenso kann ich den Ausführungen von Frederiksen, 89-90, die
   eine Modifikation der These Schultens darstellen, nicht zustimmen.

64 CIL I^2 681 = Dessau ILS 3609 (98 v.u.Z.).

65 Die Zahl dieser ministri ist unsicher, s. dazu Bömer, Untersuchungen, 43.

66 CIL I^2 675, 677, 678.

67 CIL I^2 1483. Siehe auch CIL X 3790 (Capua. 24 v.u.Z.).

68 Diese Inschriften wurden zum erstenmal von J. Johnson, Excavations at Minturnae 2: Inscriptions 1, Philadelphia 1933, 18-48

veröffentlicht. Sie werden in CIL I^2 unter den Nummern 2678–2708 abgedruckt.

69 Siehe aber gegen diese Ansicht Latte, Röm. Religionsgeschichte, 273 Anm. 1.

70 Es sind nämlich die Widmungen für V(enus) oder V(esta) (CIL I^2 2685), Spes (2689, 2698, 2700), Ceres (2699), Mercurius Felix (2702) erhalten.

71 Johnson, Excavations, 123–125; derselbe, Minturnae, RE Suppl. 7, 1940, 472–473.

72 Zu den 29 neu aufgefundenen Inschriftstelen von Minturno [sic!], Hermes 77, 1942, 161–169. Die These Staedlers ist von F. Zucker, Hermes 78, 1943, 200 und E. Bickel, Rh. Mus. 97, 1954, 6 angenommen.

73 Staedler, 180. 190 Anm. 1.

74 A. Degrassi, Inscriptiones Italiae, XIII 1, 1947, 57. 488.

75 Siehe jetzt die grundlegende Arbeit von L.R. Taylor und T.R.S. Broughton, The Order of the Consuls' Names in the Yearly Lists, Mem. Am. Acad. Rome 19, 1949, 3–14.

76 Es ist noch zu bemerken, daß in drei anderen Inschriften aus Minturnae, in denen die Datierung nach den duoviri angewendet ist (Nr. 8 = CIL I^2 2685; 25 = 2702; 29 = 2706), die Namen derselben immer am Anfang und nie am Ende der Inschrift genannt sind.

77 Über diese Form der Sklavennamen s. A. Oxé, Zur älteren Nomenklatur der römischen Sklaven, Rh. Mus. 59, 1904, 108 ff.; W. Schulze, Zur Geschichte lateinischer Eigennamen, Berlin 1904, 510–515.

78 Johnson, Excavations, 63; derselbe RE Suppl. 7, 1940, 475. Die Auslegung Johnsons wurde von F. Münzer, Zu den Magistri von Minturnae MDAI Röm. Abt. 50, 1935, 321 ff. angenommen.

79 Nr. 12 = CIL I^2 2689; 18 = 2695; 22 = 2699.

80 Plut. Marius 38; Val. Max. VIII 2,3. Vgl. Münzer a. O.; M. Bang, Marius in Minturnae, Klio 10, 1910, 178 ff.

81 Siehe auch Bömer, Untersuchungen, 102–103.

82 Nr. 8 = CIL I^2 2685. Es sind in Minturnae noch fünf andere ausschließlich aus Frauen zusammengesetzte Kollegien von magistrae bezeugt (CIL I^2 2680, 2681, 2686, 2688, 2694).

83 Siehe diesbezüglich die Besprechung von R. Meigs JRS 24, 1934, 96–97. Es ist auch zu betonen, daß in der Inschrift Nr. 25 =

CIL I^2 2702 nur 9 magistri auftreten, was mit der Theorie Johnsons nicht übereinstimmt.

84 CIL I^2 594 cap.128; vgl. A.D'Ors, Epigrafia juridica de la Espana Romana, Madrid 1953, 267-268.

85 RE Suppl. 7, 1940, 474.

86 Clodius erneuerte die ludi compitalicii nur für kurze Zeit; dann wurde ihre Veranstaltung wieder eingestellt. Erst Augustus belebte sie wieder. Siehe Suet. Aug. 31.

87 Inscr. de Délos 1760-1770. Siehe dazu Bömer, Untersuchungen, 43-44 mit weiterer Literatur.

88 F. Durrbach, Choix d'inscriptions de Délos, Paris 1921, 233.

89 Inscr. de Délos 1731.

90 Ebenda 1751.

91 Ebenda 1753.

92 F. Poland, Geschichte des griechischen Vereinswesens, Leipzig 1909, 375; Hatzfeld, Bull. Corr. Hell. 36, 1912, 177.

93 Kornemann, Conventus, RE 4, 1900, 1188.

94 Vgl. auch J. Linderski, Zum Namen Competalis, Glotta 39, 1960, 148.

95 Für die Literaturangaben s. K. Meuli, Mus. Helv. 12, 1955, 219 Anm. 51; Bömer, Untersuchungen; 43 Anm. 3.

96 M. Bulard, La religion domestique dans la colonie italienne de Délos, Paris 1926, 82 ff. 417 ff.; Meuli, 230-232; Bömer, Untersuchungen, 45.

97 Diese Tatsache steht nicht im Widerspruch mit dem, daß die Compitalia zu den sacra popularia quae omnes cives faciunt gezählt wurden (vgl. oben Anm. 49). Die collegia magistrorum und die magistri vicorum sorgten ständig für die sacella der Laren, sie standen den Spielen vor, aber am Kultus selbst und an den Spielen nahmen alle teil. Wenn hingegen ein Kult im ganzen einem bestimmten Kollegium oder einer Familie anvertraut war, so beteiligten sich an denselben nur diese Organisationen. So z. B. nahmen an dem wichtigsten Teil der Luperkalien, dem Lauf um den Fuß des Palatin, nur Mitglieder der Bruderschaft der Luperken teil.

98 J. Marquardt, Römische Staatsverwaltung, 3, 2. Aufl. Leipzig 1885, 204.

99 Wissowa, RuK^2 171; Boehm, Lares, RE 12, 1925, 810; Accame, 15; Bömer, Historia 3, 1954, 252; Bickel, Rh. Mus. 97, 1954, 29;

Niebling, Historia 5, 1956, 309; J. Bleicken, Vici magister, RE 8 A, 1958, 2480.

100 Die Quellen, auf welche sich in diesem Zusammenhang die oben genannten Forscher berufen (Cic. In Pis. 9; de domo 54; de har. resp. 22; Cass. Dio LV 8; CIL IV 60, VI 12, 335, 1324, 2221, 30888, X 3789), beweisen nur das, was augenscheinlich ist, nämlich daß es magistri vicorum und collegia Larum gab, sagen aber nichts von einem Zusammenhang der einen mit den anderen aus.

101 A.D. Nock, Cambridge Ancient History 10, 1934, 479-480; P. Lambrechts, La politique apollonienne d'Auguste et le culte imperial, N. Clio 5, 1953, 65-82.

102 Niebling, Historia 5, 1956, 303-331 passim.

103 Siehe z. B. CIL II 1133, 4293, 4297, 4304, 4306, 4307, XI 2835, V 3257, X 1582, XII 406. Ich kann auf diese Inschriften an dieser Stelle leider nicht näher eingehen und verweise auf eine andere Arbeit. Vgl. auch Bömer, Untersuchungen, 42-54.

104 Ein Verzeichnis der privaten Verbände von Anbetern der Laren gibt Waltzing, Étude historique sur les corporations professionelles chez les Romains, 4, Louvain 1900, 190-192. Über die cultores s. auch L. Schnorr v. Carolsfeld, Geschichte der juristischen Person, 1, München 1933, 267-271. Diese Verbände trugen meistens den Namen collegium Larum, aber auch collegium cultorum Larum, cultores collegii Larum. Oft war zu dem Namen noch eine nähere Bezeichnung hinzugefügt, z. B. CIL VI 671: collegium magnum Lar(um)... Antonini Pii.

105 In diesem Zusammenhang ist auf die Tatsache hinzuweisen, daß schon im zweiten Jh. bakchische Vereinigungen und sodalitates Magnae Matris existierten. In den letzten Jahren der Republik verbreiteten sich besonders Verbindungen der Bekenner der ägyptischen Gottheiten; sie nahmen an den politischen Kämpfen sehr aktiv teil und wurden durch den Senat aufgehoben. Siehe dazu A. Alföldi, Isiskult und Umsturzbewegung im letzten Jahrhundert der römischen Republik, Schweizer Münzblätter 5, 1954/55, 25-31.

106 Dir. ass., 85-86.

107 Cohn, Zum römischen Vereinsrecht, Berlin 1873, 40; De Robertis, Dir. ass., 84.

108 Über die tibicines s. J. Linderski, Państwo a kolegia, Kraków 1961, 9 Anm. 10, wo die weitere Literatur angeführt ist.

109 Vgl. Waltzing, 1, 237–238.

110 CIL VI 1872. Vgl. J. Le Gall, Le Tibre dans l'antiquité, Paris 1953, 268–270.

111 In Pis. Clark 6.

112 Waltzing 1, 103.

113 CIL I^2 687 (nur im Falle der Richtigkeit der von Heurgon, Mél. d'arch. et d'hist. 56, 1939, 14 Anm. 1 vorgeschlagenen Ergänzung horto[lanorum]).

114 Siehe aus der Zeit der Republik: inter figulos, inter falcarios, inter lignarios, vicus argentarius, bubularius, lorarius, materiarius, sandalarius, vitriarius, campus pecuarius (H. Jordan, Topographie der Stadt Rom im Altertum, 1, Berlin 1871, 515–517 und 2, 1885, 597; O. Richter, Topographie der Stadt Rom, 2. Aufl. München 1901, 401–403; Platner-Ashby, A Topographical Dictionary of Ancient Rome, London 1929, s. v.v. Daß die Handwerkerkollegien sich tatsächlich in den einzelnen Bezirken organisierten, beweist das Beispiel des Vereins von lanii piscinenses (CIL I^2 978), so genannt nach dem öffentlichen Teich, Piscina Publica in der XII. Region.

16

CICEROS REDE PRO CAELIO
UND DIE AMBITUS- UND VEREINSGESETZGEBUNG
DER AUSGEHENDEN REPUBLIK

Der Person des M. Caelius Rufus und der Caeliana Ciceros haben in dieser Zeitschrift bereits F. MÜNZER[1] und R. HEINZE[2] ihre Untersuchungen gewidmet; durch eine Kette von scharfsinnigen Feststellungen haben sie unser Wissen in dieser Hinsicht so bereichert, daß damit ein fester Grund für alle weiteren Arbeiten geschaffen wurde. Wenn wir uns aber das rege Interesse für die Geschichte des römischen Vereinswesens und zugleich den rudimentären Zustand der diesbezüglichen Überlieferung gegenwärtig halten, muß es uns erstaunlich erscheinen, daß die Caeliana von diesem Standpunkt aus niemals einer eingehenderen Prüfung unterworfen wurde. Es ist nicht unsere Absicht, eine vollständige Darstellung des römischen Vereinswesens zur Zeit der ausgehenden Republik zu geben; wir wollen nur versuchen, auf Grund der Rede Ciceros Pro Caelio einige Streitfragen von neuem zu erörtern.

Wie bekannt, wurde im April des Jahres 56 M. Caelius Rufus von dem jungen L. Sempronius Atratinus vor Gericht gefordert. Die Klage lautete *de vi*, zu den Anklagepunkten gehörten aber auch die *crimina sodalium ac sequestrium*, deren Caelius sich schuldig gemacht zu haben scheint. Man verweist auf die diesbezügliche Stelle der Caeliana oft genug, hat sich aber bisher sehr wenig bemüht, sie eingehender zu analysieren und mit anderen Quellen zusammenzustellen[3]. Der größeren Anschaulichkeit halber soll diese Stelle im ganzen Umfang wiedergegeben werden. Pro Caelio 16:

Quod haud scio an et de ambitu et de criminibus istis sodalium ac sequestrium, quoniam huc incidi, similiter respondendum putem. Numquam enim tam Caelius

---

[1] Aus dem Leben des M. Caelius Rufus, Hermes 44, 1909, 135 ff., siehe auch dens., RE II A 1366.   [2] Ciceros Rede Pro Caelio, Hermes 60, 1925, 193 ff.

[3] F. M. DE ROBERTIS zitiert diese Stelle in seinem großen Werke über die Geschichte des römischen Vereinswesens, Il diritto associativo romano (Bari 1938), nur einmal, und zwar nur gelegentlich in einer Anmerkung (S. 118 Anm. 41); auch MOMMSEN ist auf dieselbe nicht tiefer eingegangen, weder in der frühen Schrift De collegiis et sodaliciis Romanorum (Kiliae 1843) noch in seinem Meisterwerk Römisches Strafrecht (Leipzig 1899). Dasselbe gilt für die Arbeiten der folgenden Autoren: A. W. ZUMPT, Das Criminalrecht der römischen Republik, Bd. II 1, 2 (Berlin 1868—69); P. KAYSER, Abhandlungen aus dem Process- und Strafrecht. II: Die Strafgesetzgebung der Römer gegen Vereine (Berlin 1873); M. COHN, Zum römischen Vereinsrecht (Berlin 1873); W. LIEBENAM, Zur Geschichte und Organisation des römischen Vereinswesens (Leipzig 1890); I. VAN WAGENINGEN im Kommentar zu seiner Ausgabe der Rede Pro Caelio (Groningae 1908); E. COSTA, Cicerone giureconsulto (Bologna 1927); PFAFF, RE s. v. Sodalicium; J. LENGLE, Römisches Strafrecht bei Cicero und den Historikern (Leipzig und Berlin 1934); S. ACCAME, La legislazione romana intorno ai collegi nel I sec. a. C., Bull. del Museo dell' Imp. Rom. 13, 1942, 13 ff.; B. ELIACHEVITCH, La personnalité juridique en droit privé romain (Paris 1942), und auch für die neueste Arbeit DE ROBERTIS', Il fenomeno associativo nel mondo romano (Napoli 1955).

amens fuisset, ut, si se isto infinito ambitu commaculasset, ambitus alterum accu-saret, neque eius facti in altero suspitionem quaereret, cuius sibi perpetuam licentiam optaret, nec si sibi semel periculum ambitus subeundum putaret, ipse alterum iterum ambitus crimine arcesseret[1].

Was die rechtliche Natur der *crimina sodalium* und *sequestrium* anbelangt und was überhaupt unter diesen *crimina* zu verstehen sei, ist nicht ohne weiteres klar. Bemerken wir zunächst, daß dieses Vergehen in der Fassung Ciceros eine besondere Art von Bestechung bildet, den *infinitus ambitus*, der dem gewöhnlichen *ambitus* entgegengestellt ist. Wenn wir diese *crimina* rein theoretisch betrachten, so ergeben sich folgende Möglichkeiten: man kann darunter verstehen: 1. das von einem Kandidaten dadurch begangene Vergehen, daß er die *sodales* und *sequestres* für sich gewonnen hat, um mit Hilfe dieser Anhänger die Wähler zu bestechen oder einzuschüchtern, 2. daß jemand bei der Bewerbung eines Kandidaten als dessen *sodalis* und *sequester* gewirkt hat.

Es ist begreiflich, daß diese Möglichkeiten keine Alternative bilden, sie sind vielmehr als verschiedene Seiten desselben Vergehens zu betrachten.

Mit welcher von diesen Möglichkeiten haben wir aber hier zu tun? Daß Caelius sich selbst um ein Amt beworben habe, wird mit Recht fast allgemein als unhaltbar erkannt[2]; es bleibt nur die Vermutung übrig, daß er die Kandidatur eines anderen mit unerlaubten Mitteln unterstützt habe. Nachdem MÜNZER die Identität des Bestia mit dem Vater des Atratinus dargetan hat[3], läßt sich nicht weiter an die Teilnahme Caelius' an der Bewerbung Bestias um die Praetur denken; HEINZE verweist dagegen sehr glücklich auf die Pontifikalwahlen[4]. Aus der betreffenden Stelle der Caeliana (19) erfahren wir, daß Caelius bei dieser Wahl einen Senator mißhandelt hat. Es läßt sich vermuten, daß es sich hier um einen Gegner des Kandidaten handelte, für den Caelius bei dieser Wahl gearbeitet hat[5]. Wenn man dieses Ereignis im Zusammenhang mit den oben erwähnten *crimina* betrachtet, paßt es sehr wohl zu der bekannten Tatsache, daß die *sodales* nicht nur mittels Bestechung wirkten, sondern auch vor der Anwendung von Gewalt nicht zurückschreckten.

Die Ambitus-Gesetze kannten vor dem Jahre 56 den Begriff der *crimina sodalium* und *sequestrium* nicht; die Vorwürfe der Ankläger konnten demgemäß nur auf zwei Rechtsakten beruhen: 1. auf einem Senatsbeschluß vom 10. Februar desselben Jahres, über den Cicero seinem Bruder gelegentlich in einem Brief (2, 3, 5) mitteilt: *senatus consultum factum est, ut sodalitates decuriatique*

---

[1] Vgl. auch 78: *non potest, qui ambitu ne absolutum quidem patiatur esse absolutum, ipse impune umquam esse largitor.*

[2] Siehe besonders HEINZE a. a. O. S. 212. Die Auffassung von DRUMANN-GROEBE, Geschichte Roms II 348, ist nicht stichhaltig.

[3] Siehe die in Anm. 1, S. 106 angeführten Arbeiten.   [4] A. a. O. 212.

[5] HEINZE a. a. O. 217ff. und bes. 218 Anm. 1 hat sehr wahrscheinlich gemacht, daß es Q. Fufius Calenus war, der bei den Pontifikalkomitien durch Caelius zurückgedrängt wurde.

discederent lexque de iis ferretur, ut, qui non discessissent, ea poena, quae est de vi, tenerentur, 2. auf dem Gesetz, das der obenerwähnte Senatsbeschluß ankündigt. Prüfen wir zunächst diese letztere Möglichkeit.

Seit dem Senatsbeschluß vom Februar 56 verflossen bis zum Prozeß des Caelius fast drei Monate, da hatte der Senat genug Zeit zur Durchführung des Gesetzes; es spricht aber alles dafür, daß zur Zeit der Verhandlung jene *lex* noch nicht in Kraft getreten war. Wäre dies der Fall, so läge die Vermutung nahe, daß man auf dieser Grundlage eine formelle Anklage gegen Caelius erhoben hätte. Cicero äußert sich dagegen (30) sehr deutlich: *Adulter, impudicus, sequester convitium est, non accusatio: nullum est enim fundamentum horum criminum, nulla sedes*. Der *sequester* ist hier also strafrechtlich dem *adulter* und *impudicus* gleichgestellt. Diese Tatsache zeigt ausdrücklich, daß die *crimina sequestrium* noch durch keine *lex* getroffen waren, denn die zwei erstgenannten sind erst unter Augustus strafbar geworden[1]. Cicero bezeichnet also diesen Anklagepunkt als *convitium*, bloße und unbestimmte Beschuldigung, nicht nur darum, weil die Ankläger keine Beweise dafür beigebracht haben, sondern vielmehr, weil überhaupt keine rechtliche Grundlage für eine solche Anklage vorhanden war. Es waren aber doch *crimina*, was Cicero keineswegs zu leugnen versucht; sie unterlagen zwar keiner Strafe, wurden aber allgemein mißbilligt und mußten, was besonders die *sodales* und *sequestres* anbetrifft, jedem als rechtswidrige Tätigkeit erscheinen. Es unterliegt keinem Zweifel, daß die Phrase *crimina sodalium ac sequestrium* ein terminus technicus ist, der allen Anwesenden bereits geläufig war und schon früher in einem Rechtsakt formuliert worden ist. Nach Ausschaltung der vermeintlichen *lex* bleibt nur das Senatsconsult vom Februar 56, dem wir die juristische Formulierung des Begriffes zuschreiben können[2].

Aus dem bisher Gesagten ergibt sich offensichtlich, daß Ciceros Bericht über den Senatsbeschluß vom Februar 56 sehr flüchtig ist. Die Analyse der Caeliana läßt uns die Tatsache feststellen, daß der Senatsbeschluß nicht nur aus drei Punkten, sondern aus mindestens vier oder fünf Punkten bestand. Zu den in dem Briefe Ciceros bereits genannten Punkten *de sodalitatibus, de decuriatis* und *de lege de iis qui non discessissent ferenda* können wir nun auf Grund der Caeliana zwei weitere hinzufügen, nämlich *de sequestribus* und *de sodalibus*[3]. Diese Feststellung zieht wichtige Folgen nach sich: sie führt nämlich zu neuer

---

[1] MOMMSEN, Strafrecht 688 ff.

[2] Zu demselben Schluß scheint auch HEINZE a. a. O. 212 gekommen zu sein; er hat aber diese Feststellung nur gelegentlich gemacht, ohne sie zu weiterer Argumentation zu verwenden.

[3] Es ist sehr wahrscheinlich, daß im Text des Senatsbeschlusses die Maßregeln gegen die einzelnen *sodales* und jene gegen die ganzen *sodalitates* gesondert formuliert waren, denn in diesem letzteren Falle handelt es sich nicht nur um die bloße Bestechung oder Erpressung, sondern vor allem um den Mißbrauch des Vereinsrechts.

Beurteilung des Inhalts dieses Senatsbeschlusses und stellt überhaupt die Absicht, in welcher der Senat sein *consultum* ergehen ließ, in ein neues Licht.

Um das Verständnis der weiteren Ausführungen zu erleichtern, scheint es nicht unangebracht, an dieser Stelle eine kurze Besprechung der bisherigen Erwägungen einzuschalten und den heutigen Stand des Problems anzugeben. Es bekämpfen sich in der Fachliteratur zwei Ansichten. Nach der einen, die von MOMMSEN[1] stammt und von COHN[2] und WALTZING[3] gebilligt wurde, gehörte der Senatsbeschluß zu den Maßnahmen, die ausschließlich gegen Wahlumtriebe gerichtet waren. Die *sodalitates* sollten in dieser Fassung die Vereinigungen vornehmer Leute, der *amici* und *sodales* eines Kandidaten sein, die allerdings nicht durch Gewalt (*vis*), sondern nur durch Bestechung (*largitio*) wirken sollten. Unter *decuriati* dürften die Zehntschaften der Wähler zu verstehen sein, die auf diese Weise organisiert waren, um ihre Stimmen leichter verkaufen zu können. ZUMPT[4] und KAYSER[5] sind anderer Meinung: das Senatsconsult beziehe sich nicht auf die Wahlvereinigungen, sondern auf die clodischen Kollegien, die, wie sich aus einigen ciceronischen Stellen ergebe, auch in Dekurien geteilt waren. Der Senatsbeschluß dürfte also die Aufhebung der von Clodius gegründeten Vereine in Aussicht genommen haben. Neuerdings ist dieser Gedanke von dem italienischen Rechtsgelehrten F. M. DE ROBERTIS aufgegriffen worden, der nach genauer Prüfung der Quellen und der bisher ausgesprochenen Ansichten den Schluß gezogen hat: Esso ... dovette completamente prescindere dalla corruzione elettorale, colpita da altre leggi speciali in questo tempo[6]. Die Ausführungen DE ROBERTIS' haben bisher keinen Widerspruch erregt und scheinen allgemein anerkannt zu sein[7]; seine Meinung darf also als die heute herrschende Lehre bezeichnet werden.

Bei unbefangener Überprüfung der von DE ROBERTIS vertretenen Theorie kann man ihm aber nicht zustimmen; wir werden sehen, daß die Quellen keinen Anhaltspunkt für eine so formulierte Theorie bieten. Es soll an dieser Stelle das wichtigste Ergebnis der bisherigen Ausführungen besonders betont werden, nämlich, daß schon im Text des Senatsbeschlusses vom Februar 56 sich ein Punkt *de sequestribus* befunden hat, und nicht, wie die herrschende Lehre stillschweigend anzunehmen scheint, erst in der *lex Licinia*. Es fragt sich, auf welche Weise die Maßnahmen gegen die *sequestres*, die Leute, bei denen die Bestechungsgelder deponiert waren, in Einklang mit der Theorie gebracht werden könnten, die jede Beziehung des Senatsbeschlusses auf die Wahlumtriebe zu negieren versucht. Diese Theorie muß also als den Quellen

---

[1] De collegiis 60.   [2] A. a. O. 58.

[3] J. P. WALTZING, Étude historique sur les corporations professionnelles chez les Romains I (Louvain 1895) 111f.

[4] A. a. O. 385.   [5] A. a. O. 165.   [6] Dir. ass. 107 Anm. 42.

[7] Siehe ACCAME a. a. O. 32ff.; L. ROSS TAYLOR, Party Politics in the Age of Caesar (Berkeley and Los Angeles 1949) 210.

widersprechend bezeichnet und als solche abgelehnt werden. Die Ablehnung der heute herrschenden Meinung bedeutet aber nicht, daß damit der Platz für die Erneuerung der Mommsenschen Lehre geräumt ist und daß diese Lehre mit allen Einzelheiten anzunehmen sei; sie bedeutet auch gar nicht, daß alle Ausführungen De Robertis' zu verwerfen seien. Es handelt sich hier nur um das Wichtigste, um die Frage, ob es irgendeinen Zusammenhang zwischen dem Senatsconsult und den Maßnahmen gegen Bestechung gegeben habe. Es liegt auf der Hand, daß nach der obigen Argumentation eine Meinung, die diesen Zusammenhang verneinen wollte, nicht mehr haltbar ist. De Robertis hat wohl Recht, wenn er den Senatsbeschluß entgegen der Ansicht Mommsens auf die clodischen Vereine bezieht[1]. Ich möchte aber dazu bemerken, daß sich aus dieser wohl richtigen Behauptung nicht notwendig ergibt, daß eine Beziehung des Senatsbeschlusses auf die Wahlumtriebe zu negieren sei.

Um die obigen Erörterungen noch etwas eingehender zu begründen, scheint es zweckmäßig, auch die in dem Brief Ciceros uns begegnenden Bezeichnungen *sodalitates* und *decuriati* einer Analyse zu unterwerfen.

Was im Text des Senatsbeschlusses unter *sodalitates* zu verstehen sei, hat schon, und im wesentlichen richtig, Th. Mommsen geklärt[2]. Es muß als unbestritten angenommen werden, daß es Vereinigungen einflußreicher Leute waren, die u. a. bei den Wahlen wirkten und gewisse Kandidaturen unterstützten. Cicero nennt solche *sodalitates* einige Mal, ihr Wesen erscheint aber mit besonderer Klarheit in dem von Q. Cicero verfaßten Commentariolum petitionis. Es heißt 19: *nam hoc biennio quattuor sodalitates hominum ad ambitionem gratiosissimorum tibi obligasti, M. Fundanii, Q. Gallii, C. Cornelii, C. Orchivii: horum in causis ad te deferendis quid tibi eorum sodales receperint et confirmarint scio, nam interfui.* Diese vier Männer sind also die Teilnehmer und vielleicht Vorsteher der einzelnen *sodalitates* gewesen; daraus ergibt sich, daß solche Organisationen eine gewisse Dauerhaftigkeit besaßen und nicht nur für eine bestimmte Wahl ins Leben gerufen wurden. Im Gegensatz aber zu den Kollegien, deren Vorhandensein von dem Wechsel der Mitglieder und der *magistri* unabhängig war, war das Bestehen einer solchen *sodalitas* eng mit der Person ihres Vorstehers verknüpft. Es gibt noch einen weiteren Unterschied zwischen *sodalitates* und *collegia* = Berufsverbänden: die innere Organisation der letzteren beruht auf demokratischen Prinzipien, ihre Vorsteher, die *magistri*, *quaestores*, *decuriones* usw., werden von allen Genossen gewählt; nirgends begegnet uns z. B. ein *collegium Cornelii*, des Cornelius, wie oben eine gleichnamige *sodalitas*[3]. Besondere Aufmerksamkeit muß auf die soziale Seite des

---

[1] Dir. ass. 102 ff., siehe auch Accame a. a. O. 34.   [2] De collegiis 60.

[3] De Robertis (Dir. ass. 23 Anm. 78 und 103 Anm. 21) hat irrtümlich die *sodalitas Cornelii*, die ihren Namen von dem Volkstribun C. Cornelius führte, mit dem *collegium Corneliorum* (Cic., Pro Corn. bei Asc. S. 75 Clark, vgl. App., B. C. 1, 100—104, CIL I² 722) identifiziert, welches aus den von Sulla freigelassenen Sklaven zusammengesetzt war

Problems gelenkt werden, die gewöhnlich unberücksichtigt bleibt. In dieser Hinsicht ist mit besonderem Nachdruck der Umstand hervorzuheben, daß die Mitglieder der *sodalitates* aus den mittleren und oberen Schichten der Gesellschaft stammten, während die der Kollegien die niederen Klassen repräsentierten, besonders die *plebs urbana*[1].

Aber die in Rede stehenden *sodalitates* haben auch mit den alten religiösen Genossenschaften, die ebenfalls denselben Namen führten, nichts gemein. Jene waren wirkliche religiöse Bruderschaften, die manchmal aus uralten Zeiten stammten und sich guten Rufes erfreuten, diese hingegen waren nicht eine Ausartung der früheren, sondern, was auch aus dem oben zitierten Zeugnis des Q. Cicero hervorgeht, ganz neue Vereinigungen, die sich um einen oder mehrere einflußreiche Politiker oder Geschäftsleute gruppierten und fast ausschließlich politischen Zwecken dienten[2]. Cicero hat diese Änderung der Bedeutung sehr richtig wahrgenommen, indem er in der Planciana (37) eine Vereinigung zur Wahlbestechung als eine *consensio* bezeichnet, *quae magis honeste quam vere sodalitas nominaretur*. Dasselbe gilt auch für das Wort *sodalis*, welches von Cicero Pro Plancio 46 als *nomen criminosum* erklärt wird. Gleichzeitig waren aber diese beiden Benennungen auch in der älteren, nicht abfälligen Bedeutung im Gebrauch; Cicero selbst verwendet sie manchmal in diesem Sinne, u. a. auch in derselben Rede Pro Plancio[3]. Einige der älteren *sodalitates* bestanden auch damals fort: Cicero bezeichnet z. B. als *sodalitas* die Bruderschaft der *Luperci*, man kann auch an die *sodalitates Magnae Matris* denken[4]. Diese religiösen *sodalitates* wurden durch den Senatsbeschluß offenbar nicht getroffen. Im weiteren wird also nur von den *sodalitates* — politischen Vereinigungen die Rede sein.

Daß die Tätigkeit solcher Verbände nicht nur auf Wahlbeeinflussung beschränkt war, hat schon MOMMSEN erkannt und auch Beispiele dafür angeführt; wenn er aber behauptet, daß die *sodalitates* bei den Wahlen und überhaupt nur *largitio* geübt haben[5], vermag ich dem Meister der Altertumswissenschaft nicht zuzustimmen. Es ist wahr, daß in den Quellen, auf welche MOMMSEN hinweist (d. h. in der Planciana), nur von Bestechung die Rede ist,

---

Zum *collegium Corneliorum* siehe jetzt J. ČESKA, Deset tisic Corneliu, Listy Filologicke III 78, 1955, 177 ff.

[1] Nicht zutreffend erscheint die Ansicht DE ROBERTIS' Dir. ass. 103 Anm. 21, der die vier oben erwähnten *sodalitates* für Vereinigungen von Freigelassenen hält. Danach wären die Freigelassenen zu *sodales* ihrer ehemaligen Herren geworden, was jedenfalls höchst unwahrscheinlich ist.

[2] Zu dieser Frage vgl. ELIACHEVITCH a. a. O. 219 ff., wo die Quellen- und Literaturangaben vollständig verzeichnet sind.

[3] Pro Plancio 29. Für die weiteren Belege siehe H. MERGUET, Lexikon zu den Reden des Cicero (Jena 1884), und W. A. OLDFATHER, H. V. CANTER, K. M. ABBOT, Index verborum Ciceronis epistularum (Urbana 1938) s. vv. *sodalitas* und *sodalis*. Siehe auch de or. 2, 197, 200; Brut. 166; de nat. deor. 80.

[4] Pro Caelio 26; de senect 13, 45.   [5] De collegiis 41—42, 47.

aber diese Tatsache darf nicht verallgemeinert werden; sie beweist insbesondere gar nicht, daß auch anderswo nur *largitio* vorliegen müsse. Wenn z. B. Cicero ad Att. 1, 14, 5 über die *barbatuli iuvenes, totus ille grex Catilinae* spricht, so paßt dieses Bild sicher nicht zu den aus Sklaven und städtischer Plebs zusammengesetzten Vereinen, sondern eher zu einer *sodalitas* vornehmer Jugend. Es ist bemerkenswert, daß anderswo dieselben *barbatuli iuvenes* als *commisatores coniurationis* bezeichnet werden[1]. Diese *barbatuli iuvenes* erscheinen in Verbindung mit den *operae Clodianae*; es kann als sicher gelten, daß die Gegner des Clodius, Milo und Sestius, von gleichartigen Vereinigungen unterstützt wurden. Daß solche Organisationen nicht nur zu Wahlbestechungszwecken gegründet wurden, ist offensichtlich. Man braucht aber gar nicht derartige Beweise anzuführen; es genügt, sich an die Tatsache zu erinnern, daß die *sodales* kraft des im Senatsbeschluß angekündigten Gesetzes von der gleichen Strafe getroffen werden sollten wie Gewaltverbrecher. Hätten die *sodales* wirklich nur *largitio* geübt, so wäre diese Bestimmung sehr eigentümlich und rätselhaft; nehmen wir dagegen an, sie hätten auch Gewalt anzuwenden gepflegt, so entfallen diese Schwierigkeiten der Interpretation.

Im Text des Senatsbeschlusses müssen wir also unter *sodalitates* die politischen Vereinigungen der Vornehmen verstehen, deren Wirkung sich auf alle Gebiete des Gesellschaftslebens erstreckte, besonders diejenigen, die die Wähler bestachen und sich an den Straßenkämpfen bewaffnet beteiligten.

Daß unter *decuriati* die *decuriae tribulium* gemeint sind, ist aus Stellen wie etwa Cicero Pro Planc. 45. 47 zu entnehmen[2], dagegen besticht die Beziehung auf die clodischen Kollegien auch wegen der uns Pro Sest. 34 und De domo 13 entgegentretenden Ausdrücke nicht wenig[3]. Die Erklärung dieser Bezeichnung bereitet also gewisse Schwierigkeiten, die aber nur zu einem Teil auf unklaren Äußerungen unserer Quellen beruhen, zu einem anderen dagegen dadurch hervorgerufen sind, daß neuere Forscher diese Interpretationsmöglichkeiten als sich widersprechend betrachten und bald die eine, bald die andere aus dem Wege räumen wollen. Ein Beispiel für derartiges Verfahren bietet COHNs Behauptung, daß, weil die clodischen Vereine rechtlich als *collegia* gestiftet wurden, der Senat, wenn er sie treffen wollte, sie bei demselben Namen nennen müßte[4], oder DE ROBERTIS' Versuch, den Dekurien ausschließlich militärische Bedeutung beizumessen[5], was offenbar falsch ist, da die

---

[1] Ad Att. 1, 16, 11.

[2] Pro Plancio 45: *decuriatio tribulium, discriptio populi, suffragia largitione devincta severitatem senatus ... excitarunt.* 47: *sic tu* (sc. Laterensis) *doce* (Plancium) *sequestrem fuisse largitum esse conscripsisse tribulis decuriavisse.*

[3] Pro Sestio 34: *servorum dilectus habebatur pro tribunali Aurelio nomine collegiorum cum vicatim homines conscriberentur, decuriarentur.* De domo 13: *cum desperatis ducibus decuriatos ac descriptos haberes exercitus perditorum.*　　　　[4] A. a. O. 61.

[5] Dir. ass. 106ff. Diese Ansicht hat schon durch ACCAME a. a. O. 35 ihre Berichtigung erfahren.

Dekurieneinteilung ein typisches Merkmal der römischen Vereine bildete. Diese sich anscheinend widersprechenden Interpretationsmöglichkeiten lassen sich aber in Wirklichkeit sehr leicht in Einklang bringen.

Was nämlich Cohns oben angeführte Meinung betrifft, so ist sie sehr formalistisch ausgedrückt. Nach der *lex Clodia*, die die freie Vereinsbildung unter Schutz der Volksversammlung gestellt hat, war jede Einschränkung der Vereinsfreiheit erst nach der Abrogation des clodischen Gesetzes möglich. Im Jahre 56 konnte also der Senat, anders als im Jahre 64, nicht gegen alle Vereine vorgehen und ihre rechtliche Stellung zu ändern versuchen, d. h. er konnte nicht die auch für die Zukunft in dieser Hinsicht alle Bürger bindenden Vorschriften einführen. Aber es ist auch klar, daß damit dem Senat und der Magistratur die polizeiliche Aufsicht über die Vereine nicht entzogen wurde[1]. Der Senat konnte also auch nach der *lex Clodia* die staatswidrigen Vereine, oder besser gesagt, die Vereine, die er als solche erkannt hatte, auflösen oder deren Auflösung der Magistratur auftragen. Cicero schildert uns die von Clodius gegründeten *collegia* als in Dekurien geteilte Scharen bewaffneter Leute, die mit den echten Kollegien nichts zu tun haben und sich nur als solche aufspielen[2]. Also streng juristisch genommen — und das war eben der Standpunkt des Senats — hatten die Organisationen, welche an den Straßenkämpfen teilgenommen haben und überhaupt entweder zu diesem Zwecke oder zur Wahlbestechung ins Leben gerufen wurden, keinen Anspruch auf den Namen der Kollegien (unter *collegia* sollen hier die durch das Gesetz des Clodius geschützten Vereine verstanden werden). Die Kollegien »der Räuber und Banditen« sowohl wie die Wahlklubs zum Verkauf der Stimmen waren schon ex definitione gesetzwidrig und konnten demgemäß nicht, wie es sonst selbst verständlich ist, unter dem Schutze des Rechts stehen. Es muß aber darauf aufmerksam gemacht werden, daß die oben gebrauchten Kunstausdrücke, wie *decuriati*, *collegia*, selbst der Begriff des Rechts, nicht absolut, sondern nur relativ zu verstehen sind; man darf nicht vergessen, daß die obige Argumentation nur den Standpunkt des Senats wiederzugeben versucht und daß die Gegner desselben ganz anderer Ansicht waren. Clodius hat seine Vereinigungen als *collegia* gestiftet, der Senat wollte sie aber als solche nicht anerkennen.

Die bisherigen Ausführungen haben uns also zu dem Schlusse geführt, daß der Senat, als er gegen die *decuriati* einschritt, damit nicht, wie De Robertis meint[3], die *lex Clodia* formell aufheben oder einschränken, sondern vielmehr sie umgehen wollte. Auf diese Weise wird meines Erachtens sowohl das von Cohn konstatierte Hindernis beseitigt als auch die Beziehung des Ausdruckes *decuriati* auf die clodischen Vereine verteidigt. Im Vergleich mit der Inter-

---

[1] In diesem Sinne auch Mommsen, Strafrecht 662 Anm. 4.

[2] Post red. in sen. 33: *simulatione collegiorum*, Pro Sest. 34: *nomine collegiorum*, Post red. ad Quir. 13, De domo 13, In Pis. 11.　　　　[3] Dir. ass. 108.

pretation DE ROBERTIS' ist aber diese Beziehung offensichtlich in einem ganz anderen Sinn gemeint.

Als *decuriati* erscheinen also in unseren Quellen nicht nur die Kollegien des Clodius; die in der Planciana erwähnten Abteilungen der Bürger, die ihre Stimmen verkauft hatten, mußten auch im Jahre 56 existieren und sollten ebensogut durch den Senatsbeschluß getroffen werden. Daß es sich in der Planciana nur um *largitio* handelt, hat nur für diesen Einzelfall Beweiskraft, anderswo konnten solche Zehntschaften ebensogut auch Erpressung üben. Die clodischen Vereine erweckten anderseits nicht nur die Straßenunruhen, sondern beteiligten sich auch an den Wahlkämpfen. Die oft ausgesprochene Meinung, daß diese letztgenannten Vereine zum größten Teil aus Sklaven bestanden und infolgedessen zu Wahlzwecken ungeeignet waren[1], beruht auf Übertreibung einiger Äußerungen Ciceros, der, gewiß auch selbst nicht ohne Übertreibung, über die Teilnahme der Sklaven ausführlich spricht, aber auch zu bemerken weiß, daß die Sklaven nur neben den Freien aufgenommen wurden: *cum in tribunali Aurelio conscribebas palam non modo liberos, sed etiam servos ex omnibus vicis concitatos*[2]. Die Sklaven machten also wohl nur eine Minderheit der Mitglieder aus. Es ist noch zu bemerken, daß Erpressung auch eine Art des Wahlkampfes bilden konnte.

Im Jahre 53 bewarb sich Clodius um die Praetur. Hinsichtlich dieser Bewerbung bemerkt Cicero: (Clodius) *convocabat tribus, se interponebat, Collinam novam dilectu perditissimorum civium conscribebat*[3]. Die Stelle — wie sie handschriftlich überliefert und hier wiedergegeben ist — ist offenbar verderbt, denn die Wendung *Collinam novam* gibt keinen befriedigenden Sinn und ist auch für MOMMSEN unerklärbar geblieben[4]. Statt *novam* sollte man wohl eher *novo* schreiben und das Wort nicht mit *Collina*, sondern eher mit *dilectus* verbinden: *Collinam novo dilectu . . . conscribebat*. Diese Konjektur empfiehlt sich sehr aus sachlichen Gründen und bereitet keine paläographischen Schwierigkeiten, da die Änderung *novo/novam* leicht verständlich ist. Im Jahre 53 hat also Clodius einen neuen *dilectus* in der *tribus Collina* vorgenommen[5]; zum erstenmal geschah es aller Wahrscheinlichkeit nach im Jahre 58, als er sein Vereinsgesetz durchgeführt hatte. In dieser Hinsicht ist es weiter sehr bemerkenswert, daß die hier von Cicero gebrauchten Bezeichnungen (*dilectus*, *cives perditissimi*, *conscribere*) sich einerseits mit den in der Planciana gebrauchten termini technici zusammenstellen lassen, wo von der *conscriptio tribulium* die Rede ist[6], anderseits aber auch mit den Benennungen, welche Cicero für die von Clodius im Jahre 58 gestifteten Vereine angewandt hat (*dilectus*, *exercitus perditorum*, *conscribere*)[7]. Nach Ciceros Angabe hat Clodius im Jahre 53 seine *conscriptio tributim* durchgeführt, wenn sie auch nur auf die

---

[1] COHN a. a. O. 60; DE ROBERTIS, Dir. ass. 105.   [2] De domo 54.   [3] Pro Mil. 25.
[4] De collegiis 59 Anm. 14.   [5] Vgl. L. ROSS TAYLOR a. a. O. 202.
[6] Pro Plancio 45. 47.   [7] Pro Sest. 34, De domo 13, In Pis. 11.

tribus Collina beschränkt war. Wir haben also hier mit demselben Verfahren zu tun, welches in der Planciana als *conscriptio tribulium* bezeichnet ist. Daß aber diese clodische *conscriptio* nicht nur Stimmzwecke im Auge hatte, kann man auf Grund der Ausdrücke *dilectus* und *perditissimi cives* vermuten, die mit bloßer *largitio* nicht vereinbar sind. Es sei noch hinzugefügt, daß die im Jahre 58 von Clodius organisierten Kollegien nach *vici* angeworben und in Dekurien geteilt waren, d. h. daß auch diese *conscriptio* zugleich *tributim* gemacht wurde, da die stadtrömischen *vici* sich mit den vier städtischen *tribus* decken mußten; eine Wahrnehmung, die nicht ohne Wert für die Beurteilung des Wesens der als *decuriati* bezeichneten Organisationen zu sein scheint, indem sie lehrt, daß kein grundsätzlicher Unterschied zwischen *decuriati* und *decuriae tribulium* bestand. In unsern Quellen erscheint bald die eine, bald die andere Seite ihrer Tätigkeit, bald *largitio*, bald *vis*.

Im Jahre 56 konnten die *sodales* und *decuriati* nur für wirklich begangene Gewaltakte bestraft werden; die bloße Zugehörigkeit zu einer *sodalitas* oder *decuria* bildete damals kein juristisch definiertes Vergehen. In Zukunft aber, kraft des neuen Gesetzes, sollte auch schon die bloße Zugehörigkeit als ein *crimen* behandelt und mit gleicher Strafe wie für *vis* belegt werden, wenn auch die *sodales* oder *decuriati* in diesem oder jenem Fall keinen Gewaltakt begangen hatten[1]. Sie haben freilich auch Bestechungen, nicht nur Gewaltakte verübt; bei der Bemessung der Strafe erkannte der Senat augenscheinlich das letztere, für die Staatsordnung gewiß gefährlichere Vergehen als maßgebend.

Es liegt auf der Hand, daß diese Strafe nur gegen die Mitglieder verbrecherischer Vereinigungen Anwendung finden sollte und nicht gegen Bewerber um Ämter. Aus den bisher analysierten Quellen ergibt sich leider nicht, ob der Senatsbeschluß Bestimmungen betreffend die Verfolgung von Bewerbern enthielt, die sich unerlaubter Wahlvereinigungen bedient hatten. Wenn wir uns aber an das Vorhandensein des Punktes *de sequestribus* erinnern, so können wir eine solche Annahme als wahrscheinlich gelten lassen.

Damit wäre die erste Aufgabe dieser Untersuchung, die Zusammenstellung der Angaben der Caeliana über die *crimina sequestrium* und *sodalium* mit dem Bericht Ciceros über den Senatsbeschluß vom Februar 56, erledigt; es bleibt noch auf Grund derselben Stelle der Caeliana eine Prüfung der in der Rede Ciceros Pro Plancio überkommenen Nachrichten über die *lex Licinia de sodaliciis* vorzunehmen und zu versuchen, den Zusammenhang des Senatsbeschlusses vom Jahre 56, der zuerst in der Caeliana bekannt gewordenen *crimina sodalium ac sequestrium* und des licinischen Gesetzes festzustellen.

---

[1] Es ist ein großes Verdienst DE ROBERTIS', die scharfsinnige Wahrnehmung gemacht zu haben (Dir. ass. 112 ff.), daß die *sodales* und *decuriati* nicht für *vis*, sondern nur mit gleicher Strafe wie für *vis* gestraft werden sollten.

Es heißt Pro Plancio 47: *Itaque haesitantem te* (sc. Laterensem) *in hoc soda-liciorum tribuario crimine ad communem ambitus causam contulisti.* Das *crimen sodaliciorum* erscheint hier also im Gegensatz zum *ambitus communis.* Man pflegt auf Grund dieser Stelle anzunehmen, daß die *lex Licinia* den Begriff des schweren *ambitus* zum ersten Male eingeführt und das Delikt abgesondert vom *ambitus communis* behandelt habe. Bemerken wir aber zunächst, daß der-selbe Gegensatz des schweren und des gewöhnlichen *ambitus* uns schon in der Caeliana begegnet, zwei Jahre vor der Rede für Plancius und ein Jahr vor der *lex Licinia.* In dieser Rede erscheinen, wie wir schon gesehen haben, die *crimina sodalium* und *sequestrium,* welche als gesteigerter, *infinitus ambitus,* aufgefaßt, dem gewöhnlichen *ambitus* entgegengesetzt werden. Es wurde oben gezeigt, daß Cicero den Begriff des *infinitus ambitus* in der Rede für Caelius nur aus dem Senatsbeschluß vom Jahre 56 geschöpft haben konnte. Ein Jahr später er-scheint das gleiche Delikt auch in der *lex Licinia.* Man sieht nun mit voller Klarheit, daß es ins licinische Gesetz aus dem Senatsbeschlusse übertragen worden sein muß. Das auf diese Weise zuerst im Senatsbeschluß theoretisch formulierte *crimen* des schweren *ambitus* wurde durch das Gesetz des Crassus auch in die Rechtspraxis eingeführt.

Damit ist auch die von Mommsen[1] abgelehnte, von Cohn[2] und neuerdings von De Robertis[3] erneuerte Vermutung, daß das licinische Gesetz mit der durch den Senatsbeschluß angekündigten *lex* identisch sei, auf einem anderen Wege endgültig erwiesen[4].

Daß die *lex Licinia* nach dem Vorgang des Senatsbeschlusses die Straf-barkeit der *sequestres* eingeführt hat, ergibt sich aus einigen weiteren Stellen der Planciana[5]. Es ist leicht zu beweisen, daß die gegen andere Anhänger der Kandidaten gerichteten Bestimmungen des Gesetzes gleichfalls aus dem Senatsconsult übernommen worden sind. Wir lesen Pro Plancio 46: *quos tu* (sc. Laterensis) *si sodalis vocas, offitiosam amicitiam nomine inquinas criminoso; sin quia gratiosi sint accusandos putas.* Es ist also hier dasselbe *crimen sodalium* versteckt, das uns schon in der Caeliana entgegentrat. Die Anhänger eines Amtsbewerbers, die ihm bei Bestechung bzw. Erpressung geholfen hatten,

---

[1] De collegiis 45.　　　[2] A. a. O. 66.　　　[3] Dir. ass. 110ff. Vgl. Accame a. a. O. 34.
[4] De Robertis verweist Dir. ass. 112 Anm. 7 auf Sch. Bob. S. 150 Stangl: *crimine de sodaliciis Vatinius coeperat accusari* und behauptet: »e poichè l'"interrogatio in Vatinium' è del 56 non può trattarsi che del senatoconsulto in questione«. Wir haben es dabei augen-scheinlich nur mit einem Versehen sowohl des antiken als auch des modernen Gelehrten zu tun. Cicero spricht an der entsprechenden Stelle (33) der Interrogatio in Vatinium nur über die *lex Licinia Iunia,* der Scholiast hat *Iunia* weggelassen und *Licinia* irrtümlich als *lex Licinia de sodaliciis* erklärt. Auf diese Weise hat der italienische Rechtsgelehrte, von einer irrtümlichen Interpretation ausgehend, dem Senatsbeschluß wohl richtig die Einführung des Begriffes des *crimen sodaliciorum* zugeschrieben und damit seine eigene Behauptung, daß der Senatsbeschluß nichts mit den Wahlumtrieben zu tun gehabt habe, negiert.　　　[5] Pro Planc. 45. 47. 48.

konnten nun vor Gericht gebracht werden. Cicero spricht Pro Plancio 37 von einer *consensio quae magis honeste quam vere sodalitas nominaretur* und durch welche die einzelnen *tribus* bestochen wurden. Diese *sodalitas* ist ohne Zweifel eine den durch den Senatsbeschluß verbotenen *sodalitates* gleichartige Vereinigung. Durch solche *sodalitates* wurden also die *decuriae tribulium* angeworben[1], deren Mitglieder (*decuriati*) aber, wie wir gesehen haben, nicht nur ihre Stimmen verkauften, sondern auch bei der weiteren Bestechung und Erpressung mitwirkten. Es ist daher nicht unwahrscheinlich, daß die *lex Licinia* die Ankündigung des Senatsbeschlusses hinsichtlich der Strafe gegen die Teilnehmer der *sodalitates* und *decuriae* verwirklicht hat, ohne von dem Prinzip abgehen zu müssen, daß nur die Bewerber um ein Amt und ihre Helfer bei der Bestechung sich strafbar machen, die bestochenen Wähler aber nicht.

Das *crimen sodaliciorum*, wie es in der Planciana erscheint, beruht auf *decuriatio* und *conscriptio tribulium*; für die Beweisführung des Mißbrauches scheint aber nur die Anwesenheit eines *sequester* und *divisor* maßgebend gewesen zu sein, da nur in diesem Falle erwiesen werden konnte, daß diese *decuriatio* Bestechung[2] zum Zweck gehabt hat und damit zu einem rechtswidrigen Verfahren geworden ist[3]. *De sodaliciis* konnte sowohl ein Kandidat belangt werden, der die *conscriptio* und *decuriatio tribulium* selbst durchgeführt und zugleich als *sequester* oder *largitor* gewirkt hatte, wie auch einer, der dieses Geschäft mittels seiner *sodales* erledigt hat. Cicero betont in der Planciana besonders diese erste Möglichkeit und bemüht sich zu beweisen, daß Plancius niemals die Zehntschaften der Wähler angeworben habe und niemals ein *sequester* oder *divisor* gewesen sei; der Bobienser Scholiast macht dagegen auf die zweite Möglichkeit aufmerksam, indem er berichtet (STANGL S. 152) · *M. Licinius Crassus . . . pertulit, ut severissime quaereretur in eos candidatos qui sibi conciliassent ⟨sodales⟩[4] ea potissimum de causa ut per illos pecuniam tribulibus dispertirent ac sibi mutuo eadem suffragationis emptae praesidia communicarent.*

Sodales conciliare wurde nur in dem Falle zum Verbrechen, wenn es als Vorbereitung zur Bestechung dienen sollte. Dieses Verfahren wird als

---

[1] Nicht überzeugend ACCAME a. a. O. 34, der die Dekurien für Unterabteilungen der *sodalitates* hält. ACCAME hat übrigens Vorgänger in E. KÖPKE, Ciceros Rede für Cn. Plancius (Leipzig 1856) 16—17, und ZUMPT a. a. O. 367 ff., deren Ausführungen bereits durch KAYSER a. a. O. 168 ff. und COHN a. a. O. 68 ff. berichtigt worden sind.

[2] Vgl. Pro Plancio 14: *modo ne largitione sis victus* und dazu W. KROLL, Ciceros Rede für Plancius, Rh. Mus. 86, 1937, 134.

[3] Siehe zu dieser Frage die scharfsinnigen Ausführungen ACCAMES a. a. O. 35 f.

[4] Zu dieser Stelle siehe MOMMSEN, De collegiis 55; TH. STANGL, Bobiensia, Rh. Mus. 65, 1910, 258 f. Im Römischen Strafrecht 872 Anm. 2 dachte MOMMSEN allerdings an »*alios*«. Mit dieser Ergänzung ist aber die nachstehende Bemerkung *ea potissimum de causa ut per illos pecuniam tribulibus dispertirent* nicht vereinbar, da sich daraus ergeben würde, daß ein Bewerber durch andere Bewerber die Bestechungsgelder verteilen durfte.

gesteigerter *ambitus* bezeichnet, es ist jedoch nicht gerechtfertigt, das *crimen sodalium* (*sodales conciliare* oder *sodalem esse*) mit dem *crimen tribuarium sodaliciorum* zu identifizieren. Vom Standpunkt des Kandidaten gesehen, bildete die Anwerbung der *sodales* nur eine Vorstufe zur eigentlichen Bestechung; diese selbst und besonders die sie sehr erleichternde *decuriatio tribulium* wurde nur selten von dem Kandidaten persönlich durchgeführt. Und erst diese *decuriatio* soll als *crimen sodaliciorum* angesehen werden.

Sind auch die die Kandidaten und nicht nur ihre Anhänger betreffenden Bestimmungen der *lex Licinia* aus dem Senatsconsult übernommen, oder sollen wir sie als eine Innovation des Gesetzes betrachten? Wir haben vorher gesehen, daß das *crimen sodalium* zweierlei Interpretationen zuläßt; man kann es auch im Sinne des vom Bewerber um ein Amt begangenen Deliktes verstehen. Die Planciana liefert uns den Beweis, daß dieses Delikt wirklich schon im Text des Senatsbeschlusses in diesem Sinne aufgefaßt war. Aber dies ist nicht alles: aus einigen Äußerungen Ciceros kann gefolgert werden, daß die Einführung der *iudices editicii* und überhaupt des für den Angeklagten ungünstigen Prozeßverfahrens in die Sodalizienprozesse schon im Senatsbeschluß vom Jahre 56 vorgesehen war. Es heißt Pro Plancio 36: *quod genus iudiciorum si est aequum ulla in re nisi in hac tribuaria, non intellego quam ob rem senatus hoc uno in genere tribus edi voluerit ab accusatore.* 37: *Quid? huiusce rei tandem obscura causa est an et agitata tum cum ista in senatu res agebatur, et disputata hesterno die copiosissime a Q. Hortensio cui tum est senatus adsensus?* und weiter: *ita putavit senatus, cum reo tribus ederentur eae quas is largitione devinctas haberet, eosdem fore testis et iudices.*

Aus den oben wiedergegebenen Stellen erfahren wir also, daß es der Wille des Senats war, in der *res tribuaria* (d. h. *crimen sodaliciorum*) die *iudices editicii* einzuführen. Bei der Debatte im Senat hatte Q. Hortensius, der auch im Prozeß des Plancius neben Cicero als Anwalt eine Rede gehalten hat, das Wort ergriffen und sich für Edition der Geschworenen ausgesprochen[1]. Sein Vorschlag fand bei der Senatsmehrheit Gehör. Die Worte *senatus voluerit, putavit, adsensus est* können sich unmöglich auf etwas anderes beziehen als auf ein Senatsconsult[2], und da kann von keinem anderen die Rede sein als von dem Senatsbeschluß vom Februar 56, dem wir schon die anderen Bestimmungen der *lex Licinia* zugeschrieben haben.

Es wurde im vorstehenden versucht, von der in der Rede Ciceros für Caelius vorkommenden Stelle über die *crimina sodalium ac sequestrium* ausgehend, den Entwicklungsgang der Vereins- und Ambitusgesetzgebung in den Jahren 56 und 55 darzulegen. Die Ergebnisse dieser Untersuchung können folgendermaßen zusammengefaßt werden: 1. alle wesentlichen Bestimmungen

---

[1] KROLL a. a. O. 136 Anm. 34 gegen DRUMANN-GROEBE III 94. VI 47 und MÜNZER, RE VIII 2478.   [2] Vgl. Sch. Bob. S. 160 STANGL.

der *lex Licinia de sodaliciis* waren schon ein Jahr vorher in einem Senatsbeschluß vom Februar 56 vorgesehen, 2. die in allen Darstellungen des römischen Vereinswesens gebrauchte Benennung dieses Beschlusses »*senatus consultum ut sodalitates decuriatique discederent*« entspricht dem wahren Inhalt desselben nicht, denn der Brief Ciceros, dem sie entnommen ist, gibt nur einen Punkt der umfangreichen Bestimmungen des Senatsconsults wieder. Das Senatsconsult erscheint uns als ein wichtiger Rechtsakt sowohl für das römische Vereinswesen wie für die Ambitusgesetzgebung.

17

Suetons Bericht über die Vereinsgesetzgebung unter Caesar und Augustus.

Suetonius, Divus Iulius (ed. Roth.) 42:

Cuncta collegia praeter antiquitus constituta distraxit. Poenas facinorum auxit ...

Divus Augustus 32:

Pleraque pessimi exempli in perniciem publicam aut ex consuetudine licentiaque bellorum civilium duraverant aut per pacem etiam extiterant; nam et grassatorum plurimi palam se ferebant succincti ferro, quasi tuendi sui causa, et rapti per agros viatores sine discrimine liberi servique ergastulis possessorum supprimebantur, et plurimae factiones titulo collegii novi ad nullius non facinoris societatem coibant. Igitur grassaturas dispositis per opportuna loca stationibus inhibuit, ergastula recognovit, collegia praeter antiqua et legitima dissolvit.

Die zwei oben wiedergegebenen Suetonsstellen haben eine umfangreiche Literatur hervorgerufen[1]; im Laufe der Polemik wurden zwar manche Streitfragen geklärt, es scheint aber, daß noch nicht alle Interpretations-

---

[1] Th. Mommsen, De collegiis et sodaliciis Romanorum (Kiliae 1843) 78—79; P. Kayser, Abhandlungen aus dem Proceß- und Strafrecht. II: Die Strafgesetzgebung der Römer gegen Vereine (Berlin 1873) 178; M. Cohn, Zum römischen Vereinsrecht (Berlin 1873) 70—73; W. Liebenam, Zur Geschichte und Organisation des römischen Vereinswesens (Leipzig 1890) 27—30; J. P. Waltzing, Étude historique sur les corporations professionnelles chez les Romains I (Louvain 1895) 112—113, 115—117; L. Schnorr von Carolsfeld, Geschichte der juristischen Person I (München 1933) 258—260; F. M. De Robertis, Il diritto associativo romano (Bari 1938) 176—180; B. Eliachevitch, La personalité juridique en droit privé romain (Paris 1942) 235, 251; S. Accame, La legislazione romana

möglichkeiten erschöpft worden sind. Nicht selten pflegte man vielmehr Folgerungen zu ziehen, die als mit dem wahren Inhalt des Textes unvereinbar erscheinen müssen. Es soll also in den folgenden Bemerkungen eine streng philologische Analyse des Textes vorgenommen werden, und erst auf dieser Grundlage wollen wir versuchen, eine Antwort auf die Frage zu geben, welche juristischen Schlüsse aus dem Bericht Suetons gezogen werden können. Um die notwendige Klarheit zu gewinnen, empfiehlt es sich, unsere Erläuterungen ausschließlich auf die innere Kritik des Suetonstextes zu beschränken und alle weiteren Probleme, die sich auf die Vereinsgesetzgebung Caesars und Augustus' beziehen, beiseite zu lassen.

Einer eingehenderen Prüfung bedürfen vor allem die von Sueton gebrauchten termini technici: *collegia antiqua* (*antiquitus constituta*), *collegia legitima*, die Phrase *titulo collegii novi*. Den Kernpunkt bildet dabei die Interpretation des Ausdruckes *collegia legitima* und überhaupt des Terminus *legitimus*. Eine scharfsinnige und inventionsreiche Erklärung wird uns von De Robertis gegeben[2]). Er ist der Meinung, daß der Terminus *legitimus* zur Zeit Suetons seine ursprüngliche technische Bedeutung ,,einem konkreten Gesetze entsprechend" noch nicht verloren habe und darum nicht als ,,der allgemein geltenden Rechtsordnung entsprechend" verstanden werden könne. Von dieser Voraussetzung ausgehend, gelangt De Robertis zu dem Schluß, daß Caesar ein Vereinsgesetz durchgeführt und Augustus dieses Gesetz nur durch einen Erlaß erneuert habe. Da Caesar alle Kollegien mit Ausnahme der *antiquitus constituta* aufgelöst hat, Augustus dagegen mit Ausnahme von *antiqua* und *legitima*, müsse der Ausdruck *legitima collegia* sich auf ein konkretes Gesetz beziehen; wenn wir an die Tatsache erinnern, daß die von der *lex Clodia* garantierte Vereinsfreiheit durch das licinische Gesetz *de sodaliciis* nur in einem gewissen Grade eingeschränkt wurde, und zwar nur mit Bezug auf eine spezifische Art von Vereinigungen, so bleibe kein anderes Vereinsverbot, auf welches der Ausdruck *legitimus* sich beziehen könnte, als das Caesars. Diese logisch durchgeführte Argumentation bedarf einer weiteren Begründung: De Robertis hat es nicht dargetan, daß wir den Begriff *legitimus* in diesem Sinne aufzufassen haben, den er ihm zuschreiben will. Der Behauptung, daß der Ausdruck *legitimus* immer (wenigstens in der vorgaianischen Zeit) im Hinblick auf eine konkrete *lex* gebraucht wurde, kann man nicht zustimmen; es genügt, einige Beispiele aus den Wörterbüchern zu schöpfen, um zu zeigen, daß das Wort sehr oft untechnisch verwendet wurde ohne Anspielung auf die staatliche Rechtsordnung oder jedenfalls ohne Beziehung auf ein greifbares Gesetz[3]). Die

---

intorno ai collegi nel I sec. a. C., Bull. del Museo dell'Imp. Rom. 13, 1942, 39ff. Die Interpretation De Robertis', von Accame weiter fortgeführt, bedeutet bei der Erforschung des Textes den größten Fortschritt; aber auch sie erweckt Bedenken.

[2]) A. a. O. 177—178 mit Anm. 20.
[3]) Siehe z. B. Cic., Fam. VII 6, 1; Brut. 21, 82; Horat., Epist. II 2, 109; Quint., IX 2, 57. Siehe auch G. Tibiletti DE IV s. v. *Lex* S. 705, wo die weiteren Belege verzeichnet sind.

324

Literatur von Mommsen an vertritt eine der Theorie De Robertis' entgegengesetzte Ansicht[4]). Damit ist aber nicht erbracht, daß das Wort an unserer Stelle sich nicht auf eine bestimmte *lex* beziehe[5]). Die Frage, die wir hier zu lösen haben, soll also vielmehr in der Weise formuliert werden, ob in unserem Falle dieser Ausdruck seine Begründung in einem Gesetze bzw. in einer anderen die Bürger bindenden Verfügung habe, oder auf die staatliche Ordnung überhaupt hinweise. Die neue Erörterung der Verwendung des Ausdruckes *legitimus* in den Rechtsbüchern kann m. E., ganz abgesehen davon, daß es nicht im Rahmen dieser Abhandlung liegen würde, bei der Interpretation der Suetonsstelle nicht behilflich sein; es ist vor allem notwendig, den Gebrauch bei Sueton selbst zu prüfen. Das Wort erscheint in den Suetonischen Biographien außer unserer Stelle achtmal: einmal hat es sicher[6]) und dreimal aller Wahrscheinlichkeit nach keine Verbindung mit irgendeinem Volksgesetze[7]), viermal aber kann es letzten Endes auf eine *lex* zurückgeführt werden[8]). In der Wendung *collegia legitima*

---

[4]) Mommsen, Iudicium legitimum, SZ 12, 1892, 268ff. = Ges. Schr. III 356ff.; Schnorr von Carolsfeld a. a. O. 258—259 und zuletzt G. Tibiletti, Sulle leges romanae, Studi Francisci IV (Milano 1956) 601 Anm.

[5]) Die Behauptung Tibilettis: *legitimus* non si riferisce alla *lex* in senso stretto (Studi Francisci IV 615 Anm. 1) scheint in einer anderen Richtung als die von De Robertis übertrieben zu sein. Es unterliegt keinem Zweifel, daß manchmal *legitimus* in Zusammenhang mit einer bestimmten *lex* oder einer Reihe der Gesetze zu bringen ist. Zu dieser Frage siehe L. Mitteis, Römisches Privatrecht (Leipzig 1908) 34ff.; M. Kaser, Das altrömische Ius (Göttingen 1949) 74 mit Anm. 48; derselbe, Das römische Privatrecht I (München 1955) 172—173; E Weiss, Lex Plaetoria, RE Suppl. V 579ff. (über die Bezeichnung *legitima aetas* hinsichtlich privatrechtlicher Handlungsfähigkeit).

[6]) Claud. 21: *legitimum tempus* (über die *ludi saeculares*); der Ausdruck bezieht sich hier augenscheinlich auf den *ordo* der Jahrhunderte.

[7]) In demselben Abschnitt Claud. 21 wird weiter das *munus gladiatorium iustum atque legitimum* dem *extraordinarium* entgegengesetzt. Wie aus der Beschreibung Suetons erhellt, beruht der Gegensatz nicht auf rechtlicher Grundlage, sondern vielmehr auf der Tatsache, daß das letztgenannte *munus* ein neueingeführtes, kurzes (*breve dierum paucorum*) und nicht so prachtvolles gewesen ist. Aug. 45 werden *pugiles legitimi atque ordinarii* und *catervarii* (d. h. nach der zutreffenden Erklärung M. Levis z. d. Stelle in seinem Kommentar zu Suetons Divus Augustus, Firenze 1951, „professionisti" und „diletanti") auseinandergehalten. Ob hier ein Volksgesetz vorliegt, ist sehr zweifelhaft. Vgl. aber Petr., Satyr. 117: *tamquam legitimi gladiatores* und *SC de sumpt. lud. glad. min.*, Dessau ILS 5163 v. 62—63 = A. D'Ors, Epigrafia juridica de la España romana (Madrid 1953) nr 3 S. 59—60. Unter *legitimi honores* (Claud. 5) ist die tatsächliche Bekleidung eines Amtes zu verstehen im Gegensatz zu den bloßen *ornamenta*.

[8]) Galba 8: *legitimum tempus* (hinsichtlich der *honores*) ist offenbar mit den *leges annales* zu verbinden. Ebenfalls muß *legitima poena* (Claud. 14) die durch ein bestimmtes Gesetz gegen ein bestimmtes Verbrechen gerichtete Strafe gewesen sein. Vesp. 8: *legitima praemia* (bez. der Soldaten); der Ausdruck wird auch hier im Hinblick auf eine gesetzliche Verfügung gebildet sein. Über *legitimus senatus* (Aug. 35) siehe Mommsen, Röm. Staats-

ist das Wort offenbar nicht in der übertragenen Bedeutung gebraucht, sondern als der Terminus des Staatsrechts. Unter *collegia legitima* sollen wir also die Vereine verstehen, die nicht nur allgemein der Staatsordnung, sondern speziell dem geltenden Vereinsrecht entsprechen. Diese „geltende Vereinsordnung" — wir müssen es uns klarmachen — dürfte aber durch eine bestimmte gesetzliche Verfügung in Kraft gesetzt worden sein. Es kann also die Vermutung naheliegen, daß der Terminus sich hier wirklich auf ein Vereinsgesetz bezieht. Daß es das des Caesar gewesen sei, muß erst bewiesen werden: es ist nur eine der gleichberechtigten Interpretationsmöglichkeiten. Unter diesen Umständen ergeben sich nämlich zwei Beziehungsmöglichkeiten des Ausdruckes *legitimus*:

1. auf die Vereinsordnung, die in der vorcaesarischen Zeit gegolten hat. Daß nach der *lex Clodia* die Vereinsfreiheit herrschte, können auch jene Schriftsteller nicht verneinen, die für die frühere Zeit die Staatskonzessionierung der Vereine annehmen[9]). Aus dem Bericht Suetons, daß Caesar *cuncta collegia praeter antiquitus constituta* aufgelöst hat, ergibt sich nicht notwendig, daß er das Vereinsfreiheitsystem ganz abgeschafft und besonders freie Vereinsbildung für die Zukunft verboten habe[10]). Aber auch wenn man einen solchen Schluß als wahrscheinlich gelten läßt, kann im Lichte der bisherigen Interpretationsversuche die Möglichkeit nicht in Abrede gestellt werden, daß sein Gesetz später abrogiert werden konnte. Augustus hätte nach dieser Interpretation nur die verbrecherischen Vereine unterdrückt, da alle anderen *legitima* sein mußten.

2. auf die Verordnung Caesars. Die *collegia legitima* wären dann die von Caesar anerkannten Vereine. Das Schwergewicht würde hier auf die Verfügung des Caesar verlegt; Augustus hätte nur dieselbe nach den Wirren des Bürgerkrieges wieder in Kraft gesetzt.

Die These, daß Caesar eine Vereinsreform vorgenommen hat, hat also viel für sich. Das Vorhandensein einer *lex Iulia Caesaris de collegiis* kann aber durch die Erörterung der Bezeichnung *collegia legitima* nicht endgültig nachgewiesen werden.

Es bleibt noch die Phrase *titulo collegii novi* einer Analyse zu unterziehen, die uns vielleicht den Schlüssel zur Lösung der Frage nach dem Zusammenhang der *collegia antiqua* und *legitima* und überhaupt zum richtigen Verständnis des ganzen Suetonstextes geben wird.

Es ist wohl an dieser Stelle nicht unangebracht, auf die Bedeutung der Ausdrücke *collegia antiqua* und *collegia nova* näher einzugehen. Nach der Ansicht De Robertis' dürfte die Bezeichnung *collegium novum* die Übereinstimmung eines Vereins mit dem von Caesar eingeführten *novus ordo* zum

---

recht III³ 924; er stellt aber nicht ausdrücklich fest, daß Augustus die Geschäftsführung des Senats durch ein Gesetz geordnet hat. Siehe doch Cass. Dio 55, 3 und dazu O'Brien Moore, *Senatus* RE Suppl. VI 766.

[9]) Siehe bes. Cohn a. a. O. 56.

[10]) Cohn a. a. O. 70—71; Eliachevitch a. a. O. 235. Siehe auch unten 400.

Ausdruck bringen[11]); diese Bezeichnung sei also nicht im Gegensatz zu den *collegia antiqua* gebraucht. De Robertis behauptet ferner, daß 1. die *collegia legitima* dieselben Vereine gewesen seien wie *antiqua*, 2. nur diese letztgenannten von Caesar regelmäßig autorisiert wurden, 3. Augustus dieselben Vereine verschont habe wie Caesar[12]). Seiner Meinung nach entsprachen also der Verordnung Caesars nur die *collegia antiqua*, welche auf Grund dieser Verordnung allein zu *legitima* wurden; wenn aber keine anderen Vereine nach der Maßnahme Caesars hätten rechtlich weiterbestehen können und wenn De Robertis zugleich das in der Phrase *titulo collegii novi* erscheinende *collegium novum* als dem caesarischen *novus ordo* entsprechend interpretiert, so würde sich aus dieser Konstruktion ergeben, daß die *collegia nova* mit den *collegia antiqua* identisch gewesen seien.

Diese Theorie ist aber unhaltbar, und zwar sowohl aus textkritischen wie sachlichen Gründen: sie findet, wie wir sehen werden, keine Begründung im Suetonstext und widerspricht allem, was wir von der Terminologie des römischen Vereinswesens wissen. Bedenken erweckt auch die Gleichstellung der *collegia antiqua* mit den *legitima*. Schnorr von Carolsfeld hat mit Recht bemerkt, daß zwar alle von Augustus verschonten Vereine (die alten mitgerechnet) *legitima*, aber nicht alle zugleich *antiqua* sein mußten[13]). Er hat aber diese Behauptung eher als ein logisches Postulat formuliert (dessen Richtigkeit als eines solchen unbestritten ist), als sie aus dem Suetonsbericht hergeleitet.

Es ist zwar zu bemerken, daß es nicht klar ist, was unter dem Begriff *collegium antiquum* zu verstehen ist. Accame bemerkt mit Recht, daß wir unter dieser Bezeichnung nicht nur die acht angeblich von Numa gestifteten Zünfte verstehen sollen, sondern auch andere Vereine, die vor dem Eingreifen der politischen Agitation ins Vereinsleben entstanden waren[14]). Man bemüht sich ferner, das Verzeichnis solcher Vereine zu rekonstruieren, was zwar für die Geschichte einzelner Vereine nicht ohne Bedeutung ist, verspricht aber keine neuen Erkenntnisse zur juristischen Interpretation unserer Stelle. Jedenfalls war die Bezeichnung *collegia antiqua* unseren antiken Berichterstattern geläufig, und zwar faßten sie dieselben, entgegen der Ansicht De Robertis, als Gegensatz zu den *collegia nova* auf. Es soll hier die Tatsache besonders betont werden, daß die *collegia antiqua* und *nova* nicht zum ersten Mal bei Sueton nebeneinander auftreten. In diesem Zusammenhang sind vor allem einige Äußerungen Ciceros anzuführen, welche man niemals zur Interpretation des Berichtes Suetons angewendet hat. Wie bekannt, hat im J. 64 der Senat eine Maßnahme gegen Vereine getroffen, die aber nach sechs Jahren durch eine *lex Clodia* abgeschafft wurde. Nun heißt diese *lex* bei Asconius (S. 16 Stangl): *lex Clodia de collegiis restituendis novisque instituendis*. An diese *collegia nova* erinnert

---

[11]) A. a. O. 179 Anm. 23.
[12]) A. a. O. 178—179.
[13]) A. a. O. 258—259. Vgl. auch Liebenam a. a. O. 30.
[14]) A. a. O. 43—44.

Cicero In Pis. IV 9: *collegia, non ea solum, quae senatus sustulerat, restituta, sed innumerabilia quaedam nova ex omni faece urbis ac servitio concitata* und Pro Sest. XXV 55: *collegia non modo illa vetera contra senatus consultum restituerentur, sed ab uno gladiatore innumerabilia alia nova conscriberentur.* Als *collegia nova* sind hier diese Vereine aufgefaßt, die erst auf Grund der *lex Clodia* gegründet wurden und sie werden diesen, *quae senatus sustulerat,* entgegengesetzt. Diese letztgenannten werden Pro Sestio als *vetera* bezeichnet. Das Adjektiv *vetus*, beachte man, weist hier nicht darauf hin, daß diese Kollegien von alters her bestanden, sondern unterstreicht bloß den Gegensatz zu den *collegia nova*. Es sind die Vereine, die vor dem J. 64 entstanden waren. Die Ausdrücke *collegia nova* und *vetera* sind hier also nur relativ genommen verständlich[15]). Diese Tatsache liefert uns eine offenbare Parallele zum Gebrauch dieser Ausdrücke durch Sueton.

Caesar hatte *cuncta collegia praeter antiquitus constituta* aufgelöst. Nach seinem Tode aber *plurimae factiones titulo collegii novi ad nullius non facinoris societatem coibant.* Augustus unterdrückte also alle Vereine *praeter antiqua et legitima.*

Aus dem ersten Satz ergibt sich, daß nach der Maßnahme Caesars nur die alten Vereine weiterlebten. Nun belehrt uns Sueton, daß die verschiedenen *factiones*, die, wie aus dem Zusammenhang erhellt, Vereinigungen von Räubern und anderen Missetätern sich unter dem Deckmantel der *collegia nova* zusammenschlossen. Daß solche *factiones* widerrechtlich waren, ist offensichtlich; es besteht aber zugleich kein Zweifel darüber, daß die *collegia nova*, als welche sie sich aufzuspielen versuchten, ganz regelrechte Organisationen waren. Auf den ersten Blick scheinen diese Testimonien widersprechend zu sein; in Wirklichkeit besteht hier kein Widerspruch.

Über die *collegia antiqua* des Sueton wissen wir nur soviel, daß sie schon einige Zeit vor der Unterdrückung der Kollegien von Caesar existiert hatten; wie alt sie wirklich waren, wissen wir nicht genau und dies Problem interessiert uns hier auch nicht. Die *collegia nova* müssen dagegen die Vereine sein, die erst nach der Verfügung Caesars ins Leben gerufen wurden. Man sieht jetzt, daß der Begriff *collegia legitima* neben den *collegia antiqua* auch die *collegia nova* umfaßt; damit ist die These widerlegt, welche die *collegia antiqua* und *legitima* völlig identifiziert.

Wir müssen uns vor allem darüber klar sein, auf welcher juristischen Grundlage die *collegia nova* gegründet werden konnten. Man kann auf folgende Möglichkeiten hinweisen. Die *collegia nova* sind:

1. die auf Grund der Maßnahme Caesars gegründeten Vereine[16]). Caesar hätte danach in seiner Verfügung die Gründung neuer Vereine vorgesehen, denen aber eine formale Genehmigung seitens der Staatsorgane erteilt werden mußte.

---

[15]) Vgl. G. M. Monti, Le corporazioni nell'Evo antico e nell'alto Medio Evo (Bari 1934) 190—191.

[16]) Vgl. Accame a. a. O. 39, der die *collegia legitima* erklärt als quelli costituiti in base alla legge di Cesare.

2. die frei gebildeten Vereinigungen. Caesar habe also nur die wider-
rechtlichen Organisationen unterdrückt; die Vereinsbildung sei, von seiner
Verfügung unangetastet, frei geblieben wie vorher.

3. die erst nach der eventuellen Abschaffung der Verordnung Caesars
entstandenen Vereine.

Es ist zu bemerken, daß diese letzte Möglichkeit zu demselben Schluß
führt wie die erste, nämlich daß Caesar eine gründliche Reform des Vereinsrechts durchgeführt hat, durch welche die Rechtsstellung der Gesamtheit
der Vereine auch für die Zukunft ganz geändert wurde. Es kann nicht
bezweifelt werden, daß zur Zeit des Augustus als *collegia legitima* nebeneinander die *collegia antiqua* und *nova* existierten. Die von Augustus aufgelösten *collegia* waren also in Wirklichkeit nur *factiones*, die als *collegia*
auftraten. Die Tatsache, daß Augustus die *collegia antiqua* speziell genannt
hat, zeigt, daß er seine Verfügung an die des Caesar anknüpfen wollte.
Wären nun die *collegia nova* erst nach Abrogation der Verordnung Caesars
gegründet worden, so wäre es sehr wahrscheinlich, daß sie alle von Augustus
aufgelöst worden wären. Auf diese Weise kann man die dritte Möglichkeit
ausscheiden. Was dagegen die zweite oben angedeutete Möglichkeit betrifft,
so ist sie, historisch genommen, sehr unwahrscheinlich. Die Aufhebung
aller Vereinigungen mit Ausnahme nur von wenigen und die Genehmigung
der freien Vereinsbildung miteinander in Einklang zu bringen, scheint unmöglich. Es ist aber zu betonen, daß eine solche Möglichkeit nichtsdestoweniger besteht und ich kein Mittel sehe, diese Frage auf dem Wege der
rein textkritischen Analyse zu lösen. Die Analyse des Suetonstextes kann
daher als ein gutes Beispiel dienen, daß man sich immer gegenwärtig halten
muß, was wirklich aus dem Texte abgeleitet wird und was nur Schlüsse sind, die
wir nur mit Rücksicht auf sachliche Wahrscheinlichkeit ziehen. Die These
also, daß Caesar das römische Vereinswesen auf neuer Grundlage geordnet
hat und daß Augustus sein Werk fortsetzte, ist durch die innere Kritik des
Berichtes Suetons nicht ausgeschlossen und durch die sachliche Wahrscheinlichkeit sehr unterstützt[17]).

Die obigen Erörterungen haben sich in einer anderen Richtung bewegt
als die bisherigen Interpretationsversuche; auch die Problemstellung war
eine andere. Es sei in diesem Zusammenhang an die schönen Worte Mommsens zu erinnern, deren Richtigkeit wir immer besser kennenlernen, daß
die Natur des römischen Vereinswesens derartig ist, daß sie *perpetuam
interpretationem vix recipiat*[18]).

---

[17]) Es ist nicht unwahrscheinlich, daß Caesar diese Reform durch ein
Gesetz durchgeführt hat, ich verstehe aber nicht, warum aus dieser wohl
richtigen Annahme sich ergeben sollte, daß Augustus nur ein Edikt ergehen
lassen konnte. Der Bericht Suetons berechtigt uns keinesfalls zu einer
solchen Folgerung.

[18]) De collegiis 128.

CICERO AND SALLUST ON VARGUNTEIUS

In the famous meeting at the house of Laeca the conspirators decided to resort to violence and to put the consul Cicero to death. Sallust's narrative of the plot is as follows: igitur perterritis ac dubitantibus ceteris C. Cornelius eques Romanus operam suam pollicitus et cum eo L. Vargunteius senator constituere ... sicuti salutatum introire ad Ciceronem ac de improviso domi suae inparatum confodere.[1] Cicero's own version, so far as the status of the would-be assassins is concerned, is divergent: reperti sunt duo equites Romani, qui ... sese illa ipsa nocte paulo ante lucem me in meo lectulo interfecturos pollicerentur.[2]

One of those equites Romani was certainly C. Cornelius, but who was the other?[3] In the modern literature Cicero's statement is simply set aside as a mere inaccuracy.[4] Consequently, in all standard works dealing with the Catilinarian conspiracy or the composition of the Roman senate there appears Vargunteius as being a member of the senate in 63.[5] This would, however, mean that Cicero made in an official report denouncing the plot a slip in so important a question as the status of the persons involved and that he repeated it later when preparing the speech for publication. This seems hardly likely. Of course, either Cicero or Sallust must be wrong, but why should we not blame the latter? It is to be stressed that neither Cicero's statement has been proved on external evidence wrong, nor that of Sallust right. Let us now consider the possibility of Sallust being inaccurate. Would it lead to rejection of his report of Vargunteius' participation in the attempt to murder Cicero? Not necessarily; but there remains one way of escape only: to prove that Cicero's unknown eques and Sallust's Vargunteius senator were, or rather could be, identical.

An important piece of evidence on Vargunteius is contained in the Pro Sulla 6: quis nostrum adfuit Vargunteio? nemo, ne hic quidem Q. Hortensius, praesertim qui illum solus antea de ambitu defendisset. Vargunteius' trial de ambitu is to be placed in any case before the passage of the lex Tullia on electoral corruption;[6] since he appears as a member of the so-called first Catilinarian conspiracy[7] it seems very likely that he was in 66 indicted under the lex Calpurnia de ambitu on a charge of electoral bribery and eventually condemned.[8] This may have induced him to join Catiline, Autronius Paetus and Sulla. The

---

[1] Cat. 28, 1.

[2] Cat. I 9.

[3] Other sources (Plut., Cic. 16, 1; App., B.C. II 3) are here apparently confused. Cf. K. Buresch, Die Quellen zu den vorhandenen Berichten von der Catilinarischen Verschwörung. Commentationes O. Ribbeck. Lipsiae 1888, 232; Münzer, RE IV 1255 No. 19 and 1278 No. 89.

[4] Cf. e.g. H. Gundel, RE VIII A 377: Wenn es bei Cic. Cat. I 9 von C. Cornelius und ihm (sc. Vargunteius) heißt duo equites Romani so mag dies Flüchtigkeit seitens des Redners sein (durch Aufregung an diesem Tage bedingt...)

[5] Cf. Drumann-Groebe, Geschichte Roms 5, 480; T. Rice Holmes, The Roman Republic I, Oxford 1923, 255; P. Willems, Le Sénat de la République Romaine III² (Registres), Paris 1885, 102; T. R. S. Broughton, The Magistrates of the Roman Republic II, New York 1952, 497.

[6] It is hardly possible that Hortensius defended one of the outstanding Catilinarians in September or October 63.

[7] Cic., Sull. 67.

[8] Cf. S. H. Rinkes, Disputatio de crimine ambitus, Lugd. Batav. 1854, 99–100; A. W. Zumpt, Der Criminalprozeß der römischen Republik, Leipzig 1871, 528; L. Lange, Römische Altertümer III², 225.

penalty provided by the Calpurnian law was exclusion from the senate and loss of ius honorum for ever.[9]

Cicero speaking of duo equites Romani may have alluded to the actual status of Vargunteius, whilst Sallust to his previous position.[10] If so, Cicero's statement cannot be longer regarded as a mistake due to his excitement: on the contrary, it was from the legal standpoint possibly the most strictly correct expression.

If our argumentation be granted, the entry on Vargunteius in the lists of the Roman republican senators: L. Vargunteius, a senator in 63, should be replaced by the following one: L. Vargunteius, a senator in 66. Convicted de ambitu and expelled from the senate.[11]

---

[9] Cass. Dio 36, 38, 1; Sch. Bob. 78 Stangl.

[10] It is worth-while to note that Cat. 17, 3 he lists (in 64 B.C.) among the men of senatorial rank P. Autronius Paetus and P Cornelius Sulla who, however, having been in 66 convicted de ambitu and expelled from the Senate, technically were not at that time senators.

[11] The present note has been compiled during my stay at Bryn Mawr thanks to a grant from the Ford Foundation. I wish to thank Professor T. S .R. Broughton for help and assistance: however, for any view expressed above I am responsible alone.

19

THE SURNAMES AND THE ALLEGED AFFINITY OF C. CAELIUS RUFUS

In an interesting and inspiring article Professor M. Brożek[1] has recently called attention to the form in which there appears in the *History* of Cassius Dio (ind. lib. 57) the name of C. Caelius Rufus (cos. A. D. 17): Γ. Καικίλιος[2] Γ. υἱ. Νέπως ἢ ῾Ροῦφος. The juxtaposition of the two cognomina Rufus (a normal cognomen in the gens Caelia) and Nepos (normally used by a branch of Caecilii, the Caecilii Metelli Nepotes) is indeed striking and various hypotheses have been advanced to explain this name-form. Professor Brożek cites with approval (and probably he is right in so doing) the opinion of Klebs[3] that this unusual name was concocted by a scribe who mistakenly added to the gentilicium Καικίλιος (which he had already found in his text: such a corruption of Caelius — Καίλιος into Caecilius — Καικίλιος is very frequent in the manuscripts) the cognomen Nepos (while retaining at the same time the cognomen Rufus of the Caelii).

M. Brożek proposes to trace back that error to its very first conception. He conjectures that the full name of C. Caelius Rufus, also including his filiation, was C. Caelius C. f. M. n. Rufus. The scribe would have erroneously understood the abbreviation n(epos) as N(epos) and M(arcus) as M(etellus). This, in combination with Καικίλιος from Καίλιος, should have produced in the extant text of Cassius Dio the strange form Γ. Καικίλιος Γ. υἱ. Νέπως ἢ ῾Ροῦφος. The author contends

---

[1] M. Brożek, *De C. Caelii Rufi nomine corrupto*, Eos LII 1962, p. 129.

[2] Cf. 57, 17, 1 Γάιος Καικίλιος. Also the fasti Lunenses call him Caecilius (CIL IX 1356; A. Degrassi, *Inscriptiones Italiae*, XIII f. 1, Roma 1947, p. 310); this is, however, only a mistake as the name of the other consul of 17 A.D. is also corrupted (L. Pontius Flaccus instead of L. Pomponius Flaccus). Cf. also E. Groag, RE III (1899), col. 1266 (*Caelius* no 33); A. Degrassi, *I Fasti Consolari dell'Impero Romano*, Roma 1952, p. 8.

[3] E. Klebs, *Prosopographia imperii Romani*, I, Berolini 1897, p. 261. Klebs rejects the explanation of Nipperdey (*Opuscula*, p. 534), that the full name of the consul C. Caelius was C. Caecilius Metellus Nepos Caelius Rufus or C. Caelius Rufus Caecilius Metellus Nepos and that this unusual accumulation of nomina was due either to adoption or to addition of the maternal name (Nipperdey's explanation has been rejected also by Groag, RE III (1899), col. 1266; *Prosop. imp. Rom.*, II², 1936, p. 27—28, but accepted by U. Ph. Boissevain in his edition of Cassius Dio, ad loc.). However, it is interesting to observe that such hybrid name-forms sporadically made their appearance already in the late republic; cf. e.g. P. Cornelius Scipio Nasica (cos. 52 B.C.) whose name after his adoption into the family of the Caecilii Metelli was Q. Caecilius Metellus Pius Scipio Nasica (cf. on him F. Münzer, RE III (1899), col. 1224—1228, s.v. *Caecilius* no 99; idem, *Aus dem Verwandtenkreise Caesars und Octavians*, Hermes LXXI 1936, p. 222 ff.; M. H. Prévost, *Les adoptions politiques à Rome sous la République et le Principat*, Paris 1949, p. 19; L. R. Taylor, *The Office of Nasica Recorded in Cicero, Ad Atticum 2.1.9*, Classical, Mediaeval and Renaissance Studies in Honor of B. L. Ullman, Roma 1964, p. 80 ff.).

further that Marcus, C. Caelius' grandfather, was none other than M. Caelius Rufus, praetor in 48 B. C. To strengthen this supposition he adduces two arguments: 1. Velleius Paterculus (who was a contemporary of C. Caelius) did not mention in his *Historia Romana* the praetorship of M. Caelius Rufus "suo loco", but only additionally in II 68,1—2; he would have added this passage in consideration of the influence of M. Caelius' grandson, the consul who *fortasse satis valuit, ut et avus eius et ipse Velleio non neglegendi viderentur*. 2. Velleius would have mentioned M. Caelius also because of *communio civitatis*. M. Brożek points out that the home -town of Velleius greatgreatgrandfather was Aeclanum and that an inscription (CIL IX 1238) testifies the existence in that town also of the Caelii Rufi.

That the praenomen of C. Caelius' grandfather was Marcus, it has been deduced by M. Brożek by subtle reasoning from a scribe's mistake; assuming as a working- -hypothesis the correctness of this theory, let us see at first if the arguments adduced to prove the identity of this Marcus with M. Caelius Rufus, Cicero's friend and praetor in 48 will stand criticism.

1. It is contended that Velleius Paterculus mentions M. Caelius in order to gain the favour of his grandson, the influential consul. But the text points to the contrary. Velleius relates that M. Caelius as praetor in 48 rebelled against Caesar, intended to cancel debts, was declared enemy by the senate and finally was killed by consular troops[4]. To mention this (and only this) would be, indeed, a very perverse method of gaining C. Caelius' favour[5]. Could not Velleius select from the deeds of M. Caelius anything more suitable to that end?

So this point proves nothing. Neither that the consul was a grandson of the orator, or that he was not. It is simply not pertinent.

2. It is contended that the home-town of Velleius and the Caelii Rufi was Aeclanum in the land of the Hirpini. If the alleged *communio civitatis* is to have any bearing on the question of the indentity of M. Caelius the grandfather with M. Caelius the orator, it is indispensable to prove on external evidence that both men descended from the same community, be it Aeclanum or any other town in Italy.

a. The origin of Velleius Paterculus. It is to be observed that it was Minatus Magius, Velleius' maternal and not paternal ancestor that was a native of Aecla-

---

[4] Vell. II 68.1—2: *M. Caelius... in praetura novarum tabularum auctor extitit nequiitque senatus et consulis auctoritate deterreri; accito etiam Milone Annio, qui non impetrato reditu Iulianis partibus infestus erat, in urbe seditionem, in agris haud occulte bellicum tumultum movens, primo summotus a re publica, mox consularibus armis auctore senatu circa Thurios oppressus est.* It may be interesting to observe that Velleius mentions Caelius in passing once before (II 36,2), but in a very appropriate place: among other prominent orators of Cicero's time.

[5] It may be amusing to observe that abolition of debts — *tabulae novae* — was also Catiline's slogan. There was nothing more repudiating to the propertied classes in Italy than projects for the cancellation of debts (cf. Z. Yavetz, *The Failure of Catiline's Conspiracy*, Historia XII 1963, p. 490 ff.). And the consul C. Caelius was certainly not a man to be pleased by such information about his ancestor.

num. The Vellei themselves were a Campanian family, with their *domus* probably at Capua[6].

b. The *patria* of M. Caelius Rufus: Aeclanum or Tusculum? But the choice is by no way confined — as M. Brożek seems to admit — only to these two municipalities. In fact, Professor Brożek is, to my knowledge, the first to propose Aeclanum. The inscription that records there a Caelius Rufus is late and suspect[7], so that this is rather a remote possibility. But in discussing the origin of M. Caelius Rufus it seems hardly possible to omit the basic text of Cicero, *pro Caelio 5*: *Nam quod est obiectum municibus esse adulescentem non probatum suis, nemini umquam praesenti ... ani maiores honores habuerunt, iudices, quam absenti M. Caelio; quem et absentem in amplissimum ordinem cooptarunt et ea non petenti detulerunt quae multis petentibus denegarunt*. The corrupt reading ... *ani* (*praetoriani* P) has become a real crux interpretum. Various emendations have been proposed, but none gained general favour. Beroaldus (in 16th century) proposed *Puteolani*, but against this conjecture cf. the just remarks of C. M. Francken, P. Groebe and R. G. Austin[8]; Orelli (in 1832) read *Praenestini*, W. Wegehaupt (in 1878) *Cumani*, F. Luterbacher (in 1905) *Formiani* and Vollenhoven *Veronenses*[9]. Some scholars were of the opinion that there was hidden no city-name at all and so Oetling (in 1868) proposed to read *oppidani*, Francken (in 1880) *praetori populi Romani* (sic!), Harnecker (in 1886) *populares* (which I adduce only for curiosity). The most plausible had long seemed the reading *Tusculani*, thus assigning the patria of M. Caelius Rufus to Latin Tusculum. This reading was proposed by J. G. Baiter and accepted, among others, by F. Münzer, P. Groebe and R. Syme[10]. But there are strong arguments against this conjecture. R. G. Austin and L. R. Taylor have rightly pointed out that Cicero's words about the excessive honours given to Caelius by his municipes would have

---

6 See the discussion and sources in R. Syme, *The Roman Revolution*, Oxford 1960 (first published 1939), p. 383; I. Lana *Velleio Patercolo*, Torino 1952, p. 55 ff., esp. p. 62; A. Dihle, RE VIII A (1955), col. 638—639 (*Velleius* no 5). There seems to be no connection between the family of the historian and C. Velleius, a senator from Lanuvium, cf. L. R. Taylor, *The Voting Districts of the Roman Republic*, Rome 1960, p. 263.

7 CIL IX 1238: D.M. /C. Caelio Rufo/ qui vixit ann. XXVI/ m. VII C. Caelius fil. /infeliciss. The editor (Th. Mommsen) comments on this inscription as follows: „Vide ne sit interpolata; certe offendit quod pater cognomine caret". Cf. Münzer, RE III (1899), col. 1267: „eine verdächtige und jedenfalls späte Inschrift".

8 C. M. Francken, *Ciceronis Oratio pro Caelio*, Mnemosyne N. S. VIII 1880, p. 204; P. Groebe, *Das Geburtsjahr und die Heimat des M. Caelius Rufus*, Hermes XXXVI 1901, p. 614; R. G. Austin, *M. Tulli Ciceronis Pro M. Caelio Oratio*[3], Oxford 1960 (2nd edition 1952), p. 147.

9 Vollenhoven (cited by Austin) thus identified M. Caelius with Caelius known from Catullus. This opinion was shared also by Francken, *o.c.* p. 204. Against this view see, however, the remarks of F. Arnaldi, *Catullo e Clodia*, Rivista di Filologia V 1927, p. 351; M. Rothstein, *Catull und Lesbia*, Philologus LXXVIII 1923, p. 17.

10 Münzer, RE III (1899), col. 1267; Groebe, *o.c.* p. 614; R. Syme, *Caesar, the Senate and Italy*, Papers of the Brit. School at Rome XIV, 1938, p. 6 n. 19; idem, *The Roman Revolution*, p. 88—89. On evidence of inscriptions the Caelii were a prominent family at Tusculum.

sounded very strange if his home-town were Tusculum, the *patria* of many distinguished aristocratic and consular families[11].

The situation changed in 1905 when A. Clark adduced the reading of Σ (a second hand in Cod. Paris. 14749 representing the tradition of the lost Cod. Cluniacensis) *Praestutiani*. This reading had, however, already been known to Gruter (in 17th century) who emended it into *Praetutiani*. This emendation (in the form *Praetuttiani*) was introduced by R. G. Austin into his Oxford edition of the *Pro Caelio*[12]. Austin points out to the existence of an ager Praetuttianus in Picenum with its chief town Interamnia (not to be confounded with Interamna on the Nar). He thinks that Cicero used *Praetuttiani* as a shortened form for the full title *Interamnates Praetuttiani*. Austin's solution has recently been adopted by L. R. Taylor in her monumental monograph on the Roman voting districts[13].

So the question concerning the origin of M. Caelius Rufus, as it stands now, is, at best: Tusculum or Interamnia? (but not Aeclanum).

c. The home-town of C. Caelius Rufus (cos. A. D. 17). An inscription from Tusculum (CIL XIV 2622) records a C. Caelius C. f. Rufus who was aedil of Tusculum together with C. Caninius Rebilus. This man has been with great probability identified with the consul[14].

So, it seems to be virtually certain that all the three men concerned, Velleius, C. Caelius the consul and M. Caelius the orator descended from three different towns and that none of them was Aeclanum[15].

It now becomes clear that the identification proposed rests only on the praenomen Marcus recovered by M. Brožek from the text of Cassius Dio as the praenomen of C. Caelius' grandfather, but not attested as such elsewhere. Let us now see if it is reasonable at all to attribute C. Caelius a grandfather named Marcus.

Theoretically (and perhaps only theoretically) it is not impossible that a scribe had misunderstood the abbreviation *M(arcus)* as *M(etellus)* and *n(epos)* as *N(e-*

---

[11] Austin, *o.c.* p. 49, 147; Taylor, *The Voting Districts*, p. 199—200. On the attitude of the *Tusculani* cf. Cicero, *pro Plancio* 19—23 where the orator contrasts the lack of interest of the Tusculani in the petitio of M. Iuventius Laterensis with the great support given Cn. Plancius by his fellow-townsmen from Atina. See esp. *pro Plancio* 20: *numquando vides Tusculanum aliquem de M. Catone illo in omni virtute principe, num de Ti. Coruncanio municipe suo, num de tot Fulviis gloriari?*

[12] Austin, *o.c.* p. 146—147. Before Austin, Gruter's emendation was accepted by Rothstein, *o.c.* p. 18 and Arnaldi, *o.c.* p. 351.

[13] Taylor, *o.c.* p. 199—200.

[14] Groag, RE III (1899), col. 1266 (*Caelius* no 33); R. Syme, *Senators, Tribes and Towns*, Historia XIII 1964, p. 114. But cf. T. P. Wiseman, *Some Republican Senators and their Tribes*, U. Q. N.S. XIV 1964, p. 126, who identifies him with C. Caelius, the tribune in 51 B. C. According to Wiseman C. Caelius (cos. suff. 4 B. C.) and C. Caelius C. f. Rufus (cos. A. D. 17) were probably son and grandson of the tribune of 51.

[15] Even if Tusculum were the patria of M. Caelius, this would certainly not have been sufficient to prove such a close parentage between the consul and the orator, as that admitted by M. Brožek.

pos), but, in view of the fact that these abbreviations were most frequently used and must have been familiar to any scribe, such a thesis seems to be highly improbable[16].

This is not all. Let us observe further that in the extant text of Cassius Dio C. Caelius is equipped with only two cognomina, Rufus and Nepos; the third alleged cognomen, Metellus, is omitted. So the scribe must have at first misinterpreted *M(arcus)* into *Metellus* and then left *Metellus* out of his text. But if so, how can we know that there stood in the original text the name Marcus? This belief depends on the reasoning that the cognomen *Nepos* [from *n(epos)*] must have been preceded (as it is normal) by *Metellus* and that that latter cognomen could have been inferred only from the abbreviation *M(arcus)*. The whole theory rests ultimately on the interpretation of *Nepos* = *n(epos)* and so the grandfather Marcus becomes a more and more elusive person; another moment and he will disappear altogether.

It is said that this misinterpretation of *n(epos)* into *Nepos* was due to a scribe's error („sive dictantis sive librarii ad dictationem parum attenti culpa"). Let us now ask which condition would absolutely have to have been fulfilled in order that such confusion could have come about. The answer presents itself: the text must have been dictated and written down in Latin. If it were in Greek the full name of the consul C. Caelius, as required by the theory under discussion, would have sounded Γ. Καίλιος (Καικίλιος) Γ. υἱ. Μ. ἔγγ. Ῥοῦφος; and from ἔγγ(ονος) to Nepos it is rather a long way. But were the indices to Cassius Dio compiled in Latin?

---

16 If this thesis is to have any degree of probability, it is necessary to show that the abbreviations M. and N. were really sometimes used to denote the cognomina Metellus and Nepos respectively. As far as the inscriptions are concerned, R. Cagnat (*Cours d'épigraphie latine*[4], Paris 1914) records no such example; also on the brick-stamps where the names are possibly most contracted, such abbreviations are not attested (although this may, of course, be due only to chance). Cf. H. Bloch, *Indices to the Roman Brick-stamps*, HSPh LVIII—LIX 1948, p. 36—39.

20

THE AEDILESHIP OF FAVONIUS, CURIO THE YOUNGER AND CICERO'S ELECTION TO THE AUGURATE

IN his monumental work on the Magistrates of the Roman Republic, Professor T. R. S. Broughton records as the aediles in 52 B.C. Cato's famous *alter ego*, M. Favonius, and a M. Aufidius Lurco; the latter entry is queried, and, as the sources apparently do not permit it, no indication is given whether they held the plebeian or the curule aedileship.[1] But the exact date of Favonius' aedileship is also open to dispute, and thus a number of modern scholars assign his tenure of that office to 53[2] (and not 52[3]). Favonius' earlier career has recently been studied by Chr. Meier[4] and L. R. Taylor;[5] I propose now also to subject a later stage of his political activity to a closer scrutiny. The aedileship of Favonius appears to be associated in a rather odd way with the person of the younger C. Scribonius Curio. But Curio is also of importance for the dating of Cicero's election to the augurate: he links together Cicero's priesthood and Favonius' aedileship.

Only two sources mention Favonius' holding of the aedileship: Cassius Dio and Plutarch, in the Life of Cato Uticensis. Let us now discuss in turn these two testimonies.

[1] T. R. S. Broughton, *The Magistrates of the Roman Republic* 2 (New York 1952) 235 and 240 n. 2.

[2] G. Schubert, *De Romanorum aedilibus* (Regimonti 1828) 421; L. Lange, *Römische Alterthümer* 3[2] (Berlin 1876) 361; P. Willems, *Le Sénat de la république romaine* 1 (Louvain 1885) 491, 513; W. Drumann-P. Groebe, *Geschichte Roms* 3 (Leipzig 1906) 34–35; 4 (1908) 319; J. Seidel, *Fasti aedilicii* (Diss. Breslau 1908) 70–71; F. Münzer, *RE* 6 (1909) 2075 s.v. Favonius 1; 2A (1921) 869 s.v. Scribonius 11. Until the publication of *MRR* this had been in fact the traditional date, going back to Pighius' *Annales Romanorum* 3 (Antverpiae 1615) 404–405.

[3] The following now also opt for 52: Ch. Meier, *Lexikon der Alten Welt* (Zürich-Stuttgart 1965) 954; H. G. Gundel, *Der Kleine Pauly* 2 (1967) 525.

[4] "Zur Chronologie und Politik in Caesars erstem Konsulat," *Historia* 10 (1961) 96–98.

[5] "The Office of Nasica Recorded in Cicero, *Ad Atticum* 2.1.9," in: *Classical, Mediaeval and Renaissance Studies in Honor of B. L. Ullman* (Roma 1964) 79–85.

I. Favonius and Pompeius Rufus: Cass. Dio 40.45.1–4

In 40.45.4 we read that Favonius, the aedile, was cast into prison "on some trifling charge" by Q. Pompeius Rufus, termed tribune in 40.45.2. The date of the tribunate of Pompeius Rufus is 52 B.C.: this date is established by Asconius (32–33, 37, 42, 49 C), and Cass. Dio also (40.49.1–2 and 55.1) assigns his tribunate unequivocally to that year. *Prima facie* this might also seem to establish beyond any reasonable doubt the date of the aedileship of Favonius as 52, and such was apparently the opinion of Broughton. He writes (*MRR* 2.240 n. 2): "Dio places Favonius' aedileship during the tribunate of Pompeius Rufus, which is dated in 52."

Let us, however, look more closely into the passage in question. Dio relates that Pompeius Rufus, although he was then serving as tribune, was put in jail by the senate, apparently for his part in the riots preceding the election of Cn. Domitius Calvinus and M. Valerius Messala to the consulship of 53, and that in revenge he later arrested Favonius. It is clear that in this passage Dio dates the tribunate of Pompeius Rufus in 53, when Calvinus and Messale were consuls, and not in 52, the year of Pompey's consulship. If Dio's narrative is treated as a separate whole, the following picture emerges: he really places the aedileship of Favonius during the tribunate of Pompeius Rufus, but a) according to the computation adopted by him in this passage the date of Rufus' tribunate was 53; and b) this would consequently also be his date for Favonius' aedileship. From the fact that Dio erred in respect to a), it does not necessarily follow that he must have been wrong also in respect to b).

It is a plausible suggestion that Pompeius Rufus was imprisoned by the senate as tribune designate in July (or August) 53, and that Dio, when dating his tribunate in 53, was confused by that circumstance.[6] But Pompeius Rufus could arrest Favonius only as tribune: either in December 53, during the first days of his tribunate, or in 52. Accordingly the date of Favonius' aedileship would be 53 or 52. Until Broughton's Magistrates appeared, it had been in fact the predominant opinion that Pompeius Rufus arrested Favonius immediately upon

---

[6] Cf. E. Meyer, *Caesars Monarchie und das Principat des Pompeius*[3] (Stuttgart und Berlin 1922) 209–210; G. Niccolini, *I fasti dei tribuni della plebe* (Milano 1934) 315. A. Clark (*M. Tulli Ciceronis Pro T. Annio Milone Oratio* [Oxford 1895] 132) argued that "the college of the tribunes to which Rufus and Plancus belonged came into office early in 53 B.C., going out at the corresponding time in 52." But this is only a curiosity.

entering office on 10 December 53.[7] This opinion presents a compromise between the actual date of Rufus' tribunate and Dio's chronology in the passage under discussion. It may therefore be preferable to opt with Broughton for 52, but at the same time it ought to be made clear that on the basis of Dio's text alone neither solution can be definitely proved or disproved. It would be better to leave the whole controversy undecided. But perhaps Plutarch can provide more definite information.

II. FAVONIUS AND CURIO: PLUTARCH, CATO MINOR 46

Plutarch's account belongs virtually to the Cato-legend. At first he tells us the story of how Cato secured Favonius' election to the aedileship: when he discovered that the balloting tablets had been forged (they were all inscribed in one hand) he appealed to the tribunes of the plebs and succeeded in annulling the results of the voting. But even after Favonius had finally been elected aedile he did not stop helping him. The fable follows of Cato's arranging the spectacles in the theater on behalf of Favonius. These performances were marked by extreme austerity. At the same time, in another theater, Curio, the colleague of Favonius in the office (Κουρίων ὁ Φαωνίου συνάρχων) was giving lavish games. But the people, so Plutarch assures us, left him and went over to Cato and Favonius.

Plutarch seems to place the aedileship of Favonius after the riots and anarchy of late 54 and the first half of 53, but before the outbreak of violence in late 53 and early 52 caused by the fierce canvassing of Scipio Nasica, Plautius Hypsaeus, and Annius Milo for the consulship of 52. So, on the basis of Plutarch's chronology, we would have to date the aedileship of Favonius (and of Curio) in 53. However, if they held the curule aedileship,[8] they could at the earliest have been elected at the end of July 53, or even later. The consular elections for 53 were not held until July or August 53,[9] and the *comitia aedilicia* could take place

---

[7] See Lange, *RA* 3². 362; Drumann-Groebe 3.35 n. 1; 4.319; Seidel 71; Münzer, *RE* 6.2075; Niccolini 317; Miltner, *RE* 21 (1952) 2252 (Miltner holds that Favonius, when he was arrested by Rufus, just "vom Tribunat abgetreten war": a typical inaccuracy of Miltner).

[8] Niccolini 315. This was apparently also the opinion of Lange, *RA* 3². 360–361.

[9] According to Dio 40.45.1, they took place in the seventh month of the year; according to Appian *B.C.* 2.71 the city was eight months without consuls. Dio's date is accepted by Niccolini 315 (with discussion) and Broughton, *MRR* 2.228.

only after the consuls had been chosen. But it is theoretically possible that Favonius[10] (and Curio) were the plebeian aediles: in that case they would have been elected in 54 and would have served in 53 their full term of office.

Now, who is this Curio? It would seem, the notorious C. Scribonius Curio, tr. pl. (suff.) in 50. But here a difficulty arises.

Against the dating of Favonius' aedileship in 53 serious objections may be raised, all connected with the person of Curio. Broughton remarks that " Curio was absent from Rome in 53 and gave his games in honor of his father in 52." Broughton's conclusion is that "Curio was not then an Aedile but was preparing for his candidacy for the aedileship of 50."[11] These arguments invite discussion.

1. *Curio's absence from Rome in 53* would, of course, preclude any possibility of his being aedile in that year. In fact, we know that he was then in Asia, and although his title is not preserved, it is a reasonable conjecture that he served there in 54 (and perhaps in 53) as quaestor under C. Claudius Pulcher.[12] Nevertheless, many scholars have thought it possible to make him aedile in 53. The point is that we do not know exactly when Curio left Asia and returned to Rome. Cicero directed six letters to him in 53 (*Fam.* 2.1–6), but none of them is dated. However, all of these letters seem to have been written during the first half of 53 (1–3), or about the middle of the year (4–6).[13] Especially interesting is the last letter in this series (Fam. 2.6), in which Cicero asks Curio to support Milo in his campaign for the consulship of 52. The opening words of this letter seem to show that Curio had at that time already

[10] This was the opinion of Pighius, Willems, Seidel, and Münzer, cited above, n. 2. The position of Drumann–Groebe is not clear in this respect. As to Curio, see below, n. 14.

[11] *MRR* 2.240 n. 2.

[12] Münzer (*RE* 2A.868) and M. Bülz (*De provinciarum Romanarum quaestoribus*, Diss. Lips. [Chemnitii 1893] 42–43) think that he was quaestor in Asia in 54, but Münzer adds that he "verweilte dort noch 53 längere Zeit." According to Broughton (*MRR* 2.224 and 227 n. 4), he may have served in Asia in 54 and until late in 53 or early in 52. Cf. also *MRR* 2.614 (Index of careers) where he appears as "Q. ? 54 or 53, Proq. ? Asia ca. 52." In *MRR Suppl.* (1960) 55 he is termed quaestor and proquaestor in Asia, and his tenure of that office is dated in ca. 54–52. Two inscriptions from Caunus in Caria published by G. E. Bean (*JHS* 74 [1954] 89 nos. 23 and 24) may allude to him, but as he is named there without any title and no date is preserved, they are of little help to us. Bean holds that he was quaestor in 55–54; so also J. and L. Robert, *Bull. ép.* 1956 no. 274 c (*REG* 69 [1956] 164).

[13] Cf. R. Y. Tyrrell–L. C. Purser, *The Correspondance of M. Tullius Cicero* 2² (Dublin 1906) nos. 166, 168, 169, 175, 176, 177; L.-A. Constans, *Cicéron, Correspondance* 3 (Paris 1950) nos. 164, 165, 166, 173, 174, 175.

left Asia and was expected in Rome. This would explain why Cicero was so anxious to gain his support for Milo's candidature.

Since Cicero's letters to Curio give no definite answer as to how long Curio remained in Asia and when he actually came back to Rome, the possibility cannot be excluded that he did, in fact, return in 53, perhaps still in time to be elected at the delayed elections to the curule aedileship of 53.[14] But this is only a theoretical possibility: it can be positively established that he was not elected aedile in 53, or in any other year.

By chance we happen to know that Cicero was elected augur when Curio was still absent from Italy. But, as the exact date of Cicero's election is not recorded, this might seem to be to little avail for our argument. In fact, we know exactly neither when Curio returned to Rome, nor what the date of Favonius' aedileship was, nor when Cicero was elected to the augurate. However, if we link all these three issues closely together, a new and unexpected light might be shed on each of them. This problem calls for a separate discussion; see below, §IV.

2. *Curio's candidacy for the aedileship of 50.* In 51 Curio was chosen tribune of the plebs[15] (for 50). This renders highly improbable his alleged tenure of the aedileship in 53. There were certainly no legal obstacles to prevent a man who had already held the aedileship from later becoming a tribune, but, at any rate, it would have been very unusual for an *aedilicius* to compete for the tribunate.[16] But this is only a minor point here. What is important is not so much the simple fact that Curio became the tribune as the circumstance that he was elected at a by-election. He seems to have originally intended to stand in 51 for the aedileship of 50; however, after one of the designated tribunes had been convicted on a criminal charge and a vacancy in the tribunician college occurred, Curio appears to have changed his mind and got himself elected to the tribunate instead of the aedileship.[17]

But if we look more closely into the matter, we detect a complication. The first, somewhat surprising fact is that Curio's actual candidacy for

[14] As the elections to the plebeian aedileship for 53 were not affected by the interregnum and took place in 54 — and Curio resided then in Asia — the contention that he was aedile of the plebs in 53 (advocated, strangely enough, by Münzer, *RE* 6.2075, and earlier by Bülz 43) entirely lacks foundation. See Seidel's criticism, *FA* 87–88. Münzer adopted later Seidel's view, see *RE* 2A.869.

[15] For sources, see *MRR* 2.249.

[16] See Th. Mommsen, *Römisches Staatsrecht* 1³ (Leipzig 1887) 551–552. The only analogy would have been the case of M. Livius Drusus, tr. pl. 91, and aedile probably ca. 94. Cf. *MRR* 1.12 and 14 n. 1.

[17] So Münzer, *RE* 2A.869.

the aedileship of 50 is nowhere expressly mentioned. The basis for that belief is constituted by two remarks of Caelius in his letters to Cicero: *Fam.* 8.9.3 (dated 2 September 51): *Turpe tibi erit Patiscum Curioni decem pantheras misisse, te non multis partibus pluris; quas ipsas Curio mihi et alias Africanas decem donavit*, and *Fam.* 8.8.10 (written in October 51): *Me tractat liberaliter Curio et mihi suo munere negotium imposuit: nam si mihi non dedisset eas quae ad ludos ei advectae erant Africanae, potuit supersederi.*

These statements are rather vague, but nevertheless the inference seems to be possible that the *ludi* referred to cannot have been any others than those Curio would have had to give as aedile (in 50) and for which he was already making preparations. After his election to the tribunate, the panthers being of no use to him, he presented them to Caelius, the *aedilis curulis* designate.

But, one may ask, why invent new *ludi* of Curio: would it not be the most natural explanation to take Caelius' remark as referring to Curio's games honoring his deceased father?[18] We know from Pliny[19] that Curio gave not only theatrical performances, but also games in the amphitheater, for which wild beasts were necessary. There is, however, an obvious difficulty inherent in this interpretation. Curio gave his games at the latest in 52 (see below), and the panthers mentioned by Caelius were sent to Rome one year later, in 51. They could not be destined for Curio's funeral *munus.*

On the other hand it seems possible to explain why Curio withdrew from the canvass for the aedileship. The reason would be his debts, which he had contracted by his extravagant manner of life and especially by his profuse games in honor of his father; the tenure of the aedileship would have strained his resources to a still greater extent. He therefore approached Caesar, hoping to receive from him financial assistance, but was rebuffed and had to give up his aedilician plans. Only at that point, profiting by the condemnation of a tribune designate, he decided to take his chance and to stand with the help of the *boni* for the tribunate.[20]

---

[18] For this interpretation, see Tyrrell-Purser 3² (Dublin 1914) 117.

[19] *N.H.* 36.116–120.

[20] See Caelius, *Fam.* 8.4.2. Curio's election to the tribunate is discussed by W. K. Lacey, "The Tribunate of Curio," *Historia* 10 (1961) 320–322; he does not, however, analyze the question of Curio's candidacy for the aedileship. We may note that if Curio really wanted to attain the aedileship, his goal was probably the aedileship of the plebs. M. Caelius, who in 51 was elected to the curule aedileship, records as his competitors M. Octavius and C. Lucilius Hirrus (*Fam.* 8.2.2; 8.3.1); of Curio no word.

Now if Curio canvassed for the aedileship in 51, it is clear that he could not have held that office previously. This conclusion may be corroborated by other arguments. As Seidel has pointed out,[21] among the witnesses to the senatorial resolutions passed on 29 September 51,[22] Curio was listed after C. Lucilius Hirrus, *tr. pl.* in 53 and unsuccessful candidate for the curule aedileship in 51; as this list was clearly arranged in order of seniority,[23] it shows that Curio had not attained the aedileship. Seidel and Broughton have been wholly justified in removing him from the lists of the aediles, where he found his place only thanks to the credulity of some, even outstanding scholars.

3. *Curio's games in honor of his father.* With respect to the alleged aedileship of Curio we have arrived at the same conclusion as Broughton, but this has no relevance to our main question, the dating of the aedileship of Favonius. The fact that Curio did not hold the aedileship does not entail in any way the conclusion that the date of Favonius' aedileship must have been 52, and not 53. It is only the games Curio gave in commemoration of his father's death that are of importance here. The profuse extravagance of these games earned them lasting notoriety. It is an attractive and convincing suggestion, put forward by Seidel and accepted by Münzer and Broughton,[24] that Plutarch refers in fact to these games, confusing them, however, with the aedilician ones and mistakenly terming Curio the colleague of Favonius. It is clear that the dating of Favonius' aedileship depends ultimately and exclusively upon the dating of Curio's games. Broughton states firmly that Curio gave his games in 52, but Seidel puts them in 53, and he is followed in that by Münzer and recently by Chr. Meier.[25] Once more, there is no direct evidence for either assertion. Plinius (*N.H.* 36.116–120) in his description of Curio's games gives no specific date; from a letter of Cicero to Curio (*Fam.* 2.3, written according to Tyrrel-Purser and Constans in the first half of 53) we know, however, that one of Curio's freedmen was ready at that time to announce the games, but he was advised by Curio's friends to defer the formal announcement until his patron's arrival in Rome. But we do not know when Curio returned to Rome: as we have seen, he may have returned in 53, but we have no means of

[21] *FA* 88.
[22] Caelius, *Fam.* 8.8.5.
[23] Cf. *MRR* 2.247–248.
[24] Seidel 88; Münzer, *RE* 2A.869; Broughton 2.240 n. 2.
[25] See Broughton, Seidel and Münzer 11.cc.; Meier, *Lexikon der Alten Welt* 2743. But Meier at the same time dates the aedileship of Favonius to 52 (ibid. 954), dissociating in that way (intentionally or not) Curio's games from Favonius' magistracy.

proving that he actually did so. Consequently, both 53 and 52 must be taken into account as possible dates for Favonius' aedileship.[26]

III. Curio and Lurco

Let us now turn our attention to Favonius' hypothetical colleague in the aedileship, M. Aufidius Lurco. Who was this personage? It is not easy to determine; much easier and much more to the point would be to determine who he was not. In the first place he certainly was not Livia's maternal grandfather, as Willems[27] believed him to have been. Whether he is to be identified with the Lurco[28] who was a tribune of the plebs in 61, or with the M. Lurco[29] who was a senator in 59, or with

[26] An argument advanced by Seidel (*FA* 70–71) to disprove the possibility of assigning the aedileship of Favonius to 52 may be worth noticing. In 52 Favonius presided (as a *quaesitor*) over the trial of Milo *de sodaliciis* (Asconius 54 C), and it was Mommsen's firm belief that the *quaestio de sodaliciis* was always directed by non-magisterial officers, *quaesitores* or *iudices quaestionis*, and that a magistrate never functioned as the presiding officer in that court (*Röm. Staatsrecht* 2³ [Leipzig 1887] 583). Broughton was, however, not disturbed by this argument, and for good reason. The presidents of the court *de sodaliciis* are known in two other cases, and in both of them the theory of Mommsen does not seem to hold. Broughton (*MRR* 2.227 n. 3) points out that since C. Alfius Flavus, who presided in 54 over the trial of Plancius, was empowered to issue edicts (Cic., *ad Q.fr.* 3.1.24, regarding the trial of Gabinius *de maiestate*), it is very probable that he was praetor, and not only *quaesitor*, as Mommsen thought (ibid. 2.³ 201 n. 4). It is true that Cicero (*pro Planc.* 43 and *ad Q.fr.* 3.3.3, the latter reference concerning Gabinius' trial) applies to Alfius only the term *quaesitor* (as also Asconius [54 C] does with respect to Favonius), but this does not preclude the possibility that at the same time they were also magistrates. Mommsen observed himself that the term *quaesitor* was a general title given to any presiding officer of a standing court; it was used also in regard to magistrates (*Staatsrecht* 2.³ 223 n. 4; *Römisches Strafrecht* [Leipzig 1899] 207 n. 1). Decisive here, however, is the case of P. Servilius Isauricus, who held the praetorship in 54 (*MRR* 2.222) and in the same year was clearly in charge of C. Messius' trial (Cic., *ad Att.* 4.15.9); there is no doubt that this was a trial *de sodaliciis*, cf. Mommsen, *De collegiis et sodaliciis Romanorum* (Kiliae 1843) 61 and D. R. Shackleton Bailey, *Cicero's Letters to Atticus* 2 (Cambridge 1965) 211–212. The fact that Favonius served as a *quaesitor* in 52 must not therefore militate against the assumption that in the same year he was an aedile.

[27] *Le Sénat* 1.491. On evidence of inscriptions (*CIL* 9.3661 = *ILS* 125, *CIL* 2.1667, *IGR* 4.983) the name of Livia's mother was Alfidia M.f., and not Aufidia, as Suetonius (*Caligula* 23) states. Cf. Klebs, *RE* 2 (1896) 2293 s.v. Aufidius 24, and especially T. P. Wiseman, "The Mother of Livia Augusta," *Historia* 14 (1965) 333–334.

[28] Cic., *Att.* 1.16.13. Cf. Klebs, ibid. Aufidius 25; Shackleton Bailey 1.323. He may well be identical with the senator M. Lurco. See the next note.

[29] Cic., *pro Flacco* 86–89.

both, is far from certain. Nor can we tell whether he was or was not identical with the M. Aufidius Lurco who made a fortune by fattening peacocks for sale.[30] Moreover, it is not certain whether he really bore the gentilicium Aufidius.[31] But there is still something more: perhaps our Lurco was not a real person at all. Suspicion is in order. He owes his existence to a conjecture by Willems,[32] who emended the reading *ΔΟΥΡΙΩΝ* in the manuscripts of Plutarch, *Cat. Min.* 46.7 to *ΛΟΥΡΚΩΝ*, and equipped him with the gentilicium Aufidius. But the real surprise is yet to come: this is the same passage in Plutarch that was adduced previously as the evidence for Favonius' connection with Curio. If we inspect not only the text of Plutarch, but also the apparatus criticus,[33] we will find that Curio too owes his existence to a conjecture, going back to J. Amyot, a sixteenth-century French bishop and statesman, famous as a classicist for his translation of Plutarch. In place of the manuscript reading *ΔΟΥΡΙΩΝ* he read *ΚΟΥΡΙΩΝ*, and this emendation has been unanimously adopted (with the exception of Willems) by all subsequent editors and commentators.

Both conjectures have been utilized in *MRR*: the entry on M. Aufidius Lurco as aedile in 52 is provided by Plutarch as emended by Willems, whereas the discussion on Favonius' association with Curio is based on Plutarch as emended by Amyot. One (or both) of them must disappear. If Amyot's conjecture is discarded and Willems' emendation is adopted, not only Scribonius Curio and his games disappear, but also an important piece of evidence that Broughton was able to adduce in support of his dating of the aedileship of Favonius in 52. But this does not change the picture too much: as we have tried to show, the association of Favonius with Curio was not conclusive in this respect. The association of Favonius with Lurco is not conclusive either; however, it would have slightly favored the attribution of Favonius' (and Lurco's) aedileship to 53, this being the most natural chronology of Plutarch's account. It seems, however, that it is rather Lurco's name, and not Curio's, that should be deleted. Normally both aediles took care of the *ludi* and shared equal responsibility for organizing them:[34] it is there-

[30] Varro, *de re rust.* 3.6.1; Plin., *N.H.* 10.45; Tert., *de Pall.* 5.6; cf. Hor., Sat. 2.4.24.

[31] In fact, only his cognomen has been recovered from the text of Plutarch (see below). However, if he really was a Lurco, it is not unlikely that he was also an Aufidius, the cognomen Lurco being used, as far as we know, only by the gens Aufidia. Cf. I. Kajanto, *The Latin Cognomina* (Helsinki 1965) 269.

[32] *Le Sénat* 1.491.

[33] Cf. the edition by K. Ziegler in the *Bibl. Teubneriana* (Lipsiae 1964).

[34] See Mommsen, *Röm. Staatsrecht* 2.[3] 519; Seidel 88 n. 7.

fore very improbable that the two aediles should have organized the theatrical performances simultaneously but separately in two different theatres.

If we retain the reading Κουρίων, we may proceed further; but the affair with Lurco adds an uncertainty to all our conclusions.

IV. CURIO AND CICERO: THE DATE OF CICERO'S ELECTION TO THE AUGURATE

The elevation to the augurate was, after the consulship, the greatest political and social success of Cicero, marking the peak of his career after his return from the exile. Surprisingly enough, modern scholars have paid no adequate attention to the possibilities of establishing the exact date of that event.

Cicero was elected augur to fill the vacancy in the augural college after the death of P. Crassus, the younger son of the triumvir, who fell in the battle near Carrhae on 9 June 53.[35] The most widespread opinion asserts that Cicero's election also took place in 53;[36] Broughton is more cautious, and rightly so. He states that Cicero was elected "probably in 53," but further on he defines the period of time available for Cicero's election more strictly: Cicero was elected "before Curio's return from Asia and Antony's departure for Gaul."[37] In other words, Cicero attained the augurate when Curio was absent from Rome and when Antony was present.[38] In later years Antonius allegedly boasted that he originally wanted to compete for the augurate at that time and that he gave up only because of his reverence for the consular, thus paving the way for Cicero's election. Now, we do not know precisely when Antonius came to Rome from Gaul, or when he returned as quaestor to Caesar's army. This depends to a large extent upon the date of his quaestorship; opinions of scholars vary on this point, 52 or 51 being the

---

[35] Drumann–Groebe 4.114ff., 129; Münzer, *RE* 13 (1926) 293 s.v. Licinius 63; Gelzer, ibid., 325–328 s.v. Licinius 68.

[36] See Drumann-Groebe 6.80; C. Bardt, *Die Priester der vier grossen Collegien aus römisch-republikanischer Zeit* (Progr. Berlin 1871) 25; E. Ciaceri, *Cicerone e i suoi tempi* 2² (Genova 1941) 159; J. van Ooteghem, *Pompée le Grand* (Bruxelles 1954) 437; D. Magnino, *Plutarchi Vita Ciceronis* (Firenze 1964) 118. This date was apparently accepted also by M. Gelzer, *RE* 7A (1939) 967 (repeated without change in his *Cicero* [Wiesbaden 1969] 206) and F. Miltner, *RE* 21 (1952) 2159 s.v. Pompeius 31.

[37] *MRR* 2.233.

[38] Cicero, *Phil.* 2.4: *Auguratus petitionem mihi te concessisse dixisti*, and further: *Poteras autem eo tempore auguratum petere cum in Italia Curio non esset . . .?*

possibilities.[39] The only fact we know for certain is that he was already in Rome some time before the death of Clodius[40] (on 18 January 52) and that he was still there during the trial of Milo *de vi*: on 7 April 52 he delivered, as subscriptor to the accusation, a speech against Milo.[41] Nor is Curio of great help here, as also the date of his return to Rome is uncertain. To approach from that side the question of the dating of Cicero's election is obviously futile.

Let us see whether the whole problem should not be reversed and looked upon at first rather from the constitutional and not only from the prosopographical point of view. The question to be asked is not when Cicero was elected augur, but when the election to the augurate could (in 53 or 52) constitutionally take place.

On 5 May 43, Cicero wrote in a letter to Brutus (1.5.3): *Ciceronem nostrum in vestrum collegium cooptari volo*. The Republic was breaking up but he was thinking about the election and cooptation of his son to the college of the pontiffs.[42] But there were difficulties, of a constitutional nature only, of course: both consuls, A. Hirtius and C. Vibius Pansa, fell fighting against Antonius, and Cicero complains (ibid. 1.5.4): *Omnino Pansa vivo celeriora omnia putabamus; statim enim collegam sibi subrogavisset, deinde ante praetoria sacerdotum comitia fuissent: nunc per auspicia longam moram video; dum enim unus erit patricius magistratus, auspicia ad patres redire non possunt: magna sane perturbatio.*

The popular election of the members of the great priesthoods,[43] replacing the earlier *cooptatio*, was introduced by the *lex Domitia* of 104 B.C., abolished by Sulla, restored by a *lex* of T. Labienus in 63, and retained by a *lex Iulia*, passed by Caesar after 49. These elections were assigned to a special assembly (which already in the third century

[39] Broughton (*MRR* 2.236) puts his quaestorship in 52, but Drumann–Groebe (1.48–49) argued that he was quaestor in 51; so also recently D. R. Shackleton Bailey, *Cicero's Letters to Atticus* 3 (Cambridge 1968) 121. Arguments can be adduced in favor of both datings, and it would be interesting to analyze them. This question cannot, however, be gone into here.

[40] From Cicero, *Phil.* 2.49–50, we learn that Antonius came to Rome *ad quaesturam petendam* in 53: it was the period of armed clashes between Milo and Clodius, and Antonius, whose candidacy was supported by Cicero, allegedly almost succeeded in killing Clodius (cf. also Cic., *Mil.* 40).

[41] Asc. 41 C. For the date, see A. C. Clark, *M. Tulli Ciceronis Pro T. Annio Milone oratio* (Oxford 1895) 127–129; T. R. Holmes, *The Roman Republic* 2 (Oxford 1923) 315–316.

[42] Cf. Drumann–Groebe 6.635.

[43] For sources and discussion, see Mommsen, *Röm. Staatsrecht* 2³. 27–32; L. R. Taylor, "The Election of the Pontifex Maximus in the Late Republic," *CPh* 37 (1942) 421–424; R. Frei-Stolba, *Untersuchungen zu den Wahlen in der römischen Kaiserzeit* (Zürich 1967) 26–27.

elected the pontifex maximus), the *comitia* of seventeen tribes, constituting formally the *minor pars populi*. This represented a compromise between the democratic principle of popular election and the religious principle of the augural law that the priesthoods cannot be given by the people. The electoral procedure, which persisted until the empire, was complicated and cumbersome. It consisted of three stages. The first was the *nominatio*. Each member of the college in which there was a vacant place had the right to nominate one candidate, but, at least until the *lex Iulia*, no candidate could be nominated by more than two members.[44] The *nominatio* took place publicly, in a *contio*.[45] The second stage was the popular election by seventeen tribes, chosen by lot, with the people having the choice only between the nominated candidates. As the third stage, the *cooptatio* followed, the members of the college being obliged to coopt by their vote the candidate (or candidates) returned by the popular assembly.[46] The election and cooptation were complemented and made formally valid by the religious ceremony of *inauguratio* performed by an augur.

From the letter to Brutus cited above we learn that at the close of the Republic the *comitia sacerdotum* occurred at a stated time, between the consular and the praetorian elections. In the preceding paragraph Cicero mentions a *lex Iulia, quae lex est de sacerdotiis proxima*, but he discusses only those provisions of that law that concerned the election in absentia.[47] There is, however, no doubt that it was not the *lex Iulia*, but one of the earlier laws, very probably the *lex Domitia*,[48] that assigned to the elections of the priests the place between the consular and the praetorian *comitia*. A clause to that effect was, at any rate, contained in the *lex Labiena*; in the letter of Caelius of 1 August 51, we find the following information: Caelius notes at first: *C. Marcellum con-*

---

[44] Cic., *Phil.* 2.4. See also below, n. 66.

[45] *Auct. ad Her.* 1.20.

[46] Cic., *leg. agr.* 2.18.

[47] *Ad Brut.* 1.5.3.

[48] It may be noted that Cass. Dio presents the law of Labienus as a renewal of the *lex Domitia* (37.37.1): τὰς αἱρέσεις τῶν ἱερέων, γράψαντος μὲν τοῦ Λαβιήνου σπουδάσαντος δὲ τοῦ Καίσαρος, ἐς τὸν δῆμον αὖθις ὁ ὅμιλος παρὰ τὸν τοῦ Σύλλου νόμον ἐπανήγαγεν, ἀνανεωσάμενος τὸν τοῦ Δομιτίου. The wording of Cicero, *ad Brut.* 1.5.3 points in the same direction: *Gaius enim Marius, quum in Cappadocia esset, lege Domitia factus est augur, nec, quo minus id postea liceret, ulla lex sanxit.* Cicero interprets the provisions of the *lex Domitia* as still valid; as the law of Domitius was repealed by Sulla, the conclusion seems probable that the *lex Labiena* provided for the reenactment of the *lex Domitia* and did not introduce any new provisions.

sulem factum . . . P. Dolabellam XVvirum factum, and then he remarks: *Praetoriis* (sc. *comitiis*) *morae quaedam inciderunt.*[49] The *comitia sacerdotum* had already taken place, and the elections of the praetors were still in prospect.

From the words of Cicero: *Pansa vivo omnia celeriora putabamus* e.q.s. L. Mercklin[50] has acutely inferred that one of the consuls had to preside over the *comitia sacerdotum*. This provision also we may safely attribute to the *lex Domitia* as reenacted by the law of Labienus.

We may conclude that Cicero's election to the augurate must have taken place under the presidency of a consul, after the consular, but before the praetorian *comitia*.[51]

In 53 there took place only the delayed elections for 53; the consular *comitia* were held probably in July, but we do not know when the praetorian elections occurred. However, taking into account the temporary restoration of order caused by Pompey's intervention and the special measures voted by the senate against the rioters, we may assume that the praetors were elected without much trouble (especially as Clodius withdrew from the race, intending to stand for 52[52]) not long after the consular elections.

Let us now return to our prosopographical considerations. In summer 53 Curio was certainly not yet in Rome; whether Antonius was already present is not easy to tell: it is possible, but perhaps not probable. The year in question was not a normal year: the city was disrupted by riots and turmoil, and still late in June 53, the elections for that year having not yet been held, there was no prospect whatsoever of elections for 52. One may expect that Antonius, who wanted to stand for the quaestorship of 52, would not have come to Rome until there was a reasonable hope that the elections for 52 would eventually be held, that is after the report reached Gaul that the consuls for 53 had already been chosen (or, at least, that order had been restored and the electoral *comitia* were about to be convened). But this is only guessing; we have no explicit evidence to settle the question.

[49] Cic., *Fam.* 8.4.1, 3.

[50] *Die Cooptation der Römer* (Mitau und Leipzig 1848) 147, accepted by Mommsen, *Staatsrecht* 2³. 32 n. 1. Whether the regulations concerning the *comitia sacerdotum* applied also to the election of the *pontifex maximus* is uncertain.

[51] We can now see that the view according to which Cicero became augur at the end of 53 (so Ciaceri, *Cicerone* 2². 159, and apparently also Ooteghem *Pompée* 437) is patently false: no elections occurred at that time.

[52] Cic., *Mil.* 24. But cf. E. Badian, *Studies in Greek and Roman History* (Oxford 1964) 150, whose interpretation of Clodius' candidature in 53 is probably preferable to that of Cicero.

But the most important question is when the news about the disaster at Carrhae reached Rome. I have not been able to find any specific information to that effect;[53] however, taking into account the speed with which news traveled at that time,[54] we have to allow for about one month or more: from about mid-June to mid-July or even the beginning of August. And it is hardly likely that the augural college would have immediately proceeded to nomination, election, and cooptation of a new member without waiting for an official and unequivocal confirmation of the news of P. Crassus' death. Of course, the possibility cannot be entirely ruled out that Cicero was, in fact, elected in 53, but there is, at the very least, room for grave doubt.[55]

[53] The views of modern authorities are very diverse. According to some scholars, it was not until close to the end of the year that the death of Crassus became known at Rome (cf. Drumann–Groebe 3.303, 4.534; Ooteghem, *Pompée* 433. We may incidentally observe that nevertheless they assign Cicero's election to 53: an impossibility on their own premise). However, they cite no evidence; nor do any of the authors who hold that the report of Crassus' death came to Rome already in July or August (cf. Lange, *RA* 3². 368; Meyer, *Caesars Monarchie* 211; F. E. Adcock, *CAH* 9 [1934] 622). The latter view seems more likely (see below, n. 54), but this does not solve the problem. Essential for our argument is whether it was after or before the consular and praetorian elections. In fact, Lange and Meyer think that at that time the *comitia consularia* were already over. In that case the date of Cicero's election would almost certainly be 52.

[54] As illustration, some recorded instances of the speed of travel in republican times may be adduced. The messenger with the news of the victory at Pydna covered the distance from Macedonia to Rome in 12 days (Liv. 45.1.11), but this was an extraordinary feat, and was recorded by Livy as such. For a private letter a journey of 46 days from Rome to Cilicia (and in the best season of the year) was regarded by Cicero as a remarkably short time (Cic., *Att.* 5.19.1), which is wholly understandable as at the same time a letter from Epirus to Laodicea in Cilicia traveled (in winter) 48 days (Cic., *Att.* 6.1.1, 22; cf. L. W. Hunter, *JRS* 3 [1913] 91). A letter sent by Cassius from Syria on 7 May 43 reached Rome some days before the end of June (Cic., *Fam.* 12.10.1–2; 12.12.5), rather a good time, especially when taking into account disturbances of the civil war. In the summer of 47 a freedman of C. Trebonius covered the distance from Seleucia Pieria (the port of Antioch) to Brundisium in 27 days (Cic., *Att.* 11.20.1). But this establishes only a general pattern: the speed of any particular travel depended upon too many unpredictable factors. Cf. W. Riepl., *Das Nachrichtenwesen des Altertums* (Leipzig 1913) 205ff; Reincke, *RE* 16 (1935) 1539–1540. On the speed of sea travel, see the fundamental study of L. Casson, "Speed under Sail of Ancient Ships," *TAPA* 82 (1951) 136–148.

[55] The technicalities concerning the election of the priests are of some importance here. As we have seen, the candidates for the priesthoods had to be nominated at a public *contio*, convened presumably under the presidency of the same officer, who was to preside over the electoral *comitia*, that is, under the presidency of a consul. But in 53, until the election of Domitius Calvinus and

There remains the year 52.[56] In that year there took place the delayed elections for 52, and, as usual, the elections for the next year. The electoral *comitia* for 51 could be summoned at the earliest in July, the normal time for elections in the post-Sullan period, but very possibly they occurred later.[57] There is no doubt that Curio resided at that time in Rome, and, as Cicero was elected in his absence, his election must have occurred at an earlier date, possibly at the *comitia sacerdotum* before the praetorian election for 52. Let us now consider this possibility.

On the 24th day of the intercalary month (*V a.d. Kal. Mart.*[58]) Pompey was elected sole consul. Now, what is of special interest for our argument is the question when the elections for other magistracies were held. And it is interesting to note that the answer to this question has never been clearly presented. It has been argued that at least two of the *quaesitores* who presided over the trials under the *lex* (*Plautia*) *de vi* and *Pompeia de ambitu* might have been praetors in that year;[59] con-

---

Valerius Messala in July or August, there were no consuls, and the *contio* for the *nominatio* of the priests could have been summoned only after they entered office (it is utterly improbable that it could be convened by an interrex). On the other hand, there is no doubt that the *comitia sacerdotum*, like any other gathering of the popular assembly, must have been announced in *trinum nundinum*, that is 24, or according to A. K. Michels (*The Calendar of the Roman Republic* [Princeton 1967] 191–206), 25 days before the date of the meeting. And it is clear that the *comitia sacerdotum* could have been announced only after the candidates had been nominated. In 53 this would have necessitated a long interval between the consular elections and the *comitia sacerdotum*; it is, however, to be noted that this does not increase the probability of Cicero being elected in 53: important here is not the date of election, but the date of *nominatio*. And the *nominatio* must have taken place immediately after the consular elections. But there are reasons to think that the *trinum nundinum* was not observed with respect to post-interregnal elections; see below, n. 63.

[56] F. Münzer once made a cursory remark that Cicero stood for the augurship in 53 (*RE* 13 [1927] 1643), but he presented no arguments, and his observation remained unnoticed. It is possible that this was also the opinion of Lange, cf. *RA* 3².372.

[57] The *comitia* for 51 could have been held only after the election of Q. Caecilius Metellus as Pompey's colleague in the consulship. Plutarch (*Pomp.* 55) says that he was appointed consul for the remaining five months of the year; at any rate he entered office between 6 July and 13 September: see A. Ép. 1959, 146 *prid. Non. Quinct.* Pompey as sole consul, *CIL* 1² 933 *Id. Sep.* Pompey and Metellus as consuls.

[58] Asc. 36 C. I accept here the intercalary month of 27 days; see the illuminating discussion by A. K. Michels, *The Calendar of the Roman Republic* 160–163.

[59] For the list of *quaesitores*, see *MRR* 2.237. Lange (*RA* 3².372) thought that A. Torquatus and [C.] Considius, who presided respectively over the *quaestio de ambitu* and the *quaestio de vi* (under the *lex Plautia*) were praetors in that

sequently, they would have been elected some time before the trials of Milo began early in April. However, as the praetorship of any of the *quaesitores* in 52 is far from being certain, this is a very circumstantial piece of evidence, whereas at the same time an important piece of information directly concerning the elections in 52 has apparently been overlooked.

Narrating the course of events between the promulgation of the *leges Pompeiae* and the beginning of Milo's trials Asconius[60] has the following story: *Idem quoque Munatius et Pompeius tribuni plebis in rostra produxerunt triumvirum capitalem, eumque interrogaverant an Galatam Milonis servum caedes facientem deprehendisset. Ille dormientem in taberna pro fugitivo prehensum et ad se perductum esse responderat. Denuntiaverant tamen triumviro, ne servum remitteret: sed postera die Caelius tribunus plebis et Manilius Cumanus collega eius ereptum e domo triumviri servum Miloni reddiderant.* The story itself need not detain us; the mention of a *triumvir capitalis*, who was in office in 52, is, however, of prime importance. The *tres viri capitales* were elected together with other minor officials by the *comitia tributa* under the presidency of the *praetor urbanus*;[61] as the elections were held in descending order, at the time when the event related by Asconius occurred, all other magistrates must have already been chosen. According to Asconius' narrative the affair with Milo's slave happened before the beginning of Milo's trial on 4 March, and very probably even before the *leges Pompeiae* were voted on by the *comitia*.[62] We may conclude that the elections for 52 took place in March, possibly in the first half of the month.[63] This

---

year (cf. also Drumann–Groebe 2.297). But it is very likely that A. Torquatus the *quaesitor* is to be identified with A. Manlius Torquatus, who held the praetorship already in 70 (see *MRR* 2.77, 127, 133, 237, with some hesitations however, as to the identity of the *quaesitor* and the praetor on p. 586; J. F. Mitchell, "The Torquati," *Historia* 15 [1966] 26); in that case he certainly was not a praetor in 52. Cf. also Mommsen, *Staatsrecht* 2.³201 n. 2, 584 n. 4. As to Considius, Broughton (*MRR* 2.240 n. 3) considers the possibility that he was praetor in 52, but his citation of Mommsen, *Strafrecht* 208 n. 1, is misleading. Mommsen notes there that the term *quaesitor* was also used with respect to presiding praetor (cf. above, note 26), but, at the same time, he states (*Staatsrecht* 2.³584) that the *quaestio de vi* was never presided over by a praetor.

[60] 37 C.
[61] Mommsen, *Staatsrecht* 2.³594–596.
[62] Asc. 37–38 C.
[63] According to Asconius (36 C), Pompeius referred to the senate the question of the legislation *de vi* and *de ambitu post diem tertium* after his election, i.e. on the 26th of the intercalary month; on the next day (*pridie Kal. Mart.*, Asc. 44 C) a senatorial decree was passed (the question of the debate in the senate

would (or, at least, could) also be the date of Cicero's election to the augurate.

Several years later Cicero asserted: *me augurem a toto collegio expetitum Cn. Pompeius et Q. Hortensius nominaverunt — nec enim licebat*

---

and of the exact relation of the *senatus consultum* to the *leges Pompeiae* has been much discussed, without reaching, however, any generally accepted conclusions, cf. e.g. divergent interpretations proposed by T. R. Holmes, *The Roman Republic* 2.168–169, E. Meyer, *Caesars Monarchie*[3] 229–232, P. Stein, *Die Senatssitzungen der ciceronischen Zeit* [Münster 1930] 53 n. 291). The laws were formally promulgated probably on 1 March (I take the *contio* of Munatius Plancus on 1 March [Asc. 44–45 C] as immediately subsequent to the publication of the proposal of the laws) and passed on one of the comitial days at the end of March, probably on 24 or 25 March, the earliest possible date. The formal language of Asconius (cf. 36 C: *duas* [*leges*] *ex S.C. promulgavit*) and his long narration of events that intervened between the promulgation and the passage of the *leges Pompeiae* strongly suggest that the *trinum nundinum* was observed in that case. But this hardly makes possible the observance of *trinum nundinum* in regard to the elections for the praetorship and the other magistracies, even if they were announced by Pompey immediately upon entering office. Positing that the announcement took place on the 25th day of the intercalary month, the *comitia sacerdotum* could have occurred (with the observance of the *trinum nundinum*) at the earliest on 21 or 25 March (March 22 through 24 being non-comitial days, and accepting the *trinum nundinum* of respectively 24 or 25 days. The *nominatio* of the candidates could have been performed in the previous year; see below). As for the election of praetors, aediles, quaestors, and minor officials (such as the *tres viri capitales*), at least three, but probably four or five days were needed (normally the elections took much more time, but we know that in 70 they were completed in nine days, only seven of them comitial, between 27 July and 4 August; cf. Ps.-Asc. 212 Stangl, Cic., *Verr.* 1.30, *Brut.* 319), the first available day for the voting on Pompey's laws would have been 28 or 29 March. Probably on the same day would also have taken place the election of the *quaesitor* for the trial *de vi* under Pompey's law. This reconstruction is theoretically possible, but practically not very likely. First of all, it would have left too little time for preliminary legal business connected with Milo's trials, and, secondly, it seems that the *tres viri capitales* had already been in office some days before the passage of the *leges Pompeiae*.

We should not lose sight of two other possibilities: a) Pompey could have been granted a dispensation by the senate from the observation of the *trinum nundinum*, both with respect to legislation and elections, and b) 52 was an interregnal year. As the single *interreges* stayed in office only for five days, the *comitia consularia* could not be announced much in advance; they had to be summoned on the first available comitial day (with the exception of the first five days, of course). Although the elections for other magistracies were presided over by one of the newly elected consuls, it is probable that no new announcement was necessary, the original announcement by an *interrex* being valid for the whole electoral period. In that case the elections of other magistrates could have been held immediately after the *comitia consularia*. As regards the year 52, this is certainly the most likely reconstruction.

a pluribus nominari.[64] It was not quite so. Cicero himself mentions C. Lucilius Hirrus as his competitor:[65] this means that at least one member of the college must have nominated Hirrus.[66] The political affiliations of Hirrus are of interest. In 53, when he was tribune of the plebs, he proposed (together with M. Coelius Vinicianus) that Pompey be named dictator. The senate, led by Cato, reacted fiercely, and Pompey, who undoubtedly stood behind the proposal of the tribunes, retreated.[67] He had it declared that he did not desire the dictatorship. Hirrus — as so many others — was dropped. In this perspective Pompey's association with Hortensius in nominating Cicero as a candidate for the augurate is highly significant: it amounted to a demonstration of political unity between Pompey and the leading faction in the senate. This would be very significant in 53, and certainly not less in 52. But, as far as 52 is concerned, there is a snag: Pompey's nomination of Cicero does not seem to be in harmony with his attitude toward Cicero at that time.

[64] *Phil.* 2.4; cf. *Brut.* 1.1.

[65] *Fam.* 2.15.1, 8.3.1. In *ad Att.* 5.19.3 and 6.8.3 the allusion is to M. Calidius, and not to Hirrus; cf. D. R. Shackleton Bailey, *Cicero's Letters to Atticus* 3.314–315.

[66] As it was to be expected, the rhetoric of Cicero did not fail to exert some influence. The best example is Ciaceri's statement (*Cicerone* 2².159): *essendosi il collegio dichiarato per lui col lasciare da parte il suo competitore, il tribuno Lucilio Irro, era stato nominato da Ortensio e da Pompeo.* This presupposes the preliminary voting within the college (in Cicero's case unanimous, of course), with eventually only one candidate nominated and presented to the *comitia.* But this is sheer fantasy: there is no doubt that the people had the choice between more candidates than there were vacant places (cf. Cic., *Phil.* 2.4; Cael., *Fam.* 8.14.1; Hirtius, *B.G.* 8.50.1–3, all referring to Antony's election to the augurate).
A similar view to that of Ciaceri seems to have been held also by Drumann, cf. 3.95; on p. 156 he propounds a slightly different, but equally unsupported contention (retained by Groebe) that all candidates were nominated in the name of the *collegium* by two of its members (but he does not explain which ones). Essentially the same view was advocated also by L. Mercklin, *Die Cooptation* 123.
Are we really to suppose that Pompey and Hortensius nominated both Cicero and Hirrus? Cicero's words, *me augurem a toto collegio expetitum,* e.q.s. are not in favor of this interpretation: they are patently informal, and the verb *expetere* hardly conveys any notion of a formal action on the part of the college preceding, and resulting in, the nomination of Cicero by Pompey and Hortensius. The view of the scholars cited above is clearly disproved by a letter of Brutus, which shows that each member of a college was entitled to nominate a candidate and that in his own name, and not on behalf of the college (*ad Brut.* 1.7, cf. *Phil.* 13.5.12). This conclusion is corroborated also by *Auct. ad Her.* 1.20, see Mommsen, *Staatsrecht* 2³.30 n. 2.

[67] On Hirrus' activities as tribune, see Niccolini, *FTP* 315–316 (with full citation of sources).

Cicero's determination to defend Milo was not to the general's liking;[68] on the other hand, however, Cicero has words of praise for Pompey's *facilitas* and *humanitas* shown him on that occasion.[69]

But nomination and election were two separate acts. This suggests a solution. If the elections for 52 had been held in 53, Cicero would certainly have been elected to the augurate at that time. The *comitia consularia* were already announced, but when they convened they were dispersed by the armed bands.[70] Of course, by that time all the pre-liminaries for the elections had long been over: the *professiones* of the candidates for the magistracies[71] and the *nominationes* of the candidates for the priesthoods. I would therefore suggest that Pompey and Hortensius may have nominated Cicero in the autumn of 53 at a *contio* convened by one of the consuls after the announcement of elections for 52; in that case the actual election would have been performed under Pompey's presidency in March 52.

* * *

Cicero's augurate and Favonius' aedileship certainly have nothing in common, except for one thing: the link between the date of Favonius' aedileship and the date of Cicero's election to the augurate, as provided by the person of C. Scribonius Curio, has served as a starting point for the present inquiry. We may summarize our conclusions as follows:

1. If the news of P. Crassus' death had not reached Rome by the time of consular and praetorian elections in summer 53, the only date available for Cicero's election to the augurate is March 52, although he may have been nominated as a candidate in autumn 53. If Cicero was chosen augur in March 52, Curio must have returned to Rome after that date, and a) if Amyot was right in his emendation of the reading *ΔOYPIΩN* in Plutarch's manuscripts into *KOYPIΩN* (as he seems to have been) and b) if Plutarch rightly associates Curio's games with the aedilician games of Favonius, then the date of the aedileship of Favonius must be 52.

---

[68] Asc. 38 C.

[69] Two years later he wrote in a letter to App. Claudius Pulcher (*Fam.* 3.10.10): *quibus ille me rebus non ornatum voluit amplissime?* (an allusion to Pompey's nomination of Cicero?) *qua denique ille facilitate, qua humanitate tulit contentionem meam pro Milone adversante interdum actionibus suis? quo studio providit, ne quae me illius temporis invidia attingeret, quum me consilio, quum auctoritate, quum armis denique texit suis?*

[70] Sch. Bob. 172 Stangl; Cic., *Mil.* 25 and 96. Cf. Clark's notes ad locc. and Lange, *RA* 3².362.

[71] It was certainly at the official *professio* that Milo was ordered to estimate the amount of his debts; see Sch. Bob. 169–170 Stangl.

2. But if P. Crassus' death became known at Rome before the elections of the priests, Cicero might have been elected in 53; in that case, as Curio may have returned to Rome as well in 53 as in 52, we have no means of establishing whether the date of Favonius' aedileship was 53 or 52.

3. If Amyot's conjecture is rejected and Willems' emendation into *ΛΟΥΡΚΩΝ* accepted, or any other new reading proposed, Scribonius Curio disappears, and with him any link between Favonius' aedileship and Cicero's augurate. The date of the former would then be 53 or 52. The acceptance of Willems' emendation does not, however, affect in any way our argument concerning Cicero's augurate.

The results achieved are purely conditional: but we should not convert possibilities into facts and pretend to know more than we do.[72]

[72] I wish to thank Professor J. F. Gilliam who kindly consented to read this paper and offered helpful suggestions. I also owe thanks to Professor W. V. Harris for his useful criticism and to Professor D. C. Lindberg who helped to make my English intelligible.

21

THE QUAESTORSHIP OF MARCUS ANTONIUS

Accordingⁿ TO T. R. S. Broughton,[1] M. Antonius was quaestor in 52. However, in his commentary on Cicero *Att.* 6.6.4 D. R. Shackleton Bailey[2] has discarded Broughton's dating and assigned Antonius' tenure of that office to 51. In this way he has reverted to an old tradition, for Drumann-Groebe,[3] Mommsen,[4] Nipperdey,[5] and Bülz[6] were of the same opinion. Of course, Broughton was not the first to date Antonius' quaestorship in 52. This dating was advocated among others by Willems, Sobeck, and Niccolini.[7]

Neither Broughton nor Shackleton Bailey found it necessary to adduce arguments for their interpretation, but it may be interesting to look more closely into the question. Is there any discrepancy in the sources that allows one to draw such divergent conclusions?

Our main sources are Cicero, Caesar, and Hirtius.[8] Shackleton Bailey[9] adduces as evidence to reject Broughton's opinion only Hirtius *BGall.* 8.2.1.[10] This passage relates to events that occurred on or shortly before 29 December 52, and Antonius is in fact there termed quaestor, as he is

---

[1] T. R. S. Broughton, *The Magistrates of the Roman Republic* 2 (New York 1952) 236, 238 and *Suppl.* (1960) 6.

[2] D. R. Shackleton Bailey, *Cicero's Letters to Atticus* 3 (Cambridge 1968) 272.

[3] W. Drumann and P. Groebe, *Geschichte Roms* 1 (Berlin 1899) 48 (quoting Mommsen); 3 (Leipzig 1906) 698 (additions of Groebe).

[4] Th. Mommsen, *Römisches Straatsrecht* 1³ (Leipzig 1887) 534 note 1. Mommsen cites with approval the study of Nipperdey.

[5] K. Nipperdey, "Die leges annales der römischen Republik," *AbhLeipzig* 5, 1 (1865) 31.

[6] M. Bülz, *De provinciarum Romanarum quaestoribus* (Diss. Leipzig, Chemnitii 1893) 23–25.

[7] P. Willems, *Le sénat de la république romaine* 1 (Louvain 1878) 568; F. Sobeck, *Die Quästoren der römischen Republik* (Diss. Breslau, Trebnitz 1909) 61 (he mentions Bülz but does not discuss his dating); G. Niccolini, *I fasti dei tribuni della plebe* (Milan 1934) 334. This was also the original opinion of Drumann, see Drumann-Groebe 1. 48 text as compared with the note in the margin.

[8] Cic. *Att.* 6.6.4; 7.8.5; *Fam.* 2.15.4; *Phil.* 2.49–50, 71; *Mil.* 40. Caes. *BGall* 7.81.6. Hirtius, *BGall.* 8.2.1; 8.24.2; 8.38.1; 8.46.4; 8.47.2; 8.48.1, 8, 9; 8.50.1–3. See also Asc. 41 C; Schol. Bob. 123 Stangl. Cass. Dio 45.40.3 mistakenly attributes the quaestorship of Antonius to 61 or 60 when Caesar was governor in Spain.

[9] *Loc. cit.* (above, note 2).

[10] *Caesar M. Antonium quaestorem suis praefecit hibernis. ipse ... pridie Kalendas Ianuarias ... proficiscitur ad legionem XIII.*

also further on in 8.24.2 and 8.38.1.[11] On this basis it may seem possible to maintain that Antonius was quaestor from 5 December 52 to 4 December 51, but the evidence is not quite conclusive. It may well have been that he came to Gaul as quaestor in 52 and continued in 51 as proquaestor, as suggested by Broughton who lists him in 51 among the promagistrates.[12] On the other hand earlier in 52 Caesar calls Antonius a legate,[13] and he reappears in that capacity in 8.46.4[14] at the end of 51. These passages are certainly not in favor of Broughton's dating, and they cannot be explained away on the theory of Antonius' promagistracy.

It may be worthwhile to examine this evidence more closely. Was it Caesar's usual practice to omit the title of his quaestor or to describe it inexactly? Caesar had with him in Gaul in 54 another quaestor, M. Licinius Crassus. When he introduces Crassus in 5.24.3 he emphasizes his office and clearly distinguishes between him and the legates: *his* (scil. *legionibus*) *M. Crassum quaestorem et L. Munatium Plancum et C. Trebonium legatos praefecit.* Crassus appears again in 5.46.1, and Caesar again underlines his quaestorship, and only a few lines below (5.47.1, 2) mentions Crassus without any title. Even when Crassus had become proquaestor in 53 Caesar continued to write (6.6.1) *Caesar partitis copiis cum C. Fabio legato et M. Crasso* quaestore.[15] The same practice is also

---

[11]Campaign against the Eburones and the events contemporary with the siege of Uxellodunum in 51, cf. T. R. Holmes, *Caesar's Conquest of Gaul*[2] (Oxford 1911) 188–191. In 8.24.2 Hirtius juxtaposes *M. Antonium quaestorem* and *C. Fabium legatum* and *C. Caninium Rebilum legatum.*

[12]*MRR* 2.242.

[13]7.81.6: *M. Antonius et C. Trebonius legati* (siege of Alesia).

[14]*(Caesar) exercitum per legatos in hibernam deduxit: quattuor legiones in Belgio conlocavit cum M. Antonio et C. Trebonio et P. Vatinio legatis.* Cf. Drumann-Groebe 3.333.

[15]It is interesting to observe that of all his quaestors (some of whom certainly remained with him in the following year as proquaestors) Caesar mentions by name only Crassus and Antonius. This is easily explicable. Most of his quaestors were undoubtedly assigned to him by lot (cf. below, note 33 on the appointment of quaestors) and may have been militarily relatively inexperienced. Caesar did not entrust important commands to them, and in consequence he had few opportunities to mention them (cf. *BGall.* 1.52.1 *singulis legionibus singulos legatos et quaestorem praefecit*; 4.13.3 *consilio cum legatis et quaestore communicato*; 4.22.3 *id quaestori legatis praefectisque tribuit.* We are nowhere told who these quaestors were).

The case of L. Roscius introduces a complication. In late 54 and early 53 he commanded the XIII legion (*BGall.* 5.53.6). The manuscripts of class α designate him as quaestor, those of class β call him a *legatus* (see O. Seel in *app. crit. ad loc.* in his edition of the *BGall.* [Teubner, Leipzig 1961]). Earlier, however, he appears twice without any title: *BGall.* 5.24.2 and 5.24.7. In 5.25.5 we read (according to the consensus of the manuscripts): *interim ab omnibus legatis quaestoribusque quibus legiones tradiderat, certior factus est in hiberna perventum.* If the reading of the MSS is retained, it would follow that in 54 Caesar had two quaestors, M. Crassus and L. Roscius, and that when mentioning Roscius in 5.24.2 Caesar omitted his title (it should, however, be noted that in the case of Antonius Caesar would have not only omitted his presumed title of quaestor but also termed him incorrectly a legate). But there are grave doubts as to the reliability of the

followed by Caesar in the *Bellum Civile*. He there mentions three quaestors, and when he introduces them he never fails to call attention to their office.[16] In view of these examples it seems highly unlikely that Caesar should have omitted in 7.81.6 Antonius' title of quaestor and termed him *legatus* if he had really been quaestor at that time. Hirtius continues Caesar's usage. Throughout 51 Antonius appears as quaestor[17] and only at the end of this year, when he of course laid down his office, is he mentioned again as a legate.[18]

---

manuscript tradition (cf. on modern conjectures, Seel *ad loc.* and H. Meusel, *Lexicon Caesarianum* [Berlin 1893] s.v. *quaestor*). In 58 and 55 Caesar had with him only one quaestor (cf. *BGall*. 1.52.1 and 4.13.3, quoted above; on 4.22.3 see below), and it is doubtful if we should attribute to him two quaestors in 54 (cf. Groebe in Drumann-Groebe 3.697–698; Holmes' criticism of Groebe [(above, note 11) 565] is not convincing). Most probably the MSS reading *quaestoribus* is due to the attraction by the following *quibus* and the preceding *legatis* strengthened by *omnibus* (cf. 4.22.3 where *a* MSS have the reading *quaestori*, β MSS *quaestoribus*, this latter reading rightly discarded by most editors). We may conclude that Roscius was probably a legate in 54 and in early 53 (the title of *legatus* being occasionally omitted by Caesar, cf. Holmes [above, note 11] 564–565) or that in 54 he received the legionary command without any specific title and formally became a legate only in 53. Broughton (*MRR* 2.226) lists him in 54 (with a query) among legates and lieutenants.

[16]Sex. Quinctilius Varus, quaestor in 49: *BCiv.* 1.23.2; 2.28.1–2. Marcius Rufus, quaestor in 49: 2.23.5 (no title a few lines below in 2.24.1); 2.43.1. P. Cornelius Lentulus Marcellinus, quaestor in 48: 3.62.4 (the title is omitted in the immediately following narrative, 3.64.1 and 3.65.1).

[17]See above, notes 10 and 11.

[18]*BGall*. 8.46.4 (quoted above, note 14). He appears without any title in the immediately following passages 8.47.2; 8.48.1, 8–9. The passage 8.50.1 concerning Antonius' *petitio* for the augurate in 50 presents no difficulty here. We read that *Caesar hibernis peractis ... in Italiam ... est profectus, ut municipia et colonias appellaret, quibus M. Antoni, quaestoris sui, commendaverat sacerdotii petitionem.* At the time of his *petitio* and Caesar's intended personal support for him Antonius was neither quaestor nor legate. But if in this context a title should have been mentioned, it certainly had to be the quaestorship as it recalled not only the personal favour of Caesar but also that of the people. Cf. Nipperdey (above, note 5) 31.

It may, however, seem unusual that Caesar should have appointed as a legate his quaestor designate, and that Antonius did not continue in 50 as proquaestor, but appears again as a legate. These considerations do not, however, immediately affect the dating of Antonius' quaestorship. It is of course possible to conjecture that the term *legatus* was used here by Caesar and Hirtius only loosely to denote a higher military charge, but it must be pointed out that this does not seem to have been Caesar's usual practice. In all other cases there is no doubt that the man termed *legatus* held a regular appointment. For a list of Caesar's *legati*, see Willems (above, note 7) 2.612–615; Groebe in Drumann-Groebe 3.696–701; Holmes (above, note 11) 563–565. Willems (2.608, note 4) asserts that only a senator (i.e., at least a *quaestorius*) could be a *legatus*, and there is no doubt that this was normal practice in the late republican period (cf. Mommsen, *Staatsrecht* 2.³ 682). There is, however, no compelling reason to assume that the *lex Vatinia* must have contained the same provision as the *lex Gabinia*, which limited in 67 Pompey's choice of his legates to senators. It is also possible that the quaestor designate could be treated as practically a member of the senate. Holmes (*loc. cit.*) points out that

The attribution (on the basis of Caesar and Hirtius) of Antonius' quaestorship to 51 may seem, however, to be inconsistent with Cicero's remarks about Antonius which appear to be rather in favour of Broughton's dating. Cicero mentions the quaestorship of Antonius in two letters to Atticus, a letter to Caelius,[19] and above all in the Philippics. The letters, interesting though they are, are only of indirect value for our present purpose. On the other hand the Philippics seem to furnish a full account of the events surrounding Antonius' *petitio* for the quaestorship.[20] We do not know exactly when Antonius left Gaul and returned to Rome *ad quaesturam petendam* but it was in the period of armed clashes between Milo and Clodius who were canvassing respectively for the consulship and the praetorship. As the consuls for 53 were elected only in July or August of that year,[21] the electoral *comitia* for 52 could only have been summoned, at the earliest, late in August or in September, and Antonius cannot have come to Rome long before that date.[22] At any rate Antonius, whose candidature (at Caesar's request) was supported by Cicero, took an active part in the street fighting, and on one occasion he allegedly almost succeeded in killing Clodius.[23] It would follow from the narrative

---

Caesar may have had at least two other legates, not yet senators, and Broughton (*TAPA* 79 [1948] 63–67) accepts that Caesar himself held a legateship before his quaestorship.

[19]On *Att.* 6.6.4 and *Fam.* 2.15.4 see below, 219. *Att.* 7.8.5 is amusing: Cicero quotes Pompey's indignant exclamation after a *contio* of Antonius: *quid censes . . . facturum esse ipsum, si in possessionem rei publicae venerit, cum haec quaestor eius infirmus et inops audeat dicere?* The letter was written on 25 or 26 December 50, and Antonius was at that time already tribune of the plebs, but Pompey had chosen to call him quaestor in order to underline his personal connection with Caesar. Unfortunately Pompey's abuse of Antonius offers no help for establishing when this "feckless nobody of a quaestor" (as Shackleton Bailey renders *quaestor infirmus et inops*) held his office.

[20]Cic. *Phil.* 2.49–50: *Venis e Gallia ad quaesturam petendam . . . Acceperam iam ante Caesaris litteras ut mihi satis fieri paterer a te: itaque ne loqui quidem sum te passus de gratia. Postea sum cultus a te, tu a me observatus in petitione quaesturae; quo quidem tempore P. Clodium approbante populo Romano in foro es conatus occidere . . . (50) Quaestor es factus: deinde continuo sine senatus consulto, sine sorte, sine lege ad Caesarem cucurristi. Id enim unum in terris egestatis, aeris alieni, nequitiae perditis vitae rationibus perfugium esse ducebas.* Cf. *Phil.* 2.21.

[21]Cass. Dio 40.45.1; App. *BCiv.* 2.71.

[22]Antonius allegedly originally wanted to stand at that time for the augurate also (Cic. *Phil.* 2.4); see on this question J. Linderski, "The Aedileship of Favonius, Curio the Younger and Cicero's Election to the Augurate," *HSCP* 76 (1972) 190–191.

[23]Most probably this event occurred no later than 53. Cicero refers to it also in *Mil.* 40 and in 41 he continues: *Quid? comitiis in campo quotiens potestas fuit! cum ille (scil. Clodius) in saepta irrupisset, gladios destringendos, lapides iaciendos curasset . . . .* If Cicero adopts here the chronological order of events it would follow that the disruption of the consular *comitia* was subsequent to Antonius' clash with Clodius. Now, in 52 (between 1 January and the death of Clodius on 18 January) no attempt could be made to convene the assembly as there were no regular magistrates and also no interrex was appointed (Asc. 30–31 C).

of Cicero that Antonius' goal was the quaestorship of 52. This inference is corroborated by the fact that in all probability Antonius reached the age of thirty in 53,[24] and so according to the *leges annales* this was *suus annus* for the *petitio quaesturae*.

The source situation has been lucidly characterized by J. D. Denniston in his commentary on the first two Philippics.[25] He agreed that on the basis of Caesar and Hirtius the only acceptable date for Antonius' quaestorship was 51 but ruefully conceded that he could not reconcile the evidence of the *Bellum Gallicum* with Cicero's statement in the Philippics. "Surprisingly enough," he wrote, "the discrepancy has not, as far as I know, been noticed." The discrepancy had, however, been noticed by Nipperdey, whose explanation won Mommsen's praise.[26] According to Nipperdey, although Antonius came to Rome around the end of 53 or during the first few days of 52, he intended from the very beginning to stand for the quaestorship of 51 "da sich Cicero schon im Juli 65 um das Consultat für 63 bewarb." Consequently Cicero's narrative in the Philippics is "durchaus nicht im Widerspruch" with the testimony of Caesar and Hirtius. Bülz[27] also found it necessary to explain why Antonius, who came to Rome with the clear purpose of obtaining the quaestorship, was finally elected not for 52 but for 51. In his opinion Antonius canvassed originally for the quaestorship of 52, but when the elections were delayed and did not take place until 52 he changed his mind and decided to stand for 51 mainly because the year 52 already *aliqua ex parte praeterierat*.

Neither the theory of Nipperdey nor that of Bülz may be regarded as convincing. It is hard to believe that Antonius, a scion of a noble family, enjoying moreover the favour of Caesar that secured him also Cicero's support, would have needed to canvass as long for his quaestorship as Cicero for his consulate. One is also reluctant to accept Bülz's supposition that Antonius did not want to be elected for 52 because as part of this year had already passed he would not have been able to serve his full term of office. Would it have been so important to him not to lose any month of his quaestorship that he would have preferred to postpone his election and so hold his office one year later? In any event he intended to return to Gaul to Caesar, and it was certainly of no great importance how long he commanded the soldiers as quaestor and how long as legate.

[24]See G. V. Sumner, "The Lex Annalis under Caesar," *Phoenix* 25 (1971) 363. Antonius had his birthday on 14 January (A. Degrassi, *Inscr. It.* 13.2.397–398) and so, as the elections for 53 were delayed, he could theoretically be elected even to the quaestorship of 53.

[25]J. D. Denniston, *M. Tulli Ciceronis Orationes Philippicae* 1, 2 (Oxford 1926) 128–129.

[26]See above, notes 4 and 5.

[27]*Op. cit.* (above, note 6) 24–25.

The question obviously requires a different approach. Let us turn again to our sources and consider the sequence of events. There took place in 52 two sets of elections: the delayed *comitia* for 52 and the regular elections for 51. The dates of these elections can be established only approximately. Pompey was chosen as sole consul on the 24th day of the intercalary month; it has often been tacitly assumed that he immediately held the elections for other magistracies, but no positive proof has ever been offered. Asconius (37 C) mentions, however, still before the beginning of Milo's trial on 4 April, a *triumvir capitalis*; as the elections were held in the descending order, by that time all the other magistrates, including the quaestors, must have already been chosen.[28] This important evidence for the date of the elections for 52 seems to have been completely overlooked in the modern literature. We may conclude that if the elections of the other magistrates began on the earliest available comitial day the quaestors for 52 may have been chosen already early in March.

As far as the *comitia* for 51 are concerned we should expect that they were preceded by the election of Scipio Nasica as Pompey's colleague in the consulship. Scipio entered office between 10 July and 11 September,[29] and this will also establish approximately the date of the *comitia* for 51. At which of these elections did Antonius become quaestor?

After Cicero had with much delight described the unfortunately abortive assult of Antonius on Clodius, he continues: *quaestor es factus*. This presentation conveys the impression that Antonius' election was a well merited reward for that glorious attack in the Forum. But despite the persuasiveness of Cicero his words cannot be taken as a conclusive proof that Antonius was in fact elected for 52. Not to mention the fact that the orator treats the career of Antonius very summarily and with many omissions and distortions, Cicero himself may be quoted to call in doubt the correctness of the inference he would like his readers to make.

The last we hear of Antonius' candidacy is in connection with his attempt on Clodius' life; when we meet him again after the turmoil following the death of Clodius he appears in the role of Clodius' avenger, as a *subscriptor* to the accusation levelled against Milo. On 7 April 52, when Cicero delivered his speech *pro Milone*,[30] Antonius, his recent protégé for the quaestorship, charged Milo with the same crime he himself had almost committed. No orator could fail to deride this amusing

[28]For a more detailed discussion, see Linderski (above, note 22) 195–197.

[29]On 6 July Pompey appears as sole consul (*AEpigr.* 1959, 146; July 7–9 are *dies nefasti*), on 13 September together with Metellus [Scipio Nasica] (*CIL* 1². 933; Sept. 12 is N.).

[30]For the date, see T. R. Holmes, *The Roman Republic* 2 (Oxford 1923) 315–316, but cf. A. W. Lintott, "*Nundinae* and the Chronology of the Late Roman Republic," *CQ* 18 (1968) 191 note 4.

situation, and so Cicero, by heaping praise on Antonius for his noble and courageous assault on that beast Clodius, showed him at the same time a despicable weathercock: *Nuper vero, cum M. Antonius summam spem salutis bonis omnibus attulisset gravissimamque adulescens nobilissimus rei publicae partem fortissime suscepisset atque illam beluam iudici laqueos declinantem iam irretitam teneret, qui locus, quod tempus illud, di immortales, fuit!* (*Mil.* 40).[31] Many lofty words but no mention of Antonius' quaestorship, and yet, on the theory assigning to him the quaestorship of 52, he must already have been elected. It is hardly likely that Cicero purposely omitted the office of Antonius. Quite on the contrary, it would have served his purpose well to point out that the man who had come close to killing Clodius received a signal favor from the Roman People, and later betrayed them, whereas Milo, the true defender of the *boni*, was facing exile. But if the Philippics offer no conclusive proof that Antonius was quaestor in 52, the *pro Milone* falls short of disproving it.

Paradoxically enough, it is only the Philippics that can help us here. We read: *Quaestor es factus: deinde continuo sine senatus consulto, sine sorte, sine lege ad Caesarem cucurristi* (*Phil.* 2.50). Cicero refers to the same event in two letters written in 50, six years before his speeches against Antonius. He apologizes to Atticus and Caelius Rufus for having left in command of Cilicia his quaestor C. Coelius Caldus, a relatively young and inexperienced man. His explanation is socially and politically very illuminating:[32] *Att.* 6.6.4: *adde illud. Pompeius, eo robore vir, iis radicibus, Q. Cassium sine sorte delegit, Caesar Antonium: ego sorte datum offenderem . . . ? Fam.* 2.15.4: *Postremo non tam mea sponte quam potentissimorum duorum exemplo, qui omnes Cassios Antoniosque complexi sunt, hominem adolescentem non tam allicere volui, quam alienare nolui.* The phrase *sine sorte* has been much discussed and much misused. The quaestorian provinces were normally assigned by lot, but the appointment of quaestors *sine sorte* but *ex senatus consulto* was a perfectly legal administrative procedure which may even have been applied much more fre-

---

[31]According to ancient authorities the text of the *pro Milone* as published by Cicero differed considerably from the speech actually delivered by him in the court (Asc. 42 C; Schol. Bob. 112 Stangl; Cass. Dio 40.54. See also J. Humbert, *Les plaidoyers écrits et les plaidoiries réelles de Cicéron* [Paris 1925] 189–197. Contra: J. N. Settle, "The Trial of Milo and the other *Pro Milone*," *TAPA* 94 [1963] 268–280). This must not militate against our argument: there is no conceivable reason why Cicero should have omitted the office of Antonius either in the speech actually delivered or in its later literary elaboration.

[32]Cicero's succession problems in Cilicia have been discussed by L. A. Thompson, "Cicero's Succession-problem in Cilicia," *AJP* 86 (1965) 375–386, and recently they have been elucidated in a broader context by A. J. Marshall, "The Lex Pompeia de Provinciis and Cicero's Imperium in 51–50 B.C.: Constitutional Aspects," *Aufstieg und Niedergang der römischen Welt* 1. 1 (Berlin–New York 1972) 887–921.

quently than it would seem at first sight.[33] Willems was therefore of the
opinion that in 44 Cicero must have been *mal servi par sa mémoire,* for
in any other case he would not have alluded to the same event in 50 as
la chose la plus légale au monde.[34] But Cicero, when he wanted, had an
excellent memory, and we had better look for another explanation of
his words.

In Cicero's phrase the rhetorical stress is on *sine senatus consulto, sine
sorte, sine lege,* but the real meaning of the whole sentence is hidden in
"*continuo,*" as rightly suggested by A. R. Hands.[35] The word is commonly
rendered as "immediately"; Cicero, however, (as is easily seen from the
examples in Merguet's dictionary) uses it often to indicate that between
two closely connected events no other event occurred bearing upon
them.[36] Thus the length of time indicated by *continuo* may vary considerably, as is also true of other similar expressions like *mox* and *nuper.* The
exact meaning of the passage would be that in the period of time between
Antonius' election and his departure from Rome no decree of the senate
was passed concerning the quaestorian provinces and no *sortitio provinciarum* took place.[37] Cicero does not say that such a decree was not passed

---

[33]Drumann-Groebe 2.130 and V. Ehrenberg, *RE* 13 (1926) 1504 interpret the appoint-
ment of Cassius and Antonius as an example of the triumvirs' "Willkür;" so also Tyrrell-
Purser, *The Correspondence of M. Tullius Cicero* 3² (Dublin 1914) 256–257. These inter-
pretations are completely mistaken. See the excellent analysis by L. A. Thompson, "The
Appointment of Quaestors *extra sortem,*" *PACA* 5 (1962) 17–25, esp. 19–20. Cf. also
Mommsen, *Staatsrecht* 2.³ 532-534; Willems (above, note 7) 2.599 ff., esp. 607–608.

[34]*Op. cit.* (above, note 7) 2.607, note 3.

[35]Quoted by Thompson (above, note 33) 21, note 23.

[36]Cf. esp. *Cael.* 9; *Vat.* 36: *quis legatos umquam audivit sine senatus consulto? Ante te
nemo: post* (i.e., after 59) *continuo* (i.e., in 58) *fecit idem . . . Clodius.*

[37]The interpreters are, however, at a loss when it comes to explain the phrase *sine lege.*
Denniston ([above, note 25] 129) remarks that he could not find any instance of a
quaestor being assigned *lege* to a province; Thompson ([above, note 33] 20) comments:
"if there had been a *lex,* it would certainly have been mentioned by Cicero or someone
else" for "it is impossible to believe that Cicero would have omitted from his contemporary correspondence such a *popularis* measure." The translators are either evasive
(e.g., "*sans loi*": A. Boulanger and P. Wuilleumier in *Collection Budé*) or unduly interpretative (e.g., "without procuring any law to be passed" in the old translation by C. D.
Yonge). Cf. also Drumann-Groebe 1.48: Antonius returned to Gaul "ohne eine Bestimmung des Senats, des Volkes oder des Loses zu erwarten." All these interpretations are
obviously going in the wrong direction. It was an exclusive prerogative of the senate
to assign the quaestorian provinces, and there is no reason why Cicero should have
criticized Antonius for not procuring a law concerning his assignment. Not to mention
the fact that Antonius as only a quaestor (designate) was not in a position to sponsor
any law, the mere allusion to such a *lex* would have implied the possibility of transferring the provincial appointments from the senate to the popular assembly, hardly a
thing one would ascribe to Cicero. *Sine lege* clearly does not mean here without the *lex
comitialis,* but stands generally for "without any legal justification," cf. the expressions
nulla lege, nullo pacto. See Forcellini-De Vit, *Totius Latinitatis Lexicon,* s.v. *lex,* page 743
no. 15: *sine lege est sine ratione, modo, ordine.*

at all; indeed the implication is that it was in fact carried out but only after Antonius had already left the city. This interpretation receives support from Cicero's remarks in the letters to Caelius and Atticus. Far from criticizing Caesar's selection of Antonius *sine sorte* Cicero uses it as an excuse for, and a parallel case to, the delegation of his *imperium* to Coelius Caldus. The procedure governing the assignment of quaestorian provinces is of importance here. It consisted of two stages. The first was the *senatus consultum de provinciis quaestorum* and the other the *sortitio provinciarum*. Some provinces were assigned *sine sorte* directly by the senate, and the others were marked out to be distributed by lot among the remaining quaestors on 5 December, the date of their entry into the office.[38] There can be no doubt that Antonius was assigned to Caesar at the latter's request in the regular way by a *senatus consultum*. As the passing of the decree was a matter of administrative routine, he had left Rome without waiting for it—certainly a minor constitutional impropriety, but misrepresented by Cicero in a masterly way.

These considerations are of immediate importance for the dating of Antonius' quaestorship. The connection has been normally overlooked, but it was seen clearly by Thompson.[39] His conclusion is, however, startling. He maintains that even on this interpretation of *continuo* the statement that Antonius rushed off to Gaul *sine senatus consulto* and *sine sorte* "would nevertheless be a lie on Cicero's part: Antonius did not leave for Gaul until April 52 (Ascon. *in Mil.* 36)." This conclusion is based on two assumptions: a) that the *S.C. de provinciis quaestorum* was passed before 7 April; b) that Antonius was quaestor in 52.

Thompson takes it for granted that the *S.C.* was voted on before 7 April, but he offers no evidence. He cannot, however, be criticized on that account, since it is possible to establish beyond any doubt that the quaestorian provinces were in fact assigned or allotted before or around 7 April. It was a duty of the urban quaestors to allot from the general *album iudicum* the panels of jurors to single *quaestiones* (or at least to the *quaestio de vi* for which this procedure is directly attested).[40] Now, for the trials of 52 there existed two distinct lists of jurors: the list of 360 jurors for the trials under the *leges Pompeiae de vi* and *de ambitu* drawn up by Pompey and the list of jurors composed as normally at the end of the previous year by the urban praetor.[41] From this list were provided

---

[38]See Mommsen, Willems, and Thompson cited in note 33. The mechanism of provincial appointments was in 52 substantially changed by the *lex Pompeia de provinciis*, but there is no indication that the law of Pompey had affected the appointment of provincial quaestors. Cf. Marshall (above, note 32) 912, note 97.

[39]*Op. cit.* (above, note 33) 21, note 23.

[40]Cass. Dio 39.7; Cic. *QFr.* 2.12 (on the text, cf. W. Sternkopf, *Hermes* 39 [1904] 395–396). See Mommsen, *Staatsrecht* 2.³ 561, and esp. J. Lengle, "Die Auswahl der Richter im römischen Quästionsprozess," *ZSav* 53 (1933) 290–292.

[41]C. Nicolet, *L'ordre équestre à l'époque républicaine* (Paris 1966) 620–623.

the jurors for the trials *lege Plautia de vi*, and here the cooperation of the urban quaestors was indispensable. As the trials under the *lex Plautia* began immediately after the condemnation of Milo,[42] the inference seems justified that around that time the quaestorian provinces must have already been assigned.

Is it not true that if the *S.C.* was passed before the trial of Milo, and if Antonius was quaestor in 52 it was a lie on Cicero's part to imply that he left for Gaul without the authorization of the senate? But let us look closer at this rather peculiar argument. That Antonius was quaestor in 52 is inferred from what Cicero seems to say in the Philippics, and this inference is not only tacitly treated as a firmly established fact but also immediately turned against Cicero to brand his statement concerning Antonius' departure as a lie. This is hardly fair. Thompson quotes with approval R. Syme's acid remark that the Philippics are an eternal monument of misrepresentation, but it is a pity that in this case he has not followed it. Why should we rather not construct a completely opposite line of argument: as a starting point we must take the fact explicitly attested by Cicero that Antonius departed from Rome *sine senatus consulto* (a misrepresentation but not a lie). Now, if in 52 the *S.C. de provinciis quaestorum* was passed (as established above) when Antonius was still in Rome, the conclusion is inescapable that he was not quaestor in 52. If Antonius was elected for 51, not only does the discrepancy between Cicero and Caesar/Hirtius disappear, but Cicero also provides the answer why he hastened to Gaul without waiting for the necessary constitutional formalities: he was hard pressed by his creditors and as soon as possible he fled from Rome, the *terra egestatis*.[43]

One question still remains unanswered: why Antonius, who undoubtedly desired to become quaestor in 52, postponed his election till summer (or autumn) 52? An *obtrectator* of Antonius would have an answer ready at hand: *vinolentia et meretrices*. This explanation would have pleased Cicero, and perhaps would not be completely devoid of truth. At least A. C. Clark[44] came close to this idea when he suggested that Antonius may have established a liaison with Fulvia (in the eyes of Cicero undoubtedly a *meretrix*) by that time, and that this may have been the ultimate reason for his appearance before the jury as Milo's accuser and Clodius' avenger. Antonius' connection with Fulvia in 52 is only a guess and not a fact, but if we examine more attentively Cicero's narrative we can discern two different periods of Antonius' *petitio*. At first there was a period when he cultivated Cicero (*sum cultus a te*), but later (still

[42] Asc. 55 C.
[43] *Phil.* 2.50. On Antonius' debts, see Drumann-Groebe 1.47–48.
[44] A. C. Clark, *M. Tulli Ciceronis Pro T. Annio Milone Oratio* (Oxford 1895) 37. So also Ch. L. Babcock, "The Early Career of Fulvia," *AJP* 86 (1965) 5–6, 13–14.

before the *comitia* as he left Rome shortly after his election) he reverted to his old style of life, to his *nequitia*. When did this sudden transformation occur? No doubt it must be connected with the death of Clodius and the changed political situation in Rome after Pompey's intervention. The murder of Clodius, far from being committed with "the approbation of the Roman People," aroused the indignation of the city plebs not only against Milo but also against other enemies of Clodius, as Cicero knew so painfully well from his own experience. In view of Pompey's professed enmity toward Milo, Antonius had to reconsider his position. The chances for his election were not bright: it was imperative to break off immediately his unnatural alliance with Cicero and to return to his old friends—if no longer to Clodius, then at least to the Clodiani. But it was already too late to think of the election for 52—Antonius preferred not to take any chances, but to wait a few months and be safely elected for 51. It is in this context that we must view his accusation of Milo: it was a shrewd political move meant to appease Pompey and the Clodiani and to pave the way for his election to the quaestorship of 51.

Now all the pieces of our source-mosaic fit well together: Antonius came to Rome in 53 with a clear plan to obtain the quaestorship of 52. The Clodius affair caused him to withdraw his candidature for 52 and to stand for 51. On his election in the summer or autumn 52 he hurried to Caesar without waiting for an appropriate *senatus consultum*. Consequently when he emerges in Gaul Caesar introduces him as a legate, but at the end of December, as is to be expected, he appears as quaestor and is so termed regularly throughout 51.[45]

[45]We are grateful to our friend, Professor C. P. Jones, for his kind help in matters of style.

22

THE MOTHER OF LIVIA AUGUSTA AND THE AUFIDII
LURCONES OF THE REPUBLIC

I.

The problems encompassed in the title of the present note are not without interest: an emperor's scornful allegation, a biographer's attempt at a learned explanation, and the imagination of modern scholars have all contributed to making the story of Livia's maternal grandfather and the Aufidii Lurcones both intricate and amusing. Suetonius seeks to refute the assertion of Caligula, expressed in a letter to the senate, that the maternal grandfather of Livia Augusta was of humble origin, only a decurion of Fundi. The biographer states: *publicis monumentis certum est Aufidium Lurconem*[1] *Romae honoribus functum (Caligula* 23. 2). There is no doubt that an Aufidius Lurco obtained *honores* in Rome (he may well be identified as one of the senatorial Lurcones of Cicero's time, see below, part II), but Suetonius and his modern followers erred in taking him for Livia's maternal grandfather: on the evidence of inscriptions the name of Livia's mother was Alfidia M. f.[2] (and not Aufidia).

A poet also has his share in the embellishment of the story: it has been argued that Horace's Aufidius Luscus,[3] praetor[4] of Fundi, might be of rele-

---

[1] The reading of the manuscripts is *Lyrgonem;* corrected by Stephanus (cf. M. Ihm *ad loc.* in his edition of Suetonius in the *Bibl. Teubneriana*, Leipzig 1908) and Lipsius (cf. Klebs, *RE* 2 [1896] 2293 s. v. Aufidius 24).

[2] *CIL* 2. 1667, 9. 3661 = *ILS* 125, *IGRR* 4. 983; cf. Klebs, *loc. cit.;* R. N. Rosborough, *An Epigraphical Commentary on Suetonius's Life of Gaius Caligula*, Diss. Pennsylvania (Philadelphia 1920) 36–37.

[3] Horatius, *Sat.* 1. 5. 34–36; cf. Kiessling–Heinze, *ad loc.* (8 ed., Berlin 1961, going back at least to the fourth edition in 1910); A. Stein, *PIR*[2] A 528 (Berolini 1933).

[4] This is another riddle: it is borne out by inscriptional evidence that the chief magistrates at Fundi were the three aediles (see Mommsen, *CIL* 10, p. 617; E. Manni, *Per la storia dei municipi fino alla guerra sociale* [Roma 1947] 123 n. 1). There has been a long dispute and excessive speculation as to whether the title of *praetor* given by Horace to Aufidius Luscus has any constitutional significance (see e. g., A. Rosenberg, *Der Staat der alten Italiker* [Berlin 1913] 5 ff.; E. Kornemann, "Zur altitalischen Verfassungsgeschichte", *Klio* 14 (1915) 199; A. N. Sherwin-White, *The Roman Citizenship* [Oxford 1939] 63) or is to be dismissed as a mere *licentia poetica* (so Mommsen, *Hermes* 13 [1878] 113 = *Ges.Schr.* 7 [Berlin 1909] 198; cf. H. Rudolph, *Stadt und Staat im römischen Italien* [Göttingen 1935] 64; E. Manni, op. cit. 114–116, 127–128). According to A. Degrassi Horace used the term *praetor* as "*il titolo convenzionale dei magistrati delle città italiane*" ("Quattuorviri in colonie romane e in municipi retti da duoviri", *Memorie dell'Accademia dei Lincei, Classe di scienze morali e storiche*, ser. VIII, vol. II, 1949 [1950] 315–316 = *Scritti vari di antichità*, I [Roma 1962] 141–142). He points out that in Horace, *Sat.* 2. 3. 180–181, the chief magistrate of Canusium,

vance here; as T. P. Wiseman[5] puts it, Caligula "could have been mischievously referring to this man". On that ground he challenges Caligula's attribution of Livia's *maternus avus* to Fundi (which is normally accepted[6]) and opts for Marruvium, where an inscription[7] was found honoring Alfidia, *mater Augustae.*

Although he displays his usual acumen in detecting the possible connections of Alfidia's husband M. Livius Drusus Claudianus with the Marsi and Marruvium,[8] it seems doubtful whether Wiseman's hypothesis will meet with greater success than that of Suetonius did. Wiseman says that if Caligula really referred to Horace's Aufidius Luscus "his evidence is as untrustworthy for the origin of Livia's mother as it patently is for her name".[9]

a town governed by the *quattuorviri*, is also called *praetor*. Degrassi's interpretation had already been foreshadowed by Kiessling–Heinze in their commentary *ad locc.*

[5] "The Mother of Livia Augusta", *Historia* 14 (1965) 334. See also his recent book, *New Men in the Roman Senate* (Oxford 1971) 57, 211.

[6] See, e. g. R. Syme, *The Roman Revolution* (Oxford 1939), 358 n. 1; L. R. Taylor, *The Voting Districts of the Roman Republic* (Rome 1960) 188–189.   [7] *CIL* 9. 3661 = *ILS* 125.

[8] M. Livius Drusus Claudianus was (as it seems) an adoptive son of the tribune of 91 M. Livius Drusus (cf. L. Petersen, *PIR*² L 294, Berolini 1970), who, as Wiseman points out, had been a close friend and *hospes* of Q. Poppaedius Silo, the famous Marsic general and hero during the Social War. Hence his hypothesis: "The honour paid to Alfidia at Marruvium may be significant" – says Wiseman, and proceeds to ask: "did Livius Drusus' son perpetuate his father's connection with the Marsi by marrying a woman of Marruvium?" (p. 334). Ingenious – and far-fetched. For the implication of this theory is that Alfidia was honored at Marruvium because (1) she was a Marruvine by birth, and (2) her husband a son of an old friend of the Marsi. Should we infer that if she did not derive from a local *gens* there would not have been sufficient reason for the Marruvini to commemorate her? In fact, Wiseman concludes (p. 334): "Thus it is at least possible that Alfidia was a Marruvine, honoured as *municeps* rather than merely as the emperor's mother-in-law".

The only thing for which we have clear evidence is the connection of M. Livius Drusus with the Marsi. It seems therefore logical to suppose (accepting for the moment Wiseman's way of thinking but reversing his approach) that the Marsi, when M. Livius Drusus Claudianus came to posthumous prominence as an ancestor of the imperial family (though he had fought to the very end against Octavianus and had taken his own life), dug out of the dim past his father's good offices to their nation, and honored him (see *CIL* 9. 3660 = *ILS* 124), along with his wife Alfidia (of Fundi, of course).

Wiseman's thesis thus ultimately rests on the fact that an inscription honoring Alfidia was found at Marruvium. But is this circumstance really so startling as to require so elaborate an explanation as that presented in Wiseman's paper? Similar honors were paid to Alfidia and her husband in the obscure town of Tucci in Baetica (*CIL* 2. 1167, mentioning only Alfidia), and at Samos (*IGRR* 4. 982, 983). As there is no detectable connection of Livia's parents with either Tucci or Samos, it was clearly due to pure chance that inscriptions commemorating them came to light there (they were certainly set up also in many other cities); and since the simplest solution is usually the best one, the same explanation will hold also with respect to Marruvium. Moreover, there are strong reasons to believe that it was precisely at Fundi that Alfidia received most exceptional honors, see below, n. 10.

[9] *Op. cit.* 334. In a less sophisticated manner the same opinion was also expressed by M. Johnstone Du Four, *C. Suetonii Tranquilli Vita Tiberii*, Diss. Pennsylvania (Philadelphia 1941) 24 n. 1:

But this argument patently misses the point. Suetonius does not cite Caligula's words in full, and we do not know whether in Caligula's letter to the senate the name of Livia's *avus* was mentioned (or in which form); it is possible that Suetonius got the name Aufidius from that source, but it is also possible that it was his own guess and mistake, and not the emperor's.

As to the origin of Livia's mother it should be stressed that it was not only Caligula who associated Livia's maternal family with Fundi. In the biography of Tiberius Suetonius notes that there were some authorities who held the mistaken view that Tiberius was born at Fundi. This error, Suetonius explains, was due to the fact that Fundi was the home town of Tiberius' maternal grandmother; he further notes that a statue of Felicitas was erected at Fundi by a decree of the senate, apparently to honor there the *mater Augustae*.[10] This tradition is certainly independent of Caligula's letter; it is hardly possible to argue that the satire of Horace influenced not only Caligula, but Suetonius and the antiquarians criticized by him as well. We should not be deterred by the Aufidius Luscus of Horace from attributing to Fundi M. Alfidius, the maternal grandfather of Livia: both Aufidii and Alfidii were at home at Fundi, and it is quite possible that both *gentes* produced local magistrates.[11]

But Wiseman himself has destroyed the main pillar of his argument. He writes that "the evidence of Caligula who was concerned to illustrate the superior nobility of the line of Antony and Octavia over that of Livia and Au-

---

"Caligula reproached Livia with being the granddaughter of Aufidius Lurco, a decurion of Fundi" – an excellent example of turning a legitimate guess into an illegitimate statement of fact. We know that Caligula reproached Livia with being *materno avo decurione Fundano ortam* (Suet., *Cal.* 23. 2), we do not know if he reproached her with being "the granddaugher of Aufidius Lurco". This is only a guess, and not the fact.

[10] Suet., *Tib*. 5: *Tiberium quidam Fundis natum existimauerunt secuti leuem coniecturam, quod materna eius auia Fundana fuerit et quod mox simulacrum Felicitatis ex s. c. publicatum ibi sit*. The full significance of this testimony seems to have been overlooked by Wiseman. It clearly shows that Fundi is to be added to the list of towns where Alfidia was honored by the erection of statues. Moreover, the fact that it was the statue of Felicitas that was set up, and that this action was taken *ex senatus consulto* (and not simply on the initiative of the local officials as presumably at Samos, Marruvium and Tucci), points to the special importance and distinction of Fundi, we may safely assume, as the home town of Alfidia. (On the goddess Felicitas and the imperial concept of *felicitas*, see Otto, *RE* 6 [1907] 2164; D. Vaglieri, *DE* 3 [1922] 43–44; and, above all, H. Erkell, *Augustus, Felicitas, Fortuna* [Göteborg 1952]. Cf. also the wording of *IGRR* 4. 983 where Alfidia is hailed as μεγίστων ἀγαθῶν αἰτίαν γεγονυίαν τῷ κόσμῳ).

[11] For Aufidii, apart from Aufidius Luscus, see *CIL* 12. 4357: *L. Aufidio L. f. . . . . aed. bis quinq. bis Fundis*; and for Alfidii (as yet not recorded epigraphically to have held magistracies at Fundi), *CIL* 10. 6248; *C. Alfidius C.* [*f.*] *Rufio*. No Alfidii occur at Marruvium; of course it is possible that the Alfii, prominent in the district, were akin to the Alfidii (this argument plays some role in Wiseman's demonstration), but this can hardly be regarded as having any direct bearing on the question of Alfidia's origin.

gustus, should not be believed without reservations".[12] Certainly not; but there is no doubt – and Wiseman does not question this[13] – that Caligula was right in stating that Livia's mother was not of senatorial origin.[14] To call attention to this disgraceful fact was Caligula's main purpose, while the question whether the mother of Livia came from Fundi or any other Italian town was obviously of only secondary, if any, importance. I see no point in substituting wrong Fundi for right Marruvium: was Marruvium any better than Fundi? Suetonius' "Aufidia of Fundi" should certainly be forgotten, but perhaps not Alfidia of Fundi.

II.

If Caligula had really been induced by the satire of Horace maliciously to change the name of his *proavia* from Alfidia into Aufidia, he walked straight into his own trap. For his main purpose was to convey the picture of a boastful municipal nonentity, and the Alfidii would serve that purpose. There were, in fact, no senatorial Alfidii. The contrary was true of the Aufidii, and Suetonius promptly pointed this out: an Aufidius Lurco held *honores* in Rome.

Caligula was at best misinformed, at worst mischievous, Suetonius, however, was simultaneously overcritical and too credulous: he rejected Caligula's assertion that the grandfather of Livia was only a municipal great man while adopting or conjecturing the false name-form Aufidius. But this is not the end of the story. Suetonius was wrong, but it would nevertheless be interesting to identify the man whom he had selected as Livia's grandfather. He asserts that the name of this man was to be found in public documents. An important and known personage, no doubt.

If so, the M. Aufidius Lurco mentioned in Pliny's *Naturalis Historia* would be an attractive candidate. In Pliny's account of various πρῶτοι εὑρεταί he occupies a place of honor in the history of Roman culinary art, along with Q. Hortensius, the famous consular, augur, orator and gourmet. Lurco

---

[12] Op. cit. 333.

[13] See his remark, p. 334: "There is no evidence that her father was ever a senator".

[14] The first known senator of the gens Alfidia is recorded as proconsul of Sicily, according to Wiseman (p. 334) in the later years of Augustus' reign. But this does not necessarily follow from Groag's remark (*PIR* I² A 527): "*aequalis videtur M'. Aemilii Lepidi cos. a. 11 p. C.*" All we learn from the acephalous *cursus* (*CIL* 8. 9247) of an *ignotus* who subsequently served as *legatus* in Sicily under Alfidius Sabinus, and in Asia under a Lepidus, is that Alfidius' tenure of the Sicilian governorship preceded the proconsulship of Lepidus in Asia. The dating depends upon restoration of Lepidus' *praenomen*: Manius or Marcus. In the former case the *terminus ante quem* for Alfidius' proconsulship in Sicily would be 21/22, in the latter 26/27. On the dating of the proconsulships of M'. and M. Lepidus in Asia and the tangled question of M'. and M. Lepidi in Tacitus, see D. Magie, *Roman Rule in Asia Minor*, 2 (Princeton 1950) 1362–1363, 1581 (unfortunately containing inaccuracies and misunderstandings), and, above all, the magisterial studies by R. Syme, "Marcus Lepidus, Capax Imperii", *JRS* 45 (1955) 22–33; *Tacitus* (Oxford 1958) 1. 382–383, 2. 751–752.

was the first to conceive the idea of fattening peacocks in order to put them on the market.[15] Pliny took this information, as much else, from Varro's treatise on the *res rusticae*. *De pavonibus nostra memoria* – says one of the interlocutors in Varro's tract – *greges habere coepti et venire magno. ex iis M. Aufidius Lurco supra sexagena milia nummum in anno dicitur capere*.[16] One may note that Varro does not specifically credit Lurco with having been the first to fatten peacocks; he is presented rather as an example of an especially successful businessman.[17] Varro, in fact, introduces M. Seius and L. Abuccius as the authorities in the art of feeding and raising of peacocks.[18]

Some generations later, Lurco, Hortensius and the peacocks once more crop up together in Tertullian's tract *de pallio*, this time not to be applauded but to serve as a telling example of Roman degeneration: *Praecidam gulam, qua Hortensius orator primus pavum cibi causa potuit occidere, qua Aufidius Lurco primus sagina corpora vitiavit et coactis alimentis in adulterinum provexit saporem (de pallio* 5. 6). They appear in the midst of an impressive collection of sadists, gourmets and squanderers, preceded by the notorious Vedius Pollio (who, to use Tertullian's words, *servos muraenis invadendos obiectabat)*, and followed by Asinius Celer (who *mulli unius obsonium sex sestertiis detulit)* and Aesopus histrio (who *centum milium patinam confiscavit).*[19]

This company does not seem to do justice to Lurco: while the other gentlemen mentioned by Tertullian dissipated money on gastronomic treats, he made a fortune profiting from the extravagances of the others – but perhaps this was, for Tertullian, even more repugnant.

At any rate the fame of Lurco was firmly established: it is a rare honor to serve as an *exemplum*. Moreover, it is quite possible that Horace not only ridiculed Aufidius Luscus of Fundi but also mentioned our Aufidius Lurco –

---

[15] Plin., *N. H.* 10. 45: *Pavonem cibi gratia Romae primus occidit orator Hortensius aditiali cena sacerdotii. saginare primus instituit circa novissimum piraticum bellum M. Aufidius Lurco exque eo quaestu reditus HS. sexagena milia habuit.*

[16] Varro, *R. R.* 3. 6. 1. The dialogue takes place in a *villa publica* during an election to the curule aedileship. The dramatic date of the third book of the *R. R.* cannot therefore be (as is often stated) 54, since in that year no elections for the curule magistracies occurred; it is probably 50, as ingeniously established by E. Badian, *Athenaeum* N. S. 48 (1970) 4–6.

[17] The information concerning Hortensius also is presented by Varro in a somewhat less positive manner than in Pliny: *primus hos (pavones) Q. Hortensius augurali aditiali cena posuisse dicitur (R. R.* 3. 6. 6).

[18] *R. R.* 3. 6. 3–6; cf. 3. 2. 1–14, 17; 3. 10. 1. Of Abuccius nothing more is known; on Seius, see Münzer, *RE* 2A (1923) 1121–1122; C. Cichorius, *Hermes* 39 (1904) 465–466; and below, n. 64 and 65.

[19] See on them, J. Keil, *RE* 8A (1955) 568–570 s. v. Vedius no. 8; Groag, *PIR²*, 1 (1933) A 1225; Münzer, *RE* 4 (1901) s. v. Clodius no. 16. On the whole passage, see also the excellent commentary by A. Gerlo, *Q. S. Fl. Tertullianus. De pallio* (Wetteren 1940) 192–201. The new commentary on the *de pallio* by S. Costanza (Napoli 1968) is, at least as far as the prosopography is concerned, totally disappointing.

not very favourably, as a matter of fact. But his reasons for criticizing Aufidius were altogether different from Tertullian's: Aufidius was not sophisticated enough in preparing the *mulsum*; he mixed it in an improper way: it
was much too strong.[20]

The identification proposed above is attractive, though it is admittedly
only a tentative one. But let us consider the following arguments:

To be reproached by Horace with a fault in so important a matter as the
preparation of *mulsum*, one had to be a celebrity in culinary circles. The Aufidius of Horace therefore was undoubtedly a gourmet of renown; does this
also apply to Aufidius Lurco? We have heard of the profits earned by him as
a peacock raiser, but nothing as yet to justify his fame as a gourmet. Is there
any independent testimony to that effect? Tertullian is here once more of
assistance.

What should happen to the soul of a *homicida*? Should it be punished by
being transferred to a beast, *pecus lanienae et macello destinatum*, in order to be
slaughtered and served up as a dish? This will not do; for it would upset the
sense of justice – so warns Tertullian. Such a soul would receive more *solacii*
than *supplicii*. It will find its funeral attended to by the best cooks, it will be
consigned to the grave by the *condimenta Apiciana et Lurconiana*, the famous
spice sauces of Apicius and Lurco.[21]

M. Gavius Apicius was credited with many epochal inventions in the field
of culinary art which, together with his luxurious style of life, have won him
an everlasting reputation as the paradigm of a Roman epicure.[22] He was famous, *inter alia*, for his *cocturae* and *condimenta*[23] but the sauce of Lurco[24] was
no worse. No greater honor could have been paid to Aufidius Lurco than to
be cited together with the two foremost culinary celebrities of the republican
and imperial ages respectively: Hortensius and Apicius.[25] This establishes

---

[20] Horat., *Sat.* 2. 4. 24–27:

> Aufidius forti miscebat mella Falerno:
> mendose; quoniam vacuis committere venis
> nil nisi lene decet: leni praecordia mulso
> prolueris melius.

[21] Tert., *De anima* 33. 3–4; Cf. the classic commentary by J. H. Waszink, *Q. S. Fl. Tertulliani de
anima* (Amsterdam 1947) 393–397.

[22] See on him Groag-Stein, *PIR*², 4. 1 (1952) G 91; J. André, *Apicius. L'art culinaire* (Paris
1965) 7–9, 19–21.   [23] Cf. André, p. 9.

[24] There can be no doubt that the *nomen gentilicium* of Lurco, the inventor of *condimentum Lurconianum*, was Aufidius. See below, n. 30.

[25] It is worth noticing that in the *de pallio* (5. 7), a few lines after Hortensius and Aufidius Lurco, Apicius also turns up: *Taceo Nerones et Apicios, Rufos*. The Rufus mentioned here is another celebrity: no doubt, none other than C. Sempronius Asellio Rufus, the man who had introduced
young storks to Rome as a gourmet dish (see on him E. Badian's brilliant article, "The Sempronii
Aselliones", *Proceedings of the African Classical Associations* 11 [1968] 3–5).

virtually beyond any doubt the identity of Tertullian's and Varro's M. Aufidius Lurco with Horace's Aufidius.[26]

Whatever opinion Tertullian or Horace might have formed of him, Lurco was undoubtedly a respectable gentleman and landowner, and a successful businessman; his daughter would be an excellent match for any noble, such as, e. g., M. Livius Drusus Claudianus, the father of Livia Augusta. M. Aufidius Lurco, the peacock breeder and gourmet, would make an excellent *avus Augustae*.[27]

It was undoubtedly Aufidius' way of life that earned him his surname – he is the first Aufidius and in general the first (if not only) person in republican times known to bear the *cognomen* Lurco[28] – glutton.[29]

We must stop here for a while. There is no evidence – apart from the notice in Suetonius, the veracity of which must first be proven (not to mention the fact that the M. Aufidius Lurco discussed here need not be identical with the one referred to by Suetonius, although he probably is) – that our M. Aufidius Lurco was ever a magistrate. This poses the question of further identifications. As usual, Cicero is of help. He twice mentions a Lurco (or two different Lurcones) – taking into account the extreme rarity of this *cognomen*,[30]

---

[26] Klebs (*RE* 2 [1896] s. v. Aufidius 26) and Kiessling-Heinze (*ad loc.*, 4th ed. in 1910) were very positive about this identification, but since they overlooked the passage from the *de anima* of Tertullian, they were not able to produce a definitive proof. (Later, in the fifth edition in 1921, R. Heinze changed his mind and came to the conclusion that no identification was possible). Gerlo, p. 195, and Waszink, p. 396, mention the *condimentum Lurconianum* in this context, but they took the identification for granted, and failed to point out the special importance of this passage.

[27] This also seems to be the opinion of T. R. S. Broughton in his *Magistrates of the Roman Republic*. He registers him (2. 535: Index of Careers) as "Aufidius Lurco" (the identity with the peacock Aufidius is established by the *RE*-number, Aufidius 26, quoted by Broughton; the omission of the *praenomen* is not justified: Aufidius' *praenomen* Marcus is attested by Varro and Pliny), and terms him "Mag., date uncertain". He identifies him both with M. Aufidius Lurco mentioned by Suetonius and with M. Alfidius attested epigraphically as the grandfather of Livia. For a detailed discussion of Broughton's reconstruction, see below, part III.

[28] Cf. I. Kajanto, *The Latin Cognomina* (Helsinki 1965) 269. The origin of the Roman *cognomina* as personal nicknames is persuasively argued by A. Alföldi, "Les *Cognomina* des magistrats de la République romaine", *Mélanges A. Piganiol* (Paris 1966), 709–722 (p. 714: Lurco). As a disparaging epithet we find the word applied to Sallust by the grammarian Lenaeus, a freedman and admirer of Pompey (Suet., *de gramm*. 15).

[29] This is the basic meaning of the word (cf. Plaut., *Pers*. 421: *lurco edax;* Serv., *Aen*. 6. 4: "*lurcho*", *id est vorax;* Lucil. 2. 75–80 with Marx' commentary), but it also could have erotic connotations (cf. Apul., *Met*. 8. 25).

[30] Apart from M. Aufidius Lurco known from Varro, Pliny and Tertullian, M. Aufidius Lurco referred to by Suetonius, Lurco, the inventor of *condimentum Lurconianum*, and the Lurcones mentioned by Cicero (who may all turn out to be one and the same person), I know of only two other persons bearing the *cognomen* Lurco: A. Petronius Lurco, *cos. suff.* A. D. 58, and M. Petronius Lurco, mentioned in A. D. 45 among the *curatores tabularum publicarum*. (for this reading of CIL 6.31201, see M. Hammond, "Curatores tabularum publicarum", *Classical and Mediaeval Studies in*

there is no doubt that it is wholly justifiable to provide them with the *nomen* Aufidius.

From a letter to Atticus written at the beginning of July 61 we learn of an anti-bribery law promulgated by the tribune of the plebs Lurco.[31] The bill contained one novel and important clause providing that any person convicted of distributing bribes should pay 3000 sesterces annually to every tribe[32] for life; he would be free from any punishment if he had only promised money but did not actually distribute it among the tribes. But Lurco's action was ill-fated from the very beginning – the lameness of its *rogator* was a bad omen. Cicero, of course, did not fail to poke fun at Lurco's bodily deformity, wittily juxtaposing *claudus homo* and *bono auspicio promulgavit*. That Lurco was lame is interesting enough,[33] but his activity as tribune must be studied in a broader political context. The Catonian flavor of his proposal then becomes unmistakable – and not only because of the awkwardness of the bill's new provision ridiculed by Cicero.[34] Apart from his predilection for making fun of what he regarded as unrealistic features in Catonian policy, Cicero had his own good reason for ridiculing Lurco: Lurco's bill, if passed, would have replaced his own law against electoral bribery; hence his evident lack of enthusiasm.

The new law *de ambitu* was clearly intended as a move in the legal warfare waged between the groups headed by Cato and Pompey the Great. Pompey, who since his return to Rome in January 61 had tried in vain to have his acts in the East ratified by the Senate, nourished hopes of achieving that goal through the agency of his new protegé for the consulship of 60, his former

---

Honor of E. K. Rand, New York 1938, 123–131). According to E. Groag (*RE* 19 [1938] s. v. Petronius 41 and 42) there is a fair possibility that they were identical with each other.

[31] *Ad Att.* 1. 16. 13: *Lurco autem tribunus pl., qui magistratus simultatem cum lege Aelia iniit, solutus est et Aelia et Fufia ut legem de ambitu ferret quam ille bono auspicio claudus homo promulgavit. ita comitia in a. d. VI Kal. Sext. dilata sunt. novi est in lege hoc, ut qui nummos in tribu pronuntiarit, si non dederit, impune sit, sin dederit, ut quoad vivat singulis tribubus HS CIƆ CIƆ CIƆ debeat.* The text ist reproduced according to the edition of D. R. Shackleton Bailey, *Cicero's Letters to Atticus,* 1 (Cambridge 1965), who, following a brilliant conjecture of A. Clark, definitely solved the *crux* at the beginning of the passage.

[32] The reading *tribubus* is clearly preferable to *tribulibus.* See Shackleton Bailey, *ad loc.,* p. 324. But cf. also A. W. Zumpt, *Das Criminalrecht der römischen Republik,* 2. 2 (Berlin 1869) 266–268, who thinks that the payment had to be made not to all the tribes, but only to those actually involved in the bribery.

[33] It establishes, for instance, that bodily deformity did not disqualify one for the tribunate, cf. Th. Mommsen, *Römisches Staatsrecht,* 1³ (Leipzig 1887) 493–494. On lameness as an unlucky sign, see Shackleton Bailey *ad loc.*

[34] Cicero continues (*ad Att.* 1.16.13; cf. above, n. 31): *dixi hanc legem P. Clodium iam antea servasse; pronuntiare enim solitum esse et non dare.* Completely erroneous is the interpretation of S. H. Rinkes (*Disputatio de crimine ambitus et de sodaliciis apud Romanos* [Lugduni Batavorum 1854] 138) that Lurco's bill was designed *"in commodum Clodii et Clodianorum".*

legate, L. Afranius. The active collaboration of the Pompeian consul of 61, M. Pupius Piso, and electoral bribery should pave the way for Afranius.[35] But the Catonians were not prepared to give up. They had a sound majority of the Senate behind them, and shortly before Lurco presented his bill, Cato and Domitius succeeded in pushing through the House two decrees aimed at electoral bribery, and indirectly at Pompey's plans. One of them made the magistrates subject to inquiries and their homes subject to search in connection with electoral malpractices; and the other, closely linked with the former, declared it a crime against the state *(adversus rem publicam)* to give shelter in one's house to *divisores*, the notorious bribery agents who distributed money among the tribes. Rumor had it that these decrees were directed against the consul Piso, who was said to harbor the divisores in his house, *quod ego non credo*, comments Cicero.[36]

These measures having obviously proved futile, the Catonians must have felt that a new anti-bribery law was needed. However, they encountered a difficulty of a legal nature. The elections had already been announced, and, according to a provision of the *leges* Aelia and Fufia passed in the mid-second century,[37] no new legislation concerning the electoral law could be voted on in the period between the announcement and the holding of the elections.[38] In order to go ahead with the plan of a new *ambitus* law special action on the part of the Senate was necessary. Lurco was exempted by a *senatus consultum* from the provisions of the Aelian and Fufian law, and was thus authorized to

[35] For an account of the political situation in 61, see W. Drumann—P. Groebe, *Geschichte Roms*, 4 (Leipzig 1908/10) 488–492; T. R. Holmes, *The Roman Republic*, 1 (Oxford 1923) 290–300.

[36] Cic., *ad Att.* 1. 16. 12.

[37] This is the traditional date, based on Cic., *In Pis.* 10. G. V. Sumner's attempt to date both laws to 132 B. C. ("Lex Aelia, Lex Fufia", *AJPh* 84 [1963] 344–350) was opposed by A. E. Astin ("Leges Aelia et Fufia", *Latomus* 23 [1964] 445), but it seems to have found some favor recently in the eyes of E. J. Weinrib, "Obnuntiatio: Two Problems", *Zeitschrift der Savigny-Stiftung für Rechtsgeschichte. Romanistische Abteilung* 87 (1970) 396.

[38] The view expressed in the text differs from the *communis opinio* (deriving ultimately from L. Lange's interpretation of *Sch.Bob.* p. 148 Stangl and Cass. Dio 36. 39; see his study *De legibus Aelia et Fufia commentatio* [Gissae 1861] = *Kleine Schriften*, 1 [Göttingen 1887] 334–340) that no new legislation (and not only, as I believe, measures concerning the electoral law) could be passed in the electoral period. But the traditional interpretation is untenable. All known exemptions from the *leges* Aelia and Fufia were granted in order to pass *ambitus* laws after the announcement of the electoral *comitia*. Moreover, it can be positively demonstrated that in 67 the tribune C. Cornelius did not need any dispensation in order to present his bill *ne quis nisi per populum legibus solveretur* for vote of the tribes during the electoral period, whereas at the same time a special exemption was required for the passage of the consular law *de ambitu*. The absence of such exemption made it impossible for Cornelius to pass his own anti-bribery law (Cass. Dio 36. 38–39; Asconius 57–59 C). Shackleton Bailey's statement (*op. cit.* 1. 324) that the *leges* Aelia and Fufia appear "to have somehow restricted tribunician legislation at election periods" is not precise: the laws dealt with tribunician legislation as well as with that of the curule magistrates. This question cannot be gone into here; I propose to treat it in detail in another study.

put the proposal of his law *de ambitu* to the vote of the tribes before the elections.[39] However, in spite of this arrangement he was not to score a success: the law did not carry.[40]

Two years later we meet a M. Lurco, *vir optimus, meus familiaris*, as Cicero calls him, testifying as a witness against L. Valerius Flaccus at the latter's trial for extortion in Asia.[41] Cicero's remark about the *legatio libera*[42] undertaken by Lurco shows that he was a senator at that time and thus very probably identical with the tribune of 61. He appears to have had some sort of business connections with the province of Asia.[43] A freedmen of Lurco was condemned in Asia, apparently on a criminal charge, during the governorship of Flaccus.[44] We may further note that C. Sextilius, the son of Lurco's sister, also is attested as having interests in Asia.[45]

There is little doubt that M. Aufidius Lurco, the senator and tribune of the plebs, was the man to whom Suetonius refers. Unfortunately nothing is known about his further career.[46] If all the Aufidii and Lurcones mentioned in the course of this paper are identified and amalgamated into one person (which, on more than one count,[47] is attractive and plausible) the following

[39] The fact that this caused the postponement of the elections seems to be sufficient proof that Lurco was not exempted from the observance of the *trinum nundinum*.

[40] Cic., *ad Att.* 1. 18. 3 (20 January 60): *facto senatus consulto de ambitu . . . nulla lex perlata*. Shackleton Bailey (*op. cit.* 1. 331) rightly points out that this probably refers to the decree by which Lurco was empowered to introduce his law *de ambitu*, and not to the decrees dealing with the searching of the houses and sheltering of the *divisores* mentioned in *ad Att.* 1. 16. 12. Lurco's law was either vetoed by a tribune or rejected by the people.

[41] Cic., *pro Flacco* 86–89. Cf. Drumann—Groebe, 5 (Leipzig 1919) 613 ff., esp. 622.

[42] *Pro Flacco* 89. On the *legationes liberae*, see Mommsen, *Römisches Staatsrecht*, 2³ (Leipzig 1887) 85–87; R. O. Jolliffe, Phases of Corruption in Roman Administration in the last Half-Century of the Roman Republic, Diss. Chicago (Menasha 1919) 77–90; J. Suolahti, "Legatio libera", *Arctos* 5 (1970) 113–119.

[43] It is interesting to note that Lurco undertook the *legatio libera* in order to attend in a province to his rights as creditor *(exigendi causa)*. Cf. Suolahti, p. 116; Wiseman, *New Men*, 200.

[44] *Pro Flacco* 87–88.

[45] *Pro Flacco* 84–89. Cf. Münzer, *RE* 2A (1921) 2034, 2036 s. vv. Sextilius 7 and 18; *RE* 8A (1955) 243–244 s. v. Valerius 391; E. Badian, *JRS* 55 (1965) 113–114; Wiseman, *New Men* 198.

[46] In *MRR* 2. 235 a M. Aufidius Lurco (identified by Broughton with Lurco the tribune) appears (with the mark of interrogation) as an aedile in 52. But almost certainly he is a phantom owing his existence only to P. Willems' emendation (*Le sénat de la république romaine,* 1 [Louvain 1885]491) of Plutarch, *Cat. Min.* 46. 7. For a detailed discussion, see my article "The Aedileship of Favonius, Curio the Younger and Cicero's Election to the Augurate", *Harvard Studies in Classical Philology* 78 (1972) 188–190.

[47] The main, and, in my opinion, decisive argument in favor of the identification is the *cognomen*. There seems to be little doubt that M. Aufidius Lurco, the peacock raiser, earned his *cognomen* as a personal nickname (and did not inherit it; cf. above, n. 28). Since, however, M. Lurco the senator and tribune, was approximately his coeval (cf. the next note) it would be rather a strange coincidence if he too should have been given quite independently the same rare *cognomen* and at the same time. The identification is the easiest and best way to remove this difficulty.

picture would emerge: a senator and a gourmet, he certainly was more successful as a businessman and innovator in Roman culinary art than as Cato's ally in politics. Peacocks and not his tribunate supplied his real title to fame. However, his greatest success would have been to serve as *avus Augustae*.[48] But for three inscriptions that have stripped him of that honor he was, thanks to Suetonius' error or credulity, very close to that mark of celebrity.

III.

But was Suetonius, after all, really wrong? Not everybody is of this opinion. Among the dissenters are T. R. S. Broughton, L. R. Taylor and D. R. Shackleton Bailey, a formidable array of names and authority. This impels one to caution – and to a careful analysis of their arguments. If there is any chance of vindicating the authority of Suetonius, and of restoring M. Alfidius to senatorial dignity, it ought to be explored.

In *MRR*, in the Index of Careers, there appears (p. 529)[49] a M. Alfidius Lurco (with the annotation "not in *RE*"); for further information we are directed to Aufidius Lurco, Aufidius no. 26 in *RE*. He is presented on p. 535 as "Aufidius Lurco (26) Mag., date uncertain". Further discussion and explanation is offered in Additions and Corrections. The addition in question refers to p. 487, Appendix III: Supplementary List of Senators. It runs as follows (p. 647):

"A magistrate whose offices (and their dates) remain unknown was Alfidius, the maternal grandfather of Livia, a municipal magistrate of Fundi,

---

[48] Chronologically he fits in quite well. Livia was born in 58 B. C. and gave birth to Tiberius when she was sixteen years old; if that pattern also prevailed in the preceding generation, her mother will have been born some twenty years previously, ca. 80–75. Aufidius Lurco must have been at that time in his early twenties; in 61 when he held the tribunate he was at least thirty three years old, but may well have been much older. On the other hand, the peacock-Aufidius *pavones saginare instituit circa novissimum piraticum bellum* (Plin., *N. H.* 10. 45), i. e. Pompey's campaign against the pirates in 67. This date is in harmony with the career of the tribune M. Lurco.

The phrase *circa novissimum piraticum bellum* causes some difficulty. It is normally taken to mean the *bellum piraticum* of Pompey, but R. Heinze refers it to the war against Sex. Pompeius in 37 and 36. B. C. (in Kiessling—Heinze, 2[8] [1961] 270, going back to 2[5] in 1921. He evidently changed his earlier interpretation in 2[4] [1910] 233). As Varro does not use this expression when he speaks of Aufidius Lurco in *R. R.* 3. 6. 1, Heinze concluded that Pliny got it from a different source, possibly from a different treatise of Varro. This is plausible, but Heinze's interpretation of *bellum piraticum* is unconvincing and improbable. The dramatic date of the dialogue in the third book of Varro's *de re rustica* is in all probability 50 B. C. (cf. above, n. 16). The peacock business had already been flourishing for some years at that time, as suggested by Varro's words that it became fashionable to raise peacocks *nostra memoria* (besides Varro, *R. R.* 3. 6. 1–6, see Cic., *ad Fam.* 9. 20, written in 45: *etiam Hirtio cenam dedi, sine pavone tamen*, and cf. Hor., Sat. 1. 2. 115–116). If Pliny took his dating *circa novissimum piraticum bellum* from Varro, it must refer to Pompey's campaign; if it was his own addition, and if he was thinking of Octavian's *piraticum bellum* against Sex. Pompeius, he was simply mistaken (and together with him also Heinze).

[49] All subsequent references are to vol. 2.

who held unnamed *honores* in Rome (Suet. *Cal.* 23, with the name Aufidius Lurco; cf. *Tib.* 5). On the name Alfidius, see *CIL* 2. 1667; *ILS* 125; *IGRP* 4. 983."

Essentially the same interpretation is also to be found in L. R. Taylor's *Voting Districts of the Roman Republic*. In her list of republican senators with tribes "Alfidius from Fundi, hence AEM", is recorded (p. 188). He is marked, surprisingly enough, as *certus*. This entry is accompanied by the following commentary (p. 188–189):

"The maternal grandfather of Livia, wife of Augustus; he was a municipal magistrate of Fundi who held *honores* in Rome. See Suet. *Tib.* 5, and also *Cal.* 23, where the name is Aufidium Lyrgonem. But Livia's mother's name is Alfidia in *ILS* 125. On the name, see Klebs s. v. "Aufidius" no. 24 *RE* and *MRR* 2, p. 647; Schulze, *LE* 119, 587."

One notes with interest her reference to the passage in *MRR* which we have reproduced above. But the authority of L. R. Taylor has in turn been invoked in *MRR Suppl*. The entry in question reads as follows (p. 4):

"ALFIDIUS, AEM. Maternal grandfather of Livia. A municipal magistrate of Fundi who held honores in Rome (Suet. *Cal.* 23, with the reading *Aufidium Lyrgonem;* cf. *Tib.* 5). The name of Livia's mother is given as Alfidia in *ILS* 125. (LRT) See additions and corrections, p. 647."

The instruction to consult additions and corrections attached to the second volume of *MRR* closes up the circle of quotations and selfquotations. As compared with the note in "Additions and Corrections" the Supplement brings only one substantial addition: the indication of Alfidius' tribe, taken from *VDRR*.

The treatment of this whole question in *MRR* and *VDRR* is both instructive and startling. To begin with, Broughton obviously identifies M. Alfidius,[50] attested epigraphically as the maternal grandfather of Livia, with M. Aufidius Lurco. The basis for this identification is less obvious. Most surprising is his choice of the man to be identified with Alfidius. Aufidius *RE* no. 26 is that gentleman who *pavones primus saginare instituit*. There is no independent evidence for his being a magistrate, apart from his identification with M. Lurco, the senator and tribune, or with M. Aufidius Lurco known from Suetonius or with both of them. Now, Broughton clearly rejects the identification of Alfidius with M. Lurco referred to by Cicero and

---

[50] It must be borne in mind that epigraphically no *cognomen* of M. Alfidius is attested; the *cognomen* Lurco given to him by Broughton is the result of his identification with M. Aufidius Lurco, i. e. of the identification that is yet to be proven. Of course, in the inscription *CIL* 9. 3661 = *ILS* 125 *Alfidia M. f. mater Augustae*, his *cognomen*, if he had any, could not be recorded.

treats him as identical only with M. Aufidius Lurco recorded by Suetonius and with M. Aufidius Lurco known from Varro and Pliny. This leaves us with two Marci Lurcones: the tribune (and senator), and another M. Lurco who held unspecified magistracies and bred peacocks. However, on Broughton's theory, only the first of them bore the *gentilicium* Aufidius; the latter was in reality an Alfidius. In common they had only the *cognomen* (and the *praenomen*).

There is certainly nothing impossible in the hypothesis that M. Aufidius Lurco and M. Alfidius Lurco simultaneously held offices at Rome, but given the rarity of the *cognomen* this does not seem to be a comfortable situation. But this is not all: Broughton seems to have overlooked the fact that on this reconstruction his M. Aufidius Lurco,[51] or rather Lurco's *nomen gentilicium*, simply disappears. Cicero mentions him by *cognomen* only;[52] his *nomen* Aufidius had been deduced from the comparison (not necessarily identification) with M. Aufidius Lurco (or Aufidii Lurcones) referred to on the one hand by Suetonius, and by Varro, Pliny and Tertullian on the other. Now, if that latter person was in reality an Alfidius Lurco, as Broughton believes him to have been, there is no source authority left at our disposal to validate the supposition that the Lurco of Cicero belonged to the *gens* Aufidia. On Broughton's own theory the conclusion seems inescapable that he too bore the *nomen* Alfidius.

This, in fact, has been the proposition tentatively advanced by L. R. Taylor;[53] however, on closer scrutiny, her reconstruction generates as many doubts as that of Broughton. M. Aufidius Lurco, the peacock breeder, does not appear in her list of republican senators with tribes; unlike Broughton she clearly declined to identify him either with M. Alfidius or with any of the other M. Lurcones (i. e. with Suetonius' M. Aufidius Lurco or Cicero's M. Lurco). Two persons result from her reconstruction: M. Aufidius Lurco, probably not a senator (attested by Varro and the Varronian tradition), and M. Alfidius Lurco, the senator, magistrate and grandfather of Livia (extracted from the epigraphical evidence, Suetonius and Cicero). This is not so discomforting as to have both of them simultaneously sitting in the *curia*; nonetheless the same objection applies to Taylor's theory as to that of Broughton: the difficulty is posed by the *cognomen*. The simultaneous occurence of a rare *cognomen* in two different *gentes* with a strikingly similar *nomen* seems to strain credulity.

---

[51] He is listed by Broughton in the following way: *MRR* 2. 535: "(M. Aufidius) Lurco (*RE* 25, cf. 27) Tr. Pl. 61", and 2. 179: "(M. Aufidius?) Lurco". This is correct, for the *praenomen* of the tribune is not directly attested; no further identification is proposed, but on p. 235 an aedile "M. Aufidius Lurco" is tentatively listed. This time his *nomen* and *praenomen* is neither queried nor parenthesized, but in all probability he was neither Lurco nor Aufidius: he did not exist at all (see above, n. 46).

[52] Actually, this applies only to Lurco, the tribune of the plebs in 61. Cicero gives the *praenomen* for the senator of 59.   [53] *VDRR* 197.

Despite obvious inconsistencies in their presentation of the problem the amassed authority of T. R. S. Broughton and L. R. Taylor did not fail to exert influence. D. R. Shackleton Bailey, normally so cautious and critical, readily accepted the line of reasoning advocated by Broughton and Taylor. He is of the opinion that Lurco, the tribune of the plebs in 61, was

"perhaps the epicure M. Aufidius (?) Lurco, who made a fortune by fattening peacocks for sale . . .; and probably the Senator M. Lurco who gave evidence against L. Flaccus in 59 . . . He in turn could well be identified with Livia Augusta's maternal grandfather Alfidius Lurco, a magistrate of Fundi who came to hold office in Rome (Suet. *Cal.* 23. 2: cf. Broughton, p. 647)."[54]

Shackleton Bailey has thus carried the argument embraced by Broughton and Taylor to its logical conclusion: all Aufidii Lurcones give way to a single person, M. Alfidius Lurco. This conclusion may be accepted or disputed, but in any event there is a truth in it: as has been shown in the course of our discussion, one can postulate the existence of either M. Aufidius Lurco or M. Alfidius Lurco; to have both of them at the same time is very unlikely. But this is not the only alternative: the old answer to the problem,[55] M. Aufidius Lurco and M. Alfidius (without any *cognomen*), may still prove to be the most attractive solution.

It is obvious that at the root of all confusion lies the discrepancy between the inscriptions and the text of Suetonius regarding the form of Livia's grandfather's name. Thus the problem facing us turns out to be not only a prosopographical riddle but also a textual puzzle.

It may therefore be interesting to analyze Suetonius' testimony particularly from the textual point of view.[56] He states that one M. Aufidius Lurco held offices in Rome and that this fact is borne out by the *publica monumenta*. If we take this statement at its face value – and there is no reason why we should not believe him – it must mean that Suetonius had seen documents pointing to the existence in the later years of the Republic of the senator and magistrate named M. Aufidius Lurco. There is certainly nothing extraordinary in that, and it is probably wholly justifiable to identify this M. Aufidius Lurco with the other Lurcones known from the literary sources.

---

[54] D. R. Shackleton Bailey, *Cicero's Letters to Atticus*, 1 (Cambridge 1965) 323. It is certainly not correct, and perhaps even misleading, to state straightforwardly, without any qualifying remark, that the name of Livia Augusta's maternal grandfather was Alfidius Lurco; the *cognomen* Lurco is not directly attested for him (cf. also above, n. 50).

[55] Cf. Klebs, *RE* 2 [1896] 2293 s. v. Aufidius 24 and 2289 s. v. Aufidius 9.

[56] It may be convenient to reproduce here the text of Suetonius in full: *Liuiam Augustam proauiam Ulixem stolatum identidem appellans, etiam ignobilitatis quadam ad senatum epistula arguere ausus est quasi materno auo decurione Fundano ortam, cum publicis monumentis certum sit, Aufidium Lurconem Romae honoribus functum (Caligula 23. 2).*

But with this statement there is coupled in the text of Suetonius another assertion: we are told that this Aufidius Lurco was Livia's grandfather. We know, however, that the real name of Livia's mother was Alfidia; the evidence of inscriptions is unassailable. On the other hand, no Alfidius is known to have held *honores* in Rome. Therefore the only possibility of saving the contention of Suetonius that the maternal grandfather of Livia was a senator is to equate the Alfidius of the epigraphical tradition with the Aufidius Lurco (or Aufidii Lurcones) recorded in the literary sources. This is precisely the way along which Broughton, Taylor and Shackleton Bailey have chosen to proceed. But Alfidius is not Aufidius. Both names are attested epigraphically as distinct *nomina*,[57] and they certainly were not interchangeable. The only escape would be to accept an early corruption in the manuscript tradition resulting in the replacement of the hypothetical original reading Alfidius (in Suetonius and in other writers) by the present *vulgata* Aufidius. Suetonius' copyists, not Suetonius, were at fault. This, in fact, is the basis on which the theory of M. Alfidius, the grandfather of Livia, holding *honores* in Rome, does ultimately rest. But this circumstance has never been clearly presented by any of the scholars named above.

If the text of Suetonius is emended,[58] we must also correct Varro, Pliny and Tertullian: otherwise we would once more find ourselves in the uncomfortable situation of being confronted with the two Lurcones: Alfidius and Aufidius. Of course, the corruption of the relatively obscure Alfidius into the prominent Aufidius is not impossible, even if the extant manuscript tradition does not seem to favor such an assumption. In all instances bearing on our question only the reading Aufidius is recorded.[59] However, an example of a similar modern text corruption is very instructive, and it should not be lightly set aside.

In Asconius' commentary on Cicero's speech *Pro Milone* a certain M. Alfidius is recorded; Alfidius (or Alphidius) is the reading of all the manuscripts.[60] The name, however, was changed by Manutius into Aufidius – a

---

[57] Cf. *Thes. Ling. Lat.* s. vv. Alfidius and Aufidius; W. Schulze, *Zur Geschichte lateinischer Eigennamen* (Berlin 1904) 119, 203, 269, 427.

[58] This possibility was contemplated by M. Ihm in his edition of Suetonius in the *Bibl. Teubneriana* (Lipsiae 1908).

[59] See the *apparatus criticus* to the editions of Suetonius by M. Ihm, of Varro's *de re rustica* by H. Keil (Lipsiae 1884), of Pliny by C. Mayhoff (Lipsiae 1875), of Tertullian's *de pallio* by A. Gerlo (Wetteren 1940 and Turnholt 1954 = *Corpus Christianorum* vol. 2), G. Säflund (Lund 1955) and S. Constanza (Napoli 1968). Cf. also H. Keil, *Commentarius in Varronis Rerum Rusticarum libros tres* (Lipsiae 1891) 248.

[60] See the editions of Asconius by A. Kiessling and R. Schoell (Berolini 1875) 49. 14 and *app. crit.*, A. Clark (Oxonii 1907) 55. 21, Th. Stangl (Vindobonae-Lipsiae 1912) 46. 14, C. Giarratano (Romae 1920) 61. 6.

perfect parallel to the postulated ancient corruption of the same name. Manutius "emendation" had been followed by many editors until Kiessling-Schoell, Clark, Stangl and Giarratano restored the original manuscript reading.

But the text of Asconius is important not only because of this example of subsequent corruption and successful restoration of the original reading. We have here, at last, a real Alfidius at our disposal, and not the elusive grandfather of Livia known exclusively through his daughter's filiation or called into being by emending of a text.

Who was this Alfidius? Very probably either himself the venerable ancestor of Tiberius or (as Wiseman suggests[61]) his son; in that latter case a brother of Alfidia and an uncle of Livia. He appears in Asconius successfully prosecuting Sex. Cloelius,[62] the notorious henchman of P. Clodius. Sex. Cloelius' counterpart on Milo's side, M. Saufeius, *qui dux fuerat in . . . Clodio occidendo*, was accused, among others, by M. Seius, already known to us.[63] It is interesting to recall that Varro records him as a foremost authority in the art of peacock breeding. As his opponent was no less an orator than M. Cicero,[64] Seius failed to score a court victory. He proved not so successful in the courthouse as in his exemplary farm. It is now indeed tempting to identify the M. Alfidius mentioned by Asconius with the M. Aufidius (= Alfidius) known from Varro and Suetonius. If this idea be granted we would meet two prominent experts on peacock problems taking an active part in the court warfare of 52, prosecuting with varying degrees of success the followers of Milo and Clodius respectively.

However nice it might be to renew our acquaintance with the peacocks and the men who owed their fame to them, the story as unfolded above is too amusing to be true. And if we reject it,[65] the theory of Broughton, Taylor and Shackleton Bailey, although we have done our best to validate it, is bound to disappear.

Asconius, when he mentions M. Alfidius, does not provide him with any *cognomen*; it is a fair inference that he had none. This is all the more probable as Asconius duly records the *tria nomina* of C. Caesennius Philo,[66] the other

---

[61] "The Mother of Livia Augusta" 334.

[62] For the name, see D. R. Shackleton Bailey, "Sex. Clodius – Sex. Cloelius", *Cl. Q.* N. S. 10 (1960) 41–42.   [63] Asc. 54–55 C. Cf. above, n. 18.

[64] Asc. 55 C. He was, however, on good terms with Cicero, see Cic., *ad Fam.* 9. 7. 1; *ad Att.* 5. 13. 2; 12. 11.

[65] Peacocks discarded, the uncommon fate of their progeny offers a more fascinating link between Alfidius and Seius, although admittedly of lesser practical importance to them: Tiberius and Seianus could trace their descent to them (if the M. Alfidius mentioned by Asconius was the father of Alfidia and not her brother, and if M. Seius was the father of M. Seius Strabo, the father of Seianus, which is very probable, cf. C. Cichorius, „Zur Familiengeschichte Seians", *Hermes* 39 [1904] 465–466).   [66] Asc. 55 C.

accuser of Sex. Cloelius.[67] On the other hand, the most prominent part of the nomenclature of M. Aufidius Lurco was clearly his *cognomen*. It was never omitted by any of the authors speaking of him. Moreover, that he commonly styled himself Lurco and not Aufidius is amply attested by the name of *condi-*

[67] Professor E. Gruen has called my attention (in a letter) to the fact that "among the accusers of M. Saufeius Asconius gives L. Cassius, L. Fulcinius and C. Valerius, as well as M. Caelius, his defense counsel". He notes that "all of them presumably had *cognomina*. Caelius certainly did". As this is an important objection to the reconstruction presented in the text, the point raised by E. Gruen ought to be dealt with in some detail.

On p. 51 C (I take this page *exempli gratia*) Asconius mentions fourteen persons (including Alfidius but not counting Clodius, Milo and Cicero). He provides only two of them with *cognomina*. Are we to believe that Asconius omitted twelve surnames? If so, it would be interesting to explore what reasons had induced him to record the *cognomina* of just two men, viz. M. Terentius Varro Gibba and M. Caesennius Philo. As far as the first of them is concerned, it is possible to argue that Asconius mentioned his second *cognomen* in order to distinguish him from his famous namesake, the antiquarian M. Terentius Varro. In doing so he would have followed the example of Gibba himself. In 43 B. C. M. Terentius Varro was proscribed. Gibba, who held in this year the tribunate of the plebs, took every precaution not to get confused with him. In order to point out that he was a different Terentius Varro, he issued a statement making known his *agnomen* (Cass. Dio 47. 11. 3; cf. Münzer, *RE* s. v. Terentius 89; Broughton, *MRR* 2. 340). No such or similar arguments can be adduced with respect to C. Caesennius Philo; most probably Asconius recorded his *cognomen* because he had one. C. Valerius, C. Fidius and T. Flacconius are known only from Asconius; this means that in any event it is not possible to prove that Asconius omitted their *cognomina*. L. Cassius (not in *RE*) was perhaps identical with L. Cassius, *RE* no. 14, for whom no *cognomen* is attested. Nor is any *cognomen* recorded for M. Seius and Sex. Cloelius. Three persons are provided by Asconius with filiation, viz. M. Saufeius M. f., L. Fulcinius C. f. and Cn. Aponius Cn. f. Asconius clearly took the information concerning their filiation from an official source (such as e. g. *acta urbis*); he could hardly have omitted their surnames if they were recorded in his source (We may note that Asconius introduces p. 32. 15 C the first of the men mentioned above simply as M. Saufeius; only as a defendant he becomes M. Saufeius M. f.). The identification of Considius (his *praenomen* is omitted in the manuscripts of Asconius), the *quaesitor lege Plautia de vi*, with either C. Considius Longus or M. Considius Nonnianus or C. Considius Nonnianus is far from certain (cf. Broughton, *MRR* 2. 240 n. 3). Asconius, when he mentions the *quaesitores* of 52, gives the *tria nomina* of two of them (L. Domitius Ahenobarbus and A. Manlius Torquatus), but attributes no *cognomina* to M. Favonius, L. Fabius and Considius. Since M. Favonius certainly did not have any surname, it is a fair inference that the same will hold also with respect to L. Fabius and Considius. The *cognomina* seem to have been especially popular (for different reasons) among the senatorial aristocracy and the freedmen, much less among the Roman and Italian gentry (including "*parvi senatores*"). As all the persons discussed here clearly belonged to that latter class, this may account the fact that most of them lacked the *cognomina*.

But the case of M. Caelius still remains to be explained. Since Asconius left out the *cognomen* of M. Caelius, he could have omitted the postulated *cognomen* of M. Alfidius as well. Logical and misleading. The name-form M. Caelius Rufus was used by Caesar, Valerius Maximus, Pliny the Elder, but not by Velleius Paterculus or Tacitus. Especially telling is Tacitus,Dial. 17. 1 and 18. 1, where he juxtaposes *Caelium et Calvum*. But most revealing is the fact that Cicero does not mention Caelius' surname at all, nor does Caelius himself. There is nothing unusual in Asconius' omission of Caelius' *cognomen*: he followed the Ciceronian (and Caelian) usage. On the other hand, it would have been very unusual if he had chosen to omit the surname of the man to whom Cicero normally referred by *cognomen* only.

mentum Lurconianum, and by Cicero's custom of referring to him by *cognomen* only.

If M. Alfidius possessed no *cognomen* he cannot be identical with the man called M. Aufidius Lurco. Any theory alleging the identity of these men, and trying to emend accordingly the texts of Suetonius, Varro, Pliny and Tertullian must take this into account; unless it is able to do away with this difficulty it is doomed to failure.[68]

There is no doubt that the man whose name Suetonius read in the public documents bore the *cognomen* of Lurco; hence almost certainly not an Alfidius. It is therefore reasonable to dissociate M. Aufidius Lurco, the senator and magistrate but not the grandfather of Livia, from M. Alfidius, the grandfather of Livia but not a senator. Of course, one can argue that this does not conclusively disprove the senatorial dignity of M. Alfidius. That is true enough in the sphere of pure theory; but when confronted with the emphatic assertion of Caligula to the contrary, and with Suetonius' error, the burden of proof must remain with those who accept the content of Suetonius' narrative but reject its original wording. After all, why should Suetonius who committed many blunders of a similar kind[69] be more trusted than Caligula?

So, after all our efforts to dispel the prosopographical clouds surrounding the maternal ancestry of Livia, we are, for the time being, left with M. Alfidius, Livia's maternal grandfather and a municipal magistrate of Fundi, and with M. Aufidius Lurco, the epicure and magistrate in Rome, as grandfather of Livia an unsuspecting impostor.[70]

---

[68] Every author should at times act as his own *advocatus diaboli* and try to destroy his own thesis; it is therefore our duty to point out possible ways of attacking our line of defence:

1) it is conceivable that the M. Alfidius of Asconius was a brother of Alfidia, and that he did not inherit any *cognomen* from his father, although the latter bore the surname Lurco (but the more obvious reason why he did not inherit any *cognomen* is that his father had none).

2) It is possible that the M. Alfidius recorded by Asconius had nothing in common with either the father or brother of Livia's mother; Livia's grandfather was another M. Alfidius, distinguished from the former by the *cognomen* Lurco (to this we may answer that it is unreasonable to multiply the Alfidii only in order to save Suetonius' muddling; a further obstacle is posed by the very probable identification of M. Aufidius Lurco with Horace's Aufidius, where the reading Aufidius is beyond any doubt).   [69] Cf. Wiseman, "The Mother of Livia Augusta" 333.

[70] I should like to thank Professor Erich Gruen for his kind comments and criticism that helped improve both substance and style of this paper. He is, however, not responsible for any of the views expressed above.

23

TWO QUAESTORSHIPS

I

C. Cassius Longinus, the tyrannicide, appears for the first time in the records of history in 53 B.C. as a gifted general immediately before and especially after the catastrophe of Crassus' army at Carrhae. All the sources unanimously term him quaestor at that time.

According to Plutarch *Crassus* 18, the army commanded by Crassus was not prepared to face the enemy and ὥστε καὶ τῶν ἐν τέλει τινὰς οἴεσθαι δεῖν ἐπισχόντα τὸν Κράσσον αὖθις ὑπὲρ τῶν ὅλων γνώμην προθέσθαι· τούτων ἦν Κάσσιος ὁ ταμίας. In Cassius Dio 40. 25. 4, C. Cassius appeared immediately after the defeat at Carrhae when the remains of the Roman army were seized with panic: καὶ αὐτῶν οἱ μὲν ἁλόντες ἡμέρας γενομένης ἀπώλοντο, οἱ δὲ ἐς τὴν Συρίαν μετὰ Κασσίου Λογγίνου τοῦ ταμίου διεσώθησαν. Similarly Velleius Paterculus 2. 46. 4: "reliquias legionum C. Cassius, . . . tum quaestor, conservavit"; Auctor De viris illustribus 83: "Gaius Cassius Longinus quaestor Crassi in Syria fuit, post cuius caedem collectis reliquiis in Syriam rediit"; Eutropius 6. 18: "reliquiae exercitus per C. Cassium quaestorem servatae sunt." Festus Breviarium 17 also mentions Cassius (with the erroneous praenomen Lucius instead of Gaius) in connection with the battle of Carrhae: "Lucius Cassius, quaestor Crassi, . . . reliquias fusi collegit exercitus." Appian BC 4. 59, describing Cassius' military exploits in Syria in 43, records the reputation he had acquired among the Parthians ἐξ οὗ Κράσσῳ ταμιεύων ἐμφρονέστερος ἔδοξε τοῦ Κράσσου γενέσθαι. This must refer, it would seem, to 53, as only in that year did Cassius have the opportunity to show himself more skillful than his commander.

On the basis of this overwhelming evidence,[1] T. R. S. Broughton had no misgivings about assigning the quaestorship of C. Cas-

sius to 53.[2] D. R. Shackleton Bailey followed in the wake of Broughton,[3] but G. V. Sumner has recently voiced disagreement:[4] Sumner argues that C. Cassius was probably already Crassus' quaestor in 54 or even 55.[5] He points out that Cassius was older than Brutus (Plut. Brut. 29, 40; App. BC 4. 89), who was born in 85. Cassius' birthdate was probably 86, and so, according to the leges annales, he was already eligible for the quaestorship of 55. Ingenious, convincing (although not fully conclusive: possibility is not reality), and superfluous.

Of course, C. Cassius could not have been —and was not—quaestor in 53. The decisive evidence, however, escaped Broughton's attention, and Sumner also failed to notice it. The battle of Carrhae occurred on 9 June 53. If Cassius was a quaestor at that time, he had to have been elected to this office at the comitia of 54. However, a glance at the chronology of Roman elections will show that no regular magistrates were chosen in 54 for 53. When the delayed elections for 53 finally took place in Rome, sometime in July or August of that year,[6] the battle of Carrhae was over. Moreover, how could Cassius have stood in those elections, since, when they were held, he was still in Syria fighting the Parthians? In sum, when he saved the remnants of the Roman legions at Carrhae, Cassius was technically a proquaestor.[7]

---

1. Cf. Liv. Per. 108 (in the description of the events of 52 and 51): "C. Cassius, quaestor M. Crassi, Parthos, qui in Syriam transcenderant, cecidit." In 52 Cassius was a proquaestor; the expression quaestor M. Crassi refers to his past relationship with Crassus. The text allows, however, no inferences as to the date of his office. The same remarks apply to Justinus 42. 4: "exercitus Parthorum . . . in Syria a Cassio, quaestore Crassi, cum omnibus ducibus trucidatur."

2. The Magistrates of the Roman Republic, II, 229. Cf. also MRR, Suppl., p. 14. The same dating was accepted by Fröhlich, s.v. "Cassius (59)," RE, III (1897), 1727.

3. D. R. Shackleton Bailey, Cicero's Letters to Atticus, III (Cambridge, 1968), 221. Cf. also J. W. Eadie, The Breviarium of Festus (London, 1967), p. 133.

4. G. V. Sumner, "The Lex Annalis under Caesar," Phoenix, XXV (1971), 365.

5. In that way Sumner has revived the pre-Broughtonian tradition. W. Drumann-P. Groebe, Geschichte Roms, II (Leipzig, 1902), 99, accepted 54 as the year of Cassius' quaestorship, but they offered no proof. So also Th. Mommsen, Geschichte des römischen Münzwesens (Berlin, 1860),

p. 636, n. 498; P. Willems, Le Sénat de la république romaine, I (Louvain, 1878), 534; F. Sobeck, Die Quästoren der römischen Republik (Diss. Breslau, 1909), p. 59; G. Niccolini, I fasti dei tribuni della plebe (Milan, 1934), p. 334. L. Lange, Römische Alterthümer, III² (Berlin, 1876), 602 (Index; cf. pp. 367 and 387), opted for 55. This seems also to have been the opinion of I. C. Orelli and I. G. Baiter, Onomasticon Tullianum, II (Zurich, 1838), 134–35, and M. Bülz, De provinciarum Romanarum quaestoribus (Diss. Leipzig, 1893), p. 66.

6. On the date of the elections in 53, see Cass. Dio 40. 45. 1; App. BC 2. 71.

7. It is impossible to decide whether he held his quaestorship in 55 or in 54. If he left for Syria together with Crassus he must have been quaestor in 55. Crassus departed from Rome before the middle of November (see Drumann Groebe, IV, 107; MRR, II, 215) and by that time the elections for 54 had not yet been held (Cic. Att. 4. 13). According to an attractive hypothesis of Sumner (op. cit. [n. 4], p. 249, n. 12), these elections did not take place until early in 54. If Cassius was elected for 54, he joined Crassus in Syria with some delay.

It is well to remember (as Sumner reminds us) that the term "quaestor" was frequently used by the sources in place of "proquaestor."[8] But it is seldom possible to prove that the terminology we find in our sources is so totally misleading as in the case of C. Cassius' quaestorship.

II

The quaestorship of Q. Cassius Longinus is attested by Cicero, the *Bellum Alexandrinum*, and Cassius Dio. He was quaestor of Pompey by special choice; selected *sine sorte*[9] (a token of a close relationship between him and the triumvir), he served in Further Spain.[10] However, as tribune of the plebs in 50/49 he deserted Pompey and eagerly embraced Caesar's cause. His quaestorship in Spain was not so eventful as that of his cousin[11] in Syria: Gaius earned fame (and envy) by repulsing the Parthians; Quintus became notorious for his extortions. Quintus' course carried its risk, too: *ex insidiis vulneratus*, he barely escaped with his life.[12]

None of the sources mentioned above provides the exact date of his office: hence a considerable amount of disagreement in the modern scholarship. The following dates have been proposed, mostly without discussion: 56,[13] 55,[14] 54,[15] 52,[16] 51,[17] and 50.[18]

Some of these dates can be discarded without much argument. Cassius could not have held his quaestorship in 50, since in that year he stood for the tribunate of 49. Nor could

he have held this office in 56, for he is attested as Pompey's quaestor in Spain, and the law of Trebonius that gave Pompey command of both Spanish provinces for five years was not carried through until 55.

As Pompey sent his legates to Spain immediately after he received the command,[19] it is conceivable that Cassius was already elected for 55, and either went to Spain immediately after the passage of the *lex Trebonia* or remained in Rome as Pompey's *quaestor consularis* and assumed his provincial appointment in 54 as *proquaestor*. But he may just as well have been elected for 54 or 53.[20]

Nipperdey opted for 51; the verdict of Broughton was 52. Why these dates? Nipperdey based his theory upon Cicero's statements concerning the appointment of Q. Cassius *sine sorte*: "Pompeius . . . Q. Cassium sine sorte delegit, Caesar Antonium" (*Att.* 6. 6. 4); "potentissimorum duorum [*sc.* exemplum], qui omnes Cassios Antoniosque complexi sunt" (*Fam.* 2. 15. 4). He concluded that Cassius held his quaestorship simultaneously with Antonius. As he assigned the office of Antonius to 51, he also found automatically the date of Cassius' quaestorship. We may surmise that a similar line of thought was followed by Broughton: when he accepted 52 as the year of Antonius' quaestorship, he consequently dated the office of Cassius to the same year.

Leaving aside the question of the date of Antonius' quaestorship,[21] the inference made

---

8. Only Cicero in the heading of a letter (*Fam.* 15. 14) sent to Cassius in 51 from Cilicia calls him *proquaestor* (and himself *imperator*).

9. Cic. *Att.* 6. 6. 4, *Fam.* 2. 15. 4 (written in August 50). Drumann–Groebe. II. 130, interpret this as an example of Pompey's *Willkür*; so also V. Ehrenberg, *s.r.* "Losung," *RE*, XIII (1926). 1504. It is true that the quaestorian provinces were normally assigned by lot, but the governors could select their quaestors *sine sorte* on the basis of a special authorization by the senate. See Th. Mommsen, *Römisches Staatsrecht*, II[3] (Leipzig, 1887), 532–34; Willems, *Le Sénat*, II, 607–608; and especially L. A. Thompson, "The Appointment of Quaestors *extra sortem*," *PACA*, V (1962), 17–25.

10. *Bell. Alex.* 48. 1, 50. 1; Cass. Dio 41. 24. 2.

11. *Frater* in Cic. *Att.* 5. 21. 2 clearly means *frater patruelis*, cf. Drumann–Groebe, II, 129–30.

12. *Bell. Alex.* 48. 1, 50. 1.

13. Drumann–Groebe, II, 130. According to Drumann–Groebe, Cassius remained in Spain until 50.

14. Mommsen, *Münzwesen*, p. 635, n. 495; Bülz, *op. cit.* (n. 5), p. 10; Sobeck, *op. cit.* (n. 5), p. 57; Niccolini, *op. cit.* (n. 5), p. 334. Bülz and Sobeck also think that he returned to Rome only in 50.

15. Münzer, *s.r.* "Cassius (70)," *RE*, III (1897), 1740 (*von 54 an*); Willems, *Le Sénat*, I, 535.

16. Broughton, *MRR*, II, 236 (but cf. Index of Careers, p 544: *ca.* 52).

17. K. Nipperdey, "Die *leges annales* der römischen Re publik," *ASG*, V.1 (1865), 32.

18. Orelli–Baiter, *Onomasticon Tullianum*, II, 137.

19. *MRR*, II. 220.

20. Thompson, *op. cit.* (n. 9), p. 19, opines that he wa quaestor in 54 or 52; why not in 53?

21. He was quaestor in 51 (as suggested by Nipperdey) not in 52 (as in *MRR*). See A. Kaminska-Linderski and J Linderski, "The Quaestorship of M. Antonius" (forthcoming

by Nipperdey (and Broughton) does not seem to have any real basis in Cicero's testimony. What Cicero says is that both Cassius and Antonius were appointed in the same way *sine sorte*, but there is no hint in his text that it happened at the same time. If the order of names has any significance here, it may even mean that Cassius held his office before Antonius, but it would not be wise to press this point.

Two other letters of Cicero may offer some unexpected help. Cicero gives the following advice to C. Cassius (*Fam.* 15. 14. 4, written in October, 51): "ego ceterarum rerum causa tibi Romam properandum magno opere censeo . . . sed, si quae sunt onera tuorum, si tanta sunt, ut ea sustinere possis, propera . . . sin maiora, considera, ne in alienissimum tempus cadat adventus tuus." A few weeks later, in a letter to Atticus (5. 20. 8, written in Cilicia on 19 December, 51), Cicero entreated his friend: "Lucceius de Q. Cassio cur tam vehemens fuerit et quid actum sit aveo scire."

The incident mentioned in the letter to Atticus is otherwise not known, but Shackleton Bailey has ingeniously combined it with the enigmatic phrase "si quae sunt onera tuorum" in the letter to C. Cassius, and has acutely (albeit tentatively) deduced from it that Q. Cassius may have been on trial at that time.[22] Cassius' extortions in Spain offer a further clue. He may have been prosecuted *de repetundis* (or at least threatened with the prosecution); in that case we may infer that in 51 he was in Rome.

The foregoing considerations may have clarified some disputed points, but above all they have shown that the evidence on the exact date of Q. Cassius' quaestorship is strictly nonexistent, and that modern conjectures are of doubtful value. Q. Cassius could have been quaestor in any year between 55 and 51, although the odds are against his holding this office in 51.

---

22. D. R. Shackleton Bailey, *Cicero's Letters to Atticus*, III, 230–31. His prosecutor would have been L. Lucceius Q. f., the historian and friend of Cicero. Cf. Münzer, *s.v.* "Lucceius (6)," *RE*, XIII (1926), 1557.

Magnus Wistrand: *Cicero Imperator*. Studies in Cicero's correspondence 51–47 B. C. Göteborg: Acta Universitatis Gothoburgensis 1979. VIII, 230 S. (Studia Graeca et Latina Gothoburgensia. 41.) 80 sKr.

'Cicero *imperator*' sounds as implausible as 'Pompeius *orator*' or 'Marius *philosophus*'. And yet Cicero was much more of a Roman and much less of a *philosophus* than we (or Petrarch) are prepared to admit. Nobody has better summed up Cicero's experience in Cilicia than the old Drumann: «die Menschen im nahen Gebirge ... hetzte er wie Tiere. Ihre Wohnungen wurden von ihm niedergebrannt und sie selbst erwürgt oder verkauft. ... So konnte er mit ihrem Blute für den Triumph zahlen.»[1]

It all came about largely by chance. Cicero achieved the peak of his career as *consul togatus*, and he steadfastly refused provincial commands. But then in 52 the *lex Pompeia de provinciis* intervened. It introduced a five year interval between city magistracies and provincial appointments, and as a result those magistrates who had not yet held provincial governorships were now called to their turn of duty. To Cicero's lot fell Cilicia, not a nice task in view of the proverb: τρία κάππα κάκιστα: Καππαδοκίη, Κρήτη καὶ Κιλικία. He received a military *imperium*,[2]

---

[1] W. Drumann - P. Groebe, Geschichte Roms 6 (Leipzig 1929) 125–126.

[2] As regards Cicero's *imperium* the major question appears to be whether Cicero (and other governors who administered provinces under the *lex Pompeia*) received the *lex curiata*. W. maintains (170–171) that «Cicero had confirmed the decree passed by the Senate in February 51 concerning his proconsular *imperium* with a *lex centuriata*, or possibly a *lex curiata*, or even a *lex tributa*». This is inane: Cicero as a *privatus* could not cause any law to be passed. A. J. Marshall in his study of the *lex Pompeia de provinciis* (ANRW I 1, 887 ff, esp. 893–895) complains that discussions of the *lex curiata* do not touch upon the question of Cicero's *imperium*. Unfortunately this is true also of the otherwise thorough book by H. Versnel, Triumphus (Leiden, 1970). Yet it is precisely in Ci-

and on 31 July 51 arrived in his province. When in October 51 Cicero or rather his legates defeated the inhabitants of the Amanus range, the soldiers honored their commander by the *acclamatio imperatoria* thus paving the way for him to a *supplicatio* and possibly a triumph. To secure a triumph was soon to become Cicero's major preoccupation. He kept his *imperium* throughout the Civil War and laid it down only in 47. The Republic was falling apart; he was musing about his *lictores laureati* and his triumphal entry. Cicero scored his victory at Issus and camped at Arae Alexandri. As Karl Marx has observed, history is enacted twice: as tragedy and as farce. This sets the stage for the schemes and tribulations of Cicero *imperator* – and for W.'s book.

W. discusses Cicero's military achievements and the question of his triumph down to the outbreak of the Civil War, his position after the *senatus consultum ultimum* of 7 January 49 and his conduct in the spring of 49, and finally his peregrination to Greece and back to Brundisium and Rome. The method of presentation is peculiar: repetitive quotations of long passages from Cicero's correspondence followed by a more or less literal paraphrase followed by a diffuse commentary. As it is hardly necessary to summarize Cicero, and Wistrand's own contribution, in addition to being flat and tedious, glitters with painstakingly elaborated commonplaces,[3] a large portion of the book evaporates on the first reading. The author's understanding of Roman politics is a marvel in this post-Symean age. On p. 13 we encounter the following analysis, not uncharacteristic of W.'s style of scholarship, of Cicero's letter to Cato, *Fam.* 15, 4, 11:[4]

«It should be noted that Cicero does not state explicitly that he is striving for a triumph; he uses the words *honorem meum*. Moreover, wishing to avoid giving Cato the impression that he is asking for his services as a friend (*rogare*) he rather reminds him of a duty. Cicero here draws an important distinction, which tells us something about Cato. Bearing in mind that Cato did not like to have his judgements in official matters influenced by personal relationships, Cicero apparently found it improper to ask Cato for a favour as a friend. Thus Cicero's distinction implies that Cato had the ambition of remaining independent of the complex obligations of *amicitia*, which pervaded and corrupted Roman politics. This is, I think, the easiest explanation of Cicero's anxiety not to ask Cato as a friend and it can be supported by Sallust's famous comparison of Caesar's and Cato's characters (*Cat.* 54).»

W.'s 'analysis' presupposes the existence of a pure, uncorrupted model of Roman politics. This was possible *in Platonis* πολιτεία, not *in Romuli faece*, Cicero would say (*Att.* 2, 1, 8). *Amicitia* (and *clientela*) formed the essence of Roman politics; as Ronald Syme put it, *amicitia* was a weapon, not a sentiment

based on congeniality.[5] W. does not distinguish between personal friendship and political *amicitia* – with disastrous consequences for his book. Cicero was never Cato's personal friend, nor did he belong to the inner circle of Cato's political allies. One wonders how, after reading the works of L. R. Taylor, Chr. Meier and P. A. Brunt[6] (which he cites in a footnote), W. could arrive at his blurred vision of Roman *amicitia* and his naively idealistic image of Cato. No mystery here. The answer resides in what Ronald Syme has diagnosed as «the influence of literature when studied in isolation from history».[7] *Cato nihil largiundo gloriam adeptus est* – so Sallust (*Cat.* 54). But don't we know that in 60 Cato engaged in electoral bribery to check Caesar and procure the consulship for Calpurnius Bibulus, the husband of his daughter? (Suet. *Caes.* 19). No matter: history pales into insignificance when confronted with a comforting literary fiction.

W.'s avowed goal is to 'examine' Shackleton Bailey's edition and commentary[8] (2). Not a mean task. His principal point of contention concerns the text and interpretation of *Att.* 8, 3, 4 (Appendix 2, 206–211). W. proposes to retain the vulgate *invite cepi Capuam*, whereas Shackleton Bailey in his text daggers *invite cepi* and in his commentary favors Lehmann's *non recepi* or Sternkopf's *hinc reieci*.[9] The controversy has obvious consequences for the reconstruction of Cicero's official sphere of responsibilities at the beginning of the Civil War.[10] W. admits that the adverbial construction (*invite* instead of *invitus*) is unparalleled, but he contends it is not «impossible Latin». The argument is devoid of any force. *Hapax legomena* are not impossible, but it is a perverse and pernicious principle for an editor to adopt unusual constructions as his guide. When on 28 February 49 Cicero wrote *cum imperatam iam Capuam . . . accipere nolui* (*Att.* 8, 12, 2 = SB 162, 2) he certainly meant to say that although the command in Capua had already been assigned to him, he did not wish to accept it and that actually he did not assume it (cf. 8, 11, D, 5 = SB 161 D, 5: *cum a me Capuam reiciebam*), especially if we read the letter in conjunction with *Att.* 7, 14, 3 = SB 138, 3 (*in ora maritima . . . cui ego prae-*

---

cero's triumph that we may seek an answer to our problem. The constitutional legality of Cicero's request for a triumph was never in doubt (except for the quality of his victory), and it seems probable that the possession of the *lex curiata* was a regular prerequisite for a triumph. Cf. Mommsen, Staatsrecht 1,[3] 126–128; Versnel, op. cit. 164ff. 350ff.

[3] A few examples: on the basis of Att. 8, 11 B, 3 the author arrives at the conclusion that «Cicero was aware that he could be criticized for his conduct» (81). W. also feels it necessary to explain that the *boni* were «the traditional backers of senatorial predominance» (82). It is important «to observe the small nuances that may affect the meaning of the text and to read between the lines», and especially so «in the correspondence between leading politicians, since the wording there is often very guarded» (108). In Roman politics «alliances of friendship, private antipathies, and ignorance of the conditions under which a decision could be brought about influenced the opinion of many senators as much as reasons that had anything to do with the matter itself» (49) – with the exception of Cato of course: see below.

[4] The text runs as follows: *Nunc velim sic tibi persuadeas, si de iis rebus ad senatum relatum sit, me existimaturum summam mihi laudem tributam si tu honorem meum sententia tua comprobaris, idque, etsi talibus de rebus gravissimos homines et rogare solere et rogari scio, tamen admonendum potius te a me quam rogandum puto.*

sum), 8, 11 B, 1 = SB 161 B, 1 (*in ea ora ubi praepositi sumus*; cf. 7, 11, 5 = SB 134, 5), and *Fam.* 16, 12, 5 = SB 146, 5 (*ego adhuc orae maritimae praesum a Formiis, nullum maius negotium suscipere volui, quo plus apud illum* [sc. Caesarem] *meae litterae cohortationesque ad pacem valerent*). In this way also *Fam.* 16, 11, 3 = SB 143, 3 of 12 January to Tiro (*nos Capuam sumpsimus*) finds a cogent explanation. *Sumpsimus* will here have the same meaning as *iam imperatam* at *Att.* 8, 12, 2: Cicero 'took' Capua in the sense that it was assigned to him by the Senate, but eventually he did not go there and assumed a lesser command (*ora maritima*). The interpretation of Shackleton Bailey still stands.

On the other hand W. is probably right in interpreting the expression *victoria iusta* (*Fam.* 2, 10, 3 = SB 86, 3) as «a legitimate victory», i. e. the victory which could form the basis for the granting of a triumph (203–205). He also rightly points out against T. R. S. Broughton, The Magistrates of the Roman Republic 2, 263, that Curio did not receive his *imperium* from the Senate – his lictors were *laureati* (132 n. 1., but cf. already Shackleton Bailey, Att. vol. 4, 404: «Propraetor by Caesar's appointment»), and on p. 101 n. 2 he presents a good criticism of Mommsen, Röm. Staatsrecht 1,³ 117 n. 1 (concerning the *imperium* of Cicero in 49).

---

⁵ The Roman Revolution 12.

⁶ W. cites Brunt's Social Conflicts in the Roman Republic (London, 1971), but not the same author's special study of *amicitia* in PapCambrPhilSoc 11, 1965, 1–20.

⁷ Op. cit. 4. Syme does not appear in W.'s book, a symptom of another fashionable disease: the cult of *res novae* («My bibliography concentrates on works published during the last ten years» [21]).

⁸ D. R. Shackleton Bailey, Cicero's Letters to Atticus 1–7 (Cambridge, 1965–1977); Cicero: Epistulae ad Familiares 1–2 (Cambridge, 1977).

⁹ Att. vol. 4, 438–440 (Appendix 2).

¹⁰ Cf. e. g. R. E. Smith, Cicero the Statesman (Cambridge, 1966), 220: district of Capua and shore of Campania; D. Stockton, Cicero (Oxford, 1971), 256: the Campanian coast and the raising of troops there.

Alas, a few correct observations cannot redeem a misbegotten book.

¹¹ The following omissions and inaccurate or questionable statements may also attract the attention of the reader: Cassius was not a lieutenant of Bibulus (37), cf. Broughton, MRR 2, 242; J. Linderski, ClPh 70, 1975, 35 ff. On the *dies comitiales* it is possible to find a better authority than Tyrrell and Purser (43). For the speed of travel (50) W. has missed the fundamental article by L. Casson, TAPA 82, 1951, 136–148, and on the lictors (passim) he ought to have consulted the excellent study by B. Gladigow, ANRW I 2, 295–313. And finally we cannot pass over the remarkable interpretation of *Att.* 7, 7, 4 of Dec. 50 (*De honore nostro, nisi quid occulte Caesar per suos tribunos molitus erit, cetera videntur esse tranquilla*): «Cicero was afraid that some manoeuvre in high politics on Caesar's part would make his triumph impossible anyway. The meaning of *occulte* seems to be that Cicero did not know whether Caesar was planning anything of this kind, but suspected that Caesar might do so without letting Cicero know» (55 n. 3). *Incredibile dictu*! Caesar would not inform Cicero of his plans?

25

Cicero. The Ascending Years. By THOMAS N. MITCHELL. New Haven: Yale University Press, 1979. Pp. XII + 259. $17.50.

Do we need another biography of Cicero? The author of the book under review obviously had no doubts. Cicero's ascending years have been less studied, he says, than the glorious misfortunes of Cicero the consular. He devotes 242 pages to scrutinizing in four chapters Cicero's Political Heritage, Cicero's Apprenticeship, Cicero the Candidate and Cicero the Consul. The result, he avers, is "a more complete and fully documented account of Cicero's political life and thought in the most significant stages of his career and a more extensive discussion of the political background of his statesmanship than can be found in standard biographies" (p. VIII). An ambitious claim: D. Stockton, the author of another recent study of Cicero (*Cicero. A Political Biography*, [Oxford:1971]), satisfied himself with professing to write "primarily for the student of Roman history, and most particularly the undergraduate student" (pp. VII-VIII). He covers the same time-span as Mitchell in 142 pages, with very scanty footnotes, however. R. E. Smith (*Cicero the Statesman*, [Cambridge: 1966]) needs 131 pages to reach the year 63/62, and he completely omits references to sources and modern literature: they can easily be found elsewhere (a sensible statement, but a practice hard on the reader). No doubt Mitchell provides more information than Stockton, Smith or Rawson (*Cicero. A Portrait*, [London: 1975]), but as these books were not conceived as encyclopedias of Ciceronian knowledge, this does not tell us much. To find a measure there is only one place to turn, M. Gelzer's *RE*-article on "Cicero als Politiker" and his masterful *Cicero: ein biographischer Versuch*, (Wiesbaden: 1969). Only 65 pages in *RE*, but what a wealth of information! Or, perhaps still better, we should turn to the massive, indispensable and awkward biography by W. Drumann (W. Drumann-P. Groebe, *Geschichte Roms oder Pompeius, Caesar, und ihre Zeitgenossen*, vols. 5 and 6, [Leipzig: 1919, 1929]). Drumann-Groebe is quite inexplicably missing from Mitchell's bibliography (does it not count as a "standard biography"?), but it is universally praised as a mine of information: 336 pages of a much larger format than Mitchell's, with copious references to sources, bring the reader to the last day of Cicero's consulate. On the face of it Mitchell should be no competition for Drumann or Gelzer, and he is not — if we are interested in easy access to a reliable chronicle of Cicero's life. But his is an important book, for it is a book not only of information, but also of interpretation.

Now — and this has to be stressed emphatically — Mitchell does not write biography in the traditional meaning at all. He writes of the influence of Roman history on Cicero and of Roman history as seen by Cicero. M. Rambaud's *Cicéron et l'histoire romaine*, (Paris: 1953), comes to mind, but the comparison is misleading. Not for Mitchell the painstaking collection and investigation of *exempla historica* or of Cicero's historical method. He is entranced by the achievements of modern prosopography and political history, and he provides the reader with generous, though erratic and idiosyncratic references (e.g. C. Nicolet's great *L'ordre équestre* is not listed in his bibliography) to recent work in this field. And so his book stands as a solid pillar of modern prosopographical orthodoxy, and as such it will be comforting to many, and irritating to some. This does not mean that he is not fighting a running battle with other historians and prosopographers, but prosopography has by now become something more than a simple tool (as it is still treated by those historians who are interested in History, and not merely in histories): it is a view of the world. Mitchell is interested in History, but caught in a web of *prosopa* he plunges with delight into Roman factional strife almost losing sight of the underlying causes which made that strife so bloody and so fatal for the Republic. He displays only modest interest in social and economic questions, and yet veterans and proletarians, land and grain were the bread and butter of Roman history, factional strife among the oligarchs only its topping. Without men, dispossessed, impoverished, disgruntled, who were ready to follow the Leader, there would have been no Marius, Cinna or Sulla; Cicero would not have had to live in his youth through various reigns of terror: his political apprenticeship would have been vastly different; nor would he have had an opportunity to savor his "apotheosis" and commit the line *O fortunatam natam me consule Romam*.

It is not possible to write history without philosophy. Drumann was well aware of this: *Geschichte ohne Philosophie* was meaningless for him (vol. 1, p. IV). The philosophical results of his work, which Eduard Meyer once described as *wohl das bizarrste Produkt deutscher Gelehrsamkeit*, were indeed profound and timely: Roman history shows that the republican system cannot in the long run satisfy the needs of men, and so (he happily confesses) his book has quite naturally become *eine Lobschrift auf die Monarchie* — as befits *der Preusse, der Unterthan eines Friedrich Wilhelm* (written in 1844 in Königsberg, today Kaliningrad). Let us not smile: others will laugh at us. A comparison with Mitchell imposes itself, although some may find it a bit mischievous. Here we have *in nuce* Mitchell's philosophy of Roman history: "the republican constitution, which in a long process of growth and adjustment to the political demands of the various segments of the society had identified basic principles of political freedom and democratic government . . . collapsed under the stress of changing social, economic, and political conditions and gave way to an opposing philosophy of government — autocracy" (p. VII). The end result of republican history is in both cases similar but not the same: monarchy for Drumann, autocracy for Mitchell, the benign grin of an *ancien régime* versus the ominous flavor of a modern dictatorship. This should not surprise us for whenever we write of the past we also write of the present. But the word "democracy," if it is to retain any meaning at all, is completely out of place with reference to Rome. The pithy phrase of Andrew Alföldi comes to mind: "the collective monarchy of the nobles." Prosopographical lists are quite eloquent in this respect. Even the vaunted "impartiality" of Roman law did not assure everyone of equality before the law: according to the republican criminal procedure the *personae viles* were subject to the summary jurisdiction of the *tresviri capitales*: not unreasonable but hardly democratic (see W. Kunkel, *Untersuchungen zur Entwicklung des römischen Kriminalverfahrens in vorsullanischer Zeit*, [Munich: 1962] 71ff.). Nor does it help to say that the political system in Rome "while it insisted on the principle of popular sovereignty, concentrated power in the hands of the executive officials and their advisory council, the senate" (p. 96). Note the curious impersonal tone: the political system acts all by itself. Why not say: "Those who created Roman political system, while occasionally professing the principle of popular sovereignty, insisted upon the concentration of power in their own hands"? Popular sovereignty without popular legislative initiative is mere fiction. Not by chance did Mommsen begin his discussion of the Roman constitution with the *magistratus*. Roman voting assemblies, it is true, were organized according to the principle one man, one vote, but individual votes carried different weight, hardly a truly democratic idea, only a facade, as Cicero himself put so aptly: (Servius Tullius) "ita disparavit, ut suffragia non in multitudinis, sed in locupletium potestate essent, curavitque, quod semper in re publica tenendum est, ne plurimum valeant plurimi" (*de rep*. 2.39). As this is no more an *arcanum imperii*, at least at Rome, why then this talk of democracy in Rome? The word "democracy" functions in contemporary western and particularly American civilization as a magic spell, and it is probably comforting to discover democracy in another great republic, for who would want to be told that the Roman Republic was able to achieve its lasting military success only because it had never known a democratic government?

If Cicero would have disapproved of Mitchell's treatment of the constitution, he would have been pleased with his love of *concordia*. There existed for instance a basic agreement between Pompey (there is almost as much of Pompey as of Cicero in the chapter on Cicero the Candidate) and the government in Rome: Pompey did not extort from the senate his consulship (and triumph): it was offered to him by his Sullan friends (pp. 116ff., esp. 129-130). Now this view is not implausible for the seventies, yet it will hardly do for the year 71. Mitchell seems to deny any co-operation between Pompey and the tribune M. Lollius Palicanus concerning the restoration of the tribunician prerogatives, but he forgets that before he entered the city Pompey spoke at the *contio* convened by Palicanus (Ps.-Asc. p. 189, 220 St.).

History, *concordia*, Pompey, but what of Cicero? "His heritage and connections bound him closely to the *via optimas*" (p. 51), and he remained a good traditional conservative throughout his life; he never espoused any popular causes (this against Syme, *The Roman Revolution* 137); if he supported Pompey, it was because he did not regard him a *popularis* (p. 106). He was no legalist: his policy "was directed by the belief that the survival of his brand of republicanism represented the highest law and that violent dissidents . . . should be viewed and treated as *hostes*" (p. 66). He practiced the policy of appeasement only when the *potentia* of his enemies "made the risks of violence unacceptable" (p. 67; on Cicero and the law, see also C. J. Classen, "Cicero, the Laws and Law-courts," *Latomus* 37 ([1978] 598-619). "The successes and achievements of Cicero's ascending years were rare and admirable by any measure of statesmanship" (p. 242), but he finally succumbed to "forces too strong for oratory" (p. 241). This is a marvellous characterization of Cicero, one that both his admirers and *obtrectatores* can embrace *con amore*. And yet how not to agree with Shackleton Bailey's *dictum*: "the immortality for which he always hungered is due to what he wrote rather than to what he did" (*Cicero* [New York: 1971], p. VIII).

To conclude: this is a competent book, written presumably for scholars, yet not completely unreadable. It is a very serious book; those who are offended by wit, irony or who think that violence can be exorcised by being ignored, will like it very much. Yes, we do need another biography of Cicero.

26

DE VILLA APPIO PULCHRO FALSO ATTRIBUTA

Amicus Palmerus, magis amica veritas. Nuperrime in ephemeridi cui Phoenici nomen inditum est, vir doctissimus amicus meus Robertus E.A. Palmer de inscriptione « AE » 1928, 108 sagacissime disseruit.[1] In commentario eius cum multa collaudo et probo, tum

[1] R. E. A. PALMER, *A Poem of All Seasons*, « Phoenix », XXX, 1976, 159-173.

errorem unum praecipue doleo. Statuit enim vir doctus Appium Claudium Pulchrum, quem consulem anno a.u.c. 700 auguremque fuisse constat, villam in extremo campo Martio sitam habuisse.[2] Admonet nos etiam Palmerus de ara, quam non longe ab ea campi extremitate magistri vici Aescleti Laribus Augustis posuerunt, et praecipue de eo, quod inter hos magistros P. Clodius aliquis P. l. nominatur.[3] Nemini dubium esse possit, porro pergit Palmerus, quin in isto Clodio quasi vestigium familiae urbanae gentis Claudiae ipsaeque villae in Campo sitae remaneat. Satis speciose: sed villa inventa et familia invenienda esset. Sed nunc est mihi properandum ad Palmeri comitem in rebus Appii Pulchri familiaribus calamo augendis, virum eruditissimum I. Shatzman, qui sibi persuaserit, ut in libro suo de villa Appii urbana paulo copiosius disputaret: Appium non solum villam magnificentissimam in campo Martio extremo habuisse, sed etiam hortos, et in hortibus aviarium.[4]

Testis quis sit mireris? Varronem citant. At non legunt. Est enim locus *Rerum Rusticarum* celeberrimus (3,2), ex quo comperimus comitiis aediliciis sole caldo Varronem ipsum cum tribule suo Q. Axio senatore umbram quaerentes in villam publicam [5] venisse. Ibi Appium Claudium augurem cum quattuor amicis, Merula et Pavone ad sinistram, Pica et Passere ad dextram, quasi in ornithone in subselliis sedisse. Comitiis transactis Appium e villa in hortos discedisse, ut ibidem candidato suo gratularetur (*R.R.* 3,17,1). Eos hortos, qui villae publicae plane iuncti essent,[6] cave ne confundas cum Appii hortis a Cicerone *De Domo* 112 commemoratis.

Sic vides lector benevole totam Appii rei familiaris fictam rationem: vides villam - erat villa publica; vides hortos - erant horti publici; vides denique aviarium - erant auguris optimi quattuor necessarii, qui cognomina ex avibus traxerant.

---

[2] Op. cit. 172.   [3] *CIL* VI, 30957.   [4] SHATZMAN, *Senatorial Wealth and Roman Politics,* Collection Latomus, 142, 1975, 323, 446.   [5] De villa publica nuperrime scripserunt G. TOSSI, *La Villa Publica di Roma nelle fonti letterarie e numismatiche*, « Atti dell'Istituto Veneto », Classe di scienze morali, lettere ed arti, 135, 1976-77, 413-426; L. RICHARDSON, JR., *The Villa Publica and the Divorum*, in *Essays in Archaeology and the Humanities in Memoriam Otto J. Brendel* (Mainz, 1976), 159-163.   [6] Cf. G. TOSSI, op. cit., 422; F. COARELLI, *Il Tempio di Bellona*, « BCAR », LXXX, 1965-67 [1968] 64. De hortis in campo Martio sitis vide etiam P. GRIMAL, *Les Jardins Romains* (Paris, 1943), 126 sqq. De errore Shatzmani vide etiam D. R. SHACKLETON BAILEY in censura libri Shatzmani, « Phoenix », XXX, 1976, 209.

27

PATIENTIA FREGIT: M. OCTAVIUS AND TI. GRACCHUS (CICERO, BRUTUS 95)

Which of the virtues was responsible for the beginning of the Roman Revolution: patience or steadfastness, *patientia* or *constantia*? Or was it the vice of stubborness, *pertinacia*? The clash between Octavius and Tiberius presents an interesting historical — and rhetorical — problem.

Octavius and Tiberius originally were friends, maintains Plutarch (*Ti. Gr.* 10.1). Not impossible, but most probably only a rhetorical device introduced to dramatize the conflict (1). Not so is the message of Cassius Dio (frg. 83.4 Boiss.): Octavius fought Tiberius διὰ φιλονεικίαν συγγενικὴν. This can mean inherited *inimicitia* or inborn contentiousness. The former interpretation is dear to the heart of prosopographers (2), always in search of *amicitiae* and *inimicitiae* stretching back and forth for generations. *Amicitae* and *inimicitae* did exist; but as actually reconstructed they are often only a product of prosopographical fancy. «Inborn contentiousness» can as easily be dismissed as a rationalization of an ancient writer at a loss to explain the fierce struggle between the fellow-tribunes (3). In any case it runs counter to Cicero's characterization of Octavius — not that Cicero is a reliable or disinterested source (4) — but still his appraisal of Octavius' style and comportment as an orator is of interest.

Cicero compares Octavius to Gaius Tuditanus, the historian and antiquarian, who was *omni vita atque victu excultus atque expolitus*, and whose *genus orationis* was *elegans*. Cicero continues (*Brut.* 95):

> Eodemque in genere est habitus is qui *iniuria accepta* fregit Ti. Gracchum *patientia*, civis in rebus optimis *constantissimus*, M. Octavius.

That *elegantia* (5) was a characteristic feature of Octavius' oratorical style was not the opinion of

---

(1) Cf. P. Fraccaro, Studi sull'età dei Gracchi, Città di Castello 1914, 93 ff., esp. 95-96, still the best study of the question. So also, and with the same argument, A.E. Astin, Scipio Aemilianus, Oxford 1967, 346. No discussion of this passage in other recent studies of Ti. Gracchus and Octavius: A. Guarino, «L'abrogazione di Ottavio», Atti dell'Accademia di Scienze Morali e Politiche (Napoli) 81, 1970, 236-266; A.H. Bernstein, Tiberius Sempronius Gracchus, Ithaca 1978, 170 ff.; D. Stockton, The Gracchi, Oxford 1979, 65-67.

(2) D.C. Earl, «M. Octavius, trib. pleb. 133 B.C., and his Successor», *Latomus* 19, 1960, 662, accepted by Astin, op. cit. 346: «almost certainly 'hereditary'». E. Badian, «Tiberius Gracchus and the Beginning of the Roman Revolution», ANRW I, 1, 1972, 701 n. 99, criticizes Earl's interpretation, and takes συγγενικός to mean 'congenital'.

(3) Fraccaro, op. cit. 94-95.

(4) Cf. J. Béranger, «Les jugements de Cicéron sur les Gracques», ANRW I, 1, 1972, 732 ff.

(5) On Cicero's usage of *elegans* and *elegantia*, see A.E. Douglas, M. Tulli Ciceronis Brutus, Oxford 1966, Introduction, p. XLII-XLIII, Commentary, p. 25, and for a definition of *elegantia*, see Auct. *ad Her.* 4.17 (cf. G. Calboli, Cornifici Rhetorica ad C. Herennium, Bologna 1969, 300-301); Cic. *Part. orat.* 21. In his rhetorical works Cicero commends the following orators and politicians for their *elegantia dicendi* or *elegantia verborum*: Cato the Censor (*Brut.* 63: his orations were *acuti, elegantes, faceti*; on the *genus orationis facetum et elegans*, cf. *de or.* 2.240-241); C. Sulpicius Galus, cos. 166 (*Brut.* 78); C. Laelius, cos. 140 (*Brut.* 89 and Douglas ad loc., 86, 211, cf. 295); C. Sempronius Tuditanus, cos. 129 (*Brut.* 95); M. Octavius, tr. pl. 133 (*Brut.* 95); M. Aurelius Scaurus, cos. suff. 108 (*Brut.* 135); L. Licinius Crassus, cos. 95 (*Brut.* 143); Q. Mucius Scaevola, pont. max., cos. 95 (*Brut.* 146, 163, 194); C. Sextius Calvinus (*Brut.* 130, probably the son of the consul of 124, see G.V. Sumner, The Orators in Cicero's Brutus: Prosopography and Chronology, Toronto 1973, 76-77); Q. Lutatius Catulus, cos. 78 (*Brut.* 133); C. Scribonius Curio, cos. 76 (*de or.* 2.98); Q. Hortensius, cos. 69 (*Brut.* 303); L. Manlius Torquatus, cos. 65 (*Brut.* 239); Ser. Sulpicius Rufus, cos. 51 (*Brut.* 153); C. Calpurnius Piso, quaest. 58 and Cicero's son-in-law (*Brut.* 272); L. Manlius Torquatus, praet. 49 (*Brut.* 265); L. Licinius Calvus, the poet and the accuser of Vatinius (*Brut.* 283, cf. Douglas ad loc.); C. Iulius Caesar (*Brut.* 252, 261). A nice company: nearly all of them good optimates. Caesar is an exception and a misunderstanding, but at the end of the Republic many other things, not only oratory, got into the wrong hands. The orators of the *popularis* bent were not expected to be endowed with *elegantia*. The Marians Cn. Papirius Carbo (cos. 85, 84, 82) and M. Marius Gratidianus (pr. probably in 85 and 82, see Sumner, op. cit.

Appian (or of his source): he speaks of the tribunes abusing each other (*B.C.* 1.12.50: λοιδοριῶν δὲ τοῖς δημάρχοις ἐς ἀλλήλους γενομένων). But in matters of style Appian is hardly a match for Cicero. Should we conclude that Octavius scolded Tiberius in an elegant manner?

But of historical importance is above all the interpretation of *iniuria* suffered by Octavius and of his *patientia*. The verdict of Ernst Badian is clear and precise: it was not Tiberius, who «by his 'impatience' brought on the crisis that marks the opening of the Roman Revolution... it was Octavius, by his patience, who did so» (6). And in another place: «The conflict came about through the *patientia* of Octavius, but it was Tiberius' reply that raised it to a new and dangerous level» (7). Thus *pace* Badian Octavius' *patientia* manifested itself in his persistent opposition to the agrarian law. Now, according to a strict grammatical analysis of Cicero's passage the *iniuria* suffered by Octavius at the hands of Tiberius should have preceded his display of *patientia*. Fraccaro points to the words of Appian, *B.C.* 1.12.49: καὶ τότε μὲν αὐτῷ πολλὰ μεμψάμενος ὁ Γράκχος and explains the *iniuria* as «improveri e insolenze di Tiberio a Ottavio» (8). But this hardly qualifies as *iniuria* (see below). It is perverse to expend ingenuity in searching after a hypothetical *iniuria* when the real one is at hand: the deposition of Octavius.

Rhetorica sunt, non leguntur: surprisingly enough no student of Tiberius seems to have observed that in the passage under discussion we are dealing with a rhetorical and philosophical *topos* and not really with a historical description.

In the *Paradoxa Stoicorum* 2.17-18 Cicero contrasts the happiness of the virtuous man (like Cicero himself) with the wretchedness of his enemies: «mihi vero quidquid acciderit in tam ingrata civitate ne recusanti quidem evenerit, non modo non repugnanti». But *virtus* cannot be broken by *inimicorum iniuria*, be it death or exile (9). On the other hand the bad man is only seemingly successful, for he has constantly to fear the consequences of his evil deeds: «quocumque aspexisti, ut *furiae* (10) sic tuae tibi occurrunt *iniuriae* quae te respirare non sinunt». The rhetorical similarity between this passage and Cicero's characterization of Octavius is striking. The *virtus* of Octavius could not be broken by the *iniuria* of his deposition. He did not fight back; he offered at best only a passive resistance (11). *Patientia* was his shield. But it was the *iniuria* of Octavius' deposition that hounded and haunted Tiberius and eventually caused his downfall. Cicero makes this clear in *de leg.* 3.24: «ipsum Ti. Gracchum non solum neglectus,

---

118-119) and *ex eodem genere complures* were as orators *minime digni elegantis conventus auribus* («the attention of an audience of cultivated taste», Douglas ad loc.) but *aptissimi ... turbulentis contionibus* (*Brut.* 223). *Elegantia* and *gravitas* often appear in conjunction (*Brut.* 143, 265; *de or.* 2.98; *Orat.* 134), and *gravitas* was a particular virtue of the *boni* (cf. below, n. 12). Octavius was on the right side of the fence both as a politician and as an orator.

(6) Badian, op. cit. 707.

(7) Ibid. 711.

(8) Fraccaro, op. cit. 96.

(9) Death, exile, deposition — this is the perspective in which we ought to view the *iniuria* of Octavius — notwithstanding Cic. *de off.* 1.33: «Exsistunt etiam saepe iniuriae calumnia quadam».

(10) In the optimate propaganda the Furiae are not associated directly with Ti. Gracchus, but they figure prominently in the story of Gaius' end: he perished in *luco Furinae* or *Furrinae* (Plut. *G. Gr.* 17.3; Auct. *de vir. ill.* 65.5) which the politically colored etymology interpreted as the Sacred Grove of the Furies, Cic. *Nat. deor.* 3.46: «Eumenides... quae si deae sunt, quarum et Athenis fanum est et apud nos, ut ego interpretor, lucus Furinae, Furiae deae sunt, speculatrices, credo et vindices facinorum et sceleris», cf. Pease ad loc. and the illuminating article by S. Eitrem, «G. Gracchus und die Furien», *Philologus* 78, 1922, 183-187.

(11) App. *B.C.* 1.12; Plut. *Ti. Gr.* 12.4-5. Octavius behaved strictly according to the Socratic rule «accipere quam facere praestat iniuriam» (Cic. *Tusc. Disp.* 5.56).

sed etiam sublatus intercessor evertit. Quid enim illum aliud perculit nisi quod potestatem intercedenti collegae abrogavit?».

A few Ciceronian definitions will be of help. First, what is *patientia*? It is nothing else but «rerum arduarum ac difficilium voluntaria ac diuturna perpessio» (*de inv.* 2.163). But *patientia* is also an ingredient of *fortitudo*, and «fortitudo est considerata periculorum susceptio et laborum perpessio» (ibid.). In *de part. orat.* 77 Cicero presents an equally telling although slightly different set of definitions. He argues that «quae *venientibus malis* obstat *fortitudo*, quae *quod iam adest* tolerat et perfert *patientia* nominatur». The picture is clear. The characteristic feature of *fortitudo* is an active resistance against coming evils; the characteristic feature of *patientia* is steadfast endurance of the present *malum*. Octavius showed his *patientia* when he nobly endured the indignity of his deposition. His fight against the lex *agraria* was not an exercise in *patientia*: it called for another quality of spirit, it called for *fortitudo* and *constantia*. And in fact Cicero praises Octavius as *civis in rebus optimis constantissimus*.

Constantia and *fortitudo* often appear in conjunction; vir *constans* is also *vir fortis, severus, gravis* and *sapiens* (12). These qualities distinguish him from *popularis civis*, a *levis* one and a mere *adsentator* (*Lael.* 95). The virtue of *constantia* shines forth most conspicuously in all those firm, grave, wise and stern men who checked the *furor* of the *audaces*, who opposed the nefarious schemes of mob-rousers (13). Q. Aelius Tubero (14) earns his characterization as *constans civis et fortis* because he opposed G. Gracchus: he was *imprimis Graccho molestus* (*Brut.* 117). *Constantia* was a particular virtue of those tribunes of the plebs who embraced the cause of the *boni*. *Constantes* were Cicero's champions the tribunes M. Cispius (*Sest.* 76) and L. Racilius (*Planc.* 77). And M. Caelius, as long as he followed the advice of Cicero «talis tribunus plebis fuit [in 52], ut nemo contra civium perditorum popularem turbulentamque dementiam a senatu et a bonorum causa steterit *constantius*» (*Brut.* 273).

Yet Cicero has to concede that when the *constantia* of an *intercessor* borders on *pertinacia* it may be the origin of a *seditio*, although of course a riot may also arise from *improbitas* of a sponsor (*lator*) of a law who tries to win over the ignorant multitude by unscrupulous promises of *largitio* (15). A rhetorical *topos* only: but also a marvellously fitting description of the clash between Tiberius and Octavius. And as an immediate cause of the Roman Revolution *pertinacia* is a better candidate for culprit than *patientia*.

---

(12) For *constans, constantia* and *gravis, gravitas*, see Cic. *Acad.* 2.53; *Fin.* 2.81; 3.1,75; *Lael.* 64, 95, cf. 99; *Nat. Deor.* 1.1; *Tusc.* 4.57,60,61; 5.13,104; *Balb.* 46; *Cluent.* 196; *Dom.* 39; *Phil.* 9.10; 10.13,41; *Sest.* 88. For *constans, constantia* and *fortis, fortitudo*, see *Brut.* 117; *de orat.* 1.80; *Tusc.* 5.13; *Flacc.* 98; *Phil.* 12.18; 13.15; 14.17; *Planc.* 77. For *constans, constantia* and *severus, severitas*, see *Lael.* 95; *Sull.* 45. For *constans, constantia* and *sapiens, sapientia*, see *Acad.* 2.23,53; *Fin.* 3.75; *Nat. Deor.* 1.1; *Tusc.* 4.55; 5.13. For a discussion of the political concepts of *iniuria, fortitudo, patientia* and *constantia*, see also J. Hellegouarc'h, *Le vocabulaire latin des relations et des partis politiques sous la république*, Paris 1963, 166-167, 247-248, 274 n. 6, 284-285.

(13) Cic. *Cat.* 2.25; *Sest.* 139. On Cicero's usage of the terms *audax* and *audacia*, cf. Ch. Wirszubski, «Audaces: A Study in Political Phraseology», *JRS* 51, 1961, 12-22; E. Badian, «Manius Acilius Glabrio and the Audacissimi», *AJP* 96, 1975, 71-75.

(14) See on him T.R.S. Broughton, The Magistrates of the Roman Republic 1.502.

(15) *Sest.* 77: «Nam ex *pertinacia* aut *constantia* intercessoris oritur saepe seditio, culpa atque improbitate latoris commodo aliquo oblato imperitis aut largitione»; cf. *Marc.* 31: «quae enim *pertinacia* quibusdam, eadem aliis *constantia* videri potest».

28

The Aediles and the *Didascaliae*

In the new *Supplement* (1986) to T.R.S. Broughton's *Magistrates of the Roman Republic* there appears on p. 144 the following entry:

L. Minucius Thermus (not in *RE*), *Aed. cur.*, uncertain date. He put on a revival performance of the *Andria* of Terence.

For information we are directed to Donatus, *Commentum Terenti* (ed. P. Wessner) 1, p. 36 (*Praefatio* 6 on the *didascaliae* to the *Andria*), and to an article by J. Heurgon.[1] There is no back-reference to *MRR*, but in vol. 1.489 under 135 B.C. we have the following pair of curule aediles (both queried): Q. Minucius and (L.) Valerius (Flaccus). For information we are again directed to Donatus' note on the *didascaliae* to the *Andria*, and in n.5 (p. 490) we read that according to Dziatzko[2] "these were Aediles at the time of a revival performance."

Thus between the original volume and the supplement Minucius changed his praenomen from Q. to L., and acquired the cognomen Thermus. An intriguing story. It leads us to the jungle of Donatus' text and its apparatus,[3] and to the thicket of constitutional history.

P. Wessner, vol. 1 (Teubner 1902) 36, lines 3-5, gives the following text:

haec prima facta est, acta ludis Megalensibus M. Fuluio M.' Glabrione [Q. Minucio Valerio] aedilibus curulibus.

Now the readings in the apparatus:[4]

a) codex A (Parisinus lat. 7920 of the XIth century):

in (corrected to m by a *munus recentior*) fuluio edile int glabrio neq; minutio ualerio curulib;

b) codices T and C (Vatic. lat. 2905 and Oxoniensis Bodl. 95, both of the XVth century, but ultimately derived from the archetype through a strain of tradition different from A):

m. (marco T) fuluio edile et m. glabrione quinto minutio termonii. L. Valerio curuli

---

[1] "Sur un édile de Térence," *REL* 27 (1949) 106-108.

[2] The reference is to K. (or C.) Dziatzko, "Ueber die Terentianischen Didaskalien," *RhM* 21 (1866) 64-92 at 64-65. But one has also to read the first part of Dziatzko's article, *RhM* 20 (1865) 570-597, esp. 572-573 and 587-591. The article of Dziatzko is still fundamental for all investigations of magistrates and *didascaliae*.

[3] In the codices of Terentius the *didascaliae* to the *Andria* are not preserved.

[4] For information on the codices, see Wessner, vol.1, pp. VII-IX, X-XII, XIII-XIV; for the stemma, see p. XXXIII. In recent years much work has been done on the manuscripts of Donatus, and Wessner's stemma has been variously refined, see O. Zwierlein, *Der Terenzkommentar des Donat in codex Chigianus H VII 240* (Berlin 1970); M.D. Reeve, *Hermes* 106 (1978) 608-618; *CP* 74 (1979) 310-326; M.D. Reeve and R.H. Rouse, *Viator* 9 (1978) 235-249.

c) codex V (Vatic. Regin. lat. 1496 of the XVth century; like T and C descended from the archetype through the postulated codex β, but through a different line of transmission):

m. fuluio et m. glabrione q. minutio termonii L. ualerio aedili curuli

From codex A (he does not seem to have used the readings of other codices[5]), Dziatzko recovered four names of the aediles: M. Fulvius, M.' (an obvious correction for M.) Glabrio, Q. Minucius[6] and (L.) Valerius. The *didascaliae* (loc. cit.) date the first performance of the *Andria* to the consulship of M. (Claudius) Marcellus and C. Sulpicius (Galus) = 166 B.C., and to this year will also belong the first pair of the aediles, M. Fulvius (Nobilior), the future consul of 159, and M.' (Acilius) Glabrio (cos. suff. 154).[7] So far no problems. But the other pair is either to be excised (as Wessner does in his text) or explained as the aediles under whose charge the (hypothetical) revival performance of the play was staged. Now that there was a revival follows (according to Dziatzko) not only from the presence in the *didascaliae* of four names of the aediles (note the circular argument) but also from the mention of two directors, L. Atilius Praenestinus and L. Ambivius Turpio. He argues that a play was always directed by one *actor* only, and hence we have to assign Ambivius Turpio to the original performance, and Atilius Praenestinus to the revival.[8]

The date of this revival can be established only very approximately. Dziatzko proposes to identify the aedile Valerius with the consul of 131, L. Valerius Flaccus, and assigns 143-134 as the possible dates for his aedileship (with the exception, however, and for no reason I can discern, of 138). Broughton lists him (under 135) in the form (L.) Valerius (Flaccus), and judiciously observes (1.490, n.5): "Dates and identifications remain exceedingly doubtful." But the praenomen should not be bracketed, for although it is missing from the codex A (and from Wessner's and Dziatzko's text), it is attested in the codices T, C and V.[9] Furthermore in the second century among the known Valerii the praenomen L. was used amost exclusively by the Valerii Flacci.[10] This considerably stengthens the case for the identification with the consul of 131 (but, needless to say, does not prove it).

---

[5] See *RhM* 20 (1865) 572-573; 21 (1866) 64, n.1.

[6] The manuscripts of Donatus have Minutius, but Minucius is the normal spelling of the name, as attested by coins and inscriptions; cf. M.H. Crawford, *Roman Republican Coinage* (Cambridge 1974) 275 (no. 243.1); W. Schulze, *Zur Geschichte lateinischer Eigennamen* (Berlin 1904) 361.

[7] In *MRR* 1.437 the name of Fulvius is given correctly as M. Fulvius (Nobilior)—his cognomen derives from the identification with the consul, but Glabrio appears as the M.' Acilius Glabrio: here the nomen Acilius should be put within parentheses for it does not figure in the manuscripts of Donatus.

[8] *RhM* 20 (1865) 587-591.

[9] In the *Supplement* (1986) 211, the praenomen is not bracketed, but it is queried. J. Seidel, *Fasti aedilicii* (Diss. Breslau 1908) 78-79, vehemently criticized the idea of Dziatzko "weil der Vorname des Aedilen fehlt." Münzer, "Minucius 15," *RE* 15 (1932) 1943-1944, endorsed this criticism wholeheartedly. The conclusion? One has to read the apparatus.

[10] As can easily be gathered from the list in F. Münzer, *De gente Valeria* (Diss. Berlin, Oppoliae 1891) 34-54 and from the Indices to *MRR* (2.628-632). Cf. Heurgon (above, n.1) 106-107. The only exception is L. Valerius Tappo, tr. pl. 195.

As to the date, if we accept the identification of the aedile with the consul, 134 must be excluded for under the lex Villia it was the latest possible year for Valerius' praetorship (cf. *MRR* 1.490). Perforce 135 must be excluded as well for this would have made him stand for the praetorship while holding the aedileship.

Now under 135 *MRR* (1.489 and 490 n.4) lists a third curule aedile (also with a question-mark), C. Sempronius Tuditanus (cos. 129, pr. 132). This year is now freed for him, perhaps in vain, since his aedileship also presents a thorny problem. The entry is based on Cic. *Att.* 13.32 (= SB 305).3 of 29 May 45. Cicero states that Tuditanus achieved his curule magistracies *legitimis annis*. Why did he choose this locution and not *suis annis*? Because he knew the year of Tuditanus' praetorship, but he clearly did not know Tuditanus' age. He argues that as Tuditanus gained his curule offices *legitimis annis*, and as he was elected to them *perfacile*, it is most unlikely that he became praetor late, *sero*. Thus *legitimis annis* must refer to the intervals between the curule magistracies. But in order to be able to say that Tuditanus achieved his praetorship *legitimo anno* one must know the interval between either the quaestorship and praetorship or the aedileship and the praetorship. Now since Cicero, when he wrote this letter, apparently did not yet know the year of Tuditanus' quaestorship (this follows from *Att.* 13.4 [= SB 311].1 of 4 June 45), only the aedileship remains. This argument reproduces the main line of Astin's admirable discussion;[11] it is logical but not entirely compelling. Cicero does not mention the aedileship explicitly, but he stresses that he had found the year of Tuditanus' praetorship in the book (*Liber annalis*) of Libo. Thus what he meant by *legitimis annis* may simply be this: Tuditanus attained the consulship at the shortest possible interval after his praetorship or conversely he held his praetorship at the shortest possible interval before the consulship, and hence he held these offices *legitimis annis* with respect to each other.

If we deny the aedileship to Tuditanus no further problem. If we grant it, and place it in 135 (assuming that Tuditanus observed the *biennium* between the aedileship and the praetorship),[12] and assume further that he held a curule and not a plebeian aedileship, we have on our hands a constitutional problem with repercussions reaching the aedileship of Minucius and Valerius.

The curule aedileship was administered by alternating pairs of patricians and plebeians, the patricians holding the office in the odd-numbered and the plebeians in the even-numbered

---

[11] A.E. Astin, *The Lex Annalis Before Sulla* (Collection Latomus 32, Bruxelles 1958) 8-9. Cf. also E. Badian, "Cicero and the Commission of 146 B.C.," *Hommages à Marcel Renard* 1 (Collection Latomus 101, Bruxelles 1969) 53-65; G.V. Sumner, *The Orators in Cicero's Brutus: Prosopography and Chronology* (Toronto 1973) 156-157, 166-170. D.R. Shackleton Bailey, *Cicero's Letters to Atticus* 5 (Cambridge 1966) 351, takes *legitimis annis* to mean *suis,* but this is clearly "wrong for the context" (Sumner 157; Badian 56 n.1). The discussion by R. Develin, *Patterns in Office-Holding 366-49 B.C.* (Collection Latomus 161, Bruxelles 1979) 87-88, is inadequate. See now Broughton's lucid note, *Suppl.* (1986) 190. He concludes that Tuditanus' aedileship "is not proved," but "if he held it, 135 is the most probable date." But the date 135 opens a can of constitutional worms; see below in the text.

[12] I do not wish here to enter into the discussion between Astin, Badian, Sumner and Develin whether in the second century the *biennium* between the curule aedileship and the praetorship was statutory or merely customary.

years. This rule seems to have prevailed from 390 (or in any case 388), but ultimately it was abandoned, and the office was each year thrown open *promiscue* to all competitors (Livy 7.1.6). It was still in force in 161-160, but it appears not to have been operative in 91 when we find a plebeian curule aedile in the year that ought to have been reserved for the patricians.[13]

Now 135 was a patrician year: it was a wrong year for the curule aedileship of the plebeian Tuditanus. If we insist on this date, this would mean that the rule of alternation ceased to be enforced by 135. This was in fact the conclusion of Seidel:[14] not impossible, but Cicero's letter is a very slender foundation to sustain a major electoral innovation. Münzer[15] was sceptical, but Cichorius[16] was enthusiastic. In the verse of Lucilius, "per saturam aedilem factum qui legibus solvat" (Marx 48, Krenkel 34), he found contemporary evidence corroborating the idea of Seidel. Somebody was elected to the aedileship "in nicht korrekter, nicht gesetzmässiger Weise" (according to Cichorius this is the meaning of *per saturam* in this passage[17]), and later was given dispensation from the law by the senate. Cichorius imagines that the verse refers to the irregular election of a plebeian to the curule aedileship in an odd-numbered "patrician" year; it would thus demonstrate that by 123, when Lucilius wrote the first book of his *Satires*,[18] the rule of alternation had already been broken. Ingenious and far-fetched, and perhaps even more far-fetched than ingenious, for we can easily imagine many other electoral irregularities[19] that required dispensation from the law.

So if we discard Tuditanus, and the testimony of Lucilius, we are finally left with Q. Minucius and L. Valerius (Flaccus), an odd pair, for one of them was patrician and the other plebeian. To whatever year we assign this pair (136 is the earliest possible date, see above), the rule of alternation did not then operate. But again if we are too timid to derive a constitutional innovation from a tentative identification, there is an easy way out: we can reject the identification of the aedile and the consul, deprive the aedile of his (hypothetical) cognomen Flaccus, and make out of him a plebeian. Then of course we have no peg from which to hang a date, and so Valerius and Minucius would be floating somewhere in the second half of the second century.[20]

---

[13]T. Mommsen, *Römisches Staatsrecht* 2³ (Leipzig 1887) 481-482; *MRR* 1.116, 444-445; 2.21.

[14]*Fasti aedilicii* (above, n.8) 41-43.

[15]*RE* 15 (1932) 1944 ("Minucius 25"); 2A (1923) 1441 ("Sempronius 90"). Broughton, *MRR* 1.490, n.4 remarks that "if the practice of alternating pairs of patricians and plebeians still continued" 136 would be the mos probable year for Tuditanus' aedileship. This is unlikely, for Tuditanus' office depends on Cicero's letter, and 13€ would hardly be a *legitimus annus*, for we would have an interval not of two but rather of three years between hi aedileship and his praetorship. The way out of this difficulty may be the suggestion of Astin ([above, n.10] ! n.3) that he may have been a plebeian aedile in 134.

[16]C. Cichorius, *Untersuchungen zu Lucilius* (Berlin 1908) 234-236 (the dissertation of Seidel was writte: under Cichorius' direction).

[17]He follows the interpretation of F. Marx, *C. Lucilii Carminum reliquiae* 2 (Leipzig 1905) 23-24. But c: Mommsen, *Staatsrecht* 3.1 (1887) 336, n.5, who found this passage baffling, as does also W. Krenkel, *Lucilius Satiren* (Berlin 1970) 119.

[18]This is Cichorius' date; Krenkel (p. 25) dates it to 125/124.

[19]In fact Cichorius himself hints at a number of them.

[20]Seidel's solution (*Fasti aedilicii* 78-79) is to reject the identification with the consul (on wrong ground.

While Valerius may be thus losing his patrician status and his cognomen Flaccus (though he retains his praenomen L.), Minucius may be gaining a cognomen and perhaps changing the praenomen. That he had a cognomen was for everybody to see in the apparatus of Wessner; but it was only in 1949 that J. Heurgon saw it. In the reading *termonii* of the codices T, C and V he recognized the name Thermus, the well-known cognomen of the Minucii.[21] Our aedile may thus have been ultimately descended from Q. Minucius Q.f.L.n. Thermus, consul in 193 (*MRR* 1.346); for his *floruit* the only secure *terminus post quem* is 166, the date of the first staging of the *Andria*.

For the prosopographical dessert the praenomen: L. or Q.? Both praenomina were used by the Minucii Thermi, but with respect to our aedile the unanimous reading of the manuscripts is the resounding Q. L. is a ghost-praenomen. We hunt it down in Heurgon's last paragraph. He points out that one of the directors who staged revivals of *Eunuchus* and *Adelphoe* was L. Minucius Prothymus,[22] probably a freedman (his cognomen Prothymus pointing to his servile origin)[23] of a L. Minucius. Whether this L. Minucius was ever aedile we of course do not know; Heurgon ventures only a supposition that he was *vraisemblablement* a brother or son of "our Quintus."[24]

For the chronology of Terence's plays and for the dates of second-century aediles the *didascaliae* are a source uncertain and confusing.[25] Hence it is important to present the textual evidence clearly and fully. But even when this is done few certain points emerge; most aediles recorded in the *didascaliae* will continue their existence on the pages of *MRR* and its *Supplements* surrounded by question-marks. This note, too, takes the shape of a question-

---

see above, n.8), but to retain the patrician status of Valerius, and to assign the aedileship of Minucius and Valerius to the period when the office was open to free competition (i.e., according to his theory after 135, see above, n.13).

[21]Heurgon (above, n.1) 107-108.

[22]Here is the evidence: a) Terent., *Didasc.* to *Adelph.* (*P. Terenti Afri Comoediae*, ed. S. Prete [Heidelberg 1954] 349): in the *codex Bembinus* Minucius is not mentioned ("egere Lucius Hatilius praenestinus Lucius Ambibius Turpio"); the reading of the *recensio Calliopiana* (on the codices of Terence, see the lucid presentation by Prete 9-44, esp. 35, 43-44) is "L.At.Praen.Minutius Prothymus;" b) Donatus, *Commentum Terenti, Eunuchus Praef.* 6 (Wessner 1.266): "agentibus etiam tunc personatis L. Minucio (*Numidio* [*munidio* T] codd.) Prothymo (various spellings in the codices) L. Ambiuio Turpione" (no mention of Minucius Prothymus in the manuscripts of Terence); c) Euanthius, *de comoedia* 6.3 (Wessner 1.26): "personati primi egisse ... tragoediam Minucius Prothymus" (again various spellings in the manuscripts); d) Donatus, *Adelph. Praef.* 6 (Wessner 2.4): "agentibus L. Ambiuio et L. <Minucio Prothymo>, qui cum suis gregibus etiam tum personati agebant" (supplied on the basis of c, b and a). It was again Dziatzko, *RhM* 20 (1865) 578; 21 (1866) 66-68, 81-82, who argued most forcefully for assigning Minucius Prothymus to revival performances. Cf. W. Kroll, "Minucius 46," *RE* 15 (1932) 1966.

[23]H. Solin, *Die Griechischen Personennamen in Rom. Ein Namenbuch* 2 (Berlin 1982) 768-769, lists Minucius Prothymus among the *incerti*, but out of his fourteen examples of the cognomen, nine belong to slaves and *liberti*, and most probably all of its bearers in the city of Rome were ultimately of servile descent.

[24]Heurgon (above, n.1) 108.

[25]A number of scholars advocate discarding the *didascaliae* altogether and relying on the prologues alone (see for all H.B. Mattingly, "The Terentian *Didascaliae*," *Athenaeum* 47 [1959] 148-173; "The Chronology of Terence," *RCCM* 5 [1963] 12-61). This is unwise; the *didascaliae* contain much doubtful information, but also much that can be well fitted into the magisterial careers of the second century (as e.g. the dates of the aediles under whose charge the *Andria* was first produced, see above in the text). The prologues on the other hand are even more unreliable a guide, since their interpretation depends so often on subjective perceptions of the reader.

mark. It is offered in the spirit of admiration for *MRR* and its Author, and as a contribution toward a next *Supplement*.

29

ROMAN OFFICERS IN THE YEAR OF PYDNA

I. LEGATES, LIEUTENANTS

In the preface to his *magnum opus* T. R. S. Broughton defines "Legates, Lieutenants" as men "who served with definite military functions," and he adds "as these are a rather indefinite group I have included among them (with a mark of interrogation) a considerable number of persons who were active in military capacities but whose title is not preserved."[1] It is, no doubt, a reasonable procedure. We must, however, be well aware of the ambiguous meaning the term *legatus* had in the annalistic tradition and, consequently, also in Livy. There were originally only two kinds of officers in the Roman army, the *tribuni militum* and the *praefecti socium*. The senatorial *legati* permanently attached to the commander of an army appear relatively late, only after the Second Punic War. Varro describes them as *qui lecti publice, quorum opera consilioque uteretur peregre magistratus.*[2] At the same time they were not only *consiliarii* but also military officers subordinated to the commander-in-chief. However, they did not derive their military authority from their status as legates, but rather from the commission given individually to each of them by the commander. As *legati* they were only potential officers. Now, the commander would normally place in charge of specific military operations the senatorial *legati*, but he did not have to. He could appoint any person he thought fit to perform the task. Such persons had no official title, but the annalists (by the extension of the meaning of the term *legatus*) called them legates.[3] Hence the confusion in our sources, and in our prosopographies. Not

---

[1] T. R. S. Broughton, *The Magistrates of the Roman Republic* 1 (New York 1951) X.

[2] Varro, *de lingua Latina* 5.87. See also Polybius, 6.35.4, and F. W. Walbank, *A Historical Commentary on Polybius* 1 (Oxford 1957) 717–18.

[3] The best discussion of the terminology and of legal aspects (especially as far as the pre–Marian period is concerned) is still that by T. Mommsen, *Römisches Staatsrecht* 2³ (Leipzig 1887) 673–701, esp. 694–701. For later developments, see R. E. Smith, *Service in the Post–Marian Roman Army* (Manchester 1958) 59–69; J. Harmand, *L'armée et le soldat à Rome de 107 à 50 avant notre ère* (Paris 1967) 368–83. Still very much worth reading is J. N. Madvig, "Die Befehlshaber und das Avancement in dem römischen Heere," in his *Kleine philologische Schriften* (Leipzig 1875) 477–560.

every man who was active in a military capacity was a *legatus* in the strict (and not annalistic) meaning of the term. It is not easy, and often it is impossible, to distinguish in our sources the senatorial *legati, lecti publice*,[4] from the "personal legates" of the commander (the commander would normally choose them from among the senators, the sons of senators and the militarily distinguished equestrians). However, it is well to remember that, when we group all the men "who served with definite military functions" under one heading of "Legates, Lieutenants," we are following in the footsteps of the annalistic tradition.

The situation would have been even more complicated if we had to accept Mommsen's contention that "als ständige Legaten scheinen den Beamten in älterer Zeit (i.e., before the last century of the Republic) nicht selten Nichtsenatoren beigegeben zu sein."[5] On the other hand Willems maintains that "on ne saurait prouver d'aucun légat qu'il ne fût point sénateur au moment de sa *legatio*."[6] In fact Mommsen's "nicht selten" is an obvious exaggeration: he adduces only two, and rather doubtful, examples of non–senatorial permanent legates attached to a commander.[7] Consequently, we should probably classify in our *fasti legatorum* only senators as permanent (*lecti publice*) legates. All other men who appear in our sources with definite military functions will rather have been personal "legates" (or, as Mommsen aptly defines them, *Beauftragte*) of the commander.

---

[4] They were appointed on the basis of a *senatus consultum*, although their actual selection was normally carried out by the presiding magistrate. See esp. Polybius, 35.4.5, and other sources listed by Mommsen, *Staatsrecht* 2³ 677–78; P. Willems, *Le sénat de la république romaine* 2 (Louvain 1883) 608–10.

[5] *Staatsrecht* 2³. 682.

[6] *Le sénat* 2. 608, n. 4.

[7] *Staatsrecht* 2³. 682, n. 3. The first case is that of C. Laelius (cos. 190). He was quaestor in 202, but Livy calls him *legatus* of Scipio already in 206 (28.19.9, and 28.28.14, *L. Scipio frater meus et C. Laelius legati*). In all probability Livy uses here the word *legatus* in its annalistic meaning: Laelius was simply a "lieutenant" of Scipio, and not a senatorial legate (on Laelius' activities as "legate, lieutenant," see *MRR* 1. 300, 314). The same explanation will apply also to L. Scipio: it is hardly possible that he had been quaestor before 207, when he is first attested in command of an important military operation (cf. *MRR* 1. 297, 300). The explanation of Willems (*Le sénat* 2. 608, n. 4) that Laelius was *quaestor iterum* in 202, and that he had held this office for the first time before 206, introduces an unnecessary complication. At 30.33.2 Livy writes: "Laelium, cuius ante legati, eo anno quaestoris extra sortem ex senatus consulto opera utebatur." In this passage *ex senatus consulto* does not refer to *legati* but only and exclusively to *quaestoris extra sortem* (on the quaestors *extra sortem*, see L. A. Thompson, "The Appointment of

With this in mind let us turn to the year of Pydna. Broughton (*MRR* 1. 431) lists eight men as certain or possible legates, lieutenants in 168. Already *a priori* it hardly seems possible that all of them should have been permanent senatorial legates, especially as seven of them served under one commander, Aemilius Paullus.

Three men are explicitly described by Livy as *legati:*

1) Cn. Anicius. Livy 44.46.3 informs us "ad Aeginium . . . oppugnandum Cn. Anicius legatus missus erat." Nothing more is known of him, but he obviously was a relative of the praetor L. Anicius Gallus who waged war in Illyria against king Gentius (*MRR* 1. 428). Anicius Gallus was the first of the Anicii to reach higher magistracies,[8] and so Cn. Anicius, if he was at all a senator, was at best a *quaestorius.*

2) C. Cluvius. He was in charge of the camp during the battle of Pydna (Livy 44.40.6). Broughton identifies him with C. Cluvius Saxula who was *praetor iterum* in 173. He points out that in 168 "many of the officers . . . were deliberately chosen from among the older men" (*MRR* 1. 432, n. 2; cf. 395, 408). Although Livy 44.21.2 refers only to the choice of the tribunes of the soldiers from among the experienced men (see below), Broughton's identification is not implausible.

3) M. Sergius Silus. He commanded at the battle of Pydna "duae cohortes . . . Marrucina et Paeligna, duae turmae Samnitium equitum"

---

quaestors *extra sortem,*" *Proceedings of the African Classical Association,*" 5 [1962] 17–25, esp. 19).

Mommsen's second example is Sp. Mummius, who according to Cicero was a legate of his brother in Corinth in 146 (Cic. *ad Att.* 13.5.1; 6.4). Mommsen appears to take Cicero's words to mean that Sp. Mummius could not have been one of the ten commissioners sent by the senate to Corinth because he was not yet a senator, but that he could serve as a permanent *legatus* to his brother. This is not, however, the point Cicero makes. Cicero argues "non solitos maiores nostros eos legare in decem qui essent imperatorum necessarii" (*ad Att.* 13.6.4). Two other solutions seem preferable: a) Sp. Mummius may have been a personal legate of his brother (Cicero knew that Spurius was in Corinth in 146, but he did not know whether he had been there as *legatus lectus publice*); b) he may have been by 146 already a *quaestorius* (nothing seems to preclude this possibility, cf. G. V. Sumner, *The Orators in Cicero's Brutus: Prosopography and Chronology* [Toronto 1973] 45), and hence a senatorial legate. On the complicated question of Cicero's historical investigations of the *decem legati* of 146 B.C., see D. R. Shackleton Bailey, *Cicero's Letters to Atticus* 5 (Cambridge 1966) 349, 351, 355, 357–60; E. Badian, "Cicero and the Commission of 146 B.C.," *Hommages à M. Renard* 1 (Collection Latomus 101, Bruxelles 1969) 54–65. Neither Shackleton Bailey nor Badian touches upon the question raised by Mommsen.

[8] Cf. E. Klebs, "Anicius 15," *RE* 1 (1894) 2196–97.

which were posted as *praesidium* on the bank of a "flumen . . . ex quo et Macedones et Romani aquabantur" (Livy 44.40.4–5). Again, we do not hear anything more of him. F. Münzer suggests that he may have been the son of the heroic M. Sergius Silus, pr. urb. in 197.[9] In this case he would have been ca. thirty–five years old in 168, probably an experienced soldier, but certainly not an eminent senator.

4) C. Sulpicius Galus. He is referred to in our sources either as *legatus* or as *tribunus militum*. Technically he was probably the latter. See on him below.

The remaining four men are queried. The precise meaning of the mark of interrogation preceding their names is, however, not always clear, and in any case it does not always mean the same thing:

5) Q. Aelius Tubero. After the capture of Perseus he was given *tuendi cura regis* (Livy 45.7.1, cf. 8.8; Plut. *Aem.* 27.1). He was married to a daughter of Aemilius Paullus, and was famous for his poverty.[10] Broughton considers the possibility of his identification with Q. Aelius, tr. pl. in 177, but the latter can be identified as well with Q. Aelius Paetus, cos. 167.[11]

6) Q. Fabius Maximus Aemilianus. He was present at the council of war, and subsequently he executed (together with Scipio Nasica) the famous flanking march which forced the Macedonians to take their stand at Pydna, Livy 44.35.14: "ipse (i.e., Aemilius Paullus) P. Scipionem Nasicam, Q. Fabium Maximum filium suum cum quinque milibus delectis militum . . . mittit" (cf. Plut. *Aem.* 15.3–6). He was then ca. eighteen years old,[12] and it was Scipio Nasica (cf. below) who was in charge of the operation. Fabius Aemilianus is obviously to be classified as a personal legate of the commander.

There is no doubt that both Aelius Tubero and Fabius Aemilianus "served with definite military functions." The mark of interrogation before their names indicates our lack of information of whether they had the title of *legatus*.

7) L. Atilius. Livy 45.5.2 describes him as *inlustris adulescens*. He persuaded the Samothracians to withdraw the right of asylum from Perseus. Livy wonders, however, whether his intervention at the *contio*

---

[9] "Sergius 41," *RE* 2A (1923) 1720.
[10] Cf. E. Klebs, "Aelius 154," *RE* 1 (1893) 535.
[11] *MRR* 2. 526 (Index of careers); cf. 1. 398.
[12] F. Münzer, "Fabius 109," *RE* 6 (1909) 1792.

of the Samothracians occurred *casu* or *consilio*. If *casu*, there is no reason to list him as a legate or lieutenant. If *consilio*, he will have acted on orders from the commander of the fleet, the praetor Cn. Octavius. The mark of interrogation reproduces here Livy's hesitation whether L. Atilius had any official function at all.

But even if we accept that he acted on orders from Cn. Octavius, this alone would still not justify his inclusion among "Legates, Lieutenants." His mission was essentially very similar to that of P. Lentulus, A. Postumius and A. Antonius, who were sent to Perseus to negotiate his surrender.[13] It was diplomatic in character, not military. Consequently, he rather ought to be listed among "Legates, Envoys."

8) M. Porcius Cato (Licinianus). He fought valiantly in the battle of Pydna. He lost his sword, but, *veritus ignominiam* (Front. *Strat.* 4.5.17) succeeded in recapturing it. Now, this is the only incident concerning Cato that our sources relate. None of our authorities attributes to him a "definite military function." Frontinus, Valerius Maximus and Iustinus speak of him as simply fighting *in acie* (as a cavalryman); Plutarch describes him turning back to his companions and calling for aid in his effort to regain his sword.[14] Even more telling is the testimony of Licinianus' father himself. Cato Licinianus first saw military service in 173 in Liguria as a *tiro* under the command of M. Popillius,[15] but in 168 he seems to have participated in the *bellum Macedonicum* still only as a *miles*. Cicero mentions (*De off.* 1.37) "Catonis senis . . . epistula ad

---

[13] Livy 45.4.7; *MRR* 1. 430.

[14] Front. *Strategemata* 4.5.17 ("in acie decidente equo prolapsus . . . gladium excidisse vaginae"); Val. Max. 3.2.16: "qui cum ab hoste in acie vehementer . . . peteretur, vagina gladius eius elapsus decidit" (A confused account. Valerius Maximus does not realize that Cato fought as an *eques*, and seems to imagine him as a commander–in–chief: the enemies impressed by his bravery "postero die ad eum supplices pacem petentes venerunt"); Iust. 33.2.1–4: "dum inter confertissimos hostes insigniter dimicat, equo delapsus pedestre proelium adgreditur . . . gladius ei e manu elapsus"; Plut. *Aem.* 21.1–6; *Cat. Mai.* 20.7–8.

[15] Cic. *De officiis* 1.36: "Popilius imperator tenebat provinciam, in cuius exercitu Catonis filius tiro militabat. Cum autem Popilio videretur unam dimittere legionem, Catonis quoque filium, qui in eadem legione militabat, dimisit. Sed cum amore pugnandi in exercitu remansisset, Cato ad Popilium scripsit, ut, si eum patitur in exercitu remanere, secundo eum obliget militiae sacramento, quia priore amisso iure cum hostibus pugnare non poterat." This passage has often been regarded as interpolation (cf. H. Jordan, *M. Catonis . . . quae extant* [Lipsiae 1860] CIIII–CV; C. Atzert, *Cicero, De officiis* [Lipsiae 1958] XXVIII–XXIX), but whatever our opinion as to that question, there is no reason to

Marcum filium, in qua scribit se audisse eum missum factum esse a
consule cum in Macedonia bello Persico miles esset. Monet igitur ut
caveat, ne proelium ineat; negat enim ius esse, qui miles non sit cum
hoste pugnare." This passage follows immediately upon the passage
reproduced in n. 15; it is shorter, less detailed, but stylistically much
superior. It is hardly likely that the Censor wrote two almost identical
letters, both concerning the military oath, one to his son's commander
in Liguria and the other directly to his son in Macedonia. The first
passage will be either an interpolation or at best Cicero's earlier version. In any case in a passage concerning technicalities of the *ius mili-
tare*[16] Cato (and Cicero) would hardly have omitted[17] the title of Licinianus, if he had had any. Hence we may be quite certain that he was not
a "lieutenant" in 168. He was too young to be a senatorial *legatus,* and
he certainly was not tribune of the soldiers: in 168 only ex–magistrates
were eligible to become military tribunes (see on this below, part II).
The son of Cato is in all probability to be removed from the roster of
"Legates, Lieutenants" at Pydna. He served as *eques,* and as the future
son–in–law of Aemilius Paullus he may have gone to Macedonia among
the *contubernales* of the consul.

II. TRIBUNES OF THE SOLDIERS

First of all it is important to note regulations concerning elections
and appointments of military tribunes in the period of the Second Macedonian War.

Twenty–four tribunes for the first four consular legions were

---

reject the information it provides about Licinianus' *tirocinium.* The *Popilius imperator*
mentioned here will be rather M. Popillius Laenas, cos. 173 than C. Popillius Laenas, cos.
172 (cf. *MRR* 1. 407–8, 410–11). The date of Cato's *tirocinium* in 173 (and consequently his
date of birth in 191 or 190) fits in well with the most probable date of his death as *praetor
designatus* in 152 or 151 (cf. W. Drumann–P. Groebe, *Geschichte Roms* 5 [Leipzig 1919] 160–
61).

   16On the *sacramentum,* cf. J. Linderski, "Rome, Aphrodisias and the *Res Gestae:*
the *Genera Militiae* and the Status of Octavian," *JRS* 74 (1984) 75–76.

   17Cato stresses his function of *legatus* in his oration *de suis virtutibus contra L.
Thermum;* see H. Malcovati, *Oratorum Romanorum Fragmenta*² (Torino 1955) 52–53,
frags. 130, 132. See also Cicero, *De sen.* 18 (Cato speaking): "qui et miles et tribunus et
legatus et consul versatus sum in vario genere bellorum." Cf. *Brut.* 304: "erat Hortensius
in bello primo anno miles, altero tribunus militum, Sulpicius legatus."

elected by the tribal assembly; the tribunes for the remaining legions were appointed by the consuls or praetors.[18]

In 171 a temporary change occurred (Livy 42.31.5): "in tribunis militum novatum eo anno propter Macedonicum bellum, quod consules (i.e., the consuls of 171 P. Licinius Crassus and C. Cassius Longinus) ex senatus consulto ad populum tulerunt, ne tribuni militum eo anno suffragiis crearentur, sed consulum praetorumque in iis faciendis iudicium arbitriumque esset."[19] *Eo anno* is ambiguous. One would expect that the tribunes for the consular year 171 had already been elected in the preceding year and entered upon their office together with the consuls. This was the practice in later times (Cic. *Verr.* 1.30); that this rule also obtained in the second century seems to follow from Livy's account referring to the consular year 191 and the army of M. Acilius Glabrio (36.1.6–7; 2.2; 3.13–14). The law would thus apply to the appointment of the tribunes (of the first four legions) for the consular year 170. But *propter Macedonicum bellum* may perhaps be taken to militate against this interpretation: the war began in 171. Still it is most natural, linguistically and constitutionally, to interpret *eo anno* as indicating that no elections of the tribunes were to take place in 171 (for 170), and that the tribunes for 170 were to be selected in 170 by the consuls of that year.

The tribunes of the remaining legions were always appointed by the consuls or praetors after the beginning of the consular year. In 171 the praetor C. Sulpicius Galba was given the task of raising four reserve legions, the *legiones urbanae,* and was instructed to select for them "quattuor tribunos militum ex senatu . . . qui praeessent" (Livy 42.35.5). If we keep the transmitted text we get four senatorial legionary commanders, an interesting innovation for normally each legion was

---

[18]For a convenient summary of the development and legal position of the military tribunate, see Mommsen, *Staatsrecht* 2³. 575–78; J. Marquardt, *Römische Staatsverwaltung* 2² (Leipzig 1884) 363–65; J. Lengle, "Tribunus militum," *RE* 6A (1937) 2439–44; J. Suolahti, *The Junior Officers of the Roman Army in the Republican Period* (Helsinki 1955) 36–42; Harmand (n. 3 above) 349–58; C. Nicolet, "Armée et société à Rome sous la république: à propos de l'ordre équestre," in J.–P. Brisson (ed.), *Problèmes de la guerre à Rome* (Paris 1969) 133–40. The classic account is of course that of Polybius 6.12.7; 19.1–9; 34.3; cf. Walbank (n. 2 above) 677, 698–700, 717 (but see below, n. 26).

[19]Cato's speech *De tribunis militum* (Malcovati, *ORF*², 58–59, frags, 150–51) is commonly dated to this year, but it may well belong to any of the following years, cf. A. E. Astin, *Cato the Censor* (Oxford 1978) 118; M. T. Sblendorio Cugusi, *Marci Porci Catonis Orationum Reliquiae* (Torino 1982) 299–301 (with ample bibliography).

commanded in turn by each of its six tribunes, separately or in pairs. But we may emend (as suggested by Crévier) to *XXIV tribunos*. This is interesting, too, since in this case the equestrians (and the sons of senators who had not yet held offices) would be excluded in 171 from the military tribunate.

Whether a similar provision also applied (in 171 or 170) to the four consular legions we do not know. In 171 there were sent (*missi*) to Greece with P. Licinius as military tribunes, along with two consulars, also *tres inlustres iuvenes* (Livy 42.49.9; *MRR* 1. 417). But *iuvenis* is a flexible term; it may well apply to young senators.[20] In any case these men were in all probability elected in 172, and not selected by Licinius himself.[21] An interesting piece of (circumstantial) evidence seems to support this conclusion. At the battle of Callinicus the right wing of the Romans was led by C. Licinius Crassus (pr. 172), the brother of the consul; the left wing by M. Valerius Laevinus (pr. 182), and the center by Q. Mucius (cos. 174). Livy (42.58.12) provides none of them with a title, but at 42.49.9 he listed Q. Mucius among the tribunes of the soldiers. Consequently in *MRR* 1. 418–19 C. Licinius Crassus and M. Valerius Laevinus are classified (and rightly so) as legates. If the appointments of the tribunes had been in the hands of the consul he certainly would have appointed (in 171 for 171) his brother a tribune. But if the tribunes for 171 were elected in 172 C. Licinius was not eligible: he was praetor in this year, and could not stand for another office *in magistratu*. When P. Licinius secured the *provincia* Macedonia, he appointed his brother as a legate. Here we see plainly how the older system of securing the senior commanders from among the military tribunes was com-

---

[20] Of the *tres iuvenes*, P. (Cornelius) Lentulus was praetor in 165 (and suffect consul in 162), and hence very likely a *quaestorius* by 172; on the other hand the two Manlii Acidini were probably not yet senators. They were the sons respectively of L. Manlius (perhaps the consul of 179) and of M. Manlius (unknown; and his praenomen is suspect since the name Marcus was forbidden among the patrician Manlii). The son of Lucius may have been quaestor in 168. Cf. *MRR* 1. 419, 428.

[21] H. H. Scullard, *Roman Politics 220–150 B.C.*[2] (Oxford 1973) 197, uses "Licinius' staff appointments" for a reconstruction of factional politics. But a careful prosopographer will have to admit that we do not know whether these men were appointed by Licinius or elected (as seems likely) by the *comitia* and assigned to Licinius' army by lot. Such cavalier procedure unfortunately gives bad odor to prosopography. This has been well seen by R. Develin, *The Practice of Politics at Rome 366–167 B.C.* (Collection Latomus 188, Bruxelles 1985) 295–96, who rightly stresses Livy's *cum eo missi;* this phrase would have to be hard pressed to yield an unequivocal sense of "appointed by Licinius."

plemented by the appointment of former senior magistrates as legates. The old system was to be formally revived in 168 (see below), but the future belonged to the flexible arrangement of legateships.

At the beginning of Livy's account of the consular year 170 there is a large gap in the manuscripts, and we have no direct information concerning the military tribunate and the levies,[22] but an odd piece of evidence throws light on the arrangements in this year. Namely C. Cassius Longinus, the consul of the preceding year, whose *sors* had been Italy, served in 170 as a military tribune in Macedonia under the consul A. Hostilius (Livy 43.5.1–9). He could not have been elected to that post *in magistratu*, in 171 (and moreover it appears that he did not return to Rome, but went directly from his *provincia* to Macedonia); hence he was appointed, and appointed under his own law. Now we know that the *lex Licinia Cassia* was in force (in 170) with respect to the appointments for 170.[23] Was it also operative with regard to the appointments for 169?

Now under 169 Livy reports (43.12.6–7): "quattuor praeterea legiones scribi iussae, quae, si quo opus esset educerentur. tribunos iis, non permissum, ut consules facerent: populus creavit." These elections took place, it would appear, in 169 for 169. Suolahti interprets this provision as a kind of compensation for the *lex Licinia Cassia*· the people were now to elect not only twenty–four tribunes for the first four legions but also the additional twenty–four tribunes (who normally were appointed by the consuls) needed for the (four) extra legions.[24] On the other hand Lange believed that the provision mentioned by Livy applied only to the four consular legions, and that it restored the regulations that obtained before 171.[25] We should, however, consider the

---

[22] A. Afzelius, *Die römische Kriegsmacht während der Auseinandersetzung mit den hellenistischen Grossmächten* (Aarhus 1944) 45, suggests that after the great levies of 171 when eight legions were conscripted (four consular and four *urbanae*, Livy 42.31.2; 35.4) no new legions were formed in 170.

[23] But with his appointments Hostilius was singularly unlucky; the war was not going well, and the senatorial envoys brought back to Rome distressing news: "exercitum consulis infrequentem commeatibus vulgo datis per ambitionem esse; culpam eius rei consulem in tribunos militum, contra illos in consulem conferre" (Livy 43.11.9–10).

[24] Suolahti (n. 18 above) 40. So also Madvig (n. 3 above) 542–43, n. 5. Willems (n. 4 above) 2. 634, n. 2, rightly refers this passage to the urban legions, but does not express any opinion as to the mode of selection of the tribunes for the consular legions.

[25] L. Lange, *Römische Alterthümer* 2³ (Berlin 1879) 288, 655. Lange also believed that this provision may have formed part of the *lex Rutilia de tribunis militum* (Fest. 316 L.). A tribune of the plebs named P. Rutilius is indeed conveniently available in 169

whole narrative of Livy about the military preparations in 169, and refrain from interpreting isolated passages. Livy's *praeterea* refers to what he had said in the immediately preceding passages, at 43.12.1–5. We learn that the senate decided *in utramque provinciam* (i.e., Macedonia and Italia), *quod res desideraret supplementi decerni*. The key word here is *supplementi*. Then follows the enumeration of the *supplementa* voted for the Macedonian war and the *provincia Italia*. It is important to realize that no new consular legions were to be conscripted. The four new legions were the *legiones urbanae* (the old *urbanae* of 171 will by now have been dismissed), two of which, however, the consul Cn. Servilius Caepio took with him to Gaul.[26] Now it is evident that the popular election of military tribunes did in fact apply in 169 to the four new legions; whether it also applied to the four consular legions that stood in the field, in Macedonia and in Gaul, remains to be seen. The selection of the tribunes for these legions (and their *supplementa*, cf. Livy 44.1.1–2) may still have been governed by the *lex Licinia Cassia* of 171, and may have continued to be in the hands of the consuls. If this was the case, we would have in 169 a reversal of the normal procedure, a

---

(*MRR* 1. 425). The idea of Lange was accorded a cautious hearing by G. Rotondi, *Leges publicae populi Romani* (Milano 1912) 478–79, and C. Nicolet, "Armée" (n. 18 above) 135, has tentatively endorsed it: "c'est peut-être de 169 . . . que date la *lex Rutilia* qui réglait définitivement le partage des compétences entre les consuls et le peuple." But it is enough to read carefully the text of Livy (and beyond the text of Livy we have nothing) to see that in 169 nothing was decided *définitivement*. Quite on the contrary we have in 169 an exceptional (and short-lived) situation of the people electing the tribunes of the urban legions, who before and after 169 were always appointed by the consuls and praetors (see below in the text). Nicolet duly notes this, but strangely enough does not see any incongruity between this fact and his general statement. Broughton (*MRR* 1. 425) and G. Niccolini, *I fasti dei tribuni della plebe* (Milano 1934) 125–27, had not allowed themselves to be swayed by Lange and his dubious idea; they do not assign to P. Rutilius tr. pl. in 169 any law concerning the military tribunes. Niccolini (405–6) rightly assumes that the law mentioned by Festus must be later than 168, and attributes it to an unknown tribune of the plebs Rutilius Rufus; but the best candidate for the *lator* of this law is still P. Rutilius Rufus, cos. 105 (cf. *MRR* 1. 555).

[26] Liv. 43.15.3–5. I take it that the two old consular legions (of 171) in Gaul were not dismissed (as postulated by Afzelius [n. 22 above] 45–46) for in this case the vote of *supplementum* for the consul whose lot was Italy (= Gaul) would have been superfluous. The basic study on the *legiones urbanae* remains T. Steinwender, "Die legiones urbanae," *Philologus* 39 (1888) 527–40. Walbank, (n. 2 above) 1. 677, 699, is unfortunately confused and inaccurate: he erroneously describes as *legiones urbanae* the four consular legions (*quattuor primae*).

situation brought about by a combination of military exigency and popular pressure. Mommsen, disliking disorder, tried to find a way out of this irregular situation. In a dogmatic footnote[27] he asserted that the *quattuor primae* were in each year always the newly formed legions. The proof? The very passage of Livy we are discussing! Developing this *circulus vitiosus* he further argued that in republican times the legions received new numbers every year, and that the new legions always received the first numbers. Unfortunately, and not uncharacteristically, Mommsen disregarded the splendid study of F. Gessler[28] who demonstrated, clearly and plainly, that although the numbers changed each year indeed, the first four numbers were always reserved for the legions commanded by the consuls. No praetor or promagistrate is on (reliable) record commanding a legion numbered 1, 2, 3 or 4. Until a consular legion was dismissed (or taken over by a promagistrate), it remained among the *quattuor primae,* with its number oscillating between 1 and 4. The fact remains: in 169 the tribunes of the four reserve legions were (exceptionally) elected by the people: Roman constitutional history cannot always be made clean and tidy.

A further change occurred in the consular year 168, when "senatus decrevit ut in octo legiones parem numerum tribunorum consules et populus crearent; creari autem neminem eo anno placere, nisi qui honorem gessisset. tum ex omnibus tribunis militum uti L. Aemilius in duas legiones in Macedoniam, quos eorum velit, eligat" (Livy 44.21.2–3).

The *octo legiones* will be (Livy 44.21.5–11): a) the four consular legions, two in Macedonia (continuing from the previous year or, more exactly, from the very beginning of the war in 171, now again replenished with the *supplementa*), and two in Italy (probably newly formed, as can be deduced from Livy's account at 45.12.10–12, and particularly from the phrase, referring to the consul C. Licinius Crassus, "cum legionibus ad conveniendum ⟨diem⟩ edixit"); b) the two legions that the praetor L. Anicius Gallus *portare in Macedoniam est iussus* (no doubt the two *urbanae* of 169); c) two legions remain to be accounted for. Now Cn. Servilius Caepio, consul of 169, continued in 168 in command in Gaul (cf. Livy 44.21.7: "Cn. Servilio Galliam obtinenti provinciam"; *MRR* 1. 428), and he obviously needed a military force. Afzelius had him

---

[27]*Staatsrecht* 2³. 578, n. 2.

[28]F. Gessler, *De legionum Romanarum apud Livium numeris* (Diss. Berlin 1866) passim, esp. 7–11, 16–17.

dismiss the consular legions (of 171) already in 169, and he also thinks that the two *urbanae* that Caepio took with him to Gaul in 169 were now taken over by the consul C. Licinius Crassus[29] (and upgraded to the rank of consular legions). But that would leave Servilius Caepio without any legions. I am inclined to allow Caepio to keep (as garrison legions) either the two former *urbanae* or the two old consular legions (which now would have lost their numbers among the *quattuor primae*). But it is very likely that the legions of Caepio did not count toward the *octo;* in this case we would have to postulate (as Afzelius does) the levy of the two new *urbanae*.

For these eight legions the people and the consuls were to select an equal number of military tribunes (i.e., twenty–four and twenty–four). This may (but need not) mean that in the previous year (169) this was not the case. Now we have seen that in 169 (for 169) the tribunes of the *legiones urbanae* were elected by the people; should it follow that also the tribunes destined for the consular legions were in 169 (for 168) elected by the people as well? On the surface of it, it should, but there is a fatal obstacle to this reconstruction: the regulation "creari autem neminem eo anno placere, nisi qui honorem gessisset." This rule was enacted by the senate in 168 with Aemilius Paullus presenting the *relatio* (Livy 44.31.1). This is the crucial point for it shows that at that time, at the beginning of the consular year 168, the tribunes of the soldiers had not yet been elected (or appointed). This means that no elections of the tribunes (for the consular legions) took place in 169 (for 168). The *lex Licinia Cassia* was still in force.

All pieces of the puzzle now fall into place. In 171 the *lex Licinia Cassia* decided that *eo anno,* i.e., in 171 for 170 (and not 171 for 171) the popular election of the military tribunes would not take place; consequently we should assume that the tribunes of the first four legions were appointed in 170 (for 170) by the consuls. If the Licinian and Cassian law had applied specifically only to the elections in 171 (for 170) it would have automatically lapsed in 170. But it appears to have been valid still in 169; hence we have to assume that either its validity was extended year by year by special legislative action or that it suspended the popular election of military tribunes (of the first four legions) for the whole

---

[29] Afzelius (n. 22 above) 46. Nicolet, "Armée" (n. 18 above) 135, speaks of "huit nouvelles légions," but in 168 the Romans conscripted either two (so Afzelius) or at best four new legions.

duration of the Macedonian war. But in 169 a compromise *sui generis* was struck with the people electing the tribunes for the reserve legions, less crucial for the conduct of the war. This was accomplished, no doubt, by a special law or plebiscite (clearly hinted at by Livy's *non permissum, ut consules facerent,* 43.12.6–7). And finally we arrive at the innovation of 168. *Senatus decrevit* says Livy, but again legislative action must have followed: a *lex* was necessary to change the rules concerning the eligibility to an office. Livy, *more suo,* adducing procedural details not for their own sake but solely as an embellishment of his narrative, recorded the preliminary decree of the senate, but omitted to mention the vote of the people.[30]

The tribunes of the *quattuor primae* were normally (i.e., before 171 and after the Macedonian war) elected in advance, in the preceding consular year, and were assigned by lot to the individual legions; and the legions themselves were assigned also by lot to the consuls. In other words under normal circumstances the consuls had no say in the selection and distribution of their tribunes; if the new legions were to be formed, the tribunes assisted at their levy; if the consul was to take over the legions from his predecessor, the old tribunes would step down and the new would take their place.[31]

Now in 168 a remarkable procedure was devised. It consisted of several stages: a) the popular election of twenty–four tribunes and the appointment by the consuls of the further twenty–four tribunes; b) the selection (in place of the customary allotment) by Aemilius Paullus of twelve tribunes for the two Macedonian legions out of the whole pool

---

[30] Willems (n. 4 above) 2. 634, n. 3, points out that "le choix accordé au consul L. Aemilius est une dérogation à la loi en vertu de laquelle le peuple élit les tribuns militaires des légions consulaires," and hence could be enacted only by a *lex*. On the other hand he believes that the stipulation "creari . . . neminem . . . placere nisi qui honorem gessisset" was only a recommendation of the senate which the people need not have followed. This is hardly convincing; we here deal with a set of regulations and not with exhortations, and consequently also this part of the senatorial decree will have been incorporated as a clause in the *lex de tribunis*. Rotondi (n. 25 above) 282, does not here see, oddly enough, any need for a law, and P. Meloni, *Perseo e la fine della monarchia macedone* (Cagliari 1953) 322, does not see any problem at all.

[31] Livy 44.1.1–2 provides a neat illustration of this principle. In 169 the consul Q. Marcius Philippus took over the legions in Macedonia from his predecessor, A. Hostilius, and brought with him only a *supplementum,* and yet "M. Popilius consularis et alii pari nobilitate adulescentes tribuni militum in Macedonicas legiones consulem secuti sunt." Cf. Mommsen, *Staatsrecht* 2³. 577, n. 7.

(as it appears) of forty–eight elected and appointed tribunes (but Livy may here be inaccurate, and Aemilius may well have selected his tribunes only out of the elective ones); c) distribution of the remaining tribunes among the remaining six legions, presumably by lot, as Livy stressed so particularly the privilege of personal selection accorded Aemilius Paullus.

All this (and all the preceding) information comes from the annalistic part of Livy's *History,* and the reliability of this tradition has often been called into doubt. M. Gelzer, in a classic article, came to the conclusion that whenever Livy's information on troop levies can be checked against older sources (i.e., mostly Polybius) it appears inaccurate and wanting. This is too harsh an opinion. Afzelius and Brunt have convincingly defended the general credibility and coherence of Livian accounts dealing with the levies. Brunt points out that the annalists adduced primarily the senatorial decrees, but were not particularly concerned (as Polybius was) with the actual strength of the armies in the field. And between the senatorial military wishes embodied in the *senatus consulta* and their implementation there was often a substantial gap.[32] This does not mean that Livy's account is without blemish. And so he piles up constitutional details concerning the changes in the election and appointment of military tribunes, but the picture is blurred. In strict procedure he is not interested; its various stages he as often mentions as omits. He may be forced to make sense, but the reconstruction of details must remain hypothetical. Still no student of prosopography can disregard legal arrangements, however tentatively reconstructed, and fish solely for names: the prosopographical catch swam in a constitutional pond.

In particular the provision "creari . . . neminem eo anno placere, nisi qui honorem gessisset" is of paramount importance for the reconstruction and interpretation of the list of the military tribunes in 168. In the first part of the second century we find among the military tribunes, especially in the years of decisive campaigns, a large number of ex–praetors and ex–consuls. In 168, for the first and last time in Roman

---

[32] See H. Nissen, *Kritische Untersuchungen über die Quellen der vierten und fünften Dekade des Livius* (Berlin 1863) 261–63; M. Gelzer, "Die Glaubwürdigkeit der bei Livius überlieferten Senatsbeschlüsse über römische Truppenaufgebote," *Hermes* 70 (1935) 269–300 = *Kleine Schriften* 3 (Wiesbaden 1964) 220–55, esp. 300 = 255; Afzelius (n. 22 above) passim; P. A. Brunt, *Italian Manpower 225 B.C.–A.D. 14* (Oxford 1971) 416–26, 645–60.

history, this trend found its formal expression in the decree of the senate (and the law). It would certainly be incorrect, both from the social and the military point of view, to describe those high personages as "junior officers." But the term *honos* is ambiguous. Should the clause *nisi qui honorem gessisset* mean that eligible for the election or appointment to the military tribunate were only the men who had administered at least the quaestorship? Some scholars endorse this view,[33] others consider the possibility that the clause could have also referred to a previous tenure of the (elective) military tribunate.[34] Now it is true that the elective *tribuni militum* were regarded as magistrates, and that every elective office could be described as *honos*.[35] On the other hand, however, Cicero, *Verr.* 1.11, speaks of the quaestorship as the *primus gradus honoris*. Livy does not use the term *honos* with respect to the military tribunes, and at 25.6.8 he even contrasts the holding of the military tribunate with *honores petere et gerere*. Certainty cannot be achieved, but it appears likely that in 168 we should postulate for the military tribunes at least the quaestorship, and understand the clause *nisi qui honorem gessisset* in the sense of *qui eos magistratus gessissent, unde in senatum legi deberent* (Livy 22.49.17). With this in mind let us turn to *MRR*.

In 168 Broughton lists one possible and six certain tribunes of the soldiers (1. 429). Let us now look more closely at those seven names:

1) A consular, C. Cassius (Longinus), cos. 171. He served in Illyria under the praetor L. Anicius. Livy 44.31.15 terms him explicitly *tribunus militum:* "in custodiam C. Cassio tribuno militum traditus (sc. Gentius)."[36]

2) Another consular, L. Postumius Albinus, cos. 173. Livy does not actually describe him as a military tribune, and this, no doubt, should have been noted in *MRR*. At the battle of Pydna he led the second legion against the *media acies* of the Macedonians (44.41.2): "secundam legionem L. Albinus consularis ducere . . . iussus." At

---

[33] Cf. W. Weissenborn and H. J. Müller, *Titi Livi Ab Urbe Condita Libri* 10² (Berlin 1880) 103 ad loc.; P. Fraccaro, "Studi sull'età dei Gracchi, I: Oratori ed orazioni dell'età dei Gracchi," *Studi storici per l'antichità classica* 5 (1912) 353, n. 2.

[34] Cf. A. E. Astin, *The Lex Annalis Before Sulla* (Collection Latomus 32, Bruxelles 1958) 35, n. 3. Surprisingly enough, Sumner (n. 7 above) 45, takes Astin's cautious remark as a statement of fact.

[35] Mommsen, *Staatsrecht* 1³. 9–10; 2³. 578, n. 1; J. Hellegouarc'h, *Le vocabulaire latin des relations et des partis politiques sous la république* (Paris 1963) 383–87, esp. 385.

[36] For his identification, cf. F. Münzer, "Cassius 55," *RE* 3 (1899) 1726.

45.27.4 he is called L. Postumius, and leads a detachment "ad Aeniorum . . . urbem diripiendam." He may have been a *legatus;*[37] but the very provision for the election of military tribunes from the ranks of former magistrates is a powerful argument for siding with Broughton and assigning to Postumius the military tribunate.[38] Still, a query would be in place.

3) A *praetorius,* C. Sulpicius Galus, pr. 169. He is credited with predicting (or explaining), on the eve of Pydna, a lunar eclipse. Cicero (*Rep.* 1.23) and Valerius Maximus (8.11.1) call him *legatus,* whereas Livy (44.37.5) and Pliny (*NH* 2.53) term him *tribunus militum* (other sources adduced in *MRR* do not mention his title). It is not unlikely that Cicero merely reproduces the usage of his epoch when a person of Sulpicius' standing would hardly have served as a tribune of the soldiers, and hence there is a sound reason to follow Livy and Pliny, who may have better preserved genuine tradition, especially as Livy describes Sulpicius very precisely as "tribunus militum secundae legionis, qui praetor superiore anno fuerat."

Madvig adduces other examples when one and the same man is termed in the sources both a *legatus* and a *tribunus militum;* with respect to Sulpicius Galus he believes that Livy confused him with Ser. Sulpicius Galba: the former will be *legatus,* the latter *tribunus militum.*[39] If any confusion occurred, it did rather the other way round; see below on Ser. Galba. Münzer suggests that Sulpicius Galus "konnte als Legionstribun durch einen besonderen Auftrag des Feldherrn . . . zum Legaten erhoben werden."[40] *Erhoben* is a wrong word. Münzer fails to take into account that throughout the first part of the second century the military tribunate ranked often as high as the position of a *legatus,* and in 168 the posts of military tribunes, filled with eminent men, clearly took precedence over the posts of legates. Sulpicius Galus was urban praetor in 169; this means that he could not stand in that year for the tribunate of the soldiers of 168. Consequently he was either an appointed tribune or, if elective, the elections had to take place (as postulated above) in 168 for 168.

---

[37] F. Münzer, *Römische Adelsparteien und Adelsfamilien* (Stuttgart 1920) 215, calls him *Consularlegat.*

[38] Cf. P. Meloni (n. 30 above) 323, n. 2. He regards the military tribunate of Postumius very probable, but does not explain why he so thinks.

[39] Madvig (n. 3 above) 545, n. 2.

[40] F. Münzer, "Sulpicius 66," *RE* 4A (1931) 809.

4) An *aedilicius*, P. Cornelius Scipio Nasica, aed. cur. 169. He played an important role in the battle of Pydna commanding five thousand of *delecti milites* with whom he carried out the famous flanking march (Livy 44.35.14; Plut. *Aem.* 15–17; cf. above, part I, on Q. Fabius Maximus Aemilianus). He spoke boldly at the council before the battle (Livy 44.36.9–14, where Livy calls him *clarus adulescens;* cf. 44.38.1, *egregius adulescens*). After the victory he was sent to Amphipolis "cum modica peditum equitumque manu . . . ut . . . ad omnes conatus regi impedimento esset" (Livy 44.46.1–2; cf. Plut. *Aem.* 26.7). *MRR* 1. 434 lists him as a tribune of the soldiers also under 167 rightly assuming that all the officers continued until their commanders returned to Rome. In that year Nasica was sent (again with Q. Fabius Maximus Aemilianus) "ad depopulandos Illyrios" (Livy 45.33.8, and 34.8). Ample evidence, but no source gives Nasica's title (which again ought to have been noted). His case is parallel to that of A. Postumius Albinus, and the same argument applies: he may have been a legate, but it is preferable to classify him (with a query) as a military tribune. Let us also observe that Nasica was curule aedile in 169 (Livy 44.18.8; *MRR* 1. 424); this again means that he could not stand for the elective tribunate of the soldiers in 169 for 168. Hence he was either appointed to that office or, as we have argued above, the elections of military tribunes for 168 took place at the beginning of the consular year 168.

So far no problem with the criterion of the eligibility to the tribunate as recorded by Livy. With respect to the three remaining men troubles abound and questions intrude.

5) C. Postumius. Unknown and unidentifiable. Livy 45.6.9 terms him explicitly *tribunus militum*. He served in the fleet, under the praetor Cn. Octavius. If he served in one of the legions we would have to regard him a quaestorius or at least postulate for him an earlier (elective) military tribunate; in the Index of Careers (*MRR* 2. 607) Broughton does not suggest for him any previous office, and rightly so, for the regulation requiring previous magistracy need not have applied (and on a strict interpretation of Livy's language did not apply) to the tribunes serving in the fleet.

6) Ser. Sulpicius Galba is introduced by Livy only in 167 when he opposed the granting of a triumph to Aemilius Paullus. Livy (45.35.8) describes him as "qui tribunus militum secundae legionis in Macedonia fuerat, privatim imperatori inimicus" (so also Plut. *Aem.* 30.5 who calls him *chiliarchos,* but does not specify the legion). Neither Livy nor Plutarch explain why Galba was the enemy of Aemilius Paullus, but Mün-

zer does: Ser. Sulpicius Galba who probably ("wahrscheinlich") was
the father of our Galba may have been one of the candidates for the
consulship of 182 defeated by Aemilius Paullus, and perhaps ("vielleicht") he bequeathed to his son his (presumed) enmity to Paullus.[41]
Perhaps. But should we accept Münzer's speculation we would perforce be treated to the wondrous spectacle of Aemilius Paullus selecting
the son of an old enemy to one of the twelve posts of military tribunes
he had available in his two legions. No better candidate was at hand? It
is perhaps not unreasonable to assume that the cantankerous Galba
became the *imperator*'s personal enemy only during the campaign: Aemilius Paullus was a harsh taskmaster. But Galba may not have been a
military tribune at all. Münzer dates Galba's birth to ca. 194; he became
praetor in 151. This would make him 26 years old in 168 and 43 years old
in 151, rather late for the praetorship. Astin estimates that he was born
by 192 (and no later than 188), and Sumner regards 191 as the *terminus*.[42]
On any count he was rather too young to have held the quaestorship
prior to 168, and consequently according to the rules that obtained in
168 he may not have been eligible to the military tribunate. And in fact
Livy 45.37.4 intimates (in a speech he puts into the mouth of M. Servilius, cos. 202) that in 167 Galba had not yet held any magistracy:
Galba should not block the triumph of Aemilius Paullus, but let him
rather, if Paullus had done anything wrong, accuse his enemy before the
people "serius paulo, cum primum magistratum ipse cepisset." Madvig
rejects this as "rhetorical embellishment,"[43] and he may well be right.
To reject information contained in a violent and rhetorical speech is
simple and easy; it would only necessitate moving Galba's estimated
birthdate upwards to 197–196, a minor adjustment. A more adventurous
proposal is this: Livy terms both C. Sulpicius Galus and Ser. Sulpicius
Galba *tribunus militum secundae legionis*. In his rhetorical zeal, trying to
show Galba's depth of ingratitude toward his commander, Livy (and his
follower Plutarch) may have erroneously attributed to Galba the position held by his elder *propinquus* (cf. Cic. *de or.* 1.228; Val. Max. 8.1.
abs. 2). If we decide to keep Galba on the roster of the tribunes we face
two choices: we have either to reject Livy's information that he had not
held any prior magistracy or to assume that Galba had previously been

---

[41] F. Münzer, "Sulpicius 57," and "Sulpicius 58," *Ibid*. 759–61.
[42] Astin, *Lex Annalis* (n. 34 above) 35; Sumner (n. 7 above) 44–45.
[43] Madvig (n. 3 above) 545–46, n. 2.

an (elective) military tribune, and that this charge was the lowest magistracy providing eligibility to the tribunate of the soldiers in 168. In this case M. Servilius would have stressed in his speech only the fact that the quaestorship was the first magistracy giving the incumbent a right to accuse his enemy before the people; for that purpose the tribunate of the soldiers did not count as a magistracy. Whatever our choice, the case of Galba again demonstrates the inseparable link between prosopography and the electoral law.

7) L. Cornelius Scipio. This entry is queried. It ought to be removed. The Cornelius Scipio in question is identified by Broughton with the man known from one of the *elogia Scipionum* (*CIL* I².13 = *ILS* 5 = *ILLRP* 314): he was a son of L. Scipio Asiaticus, tribune of the soldiers, quaestor, and died at the age of 33. He was apparently the quaestor L. Cornelius Scipio who toward the end of 167 entertained in Rome king Prusias of Bithynia (*MRR* 1. 433). If so he was tribune of the soldiers in one of the preceding years, but this year cannot have been 168: he had not yet been a magistrate, and in this year only former magistrates were eligible to the tribunate. Even if the clause "nisi qui honorem gessisset" covered former (elective) military tribunes, Scipio still does not qualify as a tribune of the soldiers in 168: this would have to be his second tribunate, and his epitaph does not mention the iteration of that office. He ought to be listed (with a query as to the precise date) under 169.

* * *

The *MRR* is a monument of scholarship. It has elevated and invigorated the study of Roman republican history. It is a living monument. A recent *Supplement* has brought a rich crop of "magisterial revisions."[44] It is with a view to a new harvest that I offer this contribution.

[44] *MRR* 3: *Supplement* (Atlanta 1986). Its apt description as "magisterial revisions" I borrow from the title of the erudite review by E. Champlin, *CP* (1989) 51–59.

30

THE DEATH OF PONTIA

In his chapter *de pudicitia*, immediately after recounting the story of Verginia (whose father chose to be *pudicae interemptor* rather than *corruptae pater*), Valerius Maximus also gives this example of the old *robur animi* (6.1.3):

Nec alio robore animi praeditus fuit Pontius Aufidianus eques Romanus, qui postquam conperit filiae suae uirginitatem a paedagogo proditam Fannio Saturnino, non contentus sceleratum seruum adfecisse supplicio etiam ipsam puellam necauit. ita ne turpes eius nuptias celebraret, acerbas exequias duxit[1]).

This passage has been thoroughly misinterpreted by eminent scholars. F. Münzer has this to say: "Fannius Saturninus, ein freigelassener Pädagog, verführte die Tochter eines römischen Ritters Pontius Aufidianus, worauf dieser beide tötete"[2]). And C. Nicolet avers that the daughter of Pontius Aufidianus was seduced "par son *paedagogus*, Fannius Saturninus", and adds "Noter cependant le nom du précepteur, peut-être un affranchi d'un Fannius"[3]).

---

1) Valerius Max. rec. C. Kempf, Lipsiae 1888, p. 271. The epitome of Iulius Paris (p. 532 Kempf) gives the following text: *Pontius Aufidianus eques Romanus, postquam conperit filiae suae uirginitatem a paedagogo proditam Fannio Saturnino, punito seruo puellam quoque necauit.*

2) RE 6 (1909) 1994, s. v. Fannius 19 (cf. Pontius 19, RE 22 [1953] 36). So also Kempf (cf. his Index, p. 643), and many other earlier scholars (see the edition of A. Torrenius [Leidae 1726]). The idea that it was the *paedagogus* who seduced Pontia, and that he bore the name of Fannius Saturninus, goes back to the famous commentary by Oliverius Arzignanensis Vicentinus. It was first published in Venice in 1487 together with the *recensio* of Valerius by Marcus Antonius Sabellicus (i. e. Marcantonio Coccio, ca 1436–1506), "arte et impensis Joannis Forliviensis, Gregoriique fratrum", and subsequently it was reprinted (and plagiarized) many times (see the list in the *Editio Bipontina* of 1806, reprinted by A. J. Valpy, London 1823, vol. III, pp. 1388–1407, esp. 1392–1393). Oliverius comments (I used the edition Venetiis 1488): "Faunus (sic) Saturninus Pontii pedagogus eius filiam per dolum uiciauerat: Pontius id ubi cognouit et pedagogum et filiam pari poena mulctauit: nam utrunque necauit maluitque acerbum filiae funus prosequi quam turpes eius nuptias celebrare." Explaining *sceleratum seruum* he continues: "Perfidum pedagogum qui filiae uicium intulerat."

3) L'ordre équestre à l'époque républicaine, vol. 2: Prosopographie des chevaliers Romains (Paris 1974) 992, and 993, n. 2. So also recently P. Voci, Storia della patria potestas da Augusto a Diocleziano, Iura 31 (1980 [1983]) 54. I. Kajanto,

As the *paedagogi* were normally slaves, the *paedagogus* Fannius Saturninus stands out as an oddity. Hence Münzer's (and Nicolet's) attempt to see in him a freedman of a Fannius. Thus Pontius Aufidianus would have hired for his daughter a freedmen preceptor, a rather unusual course of action[4]. And as Fannius was a former slave, Valerius Maximus was perhaps justified in calling him (in anger) *sceleratus servus*. But if our *paedagogus* was a freedman, one wonders how he acquired his cognomen Saturninus which does not look at all like his former servile name[5].

The *paedagogus* Fannius Saturninus is a figment. The *virginitas* of Pontia was not *prodita* to the *paedagogus* Fannius Saturninus, but rather to a Fannius Saturninus by an (unnamed) *paedagogus (a paedagogo)*. This restores sense and Latin: *prodere* with a dative regularly means "to betray something to somebody"[6]. That Münzer "quite misread this edifying anecdote" did not escape the sharp eye of D. R. Shackleton Bailey[7]. But much

---

The Latin Cognomina (Helsinki 1965) 213, also lists Fannius Saturninus as a freedman (see also below, n. 5).

4) On the *paedagogi*, see E. Schuppe, Paidagogos, RE 18 (1942) 2380–2385; S. F. Bonner, Education in Ancient Rome (Berkeley 1977) 40–46, and, in greater detail, R. Boulogne, De Plaats van de Paedagogus in de romeinse Cultuur (Diss. Groningen 1951). A good collection of evidence (also inscriptional evidence on the *paedagogi* of the *puellae*) in TLL s. v. For a *paedagogus* of a *sponsa*, see CIL 10.6561 = ILS 199.

5) The data in Kajanto (above, n. 3) 213 show clearly that the cognomen Saturninus was used predominantly by the *ingenui*. H. Solin, Beiträge zur Namengebung der Senatoren, Epigrafia e Ordine Senatorio 1 = Tituli 4 (Roma 1982) 422–423, points out that although the cognomen Saturninus was especially popular in the nomenclature of the *ordo senatorius*, it was also "in allen Volksschichten schon früh eingedrungen". This is correct, but the example Solin chose to adduce is unfortunate: "Val. Max. VI. 1, 3 erwähnt einen Freigelassenen Fannius Saturninus, der irgendwann gegen Ende der republikanischen Zeit lebte". It is important to point out emphatically that Valerius Maximus does not describe the *paedagogus* as a *libertus*: he calls him *servus*.

6) For examples, see OLD s. v., and for the usage in Valerius Maximus, see esp. 6.5.7: *L. Sulla ... cum (Sulpicium Rufum) proscriptum et in uilla latentem a seruo proditum conperisset, manu missum parricidam, ut fides edicti sui constaret, praecipitari protinus saxo Tarpeio cum illo scelere parto pilleo iussit.* Cf. also below, n. 14.

7) Two Studies in Roman Nomenclature (American Classical Studies 3 [1976]) 14–15, 125. So also, correctly (and in passing), Bonner (above, n. 4) 41, and W. V. Harris, The Roman Father's Power of Life and Death, Studies in Roman Law in Memory of A. Arthur Schiller (Leiden 1986) 87. But, as so often, light had been seen a long time ago: in the German translation of Valerius Maximus by Friedrich Hoffmann (Stuttgart 1829) we read (p. 366): "(Pontius Aufidianus) erfuhr, daß der Erzieher seiner Tochter ihre Unschuld an Fannius Saturninus verkauft hatte". Also this interpretation goes back to the early days of classical scho-

more can be said; Valerius Maximus' story opens up intriguing legal and prosopographical avenues.

It might appear that we here have an old tale, the lovers' union facilitated by a slave, a tale worthy of Plautus' pen, with a Caecilian *durus pater*. But this is not so: in comedy crafty slaves abet and facilitate love affairs of their young and foolish masters with *meretrices* or putative *meretrices*; they do not conspire *ad virginitatem prodendam*. Virginity was a serious matter, a matter of passion, law and religion, and this spells tragedy and unreason. The epithet *sceleratus servus* well conveys this murky atmosphere. Lapsed Vestals were buried alive in *campus sceleratus*; though often employed as a general term of abuse, *sceleratus* retained its primary association with the violation of religious norms, with taboo and pollution[8]).

The injured father had the *sceleratus servus* executed. This is not surprising: the *paedagogi* were the *custodes* of their young

---

larship. In 1513 there appeared in Paris the famous edition of Valerius Maximus "cum duplici commentario: historico videlicet ac literato Oliverii Arzignanensis et familiari admodum ac succincto Iodoci Badii Ascensii. Venumdatur ab Ascensio et Ioanne Paruo." The commentary of Ascensius (i. e. Iodocus Badius, 1462–1535) reads as follows (p. 196): "(Pontius Aufidianus) postquam comperit virginitatem filiae suae proditam i. e. prostitutam, et iniquo pretio venditam Faunio Saturnio (sic) a paedagogo, i. e. eius ductore in ludum literarum (Oliverius intelligit Faunium Saturnium esse paedagogum, ut dicat proditam i. e. vulgatam. ego quia separat interponendo proditam credam Saturnium esse divitis et civis Romani qui eius pudicitiam a paedagogo emerat nomen) non contentus affecisse supplicio servum sceleratum, s(cilicet) paedagogum illum: necavit etiam ipsam puellam: et ita duxit acerbas exequias, ne celebraret turpes nuptias eius, s(cilicet) cum corruptore: quia potuisset Saturnium cogere, quam vitiarat ducere." The interpretation of Ascensius was almost totally forgotten. It is in 1823 that we hear the last of it, and we get a glimpse peculiar and distorted. In A. J. Valpy's London edition (1823) of Valerius Maximus (i. e. the edition of J. Kapp with the notae in usum Delphini and notae variorum) we have (vol. II, p. 1212) a note attributed to Badius (i. e. Ascensius): "Oliverius intelligit Fannium Saturninum fuisse paedagogum". This note was lifted from some earlier commented edition; it recurs verbatim in Valerius Maximus cum selectis Variorum observationibus et nova recensione A. Thysii (Lugduni Batavorum. Ex Officina Hackiana anno 1670), p. 513. The opinion of Oliverius is thus quoted through the intermediary of Ascensius; there is no word of Ascensius' own (and correct) explanation. In another seventeenth century commentary of Valerius, "in usum studiosae iuventutis," by Johannes Minellius [Jan Minell, 1625–1683] (Roterodami 1662), the comments are indiscriminately and confusingly lifted from Oliverius and Badius without either of them ever being mentioned (Minell, pp. 314–315, did not even realize that the interpretations of Oliverius and Badius are mutually exclusive).

8) Cf. A. Ernout and A. Meillet, Dictionnaire Étymologique de la Langue Latine[3] (Paris 1951) s. v. *scelus*. This also clearly follows from the examples cited by OLD and Forcellini.

charges, and probity was required of them[9]). Horace (Sat. 1.6.81–84) describes his father as *incorruptissimus custos*: fearing that a *paedagogus* might easily be bribed, he personally conducted his son to and from school, and so *pudicum, qui primus virtutis honos, servavit ab omni non solum facto, verum opprobrio quoque turpi.*

Executions of slaves were an affair common enough, for one could hire for that purpose (at least in Puteoli, but presumably also in other Italian towns) the services of a private entrepreneur[10]). The expression *adfecisse supplicio* shows indeed that Pontius did not kill the *paedagogus* in a fit of rage, but rather handed him over for execution to his own servants or to a professional *manceps*, as he is called in the *lex Libitinaria* from Puteoli. For the phrasing, Cic. Verr. II.3.119 provides a good parallel, for it also refers to a slave: *cum audierit* (sc. *dominus*) *eas res, quibus fundi fructus et cultura continetur, amotas et venditas, summo supplicio vilicum adficiat,* but most telling is a further example from Valerius Maximus, 8.4.1: an innocent slave admitted under torture to having killed a slave belonging to another owner; delivered (*deditus*) to the latter *supplicio adfectus est*[11]).

On the other hand Pontius *puellam necavit*. The embodiment of the *prisca severitas*, the father's *ius vitae necisque* figured prominently in Roman national mythology. That the father had the right to put to death his son or daughter no Roman ever doubted; what has been disputed, then and today, is how serious the offence had to be to justify the execution, and whether the father could act entirely on his own or only after consulting his *propinqui* and *amici*. It would appear that the *pater familias* or the husband could without any formal proceedings kill a son, a daughter or a wife solely if they were apprehended committing a grave crime, including adultery or *stuprum*. But if the transgression was not manifest the father had to institute an inquiry and render a formal verdict (and he was directed by custom though not by law to act with the cooperation of a *consilium* or *iudicium domesticum*)[12]). One thing,

---

9) Suetonius (Aug. 67.2) reports that Augustus executed by drowning in a river the *paedagogus* and the *ministri* of Gaius Caesar who profiting from Gaius' illness and death committed acts of arrogance and greed in his province.

10) Cf. the *lex Libitinaria*, A.E. 1971, 88, col. II, lines 8–10.

11) For further examples from Valerius Maximus, see E. Otón Sobrino, Léxico de Valerio Máximo 1 (Madrid 1977) 60–61, s. v. *adficio*.

12) Two classical and contradictory studies of the problem are E. Volterra, Il pretese tribunale domestico in diritto romano, RISG 2 (1948) 103–153 (the father was not legally obliged to convene a domestic court), and W. Kunkel, Das Kon

however, is certain: if the father had killed his son surreptitiously, he could be prosecuted for murder[13]).

The verb *conperit* indicates that Pontius learnt of the affair in an indirect way[14]), and hence we have to postulate an investigation, a verdict and a formal execution, of the slave *paedagogus* by crucifixion[15]), and of Pontia by strangulation[16]).

However it might have happened, and whatever the legal ground, the unfortunate Pontia was dead. And thus, Valerius Maximus concludes, Pontius Aufidianus *ne turpes eius nuptias celebraret, acerbas exequias duxit*. The mention of *nuptiae* evokes surprise; any future wedding of Pontia would indeed be a shameful affair, but the case gains poignancy and the crushing weight of an *exemplum* if Fannius Saturninus was Pontia's fiancé. If this was so, the father's *robur animi* glows with even more commendable severity, and the symbolic association of *nuptiae* and *funera* becomes stark reality. For technically Pontia had committed a *stuprum*: that her lover was also her *sponsus* was not an attenuating circumstance[17]).

---

silium im Hausgericht, ZSS 83 (1966) 219–251 = Kleine Schriften (Weimar 1974) 117–149 (the father could put a son or a daughter to death only *ex consilii sententia*). The view of Kunkel is too rigid: see now the judicious study by Harris (above, n. 7) 81–95.

13) See Oros. 5.16.8 (cf. Val. Max. 6.1.5; Ps.-Quint. Decl. Mai. 3.17, and see Harris [above, n. 7] 84–85); Dig. 48.9.5.

14) In Valerius Maximus *comperio* very often denotes a result of an inquiry or investigation (he uses only the forms *comperit* and *comperisset*, cf. Sobrino, Léxico [(above, n. 11] s. v.). This sense is common (cf. OLD s. v.); Cic. Mil. 73 offers a good parallel: *eum (sc. Clodium), quem cum sorore germana nefarium stuprum fecisse L. Lucullus iuratus se quaestionibus habitis dixit comperisse*. *Deprehendo* appears in the *Digest* (48.5 passim, esp. 24) as a technical term if the lovers were caught in the act. This usage goes back to Cato the Elder (frg. 221 Malcovati, ORF²), and it was also the usage of Valerius (Sobrino, Léxico 1.522); see esp. 6.1.13 (adduced below, n. 18); 8.1.12.

15) A normal form of execution for slaves, see T. Mommsen, Römisches Strafrecht (Leipzig 1899) 919–920; and see now also the *lex Libitinaria* from Puteoli, loc. cit. (above, n. 10).

16) *Neco* was a general term for execution, but it was particularly often employed for the killing without the shedding of blood, cf. J. N. Adams, Two Latin Words for 'Kill', Glotta 51 (1973) 280–290. The usage of Valerius Maximus conforms to this rule (cf. Sobrino, Léxico [above, n. 11] 3 [1984] 1335). For *necare* in the sense of *strangulare* see especially 5.4.7; 6.3.8 (with Liv. Per. 48). This was the normal mode of execution of women.

17) See Mommsen, Strafrecht (above, n. 15) 695: "Die Geschlechtsgemeinschaft zwischen Brautleuten scheint stets als Stuprum behandelt worden zu sein". The case of Pontia is a welcome and unpleasant illustration of this principle (Mommsen himself adduces no examples).

But who was her lover, and what has become of him? If
Fannius Saturninus and Pontia had been surprised together by the
vigilant father, Saturninus would have hardly escaped unscathed –
and Valerius Maximus would have hardly omitted to describe his
punishment[18]).

The identity of Fannius Saturninus eludes us. No other Fannius with the surname Saturninus is on record, but we know from
Cicero (Att. 5.1.2, May 50) an Annius Saturninus. Whether we
have to identify the two Saturnini, and if so, whether we have to
correct the text of Valerius Maximus or that of Cicero, must
remain *sub iudice*. However, as Shackleton Bailey notes, *Fannio* in
Valerius Maximus has the support of the epitome of Iulius Paris[19]).

The would-be tie between the Pontii and Fannii (provided
that this was the nomen gentile of Saturninus) was thus severed,
but there may have existed some distant affinity between the two
families, with the Titinii serving as the connecting link.

Q. Titinius was a juror in the trial of Verres (Cic. Verr.
II.1.128); his son appears in a letter of Cicero (Att. 9.19.2) as
Pontius Titinianus – he was thus adopted by a Pontius[20]). Now in
the *Verrines* (II.1.128,130) Cicero introduces also a *frater ger-
manus* of Q. Titinius, an *eques* Cn. Fannius (but see on his name
below). This brings to mind the notorious marriage of Fannia and
C. Titinius of Minturnae (Val. Max. 8.2.3, cf. 1.5.5, Plut. Mar.
38.3–9). Münzer[21]) in fact thought that Cn. Fannius may have
been an illegitimate son of Fannia, but Cicero (as Shackleton

---

18) Cf. the delightful list at 6.1.13: *Sempronius Musca C. Gellium deprehensum in adulterio flagellis cecidit, C. Memmius L. Octauium similiter deprehensum
pernis contudit, Carbo Attienus a Vibieno, item Pontius a P. Cerennio deprehensi
castrati sunt. Cn. etiam Furium Brocchum qui deprehenderat familiae stuprandum
obiecit.*

19) Textual Notes on Lesser Roman Historians, HSCP 85 (1981) 164; cf.
Nomenclature (above, n. 7) 14. In his Cicero's Letters to Atticus 3 (Cambridge
1968) 189, Shackleton Bailey opines that Annius Saturninus may have been a con-
nection or client of Annius Milo (the letter concerns the sale of Milo's property).
On the other hand Cicero wrote this letter in Minturnae, the home of the Fannii.
Hence perhaps the remark in Textual Notes 164: "But more likely *Fannio* in Cic.
Att. 5.1.2" [i. e. more likely than *Annio* in Val. Max.].

20) Cf. F. Münzer, RE 6A (1937) 1549 s. v. Titinius 17; 22 (1953) 38 s.v.
Pontius 22; T. P. Wiseman, New Men in the Roman Senate 139 B.C.–14 A.D.
(Oxford 1971) 266; Shackleton Bailey, Nomenclature (above, n. 7) 125.

21) RE 6 (1909) s. v. Fannius 11; 6A (1937) 1549 s. v. Titinius 17. F. Càssola
in his excellent study I Fanni in età repubblicana, Vichiana N.S. 13 (1983 [= Miscellanea di studi in memoria di Francesco Arnaldo]) refers to this Fannius only in
passing (p. 99) and has no mention of Fannius Saturninus.

Bailey reminds us)[22]), would hardly have referred to sons of different fathers as *fratres germani*. C. Nicolet proposed an elegant solution: Cn. Fannius (originally Cn. Titinius) was adopted by a member of his mother's family[23]). Another scenario is possible: perhaps it was Q. Titinius who bore the adoptive name. This would produce an even closer connection between the Pontii and Fannii: a Fannius adopted by a Titinius gave his own son for adoption to a Pontius. All these considerations may be written on prosopographical quicksand: Shackleton Bailey points out that in the *Verrines* the manuscript authority supports the reading *Faenius* and not *Fannius*[24]). The attested connection between the Fannii and Titinii[25]) makes the reading Fannius prosopographically attractive, but is it attractive enough to outweigh paleography?

We are not yet at the end of our file. In the *consilium* of Pompeius Strabo (CIL 6.37045, line 10 = ILLRP 515) there appears *L. Ponti(us) T.f. Qui(rina)*, judging by his position on the list, an *eques*. His tribe, the Quirina, was also the tribe of Amiternum in the land of the Sabines[26]). And from Amiternum we know a P. Aufidius Pontianus (a nice counterpart to our Pontius Aufidianus), an entrepreneur who organized the transport of herds of sheep from the "furthest Umbria" to "the pastures of Metapontum and to market at Heraclea"[27]).

It is in one of the small towns of the Sabines, of Samnium or

---

22) Nomenclature (above, n. 7) 38. Cf. also R. Syme, Senators, Tribes, and Towns, Historia 13 (1964) 116 = Roman Papers 2 (Oxford 1979) 594.

23) L'ordre équestre 2 (above, n. 3) 872–874, 1039–1040; Les noms des chevaliers victimes de Catilina dans le Commentariolum Petitionis, Mélanges d'histoire ancienne offerts à William Seston (Paris 1974) 390–392.

24) Nomenclature (above, n. 7) 38. C. Nicolet, L'ordre équestre 2.874 n. 10), was aware of this *lectio*, but ultimately retained the traditional reading.

25) But we should not forget that the descent of Q. Titinius and Cn. (Fannius) from C. Titinius and Fannia is only conjecture and not fact.

26) Cf. Nicolet, L'ordre équestre 2 (above, n. 3) 993–994. He writes that this Pontius "peut très bien avoir eu des liens avec les Titinii: la tribu Quirina est celle d'Antium, assez proche de Minturnes". But it is not certain at all that the Quirina was the tribe of Antium in the republican times: see L. R. Taylor, The Voting Districts of the Roman Republic (Rome 1960) 274, 319–321. On L. Pontius, see also N. Criniti, L'epigrafe di Asculum di Gn. Pompeo Strabone (Milano 1970) 155–158.

27) Varro, de re rust. 2.9.6. Cf. Ö. Wikander, Senators and Equites I. The Case of the Aufidii, Opuscula Romana 15 (1985) 158, 159 n. 41; Nicolet, L'ordre équestre 2 (above, n. 3) 796. According to Münzer (RE 22 [1953] 36 s.v. Pontius 19) he was "gewiß ein Verwandter" of our Pontius Aufidianus. He may be identical with the Pontianus mentioned by Cicero, Att. 12.44.2.

of Campania that we have to seek the domicile of Pontius Aufidianus and Fannius Saturninus. Of this Italy of local notables, of family alliances and family feuds, of business and passion, two evocations exist: Cicero's *Pro Cluentio* and Varro's *De re rustica*. For Valerius Maximus it was the Italy of *exempla*.

31
TWO SPEECHES OF Q. HORTENSIUS.
A CONTRIBUTION TO THE *CORPUS ORATORUM*
OF THE ROMAN REPUBLIC*

In the year 54 B.C. Cn. Plancius was accused by his unsuccessful rival to the aedileship M. Iuventius Laterensis of having secured the election by means of bribery and forbidden electoral clubs.[1] He was tried under the *lex Licinia de sodaliciis*, a consular law of M. Licinius Crassus.

In Cicero's speech *Pro Plancio* there is an interesting testimony concerning the activity of Q. Hortensius as orator and statesman in connection with the Licinian law and the trial of Plancius.[2] After having briefly discussed the controversial question of the *iudices editicii* who according to the *lex Licinia* made up the jury in the *quaestio de sodaliciis* Cicero continues: "Quid? huiusce rei tandem obscura causa est an et agitata tum cum ista in senatu res agebatur, et disputata hesterno die copiosissime a Q. Hortensio cui tum est senatus adsensus?".[3]

The exact meaning of this somewhat obscure passage has been disputed:[4] a penetrating explanation of some difficulties presented by the text was given lately by W. Kroll,[5] but, to my mind, the full implication of the passage was missed also by him. The passage being discussed by renowned scholars, it is perhaps worth noting that this striking evidence for the oratory of Q. Hortensius is not recorded in H. Malcovati's accurate and indispensable collection of the fragments of Roman orators.[6] It seems therefore

---

* This article was originally published in *La Parola del Passato* 16, fasc. 79 (1961) 304–311. It is reproduced here in a revised form, but the original argument and (for the most part) original footnotes have been retained. For further remarks, see *Addenda*.

[1] On Plancius and Laterensis, see F. Münzer, "Plancius 4", *RE* 20 (1950) 2013–2015, esp. 2014–2015; "Iuventius 16", *RE* 10 (1919) 1365–1367.

[2] On Hortensius, see W. Drumann-P. Groebe, *Geschichte Roms* 3 (Leipzig 1906) 78–101, esp. 94; [F.] Vonder Mühll, "Hortensius 12", *RE* 8 (1913) 2470–2481, esp. 2478; M. Schanz-C. Hosius, *Geschichte der römischen Literatur* 1[4] (München 1927) 385–387.

[3] *Pro Plancio* 37 (ed. A. Klotz, Bibl. Teubn., Lipsiae 1916).

[4] Drumann-Groebe, 3.94; Vonder Mühll, 2478; Münzer, *RE* 20.2014.

[5] W. Kroll, "Ciceros Rede für Plancius", *RhM* 86 (1937) 127–139, esp. 136, n. 34. Cf. Münzer, loc. cit.

[6] H. Malcovati, *Oratorum Romanorum Fragmenta*[2] (Augustae Taurinorum 1955) 310–330 (no 92).

justified to draw attention once more to this important testimony, and to make a new attempt at its interpretation.

At first sight it must appear uncertain whether Cicero mentions in the passage quoted above only one speech of Hortensius or is hinting at two different orations. In the first case there is no doubt that this speech was delivered in the senate ("cui ... est senatus adsensus"). If, however, the other supposition be granted, we face a new difficulty: it is not clear whether Hortensius delivered the other speech also in the senate or before the court when defending Plancius against the charge brought by Laterensis.

These are the preliminary questions which should be solved before further analysis of the Ciceronian evidence is attempted.

Some scholars assert that only the first solution holds good: according to their view it is the speech delivered by Hortensius in the senate to which Cicero refers.[7] To support this view one may call attention to the fact that sometimes an important trial gave occasion for a discussion in the senate. In our case Hortensius would have spoken in the senate, after the trial of Plancius had already begun, about some procedural questions of the legal process provided by the Licinian law, especially with regard to the *iudices editicii*. Such a solution is in itself not improbable, but it can hardly be deduced from the passage quoted above.

The exact date for Hortensius' speech is given by the phrase "hesterno die". The passage containing the phrase "hesterno die" and mentioning the speech of Hortensius is introduced by an *et*, being clearly opposite to the preceding *tum cum*. It follows that the senate had discussed the question of the *iudices editicii* already some time before the trial of Plancius and the oration of Hortensius. If we accept the view of the scholars mentioned above the final words "cui tum est senatus adsensus" should be referred to the speech delivered by Hortensius "hesterno die". The evidence for such an opinion is, however, very weak. Cicero would hardly have said "cui tum est senatus adsensus" if he wanted the sentence to refer to the speech delivered by Hortensius on the preceding day. It has been pointed out that such locution corresponds well with the *tum cum* phrase of the first passage and, consequently, makes the words "cui tum est senatus adsensus" refer rather to that passage than to the following one which contains no explicit mention of a discussion in the senate.[8] It follows that there is not one, but two speeches of Hortensius to which Cicero refers: one delivered by him in the senate when discussing some questions concerning the problem of the *iudices editicii* and the other before the court when defending Plancius.

---

[7] Drumann-Groebe, 3.94; 6 (Leipzig 1929) 47, n. 2; Vonder Mühll, 2478.

[8] Klotz in *apparatu critico* ad loc. against H. Keil, *Observationes criticae in Ciceronis orationem pro Plancio* (Erlangae 1864) 8; Kroll, 136, n. 34.

Up to this point our argumentation has been following in general lines the explanation presented by Kroll; it is, however, tempting to go further and to reconstruct, as far as possible, the content of the orations under discussion, and to make an attempt at providing them with possibly precise dates.

Since the *Pro Plancio* of Cicero is dated to the end of August or the beginning of September 54 B.C.[9] the same holds good also for the *Pro Plancio* of Hortensius; the dating of his oration *In senatu* is, however, attended with remarkable difficulties which can only be solved in connection with the more general question of the *lex Licinia*.

There has been a vigorous discussion of the Licinian law and there is no need to repeat it here;[10] some propositions put forward in that discussion which may prove useful for our purpose require, however, careful consideration.

It has been argued[11] that the *Lex Licinia de sodaliciis* had been foreshadowed by a decree of the senate of February 10, 56 B.C.[12] The decree of the senate was, in my opinion, designed not only, as has been generally maintained for some time, to dissolve the political associations that were said to have acted against the state, especially the *collegia* founded by the tribune Clodius,[13] but attempted also to check the bribery at elections.[14] This supposition results incontestably from a passage in the *Pro Caelio* where Cicero mentions the *crimina sodalium ac sequestrium*.[15] The connection of these offenses with electoral bribery is apparent. Since the speech *Pro Caelio* is dated to April 4, 56 B.C.,[16] these *crimina*, about which

---

[9] Drumann-Groebe, 6.39–41.

[10] Cf. Th. Mommsen, *De collegiis et sodaliciis Romanorum* (Kiliae 1843) 40–73; M. Cohn, *Zum römischen Vereinsrecht* (Berlin 1873) 58–70; F.M. De Robertis, *Il diritto associativo romano* (Bari 1938) 110–124; S. Accame, "La legislazione romana intorno ai collegi nel I sec. a. C.", *Bull. dell'Museo dell'Imp. Rom.* 13 (1942) 32–38. A full discussion is also presented in J. Linderski, *Państwo a Kolegia. Ze studiów nad historią rzymskich stowarzyszeń u schyłku republiki / Staat und Vereine. Studien über die Geschichte des römischen Vereinswesens am Ende der Republik* (Kraków 1961) 81–92.

[11] Cohn, 65–70; De Robertis, 111–116; Linderski, 89–91.

[12] Cicero mentions some provisions of that decree in *Ad Q. fr.* 2.3.5: "senatus consultum factum est, ut sodalitates decuriatique discederent, lexque de iis ferretur, ut qui non discessissent ea poena quae est de vi tenerentur".

[13] Cf. esp. De Robertis, 102–108.

[14] J. Linderski, "Ciceros Rede pro Caelio und die Ambitus- und Vereinsgesetzgebung der ausgehenden Republik", *Hermes* 89 (1961) 109–112.

[15] *Pro Caelio* 16.

[16] See R.G. Austin, *M. Tulli Ciceronis Pro M. Caelio Oratio*[3] (Oxford 1960) 151.

the previous *leges ambitus* are silent, could have been juridically defined
only by the *senatus consultum* under discussion.[17]

Speaking of the procedural questions of the trial under the Licinian
law, Cicero asserts that it was in fact the senate which "hoc uno in genere
tribus edi voluerit ab accusatore" (*Pro Plancio* 36). Then follows the passage quoted at the beginning of the present remarks which contains an
implicit mention of a decree ("cui est ... senatus adsensus") concerning the
iudices editicii. The same decree of the senate seems to be mentioned also
in other paragraphs of the speech: 37: "ita putavit senatus"; 42: "senatus
censuit"; 44: "consilium ... senatus". It would thus appear that also those
provisions of the *lex Licinia* that stipulated that the jury for the trial *de
sodaliciis* be composed of the *iudices editicii* had been anticipated by a
decree of the senate.[18] We have just seen that the *senatus consultum* of
February 56 was directed also against the bribery at elections. Hence it
seems probable that it was this decree that contained dispositions concerning the *iudices editicii*. Thus the evidence clearly tends to support the
identification of the *senatus consultum* of February 10, 56 recorded by
Cicero in a letter to his brother and the *senatus consultum* known from the
Pro Plancio. The implication of this supposition is apparent: the speech of
Hortensius *In senatu* should be dated to February 56, probably to the very
day on which the decree concerning the *sodalitates* and *decuriati* was
passed.

There is, however, a difficulty. The *Scholia Bobiensia* comment on the
passage in question as follows (p. 160, ed. Stangl): "facta senatus consulti
mentione, qui secundum legem Liciniam quattuor edi tribus ab accusatore
voluerit". The scholiast speaks of the *senatus consultum* as being an interpretive decree, a decree that aimed at interpretation of some obscure points
of the law. According to his explanation the *senatus consultum* followed
the law and did not precede it. If it was subsequent to the *lex Licinia*, the
speech of Hortensius in the senate should be dated to 55 or even 54 B.C.
— and not to 56 as we had been inclined to think. Probably in consideration
of this notice of the *Scholia* some scholars have been induced to set aside
the statements of Cicero in which he insists on the senate's authorship of the

---

[17] See Linderski, (above, n. 14) 107–108.

[18] It is to be stressed that also those scholars who accept a connection between the
lex Licinia and the earlier action of the senate do not discuss in this context the problem
of the *iudices editicii*. Only A.W. Zumpt, *Das Criminalrecht der römischen Republik* 2.2
(Berlin 1869) 395, expressed the opinion that Crassus' law had been foreshadowed also
in this respect by a decree of the senate; he sees in this senatorial measure a decree
different from that of February 56. Cf. E. Wunder, *M. Tulli Ciceronis Oratio Pro Cn.
Plancio* (Lipsiae 1830), proleg. p. LXXV.

provisions of the *lex Licinia* concerning the *iudices editicii*.[19] There is, however, explicit and strong evidence that does tend to support our previous view and to contradict the explanation given by the *Scholia*. We read *Pro Plancio* 42: "Et illud acerbum iudicium si quemadmodum senatus censuit populusque iussit ita fecisses, ut huic et suam et ab hoc observatas tribus ederes, non modo non quererer, sed hunc iis iudicibus editis qui idem testes esse possent absolutum putarem". This statement of Cicero is so explicit that it cannot be misinterpreted. "Senatus censuit populusque iussit": the senate decreed, the people ordered, or more exactly: the senate passed a decree, the people voted a law. The sentence leaves no doubt about its real meaning: the prescriptions of Crassus' law concerned with the composition of the jury for the trial *de sodaliciis* had been prepared by a senatorial decree: it is very probable that this was the same decree that ordered dissolution of the political associations in February 56. There is in our sources no hint of another *senatus consultum* conerned with these questions. The review of the evidence leads thus to the conclusion that Cicero's clear statements as to the senate's authorship of the measures concerning the *iudices editicii* have been wrongly discredited by most modern scholars who following the misinterpretation of the *Scholia* have considered the *senatus consultum* referred to by Cicero to have been an interpretive decree enacted after the law was passed.

In the foregoing remarks we have been trying to prove the incorrectness of the current opinion based on the false interpretation given by the *Scholia*: we now may return to further analysis of Hortensius' speech. Since Hortensius discussed the problem of the *iudices editicii*, some words of explanation with regard to that kind of jurors seems desirable.

As *iudices editicii* there were defined the jurors who were appointed by one party.[20] Such procedure is known in detail from the epigraphically preserved *lex repetundarum*. Out of the list of 450 jurors the accuser appointed one hundred. The accused struck out fifty and the remaining made up the jury. In the Sullan period the *editio iudicum* was abandoned and replaced by *sortitio*, the appointment of juries by lot, which remained in force from that time onwards. The only occurrence of the *editio* in the post-Sullan period appears in the trial *de sodaliciis*, as provided by the Licinian law. The panel was divided *tributim* into 35 sections. The accuser named four tribes and the defendant might reject only one. It seems, however, that

---

[19] So, especially, Mommsen, *De collegiis* 45.

[20] See Th. Mommsen, *Römisches Strafrecht* (Leipzig 1899) 216–217; J.L. Strachan-Davidson, *Problems of the Roman Criminal Law* 2 (Oxford 1912) 98–111, esp. 108–110; J. Lengle, "Die Auswahl der Richter im römischen Quästionsprozess", *Zeitschrift der Savigny-Stiftung* 53 (1933) 275–296, esp. 290.

the *senatus consultum* mentioned by Cicero contained more accurate dispositions with regard to the *editio* of the tribes. Immediately after the passage which has served as a starting point for the present remarks Cicero states: "hoc igitur sensimus: 'cuiuscumque tribus largitor esset, et per hanc consensionem quae magis honeste quam vere sodalitas nominaretur, quam quisque tribum turpi largitione corrumperet, eum maxime iis hominibus qui eius tribus essent esse notum'". The orator cites here apparently the *sententia* of the senate which he explains in the following way: "ita putavit senatus, cum reo tribus ederentur eae quas is largitione devinctas haberet, eosdem fore testis et iudices" (*Pro Plancio* 37).

The term *sodalitas* denotes here the association through the agency of which bribes were distributed throughout the tribes. As we have seen the dissolution of *sodalitates* was ordered by senatorial decree in February 56. It is highly significant that the mention of a *sodalitas* appears here in connection with the *editio iudicum*. This conjunction may serve as the ultimate argument for the view expressed above that the *senatus consultum* of February 56 was concerned also with the *editio* of the tribes.

One may observe further that the passage "hoc igitur sensimus" points directly to Hortensius' speech and especially to his proposal put forward during the discussion in the senate. Simultaneously, however, the same passage appears as a link between the proposal of Hortensius and the opinion of the senate quoted by Cicero. The proposal of Hortensius was accepted by the majority ("cui tum est senatus adsensus") and incorporated into the text of the decree. It results from this argumentation that the *sententia senatus* cited by Cicero presents in fact the original wording of the proposal of Hortensius. In accordance with his opinion approved by the senate the prosecutor should appoint the jurors belonging to those tribes he claims to have been corrupted by the defendant.

Thus, if our argumentation be granted, there is preserved in the *Pro Plancio* not only a testimony concerning two distinct orations of Hortensius, but also — and this is especially to be emphasized — a fragment of his *Oratio in senatu*.

Now let us pass to Hortensius' speech *Pro Plancio* beginning our discussion with some more general observations.

Laterensis sought to prove that Plancius had corrupted the tribes of Teretina and Voltinia. He did not, however, choose for the jury, as one might have expected, the tribes named above: he appointed the Lemonia, Ufentina, Clustumina and Maecia;[21] the latter was perhaps his own tribe.[22]

---

[21] *Pro Plancio* 38; 43.

[22] This conclusion may be inferred by combining two statements of Cicero: "Quid Plancio cum Lemonia, quid cum Ufentina, quid cum Clustumina? Nam Maeciam, non

Cicero insists that Laterensis having done so did not observe the "consilium senatus" and the "sententia legis".[23] These are, however, somewhat vague and indefinite expressions. The very fact that Laterensis apparently did not take into account the disposition of the senate indicates clearly enough that he was not bound by any legal provision to observe it strictly. There is an apparent contradiction between what Cicero and, we may add, Hortensius are trying to give out as the only legally valid principle for the appointment of the jurors and the actual procedure adopted in the trial of Plancius, as set in train by Laterensis. The explanation of this contradiction may be, I think, as follows:

The clause of Crassus' law dealing with the jury for the *quaestio de sodaliciis* must have been formulated rather ambiguously. The law adopted in general the provisions introduced by the decree of the senate. It did not, however, contain any clear disposition as to which tribes were to be chosen and, in particular, it apparently did not impose on the accuser the obligation to appoint those tribes he suspected of having been corrupted by the accused. On the other hand, since Hortensius and Cicero could contest the validity of the procedure adopted by Laterensis, the law must not have said expressly that the prosecutor could choose whatever tribe he wanted. Hence the field was open to various interpretations, and the question may have arisen whether Laterensis was right in his interpretation of this point of the law.

Dispositions concerning the *editio* of the tribes being the matter of controversy, it was very clever to ask Hortensius, who as the author of the relative point of the senatorial decree must have gained considerable authority in this respect, to defend Plancius. He could speak not only in his own name, but also in the name of the senate.

Cicero devotes to this question relatively not much space and for the more detailed refutation of Laterensis' view he refers his audience to the speech of Hortensius. It is very probable that in this part of the speech (paragraphs 36-44) he is repeating only the arguments used already by Hortensius.[24] He states at the beginning that the problem of the *iudices*

---

quae iudicaret, sed quae reiceretur, esse voluisti", and "...ut huic et suam et ab hoc observatas tribus ederes, non modo non quererer..." (*Pro Plancio* 38 and 42). L.R. Taylor in her recent book, *The Voting Districts of the Roman Republic* (Rome 1960) 222, argues that the tribe of Laterensis was Papiria. The argument is based on the fact that the Iuventii were of Tusculan origin and Tusculum belonged to the Papiria tribe. The problem deserves further discussion.

[23] *Pro Plancio* 39; 42; 44.

[24] Cf. *Pro Murena* 54 where Cicero tells us he will be dealing with the points of accusation already discussed by Crassus and Hortensius.

editicii had been disputed for a long time and that on the previous day Hortensius had discussed it exhaustively. Hortensius in his speech before the jury must have at first tried to explain why the senate "hoc uno in genere tribus edi voluerit ab accusatore", the question which is mentioned by Cicero simply as an "obscura causa", with reference, however, to the speech of Hortensius. Then he presented the motives which had induced him to bring the proposal (and the senate to accept it) that the jurors should be selected from the strictly determined tribes, namely those suspected of having an unfair connection with the accused. He must have insisted on this principle as being still valid and not abrogated by the *lex Licinia*. He asserted further that only when the selection of the jurors is made with observation of this principle can the jury be well informed about the case because only then can the jurors be simultaneously *iudices* and *testes*.

If we are right in our arguing we have in this way reconstructed a considerable and the most important part of Hortensius' oration *Pro Plancio*.

All this should add up to the conclusion: in February 56 B.C. Hortensius delivered a speech in the senate which may be denominated *In senatu de iudicibus editiciis*. A fragment of this oration is preserved in the *Pro Plancio*. In August or September 54 he defended Plancius against Laterensis. His speech *Pro Plancio* was concerned in a considerable part with the same juridical problems as his speech *In senatu*.

32

VERGIL AND DIONYSIUS[1]

Archaic Rome: is it history or literature? If history, is it possible to recover facts from fiction? Are modern theories superior to ancient legends? But fictions themselves and legends are history too. "La grande Roma dei Tarquini" mirrors, evokes and justifies *la grande Roma* of Mussolini,[2] and Roman stories of early Rome reflect the successive layers of Roman history, from the Punic Wars through the Gracchi to Augustus. It was at the time of the first Princeps that the new and lasting edition of Rome's past was compiled. Two names stand out: Livy and Vergil; in their shadow languishes Dionysius of Halicarnassus. The *vates* and his prose counterpart boast innumerable modern treatments; Gabba's bibliography covers twenty three pages and yet one searches in vain for an earlier book entirely devoted to Dionysius. *Incredibile dictu*, and yet true, the monograph of Gabba appears to be the first book with Dionysius' *Antiquitates* as its sole subject. Domenico Musti's *Tendenze nella storiografia romana e greca su Roma arcaica. Studi su Livio e Dionigi d'Alicarnasso* (Rome, 1970) dealt equally with Livy's and Dionysius' image of early Rome;[3] it is striking that nobody seems to have been interested in the con-

---

[1]These comments have been prompted by the book by Emilio Gabba, *Dionysius and the History of Archaic Rome* (Berkeley, University of California Press, 1991). Pp. XI + 253. Cloth, no price stated. (Sather Classical Lectures, vol. 56). ISBN 0-520-07302-9. They are offered in lieu of a formal review. The book is composed of six erudite chapters: 1) Greek Historiography and Rome before Dionysius 2) Political and Cultural Aspects of the Classicistic Revival in the Augustan Age 3) Dionysius's Historical Tenets and Methods 4) History and Antiquarianism 5) Dionysius on the Social and Political Structures of Early Rome 6) The Political Meaning of Dionysius's History. The remarks here presented deal mostly with issues raised in chapters four and six, and they deal with them, as befits this journal, through the prism of Vergil and Vergilian commentators. The book of Gabba is an outgrowth of a long-standing interest: he has devoted specifically to Dionysius no less than eight articles, the first dating from 1966.

[2]On this concept (though he does not discuss its ties with contemporary politics), see A. Alföldi, *Early Rome and the Latins* (Ann Arbor 1965) 318-35. Detached from political propaganda this catchy phrase (it was invented in 1936) continues to flourish: see the recent exhibition catalogue: M. Cristofani, *La Grande Roma dei Tarquini* (Rome 1990).

[3]The interest in Dionysius in Italy continues: see the recent monograph by L. Fascione, *Il mondo nuovo. La costituzione romana nella storia di Roma arcaica di Dionigi d'Alicarnasso* (Naples, 1988, 222 pp.). Its topic coincides with Gabba's fifth chapter; as Gabba's preface is dated 1987, he was not able to take notice of Fascione's book. In general, Gabba unfortunately devotes little attention to Dionysius' terminology; one can still consult with profit (missing from Gabba's bibliography) the monograph by V. Nordstroem, *De institutionum Romanorum vocabulis Dionysii Halicarnassensis* (Diss. Helsingfors, 1890). Here we should also record the conference at the University of Dijon in 1988 devoted entirely to Dionysius. The papers of this conference appeared in *MEFRA* 101 (1989) 7-242. Three contributions deal directly with the issues raised in Gabba's book and in the present article: J. Poucet, "Denys d'Halicarnasse et Varron: le cas des voyages d'Enée" (63-95); D. Briquel, "Denys, témoin de traditions disparues: l'identification des Aborigènes aux Ligures" (97-111); P.M. Martin, "Enée chez Denys d'Halicarnasse. Problèmes de généalogie" (113-42).

ceptual links between Dionysius and Vergil.

In Gabba only two (but dense) pages (116-17) explore those links, and only two passages from the *Aeneid* are called for comparison: they concern the "return" of the Trojan Dardanidae to the country of their ancestor.[4] The problem is a central one: nothing less than the origins of the Roman *ethnos*. Where do the Aborigines, the Trojans, the Sabines, the Etruscans, and most importantly (for Dionysius) the Greeks fit in?

The Rome of Dionysius was ultimately a Greek city; even the Aborigines came from Greece. This entailed various consequences: first of all Dionysius had to reject the theory of autochthony (and the etymology *ab origine*) propounded (so the *communis opinio*) by the greatest *lumen* of Roman antiquarian science, by Varro in his various works.[5]

Here we have our first link with Vergil, or rather with the Vergilian antiquarian lore for Vergil himself at the outset of his poem does not mention the Aborigines at all; he introduces Aeneas to Latium already in the sixth line: "inferretque deos Latio; genus unde Latinum / Albanique patres atque alta moenia Romae" (1.6-7; cf. 1.31: "arcebat longe Latio"); and over Latium rules the *rex* Latinus (7.38, 45). For the commentators this posed a problem. The canonical version was enshrined by Livy: the *loca* where the Trojans disembarked were held by "Latinus rex Aboriginesque" (1.1.5); and it was only after the death of Latinus that Aeneas "Latinos utramque gentem appellavit" (1.2.4).[6]

On the phrase "genus unde Latinum" Servius remarks sensibly: "si iam fuerunt Latini et iam Latium dicebatur, contrarium est quod dicit ab Aenea Latinos originem ducere." A two-pronged disquisition follows, grammatical and historical. The grammatical argument centers on the meaning of the adverb *unde*: it does not apply to persons but to places. So Servius; but a grammarian

---

génealogie" (113-42).

[4]*Aen.* 7.205 (in fact 206-8), 240. We may add that Gabba adduces only four passages of Servius and Servius *auctus*: *ad Aen.* 1.378 and 3.148 (dealing with Varro's ideas of the Penates); 7.176 (Varro on the Roman borrowings from other nations); 8.638 (the origin of the Sabini). This neglect of the scholiast in modern literature is not unusual. A pity: antiquarian controversies about the early history of Italy continued to live in the exegesis of Vergil as practiced in schools. There is still much work to be done. For an appraisal of Servius and of his commentary (and of Servius *auctus*), see R. A. Kaster, *Guardians of Language. The Grammarian and Society in Late Antiquity* (Berkeley 1988) 169-97.

[5]Gabba (114) mentions only the *Antiquitates rerum humanarum* (cf. Dion. Hal. 1.14.1; Servius and Servius *auctus, ad Aen.* 8.51), but Varro discussed the Aborigines also in the *De lingua Latina* (5.3) and in the *De gente populi Romani* (Servius, *ad Aen.* 7.657); and he also wrote a *satura* entitled *Aborigines*, on which see J.-P. Cèbe, *Varron, Satires Ménippées. Edition, traduction et commentaire* 1 (Rome 1972) 1-35. For a dissenting view, see below, n. 20.

[6]On Livy's version, cf. R.M. Ogilvie, *A Commentary on Livy. Books I-V* (Oxford 1965) 38.

hiding in the text of Servius *auctus* rightly adverts: "sed veteres *unde* etiam ad personam adplicabant." Thus in the school edition of the commentary the meaning of *unde*, and hence also the question of the origin of the *genus Latinum* was neatly solved, and it was solved in conformity with the Livian account; in the more extended edition containing *opiniones variorum* it was left hanging in the air, as it should: the verbal ambiguity is genuine, and it cannot be conjured away solely by the grammatical learning.[7]

Hence the historical disquisition. Here Servius invokes the mighty names of Cato and Sallust: "Cato in originibus hoc dicit, cuius auctoritatem Sallustius sequitur in bello Catilinae,[8] *primo Italiam tenuisse quosdam qui appellabantur Aborigines. hos postea adventu Aeneae Phrygibus iunctos Latinos uno nomine nuncupatos.*"[9] Thus the *pueri* in the school learned this: "ergo descendunt Latini non tantum a Troianis, sed etiam ab Aboriginibus."

This presupposes *unde* applying to *loca*; but what if the poet really meant the adverb to refer directly to Aeneas? Was he historically wrong? Of course not; an iron tenet of Vergilian *interpretes* was that the *vates* was always right. But Cato could not be wrong either. Hence this piece of sophistic explanation: Aeneas and his Trojans were the victors;[10] consequently Aeneas could impose on the Latins the name of his people: "novimus quod victi victorum nomen accipiunt." Aeneas chose a different course: to conciliate the Latins he not only did not deprive them of their name but even extended it to the Trojans. Aeneas could rightfully obliterate the *nomen Latinum*; he chose to preserve it.[11] In this

---

[7]No progress in modern commentaries; cf. e.g. R.G. Austin, *P. Vergili Maronis Aeneidos Liber Primus* (Oxford 1971) 30 ad loc.: 'The reference in *unde* could be to the whole process just described, but *uirum* is the more natural antecedent" (examples of *unde* with a personal reference follow). Observe that the modern commentator, unlike his ancient colleague, entirely disregards the only point of real importance, the controversy over the historical substance of Vergil's line.

[8]The text of Sallust (*Cat.* 6.1) reads: "Urbem Romam, sicuti ego accepi, condidere atque habuere initio Troiani qui Aenea duce profugi sedibus incertis vagabantur, cumque iis Aborigines, genus hominum agreste, sine legibus, sine imperio, liberum atque solutum. Hi postquam in una moenia convenere . . . incredibile memoratu est quam facile coaluerint." Sallust's *una moenia* finds an echo in Vergil's *alta moenia* (curiously not observed by Austin ad loc.). On Sallust's characterization of the Aborigines, cf. P. McGushin, *C. Sallustius Crispus, Bellum Catilinae. A Commentary* (Leiden 1977) 70-1.

[9]Frg. 1.5 in H. Peter, *Historicorum Romanorum Reliquiae I*[2] (Lipsiae 1914) 52. For a detailed commentary, see W.A. Schröder, *M. Porcius Cato. Das erste Buch der Origines* (Meisenheim am Glan 1971) 102-8.

[10]This presupposes the version mentioned in passing by Livy (1.1.5): "alii proelio victum Latinum . . . tradunt." Livy, Cato and Varro favored the story of an amicable encounter of Aeneas and Latinus (cf. Ogilvie, *Commentary* [n. 6 above] 38). Vergil's story is more complicated: first a friendly encounter, (170 ff.), then the ravages of war, Aeneas' victory, and divine command that the Latins should not perish, but preserve their name and their language, and absorb the Trojans (*Aen.* 12.819-40).

[11]Servius, *ad Aen* 1.6: "volens sibi favorem Latii conciliare (this echoes Livy, 1.2.4) nomen Latinum non solum illis non sustulit sed etiam Troianis imposuit. merito ergo illi tribuit quod in ipso fuerat ut posset perire."

5

perspective he takes the place of a new founder of the *nomen Latinum*, the *vir* from whom the Latins descended. Whatever the application of *unde*, Vergil was right.

But invoking and quoting Cato, the commentators also edited him. For Cato, if we are to believe Dionysius (1.1.11), saw in the Aborigines not an autochthonous population but, surprisingly, arrivals from Greece, and this view was shared also by another early annalist, C. Sempronius Tuditanus.[12] They dated the arrival of the Aborigines to a time before the Trojan War, and led them to Italy from Achaia; Dionysius devoted a lengthy excursus to the refinement of this theory ultimately opting for the Aborigines being a colony of the Arcadians, and connecting their migration with the story of Oenotrus (1.11-13). But in the end he expresses doubt, and asks his readers to suspend judgement (1.13.4); as Gabba (115) observes, it was not an easy task to displace Varro's autochthonous theory. And it was this theory that was to live on in Pliny, in Johannes Lydus, in the compilers of the *Glossae*, and in the Vergilian commentaries.[13]

In the *Aeneid* the crucial passage comes in Book 7 (170-248). Latinus receives the Trojans in his palace, the ancient *regia Pici* (171); in the *vestibulum* there stood the *imagines* of Italus, Sabinus, Saturnus, Ianus, "aliique ab origine reges" (181). The commentator explains "ab origine" as "pro *Aboriginum reges.*" He may well be right; Picus and Saturnus were in fact explicitly described as *reges Aboriginum.*[14] The ancestors of Latinus were Italian gods and kings, not any Greek arrivals (*Aen.* 7.47-9): "hunc Fauno et nympha genitum Laurente Marica / accipimus; Fauno Picus pater, isque parentem / te Saturne refert, tu sanguinis ultimus auctor."

Were all other etymological efforts effectively excluded from the Roman schools? Dionysius writes that some authorities described the Aborigines as

---

[12]C. Sempronius Tuditanus was consul in 129, and the author of the *Annales* (in which he will have dealt with the Aborigines), and of a treatise *de magistratibus*, in at least thirteen books. See Peter, *HRR* 1. 142-46.

[13]For a collection of references, see *TLL* s.v. "aborigines."

[14]Festus 228 Lindsay (Picus); Iustinus 43.1.3: "Italiae cultores primi Aborigines fuere, quorum rex Saturnus"; Suet., *Vit.* 1, and Dion. Hal. 1.31.2 (Faunus; at *Aen.* 7.213 Latinus is addressed as "genus egregium Fauni"). Varro (*De ling. Lat.* 5.53) derived the Aborigines from his native Reate in the land of the Sabines: hence the *rex* Sabinus. Cf. B. Rehm, *Das geographische Bild des alten Italien in Vergils Aeneis* (=*Philologus* Suppl. 24.2 (Leipzig 1932)) 63, n. 135 (sceptical if Vergil really hints at the Aborigines); G.J.M. Bartelink, *Etymologisering bij Vergilius* (=Mededelingen der Koninklijke Nederlandse Akad. van Wetenschappen, Afd. Letterkunde, N.R. 28, 3 (Amsterdam 1965) 61-2. On the tradition concerning the *reges Aboriginum* (= the *reges Laurentum*), see P. Fraccaro, *Studi Varroniani. De gente populi Romani libri IV* (Padova 1907) 175-83.

wanderers and vagabonds, and suitably called them Aberrigines (1.10.2). Who were those Roman authorities?

Gabba avers (114): "The damaging theory of the people with no fixed abode was championed by Saufeius." As his source Gabba adduces Cornelius Nepos' *Life of Atticus* (12.3).[15] From the passage of Nepos we learn that L. Saufeius was a rich *eques*, a friend and *aequalis* of Atticus. We learn of his philosophical studies in Athens, and of his *pretiosas possessiones* in Italy (which were confiscated by the triumvirs and restored to him through the efforts of Atticus), but Nepos has no word of Saufeius' etymological pursuits.[16] It is Servius *auctus* who provides this information in his notice on *Aen*. 1.6. He writes: "Saufeius Latium dictum ait, quod ibi latuerant incolae qui, quoniam in cavis montium vel occultis caventes sibi a feris beluis vel a valentioribus vel a tempestatibus habitaverint, Casci vocati sunt, quos posteri Aborigines cognominarunt, quoniam + aliis ortos esse recognoscebant, ex quibus Latinos etiam dictos."

Thus Saufeius, who probably descended from the family of Saufeii domiciled and influential at the Latin Praeneste, was above all interested in the etymology of the name of his native region; a follower of Epicurus, he may have written an Epicurean account of the development of civilization from the cave-dwellers to the higher forms, but a work of a purely antiquarian character is also possible.[17] Saufeius was not the first to connect Latium with *lateo*; but according to the more popular explanation it was Saturn who was there hiding after he was expelled from Olympus. The Epicurean Saufeius substituted in a rationalistic vein the *incolae* for the god. In the shorter edition of the commentary the reference to Saufeius was excised, and only this information was offered to the *pueri*: "Latium autem dictum quod illic Saturnus latuerit." Oddly enough, the commentator does not remark in this place that it was this explanation that was favored by Vergil, *Aen*. 8.319–23: Saturnus . . . / . . . Latiumque vocari / maluit, his quoniam latuisset tutus in oris."[18]

---

[15]The reference (114, p. 45) reads: Nepos, *Att*. 12.3 = Fr. 2 Peter. This is doubly inaccurate. On Nepos, see above in the text; and in Peter's *HRR* (vol. 2, p. 8) there is only one fragment of Saufeius listed (culled from Servius *auctus*, *ad Aen*. 1.6).

[16]On Saufeius' possible family connections, and his philosophical interests and attachments (he was, like Atticus, an Epicurean), see F. Münzer, "Ein römischer Epikureer," *RhM* 69 (1914) 625-29; A.E. Raubitschek, "Phaidros and his Roman Pupils," *Hesperia* 18 (1949) 96-103; C. Nicolet, *L'ordre équestre à l'époque républicaine*, vol. 2: *Prosopographie des chevaliers Romains* (Paris 1974) 1012-13.

[17]Cf. E. Rawson, *Intellectual Life in the Late Roman Republic* (Baltimore 1985) 9, n. 26.

[18]Servius ad loc. records the etymology of Varro, "quod latet Italia inter praecipitia Alpium et Apennini," and Servius *auctus* returns to the troubling question of Latinus: "quidam

7

The passage concerning the Aborigines is corrupt; Thilo obelizes it, the *Editio Harvardiana* accepts the reading "quoniam < nullis > aliis ortos" proposed in 1879 by A. Riese. Thus this emendation (as also all other emendations listed by Thilo in his apparatus)[19] presupposes the etymology *ab origine*; no Aberrigines in Saufeius.[20]

Thus Vergil, and his commentators, stood firmly in the camp of Varro; they embraced his interpretation to the exclusion and oblivion of all others. The contrast with Dionysius is perfect.

In his *Antiquitates* the Pelasgians form the next wave of immigrants to Italy (1.17-30). They came from Thessaly, but originated in the Peloponnesus, and thus were bound by ties of kinship to the Aborigines. Together with the Aborigines they made a war on the Sicels, and expelled them from their abodes (in the territory of the future Latium, Campania and Etruria).[21] But they suffered the wrath of gods, and only small relics of them remained in Italy. Vergil mentions the Pelasgi seven times, and he, and the commentators, firmly identify them as the Greeks; but in six passages (1.624; 2.83, 106, 152; 6.503; 9.154) they are the Greeks at Troy and their treacherous arts. It is only once, at 8.600–2,

---

ferunt a Latino dictum Latium (this was the opinion of Livy), alii ipsum Latinum a Latio" (this was in fact the interpretation that Vergil embraced). Cf. Bartelink (n. 14 above) 49-50; R. Maltby, *A Lexicon of Ancient Latin Etymologies* (Leeds 1991) 329.

[19]Maltby in his very useful book (n. 18 above) 2, attributes this phrase directly to Servius *auctus* (and not to Saufeius), and prints "ab iis ortos" (he does not indicate that this is a conjectural reading).

[20]We do not know who was the originator of this curious interpretation; in addition to Dionysius it is recorded in *Origo gentis Romanae* 4.2: "Alii volunt eos, quod errantes illo (= *in Italiam*) venerint, primo Aberrigines, post mutata una littera altera adempta Aborigines cognominatos"; cf. Festus 328.9-10 L.; Paulus ex Festo 17 L. J.-C. Richard, "Varron, l'Origo gentis Romanae et les Aborigènes," *RPh* 57 (1983) 29-37, argues that it was in fact Varro who invented this etymology. I do not see how this conclusion can be reached on the basis of Macrobius, *Sat.* 1.7.28 (quoting Varro), where the phrase "cum Latium post errores plurimos adpulissent" refers to the Pelasgi and not to the Aborigines; on the other hand Varronian echoes reverberate in the *Origo*: in particular the etymological method of this treatise closely resembles the practice of Varro (see the examples adduced by Richard 35-6). In the *Origo* the newcomers are greeted by Picus; they may have come *errantes*, but they were the first human occupants of Italy (cf. Paulus ex Festo 17 L.: "fuit enim gens antiquissima Italiae"), and thus it was in Italy that they changed from Aberrigines to Aborigines. This scheme we perhaps can ascribe to Varro, who would thus become the originator (or at least propounder) of both etymologies. But this should not mean that Varro regarded the Aborigines as the Greeks: so P.L. Schmidt, "Das Corpus Aurelianum und S. Aurelius Victor," *RE Suppl.* 15 (1978) 1617 (again one wonders how this conclusion can be derived from Varro, *De gente populi Romani* frg. 25 Fraccaro (n. 14 above) = August., *De civ. Dei* 18.15).

[21]Servius, preserving the autochthony of the Aborigines in Italy, has a curious construction of the Siculi (Sicani) expelling the Aborigines and being in turn "pulsi ab illis quos ante pepulerant" (*ad Aen.* 8.328, cf. 7.795). Cf. Briquel (n. 3 above) 108-9. Gabba (114) disregards this version.

8

that Vergil mentions the Pelasgians in Italy: "veteres Pelasgos . . . qui primi finis aliquando habuere Latinos" (we also learn that the Pelasgians possessed a sacred grove near the city of Caere, historically a major Etruscan city[22].

Commenting on these lines Servius (and Servius *auctus*) adduce various theories concerning the origin of the Pelasgians (the commentators opt for Thessaly), and aver: "hi primi Italiam tenuisse" (apparently not perceiving any contradiction between this statement and their comments on the Aborigines).

Again a stark contrast with Dionysius: as the allies of the Aborigines, the Pelasgians are for Dionysius an important ingredient of the early history of Italy and of Roman ethnogenesis; in the *Aeneis* they are totally insignificant, and they are largely neglected also by the scholiasts.[23]

Next came the celebrated Evander with his Arcadians; they were peacefully accepted by the Aborigines, and established themselves on the Palatine. It was they who brought to Italy ingredients of higher civilization: music, crafts, and laws, and the Greek alphabet.[24] So Dionysius (1.31–33). Now Vergil mentions Evander twenty-eight times; if the Pelasgians only tangentially touched upon the history of Rome, Evander, the possessor of the Palatine, was an essential part of Rome's past. But in Vergil the stress is on the description of the future site of Rome (*Aen.* 8.50ff.); furthermore whereas in Dionysius the Arcadians live in peace with the Aborigines, in Vergil they "bellum adsidue ducunt cum gente Latina" (8.55); the story of their future amalgamation with the Latins and the Trojans is not told.

In Vergil (and in Livy) Hercules comes to Italy and Pallantium alone with his cattle;[25] in Dionysius (1.39–44) he and his followers constitute another wave of Greek immigrants; when Hercules departed from Italy he left behind him the Epeans (from Elis) and the Arcadians from Pheneus, who ultimately mingled with the Arcadians of Evander and the Aborigines.

And finally there arrived the Trojans: for Dionysius (1.57–8, 61–2, 68–9) unmistakably still another group of Greeks. For Vergil (and the Romans of the Augustan age) this was heresy. Aeneas and his line was connected (through gods) with the line of Evander: Aeneas stresses this himself in his address to the

---

[22]No comment here, but *ad Aen.* 10.183 Servius *auctus* attributes to the Pelasgians the foundation of Caere. Cf. also *ad* 8.479 where he hesitates between Pelasgus, Telegonus and Tyrrhenus.

[23]We will be able to appreciate better how little Vergil and his interpreters have to say of the Pelasgians in Italy if we consider that D. Briquel, *Les Pélasges en Italie. Recherches sur l'histoire de la légende* (Rome 1984) devoted to the subject full six hundred fifty-nine pages.

[24]That the letters were Greek Dionysius states explicitly (1.33.4); in Livy (1.7.8) Evander is "venerabilis vir miraculo litterarum," and in Tacitus (*Ann.* 11.14.3) "litterarum formas . . . Aborigines Arcade ab Evandro didicerunt."

[25]*Aen.* 8.190-265; Livy 1.7.3-12, and cf. Ogilvie, *Commentary* (n. 6 above) 55-61.

9

Arcadian king (*Aen.* 8.134–142), but he was not a Greek. Vergil and the commentators emphasize the overriding fact that Dardanus, the ancestor of Aeneas, originated in Italy.[26] Dionysius, on the other hand, is firm in asserting the Arcadian origin of Dardanus (1.61, 68). He could look upon an illustrious Roman predecessor: "Graeci et Varro humanarum rerum Dardanum non ex Italia, sed de Arcadia, urbe Pheneo, oriundum dicunt."[27]

Gabba (117) points out that the story of the Italian origin of Dardanus may have been based "on traditions of Etruscan nobility."[28] This leads us to the role of the Etruscans in Dionysius and in Vergil. More differences here: Dionysius is a notorious champion of Etruscan autochthony in Italy (1.16–30); Vergil remains firmly anchored in the Herodotean tradition deriving the Tyrrhenians from Lydia, and so are his commentators.[29]

Gabba stresses (117) that the Etruscans "are assigned a decidedly positive role by Dionysius" whereas they "are divided by Vergil into friends and enemies of Aeneas." But in the *Aeneid* the enemies of Aeneas are not the Etruscans per se but rather the Etruscan outcasts: the cruel Mezentius was chased away by the inhabitants of Caere, and found refuge with Turnus in the Rutulian Ardea (*Aen.* 8.479–93). To fight Mezentius and Turnus Aeneas acquired as allies the whole of Etruria (*Aen.* 10.148–214), including Mezentius' native Caere.[30] Vergil here stands strikingly opposed to the annalistic tradition: in Livy (1.3–4; 3.4–5) Mezentius is not an exile, but rules the opulent Caere; the Aborigines and the Trojans have to cope with the overbearing power of Etruria, the *florentes opes Etruscorum.* And Dionysius sides with Livy, not Vergil: his Mezentius is a powerful king of the Tyrrhenians (1.64–65).

The alignment pitting Livy and Dionysius against Vergil (and in the case of the all-important origin of Aeneas also Dionysius and Varro against Vergil) should serve as a warning to those scholars who would wish to detect in often

---

[26]*Aen.* 3.94-6, 166-8; 7.205-7, 239-40; Servius and Servius *auctus, ad locc.*

[27]Servius *auctus ad Aen.* 3.167. Cf. H. Hill, "Dionysius of Halicarnassus and the Origins of Rome," *JRS* 51 (1961)) 88–93 at 92. But as Poucet (n. 3 above) 73, points out, this does not mean that Dionysius directly follows Varro; he may have used one of the unnamed *Graeci scriptores.* On the stemma of Aeneas in Dionysius, see now Martin (note 3 above) esp. 120–22, 140–41.

[28]As argued by G. Colonna, "Virgilio, Cortona e la leggenda etrusca di Dardano," *Arch. Class.* 32 (1980) 1-15. Cf. Briquel, *Les Pélasges* (n. 23 above) 161-65.

[29]*Aen.* 8.479-80, 499, and Servius and Servius *auctus,* ad loc. Cf. also the comment on 2.781. See now the voluminous treatment (576 pp.) by D. Briquel, *L'origine Lydienne des Etrusques. Histoire de la doctrine dans l'Antiquité* (Rome 1991), and specifically on Dionysius, see the article of the same scholar, "L'autochtonie des Etrusques chez Denys d'Halicarnasse," *REL* 61 (1983) 65-83.

[30]See the scholiast's comment on 10.183: at 7.652 "ducit Agyllina nequiquam ex urbe secutos / mille viros" (of Mezentius' son Lausus) refers to those who followed Mezentius and Lausus when they had fled from Caere (= Agylla).

minor divergences in mythical history either signs of Augustan ideology or of veiled opposition to Augustus.[31] The truth of the matter is that Dionysius represents the pre-Augustan layer of Roman mythology of the *origines*; he does not criticize Vergil's vision or the official version of the new regime: he disregards them.[32]

As Gabba demonstrated in his marvelous chapter on "The Political Meaning of Dionysius's History" (190–216), the aim of the Greek historian was to bolster the pride of the Greeks: Greece was not ruled by a barbarian nation but by a city that was a Greek colony.

Gabba concludes (117): "within the overall framework of Italian ethnography the distance separating Virgil and Dionysius may indeed be smaller than one might expect at first glance." We have tried to take a second glance, and the distance is as great as ever.[33]

[31]As does, e.g., Hill (n. 27 above) 92.

[32]Cf. Poucet (n. 3 above) 93: "l'historien d'Halicarnasse traite son sujet, comme si l'Énéide de Virgile n'existait pas." Martin (n. 3 above) 136, concludes: "Le récit de Denys est donc un récit à l'usage du monde grec."

[33]American university presses notoriously overedit manuscripts, but at the same time in the case of Gabba's book the California Press was not able to create a decent index. The indices bristle with irritating mistakes: p. 249: Diocles of Peparethus is presented as Diocles Peparethus; p. 251: Festus and Pauli *excerpta ex* Festo are conflated; Livy's *Praefatio* to his *Ab urbe condita* is listed as a separate work; p. 252: no distinction between Servius and Servius *auctus* although Gabba in the text of his book distinguishes them carefully; p. 253; the compiler of the index conflated Mirsch's edition of Varro's *Antiquitates rerum humanarum* and Cardauns' edition of *Antiquitates rerum divinarum*; p. 253: we note the entry: Xanthus of Lydia, *Lydiaca* I. 28.2. As should be clear from Gabba's discussion (p. 112), and as was easy to check, the reference I.28.2 is not to Xanthus but to Dionysius' *Antiquitates* (where Dionysius mentions Xanthus).

33

TWO *CRUCES* IN SENECA, *DE VITA BEATA* 25.2

As there is no difference between pleasure and hardship, why not demonstrate one's virtue in prosperity rather than in adversity and poverty? *Quid ergo est?*—asks Seneca.

> Malo quid mihi animi sit ostendere praetextatus et † causatus
> quam nudis scapulis aut † sententis.

In a recent issue of *AJP* (101 [1980] 446) A. W. Camps rushed to rescue this text from the *tormentum crucis*. In place of the nonsensical *causatus*, the reading of our best authority, the *codex Ambrosianus*, he proposes to read *canusinatus*. The wool of Canusium was indeed famous, and it was used, as Camps notes, "for the warm outergarment, called the *paenula*." I object to this *sanatio*, for however captivating it might appear, it is guilty of three *crimina*.

First, *nihil novi sub sole.* The reading *canusinatus* appears in Muretus' edition of Seneca, Rome 1585; and Muretus claims to have derived it from a *codex Siculus.*[1] The first reaction of the present writer to Camps' idea was to attempt a counter-emendation: *causiatus* (*causia* or *causea* was a Macedonian head-gear, but it was also known at Rome, cf. Mart. 14.29). A glance at L. D. Reynolds' *OCT* apparatus (Oxford 1977) saved this writer from rushing this old[2] (and indefensible) emendation into print. As the German saying goes, *hier ist der Hund begraben:* Reynolds does not list the reading *canusinatus,* nor is it to be found in any recent edition of Seneca. To come across it one has to go to older books, for instance the edition by C. R. Fickert (see n. 1),[3] the famous fourth edition of Lipsius (Antverpiae 1652) or, surprisingly enough, the school edition by J. F. Hurst and H. C. Whiting (New York 1877).

Second, a credible emendation must fit smoothly into the rhetorical structure of the sentence. Camps' emendation violates this rule. There are two *cruces* in the text; while trying to remove the first of them Camps states expressly that the merits of Lipsius' *semitectis* (which he prints in lieu of the other *crux*) "are irrelevant here." Now, quite to the contrary, the merits or demerits of Lipsius' conjecture are very relevant here.

The sentence in question has either chiastic or parallel structure. In the former case Seneca is contrasting *praetextatus* with †*sententis* and †*causatus* with *nudis scapulis;* in the latter *praetextatus* is opposed to *nudis scapulis* and †*causatus* to †*sententis.* If we take, for

---

[1] For the reading of Muretus, see C. R. Fickert, *L. Annaei Senecae Opera* 3 (Lipsiae 1844) 187, in app. This obviously is not the place to enter into a discussion of the mysterious *codex Siculus;* see M. C. Gertz, *Studia critica in L. Annaei Senecae Dialogos* (Hauniae 1874) 9–11.

[2] Reynolds attributes it to Brakman, (i.e. C. Brakman, *Annaeana nova* [Leiden 1910] 8–9; cf. Idem, "Annaeana," *Mnemosyne* 56 [1928] 151), but according to Fickert's apparatus the reading *canusinatus* appears already in some of the *codices Pinciani.* That *causiatus* might be *the* reading also occured to H. Wagenvoort, "Ad Senecae Dialogorum Libris VII-XI adnotationes criticae," *Studi Luigi Castiglioni* 2 (Firenze 1960) 1084–85, but he discovered in time that the same conjecture (in the form *causeatus*) had been proposed by M. Leumann in *TLL* s.v. "gausapatus" (1934). Apparently neither of them consulted Fickert (or Lipsius), and in addition Wagenvoort missed Brakman and T. Birt, "Marginalien zu lateinischen Prosaikern," *Philologus* 83 (1927) 49–50, who also read *causeatus* (and Birt in turn missed Brakman's study of 1910).

[3] In addition to *canusinatus* and *causeatus* Fickert lists the following readings (emendations or the readings of the *deteriores*): *camisatus, catus, gausapatus, chlamydatus, clamidatus, candidatus.*

example, Camps' *canusinatus* (to which Lipsius' *gausapatus* corresponds[4]) and Lipsius' *semitectis* (sc. *scapulis*) we would conjure up the following picture: take off your *praetexta* and your shoulders are bare; take off your fine Canusian *paenula* and your shoulders are half-covered (or vice versa in the chiastic arrangement). Rhetorically it is a lame figure: *nudae scapulae* and *semitectae scapulae* are ill-matched and awkward as the opposing pair to *praetextatus* and *canusinatus*. One wonders why the *praetexta* and the *paenula*—or rather the lack of them—should have produced different results with respect to the degree of nakedness of the poor man's back.

This leads us to our third and crucial point. Camps' conjecture disregards the *realia* of the Roman *res vestiaria*. Roman mantles, and in particular the *paenula*, have been the subject of a long and erudite study by Frank Kolb. As he points out, the *paenula* was steadily gaining popularity in the Roman world, but even at the time of Trajan it was socially an inferior dress as compared with the toga. On the *Anaglypha Traiani* the senators and the knights appear dressed in the togas; *paenulati* are the common citizens.[5] Gellius, *Noct. Att.* 13.22(21).1, speaks of *toga, paenula* and *lacerna*, in this order of social respectability. The magistrate's *praetexta* and the common citizen's *paenula* are again an ill-matched pair. Of course one can argue that the magisterial *praetexta* is here associated not with the common *paenula*, but rather with the rich man's expensive *paenula Canusina*. This would indeed be a possibility were not the syntax and the dressing habits of the Romans against it.

In the text of Seneca the conjunction *et* springs to one's eyes.[6] If we print *canusinatus* we tacitly assume that Seneca's rich philosopher

---

[4] Lipsius (4th ed., Antverpiae 1652) prints *praetextatus et candidatus*, but in his annotation to *praetextatus* he opts for *pexatus* (slavishly reproduced in the *Dictionary* of Lewis and Short), a good example of how fondness for conjectures leads to the disfiguration of a perfectly sound text. In his annotation to *candidatus* he changed his mind and decided to read *petasatus et gausapatus*. In Lipsius' defense it ought to be said that he perceived the incongruity of the *praetexta* and the *paenula*, see below in the text.

[5] F. Kolb, "Römische Mäntel: *paenula, lacerna,* μανδύη," *Röm. Mitt.* 80 (1973) 69–167, esp. 93–94, and plate 24. Cf. T. Mommsen, *Römisches Staatsrecht* 3 (Leipzig 1887) 217–23.

[6] W. H. Alexander, "Seneca's Dialogues I, II, VII, VIII, IX, X. The Text Emended and Explained," *University of California Publications in Class. Phil.* 13.3 (1945) 65–66, attempted to defend Lipsius' *gausapatus* and *semitectis* with the following argument: "just as *semitectis* gives a contrast with *nudis, gausapatus* . . . suggests the contrast between the dignity of the official *praetexta* and the informality of the outing suit." But Seneca's *et* is a stumbling block for any such interpretation: it suggests complimentarity,

wore at the same time both the toga and the *paenula* (as an overcoat). Now on the basis of literary and monumental testimonies F. Kolb was able to establish that the *paenula* was worn "direkt über der Tunica und nicht über der Toga."[7] As Nonius (861 L.) says, *paenula est vestis, quam supra tunicam accepimus.*

There exists, it seems, sufficient evidence to dispose, once and for ever, of all emendations that assume a garment hiding in †*causatus.* And so it goes and *canusinatus*, and *gausapatus*, and *chlamydatus*, and *camisatus.*

The *veteres*, and nowadays Camps, looked for an answer to the shoulders. The *moderni* transferred their attention to the head and the feet. As far as the head-cover is concerned only one conjecture seems to have been proposed, our old acquaintance, *causiatus* (but see n. 4). Yet it is not obvious at all why Seneca should have selected this rare and non-Roman head-cover as his example. The Romans *praetexta* and the Macedonian *causia* are an odd pair.[8] *Coronatus* would be a better choice, for it could point to the status of personal felicity.[9] Yet it is too far removed from the word-form we are supposed to emend, and above all, we have to remember that among the Romans the uncovered head was not a symbol of poverty or adversity.[10]

The head being of no help, let us now turn to the feet. Here the prospects seem brighter. The senatorial shoes, the *calcei*,[11] are a

---

not contrast. Alexander perceived this clearly. His solution? "It would improve the text from this point of view to read *aut* for *et* after *praetextatus.*" Again, the old *morbus philologorum:* the readiness to sacrifice a sound text for the sake of a doubtful conjecture. The reading *semitectis* must go: as Birt, op. cit. (above, n. 2) 50, observed, it brings "für das, was Seneca will, nichts wesentlich Neues."

[7] Op. cit. (above, n. 5) 79–80.

[8] Cf. the critique of this emendation by A. Klotz in his review of Brakman's *Annaeana nova* in *Berliner Philologische Wochenschrift* 31 (1911) 834.

[9] Cf. the curious phrase *vulgum tam chlamydatos quam coronatos voco (de vita beata* 2.2), now brilliantly elucidated by H. Dahlmann, *Bemerkungen zu Seneca, De Vita Beata* (= Abh. Akad. Mainz, 1972, 6) 5–8 (= 309–314). *Chlamys* and *corona* are here the symbols of *felicitas,* cf. Cic. *Phil.* 2.85 of Caesar: *sedebat in rostris . . . amictus toga purpurea . . . coronatus,* and see other examples collected by Dahlmann (Suet. *Cal.* 19; *Ner.* 25; *Domit.* 4.4, and already Auctor *ad Her.* 4.60). Yet all this is of little help for the conjecture *coronatus.* As Dahlmann saw, Seneca alludes to the *felicitas* of a *triumphator,* and under the Empire this was an exclusive privilege of the ruler, cf. Mommsen, *Staatsrecht* 1[3] (1887) 426–29, and 432 n. 5 (*chlamys* as the Greek term for the Roman *paludamentum*).

[10] Cf. Mommsen, *Staatsrecht* 3.217. See also 1[3].426: "Kopfbedeckung trägt der Beamte in der Friedenstracht in der Regel nicht."

[11] See Mommsen, *Staatsrecht* 3.2 (1888) 888–92, esp. 888: "Der Schuh scheidet die Senatoren von den übrigen Bürgern."

splendid counterpart to the magisterial *toga praetexta*. *Calceatus* is the conjecture we owe to the *ingenium* of F. Schultess.[12] We ought to have embraced it unreservedly but for one obstacle: how are we to solve the other *crux?* Schultess proposed to read *sectis plantis*, quoting Verg. *Ecl.* 10.49: *tibi ne teneras glacies secet aspera plantas*, but this is far-fetched indeed. As a result no editor with the exception of J. W. Basore in *LCL* (1932) admitted Schultess' conjectures into his text, and Reynolds does not quote them even in his apparatus. He may be right for it cannot be stressed enough that a successful emendation must take care of both daggers at once. So there is no happy end to this story, but there is a morale to it: better two daggers than one placebo.

*   *   *

Strictly as an *obiter dictum* may I be permitted to offer a sugges-tion. Perhaps we ought to change the direction of our search. Seneca's argument consists of a series of three rhetorical expositions, questions and answers (or conclusions). Our *cruces* come in the second segment. In the first part (25.1) he contrasts the *opulentissima domus* and the *pons sublicius*, the 'domicile' of the *egentes*, and concludes: *Domum illam splendidam malo quam pontem.* In the third part (25.3) he jux-taposes felicity and adversity. His conclusion is: *Malo gaudia tempe-rare, quam dolores compescere.* This demonstrates clearly that also his conclusion in the second segment ought to be closely connected with the preceding *expositio*. This *expositio* runs as follows (Reynold's text):

> Pone <in> instrumentis[13] splendentibus et delicato apparatu: nihilo me feliciorem credam quod mihi molle erit amiculum,[14] quod purpura conuiuis meis substernetur. Muta stragula mea:[15] nihilo miserius ero si

[12] F. Schultess, *Philologischer Anzeiger* 17 (1887) 302 (review of the edition by M. C. Gertz). He regards *calceatus* as *sicher; sectis plantis* "würde wenigstens dem Sinne entsprechen." A. Klotz (loc. cit. [above, n. 8]) describes Schultess' *calceatus* as *glänzend;* "ingeniose Schultess" remarks E. Hermes in his Teubner edition (1905).

[13] *instrumentis* A. F. Haase (Bibl. Teubn. 1851) following some *dett.* (R and V, Reynolds) reads *in stramentis*, not without some justification. See below in the text.

[14] A. Bourgery (Coll. Budé, Paris 1951), endorsed by W. H. Alexander, op. cit. [above, n. 6] 65, reads *adminiculum*, "cushion." He follows the *manus quinta* in the *Ambrosianus* (cf. the edition by M. C. Gertz, [Hauniae 1886] 245 in app.). But there is no doubt that *amiculum* is the correct reading: it has manuscript authority and is required by the following *praetextatus* and *nudis scapulis.* Cf. Varro, *Men.* 212 (Non. 864 L.): *cubo in Sardianis tapetibus; clamidas et purpurea amicula.*

[15] So Madvig combining the conjectures of Agricola (*Malo stragulam meam*) and Fickert (*Muta magnam rem meam*); *multas magnam meam* A.

> lassa ceruix mea in maniculo faeni adquiescet, si super Circense
> tomentum per sarturas ueteris lintei effluens incubabo.

Now as a companion to *praetextatus* (cf. *molle amiculum, purpura . . . substernetur*) one would expect a word conveying a sense of
luxury, perhaps *delicatus*.[16] Seneca's usage of the word is not against
this idea, and may even be taken to support it.[17] As to †*sententis*, I
doubt if this *paradosis* contains a word referring to *scapulae;* if this
were the case one would rather expect the word-order *scapulis nudis
aut. . . . Nudis scapulis* expresses an absolute concept: the lack of a
garment.[18] A similar concept, expressing the want of something essential, will also be hidden in †*sententis*. Consider what Seneca says in
Ep. 20.9:

> Ego certe aliter audio, quae dicit Demetrius noster, cum illum uidi
> nudum,[19] quanto minus quam [in] stramentis incubantem . . . Quid
> ergo? . . . Et ille ingentis animi est, qui illas circumfusas sibi . . . ridet
> suasque audit magis esse quam sensit. Multum est non corrumpi diuiti-
> arum contubernio; magnus ille, qui in diuitiis pauper est.

The perfect philosopher shows his virtue *nudus* and without
stramenta, and still better when he does not let himself *corrumpi*
diuitiarum contubernio. The same image, the same morale, and nearly
the same wording as in *de uita beata.* In view of this text and of the
preceding disquisition about the *stragula* (and probably also *stramenta*), *maniculum faeni* and *tomentum,* one may ask: is it too adventurous to read *nudis scapulis aut sin <e stra> mentis?*[20]

[16] One of the *deteriores* (cf. Fickert in app.) has *catus;* not that this *per se* is *magni
momenti.*

[17] Cf. esp. *Ep.* 66.49; 114.4 *(quam delicatus fuerit,* sc. Maecenas); *de ira* 1.18.2; *de
tranqu. animi* 2.13; *de const. sap.* 10.2 *(delicati et felices)*; cf. also Cic. *de off.*
1.106 *(delicate ac molliter vivere).*

[18] Cf. *Ep.* 63.11.

[19] Cf. *Ep.* 62.3: *Demetrium . . . mecum circumfero et relictis conchyliatis* (= *pur-
puratis,* cf. Dahlmann, op. cit. [above, n. 7] 6) *cum illo seminudo loquor. Seminudus =
nudis scapulis.*

[20] T. Birt, op. cit. (above, n. 2) 49–50, read *nudis scapulis aut sine tegmentis.* He
introduced *tegmentis* as a counterpart to his reading *causeatus,* and adduced as a com-

parison *Consol. ad Helv.* 7.9, *tegmenta capitum.* But *tegmentum* does not *per se* point to the head-gear; and objections to the reading *causeatus* (see above) still hold. Yet it was a great idea to discover *sine* in the first part of † *sententis.* Cf. also P. Grimal, *L. Annaei Senecae De Vita Beata* (*Collection Érasme*, Paris 1969) 112 in app. "A titre d'hypothèse" he proposes to read *praetextatus et loricatus quam nudis scapulis et sine tegumentis.* *Sine tegumentis* reproduces basically the reading of Birt (without quoting him), and *loricatus* is better passed over with silence, even *á titre d'hypothèse.*

I should like to thank my friend Deedra Keller for her unfailing help.

34

AES OLET:
PETRONIUS 50.7 AND MARTIAL 9.59.11

T RIMALCHIO boasts that he alone possesses true Corinthian
bronzes. A (feeble) joke only: he buys his bronzeware from a
smith named Corinthus. But bronzes, he confesses, are not his favorite
objects:

ignoscetis mihi quod dixero: ego malo mihi vitrea, certe non olunt.[1]

[1] *Sat.* 50.7. The reading of the Traguriensis (H) is *certe nolunt*; *certe non olunt* was
proposed by F. Bücheler in his Berlin 1862 edition (in his apparatus he notes the *adscrip-
tio* of Jahn, *certe non olent*; see also his *praefatio*, p. XXXIII), and has been accepted by
(it appears) all subsequent editors. It is obvious paleographically, unassailable linguistically (the third conjugation form *olo, -ere*, was used in popular speech; it is attested in
Plautus, Afranius and Pomponius, cf. *OLD* s.v., and Nonius 147 M. = 214 L.), and it
makes excellent sense. G. C. Whittick, "Petronius, 50.7," *Latomus* 17 (1958) 545, notes
that the Traguriensis "nowhere goes wrong on the negative *non*," and proposes to read
certe inolunt, the existence of the negative form *inolere* to be derived from Lucr. 2.850
inolentis olivi. Certainly ingenious, but it is difficult to imagine Trimalchio using the
Lucretian idiom. Bücheler's predecessors kept *nolunt*, but some editors objected to *certe*.
C. G. Antonius, *Petronii Arbitri Satyricon ex recensione Petri Burmanni passim reficta*
(Lipsiae 1781), conjectured *certi nolunt*, and commented in his *apparatus* (p. 147): "*certi*
autem sunt *notissimi*, qui possint nominari." Scheffer (as Antonius puts it) "olim suspi-
catus est *ceteri*, postea haesit." His idea was picked up by N. Heinsius who read *caeteri
nolint*. P. Burmann, *Titi Petronii Arbitri Satyricon* (Amstelodami 1743) is more detailed;
he quotes Scheffer as writing: "suspicabar olim *caeteri nolunt*, nunc haereo, vereorque,
altius subesse malum" (p. 332; cf. Bücheler's judgment on the merits of Scheffer and
Heinsius, p. XXXXI). Orelli proposed *certae nolunt*, "cauillari Trimalchionem Fortunatam suam opinatus" (Bücheler 1862 in app.). Cf. also the apparatuses in the editions of
L. Friedländer, *Petronii Cena Trimalchionis* [2] (Lipsiae 1906), K. Müller (1st and 3rd
edd., München 1961 and 1983), C. Pellegrino (Roma 1975), all *minus accurate*. Scheffer
was right: "altius subesse malum." It is against the background of those emendations
that Bücheler's *ingenium* brightly shines: for what should have been the point of
Trimalchio's remark that he cherishes glass more than bronze, but others do not?

If we wished to develop the thought of the genial host (without, however, imitating his grammar), we would be tempted to exclaim: "aenea olunt." But "the smell of bronze" is a concept so peculiar that modern Petronian commentators refuse even to try to sniff. In this respect they are quite unlike Martial's (9.59.11) Mamurra who

consuluit nares an olerent aera Corinthon.

In his recent commentary on the *Cena Trimalchionis* M. S. Smith has this to say: "The belief that a connoisseur could identify Corinthian bronze by its smell is mocked by Martial."[2] This indeed may seem (see below) to be the point Martial makes, but it is assuredly not the point of Trimalchio's remark: he does not identify his "Corinthian" ware by its smell; he merely observes that he prefers glass to bronze because the former (unlike the latter) does not smell.

---

[2] *Petronii Arbitri Cena Trimalchionis*, edited by M. S. Smith (Oxford 1975) 136. Smith's comment reproduces the communis opinio of Petronian interpreters, cf. Friedländer (above, n. 1) 280; A. Maiuri, *La Cena di Trimalchione di Petronio Arbitro* (Napoli 1945) 183; P. Perrochat, *Le Festin de Trimalcion*[3] (Paris 1962) 109–110; Pellegrino (above, n. 1) 309. Smith also adduces ad loc. Plin. *Ep.* 3.6.1, but although in this passage Pliny mentions indeed a *Corinthium signum*, he says nothing about its smell. In his note on this passage of Pliny, A. N. Sherwin-White, *The Letters of Pliny. A Historical and Social Commentary* (Oxford 1966) 225, displays the same misunderstanding of Trimalchio's words: "Petronius ... robustly mocks the pretensions of amateurs of Corinthian bronzes, such as Martial's Mamurra who tested his bronzes by smell." So also W. C. A. Kerr in his Loeb (1920) Martial (2.116, n. 2): "Connoisseurs professed to detect an odour in genuine Corinthian bronze: *Petr.* 50" — not quite accurate even as a comment on Martial, and as interpretation of Petronius not better than the ideas of Trimalchio himself. The same opinion in E. V. Marmorale, *Petronii Arbitri Cena Trimalchionis* (Firenze 1947) 83 (ad loc.): "Trimalchione non poteva sopportare l'odore dei vasi corintii, attestatto da Mart. 9,59,11." It is worth noting that L. Friedländer in his venerable edition and commentary (*M. Valerii Martialis Epigrammaton Libri*, vol. 2 [Lipsiae 1886] 82, ad loc.) takes the words of Martial at their face-value: "Die Corinthischen Bronzen hatten einen eigenthümlichen Geruch, der als Merkmal der Aechtheit galt." To support this statement he refers to A. W. Becker, *Gallus; oder, römische Scenen aus der Zeit des Augustus,* neu berbeitet von H. Göll, 1 (Berlin 1880) 43–44, who quotes solely Martial and Petronius, and believes that the peculiar odor derived from oxidation. The circle of non-information is thus tightly closed. But its classical form this interpretation received already in 1800 in an erudite article by the then famous but today utterly forgotten C. A. Böttiger, "Der Geruch, ein Kennzeichen des Metalls," reprinted in his *Kleine Schriften* 3 (Leipzig 1850) 422–425. Cf. below, n. 6.

Now in antiquity bronze did smell indeed, and it smelled because it was greased—a sensible precaution against bronze rust. Cato prescribes "ahenea omnia unguito (sc. *amurca*), sed prius extergeto bene. postea, cum unxeris, cum uti voles, extergeto: splendidior erit et aerugo non erit molesta,"[3] advice repeated by Pliny the Elder (*NH* 15.34): "aeramenta (sc. *amurca ungui*) contra aeruginem, coloris gratia elegantioris." At *NH* 34.99 Pliny observes "aera extersa robiginem celerius trahunt quam neglecta nisi oleo perunguantur." Observe that here Pliny speaks of *oleum* itself, and not of *amurca*; in the next sentence he remarks on the use of bronze to ensure the *perpetuitas monimentorum*, in particular of the bronze tables "in quibus publicae constitutiones inciduntur." It is thus most likely that these *tabulae* were also periodically cleaned and oiled.[4] But to fight rust not only *amurca* and *oleum* were used.

The *lex metalli* from Vipasca in Lusitania, in the chapter containing the baths regulations, prescribes that once a month the overseer ought to wash, clean and grease with fresh animal fat the bronze vats used for heating the water, *CIL* 2.5181 = *ILS* 6891, lines 25–26: "Aena quibus utetur lavare tergere unguereque adipe e recenti tricensima quaque die recte debeto."[5] The commentators of this document neglect Cato and

---

[3] Cato, *Agr.* 107 [= 98].2. On the preparation and the uses of *amurca*, the lees or dregs of olive oil, see also 104–106, 107–110 (= 95–97, 99–101), and the notes ad locc. by R. Goujard, *Caton. De l'agriculture* (Paris 1975 [Coll. Budé]) 259–262; H. Blümner, *Technologie und Terminologie der Gewerbe und Künste bei Griechen und Römern* 1 [2] (Leipzig 1912) 335; 4 (1887) 338.

[4] C. Williamson, "Monuments of Bronze: Roman Legal Documents on Bronze Tablets," *Class. Ant.* 6 (1987) 160–183, refers to Pliny *NH* 34.99, and remarks on the polishing of bronze tablets (p. 166, n. 23), but has no word of oiling, whereas Pliny insists that polished bronze (*aera extersa*) must be oiled for otherwise it will soon be covered with rust.

[5] See R. Shaw-Smith, "Metal Polish," *CQ* 31 (1981) 469. He does not mention Petronius or Martial. See now the edition and commentary by C. Domergue, *La mine antique d'Aljustrel (Portugal) et les tables de bronze de Vipasca* (Paris 1983) 52–53 (text and translation), 83 (commentary). His translation is straightforward: "Tout les trente jours, il devra convenablement laver, frotter et enduire de graisse fraîche les chaudières en usage," but in his commentary he writes that it was not only the vats (*chaudières*) that were to be greased but also and in particular "les robinets qui y étaient adaptés et commandaient la distribution de l'eau chaude." He argues that for the greasing of the vats no *adeps recens* was necessary; fresh grease was on the other hand essential for keeping in service the *robinetterie*. That may be so; but in the text itself only vats are mentioned and no faucets and taps: Domergue conjures them up, so to speak, from fresh fat. D. Flach, "Die Bergwerksordnungen von Vipasca," *Chiron* 9 (1979) 435, believes that the vats were to be cleaned "damit sich kein Kalkstein festsetzte." Oddly enough, he does not

Pliny; but it is in the light of their remarks that the prescription of *unguere* after *tergere* finds its natural explanation.

But there is more to the rust, the Corinthian bronzeware, Trimalchio and Mamurra that meets the nose. At *Tusc.* 4.32 Cicero draws a peculiar parallel between the types of men and the types of bronze:

> Inter acutos autem et inter hebetes interest, quod ingeniosi, ut aes Corinthium in aeruginem, sic illi in morbum et incidunt tardius et recreantur ocius, hebetes non item.

Cicero's medical expertise may be questioned, but he knew his bronzes: the Corinthian bronzes were more resistant to the rust than the other cheaper kinds,[6] and apparently they could be cleaned with

---

mention the bronze rust (and cf. Domergue, p. 83, who points out that the water of Aljustrel "n'est pas calcaire").

[6] Blümner 4.185 (above, n. 3) states (referring to Cicero) that with respect to the Corinthian bronzes "galt als ein besonderer Vorzug, dass es keinen Grünspan ansetze." "No rust" would be ridiculous, but this is not what Cicero says. See now the excellent article by D. Emanuele, "*Aes Corinthium*: Fact, Fiction and Fake," *Phoenix* 43 (1989) 347–357, with full collection of ancient references and modern discussions. He points out that the genuine Corinthian bronzes apparently were high-tin bronzes, and "a high tin-content . . . increases the alloy's resistance to corrosion" (p. 352). As to the smell of bronze he has this to say: "Martial and Petronius suggest that some of their contemporaries thought they could recognize genuine Corinthian bronze by its smell [certainly incorrect with reference to Trimalchio, see above in the text, and n. 2]. This seems a most unreliable method, but if there was any difference, perhaps the patina itself, produced by the chlorides in Corinthian water, had a distinct odor [but this does not apply to Trimalchio's bronzes for although they were produced by a Corinthus they were not produced in Corinth]. It is more likely that Martial . . . and Petronius . . . meant to satirize the notion of olfactory authentication" [again, this does not apply to Petronius]. With respect to Martial this remains a possibility, but *amurca* and *oleum* are better choices. Professor J. Bodel points out (in a letter) that W. D. Lowe in his edition of the *Cena* (Cambridge 1905) commenting on "assellus Corinthius," (31.9, p. 18) adduces (in addition to Petr. 50.7 and Mart. 9.59.11) also Arrian, *Epict.* 1.20; the passage (it figures also in the article by Böttiger [above, n. 2] 423–424) describes the methods applied by the testers of coins: ὁ ἀργυρογνώμων προσχρῆται πρὸς δοκιμασίαν τοῦ νομίσματος, τῇ ὄψει, τῇ ἀφῇ, τῇ ὀσφρασίᾳ, τὰ τελευταῖα τῇ ἀκοῇ. Lowe concludes in the familiar vein: "Corinthian bronze was supposed to possess a peculiar odour." Arrian talks of testing a *denarius*, a silver coin: the tester tried to discover whether the coin was adulterated with bronze. Pure silver and an alloy of silver and bronze would have thus possessed a distinct smell; we should rather follow the finding of Vespasian that money, even that acquired from the *urinae vectigal*, had no smell at all (Suet. *Vesp.* 23.3). According to Ps.-Arist. *Mirab.* 49 (834 a) among the cups of Darius (captured by Alexander) there was

less effort (so as sharp-witted men would get well again faster than the dull). And that means that the real Corinthian ware needed to be greased less frequently, and less thoroughly.

Now, if Trimalchio could detect on his bronzes the rancid smell of old grease that was unpleasant even to him, the ware he was purchasing from Corinthus was of poor quality indeed. Or conversely: if the bronzes produced by Corinthus lived up to the name of their creator, then Trimalchio, by excessively greasing them, failed to recognize their real quality. Either way, he was a vulgar upstart.

At least he was rich. Martial's Mamurra was poor, vulgar, and an impostor: he spent a whole day in rich shops pretending not to have found anything to his liking, and at the closing hour carried off two cups bought for a penny. The bronzes did not pass the test of his nose: they did not smell enough of Corinth. But we should read Martial's mockery of Mamurra in the light of ancient practice of *aera unguere*:[7] if a bronze piece was not covered with thick rust, and did not exude the smell of oil, it could be a Corinthian ware. The smell of Corinth was no smell at all.

---

a good number ἃς εἰ μὴ τῇ ὀσμῇ, ἄλλως οὐκ ἦν διαγνῶναι πότερόν εἰσι χαλκαῖ ἢ χρυσαῖ. Here we are in the land of the *mirabilia*: not a reliable guide for the students of Petronius.

[7] Received notions often cloud the perception of even very diligent scholars: Blümner (above, n. 3) conscientiously notes that an *Oelanstrich* was put on bronzes (4.338), but at the same time he interprets the passage of Martial as pure fable (4.185).

35

ALFRED THE GREAT AND THE TRADITION
OF ANCIENT GEOGRAPHY

AMONG various works translated from Latin by Alfred, or on his behalf, there was a history written in the early fifth century by a Spanish priest, Orosius: *Historiae adversum paganos*. Orosius preceded his history by a geographical description of the world. This part, as extant in Alfred's Anglo-Saxon version, is not simply a translation of Orosius' text, but an almost entirely new work, with many and important additions. Alfred's aim was to bring up to date the Orosianic description, which for the ninth century, especially in regard to north and middle Europe, was completely anachronistic. His Geography constitutes thus a monument of Anglo-Saxon scholarship and a real treasure of historical information. Owing to the efforts of generations of scholars the general picture of Alfred's Europe seems now to be clear.[1] There is, however, a problem that has never been studied in detail: the problem of classical tradition in his work. Had Alfred at his disposition, apart from Orosius, other ancient geographical works, and, if so, is it possible to discover which ones? The present paper is intended as a contribution to this particular issue.

Let us analyze the following passage to which nothing in Orosius' text corresponds:

Ond hie Maroara habbað be westan him þyringas ond Behemas ond Begwara healfe; ond be suþan him, on oþre healfe Donua, þaere ie, is þaet land Carendre, suþ oþ þa beorgas, þe mon Alpis haet. To þaem ilcan beorgan licgað Begwara landgemaero ond Swaefa. / Ond / þonne be eastan Carendran londe, begeondan þaem westenne, is Pulgara land. Ond be eastan þaem is Creca land. Ond be eastan Maroara londe is Wisle lond; ond be eastan þaem sint Datia, þa þe iu waeron Gotan.[2]

/ And these Moravians have west of them the Thuringians, and Bohemians, and part of the Bavarians; and south of them, on the other side of the Danube, is the country of Carinthia, south to the mountains called the Alps. Towards the same mountains lie the boundaries of the Bavarians and the Svabians. Then east of the country of Carinthia, beyond the wilderness, is Bulgaria and east of it is Greece; and east of Moravia is the Vistula country, and east of it are the Dacians, who were formerly Goths[3] /.

Here the point of orientation for Alfred is Moravia — today a part of Czechoslovakia with its center around the city of Brno, in the ninth century the most important Slavic state (the so-called Great Moravian state) in this part of Europe including also a northern part of ancient Pannonia. Carinthia is said to have lain

---

[1] See especially from the recent literature K. Malone, "King Alfred's North," SPECULUM, v. (1930), 139–167; R. Ekblom, "Alfred the Great as Geographer," *Studia Neophilologica* XIV (1941/42), 115–144; G. Labuda, *Źródla, sagi i legendy do najdawniejszych dziejów Polski* [Sources, sagas and legends concerning the earliest history of Poland] (Warsaw, 1960), pp. 13–90; *Źródla skandynawskie i anglosaskie do dziejów Slowiańszczyzny* [Scandinavian and Anglo-Saxon sources illustrating the history of the Slavs] (Warsaw, 1961), pp. 7–118 (edition of Alfred's Geography with an important commentary). Labuda's works are cited hereafter as Labuda I and Labuda II.

[2] H. Sweet, *King Alfred's Orosius* (London, 1883), p. 16; Labuda II, 66.

[3] The translation is that of Ekblom, p. 117.

south of Moravia, the deviation from real south being here, according to Ekblom, about 19°. Ekblom locates Alfred's Carinthia in the district west of Graz,[4] far from the Danube, identifying it in this way with the mediaeval Carinthia. But Alfred says explicitly that it is to be located "on the other side of the Danube"; as he mentions no other country between Moravia and Carinthia, he obviously means to say that the latter extended as far north as the Danube. His Carinthia thus corresponds roughly to ancient Noricum. The real trouble begins, however, only when one attempts to determine the positions of the Vistula country and Dacia. Alfred speaking of Dacia and of the Goths who lived there is strikingly anachronistic; he may have been influenced here by the preceding chapter of Orosius providing the information on the same subject.[5] The relevant passage left by Alfred untranslated, reads: "ab oriente Alania est, in medio Dacia ubi et Gothia, deinde Germania est, ubi plurimam partem Suebi tenent."[6] The mention of Dacia and Gothia appears here, however, in an entirely different context; still more important is the fact that Alfred is aware of the disappearance of the Goths. It is to be observed that Dacia and Gothia linked up together are to be found also in other sources[7]; it cannot at least be excluded, although at the same time it cannot yet be positively proved, that Alfred derived this information from some other source.

In Alfred's Europe east of Moravia lies the Vistula country; whether his statement "and east of it is Dacia" is to be understood as implying that Dacia lies east of the Wisle lond or east of Moravia has been disputed. The former meaning had been generally accepted[8] until Ekblom argued that, Moravia being for Alfred the starting point, only the latter interpretation makes sense.[9] The discussion seems to me, however, a little superfluous. According to Alfred, both Dacia and the Vistula country lie east of Moravia, and, if so, Dacia is necessarily to be located east of the "Wisle lond." It was Malone's theory that the positions given by Alfred are in most instances deviated from the real ones about 45°; as his "east" means "southeast," the items indicated by him are to be shifted 45° clockwise.[10] But, as Ekblom rightly pointed out, Malone's shifting-system does not work in our case. Dacia should have to be shifted clockwise, but the Vistula country counter-clockwise.[11] The Swedish scholar, although claiming that he "unlike Malone, has not been misled into presuming that Alfred means to say that Greece (the Eastern Empire) lies to the east of Bulgaria and Dacia to the east of the

[4] Pp. 131 and 141 (map).

[5] Cf. Labuda, I, 41.

[6] *Oros.* I 2, 53 (ed. C. Zangemeister)

[7] See Iordanes, *Get.* XII 74 (ed. Th. Mommsen): "Daciam dico antiquam, quam nunc Gepidarum populi possidere noscuntur, quae patria in conspectu Moesiae sita trans Danubium corona montium cingitur, duos tamen habens accensus, unum per Boutas, alterum per Tapas. Haec Gotia, quam Daciam appellavere maiores, quae nunc ut diximus Gepidia dicitur."

[8] See esp. Malone, p. 153.

[9] P. 122.

[10] Malone, pp. 151 ff., esp. 166.

[11] Ekblom, pp. 126 ff. Malone (p. 153) resorted in that case to an emendation reading "norþan" instead of the "eastan" of the text, in this way placing the Vistula country north of Moravia. He observed himself, however, that the emendation was very drastic.

Vistula country,"[12] was never-the-less compelled to confess that no reasonable explanation could be adduced: "it need not astonish us that minor mistakes were made about countries so far from England as the Vistula country, Dacia and the Eastern Empire."[13]

According to Labuda's opinion, many inconsistencies and inaccuracies in Alfred's description may be explained on the theory that he had at his disposition a map by the help of which he determined the positions of countries and tribes mentioned by him, but at the same time he reproduced geographical errors and misconceptions contained in that map.[14] This is the most ingenious theory ever put forward for the interpretation of Alfred, but even Labuda came short of solving definitely this intricate question. His conclusion is that only a map could have given Alfred an idea of what the position of Dacia in respect to Moravia was. It is, however, to be stressed that the main difficulty here is presented not by the position of Dacia but by that of the Vistula country. The position of Dacia can be explained on Malone's theory, that of the "Wisle lond" cannot.

The Vistula river, or at least its name, if not always its exact localization, was well known to the ancient geographers. There is no doubt that it must have been indicated on Alfred's map. It was quite natural that he associated the Vistula country, the information about which he apparently received from contemporary, anonymous and perhaps oral sources, with the river Vistula of ancient tradition. So far he was right. The "Wisle lond," the country of the tribe of Wislanie, did in fact have its center around the upper Vistula. For some ancient geographers, however, the Vistula constituted the western boundary of Dacia. This was the viewpoint of the two late-Roman geographical descriptions, the *Divisio orbis terrarum* and the *Dimensuratio provinciarum*, and also of Pliny, though he did not mention Dacia by name:

Divisio orbis 14: Dacia finitur ab oriente desertis Sarmatiae, ab occidente flumine Vistla. Dimens.provinc. 8: Dacia, Getica finiuntur ab oriente desertis Sarmatiae, ob occidente flumine Vistula.[15]
Plin. N.H. IV 81: Agrippa totum eum tractum ab Histro ad oceanum bis ad decies centenum milium passuum in longitudinem, quattuor milibus minus CCCC in latitudinem, ad flumen Vistlam a desertis Sarmatiae prodidit.

The picture given by the sources cited above is exactly the same as Alfred's: the Vistula is west of Dacia, that is, reckoning from Moravia, as Alfred does, Dacia lies directly to the east of the Vistula. Pliny, the *Divisio* and the *Dimensuratio* are based on the most famous Roman geographical work, which exercised tremendous influence on the picture of the world in subsequent centuries: on the *Commentarii* of Agrippa and perhaps on his *Mappa Mundi*.[16] Thus the map (or the description)

---

[12] Ekblom, p. 128–129.

[13] Ekblom, p. 142.

[14] Labuda, I 38 ff.

[15] The *Divisio* and the *Dimensuratio* are cited in the edition of P. Schnabel, *Philologus*, cx (1935), 425–440.

[16] See D. Detlefsen, *Ursprung, Einrichtung und Bedeutung der Erdkarte Agrippas* (Berlin, 1906), Quellen u. Forschungen zur alten Geschichte u. Geographie, Heft 13, *passim*, esp. p. 34; A. Klotz, "Die geographischen commentarii des Agrippa und ihre Überreste," *Klio* xxiv (1931), 38–58, 386–466, esp. 421–422; H. Lowmiański, Początki Polski [The Origins of Poland] (Warsaw 1963), I, pp. 145–149.

Alfred used was almost certainly a late ancient offspring of Agrippa's work. On this theory the hindrances that faced scholars interpreting our passage, the strikingly inaccurate localization Moravia-Wisle lond-Dacia, can be for the first time reasonably explained.

The thesis presented above sheds new and unexpected light on still another item in Alfred's description. In a passage we have already cited Alfred speaks of a wilderness between Carinthia and Bulgaria. The same wilderness is mentioned by him in another context also:

> ond be suðan Istria is se Wendelsae þe man haet Atriaticum; ond be westan þa beorgas þe man haet Alpis; ond be norðan þaet westen þaet is betux Carendran ond Fulgarum.[17]
> / On the south of Istria is that part of the Mediterranean Sea, which is called Adriatic; and on the west, the Alpine mountains; and on the north, that waste, which is between Carinthia and the Bulgarians[18] /.

In the ninth century the Bulgarians reached the peak of their power ruling even over a part of ancient Dacia and Pannonia. Bulgaria and Moravia became thus neighbouring powers. For this reason the localization of the "wilderness" has been of interest to the historians. Hampson, who published a chapter on Alfred's geography in Bosworth's edition of Orosius, maintained that Alfred meant here "the desolate tract on the north of the Drava and eastward of Clagenfurt, the capital of Carinthia,"[19] thus implying the mention of the wilderness to be an authentic contribution by the Anglo-Saxon writer to the geography of the Danubian territories. Malone expressed the same view even more explicitly, listing among the items added by Alfred the wilderness between Carinthia and Bulgaria.[20] Malone identifies it with Pannonia, and Ekblom too seems to have placed it there. According to Ratkoš and Dekan, Alfred's wilderness was a waste land on the border between Moravia and Bulgaria, somewhere in the region of the river Theiss.[21] Labuda tried to explain the desert as the land devastated by the incursions of the Avars and especially as the effect of the destruction of the Avarian state by Charlemagne.[22] This might be, however, only a modern explanation: as Alfred knew neither Huns nor Avars, it could not have been his. There can be little doubt that the Hungarian plains were scarcely populated in the ninth century, but the question is whether Alfred's information is at all to be taken as depicting the actual situation.

The "northern deserts" were a commonplace of ancient geography and rhetoric. The best known were the *Scytharum deserta* or Σκυθέων ἐρημία. The tradition of a northern, Scythian wilderness goes down from Herodotus through Pliny to

---

[17] Sweet, p. 22; Labuda, II, 72.

[18] The translation is that of Bosworth.

[19] R. T. Hampson, "An Essay on the Geography of King Alfred the Great," in J. Bosworth, *King Alfred's Anglo-Saxon Version of the Compendious History of the World by Orosius* (London, 1859), p. 48.

[20] P. 150.

[21] J. Dekan, "Príspevok k otázke politýckych hranic Vel'kej Moravy" [Le problème de la frontière politique de la Grande-Moravie], *Historica Slovaca*, v (1948), 209; P. Ratkoš, "K otázke hranice Vel'kej Moravy a Bulharska" [Zur Frage der Grenzen Gross-Mährens mit Bulgarien], *Historický Časopis* (Bratislava) III (1955), 213–214.

[22] Labuda, I, 30, 41.

late and even Byzantine writers such as Procopius from Caesarea.[23] Antiquity knew not only the wasteland north of the Black Sea, where the Scytharum deserta are to be located, but also a wilderness in the Danubian region. Arrian, speaking of the Danubian campaign of Alexander the Great, reports that the Getae fled ἐς τὰ ἔρημα (ι 4, 5) and Strabo knows in the same area, north of the Lower Danube, ἡ τῶν Γετῶν ἐρημία (VII 305). There was, however, still another waste land in the Danubian region.

About the middle of the first century B.C. an important event took place in the history of Dacia and Pannonia: a bitter war between the Dacians and a Celtic tribe, the Boii. The former built up a strong belligerent state in the Transylvanian mountains while the latter created a confederation of Celtic tribes living in Pannonia, Noricum and present-day Czechoslovakia. The war ended with the disastrous defeat inflicted upon the Boii by the Dacian ruler Burebista. Strabo reports that Burebista Βοῖος δὲ καὶ ἄρδην ἠφάνισε (VII 3, 11) and that μέρος μέν δή τι τῆς χώρας ταύτης (i.e. of Pannonia) ἠρήμωσαν οἱ Δακοὶ καταπολεμήσαντες Βοίους καὶ Ταυρίσκους (VII 5, 2). The events referred to were so impressive that they gave rise to the tradition of the *deserta Boiorum*.[24] The expression is used by Strabo, Pliny and the *Dimensuratio provinciarum*. The pertinent passages run as follows:

Strabo VII 1,5: Ἐλουήττιοι καὶ Ὀυιδολικοί . . . καὶ ἡ Βοίων ἐρημία.
Plin. N.H. III 146: Noricis iunguntur lacus Pelso, deserta Boiorum; iam tamen colonia Divi Claudi Savaria et oppido Scarabantia habitantur.
Dimensuratio 18: Ilyricum, Pannonia ab oriente flumine Drino, ab occidente desertis, in quibus habitabant Boi et Carni.

The wording both of Pliny and the *Dimensuratio* is interesting: the *Dimensuratio* speaks of "deserta, in quibus habitabant Boi et Carni"; Pliny knows two towns, Savaria and Scarabantia, flourishing in the area depicted by him as *deserta*. Pliny may have been alluding to a subsequent development, but in any case it is evident that the term is not to be understood in the modern meaning of the word

---

[23] For the citation of sources see S. Borzsak, "Die Kentnisse des Altertums über das Karpatenbecken," / *Diss. Pannonicae*, I, 6 / (Budapest, 1936), p. 31. Cf. also *Thes. ling. lat.*, *s.v.* "deserta."

[24] It is to be noted that some of the recent scholars refuse to accept any connection between the extermination of the Boii and the *deserta* named after them. They argue that the decisive battle took place somewhere in the area close to the river Theiss, while the *deserta Boiorum* lay in the borderland between Pannonia and Noricum. It cannot, however, be denied that from the powerful tribe only remnants survived into the Roman period and that the sudden disappearance of the political power of the Boii must have influenced in some way or other the geographical denomination. The language of Strabo (cf. also V 1, 6: μεταστάντες/sc. the Boii/δ᾽ εἰς τοὺς περὶ τὸν Ἴστρον τόπους μετὰ Ταυρίσκων ὤκουν πολεμοῦντες πρὸς Δακοὺς, ἕως ἀπώλοντο πανεθνεί· τὴν δὲ χώραν οὖσαν τῆς Ἰλλυρίδος μηλόβοτον τοῖς περιοικοῦσι κατέλιπον) is not in favor of the view referred to above. For detailed discussion see esp. A. Alföldi, "Zur Geschichte des Karpatenbeckens im I Jh. v. Chr.," *Archivum Europae Centro-Orientalis*, VIII (1942), 1 ff., esp. 16 ff. Cf. also K. Müllenhoff, *Deutsche Altertumskunde*, II, 267; III, 79 ff.; A. Graf, *Übersicht der antiken Geographie von Pannonien Diss. Pannonicae*, I, 5 (Budapest, 1935), pp. 20, 22, 26 ff.; A. Mocsy, *Die Bevölkerung von Pannonien bis zu den Markomanenkriegen* (Budapest, 1959), p. 31; *Pannonia.*, RE Suppl. IX (1962), pp. 521, 531 ff.; M. Macrea, "Burebista şi Celţii da la Dunărea de mijloc" [Burébista et les Celtes du Moyen-Danube], *Studi şi cercetări de istorie veche*, VII (1956), 118–134; I. Degmedžić, Poraz Boia i Tauriska na Tisi [La chute des Boiens et des Taurisques sur la Tisa], *Rad voyvodanskikh muzeya* (Novi Sad), VIII (1959), 27–28.

as a complete wasteland. The most important fact is, however, that Pliny and the Dimensuratio place the *deserta* east of Noricum — and this is exactly the same area where Alfred's wilderness lay — east of Carinthia. Pliny and the *Dimensuratio*:[25] the same sources, based on Agrippa's *Commentarii*, to which we have previously attributed Alfred's localization of Dacia and the Vistula. This coincidence is too striking to be mere chance.

Thus we have traced back to the *Commentarii* and the map of Agrippa important elements in Alfred's description of the Danubian region.[26] This stresses once more the persistence of classical tradition in the mediaeval geographical treatises, especially the persistence of data derived from the work of Agrippa. Classical elements are presumably still to be discovered in many places, in Alfred and elsewhere, where nobody suspects their presence, as has been the case also with our passage.[27]

[25] On the passages cited above see D. Detlefsen, *Die Anordnung der geographischen Bücher des Plinius und ihre Quellen*, Quellen u. Forschungen zur alten Geschichte u. Geographie, 18 (Berlin, 1909), pp. 11ff., 47–48; *Ursprung*, p. 30; Klotz p. 412–413.

[26] Incidentally, should it be remarked that since Alfred's wilderness is derived from ancient tradition, it cannot be of any help in determining the boundaries between Moravia and Bulgaria.

[27] I should like to express my thanks to Professors Andrew Alföldi and Sterling Dow for encouragement and helpful criticism. I am indebted also to Mr C. P. Jones for correcting my English.

36
NOTES ON *CIL* I² 364*

The so-called inscription of Faliscan cooks engraved on both sides of a bronze plate found at Falerii presents an important monument of old Latin and at the same time a precious source for the history of the Faliscan dialect;[1] it may also serve as evidence for the first steps of literary activity on Italian soil.[2] It has evoked a considerable number of modern studies concerning chiefly various linguistic problems, historical questions remaining relatively less elucidated.

Yet for both a linguist and a historian it is imperative to solve the following question, of crucial importance for the proper understanding of the document: did the "Falesce quei in Sardinia sunt" (named in inscription *a*) issue the inscription *b* too?, or, in other words: can they be identified with the cooks mentioned in the latter?

Almost all scholars who dealt with these inscriptions have admitted the identity of cooks and *Falesce*;[3] however, only few of them discussed this particular point, the majority repeating the received opinion. H. Dessau was

---

* This note was originally published in *La Parola del Passato* 13, fasc. 58 (1958) 47–50. It is here presented in a revised form, but the original argument is retained (and also, for the most part, the original footnotes). For further remarks, see *Addenda*.

[1] It will be convenient to adduce here the full text of the inscription: On one side (*a* hereafter): "Iovei Iunonei Minervai / Falesce quei in Sardinia sunt / donum dederunt. Magistreis / L. Latrius K. f., C. Salv[e]na Voltai f. / coiraveront". On the other side (*b* hereafter; *versus saturnius*, cf. F. Leo, "Das saturnische Versus", *Abh. Göttingen*, Phil.-hist. Kl., N.F. VIII 5 [1905] 70; W.J.W. Koster, "Versus Saturnius" *Mnemosyne* 57 [1929] 344–345): "Gonlegium quod est aciptum aetatei age(n)d[ai] / opiparum a[d] veitam quolundam festosque dies, / quei soveis aastutieis opidque Volgani / gondecorant sai[pi]sume comvivia loidosque, / ququei huc dederu[nt i]nperatoribus summeis / utei sesed lubent[es be]ne iovent optantis".

[2] See the remarks by Z. Żmigryder-Konopka and K. Rozenberg, in: *Munera Philologica L. Ćwikliński oblata* (Posnaniae 1936) 341–346, who are inclined to see in the verse a specimen of Italian literature, influenced, however, by the Greek style. On the latinization of the Faliscan territory, see J. Safarewicz, *Eos* 47 (1954–55) 184–190.

[3] This is the opinion of Deecke, Bormann, Mommsen, Buecheler, Aust, Waltzing, Kornemann, Diehl, Lommatsch, Frank, Żmigryder-Konopka, Rozenberg, Pisani, Warmington, and others. The most detailed discussion is given by E. Lommatsch in *CIL* I², p. 404.

the first to reject this hypothesis, and to give a new interpretation: "hos cocos diversos esse apparet a Faliscis in Sardinia degentibus qui titulum in parte opposita laminae incidendum curaverunt".[4] Unfortunately Dessau did not disclose the full train of his argument, and as a result his idea failed to gain approval. Nevertheless the effort of this great epigraphist should not be abandoned without further discussion.

At each corner of the plate on which the inscriptions were engraved there are still extant the holes that were apparently destined for the hooks by which the plate was affixed to a votive offering.[5] Thus only one side of the plate, and only one dedication, was visible.

This circumstance did not escape the attention of Lommatsch. Yet he still asserts that both inscriptions were engraved by the same group, the Faliscan cooks. He argues that the inscription compiled in the saturnian verse carries the principal meaning, the dedication on the other side being auxiliary and of only minor interest. Accordingly he assumes that the former was exposed, the latter covered. It is an explanation logically faulty, and historically unlikely.

The dedication in the saturnians declares that a votive offering was bestowed by a guild of cooks on their All-Highest-Commanders ("inperatoribus summeis"); in the inscription on the other side a gift is declared as offered to Iuppiter, Iuno and Minerva by the Faliscans living in Sardinia;[6] further the names of the *magistri* are given who supervised the erection of the offering. This inscription may be less interesting to us, but it is doubtful whether this was the case also for the members of the guild. In the votive inscriptions set up under the Republic by professional guilds the names of foremen are for the most part carefully spelled out.[7] This practice is easily understandable especially when we consider the pride with which guild officials of the Empire speak of their filling all the posts in

---

[4] *ILS* 3083 (in commentary).

[5] The holes are distinctly conspicuous on the photographs of the plate published by E. Lommatsch in *CIL* I², p. 404, and E. Diehl in *Inscriptiones Latinae* (Bonnae 1912), tab. 3 a, b (cf. p. VIII). If there were only two holes we could imagine that the plate was suspended, and that in this way both inscriptions were simultaneously exhibited.

[6] Most scholars assume that "imperatores summi" (*b*, line 5) are the same deities as Iuppiter, Iuno and Minerva (*a*). Iuppiter Imperator is attested: Livy 6.29.8; Cic. 2 *Verr.* 4.128–129; cf. [E] Aust in *Myth. Lexikon* (Roscher) 3 (1890–94) 643–645, but there is no independent attestation of the epithet with respect to Iuno and Minerva. On the cult of Minerva at Falerii, see G. Wissowa, *Religion und Kultus der Römer*² (München 1912) 253; F. Altheim, *Römische Religionsgeschichte* (Baden-Baden 1951) 1.202–204; Idem, *Geschichte der lateinischen Sprache* (Frankfurt a. M. 1951) 406–408. On Minerva Capta, see Ovid. *Fast.* 3.835–848.

[7] Only occasionally are they omitted as in our metric inscription.

various corporations.[8] It was not otherwise under the Republic. Thus the content of this inscription was of more than passing interest, and it is absurd to assume that the inscription was engraved in order to be immediately turned to the wall, and hidden from view. There is every reason to believe that each of these inscriptions belonged to a different guild, and that each of them was engraved separately.

Under what circumstances might these dedications have been compiled? The exact dating of the monument is attended with remarkable difficulties: the peculiarities of language permit the attribution of each of the dedications to a period lasting from the second half of the third century to the Gracchan times.[9] Since the sojourn of the Faliscans in Sardinia during the period of the Punic domination seems improbable the terminus post quem is provided for inscription *a* by the date of the Roman capture of the island: 238 B.C. Three years earlier (241 B.C.) Falerii (Falerii Veteres) was destroyed by the Romans, and its inhabitants were moved to a new site near by (Falerii Novi). The content of the first dedication (*a*) thus seems to fit well with the course of political events. It is not unlikely that after the destruction of Old Falerii a throng of Faliscans settled down in Sardinia; but one may doubt that they formed a corporation of cooks.

The cooks of the inscription *b* are speaking with evident conceit and self-praise (ἀλαζονεία), the features so characteristic of the Greek μάγειροι.[10] Their profession is indispensable to human society: the making of holidays agreeable to gods, garnishing of banquets and games—all these depend on their cleverness. On an island retarded in its economic development, where towns did not play as important a part as in other regions of the Mediterranean, where moreover permanent struggles and combat against aboriginal tribes lasted throughout the republican period and did not cease even under the early Empire, prevailed conditions uncomfortable for the cultivation of the so vividly depicted culinary activities.[11] I am therefore

---

[8] See J.P. Waltzing, *Étude historique sur les corporations professionnelles chez les Romains* 4 (Louvain 1900) 341–342. Cf. *CIL* V 4449: "in omni(bus) coll(egiis) magisterio perfunct(i)".

[9] Of the two last collections of old Latin remains V. Pisani (*Manuale storico della lingua latina* 3: *Testi latini, arcaici e volgari* [Torino 1950] 15–17) appears to date them to the end of the third century, E.H. Warmington (*Remains of Old Latin* 4.151 [1940; Loeb Class. Library], pp. 124–125) ultimately attributes them to the Gracchan period.

[10] See E. Moore Rankin, *The role of the μάγειροι in the Life of the Ancient Greeks as Depicted in Greek Literature and Inscriptions* (Chicago 1907) 35; Żmigryder-Konopka and Rozenberg (above, n. 2) 342–343. The cooks were ubiquitous in republican Italy, but Plautus' "qui mi intro misti in aedis quingentos coquos" (*Aulul.* 553) is a comic exaggeration.

[11] It is worthwhile to note that none of only three other guild inscriptions found in Sardinia belongs to a professional guild.

inclined to think that the Faliscans in Sardinia did not form a guild of cooks, but expelled from their native city came together into a club similar to the numerous associations of Roman and Italian businessmen and adventurers spread over Sicily and the eastern part of the Mediterranean.[12] The guild of cooks on the other hand will have existed at the city of Falerii (Novi) itself. This supposition corresponds well with the content of the poem and the reputation of Falerii as a center of the culinary art.[13]

The plate had originally belonged to one of these corporations, and subsequently it came into the possession of the other which — new bronze plate being expensive — inscribed its own dedication on the back side.

The similarity of letter forms would seem to indicate a relatively short interval between these inscriptions. But to divine which of them was inscribed first would be mere guesswork.[14]

---

[12] The phrase "Falesce, quei in Sardinia sunt" is very similar to the set expressions "Italici (or cives Romani) qui in ... consistunt (or negotiantur)"; Ἰταλικοί (or Ῥωμαῖοι) ὁι κατοικοῦντες (or παρεπιδημοῦντες). Cf. J. Hatzfeld, *Les trafiquant italiens dans l'orient hellénique* (Paris 1919) 257–290.

[13] *Faliscus venter*, a sort of sausage, was a famous dish (Varro, *de ling. Lat.* 5.111; Mart. 4.46.8; cf. Stat. *Silv.* 4.9.35).

[14] It is, however, very likely that both times the plate was attached to a gift deposited in the same temple, very probably the famous shrine of Iuno Quiritis (Curritis) left untouched by the Romans.

37

Libiis or *Libens* ?

A Note on a New Dedication to Liber Pater from Dacia

A. Popa and J. Al. Aldea have recently published [1] (with an excellent photograph) a new (already thirty fifth [2]) inscription recording the cult of Liber Pater in Dacia. They give the following text : *Libiis | votu | Libro P|atri · s | Paulinu*. The inscription displays some rather well known vulgar Latin features, duly noted by the editors, as the lack of the final *-m* in *votum* or the syncopated form *Libro* instead of *Libero*. It would have hardly required any additional comment but for an intriguing although largely non-existent epigraphical problem conjured up by the editors.

According to Popa and Aldea the main interest of the inscription lies in the opening word of the dedicatory formula. They transcribe it as *Libiis* and interpret as *abl. pl.* of the word *libum, -i*, «offrande, gâteau». The correct form would be *libis*, but the authors point out that the gemination of the letter I is quite common in (vulgar) Latin inscriptions. On this basis they put forth the following theory (p. 624) : «C'est là, autant que nous sachions, le seul cas où ce terme a été utilisé dans une inscription et placé sur un fronton, dans l'intention évidente de préciser que l'auteur de la dédicace a déposé une offrande au dieu qu'il adorait, offrande représentée, en l'occurence, ... par une urne renfermant des grains. Ce fait constitue, à notre avis, une nouveauté intéressante, tant en ce qui concerne les études d'épigraphie latine que la connaissance approfondie de certain détails du culte de Liber Pater dans la province de Dacie et même dans l'ensemble de l'Empire romain.» They also offer a translation of the text : «Paulinus a accompli par des offrandes le vœu qu'il avait fait à Liber Pater».

This interpretation and translation raises serious doubts. To begin with it is hardly correct to render the word *libis* by the phrase «par des offrandes». The term seems to have always been used in its concrete meaning «cake of meal» or «sacrificial cake», and not generically as «offering» [3].

---

(1) *Une nouvelle inscription dédiée à Liber Pater* in *Latomus*, 32, 1973, p. 623-625.
(2) Cf. A. BODOR, *Der Liber- und Libera-Kult. Ein Beitrag zur Fortdauer der bodenständigen Bevölkerung im römerzeitlichen Dazien* in *Dacia*, N.S. 7, 1963, p. 211-239.
(3) The editors quote (p. 624, n. 6) A. ERNOUT and A. MEILLET, *Dictionnaire étymologique de la langue latine*⁴, Paris, 1959, p. 356, but Ernout and Meillet do not say that *libum* means «offrande» ; they correctly define it as «gâteau de sacrifice offert aux dieux, ... puis, dans la langue commune, gâteau en général». See also FORCELLINI-DE VIT, *Totius Latinitatis Lexicon* and LEWIS-SHORT, *A Latin Dictionary*, *s.v. libum*.

The use of cakes was common in the Roman cult [4] ; some literary texts explicitly link the offering of the *liba* with the cult of Bacchus or Liber Pater, see Varro, *de lingua Latina*, VI, 14 : *Liberalia dicta, quod per totum oppidum eo die sedent sacerdotes Liberi anus hedera coronatae cum libis et foculo pro emptore sacrificantes* ; Ovid, *Fasti*, III, 725 f. (description of the Liberalia), esp. 735 : *liba deo fiunt*, and 761-2 : *melle pater fruitur, liboque infusa calenti iure repertori candida mella damus* ; Vergil, *Georg.*, II, 393-6 : *ergo rite suum Baccho dicemus honorem* | *carminibus patriis lancesque et liba feremus,* | *et ductus cornu stabit sacer hircus ad aram,* | *pinguiaque in ueribus torrebimus exta colurnis*. These texts may seem to lend some support to the interpretation advanced by Popa and Aldea, but it is in fact only a seeming support. The *liba* were used as a normal, habitual offering to Liber Pater, especially at the feast of Liberalia [5], and it is very doubtful if a vow could be fulfilled by a mere gift of cakes. It called for something more special, e.g. the erection of an altar. The god expected to get his cakes anyway [6].

A basic rule in epigraphical studies is not to search after rare words or unusual turns of speech when a habitual formula is at hand. Popa and Aldea are aware of this precept. Hence, as a (distant) alternative they admit, albeit reluctantly, that the first word of the inscription could be read as *Lib(e)ns*. This is, no doubt, the only plausible interpretation, and the authors had better forget their fantasy about the *liba*. However, their reading of the word in question still requires a correction. This time they seem to take the two vertical strokes as the letter N (and not as a geminated I). However, as the photograph does not show any trace of a bar connecting the two verticals, this reading is impossible, unless one would like to admit,

---

(4) See esp. VARRO, *de re rustica*, II, 8, 1 ; HORACE, *Epist.*, I, 10, 10 ; SERVIUS, *Aen.*, VII, 109. The cake offering was normally only a preliminary sacrifice, cf. VERGIL, *Georg.*, II, 393-6 (quoted in the text), and K. LATTE, *Römische Religionsgeschichte*, München, 1960, p. 387 (Voropfer) See also HUG, *Libum* in *R.E.*, XIII, 1927, col. 143 ; M. SORDI, *Libarius* in *D.E.*, IV, 1957, p. 795.

(5) Cf. G. WISSOWA, *Religion und Kultus der Römer* ², München, 1912, p. 209 ; A. BRUHL, *Liber Pater*, Paris, 1953, p. 15-16.

(6) In any case this was the expectation of Priapus, VERGIL, *Ecl.*, 7, 33-36 :
> *Sinum lactis et haec te liba, Priape, quotannis*
> *exspectare sat est : custos es pauperis horti.*
> *nunc te marmoreum pro tempore fecimus ; at tu,*
> *si fetura gregem suppleuerit, aureus esto.*

It is true, however, that a lesser deity, like *Lar patrius*, could be less fastidious, TIBULLUS, I, 10, 21-24 :
> *hic placatus erat, seu quis libauerat uuam,*
>   *seu dederat sanctae spicea serta comae.*
> *atque aliquis uoti compos liba ipse ferebat*
>   *postque comes purum filia parua fauum.*

But this was in good old times *cum paupere cultu stabat in exigua ligneus aede deus* (*ibid.*, lines 19-20). And if any *uoti compos* because of his poverty brought to the god only holy cakes, he could have hardly had the means or reason to record this on stone. With the poets was a different question.

as the editors are inclined to do, an error of the lapicide. This is not necessary. It is well known to any student of Latin epigraphy that in inscriptions two verticals often stand for the letter E ([7]) ; this is of course the correct reading also in our case ([8]). This is a pity for instead of discovering «une nouveauté intéressante» we must content ourselves with a normally dull although rather unusually phrased ([9]) dedication : *Libe(n)s | votu(m) | Lib(e)ro P | atri · s(olvit) | Paulinu(s)* ([10]).

(7) See e.g. R. CAGNAT, *Cours d'épigraphie latine* [4], Paris, 1914, p. 14 ; cf. the remark in *CIL*, III *Suppl.*, p. 2567 : II = E *passim*.

(8) The form *libes* (instead of *libens*) is so frequent in inscriptions that no argument is necessary here ; see e.g. DESSAU, *ILS*, III, 2, p. 826 (index), and especially for Dacia, S. STATI, *Limba latina in inscriptiile din Dacia şi Scythia Minor*, Bucuresti, 1961, p. 64.

(9) The structure of the formula *libens uotum* (name of the deity) *soluit* (name of the dedicant) seems to be unusual. At any rate among the dedications collected by Dessau I was not able to find any direct parallel (cf. however *ILS*, 4673).

(10) Popa and Aldea are of the opinion that the S at the end of line 4 does not stand for *s(oluit)*, but represents the termination *-s* of the name Paulinus, for which there was no place in line 5. This is of course not impossible (cf. *ILS*, 4739), we should, however, take into account that the formula *libens uotum* was normally rounded off by the verb *soluit*. Especially in view of the «vulgar» character of the inscription it seems legitimate to see here another feature of popular Latin, the omission of the S at the end of the word. Cf. S. STATI, *op. cit.*, p. 59-61.

38

NATALIS PATAVII

In a remarkable article, "The Era of Patavium", ZPE 27, 1977, 283-293, W.V. Harris addressed himself to a Patavine epigraphical peculiarity attested by eleven inscriptions,[1] the notation N (normally with a bar over it), followed by a numeral. If the Patavine N̄ "possesses a pleasing riddle-like quality", Harris' solution of it possesses a pleasing intellectual quality: it would denote the era of Patavium. Harris dates its beginning to 173 B.C., one year after the consul M. Aemilius Lepidus "Patavinorum in Venetia seditionem comprimeret" (Liv. 41,27,3). It is an elegant and economical theory, vastly superior to the idea of Kubitschek that N̄ stood for 'nummi'[2] or Svennung's 'desperate' proposal that it denoted serial numbers from a stonemason's workshop.[3] It may even be superior to Sartori's erudite resignation whose conclusion was that no certain conclusion was possible.[4]

But what did the abbreviation N̄ actually stand for? Mommsen's 'numero' (cf. his note on CIL V 2787) need not militate against Harris' idea. Harris himself observed in passing that "'N'... might stand ... for 'nostro [sc. anno]'" (p. 291). 'N' for 'noster' is of course a common epigraphical abbreviation, but 'n(ostro anno)' is unusual, as F. Sartori was quick to point out in his new contribution to the subject.[5] A more satisfactory solution, and one that would place Harris' theory on terra firma, may be at hand. I should like to suggest that the abbreviation N̄ stands for n(atali [sc. die]).[6]

---

1. In an appendix, p. 293, Harris conveniently reproduces all the eleven inscriptions in question.

2. W. Kubitschek, Eine Stiftung aus Feltre, Num. Zeitschr. 42, 1909, 56; cf. E. Ghislanzoni, Not. Sc. 1926, 352; C. Gasparotto, Padova Romana, Roma 1951, 59 n. 39 (indication of prices).

3. J. Svennung, Numerierung von Fabrikaten und anderen Gegenständen im römischen Altertum, Arctos 2, 1958, 164-186. This idea has recently gained new adherents: see the works quoted by Sartori (below, n. 5), p. 219 n. 5. A novel variation of the numbering theory was proposed by G. Manganaro, Pankarpeia di epigrafia latina, Siculorum Gymnasium 23, 1970, 82-83: the numbers would refer to documents emanating from the municipal tabularium (Most improbable: why should the municipal authorities be interested in numbering simple dedicatory or funerary stones?). For a similar idea, see S. Mrozek, Munificentia privata in den Städten Italiens der spätrömischen Zeit, Historia 27, 1978, 362.

4. F. Sartori, Una particolarità epigrafica di Patavium, Memorie dell' Accademia Patavina di Scienze, Lettere ed Arti, Classe di Scienze Morali, Lettere ed Arti 75, 1962-63, 61-73.

5. F. Sartori, Epigraphica Patavina Minima, Atti e Memorie dell'Accademia Patavina 90, 1977-78, 217-222 at 221. I am thankful to Professor Sartori for kindly sending me offprints of his articles.

6. This idea occurred to me early in 1978 during a pleasant talk with Professor Harris in the cafeteria of the Institute for Advanced Study in Princeton. I soon learnt that Professor R.E.A. Palmer had arrived simul-

It is well known that not only homines and dei, but also collegia, templa and urbes had their dies natales.[7] First of all we have the natalis of Rome on April 21, the feast of Parilia.[8] The case of Rome was most prominent, but not unique. When in 57 B.C. Cicero was coming home from his exile he landed on 5 August in Brundisium: "ibi mihi Tulliola mea fuit praesto natali suo ipso die, qui casu idem natalis erat et Brundisinae coloniae et tuae vicinae Salutis" (Att. 4,1,4). In a later period, in 185 A.D., an inscription from Simitthus in Africa Proconsularis records the natalis civitatis, no doubt of Simitthus.[9] In the fourth century we hear that Constantine celebrated the natalis of Trier,[10] but above all we should not forget the birthday of the New Rome, the γενέθλια of Constantinople on 11 May.[11] And finally an entry in the lexicon of Souda (1, p. 393, no 4266, ed. Adler) contains information about the feast of Astydromia which was celebrated παρὰ Λίβυσιν to commemorate τῆς πόλεως γενέθλια, presumably of Cyrene.[12]

The evidence seems unequivocal, though sparse. Yet F. Bömer attempted to discredit it as late (including the case of Brundisium) and inaccurate. He concludes: "Nur für Rom [ist] ein Geburstag bekannt": all other cities celebrated only "einen Gründungstag"; all other attested natales were simply "Nachahmungen" of Rome.[13] Now the distinction between the dies natalis of a

---

taneously at the same solution. If this note is in need of correction I do hope he will be persuaded to open to the reading public his vast store of erudition.

7. W. Schmidt, Geburtstag im Altertum (Religionsgesch. Versuche u. Vorarbeiten VII 1), Gießen 1908, passim and esp. 79-83.

8. For the sources, see A. Degrassi, Fasti Anni Numani et Iuliani (Inscr. It. XIII 2), Romae 1963, 443-445.

9. CIL VIII 14683 a = ILS 6824, a decree of the curia Iovis. The prescript reads as follows: curia Iovis. acta / V k. Decembres / Materno et [A]ttico cos./ natale civi[t]atis. J. Schmidt, Statut einer Municipalcurie in Africa, RhM 45, 1890, 599-611, esp. 606, 610, points out that the concilium of the curiales took place on 27 November, the anniversary of the foundation of the colonia (natale is here an abl. = natali). Simitthus was established as a colony by Augustus, see F. Vittinghoff, Römische Kolonisation und Bürgerrechtspolitik unter Caesar und Augustus, Abh. Mainz 1951, Heft 14, 112 n. 2.

10. Paneg. Lat. 6 (7), 22,4 Mynors: video hanc fortunatissimam civitatem, cuius natalis dies tua pietate celebratur.

11. For a discussion, sources and modern literature, see G. Dagron, Naissance d'une capitale. Constantinople et ses institutions de 330 à 451, Paris 1974, 29-34. 11 May is the date of what most scholars commonly describe as dedicatio; it is, however, interesting to observe that the old Roman ritual did not know the ceremony of the dedicatio of cities, but rather the ceremony of the inauguratio of the pomerium. See below in the text and note 15.

12. Cf. P. Stengel, RE 2, 1896, 1868.

13. F. Bömer, P. Ovidius Naso. Die Fasten 2, Heidelberg 1958, 271-273.

city and the day of its foundation is artificial, unjustified and misleading.
It rests on no solid ground, but only on conclusions derived from the etymology of Parilia and the meaning of the verb pario: the feast of Parilia was
celebrated only in Rome, not in other cities, hence only Rome was 'born'.

The wording of Cicero, de div. 2,98 (cf. Pease ad loc.), points exactly
to the contrary: "[L. Tarutius Firmanus] urbis etiam nostrae natalem diem
repetebat ab iis Parilibus quibus eam a Romulo conditam accepimus". For
Cicero the natalis urbis was the day on which eam a Romulo conditam accepimus; in other words the Geburtstag was for him the same thing as the Gründungstag, and there is no reason why this equation should not apply to other
cities as well. Of course in Rome the idea of the natalis urbis, and
especially of its date, may have been re-inforced by the derivation of
Parilia from pario (although the popular connection of Parilia with Pales
was always very much alive), yet this consideration should not affect our
argument in any way.

Secondly, if temples had their natales, then why not cities? Surely we
cannot hold that the natales templorum were nothing but mere imitation of
the natalis urbis. To Cicero the natalis of Tullia, of Brundisium, and of
the temple of Salus, all appeared to be very akin to each other.

But above all Römer failed to pose a very pertinent question: which act
technically constituted the 'birth' of a city or a temple?

As far as temples are concerned this was, no doubt, the act of dedica-
tio/consecratio but it is important to remember that when a temple was
rebuilt it was in a sense reborn. In this case its natalis was frequently
transferred to the day of the re-dedication.[14] A Roman city, however, was
not the property of a deity, it was not a res sacra, and consequently the
rite of consecratio/dedicatio could not find any application at the foundation ceremony. In a famous passage Varro writes (Ling. Lat. 5,143):
"oppida condebant in Latio Etrusco ritu multi, id est iunctis bobus, tauro
et vacca, interiore aratro circumagebant sulcum. hoc faciebant religionis
causa die auspicato, ut fossa et muro essent muniti". Varro points out that
murus et fossa are to be understood in a ritual sense: "terram unde exculp-
serant 'fossam' vocabant et introrsus iactam 'murum'". Tarutius Firmanus concurs. According to Solinus 1,18 this mathematicus maintained that "Romulus
... auspicato murorum fundamenta iecit ... XI K. Mai., hora post secundam

---

14. G. Wissowa, Religion und Kultus der Römer, [2]München 1912, 65-67,
475, 477; Idem, Gesammelte Abhandlungen zur römischen Religions- und Stadtge-
schichte, München 1904, 268-279; K. Keyssner, Natalis templi, RE 16, 1935,
1801-2. On consecratio/dedicatio, see Wissowa, RE 4, 1900 s.v. consecratio.
The diffuse divagation by H. Bardon, La naissance d'un temple, REL 33, 1955,
166-182, contains nothing of use.

ante tertiam". That the drawing of sulcus primigenius was *the* act of foundation has always been clear to students of disciplina Etrusca and res
augurales;[15] they did, however, a poor job persuading the others. This
legendary act was in historical times repeated time and again at the foundation of Roman colonies, and yet Mommsen maintained that the official date
of Coloniegründung was the date of the lustrum,[16] and E.T. Salmon believed
that the colonia dated officially from the day when the groma was removed
and the forma and the lex colonica were set up in the forum. In a perceptive
article A.M. Eckstein has recently refuted these theories, and persuasively
established or re-established, it is hoped once and for ever, that the foundation day of a Roman colonia was the day on which the plowing ritual was
performed.[17] A Roman colony celebrated its natalis on the real anniversary
of its foundation; for most cities in Italy, including Rome, this was a
fictitious anniversary of a legendary foundation.

Now Patavium was neither founded nor re-founded in 174 or 173:
its legendary founder was Antenor and it did not become a municipium until
49 B.C.[18] Yet an important event in the life of a city was apt to be regarded as a new beginning. Livy (6,1,3) speaks of a secunda origo, of renata
urbs when Rome was rebuilding after destruction wrought by the Gauls. And
Cicero (Flacc. 102) exclaims "O Nonae illae Decembres quae me consule
fuistis! Quem ego diem vere natalem huius urbis aut certe salutarem appellare
possum". Patavium we learn from Livy (41,27,3) was torn apart by certamen
factionum and intestinum bellum. Livy mentions that the legati from Patavium
were received by the senate: apparently the pro-Roman party turned for help
to the imperial city. It should not come as a surprise that the victors in
civil strife should celebrate the re-establishment of peace, tranquillity
and their domination as a new birth of their city: Patavinis adventus consulis saluti fuit.

---

15. See C.O. Thulin, Die etruskische Disciplin III 3-17 (Göteborgs
Högskolas Årsskrift XV, 1909, reprint Darmstadt 1968); P. Catalano, Contributi allo studio del diritto augurale 1, Torino 1960, 575-583. See now also
W.A. Schröder, M. Porcius Cato. Das erste Buch de Origines (Beitr. zur
klass. Phil. 41), Meisenheim 1971, 171-176.

16. Th. Mommsen, Römisches Staatsrecht 2[3], Leipzig 1887, 636-638;
E.T. Salmon, Roman Colonization under the Republic, London 1969 [Ithaca
1970], 26.

17. A.E. Eckstein, The Foundation Day of Roman Coloniae, California
Studies in Class. Antiquity 12, 1979, 85-97.

18. H. Philipp, Patavium, RE 18, 1949, 2114-15, 2117; U. Ewins, The
Enfranchisement of Cisalpine Gaul, PBSR 23, 1955, 91.

The abbreviation N appears relatively frequently as the littera singularis for n(atalis),[19] but we have to remember that natalis almost invariably means dies not annus. I know of only one exception to this rule. Reporting on the famous vinum Opimianum Pliny (NH 14,102) writes: "anno fuit omnium generum bonitate L. Opimio cos., cum G. Gracchus tribunus plebis seditionibus agitans interemptus est; ea caeli temperies fulsit (cocturam vocant) solis opere natali urbis DCXXXIII". Here natalis urbis denotes the whole year of L. Opimius' consulship, and not merely 21 April 633 a.u.c. But it is n(atali die), and not n(atali anno) that makes sense for Patavium. In the latter case we surely would have expected more inscriptions than the paltry eleven to carry the notation N̄. I should like to suggest that all the stones in question commemorate events that took place on the very dies natalis of Patavium. This would explain very well their relative paucity.

Leges templorum and leges collegiorum contained regulations concerning sacrifices to be offerred and festivities to be celebrated on their dies natales;[20] and, as we have seen (above, n. 9), the curia Iovis in Simitthus took care to record that its decree was passed natali civitatis. The Patavine local foible, as Harris calls it, will manifest itself in a greater number of such inscriptions, the persistent application of the notation N, and, above all, in the numeral appended to this notation. Yet, even this is not totally unparalleled. Pliny offers a combination of natalis urbis followed by a numeral, and a similar phrase appears on a curious coin from the reign of Hadrian: "ann(o) DCCCLXXIIII nat(ali) Urb(is) P(arilibus) cir(censes) con(stituti)".[21]

Let us now turn again to the inscriptions from Patavium and investigate whether they bear out our theory. Of the eleven inscriptions exhibiting the notation N̄ (or Ñ) two refer to the ludi, rather a high percentage, but the really striking fact is that these are the only two inscriptions of this character from Patavium. ILS 5650 mentions a theatrical performance; CIL V 2787 = ILS 5202 is a dedication set up by certain Q. Magurius Felix, "lus(or)[22] epidixib(us) et cetaes". Here we have no doubt an allusion to the

---

19. In the calendar of Filocalus the standard abbreviation for natalis is N̄, including n(atalis) Urbis; Degrassi, Fasti, pp. 237ff. The remaining fasti, however, use the abbreviation nat(alis) or no abbreviation at all. For the epigraphical evidence, see esp. the lex collegii Aesculapi et Hygiae, CIL VI 10234 = ILS 7213, lines 9, 11; CIL VI 29691.

20. For temples, see A. Aust, De aedibus sacris populi Romani, Diss. Marpurgi 1889, passim, esp. 34ff.; and for collegia, J.P. Waltzing, Étude historique sur les corporations professionnelles chez les Romains 4, Louvain 1900, 434-5.

21. P. Strack, Untersuchungen zur römischen Reichsprägung des zweiten Jahrhunderts 2, Stuttgart 1933, 102-105.

22. Dessau expands lusit (vel: lusor); for the reading lusor, see F. Bücheler, Artisten-Wörter, RhM 58, 1903, 318.

ludi cetasti, reputedly instituted by Antenor.[23] This makes it very likely
that both theatrical and other performances were staged on the natalis of the
city. The new natalis may have been celebrated on the same day as the old --
so as after the refectio of a templum the ceremony of re-dedication was often
performed on the old natalis of the temple.[24] But it is not impossible that
the ludi cetasti were organized only after the Roman intervention, and that
it was about the same time that the Patavini started to advertize (as did
some other cities) their Trojan syngeneia with the Romans.[25] Two inscriptions
refer to activities of public figures: CIL V 2864 = ILS 5406 records that
"M. Iunius Sabinus IIII vir aediliciae potestat(is) e lege Iulia municipali
... frontem templi vervis et hermis marmoreis pecunia sua ornavit" -- the
natalis civitatis will have been a suitable day for the unveiling of these
gifts before the gathered multitude (cf. Cic. Att. 4,1,4). CIL V 2794 is a
dedication to G(enius) c(ollegii) d(endrophorum) by a VI vir "ob honorem
q(uin)q(uennalitatis)"; perhaps this was the day on which the quinquennales
of the collegium entered their office or simply the day when the dedication
was set up. In fact I suspect that CIL V 2797 (a dedication to Isis Regina)
and Not. Sc. 1926, 352 (a solutio votis) contain the notation N̄ because they
happened to be put up on the dies natalis civitatis. This explanation will
also hold for four funerary stones (CIL V 2873, 2885, 2943, 3031): either the
persons in question died or the stones were erected natali civitatis. And
finally CIL V 3019 would indicate that the construction of a building was
concluded on the CCC[...] birthday of the city.

A much discussed inscription from Feltria, ILS 9420, exhibits a similar
notation: N̄ CCCLXII. The mention of a consular pair assures its date: 323
A.D. Harris argues persuasively (p. 290) that here we are in the presence of
a local era of Feltria: the city may have become a municipium in 39 B.C. The
inscription contains regulations of a funerary foundation. The decree of the
curia Iovis from Simitthus offers a parallel: it was enacted natali civitatis
and so will have been the document from Feltria. The only difference is this:
in Simitthus we are given the calendar date of the natalis dies; in Feltria
(and in Patavium) its number.[26]

---

23. Tac. Ann. 16,21,1 and Koestermann ad loc. p. 378.
24. Keyssner, loc. cit. (above, n. 14).
25. Cf. Cato, fr. 42 Peter (Plin. NH 3.130); R.M. Ogilvie, A Commentary
on Livy. Books 1-5, Oxford 1965, 36.
26. A comment on two funerary inscriptions from Numidia which seem to
display a similar formula is in order. CIL VIII 4375 (Seriana) is a stone set
up for an imm(unis) leg(ionis) III Aug(ustae). The first two lines read: D M
S / N (hedera) CC (hedera). This may be an indication of a local era (cf.
Harris, p. 290), but it is also possible that CC does not represent any
number at all but an abbreviation. In CIL VIII 5585 = ILAlg. 5635 (Thibilis)
I am inclined to follow Svennung (above, n. 3), pp. 172-3, and take N̄ C III
as the indication of the age of the deceased (however, as Svennung points out,
we have to keep in mind "daß gerade in dieser Gegend von Afrika ein numero
vor der Jahreszahl sich nicht finden läßt").

39

JULIA IN REGIUM

I.

Iulia, diui Augusti filia -- so is Julia styled in an inscription, found many years ago, and missed by all those who recently wrote about her ambitions and misfortunes. It reads:

C(aius) Iulius Iuliae diui
  Aug(usti) f(iliae) l(ibertus) Gelos [si]bi et
C(aio) I(ulio) Iul[iae diui] Aug(usti) f(iliae) l(iberto)
  Thiaso patr[i sexuir(o) a]ug(ustali)
[et Iu]liae diuai Au[g(ustae) l(ibertae) ...]
         matr[i]
       ex testament[to]

This remarkable document is made even more remarkable by the place of its discovery; the city of Regium where Julia lived in exile and where she found her death.[1] Her journey to Regium began in 2 B.C. when "a foul and

1) The inscription was found in November 1949 and published by C.Turano, with a short commentary and a serviceable photograph, "Note die epigrafia classica II", Klearchos 5, fasc. 19, 1963, 76-81. AE reproduced it (without comment) only in the issue for 1975 (1978),289. In AE 1952,25-26 (after no.61) there is a report of an incomplete report by G.Iacopi in Fasti Archaeologici 4, 1949 (1951), 382, no. 3910 ("Due iscrizioni frammentarie con la menzione di Giulia figlia di Augusto, e di due trierarchi". Cf. below, n.10). The inscription has also been reproduced (on the basis of autopsy) by F.Costabile, Istituzioni e forme costituzionali nelle città del Bruzio in età Romana, Napoli 1982, 172, n.55, and by M.Buonocore,"L'epigrafia latina dei Bruttii dopo Mommsen ed Ihm", Rivista Storica Calabrese N.S. 6, 1985 = Studi storici e ricerche archeologiche sulla Calabria antica e medioevale in memoria di Paolo Orsi, 327-356 at 329. I should like to thank Dr.Elena Lattanzi of the Soprintendenza Archeologica della Calabria for drawing my attention to the works of Costabile and Buonocore, and for kindly inspecting the stone for me. I am thankful to my colleagues and friends, to Prof.J.F.Gilliam and Prof. Christian Habicht of the Institute for Advanced Study in Princeton, for providing photocopies of the articles in Klearchos, to Prof.Umberto Laffi of the University of Pisa, for procuring a copy of the article by Buonocore, and to Prof.William Harris of Columbia University for xeroxing the relevant pages from the book of Costabile.
Lines 2 and 4 are slightly indented; the text in lines 6 and 7 is placed approximately at the center of the line; in line 2 there is an empty space left between [si]bi and et. Also note:
line 2: Turano reads Celos and interprets this name (p.77, n.4) as signifying niger (Κελαινός); the Editors of AE observe: "Celos pour Gelos". Dr.Elena Lattanzi informs me that the correct reading is indeed Gelos (cf. below, n.16). So also Costabile (172, n.55) and Buonocore (329, and 349,n.27).
line 3: A]ug(usti) Turano, AE, but a trace of the upper part of A is visible on the photograph. Costabile and Buonocore read Aug(usti).
line 4: Turano restores the text alternately as patr[i mag(istro) a]ug(ustali). Cf. below, n.18.
line 5: diuai Turano, AE, Costabile, Buonocore, Lattanzi, but the photograph does not seem to exclude the reading diuae; Au[gustae Turano, AE; Au[g(ustae) Buonocore (Costabile gives two readings of this line, both incorrect, without proper indication of the length of the lacuna). At the end of the line we probably should leave space for the cognomen (so Costabile and Buonocore; Turano does not leave any space).

sudden storm erupted in the house of Augustus" (Vell. 2. 100. 2). The beloved daughter of the Princeps was banished to the island of Pandateria,
a cloud of rumor and propaganda hanging over her to these days.[2] There she
was kept in strict confinement, her mother Scribonia her lone and voluntary
companion.[3] The populace of Rome, we are told, frequently and vociferously
remonstrated with Augustus to bring her back. It was only after some time
that the emperor bowed to the pressure (so Cass. Dio [Xiph.] 55. 13. 1) and
transferred her to the mainland. According to Suetonius this happened post
quinquennium (Aug. 65. 3), which leads us to A.D. 3 (counting inclusively)
or to A.D. 4 (counting exclusively). The former is the traditional date, but
a word can be put forth also for the latter.[4]

In A.D. 2 Tiberius was allowed to return to Rome, for the time being
strictly as a private person. In her admirable study of the years 2-8 A.D.,
B.Levick interprets the new intensity of agitation in Julia's favor, the

R.Hanslik, Der Kleine Pauly 2, 1975, 1540, seems to have been the only
scholar to notice this document in connection with the story of Julia, but
he described it erroneously as the "Grabinschrift zweier Sklavinnen der
Iulia", and failed to realize its historical and legal significance. H.
Chantraine utilized our inscription in his valuable "Freigelassene und Sklaven kaiserlicher Frauen", Studien zur antiken Sozialgeschichte. Festschrift
Friedrich Vittinghoff, Köln-Wien 1980. He lists the two freedmen of Julia
(391, and 405, n.41), but in place of the freedwoman of Livia he has an
entirely spurious M. Iulius divae Aug. 1. (390, and 405, n.27). She is also
missing from M. Buonocore's list of gentilicia attested in Regium: "Vecchie
e nuove iscrizioni da Regium Iulium", Klearchos 24, 1982 (1984), 143.

2) I do not propose to go in this place into the story of Julia's
catastrophe in 2 B.C. The sources on her fall and banishment are conveniently
assembled in PIR[2] IV 3, 1976, 300. That conspiracy was afoot (or that at
least Augustus feared a conspiracy) is the theory put forward by E.Groag,
("Studien zur Kaisergeschichte. III. Der Sturz der Iulia", Wiener Studien 40,
1918, 150-167; 41, 1919, 74-88) and brilliantly elaborated by B.Levick
("Tiberius' Retirement to Rhodes", Latomus 31, 1972, 779-813) and R.Syme
(The Crisis of 2 B.C., Sb. München, 1974, 7 = Roman Papers III, Oxford 1984,
912-936; History in Ovid, Oxford 1978, 193-198). Cf. now also P.Green,
"Carmen et Error: πρόφασις and αἰτία in the Matter of Ovid's Exile", Clas-
sical Antiquity 1, 1982, 202-220. Some still believe that only concern for
"morals" informed the action of Augustus (cf. A.Ferrill, "Augustus and his
Daughter: a Modern Myth", Studies in Latin Literature and Roman History II =
Collection Latomus 168, 1980, 332-346; W.K.Lacey, "2 B.C. and Julia's Adultery"
Antichthon 14, 1980, 127-140; G.P.Goold, "The Cause of Ovid's Exile",
Illinois Classical Studies 8, 1, 1983, 94-107). But morals do not exist in a
Platonic void divorced from politics and the quest for power -- as every
historian might be expected to know.

3) Vell. 2. 100. 5; Suet., Aug.65; Cass. Dio 55. 10.14.

4) This is the only example of the construction post quinquennium in
Suetonius. If used with the genitive it expresses the point from which the
period is reckoned, as in Dig. 49. 16. 13. 6: "post quinquennium desertionis"
(cf. OLD s.v.). Sometimes this point has to be supplied from the context,
as e.g. in Cic. 2 Verr. 2. 143: "quis erit ... qui te ... post quinquennium
(i.e. from the date of the acquittal) statuarum nomine arcessat?". Nothing
prevents us from interpreting Suetonius' phrase in this sense, but the
linguistic ambiguity remains.

agitation that proved effective in A.D. 3, as an answer to the return of
Tiberius.[5] But it is doubtful that Augustus simply retreated when confronted with a faceless opposition behind which the partisans of Julia were
hiding. It was the following year that was memorable for the design of the
Principate. On 21 February A.D. 4 Gaius Caesar died in Lycia, and when the
news of his demise reached Rome the political situation changed dramatically.
A new arrangement of succession was effected by a peculiar set of adoptions.[6]
On 26 June Tiberius was adopted by Augustus, given the tribunitial power
for ten years, and thus elevated to the position of co-regent and anointed
as heir apparent. On the same day Augustus also adopted Agrippa Postumus,
but, unlike his elder brothers, he was given no honors and no public and
formal assurances of a speedy advancement.

Now Zonaras 10. 36 (vol. 2, p. 449 Dindorf) in his very confused excerpt
from Cass. Dio (55. 13. 1a) intimates that Augustus adopted Tiberius
yielding to the persuasion of Julia, who had now been recalled from
banishment. Zonaras apparently mistook the transfer of Julia from Pandateria
to the mainland (correctly reported by Xiphilinus = Cass. Dio 55. 13. 1) for
her complete restoration; his story of Julia's intercession for Tiberius is
a wild fabrication,[7] but it may contain a garbled reminiscence of a
chronological link between the adoption of Tiberius and Julia's removal
from the island. Thus Augustus will have combined the elevation of Tiberius
and Agrippa with a show of leniency towards Julia.

Through the adoptions of A.D. 4 the seeds were sown of a vicious struggle
that soon ended with the triumph of Livia's son and the disgrace and
banishment of Julia's children, Julia the Younger and Agrippa. Julia's
personal situation improved considerably, but her political hopes sank
lower and lower. When the populace of Rome continued to clamor for her
complete restoration, the Princeps proved intransigent (Suet., Aug. 65. 3).

Julia now lived confined to one town, "uno oppido clausa" (Suet., Tib.
50), oppido Reginorum, Tacitus informs us (Ann. 1. 53), and the new inscription offers welcome corroboration.

Why Regium? Long distance from Rome may have been one reason -- Tacitus
is careful to stress that the Regini inhabit the straits of Sicily. But
there was much more to Julia's new place of exile than mere remoteness. The
Triumvirs had originally included Regium among the eighteen cities of Italy

---

5) "The Fall of Julia the Younger", Latomus 35, 1976, 301-339 at 310.

6) For all details, see B.Levick, "Drusus Caesar and the Adoptions of A.D.
4", Latomus 25, 1966, 227-244; cf. Eadem, Tiberius the Politician, London
1976, 47-50.

7) Though recently it was accorded some credence: Julia put in a word
naturally not for Tiberius but rather for Agrippa! (Green, op. cit. [above,
n.2], 214, n.73. In the course of his argument he confuses the two Julias).

destined for veterans as prizes of victory (App., BC 4. 3). But then Sal-
vidienus Rufus unsuccessfully fought a naval engagement against Sex. Pompeius
(42 B.C.), and Octavian, stopping at Regium on his way to Brundisium and
Philippi, found it advisable to assure the inhabitants of Regium and of Vibo
that they would be exempted from the confiscations. The two cities occupied
a strategic position at the straits, and it was imperative to gain their
loyalty against the allurements of Pompeius (App., BC 4. 86). Octavian
almost kept his word. No legions were settled at Regium, but when Sex. Pompeius was finally defeated, part of the cíty was assigned to the sailors of
the victorious fleet (Strabo 4. 259). The municipium now carried the proud
name Regium Iulium, and its citizens were bound to Augustus by the manifold
ties of gratitude.[8] The old inhabitants owed to the Emperor their preservation from the disaster he himself had been instrumental in preparing; the
new settlers owed to him all the possessions they had. The magistrates of
the city, mindful of the past dangers and the present peace, could be
trusted to keep a watchful eye on Julia and not allow her to brew any trouble.

   Another inscription from Regium may be of importance, a funerary stone
set up by the trierarchus C. Iulius C. f. Niger for his fellow trierarchus
C. Iulius Euandrus, son of Neoptolemus.[9] The two men seem to have been
officers in active service and not retired captains settled in Regium among
the other classiarii. Hence the suggestion that a detachment of the fleet
of Misenum may have been stationed at Regium.[10] If this was the case, Julia
was well protected indeed.

II.

   The literary sources now fall silent until Julia's last days. The welcome

---

   8) Cf. Th.Mommsen, CIL X, 1, pp.3-4.

   9) It was found in 1949 together with the inscription set up by Iulius
Gelos, and was also published by C.Turano, "Note di epigrafia classica I",
Klearchos 2, fasc. 7-8, 1960, 65-68 = AE 1975, 284 (where the volume and
date of the publication is given mistakenly as Klearchos 1, 1959).

   10) G.Iacopi in his preliminary notice of the find, Fasti Archaeologici
4, 1949 (1951), 382, no.3910; the Editors of AE incline to the same view.
So also G.Schmiedt, Antichi porti d'Italia, Firenze 1975, 110-111, but M.
Reddé, Mare nostrum, Rome 1986, 204-205, n.181, finds this idea unlikely;
however, he alludes to our inscription only in passing. Thus, despite its
obvious interest to students of the Roman navy, the inscription was accorded no discussion by Reddé, and was missed by D.Kienast, Untersuchungen
zu den Kriegsflotten der römischen Kaiserzeit, Bonn 1966. Observe that
neither man was a freedman: the patronymicon of C. Iulius Euandrus shows
that he was a peregrine who received the citizenship as a reward for his
services to Octavian; his case thus parallels that of the famous Seleucus
of Rhosos. C. Iulius Niger will on the other hand belong to the next generation of the trierarchi; his father was either a peregrine or a freedman
in the service of Octavian, and his own cognomen demonstrates the progress
of romanization.

exception is the report of Suetonius (Tib. 50) that Augustus granted Julia
for her use a property (peculium) and a yearly allowance in cash (praebita
annua).[11]

The peculium of Julia leads us back to those semi-promising days when she
left Pandateria. On that island her regime had been harsh: Augustus denied
her all the amenities ("delicatiorem cultum ademit"), including the use of
wine; in Regium her treatment was less rigorous (Suet., Aug. 65. 3). Thus,
no doubt, it was at that time that Augustus conceded Julia the use of peculium (which will have comprised her house, her slaves and the instrumentum
domesticum) and provided her with a monetary allowance. It was an arrangement
not dissimilar to that many other young nobles -- and exiles -- used to
enjoy.[12]

Few students of Augustus realize that the mention of peculium is the only
certain clue we have concerning the legal status of Julia. Had she been
married to Tiberius cum manu, as one might perhaps have expected considering
the traditionalist leanings of her father and her husband, she would have
become, on her divorce, a person sui iuris, owning her own property. Her
peculium defines her as a filiafamilias. It also throws light on the dark
days of her relegation in 2 B.C. On Pandateria she apparently had no
possessions of her own; this explains very well why the compassionate
Scribonia chose to accompany her unfortunate daughter.

Paradoxically enough, in civil law the position of Julia and Tiberius was
now identical: both were in potestate and owned no property.[13] After his
adoption Tiberius paraded his dutiful observance of the legal restrictions
imposed upon him as a filiusfamilias. As Suetonius puts it (Tib. 15. 2), "he

11) Here will also belong the statement of Cassius Dio (Xiph.) 56. 32. 4
that although Augustus did not recall Julia from exile, he nevertheless
regarded her worthy to receive gifts (καίπερ καὶ δωρεῶν ἀξιώσας). As
this remark comes in Dio's enumeration of the provisions of Augustus' will,
E.Hohl ("Primum facinus novi principatus", Hermes 70, 1935, 352, n.5) took
it as a mistaken reference to a legacy which Dio or his excerptor imagined
was left to Julia by Augustus (in fact Augustus left Julia no legacy, see
below, III). But the closer context of this enunciation is not the will of
Augustus but Julia's continuing exile; we should rather see here a garbled
reference to her peculium.

12) Cf. Thomas, (below, n.13), 547-549. The closest parallel to the annua
of Julia is provided by the story in Seneca, de clem. 1. 15. 2-7. The son of
L. Tarius Rufus (cos. suff. 16 B.C.) was convicted by the iudicium domesticum
(in which also Augustus himself participated) of plotting against his
father's life, and was relegated to Massilia. Nevertheless Tarius extended
to him the same liberal yearly allowance that he had been wont to give him
previously.

13) On the administration and legal aspects of the peculium, see M.Kaser,
Das römische Privatrecht I^2, München 1971, 64, 267, 287-288, 343-344, 392-393;
B.Albanese, Le persone nel diritto privato romano, Palermo 1979, 271-281;
and especially on the peculium of the filiafamilias, M.García Garrido, Ius
uxorium. El régimen patrimonial de la mujer casada en derecho romano, Roma-
Madrid 1958, 13-28. The social consequences of this peculiar institution
are discussed in a spirited study by Y.Thomas, "Droit domestique et droit
politique à Rome", MEFRA 94, 1982, 527-580.

ceased to act as paterfamilias, and did not retain in any particular the
rights he had given up. For he neither made gifts nor freed slaves, and he
did not even accept an inheritance or any legacies without expressly entering
them as an addition to his peculium" ("Nec quicquam postea pro patre familias
egit aut ius, quod amiserat, ex ulla parte retinuit. Nam neque donavit neque
manumisit, ne hereditatem quidem aut legata percepit ulla aliter quam ut
peculio referret accepta"). Upon his adoption his former property became
technically the property of Augustus, and was given back to him to be enjoyed solely as a peculium. Although the concessio peculii implied the
right to administer it, fully and freely, there were some strictly defined
and unpleasant limits to that freedom. The filiusfamilias was not entitled
to perform any formal acts of the ius civile, and in particular, Cicero and
the jurists inform us, he could not make gifts or manumit slaves without
permission from his father.[14] As a result, Suetonius avers, Tiberius will
have altogether refrained from manumitting slaves.[15]

Julia was less squeamish and more generous. In the new inscription from
Regium her freedmen stand before us; it is high time to get acquainted with
them.

The stone was set up by C. Iulius Gelos,[16] on the basis of the testamentary disposition of his father.[17] Both Gelos and his father Thiasus,

---

14) For donatio, see Cic., de leg. 2. 50; Dig. 39. 5. 7 pr. (Ulpian, 44
ad Sab.); and for manumission, Dig. 37. 14. 13 (Modestinus, 1 pand.); 33.
8. 19. 2 (Papinian,7 resp.); 40. 1. 7 (Alfenus Varus, 7 dig.; cf. A.Watson,
The Law of Persons in the Later Roman Republic, Oxford 1967, 187-90); 40. 2.
4 pr. (Iulianus, 42 dig.); 40. 2. 22 (Paulus, 22 quaest.); 40. 15. 1 (Paulus,
1 ad leg. Iul.). In addition to the literature cited in the preceding note,
see also W.W.Buckland, The Roman Law of Slavery, Cambridge 1908, 458-459,
718-723.

15) Whether the picture presented by Suetonius corresponds to reality is
another question. Epigraphy might be of help, but two major studies of the
nomenclature of the imperial slaves and freedmen, H.Chantraine, Freigelassene
und Sklaven im Dienst der römischen Kaiser, Wiesbaden 1967, and P.R.C.Weaver,
Familia Caesaris, Cambridge 1972, are silent on that point; the passage of
Suetonius is missing from their indices. Tiberius was frugal and skimpy
(cf. Tac., Ann. 4. 6. 4), and he may indeed have manumitted no slaves; it is
telling that Chantraine (p.36) was not able to find any certain evidence for
freedmen of Tiberius as a privatus (i. e. before his adoption). On the
other hand it is not altogether likely that all freedmen of Tiberius we
encounter in inscriptions were manumitted after the death of Augustus; one
can legitimately entertain the notion that at least some of the freedmen who
style themselves Ti. Caes. lib. (cf. Chantraine, 18, 144; Weaver, 44, 49)
were freed when Tiberius was not yet Augustus. The subject requires a separate
treatment.

16) Oddly enough, we know from approximately the same period (26 A.D.)
another imperial freedman bearing the same surname, C. Iulius divi Augusti
l. Gelos, a notable in Veii, admitted by the Veientes inter Augustales
(CIL XI. 3805 = ILS 6579).

17) As a woman did not have the legal capacity to make a will (unless she
had undergone capitis deminutio), it is very unlikely that this was the
joint testamentary disposition of Gelos' parents. Cf. Watson, The Law of
Persons (above, n.14), 152-154.

who as a sevir Augustalis reached some prominence in Regium,[18] took their
praenomina after that of the father of the manumitrix. Nothing unusual so far,
but Gelos' mother (whose cognomen presumably stood in the lacuna at the end
of line 5) is a surprise: she was a freedwoman of Livia, diva Augusta. This
raises a host of legal and historical questions. In line 5 Iu]liae is
clearly legible on the photograph, and hence the mother of Gelos was manumitted only after Livia had been admitted "in familiam Iuliam nomenque
Augustum" (Tac., Ann. 1. 8. 1). This happened in virtue of Augustus' last
will that was opened and read in the senate early in September of A.D. 14
(cf. below, n. 26). On the other hand Thiasos and Gelos must have been
manumitted before that date: in his will Augustus left no property to Julia,
and as a consequence she lost her peculium to which also her slaves belonged
(see below, III).

The picture that seems to emerge is not unfamiliar: the jolly and
generous Julia freed her slaves early, the father and the son; the mother
remained the slave of the tight Livia until her services were needed no
more. Tacitus places the death of Julia shortly after the accession of
Tiberius (below, IV), hence late A.D. 14 or early 15 may be the date of the
manumission of Gelos' mother.

But what was the slave of Livia doing in the household of Julia? The
contubernium between slaves belonging to various members of the imperial
domus was a common occurrence, but there may be much more to our inscription
than the simple cohabitation of the two slaves. Was the mother of Gelos,
the Ignota, Livia's spy in Julia's household, keeping her mistress con-
fidentially informed about the behavior of the exile? If this was so, her
manumission at the end of Julia's life was a reward well-earned, and not
unexpected.

There is a simpler explanation, much less generous to Julia, and much
more favorable to Livia. The Ignota may have been a slave of Julia. Her
husband and her son were freed, but she remained in slavery. When the
peculium of Julia was taken by Augustus' heirs, Tiberius and Livia, she may
have ended up in Livia's share, and was ultimately manumitted by her new
owner.

In the inscription Livia appears as diva Augusta. This establishes the
terminus post quem for the setting up of the stone: A.D. 42 (or 41), when
Claudius, compensating for Tiberius' and Caligula's lack of piety, had the

---

18) That he was an Augustalis Turano and AE assume on the strength of the
letters]ug in line 4; it cannot be a reference to Augustus as the status
of Thiasus as Aug(usti) f(iliae) l(ibertus) was already given in line 3.
In his list of Augustales, R.Duthoy, Epigraphische Studien 11, 1976, 143–
214, esp. 156, takes no notice of Thiasus.

senate consecrate Livia as diva.[19] Thus the parents of Gelos could have
died at the earliest in 42 (41); now we can make various computations.

The lex Aelia Sentia introduces a complication. This law, passed in A.D.
4, prohibited the owners from manumitting slaves under thirty years of age
unless a iusta causa for manumission was shown, and approved by the consilium of a magistrate consisting of five senators and five knights.[20] Now
in order to reach the required age by A.D. 14 Gelos must have been born at
the latest in 17 B.C. If we assume that his parents were at that time twenty
years old or so, they will have died at the earliest in their late seventies;
not likely. We can imagine that Thiasos and his contubernalis came to Julia
as the servi peculiares together with their son, though he may very well
have been born later in Julia's household in Regium.[21]

As a filiafamilias Julia was obliged to ask her father for permission to
free Thiasos and Gelos; but now we know she had also to prevail upon
Augustus to allow her to free Gelos against the letter of the law. It is
true that the causa seems to have been treated very flexibly, and the inscriptions record freedmen, also imperial freedmen, who were manumitted
before the legal age.[22] Still it is well to see that Augustus was ready to
accomodate his daughter -- in small matters. For soon the modest comfort she
enjoyed was to come to a grievous end.

The eyes of our greatest historians, of Cornelius Tacitus, of Ronald
Syme, are riveted on the Princeps and the exercise of power: law is only a
dressing. Dressing it is, but potent and poisonous, as Tiberius, and Julia,
and Augustus, knew so well.

Tiberius "fraudulently deprived Julia of the property (peculium) and the
yearly income (praebita annua) which her father had granted her. This he did
under the pretext of observing public law (per speciem publici iuris) as
Augustus made no provision concerning this matter in his will". So Suetonius
(Tib. 50).

Through rumor and misinformation an occasional document fortunately

19) PIR[2] V, 1970, 77. For Costabile (above, n.1), 172, n.55, the terminus
post quem is 29, "anno della morte di Livia". So also Buonocore, "L'epigrafia
latina dei Bruttii" (above, n.1), 239. They forget that Livia did not become
diva on her death but only under the reign of Claudius. For the nomenclature
of her slaves and freedmen, see Chantraine, "Freigelassene und Sklaven kaiserlicher Frauen" (above, n.1), 390; Weaver, op. cit. (above, n.15), 24, n.1;
28-29.

20) Gaius, Inst. 1.17-20, 38-9. Cf. Buckland, op. cit. (above, n.14),
537-44; Kaser, Privatrecht (above, n.13), 297.

21) If the Ignota was a slave of Livia there is a complication for in
this case her son should have belonged to Livia as well (cf. Kaser, Privatrecht (above, n.13), 114), although if he was born in the household of Julia
it is possible to argue that he became Julia's property through usufruct:
see J.Linderski, "Partus Ancillae", Labeo (forthcoming).

22) Cf. Weaver, op. cit. (above n.15), 97-104.

shimmers. The imperial librarian and secretary Suetonius was fond of gossip, but he also knew the value of legal texts: Tiberius insisted on a strict observance of Augustus' last will and testament.[23] We can expect indeed that the new Princeps followed the letter of the law as scrupulously as he himself had observed the patrimonial restrictions of the filiusfamilias.

What was then Julia's status in civil law now and her patrimonial position? Augustus died on 19 August A.D. 14. At the moment Julia became a person sui iuris, but a woman normally needed a guardian. Unless Augustus appointed a tutor for Julia in his last will (and we have no information that he did), the guardianship would have devolved on the closest agnatus, and the closest (and only) male relative of Julia was Tiberius (Agrippa Postumus being an un-person). The duty of the guardian was in particular to refuse to give his consent (auctoritas) to any transaction that could diminish the woman's patrimony. This is not exactly what Tiberius did, but we can also be certain that he did not do anything legally reprehensible. For Julia needed no guardian. Through the leges Iulia de maritandis ordinibus (18 B.C.) and Papia Poppaea (9 A.D.) the woman who had borne three children was freed from the tutela, and Julia, as the mother of Gaius and Lucius, of Julia the Younger and Agrippina, and of Agrippa Postumus (not counting her son by Tiberius who died as an infant), amply earned the ius trium liberorum.[24] Thus Tiberius was spared being placed in a quandary between the strict interpretation of Augustus' will (and his pleasure to do harm to Julia) and the obligations to his potential ward.

Augustus composed the last version of his testament on 3 April A.D. 13 (Suet., Aug. 101. 1);[25] it was opened and read at the session of the senate de supremis Augusti (Tac., Ann. 1.8.1) convoked by Tiberius in virtue of his tribunitial power (Tac., Ann. 1.7.3; Suet., Tib. 23). Curiously enough, the exact date of this meeting is not transmitted, but it will have preceded by a few days the dramatic meeting of 17 September at which the senate formally

---

23) But contrary to the long held opinion (cf. e.g. A.Macé, Essai sur Suétone, Paris 1900, 110-198) it appears that Suetonius did not conduct for his Lives any systematic archival researches and used archival material only occasionally: see the careful study by L.De Coninck, Suetonius en de Archivalia, Brussel 1983.

24) For the tutela mulierum, see Watson, The Law of Persons (above, n.14), 146-154; Kaser, Privatrecht (above, n.13), 367-369; Albanese, op. cit. (above, n.13), 529-537; and for the ius trium liberorum, Gaius, Inst. 1. 45. 94; Paulus, Sent. 4. 9. 9 (FIRA II, 380); cf. R.Astolfi, La lex Iulia et Papia, Padova 1970, 174-179.

25) The best study of the successive testaments of Augustus remains E. Hohl, "Zu den Testamenten des Augustus", Klio 30, 1937, 323-342; cf. also D.Timpe, Untersuchungen zur Kontinuität des frühen Prinzipats, Wiesbaden 1962, 40-45; J.Ober, "Tiberius and the Political Testament of Augustus", Historia 31, 1982, 306-328. None of them discusses the position of Julia or analyzes the will in detail as a document of civil law.

offered the principatus to Tiberius.[26]

Suetonius intimates that Tiberius was able to deprive Julia of her peculium and her praebita annua only because Augustus made no mention of this
matter in his will ("quod nihil de his Augustus testamento cavisset"). This
should not, however, be taken to mean that Julia was not mentioned in the
will at all. Historians, innocent of the law as they often are, have for too
long allowed this nonsense to plague their scripts.

In a Roman will the heredes sui had to be either expressly instituted
heir or expressly disinherited. In particular the sons in potestate had to
be instituted or disinherited nominatim; the daughters and other more distant
heredes sui could be disinherited by a general clause of disinherison:
ceteri omnes exheredes sunto. If a son was neither instituted nor disinherited the will was void; if a daughter and other heredes were passed over
in silence the will was valid, but the overlooked persons would automatically
qualify for their share of inheritance as if on intestacy.[27] Augustus
instituted as his heirs Tiberius and Livia (the latter needed, however, the
exemption, to be voted by the senate, from the lex Voconia which enacted
that the person belonging to the first census class could not appoint a woman
as his heir). The testamentary dispositions of Augustus are unanimously
reported by our sources which equally unanimously omit to mention the disinherison of Julia.[28] And yet Augustus must have formally disinherited her;
if he did not wish to mention her by name, then in any case inter ceteros.
For should he have failed to do so, Julia would have qualified, without
needing any exemption from the Voconian law, for her share of the patrimony.
In effect, through the rules of adcrescere (Gaius, Inst. 2. 124), she would
have ended up receiving more than Livia. The clause of disinherison must
have stood, as usual (Gaius, Inst. 2. 128), immediately after the enumeration
of all heredes, including those secundo and tertio gradu.

This clause of disinherison, general or specific, must not be confounded
with the injunction, also contained in the will, that neither Julia nor
Julia the Younger be buried in the Mausoleum (Suet., Aug. 101. 3; Cass. Dio
56. 32. 4). This part of Augustus' testament has been greatly elucidated by

---

26) For the controversies concerning this meeting, see R.D.Goodyear, The
Annals of Tacitus I,Cambridge 1972, 169-176; M.M.Sage, "Tacitus and the
Accession of Tiberius", Ancient Society 13-14, 1982-3, 293-321.

27) Gaius, Inst. 2. 123-4, 127-8; cf. A.Watson, The Law of Succession
in the Later Roman Republic, Oxford 1971, 42-52, 173-177; Kaser, Privatrecht (above, n.13), 703-707.

28) Tac., Ann. 1. 8; Suet., Aug. 101; Tib. 23; Cass. Dio 56. 32 (cf. 56.
10. 2 for earlier exemptions from the Voconian law).

Fernand De Visscher's studies on the Roman law of sepulchres.[29)]

There existed in Roman law two basic kinds of tombs, sepulcra familiaria and sepulcra hereditaria. Access to the latter was open to all heredes scripti, and to all those who would have acceded to the inheritance on intestacy. Moreover, this right was not denied even to the exheredati, unless the testator specifically excluded them from the tomb.[30)] This was precisely the position of Julia. But the right of burial extended also to the children of the disinherited, hence the specific exclusion of Julia the Younger despite the fact that she did not belong to the category of heredes sui of Augustus, and on intestacy would not have qualified for any portion of his property. But it is doubtful whether Augustus intended the Mausoleum to be a hereditary tomb in the technical sense of the word. The descriptions of Tacitus, tumulus Augusti (Ann. 3. 4. 1), tumulus Caesarum (3. 9. 2) and tumulus Iuliorum (16. 6. 2), point clearly to a sepulcrum familiare.[31)] But again it was hardly a usual family tomb destined solely for the agnatic descendants: Julia the Younger, despite her name, it is generally maintained, did not belong to the gens Iulia.[32)] And yet, as the injunction of Augustus shows, she had full right to be buried in his tomb. As De Visscher points out, "a tomb was not necessarily either a family or a hereditary tomb. Its legal position depended on the will of the founder. The founder could reserve the tomb exclusively for himself or he could reserve it for certain specifically

---

29) F. De Visscher, Le droit des tombeaux romains, Milano 1963, esp. 93-138. He follows the lead of A.Albertario, Studi di diritto romano II, Milano 1941 (original publication in 1910),1-27. For a succinct summary, see A.Watson, The Law of Property in the Later Roman Republic, Oxford 1968, 8. The most important recent study of the subject is M.Kaser, "Zum römischen Grabrecht", ZRG 95, 1978, 15-92, esp. 57-60. The principal legal texts are Dig. 11. 7. 5 (Gaius, 19 ad edictum provinciale) and 11. 7. 6 (Ulpian, 25 ad edictum).

30) Ulpian (above, n.29): "exheredatis autem, nisi specialiter testator iusto odio commotus eos vetuerit, humanitatis gratia tantum sepeliri, non etiam alios praeter suam posteritatem inferre licet". Cf. Kaser, "Grabrecht" (above, n.29), 56-57. Ulpian may be right that this rule was introduced for humanitarian reasons, especially with respect to the punitive disinherison of the filiifamilias, but this cannot have been exclusively so as regards the filiaefamilias. For, according to the lex Voconia, in rich families the daughters had to be disinherited and given only legacies, but it would have been unfair to prohibit them also from burial in the hereditary tomb. On the application of the lex Voconia under the Empire, see Astolfi, op. cit. (above, n.24), 337-340.

31) Especially telling is the last passage: the embalmed body of Poppaea "tumulo Iuliorum infertur". Tacitus intimates that Nero committed two outrages: the body of Poppaea was embalmed against the mos Romanus and in imitation of foreign kings (cf. De Visscher, op. cit. (above, n.29), 9, 25), and the tomb of the Julii was violated by the introduction, to use the language of epigraphical injunctions, of a corpus extraneum (cf. De Visscher, 103-106). A full legal study of the imperial tombs is a desideratum.

32) There is no trace of her adoption by Augustus; her full name (which is not attested) was probably Vipsania Iulia (cf. PIR^2 IV, 301).

designated **persons**, outside of any particular system of devolution".[33] The
Mausoleum was apparently open to all descendants of Augustus, agnatic or
not, and to all those whom the Princeps thought worthy of burial in this
hallowed place, as Marcellus, Agrippa and Drusus. Thus the tomb of Augustus
and of the Julii was at once transformed into the monument of that new
entity, the domus Augusta.[34] Both Juliae belonged there on account of the
laws of inheritance and through the ties of blood; they had to be forbidden
entry individually and by name.[35]

But for the time being the fate of her bones was only a minor worry for
Julia. Property mattered. The lex Voconia forced even a loving father to
disinherit his daughter, but he would normally leave her a legacy of her
peculium.[36] Augustus did not. A response of Papinian (12 resp. = Frg. Vat.
294, FIRA II. 529-30) provides legal illustration to the decision of
Augustus:

> Quod pater filiae, quam habuit ac retinuit in
> potestate, donauit, cum eam donationem testamento non
> confirmasset, filiae non esse respondi; nam et peculia
> non praelegata communia fratrum esse constabat.

What the father gave to his daughter was her peculium; legally it still
belonged to the donor, but was separated from his property. If the father
failed to confirm the gift of the peculium in his will, the jurists interpreted this as indicating his intention to take it back (ademptio peculii).
In favor of this interpretation Papinian adduces the following argument: it
was generally regarded (constabat) that the peculia which belonged (separately)
to the brothers (and which could be of varying size) would become the common
property of the brothers (to be equally divided between them) if they were
not praelegata by the testator (i.e. given to each brother in addition to
his share of inheritance). The text of Suetonius demonstrates that this
interpretation of the testator's intent was current already at the time of
Augustus; it may well go back to the republican jurists.

On the part of Augustus it was no oversight. During his long reign he had

---

33) Op. cit. (above, n.29), 96: "Un tombeau n'est pas nécessairement,
soit de famille, soit héréditaire. C'est de la volonté du fondateur que
dépend le régime du tombeau. Le fondateur peut s'être réservé la tombe de
façon exclusive à lui-même ou la réserver à certain personnes nommément
désignées par lui, en dehors de tout système particulier de dévolution".

34) Cf. the fine study by R.P.Saller, "Familia, Domus, and the Roman
Conception of the Family", Phoenix 37, 1984, 336-355, esp.345-347 (the
domus Caesarum).

35) The injunction of Augustus finds numerous epigraphical parallels, cf.
De Visscher, op. cit. (above, n.29), 97.

36) García Garrido, op. cit. (above, n.13), 112-113, 121-122.

sponsored major legal innovations concerning wills,[37] had rendered decisions
concerning the validity of various testamentary dispositions,[38] and in his
own will he left numerous legacies to be paid out by his heirs. When he in
his own hand wrote his testament he must have been well aware how his
silence about Julia's peculium might be interpreted.

It was a political decision. Julia was his daughter, but she was also an
embarrassment and potential incitement to riot. Tiberius, as the possessor
of imperium and tribunitial power, was free to deal with her on the level
of politics and public law as he wished; his hands were not to be tied at
civil law.

At the moment Tiberius and Livia entered upon the inheritance of Augustus
the peculium of Julia ceased to be her property and reverted to the general
patrimony of Augustus. At the division of this patrimony it could have ended
up in the share of Tiberius or of Livia, or could be divided between them
(cf. above, II). Another outcome was possible: the heirs, acting together
or individually, were free to leave the peculium, technically as their gift,
to its current holder. There was nothing in the law to prevent them from
from doing so. Here comes into play the presumed intent of the testator.
Tiberius argued that the intent of Augustus was to deprive Julia of her
peculium and of her allowance, and that he had no choice but to follow the
will of the testator. Some perceived this as malice, and Suetonius summed
up this opinion when he wrote that Tiberius defrauded (fraudavit) Julia "per
speciem publici iuris".[39]

It so happens that only two legal decisions of Tiberus are mentioned in
the Digest;[40] one of them concerns a will (Dig. 28. 4. 42 = Pomponius, 12
ex variis lect.). A pater familias instituted as his heir a certein Parthenius, and, in the event Parthenius should not be heir, he appointed a substitute heir. The testator believed that Parthenius was an ingenuus, but in
fact he was a slave, a slave of Tiberius. On the orders of Tiberius Parthe-

37) See the texts in G.Gualandi, Legislazione imperiale e giurisprudenza
I, Milano 1963, 3-5. Cf. Watson, The Law of Succession (above, n.27), 35-39.

38) Val. Max. 7. 7. 3-4; 9. 15. ext. 1. Cf. F.Millar, The Emperor in the
Roman World, London 1977, 529-530.

39) A confusing phrase. M.Kaser, "Ius publicum und ius privatum", ZRG
103, 1986, 59, n.253, rightly observes that "Tiberius hat nicht versucht,
das Testament des Augustus als ius publicum hinzustellen, sondern hat, weil
dieser zugunsten der Tochter Julia über das vom Vater erworbene Pekulium und
die Renten nichts angeordnet hatte, ihr unter Hinweis (oder dem Vorwand) der
zwingend geltenden Testamentsordnung nichts von diesen Gütern zukommen lassen". At Dig. 28. 1. 3 (Papinian, 14 quaest.) we read: "Testamenti factio
non privati, sed publici iuris est", but we have to interpret this passage
in the sense suggested by Kaser (pp.93-94): "Als einseitiger Rechtsakt mit
weitragenden Folgen ist das Testament an strenge Erfordernisse gebunden, die
namentlich die Form und den Kreis der zulässigen Inhalte begrenzen, aber
auch den der zur Errichtung Befähigten. Vieles, was das Testament angeht,
mußte daher in zwingenden Rechtsvorschriften geregelt sein". Cf. also P.
Leuregans, "Testamenti factio non privati sed publici iuris est", RHD 53,
1975, 239.

nius accepted the inheritance. But the person who was named in the will as
the substitute disputed Parthenius' rights to the inheritance. He argued, it
appears, that if the testator had known that Parthenius was a slave he
would not have appointed him as heir (for in strict law a slave acquires
everything for his master and not for himself), but would rather have named
the substitute as his heir. The case was decided by Tiberius himself.[41] The
choice was between the presumed intent of the testator (as argued by the
substitute heir) and the letter of the will. Tiberius granted equal force
to both considerations: he ruled that the inheritance be divided between
himself and the substitute. This decisison was hailed by Roman jurists as
exemplary; modern commentators often take it as a sign of Tiberius' rapacity
(he ought to have left the whole inheritance to the substitute) or as a sign
of his generosity (according to the wording of the will he was fully entitled
to take everything for himself).[42] One thing is manifest: it was not the
intent of the testator to give anything to Tiberius. And there was another
choice open to Tiberius: he could free Parthenius and concede to him at least
part of the inheritance. Both in the case of Julia and that of Parthenius
we see the same mind at work, legalistic and unpleasant.

When Tiberius thus acquired the possessions of Julia and stopped paying
her the allowance, not a few people may have wished to hide even deeper in
their memory the recollection of those days in 2 B.C. when Tiberius,
uncertain of the future, languished on the island of Rhodes, his intimate
ties with the house of the Julii severed after the Princeps ordered the
banishment and divorce of Julia. At that time he is said to have interceded
with Augustus in favor of the exile: he bade his former father-in-law to
allow Julia to keep all the gifts he had made out to her (Suet., Tib. 11. 4).
Now, entrenched in power, ungenerous and vengeful, he took away from her
everything she had.

IV.

But even so Julia was not totally destitute or alone. She had her freedman, we have learned. And the most hallowed obligation of the libertus was
to give help to the patron in need. They may have been afraid. There was
also Scribonia, not easily scared. Velleius (2. 100. 5) asserts that Scribonia "exilii permansit comes", which may be taken to mean (on the strength
of permansit) that Scribonia not only went with Julia to Pandateria but

40) Gualandi, op. cit. (above, n.37), 7.

41) Whether on appeal of in first instance, we cannot tell. For the
possibilities and uncertainties of the procedure in civil matters before the
Emperor, cf. e.g. J.M.Kelly, Princeps Iudex, Weimar 1957, 79-102; Millar,
op. cit. (above, n.38), 507-537.

43) Dig. 28. 5. 41 (Julian, 30 dig.); Inst. 2. 15. 4. For modern interpretations, see Buckland, op. cit. (above, n.14), 143-144; H.J.Wieling,
Testamentauslegung im römischen Recht, München 1972, 138-140.

also to Regium, and remained with her to the very end. Direct proof was
lacking. The light comes from an inscription, and it comes again from Regium.[43] We read:

> L(ucius) Scrib[onius]
> Scribon[iae]
> Caesari[s l(ibertus)]...

The exact provenance of the inscription is unknown, but it is preserved
in the Museo Nazionale di Reggio Calabria. In fact we can hardly doubt that
it was found in that city or its vicinity. This stone and the text of Velleius
form two parts of the puzzle; separately they are inconclusive, but if put
together the picture is not to be missed. We have before us the epigraphical
record of Scribonia's sojourn in Regium. Julia was in caring hands; she could
take refuge in the household of her mother.

She could not: Tiberius did not limit himself solely to the weapon of
civil law. He not only did not show any kindness to Julia, officium or
humanitas, so Suetonius commiserates (Tib. 50), but on the contrary although
"on her father's orders ("ex constitutione patris") Julia was confined to
one town, Tiberius prohibited her from leaving the house and associating
with the people"("domo ... egredi et commercio hominum frui vetuerit"[44]). If

---

43) Also this inscription was published (with a good photograph) by C.
Turano, "Note di epigrafia classica I", Klearchos 2, fasc. 7-8, 1960, 71-73,
and reproduced in AE 1975 (1978), 75, no.286. Lines 2 and 3 are slightly
indented, and the size of the letters decreases by about one third from line
1 to line 3. Turano interprets the inscription as referring to Scribonia and
her brother Lucius and recording their joint construction or restoration of
a monument; consequently in line 2 he supplies Scribon[ia], and at the end
of line 3 postulates an abbreviation of fecerunt, restituerunt or of a
similar verb or phrase. He believes that the inscription must be dated to
40-39 B.C. when Scribonia was actually the wife of Octavian. The editors
of AE provide the following text: "L. Scrib[onius] / Scribon[iae] /
Caesari[s ...]". They say that the plaque commemorates the building activity
of L. Scribonius Libo; Scribonia disappears as a co-dedicator, her name and
her position as Caesaris uxor serving only to enhance the status of her
brother. If so, we should read in line 3 Caesari[s frater], but the editors
of the AE apparently preferred to leave the mystery of that line unsolved.
All these readings are inadmissible. It is odd that Scribonius appears
without the cognomen; this perhaps can be remedied, space permitting, by
supplying Libo in line 1. But above all it is hardly likely that Libo would
have identified himself solely as the brother of "Caesar's wife", either in
40-39, when he was a partisan of Sex. Pompeius, or in later years, when
Scribonia ceased to be the wife of Octavian. On the other hand such status
indications are normal with the slaves or freedman of imperial ladies. This
was clearly seen by Chantraine, "Freigelassene und Sklaven kaiserlicher
Frauen", (above, n.1), 390 and 404, n.11;·he firmly identifies the author
of our inscription as a freedman of Scribonia.

44) Goodyear, The Annals of Tacitus (above, n.26), I, 325, n.3, writes
that "in this too Tiberius could have appealed to the authority of Augustus",
and quotes Suet., Aug. 62. 2. We read there that Augustus brought up his
daughter and his granddaughters very strictly, and that he even kept them
from meeting strangers ("extraneorum ... coetu ... prohibuit"). This refers
obviously to the time when they lived in his house and were not yet married.
Augustus exercised patria potestas over Julia, and (no doubt) guardianship

we take the last phrase literally, as we probably should, Julia will have
also been deprived of the company of her mother, remaining alone with the
guards, prisoner in her own house that now belonged to Tiberius.

About her death Tacitus harbors no doubt: "In the same year (A.D. 14)
Julia died. Many years previously her father confined her for immorality
first to the island of Pandateria and then to the town of Regium... When
Tiberius assumed power Julia lived in exile, disgraced, and, after the
slaughter of Agrippa Postumus, bereft of all hope. Tiberius destroyed her
by depriving her of the necessaries of life and letting her slowly waste
away to death. Because of the length of her banishment he thought the murder
would pass unnoticed ("infamem, extorrem et post interfectum Postumum
Agrippam omnis spei egenam inopia ac tabe longa peremit, obscuram fore necem
longinquitate exilii ratus").[45]

Cassius Dio is equally blunt: "Tiberius did not recall his wife Julia
from the exile ... but even kept her locked up until she perished from
maltreatment and hunger (ὑπὸ κακουχίας καὶ λιμοῦ)".[46]

Summing up three decades of pro-Tiberian partisanship R.S.Rogers wrote:
"we believe that ... Augustus' daughter Julia, her son Agrippa Postumus,
and her long-time paramour, Sempronius Gracchus, died natural deaths in the
last four and a half months of A.D. 14".[47] What an opportune coincidence!
Three potential rivals, three enemies of the new Princeps die a natural
death within a few months of his accession to power. And, to top the odds,
at the time of their disappearance Agrippa Postumus and Sempronius Gracchus
were incarcerated on remote islands, and Julia was kept under house arrest
in a distant town on the southern tip of Italy. Few students of history will
be ready to admit that Agrippa and Gracchus quietly passed away in their own

over Julia the Younger and Agrippina; Tiberius had with respect to Julia
neither prerogative. The two situations are not comparable.

45) Ann. 1. 53. 1-2. On peremit, see R.Syme, Tacitus, Oxford 1958, I, 358;
II, 727; Goodyear, The Annals of Tacitus (above, n.26), I, 324-325. On
longinquitate, see Goodyear, 326. Tacitus continues (1. 53. 3): "Par causa
saevitiae in Sempronium Gracchum...", and goes on to describe the murder of
Gracchus on the island of Cercina to which that pervicax adulter of Julia
had been relegated. Saevitia is a cruel and expressive word; it links the
fate of Julia and Gracchus. R.S.Rogers,"The Death of Julia and Gracchus, A.D.
14", TAPA 98, 1967, 387, thinks that "the saevitia is of Augustus, not of
Tiberius", and that it refers to Gracchus' trial and relegation and not to
his death: a fanciful interpretation.

46) Cass. Dio 57. 18. 1a = Zonaras 11. 2 (vol. 3, p.5 Dindorf):

τὴν δὲ γυναῖκα Ἰουλίαν οὔτε ἐπανήγαγεν ἐκ τῆς ὑπερορίας ἣν παρὰ
τοῦ πατρὸς αὐτῆς τοῦ Αὐγούστου κατεδικάσθη δι' ἀσέλγειαν, ἀλλὰ καὶ
κατέκλεισεν αὐτήν, ὥσθ' ὑπὸ κακουχίας καὶ λιμοῦ φθαρῆναι.

Cassius Dio (or Zonaras) dates the death of Julia to 17 A.D.; she was of
course not the wife but rather the former wife of Tiberius (cf. a similar
use of uxor in Suet., Tib. 50). The term κακουχία is of interest; it is
often used particularly of maltreatment of a wife, see LSJ s.v.

47) Rogers, op. cit. (above, n.45), 390.

beds, but the death of Julia, and its mode, sparked an emotional controversy.[48]

But whether she was murdered, starved to death,[49] or killed by despair,
Tiberius was the manifest author of her demise. The task and duty of the
modern historian is not to apportion blame -- this we can leave to Tacitus --
but not to shun unpleasant facts.

It is therefore perhaps not otiose to inquire after Tiberius' grounds
for his action, and his motives. The Roman Empire was a Rechtsstaat, and some
legal ground always lurks somewhere.

Originally Julia was sent to Regium "ex constitutione patris" (Suet.,
Tib. 50). This is unhelpful for it can denote the decision taken by Augustus
in virtue of his patria potestas or in an official capacity.[50] When in 2
B.C. Julia was relegated to Pandateria, Augustus "de filia ... notum senatui
fecit" (Suet., Aug. 55. 2); whether the senate was asked to take any action,
we do not know.[51] As there are on record other cases of relegations decreed by patresfamilias,[52] we need not assume any offical act, though this
would be the first case of a private banishment to an island. On the other
hand Agrippa Postumus was confined in perpetuum to the island of Planasia

---

48) For a catalogue of opinions and pronouncements, see Rogers 306, n.9;
E.Meise, Untersuchungen zur Geschichte der Julisch-Claudischen Dynastie,
München 1969, 34, n.201.

49) E.F.Leon, "Scribonia and her Daughters", TAPA 82, 1951, 174, points
out that the proper word for starvation is inedia, not inopia. But inopia
may suggest not only general lack of means but also hunger and lack of food.
Cf. Caes., BG 7. 20. 10: "fame et inopia"; Cic. (D. Brut.), Fam. 11. 10. 4:
"ut inopia potius quam ferro conficeretur"; Petr., Sat. 88.5: "inopia ex-
tinxit". And Tacitus writes that Anicetus "non inops exilium toleravit et
fato obiit" (Ann. 14. 62. 4). The intimation is that if he were inops his
death would not have been fato but rather brought about by his wretched
circumstances. Cf. TLL s.v. 1742. 77-80, 1743-4, 1746. 4-44.

50) The only other instance of the term in Suetonius, "constitutiones
senatus quasdam rescidit" (Tib.33), is equally vague; it denotes in general
"decisions of the senate".

51) On the basis of the passage of Cass. Dio (55. 10. 14) that Augustus
did not keep to himself the affair of Julia ἀλλὰ καὶ τῇ γερουσίᾳ κοινῶσαι
J.Bleicken, Senatsgericht und Kaisergericht, Göttingen 1962, 33-34, n.3,
inclines to assume a decision of the senate, perhaps the iudicium senatus.
He argues that in Cassius Dio κοινοῦν τινι does not simply mean "to inform"
but rather "to deliberate together" or "to carry a measure together". If
a decree of the senate concerning Julia was indeed passed in 2 B.C. she
would have to be recalled from Pandateria and confined to Regium technically
also by a senatus consultum.

52) In fact only three cases are known. On the case of Tarius, see
above, n.12, and for the procedure, W.Kunkel, "Das Konsilium im Hausgericht",
Kleine Schriften, Weimar 1974, 118-122 (originally published in ZRG in 1966).
Two other cases (one of them possibly legendary) concern the relegation of
sons to the countryside; see the sources in P.Voci, "Storia della patria
potestas da Augusto a Diocleziano", Iura 31, 1980 (1983), 53-54, nos. 3 and 5.

by a decree of the senate (Suet., Aug. 65. 4; cf. Tac., Ann. 1. 6. 2). As
Augustus had earlier abdicated his adoptive son, this may mean that he had
no patria potestas over Agrippa at that time.[53]

Julia was not under Tiberius' potestas, and as he does not seem to have
consulted the senate, he must have acted in virtue of his imperium. Here
we have to keep apart Julia's continuing confinement to Regium and her newly
imposed house arrest. If she had been relegated to Regium (and previously
to Pandateria) through an official act of the senate or of Augustus, Tiberius did not need to take any action to keep her there, all public acts of
Augustus automatically validated by his deification. The patria potestas
on the other hand did not reach beyond the grave. Thus if Augustus had
ordered the banishment of Julia solely on the basis of his fatherly prerogatives, upon his death, as a person sui iuris, she would have been free
from all restrictions, free to leave Regium and return to Rome. Once the
question is posed in this way, the improbability of this scenario is manifest.
Augustus, who took pains to bar Julia from his tomb, to disinherit her, and
to take away her peculium, would hardly have left his daughter so dangerously
close to freedom. We have to conclude: Julia was kept in Regium iure publico.
It was now up to Tiberius either to do nothing or to have her recalled. That
he did not recall her is understandable; but why the house arrest? Malice is
the answer assumed by many, but in the struggle for power there are often
good grounds for being unpleasant.

For Julia spelt danger. A few years previously an attempt had been made
to free her and Agrippa and transport them to the armies.[54] And she had
her hopes now. For on learning of the death of Augustus, a certain Clemens,
a (former) slave of Agrippa, conceived a bold plan of rescuing his master,
perhaps not without the knowledge and support of some highly placed persons.
Plying a cargo vessel he reached Planasia -- too late: the guards had
already slain Agrippa, and Clemens was able to snatch away only the ashes.
Subsequently, posing as Agrippa, he was able to collect a large band, and for
two years elude capture.[55] It was evidently in response to Clemens' attempt
that Tiberius placed Julia under arrest; it was his duty as an imperium-
holder to do everything to prevent riot and rebellion.

When Julia thus wasted away, the verse of the poet, for us strangely

---

53) For this interpretation, see B.Levick, "Abdication and Agrippa
Postumus", Historia 21, 1972, 674-697, esp. 692-694.

54) Suet., Aug. 19; cf. Levick, "The Fall of Julia the Younger" (above,
n.5), 337-338.

55) Tac., Ann. 2. 39-40 (and Goodyear ad loc.); Suet., Tib.25; Cass. Dio
57. 16. 3. Of the affair there are many interpretations; cf. e.g. P.M.D.
Swan, A Study of the Conspiracies Against Emperors of the Julio-Claudian
Dynasty, Diss. Harvard 1964, 71-83; Levick, Tiberius (above, n.6), 150-152;
M.Sordi, "La morte di Agrippa Postumo e la rivolta di Germania del 14 d.C.",
Scritti in onore di Benedetto Riposati II, Rieti 1979, 481-495.

evoking the lines of Tacitus, may have come to the lips of the learned prisoner:[56]

multis sum modis circumventus, morbo exilio atque inopia.

If Scribonia could communicate with Julia she would encourage her not to surrender to pavor, of which Ennius also speaks, but to endure cruciatus and nex, and not oblige her persecutors with a self-inflicted death. For this gravis femina two years later sternly advised her grand-nephew M. Scribonius Libo against committing suicide when his alleged (or real) conspiracy was denounced in the senate: "Quid te delectat alienum negotium agere?" (Seneca, Epist. 70. 10). She did not succeed in persuading Scribonius or Seneca ("manus sibi attulit nec sine causa").[57] Julia also had a good causa not to listen to her mother. After the death of Agrippa Postumus she was omnis spei egena.

The day of Libo's suicide was declared a public feast;[58] the death of Julia Tiberius preferred to keep veiled in obscurity.

V.

The story of the daughter of Augustus does not end with her death. Selective posthumous rehabilitation is a useful device in all authoritarian regimes. Caligula rendered honors to his mother and his brothers, and deposited their ashes in the Mausoleum, next to the remains of Tiberius; and he recalled from banishment other victims of persecution (Suet., Cal. 15; Cass. Dio 59. 3. 5-8, 6. 2). As so often, this "thaw" was but a prelude to a new round of repression. Claudius followed in the footsteps of Caligula extending political rehabilitation even to Marcus Antonius (who, after all, was his grandfather). But he also honored Tiberius and Germanicus, his parents Drusus and Antonia, and Livia, whom he elevated to the position of a diva (Suet., Claud. 9). Outwardly and officially the past history of the domus Augusta appeared as a monolith, again a phenomenon not unknown in the history of modern totalitarian parties. It is in that atmosphere of embellishing and expurgating history that we have to place our inscription. It belongs, we have seen (above, II), to the age of Claudius. If Julia had

---

56) Ennius, Scaen. (Alcmeo) 24-28 Vahlen = 25-29 Warmington = 16-20 Jocelyn. Only, unlike Alcmeo, she had no reason to feel remorse. Cf. Plaut., Bacch. 519c: "mori me malim excruciatum inopia". On Julia's "litterarum amor multaque eruditio", see Macr., Saturn. 2. 5. 2.

57) On the affair of Libo, see Tac., Ann. 2. 27-32; Goodyear, The Annals of Tacitus II, Cambridge 1981, 262-283. Libo committed suicide on the Ides of September of 16 A.D. (Tac., Ann. 2. 32); at that time Scribonia must have resided in Rome. Thus this story indirectly confirms Tacitus' dating of Julia's death to 14 A.D. as against Cassius Dio (Zonaras) who puts it in 17 A.D. (above, n. 46) -- unless Tiberius, after he placed Julia under house arrest, ordered Scribonia to leave Regium.

58) Tac., Ann. 2. 32; Fasti Amit. (A.Degrassi, Inscr. It. XIII, II, 192-193, 509).

remained a discarded un-person her freedmen would hardly have dared so
proudly to display her name and unite it with that of her father who had
banished her and had never relented. Literary sources know nothing about her
posthumous fate. She certainly was not rehabilitated with such pomp as her
daughter Agrippina. But she undoubtedly partook in the rewriting of history.
If by some chance all literary sources pertaining to her catastrophe had
perished, our humble inscription would have stood for all times as a
document of cooperation between the Princess, her father and her stepmother.
Iulia, diui Augusti filia, diuus Augustus and diua Augusta form a happy
family. Such was the Fairyland of the diui.

40

CERTIS CALENDIS

In *Supplementa Italica*, II, Roma 1983, pp. 87-89, n. 71, Rita Volpe republishes an intriguing Christian inscription from Velitrae. The stone was unearthed in 1922, published by G. Mancini in «Notizie degli Scavi», 1924, p. 351, n. 3, and duly reprinted in *AEp*, 1925, 90. When the stone was found (and recomposed out of twenty-two fragments) only the right edge and the upper left corner were missing; stored in the Musco Civico at Velletri it suffered devastating damage: today only a small fragment of the bottom part survives, displaying a few letters only, the drawing of a dove and the chrismon (see the photograph, p. 88). The text (with many «vulgar» features) commemorates the death of a young girl; it is an acrostic (1), with the name of the deceased hidden at the beginning of lines 2-7. I reproduce it below with the supplements of Volpe:

> [*Quaerat per capi*]*ta versorum nomen scire qui* [*velit?*].
> [*Parva per*] *merita quesquet* (!) *in pace fideles* [*puella*]
> [*Rei pa*]*rentes ut possunt fletus optutib*[*us dant*]
> [*Iam*] *ecce venit tempus ubi merita pecca*[*torum*]
> [*S*]*empiterne Deus, misereri ossibus is*[*tis ---*]
> *Certis calendis diem mor*[*i*]*tur* [*postquam?*]
> *Annus octo vixit, venit die Nove*[*mbris*]
> *septima pos decima, in* [*s*]*omnio* [*pacis?*] (2).

---

(1) Cf. G. Barbieri, *Una nuova epigrafe d'Ostia e ricerche sugli acrostici*, «Quarta Miscellanea Greca e Romana», Roma 1975, p. 325, n. 14; p. 369, n. 66. The supplements of Volpe produce the name Prisca. On the place of the acrostics within the *carmina epigraphica* and on their funerary ideology, see G. Sanders, *L'au-delà et les acrostiches des Carmina Latina Epigraphica*, «Roczniki Humanistyczne», XXVII, 3 (1979 [1982]), pp. 57-75.

(2) Line 1:]*ta versorum* Mancini; [*per capi*]*ta versorum* Barbieri, op. cit., (above, note 1), p. 325, n. 14. Line 2: *fideles* = *fidelis*. Line 3: *optutibus* = *obtutibus*. Mancini reads *optu tib*[*i*

In line 6 comes the enigmatic phrase *Certis calendis diem mor[i]tur* (3).

R. Volpe offers this comment (p. 89): «L'espressione *certis calendis* non trova confronti, e non ha attinenza con la datazione seguente; se non si tratta di un errore di lettura del Mancini (sulla cui lettura si basa anche la nostra, in quanto la foto della Soprintendenza è molto poco attendibile, e anche in questo caso dà una parola senza senso), si potrebbe ipoteticamente pensare ad un significato di 'momento stabilito, fissato', intendendo forse che la morte giunge quando è il momento destinato».

An excellent intuition! It will turn into certainty if we consider the following:

First of all we have to remember that it was on the Kalends that the outstanding debt (and interest) was to be paid (4). The lines of Horace come to mind,

---

dare]. Volpe's [*dant*] is clearly preferable, cf. *CLE*, 629, 8-9 = Pais, *Suppl It*, 384 (Iulium Carnicum): *et misera mater... / cottidie fletus dat*; *CLE*, 59, 10-11 = *CIL*, I², 1215 = VI, 25369: *prae deside]rio gnatae fletus in dies / edunt* (sc. *parentes*). *Optutibus* is ingenious, but is it right? No *loci similes* seem to be available. Line 4: For the phrase *venit tempus*, cf. *CLE*, 815, 2 (=) *CIL*, X, 2533, 7-8 (Puteoli): *ven]erit summa dies et [ineluctabile t]empus*, imitating Verg., *Aen*, II, 324. *meriti pecca* [Mancini. Line 5: *misereri* = *miserere*. Line 6: see below, note 3. Line 7: [*die*] *Nove[mbres*] Mancini. As the stone is lost, and as on the negative of the photograph (see below, note 3) there is indicated a lacuna, Mancini's brackets are to be retained. *Venit*, in the sense of «to pass away», and used absolutely (or in combination with the expression *in somno pacis*), does not seem to be attested. Line 8: *pos* = *post*. There seems to exist in the *carmina epigraphica* only one parallel to this numbering of the days of a month, a late inscription from Salonae in Dalmatia dated to 559, *CLE*, 719, 9 = Diehl, 79 = *CIL*, III, 9527, 12-13: *tertio post decimum / Augusti numero mens(is)*. For the expression *in somnio pacis* (in place of the expected and regular locution *in somno pacis*), cf. Diehl, 3192 A; 3444. I wish here to record my continuing debt to *Concordanze dei Carmina Latina Epigraphica* by P. Colafrancesco, M. Massaro and M.L. Ricci (Bari 1986).

(3) So read without hesitation by Mancini, and reproduced in *AEp*. The negative in the possession of the Soprintendenza Archeologica of Lazio covers the whole inscription, but, as R. Volpe observes (p. 88), «le lettere sono state rubricate modernamente e male falsando la lettura». Line 6 according to the reproduction given by Volpe (p. 88) reads CERTACNENDI-SDIEMMO, then a trace of a letter, empty space, and the letter B. The phrase *diem moritur* is unusual, though not impossible. The normal idiom was *diem obire* or *fungere* or *mortem obire*. I doubt that we here have the expression *dies moritur* (cf. *TLL*, s.v. *dies*, col. 1045, 72-73), «the day (sc. of life) comes to an end». The supplement *postquam* is unlikely: each of the preceding lines forms a distinct conceptual and syntactic unit. That this is true also of line 6 is demonstrated by the present tense of *moritur* (provided of course that this is the correct reading). Volpe refers *moritur* to the deceased girl, and through *postquam* connects it with the next line, but *moritur* and *vixit* are strange tense-fellows. We rather have in line 6 a gnomic statement: one has to die *certis calendis*. However, in place of *mor[i]tur*, I am inclined to read: *Certis calendis diem mor[i] tu[*. Or should we postulate the reading *diem morti[s...*?

(4) J. Marquardt, *Römische Staatsverwaltung*, II, Leipzig 1884², p. 60, n. 3 To his examples add *Dig.*, XLV, 1, 47 (Ulp., 50 *ad Sab.*): *Qui sic stipulatur:* «*quod te mihi illis kalendis dare oportet, id dare spondes?*» *Videtur non hodie stipulari, sed sua die, hoc est kalendis.*

cum tristes misero venere calendae,
mercedem aut nummos unde unde extricat (5),

and of Ovid:

qui ... timet celeres Kalendas,
torqueat hunc aeris mutua summa sui (6).

And, a century earlier, Afranius:

Septembris heri Kalendae, hocedie ater dies (7).

In Roman cult and calendar the days following the Kalends (also Nones and Ides) were *insignes* by past military disasters, and hence *atri* (8). So also they were for a debtor: on the Kalends he paid his interest, and the next day he faced his own *dies ater* of penurious calamity. Debt you cannot escape for

centum explicentur paginae Kalendarum,

the pages in the *Kalendarium*, the creditor's account book (9). There will come the Kalends on which you will have to pay not merely the interest, but pay off your whole debt. Plutarch complains that although the Kalends are holy, the money lenders made this day accursed and detested (10). The same business customs, the same sentiment, and the same phrases were current in Christian antiquity, in the milieu to which our inscription belongs. Jerome, fulminating against the usurers, exclaims:

---

(5) Horat., *Sat.*, I, 3, 86-87; cf. *Epod.*, II, 69-70.
(6) Ovid., *Rem. am.*, 561-562. Cf. ad loc. P. Pinotti, *P. Ovidio Nasone, Remedia amoris: Introduzione, testo e commento*, Bologna 1988, pp. 253-254.
(7) Afr., *Com.*, 163 (O. Ribbeck, *Scaenicae Romanorum poesis fragmenta*, vol. II: *Comicorum fragmenta*, Lipsiae 1878², p. 185).
(8) Cf. G. Wissowa, *Religion und Kultus der Römer*, München 1912², p. 444.
(9) Mart., VIII, 44, 11. Cf. *Dig.*, XLV, 1, 46, pr. (Paul., 12 *ad Sab.*): «*Centesimis kalendis dari*» *utiliter stipulamur, quia praesens obligatio est, in diem autem dilata solutio*; J. Oehler, *Kalendarium*, PW X (1919), coll. 1564-1565.
(10) Plut., *De vitando aere alieno*, 2 (828).

Qui expectatis kalendas, ut negotiemini, et usuras augeatis de usuris (11).

And Ambrose brands the usurers for taking on each Kalends one percent interest on their capital:

Veniunt Kalendae, parit sors centesimam. Veniunt menses singuli, generantur usurae (12).

Next, let us not forget a favorite saying of the emperor Augustus. Suetonius reports that Augustus,

cum aliquos numquam soluturos significare vult, «ad Kalendas Graecas soluturos» ait (13),

«they will pay on the Greek Kalends», i.e. never, as the Greeks had no Kalends. A. Otto adduces for this saying only the passage of Suetonius, and asks: «War das Wort Eigentum des Kaisers?» (14). This is unlikely for Suetonius introduces this phrase among other colloquialisms of the Emperor; the ultimate origin we will have to seek in Latin comedy. No further enlightenment comes from Forcellini, *TLL* or *OLD*, but it is well to remember that the saying of Augustus, undoubtedly propagated directly by Suetonius, was appropriated by a number of modern European languages (15).

Third, and decisive, the widespread idea of death as repayment of debt, as *debitum naturae*; when we are born we receive our life as a loan, and we have to return it, *debitum solvere, persolvere* or *reddere*. This concept has received some

---

(11) Hieronym., *Comment. in Amos*, III, 8, (Migne, *Patr. Lat.*, XXV, p. 1080 C).
(12) Ambrosius, *De Tobia*, XII, 42 (Migne, *Patr. Lat.*, XIV, p. 812 B).
(13) Suet., *Aug.*, 87.
(14) *Die Sprichwörter der Römer*, Leipzig 1890, p. 65.
(15) It also appears in early modern Latin. In the *Glossarium* of Du Cange (Editio Nova, IV, Niort 1885 [= Paris 1938], p. 485) we find the following passage from the Life of S. Rosa: *Apage, sat nugarum, ad Calendas Graecas haec impleta videbimus* («*Acta Sanctorum*», Augusti tomus quintus, p. 971, col. 2). S. Rosa lived in Lima, Peru; the saying (attributed to her mother) is dated to 1629.

attention as a literary topos (16), but it is instructive and illuminating first to consider it as a (quasi)legal construct.

In Roman law an obligation could arise either *ex delicto* or *ex contractu*. A contract could be concluded in several ways. One way was to conclude it through *res*: one party, the future creditor, handed over a thing to the other, the future debtor. A subspecies of this *obligatio re facta* was loan, in its two forms of *mutuum* and *commodatum*. As no solemn words were pronounced, it was technically an informal contract. Peering through this legal looking glass one can easily imagine a child as signifying by the very act of its birth the acceptance of the loan of life (and a stillborn child as rejecting that offer). Now in the law of obligations a fundamental distinction existed between *certum* and *incertum* (or *dubium*). A life was a specific commodity, a loan exactly determined, a *res certa*. And a loan of a *res certa* created *obligatio certi*: the creditor, whoever that being was, Nature, Fate, Gods or God, had an action for the recovery of the loan, the *condictio certae rei*. And the *debitor* had no exception available against the creditor's claim. However, this being a formless contract, no interest could be charged; the charging of interest would have required a separate and a formal stipulation. The capital of life, *sors*, was given free to be used freely, but it had to be repaid in full, in the same form, with no substitutions allowed (17).

---

(16) The theme was first treated by B. Lier, *Topica carminum sepulcralium Latinorum*, «Philologus», 62 (1903), pp. 578-583 (he traces it back to Simonides, Euripides and Krantor), touched upon by E. Lissberger, *Das Fortleben der römischen Elegiker in den Carmina Epigraphica*, Diss. Tübingen 1934, p. 37, and by A. Brelich, *Aspetti della morte nelle iscrizioni sepolcrali dell'impero romano*, Budapest 1937, pp. 40-41, and discussed briefly but incisively by R. Lattimore, *Themes in Greek and Latin Epitaphs*, Urbana 1942, pp. 170-171, and more recently and more amply by D. Pikhaus, *Levensbeschouwing en milieu in de latijnse metrische inscripties*, «Verhandelingen van de Academie voor Wetenschappen... van Belgie. Klasse der Letteren», Jaarg. XL, n. 83, Brussel 1978, pp. 54-84. See also *TLL*, s.v. *debitum*, col. 106, 24 ff.

(17) Technically speaking the loan of life is to be classified as part *mutuum* and part *commodatum*. It was a loan for use, and it shared this quality with *commodatum*. Also the thing itself was to be returned and not only its equivalent. A detailed legal study of this peculiar construct will repay the effort. The principal legal texts are Gaius, *Inst.*, III, 90; IV, 88-89; Iust., *Inst.*, III, 13-14 (*obligatio* and *contractus*; cf. the commentary of J.B. Moyle, *Imperatoris Iustiniani Institutionum Libri Quattuor*, Oxford 1912, pp. 391-400); *Dig.*, XII, 1 and XIII, 3 (*res creditae in certum* and *condictio certae rei* or *triticiaria*); XIII, 6 (*commodatum*); XLIV, 7 (*obligationes* and *actiones*); XLV, 1, 74 (a definition of *certum*); L, 16, 108 and L, 17, 66 (a definition of *debitor*). Cf. A. Berger, *Encyclopedic Dictionary of Roman Law*, «Trans. Amer. Philos. Soc.», XLIII, 2, Philadelphia 1953, pp. 387, 399, 405, 413, 591, 603; H.F. Jolowicz and B. Nicholas, *Historical introduction to the study of Roman law*, Cambridge 1972³, pp. 271 ff., esp. 284-287; A. Watson, *The law of obligations in the Later Roman Republic*, Oxford 1965, pp. 10-17, 166-171, 208-213; M.

The sentiment that life was but a loan was voiced not only in philosophy and literature, Greek and Latin, but it also penetrated to popular culture. In Rome we meet it not only in Lucretius' verses:

> *rerum primordia pandam,*
> *unde omnis natura creet res auctet alatque*
> *quove eadem rursum natura perempta resolvat* (18),

or in Valerius Maximus' disquisition reporting the words, the *voces*, of Anaxagoras:

> *quas si quis efficaciter auribus receperit, non ignorabit,*
> *ita liberos esse procreandos, ut meminerit his a rerum*
> *natura et accipiendi spiritus et reddendi eodem momento temporis legem dici* (19),

or in Cicero's terse statement:

> *mors ... naturae debita* (20),

but also in numerous funerary monuments. These inscriptions are particularly important as the concept of repaying a debt of life stands in them preeminent.

The earliest of these texts comes from Rome, is dated to 10

Kaser, *Das römische Privatrecht*, I, München 1971², pp. 479 ff, 522-527, 530-534.

(18) Lucr., *De rerum natura*, 1, 55-57. Surprisingly, no comment ad loc., in C. Bailey, *Titi Lucreti De Rerum Natura Libri Sex*, II, Oxford 1947, p. 61. Lucretius' *resolvat* is echoed in *resoluta* of CLE, 1567, 2, quoted below in the text (note 36), and for *perempta*, cf. esp. CLE, 1522, 15 = CIL, XII, 1122: *die sua peremptus* (referring to a horse, *veredus*). Cf. also Cic., *De senectute*, 72.

(19) Val. Max., V, 10, 3. Observe that Valerius intimates a sort of a formal agreement, with nature pronouncing a *lex* for the contract, the loan of *spiritus* to the child. The phrase *spiritum reddere* is Ciceronian, cf. *Phil.*, X, 20: *cum vero dies et noctes omnia nos undique fata circumstent, non est viri minimeque Romani dubitare eum spiritum, quem naturae debeat, patriae reddere* (observe the juxtaposition of *fata* and *natura*). In due course, it was appropriated by the Christians, see below, note 21. The same image in Venantius Fortunatus, V, 7, 17: *hac nati morimur damnati lege parentum*. Cf. Pikhaus, op. cit., (above, note 16), p. 77.

(20) Cic., *Phil.*, XIV, 31. So also Tert., *De anima*, 50, 2: *mortem naturae debitum pronuntiamus*. Cf. A. Pellicer, *Natura. Étude sémantique et historique du mot latin*, Paris 1966, esp. pp. 170, 277-278. The literary examples quoted in the text I owe to Pellicer. But, as B.L. Hijmans rightly points out in his review («Mnemosyne», 23, 1970, pp. 339-340), Pellicer completely neglected to utilize the epigraphical evidence.

C.E., and displays the verb *reddere* (21), popular in this context both in classical and Christian inscriptions:

debitum reddidit X K. Sept. Maluginense (sic) *et Blaeso cos.* (22).

On other stones we read:

debitum reddidi; *debit[um re]ddidi in patria* (23);
nec patrio potui gremio mea debita fatis / reddere nec manibus lumina contegere (24);
debit(um) / natur(ae) reddi/dit; *tam su[bi]/to debitum natur(a)e / [cum redd]eret* (25).

The theme was also current in Christian epitaphs:

fidelis in Chr(ist)o ... / ... reddidi nunc d(omi)no rerum debitum communem / omnibus olim (26);
pridie n[a]tali suo serotina hora reddit debitum vit[a]e suae (27);
debitum vite (sic) *finem r/eddidit* (28);
reddidit qui/escens devitum (= *debitum*) *in pace / naturae* (29).

---

(21) In addition to *debitum*, it was frequently used with *anima, vita, corpus, caro, spiritus, lumen, obitus* or absolutely (as it seems only in Christian inscriptions). See the texts in Diehl (especially vol. II, pp. 173-180), and Pikhaus, op. cit., (above, note 16), pp. 63-65, 79-83, 479 and notes 139-143, 194, 199-201, 205. Cf. also H. Krummrey, *Das Grabgedicht für Carice im Museum von Urbino*, «Klio», 49 (1967), pp. 113-114.

(22) *CIL*, VI, 25617, 2 (= the prescript to *CLE*, 965).

(23) *CIL*, IX, 5860, 2 (Auximum); *AEp*, 1933, 74, 6 (Salona).

(24) *CLE*, 1168, 3-4 = *CIL*, III, 423, 6-7 (Teos in Lydia). The theme of *debitum reddere* is here combined with the theme of death in a foreign land, cf. P. Cugusi, *Aspetti letterari dei Carmina Epigraphica Latina*, Bologna 1985, p. 210.

(25) *CIL*, VIII, 16374, 4-6 (Aubuzza, Africa Proconsularis); 16410, 3-5 (El-Ghorfa, Africa Proconsularis). But the phrase itself is literary: it recurs in Cornelius Nepos, *Vitae*, XXI, 5: *morbo naturae debitum reddiderunt*; Hyginus, *Astr.*, II, 20, 2: *Hellen decidisse et ibi debitum naturae reddidisse*. Cf. Lier, op. cit., (above, note 16), p. 582, note 1; Diehl in his annotation to *ILCV*, 3302.

(26) *CLE*, 693, 1, 4-5 = Diehl, 1347 = *ICUR*, II, 4985 (Rome, a. 483). Cf. below, note 35.

(27) Diehl, 1524, 3 = *ICUR*, VI, 15634.

(28) *AEp*, 1946, 116, 12-13 (Mactaris).

(29) N. Duval, *Inscriptions byzantines de Sbeitla (Tunisie)*, MEFRA, 83 (1971), pp. 245-248 = *AEp*, 1971, 493, 11-13 (Sbeitla = Sufetula).

Next to *reddere*, another favorite verb was *(per)solvere*, with an even stronger intimation of a legal contract. We read:

debitu(m) persolvit (30);
hoc titulo tegeor, debita persolvi (31);
debitum / naturae persolvit (32);
debitum naturae solvit (33).

So also in Christian texts:

dibitum (sic) / *naturae solvit* / *III Kal. Maias* / *in pace* (34);
ultimum iam solvi devitum (sic) *comunem omnibus unum* (35).

The length of life, we read in an epitaph from Rome, was prescribed by nature at birth:

Tempore quo sum genita, natura mihi bis denos tribuit annos, quibus completis septima deinde die resoluta legibus otio sum perpetuo tradita: haec mihi vita fuit.

And further:

mors etenim hominum natura, non poena est; cui contigit nasci, instat et mori (36).

This sentiment was repeated again and again (37): that

---

(30) *CIL*, VI, 11693, 6-7.
(31) *CLE*, 1316, 4 = *CIL*, II, 1235, 7 (Hispalis).
(32) *CIL*, VI, 3580, 12-13. Also this phrase occurs in literature, in Hyginus, *Fab.*, XXVI, 3: *debitum naturae persolvit*.
(33) *CIL*, VI, 37317, 13. Cf. 15696, 6: *debitum] naturae solvero*; Hyginus, *Fab.*, LII, 2: *debitum naturae solvebat*.
(34) Diehl, 3302 (Rome, a. 352).
(35) *CLE*, 718, 5 = Diehl, 1521 (Ebora in Lusitania, a. 593). Cf. above, note 26.
(36) *CLE*, 1567, 1-3, 7-8 = *CIL*, VI, 11252, 7-9, 12-13. For *resoluta legibus* (lines 2-3), cf. Sil. It., *Pun.*, XI, 36: *resoluta legibus urbs*.
(37) Cf. esp. the parallels from Seneca, first pointed out by C. Hosius, *Inschriftliches zu Seneca und Lucan*, «Rh. Mus.», 47 (1892), pp. 462-463, esp. *Epist.*, XCIX, 8: *cui nasci contigit, mori restat*; *De remediis fortuitorum*, II, 1 (p. 447 Haase): «*Morieris*». *Ista hominis natura est, non poena*. Cf. also Manilius, *Astronomica*, IV, 16, repeated verbatim in *CLE*, 1489, 3 = *CIL*, II, 4426 = G. Alföldy, *Die römischen Inschriften von Tarraco*, I, Berlin 1975, p. 342, n. 693: *nascen-*

the debt will be exacted, there was no doubt; but when and where the final payment was to be made, was not stated explicitly in the original contract. And the contractual nature of life nowhere stands clearer than in the urban epitaph for Plocamus:

> *Desinite, aequales, Plocami lugere sepulti*
> *fata...*
> *in requiem excessi; quod quaeritis, id repetitum*
> *apstulit iniustus creditor ante diem* (38).

The creditor may be perceived as unjust, requesting the payment too soon. On the topos of *mors immatura*, often discussed, we need not dwell; nor is there any need to adduce numerous examples from funerary poetry for death that came *ante diem* (39). But the idea of a creditor (his identity not revealed in our inscription) is all important; and the phrase *ante diem* points perforce to a day on which the creditor had all legal and moral right to request, *repetere*, the *debita*. Legal illumination comes from Cicero's disquisition at *Tusc.*, I, 93:

> *Pellentur ergo istae ineptiae paene aniles, ante tempus*
> *mori miserum esse. Quod tandem tempus? Naturaene?*
> *At ea quidem dedit usuram vitae tamquam pecuniae*
> *nulla praestituta die. Quid est igitur querare, si repetit,*
> *cum vult? Ea enim condicione accepeus.*

Cicero makes two legal points. First, nature bestows not life itself but solely *usuram vitae*, its enjoyment. This concept recurs in an early imperial inscription from Nola:

> *Usurae vitae sortem morti reddidit* (40).

---

tes morimur, finis ab origine pendet, and other examples collected by Otto, op. cit., (above, note 14), pp. 237-238; M.C. Sutphen, *A further collection of Latin proverbs,* «Amer. Journ. Philol.», 22 (1901), p. 251; Lier, op. cit., (above, note 16), pp. 583-586; Pikhaus, op. cit., (above, note 16), pp. 57-61; G. Sanders, *Licht en duisternis in de christelijke grafschriften,* «Verhandelingen van de Academie voor Wetenschappen ... van Belgie. Klasse der Letteren», Jaarg. XXVII, N. 56, Brussel 1965, vol. I, pp. 194 ff. See also above, note 19.

(38) *CLE,* 1001, 1-4 = *CIL,* VI, 6502.
(39) Seven instances in the collection of Bücheler-Lommatzsch.
(40) *CLE,* 183 = *Eph Ep,* VIII (1889), p. 90, n. 334, 6-7. Cf. Bücheler ad loc.; Lier, op. cit., (above, note 16), pp. 578-579.

In view of Cicero's text we have to take both *sortem* and
usurae as depending on *vitae*: the deceased returned to death
sortem vitae, the principal or capital of his life. And what kind
of life? *Usurae vitae*, life granted only for use, not for ownership. The thought that life does not belong to us appears also in
the celebrated line of Lucretius, and he expressed it, like Cicero,
in a way typically Roman, through a legal formula:

vitaque mancipio nulli datur, omnibus usu (41).

Among the *res mancipi*, the ownership of which was transferred through a solemn legal ceremony of *mancipatio*, the jurist
Gaius enumerates slaves, oxen, horses, mules, asses, Italic land
and rustic servitudes (42). *Vita* is not on this list. In fact it could
not be owned at all, in any way, and in particular it could not be
acquired by *usucapio*. For Lucretius' *usu*, as the opposition to
mancipio demonstrates, does not refer to the mode of acquisition. It denotes the usufruct of life, or legally speaking *ius alienis
rebus utendi, fruendi, salva rerum substantia* (43). One's life was
always a *res aliena*.

Technically, usufruct and loan were two different and separate institutions, but in the moralistic literature the concept of
life as a loan and the concept of life as un usufruct appear side
by side. Especially telling is Seneca:

*Itaque non est quod nos suspiciamus tamquam inter
nostra positi; mutua accepimus. Usus fructusque noster
est, cuius tempus ille arbiter muneris sui temperat; nos
oportet in promptu habere quae in incertum diem data
sunt et appellatos sine querella reddere: pessimi debito-
ris est creditori facere convicium* (44).

---

(41) Lucr., *de nat. rer.*, III, 971. Bailey in his commentary ad loc. (op. cit., [above, note
18]) disregards the inscriptional evidence, does not know the study of Lier (op. cit., [above, note
16]), but succeeds in adducing (while missing all other texts) three additional parallels for the
idea of life as a loan.

(42) Gaius, *Inst.*, I, 120; II, 29.

(43) *Dig.*, VII, 1, 1. Cf. Bailey, op. cit., (above, note 18), ad loc.; Watson, *The law of property in the later Roman Republic*, Oxford 1968, pp. 16-18, 21 ff, 203, note 2.

(44) Seneca, *Cons. ad Marc.*, X, 2. Lier, op. cit., (above, note 16), p. 579, aptly compares
Plut., *Cons. ad Apoll.*, 10 (106 F); 28 (116 A). Cf. R. Kassel, *Untersuchungen zur griechischen
und römischen Konsolationsliteratur*, München 1958, pp. 74, 91-92.

And in another passage (*Cons. ad Polyb.*, X, 4-5):

Rerum natura illum tibi sicut ceteris fratres suos non mancipio dedit, sed commodavit; cum visum est deinde repetit nec tuam in eo satietatem secuta est sed suam legem. Si quis pecuniam creditam solvisse se moleste ferat, eam praesertim, cuius usum gratuitum acceperit, nonne iniustus vir habeatur? Dedit natura fratri tuo vitam, dedit et tibi: quae suo iure usa si a quo voluit debitum suum citius exegit, non illa in culpa est, cuius nota erat condicio, sed mortalis animi spes avida.

For Seneca life was both an usufruct and a loan. As to what kind of loan it was (a very Roman preoccupation), he wavered: once he defined it as *mutuum*, and in another place as *commodatum*. In regard to life all three constructs have some plausibility, though rather as a legal paraphrase than a precise definition. But whatever the precise legal term, the important rule was always the same: the *res ipsa* had to be returned.

Another important rule was that life was given to us *nulla praestituta die* or *in incertum diem*. This is the second point Cicero and Seneca (and Plutarch) make. And indeed in Roman law «unless a date for repayment was agreed upon either expressly or by implication, it could be demanded at any time» (15).

The concepts of *mutuum*, of *usus*, of a loan without interest, of *dies incerta*, and of the iniquity of Fortune, all of them reappear crowded into three lines of the *Consolatio ad Liviam* (*Epicedium Drusi*), 369-371:

vita data est utenda, data est sine faenore nobis
    mutua nec certa persolvenda die.
Fortuna arbitriis tempus dispensat iniquis.

But on the other hand

<hr>

(45) J.B. Moyle, *Imperatoris Iustiniani Institutionum Libri Quattuor*, Oxford 1912, p. 394.

Stat sua cuique dies.

Innumerable texts echo this line and this thought, and refer to the day of death as *dies meus, suus, tuus,* or *noster* (46).
That day or hour belonged to Parcae or to Fata, and was given
back to them (47). It was a *dies incertus* only for the debtor; it
need not have been so for the creditor:

fatis certa via est neque se per stamina mutat
Atropos: ut primo coepit decurrere filo,
crede, Secunde, mihi, pensatos ibis in annos (48).

The *certa via* of *fatum* leads inevitably to the day on which
the payment of the loan was due. A phrase in Cicero catches the
eye: *alios non solvere, aliorum diem nondum esse* (49). The *dies
aliorum* is a fixed date on which some of the debtors were
expected to pay their debt; it corresponds to *dies suus* or *noster*
of the epitaphs. And in Latin idiom a fixed date was called *dies
certus.* Loans were customarily paid off on the Kalends: a *dies
certus* for a debtor. The payment of the loan of life one could
not postpone *ad Kalendas Graecas.* This loan had to be paid off
and in full on a fixed day, *certis Kalendis* (50).

---

(46) Verg., *Aen.*, X, 467. Cf. the explication of Servius (*ad Aen.*, IV, 696) and the parallels collected ad loc. by A. Forbiger, *P. Vergili Maronis Opera*, II, Lipsiae 1875, p. 377; Otto, op.
cit., (above, note 14), p. 228; *TLL*, s.v. *dies*, cols. 1032, 32 ff; 1033, 14 ff.

(47) Cf. *CLE*, 464, 1-2 = *CIL*, X, 1920 (ager Puteolanus): *Fata suum petiere diem: qui
reddidit, / hic situs est*; *CLE* 1120, 2 = *CIL*, V, 3143, 3 (Vicetia): *debita cum fatis venerit hora tribus*; *CLE*, 2177, 4-5 (Rome): *fatis red / didi, quod dederunt*; *CLE*, 2156, 1 = *CIL*, V, 1721 (Aquileia): *Debita, non optata dies iuvenili advenit aetati.*

(48) *CLE*, 1552 A, 69-71 = *CIL*, VIII, 212 (Cilium).

(49) Cic., *ad Att.*, VIII, 10, 1. Cf. the locution *dies solvendi, Dig.*, XXXV, 1, 40, 2.

(50) A welcome parallel to the expression *certae Kalendae* we find in Martial: at VIII, 64,
4 he mentions the *Kalendae nataliciae.* The birthday was in Rome often celebrated not on the actual anniversary but on the Kalends, that is «either on the first of the month in which the birthday fell or else on the first of the month following» (H. Lucas, *Martial's 'Kalendae Nataliciae'*,
«Class. Quart.», 32, 1938, pp. 5-6). We celebrate our birthday on the Kalends, and figuratively
we die on the Kalends.

41

Updating the *CIL* for Italy

SUPPLEMENTA ITALICA, NUOVA SERIE, vol. 1, 2, 3 (Edizioni di Storia e Letteratura, Roma 1981, 1983; Edizioni Quasar, Roma 1987). Pp. 205, 214, 240. ISBN for vol.3 is 88-85020-84-4.

The modern era in the collecting and editing of Latin inscriptions begins with Theodor Mommsen and his brain-child, the *Corpus Inscriptionum Latinarum*, both immortal. But immortal also means old, and often antiquated. Few scholars systematically consult today earlier epigraphical collections, but future generations will ponder, as we do, over the volumes of *CIL*, for a replacement is not in sight, and (we can safely venture a prophecy) never will be. This applies also to the volumes concerning Italy. Leaving aside 2 successive editions of volume 1, in which the inscriptions predating the death of Caesar have been collected (1863 and 1893-1986), 8 volumes (in 27 fascicules) of the *Corpus* have been devoted to the inscriptions from Italy; they contain some 96,000 entries — a prodigious achievement, and an achievement completed in a span of time prodigiously short: the overwhelming bulk of the work (over 74,000 entries) was published in just 28 years, between 1871 and 1899. The burning question of supplements presented itself almost immediately; the periodical *Ephemeris Epigraphica* was established to publish new finds and present epigraphical discussions. It died after 9 volumes (1872-1913). In a relatively short time almost all the original volumes of *CIL* were enriched by bulky supplements, and this process still continues, but, with the exception of vol. 4 containing the inscriptions from Pompei (the last supplement in 1970), all other volumes are falling hopelessly behind the tide of new finds. Currently, thanks to the efforts of Silvio Panciera and his school, a new supplement to vol. 6 is under preparation, and Heikki Solin is hard at work on a new edition of vol. 10. And there continue to appear new volumes of this grand and lavish series, the *Inscriptiones Italiae*, but at the current pace it will take more centuries to publish and republish epigraphical monuments from Italy than it took to erect them. Hence the idea of *Supplementa Italica*. The name is somewhat misleading, for the *Supplementa* contain only Latin texts; texts in Italic dialects are excluded. But it is a telling name, and still more telling is the subtitle: *Nuova serie*. The original *serie* was stillborn more than 100 years ago; only 1 fascicule appeared, the work of the great Ettore Pais: *Corporis Inscriptionum Latinarum Supplementa Italica. Fasciculus 1. Additamenta ad vol.V Galliae Cisalpinae* (Romae 1888). The new series, guided by the *spiritus movens* of Silvio Panciera, and nourished by the efflorescence of epigraphical studies in Italy, is off to an auspicious start, but the road ahead is long, arduous and infested with financial wolves (in the preface to vol.3, p.7, M. Guarducci and S. Panciera darkly allude to "Qualche problema di finanziamento", but announce that "la crisi sembra fortunamente superata").

The aim of the *Supplementa Italica* is not only to produce supplements to *CIL*, but also to review the whole *patrimonio epigrafico* of Italy. To achieve this goal, the only practical approach was to concentrate not on the whole regions but rather on individual cities and territories. Thus each volume contains contributions dealing with separate cities from various parts of Italy. When all *coloniae*, *municipia* and *territoria* are dealt with, we shall have achieved the final *aggiornamento*, and the time will be ripe to start a new one. Each contribution is composed of the following parts:

Raccolte che si aggiornano. Here are listed the *CIL* numbers (or *Eph.Ep.* or *I.It.* numbers) of all inscriptions under review.

Bibliografia epigrafica and (separately) *Altra bibliografia essenziale*. The distinction is often difficult to grasp, but the entries listed in the *altra bibliografia* do not seem to contain the editions of inscriptions. In both lists the order of entries is alphabetical and not chronological.

Aggiunte e correzioni alle notizie storiche fornite nelle raccolte che si aggiornano. This refers to the historical, archaeological, topographical and antiquarian introductions given in *CIL* (or in *I.It.*) to each city or territory covered. Particularly important are the topographical *aggiornamenti*, indications concerning the exact provenience of inscriptions, and general information on the museums and other places where the inscriptions are currently preserved (in many cases simply extant rather than preserved).

Aggiunte e correzioni ai monumenti epigrafici compresi nelle raccolte che si aggiornano. All inscriptions published in *CIL* and other collections are listed according to the numbering of *CIL* or *I.It.* For each entry the following information is provided: whether the inscription is still extant (a picture of epigraphical carnage emerges); if it is extant, where it is to be found; the extant stones are described and often corrections offered to the readings in *CIL* (many documents still extant have markedly deteriorated); information is also given whether there exists a photograph of the inscription and where it was published (particularly important for stones that have disappeared); concordances with *ILS, ILLRP* and other collections are given, and essential, often exhaustive, bibliography is provided. As the text itself is (understandably) not reproduced, this part can meaningfully be used only if one has at hand a full edition in *CIL* or in some other collection. The textual corrections, the new and often more accurate descriptions of the monuments, and the bibliography, will make the life of an epigrapher both easier and more complicated: when quoting texts in *CIL* it is now imperative never to forget to consult the *Suppl.It.*

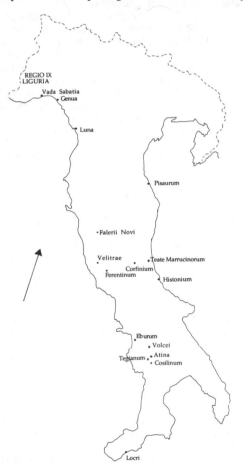

Map showing areas covered by *Supplementa Italica* vols.1-3.

e. *Nuovi testi.* These are either the *inedita* proper or texts published after the appearance of the last supplement to the volume of *CIL* in question, or after the publication of the relevant volume of *Ephemeris Epigraphica* or the volume of *Inscriptiones Italiae.* A good number of these inscriptions appeared in *Notizie degli Scavi,* but many were published in various local periodicals and monographs either difficult to obtain or unavailable in most libraries. And it is instructive and sobering to observe that many of these texts, especially short and fragmentary, never found their way to *L'Année épigraphique.* Some of these *nuovi testi* are already lost; but all that could be located and all that were photographed before their disappearance are accompanied by a photograph. Unfortunately the photographs are substantially reduced in size, and not always easily legible (they do not approach the quality of the photographs in the various museum catalogues of inscriptions, as e.g. in the magnificent volumes of F. Broilo, *Iscrizioni lapidarie latine del Museo Nazionale Concordiese di Portogruaro* 1-2 [Roma 1980-84]).

f. *Indici*: the standard epigraphical indices of *nomina* and *cognomina*, tribes, divinities, *sacerdotes* and religious institutions, geographical names, emperors and their *domus*, municipal organization, of *parole* and *cose notevoli* (abbreviations, *carmina* and sim.). These indexes refer in principle only to the "new texts"; the "old" texts are indexed only if they had been re-edited (and then they count as "new texts").

I give a list of the *aggiornamenti* published in the first 3 volumes of the *Supplementa Italica*, and offer comments on various epigraphical and historical *notabilia*. I also note the number of inscriptions listed in *CIL* for each community in question, and the number of texts now lost (aiming at a general picture, not at mathematical accuracy).

Vol.1, 23-69: FERENTINUM (Regio 1, Latium et Campania) by Heikki Solin. The inscriptions from Ferentinum (today Ferentino), originally a town of the Hernici in southern Latium, were published in *CIL* 10 (1883) by Mommsen himself. That volume contains 86 inscriptions attributed to Ferentinum by Mommsen (and 2 now attributed by Solin); and 16 *falsae* (none is rescued). Of these texts, 36 are lost, and another 5 partially damaged. Solin introduces corrections (exclusively minor and often exceedingly so) in 23 or so texts; he disqualifies 2 as mediaeval or modern, and assigns 4 to the *urbanae*. Of particular importance are his comments on 5837-40 (the local censor appearing in 5837 is probably the grandfather of A. Hirtius, *cos.* in 43, cf. Solin, "Borghesi e Ferentino," *Epigraphica* 44 [1982] 123-26) and 5853 (especially on the expression *in avitum*, "locazione perpetua"; cf. below, *Nuovi testi* no.5).

NUOVI TESTI: here Solin prints 62 additions to *CIL* (many of them tiny fragments); of these 12 are already lost. For the first time he edits some 20 texts, and corrects a good number of others, most of which had been published (or republished) by A. Bartoli in *RendLinc* 9 (1954) 470-507. Of all these documents only 4 found their way to *AEp*. On the other hand, *AEp*. 1982 [1985] nos.304-24, reproduces 21 particularly important inscriptions from Solin's *aggiornamento*. Solin's *aggiornamento* sets a standard of accuracy and completeness. A few observations:

No.5, a decree of the senate of Ferentinum. Line 10: *adicere in ius avitarium fundum*; *avitarium* is new, and the whole phrase, as Solin points out, explains *in avitum* of 5833 as the ellipsis of *in (ius) avitum*.

No.16, lines 3 and 5: for the phrases (already known from 5849 and 5853): *q(uibus) i(us) e(st) [u(na)] v(escendi)]* and *q(uibus) u(na) v(esci) [i(us) e(st]*, i.e. the right to dine respectively with the decurions and the Augustales, cf. Statius, *Silv*.1.6.43-44: *una vescitur omnis ordo mensa, / parvi, femina, plebs, eques, senatus*; here *una* qualifies *mensa*, but the point of the verse is worth noting: only during the Saturnalia could everybody eat at the same table, for normally at the official banquets every *ordo* (as the decurions and Augustales of our inscription) dined separately.

No.19, a fragment of a (metrical) text. Line 2: *sub honore pol*, cf. *CLE* 1552, A, 37 = *CIL* 8.212: *sub honore deorum*. Line 3: supply *[sac]rata deis*.

No.20, a *tabula lusoria* with an enigmatic inscription: *cimis perdas / non binionis / seoclus*. Solin remarks (50) "binionis sembra riferirsi ai punti"; cf. Isid. *Etym*.18.65: "*Iactus quisque apud lusores veteres a numero vocabatur, ut unio, binio, trinio, quaternio, quinio, senio*". *Perdo* is often found on the *tabulae lusoriae*, though normally in the phrase *perdis ploras* (see M. Ihm, "Delle tavole lusoriae romane," *RömMitt* 6 [1891] 215, no 68; A. Ferrua, "Tavole usorie scritte," *Epigraphica* 10 [1948] p.33, nos. 81, 82; p.45, no.114; p.47, no.16; Idem, "Nuove *tabulae lusoriae* iscritte," *Epigraphica* 26 [1964] pp.10-11, no.140; p.19, no.154); *cimis* is in this context a hapax, but (on analogy with *perdas*) it may be a verbal form. Its meaning can be divined from 2 entries in the *Corpus Glossariorum Latinorum* 2.353.44 and 400.42 (=*Thesaurus Glossarum Emendatarum* = *CGL* 6.212.17-18) where the forms *cimico* and *cimis* are both explained as κορίζω, "to be infested with bugs" (not to be confused with κορίζω,"to sweep, to clean"; Lewis and Short understand *cimico* as "to purify from bugs", no doubt wrongly). Hence *cimis* is perhaps to be understood as the second person singular indicative of *cimo, -ere* (a contracted form of *cimico*). In line 3, we should read *se (h)oc es(isti)*; for the form *oc*, cf. Ferrua, "Nuove *tabulae*" p.6 no.136: *occest vivere*. The whole text we may translate as follows: "You are infested with bugs. (May) you lose! Not (even) a two (have you thrown). So did you play."

No.32 line 2. Solin reads *[Popi]liae*, and comments (55): "l'integrazione [Pompi]liae dal Bartoli e da respingere perché *Pompilius* non esiste". This is true of epigraphy — but what about Numa Pompilius?

Vol.1, 73-98: PISAURUM (Regio VI, Umbria) by Giovanni Mennella and Giovannella Cresci Marrone. Pisaurum (Pesaro), a Roman colony founded in 184 in the *ager Gallicus*, famous among the archaeologists and epigraphers for its Museo Oliveriano, provided a rich crop of inscriptions collected by E. Bormann in *CIL* 11, pars 2, and Suppl. (1901 and 1926), and by Kaibel in *IG* 14 (1890), altogether 192 Latin and 2 Greek texts (and 21 *falsae*). A good number of these texts has been published in *CIL* on the basis of the antiquarian manuscript tradition; of those seen by Bormann only 1 appears to be lost, and very few are damaged. One inscription is removed from Pisaurum and assigned to the *ager* of Fanum Fortunae. Of the *falsae*, 1 is possibly authentic. The "old" *CIL* inscriptions were inspected by Cresci Marrone; she introduces very few corrections, mostly minor. Occasionally she is reticent or confusing as to her own readings: 6302 (line 1) reads *Nome[llia]*; this (or *Nome[cia]*) is also the reading of De Bellis Franchi in

1965, but in 1967 that scholar read *Nomelia*, and this was also the reading of Dessau in *ILS* and Degrassi in *ILLRP*. But Cresci Marrone does not say what her own reading is (although she saw the stone). Are the 3 last letters legible or not (or is the right upper corner broken off)? Cresci Marrone offers no comments on texts known only from manuscript tradition: a pity, for important improvements are also being made with respect to these documents. And so, for instance, G. Mennella, "La *pecunia Valentini* di Pesaro e l'introduzione dei *curatores calendarii*," *Epigraphica* 43 (1981) 237-41, shows convincingly that in 6369 we should read in line 9 *ex divisione epularum* (and not *ex divi Nervae epularum*), with the important consequence that the *curator calendar(ii) pecuniae Valentini* mentioned in lines 4-5, and the whole institution of *curatores calendarii* (the supervisors of municipal account-books) is now to be assigned to the age of Trajan (cf. *AEp.* 1982, 266). See now also G. L. Gregori, *Epigrafia anfiteatrale dell'Occidente romano* II, *Regiones Italiae VI-XI* (Vetera 4, Roma 1989) 28-29, who suggests to read *pecuniae Valentini[a]n(ae)*.

The *NUOVI TESTI* contain 15 items, 2 *inedita*, and 9 texts published previously (7 of them listed in *AEp.*, although Mennella and Cresci Marrone inexplicably record this only in 2 cases. See now *AEp.* 1982 [1984] 262-65). Four texts are re-editions of inscriptions published in *CIL*, notably 6319 commemorating C. Octavius, probably from a *sacrarium* of the *gens Iulia*, and 6327 where Cresci Marrone (following L. Braccesi) reads (lines 1-2) *Ma]gnus M[aximus / [Brita]nnicus M[aximus]*. Bormann hesitated between Magnus Magnentius and Magnus Maximus; P. Kneissl, *Die Siegestitulatur der römischen Kaiser* (Göttingen 1969), missed the stone, and does not list any victorious surname either for Magnentius or Magnus Maximus.

Vol.1, 101-76: FALERII NOVI (Regio VII, Etruria) by Ivan Di Stefano Manzella (an excellent contribution). He points out (107) that "molti hanno scritto su Falerii N. senza alcuna conoscenza diretta dei luoghi"; above all, one has to distinguish carefully between the Falerii Veteres and Novi. The inscriptions from Falerii Novi were collected for *CIL* 11, pars 1 (1888) by E. Bormann, altogether 154 texts of which some 79 are now lost and 6 or so seriously damaged — nothing short of a catastrophe. The cause above all, the lack of a local archaeological museum. The comparison with Pisaurum, and its Museo Oliveriano, imposes itself. Di Stefano Manzella offers important comments on several inscriptions, esp. 3090 II: in line 3 read *[theat]rum lapid[eum]*; 3095 a: rather *[Vespasi]ano*, and not *[Valeri]ano* (on the basis of the lettering); 3100, lines 2-3: *[---praef(ectus) al(ae)] / [---Arv]acorum*; 3116 (on the *praefectus perpetuus*); 3156 (on the *portus vinarius superior*); 3185 (a branch of the *gens Stertinia* comes from Falerii Novi).

NUOVI TESTI: 21 published after the conclusion of *CIL*, 34 *inedita*, and 11 re-editions of texts published in *CIL* (esp. no.15, the combination of 3150, 3105 and 3148b into one text; no.17: CIL 6.3578* = 32967a, now lost, belongs in fact not to Rome but to Falerii Novi; no.25: combination into one text of 11.3183 and 2 unpublished fragments; no.27: 11 3139 a, b, c + 2 new fragments). Of these texts, almost all are now in *AEp.* 1982 [1985] 269-302 and 1979 [1982] 21726. A few comments:

No. 2 (re-edition of 11. 3075): the phrase *[F]ortunae / imperio / aram po[suit]* will refer to the command of the goddess seen in a dream, cf. Artem., *Oneir.* 2.37.

No. 21. A gravestone of a *miles torquatus legionis primes* (sic) *Italicae*. A curious text: it displays vulgar form *primes, vissit*; contains a second attestation of the phrase *miles torquatus*; and the stone was set up by an *Arborius*, rare name. But the most curious fact is that 2 copies of the stone might appear to exist: one published by Di Stefano Manzella, and the other published almost simultaneously in *Il lapidario Zeri di Mentana* (Roma 1982), ed. G. Barbieri (*et alii*) 104, no.46. Even more curious is the fact that the stone was twice recorded in *AEp.* (1982, 274 under Falerii Novi, and 1983, 59 under Rome). But the mystery resolves itself into a banal story: "come appare dal confronto del foto, si tratta della stessa lastra evidentemente passata per acquisto dal privato presso il quale la vide il Di Stefano alla collezione Zeri di Mentana" (S. Panciera, *per litteras*).

No. 40. A republican funerary inscription, found in 1973, now illegible, with the consular date C. *Atilio Q. Servio c* The date is 106 B.C., and *Servio* is a mistake (of stone mason or modern copyist) for *Servilio*. Of 12 previous attestations of this consular date, in 5 cases Servilius occupies the first place (including the *Fasti Antiates*) and in Atilius (including the *Fasti Capitolini*); cf. A. Degrassi, *Fasti consulares et triumphales* (*I.It.* 13.1), 476-77.

Vol.1, 179-205: SUPPLEMENTO AGLI INDICI ONOMASTICI DI *CIL V* by Giovanni Mennella. These are the indices of names to the inscriptions from Liguria and the Alpes Maritimae (Regio IX) published since the conclusion of *CIL* 5 (1877). It is to be hoped that Mennella will soon republish the *inscriptiones ipsae* as well.

Vol.2, 11-94: VELITRAE (Regio 1, Latium et Campania) by Heikki Solin and Rita Volpe. The indefatigable Solin provides again a most erudite historical introduction and reviews the inscriptions published in *CIL*; both authors contribute to the *Nuovi testi*. The inscriptions from Velitrae, a city in eastern Latium, were collected by Mommsen in *CIL* 10 (1883), altogether 101 texts (of which 8 *falsae* and 6 *alienae*); to this number add one text in *CIL* 15, and one in *Eph.Ep.* 8 (1889). Since Mommsen, 48 texts have been lost, and one (6608) revealed itself as false. In 10.6555 it is most unlikely that the term *curator lusus iuven(um)* or *iuven(alis)* refers to an office that was administered by M. Cossinus "per mandato imperiale"; he was at first *praefectus fabrum* and *tribunus militum*; then came his municipal career beginning (quite appropriately for a military man) with the supervision of the *iuvenes*, followed by the duovirate, and crowned with his selection as *patron(us) colon(iae)*.

There are 73 *NUOVI TESTI*: 35 published previously (only 11 recorded *suo tempore* in *AEp*.); 34 *inedita* (21 longer texts or deemed more important are now reproduced in *AEp*. 1984 [1987]); and 4 re-editions of texts printed in *CIL*. Of these "new texts", 40 have already vanished (a good number were destroyed during the war), and 9 are damaged. To comment:

No. 10 (= *CIL* 10. 6571). This inscription, which Mommsen published on the basis of a manuscript copy, has been rediscovered. In line 3 Mommsen prints *proc(urator) Asia(e)*; the actual text has *proc. a sac. k.*, probably to be resolved as *proc(urator) a sac(ris) k(astrensibus)*. This would be the first attestation of this office.

No. 24. Solin gives the following text: "C. Baebius C. C. l. P+[---] / idem danista. Hoc [---] / commodum est [---] / factum ex testamento ar[bitratu---] / Pamphili." He claims that in line 1 "P è seguita da un'asta verticale"; the photograph, however, does not show any vertical bar but rather a trace of the lower part of an A. This squares well with the overall sense of the inscription, for it is evident that the *cognomen* of Baebius is to be supplied from *Pamphili* in the last line. In line 4 Solin proposes (in his commentary) to read *ar[bitratu heredum]*, better *omnium heredum*; there is no place in this line for any additional word, hence *Pamphili* must refer to the deceased *testator*. In line 2 *danista* can be either a second surname or an indication of Baebius' profession. Solin quite rightly opts for profession and not a *supernomen*. Festus (Paulus [60 Lindsay]) and the *glossae* (*Corp. Gloss. Lat.* 6.304) explain *danista* as *fenerator*. On the strength of *idem* in line 2, another word describing the occupation of Baebius must have stood at the end of line 1. Now in Plautus the *danistae* appear in a close association with *argentarii* (cf. J. Andreau, *La vie financière dans le monde romaine. Les métiers de manieurs d'argent* [Roma 1987] 350). I propose to supply in line 1 *argentarius*. Thus the supplements in lines 1 and 4 will amount to 19 and 20 letters. This is the first epigraphical attestation of a *danista*. No wonder: this was an occupation everybody despised. In Plautus' words (*Most.* 126) *'nullum ... genus est hominum taetrius ... quam danisticum"*. It is amusing that this inscription should have come from Velitrae, the *patria* of the Octavii: M. Antonius claimed that the grandfather of Octavian was an *argentarius* (Suet. *Aug.* 2.3).

No. 71 (= *AEp*. 1925, 90). Line 5: *Certis calendis diem mor[i]tur*. A mysterious phrase. R. Volpe suggests that "si dotrebbe ipoteticamente pensare ad un significato di 'momento stabilito, fissato', intendendo forse che la morte giunge quando é il momento destinato". This suggestion turns into certainty if we consider the favorite saying of Augustus, *ad Kalendas Graecas soluturos* (Suet. *Aug.* 87), "they will pay on the Greek Kalends", i.e. never, as the Greeks had no Kalends (cf. A. Otto, *Die Sprichwörter der Römer* [Leipzig 1890] 65). Another literary and funerary phrase comes to mind, *debitum naturae solvere* or *persolvere* (cf. B. Lier, "Topica carminum sepulcralium Latinorum," *Philologus* 62 [1903] 575-83; R. Lattimore, *Themes in Greek and Latin epitaphs* [Urbana 1942] 170-71). When you die you pay your debt. And the day of your death you cannot postpone indefinitely: it comes when the final payment is due, *certis calendis*.

Vol.2, 97-144: HISTONIUM (Regio VI, Sabina et Samnium) by Marco Buonocore. The inscriptions from Histonium (today Vasto), the old city of the Frentani on the Adriatic coast, were collected in *CIL* 9 (1883) by Mommsen, altogether 121 numbers (plus 7 texts published in *Eph.Ep.* 8 [1891]), and 14 *falsae*. Of these texts only 25 are lost — relatively not a high number; the preservation of the remainder is mostly due to the existence of the local Museo Comunale. Buonocore offers textual observations or corrections to some 67 texts (in particular he corrects rather numerous errors in A. Marinucci, *Le iscrizioni del Gabinetto Archeologico di Vasto* [Roma 1973]).

The *NUOVI TESTI* are not particularly numerous: only 21, all published previously (all 11 longer texts reproduced in *AEp*.; in *AEp*. 1984 [1987] 366, the article of Buonocore is mistakenly referred to as published in *Tituli* 2; no additional inscriptions are admitted; they are too fragmentary for inclusion in *AEp*.); 5 are lost. To all these texts Buonocore provides an excellent epigraphical and historical commentary, and an exemplary bibliography. Most interesting is no.3 (=*AEp*. 1967, 109), a *tabula patronatus* of 384, with its tortuous style and curious vulgar forms (e.g.

habintes = *habentes*, *hubus* = *avus*, *ortato* = *hortato*); also no.5 (= *AEp*. 1976, 189), recording a *fucinalis* (a new word in Latin), probably (on analogy with the *urbani ceriales*), a priest (or former priest) of the god Fucinus; the *sacerdos* in question was only 13 years old and belonged to the powerful local family of the Hosidii.

Vol.2, 145-94: TEATE MARRUCINORUM (Regio IV, Sabina et Samnium) by Marco Buonocore. Another excellent contribution by this author. Teate Marrucinorum (today Chieti), in whose name the old tribal denomination, Touta Marouca, can still be heard, became a Roman *municipium* probably only after the Social War. It produced inscriptions both in Latin and in its own language, the latter texts to be used in the edition of E. Vetter, *Handbuch der italischen Dialekte* 1 (Heidelberg 1953) 153-55, with the supplement by P. Poccetti, *Nuovi documenti italici* (Pisa 1979) 151-54. It was again Mommsen who collected the Latin inscriptions for *CIL* 9 (1883): 36 texts (to which add 12 published in *Eph.Ep.* 8 [1891]); 6 *falsae*. Of these documents 37 are now lost.

NUOVI TESTI: 45 inscriptions (8 already lost): 25 published previously, mostly in local publications (only 6 recorded in *AEp.*), 20 *inedita* (cf. now *AEp.* 1984 [1987] 334-50).
Very interesting is **no.12** (=*AEp*. 1976, 191) commemorating a *decurio Marruci[n]orum*: in this denomination "perdura tenacemente, anche nel I secolo d.C., l'uso tribale, anteriore alla costituzione del municipio di Teate".
No.17 (= *AEp*. 1980, 368) is a long list of the *soci monumenti*; in line 30 we read "L. Mamilius Celer, << selectus>>", i.e. *selectus* was inscribed in *litura*. It is worthwhile to observe that in his earlier edition of the text ("Ricerca onomastica di un "collegium funeraticum", *Settima miscellanea greca e romana* [Roma 1980] 431), Buonocore printed *(selectus)*, which both in the Leiden system and the system of Krummrey and Panciera denotes letters expunged by the editor as "errore adiectae". The editors of *AEp.* have [[*selectus*]], and offer this comment: "le titre de *selectus* ou bien a été martelé mais reste lisible, ou bien a été regravé dans un martelage". In *Suppl.It.* Buonocore decisively embraces the latter interpretation. He takes *selectus* to mean *iudex selectus ex quinque decuriis*. This is most unlikely. E. S. Staveley, "Iudex selectus," *RhM* 96 [1959] 201-13, esp. 209, argued that only the *equites* were appointed as *iudices selecti*. Our *selectus* appears in a list in which the highest dignitaries are the *seviri Augustales* and a *decurio* — unlikely company for an *eques Romanus*. But in a recent study S. Demougin, "Les juges des cinq décuries originaires de l'Italie," *Ancient Society* 6 (1975) 143-202, esp. 187-89, found that Staveley's rule did not obtain; still there are only 2 certain examples of the non-equestrian *iudices selecti* from Italy. Thus, it would appear that Mamilius Celer was either an equestrian *iudex selectus* in unlikely company, or a rare non-equestrian *iudex selectus*. In fact, we can safely discard either solution. To bolster his interpretation, Buonocore points out that in Teate we have another Mamilius, L. Mamilius Modestus who is styled *selectus et decurio* (*CIL* 9. 3023). But as Demougin (p.144 n.8) demonstrated, Modestus, who was a freedman (a decisive point omitted by Buonocore), could not have been a *iudex* freedmen were not eligible for service on the juries (cf. Pliny *NH* 33.30). Furthermore, the expression *selectus* to indicate a *iudex* never appears alone but always in the form *iudex selectus ex V decuriis, iudex selectus* or *iudex e selectis* (it is interesting to observe that Buonocore conscientiously adduced Demougin's article in his bibliography to 3023, but omitted to consider it in his explication of no.17). Hence, unless *selectus* was a municipal office or an officer in a *collegium*, the easiest solution is to assume that the word was engraved by mistake, and erased (and no written in the erasure after a hypothetical previous title had been obliterated).

Vol.2, 197-214: VADA SABATIA (Regio IX, Liguria) by Giovanni Mennella. Vada Sabatia (today Vado Ligure), a city on the coast of Liguria, and a Roman *municipium*, furnished only few inscription collected in *CIL* 5 (1877) by Mommsen (7 texts, and 3 *falsae*). Of those texts 3 are lost, and 1 probably belongs to Genua. In *CIL* 7776, the expansion of the abbreviation *c.c.s.* as *c(ollegium) c(entonariorum) S(abatium)*, Mennella ascribes to N. Lamboglia in 1939; but cf. already J. P. Waltzing, *Étude historique sur les corporations professionnelles chez les Romains* 3 (Louvain 1899) 164, no.602: *c(ollegium) c(entona iorum) S(abatinorum)*.

NUOVI TESTI. 11 inscriptions: 1 re-edition of *CIL*; 9 published previously (1 lost, and only 1 recorded in *AEp.*) *ineditum* (7 are now republished in *AEp.* 1984 [1987] 417-23). Two texts attract attention:
No.3 recording the tribe *Stel(latina)*; until this find, it was believed on the basis of *CIL* 5. 7779 that the tribe of Va Sabatia was the Camilia; now the question is open.
No.7, a Christian inscription dated to the consulship of Mamertinus and Nevitta, i.e. to 362, and thus the old Christian inscription from Liguria, taking this honor from *CIL* 5. 7530 dated to 432.

Vol. 3, 11-36: LOCRI (Regio III, Lucania et Bruttii) by Marco Buonocore. The Greek Lokroi (Torre Gerace, and from 1934 again Locri), became a Roman *civitas foederata* in 272, and a *municipium* probably only after 89. It produced inscriptions both in Greek and in Latin. For the pre-Roman Greek inscription and in particular for the famous archive from the temple of Zeus, see A. De Franciscis, *Stato e società in Locri Epizefiri* (Napoli 1972) and *Le Tavole di Locri. Atti del Colloquio sugli aspetti politici, economici, culturali e linguistici dei testi dell'archivio Locrese* (ed. D. Musti) (Roma 1979). The Latin inscriptions from Locri were collected for *CIL* 10 (1883) by Mommsen (27 texts), and the Greek for *IG* 14 (1890) by Kaibel (4 texts); a supplement by Ihm in *Eph.Ep.* 8 (1891) contains 10 texts; altogether 41 texts of which 18 are lost. On the basis of autopsy Buonocore provides important corrections particularly to *CIL* 10.35 and 36.

NUOVI TESTI: 21 inscriptions (3 lost); 16 published previously (15 recorded in *AEp.*) and 5 *inedita*. In nos.6 (= *AEp.* 1902, 83) and 7 (= *AEp.* 1965, 154) Buonocore reads *collecius* in place of *collegius*.

Vol. 3, 37-90: *aggiornamenti* of inscriptions from FIVE COMMUNITIES IN REGIO III (Lucania et Bruttii) by Vittorio Bracco. This is in fact an *aggiornamento* not so much of Mommsen in *CIL* 10 (1883) as rather of *Inscriptiones Italiae* 3.1 (1974): *Civitates vallium Silari et Tanagri*, published by Bracco himself. The reader of this volume of *I.It.* and of Bracco's *aggiornamento* will do well to consult frequently H. Solin, *Zu lukanischen Inschriften* (Commentationes Humanarum Litterarum 69, fasc.2, Helsinki 1981). The communities in question are as follows:

37-41: TEGIANUM (Teggiano): 48 inscriptions (and 10 *falsae*) in *CIL* 10; 1 in *Eph.Ep.* 2 (1875); 32 (and 8 *falsae*) in *I.It.* 3.1. A substantial decrease of texts in *I.It.* is explained by the fact that many inscriptions assigned by Mommsen to Tegianum are now proven to belong to Cosilinum and Atina; see below. Unfortunately, the author does not indicate which texts are still extant and which are lost; for this, one has to consult *I.It.* No "new texts" (i.e. texts published or found after 1974).

43-52: COSILINUM (La Civita presso Padula): 34 inscriptions (and 3 *falsae*) in *I.It.* The exact localization of Cosilinum (the name of which was known from a few inscriptions and literary texts) was definitely established only in 1900 on the basis of the inscription I.It. 3.1.210 (= *ILS* 9359) found *in situ*; it records the construction of a *porticus Herculis* by a *cur(ator) r(ei) p(ublicae) Cosilinatium*.

There are 7 *NUOVI TESTI* (3 re-editions of *I.It.*, 3 published previously, 1 *ineditum*), among them the mysterious text (and the only one recorded in *AEp.*) referring to *Sanctum mundum Attinis p.r.* According to Solin and Panciera, *p.r.* is to be solved as *p(opuli) R(omani)*. Still, Attis of the Roman People is rather surprising.

53-62: ATINA (Atena Lucana): 50 texts (and 5 *falsae*) in *CIL* 10; 1 in *CIL* 1²; 1 in *Eph.Ep.* 8 (1891). In *I.It.* 3.1 a substantial increase: 91 inscriptions (and 6 *falsae*).

NUOVI TESTI: 3 (all unpublished). Very important for the history of the city, although very fragmentary, is no.3: mentions a *]pr(aetor) IIv[ir---]*.

63-87: VOLCEI (Buccino): 80 inscriptions (and 6 *falsae*) in *CIL* 10; 2 in *IG* 14 (1890); 1 in *Eph.Ep.* 8 (1891). Many more texts in *I.It.*: 113 (and 9 *falsae*). Two notes:

no.17 (=*CIL* 10. 407), the famous land-register. A new fragment (no.5; see below) contains in line 3 *p]retio;* this shows that we deal in fact with "un'imposizione fiscale" (p.68), and this in turn corroborates the solution of the abbreviation *i.* as m(illenae), as proposed by Déléage (and earlier by Seeck, cf. Solin, *Zu lukanischen Inschriften* 23-26), against Mommsen's *m(odii)*.

no.22 (= *CIL* 10.416), lines 4-6 read as follows: *curatori calendari r(ei) p(ublicae) | Aeclanensium electo a divo Pio | patrono municipii/.* Bracco in his edition in *I.It.* and J. Nicols, "The emperor and the selection of the *patronus civitatis*," *Chiron* 8 (1978) 431, put a comma after *Aeclanensium*, and believe that P. Otacilius Rufus, the municipal patron in question, was "approved" (*electus*) by the emperor. Nicols concludes that "if there is little evidence that matters of patronage were submitted to the emperor for approval, it is not because there was a lack of interest in obtaining imperial confirmation, but because he generally refused to confirm the petition and the communities did not record the refusal". This interpretation received a convincing rebuttal from W. Eck, "Wahl von Stadtpatronen mit kaiserlicher Beteiligung?," *Chiron* 9 (1979) 489-94 (seconded by Solin, *Zu lukanischen Inschriften* 27). Now Bracco reports in *Suppl.It.* that Eck and Solin "attribuiscono l'intervento imperiale alla carica che precede, ossia a cura del calendario d'Eclano" (68-69). The non-committal "attribuiscono" is gravely misleading. In his article Eck did not merely "attribute" the intervention of Antoninus Pius to the selection of Otacilius as *curator calendarii*, but proved it: careful consideration of similar epigraphical formulas demonstrates that the participle (*datus* or *electus*) always follows and never precedes the mention of the *curatela calendarii*. This is a text-book illustration of the old epigraphical principle: if you jump to conclusions without comparing the epigraphical usage, you are likely to fault your jump.

NUOVI TESTI. 16 inscriptions since 1974: 5 *inedita*, 11 published previously (4 recorded in *AEp.*). Particularly important is no.5, a new fragment of the land-register *CIL* 10.407 = *I.It.* 3.1.17, listing the names of 4 new *fundi*, the *f(undus) Gentian[us], Siccit[ianus], Cagati[anus] and Silecia[nus]*. Of the 4 *gentilicia* from which these denominations are derived, only Gentius is relatively common. *Siccitius* will be an orthographic variant of *Sicitius* (*CIL* 6. 1058, col.1, line 132), and *Silecius* a variant of *Silicius* (see the evidence in W. Schulze, *Zur Geschichte lateinischer Eigennamen* [Berlin 1904] 232). On the other hand, the *gentilicium Cagatius* (assumed without any discussion by Bracco) is unattested (it is not listed in H. Solin and O. Salomies, *Repertorium nominum gentilium et cognominorum Latinorum* [Hildesheim 1988]).

89-90: EBURUM (Eboli). 6 inscriptions (and 11 *falsae*) in *CIL* 10; 9 texts (plus 3 assigned to Salernum) in *I.It.* 3.1. No *nuovi testi*.

Vol.3, 93-222: CORFINIUM (Regio IV, Sabina et Samnium) by Marco Buonocore. Another industrious and erudite contribution by this author. In Roman history Corfinium (Corfinio; until 1923 Péntima), a city of the Paeligni, was immortalized as a capital of the Italics in their fight against Rome during the Social War, and a generation later it gained fame on the pages of Caesar's *Bellum Civile*. It produced a rich crop of inscriptions, both in Paelignian and in Latin, collected for *CIL* 9 (1883) again by Mommsen: some 219 Latin texts, including 3 *falsae* (108 now lost), to which add 17 (4 lost) in *Eph.Ep.* 8 (1891). For each inscription Buonocore provides exhaustive bibliography; he also proposes a number of corrections, mostly minor, to Mommsen's readings. In particular, in 3156 the stone has *[---]viae* and not *[---]iae*; this precludes the generally accepted restoration *Lucil]iae* and identification with Lucilia C. f. Benigna, a daughter of a senator from Corfinium, C. Lucilius C.f. Benignus Ninnianus.

NUOVI TESTI. Again a rich crop: 111 texts (34 already lost), 20 *inedita*, 11 re-editions of *CIL* or *Eph.Ep.*, 80 published previously (34 recorded in *AEp.*). Observations:
No.17 (= *AEp.* 1983 [1985] 324). The comments of Buonocore are insufficient, and possibly misleading. As the original editor, G. Paci ("Nuovi documenti epigrafici dalla necropoli romana di Corfinio," *Epigraphica* 42 [1980] 46-64, esp. 48-51), points out (and after him the editors of *AEp.*), the stone, containing a *carmen* in 10 elegiac distichs, was set up for Lucilia (mulieris) l. Calybe by her husband T. Petiedius T. l. Stephanio and her son C. Lucilius Ichimenus (that he was Calybe's son follows from *nato* in line 12). The *nomen gentile* of the son cannot be explained "con la nascita in servitù" (so Paci 50), for he was not a *libertus*: rather he will be Calybe's son from a previous marriage (so rightly *AEp.*); her husbands are alluded to in line 10: "coniugibusque meis semper amanda fui". At a later time on the upper and lower edge of the stone, an inscription was added for T. Petiedius T. l. Nyctaeus. He was either a freedman of Stephanio or his patron or his father (in this case Nyctaeus and Stephanio will have been manumitted together by the same owner); so rightly Paci; the statement in *AEp.* "un parent" is too dogmatic.
No. 29, lines 2-3: *Vieida T. l. Dioclia*. So published in *NotSc.* 1902, 125. Buonocore emends to *Vieidia*. This would be a new *gentilicium* (not recorded in the *Repertorium* of Solin and Salomies). Perhaps we should read *Veidia*; the *nomen Vidius* is attested in inscriptions (cf. *Repertorium* 208) and in Cic. *Fam.* 9.10.1, where R. Syme, "Missing persons II, *Historia* 8 (1959) 211 = *Roman Papers* 1 (Oxford 1979) proposes to read *Veidium = Vedium* (cf. ILS 109; P. Veidius P. Pollio, i.e. the notorious P. Vedius). D. R. Shackleton Bailey, *Cicero. Epistulae ad Familiares* 2 (Cambridge 1977) 6. 216-17, pointing to the inscriptional evidence, retains *Vidium*. To conclude: if the nomen of Dioclia was in fact *Veidi* we can see in it a new *gentilicium* or an archaic form of either *Vedia* or *Vidia*.
No. 56 (= *CIL* 1² 3241), no doubt from the last century of the republic. Line 2 reads *Polipi T. s(ervo)*. Buonocore postulates the name *Polipius*; Solin and Salomies (*Repertorium* 145) admit it among the *gentilicia* but with a query. The *cognomen Polipus* remains a possibility. Either form is a hapax.
No. 78, lines 1-2: *Seneiia T. l. / Vettia*. The first attestation of the *gentilicium Seneius*, and of *Vettius* used as *cognomen*. Solin and Salomies (*Repertorium* 167) query *Seneius*, and do not list *Vettius* (cf. 421).

Vol. 3, 225-40: GENUA; ORA A LUNA AD GENUAM (Regio IX, Liguria) by Giovanni Mennella. Genua, of little importance until late antiquity, furnished few inscriptions: Mommsen records 37 texts *CIL* 5 (1877), and E. Pais 2 texts in his *Supplementa Italica* (1888). Of these texts 15 are now lost, 3 are *urbanae*, 3 belong to Luna, and 1 to Libarna.

NUOVI TESTI: 3 texts published previously (none recorded in *AEp.*), 1 re-edition of *CIL*.

In 3 volumes, on 654 pages, we have before us the *patrimonio epigrafico* from 15 communities, painstakingly enlarged and reviewed. Let us hope that this undertaking will not, as many other grand schemes, be remembered as a great beginning only. The stones are disappearing.

42

Zum Namen *Competalis*

Im Jahre 1955 erschien der erste Teil des Meisterwerks von
H. Krahe „Die Sprache der Illyrier" und kurz danach folgte das
erst nach dem Tode des Verfassers veröffentlichte Werk A. Mayers,
„Die Sprache der alten Illyrier". Jede weitere Bearbeitung der
illyrischen Sprachreste wird auf den uns von Krahe und Mayer
geschenkten Werken aufbauen; die indoeuropäische Sprachwissen-
schaft erhielt davon manche Anregung zur weiteren Forschung.

Auch dieser Aufsatz ist durch das Werk Krahes angeregt, wenn ich mich auch mit einer von Krahe vorgeschlagenen Etymologie kritisch auseinandersetzen möchte.

Unter anderen von Krahe als illyrisch erklärten Personennamen erscheint der Name *Competalis* (S. 56); in A. Mayers Verzeichnis der illyrischen Sprachreste ist dieser Name nicht angeführt. Ob wir es hier wirklich mit einem illyrischen Personennamen zu tun haben, erscheint uns bedenklich: wir wollen in diesem Aufsatz eine neue Erklärung des Wortes darbieten und zwar mit Heranziehung eines neuen, von Krahe nicht analysierten Materials.

Bevor wir aber das Wort einer Analyse unterwerfen, scheint es uns zweckmäßig, um dem Leser das Verständnis unserer Ausführungen zu erleichtern, an dieser Stelle die von Krahe vorgelegte Erklärung des Namens wörtlich wiederzugeben. Die Erklärung Krahes lautet S. 56—57:

Com-petalis (CIL V 1142; Aquileia), so zu analysieren wegen *Petale*, f. (CIL V 2123; Tarvisium), und *Petalus* (ebd. 5477; Angera), enthält idg. **kom* „neben, bei, mit" (Walde-Pokorny I 458, Pokorny 612; lat. *com-* und *cum*, gall. *com-* usw.), das J. Pokorny, Vox Rom. 10 (1950) 227, auch in einigen von ihm für illyrisch gehaltenen ON. erkennt: *Com-beranea* (Bachname bei Genua), *Com-pleutica* und *Com-plutum* in Spanien, ähnlich auch (ebd. 228) *κο-πλάνιον πεδίον* „die Ebene von Palencia (Altkastilien)". — Zweifelhaft ist Zugehörigkeit von messap. *kon* und *kum*; H. Krahe, IF 49 (1931) 268 und 56 (1938) 132. — Zu *Petale* und Zubehör: V. Cocco, Caballus (Coimbra 1945) 39 f.

Daß *Competalis* zu den zweistämmigen Personennamen gehört und als *Com-petalis* zu lesen ist, ist unbestritten. Das Praefix *com-* kann aber so gut lateinisch wie illyrisch sein. Weil aber neben den lateinischen Bildungen mit *com-* auch die illyrischen vorhanden sind, läßt die Analyse dieses Namengliedes keine endgültige Entscheidung hinsichtlich der Zugehörigkeit des ganzen Namens zu dem illyrischen oder lateinischen Sprachstoff erreichen.

Für die Erklärung des zweiten Gliedes zitiert der Verfasser zwei ebenfalls den italischen Inschriften entnommene Personennamen, *Petale* und *Petalus*. Diese Namen sind leider mit einem f. versehen; selbst der Verfasser läßt die Möglichkeit zu, daß sie eher einen anderen als illyrischen Eindruck machen können. Für die eingehendere Erklärung solcher Wörter und Rechtfertigung ihrer illyrischen Etymologie sind wir auf die nächsten Bände des Werkes verwiesen.

Um das mögliche Mißverständnis zu vermeiden: ich bestreite hier nicht, daß *Petale* und *Petalus* mit dem Illyrischen in Zusammenhang gebracht werden können; die Frage lautet, ob sie wirklich in Com-petalis zu entdecken sind. Infolge der lautlichen Übereinstimmung liegt zwar solche Vermutung nahe; sie führt uns aber irre. Viel leichter und natürlicher ist es, das Wort aus dem lateinischen Sprachgut herzuleiten und seine Etymologie mit Hilfe des lateinischen Sprachmaterials zu beleuchten.

Es scheint mir ganz gesichert, daß *competalis* ein adj. ist[1]), von dem subst. *compitum* regelmäßig abgeleitet; in unserem Falle ist es zum cognomen geworden. (Die tria nomina des Mannes lauten: *M. Valerius Competalis.*)

Das ganze einschlägige Material ist im Thes. 1. 1. s. vv. *compitalis, compitalia, compitum*[2]) seit langem vollständig zusammengestellt. Man braucht nur, für die Beweisführung unserer Interpretation, einige Beispiele daraus zu schöpfen.

Wir lesen zwar auf dem Steine *Competalis* und nicht *Compitalis,* wie man erwartet haben könnte; diese Tatsache bereitet aber keine Schwierigkeiten, da der Wechsel dieser Vokale besonders oft in den Inschriften begegnet[3]) und leicht zu erklären ist. Die Etymologie des Wortes *compitum* belehrt uns sogar, daß die Form mit *e*, wenn auch nicht als richtiger angesehen werden darf, jedenfalls ebenso richtig ist, wie diejenige mit *i*. Varro bringt das Wort *compitum* mit *competo, -ere* in Zusammenhang, indem er L. L. 6, 25 behauptet: *ubi viae competunt, tum in competis sacrificatur.* Diese Etymologie wurde von Porphyrius und Isidorus wiederholt und auch von den neueren Forschern übernommen[4]). Es soll an dieser Stelle an die bekannte Lautentwicklung erinnert werden, daß die offenen Mittelsilben, welche kurze Vokale enthielten, durch die Anfangsbetonung geschwächt wurden. *Compitum* mußte also aus **competom* entstanden sein. Diese Lautentwicklung ist schon im 3. Jh. v. Chr. abgeschlossen worden. Bei Varro erscheint aber *compitum* als *competum* vokalisiert. In dieser Form ist es auch durch die anderen

---

[1]) Man kann zwar auch an subst. *competalis, -is* denken (cf. CIL XI 4810, 4815, 4818, 4914); es ist aber augenscheinlich erst nach dem Muster des Adjektivs gebildet.

[2]) S. auch Thes. 1. 1., Onomasticon Bd. II s. vv. *Competalis* und *Competum,* wo auch unser *Valerius Competalis* zitiert ist.

[3]) Vgl. H. Dessau, ILS vol. III pars 2 Indices, S. 813.

[4]) Siehe Walde-Hofmann, Lat. etymologisches Wörterbuch s. v. *compitum,* Ernout-Meillet, Dictionnaire étymologique de la langue latine s. v. *peto.*

10 *

Schriftsteller vermittelt; für die hierher einschlägigen Stellen-
angaben verweise ich auf Thes. 1. 1 loc. cit. Als wichtige Tatsache
ergibt sich, daß diese Nebenform von den Zeiten der Republik bis
zum späteren Kaiserreich und früheren Mittelalter im Gebrauch
war. Wir haben gesehen, daß die Formen mit *i* lautgesetzlich sind;
diejenigen mit *e* sind dagegen in der Weise zu erklären, daß sie nach
dem Muster des selbständigen *peto* wiederhergestellt sind[1]). Es ist
zu betonen, daß in den Zusammensetzungen mit *peto* fast auschließ-
lich die restituierten oder die später gebildeten *e*-Formen hervor-
treten. Nur in *compitum* und *propitius* macht sich das Vokal-
schwächungsgesetz geltend. Die Rekomposition ergriff aber auch
compitum und seine Ableitungen; sie wurde durch den Umstand
gefördert, daß die dem *compitum* sehr nahestehenden Komposita,
wie *competo, competenter, competentia* und dgl. stets als *e*-Formen
erscheinen. Man darf schließlich nicht vergessen, besonders wenn
es sich um die Inschriften der Kaiserzeit handelt, daß neben der
Rekomposition auch die vulgärlateinische Lautentwicklung ganz
regelrecht, besonders in den Zusammensetzungen, von den *i*-haltigen
zu den *e*-haltigen Formen führte.

Die Inschriften liefern uns für die *e*-haltigen Formen einige weitere
Beispiele. In einigen auf Delos aufgefundenen und griechisch
geschriebenen Inschriften kommen die κομπεταλιασταὶ γενόμενοι[2])
zutage, die offenbar den Larenkultus auf einem *compitum* besorgten.
Der griechische Text gibt ohne Zweifel die lateinische Volksaus-
sprache dieser Zeit wieder, da die κομπεταλιασταί Freigelassene oder
Sklaven waren[3]). Also diese griechische Neubildung[4]) wurde von

---

[1]) Vgl. F. Stolz, Lat. Grammatik, München 1910, S. 167 (vgl. auch
5. Aufl. von M. Leumann, München 1926, S. 81ff.); J. Safarewicz, Zarys
gramatyki historycznej języka łacińskiego. Warszawa 1953, S. 76ff.

[2]) Inscr. de Délos 1760—1770.

[3]) Es ist unnötig, an dieser Stelle die umfangreiche Literatur zu der Kom-
petaliastenfrage anzuführen; ich verweise nur auf die neueren Arbeiten von
K. Meuli, Altrömischer Maskenbrauch, Mus. Helv. 12, 1955 S. 219ff. mit
Anm. 51 und F. Bömer, Untersuchungen über die Religion der Sklaven in
Griechenland und Rom, Abh. Mainz 1957 nr. 7, S. 43ff., wo die ausführlichen
Literaturangaben zu finden sind.

[4]) Lat. *competaliasta,-ae* ist nur eine künstlich durch Thesaurus gegebene
Latinisierung des griechischen Terminus und findet sich in den Quellen
nicht; lateinisch hätten diese κομπεταλιασταί etwa *magistri* oder *ministri*
compitales heißen müssen. Die oft gegebene Erklärung „*magistri collegii*
compitalicii" trifft das Richtige nicht; für die eingehendere Rechtfertigung
meiner Behauptung muß an dieser Stelle verzichtet und auf eine weitere
Arbeit hingewiesen werden.

competum und nicht compitum abgeleitet. Daß es sich hier nicht um eine eigentümlich griechische Aussprache des lateinischen Wortes handelt, zeigt ausdrücklich die oben angeführte Stelle Varros, wo wir *competum* lesen. Selbst das Fest der Kompitalien, das an den compita gefeiert wurde, wird uns durch Festus p. 257 Mueller als *Competalia* überliefert.

Den entscheidenden Beweis für unsere Ansicht dürfen wir aber den Inschriften der Kaiserzeit entnehmen, zu denen auch die Inschrift des *Competalis* gehört. Adj. *compitalis* erscheint in diesen Inschriften zweimal in der Form *competalis*; diese Tatsache ist von besonderem Wert für unsere Interpretation, indem sie die unmittelbare Parallele für den Namen *Competalis* gibt. Die hier in Frage stehenden Inschriften lauten: CIL XIII 6731 = Dess. 3635: *Laribus competalibus sive quadrivialibus* ...; AÉp. 1903 nr. 235 (cf. CIL II 5810): *Mercurio competali Flavius Flavianus veteranus v.s.l.m.*

Dürfen wir hier auch ein illyrisches Wort entdecken? Es ist ein Glück, daß der Kontext hier so klar ist, daß er keine derartige Erklärung zuläßt.

Es kann noch hinzugefügt werden, daß in der Inschrift CIL VIII 21873 eine *Gabinia Compitaria* erscheint; das cognomen ist nach demselben Muster wie *Competalis* gebildet[1]).

Alles bisher Gesagte führt also zum Schluß: das in der Inschrift CIL V 1142 hervortretende cognomen *Competalis* darf als ein lat. Adjektiv erklärt werden, das in diesem Falle zum Personennamen wurde. Auf jede illyrische Etymologie des Namens muß man verzichten.

---

[1]) Es ist wohl nur eine Schreibweise für *Compitalia*.

43

Two Studies in Roman Nomenclature. By D. R. Shackleton Bailey. The American Philological Association (American Classical Studies 3). 1976. Pp. viii, 135. ($5.00)

The new book by D. R. Shackleton Bailey is composed of two parts: *Onomasticon Pseudotullianum* (1–77) and *Adoptive Nomenclature in the Late Roman Republic* (79–134). The *Onomasticon* contains over one hundred eighty entries and includes wrong names or names parts of which (e.g., the *praenomen*) are wrong (such names are put in quotation marks), dubious names, and finally the names that are wrongly attributed (i.e. the cases of amalgamation of two persons or splitting up of one person). Part II contains a study of the adoptive nomenclature followed by a register of adoptions (over ninety entries arranged alphabetically according to the adoptive name and covering the period from *ca* 130 to 43).

The two lists contain a wealth of information on disinformation, and all *Ciceroniani* will constantly have to refer to them. The lover of prosopography will find there generously presented to him veritable gems of erudition and critical acumen from T. "Accius" to the famous case of Sex. "Clodius" (cf. now Shackleton Bailey's delightful "Mumpsimus— Sumpsimus," *Ciceroniana* N.S. 1 [1973, published 1976] 3–9: let's hope that the last stronghold of Sex. "Clodius," the *Collection Budé*, will finally fall) to Zosippos of Tyndaris, and from C. Aelius Paetus Staienus to C. Visellius Varro. There is no better way of expressing one's appreciation of Shackleton Bailey's ghost-names hunt than by offering some (admittedly random) observations on his list: *4* T. "Accius" (the prosecutor of Cluentius). Shackleton Bailey points out that the mss are divided between *Attius, Actius* and *Accius*, but preponderate in favor of the first. For a similar case, cf. Cic. *Att.* 8.4.3 *C. Atium Paelignum*, where *Atium* is the conjecture made by Malaespina, the mss having *Attium* or *Actium*. It is not quite clear to me why Shackleton Bailey opts in this case for *Atium* (see his edition no. 156), especially as the mss of Caesar, *BC* 1.18.1–4, seem to favor the reading Attium (cf. A. Klotz *in app. crit.*). On the other hand an inscription from Corfinium (i.e., also from the territory of the Paeligni) has *T. Ac[cio] T. l. Paelino* (*CIL* 9.3187 line 13; cf. C. Nicolet, *L'ordre équestre* 2 [Paris 1974] 756). *8* Ambivius (Cic. *pro Cluent.* 163): cf. *AÉp.* 1960, 60: *L. Ambeivius L. f. Paetus* from the vicinity of Frascati (dated to the first century b.c.). *8* Amianus (Cic.

Att. 6.1.13): "the name may be corrupt (for Amiantus?)." The name is in perfect order. As Shackleton Bailey observes, Amianus was probably Atticus' runaway slave who took refuge in the territory of the local chieftain Moeragenes in Cilicia (cf. Cic. *Att.* 5.15.3 [= 108] and Shackleton Bailey *ad loc.*). It is not impossible that he was a native of Asia Minor. In fact, L. Zgusta, *Kleinasiatische Personennamen* (Prag 1964) 66 n. 155, notes two epigraphical occurrences of the name in Asia Minor: Ἀμιανῆς (*Altertümer von Hierapolis* [= *Jb. d. dt. arch. Inst., 4 Ergänzungsheft*, Berlin 1898] 147 no. 244) and Αὐρηλίῳ Ἀμιανῷ (*MAMA* 4.27 line 7–8, probably from Prymnessos, early third century A.D.). *62–63* P. (Quinctius?) Scapula (Cic. *pro Quinct.* 17). It seems virtually certain that he was a Quinctius, cf. C. Nicolet, "Amicissimi Catilinae," *REL* 50 (1972) 182–186, especially on the conjecture *Scapulas* (Gruter ascribes it to Puteanus [C. Dupuy], but Nicolet notes [182]: "Je n'ai pu, à la Bibliothèque Nationale, retrouver la trace du manuscript de Dupuy qui doit porter en marge cette note") in *Comm. Pet.* 10: *ab atriis* (Nicolet observes that this expression occurs only in this place and at *pro Quinct.* 12 and 25) *Sapalas et Carvilios . . . sibi amicissimos comparavit* (sc. *Catilina*). Cf. also J. M. Flambard, C. Nicolet, J. M. David, "Le 'Commentariolum Petitionis' de Q. Cicéron," *ANRW* I 3 (Berlin 1973) 268–270. According to Nicolet (*L'ordre équestre* 2.998–999) he was *sans doute* (Shackleton Bailey writes "perhaps") the father of the ἀνὴρ ἱππεὺς T. Quin(c)tius Scapula (Cass. Dio 43.29.3) who rebelled in Spain against Caesar in 46, and committed suicide soon after Munda (*Bell. Hisp.* 33). Nicolet identifies this Scapula with the proprietor of the *horti Scapulani* (Cic. *Att.* 12.40.4), but Shackleton Bailey rightly notes that the property of the rebel "would surely have been forfeit to the state," and there would be no talk of the *heredes*. He ingeniously postulates the existence of an elder brother as the estate owner, but still it would rather be a strange coincidence that he should have died about the same time as the rebel. *65* Cic. *Att.* 5.20.8 reads as follows: *incendio Plaetoriano quod †leius† adustus est, minus moleste fero. Lucceius de Q. Cassio cur tam vehemens fuerit et quid actum sit aveo scire.* Some years ago Shackleton Bailey successfully discarded the vulgate *Seius*, but has not yet found a suitable candidate for scorching. Now H. Kasten, "Zu Ciceros Atticus-Briefen," *Hermes* 99 (1971) 253, has made a bold attempt at solving the name-riddle in the first sentence by attacking a name in the next. He feels that *vehementem esse de aliquo* is *untragbar* (perhaps; but how a non-native reader of Latin can feel that, is not clear to me), and consequently interprets *Lucceius* as a *Randkorrektur* for †leius†. He accepts it as the correct reading, and finds Cicero's lack of concern for the *adustus* easily explicable as it is well known that Lucceius refused to compose a monograph about the *annus mirabilis*. Such a villain, and only scorched! Kasten's solution hardly carries conviction—the glosses are after all not infallible. But accepting *Lucceius* as a gloss Kasten set into motion (without fully realizing it) an interesting chain reaction. First of all there disappears any connection between Lucceius and Q. Cassius (according to the traditional interpretation Cassius was standing trial at that time, and Lucceius may have been his accuser, cf. Constans-Bayet and Shackleton Bailey *ad loc.*, and J. Linderski, "Two Quaestorships," *CP* 70 [1975] 38 n. 22). Secondly, in the new context (*de Q. Cassio cur tam vehemens fuerit . . . aveo scire*), it would be most natural to interpret Cassius' *vehementia* as referring to the unfortunate person tormented behind the crux. And this in turn would strongly argue in favor of attributing to the phrase *incendium Plaetorianum* the metaphorical sense of *iudicium* (in any case it seems doubtful that Cicero is here speaking of a real fire). The story is instructive for it shows that ghost-names and misplaced names can easily get out of hand.

Most interesting is Shackleton Bailey's discussion of the thorny problem of testamentary adoption (92 ff.), especially his critique of the view (recently maintained by Schmitthenner and Weinrib) that this kind of adoption did not involve a change in agnatic position. As Shackleton Bailey rightly points out, the fact that Antonius did not attack in his propaganda Octavian's filial claims with respect to Caesar seems to show that he acknowledged his rival's passage into the *gens Iulia*. There also are notorious problems with the adoption of Clodius. Clodius did not use the name Fonteius, and did not accept (at least according to Cicero) the *sacra* of his new *gens*. On this basis Cicero argued that his adoption was invalid, and his tribunate null and void. Cicero's contention was not accepted, and Shackleton Bailey remarks "so permissive was Roman custom in this matter" (89). But behind this "permissive custom" were hidden Caesar's political interests, and, last but not least, also that of Cato (as Shackleton Bailey himself recognizes). Of course nobody was in doubt that the *adrogatio* of Clodius violated the spirit of the institution, but at the same time we have to remember that the *lex curiata* was proposed by the *Pontifex maximus*, and was passed strictly according to all rules, with an augur in attendance. From a formal point of view there cannot have been even the slightest doubt that Clodius legally became a plebeian, and his handling or mishandling of his old or new *sacra* could not alter that fact.

A great number of corrections proposed by Shackleton Bailey are based on the evidence of Cicero's MSS which sometimes "has been inaccurately or inadequately reported" (3). The MSS for the Letters *ad Atticum* and *ad Familiares* Shackleton Bailey has collated and reviewed for his monumental editions, and for the present work he has also checked some selected readings for the speeches, but as he writes "the Speeches as a whole

have still to be properly edited" (3). There is no doubt about this, nor is
there any doubt as to who should undertake this task.

44

AMIANUS

In a letter to Atticus from Cilicia Cicero informs his friend: de Amiano, spei nihil
putat esse Dionysius (ad Att. 6.1.13 = SB 115). D.R.Shackleton Bailey (Cicero's Letters
to Atticus 3, Cambridge 1968,246) thinks that Amiano "may well be corrupt (for Amianto?)",
and he repeats the same opinion in his recent Two Studies in Roman Nomenclature (American
Classical Studies 3), 1976,8. But there is no need for a conjecture. The name-form Amianus
(without gemination) is attested in three Latin inscriptions (CIL 8.19942 from Numidia,
13,4583 from Gallia Belgica, 13.10010,18 vasculum Gallicum, all listed in TLL s.vv.
Amianus, col. 1889 and Ammianus, col. 1938), but above all it is also known from Asia
Minor. As Shackleton Bailey observes, Amianus was probably Atticus' runaway slave who
took refuge in the territory of the local chieftain Moeragenes in Cilicia (cf. ad Att. 5.15.3
= SB 108, and Shackleton Bailey ad loc. p.216). It is not impossible that he was native of
Asia Minor. In fact, L.Zgusta, Kleinasiatische Personennamen, Prag 1964, 66 n.155,
notes two epigraphical occurrences of the name in Asia Minor : 'Αμιανῆc (Altertümer von
Hierapolis/ = Jb.d.dt. arch.Inst., 4 Ergänzungsheft, Berlin 1898/ p.147 no 244), and
Αὐρηλίω 'Αμιανῶ (MAMA 4.27 lines 7-8, probably from Prymnessos, early third century
A.D.).

45a

Fumum vendere and *fumo necare*

To the Memory of Smokey

The delightful expression *fumum vendere* has intrigued the philologians since the days of Erasmus, Casaubonus, Gothofredus and Salmasius.[1]) Recently B. Baldwin in his erudite article, *"Fumum vendere* in the *Historia Augusta"*, *Glotta* 63 (1985) 107–109, has dispelled most of the remaining smoke. In the *Iudicium Coci et Pistoris* of Vespa (*Anth. Lat.* 199 Riese; 190 Shackleton Bailey) the baker is characterized as a man who "semper multis se dicit vendere fumum" (line 61). Baldwin points out that the baker is a braggart, that "a joke on his peddling influence[2]) admirably suits the context", and that on

---

[1]) For Erasmus, see Baldwin 107. The comments of Casaubonus and Salmasius are easily available in the edition *Historiae Augustae Scriptores VI cum notis selectis Isaaci Casauboni, Cl. Salmasii et Jani Gruteri accurante Cornelio Schrevelio* (Lugduni Batavorum 1661; the edition *cum notis integris* appeared in 1671); see *Ant. Pius* 11 (Casaubonus), *Avid. Cass.* 4 and *Alex. Sev.* 36 (Salmasius). Iacobus Gothofredus commented on the *fumi venditio* in a note on Libanius, *Or.* 5.3 = 51.7 Foerster; see his *Opera juridica minora*, ed. Ch. H. Trotz (Lugduni Batavorum 1773) 443 n. 6, and below, n. 18. A similar expression is *fabulas vendere* (*Gord.* 24.4) for which I was not able to find any parallels. *Fumum vendere* survives in contemporary Italian as *vender fumo*: "raccontare fandonie, vantarsi di un credito che non si ha" (cf. *Il nuovo dizionario Italiano Garzanti* [Milano 1984] s.v.). Cf. also A. Otto, *Die Sprichwörter der Römer* (Leipzig 1890) 149.

[2]) In fact what the baker is peddling is not his influence but rather his, in the eyes of the cook, nugatory concoctions, made of trifling ingredients, nuts, honey and flour. He boasts much (*iactat,* line 65), but delivers only smoke. Cf. A. J.

424

this interpretation "the *HA's* monopoly on *fumum vendere* in the sense of trafficking is broken" (p. 108). This sense, he notes, may well be present already in Martial 4.5.7 (*vendere nec vanos circum Palatia fumos*). And there is also no doubt that the Greek proverbial καπνοὺς καὶ σκιάς formed the ultimate model for the Latin phrase.

We can be more precise. Arist. *Aves* 822 mentions τὰ Θεογένους τὰ πολλὰ χρήματα, and the scholion gives the following explanation: προείρηται ὅτι πένης οὗτος, ἔλεγε δὲ ἑαυτὸν πλούσιον. The compiler of the scholia also adduces the opinion of another commentator (ἄλλως): λέγεται ὅτι μεγαλέμπορός τις ἐβούλετο εἶναι περαίτης ἀλαζὼν ψευδόπλουτος, ἐκαλεῖτο δὲ 'Καπνός' ὅτι πολλὰ ὑπισχνούμενος οὐδὲν ἐτέλει. Εὔπολις ἐν Δήμοις.[3]) This Theogenes was one of the "new politicians" in Athens, and a butt for the comedians' ridicule.[4] At *Aves* 1125-1129 he appears in the company of Proxenides ὁ Κομπασεύς ("the Bragsman", a jocular demotic), and the scholiast (at line 1128) characterizes them as καπνοὶ... καὶ κομπασταί. This establishes the meaning of καπνοί as "braggarts", a sense of καπνός missing from *LSJ*, but recorded in J. W. White's edition of the scholia (p. 334)[5]). That Theogenes was a braggart, and that as such he was called "Smoke" – "because having promised all the things he performed nothing", is of immediate interest to the students of *fumus*,

---

Baumgartner, *Untersuchungen zur Anthologie des Codex Salmasianus* (Diss. Zürich 1961, Baden 1961) 50-51; A. Ronconi, "Nota critica e esegetica a Vespa, vv 60-65", in his *Da Omero a Dante. Scritti di varia filologia* (Urbino 1981) 212 (originally published in *Scritti in onore di B. Riposati,* Rieti 1979). In line 64 I read *de nuce* (*denuce* Mss.; *de nuce* Baehrens; *denique* Riese, Baumgartner and Shackleton Bailey) following the erudite argument of G. Bernardi Perini, "Il fornaio millantatore (Vespa 60-65)", *Atene e Roma* 28 (1973) 164-171 (at 169). Ronconi and Perini take exception to the arrangement of lines 60-62, and especially to *se* in line 61, but the text they produce is exceedingly tortuous.

[3]) J. F. White, *The Scholia on the Aves of Aristophanes* (Boston and London 1914) 154. Suid. s. v. Θεαγένους (observe the incorrect form of the name) χρήματα (Vol. 2, [Lipsiae 1931], p. 688, ed. Adler) contains the practically identical text: οὗτος δὲ πένης ὢν μεγαλέμπορος ἐβούλετο εἶναι, ἀλαζών, ψευδόπλουτος. ἐκαλεῖτο δὲ Καπνός, ὅτι πολλὰ ὑπισχνούμενος οὐδὲν ἐτέλει.

[4]) Fiehn, *RE* 5A (1934) s. v. "Theogenes 3"; K. Plepelits, *Die Fragmente der Demen des Eupolis* (Wien 1970) 34-35, 46-49; F. Sartori, *Una pagina di storia Ateniese in un frammento dei "Demi" Eupolidei* (Roma 1975) 28.

[5]) *LSJ* adduces *Kapnos* as "nickname of a man", but does not explain its precise meaning. W. R. Connor, *The New Politicians of Fifth-Century Athens* (Princeton 1971) 139 n. 3, translates the nickname of Theogenes as "Smoky", but again fails to explain its full significance.

for as a politician he was peddling vain promises just as the *venditores fumi* were later selling imaginary favors.[6])

The scholiast ascribes this passage to Eupolis, and we should not doubt that Eupolis indeed described Theogenes as "*καπνός*", but the concluding sentence ὅτι πολλὰ ὑπισχνούμενος οὐδὲν ἐτέλει reads like a scholiast's comment[7]) rather than as a verse (however distorted) from the *Demoi*.[8]) If this sentence belongs to a scholiast we have to inquire about his age. The early Byzantine compiler of the scholia on the *Aves* notes in his subscription παραγέγραπται ἐκ τῶν Συμμάχου καὶ ἄλλων σχολίων.[9]) There are in the Scholia thirteen references to Eupolis;[10]) now Symmachos used extensively the commentary of Didymos, and Didymos, among his many other works, seems to have also compiled a commentary on Eupolis, and in any case will have used Eupolis extensively in his book on the comic diction.[11]) Thus, *prima facie,* there are compelling reasons for attributing the explication of καπνός to Didymos. In the scholion to line 1294 it is Didymos who mentions Eupolis, whereas to Symmachos are ascribed quotes from Pherekrates and Kratinos. In the scholion

------

⁶) The first scholar to call attention to the notice in the scholia in connection with the expression *fumum vendere* seems to have been Casaubonus in his note on *Ant. Pius* 11.1 (above, n. 1) and esp. in his *Animadversiones ad Athenaeum* VI 9 = 6.238 c (= Aristophon, Kock 2.277): see *Athenaei Deipnosophistarum libri quindecim,* editio iuxta Isaaci Casauboni recensionem (Lugduni 1657) 421, lines 9 ff. I owe this reference to Isaac Telting, *Disputatio de crimine ambitus et de sodaliciis apud Romanos* (Groningae 1854) 281 n. 2, and Telting owed it in turn to L. G. A. Pernice, "De fumi venditoribus observationes" in his *Dissertatio de furum genere* (Göttingen 1821) 48 n. 6 (not available to me). Casaubonus also remarks on *kapnoi = dosontes et pollicitatores magni,* an explanation for which he gives credit to Petrus Victorius.

⁷) Cf. Suid. (ed. Adler) 2.213, E 361, where we read of Theogenes: ὃς Καπνὸς ἐκαλεῖτο.

⁸) White, (above, n. 3) 154 in app., interprets this line as belonging to Eupolis, but Th. Kock, *Comicorum Atticorum Fragmenta* I (Lipsiae 1880) 290–291, fr. 122, rightly (cf. below, n. 13) leaves it out as a scholion. He prints the nickname *Kapnos* as part of the fragment, but observes that it "etiam ex alia parte fabulae potest excerptum esse". A. Meineke, *Fragmenta Comicorum Graecorum* II 2 (Berolini 1839) 474–5, fr. 35 and J. M. Edmonds, *The Fragments of Attic Comedy* I (Leiden 1957) 338–339, fr. 94, are non-committal.

⁹) White (above, n. 3) 302; cf. pp. LXIV ff. on the date of the final redactor and his sources, and pp. XXV ff. and XLIX ff. on Didymos and Symmachos.

¹⁰) See White, Index, p. 376 (there are two references to Eupolis in commentary to line 1556).

¹¹) M. Schmidt, *Didymi Chalcenteri grammatici Alexandrini fragmenta* (Lipsiae 1854) 308–309; L. Cohn, "Didymos 8", *RE* 5 (1905) 455, 458, cf. 461–462.

to line 876 we have first the comment of Symmachos opening with
the verb προείρηκεν which immediately reminds us of προείρηται at
the head of the first explication to line 822. Then follows the comment of Didymos who refers to the *Demoi* and the *Kolaks* of Eupolis. But caution is in order: in the scholion to line 1379 the quotation
of Eupolis stands unattributed to any scholar; a further explanation
is introduced by ἄλλως (as at 822), and the compiler presents in turn
the opinions of Didymos and Symmachos. Thus we can be reasonably certain that on that occasion neither Didymos nor Symmachos
quoted Eupolis, and that the redactor owes his reference to some
other authority.[12]) Still Didymos (ca. 80–10 B.C.) remains the most
likely source both for the quotation of Eupolis at 822 and the explication of the nickname Kapnos.[13])

The scholiasts describe Theogenes as ψευδόπλουτος, and stress his
poverty; through his impostures, unlike many Roman "sellers of
smoke", he did not gain any wealth. Nevertheless the passage from
the Scholia is the closest Greek parallel we have to Latin *fumum vendere.*

We should not wonder at the absence of the "selling of smoke" in
Plautus or Cicero; the phrase, and the practice it describes, reflects
the imperial dispensation and corruption.[14]) In fact it is not at all
unlikely that Martial picked it up from the popular idiom, and did
not himself coin it. Here the testimony of Apuleius is especially precious. In the speech he delivered in his defense before a proconsul of
Africa[15]) the phrase *fumum vendere* carries a double pun, which sug-

---

[12]) For the names of scholars to whom notes are ascribed in the scholia to
Aves, see White LXVI ff.

[13]) Schmidt (above, n. 11) does not list this passage among the fragments of
Didymos. But that the incriminated passage is prose and not poetry, and that it
belongs to a scholion, is made all but certain by Thuk. 2.95: Περδίκκας αὐτῷ
ὑποσχόμενος ..., ἃ ὑπεδέξατο οὐκ ἐπετέλει. The similarity of the phrasing will be
the more striking if we consider that Didymos was very well acquainted with
Thukydidean diction and may well have been influenced by it (although it is
unlikely that he composed a biography of Thukydides or a commentary on the
History, cf. Cohn [above, n. 11] 460–61).

[14]) For the selling of imperial favors, cf. Tac. *Ann.* 14.50; Cass. Dio (Xiphil.)
69.7.4; W. Eck, "Einfluß korrupter Praktiken auf das senatorisch-ritterliche
Beförderungswesen in der Hohen Kaiserzeit", in *Korruption im Altertum,* ed. W.
Schuller (München 1982) 135–151. See also below, n. 17.

[15]) Claudius Maximus. His tenure as governor of Africa is dated to 157/158
or 160/161 or (most likely) 158/159; cf. B. E. Thomasson, *Die Statthalter der
römischen Provinzen Nordafrikas von Augustus bis Diokletianus* 2 (Lund 1960)
74–75; Idem, *Laterculi praesidum* 1 (Göteborg 1984) 382.

gests that at least by the middle of the second century it attained the status of a colloquial expression (*Apol.* 57–60). Iunius Crassus stated in his deposition that during his absence Apuleius used his house for nocturnal and hence magical sacrifices, and that these offerings produced *fumi tantam uim ... ut parietes atros redderet* (58, p. 66. 16–17 Helm). Apuleius perorates that Crassus is a *lurco* and *helluo* who squandered all his patrimony and sold his *testimonium* to Apuleius' accuser, (Sicinius) Aemilianus: "temulentum istud mendacium tribus milibus nummis Aemiliano huic uendidit, idque Oeae nemini ignoratur" (59, p. 68. 7–8). Apuleius concludes that he discussed the testimony of Crassus "non quod ... fuliginis maculam te praesertim iudice timerem, sed ut ne impunitum ⟨Crasso⟩ foret, crassum quod Aemiliano, homini rustico, fumum uendidit" (60, p. 69.2.5). Thus Apuleius presents Crassus' deposition as worthless smoke sold for good money, and this leads us directly to the selling of non-existent favors in the *Historia Augusta*.

In that work the phrase *fumum* (or *fumos*) *vendere* occurs six times (*Ant. Pius* 11.1; *Elag.* 10.3; 15.1; *Alex. Sev.* 23.8; 36.2; 67.2). It has been suggested that the author of the *HA* "lifted the phrase from Martial and wilfully extended its meaning".[16] He may indeed have lifted it from Martial or Apuleius, but in view of its usage in Apuleius and Vespa he hardly extended its meaning; in fact nothing precludes the possibility that *fumum vendere* was a living idiom in the fourth century as it was in the second. But there is more to be said. The fraudulent selling of imperial favors seems to have been most prevalent in the fourth century; this would account for the frequent appearance of *fumum vendere* in the *Historia Augusta*. Writing of Elagabalus and Alexander Severus the author was hinting at contemporary practices.[17]

---

[16] R. Syme, "The Composition of the Historia Augusta: Recent Theories", *JRS* 62 (1972) 129 = *Historia Augusta Papers* (Oxford 1983) 22. Syme quotes (not altogether accurately, cf. Baldwin 107) the article by W. Goffart, "Did Julian combat venal *suffragium*? A Note on *CTh* 2.29.1", *CP* 65 (1970) 149–150. Goffart leans toward regarding the expression *fumum vendere* in the *HA* as a piece of antiquarianism (he points out that at *Alex. Sev.* 38.2 we have a direct quotation from Martial), but at the same time admits the possibility that the locution may have been in current use in the fourth century.

[17] Cf. C. Collot, "La pratique et l'institution du *suffragium* au Bas-Empire", *RHD* 43 (1965) 185–221, esp. 189–190, 205; D. Liebs, "Ämterkauf und Ämterpatronage in der Spätantike", *ZSS* 95 (1978) 158–186; Idem, "Alexander Severus und das Strafrecht", *Bonner Historia-Augusta-Colloquium 1977/1978* (Antiquitas

In particular the practices castigated by Libanius in his oration *Adversus assidentes magistratibus* (51.7 Foerster)[18] mirror the method employed by "Verconius Turinus" (*Alex. Sev.* 35–36). This character, true to his name, *fumis venditis ingentia praemia percepisset*: he would promise his *suffragium*, would say nothing to the emperor, and would pocket his reward if *impetratum ... esset quod petebatur.* His corruption uncovered, the emperor condemned him to die, quite appropriately, by inhaling smoke, the herald proclaiming: "fumo punitur, qui vendidit fumum". Turinus is a fiction,[19] but the mode of his execution the learned and jocular author of the *Historia Augusta* owes to Cicero. Read the description of "Turinus'" punishment: "in foro Transitorio ad stipitem ill⟨um⟩ adligari praecepit (sc. Alexander Severus), et *fumo adposito,* quem ex stipulis atque *umidis lignis fieri iusserat, necavit".*[20] Now compare Cic. *Verr.* 2.1.45, where the orator expatiates on the inhuman *genus animadversionis* employed by Verres: "ignem ex *lignis viridibus*[21] atque *humidis* in

---

4,14, Bonn 1980) 115–147, esp. 143–145, 147; W. Schuller, "Ämterkauf im römischen Reich", *Der Staat* 19 (1980) 57–71; K. L. Noethlichs, *Beamtentum und Dienstvergehen* (Wiesbaden 1981) passim.

[18] The text of Libanius reads as follows: λέγουσι μέν τινες οὐδὲν τοιοῦτον πρὸς τὸν δικαστήν, φασὶ δὲ εἰρηκέναι (cf. the wording of *HA Alex. Sev.* 36: Turinus ... dixissetque se quaedam imperatori dixisse, cum nihil dixisset), καὶ ὁ μισθὸς ὡμολόγηται. εἶτ' ἐλθὼν φήσας εἰρηκέναι τι παρακάθηται τῷ δικαστῇ τὴν ψῆφον ἀναμένων, κατὰ δὲ τὸ δίκαιον ἐκείνης ἐνεχθείσης μισθὸν ἀπαιτεῖ ψήφου δικαίας πεπονηκὼς οὐδὲν οὐδέ γε φθεγξάμενος. The speech was delivered shortly after 388, cf. Foerster IV p. 3.

[19] R. Syme, "Missing Persons", *Historia* 5 (1956) 211 = *Roman Papers* 1 (Oxford 1979) 323.

[20] On the semantic development of *neco,* see J. N. Adams, "Two Latin Words for 'Kill'", *Glotta* 51 (1973) 280–290. He points out that "*neco* was a generic term for execution, whatever its method of infliction" (p. 284), but that "the word was becoming disproportionally common by the end of the Republic in application to murder without the use of weapon" (p. 284). Adams does not discover in *neco* any particular sense of 'suffocating', 'smothering', as postulated by W. Schulze (*Kleine Schriften* [Göttingen 1933, ²1966] 148–160, esp. 154–159 [originally published in *Sb* Berlin 1918, 320–332]) and E. Löfstedt (*Syntactica* II [Lund 1956] 380–381; *Late Latin* [Oslo 1959] 191–194), but still it is interesting that *fumus* seems to have attracted solely *neco* and not *occido* or *interficio*. Perhaps the connection is that of a particularly cruel death; I. Opelt, "'Töten' und 'Sterben' in Caesars Sprache", *Glotta* 58 (1980) 111, observes that in Caesar *neco* denotes "die grausame Tötung ohne Gegenwehr", e. g. *igni* or *cruciatu necare*. The locution *fumo necare* was also used for the killing of insects and animals (Adams 285–286), see Plin. *NH* 22.157: "fumus crematorum culices necat"; 24.116: "taxi arboris fumus necat mures".

[21] Cf. Lukian, *De morte Peregr.* 24 (below in the text).

loco angusto *fieri iussit*; ibi hominem ingenuum, domi nobilem ...
fumo excruciatum semivivum reliquit".

But Alexander Severus was not the first to employ this method of
execution. This honor goes in the *HA* to Avidius Cassius, who "primus id supplicii genus invenit, ut stipitem grandem poneret pedum
octoginta et centum et a summo usque ad imum damnatos ligaret et
ab imo focum adponeret incensisque aliis alios *fumo,* cruciatu,
timore etiam *necaret*" (*Avid. Cass.* 4.3). Here the author of the *HA* is
at the best of his worst, but his juxtaposition of burning the condemned alive and smoking them to death reminds one of the cruel
practices of the Thracians[22]) and, above all, the peevish words of
Quintus Cicero which so angered Marcus: "illum (sc. Catienum) cru-
cem sibi ipsum constituere, ex qua tu eum detraxisses; te curaturum
fumo ut combureretur plaudente tota provincia".[23])

The author of the *HA* knew his Cicero;[24]) still in Cicero the victim of Verres was left *semivivus,* whereas "Turinus" was *necatus,* as

---

[22]) Flor. 3.4.2 (= 1.39.2): "cuiusque modi ludibriis foedare mortem tam *igni*
quam *fumo*". Cf. *Vulg. Iud.* 9.49: "atque ita factum est ut *fumo* et *igne* mille
homines *necarentur*", and see below, n. 27.

[23]) Cic. *Q.fr.* 1.2.6, but cf. Plaut. *Curc.* 54: "fumo comburi nil potest, flamma
potest". In view of the Plautine dictum various emendations have been proposed
to replace *fumo* in the text of Cicero, most notably *furno* or *in furno*; this has a
nice touch of Phalaris, but does not make sense in the context, for Catienus
could not at the same time be bound to the cross and burned in the oven. D. R.
Shackleton Bailey, *Cicero. Epistulae ad Quintum Fratrem et ad Brutum* (Cambridge 1980) ad loc., p. 161, rightly defends *fumo* pointing to the passages from
the Verrines and the life of Alexander Severus; the passage from the life of Avidius Cassius offers additional support. In a recent note in *AJP* 106 (1985) 114
Shackleton Bailey produced another arresting illustration, a passage from
Lukian's *Vera historia* 2.31, where Kynyras is depicted as καπνῷ ὑποτυφόμενον
ἐκ τῶν αἰδοίων ἀπηρτημένον; καπνῷ ὑποτυφόμενον, "burnt with a smouldering
fire", corresponds very well indeed to *fumo ut combureretur*.

[24]) Cf. E. Klebs, *RhM* 47 (1892) 34 ff.; R. Syme, *Emperors and Biography*
(Oxford 1971) esp. 256–257, 274. For the passages in the *Vita Avidii* and the
Vita Alexandri Severi, see above all A. Chastagnol, "Le supplice inventé par Avidius Cassius: remarques sur l'Histoire Auguste et la lettre 1 de Saint Jérôme",
Bonner Historia-Augusta-Colloquium 1970 (Antiquitas 4, 10, Bonn 1972) 95–107,
who collected a great number of further parallels from the Verrines and especially from Jerome, *Ep.* 1, but did not discuss in detail the expression *fumo
necare*. For the mode of execution an especially good parallel is Euseb. *Hist. eccl.*
8.12.1: καὶ ποτὲ μὲν κατὰ κεφαλῆς ἐκ τοῖν ποδοῖν εἰς ὕψος ἀναρτωμένων καὶ μαλ-
θακοῦ πυρὸς (on this expression, see F. J. Dölger, *Antike und Christentum* 1
[1929] 244) ὑποκαιομένου τῷ παραπεμπομένῳ καπνῷ τῆς φλεγομένης ὕλης ἀπο-
πνιγομένων (cf. Lukian, *De morte Peregr.* 24, below in the text).

were also the unfortunates who fell into the hands of Avidius Cassius. The passage of Cicero made an impression on two other late literati: a scholiast profusely commented on it as an example of τὸ αὐξητικὸν (*Schol. Gron.* A, 344 Stangl), and Macrobius (*Sat.* 4.4.17) adduced it to show that "et materia apud rhetoras pathos movet, ut dum quaeritur Cicero flammam ex lignis viridibus factam atque ibi inclusum *fumo necatum*". The expression *fumo necatum* (quite incorrect as a summary of Cicero) parallels *fumo necavit* of the *HA*; this may perhaps point to a connection between the two writers.[25]) But the author of the *HA* was also a connoisseur of Apuleius,[26]) and indeed the locution *fumo necare* recurs in Apul. *Met.* 9.27 (a *pistor* addressing the lover of his wife): "non sum barbarus ... nec ad exemplum naccinae truculentiae (i.e. *ad exemplum fullonis*) sulpuris te letali *fumo necabo*".[27]) In fact the lover of *fullo's* wife was not really *necatus*: like the victim of Verres he escaped *semivivus* (*Met.* 9.25). A contemporary parallel is at hand, although the context is different. Ammianus Marcellinus, "a source and inspiration of the *HA*",[28]) so describes the dislodging of a Persian force from the caves in the town of Maiozamalcha (24.4.30): the Roman soldiers assembled straw and faggots at the entrance to the caves (*stipulam et sarmenta specuum faucibus aggesserunt*) and ignited them, and then "*fumus* angustius penetrans ... quosdam vitalibus obstructis *necavit*, alios ignium adflatu semustos[29]) prodire in perniciem cogit abruptam".[30])

---

[25]) The most probable date for the *HA* is the last quinquennium of the fourth century (R. Syme, *Ammianus and the Historia Augusta* [Oxford 1968] 72 ff, esp 75) although, as Syme cautiously notes, "nobody can disprove a later date". E. Birley, "Fresh Thoughts on the Dating of the Historia Augusta", *Bonner Historia-Augusta-Colloquium 1975/1976* (Antiquitas 4,13, Bonn 1978) 99–105, favors a date in the first half of the fifth century. The last decennium of the fourth century was traditionally accepted as the date of the *Saturnalia*, but Alan Cameron, "The Date and Identity of Macrobius", *JRS* 56 (1966) 25–38, would place, on good grounds, the composition of Macrobius' work in the 430's; Syme, op. cit. 146, opts for a time "about 404".

[26]) Cf. R. Syme, *Ammianus* 199–200.

[27]) For the phrase, cf. *Vulg. Apoc.* 9.18: "occisa est tertia pars hominum de igne et de *fumo* et *sulphure*"; Cf. also Val. Max. 9.6. ext. 2: "Hannibal ... Nucerinos ... *fumo* et *vapore* balnearum *strangulando*"; Tac. *Ann.* 14.64.2: "(Octavia) praefervidi balnei *vapore enecatur*".

[28]) Syme, *Ammianus* 72. But T. Barnes, *The Sources of the Historia Augusta* (Collection Latomus 155, Bruxelles 1968) 108, 125, would severely restrict the influence of Ammianus Marcellinus on the *HA*.

[29]) A very appealing conjecture by Günther (cf. the editions of Rolfe, Seyfarth or Fontaine in app.) recalling *semivivus* of Cicero and Apuleius. Cf. also Chastagnol (above, n. 24) 106 n. 20.

Yet the most vivid illustration to "fumo punitur, qui vendidit fumum" we find in Lukian, *De morte Peregrini,* duly observed by Salmasius in his commentary to *Historia Augusta (Avid. Cass.* 4.3), and duly forgotten.

The cynic philosopher Peregrinus resolved to burn himself alive in front of the crowd gathered for the Olympic games. But this will show no real fortitude, says Lukian, for it is a quick death. To pay a fitting penalty for his misdeeds Peregrinus ought to have been thrown long ago into the bull of Phalaris "instead of opening his mouth to the flames only once and expiring in an instant" (*ἀλλὰ μὴ ἅπαξ χανόντα πρὸς τὴν φλόγα ἐν ἀκαρεῖ τεθνάναι*). Lukian explains: "many people tell me that no other form of death is swifter than that by fire; you have only to open your mouth, and die at once" (*οἱ πολλοί μοι λέγουσιν, ὡς οὐδεὶς ὀξύτερος ἄλλος θανάτου τρόπος τοῦ διὰ πυρός· ἀνοῖξαι γὰρ δεῖν μόνον τὸ στόμα καὶ αὐτίκα τεθνάναι* [*De morte Peregr.* 21]). Lukian continues ironically (ibid. 24): "One should strive after the ultimate consummation and culmination and build a pyre of logs, as green as possible, of fig-wood, and be suffocated by the smoke" (*τὸ τέλος δὲ καὶ τὸ κεφάλαιον χρὴ ζηλοῦν καὶ πυρὰν συνθέντα κορμῶν συκίνων ὡς ἔνι μάλιστα χλωρῶν[31]) ἐναποπνιγῆναι[32]) τῷ καπνῷ*). This would produce slow fire and slow death, and would allow one to demonstrate his courage.[33]) Furthermore "fire itself belongs not only to Herakles and Asklepios [whom Peregrinus strove to imitate in the mode of his death] but also to perpetrators of sacrilege and to murderers, who can be seen suffering it by judicial verdict".[34])

---

[30]) There is in Ammianus an echo of Livy, cf. Liv. 10.1.6: "altero *specus* eius ore ... invento utraeque *fauces* congestis lignis accensae. Ita intus *fumo ac vapore* ad duo milia armatorum, ruentia novissime in ipsas flammas, dum evadere tendunt, absumpta".

[31]) Cf. Cic. *Verr.* 2.1.45: *ignis ex lignis viridibus* (above in the text).

[32]) Cf. Euseb. *Hist. eccl.* 8.12.1 (above, n. 24).

[33]) Cf. *De morte Peregr.* 25 where Lukian expatiates on the fortitude of the Brahmans who endure the slow death by burning without even the slightest motion.

[34]) For the execution by burning, see T. Mommsen, *Römisches Strafrecht* (Leipzig 1899) 923, but above all one has to consult that mine of abstruse information, F. J. Dölger's *Antike und Christentum* (1 [1929] 243–253) where he collected a great number of examples for "Die Verkürzung der Qualen durch Einatmung des Rauches". In fact the sources he quotes do not speak of inhaling smoke, but rather of inhaling flames; see esp. Euseb. *De mart. Palaest.* 11.19: *κἀκεῖθεν ἀφαρπάζοντα τῷ στόματι τὴν φλόγα*; Seneca in Lact. *Div. inst.* 6.17.28: "flamma ore

"Therefore more appropriate is the consummation by the smoke, which would be peculiar and belong only to you [i.e. the Cynics]" (ὥστε ἄμεινον τὸ διὰ τοῦ καπνοῦ· ἴδιον[35]) γὰρ καὶ ὑμῶν ἂν μόνων γένοιτο). Or as Salmasius put it elegantly: "ut fumo scilicet perirent, qui fumum per totam vitam venditarent".

Cicero with a touch of Macrobius, Ammianus Marcellinus and Apuleius, of Lukian and the *acta martyrum,* this is the literary ambience of *fumo necare* in the *Historia Augusta.*

---

rapienda"; Prudent. *Peristephanon* 1.50: "ore flammam sorbuit"; 3.159–160: "virgo citum cupiens obitum / adpetit et bibit ore rogum". Here also belongs the text of Lukian; Dölger quotes (incompletely) the passage from *De morte Peregr.* 21, but he has missed the crucial argument at 24. We have to distinguish between the slow and excruciating death by asphyxiation, and the painful but quick death by voluntarily inhaling fire.

[35]) For the Cynics this would be ἴδιος θάνατος (for the locution, see LSJ s.v., p. 818, 6b; Schulze, *Kleine Schriften* [above, n. 20] 159–160), their own kind of natural death.

45b

Fumo necare: an Addendum

All the examples for death by inhaling smoke and for the locution
fumo necare listed in my article in Glotta 65 (1987) referred to execution and murder. To these examples we have to add the bizarre
death of Q. Lutatius Catulus (cos. 102) who in 87 under the reign of
terror of Cinna and Marius committed suicide,[1]) as Diodoros 38.4.2
says, ἰδίῳ τινὶ καὶ παρηλλαγμένῳ τρόπῳ, "in a singular and extraordinary manner," namely "locking himself in a freshly plastered room,
he intensified the fumes from the lime with fire and smoke:[2]) his
breathing impaired, he ended his life by suffocating himself" (συγ-
κλείσας ἑαυτὸν εἰς οἶκον νεόχριστον καὶ τὴν ἐκ τῆς κονίας ἀνα-
φορὰν πυρὶ καὶ καπνῷ συναυξήσας τῇ τῆς ἀναπνοῆς φθορᾷ περι-

---

[1]) On the political circumstances of Catulus' death, see F. Münzer, "Lutatius
7," RE 13 (1927) 2079. I should like to thank my friend and former student Prof.
Christoph Konrad for calling my attention to the case of Catulus.
[2]) On lime and its use, see H. Blümner, *Technologie und Terminologie der
Gewerbe und Künste bei Griechen und Römern* 3 (Leipzig 1884), 99–110.

πνιγὴς γενόμενος μετήλλαξεν). A number of other authors tell a similar story,[3]) but linguistically the most interesting are two late sources, the *Adnotationes super Lucanum* 2.174 (p. 51 Endt) where we read that Catulus "fumo se calcis occidit" and especially the *Commenta Bernensia* to Lucan 2.173 (pp. 61–2 Usener): "Catulus ... fumo se necauit."

---

[3]) The fumes of fresh plaster intensified by fire are mentioned by Velleius 2.22.4 (Catulus "conclusit se loco nuper calce harenaque perpolito inlatoque igni, qui vim odoris excitaret ... exitiali hausto spiritu [cf. Flor. 2.9.15 *ignis haustu*; in Aug. *Civ. Dei* 3.27 we have rather trite *hausto veneno*] ... mortem ... obiit") and Val. Max. 9.12.4 ("recenti calce inlito multoque igni percalefacto cubiculo se inclusum peremit"). So also Appian *BC* 1.74.342 (ἐν οἰκήματι νεοχρίστῳ τε καὶ ἔτι ὑγρῷ καίων ἄνθρακας ἑκὼν ἀπεπνίγη); on the other hand Plutarch *Mar.* 44.5 intimates only the fumes of charcoal (κατακλεισάμενος εἰς οἴκημα καὶ πολλοὺς ἄνθρακας ἐκζωπυρήσας ἀπεπνίγη). All these accounts clearly flow from a common source, most probably Livy or the *Histories* of Sallust (Cicero frequently mentions the suicide of Catulus, but does not indicate its exact manner). Cf. E. Rawson, "Sallust on the Eighties?", *CQ* 37 (1987) 163–180, an excellent study of the Sallustian material in the Scholia to Lucan (pp. 174–177, the death of Catulus).

46

THE SURNAME OF M. ANTONIUS CRETICUS
AND THE COGNOMINA *EX VICTIS GENTIBUS*

M. Antonius Creticus, the son of a famous father and the father of a famous son,[1] had a bad press in antiquity — and still worse in modern times. In 74 as praetor he was appointed by the senate to an extraordinary command to combat the pirates in the whole of the Mediterranean; initially he operated in the West, but in 72 he invaded Crete, suffered a defeat, and died shortly afterwards.[2]

In 'Der Kleine Pauly' H.G. Gundel introduces him as "M. Antonius mit dem Spottnamen Creticus",[3] and in this he follows a long and persistent tradition of abuse. For so Antonius also appears in Klebs' article in the RE: "mit dem Spottnamen Creticus", and further: "Wegen seiner Misserfolge wurde er zum Spott Creticus genannt".[4] The same wording reappears in an article by A. Wilhelm: Antonius gained "den Spottnamen Creticus" through his "schimpfliche Misserfolge".[5] H.A. Ormerod concurs: "His principal achievement ... was the invasion of Crete in the year 72 for which in mockery he was given the title of *Creticus* ".[6] So also Maurenbrecher: "Ludibrii causa antea (i.e. before his death) Cretici cognomen acceperat".[7] P. Foucart speaks of "le surnom derisoire de Creticus",[8] and E. Courtney of the "ironical conferment" of the name Creticus on Antonius.[9] The phraseology goes back to

---

[1] His son was the Triumvir, and his father M. Antonius, the orator.

[2] For sources, see T.R.S. Broughton, The Magistrates of the Roman Republic 2, New York 1952, 101-102, 108, n.2, 111, 117, 123 (add Flor. 1.42). Cf. also below, n. 38. F.T. Hinrichs, Hermes 98, 1970, 501, argued (on the basis of the inscription from Epidauros, IG IV 2.1.66, line 25 [cf. SEG 11.397]: Μάρκου Ἀντωνίου τοῦ ἐπὶ Κρητῶν στραταγοῦ that the command of Antonius was limited solely to Crete. This flies in the face of all other evidence, cf. E. Maroti, "On the Problem of M. Antonius Creticus' Imperium Infinitum", Acta Antiqua Acad. Scient. Hungaricae 19, 1971, 259-71. The title given to Antonius in the Epidauros inscription is perplexing, but we have to remember that this is a local honorific inscription and not a translation of a Roman document; the text is replete with errors and in many places barely legible, cf. W. Peek, Inschriften aus dem Asklepieion von Epidauros, Abhandl. d. Sächs. Akad. d. Wiss., Phil.-hist. Kl. 60,2 Leipzig 1969, 16-17, nr. 21. On the photograph reproduced by Peek the reading ἐπὶ παντῶν accepted by earlier scholars, seems indeed to be excluded; ἐπὶ Κρητῶν, printed confidently by Peek, is likely but by no means definitely assured.

[3] H.G. Gundel, KP 1, 1970, 410 s.v. "Antonius 8".

[4] E. Klebs, RE 1, 1894, 2594 s.v. "Antonius 29". In fact Gundel's phrase is taken verbatim from the opening statement of Klebs.

[5] A. Wilhelm, "Zu einer Inschrift aus Epidaurus", MDAI Ath. Abt. 26, 1901, 419.

[6] H.A. Ormerod, Piracy in the Ancient World, Liverpool 1924, 225.

[7] B. Maurenbrecher, C. Sallustii Historiarum Reliquiae 1, Prolegomena, Lipsiae 1891, 72.

[8] P. Foucart, "Les campagnes de M. Antonius Creticus contre les pirates en 74-71", Journal des Savants N.S. 4, 1906, 569-581 at 581. As his source Foucart quotes Livy, Per. 97, who, however, does not mention the cognomen of Antonius at all ("M. Antonius praetor bellum adversus Cretenses parum prospere susceptum morte sua finivit").

[9] E. Courtney, A Commentary on the Satires of Juvenal, London 1980, 391.

the old Drumann:" Man nannte ihn aus Spott Creticus",[10] and beyond him to the antiquarian tradition summarized in the Onomasticon of Orelli and Baiter: "Propter ignominiosam in Cretam expeditionem per irrisionem nominatus est Creticus".[11]

As their source Orelli-Baiter, Drumann, Klebs and Courtney cite Plutarch, Ant. 1, a surprising witness for Plutarch writes: "his father (i.e. of the Triumvir) was Antonius surnamed Creticus (ὁ Κρητικὸς ἐπικληθεὶς 'Αντώνιος), a man of no great renown in public life nor illustrious (οὐχ οὕτω μὲν εὐδόκιμος ἐν τοῖς πολιτικοῖς ἀνὴρ οὐδὲ λαμπρός), but kindly and honest". No *Spott* here. Appian (Sic. 6.1-2) reports that Antonius καὶ οὐ πρᾶξαι καλῶς, χρηματίσαι δ' ὅμως διὰ τὴν πρᾶξιν Κρητικός —" although he did not perform well, he gained the name of Creticus for his work", and further: Metellus "was called Creticus with more justice than Antonius, for he actually subjugated the island". Antonius' honorific surname was unmerited, but Appian does not intimate in any way that it was given to him in mockery. Other sources do not mention the surname at all.[12]

Yet although there is no evidence for mockery there is ample room for doubt. For how could a man who had achieved nothing be given an honorific agnomen *ex virtute* ? Accordingly E. Badian prints his surname in quotation marks.[13]

Now a classic statement on the origin of the honorific cognomina we owe to Livy. On the cognomen Africanus of the elder Scipio he has this to say (30.45.7): "Africani cognomen militaris prius favor an popularis aura celebraverit an, sicuti Felicis Sullae Magnique Pompei patrum memoria, coeptum ab adsentatione familiari sit, parum compertum habeo; primus certe hic imperator nomine victae ab se gentis est nobilitatus".[14] This is normally interpreted to mean that the cognomen of Africanus was not bestowed on Scipio by an official act, a decree of the senate or the vote of the people. This would indeed be a welcome piece of information for the notice in the Fasti Consulares Capitolini is ambiguous. Under the year 205 we read "cos. P. Cornelius P.f. P.n. Scipio qui postea African(us) appell(atus) est." By whom we are not told. Similar notices we find under the years 190 (referring to L. Cornelius Scipio, "qui postea Asiaticus appellatus est"), 138 (D. Iunius Brutus, "[qui postea] Cal[l]aicus appel[latus est]"), and 79 (P. Servilius Vatia, "qui postea Isauricus appellatus est").

---

[10] W. Drumann, Geschichte Roms 1, (second edition by P. Groebe), Leipzig 1899, 46.

[11] I.C. Orellius et I.G. Baiterus, Onomasticon Tullianum, pars 2, Turici 1838, 47-48.

[12] Cic. 2 Verr. 2.8; 3.212-18; Sch. Bob. 96 St.; Ps.-Asc. 202, 259 St.; Flor. 1.42.7; Liv. per. 97; Diod. 40.1; Vell. 2.31.3-4; Lact. Inst. Div. 1.11.32.

[13] E. Badian, OCD[2], 1970, 76 s.v. "Antonius 'Creticus' ". D.R. Shackleton Bailey, Onomasticon to Cicero's Speeches, Norman 1988, 16, also has "Creticus", but he prints Creticus in his Cicero, Philippics, Chapel Hill 1986, 117, n.13.

[14] The last statement is not correct: in the Fasti as the first commander so nobilitated appears M. Valerius Maximus, cos. 263, see below in the text and nn. 19 and 20.

Under 88 we have a notice concerning L. Cornelius Sulla, "qui postea [Felix appellatus est]".[15] Since this cognomen was closely connected with the idea of the *felicitas imperatoria* , it expressed (only in a more generalized and more potent form) the same concept as the cognomina acquired *ex victis gentibus*. According to Velleius (2.27.2) and the Auctor de vir. ill. (75.9) Sulla assumed his honorific surname (immediately) after the fall of Praeneste and the death of the younger Marius in 82. And in Appian (BC 1.97.451) we read that in order to honor Sulla the senate voted (in 82) to erect a gilded equestrian statue with the inscription Κορνηλίου Σύλλα ἡγεμόνος Εὐτυχοῦς = *Cornelio Sullae Imperatori* (or *Dictatori*) *Felici* .[16] In this way, Appian comments, the epithet which the flatterers had given to Sulla on account of the unbroken chain of his victories now became permanent and official.

On this basis Doer argues that after Sulla all honorific epithets were formally given by the senate,[17] whereas Fetzer and Kneissl believe that Sulla's case was an exception and that in republican times the senate never formally bestowed the *cognomina ex virtute*. Kneissl writes: "Jene Beinamen wurden den militärischen Führern vielmehr durch private Initiative zuteil, allerdings scheint der Triumph die Voraussetzung für die Verleihung eines Siegerbeinamens gewesen zu sein. Es begegnet kein Träger eines Siegernamens, dem nicht auch ein Triumph zugestanden worden wäre".[18]

The formulation of Kneissl contains some truth, but misses the point. The Fasti Consulares assiduously distinguish between the men who acquired an honorific cognomen during their tenure of an office or subsequently (*postea*). Under 263 we read: "M.' Valerius M.f. M.n. Maximus qui in hoc honore Messall(a) appell(atus) e(st)".[19] Valerius gained this cognomen because of his capture of Messana (Seneca, de brev. vitae 13.6; Eutrop. 2.19). He celebrated his triumph still in the same year (263), and in the Fasti Triumphales he appears duly adorned with his new cognomen.[20] On the other hand the four men who are listed in the Fasti as having received their "victorious" cognomina subsequent to their consulship (*postea*) also celebrated their triumphs as proconsuls subsequent to their consulship: P. Cornelius Scipio (Africanus) in 201, L. Cornelius Scipio (Asiaticus) in 189, D. Iunius Brutus (Callaicus) in 136 or 135 (at the latest in 133), and P. Servilius Vatia

---

[15] For references, see A. Degrassi, Inscriptiones Italiae XIII, 1: Fasti Consulares et Triumphales, Roma 1947, 46-47, 48-49, 54-55 and (commentary) 120, 122, 129, 130.

[16] Cf. E. Gabba, Appiani Bellorum Civilium Liber Primus, Firenze 1958, 263-264 ad loc.; M. Crawford, Roman Republican Coinage, Cambridge 1974, 397 (both with further literature).

[17] B. Doer, Die römische Namengebung, Stuttgart 1937, 46-52, 68-71.

[18] P. Kneissl, Die Siegestitulatur der römischen Kaiser, Göttingen 1969, 21. He accepts the conclusions reached by K. Fetzer in his unpublished dissertation Historische Beinamen im Zeitalter der römischen Republik, Diss. Tübingen 1952.

[19] Degrassi (above, n. 15) 40-41, 115.

[20] Ibid. 74-75, 547-48.

(Isauricus) in 74.[21] The text of the Fasti Triumphales is lost for Africanus, Callaicus and Isauricus, but it is preserved for L. Scipio: he is duly styled Asiaticus.

The picture is clear. In the Fasti the phrase *postea appellatus est* attached to a cognomen *ex victoria* points to the year of the triumph, and to the decree of the senate granting this honor.

This was well perceived (though not expressly articulated) by T.R.S. Broughton. Of D. Iunius Brutus he writes (MRR 1.487): "He returned to celebrate a triumph ... over the Callaeci and Lusitani ... and assume the cognomen Callaicus". And of P. Scipio (1.321): "He took the title Africanus and celebrated his triumph". (He gives no comment on the surname of L. Scipio [1.362]). Consequently, until the year of the triumph, the honorific surnames of P. and L. Scipio, and of D. Iunius Brutus are given in parentheses — another example of the astounding *akribeia* of the MRR. Unfortunately, this principle was not carried out uniformly: Isauricus of P. Servilius loses its parenthesis already in 75 when Servilius was saluted as imperator (2.99), and not (as it should) in 74 when he celebrated his triumph (2.105). None of the sources adduced in MRR shows that Servilius was formally called Isauricus already in 74. In particular CIL I^2 741: "P. Servilius C. [f.] / Isauricus / imperator cepi[t]" argues against this assumption. This inscription, found in Rome and now lost, was engraved on the basis of one of the statues which Isauricus brought to Rome as his *praeda bellica*, and which he will have paraded in his triumphal procession. In other words, at this moment Servilius already had a decree of the senate addressing him as Isauricus.[22] Unexpected proof, clear and decisive, was furnished a few years ago by an inscription unearthed in Asia Minor:[23] it was set up by P. Servilius immediately after the capture of Isaura Vetus. He styles himself "Serveilius C.f. imperator". He is already acclaimed imperator, but does not yet carry the surname Isauricus.

Still it would be false to assume that the senate was granting the honorific cognomina on its own initiative. As a first prerequisite for a "victorious" surname we should posit not the triumph itself (as Kneissl does) but rather the *acclamatio imperatoria* or more generally, to use the words of Livy, the *militaris favor, aura popularis* or *adsentatio familiaris*. Thus the *fons et origo* of the honorific surnames was the private *appellatio* of the (victorious) general (which naturally enough may have been engineered by the general himself). But there was a sequel. A general acclaimed *imperator* by his soldiers remained the holder of this title whether or not the senate approved his request for a triumph. Similarly a general *appellatus*

---

[21] Ibid. 201: 80-81, 554; 558; 564.

[22] Cf. A. Degrassi, Inscriptiones Latinae Liberae Rei Publicae 1, Firenze 1957, 216 in his comment on this inscription (no. 371): "C. Servilius Vatia ... de Isauris a. 74, ut videtur, triumphavit et Isauricus appellatus est". So also Dessau, ILS 36.

[23] It was published by A. Hall, "New Light on the Capture of Isaura Vetus by P. Servilius Vatia", Akten des VI. Internationalen Kongresses für Griechische und Lateinische Epigraphik, München 1973, 568-71 at 570.

Creticus remained Creticus regardless of whether he received a triumph or not. But as *imperator* did not equal *triumphator*, so also the surname *ex virtute* was hollow without a triumph. It was a great honor if the senate acknowledged the honorific surname by including it in the decree granting the triumph; only then would the general appear on the official roster of the *triumphatores* in the full splendor of his name *ex victa ab se gente*.

This leads us back to M. Antonius Creticus. He was a prime example of those who in vain emulation of Scipio Africanus "nequaquam victoria pares insignes imaginum titulos claraque cognomina familiarum fecerunt" (Livy 30.45.7). His surname was hollow and fraudulent. But how did he get it? Perhaps through *adsentatio familiaris*. As Antonius died without returning to Rome one might well imagine that he was styled Creticus in a funeral *laudatio*, and that his honorific cognomen was displayed below his *imago* in the atrium of the Antonii. Yet Appian's comparison of Antonius and Metellus seems to presuppose something more solid than a fleeting *laudatio*. Maurenbrecher may have been on the right track: if indeed Antonius got his surname before his death, he was so *appellatus* by his soldiers. This in turn presupposes an achievement that could pass for victory. Such an achievement is hard to come by. In fact modern scholars are unanimous in condemnation: Antonius suffered a disastrous defeat. How disastrous ? Enough to cause his death: "bald darauf starb er von Scham und Kummer aufgerieben". So Drumann.[24] Foucart makes the fate of Antonius still worse: not only defeated but also taken prisoner by the Cretans.[25] The main source is Florus 1.42.3, but there is not the slightest intimation in Florus or in any other author that Antonius himself was captured. Still his defeat was painful enough. Antonius was so confident of victory that, as Florus writes, he "carried on board of his ships more fetteres than arms", "pluris catenas in navibus quam arma portaret". Hostile slander perhaps, but the fact remains that "plerasque naves intercepit hostis, captivaque corpora religantes velis ac funibus suspendere, ac sic velificantes triumphantium in modum Cretes portibus suis adremigaverunt" ("the enemy captured many ships, and hung the bodies of their prisoners from the sails and tackle, and sailing with such sails the Cretans, as if celebrating a triumph, rowed back to their harbors").[26] As a result, "Antonius was compelled to conclude a humiliating peace before his death".[27]

---

[24] Op. cit. (above, n. 10), 46.

[25] Op. cit. (above, n.8), 581: "Le préteur lui-même fut pris et conduit en Crète; il mourut bientôt d'après, non sans avoir signé une paix honteuse avec ses vainqueurs". So also J. Van Ooteghem, Les Caecilii Metelli de la République, Bruxelles 1967, 232.

[26] A fragment of Sallust probably (on account of *malo*) refers to this events: "In quis notissimus quisque aut malo dependens verberatur aut immutilato corpore improbe patibulo eminens affigebatur" (Hist. 3.9, with Maurenbrecher's note ad loc.). E.S. Forster's translation of Florus in Loeb Classical Library (1929): "and then spreading their sails the Cretans returned ... to their harbours" disregards the poignant force of *sic* and ignores the precise meaning of *adremigare*.

[27] Ormerod, (above, n.6), 227.

Of ancient authors only Diodoros mentions the peace, but he does not attach to it any derogatory epithet (40.1-2). He says that Antonius concluded an agreement with the Cretans (συνθέμενος πρὸς Κρῆτας εἰρήνην), and that for a while they observed the peace (μέχρι μέν τινος ταύτην ἐτήρουν).[28] This can only mean that the Cretans refrained from dealing (at least openly) with the pirates and Mithradates. In fact, the avowed reason for Antonius' invasion was the support the pirates and Mithradates were receiving from Crete: to his envoys the Cretans gave an arrogant answer, whereupon he attacked the island (App. Sic. 6.1.). As his goal was the pursuit of the pirates and not the conquest of the still independent Crete, Antonius could indeed maintain that he had achieved his objectives.

Under what circumstances was this agreement reached? Cicero (2 Verr. 3.312), writing a few years after Antonius' demise, is both critical and vague: "Antonium, cum multa contra sociorum salutem, multa contra utilitatem provinciarum et faceret et cogitaret, in mediis eius iniuriis et cupiditatibus mors oppressit". In any case no intimation here of a catastrophical military disaster.[29] Similarly the Scholiast of Bobbio (96 Stangl): "Coeperat ... M. Antonius piratas persequi, sed rebus nondum confectis morte praeventus est". So also Ps.-Asc. (259 St.): "M. Antonius ... Siciliam et provincias omnes depopulatus est et ad postremum inferens Cretensibus bellum morbo interiit". In another passage the Scholiast is firmer in condemnation but still relatively mild (202 St.): M. Antonius "indicto Cretensibus bello male re gesta ibidem periit". That Antonius died *ibidem* , in Crete,[30] is of interest and importance. As in this passage the Scholiast preserved much that derives from Sallust's Histories,[31] also the indication *ibidem* may be a genuine piece of information. If so, despite the initial naval debacle, Antonius will have ultimately effected his landing on the island.[32] But the Cretans

---

[28] A. Passerini, "La preparazione della guerra contro Creta nel 70 a.C.", Athenaeum 14, 1936, 45-53, tried to discredit the notice in Diodorus and maintainded (p.49) that "Antonio non ha concesso ai Cretesi nessun trattato". Proof? "Ciò si accorda col fatto che egli morì di malattia in Creta stessa: altrimenti si sarebbe allontanato dal teatro della sua sconfitta al più presto, specialmente essendo un uomo, come dice Sallustio [3.3 M.], *vacuus a curis nisi instantibus* ". No comment.

[29] It is certainly worth noting that of all possible abuses to be hurled at Antonius' father Cicero entertains in the Philippics only these two: still as a *praetextatus* , Antonius became bankrupt *culpa patris* (2.44); the first wife of his father was a daughter of the "traitor" Q. Numitorius of Fregellae (3.17). These examples are calculated to show that in squandering money and in matrimonial impropriety the son followed in the footsteps of his father. Again no mention of Creticus' military misfortunes, but this is hardly conclusive: at least as a general the son was very much unlike the father.

[30] Klebs, RE 1 (1894) 2594, adduces also Liv. Per. 97, but this passage contains no information as to the exact place of Antonius' death (see above, n.8). But as Professor W. Eck kindly points out to me, this interpretation may be too forced. *Ibidem* could simply mean "in den Gewässern vor Creta".

[31] On the basis of the fragment preserved nominatim by the Juvenal Scholia 8.105 (ed. Wessner), Maurenbrecher (2 [1893], p. 108, and frgs. 3.2,3) recognized in Ps.-Asc. (202 St.) the following Sallustian words and phrases or their echoes, here given in italics: "<M.> Antonius *curator* tuendae *totius orae maritimae, qua Romanum erat imperium* non solum ipse *nequam* verum etiam comitibus pessimis, rem inauditam invasit et indicto Cretensibus bello male re gesta ibidem periit".

[32] So also Maurenbrecher 2, p. 109: "Tamen Antonius ad insulam naves adpulit". Maurenbrecher refers to the campaign of Antonius in Crete also the fragments of Sallust concerning the geography and mythology

were not to be conquered: for this the forces of Antonius were quite insufficient. Both sides had good reasons for coming to terms: Antonius wished to save face and the Cretans prudently did not wish to engage in a protracted war with the Romans. Shortly afterwards Antonius died, and the Romans withdrew from the island.

Some time after the death of Antonius the Cretans sent an embassy[33] to Rome "to offer a defense against the accusations levelled against them" (Diod. 40.1) — no doubt an oblique reference to their dealings with the pirates and perhaps to the execution and torture of the Roman capitives so vividly described by Sallust and Florus. They must have argued that they had been unjustly accused and unjustly invaded by Antonius; they fought in self-defense, and exercised great restraint in their actions. In particular the envoys expected some consideration for "saving the quaestor and his soldiers" (Cass. Dio. frg. 111). Apparently a detachement of Antonius' army led by a quaestor was either captured or trapped by the Cretans. By agreeing to a treaty Antonius saved his men.

This reminds us of another, more famous defeat and of another general who received his cognomen after the place of his *clades*. A. Alföldi in his study of the cognomina has this to say: "La débâcle catastrophique de 321 av. J.-C. a valu le surnom, de *Caudinus* à un Postumius, général vaincu; un Antonius a reçu le surnom de *Creticus* pour ces manœuvres malheureuses entre 73 et 71".[34] But the story of the surname Caudinus is not that simple. The Fasti Consulares for the year 321 are lost but under 332 we read: "[cens(ores) Q. Poblilius Q.f. Q.n. Philo, Sp. Postumius - f. - n. Albinus] qui postea [C]audinus appell(atus) [est". The structure of this notice is identical to that of the notices recording the honorific cognomina. With his keen eye, Degrassi saw this well. His argument is as follows: "mirum est cognomen ex clade impositum in fastos receptum esse atque loco honoris habitum, tamquam Sp. Postumio non ignominiae causa inditum esset, sed ea magnanimitate qua patribus suasisset ut cum collega Samnitibus dederetur, ut populus religione exsolveretur". And Degrassi goes on to quote Livy 9.10.3: "Postumius in ore erat, eum laudibus ad caelum ferebant, devotioni P. Decii consulis, aliis claris facinoribus aequabant". Degrassi concludes: "Scilicet posteriores Postumii cladem a gentili suo acceptam decori vertere studebant".[35] Who can doubt that this is the right explanation? Its elegance springs to one's eyes.

---

of the island (3.10-15), but for this there is no compelling reason: why not connect them with the victorious campaign of Q. Caecilius Metellus Creticus?

[33] At the latest in 69. On this embassy, and the sources recounting it (App. Sic. 6; Diod. 40.1-3; Cass. Dio frg. 111), see A. Passerini (above, n. 28) 45-53. His analysis is often disappointing.

[34] A. Alföldi, "Les Cognomina des magistrats de la République romaine, "Mélanges offerts à André Piganiol, Paris 1966, 717.

[35] Degrassi (above, n. 15) 34-35, 107. The explanation of Degrassi was accepted by Broughton, MRR 1.152, n.1. I. Kajanto, The Latin Cognomina, Helsinki 1965, 186-87, has unfortunately disregarded Degrassi.

With the origin of the cognomen *Caudinus* thus illuminated, the surname *Creticus* of Antonius would remain the sole example of a cognomen *e clade acceptum* . The conclusion? The cognomen of Antonius was meant to be honorific — not derogatory. After all Antonius could well claim that he detached the Cretans from their previous association with the pirates and Mithradates, and that he saved his quaestor. Whether his surname was given to him by his soldiers or was propagated after his death by his *familiares* we cannot tell. One thing is, however, certain: it was an *appellatio privata*, never acknowledged by the senate.[36] Maurenbrecher is quite wrong when, forgetting what he wrote in his Prolegomena, he so opines in his commentary: "Sed Antonius turpiter cum Cretensibus foedere facto tamen postea Cretici cognomen a senatu accepit".[37] But the senate could have given this surname to Antonius only in the context of his request for a triumph; and we do not know whether he had made such a request, and indeed whether he was at all acclaimed imperator. And in any case Antonius' death made the whole question moot. Furthermore if the senate had in any way acknowledged the cognomen Creticus, it would have also had to acknowledge the arrangements Antonius made with the Cretans. It is true that the Cretan envoys almost got (through bribery) a decree proclaiming them friends and allies of Rome, yet ultimately the senate decided to assume an unforgiving posture and oredered the Cretans to deliver all their ships, send hostages, pay a large indemnity, and surrender Lasthenes and Panares, their leaders in the war against Antonius (Diod. 40.1-3; Cassius Dio frg. 111). The Cretans refused to comply. Q. Caecilius Metellus, the consul of 69, was now entrusted with the war; he brutally conquered the island, was acclaimed imperator (in 67), and after a long delay celebrated a triumph (in 62). Unlike Antonius he merited his cognomen of Creticus[38] "confecto bello ... ex virtute" (Sch. Bob. 96 St.).

---

[36] Broughton prints his surname Creticus in a parenthesis under 74 when Antonius was praetor (MRR 2.101), but without any parenthesis under 73, 72, 71 (2.111, 117, 123). But since in 73 Antonius had probably not yet invaded Crete (cf. J. Hatzfeld, Les trafiquants Italiens dans l'orient hellénique, Paris 1919, 80-82) he could not in this year have carried the surname Creticus even unofficially; and as no triumph was accorded to him, his surname ought to have been printed in parentheses also under 72 and 71.

[37] Op. cit. (above, n.7), vol. 2, 109. Cf. D. Magie, Roman Rule in Asia Minor 1, 1950, 293: "An attempt was made to gloze over his disgraceful failure by conferring on him posthumously the surname of Creticus".

[38] For sources, see Broughton, MRR 1.131, 139, 145, 154, 159, 163, 168-69, 176. The Fasti Consulares are not extant for 69, and from the Fasti Triumphales for 62 only a few letters remain. Broughton prints the surname Creticus in parentheses under 69 and 68 but without a parenthesis from 67 onwards; he dates to this year Metellus' *salutatio* as imperator (Degrassi, ILLRP 374, vol. 1, p. 217, favors 68). But in the inscriptions recording Metellus' *acclamatio imperatoria* (CIL 1².746 = ILS 867 = ILLRP 374; Inscr.Cret. 2.252, no. 14; IG 3.565) he still appears (like Servilius Isauricus before him) without his honorific cognomen. In view of the inscriptional evidence F. Münzer, "Caecilius 87", RE 3, 1899, 1211, points out that Metellus used his Siegerbeiname only after his triumph; this is also the view of Ooteghem (above, n. 25) 236, and Appian (Sic. 6.2) connects indeed the triumph and the grant of the cognomen: καὶ ἐθριάμβευσε, καὶ Κρητικὸς ἐκλήθη. But it would be more exact to say that Metellus officially received his victorious cognomen not after the triumph itself but rather after the senatorial decree granting him this honor.

47

Römischer Staat und Götterzeichen:
zum Problem der obnuntiatio*

Qui malam rem nuntiat, obnuntiat – heißt es in einem Scholion (Donat. ad Ter. Ad. 547). Im Bereiche der Staatsverfassung bedeutete die Obnuntiation die Meldung von ungünstigen Zeichen mit rechtsverbindlicher Kraft. Das Problem, das ich zur Diskussion stellen möchte, gehört somit gewiß nicht zu den wichtigsten Fragen der römischen Geschichte, es ist aber zweifellos interessant, lehrreich und sehr verwickelt.

Es war ein seltsamer und merkwürdiger Vorgang – mindestens für unser politisches Gefühl –, daß, wenn ein Magistrat eine öffentliche Handlung zu unternehmen im Begriffe war oder sie sogar schon begonnen hatte, da vor ihm plötzlich ein anderer Beamter oder ein Staatspriester, in diesem Falle ein Augur, erscheinen und erklären konnte, er habe ein von den Göttern gesandtes böses Zeichen gesehen; es durfte dann nichts unternommen, das Begonnene mußte unterlassen werden. Bestand der durch die Obnuntiation betroffene Magistrat auf seiner Amtshandlung, dann zog er nicht nur den Zorn der Götter auf sich, sondern beging auch einen sakral- und verfassungsrechtlichen Fehler, ein vitium, was unter Umständen zu dem Ergebnis führen konnte, daß der Senat auf Grund eines Gutachtens des Augurenkollegiums die auf diese Weise gegen die Auspizien durchgesetzte Handlung, sei es ein Gesetz oder eine Wahl, als nichtig erklären konnte. Somit bildete die Obnuntiation keineswegs nur eine antiquarische Kuriosität, ganz im Gegenteil: gerade im letzten Jahrhundert der Republik spielte die Meldung von ungünstigen Zeichen eine nicht geringe Rolle in den politischen Auseinandersetzungen, indem man in der Obnuntiation ein wirksames Mittel zur Verhinderung von Volksversammlungen fand. Man denke in diesem Zusammenhang vor allem an den bekannten Fall der Himmelsbeobachtungen, die im Jahre 59 CAESARs Kollege im Konsulat, M. CALPURNIUS BIBULUS, angestellt hat, um auf diese Weise der Gesetzgebung CAESARs und der caesarfreundlichen Tribunen

---

* Auf Einladung des Seminars für Klassische Philologie der Universität Düsseldorf am 6. Mai 1970 gehaltener Vortrag in geringfügig erweiterter und revidierter Fassung; der Vortrag wurde außerdem an den Universitäten Basel, Heidelberg, Mannheim und Köln gehalten.

309

ein Hindernis in den Weg zu legen, und an den sich daran anknüpfenden Streit, ob die leges Iuliae, Vatiniae und Clodiae rechtmäßig durchgeführt worden seien und ob sie infolgedessen de jure gültig waren – ein Streit, der in der modernen Forschung von neuem entbrannte. Dieses und andere, ähnliche Beispiele können die politische Bedeutung veranschaulichen, welche damals die Obnuntiation erlangt hat.

Das Obnuntiationsrecht, das im letzten Jahrhundert der Republik gegolten hat, wurde bekanntlich auf dem Wege der Volksgesetzgebung durch zwei aus etwa der Mitte des zweiten Jahrhunderts stammende Gesetze, die lex Aelia und lex Fufia, näher geregelt. Eine neue Regelung wurde auf diesem Gebiet im J. 58 durch den Volkstribun P. CLODIUS durchgeführt. Das Hauptinteresse der Forscher, die sich mit den Problemen der Obnuntiation befaßten, galt der Untersuchung und Rekonstruktion einzelner Vorschriften der lex Aelia und lex Fufia, weiter der Frage, ob durch die lex Clodia die genannten Gesetze ganz oder nur teilweise ersetzt wurden, und in diesem letzteren Falle, welche Bestimmungen abgeschafft, welche verändert wurden und welche unangetastet blieben. Man untersuchte ferner einzelne Fälle der Obnuntiationsanwendung und wollte auf diese Weise einerseits das allgemein geltende Obnuntiationsrecht rekonstruieren, andererseits Einblicke in die Geschichte der Obnuntiation als einer politischen Waffe gewinnen und nicht zuletzt eine Antwort auf die politisch wichtige Frage finden, ob die lex Aelia und lex Fufia im Dienste der konservativen, oder umgekehrt, der „popularen" Strömung durchgeführt seien. Es sind hier vor allem aus der neueren Zeit die Arbeiten von McDONALD, WEINSTOCK, L. R. TAYLOR, BLEICKEN, BALSDON, CH. MEIER, SUMNER und ASTIN zu nennen. Die genannten Forscher haben beachtenswerte Ergebnisse erzielt; wir besitzen jetzt glänzende Analysen einzelner Ereignisse und einzelner Quellen und ansprechende Rekonstruktionen des Ganzen. Stellt man aber die endgültigen Ergebnisse der bisherigen Forschung zusammen, so sieht man nicht ohne Erstaunen, daß dabei nicht *eine* lex Clodia oder Aelia und Fufia herauskam, sondern *einige* und zwar verschiedene.

Es wäre aber grundverfehlt, die Obnuntiation nur als eine politische Erscheinung oder nur als eine Art Manipulierung der Staatsreligion betrachten zu wollen. Die einzelnen Obnuntiationsvorgänge spielten sich natürlich auf der politischen Bühne ab; die obnuntiatio als eine Institution des öffentlichen Rechts beruhte aber letzten Endes auf sakralen Vorstellungen und sakralrechtlichen Verordnungen.

Im Rahmen dieses Vortrages können wir nicht alle verfassungsrechtlichen und politischen Fragen, die in den letzten Jahren so eifrig erörtert wurden, von neuem aufwerfen; außerdem wäre man auch kaum berechtigt, dies zu tun. Vielmehr soll das ganze Problem von einem anderen Gesichtspunkt aus betrachtet werden: es ist zuerst nach den religiösen und sakralrechtlichen Grundlagen der obnuntiatio zu fragen und von dieser Seite her zu versuchen, ein besseres Verständnis zu gewinnen. Damit soll aber nicht gesagt werden, daß auf diesem Wege alle bisher strittigen oder unklaren Fragen sich lösen lassen. Durch neue Fragestellungen kann manches Problem in ein neues Licht gerückt werden, vor allem aber geht es mir um den Nachweis, daß manche geläufigen Behauptungen und Vermutungen sich mit dem sakralrechtlichen Inhalt der obnuntiatio nicht vereinbaren lassen.

310

Das „ungünstige Götterzeichen" heißt auspicium malum, infaustum oder adversum. Die Obnuntiation bildet somit ein besonderes Kapitel des römischen Auspizienwesens. Die von den Auguren entwickelte Lehre von den Auspizien stellt eine ungemein komplizierte Doktrin dar, und da keine von den zahlreichen römischen Spezialschriften über das Auspizienwesen und Auguralrecht uns erhalten ist, muß das ius augurale auf Grund von zwar verhältnismäßig vielen, aber sehr verstreuten und oft untereinander widersprechenden Autorenangaben rekonstruiert werden. Es liegt also in der Natur der Sache, daß hier keine weitgehende Übereinstimmung zwischen den Gelehrten zu erwarten ist; manchmal aber fällt es schwer, sich dem Verdacht zu entziehen, daß das ius augurale nicht so hoffnungslos kompliziert und verwickelt war, wie es auf Grund mancher modernen Arbeit aussieht; gewiß aber war es auch nicht so einfach, wie es mehrere allgemeinere Darstellungen der römischen Religions- oder Verfassungsgeschichte glauben machen wollten. Daß man sich im Augurallabyrinth verhältnismäßig gut orientieren kann, ist vor allem den klassischen Arbeiten von MOMMSEN, WISSOWA und VALETON zu verdanken; in der letzten Zeit haben besonders wichtige und gedankenreiche Untersuchungen zum Thema des Auguralrechts DE FRANCISCI, CATALANO, KUNKEL und zuletzt MAGDELAIN vorgelegt.

Der Umstand, daß die Obnuntiation sowohl im Bereiche des Staats- wie des Sakralrechts lag, trägt, wiewohl in methodischer Hinsicht sehr lehrreich, erheblich zu den Schwierigkeiten der Interpretation bei, die durch den dürftigen Zustand und die oft sehr unklaren Aussagen der Quellen noch vermehrt werden. Da also unsere römischen Gewährsmänner, die späteren Scholiasten oder die griechisch schreibenden Autoren, wie PLUTARCH oder APPIAN, selbst keine klare Vorstellung von der sakralen Grundlage der Obnuntiation hatten, tritt in unserer Überlieferung das Politische und das Verfassungsrechtliche stark in den Vordergrund, während das Sakrale oft unberücksichtigt bleibt. Dasselbe läßt sich aber auch von der modernen Forschung sagen, die besonders in den letzten Jahren die sakrale Seite des Problems stiefmütterlich behandelt hat.

Dem Problem der obnuntiatio im Zusammenhang mit dem Auguralrecht hat bisher, abgesehen von dem, was MOMMSEN im „Staatsrecht" zu diesem Thema ausgeführt hat und was in mancher Hinsicht noch unübertroffen ist, nur VALETON als einziger Forscher eine spezielle Untersuchung gewidmet. Die aus dem Ende des vorigen Jahrhunderts stammenden gelehrten Arbeiten VALETONs sind aber höchst unsystematisch angelegt und enthalten neben glänzenden Einfällen auch eklatante Fehlschlüsse. In diesem Zusammenhang ist auch eine interessante Studie von J. BLEICKEN über Kollisionen zwischen sacrum und publicum zu nennen.

Da das ius augurale weder in all seinen Einzelheiten noch in den Grundbegriffen schon völlig erschlossen ist, könnte man leicht einwenden, daß unser Vorhaben, die Obnuntiationsprobleme gerade von dieser Seite her anzugehen, ein verzweifelter Versuch sei. Es gibt jedoch einige feste Punkte, auf die sich eine Untersuchung in dieser Richtung stützen kann. Bevor wir dies zu zeigen suchen, sei noch in Parenthese vermerkt, daß wir – wenn wir von der sakralen Seite oder vom sacrum in bezug auf die obnuntiatio reden – uns der modernen und nicht der römischen Terminologie bedienen, denn die Römer unterschieden streng zwischen sacra und auspicia: omnis populi

311

Romani religio in sacra et in auspicia divisa est – sacris pontifices... auspiciis augures praesunt, sagt CICERO (de nat. deor. 3.5; 1.122).

Die römische Augurallehre unterscheidet impetrative und oblative Auspizien. Jeder römische Magistrat war vor dem Beginn einer Staatshandlung verpflichtet, sich an die Götter mit der Anfrage zu wenden, ob sie der von ihm beabsichtigten Handlung ihre Zustimmung geben würden oder nicht; ferner mußte er stets seine Aufmerksamkeit darauf lenken, ob etwa die Götter durch zusätzliche Zeichen kundtaten, daß sie ihre bisherige günstige Haltung geändert hatten. Die Auspizien, welche die unmittelbare Verbindung mit den Göttern sicherstellten, galten als die eigentliche Grundlage des römischen Staates. Aller Wahrscheinlichkeit nach hat zur Zeit des Königtums das Recht zur Auspikation nur dem König zugestanden, Augurationen auch den Auguren. Nach dem Sturz des Königtums ist dieses Recht auf die höchsten republikanischen Magistrate und auf den (patrizischen) Senat übergegangen. Bekanntlich wird der Senat im Falle des Erlöschens aller Kurulämter zum einzigen Inhaber von Auspizien. Auspicium und Imperium sind untrennbar: die lex curiata de imperio gibt dem Magistrat nicht nur die Gewaltattribute, sie verleiht ihm auch das Recht zur Auspikation. Fragen an die Götter konnte zwar jeder Bürger richten, jeder hatte also das Auspizienrecht, aber nur in eigener Sache. Es sind dies die auspicia privata, die freilich nach dem Zeugnis CICEROs am Ende der Republik schon außer Gebrauch gekommen waren. Die Auspizien, welche die Staatsangelegenheiten betrafen – die auspicia publica –, konnten dagegen nur von den Beamten, in bestimmten Fällen wahrscheinlich auch von den Staatspriestern, eingeholt werden. Die Götter offenbarten ihren Willen durch Zeichen verschiedenster Art, und es war die Aufgabe des Priesterkollegiums der Auguren, darüber zu wachen, daß die göttlichen Offenbarungen richtig interpretiert wurden.

Die Vorzeichen, welche IUPPITER sandte, waren untereinander nicht gleich, und zwar weder in ihrem Wirkungsbereich, noch in ihrer Wirkungskraft und Wirkungsdauer: notum est esse apud augures auspiciorum gradus plures (Dan. Aen. III 374). Und es war ein fester Grundsatz der Augurallehre, daß die wichtigeren Vorzeichen den Vorrang vor den weniger bedeutsamen innehatten: minora auguria maioribus cedunt nec ullarum sunt virium, licet priora sint (Serv. Ecl. IX 13).

Als mächtigste von allen göttlichen Zeichen galten Blitz und Donner. In der Auguralterminologie hieß ein signum de caelo „auspicium maximum" (Dan. Aen. II 693), DIONYSIOS VON HALIKARNASSOS bezeichnet es als χράτιστον (2.5.5). Im Falle des Auspizienkonfliktes schlagen Blitz und Donner – wie es besonders ausführlich CASSIUS DIO (38.13.3–4) darstellt – alle anderen Zeichen. Die Wirkung des Blitzzeichens erstreckte sich ferner – im Gegensatz zu anderen Auspizien – auf den ganzen Tag, an welchem es gesehen wurde.

Diese Regeln sind wichtig in bezug auf die obnuntiatio, aber von entscheidender Bedeutung ist noch ein anderer Umstand. Der Blitz, besonders der von links nach rechts, galt nämlich als ein günstiges Zeichen für alle Privat- und Amtshandlungen – mit einer einzigen Ausnahme: für alle Volksversammlungen galten Blitz und Donner als böse Omina. Fulmen sinistrum auspicium optumum ... habemus ad omnis res praeterquam ad comitia – itaque in nostris commentariis scriptum habemus: „Iove tonante, fulgurante comitia populi habere nefas" sagt der Augur CICERO (de div. 2.74; 2.42). Blitz und Donner lösten jede Volksversammlung sofort auf und machten den ganzen Tag für Verhandlungen mit der Gemeinde religiös ungeeignet.

Die Vogelzeichen, die in der römischen Frühgeschichte eine entscheidende Rolle spielten – man denke an das berühmte Geierauspizium des Romulus – und die den eigentlichen Gegenstand der Auguraldisziplin darstellten, waren in der späteren Zeit allem Anschein nach nicht mehr üblich. Im Gegensatz zu dem Bereich militiae, wo fast ausschließlich die Auspizien de tripudiis (d. h. auf Grund der Beobachtung des Fressens der heiligen Hühner) Anwendung fanden, war im Stadtbereich die Einholung von Himmelszeichen am meisten verbreitet. Dies aber bedeutet, daß die Auspizien, die der Vorsitzende für die Abhaltung der Volksversammlung von den Göttern zu erbitten hatte, immer schwächer sein mußten als die, die den geschäftsführenden Beamten für alle anderen Amtshandlungen zuteil wurden. Auf der verfassungsrechtlichen Stufe sicherte dieser Auspizienkonflikt fast allen Staatshandlungen Vorrang vor den Komitien.

Es ist nun nach dem Ursprung dieser sonderbaren Einrichtung zu fragen. CICERO bemerkt dazu: hoc fortasse rei publicae causa constitutum est; comitiorum enim non habendorum causas esse voluerunt (de div. 2.43). An einer anderen Stelle drückt er sich ähnlich aus: ut comitiorum ... principes civitatis essent interpretes (de div. 2.74). Es war dies CICEROs Wunsch, optimatische Parteidoktrin und zum Teil auch die tatsächliche Lage der Dinge zur Zeit der klassischen Republik; ob es aber auch der ursprüngliche Zustand gewesen ist, scheint sehr zweifelhaft. Vielleicht ist hier eine andere Erklärungsmöglichkeit zu erwägen. Da ein Unwetter auf die unter freiem Himmel tagenden Versammlungen sich störend auswirken mußte, lag der Gedanke nahe, es kündige in diesem besonderen Falle der Vater IUPPITER durch Gewitter, Blitz und Donner seinen Einspruch gegen die Abhaltung der Volksversammlungen an. Wir haben es hier offensichtlich mit einem alten Grundsatz der Augurallehre zu tun, der schon in frührömischer Zeit entstanden sein muß und von den Auguralbüchern als Petrefakt bewahrt wurde, um erst später unter geänderten Umständen auch politisch ausgenutzt zu werden. CICEROs Aussage ist aber insofern richtig, als die alte augurale Vorschrift eine verfassungsrechtliche Formulierung erhalten mußte, wenn der oben angedeutete Auspizienkonflikt überhaupt in der Politik eine Rolle spielen sollte. Es mußte festgelegt werden, wem das Recht zustand, das Blitzzeichen mit verbindlicher Kraft zu melden. Ehe wir aber auf diese Frage näher eingehen, wäre es vielleicht nicht unangebracht, die Aufmerksamkeit noch auf eine andere Auspizienabstufung zu lenken, die manchmal auch zum Konflikt von Auspizien führen konnte.

Das auspicium bildet, wie gesagt, ein Gegenstück zum Imperium. Das Imperium besitzen zwar nur die höchsten Magistrate; da aber alle Beamten ihre Amtshandlungen, zumindest die wichtigsten, erst nach der Einholung der göttlichen Bewilligung vornehmen durften, kommt das Recht zur Auspikation allen Magistraten, sogar den niedrigsten, zu. Wie es der Augur MESSALA in einem bei GELLIUS (13.15) bewahrten Fragment ausführt, waren die Auspizien der Magistrate untereinander nicht gleich; sie waren geteilt in „größere" und „kleinere": auspicia maxima und minora. Zu den ersteren waren nur die eigentlichen Imperiumsträger befugt, also vor allem die Konsuln, ferner Praetoren, Zensoren, auch der Diktator und Interrex; die niederen Magi-

313

strate waren dagegen nur im Besitz von auspicia minora. Hatten zwei Beamte Auspizien hinsichtlich derselben Angelegenheit angestellt und hatten ihnen die Götter verschiedene Antworten gegeben, so trat in einem solchen Fall das Auspicium des niederen Magistrats vor dem des höheren zurück. Da aber die Magistrate meistens getrennte Funktionen ausübten, ergab sich nur selten Gelegenheit zu einer derartigen Auspizienkollision. Anders verhält sich die Sache freilich, wenn die auspizierenden Beamten die gleiche Stellung hatten, wie z. B. die Konsuln im Lager. Aber dann wechselte normalerweise das Auspicium wie auch das Imperium von Tag zu Tag. Diese Art von Auspizienkollision hat jedoch mit der rechtsverbindlichen Obnuntiation, wie sie bei den Komitien vorkommt, nur wenig zu tun. Die Vorzeichen, die den Magistraten bei der Götterbefragung zuteil wurden, waren in den meisten Fällen, ihrer Wirkungskraft nach, gleich, die magistratische Kompetenz dagegen ungleich. Man könnte also sagen, daß hier, bei der Beseitigung bzw. Überwindung einer Kollision, die entscheidende Rolle nicht das Götterzeichen, sondern der magistratische Rang bzw. die magistratische Kompetenz spielt. Diese Sachlage hatte wahrscheinlich MESSALA im Sinne, wenn er schrieb: praetores consulesque inter se et vitiant et obtinent (a.O. § 4).

Nun unterscheidet, wie wir gesehen haben, die Augurallehre zwischen den auspicia maxima, für die man die signa de caelo ansah und die mit den auspicia maxima der Magistrate nicht zu verwechseln sind, und den anderen schwächeren Zeichen. Es bestand also eine doppelte und zwar sich durchkreuzende Teilung: auf der Auguralebene nach Auspizienarten, auf der verfassungsrechtlichen Ebene nach Vorrang und Kompetenz der Magistrate. Erst dieser Sachverhalt, im Verein mit der Doppelnatur des Blitzzeichens, schuf die Möglichkeit einer schweren und wirklichen Auspizienkollision, die sowohl das Staatsrecht wie auch das ius augurale betraf.

Die Dinge lassen sich am besten durch ein Beispiel illustrieren. Holten am selben Tage ein Quästor das Blitzauspizium für sein Vorhaben und ein Konsul die Auspizien für die Zusammenkunft von Komitien ein, dann entstand eine in rechtlicher und religiöser Hinsicht komplizierte Lage: wenn der Quästor, dem verfassungsmäßig nur die auspicia minora zukamen, einen Blitz beobachtete, so erhielt er damit von den Göttern ein auspicium maximum; dem Konsul dagegen, obwohl er verfassungsrechtlich ein Träger von auspicia maxima war, konnten die Götter ihre Billigung für die Abhaltung der Volksversammlung nur durch die Zeichen bekanntmachen, die schwächer als die signa de caelo waren. Dies ist der augurale Kern der Obnuntiation. Es erhellt zugleich, daß die obnuntiatio in dem hier dargestellten Sinne nur die Volksversammlungen betraf.

Doch wäre das alles noch nicht ausreichend gewesen, um – aus bloßer Auspizienkollision – eine wirksame politische Waffe schmieden zu können. Es fragt sich vor allem, ob und warum der leitende Magistrat der Nachricht Glauben schenken mußte, daß man den Blitz gesehen habe. Um auf diese Frage antworten zu können, wird es jetzt notwendig, auf die schon früher erwähnte Scheidung der Auspizien – in impetrative und oblative – etwas näher einzugehen.

Das Hauptmerkmal des auspicium impetrativum bildet die an die Gottheit gerichtete Frage und die von dieser gegebene Antwort. Diese Frage sollte in einer bestimmten Form (legum dictio) vorgelegt werden: darin wurde sowohl die Handlung genau

314

bezeichnet, welche die Götter gutheißen sollten, wie auch die Art der Antwort, die man von ihnen erwartete. Daraus geht mit aller Deutlichkeit hervor: erstens, daß die Impetrativauspizien nur vor dem Beginn jeder auspicato vorzunehmenden Handlung angestellt werden konnten, und zweitens, daß die göttliche Antwort ausschließlich für die auspizierende Person bestimmt war. Nur der Auspizierende wußte, was der Gott ihm offenbarte.

Das Recht, die Zeichenbeobachtung vorzunehmen, oder, wie es in der Auguralsprache hieß, die spectio, konnte wohl niemand abgesprochen werden. Wahrscheinlich durften es auch Private tun, aber natürlich nur in eigener Sache. Im Besitz der spectio bezüglich der Staatshandlungen scheinen nur die Magistrate gewesen zu sein; den Auguren ist dieses Vorrecht von dem Augur CICERO, der es wissen mußte, unzweideutig abgesprochen worden: nos enim nuntiationem solum habemus, consules et reliqui magistratus etiam spectionem (Phil. 2.81), wovon noch die Rede sein wird. Wie ich schon betonte, sind für das Problem der obnuntiatio nur jene Impetrativauspizien von Wichtigkeit, die auf der Himmelsbeobachtung beruhten, weil nur die Wahrnehmung eines Blitzes die Komitien verhindern konnte. Die Tätigkeit der Himmelsbeobachtung wird in der Auguralterminologie durch zwei Fachausdrücke bezeichnet: „de caelo auspicari" oder häufiger „de caelo servare" – Ausdrücke, die nicht miteinander zu identifizieren sind. „De caelo auspicari" ist offensichtlich als der allgemeinere Begriff aufzufassen. Dies geht aus den folgenden Worten CICEROs hervor: Iam de caelo servare non ipsos censes solitos qui auspicabantur? Nunc imperant pullario; ille renuntiat... (de div. 2.74). Die auspicatio de caelo setzt die Himmelsbeobachtung voraus; ihre Ausführung erfolgt durch das servare de caelo.

Im letzten Jahrhundert der Republik ist die Himmelsbeobachtung, was die Prozedur betrifft, zu einer reinen Formsache geworden: dem de caelo auspizierenden Beamten wurde immer gemeldet, daß das fulmen sinistrum, der von links nach rechts fahrende Blitz, gesehen worden sei. Da die Wahrnehmung des Blitzes eine Selbstverständlichkeit geworden war, ist es dazu gekommen, daß in der Umgangssprache die Formel „de caelo servare" dem Ausdruck „fulmen vidisse" äquivalent wurde. In der spätrepublikanischen Zeit wurde die Einholung von Himmelsauspizien vornehmlich Instrument zur Vereitelung der Volksversammlung; diese Entwicklung spiegelt sich in der Bedeutungsveränderung des Ausdruckes „de caelo servare" wider, der jetzt nicht nur für die Bezeichnung der Himmelsbeobachtung im allgemeinen, sondern in erster Linie im Sinne von „durch die Himmelsbeobachtung die Komitien verhindern" angewandt wurde – und zwar nicht nur in der Umgangssprache, sondern, wie es scheint, auch in den Gesetzestexten. Es war dies aber zweifellos nur eine erweiterte bzw. spezialisierte Bedeutung; der Ausdruck „de caelo servare" wird von CICERO auch für die Himmelsauspizien gebraucht, die ohne irgendeine Absicht der Komitienverhinderung vorgenommen wurden.

Es drängt sich nun die Frage auf: wem stand das Recht zu, gegen die Volksversammlung mit verbindlicher Kraft zu obnuntiieren? Nach dem bisher Ausgeführten dürfte die Antwort, vielleicht allerdings nur scheinbar, nicht schwierig sein: das Recht zur Obnuntiation sollte all denen zustehen, die im Besitz von Impetrativauspizien für die Staatsangelegenheiten waren. Es kommen hier also nur Magistrate in Betracht, und zwar alle Magistrate.

315

Was religiös die Abhaltung von Komitien verhindert, ist der Göttereinspruch, der sich durch den Blitz offenbart. Staatsrechtlich aber werden die Komitien nicht eigentlich durch die Wahrnehmung des Blitzes vereitelt, sondern durch die Meldung, daß der Blitz gesehen worden sei – und das ist etwas ganz anderes. Entscheidend ist dabei der schon früher erwähnte Umstand, daß bei den Impetrativauspizien das göttliche Zeichen nur an einen bestimmten Empfänger gerichtet ist; es besteht also keine Möglichkeit zu prüfen, ob ein auf Grund seiner spectio den Himmel beobachtender Magistrat wirklich einen Blitz gesehen oder ihn nur erfunden hat. Man war sich natürlich wohl bewußt, daß die Wahrnehmung des Blitzes in (fast) allen Fällen fiktiv war – ein beredtes Zeugnis legt hier CICERO ab: retinetur autem et ad opinionem vulgi et ad magnas utilitates rei publicae mos, religio, disciplina, ius augurium, collegi auctoritas (de div. 2.70). Und kurz darauf schreibt er: auspicia... haec certe quibus utimur, sive tripudio, sive de caelo, simulacra sunt auspiciorum, auspicia nullo modo (2.71). Es gab Auguren, die der Meinung waren, ihre Lehre enthalte nur sapienter... ad opinionem imperitorum... fictas religiones (1.105).

Es war dies aber nur die Privatmeinung der Gelehrten; der Staat als solcher konnte a priori in keiner Verordnung annehmen, daß ein durch den dazu berufenen Beamten angestelltes auspicium impetrativum falsch sei oder auch nur falsch sein könnte. Demzufolge mußte jede solche Meldung als wahr angenommen werden. Es war also vom Standpunkt der staatlichen Auguraldoktrin nicht die bloße Form, der Akt der Meldung, sondern der Inhalt des Gemeldeten, die tatsächliche Beobachtung des Blitzes, wodurch die Volksversammlung aufgelöst wurde. Und diese Auffassung ist auch bei CICERO zu finden, zwar nicht bei CICERO dem Gelehrten, wohl aber beim Anwalt und Politiker CICERO; und so lesen wir in der Sestiana (83): cumque [sc. Sestius] auspiciis religionique parens obnuntiaret quod senserat.

Dies ist die augurale Basis der Rechtsverbindlichkeit der obnuntiatio. Theoretisch konnte also jeder Magistrat durch Meldung eines impetrativen Blitzzeichens die Abhaltung der Volksversammlung verhindern. Das ius augurale deckt sich aber dabei nicht völlig mit dem Staatsrecht. Die Konsuln pflegten nämlich den niederen Magistraten zu verbieten, an den Tagen, für welche die Komitien angesagt wurden, die Himmelsbeobachtungen vorzunehmen.

Wenden wir jetzt unsere Aufmerksamkeit der anderen Kategorie von Götterzeichen, den auspicia oblativa, zu, so wird sich ein ganz anderes Bild ergeben. SERVIUS erklärt im Kommentar zur Aeneis den Unterschied zwischen oblativen und impetrativen Zeichen folgendermaßen: auguria aut oblativa sunt, quae non poscuntur, aut inpetrativa, quae optata veniunt (6.190). Man bemerkt, daß SERVIUS sich hier, wie sonst oft, ungenauer Terminologie bedient, indem er augurium und auspicium vermengt und den Ausdruck augurium an der Stelle braucht, wo in der technischen Auguralsprache auspicium stehen müßte. Auf diese Frage, die zuletzt von CATALANO ausführlich behandelt wurde, brauchen wir hier nicht einzugehen.

Die Oblativzeichen werden also von den Göttern ohne vorhergehende Anfrage gesandt. Der Gott sendet sie, wann er will und wem er will. Sie sind an keinen bestimmten Empfänger gerichtet, sondern wenden sich an alle. Für die Interpretation von Oblativzeichen ist der Grundsatz besonders wichtig, daß es durchaus von der

316

Entscheidung des Handelnden abhing, ob er ein solches sich zufällig anbietendes Zeichen auf seine Handlung beziehen oder es als ihn nicht betreffend verwerfen wollte: in oblativis auguriis in potestate videntis est, utrum id ad se pertinere velit, an refutet et abominetur. Diese Formulierung von SERVIUS (Aen. 12.260), obwohl grundsätzlich richtig, gibt jedoch nicht genau den vollen Inhalt der Auguralvorschrift wieder. Was hier Schwierigkeiten bereitet, ist die Wendung „in potestate videntis". Es ist in diesem Zusammenhang an den festen Grundsatz der Augurallehre zu erinnern, daß der Blitz sowohl als göttliche Antwort bei den Impetrativauspizien, wie auch als Oblativzeichen, immer auf die Volksversammlung als ein störendes Zeichen zu beziehen war. Wenn also der den Vorsitz führende Magistrat einen Blitz gesehen hatte oder ihn als von einem anderen wahrgenommen anerkannte, mußte er diese Wahrnehmung iure augurali unbedingt auf sich beziehen und als Einsprache der Götter gegen die Abhaltung von Komitien betrachten. Es lag also in diesem Falle keineswegs in potestate videntis zu erklären, das Blitzzeichen habe mit seiner Handlung nichts zu tun, wie es VALETON anzunehmen scheint. Glücklicherweise hat uns auch PLINIUS die von SERVIUS zitierte Regel überliefert, und zwar gibt er deren Inhalt, jedenfalls was die Interpretation des Blitzzeichens angeht, zweifellos korrekter wieder. Wir lesen bei ihm nämlich (28.17): in augurum ... disciplina constat neque diras neque ulla auspicia pertinere ad eos, qui quamcumque rem ingredientes observare se ea negaverint. Hier liegt der Nachdruck auf „observare se ea negaverint". Zu vergleichen ist, was der ältere CATO in einem ähnlichen Zusammenhang sagt: quod ego non sensi, nullum mihi vitium facit (Fest. 234). Es mag hier noch an den anekdotisch gewordenen Fall des berühmten HANNIBAL-Gegners M. MARCELLUS erinnert werden, der, um durch keinerlei böse Vorzeichen gehemmt zu werden, sich vor der Schlacht in einer bedeckten Sänfte tragen ließ. Aber es war weder notwendig noch üblich, so weitgehende Sicherheitsmaßnahmen zu treffen. Es geht aus den oben angeführten Stellen klar hervor, daß es im freien Ermessen des handelnden Beamten lag, ein tatsächlich eingetretenes Oblativzeichen, in unserem Falle den Blitz, als nicht geschehen zu behandeln.

Für alltägliche Staatsgeschäfte war die reguläre Verbindung mit den Göttern durch die auspicia impetrativa gesichert. Aber es konnte leicht vorkommen, daß in der legum dictio ein wichtiger Umstand aus Nachlässigkeit oder auch absichtlich verschwiegen, beim Vortragen der Formeln ein Fehler begangen, oder endlich das dem Auspizierenden zuteil gewordene Vorzeichen falsch interpretiert wurde. Und dann sind es vor allem die Oblativzeichen gewesen, auf welchen das Wohl des römischen Staates beruhte. Durch sie war die Möglichkeit gegeben, die Gemeinde vor den schlimmen Folgen der Verfehlungen einzelner Magistrate bei der Einholung von Impetrativauspizien zu schützen. Alle Bürger durften die göttlichen Warnungen entgegennehmen und dem Magistrat melden. Aber, wie wir gesehen haben, der Magistrat konnte diese Warnungen mißachten. Es mußte also auf dem verfassungsrechtlichen Wege entschieden werden, wem das Recht zustehen sollte, den geschäftsführenden Beamten von der Wahrnehmung eines augurium malum mit verbindlicher Kraft in Kenntnis zu setzen und auf diese Weise den Abbruch der Handlung, gegen welche die Götter ihren Einspruch erhoben, herbeizuführen.

Vom Standpunkt des Staatsrechts verhält sich hier die Sache ähnlich wie bei der Ob-

317

nuntiation auf Grund der Impetrativauspizien. Die Frage lautet nämlich nicht, ob der Blitz gesehen war, sondern wem der Magistrat Glauben schenken mußte. Daß die Meldung eines Privaten keine Rechtsverbindlichkeit beanspruchen konnte, ist klar. Hingegen wurde bisweilen die Ansicht vertreten, der leitende Magistrat habe nicht umhin gekonnt, die von einem anderen Beamten erstattete Meldung des oblativen Blitzzeichens zu beachten. Aber schon aus theoretischen Gründen scheint diese These bedenklich zu sein. Es ist nämlich zu überlegen, auf welche Weise ein niederer Magistrat dem Konsul gegenüber hätte nachweisen können, daß gerade er durch die Gottheit auserwählt worden sei, ein augurium malum zu empfangen. Ein Zeichen, das ex definitione an alle gerichtet war, sollte auch allgemein beobachtet werden: warum sollte also nur ein Quästor den Blitz wahrnehmen können, während der die Volksversammlung leitende Konsul oder Praetor nichts gesehen hatte? Von diesem Gesichtspunkt aus war die Rechtslage genau umgekehrt wie bei der Meldung von Impetrativzeichen: bei den letzteren war das Blitzzeichen nur an eine bestimmte Person gerichtet, und aus diesem Grund konnte der leitende Magistrat die Wahrheit der Meldung nicht in Zweifel ziehen; dagegen verfügte bei den Oblativauspizien der Meldende über keine Mittel, die Wahrheit seiner Meldung zu begründen.

In bezug auf die niederen Magistrate bestand allerdings in der praktischen Handhabung des Obnuntiationsrechts kein großer Unterschied: den Konsuln stand es kraft ihrer maior potestas frei, die Einholung von impetrativen Auspizien für einen bestimmten Tag den magistratus minores zu untersagen, oder, kraft derselben potestas, dem von einem niederen Magistrat gemeldeten Oblativzeichen keinen Glauben zu schenken. Und schon mit Rücksicht auf das von den Konsuln erlassene Verbot des „de caelo servare" wäre die zuletzt von BLEICKEN verfochtene These von der Verbindlichkeit jeder magistratischen Obnuntiation auf Grund der oblativen Blitzzeichen unannehmbar: denn hätte jeder magistratus minor durch Wahrnehmung oder Erfindung des Blitzes die Komitien in jedem Moment verhindern können, wäre das Verbot, die auspicia impetrativa einzuholen, ganz sinnlos gewesen.

Es ist in diesem Zusammenhang die Tatsache von Interesse, daß uns, in voller Übereinstimmung mit den obigen Überlegungen, kein Fall einer von einem Quästor oder Ädilen vorgenommenen obnuntiatio bekannt ist. Noch auffallender und bedeutsamer ist aber der Umstand, daß uns auch kein Bericht vorliegt über eine konsularische oder prätorische Nuntiation des oblativen Blitzzeichens. Man könnte daran denken, daß dies der Zufälligkeit unserer Überlieferung zuzuschreiben ist, wäre nicht diese Erklärungsmöglichkeit durch den Bericht CICEROs (Phil. 2.79–82) über die Obnuntiation des ANTONIUS gegen die Wahl DOLABELLAs im J. 44 klar und deutlich widerlegt. Demnach konnte ANTONIUS die Wahlversammlung in seiner Eigenschaft als Konsul nur durch das „servare de caelo", also auf Grund von Impetrativauspizien verhindern: auf Grund der Oblativauspizien dagegen nur als Augur.

Wie aus der Polemik CICEROS gegen ANTONIUS erhellt, war es ein spezifisches Vorrecht der Auguren, auf Grund der Wahrnehmung der oblativen Zeichen mit den Worten „alio die" einzugreifen und rechtsverbindlich die Fortführung der Verhandlungen mit der Gemeinde zu verbieten. Es ist wohl verständlich und logisch, daß man die Entscheidung über die Natur und Gültigkeit der von IUPPITER unbefragt und

318

unerwartet gesandten Zeichen und Warnungen den besonders dazu berufenen Sachkundigen überließ.

Die obnuntiatio auf Grund der Impetrativauspizien beruhte auf Auspizienkollision von zwei oder mehreren Beamten. Bei den Oblativauspizien gibt es dagegen keine Kollision von Magistratsauspizien. Es ist der Gott selbst, der seinen Einspruch erhebt.

Das Bild scheint somit klar und einfach. Aber das römische Verfassungssystem war nicht einfach; es hat durch die Institution des Volkstribunats seine besondere Prägung erhalten. Nun besaßen, gemäß der herrschenden Lehre, die Volkstribunen kein Auspizienrecht. Das plebiscitum hieß lex inauspicata (Liv. 7.6.11); DIONYSIOS VON HALIKARNASSOS bezeugt, daß, bis zu seiner Zeit, kein Tribun auspicato gewählt worden ist (9,49; vgl. Liv. 6.41.5), und wir haben keinen Anlaß, die Richtigkeit dieser Angaben zu bezweifeln. Mit diesem Sachverhalt scheint die Tatsache in schroffem Widerspruch zu stehen, daß die Tribunen offensichtlich das Obnuntiationsrecht hatten und bei den Obnuntiationsvorgängen der späten Republik sogar eine prominente Rolle spielten. Theoretisch konnte die tribunizische Obnuntiation entweder auf imperativen oder auf oblativen Zeichen beruhen. Und es ist in der Tat bezeugt, daß die Tribunen Himmelsbeobachtungen anstellten. Das servare de caelo bedeutete aber die Einholung von Impetrativauspizien, jenen Auspizien also, die den Volkstribunen fehlten. Ist es überhaupt möglich, hier eine Lösung zu finden?

In dieser Hinsicht ist die Stellungnahme MOMMSENs besonders lehrreich. Sie ist sehr uneinheitlich und zeigt deutlich, welche Schwierigkeiten hier vorliegen. MOMMSEN hat richtig erkannt, daß die magistratische Obnuntiation an die spectio anknüpfte, d. h. auf der Meldung von imperativen Blitzzeichen beruhte. An einer anderen Stelle im „Staatsrecht" (I³ 113) finden wir aber die Bemerkung, daß die Obnuntiation „nicht auf die im Wege der spectio erlangten Zeichen beschränkt" sei; MOMMSEN bezeichnet sie dort als „nur insofern magistratisches Recht, als der Beamte die Mitteilung des anderen Beamten nicht . . . befugt ist zu ignorieren". Er hat hier offensichtlich die Meldung der oblativen Zeichen im Sinne. Diese an sich etwas unbestimmte Behauptung dient MOMMSEN als Stütze für die Erklärung des Obnuntiationsrechtes der Volkstribunen. Er sagt nämlich: „Es erklärt sich daher leicht, daß die Tribunen, obwohl sie keine Impetrativauspizien einholen, dennoch späterhin die Obnuntiation ausüben." Wir haben also bei MOMMSEN drei Kategorien von Personen, die das Obnuntiationsrecht besaßen: die Magistrate auf Grund sowohl der auspicia impetrativa (was richtig ist) wie oblativa (was mit den Ausführungen CICEROs im Widerspruch steht); die Volkstribunen und die Auguren nur auf Grund der signa oblativa. MOMMSEN scheint auch anzunehmen, daß die concilia plebis nur durch oblative Zeichen unterbrochen werden konnten (I³ 109, 113, II³ 284); die Obnuntiation auf Grund der auspicia impetrativa wäre demnach nur gegen die Versammlungen des Gesamtvolkes statthaft: eine schöne Konstruktion, nur leider ohne Fundament.

Tatsache ist, daß die Tribunen zum Zweck der Obnuntiation die Himmelsbeobachtungen vornahmen, und zwar *auch* in bezug auf die concilia plebis, nicht nur gegen die comitia. Diese Tatsache ist natürlich der Aufmerksamkeit MOMMSENs nicht entgangen; doch er beschränkt sich auf eine etwas resignierend klingende Bemerkung:

319

„darin ... liegt eine Anomalie", sagt er, „daß die Tribunen die Blitzbeobachtung angestellt haben, die auf der spectio ruht und zu den Impetrativauspizien gehört" (II³ 284–5). Mit dieser Anomalie wird aber seine ganze Theorie hinfällig.

Innere Widersprüche, die im „Staatsrecht" nur im Keime zu finden sind, treten in Arbeiten anderer Forscher noch deutlicher hervor. Auch WISSOWA, der sonst zwischen den auspicia impetrativa und oblativa streng unterscheidet, vermengt sie im Falle der obnuntiatio. Er bemerkt, daß die Volkstribunen das ius obnuntiandi zweifellos besessen haben, obwohl sie der spectio entbehrten (RE I 2585). Die spectio definiert er als das Recht, die signa impetrativa einzuholen. Sein Schluß ist, daß die tribunizische Obnuntiation auf der Meldung von Oblativzeichen beruhte. Dieselbe Ansicht, obzwar mit verschiedenen Modifikationen, wird auch von MARBACH, WEINSTOCK, BLEICKEN und MAGDELAIN vertreten. BLEICKEN nimmt sogar an, daß jede Obnuntiation, auch die von den ordentlichen Magistraten vorgenommene, auf Grund von Oblativauspizien erfolgte. Es ist hier nicht der Ort, sich mit den Interpretationen der genannten Gelehrten in allen Einzelheiten auseinanderzusetzen; wir müssen uns auf einige allgemeinere Bemerkungen beschränken.

Die Hauptschwierigkeit bildet dabei die Interpretation des Ausdruckes „de caelo servare". Es steht fest, daß die Tribunen die servationes de caelo vornahmen. Wenn man also den Volkstribunen die obnuntiatio oblativorum zuschreiben will, muß man unbedingt den Ausdruck „de caelo servare" auch auf die Wahrnehmung von Oblativzeichen beziehen. Diese Folgerung wird manchmal von den Anhängern der hier kritisierten These stillschweigend übergangen, WISSOWA und BLEICKEN formulieren sie aber eindeutig. WISSOWA behauptet nämlich, daß die Wendung „de caelo servare" zum allgemeinen Ausdruck für den Empfang impetrativer oder oblativer Auspizien wurde. Die Stellen, durch welche WISSOWA seine Auslegung des Terminus „de caelo servare" begründen will, sind aber nicht schlüssig (Cic. de div. 2.74; de domo 40). Der Ausdruck „de caelo servare" steht dort ganz eindeutig im Zusammenhang mit der Einholung von Impetrativauspizien. Noch wichtiger ist die Tatsache, daß CICERO (Phil. 2.79–82) in seiner Polemik gegen ANTONIUS sowohl die spectio wie auch das „de caelo servare" als den Auguren nicht zustehend schildert und als ausschließliches Vorrecht der Magistrate darstellt. Den Auguren kommt nur die Wahrnehmung und Meldung von sich zufällig darbietenden Oblativzeichen zu. Spectio und „de caelo servare" werden also von CICERO in einen engen Zusammenhang gebracht und der bloßen Wahrnehmung von Oblativzeichen entgegengestellt. Danach ist die spectio am besten als das den Magistraten allgemein zustehende Recht aufzufassen, die Himmelsbeobachtung vorzunehmen, „de caelo servare" hingegen als tatsächliche, praktische Anwendung und Ausführung dieses Rechtes.

Die magistratische Beobachtung des Himmels, wie auch die Meldung (nuntiatio) des Blitzes mußte dabei – wie es CICERO formuliert – gemäß den Gesetzen (per leges) vor Beginn der Verhandlungen stattgefunden haben. Was dabei unter leges zu verstehen sei, ist freilich unklar. Meistens denkt man an ein Volksgesetz, seien es die lex Aelia und lex Fufia oder die lex Clodia. Es bleibt aber auch zu erwägen, ob die Möglichkeit besteht, den Ausdruck im Sinne der auguralen Verordnung aufzufassen. Auf diese vielumstrittene Frage, deren Lösung interessante Aufschlüsse gewähren könnte, können wir aber an dieser Stelle nicht eingehen.

320

Aus dem CICERO-Text ergibt sich zugleich, daß den Auguren, im Gegensatz zu den Magistraten, in jedem Moment der Verhandlungen, auch nach dem Abschluß der Abstimmung, freistand, auf Grund der Wahrnehmung eines oblativen Blitzzeichens mit dem Spruch „alio die" einzugreifen. Diese Interpretation wird durch zwei andere CICERO-Stellen durchaus bestätigt. In der Schrift de legibus (2.31) preist CICERO die Größe der Augurenwürde und erwähnt dabei als eine außerordentliche Befugnis (die offensichtlich nur die Auguren besaßen) das Recht, begonnene Volksversammlungen auflösen zu können: comitiatus et concilia vel instituta dimittere – rem susceptam dirimere. In einem Brief an ATTICUS (4.3.3–5) schildert er den Verlauf der von dem Volkstribun ANNIUS MILO gegen die Wahl des CLODIUS zur kurulischen Ädilität vorgenommenen Obnuntiationen. Es erhellt daraus, daß die sich an die Himmelsbeobachtung anknüpfende tribunizische Obnuntiation, um gültig zu sein, vor Beginn der Volksversammlung vorgebracht werden mußte. Es ist interessant, auf solche Weise feststellen zu können, daß in dieser Hinsicht für die tribunizische Obnuntiation dieselben Vorschriften galten wie für die der ordentlichen Magistrate.

Fassen wir den ganzen Sachverhalt zusammen, so ergibt sich für die tribunizische Obnuntiation das folgende Bild: 1. die Volkstribunen besitzen kein Auspizienrecht, 2. sie haben kein Recht, die signa oblativa verbindlich zu melden, 3. sie nehmen die Himmelsbeobachtungen vor, die bei den ordentlichen Magistraten mit dem allgemeinen Auspizienrecht verbunden sind.

Diese Tatsachen sind einwandfrei erwiesen, lassen sich aber anscheinend in keine vernünftige Konstruktion einordnen. Dies bedeutet aber nur soviel, daß die bisherige Fragestellung, wonach man den Tribunen entweder das allgemeine Auspizienrecht oder die Meldung von Oblativzeichen zuschrieb und dabei jedesmal einen Teil der Überlieferung weginterpretieren mußte, falsch ist.

Da die Volkstribunen keine Handlung auspicato vornahmen, ist das tribunizische ius obnuntiandi kein Auspizienrecht, jedenfalls wenn wir unter Auspizien die Einholung von göttlicher Zustimmung für eigene Handlungen verstehen. Daraus folgt, daß die tribunizischen servationes de caelo von den durch Magistrate angestellten auspicia impetrativa sakralrechtlich grundverschieden sein mußten. Der Hauptirrtum landläufiger Interpretationen scheint darin zu stecken, daß man die Tätigkeiten „auspicari de caelo" und „servare de caelo" völlig gleichsetzt. Wie wir zu zeigen versuchten, waren die Begriffe „spectio", „auspicari de caelo" und „servare de caelo" zwar eng verwandt und untereinander verbunden, aber doch durchaus nicht identisch. Dies erhellt am besten aus der folgenden Tatsache: die auspicatio de caelo mußte von einem Auspizieninhaber, also einem Magistrat, angestellt werden, das servare konnte dagegen in seinem Auftrage auch ein Diener durchführen. Der Schluß scheint somit unausweichlich, daß die Tribunen nicht das Auspizienrecht als solches, sondern nur das aus dem Auspizienkomplex abstrahierte ius de caelo servandi erhielten. Man wäre also in dieser Sache gemäß der von den Römern in staatsrechtlichen Angelegenheiten mit Vorliebe praktizierten Methode verfahren, abstrakte Begriffe aus konkreten Magistraturen und Funktionen abzusondern und zu verselbständigen. Man darf in diesem Zusammenhang etwa an die tribunicia potestas der römischen Kaiser erinnern, die keine Tribunen gewesen sind, oder im Bereich des Auspizienwesens an den sehr charakteristischen Vorgang der Auspizienleihe.

321

Eine endgültige und in jeder Einzelheit begründete Lösung des Obnuntiationsproblems ist aber kaum erreichbar; wir haben es immer nur mit Interpretationsmöglichkeiten zu tun. So wird es abschließend nicht unangebracht sein, an die Worte MOMMSENs zu erinnern, der einmal geäußert hat, daß, „was die die Obnuntiation betreffenden Gesetze festsetzten und nicht festsetzten, vorsichtige Forscher nicht zu wissen sich bescheiden werden". Wie auch dieser Vortrag letztlich zeigt, hat die MOMMSENsche „Obnuntiation" ihre Geltung noch nicht eingebüßt.

48

CICERO AND ROMAN DIVINATION *

Cicero regarded his elevation to the augurate, in 53 or 52,[1] as the high point of his life, second only to the *annus mirabilis*. A few years later, under the dictatorship of Caesar, removed from public life, he composed his treatise on divination.[2] In the second book the augur Cicero proceeds to demolish the view of those politicians and philosophers who, like his brother Quintus, the speaker in the first book of the dialogue, believed in the validity and truthfulness of divination. He goes on to demonstrate that there is no substance in the claims of the haruspices, augurs, interpreters of dreams or seers. Birds do not predict the future, and the belief

* The text of this article reproduces with some minor changes the paper delivered in April 1979 in Princeton at the Ciceronian Conference organized by the Department of Classics of Princeton University. To Professors T.J. Luce, J.E.G. Zetzel and E. Champlin I should like to express my warm thanks for their kind hospitality.

[1] For the date and circumstances of Cicero's election, see J. LINDERSKI, *The Aedileship of Favonius, Curio the Younger and Cicero's Election to the Augurate*, « HSCP », 76, 1972, 190 ff. After the death of Tullia Servius Sulpicius Rufus consoled Cicero: ' [Tullia] te, patrem suum, praetorem, consulem, augurem vidisse ' (*Fam.* 4.5.5).   [2] For the date of the composition, see A. S. PEASE, *M. Tulli Ciceronis De Divinatione Libri Duo* (Urbana, 1920-1923, repr. Darmstadt, 1963), pp. 13-15, who lucidly summarizes the conclusions reached by R. DURAND, *La date du De Divinatione, Mélanges Boissier* (Paris, 1903), pp. 173-183. Cf. also R. GIOMINI, *Problemi cronologici e compositivi del ' De Divinatione' Ciceroniano* (Roma, n.d. [1974?]). The text of the *De divinatione* was certainly composed before the death of Caesar; after the Ides of March Cicero undertook some revisions, added a few short passages, and above all composed the preface (or a new preface) to Book ii.

that extraordinary occurrences, *monstra* and *ostenta,* portend calamities, is nothing but superstition. For instance, shortly before the
outbreak of the Social War mice were found gnawing the sacred
shields at Lanuvium; the haruspices, following the old tradition of
their art and the popular belief, pronounced it a most serious portent. What nonsense, exclaims Cicero. Just recently — he continues
— mice gnawed his copy of Plato's *Republic.* Should one be therefore filled with fear for the fate of the Roman Republic? [3] No
doubt these words were written after the assassination of Caesar
when the future looked bright.

When Cicero was forced to go into exile, Aulus Caecina (most
probably the son of the man whom Cicero defended in 69), a
great expert in the Etruscan discipline,[4] confidently predicted Cicero's imminent and glorious return. Now in 46 Caecina, who had
fought against Caesar with arms — and still worse — with pen,
was himself an exile. Cicero assures him in a letter[5] that he will
as speedily be restored as Cicero was in 58/57. Caecina had based
his prediction on his knowledge of the marvellous Etruscan discipline; Cicero's conviction as to the restoration of Caecina derives
not from his knowledge of the art of augury, but rather from his
experience in the art of politics which he had acquired through
assiduous study and long practice. His skills in political prophecy
had not even once deceived him — rather a startling statement
in view of his own exile. Though an *augur publicus,* he need not
study the cry of a bird on the left or observe whether the sacred
chickens are eating greedily and whether crumbs fall down from
their beaks. He makes his prediction concerning Caecina from his
knowledge of Caesar's character and the study of present political
circumstances. Unfortunately we do not know whether Caesar recalled Caecina from exile, but in any case signs indicating Caesar's

---

[3] *Div.* 2.59. Cf. also PEASE's comment ad 1.99.   [4] See on him F. MÜN-
ZER, Caecina no. 7, *RE* III (1899), 1237-8; D. R. SHACKLETON BAILEY, *Cicero,
Epistulae ad Familiares,* II (Cambridge, 1977), pp. 399 ff.; E. RAWSON, *Caesar,
Etruria and the Disciplina Etrusca,* « JRS », 68, 1978, 137-138.   [5] *Fam.* 6.6.
The jesting character of Cicero's remarks was missed by J. FERGUSON, *The Re-
ligion of Cicero, Studies in Cicero* (Collana di Studi Ciceroniani 2, Roma,
1962), p. 89.

nature were easier to read than those pertaining to his heir, whom Sir Ronald Syme has aptly characterized as a chameleon. He deceived not only posterity, but also Cicero. Of course the augurs were specialists in birds, not in chameleons, and it would be unfair to blame the augur Cicero too much.

Polybius was struck by the elaborateness of Roman religious ritual (6.56.6 ff.), and Sallust, more than one century later, described the *maiores as* ' religiosissumi mortales ' (*Cat.* 12,3). Augury and other kinds of divination formed a fundamental component of Roman state cult. The essential role of divination in Roman public life was well perceived by Stoic students of Roman history and religion. Roman practice was in perfect agreement with their philosophical views on the nature of gods and divination. According to the Stoic creed as presented by Cicero, there exists a close and reciprocal relationship between the existence of gods and the belief in divination. If there exists true divination, gods must exist, and if there are gods, there must exist men who have the power of divination. Consequently an attack on divination must ultimately lead to the undermining and destruction of the belief in gods.[6] On the level of philosophical argument Cicero had little difficulty in dismissing this proposition as naive and childish.[7] Politically, however, he felt ill at ease in attacking this, as he says, very citadel of the Stoics (*Div.* 1.10). He finds it necessary to state repeatedly and emphatically that he supports *religio* and opposes *superstitio*, and that divination is nothing but the latter and has no legitimate place in the former.[8] Yet it could hardly have escaped his attention that

---

[6] *Div.* 1.9, 82-84; cf. *Leg.* 2.32-33, and many other passages collected by Pease in his notes on *Div.* 1.10 and *N.D.* 2.12. For a lucid discussion of the Stoic argument, see M. DRAGONA-MONACHOU, *Posidonius' 'Hierarchy' Between God, Fate and Cicero's De Divinatione*, « Φιλοσοφία », 4, 1974, 286 ff., esp. 295 ff.; Eadem, *The Stoic Arguments for the Existence and the Providence of the Gods* (Athens, 1976), pp. 74 ff., 126 ff.   [7] *Div.* 1.10; 2.41, 101-102, 104-06.   [8] *Div.* 2.148 (with Pease's commentary): ' Nec vero (id enim diligenter intellegi volo) superstitione tollenda religio tollitur ... maiorum instituta tueri sacris caerimoniisque retinendis sapientis est ': 2.149; ' religio propaganda ... est, ... superstitionis stirpes omnes eligendae '. On the Roman concept of *religio*, see now A. K. MICHELS, *The Versatility of religio. The Mediterranean World. Papers Presented in Honour of Gilbert Bagnani* (Peter-

gods who give no signs can easily be construed as having no interest in men, and thus are dangerously close to the silent gods of
Epicurus.

It would seem that for the sake of his philosophical beliefs
Cicero was ready to take political risks. But did he really run any
risk? The *De divinatione* was an esoteric treatise, and Cicero was
wise enough not to harbour any hopes that his philosophical works
would be read by the masses. He did not even expect that all young
men, of the upper classes of course, would turn to the study of
philosophy. ' Pauci utinam! ' (*Div.* 2.5).

The opening words of his diatribe against haruspicine are very
characteristic from this point of view. ' We are alone ' — Cicero
says to his brother — ' and therefore we may inquire without causing
ill will into the truth of soothsaying '. Whereupon he proceeds to
demonstrate that there is no truth in it. At the same time he stresses
that the practice of haruspicine is to be cultivated ' rei publicae
causa communisque religionis ' (*Div.* 2.28 ff.). Cicero pursues the
same argument also with respect to augury. Divination by the flight
of birds is a mixture of error, superstition and above all fraud
(*Div.* 2.83). Yet augury is to be maintained for two reasons: its
rituals and regulations and the authority of the college of augurs
render great services to the state. And secondly, the mob super-

---

borough [Ontario], 1975), pp. 36-37, who distinguishes as two major com-
ponents of *religio* the element of fear and the sense of obligation; R. MUTH,
Vom Wesen römischer religio', ANRW, II. xvi. 1 (1978), pp. 290-354, esp.
342 ff. On *superstitio* (and its connection with divination), see É. BENVENISTE,
Le vocabulaire des institutions indo-européennes 2 (Paris, 1969), pp. 273-279;
S. CALDERONE, *Superstitio, ANRW*, I. ii (1972), pp. 377-396; D. GRODZYNSKI,
Superstitio, « REA », 1974, 36-60, esp. 37-44; L. F. JANSSEN, *Die Bedeutungs-
entwicklung von superstitio/superstes*, « Mnemosyne », 28, 1975, 135-188, esp.
145-157. The authors mentioned above do not pay attention to the fact that
Cicero directs his attack not only against private ' superstitiosi vates inpuden-
tesque harioli ' (*Div.* 1.132), but also against the official state divination. To
scold the former was in vogue at Rome at least since the time of Ennius,
Plautus and Cato (cf. H. D. JOCELYN, *The Tragedies of Ennius*, Cambridge,
1967, pp. 396-398). To criticize the latter could be dangerous politically, for
as Cotta says in *N.D.* 1.117 ' superstitione ... facile est liberare, cum sustuleris
omnem vim deorum '. Cf. F. SOLMSEN, *Cicero on Religio and Superstitio*,
« CW », 37, 1944, 159-160.

stitiously believes in it. Therefore those who openly disdain augury are deserving of all punishment for they undermine the basis of social stability. The consul of 249, P. Claudius Pulcher, was rightly condemned by the vote of the people when he set sail contrary to the auspices. When the sacred chickens refused to eat he reportedly exclaimed ' if they don't like to eat, let them drink ', and had them thrown into the sea. The gods promptly punished the arrogant Claudius, and he lost most of his fleet at Drepanum.[9]

Whatever the philosophical relationship between the gods and divination, Cicero was acutely aware of the constant political interconnection between divination, the belief in gods and the rule of the nobility. He tries therefore to draw a clear dividing line between *religio* and philosophy. When we wish to investigate what is *bonum* and what is *malum,* what is morally right or morally wrong, we do not turn to diviners, but to philosophers, to whom such problems rightly belong (*Div.* 2.10-11). But whether we believe in gods and divination or not, it is our civic duty to maintain the state religion, and divination forms part of it. No Roman critic of divination had ever disputed this proposition. Politically the only important question was who exercised control over the state cult.

In this respect Cicero fully agrees with the opinion of Gaius Marcellus, his colleague in the augural college. According to Marcellus the founders of the augural law at the beginning of Roman history believed in divination, yet later augury was maintained and preserved for political reasons only, ' rei publicae causa ' (*Div.* 2.75, cf. 2.70; *Leg.* 2.32). Take for example the augural theory of lightning. The *fulmen sinistrum,* literally lightning on the left but in augural reality lightning observed in the east, was the most favourable sign for all enterprises, public and private, except for the *comitia.* This regulation, Cicero assures us, was undoubtedly promulgated *rei publicae causa,* so that the rulers of the state, the *principes civitatis,* would be able to control the popular assemblies, whether they convened to pass judgements in criminal cases, to vote on laws or to elect magistrates.[10]

---

[9] *Div.* 2.70 ff. (cf. *Rep.* 2.16). For the case of P. Claudius Pulcher, see also *Div.* 1.29, N.D. 2.7, and for a discussion of its augural and legal aspects, J. LINDERSKI, *The Augural Law, ANRW,* II.xvi.3 (forthcoming).   [10] *Div.*

In professing these views Cicero was neither an eccentric philosopher nor an irresponsible statesman. He stood at the very end of a long and remarkable political and philosophical tradition. Three years before the composition of the *De divinatione* Marcus Terentius Varro propounded in 47 similar views in his *Antiquitates rerum divinarum,* which he quite characteristically dedicated to Caesar, who certainly was not a paragon of blind piety. Varro took up and elaborated the doctrine of the three kinds of theology formulated by the eminent *pontifex maximus* and jurisprudent, Q. Mucius Scaevola, probably to be identified with the consul of 95. According to Scaevola and Varro there exist three kinds of teachings about the gods: the teaching of the poets, of the philosophers, and of the *principes civitatis.* The *genus mythicon,* the tradition about the gods handed down by the poets, is utter nonsense. The *genus physicon,* the teaching of the philosophers, may contain truth, but it is hardly of any use for the commonwealth, and the common people may be disturbed and confused by it. What the philosophers say often runs counter to common practices and beliefs, and thus sows scepticism and undermines authority. In philosophy there are many questions that can be tolerated within the walls of the lecture room, but not in the market place.[11] Common people ought to be encouraged to honour gods, not to despise and disregard them. On the other hand the *genus civile,* the state religion directed by the *principes civitatis,* may sometimes be false, but it always is good and useful for the state.

Varro in his *Antiquitates* discussed the *res humanae* before the *res divinae.* He justified this procedure by pointing out that the painter exists before the picture, the builder before the building. Similarly human communities exist before their institutions. This does not mean, however, that he discarded the gods altogether.

2.42-43,74. Cf. J. LINDERSKI, *Römischer Staat und Götterzeichen: zum Problem der obnuntiatio,* « Jahrb d. Universität Düsseldorf », 1969-70, pp. 312 ff.; for an interpretation of the term *fulmen sinistrum,* see I.O.M. VALETON, *De modis auspicandi Romanorum,* « Mnemosyne », 17, 1889, 292-308. [11] Varro in August. *C.D.* 6.5: ' Sic alia, quae facilius intra parietes in schola quam extra in foro ferre possunt aures '. Cf. Cic. *Div.* 2.28: ' soli sumus; licet verum exquirere sine invidia, mihi praesertim de plerisque dubitanti '.

Varro did not treat of what he regarded as the real nature of the
gods, but only of Roman religious institutions as they had developed in the course of Roman history. He says that if he had not
been merely describing the customs of Rome, but were himself
founding the Roman state anew, he would have introduced the
gods and the worship of them according to the rules of nature
(he does not explain what those rules are). But in an existing society one is bound to uphold traditional customs and traditional
beliefs.[12]

Polybius, like de Tocqueville [13] in nineteenth century America,
found in the cult of gods that quality in which the Romans were
most distinctly superior to other nations. It is *deisidaimonia* or
superstition that maintains cohesion of the Roman state. If the
society were composed of sages this would not be necessary. The
fickle multitude is, however, full of lawless desires, irrational anger
and violent passion, and it can be held in check only by unseen
terrors and religious mummery. The ancients acted wisely, Polybius
concludes, in introducing among the poeple beliefs in gods and in
terrors in the afterlife. The moderns are foolish when they try to
abolish such useful superstitions.[14]

---

[12] For the views of Scaevola and Varro, see the polemical accounts of
Augustine, *C.D.* 4.27,31; 6.5-6,12; 7.5-6 and Tertullian, *Ad nat.* 2.1.8-15. For
a recent edition with commentary of the fragments of Varro, see B. CARDAUNS,
M. Terentius Varro: Antiquitates Rerum Divinarum I.18-21; II.139-145 (« Abh.
Mainz », Einzelschriften, Wiesbaden, 1976), and for a detailed discussion of
modern interpretations of the *theologia tripertita*, see G. LIEBERG, *Die 'theologia tripertita' in Forschung und Bezeugung, ANRW* I.IV (1973), pp. 63-115.
Cf. also H. D. JOCELYN, *The Roman Nobility and the Religion of the Republican State*, « Journal of Religious History », 4, 1966, 89 ff., esp. 90-93.

[13] *De la Démocratie en Amérique* vol. I, part II, ch. 9; vol. II, ch. 5.
Cf. B. FABIAN, *Alexis de Tocquevilles Amerikabild* (Heidelberg, 1957), pp. 58 ff.

[14] Polyb. 6.56.6-12 (with Walbank's commentary ad loc.); cf. 16.12. P. PÉ-
DECH, *Les idées religieuses de Polybe,* « Revue de l'hist. des religions », 167,
1965, 35-68, comes to the conclusion that ' la religion de Polybe est-elle moins
une position personnelle que l'adhésion à un fait social dont on saisit les
multiples aspects dans les milieux qu'il a fréquentés ' (p. 63); at the same time
Polybius ' n'est donc pas un esprit irréligieux ni même indifférent ' (p. 67).
Not very illuminating. Cf. the polemic by A. J. L. VAN HOFF, *Polybius' Reason
and Religion*, « Klio », 59, 1977, 101-128, esp. 115 ff. Certainly a great majority

The ideas about the character of the popular religion held by Polybius, Scaevola, Varro, Marcellus and Cicero, were for the first time expressed and widely discussed in fifth and fourth century Athens. The author of the drama *Sisyphos*, whether Euripides or Kritias,[15] the notorious leader of the Thirty Tyrants, puts into the mouth of Sisyphos the statement that the gods were a tricky contrivance of a certain crafty and clever man in order to terrorize the multitude into blind submission. Laws and punishments — he continues — are not a sufficient basis for a stable human society. Fear of gods, who hear and see everything, is necessary to prevent men from committing hidden crimes. In the preserved fragment the author does not say anything about the origin of divination; he mentions, however, superstitious fear caused by thunder and lightning, the divinatory interpretation of which was introduced, as Cicero says, only *rei publicae causa*.

Of importance in this theory is the idea of deception practiced by some superior men, the *principes civitatis* of Varro and Scaevola,

---

of Roman *principes civitatis* were not conscious (cynical, some would say) 'manipulators' of religion in the sense of L. R. TAYLOR (cf. her book *Party Politics in the Age of Caesar*, Berkeley, 1949, ch. iv: 'Manipulating the State Religion', pp. 76-97). Polybius attributes also to the aristocrats a great deal of δεισιδαιμονία. As a class they did not distinguish between belief and manipulation, as has been true of every successful social group which saw in religion, secular (as Marxism) or 'revealed', the mainstay and legitimation of their rule. Cf. the illuminating remarks by H. D. JOCELYN, op. cit. (above, n. 12), 98 ff. On the religious climate of the second century, see E. RAWSON, *Scipio, Laelius and the Ancestral Religion*, « JRS », 63, 1973, 161-174; Eadem, *Religion and Politics in the Late Second Century B.C. at Rome*, « Phoenix », 1974, 193-212.   15 H. DIELS and W. KRANZ, *Die Fragmente der Vorsokratiker*, II⁹, 88 B 25 (pp. 386-389). The fragment has traditionally been attributed to Kritias; A DIHLE, *Das Satyrspiel Sisyphos*, « Hermes », 105, 1977, 28-42, ascribes it to Euripides. A. HENRICHS, *Two Doxographical Notes: Democritus and Prodicus on Religion*, « HSCP », 79, 1975, 93-123, esp. 109-113, has demonstrated that for Prodikos too ' there had been a time when there was man but no gods yet ' (p. 112). He rightly stresses the connection between the theories of Kritias and Prodikos and the then current ' emphasis on language as a convention which enabled man to name and thus to create and to dictate new social values, including (for Protagoras) religion or even (for Critias and Prodicus) the very gods ' (p. 112 n. 67). Yet the idea of deliberate deception seems to have been absent from Prodikos' theory of religion.

with respect to uneducated and disorderly masses. But for this mode of thought it is possible to find a more venerable and influential archegetes than Kritias or even Euripides. It is none other than Plato. It has recently been pointed out that there exists a striking similarity between Plato's famous doctrine of γενναῖον ψεῦδος and the ideas of Kritias, Polybius or Cicero.[16] Plato condemns on the one hand the relativistic teachings of the nature of gods, for this is the beginning of all disorders and leads to the rule of the stronger, not better (*Leg.* 10.889c-890a). On the other

---

[16] Plato, *Rep.* 3.414-415d. See K. Döring, *Antike Theorien über die staatspolitische Notwendigkeit der Götterfurcht*, « Antike u. Abendland », 24, 1978, 43-56, an excellent study, to which I am indebted in more than one way. Cf. also B. Farrington, *Science and Politics in the Ancient World* (London, 1939), pp. 88 ff.; W. K. Guthrie, *A History of Greek Philosophy*, III (Cambridge 1969), pp. 243 ff.; W. Burkert, *Griechische Religion* (Stuttgart, 1977), pp. 371-373. Of course we have to distinguish between the outright invention of gods by a lawgiver and the more moderate ideas concerning the social usefulness of religion. To many minds traditional or popular religion was a fiction, but a useful one. Cf. Cic. *N.D.* 1.118 (Cotta speaking): ' Ii qui dixerunt totam de dis immortalibus opinionem fictam esse ab hominibus sapientibus rei publicae causa, ut quos ratio non posset eos ad officium religio duceret, nonne omnem religionem funditus sustulerunt? ', and for a collection of passages, see Pease ad loc. (pp. 513-514) and Walbank ad Polyb. 6.56 (pp. 741-742). F. Solmsen, *Theophrastus and Political Aspects of the Belief in Providence*, « GRBS », 19, 1978, 91-98, esp. 93, calls attention to the hitherto rather neglected (but cf. Pease, loc. cit. and Döring, op. cit. 50) opinion of Aristotle on the subject, *Met.* 12.8.19 (1074 b): part of religious tradition was added πρὸς τὴν πειθὼ τῶν πολλῶν καὶ πρὸς τὴν εἰς τοὺς νόμους καὶ τὸ συμφέρον χρῆσιν. Solmsen also adduces (pp. 91-92) the text of Damascius, who, commenting on Plato, *Phaedo* 113e, and trying to explain why the worst souls will never leave Tartarus, expresses the following thought: πῶς οὐδέποτε ἐξίασιν; ἢ πολιτικῶς ἔψευσται ἵνα εὐλαβῶνται αἱ ψυχαὶ τὰ ἀνήκεστα τῶν ἁμαρτημάτων (L. G. Westerink, *The Greek Commentaries on Plato's Phaedo: II, Damascius*, Amsterdam, 1977, p. 147). Not without interest in this context is the opinion of Augustine expressed in a letter to Jerome (Hier. *Ep.* 56.3): ' Alia quippe quaestio est sitne aliquando mentiri viri boni, et alia quaestio est utrum scriptorem sanctarum scripturarum mentiri oportuerit '. On the idea of deception, see also A. Wacke, *Circumscribere und dolus*, « Zeitschr. d. Savigny-Stiftung f. Rechtsgeschichte », 94, 1977, 221-228, who especially discusses the concept of *dolus bonus* (Ulp. *Dig.* 4.3.1.3) in Roman law, but does not touch upon the problem of deception in religion (except the praiseworthy deception of demons by honest people).

hand to govern his ideal state he employs deception in a way that can hardly be surpassed. But his premise is that in his *Politeia* the rulers govern because they are wise and good, not because they are wily and strong.[17] Good and wise rulers will employ fiction and deceit for the benefit of their subjects in the same way doctors apply medicine for the benefit of their patients. For eugenic purposes in order to mate the best of men with the best of women as often as possible, and the inferior men with the inferior women as seldom as possible, the rulers will have to employ fiction and deceit. They will have to devise an ingenious system of drawing lots so that inferior guardians who will go empty-handed would blame the lot and not the ruler. The lot was commonly regarded as an expression of impartial divine will, and Plato enacts that the mating or marriage festivals be accompanied by religious sacrifices.[18]

The Roman state did not advance that far in the use of the lot for the benefit of its citizens, but some remarkable cases show that the *principes civitatis*, presumably without having ever read Plato, knew well how to manipulate the lot to their advantage at election and distribution of provinces.[19] But it was above all Roman writers of historical fiction, and most particularly those whose works dealt with Roman origins, who were busy composing a Roman version of Plato's *gennaion pseudos*. Many of them, the servants of the *principes civitatis*, tried to show that the state would be ruined if its guardians were not of gold but of bronze, that is if the lower classes reached the pinnacle of power occupied by the nobles.[20]

---

[17] As J. ANNAS points out in an inspiring article (*Plato and Common Morality*, « CQ », 28, 1978, 435-451), modern philosophy 'tends to give prominence to act-centered theories' (p. 444), whereas Plato was interested in the moral quality of the agent. For Plato just acts are the acts of the just agent.
[18] *Rep.* 5.459c-460b; cf. 3.382b-d, 3.389b-c. At *Leg.* 5.741b Plato characterizes the lot as a god. On the religious aspects of the lot, see V. EHRENBERG, *Losung*, RE, XIII (1927), 1461-1465.   [19] Cf. L. R. TAYLOR, *Roman Voting Assemblies* (Ann Arbor, 1966), pp. 73-74, 143-144; E. BADIAN, *Titus Quinctius Flamininus* (Lectures in Memory of L. Taft Semple, Cincinnati, 1970), pp. 30-32.   [20] This is the political message of Cicero's *De re publica* and of Livy's *History*. According to Cicero the best political system is such

Students of Cicero have often been bewildered by what seems at first sight a striking incongruity between the second book of the *De legibus* and the second book of the *De divinatione*. In the former Cicero appears as a staunch defender of received religion including divination and augury, but in the latter he declares divination to be nothing but superstition. Some scholars are inclined to interpret Cicero's attitude in *On Divination* as only a temporary lapse into scepticims, while others attempt to discover traces of scepticism even in the *De legibus*. Still others endeavour to find in Cicero's discourse on the *Laws* a proof of his genuine religious belief, but normally they do not bother to explain how one distinguishes genuine and non-genuine beliefs.[21] Or we are presented with the assertion that ' Cicero's religious views never touched the inner core of the man ' (whatever that means), and that, consequently, ' he did not have deep religious feelings ', which, however, should not surprise us, for as the author in question decides ' few could have them in that era without being superstitious '.[22] The meaning of all this is quite mysterious for it is only a declaration of irrational belief, not an argument. If we take one religion as an objective and true measure of the genuineness of the religiosity of another doctrine, we obviously prejudice the outcome of our inquiry.

Or we are told that Cicero had religious convictions, but not a religious mentality.[23] This is close to the mark, provided that we identify religious mentality with blind emotions and credulity, and

---

' ubi in suo quisque est gradu firmiter collocatus ' (*Rep.* 1.69). Livy praises Numa for having introduced into the commonwealth ' rem ad multitudinem imperitam et illis saeculis rudem efficacissimam, deorum metum ' (1.19.5, and cf. Ogilvie ad loc.).   [21] See A. S. PEASE, op. cit. (above, n. 2), pp. 10-12, who quotes a host of modern opinion. Cf. also R. J. GOAR, *Cicero and the State Religion* (Amsterdam, 1972), pp. 96 ff., esp. 102-104, 108-109.   [22] GOAR, op. cit., p. 111. H. DÖRRIE, *Ciceros Entwurf zu einer Neuordnung des römischen Sakralwesens. Zu den geistigen Grundlagen von de legibus, Buch 2, Classica et Mediaevalia Francisco Blatt dedicata* (Copenhagen, 1973), p. 240, has reached another extreme. We are invited to believe that ' Cicero, dessen Verständnis von *religio* durch das Ja! zu einer absoluten Werte-Ordnung bestimmt ist, wird damit zum Vorläufer dessen, was Platonismus und Christentum verwirklichen sollten '.   [23] M. VAN DEN BRUWAENE, *La théologie de Cicéron* (Louvain, 1937), p. 245.

discard logical argument and intellectual reflection as a form of religious thought.

The theory of the *genus civile* and the *genus physicon* or *naturale* of religion offers a sufficient basis for explaining and comprehending Cicero's attitude to religion and divination. In the *De re publica* and *De legibus* Cicero discourses and legislates as a *princeps civitatis*; in the *De natura deorum* and *De divinatione* he presents his views as a philosopher.

His argument in his books on divination does not apply exclusively to the validity of divination, but in fact it also pertains to the philosophical validity of the whole *genus civile*. When Cicero ridicules the story of Tages, the discoverer of the Etruscan discipline, when he discards *exta, ostenta* and *fulgura* (*Div.* 2.28-69, esp. 42,50), he does not demolish something that is accidental to the Etruscan religion, he demolishes its very essence. He abolishes the Etruscan religion as it was maintained by the *lucumones*, the Etruscan *principes civitatis*. No protestations to the contrary will help to alter this obvious fact.

In arguing against divination from the flight of birds Cicero points to the great variety among different nations as to the kinds of birds observed and the method of observation. Often the same signs have the opposite meaning (*Div.* 2.76). For the Greeks thunder on the right is a favourable sign, for the Romans on the left.[24] It is not difficult to see that this argument may easily be extended to embrace all forms of popular cults, all *genus civile*. In fact in the third book of the *De re publica* Cicero has L. Furius Philus reproduce the argument of Karneades that religion and justice as practised in various countries are based on convention and not on nature.[25] Varro also was of the opinion that received religion

---

[24] *Div.* 2.82-83. Unfortunately we cannot discuss here the fascinating but commonly misunderstood system of augural orientation; for a detailed study, see J. LINDERSKI, *The Augural Law*, ANRW II.xvi.3 (forthcoming). [25] *Rep.* 3,8-31. Cf. J.-L. FERRARY, *Le discours de Philus et la philosophie de Carnéade*, « REL », 55, 1977, 128-156. For a collection of the fragments of Karneades, see B. WIŚNIEWSKI, *Karneades. Fragmente, Text und Kommentar* (Wroclaw, 1970).

did not conform to the exigencies of the *genus naturale*. In other
words, it was false (August. *C.D.* 4.27,31). Cicero the philosopher
was of one mind with Varro. Of all Roman cults he ultimately
retains as conforming to nature only the belief in gods, and he formulates it in most general terms: ' The beauty of the universe and
the celestial order compel me to confess that there exists some
superior and eternal Being who deserves human acknowledgement
and admiration ' (*Div.* 2.148). The worship which springs from the
knowledge of nature is to be cultivated, but all forms of superstition (like divination) should be extirpated (*Div.* 2.143).

Two problems arise in this connection. First, the kind of natural religion Cicero had in mind. Second, why he was so violently
opposed to divination. In the *De divinatione* Cicero does not present
any system of natural religion, nor does Varro in his *Divine Antiquities*. In his treatises *De re publica* and *De legibus* Cicero, imitating Plato, was engaged in constructing if not an ideal then
at least the best possible state. It so happened that this state
proved to be the Roman state, only slightly improved according
to the precepts of the optimate political doctrine, purged of demagogues, seditious tribunes and all other undesirable elements,
with the *boni* in full control at the helm of the government. Since
Scipio offered in the *De re publica* a clear proof that the early
Roman state was the best in the world, it had also to be provided
with the best laws (*Leg.* 1.20; 2.23). The best laws are such laws
as are congruous with the law of nature (*Rep.* 3.33), and that law
is of universal application, unchanging and everlasting (*Leg.* 2.8).
Not all statutes put in force by various nations deserve to be called
laws. In fact not all Roman laws are true laws made in agreement
with nature and containing a right distinction between things just
and unjust (*Leg.* 1.42; 2.13).

It is of some interest to look more closely at those laws which
according to Cicero deviated from that conformity to nature that
was so characteristic of the Roman state. As an example Cicero
adduces the *lex Valeria* concerning the dictatorship of Sulla, which
authorized the dictator to put to death with impunity any citizen,
and he compares it to the notorious laws passed by the Thirty

Tyrants in Athens.[26] The *lex Valeria* was indeed the ultimate basis of Sullan proscriptions; in this connection it may not be amiss to mention that in 63 Cicero as consul successfully opposed an attempt to allow the sons of the proscribed to stand for offices. This measure, he argued, would threaten the political stability of the republic.[27] The *utilitas rei publicae* and the lofty principles of natural law obviously were not one and the same thing. And Cicero spoke a different language in his speeches and his theoretical works. But for our purpose more instructive is the case of the *lex Titia,* and the *leges Appuleiae* and *Liviae.* Cicero regarded them as null and void, which is of course understandable for they were passed by wicked and seditious tribunes. They were abolished by the senate ' in one sentence and in a single moment '. How different are the laws of nature: they cannot be abolished or abrogated, nor can be abolished those statutes that conform to the principles of nature, like the laws which Cicero promulgated for his ideal state (*Leg.* 2.14).

The circumstances of the annulment of the Titian, Appuleian and Livian laws deserve attention. The first of them was an agrarian bill proposed by Sex. Titius, tribune of the plebs in 99, an admirer of Appuleius Saturninus, ' gratiosus apud populum ', and hence for Cicero ' seditiosus civis et turbulentus '.[28] He pushed his bill through the *concilium plebis* despite a very bad omen: two ravens fighting with each other flew over the assembly. The haruspices interpreted this as a *prodigium* and advised a *procuratio,* the augurs were also called in and on the recommendation of the college the senate invalidated the *lex Titia* as carried against the auspices.[29]

---

[26] *Leg.* 1.42; *Leg. agr.* 3.5. On the *lex Valeria,* see the clear exposition of E. GABBA, *Appiani Bellorum Civilium Liber Primus* (Firenze, 1958), pp. 341-342.   [27] Cic. *Pis.* 4; Plut. *Cic.* 12.2; Cass. Dio 37.25.3; Quint. 11.1.85. Cf. W. DRUMANN-P. GROEBE, *Geschichte Roms* 5 (Leipzig, 1919), pp. 461-462.   [28] Cic. *De orat.* 2.48; Val. Max. 8.1 Damn. 3.   [29] Obseq. 46; Cic. *Leg.* 2.14 in conjunction with 2.31. G. ROTONDI, *Leges Publicae Populi Romani* (Milano, 1912, repr. Hildesheim, 1962), p. 333; G. NOCERA, *Il potere dei comizi e i suoi limiti* (Milano, 1940), p. 238 and J. BLEICKEN, *Lex publica* (Berlin, 1975), p. 465, mistakenly speak of the *obnuntiatio* of the haruspices. Cf. E. J. WEINRIB, *Obnuntiatio: Two Problems,* « Zeitschr. d. Savigny-Stiftung f. Rechtsgeschichte », 87, 1970, 398 n. 13.

Appuleius Saturninus also carried his laws *per vim* and *contra auspicia*. His agrarian law was passed amid a storm, a notoriously adverse omen for popular assemblies. When the voting was to commence, thunder was heard.[30] The nobles demanded that Saturninus dissolve the gathering and abandon his project, whereupon he retorted: ' It is going to hail, if you don't quiet down '.[31] His jest was not only ' a veiled threat of a *lapidatio* ',[32] always a potent argument at Roman votings, but also a deft pun upon an augural rule. Thunder was classified by the augurs as *vitium,* but if it simultaneously thundered and hailed, they used to call it *vitium et calamitas.*[33] Jupiter sent thunder, and Saturninus, for his part, was ready to produce hail in the shape of a *lapidatio,* and in this way to create conditions for the occurrence of augural *calamitas.* In a sense his joke came true for ultimately he was stoned to death.[34] The Livian laws were also passed against the auspices.[35]

The laws singled out by Cicero for criticism were *nullae leges* not only because of their anti-optimate character, but above all because their rogators disregarded the auspices. Thus thunder, storm, lightning or the fighting ravens turn out to be genuine divine signs, and to disregard them means to disregard the will of the gods. And so divination is not superstition at all; it conforms to the law of nature. Consequently Cicero admits to his ideal state the Sibylline books, the haruspices, and naturally the augurs, about whose elevated position he sings a eulogy (*Leg.* 2.31).

On a theoretical level we have the following train of argument: a) the laws and institutions of the Roman state are the best in the world b) they are practically in full agreement with the law of nature c) divination forms an integral and legitimate part of

---

[30] App. *Bell. Civ.* 1.133, cf. 136, and see GABBA (above, n. 26), ad loc.
[31] Auct. *De vir. ill.* 73.7: ' Huic legi multi nobiles obrogantes (obnuntiantes?), cum tonuisset, clamarunt: Iam, inquit, nisi quiescetis, grandinabit '. A. W. LINTOTT, *Violence in Republican Rome* (Oxford, 1968), p. 136, erroneously connects this anecdote with ' the bill for Metellus' outlawry '.   [32] So LINTOTT, op. cit., p. 136 n. 3.   [33] Donat., *Comm. Terent., Hecyra* 2, p. 193 Wessner: ' « vitium » enim est, si tonet tantum, « vitium et calamitas » vero, si tonet et grandinet simul vel etiam fulminet '.   [34] Auct. *De vir. ill.* 73.11; Flor. 2.4.6.   [35] Cic. *Leg.* 2.14,31; Ascon, *in Corn.* 68-69 C.

Roman religious system d) it follows that divination conforms to nature, and Cicero's task in his capacity as a statesman was to prove the correctness of this conclusion. He falls back upon two standard Stoic arguments. If we admit that the gods exist, that they rule the universe, and give advice to men by sending signs of future events, then we cannot deny the existence of divination (*Leg.* 2.32-33; cf. *Div.* 1.82). In the second book of the *De divinatione* (2.101-102, 104-106) Cicero ridiculed this train of reasoning, and its inanity is indeed obvious. Yet the statesman who wanted to maintain and justify the existing order had no other choice but to accept its validity.

The other argument in favour of divination which Cicero embraces in the *De legibus* was also combatted by him in the *De divinatione*. It is a staple Stoic argument *e consensu omnium*. The validity of augury is borne out by the historical experience of Rome, and of all kingdoms, peoples and nations. Ancient seers, and finally Romulus himself and Attus Navius, testify to its truthfulness.[36] A Roman statesman could disregard opinions of foreign nations and deride the beliefs of the mob, but he could not ignore Romulus and Attus Navius.[37] He could not dismiss the *augustum augurium* which in popular belief and in learned tradition was both the beginning of Rome and the basis of her greatness.[38] Even Cicero the sceptical academician concedes that Romulus believed in divination by augury; of course he erred in this, as in general the ancients held erroneous views on many subjects (*Div.* 2.70). This is an interesting statement if we compare it with the praise of the

---

[36] *Leg.* 2.33. Cf. above, n. 6 and R. SCHIAN, *Untersuchungen über das 'argumentum e consensu omnium'* (Hildesheim, 1973), pp. 142 ff.   [37] As Cicero the philosopher does, *Div.* 2.80-81.   [38] Ennius, *Ann.* 77 ff., 501-502 V.²; Cic. *Div.* 1.107. Cf. H. D. JOCELYN, *Urbs augurio augusto condita*, « PCPS », 17, 1971, pp. 44-51. See also Cic. *N.D.* 3.5 (Cotta speaking): 'Cumque omnis populi Romani religio in sacra et in auspicia divisa est, tertium adiunctum sit si quid praedictionis causa ex portentis et monstris Sibyllae interpretes haruspicesve monuerunt, harum ego religionum nullam umquam contemnendam putavi mihique ita persuasi Romulum auspiciis, Numam sacris constitutis fundamenta iecisse nostrae civitatis, quae numquam profecto sine summa placatione deorum immortalium tanta esse potuisset'.

mos maiorum and wisdom of the ancients constantly flowing from the mouth of Cicero the orator.

The aim of the legislation about the augurs which Cicero promulgates in the *Laws* (2.20-21) was to restore augury to its pristine state. He admits that the real agural art by means of which it was possible to make truthful predictions, such as did exist in the times of Romulus and Attus Navius, has by now faded out of existence because of negligence and the great lapse of time. Also in his treatises on the nature of gods and on divination Cicero assails the negligence of the college of augurs in maintaining the augural tradition.[39] But his complaint that ' ars ' and ' disciplina vetustate evanuerit ' is rather surprising. For it was a firm tenet of Stoic philosophy that the so-called artificial divination, of which augury was one branch, was precisely a result of *observatio diuturna*, the process of long-continued observation. Such an empirical observation of the signs and the events that followed upon them is the foundation of divinatory knowledge, the *scientia*. And it is *vetustas* that produces this knowledge.[40] In the *De divinatione* Cicero fully accepts the opinion of Claudius Marcellus, who maintained that augury had no divinatory value and was established solely for reason of State.[41] In the *De legibus* he states on the other

---

[39] *Leg.* 2.33: ' Sed dubium non est quin haec disciplina et ars augurum evanuerit iam et vetustate et neglegentia '; *N.D.* 2.9: ' Sed neglegentia nobilitatis augurii disciplina omissa veritas auspiciorum spreta est, species tantum retenta '; *Div.* 2.76-77.   [40] On the concepts of a) artificial divination, see Cic. *Div.* 1.11,34,72; 2.26 (and Pease's comments ad locc.); A. BOUCHÉ-LECLERCQ, *Histoire de la divination dans l'antiquité* I (Paris, 1879), pp. 58-63; P. FINGER, *Die zwei mantischen Systeme in Ciceros Schrift über die Weissagung (De Divinatione I)*, « RhM », 78, 1929, 371-397; F. PFEFFER, *Studien zur Mantik in der Philosophie der Antike* (Meisenheim, 1976), pp. 88-95; b) *observatio diuturna*, see Cic. *Div.* 1.12,34,72; 2.26,28,42,146; *N.D.* 2.166; c) *scientia* and *vetustas*, see Cic. *Leg.* 2.33; *Div.* 1.1-2, 34 and esp. 109: ' Quae enim extis, quae fulgoribus, quae portentis, quae astris praesentiuntur, haec notata sunt observatione diuturna. Adfert autem vetustas omnibus in rebus longinqua observatione incredibilem scientiam '. For a comprehensive discussion of all these concepts, see P. REGELL, *De augurum publicorum libris* (Diss. Vratislaviae, 1878), pp. 3-7; J. LINDERSKI, *The Augural Law, ANRW*, II.xvi.3, chapter 4 (forthcoming).   [41] *Div.* 2.75: ' Equidem adsentior C. Marcello [praet. 70] potius quam App. Claudio [cos. 54, cens. 50], qui ambo mei collegae fuerunt,

hand that in ancient times (*apud maiores*) the science of augury was of double character. It was used most often *ad agendi consilium,* and occasionally *ad rei publicae tempus.*[42] This distinction is most revealing. The *consilium agendi* refers to the use of the auspices in connection with magisterial activities, that is, it refers to the observation and announcement of both solicited and unsolicited or impetrative and oblative signs. The context seems to indicate that in this place Cicero embraces the view of Appius Claudius, according to whom the art of augury was at least to some extent capable of divination.[43] Yet in the *De divinatione* Cicero upholds a diametrically opposite view. It is not difficult for him — he says — though he himself is an augur, to argue against the auspices. For the Roman augurs are not like the augurs of the Marsi; the Roman augurs do not claim to foretell the future by observing the flight

existimoque ius augurum, etsi divinationis opinione principio constitutum sit, tamen postea rei publicae causa conservatum ac retentum '; 2.70: ' retinetur autem et ad opinionem vulgi et ad magnas utilitates rei publicae mos, religio, disciplina, ius augurium, collegi auctoritas '; *Leg.* 2.32 (Atticus speaking): ' est in conlegio vestro inter Marcellum et Appium optimos augures magna dissensio — nam eorum ego in libros incidi —, cum alteri placeat auspicia ista ad utilitatem esse rei publicae composita, alteri disciplina vestra quasi divinare videantur posse '. [42] *Leg.* 2.33: ' Ita neque illi [sc. Marcello] adsentior, qui hanc scientiam negat umquam in nostro collegio fuisse, neque illi [sc. Appio], qui esse etiam nunc putat. Quae mihi videtur apud maiores fuisse duplex, ut ad rei publicae tempus nonnumquam, ad agendi consilium saepissime pertineret '. On the expression *rei publicae tempus,* see A. Du Mesnil, *M. Tullii Ciceronis de legibus libri tres* (Leipzig, 1879), ad loc., p. 138.

[43] Cicero characterizes Appius as ' cum auguralis tum omnis publici iuris antiquitatisque nostrae bene peritus ' (*Brut.* 267). For his augural views and theories, see *Div.* 1.27-28 (with Pease's note, p. 133), 29 (Pease, pp. 137-140; J. Bayet, *Les malédictions du tribun C. Ateius Capito, Hommages à G. Dumézil* [Collection Latomus 45, Bruxelles, 1960], pp. 31-45), 105 (Quintus speaking): ' Cui quidem auguri (sc. Appio Claudio) vehementer adsentior; solus enim multorum annorum memoria non decantandi auguri sed divinandi tenuit disciplinam. Quem inridebant collegae tui eumque tum Pisidam, tum Soranum augurem esse dicebant; quibus nulla videbatur in auguriis aut praesensio aut scientia veritatis futurae; sapienter, aiebant, ad opinionem imperitorum esse fictas religiones ' (cf. Pease ad loc., pp. 288-289). R. Syme's memorable judgement of Appius is worth recalling (*The Roman Revolution,* Oxford, 1939, p. 45): ' proud, corrupt and superstitious '.

of birds and other signs (*Div.* 2.70). It is important to note that
Cicero here speaks as an augur, and not as a sceptical philosopher.
The discrepancy between this passage and his views expressed in
the *Laws* assumes a special significance. It is not a discrepancy
between a philosophical and an augural theory, but rather a discrepancy between two rival augural doctrines.

We have to keep in mind that augural signs referred only
to action and not to status. It was the *prodigia* which indicated
the status of things, and the interpretation of the prodigies was
in the charge of the haruspices and *decemviri.* The distinction
between action and status constitutes a basic concept of Roman
divination. The auspices were valid for one day only; the validity
of the prodigies had no strict time limit.[44] The wrath of the gods
portended by a prodigy could be averted by a proper action, a
procuratio or *supplicatio,* which was normally ordered by the senate
on the basis of advice from the pontiffs and the technical expertise
provided by the haruspices or *decemviri.* The augurs had nothing
to do with the prodigies and their *procurationes.* A sign could,
however, function at the same time as an *auspicium malum* and a
prodigy. It could simultaneously refer to an official action and to
the status of the republic. As far as the action was concerned the
gods either allowed or prohibited it. The positive outcome of an
auspication was hardly a prediction of the future for it did not
automatically guarantee a success. It only indicated divine permission to proceed with the proposed action.

Doctrinally and theologically more interesting are negative
signs. If a negative sign occurred at the auspication itself the magistrate was obliged to abandon his undertaking. If it appeared
after the beginning of an action the magistrate in charge was obliged
to discontinue his undertaking immediately. Thus the negative sign
could be taken to function as a simple prohibition without any
divinatory ingredient. And it seems to be this interpretation that

---

[44] This is typified by the augural formula ' alio die ' (Cic *Leg.* 2.31; *Phil.*
2.82,84. For other sources, see P. CATALANO, *Contributi allo studio del diritto
augurale,* I [Torino, 1960], pp. 42 ff.). On the prodigies, see above all L.
WÜLKER, *Die geschichtliche Entwicklung des Prodigienwesens bei den Römern*
(Diss. Leipzig, 1903).

Cicero put forth in the *De divinatione*. The augural sign was not a disclosure of an inflexible verdict of fate, nor was its announcement by the augur a prediction of the future. It was only a warning. However, it is possible to argue that the warning given by the *auspicium infaustum* or *malum* was also a premonition disregard of which would result in calamity. Thus the negative sign could be held to offer a glimpse of the future, to function as a qualified prediction, which was fulfilled only in case the warning was disregarded. This was the view defended by Appius Claudius and adopted by Cicero in the *De legibus*.[45]. The augural doctrine like most theological systems was not a monolithic theory and it allowed for divergent interpretations of even its essential tenets. This throws an interesting light on Cicero's argument in the *Laws* and in *On Divination*. When Cicero states in the former work ' non video cur esse divinationem negem ' (2.32), it is hardly possible to find in this guarded statement an echo of academic scepticism. It is rather a critical allusion to the rival augural theory, which Cicero so emphatically accepts in the *De divinatione,* according to which the Roman augurs did not claim to predict the future.

But politically most significant is Cicero's admission that the *auspicia* and *scientia augurum* also pertained to *rei publicae tempus,* that they were of particular use in critical times for the state. This aspect of the role of the auspices completely overshadows in Cicero's presentation their function as *consilium agendi.* In his legislation Cicero grants to all magistrates the right to auspices, ' omnes magistratus auspicium habento ' (*Leg.* 3.10). One would expect that the magistrates are given the auspices in order to be able to perform their actions *auspicato,* with the approval of the

[45] *Leg.* 2.21: '(augures) divorum iras providento sisque apparento '; *N.D.* 2.163: ' multa cernunt haruspices, multa augures provident, multa oraclis declarantur, multa vaticinationibus, multa portentis; quibus cognitis ... multa ... pericula depulsa sunt ' (for *pericula depellere*, cf. Val. Max. 1.1.1; Plin. *N.H.* 28.11; Verg. *Aen.* 3.327-328 and Serv. auct. ad loc.); *Div.* 1.29: ' etenim dirae, sicut cetera auspicia, ut omina, ut signa, non causas adferunt cur quid eveniat, sed nuntiant eventura nisi provideris '. Crassus did not obey the *obnuntiatio dirarum* of Ateius, and he perished with his army. For a detailed discussion, see J. LINDERSKI, *The Augural Law, ANRW,* II.xvi.3, esp. n. 198 (forthcoming).

gods. But in Cicero's state the magistrates have the auspices primarily in order to impede *inutiles comitiatus*.[46] This throws bright light on Cicero's political preoccupations and expectations; he did not believe that even his ideal Rome would be free from popular demagogues. Cicero develops this thought in a remarkable passage, *De legibus* 3.43. A good augur has to remember that in great emergencies (*maximis rei publicae temporibus*) he ought to be at hand to rescue the state from danger. By what means could he achieve this task?

He was able to save the Republic thanks to his position as *consiliarius et administer Iovis*. The meaning of this statement is not immediately clear, and Cicero felt he had to explain it. He elucidates the position of the augur as 'advisor' of Jupiter by comparing him to the person who assisted at the auspication. The augur performs with respect to Jupiter the same role as the assistant with respect to the auspicant. Once the auspicant had selected his assistant, and entrusted him with material observation of signs, the assistant's *nuntiatio* was binding on the celebrant.[47] The assistant's report was valid even if it was faked, even if he reported signs that had never appeared.[48] In a similar way Jupiter was bound by the augur's announcement. There is nothing primitive in this way of thinking. It expresses an active, bold but careful attitude of the Romans toward supernatural powers; one should do whatever one can to appease them, but also whenever it was possible one should try to gain control over them. This attitude is very revealing for the proper understanding of Roman augural religion. Like everybody else, the deity had to serve the state. Jupiter had to help the *boni* to suppress subversive elements.

---

[46] *Leg.* 3.27: 'Deinceps igitur omnibus magistratibus auspicia et iudicia dantur, ... auspicia ut multos inutiles comitiatus probabiles impedirent morae. saepe enim populi impetum iniustum auspiciis dii immortales represserunt'.

[47] T. MOMMSEN'S statement to the contrary, *Römisches Staatsrecht* I[3] (Leipzig, 1887), p. 106, is not correct. The auspicant could disregard the *nuntiatio* of the *pullarius*, but he did this at his own risk, see Cic. *Div.* 1.78; Livy 41.18.14.   [48] The *locus classicus* is Livy 10.40.11 (the consul L. Papirius speaking): qui auspicio adest, si quid falsi nuntiat, in semet ipsum religionem recipit; mihi quidem tripudium nuntiatum, populo Romano exercituique egregium auspicium est'.

Cicero's speeches can be read as a running commentary to this doctrine.[49] The auspices are proclaimed the foundation stone of the Roman state (*Vat.* 23). The *principes civitatis* are exhorted to protect and defend the auspices even at the risk of their lives (*Sest.* 98). The *leges Aelia* and *Fufia* which regulated the use of *obnuntiatio*,[50] the binding announcement of unfavourable signs by magistrates and tribunes, Cicero describes as ' propugnacula murique tranquillitatis atque otii ' (*Pis.* 9) and as ' certissima subsidia rei publicae contra tribunicios furores ' (*Post red. in sen.* 11). They indeed very often checked and crippled the furor of subversive tribunes (*Vat.* 18). They endured amid the *ferocitas* of the Gracchi, the *audacia* of Saturninus, the *colluvio* under Drusus, the *contentio* of Sulpicius, the *cruor* under Cinna and the *arma* under Sulla (*Vat.* 23) .

The story of Attus Navius and Tarquinius Priscus offers a good illustration of the augural ethos of Roman optimates. Tarquinius wanted to increase the number of the *centuriae equitum,* and to name them after himself.[51] Attus Navius, ' inclutus ea tempestate augur ', warned the king, ' neque mutari neque novum constitui nisi aves addixissent posse '.[52] The original centuries were constituted by Romulus *inauguratio*, and now a new inauguration was necessary. It is not clear whether Tarquinius was represented as wanting to organize the new centuries without any augural ceremonies, but it is obvious that the augural validity of his undertaking was contested, and that Tarquinius nevertheless persisted in his project. Attus Navius then informed the king that he had consulted the

---

[49] Cf. U. HEIBGES, *The Religious Beliefs of Cicero's Time as Reflected in his Speeches* (Diss. Bryn Mawr, 1962), esp. pp. 86-128,137-146. [50] On the *leges Aelia* and *Fufia* and the *obnuntiatio*, see G. V. SUMMER, *Lex Aelia, Lex Fufia*, « AJP », 84, 1963, 337-358; A. E. ASTIN, *Leges Aelia et Fufia*, « Latomus », 23, 1964, 421-445; E. J. WEINRIB, op. cit. (above, n. 29), 395-425, and the still basic study by L. LANGE, *De legibus Aelia et Fufia commentatio, Kleine Schriften*, I (Göttingen, 1887), pp. 275-341 (originally published as *Universitätsprogramm* Giessen, 1861). [51] Livy 1.36.2-7 (with OGILVIE's commentary ad loc., pp. 150-151); Dion. Hal. 3.71; Cic. *Rep.* 2.36. [52] Livy 1.36.3; Cic. *Div.* 1.32-33 (cf. PEASE ad loc., pp. 145-148). For other sources, see G. PICCALUGA, *Attus Navius*, « Studi e Materiali di Storia delle Religioni », 40, 1969, 179 ff.

aves about the plan, and that the outcome of his consultation was
negative. Tarquinius was incensed, and wished to ridicule Attus'
augural skills. He asked him whether the thing of which he was
thinking could be done or not. Attus performed the augury and
answered that it could be done. And now Tarquinius triumphantly
revealed that he was thinking of cutting a whestone in two with
a razor. The whetstone was brought, and it was easily cut in two
with a razor. Jupiter did not abandon his *administer,* and restrained
the *impetus iniustus* of the king.[53] No wonder Attus Navius became
a paragon of an *optimus augur,* and his miracle inspired the *boni
augures* of the Ciceronian epoch in their struggle against encroach-
ment by the dynasts, the would-be kings of Rome. No miracle
happened this time.

But there is no doubt that the auspices and the augurs, the
portents and the haruspices had rendered great services to the *boni*
and the Republic. Why then was Cicero so determined to abolish
the belief in all forms of divination? Did he write his treatise on
divination only as a philosopher who with a Lucretian fervour
wished to free the minds of men from the shackles of superstition?
(cf. *Div.* 2.148). Or was he motivated by some political consideration as well?

Tarquinius Priscus may have respected the auspices. Caesar
and Antonius, Clodius and Vatinius did not. Caesar as consul and
Vatinius as tribune of the plebs disregarded in 59 the *obnuntiationes*
of the consul Bibulus and of three tribunes. Caesar wan an accomplished manipulator of men, gods and laws, and masterfully utilized the prescription of the augural law according to which the
announcement of an adverse omen had to be made in person. He
chased Bibulus by force from the Forum, and could claim that his
colleague failed to deliver personally the notice of *obnuntiatio.*[54]
As consul and *pontifex maximus* Caesar presided over the transition of Clodius to the plebs and, to use Cicero's expression, he
'released a foul and monstrous beast which had hitherto been bound

[53] See the sources in PICCALUGA, op. cit., 181 ff. For an augural interpretation, see I. O. M. VALETON, « Mnemosyne », 18, 1890, 440; 19, 1891, 411 n. 2.

[54] For this interpretation, see J. LINDERSKI, *Constitutional Aspects of
the Consular Elections in 59 B.C.,* « Historia », 14, 1965, 425-426.

by the auspices' (*Sest.* 16). During his tribunate in 58 Clodius passed a law which substantially restricted the use of *obnuntiatio* at legislative assemblies, and greatly facilitated his legislative program. P. Clodius, ' this fatal portent for the Republic' (*Pis.* 9), abolished the *lex Aelia* and *Fufia,* and in this conflagration, exclaims Cicero, ' perished the auspices and all public law ' (*Vat.* 18). Genuine anger and anxiety speak through these words, but certainly not genuine religious feeling, as some interpreters would like us to believe. Cicero regards with anger and apprehension the loss of auspices as the weapon of the *boni.* Caesar had won the battle for control of auspices before he won the battle of Pharsalos. And when he achieved supreme power, Lucan (*Phars.* 5.395-396) so describes the first elections under Caesar's dictatorship: ' Nobody is allowed to watch the sky for unfavourable omens; it thunders, but the augur is deaf. The calamitous owl appears on the left, but the auspices from the flight of birds are proclaimed to be most favourable '.

Augural symbolism, dreams, and predictions of the haruspices played a conspicuous role in the political propaganda throughout the course of civil wars.[55] Sulla placed augural symbols on his coins, Marius stressed his position as an augur. Cicero in his poem *Marius* describes his great compatriot as ' divini numinis augur ' who from the eastward flight of an eagle after a victorious struggle with a serpent drew the correct prediction of his glorious return to Rome (*Div.* 1.106). But excessive piety and belief in the *omina* over

---

[55] Cf. A. ALFÖLDI, *The Main Aspects of Political Propaganda on the Coinage of the Roman Republic, Essays in Roman Coinage Presented to Harold Mattingly* (Oxford, 1956), pp. 85-87; P. JAL, *La propagande religieuse à Rome au cours des guerres civiles,* « Ant. Class. », 30, 1961, 401 ff.; E. BADIAN, *Sulla's Augurate,* « Arethusa », 1, 1968, 26-46, and « Arethusa », 2, 1969, 199-201; J. R. FEARS, *The Coinage of Q. Cornificius and Augural Symbolism on Late Republican Denarii,* « Historia », 24, 1975, 592-602; Idem, *Princeps a Diis Electus* (Rome 1977), pp. 102 ff. Unfortunately most studies of the late republican augural symbolism are marred by the incorrect assumption that although the magistrates took the auspices only the augurs could interpret them. In fact the *magistratus cum imperio* entirely controlled their *auspicia impetrativa*; the *peritia* of an augur was, however, most helpful in the explication of the unsolicited divine signs.

which one lost control could be damaging. For instance, Cicero
remarks sarcastically, Pompeius placed great reliance on predictions
furnished by portents and the inspection of entrails. What assurances the haruspices gave to him, and what responses they sent
from Rome to the *boni* in the Pompeian camp in Greece! All of
them proved false, the result being nearly always contrary to the
prediction. Caesar on the other hand crossed over to Africa before
the winter solstice, although a famous haruspex, no doubt the notorious Spurinna, warned him not to do so. As a result he won a
victory for he landed before his enemies combined their forces
(*Div.* 2.52-53).

It is interesting to observe that Caesar in the *De bello Gallico*
and *De bello civili,* which were addressed to educated upper classes,
does not mention the auspices, omens or haruspices at all. Unlike
Sulla, who stressed his *felicitas* and intimate connection with the
gods who guided his steps through dreams, Caesar emphasized his
personal qualities as a leader in war and peace. He owed his victory
to himself and not to blind fortune. Yet for the benefit of his
soldiers and the *vulgus* he was wise enough to arrange miraculous
happenings as at the crossing of Rubicon, and the divinatory skills
of his personal haruspex Spurinna form a nice counterpart to the
prophetic fame enjoyed by Postumius, the haruspex of Sulla.

In Rome the fight for political power was also a fight for control over the gods.[57] It is important to realize that one can use
religion as a tool to maintain his domination regardless of whether
one treats religion only as a sham or finds in it divine and transcen-
dental values. But both sceptical-utilitarian and mystical-utilitarian
attitudes as represented respectively by Claudius Marcellus and
Appius Claudius presuppose the existence of a cohesive group of
principes civitatis who firmly keep in their grip both the society
and the gods. This condition, however, did not obtain any more
in the period of civil wars. Along with the old republic its religious
system too was torn apart.

---

[56] Suet. *Caes.* 32; 81.2. Cf. S. WEINSTOCK, *Divus Julius* (Oxford, 1971),
p. 344.   [57] Cf. P. JAL, *Les dieux et les guerres civiles dans la Rome de la
fin de la république,* « REL », 40, 1962, 170-200.

But if religion had lost its function as mainstay of the optimate republic, why did Cicero resolve to attack only divination ? He does not explicitly direct his criticism against *sacra* and *caerimoniae* (cf. *Div.* 1.148). In fact Cicero was not alone in this attitude. Not only the enlightened Euripides but also Plato spoke with sarcasm and hostility about diviners.[58] Cato the Elder ridiculed itinerant haruspices (Cic. *Div.* 2.51), and Ennius castigated ' superstitious prophets and shameless gut-gazers, clumsy or crazy ... men who don't know their own path yet point the way for another '.[59] The Roman senate on many occasions instructed the magistrates to burn subversive books containing dangerous philosophical or religious doctrines and to expel from the city philosophers and astrologers.[60]This criticism always referred, however, only to private unauthorized divination. It did not extend to divination as part of Roman state religion. But the fight for the gods reveals itself as a fight for control over the lines of communication between gods and men, and in this respect there is a profound difference between *sacra* and *auspicia*. As G. Dumézil put it, ' the auspices descend from the heaven; the *sacra* rise from the earth. Men are the recipients of the former and originators of the latter '.[61] The gods of sacrifice and prayer are the silent gods; they may be a source of personal comfort; politically, however, they are neither particularly helpful nor particularly troublesome. On the other hand the gods of the auspices talk to the people through their signs, and talking gods are politically most important. So far in all the history of mankind they have always talked through the intermediary of men — augurs, prophets, haruspices —, and in Roman history they had normally talked in one voice: the voice of the ruling class. When Cicero could not control the augur Antonius or the haruspex Spurinna, when the gods started talking the language

---

[58] Eurip. *I.A.* 520-521, 956-958; *Hel.* 744-751; Plato *Leg.* 11.913b; cf. *Rep.* 2.364b-e.   [59] Cic. *Div.* 1.132; Ennius, *Scen.* 319-323 Vahlen[2], 332-336 Warmington, 266-269 Jocelyn.   [60] See e.g. Livy 40.39.3-14; Plin. *N.H.* 13.84-87; Suet. *Rhet.* 1; Gell. 15.11.1; cf. W. SPEYER, *Bücherfunde in der Glaubenswerbung der Antike* (Göttingen, 1970), pp. 51-55; F. H. CRAMER, *Astrology in Roman Law and Politics* (Philadelphia, 1954), pp. 46 ff.   [61] *Mythe et épopée*, I (Paris, 1968), p. 277.

of Caesar, he preferred not to believe in their enunciations. This stance was philosophically sound and politically prudent. It was also politically reasonable, although philosophically rather inconsequential, to stop half-way, to abolish divination and retain the gods. Yet despite all the eloquence and persuasiveness of Cicero the sceptic, one is entitled to wonder whether he was right in dismissing the prophecy of mice destroying Plato's *Politeia* and his own *res publica*.

49

WATCHING THE BIRDS: CICERO THE AUGUR
AND THE AUGURAL *TEMPLA**

In his famous letter of consolation Servius Sulpicius reminded Cicero that Tullia had enjoyed in her life almost all *bona:* she had been married to *adulescentes primarii,* and she had seen her father as praetor, consul, and augur (*Fam.* 4. 5. 5). Coming from the pen of a jurist and aristocrat, this mode of consolation is doubly characteristic: Tullia's past happiness appears as a mere reflection of her father's political success, and the office of an augur as the pinnacle of Cicero's career. To this pinnacle, guarded by the nobility even more jealously than the consulate, Cicero attained ten years after the *annus mirabilis,*[1] and he never tired of extolling the power and influence of the augurs. In the *De legibus,* composed shortly after his election to the augurate, Cicero describes the *ius augurum* as "maximum ... et praestantissimum in re publica." And he says he feels so not because he himself is an augur, but because such are the facts (*Leg.* 2. 31):[2]

Philosophe et augure: Recherches sur la théorie cicéronienne de la divination. By FRANÇOIS GUILLAUMONT. Collection Latomus, vol. 184. Brussels: Latomus (Revue d'Études Latines), 1984. Pp. 214. FB 950 (paper).

Templum. By PALMIRA CIPRIANO. Biblioteca di ricerche linguistiche e filologiche, 13. Rome: Prima Cattedra di Glottologia, Università "La Sapienza," 1983. Pp. 156. L. 25,000 (paper).

1. The traditional date is 53 B.C., but 52 cannot be excluded; see J. Linderski, "The Aedileship of Favonius, Curio the Younger and Cicero's Election to the Augurate," *HSCP* 76 (1972): 181-200. Guillaumont is quite inaccurate in his description of the regulations governing the elections to the priesthoods. The popular election of *sacerdotes,* replacing the earlier *cooptatio,* was introduced in 104 by the *lex Domitia,* was abolished by Sulla, and was restored, as G. puts it, "par la loi Atia de 63" (p. 82). But the law called *Atia* (and its sponsor Atius) is an apparition, perhaps not out of place in musty books such as J. K. von Orelli and J. G. Baiter's *Onomasticon Tullianum,* pars 2 (Zürich, 1838), p. 82, or G. Rotondi's *Leges Publicae Populi Romani* (Milan, 1912), p. 380, but which one hardly expects to encounter in 1984. The sponsor of the law was the tribune of the plebs T. Labienus; Labienus was his *nomen gentilicium* (for *nomina* of this type, see W. Schulze, *Zur Geschichte lateinischer Eigennamen,* Abh. Göttingen [Berlin, 1904], pp. 104-5, 163), and there is not a shred of evidence (as already in the seventeenth century E. Spannheim saw clearly; cf. Klebs, *RE* 2 [1896]: 2254-55) that he ever bore the name Atius. The attribution of this name to Labienus seems to stem from the reading at Cic. *Att.* 7. 15. 3 "Pompeius ad legiones At(t)ianas est profectus; Labienum secum habet," where the manuscript tradition is confused and where Lipsius and Münzer, on the basis of Plut. *Pomp.* 57, conjectured *Appianas,* rightly accepted by D. R. Shackleton Bailey in his text (*Cicero's "Letters to Atticus,"* vol. 4 [Cambridge, 1968]) and ably defended in his commentary ad loc., p. 311. If this inadvertence to matters prosopographical is distressing, even more distressing is G.'s confusion of the various stages in the elections to the priesthoods, especially his apparent amalgamation of the *nominatio* and *cooptatio* (p. 82 and nn. 92 and 93; for the procedure, see Linderski, "Aedileship," pp. 191-93).

2. Since it bristles with technical terms I give also the Latin text: "Quid enim maius est, si de iure quaerimus, quam posse a summis imperiis et a summis potestatibus [i.e., the magistrates with *imperium* and the tribunes of the plebs] comitiatus et concilia vel instituta dimittere vel habita rescindere? [On the distinction between *instituta* and *habita,* see below in the text.] Quid gravius quam rem susceptam dirimi, si unus augur 'alio <die>' dixerit? Quid magnificentius quam posse decernere, ut magistratu se abdicent consules? [This is not quite accurate: see below in the text.] Quid religiosius quam cum populo, cum plebe agendi ius dare aut non dare? Quid leges non iure rogatas tollere?" The last sentence is often printed in the form "quid legem si non iure rogata est tollere?"

485

For what right (*ius*) is greater than to be able to dismiss assemblies (*comitiatus et concilia*) convened by the highest officials or to declare null and void the acts of such assemblies? What is of graver import than to effect the abandonment of any business already begun, if a single augur says "On another day" (*alio die*)? What is more magnificent than to be able to decree that the consuls resign their office? What is more binding (*religiosius*) than to give or to refuse permission to hold the assembly of the people or of the plebs or indeed to annul laws illegally (*non iure*) passed?

How puny, by comparison, look the concerns of the philospher and his position in the state! In the *Republic* the statesman is preeminent. When discoursing on the best state, Plato was forced to excogitate a fictitious construct; to demonstrate the *optimus status civitatis*, Scipio Aemilianus needed only to point to Rome nurtured into greatness by a succession of kings and statesmen (*Rep.* 2. 3). Cicero himself was able to save the state because he was consul at the time of the crisis and not merely a theoretical philosopher; had he not devoted himself since his young years to public life he could never have reached the consulship, and despite all the philosophizing the Republic would have been lost (*Rep.* 1. 7–11). Cicero the politician felt compelled to justify his literary frivolities: he composed them using odds and ends of time only, *subsiciva tempora,* a few days of vacation in the country (*Leg.* 1. 9). This sets the stage for confrontation between Cicero the philosopher and Cicero the augur—and for the book of Guillaumont.

The book falls into three parts, devoted to rhetoric and divination (pp. 17–42), to divination and politics as reflected in philosophical treatises, speeches, and letters (pp. 44–118), and finally to divination and philosophy (pp. 123–69). This organization is a marvel of mechanical division, and it produces ample repetition: *De republica* and *De legibus* are first treated (each separately) under the heading of politics and, in another part of the book, under the heading of philosophy. On the other hand, *De natura deorum,* despite its numerous references to the politics of augury, earns its place only as a statement of philosophy, and *De divinatione,* no less surprisingly, appears solely as politics and is accorded only five pages of cursory comment (pp. 45–49). G.'s *politique* is a vague word: it embraces both the political theory of divination and of augury and their application in political life. And he does not always distinguish rigorously enough between augury and other forms of divination, certainly a grave sin in a book about a famous augur. Still, on occasion, G. displays a fine grasp of augural niceties; but alas, his horror of detail and penchant for generalities too often leave the reader uninformed or confused.

G. (pp. 46–48; cf. 57–58) finds the hub of Ciceronian ideas about augury in the famous enunciation at *De divinatione* 2. 75, in which Cicero expresses the opinion that, although the augural law was originally conceived from a belief in divination, it was later maintained and preserved solely from considerations of political expediency (*rei publicae causa*).[3] In particular, this is true of the rule prohibiting the holding of popular assemblies when Jupiter thunders or lightens: the *maiores* wished to have an excuse for impeding the *comitia* (*Div.* 2. 42–43). Why the need

---

3. This philosophical stance of Cicero's had a long and illustrious pedigree, going back through Varro to Mucius Scaevola, to Polybius, and ultimately to the fifth-century Athenian enlightenment. Cf. K. Döring, "Antike Theorien über die staatspolitische Notwendigkeit der Götterfurcht," *A&A* 24 (1978): 43–56; J. Linderski, "Cicero and Roman Divination," *PP* 37 (1982 [1983]): 12–28, esp. pp. 17 ff. G., strangely enough, omits to place Cicero's views in this perspective.

for such a ruse? The Republic was teeming with demagogues who were always ready to sway the people with their pernicious *popularis eloquentia;* even Cicero's ideal Rome of the *Laws* was not completely free from this pest. To hold in check the *impetus iniustus* of the populace Cicero gives the *auspicia* to all magistrates: in this way they will be able to bring about the adjournment of many *inutiles comitiatus,* injurious meetings of the assembly (*Leg.* 3. 27). Thus the augural rules were excogitated to establish the *principes civitatis* as the interpreters of popular assemblies (*interpretes comitiorum*), whether these were held to pass judgments, to vote on laws, or to elect magistrates (*Div.* 2. 74).

In this passage the expression *interpretes* attracts attention. G. explains it as "une brachylogie," for "les *principes* sont non pas les interprètes des comices, mais les interprètes du *ius comitiorum*" (p. 48, n. 18). This is obvious and does not require any comment. What does require a comment is the augural connotation of the term *interpres,* and here G. offers little help. At the consular elections in 163 the *primus rogator,* an official who recorded the votes of the *centuria praerogativa,* suddenly died. This was a dire prodigy, and the senate decided to consult the Etruscan haruspices. In their *responsum* they declared that the presiding officer, the consul Ti. Gracchus (the father of the tribunes), was not a *iustus comitiorum rogator.* Gracchus, a paragon of a *princeps civitatis,* angrily exclaimed, "itane vero? ego non iustus, qui et consul rogavi et augur et auspicato? an vos Tusci ac barbari auspiciorum populi Romani ius tenetis et interpretes esse comitiorum potestis?"—and had them dismissed. But Gracchus was an assiduous augur, and next year, when he was the governor of Sardinia, reading the augural books, he discovered that he had indeed committed a technical error: having taken the auspices for the holding of the *comitia,* he returned to the city to preside in the senate, and on his way back to the Campus Martius he forgot to auspicate when recrossing the *pomerium.* As a result he lost his original *auspicia,* the divine permission to hold the elections on this day, and became a *non iustus rogator.* Jupiter observed this and sent a warning in the shape of the death of the *primus rogator.* Gracchus wrote a letter to the college of augurs and confessed his *peccatum;* the augurs presented the matter to the senate, and the senate decreed that the consuls must abdicate as *vitio creati* (Cic. *Nat. d.* 2. 10–11).

This famous affair, to which Cicero and other authors returned many times,[4] is most instructive. It casts sobering light on Cicero's rhetorical claims at *De legibus* 2. 31 (paraphrased above). In particular, the augurs were not entitled to decree *ut magistratu se abdicent consules;* their task was to establish whether a ritual error had been committed and to apprise the senate of their findings. They could do this on their own initiative,[5] as in the case of Gracchus, but normally the *collegium* conducted the investigations on the instructions of the senate.[6] But when the augurs had found that a *lex* was *vitio lata* or that the consuls were *vitio creati,* the

---

4. For references, see A. S. Pease, *M. Tulli Ciceronis "De Natura Deorum" Libri III* (Cambridge, Mass., 1958), pp. 572–78 ad locc.

5. Technically the report of the priests to the senate was called *nuntiatio sacerdotum;* cf. T. Mommsen, *Römisches Staatsrecht,* vol. 3 (Leipzig, 1888), pp. 958–59. Very often it consisted of the announcement of a *prodigium;* cf. ibid., pp. 1059–60.

6. The technical phrase was *ad augures referre* (Livy 45. 12. 10) or *ad collegium (augurum) deferre* (Cic. *Phil.* 2. 83). Cf. *ad collegium pontificum referre* at Livy 29. 19. 8, 29. 20. 10, 31. 9. 8, 38. 44. 5.

senate had hardly any other choice but to accept the report of the college, annul the law in question,[7] and instruct the consuls to abdicate.

But when speaking of the activities of the augurs we have always carefully to distinguish between the prerogatives, obligations, and privileges of the individual augurs and those of the *collegium augurum*.[8] Lack of attention to this fundamental division has bedeviled the study of the *res augurales* from Wissowa to G. The college of augurs functioned as a group of experts, *periti;* its main obligation was to uphold the augural law, *disciplinam tenere* (Cic. *Leg.* 2. 20). When called upon to investigate suspected violations of augural rules, they were supposed to go about their task dispassionately and scientifically, not unlike modern experts investigating a plane crash. It is not difficult to observe that the intervention of the college always took place *post actionem,* whereas the single augurs intervened *inter actionem.* Thus it lay within the prerogatives of the college (or more exactly within the prerogatives of the senate, although it normally acted after consultation with the college) "comitiatus et concilia *habita* rescindere," that is, to annul the effects of the voting in the assemblies, whether legislative or electoral. On the other hand, neither the *collegium augurum* nor the senate held the auspices or observed the sky for divine signs. Only the magistrates and individual augurs did. Whereas Cicero was hyperbolic in describing the powers of the college, he was very accurate in assessing the role of *unus augur.* Indeed, if a single augur uttered the hallowed formula "alio die," the magistrates and tribunes were forced to abandon the *res suscepta,* and in particular they were obliged to dismiss "comitiatus et concilia *instituta.*"[9]

This prescription of the augural law appears nowhere more clearly than in "the clash of the two augurs," as G. (pp. 86–91) aptly calls it, the polemic between Cicero and Antonius concerning Antonius' *obnuntiatio* in 44 against Dolabella's election to the consulship (Cic. *Phil.* 2. 79–84; cf. 1. 31, 3. 9, 5. 9). G. summarizes Cicero's train of thought correctly enough (see esp. p. 87), but he does not inquire into the theory of auspices upon which Cicero's argument was based, rather a surprising omission in a book about "la théorie cicéronienne de la divination."

The augural doctrine distinguished between solicited and unsolicited signs (*auspicia impetrativa* and *auspicia oblativa*). The crucial passage is *Philippics* 2. 81 "nos [i.e., the augurs] enim nuntiationem solum habemus, consules et reliqui magistratus etiam spectionem." With respect to the *comitia* the augurs had the right of *nuntiatio* only: they could only report unsolicited signs, and only after the beginning of the proceedings (cf. *Leg.* 2. 31 "rem susceptam dirimi, comitiatus et concilia instituta dimittere"). The magistrates, on the other hand, had both *spectio* and *nuntiatio:* the right to take impetrative auspices and to announce adverse omens (this is the famous procedure of *obnuntiatio* based upon *servare de*

---

7. The standard expression was "quae lex lata esse dicatur, ea non videri populum teneri" (Cic. apud Asc. *Corn.* 68 C.). Cf. Mommsen, *Römisches Staatsrecht,* 1³:115-16 and 3:363-68. The interpretation of A. W. Lintott, *Violence in Republican Rome* (Oxford, 1968), pp. 133 ff., and of J. R. Fears, *"Princeps a Diis Electus": The Divine Election of the Emperor as a Political Concept at Rome* (Rome, 1977), pp. 106-7, is inaccurate and conceptually mistaken.

8. See now the full exposition in J. Linderski, "The Augural Law," *ANRW* 2.16.3 (1986): 2151-225.

9. The sentence "cum populo, cum plebe agendi ius dare aut non dare" describes the same prerogative — but with rhetorical overstatement: if the augur intervened, he was quite obviously taking away the *ius agendi;* and if he did not, he could be hyperbolically depicted as giving it.

caelo, "watching the sky"). But the magistrate had to make his announcement before the beginning of the proceedings: "qui servavit [sc. de caelo], non comitiis habitis, sed priusquam habeantur, debet nuntiare" (Cic. *Phil.* 2. 81). Whence this peculiar set of regulations?

The impetrative signs the deity was sending in response to a request; hence they had a clearly defined recipient and a clearly defined meaning specified in the *legum dictio,* the formula pronounced by the auspicant.[10] They were valid for one day only.[11] The magistrate was asking the deity whether it gave him the permission to go ahead with his undertaking, for instance, the holding of the assembly. Now lightning (and thunder) was an excellent sign for all undertakings, but it impeded the *comitia* (Cic. *Div.* 2. 42–43, 74). Thus the magistrate in charge of the *comitia* would implore the deity to send him a propitious bird or induce propitious behavior in the sacred chickens (they were expected to eat greedily so that crumbs would be falling down their beaks; to achieve this they were kept hungry in a cage; cf. Cic. *Div.* 2. 71–74). At the same time the *auspicia de caelo, fulmen* and *tonitru,* were regarded as *auspicia maxima* (Serv. auct. ad *Aen.* 2. 693); they were stronger than the auspices from the flight of birds or from the observation of the sacred chickens (*auspicia ex avibus* and *ex tripudiis*).[12] Thus if another magistrate took auspices for any action of his and received from Jupiter the flash of lightning, this made the whole day unsuitable for popular assemblies.[13] This explains the customary edict the consuls issued on the day of the assembly: "ne quis magistratus minor de caelo servasse velit" (Gell. *NA* 13. 15. 1). The consuls could prohibit the *magistratus minores* from taking the auspices, but they could not deny this right to other holders of *imperium* or to the tribunes of the plebs. And as the auspicant established a direct line of communication with Jupiter, nobody could question the veracity of his report. The magistrate who was to convene the *comitia* was obliged to obey the *nuntiatio* of *fulmen* and refrain from further action on this day. This is the constitutional and augural basis of the magisterial and tribunician *obnuntiatio.* As the *auspicia impetrativa* concerned a future action, the announcement of the *fulmen* had perforce to be made before the beginning of the *comitia.*

But Jupiter could change his mind at any time. He could give his permission for an action, and later he could withdraw it. Here the oblative signs come into play. As they were not asked for, they had no specific recipient. How, then, could one know what an oblative sign meant and to what action it referred? The *vinculum temporis* is the answer elaborated by the Dutch scholar I. M. J. Valeton: the oblative adverse sign had to appear in the course of the undertaking Jupiter

---

10. Serv. auct. ad *Aen.* 3. 89; Plaut. *Asin.* 259–61; Livy 1. 18. 10 "tum peregit verbis auspicia quae mitti vellet." This procedure is also attested in Iguvium: see J. W. Poultney, *The Bronze Tables of Iguvium* (Baltimore, 1959), pp. 234–38 (table VIa, 1–18).

11. The evidence has been collected by P. Catalano, *Contributi allo studio del diritto augurale,* vol. 1 (Turin, 1960), pp. 42–45.

12. They were also stronger than any indications derived from the inspection of entrails. In the course of his polemic against the augural doctrine of *maiora* and *minora auspicia,* Seneca writes that, according to the augurs, "fulminis interventus submovet extorum vel augurii indicia" (*QNat.* 2. 34).

13. The technical term was *diem vitiare* or *tollere;* see Cic. *Att.* 4. 9. 1, 4. 17. 4, *QFr.* 3. 3. 2.

wished to stop.[14] Any person could observe such a sign and report it to the presiding magistrate. But the report of a *privatus* or even of a magistrate was not binding on the president of the assembly. Only the *nuntiatio* of an augur was binding. For the meaning of an oblative sign was often ambiguous: to interpret it properly, special knowledge was necessary; and it was not the magistrates—still less the *privati*—who possessed that knowledge. Its sole possessors were the augurs, the official *interpretes* and *internuntii* of *Iuppiter Optimus Maximus*. They read his signs and transmitted his commands.[15]

In the *Philippics* (2. 78–84) Cicero displays his augural knowledge and disqualifies Antonius as an *interpres* of Jupiter. Antonius, who was consul and augur, could obnuntiate in either capacity. On the Kalends of January he proclaimed in the senate *se Dolabellae comitia aut prohibiturum auspiciis* [thus implying he would resort to *servare de caelo* based on the consul's right to *spectio* and prevent the assembly from being convened] *aut id facturum esse quod fecit* [i.e., threatening to obnuntiate as augur]. Indeed, when he reported the adverse omen he did it in the latter capacity, for he uttered the words "alio die" after the beginning of the *comitia*. Thus he obnuntiated on the basis of an oblative sign, the occurrence of which it was impossible to predict. Hence Cicero's accusation: either the augur Antonius did not know anything of the augural law, or he reported a faked omen, which nonetheless had to be obeyed—"tua potius quam rei publicae calamitate."

Not long before his augural diatribe against Antonius, Cicero composed his dialogue *De divinatione*,[16] in which he discourses at length on the auspices. He does it in a peculiar way. In Book 1, through the mouth of his brother, Quintus, he argues in favor of the existence and efficacy of divination. In Book 2, donning the mantle of an Academic philosopher, he demonstrates that gods send no signs and that divination is merely fraud and politics. G. neatly summarizes Cicero's philosophical views, but again he shows no interest in the doctrine of divination and augury as presented by Cicero the augur.[17]

And the observation of divine signs required expert knowledge indeed. Take for instance the concept of *templum*. The most recent attempt to solve this augural riddle comes from a linguist, P. Cipriano. In the final chapter of her book

---

14. "De modis auspicandi Romanorum," *Mnemosyne* 18 (1890): 447–48. The researches of Valeton published in *Mnemosyne* between 1889 and 1898 form a solid basis for modern augural studies, but they are written in difficult Latin and are extremely involved: one has to study them and not merely consult. G. does not quote Valeton even once.

15. Cic. *Leg.* 2. 20, *Phil.* 13. 12 (cf. 5. 9); Arn. *Adv. nat.* 4. 35. For a detailed discussion, see Linderski, "The Augural Law," pp. 2226–29.

16. The whole text was certainly completed before the assassination of Caesar; after the Ides of March Cicero introduced some minor changes and composed the preface to Book 2. See R. Durand, "La date du *De divinatione*," *Mélanges Boissier* (Paris, 1903), pp. 173–83; A. S. Pease, *M. Tulli Ciceronis "De Divinatione" Libri Duo* (Urbana, 1920–23; repr. Darmstadt, 1963), pp. 13–15.

17. Major works on the theory of divination are missing from G.'s bibliography, above all P. Finger, "Die zwei mantischen Systeme in Ciceros Schrift über die Wahrsagung (*De divinatione* I)," *RhM* 78 (1929): 371–97, and P. Regell, *De Augurum Publicorum Libris* (Ph.D. diss., Vratislaviae, 1878), esp. pp. 3–7. Regell, a student of A. Reifferscheidt and later for many years a *Gymnasialprofessor* in Hirschberg in Lower Silesia, published many other important contributions to augural studies between 1881 and 1904, mostly in *Gymnasialprogramme* in Hirschberg and in *Jahrbücher für classische Philologie*.

(pp. 121–42) she firmly rejects the traditional etymologies connecting *templum* either with the root **tem-*, "to cut," "(ri)tagliare," or the root **temp-*, "to extend," "tendere." According to the former etymology, *templum* was a "spazio ritagliato," "a piece cut out of the surrounding space"; according to the latter, "spazio teso = spazio misurato," "the space extended or measured out."[18] Whether C.'s own effort will gain applause remains to be seen. Her starting point (as it was also for a number of scholars before her) is the notice in Festus (Paulus) 505 L.: "templum significat . . . et tignum quod in aedificio transversum ponitur." And it follows from Vitruvius (4. 2. 1 *supra cantherios templa*) that the precise meaning of *templum*, "plank," is that of a "traversa," i.e., "trave che incrocia un altro trave collocato precedentemente" (pp. 123–24), and not that of "legno tagliato" as earlier scholars believed (pp. 30–31). The sense of *templum* as "traversa" cannot be explained on the basis of the root **tem-*, but it can be explained on the basis of the root **temp-*, which according to C. "esprimeva già in fase preistorica non solo la nozione del *tendere* ma anche quella del *tendere intrecciando* e cioè del *tendere un elemento trasversalmente a un altro*" (p. 123). How does one arrive at this notion? No problem. The root **temp-* was in fact a "forma ampliata" of **ten-*, and it finds its place and explanation in the series **tend-*, **tens-*, and **tengh-* (p. 129). Thus *templum* would be "ciò che è teso (o si estende) trasversalmente" (p. 127).

This etymology is fraught with a fatal fiction. It is indeed not impossible to collocate **temp-* and **ten-*, but on the basis of ancient and recent Indo-European parallels (which C. collects in profusion) it is impossible to decide whether the original sense of *templum* was "stretch and cross" or "stretch" alone, the latter being undoubtedly the principal connotation of both roots. C.'s etymology ultimately rests on a slender reed, the word *templum* as used by Roman architects. And there is no reason why *templa* employed in the construction of roofs should not be interpreted as "cut planks," i.e., shorter planks placed upon the principal rafters, *cantherii*.

But whatever the linguistic value of C.'s etymology, does it tell us anything of value about the augural *templa*? For very often etymologies are transparent (a quality that one would not immediately assign to C.'s proposition) but nevertheless tell us little about the actual meaning of the word and still less about the thing or procedure denoted by the word. The neo-English word "logistics" is a good case in point; and though the game of British football (soccer) is really played with feet, this part of the body is only occasionally employed in American football.[19] But C. is adamant: her etymology of *templum* squares exquisitely with what we know about augural practices. The primary meaning of *templum* in the language of the augurs was "spazio quadripartito all' incrocio delle due linee Nord-Sud e Est-Ovest" (p. 121). This theory runs counter to the ideas of Valeton

---

18. On pp. 29–45 C. lists and discusses various etymologies proposed.

19. Cf. M. Morani, "Sull' espressione linguistica dell' idea di santuario nelle civiltà classiche," *Contributi dell' Istituto di Storia Antica dell' Università di Sacro Cuore* 9 (1983): 3–32. He warns that linguistic analysis in itself does not allow one to interpret such terms as *templum* or *fanum*. We have to consider history and archaeology. Morani quite sensibly embraces the traditional derivation of *templum* from the root **tem-* and offers a succinct analysis of the augural sense of the word.

and Catalano,[20] and C. charges these two *lumina* of augural studies with misreading the sources (pp. 43–44). Not all constructions of Valeton and Catalano are acceptable, but the impartial reader cannot fend off the impression that it is C. who forces the augurs into the torture chamber of her linguistic instruments.

Language is a very imprecise means of communication, for it freely mixes colloquial and technical senses of a word. Varro was well aware of this problem, and at *De lingua Latina* 7. 5–13 he discussed various poetic and transferred senses of *templum*. In everyday speech *templum* was any place of cult, but the augurs strictly distinguished between *templa* and *aedes sacrae*. In his *Commentarius ad Pompeium* (paraphrased by Gellius *NA* 14. 7. 7), Varro "docuit confirmavitque, nisi in loco per augurem constituto, quod *templum* appellaretur, senatus consultum factum esset, iustum id non fuisse." For that reason the successive *curiae senatus* were made *templa* by the augurs. And Varro added that "non omnes aedes sacras templa esse ac ne aedem quidem Vestae templum esse" (see also *Ling.* 7. 10; cf. Serv. ad *Aen.* 7. 153, 174; 11. 235; Serv. auct. ad *Aen.* 1. 446, 4. 200, 9. 4). There is no shred of evidence that these *templa* were ever divided into four parts; this would appear fatal to C.'s etymology, but she presents it as fatal to Varro and Cicero, Livy and Servius. All these authors imply that the *templa* in which the senate met or the Republic was administered (as the *Rostra*) were the *loca inaugurata* (see the passages in C., pp. 19–25, 88–90). She distinguishes between the *loca inaugurata* and "i *templa* veri e propri" (p. 113) that the augurs and the magistrates used for their observations. The latter were indeed divided into four (or more parts), and the former were called *templa* only *per translato* (p. 115). Thus C. rejects all sources that do not agree with her etymology—although, we should add, they find a perfect home in the traditional explanation linking *templum* (and *temenos*) with the notion of a *locus finitus* cut out from the surrounding space. But it is not easy to get out of the snares of a fictitious principle—a pity, for in the course of her argument C. offers many a perceptive observation.

She rightly points out that not all *loca inaugurata* were *templa* (the *pomerium* was inaugurated but was never referred to as *templum*) and not all *templa* were *loca inaugurata,* in particular the *auguratoria* in military camps (pp. 85–96). We have in fact to keep strictly apart two types of earthly *templa,* the places in which "auspicato et publice res administrarentur et senatus haberi posset" (Serv. auct. ad *Aen.* 1. 446), which had to be inaugurated, and the places from which auspices were taken, for which the inauguration was not necessary.[21]

What then was the function of *inauguratio?* In this connection C. offers interesting remarks on the opposition between *auspicia* and *auguria,* arriving at conclusions very similar to those of Catalano and the present writer (see n. 20).

20. Valeton, "De templis Romanis," *Mnemosyne* 20 (1892): 338–90; 21 (1893): 62–91, 397–440; 23 (1895): 15–79; 25 (1897): 93–144, 361–85; 26 (1898): 1–93; Catalano, *Contributi,* pp. 247 ff.; idem, "Aspetti spaziali del sistema giuridico-religioso romano. Mundus, templum, urbs, ager, Latium, Italia," *ANRW* 2.16.1 (1978): 440–553, esp. pp. 467–79. On the ritual of inauguration and the concepts of *templum, auspicium,* and *augurium,* see now also Linderski, "The Augural Law," pp. 2257–96.

21. I am happy to note that here C.'s argument to a great extent coincides with the exposition in Linderski, "The Augural Law," pp. 2271ff. Cf. also A. Magdelain, "L'inauguration de l'*urbs* et l'*imperium,*" *MEFR* 89 (1977): 15.

Auspicium was "un segnale dal quale si deduce se è opportuno o meno iniziare una certa impresa, l'*augurium* mostra un'influenza diretta degli dei sullo sviluppo dell'evento sottoposto alla loro attenzione e al loro intervento" (p. 105). Through *auspicium* the deity indicated whether an action could or could not be carried out on a given day, but it expressed no opinion about the merits or demerits of the undertaking itself. If the magistrate received a negative response, he could already on the following day present to Jupiter the same question and repeat it each day again and again until he received a propitious sign (cf. Livy 9. 38. 15–39. 1). The *augurium* was, on the other hand, an augmentative and charismatic act: places, persons (*reges* and *sacerdotes*), and ceremonies (as the *augurium salutis,* on which C. offers fine comments) were transferred through this rite into a special, permanently "inaugurated" state. To remove the effects of *inauguratio* the ceremony of *exauguratio* was necessary. The negative answer at an augury (whether for the purpose of *inauguratio* or *exauguratio*) was given once and for ever; the request could not be repeated. The *fanum Termini* enclosed within the temple of the Capitoline Jupiter was a lasting testimony to this augural principle: it was an inaugurated place, and at its *exauguratio* "aves . . . non addixere" (Cato *Orig.* 1, frag. 24 Peter; Livy 1. 55. 3). The *auspicia* were consulted by both the magistrates and the augurs, but the *auguria* were the exclusive province of the latter.

But *templum* denoted not only an earthly *locus,* inaugurated or not; in augural parlance it denoted also the field of vision within which the auspices were observed. Here we have carefully to distinguish between the *templa* for the observation of *signa caelestia,* the flashes of lightning, and the *templa* for the observation of the flight of birds. C. does not pay sufficient attention to this fundamental dichotomy. Varro (*Ling.* 7. 6–7) derives *templum* "a tuendo" and explains: "quocirca caelum qua attuimur dictum templum." And quoting a poet he describes this *templum* as a *hemisphaerium* bound (*septum*) by "the vault of blue." It was *ab natura,* for no formula was needed to delimit it. This hemispherical *templum* was divided into four parts, "sinistra ab oriente, dextra ab occasu, antica ad meridiem, postica ad septemtrionem."[22] Whence this orientation? Varro again provides a clue. As Festus 454 L. records, he wrote in the fifth book of his *Epistolicae quaestiones:* "a deorum sede cum in meridiem spectes, ad sinistram sunt partes mundi exorientes, ad dextram occidentes; factum arbitror, ut sinistra meliora auspicia quam dextra esse existimentur." Thus this celestial *templum* was oriented from the point of view of the gods who sat in their northern abode and gazed southwards.

Regell argued in 1881 that it was in this *templum* that the *signa ex caelo* were observed; the birds, on the other hand, were watched for in the *Lufttemplum* that extended over the city from the *arx* to the *pomerium.* Valeton severely criticized this theory and claimed that one and the same *templum,* the *templum aerium,* was used for the observation of both *fulmina* and *aves.*[23]

22. Some scholars assume a circular *templum caeleste,* but this view is augural nonsense: the field of vision was in front of the observer. See below in the text on the augural temple in Bantia.
23. Regell, "Die Schautempla der Augurn," *Jahrb. f. cl. Phil.* 123 (1881): 597ff.; Valeton, "De templis Romanis," *Mnemosyne* 17 (1889): 282ff. See now also A. Magdelain, "L'*auguraculum* de l'*arx* à Rome et

A recent, sensational archaeological find (to which C. devotes only a meager footnote), the discovery of the inscribed stones from the augural *templum* on the citadel of Bantia in southern Italy, definitely adjudicated this old dispute. During construction work in 1962 six cippi came to light; five years later followed the masterful publication by M. Torelli. Torelli ingeniously recognized in the stones the remnants of an augural *templum* and postulated that three more cippi should still be hidden under the earth. And indeed, systematic excavations revealed those three missing stones, perfectly oriented: they formed the northern line of the *templum*, measuring nine meters and twenty centimeters from the eastern to the western cippus. This triumph of scholarly divination was not without cost: as often happens in epigraphical studies, Torelli found that the new inscriptions disproved some of his earlier interpretations.[24] These nine cippi (of a height between thirty-four and fifty-six centimeters, and between twenty-nine and thirty-four centimeters in diameter) were thus placed in three rows forming a rectangular *templum;* Torelli noted that the stones were inclined to the west, so that the letters on them (measuring on the average six and a half centimeters) could be read only by the observer looking eastward. And in fact to the west of the cippi were found the remains of a structure that Torelli persuasively interpreted as an *auguratorium,* the post from which the auspicants viewed the signs. The inscriptions on the stones read as follows (the expansions of the abbreviations are Torelli's). First, the northern *finis,* on the cippi found *in situ:* northeast, *B(ene) I(uvante) AV(e);* north, *TAAR,* perhaps *T (. . .) A(ve) AR(cula);* northwest, *C(ontraria) A(ve) A(ugurium) P(estiferum).*[25] Then the remaining six cippi, which Torelli distributed along the central east-west line—east, *IOVI;* center, *SOLEI;* west, *FLUS(ae)* (an Oscan deity corresponding to Roman Flora)—and on the southern *finis:* southeast, *SIN(istra) AV(e);*[26] south, *R(emore) AVE;* southwest, *C(ontraria) A(ve) EN(ebra).*

This *templum* (dated to the last century of the Republic) was adapted only to the observation of birds; consequently, the existence of the two separate types of *templa,* one for the *signa ex avibus* and the other for the *signa ex caelo,* is virtually certain. But even more remarkable is the contribution of the Bantine *templum* to the thorny questions concerning the orientation at the auspication and the denomination of the signs observed. As the *templum* in Bantia amply demonstrates, the auspicant looked eastward, whereas the gods, as Varro informs us, looked southward. It is fitting to conclude these observations by turning back to the augural wisdom of Cicero. At *De divinatione* 2. 82 he makes in passing the following remark: "haud ignoro quae bona sint sinistra nos dicere, etiamsi dextra sint." We have to find a system of orientation in which *sinistra* = *dextra.* We shall achieve this result if we amalgamate into one system the orientation of the gods and the orientation of the auspicant. If a bird appeared in the southeastern part of

---

dans d'autres villes," *REL* 47 (1969): 253–69, esp. pp. 262–63 (his *champ visuel* corresponds to Regell's *Lufttemplum*), and F. Coarelli, *Il foro romano: Periodo arcaico* (Rome, 1983), pp. 100–107.

24. "Un *templum augurale* d'età repubblicana a Bantia," *RAL* 21 (1966 [1967]): 293–315; idem, "Contributi al supplemento del *CIL* IX," *RAL* 24 (1969): 39–48.

25. *A(uspicium) P(estiferum)* seems preferable; cf. Festus 286, 287 L.

26. But this abbreviation has certainly to be expanded as *SIN(ente) AV(e):* see Linderski, "The Augural Law," pp. 2284–85, where the reader will find discussion detailed and abstruse.

the *templum aerium,* which was the projection from the *arx* to the *pomerium* of the earthly *templum* demarcated by the cippi, it was a right-hand sign for the auspicant and a left-hand sign for the gods, *auspicium dextrum* and at the same time *sinistrum.*

The Romans derived the term *arcanum* from secret ceremonies performed by the augurs on the *arx* (Fest. [Paulus] 14–15 L.), and indeed to us the precepts of the augurs are arcane enough. We can only regret that Cicero's own treatise *De auguriis* met on its way to posterity an *avis contraria.*[27]

Neither G. nor C. does justice to Cicero the augur or to the concept of *templum,* but the strictures here presented are squabbles among the cognoscenti. Ignorance of the tenets of Roman religion (still regularly and disparagingly described as "pagan") among most classicists is profound. It demonstrates a disconcerting inability to confront on its own terms a system of thought so different from that in which most classical scholars have been brought up.[28] But we should not disparage the augurs and the pontiffs because they did not fight bloody religious wars for the iotas of their discipline. They presided over the *pax deorum*—the foundation of Rome's success.

---

27. The only direct quotation we have reads "omnibus avi incerta"(Charisius, *GL* 1:122. 22 = 156. 23 Barwick). He certainly treated also of the *aves contrariae.*

28. Cf. the penetrating remarks by J. A. North, "Conservatism and Change in Roman Religion," *PBSR* 44 (1976): 1–12.

50

THE *LIBRI RECONDITI*

T HE expression *libri reconditi* occurs three times in our sources:

Cicero, *de domo* 39:

> Venio ad augures, quorum ego libros, si qui sunt reconditi,
> non scrutor; non sum in exquirendo iure augurum curiosus;
> haec quae una cum populo didici, quae saepe in contionibus
> responsa sunt, novi. Negant fas esse agi cum populo cum de
> caelo servatum sit.

Servius *auctus, ad Aen.* 1.398:

> Multi tamen adserunt cycnos inter augurales aves non
> inveniri neque auguralibus commentariis eorum nomen inla-
> tum, sed in libris reconditis lectum esse posse quamlibet
> avem auspicium adtestari, maxime quia non poscatur.

Servius *auctus, ad Aen.* 2.649:

> Sane de fulminibus hoc scriptum in reconditis invenitur quod
> si quem principem civitatis vel regem fulmen afflaverit et
> supervixerit, posteros eius nobiles futuros et aeternae gloriae.

These texts present a number of difficult problems; I shall discuss
them in turn, beginning with Cicero.

First, the context of Cicero's enunciation. The speech concerning
his house Cicero delivered on 29 September 57 before the college of
pontiffs.[1] Eighteen months previously, bowing before the threats of
Clodius, he fled from Rome. Whereupon, in March 58, Clodius
promulgated the law *de exilio Ciceronis*, which next month was duly
accepted by the *concilium plebis*. One of its provisions ordered the
confiscation of Cicero's property; his house was razed to the ground,

---

[1] Cic. *Att.* 4.2.2.

and on part of its site Clodius erected a shrine of the goddess Liber-
tas, which he formally consecrated with the help of a relative of his,
the pontifex L. Pinarius Natta.[2] By this act he transferred the site of
Cicero's house from the sphere of *ius humanum* into that of *ius divi-
num*. Cicero's goal was to regain his property and to strike a mortal
blow at his hateful enemy. Accordingly, his argument was two-
pronged. On the one hand, he argued that Clodius's consecration of
the temple was illegal and invalid and, on the other, that the whole
tribunate of Clodius and all his acts as a tribune of the plebs were
likewise illegal and invalid. The former argument lay in the province
of the pontiffs, the latter primarily in that of the augurs.

Now, a *lex Papiria* prohibited the consecration of "any edifice, land
or altar" without the authorization of the people (*iniussu plebis*).[3] Clodius evidently did not bother to comply with this formality, and as a
result the *collegium pontificum* decided in Cicero's favor.[4] Cicero boasts
in his speech that "sacrorum iure pontifices et auspiciorum religione
augures totum evertunt tribunatum tuum" (*de domo* 41), but the verdict of the pontiffs concerned solely the validity of Clodius's consecration of Cicero's house, a thing vastly different from the validity of his
totus tribunatus. Suspicion is warranted that the action of the augurs
was also much less drastic than Cicero would like us to believe. In
fact the augurs as a college took no action at all.

In the passage concerning the augurs Cicero contrasts the *libri
reconditi* and the *responsa* of the augurs. But observe the curious way
in which he mentions these books: he does not really say that the
augurs possess them. He says only that should the augurs have any
books of recondite character, he is not prying into them. This is
revealing: the very existence of a secret book is a secret. It is not wise
to inquire even into this preliminary matter, let alone into the content
of such *libri*, should they exist. "Non sum in exquirendo iure

---

[2] For a detailed description of events and an introduction to the *de domo
sua*, see W. Drumann-P. Groebe, *Geschichte Roms* II (Leipzig 1902) 208ff., esp.
219–222, 228–231, 262–266, 553; VI (1919) 628ff., 649–650; R. G. Nisbet,
M. Tulli Ciceronis De Domo Sua ad Pontifices Oratio (Oxford 1939) viiff., 206–
209.

[3] Cic. *de domo* 127–128. On the *lex Papiria* and the *consecratio/dedicatio*, see
Nisbet 209–212; G. Niccolini, *I fasti dei tribuni della plebe* (Milan 1934)
403–404; T. R. S. Broughton, *The Magistrates of the Roman Republic* II (New
York 1952) 471.

[4] Cic. *Att.* 4.2.3.

augurum[5] curiosus,"[6] Cicero protests.

A parallel passage, referring to the pontifical law, throws light on *curiosus*, with its strong pejorative tone. *De domo* 121 Cicero writes:

Nihil loquor de pontificio iure, nihil de ipsius verbis dedicationis, nihil de religione, caerimoniis; non dissimulo me
nescire ea quae, etiam si scirem, dissimularem, ne aliis molestus, vobis etiam curiosus viderer; etsi effluunt multa ex
vestra disciplina quae etiam ad nostras auris saepe per-
manant.

A marvelous statement! Cicero says he will not discuss the details of the pontifical law (in fact he does: this statement introduces the figure of *occultatio*) because he is ignorant of them; and even if he were not, in order not to appear to other listeners (*alii*)[7] unbearably pedantic (*molestus*) and to the pontiffs themselves unduly inquisitive, he would have concealed his knowledge. Nisbet remarks[8] that for a Roman statesman it was expedient at times to affect ignorance of Greek art and philosophy, but in this place Cicero is not alluding to Greek philosophy but to something much graver: the secrets guarded by the *sacerdotes populi Romani*. A Roman statesman could well ridicule Greek philosophy,[9] but he would never ridicule in public[10] the augural or pontifical discipline; quite on the contrary it was to his great advantage to be well versed in the sacral law, but at the same time he had to

---

[5] On the concept and content of the *ius augurum* (or *ius augurale*), see J. Linderski, "The Augural Law," *ANRW* 2.16.3 (forthcoming).

[6] *Oxford Latin Dictionary* adduces this passage under the heading "excessively careful, fussy"; its rightful place is under 3b "inquisitive." Plautus, *Stich.* 198 characterizes *curiosi* as those who "alienas res curant studio maximo." The same definition in Augustinus, *de utilitate credendi* 22 (*Corp. Script. Eccles. Lat.* XXV 27,2): "curiosus ea requirit, quae nihil ad se attinet." See also *de domo* 33, adduced below, p. 217.

[7] The mention of *alii* would seem to indicate that the hearings before the pontifical college were open to the public.

[8] Ad loc. 170. But the real parallel is provided by a passage of Paulus referring to the *exceptio doli* in connection with *delegatio*, *Dig.* 46.2.19: "ideo autem denegantur exceptiones adversus secundum creditorem, quia in privatis contractibus et pactionibus non facile scire petitor potest, quid inter eum qui delegatus est et debitorem actum est aut, etiamsi sciat, dissimulare debet, ne curiosus videatur."

[9] The *locus classicus* is Cic. *pro Murena* 60–66.

[10] In private, he could be highly skeptical, as Cicero was: cf. J. Linderski, "Cicero and Roman Divination," *PP* 37 (1982) 15ff.

avoid giving the impression of having acquired his knowledge through unauthorized channels or leaks as we would call them today. Some information would inevitably come to the ears of the layman, but he should not seek it out. *Curiosa mens* was almost as pernicious as the *curiosi oculi*, of Clodius of course, which polluted the *sacrificium occultum* of Bona Dea.[11]

In Cicero's time the pontifical law contained only the *ius sacrorum*, but in the early republic, we are told, it embraced also the *ius civile*. According to the tradition, the formulae of the *legis actiones* in particular had been the secret domain of the pontiffs until the end of the fourth century when, as Livy (9.46.1,5) puts it, "Cn. Flavius scriba . . . civile ius, repositum in penetralibus pontificum evulgavit."[12] A variant tradition[13] has Appius Claudius Caecus compose a book of formulae; Cn. Flavius stole this book and made it public. The story is scarcely credible;[14] if the *ius civile Flavianum* was not a figment of the annalists, the book under this title will have contained a collection of the *legis actiones* culled from the *responsa pontificum*. It would thus form an early parallel to the treatises *de sacris* and *sacrificiis* of the later age.

Still it is interesting that according to Livy the pontiffs kept their books in the *penetralia*. Servius, *ad Aen.* 6.71, explains *penetralia* as "templorum secreta," and Servius *auctus, ad Aen.* 2.484, as "domorum secreta, dicta penetralia ab eo quod est penitus aut a Penatibus."[15] When Clodius entered the house of Caesar he violated, *inexpiabili scelere pervertit*, not only the *occulta sacra* of Bona Dea but

[11] Cic. *de har. resp.* 37. Afranius, *comoed.* fr. 109 (Ribbeck[3]) juxtaposes *sceleratus* and *curiosus*.

[12] For *repositum in penetralibus*, cf. *Res Gestae* 29.3: "in penetrali . . . reposui" (cf. below n.18). To Livy's phrase corresponds in Val. Max. 4.5.2 "Ius civile . . . inter sacra caerimoniasque . . . abditum solisque pontificibus notum."

[13] Pomponius in his *liber singularis enchiridii, Dig.* 1.2.7.

[14] Cf. F. Schultz, *Geschichte der römischen Rechtswissenschaft* (Weimar 1961) 11–13. For Flavius's publication of the calendar, see A. K. Michels, *The Calendar of the Roman Republic* (Princeton 1967) 108ff.

[15] Cf. Isid. *Etym.* 8.11.99 and Serv. *auct. ad Aen.* 3.12. For *penetralia* = *secreta*, cf. *Corp. Gloss. Lat.* 7 (= *Thes. Gloss. Emend.*) 65 s.v. On the whole subject of *penetralia* and *adyta* in Roman cult, see the excellent study by F. Cassola, "Livio, il tempio di Giove Feretrio e la inaccessibilità dei santuari in Roma," *Rivista Storica Italiana* 82 (1970) 5–31. Cf. also M. Van Doren, "Les sacraria," *Ant. Class.* 27 (1958) 31–75 and A. S. Pease, *M. Tulli Ciceronis De Natura Deorum* (Cambridge, Mass. 1958) ad 2.68, II 727–728.

also the sanctity of the *domus*, its *abditos ac penetrales focos*.[16] Vergil (*Aen.* 2.297) speaks of the *adyta penetralia* [17] of Vesta, thus identifying *penetrale* and *adytum*. [18] Servius ad loc. comments: "adytum est locus templi secretior, ad quem nulli est aditus nisi sacerdoti."[19] Among other miraculous happenings portending the victory at Pharsalos, Caesar reports (*BC* 3.105.3) "Pergami in occultis ac reconditis templi[20] locis, quo praeter sacerdotes adire fas non est, quae Graeci ἄδυτα appellant, tympana sonuerunt."[21]

It stands to reason to assume that the *libri reconditi* were the books kept in the *loca recondita, occulta, abdita*, and *secreta*. This was in any case true of the *libri Sibyllini*: in republican times they were hidden in a stone chest in a chamber under the Capitoline temple of Jupiter.[22] As they contained the *fata et remedia Romana*[23] they could be approached (the technical terms were *libros inspicere* or *ad libros adire*) only by the priests, the *quindecimviri* (earlier *duoviri* and *decemviri*) *sacris faciundis*, and the priests had to be ordered to do so by the Senate,[24] which, as Livy says (22.9.8), "non ferme decernitur, nisi cum taetra prodigia nuntiata sunt." Thus the *libri Sibyllini* were the *libri reconditi* in the full sense of the word, although this term was never used with respect to them. Moreover, according to the Varronian tradition transmitted by Dionysios of Halikarnassos (4.62.5–6, cf. Zonaras 7.11), the person who revealed their content was punished

[16] Cic. *de har. resp.* 57.

[17] Imitated by Lucan 5.146 and Silius 3.21.

[18] This identification is even clearer in the *Res Gestae* 29.3. Augustus writes about the standards recovered from the Parthians: "ea autem s[ig]na in penetrali quod e[s]t in templo Martis Ultoris reposui." The Greek text renders *in penetrali* as ἐν τῶι ... ἀδύτωι. See also Agroecius, *de orthogr.* (*Gramm. Lat.* 7 Keil) 123,29.

[19] E. Fraenkel in his review of the *Editio Harvardiana* of Servius, *JRS* 39 (1949) 152, has shown that this explanation derives from a Homeric scholion. He argues that in Caesar's text the phrase "quo praeter sacerdotes adire fas non est, quae Graeci adyta appellant" is "an interpolation from Servius or, perhaps, from some earlier commentary on Virgil" (153). For *adytum = locus templi secretior*, see also *Corp. Gloss. Lat.* 5.549,5, and cf. Isid. *Etym.* 15.4.2.

[20] It was a temple of Dionysos, Cass. Dio 41.61.3.

[21] Val. Max. 1.6.12 referring to the same omen speaks of *abdita delubri*.

[22] Varro in Dion. Hal. 4.62.5–6; Plut. *Sull.* 27. Augustus transferred them to the temple of Apollo on the Palatine, Suet. *Aug.* 31.1. Cf. Cassola (above n.15) 23.

[23] Varro in Serv. *ad Aen.* 6.72; Plin. *NH* 11.105.

[24] For the sources, see Rzach, "Sibyllinische Orakel," *RE* 2A (1923) 2107–08; G. Radke, "Quindecimviri," *RE* 24 (1963) 1117–18.

as a parricide, but it gives one pause to observe that the only example
Varro was able to adduce was the (legendary) case of M. Atilius under
the first Tarquin.

In each religion there are various grades of secrecy: the augural and
pontifical books apparently were not as secret and holy as the *libri
Sibyllini*: the augurs and pontiffs did not need any senatorial instruction to open them. The archive of the pontiffs was probably housed
in the *regia*,[25] which was their meeting place and where they kept various holy objects. How inaccessible the pontifical books really were we
cannot tell; there were in the *regia* two veritable *adyta*, the *sacrarium*
of Mars and the *sacrarium* of Ops Consiva, but neither of them is a
likely candidate for housing the books.[26]

Wissowa[27] maintains that the augurs did not have a permanent
meeting place, and if this were true it would have been very difficult,
if not impossible, to establish where they kept their *libri reconditi*.
Wissowa based his opinion on two passages of Cicero in which is mentioned the augural custom of holding meetings *commentandi causa* on
the Nones of each month. On one occasion Cicero represents the
augurs as gathering in a private house, in the gardens of a member of
the college (*de amic.* 7). In the other passage the speaker, Q. Cicero,
compares the augurs to "magi, qui congregantur in fano commentandi
causa atque inter se conloquendi, quod etiam vos quondam[28] facere
Nonis solebatis" (*de div.* 1.90). In this passage *in fano* may refer both
to the *magi* and the augurs; *fanum* was a piece of consecrated
ground,[29] not an *aedes*, and thus it was aptly chosen not only with
respect to the *magi*, who did not have roofed temples, but also with

---

[25] G. Wissowa, *Religion und Kultus der Römer*[2] (München 1912) 502. But
Wissowa's argument that this follows from the fact that the consular list was
affixed to the walls of the *regia* is faulty and unnecessary: as A. Degrassi has
shown ("L'edificio dei Fasti Capitolini," *Rendiconti della Pontificia Accademia di
Archeologia* 21 [1945–46] 57–104 = *Scritti vari di antichità* I [Roma 1962]
239–281) the *fasti consulares* graced the *arcus Augusti*. The pontifical *tabula* was
displayed each year in the *domus publica*, the official residence of the *pontifex
maximus*; perhaps the pontifical books were kept in the *domus publica* as well.
Cf. B. W. Frier, *Libri Annales Pontificum Maximorum: The Origins of the Annalistic Tradition* (Rome 1979) 87–88, 100.

[26] Cf. S. B. Platner–T. Ashby, *A Topographical Dictionary of Ancient Rome*
(Oxford 1929) 441; Van Doren (above n.15) 35–38; Cassola (above n.15) 21,
23.

[27] "Augures," *RE* 2 (1896) 2323.

[28] This seems to indicate that by Cicero's time this custom had fallen into
oblivion.

[29] Cf. esp. Livy 10.37.16: "fanum tantum, id est, locus templo effatus."

respect to the augurs, who after all were interested in interpreting the flight of birds. Thus *horti* and *fana* were ideal meeting places for them. But above all here we do not deal with official meetings which were convened to pass a decree or give a *responsum* to a magistrate but rather with informal seminars and colloquia, discussions concerning various theoretical tenets of the *disciplina auguralis*. Such gatherings could very well take place in private houses of the *collegae*.

P. Catalano[30] ingeniously surmises that the augurs may have kept their archive in close proximity to the *auguraculum* on the *arx*, in a building erected in one of the "loca publica, quae in circuitu Capitoli, pontificibus, auguribus, decemviris et flaminibus in possessionem tradita erant" (Oros. 5.18.27). This is not very likely, for neither the pontiffs nor the *decemviri* (*quindecimviri*) kept their books *in circuitu Capitoli*; and second we would expect the *libri* to be housed in a consecrated *aedes*.[31] One such *aedes* in the vicinity of the *auguraculum* offers itself: the temple of Juno Moneta, which rose immediately to the north of the *auguraculum*.[32] If we are to trust Licinius Macer, the *libri lintei*[33] from which he drew his list of eponymous magistrates and some other information concerning the elections reposed in it. It could also very well contain the archive of the augurs; the name of Juno Moneta, whether it be interpreted as "Warner" or, more likely, "Remembrancer,"[34] fits the augurs exquisitely. The *scientia augurum* was based upon *observatio*, and its results, as Cicero tells us, were enshrined, for the instruction of future generations of augurs, in the

[30] *Contributi allo studio del diritto augurale* I (Turin 1960) 109 n.7.

[31] And we may add that according to Orosius these *loca* were sold by the state under Sulla; Catalano maintains (on no grounds) that only "parte di questi terreni fu venduta sotto Silla."

[32] This temple was dedicated in 344, but it appears to have been erected on the site of an earlier shrine, presumably also of Juno, which seems to go back to the very beginning of the republic. See G. Giannelli, "Il tempio di Giunone Moneta e la casa di Marco Manlio Capitolino," *Bull. Com.* 87 (1980–81 [1982]) 7ff.

[33] On the *libri lintei*, see R. M. Ogilvie, "Livy, Licinius Macer and the Libri Lintei," *JRS* 48 (1958) 40–46, and *A Commentary on Livy: Books 1–5* (Oxford 1965) 7–12, 544–545; R. E. A. Palmer, *The Archaic Community of the Romans* (Cambridge 1970) 234ff.; Frier (above n.25) 155ff.

[34] As A. Ernout and A. Meillet, *Dictionnaire étymologique de la langue latine*[3] (Paris 1951) 731–732, point out, both senses are present in *moneo*: that of "faire penser, souvenir" (original) and that of "appeler l'attention sur, avertir" (secondary). The original sense of *Moneta* was clearly "Remembrancer" or "Recorder": Livius Andronicus chose *Moneta* to translate Μνημοσύνη. Cf. R. E. A. Palmer, *Roman Religion and Roman Empire* (Philadelphia 1974) 29–30.

monumenta.[35] The only objection to this theory is this: although Juno was occasionally associated with the auspices,[36] the god of the auspices *par excellence* was Jupiter; the augurs were his *interpretes.* Thus one would expect them to keep their *monumenta* under the protection of Jupiter himself. But we have to remember that Jupiter was the god not only of the Capitoline temple but also of the *arx.*[37]

In either case the *libri* would be deposited in a place inaccessible to outsiders. But what was their content: was it as inaccessible as the books themselves? The way to the *libri reconditi* leads through the *responsa.* The latter were open to the general public: Cicero intimates that they were given at the *contiones.* If we establish the nature of *responsa* we ought at least to be in a position to find out what the *libri reconditi* were not.

First, the *libri* and *responsa* of the pontiffs. We read *de domo* 138:

> Dixi a principio nihil me de scientia vestra, nihil de sacris, nihil de abscondito pontificum iure dicturum. Quae sunt adhuc a me de iure dedicandi disputata, non sunt quaesita ex occulto aliquo genere litterarum, sed sumpta de medio, ex rebus palam per magistratus actis ad conlegiumque delatis, ex senatus consulto, ex lege. Illa interiora iam vestra sunt, quid dici, quid praeiri, quid tangi, quid teneri ius fuerit.[38]

The *absconditum ius pontificum* contained in an *occultum genus litterarum* corresponds to the *ius augurum* contained in the *libri reconditi.* Cicero derives his knowledge "ex senatus consulto, ex lege." The *lex*

---

[35] Cic. *de div.* 1.72. On the augural concept of *observatio*, see P. Regell, "De augurum publicorum libris," diss. Vratislaviae 1878, 3–7; J. Linderski, "The Augural Law" (above n.5) chap. 4.2.

[36] Giannelli (above n.32) 22 n.76 quotes Servius *auctus, ad Aen.* 4.45: "(Iuno) in libris augurum praeesse dicatur auspiciis," but he takes this passage out of context: the auspices in question are the *auspicia nuptiarum*, and Juno appears as Juno Pronuba.

[37] The augurs as *interpretes* of Jupiter: Cic. *de leg.* 2.20; *Phil.* 13.12. Jupiter as the god of the *arx*: Serv. *ad Aen.* 3.20; Ovid. *Fast.* 2.70. The inscription *ILS* 9337 containing a list of *auguria* performed between C.E. 3 and 17 was found in 1910 at the foot of the *arx*, from which it apparently had fallen down. Thus the augurs kept on the *arx* records of their activities; this seems to tilt the argument about the location of augural archives in favor of the *arx*.

[38] On *absconditum*, "secret," and *sumptum de medio*, "taken from what is accessible to all," see Nisbet ad loc. For *interiora*, cf. Cic. *ND* 3.42, and Pease ad loc. 1051–52 with a wealth of parallels.

in question is the *lex Papiria* [39] and the *senatus consultum* refers to the
famous case of the Vestal Licinia, who on her own authority dedicated
in 123 on the Aventine "aram et aediculam et pulvinar" (*de domo*
136–137). Concerning this act the praetor Sex. Iulius "ex
auctoritate [40] senatus ad . . . conlegium (the College of Pontiffs) rettu-
lit," and "P. Scaevola pontifex maximus pro conlegio respondit": the
pontiffs disallowed the dedication because it was made "iniussu
populi." On the basis of this *responsum* a *senatus consultum* was
passed by which the urban praetor was instructed to see to it that the
objects dedicated not be regarded as sacred and that any inscribed
letters of dedication be erased. This decree was extant: the *severitas*
and *diligentia* with which the Senate handled this matter "ex ipso
senatus consulto cognoscetis." The *responsum pontificum* will have
been incorporated in the senatorial decree; was it all a nonpontiff was
ever able to see? A complication is around the corner. Cicero also
derived his knowledge "ex rebus palam per magistratibus actis ad con-
legiumque delatis." The immediate context of this enunciation is this:
in 154 the censor C. Cassius Longinus placed in the Senate house and
dedicated a statue of Concordia. He apparently encountered opposition and to defuse it he turned to the College of Pontiffs. But the
pontiffs turned him down. Cicero writes gleefully (*de domo* 136):

> habetis in commentariis vestris C. Cassium censorem de
> signo Concordiae dedicando ad pontificum collegium rettu-
> lisse, eique M. Aemilium pontificem maximum pro conlegio
> respondisse, nisi eum populus Romanus nominatim praefec-
> isset atque eius iussu faceret, non videri eam posse recte
> dedicari.

The phrase "habetis in commentariis vestris" attracts attention.[41] It

---

[39] See *de domo* 127, 128, 130, and above n.3.

[40] As Nisbet ad loc. rightly notes, *auctoritas* here does not denote an inferior
(or vetoed, cf. Caelius in Cic. *Fam.* 8.8.4–8) *senatus consultum*, but in general
the opinion of the Senate. In other words it is an untechnical expression for
the technical *senatus consultum*, cf. Th. Mommsen, *Römisches Staatsrecht* III
(Leipzig 1888) 1033 n.2.

[41] G. Rohde, *Die Kultsatzungen der römischen Pontifices* (Berlin 1936) 18, suggests that Cicero may have derived this information from the *acta magistratuum*. This is unacceptable. There was hardly any reason to record in the *acta
censorum* a failed attempt to perform a dedication. Cicero quotes the *commentarii pontificum* because this was the only source available; upon the verdict of
the pontiffs C. Cassius abandoned his plan. As it was C. Cassius himself who
consulted the pontiffs in his capacity as censor and not the Senate acting

would appear that the past *responsa* of the college were collected in the *commentarii pontificum*, and as the *responsa* were given publicly, so also the *commentarii* were open to the public, at least to the senators. Thus they would form a clear counterpart to the *occultum genus litterarum* or the *libri reconditi*. This impression is strengthened by Cicero's asseverations that he discusses the *ius publicum* solely: "Neque ego nunc de religione . . . nec de pontificio sed de iure publico disputo" (*de domo* 128, cf. 32). The *ius publicum dedicandi* was a cross between the *caerimoniae pontificum* and the *iussa populi*.[42] The latter concerned the status of a dedication in public law, the former the religious ritual. Legally valid were only the dedications performed *iussu populi*; religiously valid were only those performed according to the prescribed ritual. The pontiffs treated the *ius dedicandi* from the standpoint both of the *ius publicum* and their own *caerimoniae*. Thus we can speak of the *ius pontificium publicum*, which dealt with legal aspects of sacral acts, and the *ius pontificium* proper, which was concerned with the ritual.

Pontifical deliberations concerning Cicero's house provide a telling example. The pontiffs decreed[43] (Cic. *Att.* 4.2.3):

> si neque populi iussu neque plebis scitu is qui se dedicasse diceret nominatim ei rei praefectus esset neque populi iussu aut plebis scitu id facere iussus esset, videri posse sine religione eam partem areae mihi restitui.

Observe the conditional nature of this *decretum*: the pontiffs do not say that the house ought to be given back to Cicero, nor in fact do they say that the dedication was invalid; they merely say that if the dedication had been performed in contravention of public law, it had no validity in pontifical law either; in this case the house could be

---

through a magistrate as its intermediary, no *senatus consultum* was necessary, and none was passed. This follows very clearly from *de domo* 137, where on the one hand "simulacrum Concordiae dedicare pontifices in templo inaugurato prohibuerunt" (referring to C. Cassius), and on the other "senatus in loco augusto consecratam iam aram tollendam ex auctoritate pontificum censuit" (referring to the Vestal Licinia).

[42] *De domo* 136: "ius publicum dedicandi, quod ipsi pontifices semper non solum ad suas caerimonias sed etiam ad populi iussa accommodaverunt."

[43] *decressent.* As a collective verdict of the college this was a *decretum*; but at the same time as a reply to the question directed to the college (cf. Cic. *Att.* 4.1.7: "de domo nostra nihil adhuc pontifices responderunt"), it also was a *responsum.*

restored to Cicero without sacrilege (*sine religione*). Next day at the meeting of the Senate one of the pontiffs, speaking *de omnium collegarum sententia*, explained (Cic. *Att.* 4.2.4):

> religionis iudices pontifices fuisse, legis <es>se senatum; se et collegas suos de religione statuisse, in senatu de lege statuturos cum senatu.

In the event the dedication should prove legally invalid, the pontiffs removed the *religio*;[44] now it was the Senate's turn to decide whether the law was violated. On the question of the law the pontiffs would express their opinions as senators and not as priests.

The picture is clear: a layman, such as Cicero, was expected to discuss pontifical matters only insofar as they pertained to the *ius publicum*; questions of ritual were the preserve of the pontiffs: *illa interiora iam vestra sunt*. In the case of *dedicatio*, the *interiora*, the esoteric knowledge of the pontiffs, comprised the words which the magistrate performing the ceremony was obliged to utter, the words which the officiating pontiff dictated to him, the objects that were to be touched and the objects that were to be held (*quid dici, quid praeiri, quid tangi, quid teneri ius fuerit*). But one may ask how esoteric this knowledge really was. Not very. The ceremony of *dedicatio/consecratio* had been repeated countless times; there was nothing secret about it: the formulas and gestures were known to anybody who cared to listen and watch. Thus Cicero felt it was safe enough to assert that Clodius "non iis institutis ac verbis quibus caerimoniae postulant dedicasse" (*de domo* 138), that he "omnia aliter ac vos in monumentis habetis et pronuntiarit et fecerit" (ibid. 140). Cicero obviously did not think that there was any conflict between this statement and the rhetorical question he posed at the outset of his argument (*de domo* 33):

> Quid est enim aut tam adrogans quam de religione, de rebus divinis, caerimoniis, sacris pontificum collegium docere conari, aut tam stultum quam, si quis quid in vestris libris invenerit, id narrare vobis, aut tam curiosum quam ea scire velle de quibus maiores nostri vos solos et consuli et scire voluerunt?

---

[44] Cf. Cic. *Att.* 4.1.7: "qui (sc. *pontifices*) si sustulerint religionem, aream praeclaram habemus."

But surely if anyone was able to consult the *libri* and if anyone was able to know what the pontiffs had in their *monumenta*, these cannot have been the secret documents. What then was the *occultum genus litterarum*? In their pursuit of neat order some nineteenth-century scholars postulated the existence of two distinct collections of sacerdotal documents, the *libri* and the *commentarii*. This view seems to go back at least to J. A. Ambrosch, the founder of modern studies in Roman religion, and B. G. Niebuhr, the founder of modern studies in Roman history.[45] The *libri* would contain general rules and precepts of the *ius sacrum*, texts of the formulae, and various instructions concerning the performance of religious acts. They would form the "interior" and original core of priestly archives. The *commentarii*, on the other hand, would incorporate the results of sacerdotal interpretive activity, the *responsa* and *decreta*. But these scholars sought order where there was none; they disregarded the vagaries of Roman terminology. It was Ambrosch's successor in Breslau, A. Reifferscheidt, who in his university lectures attacked this simplistic view. Two of his pupils, P. Preibisch, and above all, P. Regell, provided a detailed refutation of the theory of Ambrosch and Niebuhr. They demonstrated that there was no difference between the *libri* and *commentarii*: the two terms were used interchangeably.[46] This new interpretation was endorsed by Wissowa and extensively corroborated by Rhode; now it forms the *communis opinio.*[47]

---

[45] J. A. Ambrosch, *Observationum de sacris romanorum libris particula prima* (*Index lectionum in Universitate Vratislaviensi* 1840) 11–12; B. G. Niebuhr, *Vorträge über römische Geschichte* I (Berlin 1846) 10–11. For a systematic exposition of this theory, see A. Schwegler, *Römische Geschichte* I (Tübingen 1853) 31–34; E. Hübner, "Die annales maximi der Römer," *Jahrbücher f. class. Phil.* 79 (1859) 407–409; F. A. Brause, "Librorum de disciplina augurali ante Augusti mortem scriptorum reliquiae," diss. Lipsiae 1875, 14–15; J. Marquardt, *Römische Staatsverwaltung* III ² (Leipzig 1885) 400–401.

[46] P. Preibisch, "Quaestiones de libris pontificiis," diss. Vratislaviae 1874, 4–5; P. Regell, "De augurum publicorum libris," diss. Vratislaviae 1878, 29–41. For the *praelectiones* of Reifferscheidt, see Regell 41.

[47] Wissowa, "Augures," *RE* 2 (1896) 2323; Rohde (above n.41) 15ff. For a summary of the discussion concerning the *libri* and *commentarii*, see now F. Sini, *Documenti sacerdotali di Roma antica. I. "Libri" e "Commentarii,"* (Sassari 1983) 45–87, and "A proposito del carattere religioso del 'dictator' (Note metodologiche sui documenti sacerdotali)," *SDHI* 42 (1976) 416–418. In his own interpretation he unfortunately returns to the theory of Ambrosch and Niebuhr.

Thus there is no one single name that would open the priestly *adyta*; it is substance that matters. If our guide is not opaque terminology but rather the form and purpose of sacerdotal documents, a lucid classification emerges: a division into those documents which were destined for the internal use of a priestly college and those which were destined for the external use.

The latter category comprised above all *responsa* and *edicta*.[48] The *responsa* were of two kinds: the official *responsa* of a college, which can also be classified as *decreta*, and the *responsa* of individual pontiffs or augurs.[49] As both the collective and individual *responsa* were based on, and derived from, the "internal" documents, they offer us good insight into various tenets of the doctrine. The *decreta* were certainly preserved in priestly archives, but this will hardly have been the case with the "replies" of individual priests. In sharp contrast to the *decreta* they were not binding explications of the doctrine but merely opinions; and the opinion of one *sacerdos* could easily be contradicted by the opinion of another. Most of them were given orally and were never committed to writing; a few became famous and found their way into various antiquarian books *de iure sacrorum, de iure pontificio, de iure augurali*, and other similar works. The authors of some of these treatises were priests: this is of importance, for as they had unlimited access to the documents closed to others, their works formed the major source of ancient knowledge about *sacra* and *auspicia*.[50] Servius *auctus, ad Georg.* 1.270, cheerfully instructs his readers "quae feriae a quo genere hominum vel quibus diebus observentur, vel quae festis diebus fieri permissa sint, si quis scire desiderat, libros pontificales legat." The author of this commentary, whom we call Servius *auctus* or Servius Danielis, probably lived in the seventh century; by his time the pontiffs and their *libri* were ghosts of the past. The source of both Servius and Servius *auctus* appears to

---

[48] For the *edicta*, see, e.g., the *edicta* of the *quindecimviri* recorded in the Augustan *acta* of the *ludi saeculares, CIL* 6.32323 = *ILS* 5050, lines 110–114, 162–163.

[49] Cf. J. Linderski, "The Augural Law" (above n.5), chaps. 2 and 3.

[50] For the fragments of these treatises, see the (unfortunately very incomplete) collection of F. P. Bremer, *Iurisprudentiae antehadrianae quae supersunt* I–II (Lipsiae 1896–1901). The studies of Brause (above n.45), P. Preibisch, *Fragmenta librorum pontificiorum* (Progr. Tilsit 1878), P. Regell, *Fragmenta auguralia* (Progr. Hirschberg 1882), and G. Rowoldt, *Librorum pontificiorum Romanorum de caerimoniis sacrificiorum reliquiae*, diss. Halis Saxonum 1906, are attempts at the reconstruction of the "original" books of the augurs and pontiffs.

have been the great commentary of Aelius Donatus;[51] when he wrote it in the middle of the fourth century the pontiffs had not yet been suppressed by the intolerant new creed, but still it is hardly likely that Donatus advised his readers to rummage in the pontifical archives. What he was thinking about was clearly the learned treatises about the *res pontificales*. This will also be true of numerous other references we find in our sources to the *libri pontificii, pontificum, pontificales, commentarii pontificum, commentarii sacrorum, libri sacrorum* or *libri sacri*, or, for that matter, the *libri auspiciorum* or *augurales*.[52] Of course in these learned treatises the original pontifical or augural documents may have been adduced or referred to directly or indirectly, as, for example, Varro quotes (*de ling. Lat.* 7.8) the formula pronounced by the augur on the *arx*. But how Varro had come by this formula is not clear; it is not clear either how to interpret his statements "tera in augurum libris scripta cum R uno" (5.21) or the phrase "in pontificiis libris videmus" (5.98). For the *libri* in question to have been the original archival documents, we would have to admit that Varro was a *quindecimvir*[53] and that the members of one collegium had access to all priestly archives. But in fact we can very well imagine that Varro quotes here at second hand from the studies written by learned augurs and pontiffs.

This also answers the question as to the identity of *vestri libri* mentioned by Cicero *de domo* 33: they will not have been any secret documents but rather "scholarly" studies written by various learned pontiffs. It was inappropriate indeed, but not criminal, to advise the pontiffs on the basis of their own scientific exertions. But above all, these books were merely expositions, divagations, and polemics and not archival documents; they may have reproduced faithfully both the doctrine and the documents they quoted, but the reader could never be sure; and moreover he could always suspect that some secret tenets of the doctrine or esoteric interpretations of ritual formulae and gestures were suppressed or remained unexpressed. Hence Cicero disclaimed in 57 any knowledge of the real content of the augural and

---

[51] A. Santoro, "Il Servio Danielino e Donato," *SIFC* 20 (1946) 79ff.; R. B. Lloyd, "Republican Authors in Servius and the Scholia Danielis," *HSCP* 65 (1961) 291ff., esp. 234–237; R. Kaster, "Macrobius and Servius: Verecundia and the Grammarian's Function," *HSCP* 84 (1980) 219ff., esp. 224ff., 255ff.

[52] Cf. Rohde (above n.41) 17ff., esp. 40–42. Servius *auctus, ad Georg.* 1.270, intimates that he derives his information from those "qui disciplinas pontificum interius agnoverunt."

[53] As proposed by C. Cichorius, *Römische Studien* (Leipzig 1922) 199.

pontifical archives: coming from the mouth of a consular, *reconditum* and *occultum* are strong words.

It is fair to assume that some of these documents were more *reconditi* and *occulti* than others; and this supposition will turn into certainty if we consider that some ceremonies were so secret that they were not recorded in writing. Festus (Paulus) 14–15 L. mentions a *genus sacrificii* "quod in arce fit ab auguribus, adeo remotum a notitia vulgari, ut ne litteris quidem mandetur, sed per memoriam successorum celebretur." If the *memoria* of each individual augur was a receptacle of this unspeakable secret, it had to be diligently protected. And in fact Plutarch and Pliny the Younger tell us that death only could deprive an augur of his priesthood.[54] Plutarch intimated that the augurs took an oath not to reveal to anybody the secrets of their office. There are reasons to suppose that these secrets and the ceremony on the *arx* concerned the *augurium salutis*: at this act the officiating augur will have been obliged to utter the secret name of the city of Rome and of its tutelary deity.[55]

Memoria leads to the *monumenta*. With the stress the Roman cult laid on the exactness of the ritual, detailed instructions were indispensable.[56] These instructions were variously called *commentarii*, *libri*, or *monumenta sacrorum*, *caerimoniarum*, or *auspiciorum*. They do not seem to have contained any general rules but rather prescriptions concerning single *sacra* or *caerimoniae*.[57] Pliny the Elder says (*NH* 27.11) "videmus . . . certis praecationibus obsecrasse summos magistratus et, ne quid verborum praetereatur aut praeposterum dicatur, de scripto praeire aliquem." The person who *praeit* was most often a priest. Cicero accuses the young and inexperienced *pontifex* Pinarius Natta that he assisted Clodius *sine libris* and that as a result Clodius performed the dedication *praeposteris verbis* (*de domo* 139–140). The

---

[54] Plut. *Quaest. Rom.* 99; Plin. *Ep.* 4.8.1. G. Crifò, "La c.d. inamovibilità dell' *augur publicus P.R.Q.*," *Latomus* 21 (1962) 689–710, seeks the explanation for this rule in the fact that the augurs "erano . . . *cives* i quali, anche se condannati o esuli, non perdevano ancora, per ciò solo, la cittadinanza romana" (707). But, if so, why did this rule not apply to other priests as well? (It applied, however, Pliny *NH* 18.6 tells us, also to the *fratres Arvales*). The explanation is to be sought in the *occulta* rather than *publica*: in the secrets to which these two priesthoods must have been privy.

[55] Cf. J. Linderski, *CP* 70 (1975) 285–286. S. Savage, "Remotum a Notitia Vulgari," *TAPA* 76 (1945) 157–165, is a competent but cursory and incomplete tour of secrecy in Roman religion.

[56] F. Bömer, "Der Commentarius," *Hermes* 81 (1953) 212–213, stresses this point very forcefully.

[57] As shown convincingly by Rhode (above n.41) esp. 169.

libri which the priests used at the actual performance of ceremonies could not be secret in any absolute sense of the word; the Arval Brethren recited their *carmen* from a *libellus*, but the *carmen* itself was also recorded in their public *acta*. [58] But as these books reproduced the pertinent parts of a particular master *commentarius*, the *commentarius dedicationis*, for instance, which must have been guarded in the pontifical archives, Cicero felt he could claim "vos in monumentis habetis" without appearing unduly *curiosus*.

Nor will he have searched in the pontifical archives to discover the *responsum* concerning the statue of Concordia. From the fact that the *responsa* were given publicly it does not automatically follow that their archival originals were accessible to outsiders. If this were the case we would have to postulate the existence of two sorts of pontifical archives, one secret and the other open to the public: not impossible but not likely either. A letter to Atticus illuminates Cicero's method of research. When Cicero was investigating the complicated question of the *decem legati* sent to Corinth in 146 he asked Atticus to find somebody who would check the pertinent information in "eo libro in quo sunt senatus consulta C. Cornelio L. <Mummio> consulibus."[59] We can safely conclude that the senatorial decrees were collected in a published *commentarius*, with each book presumably covering one consular year. It is possible that there existed a similar *commentarius* containing the *responsa pontificum*. But in this case we would rather expect Cicero to come up with more examples of the pontifical invalidation of a *dedicatio* than the paltry two he adduces. He probably got his information either from a book on the pontifical law which quoted some more significant *responsa* or from an annalistic source, especially as the affair of the censor L. Cassius and the statue of Concordia must have been a *cause célèbre*. But as the *decreta* and *responsa* of the pontifical college were public documents and as they were deposited in the pontifical archives, Cicero was again fully entitled to claim: "habetis in commentariis vestris"—whatever his immediate source might have been.

Venimus ad augures. It strikes the reader that the responsa of the augurs were given orally at the *contiones*, a most unusual thing, for one would rather expect the *responsum* to be read in the Senate or

[58] On the book in Roman cult, see Rohde 64–70.

[59] Cic. *Att.* 13.33.3. On Cicero's historical investigation of the *decem legati*, see D. R. Shackleton Bailey, *Cicero's Letters to Atticus* V (Cambridge 1966) 349, 351, 355, 357–360; E. Badian, "Cicero and the Commission of 146 B.C.," *Hommages à M. Renard* I (*Collection Latomus* 101, Brussels 1969) 54–65, esp. 63–64.

addressed in writing to the magistrate who consulted the college. In addition to the *de domo* 39, reproduced at the beginning of this article, two other texts also belong here:

> *de domo* 40: Sed haec de auspiciis . . . acta sunt a te (sc. Clodio). Tu tuo praecipitante et debilitato tribunatu auspiciorum patronus subito extitisti; tu M. Bibulum in contionem, tu augures produxisti; tibi interroganti augures responderunt, cum de caelo servatum sit, cum populo agi non posse; tibi M. Bibulus quaerenti se de caelo servasse respondit, idemque in contione dixit, ab Appio tuo fratre productus, te omnino, quod contra auspicia adoptatus esses, tribunum non fuisse.

> *de har. resp.* 48: producebat (Clodius) fortissimum virum M. Bibulum, quaerebat ex eo C. Caesare leges ferente de caelo semperne servasset. semper se ille servasse dicebat. augures interrogabat quae ita lata essent, rectene lata essent. illi vitio lata esse dicebant.

The political and augural context of this affair was as follows. M. Bibulus, Caesar's colleague in the consulship, attempted to prevent the passage of the *lex agraria*; when he was chased away from the forum by Caesar's thugs, he shut himself up in his house and proclaimed he would "watch the sky" for unfavorable omens to vitiate any legislation Caesar might propose. He also watched for the omens on the day on which the *comitia curiata* passed the law *de arrogatione Clodii.*[60] Now, toward the end of his tribunate P. Clodius, terrified by the prospect of Cicero's return, attempted to put pressure on Caesar to prevent this from happening. He pretended to side with those enemies of Caesar who, like Bibulus, claimed that all the *leges* sponsored by Caesar and by the tribunes who cooperated with him were *vitio latae*. This was a suicidal bluff, for if this view had prevailed not only would the legislation of Caesar have been mortally jeopardized but also the very tribunate of Clodius himself.[61] Some scholars believe that he almost succeeded in perishing in this self-induced

[60] For a synopsis of events, see W. Drumann-P. Groebe, *Geschichte Roms* II (Leipzig 1902) 191ff.

[61] For a discussion of Clodius's position, see L. G. Pocock, "Publius Clodius and the Acts of Caesar," *CQ* 18 (1924) 59–65, and "A Note on the Policy of Clodius," *CQ* 19 (1925) 182–184; E. S. Gruen, "P. Clodius: Instrument or Independent Agent?" *Phoenix* 20 (1966) 120–130; T. Loposzko, *Trybunat Publiusza Klodiusza* (Warsaw 1974) 261ff.

conflagration. S. Weinstock writes that "the Senate instituted an enquiry . . . ; it took the deposition of Bibulus and asked the augural college to give a verdict." [62] This is pure fantasy. Cicero does not mention any senatorial inquiry, nor does he say that the Senate referred the question of the validity of Caesar's laws to the augural college. He says very explicitly that it was Clodius who in his capacity as the tribune of the plebs *produxit in contionem* M. Bibulus and the augurs. But *in contionem producere* [63] is a thing very different from *ad collegium referre*. A magistrate or a tribune of the plebs convenes a public meeting, the *contio*; he may either himself address the crowd or allow others to speak. He also may summon any individuals and demand answers to the questions put to them. This is precisely what Clodius did. It is *luce clarius* that the augurs were *producti* by Clodius as individuals, not as the *collegium* and that their *responsa* were their personal opinions only and not the official *responsum/decretum* of the college. The augurs in question were obviously the *inimici* of Caesar and wished to see his legislation (and the legislation of Clodius himself as well) invalidated. But the *collegium augurum* as such passed no resolution in this matter, nor did the Senate. If it had we would hear even today the triumphant perorations of Cicero.

But why was Cicero so fervent in promoting the importance of the oral enunciations of a few augurs and so adamant in disclaiming any interest in the "recondite books" (let alone any knowledge of them)? It was not modesty that spoke through his words but self-interest hiding under the mask of ignorance. For the augural doctrine as upheld by the College, the Senate, and applauded by Cato, was not on his side. It distinguished strictly between the "watching of the sky" and the report of this observation. Lightning was the omen that disrupted the assemblies. As the person who was watching the sky always managed to see a flash of lightning, the very announcement *se de caelo servaturum* was sufficient to cause the magistrate who intended to convene an assembly to abandon his plan. But in strict doctrine *de caelo servare* was not one and the same thing as *fulmen videre*. The report of an adverse omen, the *obnuntiatio*, was to be made in person to the presiding officer. Caesar found an ingenious way of coping with this obstacle to his legislation. He used force and prevented his

---

[62]S. Weinstock, "Clodius and the Lex Aelia Fufia," *JRS* 27 (1937) 220. For a criticism of Weinstock's theory, see the judicious remarks of L. R. Taylor, *Party Politics in the Age of Caesar* (Berkeley 1949) 95–96, 213–214. Cf. also A. W. Lintott, "P. Clodius Pulcher—Felix Catilina?" *Greece and Rome* 14 (1967) 167.

[63]Th. Mommsen, *Römisches Staatsrecht* I[3] (Leipzig 1887) 201.

enemies from making the report of *obnuntiatio* in person to him or to the tribunes legislating in his behalf. Bibulus's *servationes de caelo* were mere show; they lacked the punch of a personal report.[64] Thus there was no augural ground for invalidating the laws of Caesar, the tribunate of Clodius, and with it Cato's mission to Cyprus which Clodius had engineered.[65] Legally Caesar's laws could only be attacked as passed by force, but this the Senate was not prepared to do.

"Dico apud pontifices, augures adsunt:[66] versor in medio iure publico" (*de domo* 34). Precisely. Both the *ius dedicandi* and the *ius obnuntiandi* formed part of *ius publicum*. *Dedicatio* and *obnuntiatio* were regulated on the one hand by the comitial laws and on the other by the pontifical or augural rules. Both these acts were performed in the open; there was nothing mysterious about them. Secret appear to have been only the pontifical and augural books pertaining to them; but again they were *occulti* and *reconditi* only in the sense that they were accessible solely to the priests. They do not seem to have contained any truly esoteric doctrine of *obnuntiatio* or *dedicatio*.

A few years after Cicero had protested in his speech *de domo* his ignorance of the *res pontificales* and *res augurales* he himself was made augur,[67] and he even produced a treatise on the auguries.[68] Knowing Cicero's habits of work and study we can safely assume that he did

---

[64] For a discussion of this principle of the augural law, see I. M. J. Valeton, "De iure obnuntiandi comitiis et conciliis," *Mnemosyne* 19 (1891) 82–83, 101–102; J. Linderski, "Constitutional Aspects of the Consular Elections in 59 B.C.," *Historia* 14 (1965) 425–426. It finds a vivid illustration in Milo's efforts to stop Clodius's election to the aedileship in 57 by personally "obnuntiating" against the consul Metellus Nepos, who was to preside over the electoral *comitia* (Cic. *Att.* 4.3.3–4). A. W. Lintott, *Violence in Republican Rome* (Oxford 1969) 144–145, arrived at the same interpretation; as he did not quote his predecessors, he received a due award: an uninformed reviewer (A. N. Sherwin-White in *JRS* 59 [1969] 287) praised him for having demonstrated this important augural rule.

[65] On Cato's defense of Clodius's tribunate, see esp. Cass. Dio 39.22.

[66] Nisbet ad loc. (96) points out that the augurs were present "in case their expert knowledge of auspices should be required." In fact Cicero claimed that Clodius performed the *dedicatio* "ominibus obscenis" (*de domo* 140). On the augural meaning of *obscaenus*, see A. Thierfelder, "Obscaenus," *Navicula Chilonensis. Studia Philologica F. Jacoby oblata* (Leiden 1956) 98–106.

[67] In 53 or 52, see J. Linderski, "The Aedileship of Favonius, Curio the Younger and Cicero's Election to the Augurate," *HSCP* 76 (1972) 181ff.

[68] See M. Schanz–C. Hosius, *Geschichte der römischen Literatur* I (München 1927) 526. The fragments in C. W. F. Mueller, *M. Ciceronis scripta quae manserunt omnia* 4.3 (Lipsiae 1904) 312.

not conduct any independent archival research; his *liber* was probably
a compilation based on published materials. Nevertheless his books
written after his election to the augurate, and touching on the *res
augurales*, possess considerable authority, especially the excursus on
the augurs in the second book of the *de legibus* [69] and the numerous
passages in the *de divinatione*.

At *de div.* 2.71–73 Cicero inveighs against reprehensible practices
currently observed at the *auspicia de tripudiis*. [70] Now the augurs
regarded it as a good sign when an object, a stone, or a tree tumbled
down all of itself or when something dropped down from the beak of
a bird. In such spontaneous happenings the will of gods obviously
manifested itself. The augurs called it *tripudium sollistimum*. The
auspicia de tripudiis thus originally belonged to the class of *auspicia
oblativa*: the gods sent them when they wished. This was uncomfortable, especially when divine will had to be ascertained swiftly and reli-
ably, as before a battle. Thus, first in military practice, chickens
started to be employed for that purpose. They were kept hungry in a
cage so that when they were given food they ate so greedily that
crumbs were bound to fall down from their beaks. This was an
ingenious method of ensuring the positive outcome of the consultation while maintaining at the same time the principle of divine free
will: if the gods wished to deny the request they were quite free to
cause the chickens to lose their appetite. The few occasions on which
Jupiter made this happen were duly recorded in Roman historical
literature, [71] but on the whole the success of the new method (which
in fact goes as far back as our sources allow us to reach) was
overwhelming. The *auspicia pullaria* became the *auspicia de tripudiis
par excellence*, [72] a manifestation if not of divine will, then in any case

[69] *De leg.* 2.20–21, 31. For a detailed commentary, see J. Linderski, "The
Augural Law" (above n.5), chaps. 1–3.

[70] G. B. Pighi, "Tripudium," *Rendiconto dell' Accad. di Bologna. Classe di
Scienze Morali*, serie 5, vol. III (1949–50), provides an erudite discussion. See
also A. S. Pease, *M. Tulli Ciceronis De Divinatione* (Urbana 1920–23, reprint
Darmstadt 1963) 131–132; E. Marbach, "Tripudium," *RE* 7A(1939) 230–232.

[71] This happened, e.g., at the battles of Aquilonia (Livy 10.40.4), Cannae
(Livy 22.42.8–10), and at the naval battle at Drepanum (Cic. *ND* 2.7; *de div.*
1.29. Pease ad locc. lists numerous passages of other authors referring to this
famous event).

[72] The augurs regarded it as a separate *genus* of *auspicia*, Festus (and Paulus)
316–317 L.: "Quinque genera signorum observant augures: ex caelo, ex
avibus, ex tripudiis, ex quadrupedibus, ex diris." Of these five *genera*, the
auspicia de tripudiis were the "impetrative" auspices *par excellence*, the auspicia
ex caelo and *ex avibus* were both "impetrative" and "oblative," *ex quadru-*

of the legalistic genius of Roman religion. But the purists complained: "simulacra sunt auspiciorum, auspicia nullo modo." The *antiquissimi augures* did not employ this *coactum* and *expressum auspicium,* and the proof is this, writes Cicero (*de div.* 2.73):

> decretum collegi vetus habemus omnem avem tripudium facere posse.[73]

Again it is hardly likely that Cicero himself unearthed this decree in the archives. In fact it can be shown that he did not. Cicero's colleague in the augural college, Appius Claudius Pulcher, consul in 54 and censor in 50, dedicated to Cicero his first book of *auguralis disciplinae libri*; Cicero studied it assiduously during his stay in Cilicia.[74] A fragment from Book I, preserved by Festus 386 L., refers to the theory of *tripudia. Tripudium sollistimum* occurs "quom avi[75] excidit ex eo quod illa fert"; as Appius does not speak specifically of the *pulli* but in general of an *avis,* it is clear that he assumed *omnem avem tripudium facere posse.* The conclusion: Cicero lifted his *decretum collegi vetus* from the *libri* of Appius Claudius. In fact his whole discussion of the *tripudia* (*de div.* 1.27–28; 2.71–74) was based on the work of Appius Claudius. To explain <*soni*>*vium tripu*<*dium*> Festus (382 L.) quotes another fragment of Appius; it is fair to assume that also his third notice (284–285 L.) concerning the *tripudia* will be of the same origin. In this passage Appius presents an etymology of *tripudium*; the same etymology recurs at *de div.* 2.72—hardly a coincidence.[76]

This discussion is of prime importance for the interpretation of Servius *auctus, ad* Verg. *Aen.* 1.398, our second passage in which the expression *libri reconditi* occurs. Servius maintains "in libris reconditis

---

pedibus only "oblative," and the *auspicia ex diris* formed a category of particularly pernicious "oblative" signs.

[73] A reference to the same decree may be hidden in the corrupt passage, *de div.* 1.28 (Q. Cicero speaking): "quod autem scriptum habetis †aut (*avi* Turnebus, *avi* or *omni avi* hesitatingly Pease, *pulte* Giomini) tripudium fieri, si ex ea quid in solidum ceciderit."

[74] Cic. *Fam.* 3.4.2; 3.9.3; 3.11.4. An incomplete collection of Appius's fragments in Bremer (above n.50) 1.243–244 and in H. Funaioli, *Grammaticae Romanae Fragmenta* (Lipsiae 1907) 426–427; a good discussion in J. Zingler, *De Cicerone historico quaestiones,* diss. Berlin 1900, 18–24, and in Pease, *M. Tulli Ciceronis De Divinatione* (above n.70) 12, 27–28, 133, 138–140, 288–289, 333–334, 471–472.

[75] *quod* †*aut*† Lindsay *quom* Mueller *avi* Ant. Augustinus.

[76] Cf. Pighi (above n.70) 154.

lectum esse posse quamlibet avem auspicium attestari, maxime quia non poscatur." This rule displays close affinity with the augural decree "omnem avem tripudium facere posse." In both cases we deal with *auspicia oblativa*; Servius makes this clear by remarking "maxime quia non poscatur." He presents the following scheme:

> hoc enim interest inter augurium et auspicium, quod augurium et petitur et certis avibus ostenditur, auspicium qualibet avi demonstratur et non petitur.

There is confusion in his terminology. What Servius *auctus* really describes is not (as he thought) a distinction between *augurium* and *auspicium* but rather between the solicited *auspicia impetrativa* and unsolicited *auspicia oblativa*. [77] In this shape this is perfectly sound augural doctrine: at the *auspicia impetrativa* the Romans employed indeed only few kinds of birds, [78] the *pulli* being one of them, but as to the unsolicited signs the augurs apparently believed that the gods could send them through the medium of any bird.

There are differences also between the augural decree and the text of Servius *auctus*. The decree speaks very specifically about *tripudium*, Servius *auctus* considers in general the *auspicia de avibus*. And in fact birds could give auspical signs not only when they ate and when crumbs were dropping from their beaks but above all through their *volatus* and *cantus*. The former the augurs called *alites*, the latter *oscines*, and Servius *auctus* goes on to speak precisely of these two categories of augural birds.

Yet his ultimate source may have treated of the *tripudia* as well. For there existed a peculiar link between this form of auspices and the *oscines*: if a feeding bird uttered a cry it functioned as an *oscen*, but at the same time it also *tripudium fecit*, as the food it carried would perforce drop down. Here obviously belongs the *oscinum tripudium* appearing in a passage of Festus (214 L.); this information will again derive from the work of Appius Claudius, for a few lines below Festus reports that Appius treated of *oscines* and *alites* and gave their lists. Thus the virtual identity of the rule ascribed by Cicero to the augural decree and by Servius *auctus* to the *libri reconditi* appears assured.

The source of Servius *auctus* explicitly opposed the *libri reconditi* to the *augurales commentarii*. Now this whole passage is a comment on Vergil's words "cantusque dedere" (*Aen.* 1.398), referring to swans,

---

[77] On the terminology of Servius, see Catalano, *Contributi* (above n.30) 80ff.
[78] Cic. *de div.* 2.76; cf. Seneca, *N.Q.* 2.32.5.

cycni. The commentator remarks that the swans were not the *aves augurales* and that they are not listed in the augural "commentaries"; on the other hand, he continues, according to the *libri reconditi* every bird was capable of giving the auspices. Vergil, he explains, "amat secretiora dicere." In other words, the poet, as a perfect augur, did not limit himself solely to the *commentarii* but also utilized the secret knowledge contained in the *libri reconditi.* Servius *auctus* points out that Vergil represents the swans both as *alites* (this he indicates by the words "stridentibus alis" (*Aen.* 1.397) and as *oscines,* as shown by the verse "et coetu cinxere polum cantusque dedere" (1.398). As *alites* and *oscines* are augural categories Vergil "totum morem augurum exsecutus est proprietate verborum."

Let us pursue the swan connection a bit further. At *Aen.* 1.390–395 Vergil writes (Venus speaking):

> namque tibi reduces socios classemque relatam
> nuntio et in tutum versis Aquilonibus actam,
> ni frustra augurium vani docuere parentes.
> aspice bis senos laetantis agmine cycnos,
> aetheria quos lapsa plaga Iovis ales aperto
> turbabat caelo.

Servius comments on line 393:

> cycnos navibus comparat, aquilam (i.e., Iovis ales) tempestati. In auguriis autem considerandae sunt non solum aves, sed etiam volatus, ut in praepetibus, et cantus, ut in oscinibus, quia nec omnes nec omnibus dant auguria: ut columbae non nisi regibus dant, quia numquam singulae volant, sicut rex numquam solus incedit; . . . item cycni nullis dant nisi nautis, sicut lectum est in *Ornithogonia*:[79]
>
>> cycnus in auguriis nautis gratissimus ales;[80]
>> hunc optant semper, quia numquam mergitur undis.

---

[79] A poem by Aemilius Macer (*obiit* 16 B.C.E.); see Schanz-Hosius (above n.68), II (1935) 164–165.

[80] So Thilo; clearly preferable to the reading *augur* adopted in the *Editio Harvardiana.* Isid. *Etym.* 12.7.19 quotes this verse in the following form:

> Cygnus in auspiciis semper laetissimus ales
> hunc optant nautae, quia se non mergit in undas.

Vergil once again appears as a *doctus augur* deftly considering distinctions between the *praepetes* (*alites*) and *oscines*. But Servius's own explanation "quia nec omnes nec omnibus dant auguria" is awkwardly confused. In this phrase two disparate ideas are coupled together. The assertion "nec omnes (sc. aves) dant auguria" alludes to the augural principle governing the *auspicia impetrativa*, but as Servius *auctus* points out in his note on line 398 Vergil must be describing an *auspicium oblativum*. Consequently Servius's *quia* is quite inane. But above all the rule "nec omnibus dant auguria" is totally alien to the Roman *scientia auguralis* — at least as practiced by the *augures publici*.

The swan connection now becomes the pigeon link which leads us to the very heart of the prophetic bird lore of the *disciplina Etrusca*. The haruspices were very much interested in various divine signs pertaining to the kings and *principes civitatis*; the *columbarum augurium*[81] finds its counterpart in the *fulgura regalia* and *exta regalia*.[82] Hence it is quite likely that they also developed a theory of a special sympathetic connection between swans and sailors. Now in their headless effort to make out of Vergil a *peritus augur* the commentators missed the obvious fact that neither Vergil nor Aemilius Macer used the term *augurium* in the technical augural sense[83] of divine approval or disapproval of an action but rather in the colloquial sense of presage. Now this colloquial usage conformed to the teaching of the haruspices, who interpreted every sign as a prodigy portending future events.[84] Toward the end of the republic this Etruscan doctrine was making headway even into the College of Augurs: Appius Claudius Pulcher believed that the task of the *disciplina auguralis* was to discover in divine signs the *praesensio . . . veritatis futurae*.[85] But there is more to the swans than the haruspices alone; the swan was the bird of Apollo, and as such he was *eo ipso* endowed with prophetic powers. The swan's last song portending his death was a topos constantly rehashed by the

---

[81] Cf. Serv. *auct. ad Aen.* 1.398: "nam et haec (sc. *columbae*) inter augurales aves dicuntur non inveniri."

[82] See C. O. Thulin, *Die etruskische Disciplin* (Göteborg 1905–09, reprint Darmstadt 1968) I 70–72; II 46–47: S. Weinstock, "Libri fulgurales," *PBSR* 19 (1951) 149–150.

[83] And in this case rather the term *auspicium* should have been used.

[84] On this aspect of the *disciplina Etrusca*, see esp. Seneca, *NQ* 2.31–32, and H. M. Hine, *An Edition with Commentary of Seneca, Natural Questions, Book Two* (New York 1981) 340ff.

[85] Cic. *de div.* 1.105. Cf. *de leg.* 2.32. For Cicero's opposition to Appius's views, see esp. *de div.* 2.70: "Non enim sumus ii nos augures qui avium reliquorumve signorum observatione futura dicamus."

poets and rhetors. Thus in the poetic and antiquarian lore of the swan as a bird of prophecy there were mixed up in various configurations Greek, Roman, and Etruscan elements. [86]

The *disciplina Etrusca* was particularly concerned with *fulgura*, *exta*, and *ostenta*. In the books dealing with the latter, the *ostentaria*, [87] various kinds of divine signs were described and interpreted. Macrobius, *Sat.* 3.20.3, mentions an *ostentarium arborarium* composed by Tarquitius Priscus,[88] and from Pliny, *NH* 10.6–42, a similar book dealing with bird signs, an *ostentarium aviarium*, can be recovered.[89] The immediate source of Pliny appears to have been his contemporary, the haruspex Umbricius Melior, but the tradition of *ostentaria* goes back deep into the republican times. Iulius Obsequens reports in his *liber prodigiorum* 14 that in 163 "in templum Victoriae cygnus inlapsus per manus capientium effugit." Prodigies were often given by birds and animals appearing in unusual places. The haruspices were normally consulted about the meaning of such happenings and about what should be done to avert divine anger.[90] When in 191 "boves duos domitos in Carinis per scalas pervenisse in tegulas aedificii . . . eos vivos comburi cineremque eorum deici in Tiberim haruspices iusserunt" (Livy 36.37.1–2). A swan in the temple of Victory was an affair even more serious; we can assume that the Senate turned to the haruspices for illumination. In their interpretation the haruspices would take account of the place in which the prodigy occurred and of various attending circumstances. The *locus*—the temple of Victoria— pointed to military operations. But, whereas the *boves* in 191 were caught and burnt alive, the swan escaped. Just as the *effugia hostia*,

---

[86] On the lore of the swan, D'Arcy W. Thompson, *A Glossary of Greek Birds*[2] (Oxford 1936) 179ff.; Gossen, "Schwan," *RE* 2A (1921) esp. 784–789; *TLL* s.v. "cycnus," col. 1585, lines 31ff.

[87] Thulin (above n.82) I 10–12; III 76ff.

[88] On this Tarquitius Priscus and the *libri Tarquitiani*, see J. Heurgon, "Tarquitius Priscus et l'organisation de l'ordre des *haruspices* sous l'empereur Claude," *Latomus* 12 (1953) 402–417; but see also the very divergent interpretation of M. Torelli, *Elogia Tarquinensia* (Firenze 1975) 105ff. Recently Heurgon changed his mind and embraced Torelli's interpretation (whether rightly, *quaeritur*), "Varron et l'haruspice Étrusque Tarquitius Priscus," *Varron, Grammaire Antique et Stylistique Latine: Recueil offert à Jean Collart* (Paris 1978) 101–104.

[89] Thulin (above n.82) III 106ff.

[90] L. Wülker, *Die geschichtliche Entwicklung des Prodigienwesens bei den Römern* (Leipzig 1903) 16–18, 36.

the victim that escaped from before the altar, was a very bad sign,[91] so also the escape of the swan portended that something dire would irrevocably happen. And it did. The consul of 163, M'. Iuventius Thalna, was victorious in Corsica, and the Senate decreed *supplicationes*, thanksgivings to the gods. When Thalna got news of this honor he was so overcome with joy that he suddenly died.[92] Thus the meaning of the prodigy is transparent. *Mortem victori portendi*, the haruspices must have declared. But they could have come upon this interpretation only if they were acquainted with the theory that swans "providentes quid in morte boni sit, cum cantu et voluptate moriantur" (Cic. *Tusc.* 1.73). The swan chased by the temple attendants must have uttered a cry; his appearance in the temple and his escape was an adverse omen, but his voice was apparently a mixed sign: both propitious and dire. The unfortunate Thalna's success in Sardinia was his "swan song." Thus the explanation of Servius or rather of his source that swans "nullis dant (auguria) nisi nautis" is manifestly incorrect even within the limits of the *disciplina Etrusca*; it is a misleading generalization of Aemilius Macer's "cycnus in auguriis nautis gratissimus ales." But we can go a bit further: Macer uses the term *ales*. As *ales* the swan was a propitious sign for the sailors, but as *oscen* it could portend death.[93]

Be it as it may, we cannot doubt that the *cycnus* occupied a place of note in the Etruscan *ostentaria*. Regell and Thulin regard the *libri reconditi* as the books of the haruspices mainly for two reasons. First, they point to the contradiction between Cicero's statement "externa . . . auguria . . . omnibus fere avibus utuntur, nos admodum paucis" (*de div.* 2.76) and the principle ascribed by Servius *auctus* to the *libri reconditi* that any bird was capable of giving augural signs. This was an Etruscan principle, they claim. No doubt; but in view of the augural decree "omnem avem tripudium facere posse" (see above) this was an augural rule as well. Thus the contradiction Regell and Thulin postulate is more illusory than real. Furthermore Servius *auctus* does not say at all that the *cycni* are listed as *aves augurales* in

---

[91] Serv. *auct.ad Aen.* 2.140.

[92] Val. Max. 9.12.3; Plin. *NH* 7.182.

[93] L. Hopf, *Thierorakel und Orakelthiere in alter und neuer Zeit* (Stuttgart 1888) 177, quotes a passage from Saxo Grammaticus, a prophetic warning in which "voce canorus Olor" portends death. In Roman reliefs the swan appears as a symbol of a happy death but also as a symbol of victory: on an altar in the Arles museum a laurel wreath is suspended between the beaks of two swans; see J. M. C. Toynbee, *Animals in Roman Life and Art* (London 1973) 260 (with further literature).

the *libri reconditi*; that they could give signs is the inference his source makes from the rule "posse quamlibet avem auspicium adtestari."

Second, Regell and Thulin[94] point to the text of Servius *auctus, ad Aen.* 2.649, the third of our texts in which the *libri reconditi* are mentioned. Here the context is unmistakably Etruscan. If a *princeps civitatis* was struck by a *fulmen* and was only scorched this signifies that his progeny would be of enduring fame. This species of *fulgura regalia* finds a close parallel in a passage of Tarquitius adduced by Macrobius (3.7.2): "est . . . liber transcriptus ex Ostentario Tusco. ibi reperitur: purpureo aureove colore ovis ariesve si aspergetur, principi ordinis et generis summa cum felicitate largitatem auget, genus progeniem propagat in claritate laetioremque efficit."

Thus Etruscan lore was indeed contained in the *libri reconditi*. Yet it is neither obvious nor necessary to assume that there ever existed a category of Etruscan books technically called *libri reconditi*. For what is the import of the enunciations of Servius *auctus*: "in libris reconditis lectum esse" and "hoc scriptum in reconditis invenitur"? Either the *libri reconditi* lived up to their name and in that case they can hardly have been consulted by a Vergilian commentator or they were *reconditi* in name only. Judging by the two passages of Servius *auctus* they treated of abstruse matters but hardly secret. Macrobius, *Sat.* 3.9.6, writes that he reproduces the two famous formulas, the *carmen evocationis* and the *carmen devotionis*, from the fifth book *Rerum Reconditarum* of Serenus Sammonicus, who in turn found them in "cuiusdam Furii vetustissimo libro." Serenus Sammonicus *floruit* under Septimius Severus and was executed in 212 by Caracalla, perhaps as a *familiaris* of Geta.[95] The author of the *Historia Augusta* (*Gord.* 18.2) equips him in jest with a library consisting of precisely 62,000 volumes, which some modern innocents take seriously. A *vir saeculo suo doctus* (Macr. *Sat.* 3.16.6), he was not neglected by Donatus, the source of Servius and Servius *auctus*, in his Vergilian commentary. Servius *auctus* twice adduces Serenus Sammonicus by name but without quoting the title of his work, once as an authority on the *miracula* of the *insula* Thyle (*ad Georg.* 1.30) and the other time as the source of explanation of the name *Gargara* (*ad Georg.*

[94] Regell, *De augurum libris* (above n.46) 35–37; Thulin (above n.82) I 5 and III 111 n.4. Cf. A. Bouché-Leclercq, *Histoire de la divination dans l'antiquité* IV (Paris 1882) 59 n.3.

[95] Kind, "Serenus 6," *RE* 2 A (1923) 1675, and above all see now the excellent article by E. Champlin, "Serenus Sammonicus," *HSCP* 85 (1981) 189–212. Cf. R. Syme, *Ammianus Marcellinus and the Historia Augusta* (Oxford 1968) 160, 171–172, 183, 186.

1.102). Sammonicus's interest in *evocatio* and *devotio* matches very well the augural and fulguratory content of the *libri reconditi* in Servius *auctus*. These *libri* are in search of an author; it would be perverse to deny them Sammonicus.[96] The shadowy Furius apart,[97] we can establish one important source of Sammonicus's knowledge: P. Nigidius Figulus. In his study of *luxuria* Sammonicus quoted Nigidius's *De Animalibus* (Macr. *Sat.* 3.16.7), and it is very likely that he also knew other works of this polyhistor. In his book *De augurio privato* Nigidius mixed freely the Etruscan and augural elements,[98] and this mixture is also the hallmark of the *libri reconditi* in Servius *auctus*.

Thus in whichever direction we turn we are confronted with layer upon layer of antiquarian tradition. And when the *libri reconditi* seem at last to be within our reach they reveal themselves as another late and confused compilation, a fitting denouement of our quest. *Tenere disciplinam*, to uphold the doctrine, was the common obligation of the augurs, pontiffs, and haruspices. We cannot doubt that the books they guarded were *occulti* indeed and *reconditi*, far removed *a notitia vulgari*. Like the inhabitants of Plato's cave we can see their shadows only.

[96] Kind, "Serenus 6," ascribed them to Sammonicus as a matter of fact, without any discussion, and Champlin observes (193): "Two abstruse items on auspices and lightning which Servius dredged out of unspecified 'libri reconditi' might well derive from Sammonicus also."

[97] Bremer (above n.50) I 29, identifies this Furius, on no apparent grounds, with L. Furius Philus, cos. 136.

[98] Thulin (above n.82) III 109. On Nigidius, see A. Swoboda, *P. Nigidii Figuli Opera* (Pragae 1889); A. Della Casa, *Nigidio Figulo* (Rome 1962) esp. 101ff.

51

EXTA AND *AVES*: AN EMENDATION IN RUFINUS, *ORIGENIS IN NUMEROS HOMILIA* 17.2

THE editors of Christian authors have naturally been much more *Christiani* than *Ciceroniani*. Yet the study of Roman antiquities, and in particular of Roman religious terminology, may often be very helpful in discovering the correct sense and correct text of hitherto unintelligible passages. The text of Rufinus, *Origenis in Numeros Homilia* 17.2, offers an instructive example. The text as printed in the authoritative edition by W. A. Baehrens, Origines, *Werke* 7 (Die Griechischen Christlichen Schriftsteller der ersten drei Jahrhunderte 30, Leipzig, 1921), 156, reads as follows (Origenes-Rufinus comment on Num. 24:1 referring to Balaam):

Denique "non abiit" [sc. Balaam] inquit [i.e. Scripture says] "ex more in occursum auspiciis"; non enim more sibi solito, stultis et inanibus sensibus rapietur in animalibus mutis et pecudibus Dei considerans voluntatem, sicut hi, qui ex istis talibus auspicia colligunt, sed agnoscet etiam ipse quia neque "de bobus cura est Deo," similiter neque de ovibus neque de avibus aliisque animalibus, sed si qua de his scripta sunt, propter homines intelliget scripta. [The same text in Migne, *Patr. Graeca*, vol. 20, col. 704]

The phrase *qui ex istis talibus auspicia colligunt* is incomprehensible.[1] We have to read: *qui ex extis et avibus auspicia colligunt.*

The expression *auspicia colligere* seems to have been an augural *terminus technicus*, although it is attested only in late Latin authors. Servius *auctus* in his comment on *Aen.* 3.246 speaks of *auspicii genus . . . secundum augures, quod de diris colligitur, quorum unum genus est quod de signis colligitur.* At *Aen.* 4.453 he mentions *genus ominis . . . de augurali disciplina translatum . . . qua e[2] diris observatur*, and informs us that *dira*

My thanks go to Professor Agnes Michels, who very kindly agreed to read a draft of this note.

[1] Baehrens does not list any variant readings or conjectures. H. Méhat (ed.), Origène, *Homélies sur les Nombres* (Sources Chrétiennes 29 [Paris 1951]) 341, follows the text of Baehrens and translates the passage in question as *qui en tirent des présages.*

[2] *qua e* ed. Harv. *quae* Thilo.

enim deorum ira est, quae duplici modo colligitur, aut ex signis aut quo-cumque modo aut quacumque ex parte (cf. also 5.7). Ammianus Marcellinus 21.1.9 uses the same expression with respect to *aves: auguria et auspicia non volucrum arbitrio . . . colliguntur . . . sed volatus avium dirigit deus.*[3] Now as we learn from Festus (Paulus) 316, 317 L. *quinque genera signorum observant augures publici: ex caelo, ex avibus, ex tripudis, ex quadripedibus, ex diris.* In Servius *auctus* and Ammianus Marcellinus the expression *colligo* assumes part of the meaning of the traditional augural term *observo.*[4] In the language of the augurs this term denoted both the perception of a sign and its interpretation and classification according to the rules codified once and for ever in the augural books.[5] In the text of Rufinus, in view of these examples the emendation *qui ex . . . avibus auspicia colligunt* suggests itself.

Although augury and extispicine formed two separate branches of divination, *exta* and *aves* appear frequently juxtaposed,[6] and the term *auspicia* was occasionally used with respect to the inspection of entrails.[7] The term *colligo* also appears in connection with the interpretation of *exta*, Serv. on Verg. *Georg.* 3.491: *Colligi enim nisi ex sana victima futura non possunt.*[8] The expression *ex extis auspicia colligere* would hardly have passed scrutiny of a republican augur, but linguisti-

---

[3] Cf. Amm. Marc. 30.5.7: *per portam voluit* (sc. Valentinianus) *unde introiit exire, ut omen colligeret, quod cito remeabit ad Gallias.*

[4] This meaning of *colligo* seems also to be present at Min. Fel. 26.1 *auspicia et auguria Romana . . . summo labore collecta*, where *collecta* means not only "collected," but also describes the *auspicia* of which the correct interpretation had been established *summo labore*, or, as Cicero would have said, *observatione diuturna* (cf. *de div.* 1.34, 72; 2.26). In his translation of *Octavius* (Coll. Budé, Paris 1974) J. Beaujeu has misunderstood this passage.

[5] At the same time in the phrase (*diras*) *quocumque modo et quacumque ex parte colligere* (Serv. *auct. Aen.* 4.453) *colligo* has the sense of *conicio*, i.e., it refers to the method of interpretation *subito ex tempore* (Cic. *de div.* 1.72) by means of *ratio* and *coniectura*. For a detailed discussion of the augural concepts of *observatio, observo, coniectura*, and *auspicia colligere*, see J. Linderski, "The Augural Law," *ANRW*, Teil II, 16.3, chap. IV, 2 (forthcoming). Cf. also *TLL* s.v. *colligo*, col. 1617, line 10 ff; P. Regell *De augurum publicorum libris* (diss. Vratislaviae 1878) 3–7; Idem, *Commentarii in librorum auguralium fragmenta specimen* (Progr. Hirschberg 1893) 20, n.52; W. Hübner, *Dirae im römischen Epos* (Spudasmata 21 [Hildesheim 1970]) 28–29.

[6] See, e.g., Liv. 2.42.10; Sen. *Quaest. Nat.* 2.42; Amm. Marc. 21.1.9–10.

[7] Festus 286 L. s.vv. *piacularia* and *pestifera auspicia*. This reflects, however, Etruscan rather than Roman divinatory lore; cf. C. O. Thulin, *Die etruskische Disciplin*, Teil 2 (Göteborg, 1906; reprint, Darmstadt, 1968) 8–10.

[8] Cf. Lact. Plac. on Stat. *Theb.* 4.468: *Ars autem haruspicina hoc habet, ut et turis motus et crepitus et fumi motus et flexus colligat, quoniam haec primum signa aut testantur extorum promissis, si bona sint, aut, si contraria, refragantur.*

cally it is a perfectly correct phrase, and we should not hesitate to restore it in the text of Rufinus.

In the following sentence Rufinus mentions *boves*, *oves*, and again *aves*; his mention of birds points back to the *auspicia ex avibus*, and of oxen and sheep to the *exta*. Sheep and oxen were two kinds of sacrificial victims which were most frequently used for extispicine.[9]

Rufinus' use of Roman divinatory terminology is quite remarkable; at 17.3 he writes: *qui divinationi et auguriis operam dedit*. The phrase *auspiciis* (*auspicio*) or *auguriis* (*augurio*) *operam dare* can be traced back to the very beginning of Roman literature. It is found already in Ennius (*Ann.* 78 V.).[10]

[9] See the passages collected by G. Blecher, *De extispicio capita tria* (RgVV II 4 [Giessen 1905]) 11 ff, and by A. S. Pease ad Cic. *de div.* 1.119 (Urbana, 1920; reprint, Darmstadt, 1963).
[10] Cf. also Cic. *Fam.* 10.12.3; Festus 276.26 L.; Varro, *de ling. Lat.* 6.91 (Bergk's emendation).

52

SANNIO AND REMUS

Ennius, *Ann.* 79-80 Vahlen reads as follows:
>   Remus auspicio se deuouet atque secundam
>   Solus auem seruat.

Auspicio se deuouet is the traditional text, but Otto Skutsch in his recent edition of Ennius proposed to read *Remus auspicio sedet*[1]). As Skutsch observes, *deuoueo* in the meaning of devoting one's attention to something is "unparalleled and impossible", but his magnificent emendation is based above all on augural terminology: *secundum augures sedere est auspicium captare*[2]). An obscure passage buried in the Terentian Scholia may provide additional and unexpected support. It seems to contain an echo of the original Ennian phrase.

In the *Eunuchus* of Terence (line 780) the *miles* Thraso prepares to storm the house of the *meretrix* Thais, and asks his slave Sanga: *Ubi alii?* Sanga answers:
>   Qui malum 'alii'? solus Sannio seruat domi.

Domi is the reading of the *codex Bembinus*, and it was naturally adopted by modern editors; the *recensio Calliopiana* has *domum*[3]), and this is also the reading in the commentary of Donatus[4]).

In our text of Donatus there are several interpretations of the passage. First Donatus points out that Terence employs the figure of παρόμοιον, alliteration, and adduces as a parallel the Vergilian verse (*Aen.* 3.183): *sola mihi talis casus Cassandra canebat*[5]). Next he interprets the phrase *solus Sannio s. d.* to mean *remanet et obseruat*, and continues: *nam 'seruat domum' rectum erat, non 'seruat domi', si custodit intellegitur*[6]). The use of *servo* (and *observo*) in the sense of *custodio* is well known, and the scholiasts and grammarians often comment on it[7]). So far nothing unusual, but the following scholion arrests attention:

Vel SERVAT pro sedet et seruat[8]), ab eo quod sequitur id quod praecedit; nam non seruat nisi qui prius in eodem loco sederit.

H. T. Karsten in his valiant attempt to separate the scholia *genuina* and *spuria* refused to attribute this note to Donatus; he assigned it to an unknown commentator, a scholar characterized by a *mira et peculiaris aliqua sapientia*[9]). Whether this note figured in the original text of Donatus or not, the explanation offered is peculiar indeed. The Scholiast asserts that "one does not keep watch unless he had first sat down in the same place". Whence this strange idea?[10]) From augury. The Scholiast alludes to the same augural principle that led Skutsch to his brilliant emendation. To appreciate fully this augural connection we have to consider the Vergilian commentary of Servius (and Servius *auctus*). At *Aen.* 9.3-4 Vergil writes:
>   Luco tum forte parentis
>   Pilumni Turnus sacrata valle sedebat.

Servius (with a few insignificant additions from Servius *auctus*) gives three explanations of *sedebat*:

a) ut Asper dicit 'erat', quae clausula antiqua est et de usu remota.

b) secundum Plautum autem 'sedere' est consilium capere[11]), qui inducit in Mostellaria[12]) servum dicentem 'sine iuxta aram sedeam, et dabo meliora consilia'.

c) sed secundum augures 'sedere' est augurium captare; namque post designatas caeli partes a sedentibus captantur auguria[13]): quod et supra ipse ostendit latenter, inducens Picum solum sedentem, ut [7.187] 'parvaque sedebat succinctus trabea', quod est augurum, cum alios stantes induxerit.

Servius concludes: erga 'sedebat' aut erat aut consilia capiebat aut augurabatur.

Of these explanations none takes account of Vergil's text. The first goes back to the renowned commentary of Aemilius Asper[14]), and attributes to *sedeo* an unprecedented sense. Tomsin argued that "Asper voulait éviter qu'on attribuât au héros une attitude oisive indigne de l'épopée et du caractère du lieu"[15]). What repelled Asper and Servius delighted modern commentators: as Forbiger aptly wrote "*sedebat* spectat ad solitudinem et otium, cui *sedendi* verbum bene convenit"[16]). For when Iris came to Turnus he was reposing; Vergil does not represent him as considering anything (explanation b) or still less as taking auspices or performing an act of augury (explanation c). It was solely the verb *sedebat* that, isolated from its immediate context, triggered in the mind of the Scholiasts those spurious but learned interpretations.

On both counts the prize goes to the augural explication. The commentators saw in Vergil not only a *poeta doctus* but above all a perfect augur. "*Vergilius amat secretiora dicere; nam totum morem augurum exsecutus est proprietate verborum*"—writes Servius *auctus* in his note on *Aen.* 1.386[17]). The Scholiasts loved to discover the *secretiora*; the more abstruse an interpretation the better. Now this procedure does not differ at all from the method of explication applied to *Solus Sannio seruat domum*. And as the commentary of Servius (and Servius *auctus*) was based on the work of Donatus[18]), there is no reason to follow Karsten and deny Donatus (or in any case his *variorum* commentary) this bit of augural lore either in the Vergilian or the Terentian Scholia.

But whereas it was natural to find *secretiora* in Vergil, such a mode of interpretation was rather odd with respect to Terence for whom nobody claimed any recondite wisdom. It must have been evoked by a very peculiar association, verbal or literary. The obvious starting point is the verb *servat*. Taken out of the context it could easily conjure up the image of augury, for as Servius *auctus* points out, *servare enim et de caelo et de avibus verbo augurum dicitur* (*Aen.* 6.198), and in fact this usage is attested by numerous examples from Ennius onwards. Still one can doubt if *servat* alone would have been sufficient to start the Scholiast on his bizarre ride of argument. Another catalyst was opportunately present: *solus*. Not only *sola ... Cassandra canebat*, not only the augur Picus was represented according to Servius as *solus sedens*, but also *Remus ... solus auem seruat*—so as Sannio *solus ... seruat domum*[19]).

But how did the Scholiast arrive at his idea that *servat* stands for *sedet et seruat?* Again *servat* alone would hardly have led him to this conclusion, but if he had read in his text of Ennius (which he presumably found quoted in an earlier commentary) *Remus auspicio sedet* and *secundam solus auem seruat*, the link between *servare* and *sedere* was firmly established[20]). Thus the phrase *solus Sannio ... seruat* evoked in his mind the image of *Remus ... solus seruat* and then *Remus auspicio sedet*, and this in turn produced the bizarre interpretation of *servat* in Terence. The circle was closed. Caught in his argument the Scholiast was more than willing to forget that Sannio watched the house and not the bird.

To a sober reader the thread connecting Sannio and Remus may appear tenuous indeed, but then we are dealing with the *sapientia mira et peculiaris*.

1) O. Skutsch, *The 'Annals' of Quintus Ennius* (Oxford 1985), 76 (Book I, lines 74-5) and 224-5 (commentary).

2) Serv. *Aen.* 9.4 (see below in the text). To this and other passages listed by Skutsch (Festus 470-2 L.; Plut. *Rom.* 22.1; *Cam.* 32.7; *Marcell.* 5.2; *Caes.* 47.3), add Liv. 1.18.7; 8.23.16; Festus 474.10 L.; *Sch. Veron. ad Aen.* 10.241; Serv. *Aen.* 6.197; Aelian. *Hist. anim.* 8.5. *Oxford Latin Dictionary* docs not record this meaning of *sedeo*; Liddell-Scott-Jones lists the augural meaning of καθέζομαι and κάθημαι only *s.v.* οἰωνός.

3) See S. Prete, *P. Terenti Afri Comoediae* (Heidelberg 1954), 222 ad loc. in app. crit.

4) P. Wessner, *Aeli Donati Commentum Terenti*, I (Lipsiae 1902), 436-437, see esp. 437, lines 1-2; Eugraphius (Wessner III.1 [1908], 134, lines 8-9) has *domi* (*doni*) in the codices L and V¹, but *domum* in all others. Nonius 61 M. = 85 L. has *domi*. F. Umpfenbach, *P. Terenti Comoediae* (Berolini 1870), 156 ad *Eun.* 780, reports the readings of the scholia inaccurately.

5) This verse was a canonical example for *paromoeon*; it is quoted by Pompeius in his *Commentum Artis Donati* (*Grammatici Latini*, ed. H. Keil, vol. V, p. 303, lines 28-31), by Sacerdos (*Gramm. Lat.* VI, p. 459, lines 1-2), by the *Scholia Bembina* (ed. J. F. Mountford, Liverpool-London 1934), 58, ad *Heaut.* 209, by Servius *ad Aen.* 2.199, and by Isid. *Orig.* 1.36.14. Cf. Wessner ad loc. I.535.

6) The words *remanet et obseruat*, and *custodit* Wessner prints *inclinatis litteris* to indicate (I, p. XLVII) *ea ... quibus integrum scholium in duas vel plures partes disiectum esse videbatur.* I do not see any compelling reason for this procedure. Cf. Eugraphius: *aut absolute dictum 'seruat domi' aut: seruat ea quae domi sunt; Scholia Terentiana* (ed. F. Schlee, Lipsiae 1893), 109 ad loc.: *servat: custodit.*

7) For the phrase *seruare domum* Nonius (387 M. = 619 L.) adduces Verg. *Aen.* 2.702 (*servate domum, servate nepotem*) and 7.52 (of Lavinia: *sola domum et tantas servabat filia sedes*), the last line also quoted by Servius in full *ad Aen.* 6.402 (SERVET: *custodiat*, to which Servius *auctus* adds *obtineat, inhabitet*), and in part (*tantas ... sedes*)

in his notes on 2.711 (SERVET: *autem custodiat*), 5.30 and *Georg.* 4.458 (where, however, he favors the sense of *tenet*).

8) The words *sedet et seruat* Wessner prints *inclinatis litteris* (see above, n. 6), but again I do not see any compelling reason for admitting an interpolation.

9) H. T. Karsten, *Commenti Donatiani ad Terenti Fabulas Scholia genuina et spuria* (Lugduni Batavorum 1912), vol. I, pp. 203 and XXI-XXII. Cf. also his *De Commenti Donatiani ad Terenti fabulas origine et compositione* (Lugduni Batavorum 1907), 9-10, 80.

10) In his annotations in the *Appendix* (I.536) Wessner was not able to adduce any parallels.

11) Cf. Serv. *ad Aen.* 1.56: SEDET *non otiatur, sed curat; apud antiquos enim 'sedet' considerat significabat, ut alio loco* [*Aen.* 9.4] *ait 'Turnus sacrata valle sedebat'*. Observe that here Servius takes this sense of *sedeo* at *Aen.* 9.4 for granted. So also Lact. Plac. *ad Stat. Theb.* 1.104: "SEDET *polysemus sermo est. significat enim* placet, *ut* [*Aen.* 2.660]: *'sedet hoc animo', aliquando* cogito, *ut* [*Aen.* 9.4]: *'Turnus secreta* [*sic*] *ualle sedebat'*, *aliquando* positum est ut hoc loco [*"Sedet intus abactis ferrea lux oculis"*], et *aliquando* curat, *ut* [*Aen.* 1.56]: *'selsa sedet Aeolus arce', et reuera* sedet".

12) This is a paraphrase not a quotation. Plaut. *Most.* 1103-4 reads: *Sic tamen hinc consilium dedero. nimio plus sapio sedens.* / *tum consilia firmiora sunt de divinis locis.*

13) Cf. Serv. *Aen.* 6.197: *ad captanda auguria post preces immobiles vel sedere vel stare consueverant. Stare* causes trouble, but the solution is at hand. *Sedere* refers to the normal posture at the *auspicatio*, i.e. to the observation of the *auspicia impetrativa*, but the person who happened to observe an *auspicium oblativum* may well have been standing as Aeneas was when he saw the *columbae* that were to lead him to the golden bough (*Aen.* 6.186-197). This also appears to have been the posture at the *augurium stativum*, see Cic. *de div.* 1.31. Cf. P. Catalano, *Contributi allo studio del diritto augurale*. I (Torino 1960), 307-317.

14) Cf. M. Schanz-C. Hosius, *Geschichte der römischen Literatur*, III³ (München 1922), 161-162; A. Tomsin, *Étude sur le Commentaire Virgilien d'Aemilius Asper* (Bibliothèque de la Faculté de Philosophie et Lettres de l'Université de Liège 225, Paris 1952).

15) Op. cit. 64.

16) A. Forbiger, *P. Vergili Maronis Opera*, III⁴ (Lipsiae 1875), 218 ad loc. So also J. Conington-H. Nettleship, *P. Vergili Maronis Opera*, III³ (London 1883), 159 ad loc.: "Turnus is represented as at ease when Iris comes to rouse him". For this meaning of *sedeo*, see the examples in *OLD s.v. sedeo* 8 (p. 1725), to which add Donatus *ad Terent. Ad.* 672 (II.135 Wessner): *'sedere' proprie ignauae cessationis est* (quoted by Tomsin).

17) Cf. J. Linderski, *The Libri Reconditi*, HSCP 89 (1985), 227-231.

18) See A. Santoro, *Il Servio Danielino e Donato*, SIFC 20 (1946), 79-104; R. B. Lloyd, *Republican Authors in Servius and the Scholia Danielis*, HSCP 65 (1961), 291 ff., esp. 334-337; R. Kaster, *Macrobius and Servius: Verecundia and the Grammarian's Function*, HSCP 84 (1980), 219 ff., esp. 224 ff., 255 ff.

19) The reading of the Scholia *domum* (instead of *domi*) was an important factor in reinforcing this connection.

20) The only passage quoted in *OLD* in which *sedeo* has the meaning of "keeping watch over something" is Mart. 12.70.2: *cum ... supra togulam lusca sederet anus.*

53

"AUSPICIA ET AUGURIA ROMANA . . . SUMMO LABORE COLLECTA": A NOTE ON MINUCIUS FELIX *OCTAVIUS* 26. 1

The text of Minucius Felix *Octavius* 26.1 reads: "Iam enim venio ad illa auspicia et auguria Romana, quae summo labore collecta testatus es et paenitenter omissa et observata feliciter." Recent translators of and commentators on *Octavius* almost unanimously follow the received opinion and construe *testatus es* both with "(auspicia et auguria) . . . et paenitenter omissa et observata feliciter" and with "(auspicia et auguria) . . . summo labore collecta."[1] This construction is, however,

1. See, e.g., G. W. Clarke, *The "Octavius" of Minucius Felix* (New York, 1974); J. Beaujeu, *Minucius Felix: "Octavius"* (Paris, 1974). G. Quispel, *M. Minucii Felicis "Octavius"* (Leyden, 1973), ad loc., comments: "*collecta* scil.: abs te." J. P. Waltzing in his classic edition of and commentary on *Octavius* (Bruges, 1909) does not discuss the meaning and construction of *collecta*. I am grateful to Prof. E. Badian for excerpting for me the relevant passages from Waltzing's commentary.

unwarranted syntactically and it produces an odd sense, for it is hardly possible to assert seriously that Caecilius "took great pains" to collect the auguries and auspices (Clarke) or that he collected them "au prix des plus grands efforts" (Beaujeu). Caecilius had adduced at 7. 4 only four exempla,[2] all of them well known, and he took three of them directly from Cicero De divinatione 1. 28–30, 1. 77–78, and 2. 20–22. A summus labor indeed! R. Arbesmann keeps closer to the text and translates the phrase in question as "collected with great labor,"[3] but this translation, while literally correct, evades rather than answers two major questions: (a) what is the precise meaning of colligo in this passage and (b) who had collected the auspices and auguries summo labore?

One ought not to forget that "to bring together, to collect, assemble" is only one of the many meanings of colligo; it also means "to collect over the period of time, accumulate" and in a more specialized sense "to deduce, infer, gather."[4] This is especially true of colligo as used in Stoic terminology. The Stoics attributed the weight of proof to the accumulation of evidence;[5] compare, for example, Cicero De divinatione 2. 33 "Ut enim iam sit aliqua in natura rerum contagio, quam esse concedo (multa enim Stoici colligunt)" (numerous examples of συμπάθεια follow). In this passage colligo has both the sense of "collect, bring together" and of "infer, gather"; the Stoics have collected ample evidence with a view to proving the existence of contagio/συμπάθεια, or conversely they infer the existence of συμπάθεια from the instances they have collected. In other words, the Stoics arrive at their conclusions on the basis of empirical observation, and then in turn they explain individual cases on the basis of their general theory. It is important to realize that a similar procedure was also applied in augury.

According to Stoic classification, augury formed a branch of artificial divination.[6] It was an empirical science. From this point of view, the augural theory distinguished between two categories of divinatory signs: (1) the veteres res, that is, those signs the meaning of which had been established already in the (remote) past empirically through the process of long-continued observation (observatio diuturna)—those signs were recorded in the books of the augurs, their meaning codified once and for ever; (2) the novae res, that is, those signs about which the augural books were silent—signs of this kind had to be explained subito ex tempore[7] by means of ratio and coniectura.[8]

---

2. "Frequentius etiam, quam volebamus, deorum praesentiam contempta auspicia contestata sunt. Sic Allia 'nomen infaustum,' sic Claudi et Iuni non proelium in Poenos, sed ferale naufragium est, et ut Trasimenus Romanorum sanguine et maior esset et decolor, sprevit auguria Flaminius, et ut Parthos signa repetamus, dirarum imprecationes Crassus et meruit et inrisit." Cf. A. S. Pease, M. Tulli Ciceronis "De diviniatione" libri duo (Urbana, 1920–23), pp. 135–40, 225–27, 379–80, who has an extensive discussion of the events mentioned by Minucius. Cicero, however, does not mention the battle of Allia in this context (but cf. Ad Att. 9. 5. 2).

3. Minucius Felix: "Octavius" (Washington, 1950).

4. OLD, s.v. "colligo." The English expression "gather," introducing an indirect statement, offers an instructive parallel.

5. Cf. Pease, "De divinatione," ad 1. 6, 1. 33, 1. 39.

6. On the distinction between natural and artificial divination, see Cic. De div. 1. 11, 1. 34, 1. 72, 2. 26; Ps.-Plut. De vita Hom. 212; A. Bouché-Leclercq, Histoire de la divination dans l'antiquité, vol. 1 (Paris, 1879), pp. 58–63; Pease, "De divinatione," pp. 70–71; F. Pfeffer, Studien zur Mantik in der Philosophie der Antike (Meisenheim, 1976), pp. 88–95.

7. I.e., "without preparation in accordance with the situation," Pease, "De divinatione," ad 1. 72.

8. See Cic. De div. 1. 34 "Est enim ars in iis qui novas res coniectura persequuntur, veteres observatione didicerunt," 1. 72 "Quae vero aut coniectura explicantur aut eventis animadversa et notata sunt, ea genera divinandi . . . artificiosa dicuntur. . . . Quorum alia sunt posita in monumentis et disciplina,

It was the accumulation of empirical observations over a long period of time, the work of generations of augurs, that had led to the establishment of *ars divinationis*.[9] This is the *summus labor* to which Minucius refers. In the passage under discussion *collecta* has the sense of both "collected" and "explained, codified":[10] "those famous Roman auspices and auguries, which were collected and explained with such great labor, and which on your evidence were neglected with remorseful consequences and observed with success."[11]

---

quod Etruscorum declarant et haruspicini et fulgurales et rituales libri, vestri etiam augurales, alia autem subito ex tempore coniectura explicantur, ut apud Homerum Calchas, qui ex passerum numero belli Troiani annos auguratus est." For the concept of *observatio* and the distinction between *ratio* and the empirical observation, see also *De div.* 1. 5, 1. 12, 1. 25, 1. 36, 1. 109, 1. 127; P. Regell, *De augurum publicorum libris* (Diss. Vratislaviae, 1878), pp. 3–7; J. Linderski, "The Augural Law," forthcoming in *Aufstieg und Niedergang der römischen Welt*, pt. 2.16.3.

9. See Cic. *De div.* 1. 12 "observata sunt haec [i.e., *signa ex avibus*] tempore inmenso et in significatione eventus animadversa et notata. Nihil est autem quod non longinquitas temporum excipiente memoria prodendisque monumentis efficere atque adsequi possit," 2. 146 "observatio diuturna . . . notandis rebus fecit artem," *De nat. deor.* 2. 166 "multa praeterea ostentis, multa extis admonemur, multisque rebus aliis quas diuturnus usus ita notavit ut artem divinationis efficeret."

10. The case for this meaning of *colligo* in Minucius Felix is strengthened by the occurrence of the word in an augural context in Servius *auctus* and Ammianus Marcellinus. The former, on *Aen.* 4. 453, tells us that "dira . . . duplici modo colligitur, aut ex signis, aut quocumque modo et quacumque ex parte" (cf. *Aen.* 3. 246, 5. 7). The *signa ex diris* formed one of the five categories into which the augurs divided the divinatory signs (Festus [Paulus] 316, 317 L.). A *dirum signum* was explained (*colligitur*) either *ex signis* or "quocumque modo et quacumque ex parte," i.e., either on the basis of the list of *dira signa* contained in the augural books or according to the situation by means of *ratio* and *coniectura*. We have here the old Ciceronian distinction between the *veteres* and *novae res*. For this interpretation, see Linderski, "The Augural Law." Amm. Marc. 21. 1. 9 argues that "auguria et auspicia non volucrum arbitrio futura nescientium colliguntur [i.e., the auguries and auspices are not effected and understood according to the will of the birds] . . . sed volatus avium dirigit deus, ut rostrum sonans aut praetervolans pinna, turbido meatu vel leni, futura praemonstret." Cf. Cic. *De div.* 1. 12 and 1. 120 with Pease, *"De divinatione,"* pp. 74–77, 313–23. On the other hand, at *De div.* 2. 67 "atque etiam a te Flaminiana ostenta collecta sunt," *colligo* has rather the simple sense of "collect, adduce": "you have also adduced the Flaminian portents," i.e., in order to show that "C. Flaminius consul iterum neglexit signa rerum futurarum magna cum clade rei publicae" (*De div.* 1. 77).

11. I should like to thank Prof. A. Michels for kindly reading a draft of this note.

54

A WITTICISM OF APPULEIUS SATURNINUS

The *Liber de viris illustribus* adduces the following example of Appuleius Saturninus' insolence (73, 6-8 Pichlmayr):

Aqua et igni interdixit ei, qui in leges suas non iurasset. Huic legi multi nobiles obrogantes, cum tonuisset, clamarunt ([1]): *Iam, inquit, nisi quiescetis, grandinabit. Metellus Numidicus exulare quam iurare maluit.*

The b o n m o t of Saturninus, *nisi quiescetis, grandinabit*, attracts attention. A. W. Lintott in his often quoted and occasionally inaccurate book, *Violence in Republican Rome*, Oxford 1968, 138 n. 3, observes that « Saturninus' jest was a veiled threat of a *lapidatio* ». That much is obvious enough ([2]), but a deeper, more sophisticated and wittier sense of Saturninus' witticism has escaped his biographers.

Lintott refers the passage under discussion to « the bill for Metellus' outlawry » and argues that not only the *lex agraria* of Saturninus, but also this bill was passed *contra auspicia*. But the Auctor of the *Liber* is so frequently unreliable (e. g. at 81,4 he says that *Cicero praetor Ciliciam latrociniis liberavit*) that one must beware of following him credulously. In our passage he achieved a remarkable confusion: *a)* he amalgamated the agrarian law of Saturninus ([3]) (which contained a clause obligating the senators and magistrates to swear an oath to uphold it) with the law concerning the *aquae et ignis interdictio* of Metellus; *b)* he did not expressly

---

([1]) The reading of A (o + p) is *et clamarent*, and so the reconstruction of P. H. Damsté, « Mnemosyne » 45, 1917, 374: *huic legi multi nobiles obrogantes cum tonuisse clamarent*, has much to recommend it.

([2]) Cf. *Vir. ill.* 73, 1: *intercedentem Baebium collegam facta per populum lapidatione submovit* (103 B. C.); Val. Max. 9, 7, 2: *idemque Q. Metellum censorem ... lapidibus prosternere conatus est* (in 102 or 101, cf. Broughton, *MRR* 1.567). This lent credibility to Saturninus' threat in 101.

([3]) On the legislation of Saturninus in 100, see the synopsis in G. Niccolini, *I fasti dei tribuni della plebe*, Milano 1934, 198-204; T.R.S. Broughton, *The Magistrates of the Roman Republic*, New York 1951, I, 575-576; E. Gabba, *Appiani Bellorum Civilium liber primus*, Firenze 1958, 101-114 (*ad* 1, 130-147).

mention the *lex agraria*, but at the same time transformed the oath clause of this law into a separate general law.

Now the course of events has been brilliantly elucidated by Emilio Gabba and Erich Gruen ([1]). When Metellus refused to swear the oath, Saturninus sent his *viator* to eject him from the senate (App. *bell. civ.* 1, 138). Metellus again refused to comply and Saturninus initiated the prosecution against him on a capital charge before (as it seems) the *iudicium populi*. Metellus did not await the outcome of the trial, or perhaps even its beginning, and went into exile. Now the assembly passed the bill calling upon the consuls to interdict Metellus from fire and water. Gruen points out that the technical validity of this law was never questioned: « it is for this reason » — he writes — « that Metellus' recall later could only be effected through another *lex* » ([2]). Hence the law *ut Metello aqua et igni interdiceretur* was not passed *contra auspicia*; in fact we do not hear of any disturbances or technical improprieties attending its passage. On the other hand the agrarian law of Saturninus was carried through force and against the auspices ([3]). Thus there is no doubt that the incriminated passage of *vir. ill.* refers to the *lex agraria* (and not to the law for « Metellus' outlawry »). We may rest assured that Saturninus uttered his witticism at the voting on the *lex agraria*.

Our next step is to reconstruct the scene of the assembly. Appian, *bell. civ.* 1, 133-134, provides a clear outline. The interceding tribunes were removed from the podium by force, and when the voting was about to begin (or perhaps when it was already in progress) the opponents of Saturninus started shouting that they heard thunder, in which case, Appian observes, it was not allowed for the Romans to take any decision. Appian's ὁ δὲ πολιτικὸς ὄχλος ἐβόα ὡς γενομένης ἐν ἐκκλησίᾳ βροντῆς corresponds almost verbatim to *huic legi multi nobiles obrogantes, cum tonuisset, clamarunt*. Appian's account is clear and logical; on the other hand *obrogantes* in the text of *vir. ill.* offers an intriguing problem.

([1]) E. Gruen, *The Exile of Metellus Numidicus*, « Latomus » 24, 1965, 576-580; E. Gabba, *Ricerche su alcuni punti di storia mariana*, « Athenaeum » n.s. 29, 1951, 21-23. There is a number of disagreements between them: e.g. Gabba opts for a trial of Metellus before the *quaestio de maiestate*, Gruen argues for the trial before the *iudicium populi*.

([2]) *Op. cit.* 580. Metellus was recalled by the *lex Calidia* of 98.

([3]) Cic. *Sest.* 37; Liv. *per.* 69; App. *bell. civ.*, 1, 133-136.

Obrogantes is the reading of our best manuscripts, and Pichlmayr rightly accepted it into his text ([1]). Yet it does not seem to make much sense — that is if one keeps in mind the definition of Ps.-Ulpian, *Reg.* 1, 3: *lex ... obrogatur, id est mutatur aliquid ex prima lege* ([2]). The enemies of Saturninus opposed the passage of his law; they did not try to alter it. In view of the following *tonuisset*, it is not *obrogantes*, but rather *obnuntiantes* that is apt to appear as the required reading. How misleading! Under the Empire the verb *obrogare* underwent a curious development and acquired a particular meaning: « to oppose (the passage) of a law ». This usage did not invade legal textbooks, and most authors avoided it as well, but it is characteristic of three very interesting sources: the *Liber de vir. ill.*, Florus and the *glossae*. The *glossae* define *obrogare* as *contra dicere uel contra legem uenire* ([3]). In Florus *obrogare* has this sense in two passages: at 2,17,7-8 (referring to the opposition of the consul L. Marcius Philippus against the legislation of M. Livius Drusus): *Aderat promulgandi dies, cum subito tanta vis hominum undique apparuit, ut hostium adventu obsessa civitas videretur. Ausus tamen o b r o g a r e legibus consul Philippus*, and at 2,15,4: *o b r o g a r e* ([4]) *auso legibus suis Minucio tribuno, [C. Gracchus] fretus comitum manu ... Capitolium invasit.* Minucius Rufus proposed to repeal the *lex Rubria de colonia Carthaginem deducenda* ([5]); it is apparent that in

---

([1]) Some other manuscripts read *abrogantes*, a common confusion. W. K. Sherwin, *Deeds of Famous Men*, Norman 1973, IX-XVI, establishes a new stemma of the *codices*, and prints *abrogantes* as the reading of V, which according to him is « a fairly accurate copy of the archetype » (p. XIV). But it is an impossible reading, for *duce Thes. l. Lat.* s.v. *abrogo* there is no clear example of the construction *abrogare legi* (*legibus*). This disposes also of Sherwin's *abrogante* at 65, 6.

([2]) Cf. *Thes. l. Lat.* s.v. *obrogo*: « terminus technicus iuris de rogatione ad quandam alicuius legis partem reformandam lata »; Flor. 2, 15, 4 and *vir. ill.* 65, 5 are wrongly classified under this heading, see below in the text.

([3]) G. Goetz, *Thesaurus Glossarum Emendatarum*, Lipsiae 1901, *s.v.*

([4]) *abrogare* codd., but Vinetus' *obrogare* is certain; cf. above, n. 1.

([5]) For sources, see Niccolini, *op. cit.*, 171-172; Broughton, *MRR* 1.521. P. Fraccaro, *Ricerche su Caio Gracco*, « Athenaeum » 3, 1925, 168 n. 4 (= *Opuscula* 2, Pavia 1967, 42) quotes the definition of Ulp. *Reg.* 1, 3 (see above in the text) and concludes: « Da questi passi [i.e. *vir. ill.* 65, 5 and Flor. 2, 15, 4] parrebbe che la colonia non

silver Latin *obrogare* could denote both the opposition to the *promulgatio* (and *rogatio*) of a law (as at 2,17,7-8) and the opposition to an existing law (as at 2,15,4) ([1]). In the latter case its meaning was very close to that of *abrogare* (with which, as we have seen, it is very often confused in the manuscripts).

Flor. 2,15,4 is a particularly interesting passage for *vir. ill.* 65,5 displays an almost identical phrase: *Minucio Rufo tribuno plebis legibus suis obrogante in Capitolium venit.* The contacts between Florus and *vir. ill.* have been much discussed ([2]), and I do not propose here to enter into a full debate of the *Quellenfrage*; it is, however, clear that either the Auctor utilized Florus or that both of them copied an *epitome* which affected the post-classical usage of *obrogare.* For the sake of clarity I give below a synopsis of their usage:

Vir. ill.	Florus
65,5 *Minucio ... legibus suis obrogante*	2,15,4 *o b r o g a r e auso legibus suis Minucio*
66,9 *Philippo consuli legibus agrariis r e s i s t e n t i*	2,17,8 *Ausus tamen o b r o g a r e legibus consul Philippus*
73,7 *huic legi ... nobiles o b r o - g a n t e s*	[In Florus nothing corresponds to this passage]

The last case — as the Auctor could not copy Florus ([3]) —

---

venisse del tutto annullata, ma in parte conservata ». Gabba, *Appiani liber primus*, p. 85, adduces the article of Fraccaro as an authority for the interpretation of *obrogare*. But it is the definition in the *Corpus Glossariorum* rather than that in the *Regulae iuris* that shows the way for the correct understanding of Florus.

([1]) Standard dictionaries (Lewis-Short, *Thes. l. Lat., Oxford Lat. Dict.*) failed to take notice of this distinction; and all of them incorrectly adduce Flor. 2, 15, 4 as an example of opposition to the passage of a bill. So also (following *Thes. l. Lat.*) M. L. Fele, *Lexicon Florianum*, Hildesheim 1975, *s.v.*, p. 428.

([2]) See now L. Braccesi, *Introduzione al De viris illustribus*, Bologna 1973, 25 n. 51, 39 ff., 62-63; L. Bessone, *Di alcuni ' errori ' di Floro*, « Riv. di filol. », 106, 1978, 421-431, esp. 424, both of them with further literature. Neither of them discusses the usage of *obrogare.*

([3]) The account of Saturninus in *vir. ill.* 73 is chronologically misplaced, and. M. M. Sage, *The De Viris Illustribus: Chronology and Structure*, « Trans. Amer. Philol. Ass. » 108, 1978, 233-234, ar-

provides a strong argument for a common source ([1]), which in all three instances employed a form of the verb *obrogare*. Both authors adapted it according to their taste, the Auctor *de vir. ill.* showing predilection for participial constructions, and Florus cherishing the infinitive. The appearance of *resistenti* at *vir. ill.* 66,9 is easily explicable. The whole passage reads as follows: [*M. Livius Drusus*] *Caepionem inimicum actionibus suis r e s i s t e n t e m ait de saxo Tarpeio praecipitaturum. Philippo consuli legibus agrariis r e s i s t e n t i* ... . In the latter passage *resistenti* is a repetition of *resistentem* from the preceding sentence; there is no doubt that the original source employed a construction of *obrogare*.

The purpose of the foregoing argument was to illustrate the rather unfamiliar usage of *obrogare*, and to show that although the text of *vir. ill.* 73,7 is sound, it nevertheless obscures the full import of Saturninus' witticism. This obfuscation goes back to the common source of the *Liber* and Florus (a Livian *epitome* ?), but hardly further back. In the sense of ' oppose ' *obrogare* is alien to Livian and Ciceronian Latin, and we should expect that in Livy (or in any other ultimately republican or Augustan source of the postulated *epitome*) a different word must have been used. With respect to Minucius Rufus versus the laws of C. Gracchus

---

gues that it may be a later addition (perhaps from a *liber exemplorum*; cf. J. Rosenhauer, *Symbolae ad quaestionem de fontibus libri qui inscribitur de viris illustribus urbis Romae*, Diss. Erlangen 1882, 27 ff.). If this is true this *liber* of *exempla* (or any other collection from which this hypothetical addition was made) would show the same predilection for the rather unusual construction *obrogare legi* (in its post-classical sense) as the Auctor himself — or should we perhaps again postulate a common source ? Structure and chronology are important, but the wording is more important still; and it is for this reason that I find the idea of a later addition of 73 both improbable and redundant.

([1]) W. K. Sherwin, *Livy and the De Viris Illustribus*, « Philologus » 113, 1969, 298-301, argues that Livy himself « should not be eliminated from consideration as a source for the *DVI* » (p. 301). However, the alleged similarity of phrasing concerns primarily set expressions. The most likely candidate for the source of both Florus and *de vir. ill.* appears to be a Livian *epitome*; is this sense Braccesi, *op. cit.*, 33-63; L. Bessone, *La tradizione liviana*, Bologna 1977, 153-159, 207-209; Idem, *La tradizione epitomatoria liviana in età imperiale*, *Aufstieg u. Niedergang der röm. Welt* II 30, 2, Berlin 1982, 1235-1236.

the required word was *abrogare*, and in fact this purer strand
of the tradition survives in Orosius 5, 12, 5: *Minucius Rufus
tribunus plebi cum maxima ex parte decessoris sui Gracchi
statuta convulsisset l e g e s q u e a b r o g a s s e t.* At *vir. ill.* 73,7
the required word is *obnuntiantes*, and this we may surmise
was the *lectio* of the original tradition. Its later distortion
to *obrogantes* need not surprise us; *obnuntio* in its non-techni-
cal application « adversum nuntium offerre » ([1]) is akin to
obrogo on its post-classical meaning of ' oppose '. In fact
Gabba in his comment on App. *bell. civ.* 1, 133 seems to assume the *obnuntiatio* against the *lex agraria* of Saturninus.
A word on the (too often misunderstood) technicalities of
obnuntiatio is in order ([2]).

The augural (and public) law distinguished between legally
binding reports of adverse omens, and reports the magistrate in charge of an action was entitled to disregard. The
binding report could be made in certain cases by the magistrates only, in certain other cases only by the augurs. As
far as the popular assemblies are concerned, the report could
be made either before the beginning of the assembly or
during its course. Before the beginning of the proceedings
the binding announcement was made on the basis of the
de caelo servare, deliberate ' watching of the sky ' for adverse
omens, primarily lightning, with the intention of impeding
the calling together of an assembly. Only higher magistrates and tribunes of the plebs could avail themselves of this
procedure. During the course of an assembly the announcement was made on the basis of unsolicited, unsought-for
' oblative ' omens; only the announcement made by an augur
was binding on the presiding officer. The presiding officer
could either obey the *obnuntiatio* and disband the assembly;
or if he chose to disregard it the results of the voting could

---

([1]) See the examples in *Thes. l. Lat.*, *s. v.* I should add that like
obrogo also *obnuntio* frequently appears with « dat. actionis vel personae agentis, cui obsistitur ».

([2]) The basic study is still I.O.M. Valeton, *De iure obnuntiandi
comitiis et consiliis*, « Mnemosyne » 19, 1891, 75-113, 229-270. S. Weinstock's article in *RE* 17, 1937, 1726-1735, is a step backwards, and
Mommsen's grand presentation in *Römisches Staatsrecht I³*, Leipzig
1887, 106-116, pays too little attention to doctrinal aspects of the
disciplina auguralis. A. W. Lintott, *Violence in Republican Rome*,
Oxford 1968, 137 n. 3, is hopelessly confused. See now J. Linderski,
The Augural Law, Aufstieg u. Niedergang der röm. *Welt* II 16, 3
(forthcoming).

be annulled by the senate, normally on the advice from the college of augurs ([1]).

Now in the case of the *lex Appuleia agraria* the assembly was in progress when thunder was heard; Saturninus disregarded it; his opponents raised a clamor; but the only constitutionally important point was whether an augur intervened. This we do not know; but it would suit well Saturninus' jest with its distinctly ' augural ' flavor. This flavor we can recapture via Terence and Donatus.

When the *Hecyra* of Terence was first staged at the *ludi Megalenses* in 165 *non est peracta* (as we learn from the *didascalia*). Terence himself explains in a new prologue what happened:

> *Hecyra est huic nomen fabulae: haec cum data*
> *Nouast, nouum interuenit uitium et calamitas*
> *Ut neque spectari neque cognosci potuerit.*
> *Ita populus studio stupidus in funambulo*
> *Animum occuparat.*

The people ran away from the theatre to admire the exhibition of a troop of tight-rope dancers; this was bad luck indeed ([2]), and Terence is wholly justified in describing it

---

([1]) Gabba, *Ricerche* (above, p. 453 n. 1), 12-24, and *Appiani liber primus* (above, p. 452 n. 3), 107, argues that « tutte le leggi Apuleie del 100 a. C., e fra queste l'agraria, furono poi cassate perché *per vim latae* ». But as we have seen the law concerning the exile of Metellus was repealed, not annulled; as to the *lex agraria* there existed legal grounds for declaring it invalid, but it is not clear whether it was actually annulled. Marius' words in App. *bell. civ.* 1,136 ὕστερον δ' οὐ δυσχερῶς ἐπιδείξειν, ὅτι οὐκ ἔστι νόμος ὁ πρὸς βίαν τε καὶ βροντῆς ὠνομασμένης κεκυρωμένος παρὰ τὰ πάτρια are certainly not conclusive. A. Passerini, *Caio Mario come uomo politico*, « Athenaeum » 12, 1934, 350-353 (= *Studi su Caio Mario*, Milano 1971, 159-161), attempted to show that Cic. *de leg.* 2.14 and *Balb.* 48 are not conclusive either. So also E. Badian, *From the Gracchi to Sulla (1940-1959)*, « Historia » 11, 1962, 219 n. 87. As to *Balb.* 48 we probably have to agree with Passerini and Badian, but as to *de leg.* 2, 14 Gabba has one important point in his favor: if none of the *leges Appuleiae* was annulled, why should Cicero have mentioned them at 2.14 alongside the *leges Titiae*? Recently Gabba changed his mind and embraced Badian's view (see the collection of his articles, *Republican Rome, the Army and the Allies*, Berkeley 1976, 199-200 n. 167), but the problem of *de leg.* 2, 14 remains unsolved.

([2]) Artemidoros, *Oneir.* 1, 76 (p. 83, line 2 Pack) says that to see (in a dream) a trapeze artist portends extreme danger (καλοπαίζοντα

as *vitium et calamitas*. Donatus (vol. 2, p. 193, lines 13-15 Wessner) (¹) praises Terence for using very appropriately an augural term:

> *VITIUM ET CALAMITAS bene secundum augures:* ' *uitium* ' *enim est, si tonet tantum,* ' *uitium et calamitas* ' *uero, si tonet et grandinet simul uel etiam fulminet.*

Saturninus was possessed of a very peculiar sense of humor indeed. And he was much better versed in augural lore than modern historians. When Jupiter thundered, *vitium* occurred; instead of giving up Saturninus reminded his enemies (and the, we should like to think, obnuntiating augurs) that for his part he was ready to co-operate with Jupiter and produce hail in the shape of stones — thus engineering the occurrence of augural *calamitas* for his foes. He kept his promise and the law was passed *per vim*. But the story does not end here. When the *senatus consultum ultimum* was enacted and the consuls proceeded against Saturninus he fled to the *curia* and *lapidibus et tegulis desuper interfectus est* (*vir. ill.* 73,15) (²). The Auctor *de vir. ill.* missed the irony of Saturninus' end, but we may be sure Livy loved it. Jupiter took his revenge; *calamitas* descended upon the tribune and he died a victim of his own witticism.

---

is here a very attractive conjecture of Pack). For Terence this came true in the waking state; incidentally his *vitium et calamitas* referring to *funambuli* indirectly confirms Pack's conjecture. F. H. Sandbach, *How Terence's Hecyra failed*, « Class. Quart. » 32, 1982, 134-135, argues that the spectators did not leave the theater, but rather chased away the actors to watch the next two events on the program, the boxers (cf. the prologue of L. Ambivius Turpio, line 33) and the tight-rope walkers.

(¹) See also vol. 2, p. 193, lines 16-17: ' *uitium* ' *translatio ab augurio, ut uitio creati consules dicuntur*; lines 21-22: ' *uitium* ' *quod non spectata est,* ' *calamitas* ' *quod non cognita*; and, on *calamitas*, cf. vol. 2, p. 193, lines 17-20 (from Probus); vol. 1, p. 283, lines 11-13 (*Eun.* 1,1,34); Serv. and Serv. auct. *georg.* 1, 151. On the augural concept of *vitium*, see D. Paschall, *The Origin and Semantic Development of Latin Vitium*, « Trans. Amer. Phil. Ass. » 67, 1936, 219-231; and on the concept and the popular and scholarly etymology of *calamitas*, see A. Ernout and A. Meillet, *Dictionnaire étymologique de la langue latine*³, Paris 1951, 153; A. Walde and J. B. Hofmann, *Lateinisches etymologisches Wörterbuch* 1³, Heidelberg 1938, 135-136.

(²) Cf. Flor. 2, 16, 6: *ibi* (i. e. *in curia*) *eum facta inruptione populus fustibus saxisque opertum in ipsa quoque morte laceravit.*

55

Religious Aspects of the Conflict of the Orders: The Case of *confarreatio*

The Conflict of the Orders touched upon all facets of life, public and private, in early Rome. The role *religio* played in this conflict offers itself as an ideal testing ground for the various methodologies and approaches devised to penetrate behind the fictional scheme of our literary sources. Institutions have their own life, and their structure can reveal much about their past. One such institutional structure was prominent in the Conflict of the Orders: that of marriage, or, more exactly, intermarriage between patricians and plebeians.

Cicero complains that if every patrician followed the example of Clodius and got himself adopted into a plebeian family, the consequences would be disastrous: very soon the Roman people would have neither the *rex sacrorum* nor the *flamines* nor the Salii; it would lose half of the other priests, and, finally, as the interrex had to be nominated by the patricians and had to be a patrician himself, the auspices too would perish.[1] The *flamines* attract attention. They will now lead us from the bright day of Cicero into the mist and fog of archaic Roman history.

The *flamines maiores* and the *rex sacrorum* form a special case, in that their status, unlike that of other priests, was inseparably connected with a particular form of marriage, the marriage *per confarreationem*.[2] In order to be eligible for the priesthood, they had to be born *ex farreatis* and had themselves to live in a marriage concluded *per confarreationem*.[3] Marriage was, in fact, an inseparable part of their *sacerdotium*: upon the death of the *flaminica* the *flamen Dialis* was obliged to resign his priesthood, and, needless to say, he was not allowed to divorce his wife.[4] As the *regina sacrorum* and the *flaminica*

1. Cic. *Dom.* 38.: *Ita populus Romanus brevi tempore neque regem sacrorum neque flamines nec Salios habebit, nec ex parte dimidia reliquos sacerdotes neque auctores centuriatorum et curiatorum comitiorum, auspicia populi Romani, si magistratus patricii creati non sint, intereant necesse est, cum interrex nullus sit, quem et ipsum patricium esse et a patriciis prodi necesse est.* Cf. R. G. Nisbet, *M. Tulli Ciceronis de domo sua ad pontifices oratio* (Oxford, 1939): ad loc.

2. The basic text is Gaius, *Inst.* 1.112: *Farreo in manum conveniunt per quoddam genus sacrificii, quod Iovi Farreo fit: in quo farreus panis adhibetur, unde etiam confarreatio dicitur; conplura praeterea huius iuris ordinandi gratia cum certis et sollemnibus verbis praesentibus decem testibus aguntur et fiunt. Quod ius etiam nostris temporibus in usu est: nam flamines maiores, id est Diales, Martiales, Quirinales, item reges sacrorum, nisi ex farreatis nati non leguntur; ac ne ipsi quidem sine confarreatione sacerdotium habere possunt* (cf. the commentary by M. David and H. L. W. Nelson, *Studia Gaiana* 3 [Leiden, 1954]: 132–33, citing further literature). Ulp. *Regulae* 9.1 does not contain any new information, but Servius Auctus, on *Aen.* 4 .103, 339, 374, and especially on *Georg.* 1.31 (ed. G. Thilo), is of importance: *tribus enim modis apud veteres nuptiae fiebant: . . . farre, cum per pontificem maximum et Dialem flaminem per fruges et molam salsam coniungebantur, unde confarreatio appellabatur.* Of modern literature, see A. Rossbach, *Untersuchungen über die römische Ehe* (Stuttgart, 1853): 95ff., 361ff.; R. Leonhard, "Confarreatio," *RE* 4 (1900): 862–64; G. Wissowa, *Religion* (1912): 118–19, 387, 506; P. E. Corbett, *Marriage* (1930): 73ff.; M. Kaser, *Privatr.* I² (1971): 76–77; A. Watson, *The Law of Persons in the Later Roman Republic* (Oxford, 1967): 23–24.

3. On the basis of Gaius, S. Brassloff, "Die Erneuerung des Flaminates," in *Studi in onore di P. Bonfante* II (Milan, 1930): 363–79, especially 372ff., argues that the *flamines* and *reges sacrorum* had to be married *per confarreationem* before they assumed their priesthood. But in practice they may have been required to undergo this ceremony in the period between their *captio* (*lectio* or *nominatio*) and *inauguratio*. Cf. below at nn. 37ff.

4. Gell. 10.15.22–24: *Matrimonium flaminis nisi morte dirimi ius non est. Uxorem si amisit, flamonio decedit* (from Fabius Pictor through the intermediary of Ateius Capito and Masurius Sabinus, cf. R. Peter, *Quaestionum pontificalium specimen* [Strassburg, 1886]: 15–16, 20–21; G. Rowoldt, *Librorum pontificiorum Romanorum de*

(in historical times this term was used almost exclusively with reference to the wife of the *flamen Dialis*)[5] fully participated in the priesthood of their husbands,[6] it is very probable that they, too, had to be born *ex farreatis*. The *flamines maiores* and the *rex sacrorum* had to be patricians, and this brings us to the heart of our problem.

So far the facts: this was the situation that obtained in the last centuries of the Republic. On this meager basis far-reaching and farfetched theories have been erected concerning the origin of the differentiation between patricians and plebeians. The facts we have can be arranged in a number of combinations, the final result being largely predetermined by our first move. Probability must be the final judge.

We can assume that *confarreatio* was the original form of Roman marriage and that it was restricted to patricians. Now Roman tradition is unanimous that there was a time when all magistracies and all priesthoods were a patrician preserve. As confarreate birth and confarreate marriage were formal requirements for the patrician *flamines*, we can surmise that at one time a similar requirement existed for all or most patrician priesthoods, and perhaps for patrician magistracies as well. Now the following development took place: the magistracies and priesthoods were gradually thrown open to plebeians, but *confarreatio* remained an exclusively patrician ceremony. As a result it was dropped as a requirement for those priesthoods to which the plebeians were admitted. It lost its political importance, and as it was a cumbersome and personally uncomfortable form of

---

caerimoniis sacrificiorum reliquiae [Halle, 1906]: 27–28; L. Strzelecki, *C. Atei Capitonis fragmenta* [Wroclaw, 1960]: 17); Plut. *Quaest. Rom.* 50 (from Ateius Capito, probably through Iuba, cf. Peter 20ff.; Strzelecki 18–19, and in greater detail, id., *De Ateio Capitone nuptialium caerimoniarum interprete* [Wroclaw, 1947]: 23ff.; but see also H. J. Rose, *The Roman Questions of Plutarch* [Oxford, 1924]: 20ff., who vigorously protests against overestimating Plutarch's use of Iuba). For other sources, see J. Marquardt, *Staatsverwaltung* III[2] (1885): 328–29. Servius Auctus, on *Aen.* 4.29, causes difficulty, for his statement runs counter to that of Gellius and Plutarch: *sane caerimoniis veterum flaminicam nisi unum virum habere non licet . . . nec flamini aliam ducere licebat uxorem, nisi post mortem flaminicae uxoris.* This is either inaccurate, represents relaxation of the original custom, or refers only to the *flamen Martialis* and *Quirinalis*, whose *castus* were less *multiplices* than those of the *flamen Dialis* (Servius Auctus, on *Aen.* 8.552).

    5. Wissowa, *Religion* (1912): 506 n. 5; *TLL* s.v. *flaminica.*
    6. Marquardt, *Staatsverwaltung* III[2] (1885): 322, 331–32.

marriage, it fell into desuetude. The twin requirements of patrician and confarreate birth survived as a relic of the past only with respect to the *flamines maiores* and the *rex sacrorum*, the priesthoods that were important in ritual but quite secondary in politics.[7]

This interpretation has two points in its favor: logic and simplicity. Yet history need not be simple or logical, and if we scrutinize the traditional theory more closely we shall easily discover two weak points: (a) we do not know for certain whether marriage by *confarreatio* was *always* restricted to patricians; (b) we do not know for certain whether *confarreatio* was ever required for any priesthoods other than the major *flamonia* and the *rex sacrorum*.

And so we arrive at the starting point of a rival theory developed some fifty years ago by Pierre Noailles[8] and Paul Koschaker.[9] They observed that our sources speak of *confarreatio* almost exclusively in connection with the major *flamonia*.[10] As Noailles put it, ancient sources restrict *confarreatio* to the "recruitment of the priestly caste of major flamines."[11] Hence the conclusion: the rite of *confarreatio* was introduced in order to limit the selection of the *flamines* to a small circle of certain privileged families. Thus the rite of *confarreatio* in conjunction with the institution of the *interregnum* played a major, perhaps decisive, role in the formation of a hereditary nobility, the future patriciate.

This is a captivating theory, but before we are seduced by it, let

---

7. Cf. above all Mommsen, *Röm. Staatsrecht* III.1 (1887): 33–36, 78–80. Very characteristic of Mommsen's way of thinking is the following argument (p. 79): "Auch zeigt uns das Recht zwei gleichberechtigte Eheformen, die bürgerliche in der Gestalt des religiösen Ehebündnisses durch Confarreation und die Consensualehe der Halbfreien. Dass jene nur bei den Patriciern begegnende dem Plebejer von Rechtswegen versagt war, wird allerdings nicht ausdrücklich überliefert, ist aber darum nicht weniger sicher."

8. P. Noailles, "Les rites nuptiaux gentilices et la *confarreatio*," *RD* 15 (1936): 401–17; "Les *dii nuptiales*," *RD* 16 (1937): 549–50; "Les tabous du mariage dans le droit primitif des Romains," in id., *Fas* (1948): 12–13 (originally published in *Annales Sociologiques*, series C, fasc. 2 [1937]: 6–34); "Junon déesse matrimoniale des Romains," in *Fas*, 29–43 (originally published in *Festschrift P. Koschaker* I [Weimar, 1939]: 386–400).

9. P. Koschaker, "Le mariage dans l'ancien droit romain," *RD* 16 (1937): 746–49; "Die Eheformen bei den Indogermanen," in *Zeitschr. für ausländ. und intern. Privatrecht* 11, suppl. vol. (1937): 77ff.

10. This is especially true of Servius Auctus, on *Aen.* 4.103, 339, 374.

11. Noailles, *Fas* (1948): 32.

us examine it in some detail. Not everybody has been convinced: Max Kaser in his celebrated *Das römische Privatrecht* described it as a "doubtful" and "artificial construction."[12] But an "artificial construction" need not be false, and in fact in his earlier and equally celebrated work *Das altrömische ius*, Kaser provided some support for the ideas of Noailles and Koschaker.[13] For Mommsen *confarreatio* was the original form of marriage; he says that there may have been a time when sacrally concluded marriage was regarded as the only valid form of marriage, particularly with respect to the legal position of children.[14] On the other hand according to Noailles and Koschaker *confarreatio* was not the oldest but rather the most recent form of *manus* marriage.[15] This is the heart and backbone of their theory, and it may indeed perplex the casual reader, for *confarreatio* has at first sight a truly archaic appearance. Yet as Kaser[16] points out very perceptively, it is *confarreatio* itself that is perplexing. From a legal point of view it is an oddity: a sacral ceremony with consequences in civil law. The legal result of *confarreatio*, i.e., of a sacral act, is the acquisition of *manus* over the wife by her husband, i.e., a civil act; it is further striking that the sources do not mention the participation in the ceremony of the previous holder of the *manus*, the father of the bride, although it was his *potestas* that was being transferred to the husband. Hence one can surmise that in fact *confarreatio* originally consisted of two separate acts: (1) the religious act that established the sacrally valid marriage, in itself a remarkable thing, for in Rome marriage was primarily a matter-of-fact arrangement—one that was naturally accompanied by religious ceremonies, but that was in no way established or validated by any religious act; (2) a civil act that transferred the *manus*. What was the character of that civil act? Kaser conjectures that originally *manus* could be established or transferred only by *coemptio*. We have to remember that we do not know the wording of the ritual formulas recited at the *confarreatio*, but they may well have contained elements taken over from the legal for-

---

12. Kaser, *Privatr.* I² (1971): 77 n. 14.
13. Kaser, *Ius* (1949): 342–45. Recently the ideas of Noailles and Koschaker have been endorsed by Richard, *Origines* (1978): 240–44. For an inspiring discussion, see also C. W. Westrup, *Recherches* (1943): 14ff.
14. Mommsen, *Röm. Staatsrecht* III.1 (1887): 34, cf. 79–80.
15. Cf. especially Noailles, *Fas* (1948): 12.
16. Kaser, *Ius* (1949): 343–44, cf. 316–21.

mula of *coemptio*.[17] Altogether the reconstruction of Noailles is quite appealing: we would have an old and primitive legal institution, the marriage by purchase, upon which at a later stage a sacral ritual was grafted. In historical times this sacral ritual overshadowed, at least in our sources (and perhaps in real practice as well), the legal side of the transaction. We may say that this theory seems to make sense of the complex double nature of *confarreatio* as a sacral and civil institution. Legally it is an impeccable construction, but let us inquire whether it gives better insight into the social history of archaic Rome.

Let us turn again to Mommsen.[18] With respect to the dichotomy between patricians and plebeians, he postulates two stages in the legal position of marriage. There was a later stage (immediately before the *lex Canuleia*) when, because of the lack of *conubium* between patricians and plebeians, for the legal validity of marriage not only the husband but the wife, too, had to be patrician. This may have been preceded by a still earlier stage during which not only the patriciate birth of both parents but *confarreatio* as well were the necessary prerequisites for the validity of marriage. Only children born of such marriages would inherit the social position of their fathers. Thus from the very beginning of the city *confarreatio* was, according to Mommsen and his followers, a patrician form of marriage; it did not play any role in the formation of the aristocracy.

To this basically static view, the new theory introduces social and sacral dynamism. We replace the original idea of a patriciate existing since time immemorial with the concept of aristocracy *in statu nascendi*. And we discover that religious institutions may have played an important role in the process of the social definition of that class. Yet we have to beware of a new schematism.

17. The phrase *certa et sollemnia verba* (Gaius 1.112, cf. *certa verba*, Ulp. *Reg.* 9.1) points to a set and unchangeable formula. Yet we do not know who pronounced the *certa verba*: the marrying parties or the priests? Nor do we know what these words represented: the consensus of the parties to conclude marriage, the formula of *coemptio*, or perhaps a prayer? All these solutions have been proposed at one time or another; Westrup, *Recherches* (1943): 11 n. 6, and Kaser, *Privatr.* I[2] (1971): 77 n. 12, prefer, perhaps wisely, to leave the matter *sub iudice*. Yet we have to remember that Gaius gives only a summary; as he himself says, *complura praeterea . . . aguntur et fiunt*—many various acts accompanied by many solemn words. The expression of the consensus of the parties, the transference of *manus* (cf. the discussion by E. Volterra, "La *conventio in manum* e il matrimonio romano," *RISG* 12 [1968]: 205ff.), and the *precationes*—all these acts will not have been missing. The marriage ceremony was a long-drawn-out and elaborate affair (cf. Marquardt, *Privatleben*[2] [1886]: 42ff.).

18. Mommsen, *Röm. Staatsrecht* III.1 (1887): 34.

First we have to look more closely at the ritual of *confarreatio*. That this complicated and plainly archaic ritual was conceived and introduced simply as a matter of political expediency defies imagination. But there are two distinct elements in the ritual of *confarreatio*: private and official. Some of the ceremonies were performed by the groom and the bride, the central act being the consumption and offering of a cake of *far*, a coarse wheat.[19] This gave the name to the whole ceremony and was plainly its most archaic layer. But what strikes the observer is the official element: the participation of the *flamen Dialis* and *pontifex maximus*.[20] Now Roman marriage was a pri-

19. Gaius 1.112 says that *farreus panis* (cf. Paul. *Epit. Festi* 65 L., *farreum libum*) was used at the sacrifice *quod Iovi Farreo* [*farreo:* Marquardt, *Privatleben*[2] (1886): 50 n. 3] *fit*. To be sure, we are not told expressly that it was the groom and the bride who performed the sacrifice, although many scholars assume this without further discussion (cf., e.g., Kaser, *Privatr.* I[2] [1971]: 77 n. 11). The text of Servius Auctus, on *Aen.* 4.374, attracts attention: *in confarreatione* the *nubentes* sat together *velatis capitibus* on two *sellae iugatae*. It is important to note that not only the bride, but also the groom was veiled; consequently this *velatio* is to be distinguished from the veiling of the bride with the *flammeum*. In all books on the *res nuptiales* I have consulted, and even in the otherwise very competent dissertation by H. Freier (see below) these two acts are commonly confused (but cf. Marquardt, *Privatleben*, 50). At the *velatio capitis* only the back of the head was veiled, the face was uncovered; this was the normal attire of the *sacrificantes ritu Romano* (see H. Freier, *Caput velare* [Tübingen, 1963]: 102ff., especially 132–33). On the other hand the *flammeum* covered the face of the bride; *obnubere* was the terminus technicus for this ceremony (cf. the passages collected by Freier, 129–30). Hence we can assume that the bride and groom were engaged in some sort of sacrifice; and indeed Gaius mentions the sacrifice of *panis farreus* and Servius Auctus (loc. cit.) the sacrifice of an *ovis*. On monumental representations either the face of the bride is covered or only the back of her head (Rossbach, *Die römische Ehe* [see n. 2 above]: 376–79; id., *Römische Hochzeits- und Ehedenkmäler* [Leipzig, 1871]: 16, 44, 96, 120, 153). This has caused some perplexity (cf. Marquardt, *Privatleben*, 45 n. 3; Freier 133). Now we have the explanation: the bride is represented either as *sacrificans* or as *nupta*. Thus Servius and monumental representations explain each other.

20. Servius Auctus, on *Georg.* 1.31, is normally adduced as the only authority attesting the participation at the *confarreatio* of the *flamen Dialis* and *pontifex maximus*, but his information goes back (through unknown intermediaries) to a very good source, Ateius Capito's *De pontificio iure*. L. Strzelecki, in *Lanx Satura N. Terzaghi oblata* (Genoa, 1963): 321–24, has ingeniously and convincingly ascribed to Ateius Capito the gloss *confarreatis nuptiis* of *Gloss. Abol.* CO 102 (*Gloss. Lat.* 3 [Paris, 1926]: 113). Its wording is almost identical with that of Servius: *multis modis nuptiae fiunt . . . farre, cum per pontificem maximum e(t) Diale(m) flaminem per fruges et molam salsam coniunguntur, ex quibus nuptiis patrimi et matrimi nascuntur*. See also W. (= L.) Strzelecki, *C. Atei Capitonis fragmenta* (Leipzig, 1967): xxvi-xxviii and 30 (fr. 6a); F. Bona, *Contributo allo studio della composizione del "De verborum significatu" di Verrio Flacco* (Milan, 1964): 90–91 n. 143. Incidentally the passage in question shows that the original

vate and family affair: there is no obvious or necessary ritual connection between the offering and sharing[21] of the cake of *far* by the groom and bride and the presence of the highest priests of the state. The participation of the state priests reveals itself as an overtly political and chronologically posterior element. Thus the historic *confarreatio* was composed of four separate intersecting components: sacral and civil, private and official. As the most primitive elements we can safely isolate the *manus* marriage by *coemptio* and the religious ceremony of the sharing and offering of *far*. These two institutions existed side by side, the ceremony of *far* being clearly outside the realm of *ius*: it was the procedure of *coemptio* that produced *manus*. The *coemptio* was not restricted to any particular class, nor should we imagine that this primitive *confarreatio* was classbound. In the ritual itself there is nothing that is patrician or aristocratic. The participation of the *flamen Dialis* and the *pontifex maximus*[22] profoundly altered the character of *confarreatio*. It transformed what had been a private institution into an institution of the state. This transformation was probably also responsible for that blending of sacral and civil elements that is so perplexing to us today.

The *confarreatio* now became a class institution and an instrument of class policy. It is obvious that the priest of Jupiter and the chief

---

meaning of *patrimi et matrimi* was "the children born of confarreate parents"; the meaning "the children whose parents are still alive" appears to be a later development. Richard in his instructive discussion (*Origines* [1978]: 241–42) unfortunately missed the studies of Strzelecki.

21. According to Wissowa, *Religion* (1912): 387 n. 3, the sharing of *far* is not directly attested; it has, however, been postulated by a number of scholars, see, e.g., A. Dieterich, *Eine Mithrasliturgie*[3] (Leipzig and Berlin, 1923): 121–22; P. De Francisci, *Primordia* (1959): 286; cf. Kaser, *Privatr.* I[2] (1971): 77. But in fact Dion. Hal. *Ant. Rom.* 2.25 speaks expressly of the κοινωνία τοῦ φαρρός, the sharing of *far* (cf. Westrup, *Recherches* [1943]: 12). Thus there is no reason to amalgamate the sacrifices mentioned by Gaius 1.112 and Servius Auctus, on *Georg.* 1.31 (= Ateius Capito, fr. suppl. 6a Strzelecki), and ascribe them either to the *nubentes* or the priests. Most probably we here deal with two separate sacrificial acts: the offering and testing of *libum farreum* by the groom and the bride, and the sacrifice of the *fruges* and *mola salsa* performed by the *flamen Dialis* and *pontifex maximus*.

22. De Francisci, *Primordia* (1959): 286–87, conjectures that the ceremony took place before the *pontifex maximus* and only later, "in seguito allo sviluppo delle credenze religiose," was transformed into a *genus sacrificii* performed in the presence of the *flamen Dialis*. This is unwarranted for it is hardly likely that the *pontifex* predated the *flamen*.

pontiff were not able to participate in each and every marriage ceremony. Thus their participation was by necessity limited to a narrow
group of select families. These families formed the nucleus of a hereditary aristocracy.

I submit that this reconstruction makes better sense of *confarreatio*
as a social institution than other theories, for it finds ample parallels
in other epochs and other social systems. For the purpose of promoting coherence within a social group and for keeping strangers away,
there is no better means than the introduction of marriage restrictions, first customary, then religious, and, finally, restrictions enshrined in law.[23]

The Twelve Tables form a watershed in this respect. They testify
to an attempt by the patricians to form a closed caste. The argument
is very straightforward here. We have to treat the prohibition of intermarriage between patricians and plebeians contained in one of

23. One can juxtapose this development with the innovations enacted by the
marriage laws of Augustus (the denomination *lex de maritandis ordinibus* is in itself
very telling) and with further changes and restrictions introduced in the course of
the Empire. Cf. R. Astolfi, *La lex Iulia et Papia* (Padua, 1970): 16–56 ("I divieti ma-
trimoniali"). In feudal Europe there was virtually no intermarriage between gentry
and peasants, and examples can be adduced from three parts of the world as disparate geographically, chronologically, and politically as ancient and medieval China,
medieval France, and early modern Russia for a tendency among the nobility to
contract marriages within their own ranks and to reach outside only for the purpose
of concluding alliances with rich or powerful upstarts; see, e.g., the recent studies
by P. Buckly Ebrey, *The Aristocratic Families of Early Imperial China* (Cambridge, 1978);
G. Duby, "Lineage, Nobility, and Chivalry in the Region of Mâcon during the
Twelfth Century," in *Family and Society: Selections from the Annales*, edited by R. Forster and O. Ranum (Baltimore, 1976): 16–40; R. O. Crummey, *Aristocrats and Ser-
vitors: The Boyar Elite in Russia, 1613–1689* (Princeton, 1983). But for direct parallels
we have to go, as in so many other cases, from Rome to India, with its legal and
religious prohibitions of intermarriage between the castes (*jāti*) and its ideal of the
purity of the three upper classes (*varna*); see J. H. Hutton, *Caste in India*[1] (Oxford,
1963); P. Kolenda, *Caste in Contemporary India* (Menlo Park, Calif., 1978). G. Dumézil, *Mariages Indo-Européens* (Paris, 1979), is, as always, stimulating, unreliable, and
replete with errors of fact and logic. He maintains (p. 48) that only patricians could
serve as witnesses at the confarreate marriage, whereas Gaius 1.112 (whom Dumézil
quotes on the same and preceding pages) speaks only of ten witnesses without speci-
fying their status. And as far as logic is concerned it is inadmissable to juxtapose the
usurpatio trinoctii in Rome and the *trirātra* in India (p. 52). The function of the former was purely legal: to break the *usus* and prevent the acquisition of *manus* by the
husband; to achieve this goal it had to be repeated each year. On the other hand the
function of the *trirātra* was ritual, not legal: it was a three-night period of conti-
nence following immediately upon the marriage ceremony.

the two last tables as a decemviral innovation. Such is the tenor of the sources, above all of Cicero: the decemvirs added two tables of unjust laws, among which was one that most cruelly prohibited intermarriage between plebeians and patricians.[24] This does not sound like a report of a codification of the existing law. This interpretation— now supported by a number of eminent scholars[25]—fits smoothly into what is the most probable model of social development after the beginning of the Republic.

As is well known, plebeian names crop up in the *fasti* and in the Senate; they are prominent among the kings and appear in Roman topography.[26] If the patriciate was not yet a closed caste, this should not surprise us. Obviously there was movement in and out: some families lost their position as a result of feuds and infighting—the relatives of the Tarquinii for instance; others may simply have died out, so that their plebeian namesakes in the later Republic had in fact nothing but the name in common with them. Yet some of those plebeian families, for instance the plebeian Claudii, would have been the junior or less fortunate branches of the original *gens*. They were left out when the patriciate was coalescing into a closed caste. Thus in a sense both the patriciate and the *plebs* were the product of division and polarization within the gentilitial society. Newcomers and descendants of *liberti* swelled the numbers of the *plebs*, but new families were also accepted into the ranks of the aristocracy, as the example of the Claudii demonstrates. This example also shows that there existed a close relationship between the aristocracy of Rome and the aristocracies of other Italian communities, especially the Latins and Sabines. The case of intermarriage between the Roman Horatii and the Alban Curiatii points to the existence of *conubium*, the right to conclude valid marriages, between Rome and at least some Latin communities. The aristocrats tended to conclude marriage alliances with the aristocracies of the neighboring commu-

---

24. Cic. *De re pub.* 2.63 (*FIRA* I: 70).

25. H. Last, *JRS* 35 (1945): 31–33; F. de Visscher, *RIDA* 1 (1952): 401–22; A. Alföldi, "Struktur des Römerstaates" (1967): 233–34; A. Watson, *XII Tables* (1975): 20ff. Of recent scholars Gjerstad and Kienast reject this interpretation (at least by implication), but to my mind they produce no valid argument: E. Gjerstad, *Early Rome* V (1973): 186–87 (the prohibition of intermarriage dates from the sixth century); D. Kienast, *BJ* 175 (1975): 98.

26. Cf. Richard, chapter IV above, at nn. 12ff., with further literature cited.

nities, and at the same time they attempted to cut themselves off from the nonaristocratic classes in their own cities.[27]

Thus we would postulate at first a natural tendency within any aristocracy to limit marriage as far as possible to its own class—that class being originally a social group, not yet a strictly defined legal entity. Then would come the introduction of ceremonial and religious marriage sanctified by the presence of the highest priests;[28] people married in this way were marked as belonging to the highest aristocracy. And as the last step came the attempt by the decemvirs to sever by law all marriage ties between patricians and plebeians. If this was an innovation, legal prohibition of intermarriage could not have existed before the Twelve Tables, whatever the social practice.

The extant testimonies concerning the Twelve Tables contain only two references to marriage regulations. One is the prohibition of intermarriage ascribed to the second, tyrannical board of decemvirs. The other is the report of Gaius, commonly attributed to table VI, referring to the *usurpatio trinoctii* in connection with the marriage by *usus*.[29] There is no mention of *confarreatio*, and our task is to fit this form of marriage into the system of the Twelve Tables.

A reminder is in order: the Twelve Tables did not treat of marriage as such, but rather of the *conventio in manum*—that is, of the methods of acquiring or avoiding *manus* in connection with marriage. But if the decemvirs treated of *usus*—as the definition goes "a formless acquisition of marital power over the wife through an uninterrupted cohabitation . . . of one year with the intention of living as husband and wife"[30]—they would certainly also have treated of *coemptio*, the acquisition of *manus* over the wife through a fictitious sale. Alan Watson[31] points out that the Twelve Tables may, in fact, have contained a reference to all three ways in which *manus* was cre-

---

27. F. De Visscher, *RIDA* 1 (1952): 412ff. For a similar tendency among the aristocrats of Gaul, see Caes. *De bello Gallico* 1.3.5; 1.8.6–7.
28. It is difficult to decide when this process began. J.-C. Richard (chapter IV above, part 2) thinks of the pre-Etruscan regal period; A. Alföldi, "Struktur des Römerstaates" (1967): 232–33, and Noailles, *Fas* (1948): 12–13, 31–32, argue for the early years of the Republic.
29. Gaius 1.111 (*FIRA* I: 44).
30. A. Berger, *Encyclopedic Dictionary of Roman Law*, Trans. Amer. Philos. Soc. 43, no. 2 (Philadelphia, 1953), s.v. *usus*, p. 755.
31. Watson, *XII Tables* (1975): 9–19.

ated. He argues that the list *usu, farreo (farre), coemptione,* found in four later authors,[32] in all probability derived from the Twelve Tables. This is an interesting and on the whole convincing proposition, but it creates new problems. Was *confarreatio* limited to patricians? If by *confarreatio* we understand the official ceremony in which the participation of the *flamen Dialis* and the *pontifex maximus* was indispensable, it is obvious that for all practical purposes it had to be.

We have already considered the possibility of the existence of private *confarreatio,* sacred rites and offerings requiring no presence of the official priests. This type of *confarreatio* would, of course, have been available to plebeians, but the important question is this: could this kind of ceremony be thought of as creating *manus?* Unfortunately this question is better left *sub iudice,* especially as extrajuridical sources are not especially helpful either. No importance can, of course, be attached to a notice in the *Historia Augusta (Alex. Sev.* 22.3), a corrupt notice at that,[33] that the *ius confarreationis* abolished by Elagabalus was restored by the Emperor Alexander Severus, but a *cursus honorum* recording a *sacerdos confarreationum et diffareationum* attracts attention.[34] The *sacerdos* in question, M. Aurelius Papirius Dionysius, was a *iurisperitus* and a high equestrian official under Marcus Aurelius and Commodus, hence not a patrician. In his capacity as *iurisperitus,* he was *adsumptus* as a *sexagenarius* into the imperial council, and subsequently was appointed, as H.-G. Pflaum puts it, to "un sacerdoce fort ancien." The task of this priest was to apply "tous les vieux précepts qui ordonnaient que certains fonctions du culte officiel ne pussent être revêtues que par des patriciens mariés selon le rituel de la *confarreatio.*"[35] But far from being an ancient *sacerdotium,* this is a priesthood of which we know nothing; and, secondly, it was the traditional duty of the pontiffs to explain the sacral law. Hence it is very unlikely that we have here a patrician form of marriage or one that required the presence of the *flamen Dialis* or chief pontiff. Most probably the inscription uses the term *confar-*

---

32. Gaius 1.110; Boethius, on Cic. *Top.* 3.14; Arnobius, *Adv. gent.* 4.20; Servius Auctus, on *Georg.* 1.31.
33. Cf. E. Hohl in his edition in app. crit. ad loc.
34. *CIL* 10.6662 = *ILS* 1455.
35. H.-G. Pflaum, *Les Carrières procuratoriennes équestres sous le Haut-Empire romain* (Paris, 1960): 473–74.

reatio in an untechnical and general sense (as Apuleius also employs the word)[36] to denote simply marriage ceremonies without any allusion to the legal aspects of marriage, and in particular without any allusion to the creation of *manus*. The inscription in question was found at Antium and was set up by the *Antiates public(e)* to honor Aurelius Papirius. This offers a clue. I would suggest that the *sacerdotium confarreationum et diffareationum* was a municipal priesthood to which the Antiates hastened to appoint the distinguished *iurisperitus* after he achieved the signal honor of being invited to join the *consilium principis* at Rome.

In this connection a curious event in the life of Julius Caesar arouses interest. Under the domination of Marius and Cinna, he was selected to become *flamen Dialis: destinatus* is the term Suetonius uses,[37] Velleius has *creatus*.[38] Now the selection of the *flamen Dialis* was a complicated process:[39] three candidates were nominated (*nominati*) by the college of pontiffs,[40] and then one of them was *captus* by the *pontifex maximus*.[41] As the third stage an augur performed the *inau-*

36. *Met.* 5.26; 10.29.

37. Suet. *Caes.* 1: *Annum agens sextum decimum patrem amisit* [to enter into the discussion concerning the date of Caesar's birth is beyond the scope of this study]; *sequentibus consulibus flamen Dialis destinatus* [possibly early in 86; M. Leone (see n. 39 below) opts for 84] *dimissa Cossutia, quae familia equestri sed admodum dives praetextato desponsata fuerat, Corneliam Cinnae quater consulis filiam duxit uxorem . . . neque ut repudiaret compelli a dictatore Sulla ullo modo potuit. Quare et sacerdotio et uxoris dote et gentiliciis hereditatibus multatus diversarum partium habebatur.*

38. Vell. 2.41: *paene puer a Mario Cinnaque flamen Dialis creatus victoria Sullae, qui omnia ab iis acta fecerat irrita, amisisset id sacerdotium.*

39. Cf. M. Leone, "Il problema del flaminato di Cesare," in *Studi di storia antica offerti a Eugenio Manni* (Rome, 1973): 193–212, with ample literature cited.

40. Tac. *Ann.* 4.16.2. Cf. Livy 40.42.8–11 (referring to the *rex sacrorum*), where in the phrase *secundo loco inauguratus* we have to read *nominatus*, as proposed by J. Rubino, *Untersuchungen über römische Verfassung und Geschichte* (Kassel, 1839): 243 n. 1, and now generally accepted.

41. Livy 27.8.4–5; Gell. 1.12.15 (who erroneously extends the procedure of *captio* to the augurs and pontiffs). Tac. *Ann.* 4.16.2 uses the term *legere* (cf. Gaius 1.112), and Livy 29.38.6 has *creatus inauguratusque*, where *creatus* clearly takes the place of *captus*. Gaius 1.113 says that *praeterea exeunt liberi virilis sexus de parentis potestate, si flamines Diales inaugurentur et feminini sexus, si virgines Vestales capiantur* (see also Ulp. *Reg.* 10.5; cf. Servius, on *Aen.* 7.303). On this basis some scholars have denied the existence of the procedure of *captio* with respect to the *flamines*, most eloquently P. Catalano, *Contributi allo studio del diritto augurale* I (Turin, 1960): 215–20, and Guizzi, *Vesta* (1968): 30–66. This is unjustified for Gaius is interested in *patria potestas*, and not in *inauguratio* or *captio*. For the Vestals the *captio* was the last stage in the process of their ordination; for the *flamines* the last stage was the *inauguratio*. It was

guratio of the new *flamen*.[42] Suetonius's *destinatus* probably refers to the stage of *nominatio*,[43] whereas Velleius's *creatus* seems to denote the *captio*.[44] At that time Caesar was engaged to Cossutia, the daughter of a rich *eques*, but he now broke this engagement and married the patrician[45] Cornelia, daughter of Cinna. The religious explanation (leaving the political one aside) is simple: as the *flaminica* had to be married by *confarreatio* and presumably had also to be born *ex farreatis*, Cossutia was apparently not eligible for this function;[46] her parents had almost certainly not been married by *confarreatio*. But on the other hand, there is no reason to suppose that a plebeian woman was at that time not capable of concluding confarreate marriage with a patrician; Caesar's mother Aurelia belonged to a plebeian *gens*, yet for Caesar to be eligible for the *flamonium* she had to have

---

only the *inauguratio* that transformed into a *flamen* the person who was *captus* (cf. S. Brassloff, "Die rechtliche Bedeutung der Inauguration beim Flaminat," *Hermes* 48 [1913]: 458–63). Consequently for the Vestals it was *captio* that caused consequences in civil law, for the flamens only *inauguratio*.

42. See Catalano, *Contributi allo studio del diritto augurale* I: 212.

43. This is borne out by Suetonius's usage at *Cal.* 12: *Deinde augur in locum fratris sui Drusi destinatus, priusquam inauguraretur, ad pontificatum traductus est.* The four stages in the ordination of an augur, at least in the practice of the late Republic, were *nominatio* by the members of the college, election (i.e., *creatio*) by the *comitia* of the seventeen tribes, *cooptatio* by the college, and, finally, *inauguratio* (*Rhet. ad Herennium* 1.20; Cic. *Phil.* 2.4; *Brut.* 1.1; *Leg. agr.* 2.18). Under the Empire the *comitia* of the seventeen tribes ceased to function, and as Caligula was certainly the sole candidate, his *nominatio* meant de facto also *cooptatio*. Thus structurally *destinatio* took the place of republican *nominatio*, the essence of which was the establishment of a binding and exclusive list of candidates. This is also the role of *destinatio* in the *Tabula Hebana*; cf. R. Frei-Stolba, *Untersuchungen zu den Wahlen in der römischen Kaiserzeit* (Zurich, 1967): 120–29.

44. According to L. R. Taylor, *CP* 36 (1941): 114–16, Caesar was *nominatus*, but he was not *captus* by the *pontifex maximus*. This is of course quite possible, but in trying to explain Velleius's *creatus*, it is important to note that the *captio* of the *flamines* structurally corresponded to the *creatio* of other priests. This *creatio* was originally achieved through *cooptatio* by the members of the college, but after the *lex Domitia* the priests were *creati* by popular election, the *cooptatio* remaining as a purely formal element.

45. There is no reason to follow Mommsen, *Röm. Forschungen* I (1864): 113–14, in denying patrician status to the Cornelii Cinnae. That Cinna was consul in 86 together with the patrician Valerius Flaccus (cf. Broughton, *Magistrates* II [1951]: 53) finds an easy explanation in the turbulent character of the times, in which many other irregularities occurred.

46. Cf. G. De Sanctis, "La data della nascita di G. Cesare," *RFIC* 62 (1934): 550–51.

been married to Caesar's father by *confarreatio*. Annia, the wife of Cinna[47] and mother of Cornelia, was also a plebeian.

Yet ultimately Caesar was not *inauguratus*, and it might not appear impossible to argue that Sulla adduced the lack of confarreate marriage between Caesar's parents (and the parents of his wife) as the formal obstacle to Caesar's flaminate. This argument is only seemingly valid. We know from Macrobius[48] that the *flamen Martialis*, L. Cornelius Lentulus Niger (praetor by 61), was married to a Publicia; Publicii were a plebeian family, and hence it follows that at least the *flamines Martiales* (and, no doubt, *Quirinales*) were not obliged to marry patrician women. This is consistent with the generally less stringent regulations governing these priesthoods[49] and also conclusively shows the possibility of confarreate marriage between patrician men and plebeian women. Thus only the *flamen Dialis* would be required to marry the *patricia* born *ex farreatis*.

In Caesar's time we would thus have had confarreate marriages between patricians and between patrician men and plebeian women; whether there existed marriages of this kind between plebeian men and patrician women is difficult to say, but appears rather unlikely.[50] But we can safely conclude that plebeians did not practice *confarreatio* among themselves; this seems to follow from Cicero, *Pro Flacco* 84. Cicero there mentions only two forms of marriage *cum manu*: *usus* and *coemptio*. The parties in question were a freedwoman and an *ingenuus* (of libertine origin), hence technically plebeians. As Cicero is at pains to enumerate every legal possibility, it seems reasonable to assume that in this case the *confarreatio* was not a legal possibility.[51] Whether this conclusion is valid also with respect to the plebeian nobility is another question; but here we enter the realm of surmises, not facts.

If *confarreatio* originally served the goal of delimiting the patrician class, informal marriage without *manus* may have had an altogether

---

47. Vell. 2.41.2.
48. Macr. *Sat.* 3.13.10. This disproves the contention of L. R. Taylor, *CP* 36 (1941): 115 (who missed the text of Macrobius, although later she dealt with it in an erudite article), that Caesar's parents could not have been married *per confarreationem* inasmuch as Caesar's mother was a plebeian.
49. Servius Auctus, on *Aen.* 8.552.
50. Westrup, *Recherches* (1943): 55ff.
51. Cf. A. Watson, *Law of Persons* (see n. 2 above): 23–24.

different purpose. We cannot here go into various theories concerning marriage by *usus*, but important for our subject is the institution of *trinoctium*. If each year the wife stayed away from the marital house for three consecutive nights, the acquisition of *manus* by her husband was interrupted, and as a result she remained under the *potestas* of her father or, if she was *sui iuris*, under the control of her agnatic guardians. The rule of the *trinoctium* is sometimes represented as an innovation introduced by the Twelve Tables, yet in the text of Gaius (1.111) there is nothing to suggest this interpretation. Most probably we are dealing here with the codification of a customary practice, which we may surmise had its roots in religion: the wife would stay away from the *sacra* of her husband and thus reaffirm her membership in her agnatic clan. Kaser remarks very sensibly that as *trinoctium* was a device to interrupt the acquisition of *manus*, it must be substantially later than the concept of *manus* marriage. He confesses, however, that the social circumstances in which a need for the institution of *trinoctium* arose are as enigmatic as ever.[52]

Now marriage without *manus* may have been in the interest of the father of the wife and of her agnates, but the cooperation of the husband was necessary too. Here the studies of the Danish scholar C. W. Westrup offer an attractive idea.[53] He conjectures that the *trinoctium* was primarily a device invented to safeguard the patrician woman from falling by *usus* under the *manus* of her plebeian husband in mixed marriages. The story reported by Livy (10.23) under the year 295 illustrates the tendency of patricians to avoid *manus* when marrying their daughters into plebeian families. Verginia, a patrician married to a plebeian, L. Volumnius, the consul of 296, was prevented by other patrician matrons from sacrificing in the *sacellum* of Pudicitia Patricia because she *e patribus enupsisset*. Now Verginia must have been married without *manus*, for if the *conventio in manum* had taken place, she would have suffered the *capitis diminutio minima*— would have become a member of the new family *in filiae loco* and a full participant in the *sacra* of the Volumnii. In this situation she would hardly have been described as a *patricia*.

To sum up: we have (not counting *coemptio*) two opposite forms of

52. Kaser, *Ius* (1949): 319–20; id., *Privatr.* I² (1971): 79–80; Watson, *XII Tables* (1975): 16–18.
53. Westrup, *Recherches* (1943): 55ff., especially 64–65.

marriage, both of them of political and religious significance: the *confarreatio*, which was surrounded by a religious aura and which a nucleus of patrician families used as an instrument to build up a closed caste; and the informal marriage without *manus*, which served the purpose of cementing alliances of presumably weaker patrician families with rich plebeians. In this perspective the prohibition of intermarriage enacted by the decemvirs reveals itself as an attempt by patrician purists and hardliners to gain undisputed ascendancy not only by fending off the plebeians, but also by weakening those of their patrician rivals who relied for their political survival on marriage alliances with plebeian families.

Reaction was inevitable. Our sources attribute the repeal of the decemviral rule to the *lex Canuleia*, a plebiscite commonly dated to 445. The Canuleian law raises a host of problems. We cannot here go into the tangled question of tribal legislation before the *lex Hortensia* or the legal validity of plebiscites. Suffice it to say that it appears highly unlikely that a plebiscite can at that early period have had the force of law. But the fact itself, the removal of the ban on intermarriages, is indisputable. The date, 445 B.C., may derive (as Ogilvie thinks)[54] from information going back to the *Annales*, yet even this is far from certain.

What attracts one's attention is that the sources, Livy primarily, but also Cicero, speak in one breath of *conubium* and auspices. This reflects a late republican doctrine, of course, but there may be a grain of truth in it. To counter the agitation of Canuleius, Livy reports (4.6.2–3), the patricians argued that the decemvirs had abolished the *conubium* (*conubium diremisse*) in order to prevent the auspices from being thrown into confusion by uncertain offspring (*ne incerta*

---

54. Ogilvie, *Comm.* (1965): 527ff. To propose any specific date would be pure guesswork. One can suspect, however, that the lifting of the ban on intermarriage would have occurred before the first appearance (or at least frequent appearance) of plebeians among consular tribunes, i.e., before the end of the fifth century. Mitchell, chapter V, part 14 above, connects the lifting of the ban with the changes caused by the *lex Ogulnia* of 300, which opened the major priesthoods to plebeians. But we should rather say that before the Ogulnian law all priests had to be born of parents married by the ceremony of *confarreatio*, and hence had to have at least patrician fathers; by admitting the plebeians to the major priesthoods (above all the colleges of pontiffs and augurs) the *lex Ogulnia* abolished this requirement, which remained in force only with respect to the major *flamines* and the "king of sacrifices."

prole auspicia turbarentur; cf. 4.2.5 *conluvio gentium, perturbatio auspiciorum publicorum privatorumque*). This they justified by the fact that no plebeian possessed the auspices (*quod nemo plebeius auspicia haberet*). "The argument is fallacious," says Ogilvie in his commentary,[55] "for in law *origo sequitur patrem.*" Yes, of course, in the developed law—but apparently not in the law of the Twelve Tables. In the marriage by *confarreatio*, the status of the bride seems to have been of legal and religious importance, and the decemvirs would simply have extended this rule to other marriages as well. If the *patres* succeeded in establishing the rule that purity of blood was a necessary requirement for the holding of certain priesthoods, it was a natural and logical step to argue that mixed marriages would ultimately lead to total contamination of the auspices used by the magistrates, for in the end there would be nobody of pure patrician blood. The argument is not fallacious—it is only perverse, for it attempts to present a patent innovation as a hallowed rule of great antiquity.

The decemviral attempt to redefine the concept of *conubium* is, in fact, no more striking or unusual than the Augustan laws *de maritandis ordinibus*. Despite a compromise on this front, the patriciate was able not only to survive undiluted but to maintain a dominant position, because it had established itself as a religious entity. The confarreate marriage, a relic of the power struggle in the distant past, remained a patrician preserve down to imperial times.[56]

55. Ogilvie, *Comm.* (1965): 532 on 4.2.5. On p. 537 (on 4.12) he corrects his argument and points out that "it is only children born of *iustae nuptiae* . . . that take the status of the father." And the patrician doctrine denied the possibility of *iustae nuptiae* between patricians and plebeians.

56. This reconstruction differs substantially from that proposed by Mitchell (chapter V above). I cannot find any compelling evidence for his identification of priests and *patres* or for his contention that all priests automatically qualified as senators. As far as we know, this may have been the case with respect to the *flamen Dialis*, but from this isolated case no safe inferences can be drawn concerning other priests. In any case Cicero *Ad Att.* 4.2.3–4 (missed or disregarded by Mitchell) shows clearly that not all pontiffs were members of the Senate. On the other hand differences between the reconstruction proposed in this paper and the ideas presented by Raaflaub (chapter VII above) are more apparent than real. As Raaflaub points out (part 6) "the closure of the patriciate" need not be imagined as the wholesale ousting of the vanquished in the political struggle from the ranks of the aristocracy, but rather as the building of fences to keep the upstarts out. The ritual of *confarreatio* was one of those fences.

56

The Auspices and the Struggle of the Orders

The Struggle of the Orders was an event fascinating and uncertain; its opposing forces, the patricians and the plebeians - clouds of fiction or probability, condensing into ancient tales or modern constructs.[1] The only thing not in contention is that it did take place.

What role did the auspices play in this momentous contest? Only an accomplished augur could divine the answer. We have to turn to 'our Roman masters' (as Mommsen called them), and ask a different question: what role did *they* envisage for the auspices? Through fable and partisan invention, in the writings of Roman antiquarians, jurists and historians, the distant past of archaic Rome still dimly shimmers. The image our sources present is clear and the message resounding: the auspices were a patricians' preserve, the bulwark and mainstay of their divinely ordained power. And this world of the early Republic, whether real or imaginary, continued to live in institutional relics, still in plain view in the day of Cicero.

Much of this traditional lore found its ultimate receptacle in the Annals of Livy. With Livy our uncertain guide, let us then embark upon our journey of divination.

Intermarriage between patricians and plebeians looms large in Livy's tale. The decemvirs imposed a ban on mixed marriages, but the plebeians' right to *conubium* with the patricians was restored only five years later by the plebiscite of Canuleius.[2]

How did the patricians try to justify the decemviral ban? By invoking the auspices - in Livy's account (4,2,5; 4,12; 6,2-3). Intermarriage, they argued, would inevitably result in *perturbatio auspiciorum publicorum privatorumque*. Why this outcome? Because no plebeian possessed the auspices (*quod nemo plebeius auspicia haberet*). Consequently, the decemvirs had abolished the *conubium* (*conubium diremisse*) in order to prevent the auspices from being thrown into confusion by uncertain

---

1 For a recent collection of such constructs, and an excellent bibliography, see K.A. Raaflaub (ed.), Social Struggles in Archaic Rome. New Perspectives on the Conflict of the Orders, Berkeley 1986.

2 Cic. rep. 2,63; Liv. 4,1-6. For an interpretation, see R.M. Ogilvie, A Commentary on Livy. Books 1-5, Oxford 1965, 526-539; J. Linderski, Religious Aspects of the Conflict of the Orders: the case of *confarreatio*, in: Social Struggles (above, n. 1), 252-261. This is the traditional date which we are not in a position to verify.

offspring (*ne incerta prole auspicia turbarentur*). The plebeians contested this argument. No confusion would arise, for the children acquire the status of the father (*patrem sequuntur liberi*). And they were particularly incensed at the intimation that they were not able to consult the auspices - as if hateful to immortal gods (*quod auspicari, tamquam invisi dis immortalibus, negarentur posse*).

The same motif and argument is prominent in the speech Livy (6,41,4-12) puts into the mouth of Appius Claudius, the grandson of the decemvir. Haranguing against the admission of plebeians to the consulship he again invokes the auspices. Rome was founded through the auspices and it is through the auspices that all affairs of the state are being conducted in war and peace, at home and abroad (*auspiciis hanc urbem conditam esse, auspiciis bello ac pace, domi militiaeque omnia geri*). And it is the *patres* who are the exclusive holders of the *auspicia, penes patres auspicia sunt*. No plebeian magistrate is elected with the blessing of the auspices (*plebeius ... magistratus nullus auspicato creatur*). On the other hand the auspices are the *propria res* of the patricians, for not only are the patrician magistrates always elected after the consultation of the auspices, but in particular the patricians select the *interrex 'auspicato'* all by themselves, without any vote of the people, and thus as private persons possess the *auspicia* which the plebeians do not have even while holding magistracies (*nobis adeo propria sunt auspicia, ut non solum, quos populus creat patricios magistratus, non aliter quam auspicato creet, sed nos quoque ipsi sine suffragio populi auspicato interregem prodamus et privatim* [3] *auspicia habeamus, quae isti ne in magistratibus quidem habent*).

The concept of the *perturbatio auspiciorum* and the remarkable assertion that the patricians *privatim auspicia habent* which the plebeians *ne in magistratibus quidem habent* evoke interest. How are we to untangle these antiquarian constructs?

The renowned author of a standard commentary made an attempt. Commenting on the *perturbatio auspiciorum,* and referring to the speech of Appius, he writes:

'Before the Lex Ogulnia of 300 only patricians could be augurs and even thereafter only patricians could hold the auspices. Hence when an *interregnum* occurred *auspicia ad patres redeunt* (Cic. *ad Brut.* 1,5,4). Since in early Rome no transaction of any kind took place without consulting the auspices, the distinction between *publica* and *privata* is anachronistic and belongs to the period after the Lex Ogulnia when plebeians by their membership of the religious colleges acquired a share in the control of those auspices which affected public transactions. But the patricians maintained an exclusive monopoly of the auspices for their own private affairs, in particular

---

[3] *privatim* is the reading of the manuscripts, but the conjecture of C.B. Crévier, *privati*, is not without merit.

for the celebration of marriages (Plautus, *Casina* 86; Cicero, *de Divin.* 1.28 with Pease's note). The consuls argue that since the auspices can only be held by patricians mixed marriages whose offspring could not validly be called patrician would in the end deprive Rome of anyone to hold the auspices. The argument is fallacious, for in law *origo sequitur patrem.*'[4]

This exposition is altogether wrong. First, the theory of an exclusive patrician monopoly of *auspicia privata*. Plautus, Cas. 86, which Ogilvie quotes in this context, does not mention patricians at all; it alludes to the *auspices nuptiarum,* but the *puella* in question is only an *ingenua*, not a *patricia*.[5] Cicero, div.1,28, says that in olden times all things of importance, including private affairs, were conducted *auspicato,* but again the incriminated passage contains no reference to patricians.[6] Thus the theory advocated by Ogilvie finds no support in the sources he quotes; it goes back to a pronouncement of Theodor Mommsen, who tried to anchor it solely in the text of Livy.[7]

The key to our puzzle is the term *privatim* in the speech of Appius Claudius. Appius stresses the exclusive prerogative of the patricians to appoint the *interrex*: they do it *auspicato*, and hence possess *privatim* the auspices which the plebeians are lacking even as magistrates. And indeed, as Cicero and Asconius eloquently attest,[8] even at the very end of the Republic only patrician senators were competent to nominate the first *interrex*, after which the chain of patrician *interreges* would perpetuate itself until the consuls were elected. Now a major division in Roman constitutional law was the opposition between *magistratus* and *privatus*. But we have to remember that senators were not magistrates; technically they were classified as *privati*. Now we see the light: in Livy's passage the contrast is not at all between private patricians and plebeian magistrates but rather between the latter and the patrician

---

4　R.M. Ogilvie, Commentary (above, n.2), 531-532.

5　The *puella expositicia ... ea invenietur et pudica et libera, ingenua Atheniensis, ... ultri ubi nuptum, non manebit auspices* (Cas. 79-86).

6　The text reads: *Nihil fere quondam maioris rei nisi auspicato ne privatim quidem gerebatur, quod etiam nunc nuptiarum auspices declarant, qui re omissa nomen tantum tenent.* In this context A.S. Pease, M. Tulli Ciceronis De Divinatione Libri Duo, Urbana 1920 (reprint Darmstadt 1963), adduces also Val. Max. 2,1,1 (*apud antiquos non solum publice sed etiam privatim nihil gerebatur nisi auspicio prius sumpto. Quo ex more nuptiis etiam nunc auspices interponuntur*), Servius, Aen. 1,346 (*nihil nisi captatis faciebant auguriis, et praecipue nuptias*; Servius adduces in turn Lucan 2,371 and Juvenal 10,336) and Liv. 6,41 quoted above in the text. Cf. also Liv. 1,36,6: *nihil belli domique ... nisi auspicato gereretur, concilia populi, exercitus vocati, summa rerum, ubi aves non admissent, dirimerentur.*

7　Th. Mommsen, Römisches Staatsrecht I (3.Aufl.), Leipzig 1887, 89 n.1, 91 n.1. The same (mistaken) view in A. Piganiol, Les attributions militaires et les attributions religieuses du tribunat de la plèbe, in: Scripta varia II (Collection Latomus 132), Bruxelles 1973 (originally published in 1919), 270: the auspices formed "un culte patricien privé".

8　Cic. dom. 38; ad Brut. 1,5,4; Asc. in Mil. 31 C.

senators - who can with all justification be discribed as *privati* ! Appius makes thus no reference to the *auspicia privata* of the patricians but rather to the *auspicia* which they use *privatim*, as senators, to appoint the *interrex*. And these auspices were, naturally, the *auspicia publica*. The idea that the *auspicia privata* of the patricians were identical with the *auspicia publica populi Romani* is a phantom which emanates from a mistranslation and misinterpretation of the term *privatim* in Livy. It is high time to chase it from the pages of Roman constitutional history.[9]

In his stimulating study of the auspices and the institution of *interregnum*, Andre Magdelain was justly suspicious of the patricians' claim to be the sole possessors of the *auspicia privata*, and of the alleged use of these auspices for the appointment of the *interrex*. He writes: "Jamais la constitution républicaine n'admit la mutation d'auspices privés en auspices publics".[10] To this clear insight our interpretation of Livy, and of the term *privatim*, offers powerful support.

Livy utilizes in his story the famous doctrine of the 'return' of the auspices: *auspicia ad patres redeunt*. According to this doctrine when there were no patrician (i.e. curule) magistrates the *auspicia populi Romani* return to the *patres* ;[11] the patres are the receptacle of the auspices which Jupiter first gave to Romulus, and which after the establishment of the Republic were transmitted from one set of the highest magistrates to another. We know this doctrine from late republican sources; in this shape it both rationalizes and reflects the situation that existed before the plebeian victories of the fourth century.

The procedure shows, however, more recent elements. In any case in the late republican period the patrician senators could not on their own

---

9 Cf. G. Lobrano, Plebei magistratus, patricii magistratus, magistratus populi Romani, SDHI 41, 1975, 247-277 at 271: "il monopolio auspicale si stabilisce ... tra *auspicia populi* e *patricii magistratus* ad esclusione dei *plebei magistratus* (non tra *auspicia* e *patricii* ad esclusione dei plebei)". But he does not stress the character of patrician senators as *privati* ; and the *auspicia populi* in Lobrano's sense is a phantom created by P. Catalano, Contributi allo studio del diritto augurale, vol.1, Torino 1960, 450 ff. Catalano defines the *auspicia populi* as "complesso degli *auspicia* dei cittadini" (pp. 453-454), i.e. as an amalgamation of the individual *auspicia privata*, and finds in them "il fondamento" of the magisterial auspices, i.e. of the *auspicia publica* (p. 463). Similarly, the *auspicia privata patrum* would form "il fondamento del potere del *rex* in quanto nominato dall'*interrex* " (p. 460). This theory constitutes a weak pillar in the splendid edifice erected by this illustrious augural scholar; it ultimately derives from a grievous misunderstanding of the term *privatim* in Livy (cf. p. 455: "direi che, stando alla lettera di Livio, sono *privata* tutti gli *auspicia* su cui si fonda o con la cui consultazione si esercita l'*interregnum*"). Also A. Heuss in his inspiring Gedanken und Vermutungen zur frühen römischen Regierungsgewalt (Nachr.Akad.Göttingen 1982, 10) 379, 397, misconstrued the meaning of *privatim*.

10 Auspicia ad patres redeunt, Hommages a Jean Bayet (Collection Latomus 70), Bruxelles 1964, 427-473 at 454.

11 Cic. ad Brut. 1,5,4: *dum unus erit patricius magistratus auspicia ad patres redire non possunt*. Cf. leg. 3,9.

activitate the auspices that had devolved upon them. A *relatio ad senatum de patriciis convocandis qui interregem proderent* [12] was necessary, and, as there were no curule magistrates, it had to be made - the height of irony and constitutional implausibility - by a tribune of the plebs! Furthermore, it is not clear how a body of patrician senators could act *auspicato* at all - if we take *auspicato* in its normal meaning, 'after the consultation of the auspices', for the auspices could be consulted solely by individual persons. It is possible that the first *interrex* was selected by lot, and as the drawing of lots depended upon divine will it was akin to the *auspicatio*.[13] But in a strict sense of the word it was only the second *interrex* who was appointed *auspicato*, and consequently it was felt that only he or his successors (but not the first *interrex*) were qualified to convene the *comitia* (or more exactly to hold the auspices for the election and the *renuntiatio* of the consuls).

Now if the auspices 'return' to the *patres*, this must mean that normally, when the magistrates are in the office, the *patres* (qua *patres*) do not have those auspices: they hold them solely in the period running from the moment the last 'patrician' magistracy had been vacated to the appointment of the first *interrex*. This consideration demonstrates *ad oculos*, again and again, that the auspices in question must have been different from the *auspicia privata*. The concept of 'return' makes no sense with respect to private auspices; it makes all sense with respect to *auspicia publica*.

Still the phrase *auspicia ad patres redeunt* is ambiguous. Should we take it to mean that the *patres* were regarded as the original and primordial source of the auspices from whom the auspices of all magistrates derived and to whom they return? Not at all! The verb *redeo* also has other meanings: 'to pass back to the control of someone', 'to devolve upon somebody'.[14] When we read in Livy (1,32,1) *mortuo Tullo ... res ad patres redierat*, this statement is certainly not meant to convey the idea that originally the state belonged to the *patres* - for the *patres* themselves according to the annalists were a creation of Romulus.

More than twenty years ago Andre Magdelain made an illuminating observation: with the exception of the few last years of the Republic all attested *interreges* were drawn from among the former holders of the

---

12 Asc. in Mil. 31 C. For the procedure and terminology, see Th. Mommsen, Staatsrecht I (3.Aufl.),   647-659.

13 All *sortitiones* pertaining to public affairs took place in a *templum*, and consequently if any *vitium* was comitted during the *sortitio*, the augurs were called upon to investigate it (cf. J. Linderski, The Augural Law, ANRW II 16.3, 1986, 2173-2175, 2193-2194, n. 173). The antiquarian descriptions of the first *interregnum* after the death of Romulus indicate the selection of *interreges* by lot, but almost all reports referring to historical times intimate the election of the first *interrex* by the vote of the patrician senators. Cf. Th. Mommsen, Staatsrecht I (3.Aufl.), 98 n.2, 656-658. The subject requires a new study.

14 Cf. Oxford Latin Dictionary, Oxford 1982, 1590, s.v. redeo, nos. 10 and 12.

highest *auspicia* and *imperia*. Hence his conclusion: during the *interregnum* the auspices did not come into the possession of all patrician senators but solely those who had previously held the highest offices.[15]

This in turn entails important consequences for our understanding of the patriciate and the struggle of the orders. Whenever the closure of the patriciate occurred, in the middle of the fifth century or toward its end, the senate was then composed, largely or exclusively, of the former supreme magistrates. They were the *patres*, the senators *par excellence*, the former holders of the *auspicia populi Romani*. During the *interregnum*, the auspices they once had held as magistrates reverted to them. Only in this sense can we speak of the 'return' of the auspices. [16]

During the regal period the (public) auspices were a prerogative of the kings, and, when the kingdom was vacant, of the *interreges*.[17] Upon

---

[15] Auspicia (above n.10), 427 ff. A. Guarino, Il vuoto di potere nella "libera repubblica", Index 3, 1972, 284-303, esp. 295, points to the irregularities of 53 and 52, especially the plebeian *interrex* Q. Caecilius Metellus Pius Scipio Nasica, and concludes that it was the whole senate (including the plebeians) that proceeded to appoint the *interrex*. His conclusion is refuted by the wording of Asconius (in Mil. 31 C.), and as to Scipio Nasica it is more economical to assume that he retained his patriciate even after his adoption into the house of Caecilii Metelli. He was probably adopted *per testamentum*, and it is very likely that this form of adoption imposed only the obligation of *nomen ferendi;* in any case we can safely assume that the *adrogatio* did not take place. Cf. M. Kaser, Das römische Privatrecht I (2.Aufl.), München 1971, 349, with further literature.

[16] A. Heuss, Gedanken (above, n. 9), 418-421, argues that "wenn die auspicia dahin kommen, wo sie hin gehören, muß ihr Aufenthalt dort ihrem 'normalen' Status entsprechen". Consequently "ist dann alles, was das Interregnum überflüssig macht, eine Trübung der Idee, die im Interregnum zum Vorschein kommt". Hence "eine grelle Paradoxie, denn diese hinderlichen Umstände machen doch genau den Mechanismus des uns geläufigen römischen Staates aus" (pp. 420-421). There is no paradox here at all once we replace the formulation 'the normal state' by 'the pure state'. When the auspices are used by the magistrates they can be rendered 'uncertain', *incerta*, by various ritual errors. During the *interregnum* they are cleansed for their return from the world of action to a passive receptable. The *patres* use them only once: to appoint the first *interrex*. The goal of the *interregnum* was the *renovatio auspiciorum* (cf. Liv. 5,31,8; 5,52,9; 6,5,6).

[17] It is in the institution of the *interregnum* that A. Momigliano sought one of the main avenues leading to the formation and delimitation of the patriciate (Osservazioni sulla distinzione fra patrizi e plebei, in: Les origines de la république romaine, Entretiens sur l'Antiquité Classique, XIII), Vandœuvres-Geneva 1967, 197-221 at 209-211 (= Quarto contributo alla storia degli studi classici e del mondo antico, Roma 1969, 419-436 at 427-428). As members of the highest aristocracy were gradually identified those senators who either had held or were capable of holding the office of *interrex*. Few scholars would now deny the regal origin of the *interregnum*, yet there is trouble with this theory. There were very few *interregna*, far too few to play a decisive role in the formation of any class. If this is so, we may still find rescue in a parallel theory of A. Magdelain, Cinq jours épagomènes a Rome?, REL 40, 1962, 201-227, esp. 220-223. He very ingeniously interprets the *interregnum* as a sacral institution, and postulates a sort of sacral *regifugium*, the ritual retreat of the

the expulsion of the Tarquins, they were vested, together with *imperium*
and the outward insignia of royal power, in the supreme magistrates of
the Republic. This magistrates were drawn, not unnaturally, from the
aristocratic *gentes,* and in turn used their magisterial *auspicium* and
imperium to set themselves apart from the lesser clans. The patriciate,
not unlike the *nobilitas,* ultimately coalesced as an aristocracy of
office.[18] In the annalistic tradition the patricians possess the auspices
because they are patricians; in fact they are the patricians because they
possess the auspices. When the time came for the plebeians to challenge
the patrician monopoly of office the dogma that the *auspicia populi
Romani* were the patrician auspices was firmly established. And the
auspices proved a most formidable barrier, a barrier that the plebeians
had never fully stormed. The late republican antiquarian terminology
offers us a glimpse into this world of strife and ultimate compromise.

The expression *magistratus patricii* is a relic of those times. It can
denote the magistrates who were of patrician birth[19] or it can refer to
the character of the office. The augur Valerius Messala in a famous
fragment preserved by Aulus Gellius (13,15,4) says that the auspices of
the patricians are divided into two classes: *patriciorum auspicia in duas
sunt divisa potestates.* The greatest (*maxima*) are those of the consuls,
praetors and censors. Other magistrates have lesser auspices
(*reliquorum magistratuum minora sunt auspicia*).[20] The augur Cicero
uses the same terminology.[21] Thus the late republican augurs not only
regarded the patrician senators and magistrates as exclusive holders of
public auspices - it is much more remarkable that they continued to
define the consulship, the praetorship and other higher and minor

---

king each year for the five days between the Terminalia and the beginning of
the New Year. During this period an interim king would hold royal auspices.
Later, upon the real and not merely ritual flight of the last king, the sacral
interreges transformed themselves into political ones - thus as a political
institution the *interregnum* was a creation of the Republic. This is an elegant
theory, and perhaps we should leave it at that. The concrete political events
are not recoverable. Cf. H. Volkmann, Das römische Interregnum und die
persische Anomia, RhM 110, 1967, 76-83; J.-C. Richard, Les origines de la plèbe
romaine, Rome 1978, 224-236. A.K. Michels, The Calendar of the Roman
Republic, Princeton 1967, 160 n. 3, remains sceptical, and perhaps rightly so.

18 This is not to deny that its distant origin lay in the regal period; for this
(obvious) proposition, see J.-C. Richard, Patricians and Plebeians, in: Social
Struggles (above, n.1), 105-129, and for a most sensible social interpretation of
the struggle of the orders, K. Raaflaub, From Protection and Defense to Offense
and Participation: Stages in the Conflict of the Orders, ibid. 198-243, esp.227-
236, 241-242.

19 As in Cic. dom. 38, often misinterpretated.

20 On this augural theory, see now J.-C. Richard, *Praetor collega consulis est* :
Contribution à l'histoire de la préture , RPh 56, 1982, 19-31; J. Linderski, The
Augural Law (above, n.13), 2178-2184.

21 Leg. agr. 2,26; ad Brut. 1,5,4.

offices as patrician magistracies - although the plebeians had administered them for more than three hundred years.

The reason for this striking terminology lies in the fact that the *auspicia publica populi Romani* were the patrician auspices. The public auspices of the plebeians did not exist. The plebeian magistrates, the tribunes of the plebs and the plebeian aediles, were elected without the preliminary consultation of the auspices; the plebiscite was the *lex inauspicata*.[22]

In the course of the fourth century the plebeians gained access to the patrician magistracies, but not the ownership of the auspices. Upon their admittance to the consulship, a strange compromise apparently was reached. The augural doctrine reflects this compromise; it hardly had invented it. As the patricians did not intend to relinquish the *auspicia*, it was agreed that the plebeians would administer their newly won offices with the help of what technically was the patrician auspices. The consulship and the other offices remained technically patrician, and they carried with them patrician auspices. A plebeian on his election to the consulate would enter as it were into patrician shoes: he would use patrician auspices, but he would not 'have' them. Here the distinction of Roman civil law between ownership, *dominium ex iure Quiritium,* and mere *possessio* comes to mind. Quite similarly the plebeians in their capacity as *magistratus populi Romani* used the auspices, but they did not own them. And that they did not own them can best be seen during the *interregnum* with the auspices devolving until the very days of the Republic solely upon the patricians in the senate. In this sense only the patrician magistrates were endowed with *iustum imperium et auspicium domi militiaeque*.[23] If we regard the political situation of the middle or the late Republic, this appears a specious technicality. But one has to

---

22 Liv. 6.41,5; 7,6,11; Dion.Hal. 9,49,5; Mommsen, Staatsrecht II (3.Aufl.), Leipzig 1887, 282-285; III 1, Leipzig 1887, 151-153. Cf. J.-C. Richard, Les origines (above, n.17), 559-562. According to Cicero (*apud* Asconius in Corn. 76 C.) the first tribunes were elected *auspicato comitiis curiatis* (cf. Dion.Hal. 6,89,1-2, who presents the election as being *curiatim* but without the attendance of the patricians; and he does not mention the consultation of the auspices. Such an assembly can hardly be described as *comitia curiata*. It should rather be classified as the *concilium plebis curiatum*). The first election of the tribunes in a tribal assembly took place in 471 (Liv. 2,56-58,2; Dion.Hal. 9,41,3. 49,5) and when the tribunate was renewed in 449 the tribunes were elected *pontifice maximo comitia habente* (Liv. 3,54,11; Cic. *apud* Asconium in Corn. 77 C.). It is difficult not to agree with R.M. Ogilvie, Commentary (above, n.2), 381: he argues that the tribunes were never elected by the *comitia curiata*, and thinks that here we deal with "an attempt by some second-century constitutionalist ... to find a respectable origin for the institution and election of tribunes". Others threat this as history: so R.E.A. Palmer, The Archaic Community of the Romans, Cambridge 1970, 219-222, 224-225, and more recently, A. Magdelain, Le suffrage universel à Rome au Veme siècle, CRAI 1979, 698-713 at 709-710. This appears far-fetched indeed.

23 Liv. 10,8,9, the speech of P. Decius Mus in support of the *lex Ogulnia* admitting the plebeians to the priesthoods, in a list of various patrician claims.

allow archaic Rome to live its own history. Even after the great compromise with the plebeians the patricians were able to retain exclusive control of two important, at the time, political tools: *interregnum* and *auctoritas   patrum*.[24] These were their last ramparts, and they were guarded by the *auspicia*.

But even if a plebeian consul merely 'possessed' but not 'owned' his consular auspices, in the administration of the consulship and in the use of the auspices there was little difference between him and his patrician colleague. Both presided *auspicato* over the *comitia   populi*, had full *auspicium* and *imperium* in the field, and could proceed to the appointment of the dictator *ave sinistra* according to the hallowed auspicial ritual. But a striking and curious fact stares us in the face: although the first plebeian consul was elected in 366, the first plebeian college of consuls appears in the *fasti* only in 172, almost two centuries later. C. Popillius Laenas and P. Aelius Ligus made history, but only a terse entry in the Fasti Capitolini, *ambo primi de plebe*, [25] indicates that the significance of this election was not lost on antiquarians and constitutional experts. The annalists took scant notice of the event; not a word in Livy.[26] The accession of the two plebeians to the consulship of 172 was apparently surrounded by no political drama, and hence was of little interest to the embroiderers of history. The absence of political and religious contention is, however, a story in itself; it demonstrates that the second century was a whole world apart not only from the plebeian and patrician struggles of the fourth century but also from the religious sensitivities of the recent war with Hannibal. For it was during the war that an attempt was made, for the first time, to have two plebeians elected to the consulship.

In 215 the consuls were L. Postumius Albinus, a patrician, and Ti. Sempronius Gracchus, a plebeian.[27] When Postumius, still as consul designate, was killed in battle, Sempronius Gracchus held the *comitia* at which the future conqueror of Syracuse, C. Claudius Marcellus, another plebeian, was elected a suffect consul *ingenti consensu*. But when Marcellus was *extemplo* entering upon his office, Livy reports, thunder was heard. The augurs were called upon by the senate to investigate the matter, and they pronounced that Marcellus' election was marred by a

---

24 Cf. G. Branca, Cic. de domo 14,38 e *auctoritas patrum*, Iura 20, 1969, 49-51.

25 A. Degrassi, Fasti Consulares et Triumphales (=Inscr. Italiae, XIII.1), Roma 1947, 50-51, 458-459.

26 He gives only a bare annalistic notice (42,9,8): *Alter consul Postumius ... comitiorum causa Romam rediit. consules C. Popillium Laenatem P. Aelium Ligurem creavit.*   Under the year 342 he mentions a plebiscite *ut liceret consules ambos plebeios creari* (7,42,2), in this form undoubtedly spurious or at least inaccurate. Cf. J.-C. Richard, Sur le Plébiscite ut liceret consules ambos plebeios creari (Tite-Live VII 42,2), Historia 28, 1979, 65-78.

27 T.R.S. Broughton, The Magistrates of the Roman Republic I, New York 1951, 247-248 (and see in particular his discussion, p.257, n.1).

ritual fault, *vitio creatum videri*.[28] Upon hearing the verdict of the
augurs Marcellus, an augur himself, stepped down. The recent example
of C. Flaminius who disregarded the auspices, and perished with his
army, made it impossible to defy the tradition and the college of augurs.
The *vitium* in question was the ritual unsuitability of the second
plebeian to become consul: by sending thunder Jupiter protested against
this violation of *fas*. The augural technicalities of the affair I have
discussed in another place,[29] but a fundamental question still remains to
be asked: why was a second plebeian unsuited for the consulate?
Because of the auspices - is clearly the answer, but we need more
precision. We can adduce two reasons - if we place ourselves in the
position of the augurs. One is similar to that propounded, in a different
context, by Cicero. Upbraiding Clodius' *transitio ad plebem*, he writes (de
domo 38) that the *auspicia populi Romani* will perish if no patricians are
left to be elected to the magistracies (*si magistratus patricii creati non
sunt*) for ultimately there will be no *interrex*, who must be a patrician
himself, and must be nominated by the patricians (*quem et ipsum
patricium esse et a patriciis prodi necesse est*). Quite similarly, should
two plebeians be elected year by year (or frequently enough) to the
consulship, the pool of available *interreges* would be greatly diminished,
and the continuity of the auspices, and of the Republic itself, would be
an jeopardy. The other reason is this: in the hands of the plebeians the
patrician auspices apparently lost their pristine purity. If the plebeian
consuls do not 'own' the auspices, and only 'administer' them, then the
auspicial continuity from Romulus to the last college of magistrates could
be secured only through the patrician chain of magistrates, and the
renovatio auspiciorum only through the *patres* and the patrician
interreges. In 172 the college of augurs must have found an ingenious
way of removing part of those religious obstacles - those concerning the
interrex remained in force.

The political implications are obvious. For almost two hundred years
after 366 the patricians held half of all consulships, and even after 172
patricians appear in the *fasti* more frequently than would be warranted
by their political stature, and far in excess of their numbers. Such was
the force of the auspical halo that surrounded them.

Until the very end of the Republic a plebeian consul was ritually the
lesser partner of the patrician: he could never become an *interrex*. If
this was so, we can safely assume that the distinction between the
orders was even more pronounced with respect to the predecessors of
the consuls, the military tribunes with consular power. There are good

---

28 Liv. 23,31,13-14: *cui ineunti consulatum cum tonuisset, vocati augures vitio
creatum videri pronuntiaverunt; volgoque patres ita fama ferebant, quod tum
primum duo plebeii consules facti essent, id dis cordi non esse. In locum
Marcelli, ubi is se magistratu abdicavit, suffectus Q. Fabius Maximus tertium.* Cf.
Plut. Marc. 12,1.

29 J. Linderski, The Augural Law (above, n.13), 2168-2172.

reasons for believing that the original supreme magistrates of the Republic were the two praetors, and that the praetor who actually held the *fasces* had the title of *maximus* (or alternatively that there was one *praetor* called *maximus* to distinguish him from the *praetores minores*).[30] These praetors were the sole holders of the *auspicia publica*. But in the second half of the fifth century Rome was in a difficult military situation. Full utilization of plebeian manpower was imperative, and thus the plebeians gained access to the new office of military tribunes.[31] The traditional denomination, military tribunes with consular power, *consulari potestate*, is either anachronistic or we have to give the term its full semantic value.[32] *Consulari potestate* would mean 'with advisory powers'. The old praetors were the 'leaders' the new military tribunes merely 'advisors'. The colleges of military tribunes were comprised of three, four or six members; according to the annalistic tradition the first college was in office in 444, and the first plebeian was elected in 400, though the possibly plebeian names appear as consular tribunes already in 444 and 422.[33] No college composed exclusively of plebeians is on record. This is hardly due merely to chance, but clearly reflects a legal regulation. The augural reason is not far to seek: only the patrician members of the college were able to transmit the auspices to their successors in their pure and pristine state. In the *fasti* there is no clear pattern in the election of the consuls and the consular tribunes. But even in the years when the consular tribunes were in office it is not unlikely that they would only supplement but not supplant the praetors. Each 'annalistic' college of the consular tribunes may have in reality been composed of two separate groups of officials: one or two posts would belong to the patrician praetors, and the remaining ones to the consular military tribunes, who could have been either patricians or

---

30 See the lucid overview of various modern theories by J.-C. Richard, Les origines (above, n.17), 455-472. On the *praetor maximus*, see esp. Th. Mommsen, Die römische Chronologic bis auf Caesar, Berlin 1858 (2. Aufl. Berlin 1859), 178-179; A. Magdelain, Practor maximus et comitiatus maximus, Iura 20, 1969, 257-268, esp. 269-272, 278-279; A. Momigliano, Practor maximus e questioni affini, Quarto contributo (above, n.17), 403-417. One of the obligations of the *praetor maximus* was to drive the *clavis annalis* into the wall of the Capitoline temple on the Ides of September. The basis text is Liv. 7,3,5: *Lex vetusta est ... ut, qui praetor maximus sit, idibus Septembribus clavum pangat.*

31 Cf. Th. Mommsen, Staatsrecht II 1 (3. Aufl.; above, n.22), 181-192; P.-C. Ranouil, Recherches sur le patriciat: 509-366 av. J.-C., Paris 1975, 28-33, with further literature.

32 Provided that *consul* and *consulo* derive from the same root (as the ancients thought). Cf. A. Ernout and A. Meillet, Dictionnaire étymologique de la langue latine (3.Aufl.), Paris 1951, 248-249; A. Walde and J.B. Hofmann, Lateinisches etymologisches Wörterbuch I (3.Aufl.), Heidelberg 1938, 264-265; A. Heuss, Gedanken (above, n.9), 448-449.

33 T.R.S. Broughton, MRR (above, n.27) I, 52-53, 84-85.

plebeians.[34] Now the annalists tell us that the consular tribunes could not celebrate triumphs (Zonaras 7,19) or appoint dictators. Indeed in the *Fasti Triumphales* no triumph of a consular tribune is recorded. As H.S. Versnel perceptively points out they shared the lack of triumphal prerogatives with the *privati cum imperio*. Consequently it would appear that the consular tribunate was not regarded as a regular magistracy which, as Versnel puts it, "by nature carried *imperium*".[35]

The inability to appoint the dictator points to their lesser *imperium* and lesser *auspicium*.[36] Under the year 426 Livy reports (4,31,4) that after a military defeat the *civitas* turned against the consular tribunes, and demanded the appointment of a dictator. But as the dictator could be *dictus* only by the consul, the augurs were consulted, and they removed this religious obstacle (*Maesta fuit civitas vinci insueta; odisse tribunos, poscere dictatorem ... Et cum ibi quoque religio obstaret ne non posset nisi ab consule dici dictator, augures consulti eam religionem exemere*). This reminds us of the situation that obtained in the historical times when the praetor, although he was a *collega* of the consuls, and was elected *isdem auspiciis*, was ritually not qualified to appoint the dictator or to preside over the election of the consuls and even the praetors. And the reason was *quia imperium minus praetor, maius habet consul* (Messala in Gell. N.A. 13,15,4). The notice in Livy tells us very little about the constitutional history of the fifth century, but it tells us much about the antiquarian and augural interpretation of that history. The college of augurs removed by their decree the ritual insuitability of a consular tribune to appoint the dictator, and this finds an exquisite parallel in the situation of 49, amply illustrated by the letters of Cicero, when the augurs removed the ritual unsuitability of the praetor M.

---

[34] For the variations on this theme, see e.g. K. Hanell, Das altrömische eponyme Amt, Lund 1946, 177-180; R. Werner, Der Beginn der römischen Republik, München 1963, 354.

[35] H.S. Versnel, Triumphus, Leiden 1980, 186-189, 350-351.

[36] R.M. Ogilvie, Commentary (above, n.2), 584, maintains that the *tribuni militum consulari potestate* did not have the auspices at all. This theory was most amply elaborated by R. Laqueur, Über das Wesen des römischen Triumphs, Hermes 44, 1909, 215-236; it is devoid of any substance. To conduct the military operations the tribunes, like the *privati cum imperio*, must have been endowed with some sort of auspices. Cf. H.S. Versnel, Triumphus (above, n.35), 186-187. For Livy's treatment of the military tribunate, see J. Pinsent, Military Tribunes and Plebeian Consuls: The Fasti from 444 V to 342 V (Historia Einzelschriften 34), Wiesbaden 1975, 34-44, and above all, the magnificent study by R. Ridley, The 'Consular Tribunate': The Testimony of Livy, Klio 68, 1986, 444-465. He writes (p.459): "as elected magistrates with consular power, able to name a dictator who could triumph, there is no reason why the tribunes could not also". Indeed; but this argument does not take account of Liv. 4,31,4 discussed below in the text. Ridley continues: "It seems, however, that they did not, and the reason is made all too clear by Livy. No tribune won a victory worthy of a triumph". This may be so (although Zonaras states emphatically that "many of the tribunes won many victories"), but: did all the triumphators win victories worthy of a triumph? Fair play is all too often a misleading guide to history.

Aemilius Lepidus to perform the *dictio* of Caesar as dictator.[37] Now in the situation excogitated by the annalists for 426 the dictator was appointed by the tribune who remained in the city; the three other tribunes were in the field, defeated and despised. Among them will have been the two praetors, one of whom would have normally performed the *dictio*. We can also assume that it was the praetors who presided over the elections, and performed all ritual functions that required a full *imperium*.

But this theory entails a wholesale re-writing of the history of the supreme magistracy by the annalists - for no good reason. Hence a different interpretation may be preferable. All members of the board (whether patrician or plebeian) were technically tribunes; there were no *praetores* hidden among them. Upon their election (and the first board was elected under the presidence of the consul-praetor) they received for their use regular patrician auspices, but they did not gain their ownership, and in consequence they were denied the quality of the *patres*, and the ability to function as *interreges*.[38] Because their auspices were not independent but as if borrowed, administered in lieu of their rightful owners, they could not celebrate triumphs or appoint dictators.

When in the middle of the fourth century the Roman government was thoroughly reshaped and the plebeians conquered the consulship, they acquired the triumphal prerogatives denied the consular tribunes, and the right to appoint dictators, but in the sphere of the auspices they remained largely an alien body. This they accepted tnemselves: the risk of angering Jupiter was too great.

Even the *lex Ogulnia* that in 300 engeneered the admission of plebeians to the priestly colleges, and in particular to the college of augurs, did not substantially improve their standing with Jupiter. Their auspicial position remained secondary and precarious. Now Ogilvie maintains that the plebeians by their admission to religious colleges "acquired a share in the control of those auspices which affected public transactions".[39] This view is totally mistaken. First, not all priestly colleges dealt with the auspices but solely the college of augurs. Secondly, we should not confuse augurs and magistrates. Their duties and responsibilities were altogether different; altogether different were their spheres of auspical competence. The Roman doctrine distinguished carefully between the *auspicia* and the *auguria*: the augurs *augurium agunt*, the magistrates (*auspiciis*) *rem gerunt*. The magistrates directed the Republic by means of auspices which they took before any and every important action. One hundred years ago the Dutch scholar I.M.J. Valeton, today almost completely forgotten, demonstrated that for the

---

[37] Cic. Att. 9,9,3. 15,2. Cf. J. Linderski, The Augural Law (above, n.13), 2180-2184.
[38] Cf. A. Heuss, Gedanken (above, n.9), 443-445.
[39] See above, n.4. On the *plebiscitum Ogulnium*, see now K.-J. Hölkeskamp, Das plebiscitum Ogulnium de sacerdotibus. Überlegungen zu Authentizität und Interpretation der livianischen Überlieferung, RhM 131, 1988, 51-67, esp. 66.

taking of auspices the magistrates did not need any help or assistance
from the augurs.[40] The augurs did not take the auspices on behalf of the
magistrates or the Republic; they did not possess the *auspicia publica*.
Their proper sphere of action was the activities technically described as
auguria and *inaugurationes*: it is in that sphere and for that purpose
only that they could solicit divine signs. At the same time as the college
they formed a board of experts: their task was to investigate the *vitia*,
mistakes in auspical ritual committed by the magistrates. On the
recommendation of the college the senate could annul the results of such
vitiated actions, nullify the laws and advise the magistrates to abdicate
their office. These distinctions are not antiquarian pedantries: it springs
to one's eyes that the admission of plebeians to the augural college had
nothing to do with the holding of auspices by plebeian consuls or
praetors. In their capacity as individual augurs the plebeians could now
proclaim oblative signs, dissolve the *comitia* and thus vitiate the
'patrician' auspices that were used to convene them. In their capacity as
members of the college of augurs they could sit in judgement over the
validity of various auspical acts. But through all these activities they did
not acquire even the slightest share in the 'patrician' *auspicia publica
populi Romani*.[41]

We cannot doubt that the plebeians had their own *auspicia privata*,[42]
but in the opinion of the patricians, at least as the argue in Livy, those
auspices were not auspices at all. In particular they were not sufficient
for concluding valid marriages with the patricians. It is easy to dismiss
all the polemics surrounding the Canuleian law as having no basis in fact
- which they certainly do not have. It is also easy to dismiss them as
making no doctrinal or augural sense[43] - which is an altogether different
proposition. The argument in Livy presupposes a closed patrician caste,
and it makes good sense if we consider marriage ritual.

Throughout the Republic the priests of Jupiter, Mars and Quirinus, the
flamines Dialis, Martialis and *Quirinalis*, had not only to be patricians,
but also had to be born of parents married by the archaic ritual of
confarreatio, and had themselves to live in a confarreate marriage. In
historical times the mothers and wifes of the *flamines* could be
plebeians (probably only the *flamen Dialis* was required to marry a

---

[40] I.M.J. Valeton, De modis auspicandi Romanorum, Mnemosyne 18, 1890, 408 ff.

[41] For a detailed analysis of the distinction between *auspicia* and *auguria*, of the
delimitation of competence between the magistrates and the augurs, and of
the duties and prerogatives of the single augurs and of the college of augurs,
see esp. A. Magdelain, Auspicia (above, n.10), 440-444; P. Catalano, Contributi
(above, n.9) passim; J. Bleicken, Zum Begriff der römischen Amtsgewalt:
auspicium - potestas - imperium (Nachr.Akad.Göttingen 1981, 9) passim, esp.
259-261; J. Linderski, Augural Law (above, n.13), 2151-2225.

[42] For the *auspicia privata* of the plebeians, see the discussion of P. Catalano,
Contributi (above, n.9), 199 ff, 451 ff.

[43] This is the view of, for instance, R.M. Ogilvie, Commentary (above, n.4), and A.
Heuss, Gedanken (above, n.9), 392-396.

patricia born of *farreatis*), and this demonstrates the existence of confarreate marriages between patrician men and plebeian women (there is no firm evidence for confarreate marriages between plebeian men and patrician women).[44] *Confarreatio* is the key to the debate in Livy. Because it was the *conditio sine qua non* for the highest priests of the state, it was not solely a private affair. In an attenuated form (by the admission of plebeian women) it continued to be the patrician form of marriage. In Roman marriage, the plebeian argue, *patrem sequuntur liberi* (Liv. 4,4,12). But this is true only of *iustum matrimonium*, and according to the patricians no *iustum matrimonium* could be contracted with the plebeians. The patrician model is that of a confarreate marriage in which not only the standing of the groom was important but also that of the bride. At the ceremony the father of both the groom and the bride will have consulted the auspices; the result was a fully patrician offspring. When the patriciate finally closed its ranks all the future consuls (or praetors) would ultimately descend from the former holders of *auspicia populi Romani*. They will also have been the offspring of confarreate marriages which effected the mixture not only of blood but also of *auspicia* (the *confarreatio* of priests was a relic of this original patrician arrangement). Hence if the plebeians were allowed to marry the patricians the *perturbatio aupiciorum* would ensue. This *conluvio gentis* would affect not so much the sons of plebeian men and patrician women - for they as plebeians were in any case not qualified for the *auspicia publica* - as the sons of patrician men and plebeian women. The auspical impurity emanating from the maternal side would make them suspect holders of public auspices.

   In the late Republic we can visit only the ruins of all those various auspical ramparts of the patricians - now inhabited by the holders of a few odd priesthoods, and occasionally by the *interreges,* and preserved for us in the tortuous constructs of antiquarians and the rhetorical exercises of historians.

---

[44] For sources, details, and discussion, see J. Linderski, Religious aspects (above, n.2), 245-258.

57

Heliogabalus, Alexander Severus and the *ius confarreationis*: A Note on the *Historia Augusta*.

Thaddeo Zawadzki
magistro optimo, optimo amico

Alexander Severus made great efforts to correct the monstrosities of Heliogabalus (*Historia Augusta, Alex. Seu.* 21, 9-22, 3):

> cum frumenta Heliogabalus euertisset, hic empta[1] de propria pe-
> cunia loco suo reponeret. ... oleum, quod Seuerus populo dederat
> quo<d>que Heliogabalus inminuerat ... integrum restituit[2]

The Author continues (22, 3):

> ius confarre[r]ationis, quod inpurus ille sustulerat, hic omnibus
> reddi<di>t.

---

[1] So the conjecture of SALMASIUS, generally accepted by the editors; *uicem pia* P(alatinus).

[2] Cf. KOHNS H.P., "Wirtschaftsgeschichtliche Probleme in der Historia Augusta (Zu AS 21 f.)", in *Bonner Historia-Augusta-Colloquium 1964/1965*, Bonn 1966, pp. 99-126, esp. pp. 104 ff.; PAVIS D'ESCURAC H., *La préfecture de l'annone: service administratif impérial d'Auguste à Constantin.* (*BEFAR* 226), Paris 1976, pp. 197-200 (who, however, missed the article of KOHNS).

So far the passage as printed in the standard Teubner edition of E. Hohl, but as his apparatus shows the text we read is due to an ingenious emendation by J.N. Madvig[3]. The reading of the P(alatinus) is *ius conferre rationes*, and in the *consensus* of other codices (Σ) we have *iussitque conferre rationes*[4]. Madvig argues that "*ius conferre* ne hi quidem scriptores dixerunt pro eo, quod est *conferendi*", and even if we had *ius rationes conferendi*[5] it would be impossible to imagine what this phrase should have signified. Madvig's *ius confarreationis* is appealing, convincing -- and surprizing. It produces an abrupt transition from *frumentum* and *oleum* to the holy and archaic marriage rites, but this perhaps need not deter us. In the jocular mind of the *Auctor* the juxtaposition may have well been evoked by the very name of *confarreatio*, the ritual of *far*. The wicked Heliogabalus took away from the people not only the grain for bread but also the grain for marriage. As Madvig puts it, "dignum Heliogabalo erat sanctissimam nuptiarum caerimoniam tollere".

The joke is exquisite indeed; the information itself invites scepticism[6]. For the ritual of *confarreatio* was hardly practiced by *omnes*; in

---

[3] *Adversaria critica*, II, Copenhagen 1873, p. 638. HOHL seems to be the first editor to introduce MADVIG's emendation into the text; in H. PETER's Teubner edition of 1884 we still read *ius conferre rationes*, with MADVIG's proposal recorded in the apparatus. MADVIG's emendation was accepted by HÖNN K., *Quellenuntersuchungen zu den Viten des Heliogabalus and des Seuerus Alexander im Corpus der Scriptores Historiae Augustae*, Leipzig 1911, pp. 129-130. MAGIE D. in his edition in the *Loeb Classical Library* (1924) does not mention the conjecture of MADVIG at all, and introduces his own emendation: *ius conferendi actiones*, "the right of bringing suit", but he justly observes (II, 218, n. 5): "the text is evidently corrupt".

[4] Also P reads *reddit*, Σ *reddidit*.

[5] According to PETER's apparatus the conjecture *conferendi* was introduced by the *editio princeps*, Milan 1475. SCHREVELIUS C. in his edition of the *HA* (Leiden 1661) prints *ius conferendi rationes*, and adduces *ad loc.* the opinion of CASAUBONUS: "Nihil est in Alagabali uita, quod hunc locum reddat clariorem".

[6] So, in passing, SYME R., "Toleration and Bigotry", in *Roman Papers*, III, Oxford 1984, p. 906, (originally published in 1978): "Alexander, it is alleged, brought back the archaic ritual of Roman marriage, the 'ius confarreationis' which Elagabalus, 'impurus ille', had abolished". Observe that MADVIG's conjecture is here tacitly admitted. BARNES T.D., *The Sources of the Historia Augusta (Collection Latomus* 155), Brussels 1978, pp. 57-58, does not include our passage among the passages "retailing authentic information about Severus Alexander".

fact already by the time of Tiberius it had become a ponderous relic of the past.

In Roman law there existed three forms of concluding marriage, or more exactly, of acquiring the *manus* over the wife: *coemptio, confarreatio* and *usus*. *Coemptio* and *confarreatio* created *manus* instantaneously; *usus* after a year of cohabitation. Hence if the wife wished to break the *usus*, and prevent the creation of *manus*, she had to stay once a year for three consecutive nights away from the marital home. But already in the second century B.C. the predominant form of marriage was the marriage *sine manu* in which the wife did not come under the power of her husband, even by *usus*[7].

The confarreatio continued, however, to be required of some priests: the *flamines maiores* (*Dialis, Martialis* and *Quirinalis*) and the *rex sacrorum* had to be born of parents married *per confarreationem*, and had themselves to live in a confarreate marriage. These priests had to be patricians (although their mothers and spouses could be plebeians). In an early period of Roman history *confarreatio* seems to have been reserved solely for the patricians, and in any case still in the late republican period it does not appear to have been available to the lower orders. Cicero, *pro Flacco* 84, offers the proof. Cicero is at pains to list every legal matrimonial possibility, and yet he mentions only two forms of marriage *cum manu*: *usus* and *coemptio*. The parties in question were a freedwoman and an *ingenuus* (of libertine origin), hence technically plebeians. We can conclude that in their case the *confarreatio* was not a legal possibility. And no wonder: the ceremony required the presence not only of ten witnesses but also of the highest priests of the state, the *pontifex maximus* and the *flamen Dialis*[8].

---

[7] For sources, discussion and literature, see ROSSBACH A., *Untersuchungen über die römische Ehe*, Stuttgart 1853, pp. 42-138 (still fundamental); CORBETT P.E., *The Roman Law of Marriage*, Oxford 1930, pp. 68-106; VOLTERRA E., *La conception du mariage d'après les juristes romains*, Padua 1940; KASER M., *Das römische Privatrecht*, I², Munich 1971, pp. 71-81, 310-325; WATSON A., *The Law of Persons in the Later Roman Republic*, Oxford 1967, pp. 19-31.

[8] For the *confarreatio*, see esp. ROSSBACH (above n. 7), pp. 95-138; LEONHARD R., *RE* 4, 1900, col. 862-864; CORBETT (above n. 7), pp. 73-78; LINDERSKI J., "Religious Aspects of the Conflict of the Orders: the Case of *confarreatio*", in RAAFLAUB K. (ed.), *Social Struggles in Archaic Rome*, Berkeley 1986, pp. 244-261. The basic sources are Gaius, *Inst.* 1, 112 and Servius *auctus, ad Georg.* 1, 31. As the *pontifex maximus* could be absent from Rome for a long period of time (as Caesar was in Gaul)

Under the year 23 A.D. Tacitus (*Ann.* 4, 16)[9] records a dispute in the senate concerning the selection of *flamen Dialis*. Only a *patricius confarreatis parentibus genitus* could be appointed, but *amissa confarreandi adsuetitudine aut inter paucos retenta* the pool of suitable candidates was very limited. For this state of things *incuria uirorum feminarumque* was blamed, but also *ipsius caerimoniae difficultates, quae consulto uitarentur*. Furthermore the person appointed to this priesthood *exiret e iure patrio* and his wife *in manum flaminis conueniret*. Now in both cases serious and adverse financial consequences ensued. The person who went out of *patria potestas* apparently was not able to receive inheritance *ab intestato*[10]; and after the *conuentio in manum* the husband acquired full legal possession of the wife's property[11]. For the wives this was particularly painful, and following the example of Augustus, who *quaedam ex horrida illa antiquitate ad praesentem usum flexisset*, it was decided to pass the law by which *flaminica Dialis sacrorum causa in potestate uiri, cetera promisco feminarum iure ageret*. Thus the *confarreatio* produced now legal consequences only in sacral law but not in civil: it ceased to create the *manus*[12].

Tacitus speaks only of the marriage of the *flamen* and the *flaminica*, but we can be certain that the *confarreatio* stopped producing *manus* also with respect to all other confarreate marriages: after all the goal of

---

he probably could be represented at the ceremony by any pontiff; we also read (Tacitus, *Ann.* 3, 58) that *saepe pontifices Dialia sacra fecisse, si flamen ualetudine aut munere publico impediretur.*

[9] Cf. the commentary by KOESTERMANN E., *Cornelius Tacitus, Annalen*, II, Heidelberg 1965, pp. 79-82.

[10] The subject is complicated and hotly debated, but this seems the only reasonable explication of the passage. For otherwise why should the *exire e iure patrio* have been regarded as an aggravation ? Cf. GUIZZI F., *Aspetti giuridici del sacerdozio romano. Il sacerdozio di Vesta*, Naples 1968, pp. 160 ff., especially p. 166 (with further literature).

[11] Cf. KASER, *Privatrecht* (above n. 7), p. 79.

[12] Cf. Gaius, *Inst.* 1, 136: ...] *Maximi et Tuberonis cautum est, ut haec quod ad sacra tantum uideatur in manu esse, quod uero ad ceteras causas proinde habeatur, atque si in manum non conuenisset.* If Maximus and Tubero are Q. Aelius Tubero and Paullus Fabius Maximus the consuls of 11 B.C., a similar regulation will have been passed already under Augustus, no doubt in preparation for the revival of the office of *flamen Dialis* in this year (Cassius Dio 54, 36, 1; cf. Suetonius, *Aug.* 31). The text, and its connection with the measures reported by Tacitus, raises a number of difficult questions, see DAVID M. and NELSON H.L.W., *Gai Institutionum Commentarii IV: Kommentar, 1 Lieferung*, Leiden 1954, pp. 168-171.

the measure was to increase in the future the *copia* of the candidates for the *flamonia*. If we need a confirmation we have it in a garbled notice of Boethius in his commentary to Cicero's *Topica* 3, 14 (*FIRA* II, 307): *Sed confarreatio solis pontificibus [= flaminibus?]*[13] *conueniebat. Quae autem in manum per coemptionem conuenerant, eae matresfamilias uocabantur: quae uero usu uel farreo minime.* Only *uxores in manu* were called *matresfamilias* (Cicero, *Top.* 3, 14). Hence, after the *confarreatio* remained only *ad sacra* and was dissociated from *manus*, the women married by this rite retained their financial independence but lost their status of *matresfamilias*[14].

As Gaius (*Inst.* 1, 112) attests, in his time also the acquisition of *manus* by *usus* either was abolished by laws or fell into desuetude. Thus *coemptio* remained now as the only means for husbands to acquire *manus* over their wives, and for the wives to gain the status of *materfamilias*[15].

The *confarreatio* lost its position as an instrument of civil law, but retained its holy status in sacral law, even if Pliny (*NH* 18, 10) writes in the past tense: *in sacris nihil religiosius confarreationis uinculo erat*[16]. That this bond was much more *religiosus* than in other forms of marriage can be seen in the procedure of divorce.

Divorce, even after the legislation of Augustus, was a relatively easy affair in Roman law[17]. Not so in the marriage contracted *per confarreationem*. To dissolve such a marriage a *contrarius actus* was necessary, the *diffareatio*. Also for this act the participation of the priests was essential. It was an unpleasant religious ceremony at which "numerous horrible, extraordinary and dismal rites" were performed[18].

---

[13] The same confusion of the regulations concerning the *flamines* and the *pontifices* (the *pontifex maximus*) in Tertullian, *de exhort. cast.* 13, 1; *de monog.* 17, 3; *de praescr. haeret.* 40, 5; *ad uxor.* 1, 7, 5.

[14] Cf. KARLOWA O., *Römische Rechtsgeschichte*, II, Leipzig 1901, pp. 156-157.

[15] Cf. Servius, *ad Aen.* 11, 581; Servius *auctus, ad Aen.* 11, 47; *ad Georg.* 1, 31, and see the discussion in LINDERSKI J., "*Usu, farre, coemptione.* Bemerkungen zur Überlieferung eines Rechtsatzes", in *ZRG* 100, 1984, pp. 301-311 at 304-305.

[16] Cf. Dionysius of Halicarnassus, *Ant. Rom.* 2, 25.

[17] See WATSON, *The Law of Persons* (above n. 7), pp. 49-56; KASER, *Privatrecht* (above n. 7), pp. 81-83, 326-328; and in greater detail, LEVY E., *Der Hergang der römischen Ehescheidung*, Weimar 1925; ROBLEDA O., "Il divorzio in Roma prima di Costantino", in *ANRW* II. 14, 1982, pp. 347-390.

[18] Plutarch, *Quaest. Rom.* 50; Festus (Paulus) 65 L. *s.v. diffareatio.* Cf. ROSSBACH (above n. 7), pp. 127-138; CORBETT (above n. 7), pp. 219-222; KNÜTTEL R., "Zum

The marriage of the *flamen* could not in principle be dissolved at all[19]; it was only under Domitian that the divorce of the *flamen* was allowed upon special request[20].

In this context an inscription recording in an equestrian *cursus* a post of *sacerdos confarreationum et diffareationum* attracts attention[21]. The inscription is acephalous, but with the help of another stone[22] the *honorandus* has been identified as M. Aurelius Papirius Dionysius, a high equestrian official under Marcus Aurelius and Commodus. Apparently because of his fame as a *iurisperitus* he was admitted (with a salary of sixty thousand sesterces) into the imperial council, and subsequently was appointed, as H.-G. Pflaum puts it, to "un sacerdoce fort ancien, dont la présence dans le cursus d'un juriste ne doit pas tellement nous surprendre, puisque cette prêtrise de *sacerdos confarreationum et diffareationum* est en vérité une charge accessible seulement à un connaisseur savant du 'droit canon', pour user de cet anachronisme. La tâche de ce prêtre consistait en effet à appliquer tous les vieux préceptes qui ordonnaient que certaines fonctions du culte officiel ne pussent être revêtues que par des patriciens mariés selon le rituel de la *confarreatio*"[23].

Prinzip der formalen Korrespondenz im römischen Recht", in *ZRG* 88, 1971, pp. 68-71.

[19] Gellius, *Noct. Att.* 10, 15, 22-23; Festus (Paulus) 79 L. *s.v. flammeo*; Servius *auctus, ad Aen.* 4, 29.

[20] Plutarch, *Quaest. Rom.* 50.

[21] *CIL* X, 6662 = (*ILS* 1455). It reads (with the supplements of PFLAUM H.-G., *Les carrières procuratoriennes équestres sous le Haut-Empire romain*, I, Paris 1960, p. 472):
[a libellis et cognitionibus Imp(eratoris) Commodi] Pii Felicis Aug(usti), ducenario | praef(ecto) uehicul(orum) a copis Aug(usti) | per uiam Flaminiam, | centenario consiliario | Aug(usti), sacerdoti confarreati | onum et diffareationum, | adsumpto in consilium ad (sestertium) LX m(ilia) n(ummum) | iurisperito, Antiates publ(ice).

[22] *CIG* III, 5895 = *IG* XIV, 1072 = (*IGR* I, 135) = (PFLAUM, *Les carrières*, I, p. 472).

[23] *Les carrières*, I, pp. 473-474. Students of law and religion are of little help. KUNKEL W., *RE* 14, 1930, col. 2270-2271 and *Herkunft und soziale Stellung der römischen Juristen*, Weimar 1967[2], pp. 222-224, offers no explanation of the *sacerdotium* of Papirius Dionysius; CROOK J.A., *Consilium Principis*, Oxford 1955, p. 154, does not mention it at all. ROSSBACH (above n. 7), p. 121, thinks that "auch hier nur die *Differeatio* des Flamen gemeint ist" -- an untenable explanation: see our argument above in the text. KARLOWA O., *Die Formen der römischen Ehe und Manus*, Bonn 1868, pp. 36-41, still not knowing the identity of the *honorandus* but realizing that he was only a *procurator*, arrived at the following conclusion (p. 40): "Für den *sacerdos confarreationum et diffareationum*... ergiebt sich... dass

But far from being an ancient *sacerdotium*, this is the priesthood of which we know nothing. And the sacral law was not expounded by the *iurisperiti* but by the college of pontiffs. In fact we do not know at all whether Aurelius Papirius in his capacity as *iurisperitus* and *consiliarius Augusti* explained the *ius sacrum* as referring to the *confarreatio;* we know only that he officiated at the rite as a *sacerdos.* Now as even a cursory perusal of equestrian careers will show, the highest priestly dignity open to the *equites* was that of a *flamen minor* or a *pontifex minor*[24]. As our *iurisperitus* was not a senator it is impossible that his *sacerdotium* had anything to do with the old and official form of *confarreatio*, the ritual for marriages of patricians, the *flamines maiores* and the *rex sacrorum.* At best it was a minor priesthood in Rome. A better solution offers. The inscription in question was found in Antium, and it was set up *publ(ice)* by the *Antiates* to honor Aurelius Papirius. Municipal priesthoods often figure in the equestrian *cursus.* Hence the obvious suggestion: the *sacerdotium confarreationum et diffareationum* was a municipal priesthood, perhaps at Antium itself. Antium was a Roman colony. And every colony was a small mirror of Rome, complete with all the priesthoods, the pontiffs, the augurs and the flamens. The colonies adopted Roman ceremonies, and it is not unlikely that for the local *flamines* an imitation of Roman *confarreatio* was conceived. In any case our incription attests the existence in the late second century of the "other" *confarreatio*, popular and plebeian.

When our sources speak of *confarreatio* they most often have in mind the marriage of *flamines*[25], occasionally of gods[26], but ultimately, as attested in the *glossae*, the word lost all its technical connotation[27].

---

er den nach altem Sacralrecht bei der *confarreatio* mitwirkenden Priestern, dem *Pontifex Maximus* and dem *Flamen Dialis* an rang durchaus nicht gleichsteht" -- a correct observation. Karlowa continues: "Es ist mir nicht unwahrscheinlich, dass nachdem die Kaiser die Würde des *Pontifex Maximus* übernommen hatten, ein besonderes Priesterthum eingesetzt wurde, welches die bisher vom *Pontifex Maximus* bei der *confarreatio* vorgenommenen Functionen statt des Kaisers auszuüben hatte". Not impossible; but it is highly unlikely (see above in the text) that this *sacerdotium* should have been entrusted to an equestrian official.

[24] For a list of "equestrian priesthoods", see MOMMSEN T., *Römisches Staatsrecht*, III, 1, Leipzig 1887, pp. 566-569.

[25] Tacitus, *Ann.* 4, 16; Gaius, *Inst.* 1, 112; Servius auctus, *ad Aen.* 4, 103; 339; 374; Boethius, *in Cic. Top.* 3, 14 (*FIRA* II, p. 307).

[26] Arnobius, *Adv. nat.* 4, 20, asks ironically: *Uxores enim dii habent. Usu, farre, coemptione genialis lectuli sacramenta condicunt ?* Apuleius, *Met.* 5, 26 gives the answer through the mouth of Amor (addressing Psyche): *"ego uero sororem*

The crime of Heliogabalus and the remedy of Alexander Severus now stand illuminated by all our knowledge of *confarreatio*. Helioga-balus may have abolished the requirement of the confarreate marriage for the *flamines*, and Alexander Severus not only restored it, but also threw the *confarreatio* open to all. In the light of our interpretation of the inscription from Antium, this appears at least not impossible. For on a strict reading of the text we should admit that Heliogabalus abolished the rite of *confarreatio* altogether, for high and low. Of course this was not beyond *inpurus ille*: he woud not hesitate to trample over the holy traditions of Roman matrimony[28]. With its strong connotation of sexual excess, the epithet *inpurus*[29] militates in favor of Madvig's conjecture.

Still the story does not make much sense, but need it ? Perhaps we should not look for sense but rather for hidden allusions. In this way we follow in the footsteps of the allegorical method of the Neoplatonists, and this procedure has been congenial to much of the *Historia-Augusta-Forschung*. The anti-Christian polemic of the *Historia Augusta* has of-ten been asseverated. Some find in our passage a critique of Constantine who "had introduced many changes into the family law of Rome"[30], others believe that the allusion may be to Theodosius' "Aufhebung der alten Priesterschaften, darunter der *flamines*, die aus konfarreierten

---

tuam... iam mihi confarreatis nuptiis coniugabo". On the other hand Amor did not seem to have bothered to go with Psyche through the ceremony of *diffareatio*, but simply recited the standard formula of divorce: "*tibi... res tuas habeto*". In this text, naturally, *confarreatae nuptiae*, is a purely literary phrase to express mock sollemnity.

[27] See GOETZ G., *Thesaurus Glossarum emendatarum*, I, Leipzig 1889 (= vol. VI of *Corp. Gloss. Lat.*), p. 253. *Confarreatio* is there explained as *sacrorum communicatio*, *confarreatus* as *consociatus* or *sociatus*. But this general and un-technical usage goes back at least to the second century: Apuleius' (*Met.* 10, 29) *talis mulieris publicitus matrimonium confarr<e>aturus* refers to the (unrealized) sexual union of the *Asinus* with the *mulier* condemned *ad bestias*.

[28] The *Vita* of Heliogabalus (6, 5 ff.) accuses him of wishing *Romanas... extin-guere... religiones*. Cf. the commentary of OPTENDRENK T., *Die Religionspolitik des Kaisers Elagabal im Spiegel der Historia Augusta (Diss.)*. Bonn 1968. BARNES T.D., "Ultimus Antoninorum", in *Historia-Augusta-Colloquium 1970*, Bonn 1972, pp. 67-69, 73, finds in this part of the *Vita* much genuine material.

[29] Cf. OPELT I., *Die lateinischen Schimpfwörter*, Heidelberg 1965, pp. 174-175; AL-FÖLDY G., "Zwei Schimpfnamen des Kaisers Elagabal: Tiberinus und Tractatitius", in *Bonner-Historia-Augusta-Colloquium 1972-74*, Bonn 1976, pp. 11-12. For the use of inpurus in the *Hist. Aug.*, see LESSING C., *Scriptorum Historiae Augustae Lexikon*, Leipzig 1906, p. 280 *s.v.*

[30] BAYNES N., *The Historia Augusta, its Date and Purpose*, Oxford 1926, pp. 133-134.

Ehen vorgegangen sein mussten"[31]. Not impossible, but only one thing is certain: the idealization of old Roman customs, and their champion, Alexander Severus.

The Author of the *Historia Augusta* lives up again to his reputation as a weaver of puzzles; but the most exquisite joke would be if the reading of the Palatinus, *ius conferre rationes*, proved to make sense after all[32].

---

[31] LIEBS D., "Alexander Seuerus und das Strafrecht", in *Bonner-Historia-Augusta-Colloquium 1977-78*, Bonn 1980, p. 115, n. 2.

[32] The *ius confarreationis* is sandwiched between *annona* and *mechanica opera* which Alexander Severus *Romae plurima instituit*. Now there are attested in Rome *mensores machinarii frumenti publici* whose task was to measure and weigh corn. The "machine" they used (as represented on the reliefs) was "une grande balance à double plateau montée sur un chevalet élevé" (PAVIS D'ESCURAC [above n. 2], pp. 233-238 at 234). Now if this qualifies as an *opus mechanicum*, the *opera* instituted by Alexander Severus may have been connected with the service of the *annona*. If so, also in the phrase *ius conferre rationes* we are entitled to see a reference to grain distribution. For MADVIG (above n. 3) "das Recht Rechnungen unter sich abzumachen" was nonsense. And indeed what should the "right to compare accounts" mean ? (for *conferre rationes* = "compare accounts", see Cicero, *Att.* 5, 21, 12). The only thing that comes to mind is this. The *rationes* will have been the accounts with the *annona*, and *conferre* would have the sense of "exchange" or "hand over". The recipients of the dole seem to have had the right of alienating (selling and bequeathing) their *tesserae frumentariae* (ROSTOWZEW M., *RE* 7, 1912, col. 179, *s.v. Frumentum*). See esp. *Dig.* 31, 1, 87 pr. (Paulus): *Titia Seio tesseram frumentariam comparari uoluit*; 32. 1. 35 pr.: *patronus liberto ... tribum emi petierat* (*i.e.* wished to buy for him a place on the list of the *plebs frumentaria*), and further: *si ei ea tribus ... comparata esset*. Should we read in the *HA: ius comparandi rationes* ? This right Heliogabalus would have abolished, and Alexander Severus restored.

58

Reden und Schweigen: Römische Religion bei
Plinius Maior. By THOMAS KÖVES-ZULAUF.
("Studia et Testimonia Antiqua," XII.)
Munich: Wilhelm Fink Verlag, 1972.
Pp. 386 + 2. Mk. 78.

It may well be that "the *Natural History*
is one of the half-dozen most interesting
books in the world" (J. W. Duff), or that only
Boswell and Saint Simon exert fascination
comparable to that of Pliny (R. T. Bruère,
CP, LI [1956], 64), but evidently this was not
the opinion of either Latte or Wissowa
Köves-Zulauf lists (pp. 337–39) some 130
passages from *NH* missing in Latte's
Römische Religionsgeschichte, and 70 passages missing even from Wissowa's great

Religion und Kultus. This oversight must appear strange, as Pliny is on all counts our major source for the history and theory of Roman official, and especially popular, religion and beliefs. But at the same time it demonstrates an urgent need for a serious study of Roman religion in Pliny.

In the labyrinth of unpredictable Plinian erudition it is easier to perish than to win. L. Robert has lucidly, albeit menacingly, outlined what one should expect of a commentator of Pliny, and his article "Philologie et géographie, II: Sur Pline l'Ancien livre II" (*Opera minora selecta*, III [Amsterdam, 1969], 1423–48) ought to be studied by anyone who is courageous enough to approach the *Natural History* (K.-Z. does not cite it). And now we have to view Roman religion through Pliny's eyes. A formidable task. It requires erudition matching that of Pliny, and casuistic skills not inferior to those of augurs and pontiffs. K.-Z. is possessed of both, and he displays them lavishly. His erudition has produced a veritable encyclopedia which will be of great use to all students of Pliny and *religio*; but, as we shall presently see, his book is a delight for the critic also.

K.-Z.'s watchword is "structural analysis." Here we have an example of it applied to *NH* 28. 11: "Es handelt sich um den Satz . . . der . . . den zweiten Punkt im ersten Teil des ersten Hauptteils darstellt (I,a,2) und der die Beweise der Intensität enthält. Wir haben auch festgestellt, dass gerade dieser Hauptteil ziemlich klar gegliedert ist, dass aber andrerseits die Art der Verknüpfung mit dem vorhergehenden ersten Punkt ('Beweis des hohen Ranges') sowie mit dem folgenden dritten ('Beweis der Intensität') logisch nicht zwingend ist. Darüber hinaus kann hier auch auf gewisse logisch irrelevante, assoziative Gedankenfäden hingewiesen werden, die den ersten mit dem dritten Punkt verbinden, den uns interessierenden zweiten Punkt somit gewissermassen überbrücken und daher von vornherein die Frage aufwerfen, inwiefern diese Vorstellungen auf irgendeine Weise auch in unserem Satz eine Rolle spielen" (pp. 34–35).

It is a pity that the author, who has dedicated his book to his Hungarian *magistri ximii* Alföldi, Kerényi, and Moravcsik,

does not follow the clarity of expression of an Alföldi. The reader who will surmount or disregard this obstacle (*depellere* in Pliny's and the author's terminology) will, however, be amply rewarded. K.-Z. has fortunately avoided the temptation to write a general monograph on Roman religion in Pliny, an impossible undertaking, and instead has concentrated upon a single but central theme: the function of religious speech, the magical power of the word and of its counterpart, silence or reticence. His book can best be described as a massive commentary on Pliny's excursus "polleantne aliquid verba et incantamenta carminum?" (28. 10–29). Pliny continues (28. 11): "Quippe uictimas caedi sine precatione non uidetur referre aut deos rite consuli. praeterea alia sunt uerba inpetritis, alia depulsoriis, alia commendationis (commentationis *codd.*) uidemusque certis precationibus obsecra⟨re sue⟩sse summos magistratus."

K.-Z. finds here a triple division of religious speech, into *precationes impetritae, precationes depulsoriae,* and *commentatio,* and correspondingly he divides his book into three parts dealing respectively with "Beschwörung" (*impetrire*), "Abwehr" (*depellere*) and "Betrachtung" (*commentari*).

The examples given for the first category (pp. 64–108) are the dedication of a temple to Ops (*NH* 11. 74; cf. recent articles by G. Morgan, *Phoenix,* XXVII [1973], 35–41; *CQ,* XXIV [1974], 140–41), the prohibition against pronouncing the name of the goddess Tutilina (18. 8), the rite of *evocatio,* and another case of religious *Schweigen,* the prohibition against uttering the secret name of the tutelary deity of Rome and the secret name of the city itself (28. 18, 3. 65). A comment on the last point. *NH* 3. 65 reads as follows: "Roma ipsa, cuius nomen alterum dicere nisi arcanis caerimoniarum nefas habetur . . ." In this text *nisi* is an addition by Mommsen; K.-Z. questions this interpretation and observes that we do not know anything about such *Geheimzeremonien* (pp. 95–102). In fact we do. The phrase *arcanis caerimoniarum* is difficult. K.-Z. points out that we can reconstruct the nominative form as *arcana caerimoniarum* or *arcanae caerimoniarum* (gen. part.). This latter form, as the author puts it (p. 98, n. 137), "kommt bedeutungsmässig einem verstärktem *arcanae caerimoniae* gleich." This offers a solution. Pliny's text would then mean "whose other name it is *nefas* to utter at all ceremonies except at the *arcanae caerimoniae*." It is perhaps not too far fetched to combine with this Festus 14–15L "arcani sermonis significatio trahitur sive ab arce . . . sive a genere sacrificii, quod in arce fit ab auguribus, adeo remotum a notitia vulgari, ut ne litteris quidem mandetur, sed per memoriam successorum celebretur," and Servius auctus *ad Aen.* 3. 265. Servius mentions "species auguralis quae invocatio appellatur," and explains it so: "invocatio autem est precatio, uti avertantur mala, cuius rei causa id sacrificium augurale peragitur." It is not impossible that it was in this invocatio *uti avertantur mala* that the secret name of the city had to be uttered (but not recorded!): only in this way could the gods be told whom they had to protect.

On pages 109–54 K.-Z. presents his discussion of *depulsio*. He analyzes in detail *NH* 11. 251 (the goddess Nemesis) and 28. 39 (the slave and the triumphator). To his numerous references two important texts can be added: Serv. auct. *Aen.* 3. 265 (quoted above), and Verg. *Aen.* 9. 326 "non augurio potuit depellere pestem" (cf. Serv. auct. *ad loc.* "'augurio' hic pro scientia augurii"). On *NH* 28. 17 (pp. 41, 55, 110, 153) cf. Serv. *Aen.* 5. 530, 12. 259, Cato in Fest. 268 L, and J. Linderski, "Römischer Staat und Götterzeichen," *Jahrbuch d. Univ. Düsseldorf* (1969–70), pp. 316–17. On Depulsor as a surname of Jupiter (p. 40, n. 50), see H.-G. Pflaum, *Mélanges I. Lévy* (Brussels, 1955), pp. 445–60.

The kernel of K.-Z.'s book (pp. 155–314), and his main contention, concerns a textual problem. Should we retain in *NH* 28. 11 (quoted above) the manuscript reading *commentatio* or emend it to *commendatio*? (pp. 42–60). The author argues with great ingenuity and learning for the former alternative: within the Plinian *Dreiteilung*, *commentatio* constitutes a logical complement of the first two notions (*impetrire* and *depellere*). The first two functions of the word are to create or to destroy the facts (p. 54: "Tatsachen schaffen oder abschaffen"; on p. 55 the author speaks of "das bewirkende und vernichtende Wort"); the logical *tertium quid* is to confirm the facts ("die Funktion der Bestätigung"). This confirmation, *commentatio*, is not to be understood, however, as a

passive acceptance of facts (hence Pliny does not call it *nuntiatio*, a simple announcement of a fact, normally an omen or other divine sign, or *acceptio*, the acknowledgment of the *nuntiatio*). It is rather a dynamic process, an explanation and interpretation. Interpretation presupposes the existence of a fact or thing, but at the same time it is interpretation that finally molds the reality ("bestimmt, was eigentlich da ist," p. 55; here K.-Z. would have profited from the discussion of interpretative formalism by F. Schulz, *Geschichte der römischen Rechtswissenschaft* [Weimar, 1961], pp. 34 ff., and of the term *interpretatio* by M. Fuhrmann, *Sympotica Franz Wieacker* [Göttingen, 1970], pp. 80–110). It is to this dynamic character of interpretation that Pliny refers in the index (to Book 28) with the words "ostenta et sanciri et depelli," and above all in his theoretical summary at 28. 17 (quoted below).

This is a captivating reconstruction, of which it can rightly be said that it creates a new reality around the term *commentatio*. This reality, however, seems to be of the same order as that produced by the augurs or haruspices: what is very logical within the closed system of the *scientia augurii* or of K.-Z.'s structural explication of Pliny may be rather untenable if viewed from a different standpoint.

K.-Z. establishes (pp. 46–48) that *commentatio* (or *commentari*) is used by Pliny 13 times in a secular context, and that its basic meaning is "description" or "consideration" (*Beschreibung, Darstellung, Betrachtung*). Pliny often refers in this way to a systematic treatise, a *Lehrbuch* (as, e.g., Cato's *De agricultura*; cf. here M. Fuhrmann, *Das systematische Lehrbuch* [Göttingen, 1960]). There is, however, a long way from a textbook, however it might transform or "corroborate" reality, to a "dynamic" religious formula, as the author is well aware. He therefore calls attention to two instances in which the term is used in a religious context. One of them is the *commentatio* of Osthanes on the magic art obviously useless for the author's purpose (again a treatise and not religious speech), but this being so, he says, *erhöhte Aufmerksamkeit* (pp. 48–49) is to be paid to the following remark of Pliny (28. 26): "Servi Sulpicii principis vir commentatio est 'quamobrem mensa linquenda non sit.' " K.-Z. considers the possibility that this *commentatio*, although its subject was a religious one, could nevertheless have constituted a kind of secular (*profanwissenschaftlich*, p. 50) explanation. He rejects, however, this obvious solution (cf. p. 57, n. 136 for a striking inconsistency), and quotes Cic. *Div.* 1. 90 and *Amic.* 7 where *commentari* refers to a priestly activity. The augurs habitually convened to "comment" on signs and omens; the results of their *commentationes* were then recorded as a binding explanation in the *commentarii*. As the *mensam linquere* constitutes an *augurium*, Servius Sulpicius was, according to the author (p. 50, n. 109), deputizing by his *commentatio* for *die beratschlagenden Auguren*. What this vague statement should mean is not at all clear; we have here a number of interconnected sentences, but not a valid argument. Nobody denies that there existed priestly *commentarii* (cf. the still basic dissertation by P. Regell, *De auguriorum publicorum libris* [Vratislaviae, 1878]), but their existence does not establish that the correct reading in Pliny is *commentationis* and not *commendationis*.

Let us look at this question from a different angle, not that of a hypothetical structural triad, *Beschwörung*, *Abwehr*, and *Bestätigung*, but that of formulaic religious speech. In fact K.-Z. himself helps reject his sweeping generalization when (p. 57, n. 136) he quite rightly observes (already not remembering exactly what he had said about the same subject on p. 50) that the words of Servius Sulpicius in his *commentatio* represented *kein rituelles Sprechen*—"sie waren kein übernatürliches Mittel mehr zur dynamischen Sanktionierung der Wirklichkeit, sondern dienten einer profan, rational gesehenen Sinngebung." It would follow from this that the *commentationes* of the augurs (and the *haruspices*) were such ritual formulas, a "supernatural means of dynamic confirmation of reality." Compare note 40 on page 74, and page 319, where the author, quoting the passage of Pliny under discussion, comments on the *Fehllosigkeit* and *Formelhaftigkeit* of the sacral language; in this case, however, Pliny's hypothetical *commentatio* must also have been a formula (or rather a set of formulas to be ritually recited). Let us investigate the validity of this claim.

As an example of augural *commentatio* K.-Z. quotes (p. 60, n. 150) Festus 152L: "pro collegio quidem augurum decretum est, quod in salutis augurio praetores maiores et minores appellantur, non ad aetatem, sed ad vim imperii

pertinere" (at p. 51, n. 111 K.-Z. seems to take this as an interpretation of *Zeichen*). Now in no way can this be taken as an example of *rituelles Sprechen*: there is no formula, there are no words that could not be expressed in a different manner. On the other hand, the *precatio* recited by the officiating augur at the *augurium salutis* (cf. F. Blumenthal, *Hermes*, XLIX [1914], 246–53; J. Liegle, *Hermes* LXXVII [1942], 249–312) did have a ritual and formulaic character, and in the text of this *precatio* were mentioned the *praetores maiores* and *minores*. The augural explanation did not change the reality or confirm it, dynamically or otherwise—this was reserved for the ritual *precatio*—it only specified that the meaning of the term *maior* did not conform to the contemporary colloquial usage. As far as divine signs are concerned, it is more to the point to quote, e.g., Cic. *Div.* 2. 73 "decretum collegii vetus habemus omnem avem tripudium facere posse" (cf. Pease *ad loc.* and P. Regell, *Fragmenta auguralia* [Progr. Hirschberg, 1882], pp. 8–9). This is not a ritual formula either, but a binding instruction that the *observatio* and *nuntiatio* of the *tripudium* applies to *omnis avis* (for the formula of *auspicium de tripudiis*, see Sabidius in *Schol. Veron. ad Aen.* 10. 241, and cf. Liv. 10. 40. 2–4).

Pliny says that *alia verba* are to be used with respect to *impetrire*, *depellere*, and *commendatio* (or *commentatio*). K.-Z. interprets this as *impetritae* and *depulsoriae precationes*. Was the *commentatio* a *precatio*? As we have seen, it was not. Hence the reading *commentatio* not only does not logically complement the two preceding notions, but it even interrupts the flow of Pliny's argument, in which he speaks of different kinds of *precationes* and *certa verba*.

What can be said in favor of the reading *commendatio*? K.-Z. too lightly discards as not relevant the text of Valerius Maximus 1. 1. 1: "Maiores . . . portentorum *depulsiones* Etrusca disciplina explicari voluerunt [derived from Cic. *Har. resp.* 18, and matching Pliny's *alia verba depulsoriis*]. prisco etiam instituto rebus divinis opera datur cum aliquid *commendandum* est, precatione, . . . cum inquirendum vel extis vel sortibus, *impetrito* . . ." (cf. Pliny *alia verba inpetritis*). That in Valerius Maximus we have the sequence *depulsiones–commen-*

dandum–impetritum, and in Pliny a different one, *impetrita(e)–depulsoria(e)–commendatio*, seems to me of slight importance as compared with the fact that the principle of division is the same (K.-Z. dwells at length on the difference of sequence, finding no *quellenmässiger Zusammenhang* and no structural similarity between Val. Max. and Pliny, pp. 42–46). Above all, the text of Valerius Maximus establishes, as required by the construction of Pliny's passage, that the *commendatio* was a *precatio*. K.-Z. also quotes in this context Ammianus 25. 2. 3, where Julian "somno . . . *depulso* . . . ventura decretis caelestis *commendabat*, . . . et numinibus per *sacra depulsoria* supplicans . . . ," only to conclude (in a not fully understandable way) in favor of the reading *commentatio*.

It would, however, be fair to adduce also other texts which clearly show that the act of *commendatio* required the pronouncement of a ritual formula, that could be placed side by side with other *precationes* mentioned by Pliny. A few examples: August. *De civ. D.* 4. 8 "cui [*sc.* Segetiae] semel segetes commendarent"; 4. 21 "quid opus erat Opi deae *commendare* nascentes." Tac. *Ann.* 15. 23 "iam senatus uterum Poppaeae *commendaverat* dis votaque publice susceperat." Apul. *Met.* 3. 7 "casumque praesentem meum *commendans* deum providentiae." *Hist. Aug.* 14. 3. 8 "cum infantis Getae natalem Severus *commendare* vellet, hostiam popa nomine Antonius percussit" (establishes the connection between *commendatio* and *sacrificium*); 18. 60. 3 "cum natalem diem *commendaret*, hostia cruenta effugit" (cf. 18. 13. 6 "cum eius natalem aruspices *commendarent*," where in view of the following mention of *hostiae*, Helm's emendation *commentarent* [accepted by Hohl] must be rejected). Plin. *NH* 25. 28 ". . . auctoritas herbae est, quam dodecatheon vocant omnium deorum potestate *commendantes*." *CIL* VI. 14000 = *ILS* 8497[a] "Sol, tibi *commendo* qui manus intulit ei" (cf. other examples of similar *execrationes* in *TLL*, III, 1884). In the last example *commendare* has a meaning akin to *devovere*; in *NH* 28. 12 Pliny mentions *Deciorum carmen* as an example of *precatio*.

But the *commendatio* was also of importance in public life. A social custom under the Republic, it became a formalized institution under the Empire, and it obtained the meaning of a binding recommendation whereby the *princeps* commended a candidate for office, or a successor to himself, to the senate, people, and army (cf. R. Frei-Stolba, *Untersuchungen zu den Wahlen in der römischen Kaiserzeit* [Zurich, 1967], pp. 33–36, 176–87). It is interesting to observe that the formal structure of *commendatio* in imperial constitutional practice had been foreshadowed by the religious *commendatio*, which was also binding and also required a set formula (i.e., at least the ritual utterance of the verb *commendo*).

On pages 155–314 K.-Z. presents his discussion of the "deutende Funktion des Wortes," i.e., of the (alleged) Plinian concept of *commentatio*. He distinguishes between two basic forms of interpretation: *Handlungsdeutung* and *Tatsachendeutung*. In the former category (pp. 156–66), of special interest is *NH* 18. 131 "serere [*sc.* napum et rapa] nudum volunt *precantem* sibi et vicinis serere se." According to K.-Z. this is "echte '*commentatio*': der Spruch ändert den Sinn der Handlung, indem er ihn ausdruckt" (p. 161, n. 33). It is, however, difficult not to observe that this *commentatio* is totally different from that of Servius Sulpicius. The *commentatio* of Sulpicius was an explanation of a formula, but it did not constitute a formula; it was not a *precatio*. In *NH* 18. 131 the formula and the explanation are one and the same thing, and the magical saying is called explicitly *precatio*. This underscores once again the fallacy of K.-Z.'s main argument.

Tatsachendeutung is simply explanation of prodigies, mostly by the *haruspices*. K.-Z. finds here four different kinds of interpretation. (1) The "open" interpretation (pp. 168–177) does not contain any hidden or obscure meaning (*NH* 17. 243, 2. 147, 11. 190 and 195, 9. 55, 8. 221). K.-Z. compares it to the authoritative explanation of an oracle by the *chresmologos*—the comparison is valid, but again it is not the words of the interpretation but the words of the oracle that constitute the unchangeable magic formula (although it is only by the intermediary of the interpretation that the true meaning of an oracle or a *prodigium* can finally be conveyed to the interested party). (2) The "double" interpretation is exemplified by the difference between Augustus' public and private explanation of the *sidus Iulium* (*NH* 2. 93–94, pp. 177–206). (3) The "alternative" interpretation (pp. 207–288) occurs at *NH* 7. 68–69 (*Valeria cum dentibus nata*), 10. 41 (the *picus* and the praetor Aelius Tubero), and 7. 22 (*Gracchorum pater* and the snakes). But the magical power of the word is best to be seen in (4), the form of interpretation which K.-Z. describes as *interrogatione decipere* (*NH* 28. 15–16, relating the *augurium* of the human head dug out *in Tarpeio*, pp. 289–314). If the Romans had answered the deceptive question of Olenus Calenus in the affirmative, the *caput imperii* would have been transferred to Etruria; by stating "non plane hic, sed Romae inventum caput dicimus," they had preserved the historical destiny of Rome. The outcome of the *augurium* depends completely upon the interpretative power of the word: the word is the reality, the world only its mirror. And so Pliny, combining magic and rationalism in a strange but agreeable way, was able to conclude with evident satisfaction: "magnarum rerum fata et ostenta uerbis permutari" (28. 14) and "haec satis sint exemplis ut appareat ostentorum uires et in nostra potestate esse ac, prout quaeque accepta sint, ita ualere."

Curiositas and πολυπραγμοσύνη mark Pliny's attitude to the world and its wonders. Köves-Zulauf renders the term *curiosus* (*NH* 21. 179) as "durch Sorgfalt Verborgenes offenbarend" (p. 328). His book is an excellent example of such veritably Plinian *curiositas*.

59

A NON-MISUNDERSTOOD TEXT CONCERNING TAGES

J. G. Préaux has recently called attention to ' un texte méconnu ' concerning Tages,[1] the discoverer of the *haruspicina*. The text in question, Martianus Capella, *De nuptiis Philologiae et Mercurii* 2.157, reads in the edition of A. Dick (*Bibl. Teubn.* 1925, pp. 66-67) as follows: 'Tages sulcis emicuit et ritum statim gentis simpuuiumque monstrauit '. 'Simpuuiumque ' is a conjecture proposed by L. Krahner (1846). It appeared so convincing to Dick that he introduced it into his text as a replacement for the vulgate reading ' sypnumque ' (or 'sipnumque '). Préaux rightly rejects ' sypnum ' and ' simpuuium ', and a score of other emendations as well (*inspiciumque, haruspicinamque, haruspiciumque*). On the basis of an exemplary analysis of the manuscript tradition he was able to show that the original reading undoubtedly was ' extispiciumque '. He points out that this reading finds a clear support in Censorinus, *De die natali* 4.13: 'Tages, qui disciplinam cecinerit extispicii '.

Alas, *nihil novi sub sole. Already* in 1881 G. Schmeisser proposed to read ' extispiciumque '.[2] In 1905 C. Thulin enthusiastically accepted in his magisterial work the conjecture of Schmeisser, and suggested we should read ' genti (and not *gentis*) extispiciumque '[3] (both Thulin and Schmeisser refer in this connection to the text of Censorinus).

[1] J. G. Préaux, *Un texte méconnu sur Tagès*, «Latomus», XXI, 1962, 379-383.
[2] G. Schmeisser, *Die etruskische Disciplin vom Bundesgenossenkriege bis zum Untergang des Heidentums* (Progr. Liegnitz, 1881), 21 n. 96.   [3] C. Thulin, *Die Etruskische Disciplin*, part 1 (= *Göteborgs Högskolas Årsskrift*, vol. 11 5; Göteborg, 1905), 3 (reprinted Darmstadt, 1968); *Scriptorum Etruscae disciplinae fragmenta* (Berlin, 1906) 1. However, as far as the reading ' genti ' is concerned, Thulin had his precedessors already in H. Grotius and C. Barth, see U. F. Kopp in his commentary *ad loc.* (Francofurti ad Moenum, 1836), 210-211.

It is pleasant to hope that the inane 'sypnum' and the impossible 'simpuuium' may now have definitely disappeared from
the text of Martianus, but it is at the same time rather disheartening
to see major modern studies of the *disciplina Etrusca* already sharing
the fate of the Etruscan *libri reconditi*. In any case they do not seem
to have been accessible to recent editors [4] of Martianus.[5, 6]

---

[4] DICK does not quote the study of SCHMEISSER, and he seems to have
consulted only the second part of THULIN's work publisched in Göteborg in
1906, see his *Praefatio*, pp. XXXI!-III. PRÉAUX does not quote in his article
either of them, nor does he mention them in his *Addenda* to the reprint of
DICK's edition (Stuttgart, 1969).   [5] After I have written this note I came
across the excellent book by L. LENAZ, *Martiani Capellae de nuptiis Philologiae
et Mercurii liber secundus*, introduzione, traduzione, commento (Padova, 1975).
LENAZ (p. 87 n. 323) duly notes and accepts SCHMEISSER's conjecture, and
remarks 'che seguo anche per quanto concerne *genti*'. In fact SCHMEISSER
says nothing about the reading 'genti'; he himself reads 'gentis'. Cf.
above, n. 3.   [6] I should like to thank Professor J. F. Gilliam for kindly
reading through a draft of this note.

60

Le délit religieux dans la cité antique (Table ronde, Rome, 6–7 avril 1978). Collection de l'École française de Rome, 48. Textes de: M. TORELLI, CH. GUITTARD, G. PICCALUGA, T. CORNELL, B. SANTALUCIA, A. FRASCHETTI, J. SCHEID, D. SABBATUCCI, G. CRIFÒ. Rome: École française de Rome, Palais Farnèse, 1981. Pp. vi + 193 + 6.

Impiety is fascinating. It appeals to the intellect. Punishment for religious infractions stirs irrational layers in the minds of onlookers and readers; the punishing of lapsed Vestals or nuns, and the tracking down of witches have been great favorites throughout the ages, in practice and in fantasy. The French School at Rome had a splendid idea to organize the *table ronde* on the subject of the *délit religieux* and to publish the papers delivered on that occasion.[1] It is a great pity that most libraries will discard the dust jacket: it reproduces the painting by Jacques Gamelin, *Le délit de la vestale découvert par le grand pontife.*[2] The very ample Vestal (with small breasts, however, one of them bare), standing in front of something that looks like a cauldron but is a tripod on which an eternal fire burns, throws up her hand in despair; her paramour kneels down, awestruck; the Chief Pontiff, very much Jehovah-like, sporting a flowing white beard, his hand raised, utters a bloodcurdling curse. This was meant to be a serious scene; it is a caricature—as are many books dealing with Roman religion. A prime example would be the (until recently)[3] only comprehensive account of Roman

1. The title of the collection is misleading: the papers it contains deal only with Italy and almost exclusively with Rome.
2. Jacques Gamelin (1738–1803) was the court painter of Pope Clement XIV and later Professor at the Academy at Toulouse. His themes were mostly biblical and classical and he seems to have particularly enjoyed scenes of death. Yet it was not *incestum* but rather innocence vindicated that was particularly popular with the painters: the Vestal Tuccia carrying water in a sieve.
3. See now J. H. W. G. Liebeschuetz, *Continuity and Change in Roman Religion* (Oxford, 1979), a book very different from Fowler's both in character and execution. Cf. the review by M. Beard, *JRS* 71 (1981): 203–5.

religion in English, the renowned *Religious Experience of the Roman People* (London, 1911) by W. W. Fowler. About two pillars of Roman religion, the pontiffs and the augurs, he has this to say: "Instead of developing, as did the wise man or seer of Israel, into the mouthpiece of God in His demand for the righteousness of man, the Roman diviner merely assisted the pontifex in his work of robbing religion of the idea of righteousness" (p. 292). A Roman gives an answer: "Sua cuique civitati religio . . . est, nostra nobis. Stantibus Hierosolymis, pacatisque Iudaeis tamen istorum religio sacrorum a splendore huius imperii, gravitate nominis nostri, maiorum institutis abhorrebat; . . . illa gens . . . quam cara dis immortalibus esset docuit, quod est victa, quod elocata, quod serva" (Cic. *Flac.* 67–69).

Sua cuique civitati religio est, nostra nobis. The book under review contributes much to discrediting and dispelling partisan interpretations of Roman cult.[4] It proposes to define "la piété antique en étudiant son contraire . . . la faute religieuse, le délit religieux" (p. vi). The way has been shown by two *lumina:* Th. Mommsen's "Der Religionsfrevel nach römischem Recht," *Gesammelte Schriften,* vol. 3 (Berlin, 1907), pp. 389–422 (originally published in 1890), and the dissertation by S. P. C. Tromp, *De Romanorum Piaculis* (Lugduni Batavorum, 1921). Now we have a third light by J. Scheid,[5] "Le délit religieux dans la Rome tardo-républicaine" (pp. 117–71) His message is loud and clear: those who criticize Roman religion should first try to understand it. "Nous nous refusons . . . à admettre l'existence d'une imperfection, d'une décadence de la religion romaine due au seul fait qu'elle aurait ignoré ou perdu la notion de piété subjective au sens chrétien du terme" (p. 118). The key term here is "subjective piety." The Roman religion was not interested in individual salvation; its only concern was *salus publica,* the preservation of the *pax deorum.* Nor was it interested in individual impiety. Scheid even maintains that "sur le plan personnel l'impiété n'existe pas" (p. 154). This formulation is open to doubt, and Scheid himself was not able to apply it consequently.[6] We should rather say that the state was concerned only with such acts of impiety as affected the well-being of the community. There existed *sacra publica* and *sacra privata;* the infringements concerning the latter need not have disrupted the *pax deorum,* and hence were of no interest to the *religio publica,* but could have had dire consequences for the *privati* involved. That an individual could indeed be guilty of personal impiety follows from the opinion of the *pontifex* Mucius Scaevola, who "consultus quid feriis agi liceret, respondit quod praetermissum noceret" (Macrob. *Sat.* 1. 16. 11, and cf. 1. 16 passim).

The principal rule governing religious infractions and their expiations was this: "si imprudens fecit, piaculari hostia facta piatur; si prudens . . . eum expiari non posse" (Varro *Ling.* 6. 30, from Q. Mucius Scaevola). According to G. Wissowa,[7] *piaculum* formed "die sakralrechtliche Parallele zu der *multa* der weltlichen Straf-

4. See also the inspiring studies by H. D. Jocelyn, "The Roman Nobility and the Religion of the Republican State," *JRH* 4 (1966): 89–104, and J. A. North, "Conservatism and Change in Roman Religion," *PBSR* 44 (1976): 1–12.
5. Scheid brings with him to the study of the theory of Roman religion a thorough knowledge of its political and prosopographical side (at least of the imperial age); cf. his *Les Frères Arvales: Recrutement et origine sociale sous les empereurs julio-claudiens* (Paris, 1975).
6. Cf. his statement on p. 141: "Certes le coupable pouvait devenir *impius,* s'il avait fauté *dolo malo.*"
7. *Religion und Kultus der Römer*[2] (Munich, 1912), p. 392.

rechts"; the obligation to offer it followed automatically *ex delicto*. On the other hand, Tromp derives the piacular obligation "e iuris sacri scripta lege."[8] Scheid proposes a novel solution. What really counted was not the transgression, the *delictum* in itself, but its consequences: "Le même acte . . . pouvait entraîner la rupture de la *pax deorum* ou non. . . . L'obligation piaculaire ne peut donc pas . . . dériver de l'infraction elle-même, mais doit être rattachée, comme la souillure, à la volonté insondable et mystérieuse des dieux, qui s'exprime à travers les vicissitudes de Rome" (p. 149). It was this unpredictable character of divine displeasure that led the Romans to offer piacular sacrifices immediately after an involuntary error in ritual was committed, even before the *ira deorum* was able to manifest itself. This frame of mind is best illustrated by the *piacula operis faciundi*, which were offered in advance in an attempt to nullify the consequences of any error that might remain undiscovered. In all these cases the *piaculum* was not meant to serve as the atonement: its goal was to preserve or to restore the *pax deorum*. The concept of sin was alien to Roman state religion (p. 150).

In what way could the state commit a religious offense? It could become guilty only through acts of its representatives, magistrates, and priests, acting in their official capacity. Here Scheid's analysis (pp. 141 ff., 151 ff.) is quite fascinating (it is based to a great extent on Tromp, *De Romanorum Piaculis*, pp. 85 ff.). The official could have committed an omission or transgression as *prudens* or *imprudens*, but as far as the state was concerned this made little difference. Rome herself could never admit to have wilfully offended the gods—such an offense would have been inexpiable and would have spelled permanent ruin to the state. Hence all public offenses were *ex definitione* involuntary. Furthermore such an offense had to be acknowledged by the state; otherwise it was regarded as non-existent. This comportment bears a close resemblance to the procedure of the *susceptio prodigiorum*. The guilty magistrate was never prosecuted for the religious offense *qua* religious offense; but he could be prosecuted for the consequences of his impiety. When in 249 the consul P. Claudius Pulcher willfully disregarded the auspices and suffered a naval defeat he was accused of *perduellio;* his position was assimilated to that of a traitor (pp. 142–43).

It attracts attention that P. Clodius was prosecuted for *incestum* when he violated the *sacra* of Bona Dea. Yet the legal situation remains puzzling, despite the efforts of Scheid (pp. 130–33, 146–47) and T. Cornell ("Some Observations on the *crimen incesti*," pp. 27–37). Nor can we claim to understand the theological significance of the weird punishment inflicted upon the lapsed Vestal. What is odd, and what seems to have gone unnoticed—even at the *table ronde*—is the rather theoretical attitude of the Romans to the *incestum*, an attitude which differs sharply from later practices. The Vestal Cornelia condemned to death by Domitian exclaims: "me Caesar incestam putat, qua sacra faciente vicit triumphavit!" (Pliny *Epist.* 4. 11. 7). It was not difficult to check; nobody tried. Here also belongs the story of Tuccia and her sieve, a rather curious way of establishing whether she forfeited her status as a *virgo*. One can suspect that stories like this point back to an epoch when the normal procedure was not a trial before the college of pontiffs or, gods forbid, before a *quaestio* set up by the people (for this development, cf. Cornell, pp. 36–37; Scheid, p. 146), but the *iudicium dei*, the ordeal.

8. *De Romanorum Piaculis*, p. 119.

The punishment of the unfortunate Vestal, who was entombed (not exactly buried) alive, displays some similarities to the notorious sacrifice of the Gauls and Greeks. This latter ceremony, which because of its flavor of human sacrifice was an embarrassment to later Roman writers, was taken up at the *table ronde* by A. Fraschetti in a long and erudite paper (pp. 51–115); the results are negligible. Fraschetti postulates "lo statuto duplice del rito—*piaculum* se si guarda al *portentum* che lo determina; 'morte rituale' se si guarda alla minaccia gallica" (p. 114). Very fine, but what are we to do with the Greeks?

The book also contains the articles by M. Torelli on the *delitto religioso* in Etruria (pp. 1–7); Ch. Guittard on "L'expression du délit dans le rituel archaïque de la prière" (pp. 9–20; a comparison of *Tab. Ig.* [esp. Ib8; VIb47; Va22–Vb7; VIa27,37,47; VIb30] with the formula of the *votum* of *ver sacrum* in Livy 22. 10. 2); G. Piccaluga on "La colpa di perfidio sullo sfondo della prima secessione della plebe" (pp. 21–25; to her examples add Cic. *QRosc.* 46); B. Santalucia on the *repressione criminale* in the regal epoch (pp. 39–49; the formulas *sacer esto* and *paricidas esto;* rather superficial); D. Sabbatucci on the *peccato "cosmico"* (pp. 173–77); and finally the concluding remarks by G. Crifò (pp. 179–84).

All in all not a bad commentary to the painting of Gamelin.

61

The Bronze Liver of Piacenza: Analysis of a Polytheistic Structure. By L. B. VAN DER MEER. Dutch Monographs on Ancient History and Archaeology, 2. Amsterdam: J. C. Gieben, Publisher, 1987. Pp. [viii] + 202 + fold-out endpaper (diagram) + looseleaf corrigenda-slip; 78 ills. in text. Dfl. 125.

The founder of the *disciplina Etrusca,* Tages, was believed to have sprung from a furrow: "sulcis emicuit et ritum statim genti[s] extispiciumque monstravit."[1] Or, as Cicero sneers, when the *bubulcus* who unearthed Tages uttered a *clamor* of amazement (for Tages was both a *puer* and a *senex*),[2] a great crowd gathered from all over Etruria; the *puer exaratus* perorated at great length, and all his *oratio,* "qua haruspicinae disciplina continetur," was committed to writing.[3]

This happened in the *ager Tarquinensis* (Censorinus *D.N.* 4. 13), at the beginning of Etruscan history. In 1877, in the vicinity of Piacenza in Northern Italy, a modern *bubulcus,* plowing a field belonging to a count, unearthed a bizarre bronze object; neither the master nor the knave recognized its value, but it found its way into the hands of local students of antiquities and soon became known to scholars, who gathered from all over Italy and Europe uttering *clamores* of amazement (cf. p. 5). The first scholarly study of the find appeared already in 1880; it came from the pen of Wilhelm Deecke, the leading Etruscologist in Germany, and the inheritor of the mantle of the great Karl Otfried Müller. Deecke first interpreted the object as a *templum,* an instrument for the observation and interpretation of celestial signs; soon, after a communication from G. Körte, he recognized its true character: a (natural size) bronze model of sheep's liver.[4] Today the prize possession of the Museo Civico in Piacenza, it once belonged to an Etruscan *haruspex:* it is inscribed with Etruscan letters. On the basis of the lettering V. D. M. suggests that the model was made around 100 B.C., probably in the region to the northwest of the Trasimene Lake (pp. 17–18).

Almost all inscriptions are on the visceral side; engraved lines divide it into forty regions, sixteen marginal and twenty-four inner, each region displaying one or two inscriptions. The parietal side has only two regions, each with one inscription. Since for any understanding of the following argument it is essential to visualize the disposition of the inscriptions on the visceral part, I reproduce below the diagram and transcription as it appears in V. D. M.'s book (p. 11).

The names engraved on the model are the names of various deities, twenty-eight in all: each in his or her own "house," or sharing it with another occupant. Some important deities occupy several houses. The liver reflected the heavens. Its regions corresponded to the abodes of gods in the sky, and thus by examining the liver of a sacrificial animal the haruspex was able to establish which gods were angry, which favorable or neutral, and what the future held.[5]

---

1. Mart. Capella *De nuptiis* 2. 157 (p. 47.11 Willis). For the text, see J. Linderski, "A Non-Misunderstood Text Concerning Tages," *PP* 33 (1978): 195–96, and, recently, D. Shanzer, "De Tagetis exaratione," *Hermes* 115 (1987): 127–28.

2. Cf. T. C. Carp, "*Puer senex* in Roman and Medieval Thought," *Latomus* 39 (1980): 736–39, who, however, has missed the case of Tages.

3. Cic. *Div.* 2. 50. Cf. Censorinus *D.N.* 4. 13 "Tages, qui disciplinam cecinerit extispicii, quam lucumones tum Etruriae potentes exscripserunt." The testimonia concerning Tages are conveniently assembled by A. S. Pease, *M. Tulli Ciceronis "De Divinatione" Libri Duo* (Urbana, 1920–23; repr. Darmstadt, 1968), pp. 435–39, and by J. R. Wood, "The Myth of Tages," *Latomus* 39 (1980): 325–44.

4. *Das Templum von Piacenza,* Etruskische Forschungen 4 (Stuttgart, 1880); *Nachtrag zum Templum von Piacenza,* Etruskische Forschungen und Studien 2.2 (Stuttgart, 1882); cf. G. Körte, "Die Bronzeleber von Piacenza," *Röm. Mitt.* 20 (1905): 348–79, esp. 349–50. V. D. M. states inaccurately (p. 19) that "only in 1905 did Körte see in the bronze the model of a sheep's liver."

5. For the technique of the haruspex, the signs he was looking for, and the terminology, see the masterly study by C. O. Thulin, *Die etruskische Disciplin,* Teil 2, Göteborgs Högskolas Arsskrift 12. 1 (Göteborg, 1906; repr. Darmstadt, 1968), pp. 4–50, esp. 24–44. In particular, the haruspex examined with greatest diligence the *caput iecoris* (= *processus caudatus lobi dextri*), represented in the diagram as the triangular shape in the right lobe (cf. Cic. *Div.* 2. 32).

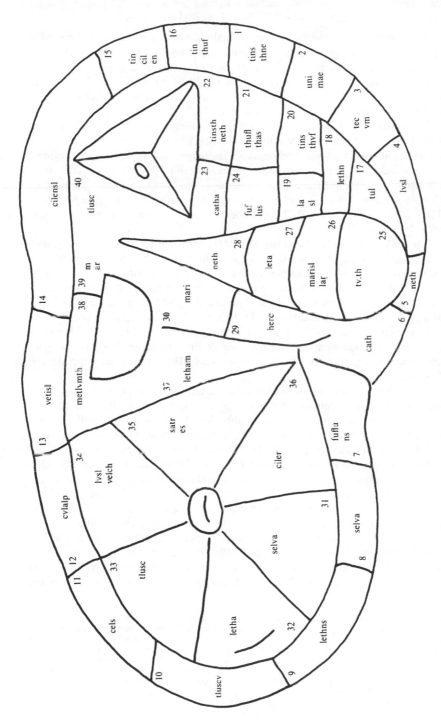

Liver of Piacenza (transcription)

597

The number of the marginal regions, sixteen, offers a first clue to the cosmic system of the liver: according to the unanimous testimony of the ancients, the division of the heaven into sixteen parts was an Etruscan invention, and indeed it has not been found anywhere outside the Etruscan world. In this way the Etruscans could easily establish "fulmen qua ex parte venisset" (Cic. *Div.* 2. 42; cf. Serv. ad *Aen.* 8. 427; Mart. Capella 1. 45).

The other clue Deecke discovered in the allegorical romance *De nuptiis Philologiae et Mercurii,* by Martianus Capella. For the wedding Jupiter invites various residents of heaven and sends his messengers through all sixteen regions, whose inhabitants Martianus records in great detail (1. 41–61). His (Latin) list is ultimately based on Etruscan lore, perhaps via Varro, Nigidius Figulus, or Cornelius Labeo.[6] After Deecke major contributions have been made by Körte, Thulin, Biedl, Weinstock, Pallotino, and Maggiani,[7] and now we have the book of V. D. M.

The bulk of his monograph (pp. 30–146) is devoted to a detailed analysis of the inscriptions; he discusses in turn the position of each theonym on the liver and provides a survey of the epigraphical, literary, and iconographical evidence. This part of the book will be much consulted, but the hottest dispute will center on the haruspical orientation of the liver and the problem of the *pars familiaris* and *pars hostilis.* Unfortunately, V. D. M.'s discussion lacks clarity; occasionally it is marred by inaccuracies (cf. above, n. 4); his presentation of the views of other scholars will often be comprehensible only to those few who keep an assortment of obscure studies within their reach. Here is his theory (pp. 19–29, 147–52).

As the point of orientation we take the incisura (between regions 6 and 7). But we have to differentiate strictly between the orientation of the liver and the orientation of the haruspex—regrettably, V. D. M. does not spell out this principle as clearly as he should. He argues that the incisura indicates an eastern point: Cath (a solar deity, pp. 48–53) and Fufluns (perhaps a moon god, although traditionally identified with Liber, pp. 53–58) face Usil (Sun, pp. 136–39) and Tiv (Moon, pp. 133–35) on the parietal side, and these bodies rise in the east (p. 23). Opposite are the regions 13 and 14 inhabited by the god of the underworld, Vetis (= Veiovis, pp. 88–90), and the goddess of Fate, Cilens[8]—no doubt in the hostile west (pp. 90–95; V. D. M. rightly rejects the identification of Cilens with the Nocturnus of Martianus Capella). The highest gods, the best and the most dreadful, live in the north. Pliny (*HN* 2. 142–44) reports that "octo ab exortu [sc. partes] sinistras, totidem e contrario appellavere dextras." *Summa felicitas* resides in the northeast, and the *partes maximae dirae* are in the

---

6. Cf. P. Mastandrea, *Un neoplatonico latino: Cornelio Labeone* (Leiden, 1979), pp. 211–14.

7. For Deecke and Körte, see above, n. 4; C. O. Thulin, *Die Götter des Martianus Capella und die Bronzeleber von Piacenza,* Religionsgeschichtliche Versuche und Vorarbeiten 3.1 (Giessen, 1906)—in many respects still unsurpassed; A. Biedl, "Die Himmelsteilung nach der disciplina Etrusca," *Philologus* 86 (1931): 199–214; S. Weinstock, "Martianus Capella and the Cosmic System of the Etruscans," *JRS* 36 (1946): 101–29; M. Pallotino, "Deorum sedes," *Studi in onore di Aristide Calderini e Roberto Paribeni,* vol. 3 (Milan, 1956), pp. 223–34; A. Maggiani, "Qualche osservazione sul fegato di Piacenza," *SE* 50 (1982 [1984]): 53–88.

8. The forms Vetisl and Cilensl are the possessives.

northwest.[9] V. D. M. places north between regions 16 and 1 (p. 149): consequently, Vetis, Cilens, and Tin (= Jupiter, pp. 30–37), in Tin's association with Cilens and Thuf (= Thufltha, a goddess of punishment[?], pp. 96–107), portend calamity; Tin-Ne(th) (pp. 37–40: Tinsth Ne(th), "Neptune in the area of Jupiter"), Uni-Mae (Juno and Maius, pp. 40–42), Tecum ("a kind of Jupiter," p. 46), and Lusa (perhaps= the Lynsa Silvestris of Martianus, pp. 46–48; Lusl is a genitive) bring felicity; the other regions are either somewhat favorable (5–8, southeast) or somewhat unpropitious (9–12, southwest). Most scholars see in the right lobe the *pars familiaris* and in the left the *pars hostilis;* V. D. M. draws the dividing line across the two lobes: the bottom (eastern) half is *familiaris,* the upper (western) *hostilis.* Thus Cilens occurs in both the *pars familiaris* (region 36) and the *hostilis* (region 14). The conclusion: "The haruspices did not take risks, they studied the intentions of a god both in his favourable and unfavourable positions" (pp. 149–50). V. D. M.'s system displays close affinity with that of Thulin; it combines well the literary sources, Martianus, and the Liver, but there is much that we still do not understand, especially in the organization of the inner regions.

V. D. M. adamantly rejects Maggiani's theory (above, n. 7) of Chaldaean astrological influences on Etruscan hepatoscopy (pp. 153–56); these influences may have been overstated, but V. D. M.'s conclusion that "liver consultation in Etruria was a phenomenon which arose spontaneously" (p. 164) will find few supporters. After the classic article of J. Nougayrol we can hardly doubt that Etruscan hepatoscopy received at least some impulse from the East.[10]

On an Etruscan mirror we see Tages depicted as a young man and attired as a *flamen* (not *haruspex!*); he holds in his hands the liver of a victim and explains to Tarchon the craft of extispicy.[11] V. D. M. is the last in a long line of scholars to claim the mantle of Tages. His audience will probably be more skeptical than that of the original prophet.[12]

9. Cf. Dion. Hal. *Ant. Rom.* 2. 5. 2–4; Sen. *QNat.* 2. 41–2; Serv. ad *Aen.* 2. 693. The same system underlies the augural *templum* in Bantia, unfortunately not utilized by V. D. M.; cf. J. Linderski, "Watching the Birds: Cicero the Augur and the Augural *Templa,*" *CP* 81 (1986): 338–40, and, in greater detail, id., "The Augural Law," *ANRW* 2.16.3 (1986): 2281–86.

10. "Les rapports des haruspicines étrusque et assyro-babylonienne, et la foie d'argile de Falerii Veteres (Villa Giulia 3789)," *CRAI* (1955), pp. 509–19. From the ancient East there are known numerous clay models of the liver; see R. D. Biggs and J.-W. Meyer, "Lebermodelle," *Reallexikon der Assyriologie* 6 (1980–83): 518–27.

11. M. Pallotino, "Uno specchio di Tuscania e la leggenda etrusca di Tarchon," *RAL* 6 (1930): 49–87; Wood, "Myth," pp. 326, 330.

12. The book is produced sloppily on glossy paper at an exorbitant price. The text was set on an inferior computer, with margins justified but with atrocious microspacing. Diacritical signs in French, Italian, German, and Etruscan produce thoroughly mutilated shapes of letters. In the bibliography a number of articles have truncated references (only the first page is listed) and, deplorably, all books appear without indication of the place of publication. There is no index. The book is redeemed, however, by a splendid set of illustrations: short of traveling to the Museo Civico in Piacenza, this is the place to go if one wishes not only to read about the *iecur* but also to see it.

62

Fratres Arvales: Storia di un collegio sacerdotale romano. By IDA PALADINO.
Problemi e Ricerche di Storia Antica, 11. Rome: "L'Erma" di Bretschneider,
1988. Pp. 317; 1 table in text.

"Or, the Pitfalls of Evidence." We miss this subtitle. It illuminates the subject
and raises it to the rank of problem or puzzle. For consider this: only five literary
sources mention the *arvales,* and yet we know by name 174 members of the
confraternity, all of them attested epigraphically, and none predating the Empire.[1]
And this: nearly all these names appear in a single category of sources, the *acta* of
the *arvales:* very few are on display in other documents. And above all consider
this: what our modern authorities suppose were the principal cult duties of the

---

1. B. Borghesi, *Oeuvres numismatiques,* vol. 1 (Paris, 1862), pp. 376-77, discovered a reference to the
membership in the college of the *fratres arvales* in the wreath of corn-ears depicted on some late
republican coins; Paladino calls his idea "affascinante" (p. 21) but remains (wisely) noncommittal. M. H.
Crawford, *Roman Republican Coinage* (Cambridge, 1974), pp. 466, 509-11, does not mention the idea of
Borghesi at all with respect to the aurei of the monetalis L. Mussidius Longus (no. 494, 44-46, dated to 42
B.C.); and with respect to the denarii of D. Iunius Albinus (no. 450, 3, dated to 48 B.C.), he observes that
the wreath is "perhaps intended to allude to action over the corn supply."

brethren do not seem to bear any resemblance to what we know of their activities from the *acta* of the college, a record painstakingly detailed and accurate.[2]

The rich quarry of names naturally attracted prosopographical game hunters;[3] this is good and right, provided we do not neglect or disparage the ceremonies of the brethren. The arvals were not merely a group of men who delighted "in dress and show and ceremonial."[4] Their cult was part of Rome; when their grove and the shrines were invaded and plundered in the fourth century, with the arvals the old Rome, too, faded away.

The stones started reappearing in the sixteenth century; in 1795 the first collection of documents pertaining to the arvals was published;[5] but the turning point in the study of the college arrived only in 1867, when the Prussian Archaeological Institute in Rome, under the direction of Wilhelm Henzen, began excavations on the site of the grove of the *arvales*, in the locality outside the Porta Portuensis known as La Magliana, or as the arvals themselves described it, "in luco Deae Diae via Campana apud lap(idem) V."[6] Soon W. Henzen produced an edition of all the fragments of the *acta*, with a copious commentary.[7] His magnificent work remains the rock on which all subsequent studies have built; in 1950 appeared a supplement by E. Pasoli, useful but vastly inferior to Henzen's original edition.[8] More recently the excavations have been resumed by the French School in Rome, under the direction of John Scheid; they produced sparse new inscriptional evidence but uncovered rich architectural remains, above all the *balneum* of the brethren (dated to the Severan age), thus disproving Henzen's contention: "balnea non fuerunt in luco."[9]

P. briefly (too briefly) discusses "la documentazione" (pp. 19–21),[10] and proceeds to a study of the organization of the college and of the ritual calendar of the *fratres* (pp. 41–84). The main part of the book deals with the *sacrum Deae Diae* (pp. 85–191); two chapters follow, on the *carmen fratrum arvalium* and the foundation myth of the college (pp. 195–263). As for the details of the ritual, P. does not progress much (if at all) beyond Henzen; her presentation of the foundation myth and the story of Acca Larentia is excellent, but the explanation is foggy: the myth has something to do with the "dissociazione mitico-rituale [never forget the hyphens!] tra Romulus e Quirinus" (p. 261).

---

2. The earliest preserved fragment dates to 21 B.C., and the record continues in abundance (some two hundred pages in the edition of Henzen) to A.D. 241, with a small stray fragment dated to A.D. 304.

3. See esp. J. Scheid, *Les Frères Arvales: Recruitement et origine sociale sous les empereurs Julio-Claudiens* (Paris, 1975); R. Syme, *Some Arval Brethren* (Oxford, 1980).

4. Syme, *Some Arval Brethren*, p. 112.

5. G. Marini, *Gli atti e monumenti dei fratelli Arvali* (Rome, 1795).

6. Cf. J. Scheid, "Note sur la via Campana," *MEFRA* 88 (1976): 639–67.

7. *Acta Fratrum Arvalium Quae Supersunt* (Berlin, 1874). For his excavations, see W. Henzen, *Scavi nel bosco sacro de'fratelli Arvali* (Rome, 1868).

8. *Acta Fratrum Arvalium Quae Post Annum MDCCCLXXIV Reperta Sunt*, Studi e ricerche, vol. 7 (Bologna, 1950). P. (p. 18) lists the fragments of the *acta* published after the supplement of Pasoli but unfortunately does not reproduce them; and, oddly enough, she missed Pasoli's own *aggiornamento*, "Additamenta actorum fratrum arvalium," *Accademia delle Scienze di Bologna. Classe di Scienze Morali, Memorie*, serie 5, vol. 6 (1956–57): 75–92.

9. *Acta Fratrum*, p. xxiii; H. Broise and J. Scheid, *Recherches archéologiques à La Magliana: Le balneum des Frères Arvales*, Roma Antica, vol. I (Rome, 1987). For the importance of this discovery for the history and cult of the *arvales*, see esp. pp. 16–18.

10. She never asks what was the purpose of the records left by the arvals; for this, see M. Beard, "Writing and Ritual: A Study of Diversity and Expansion in the Arval Acta," *PBSR* 53 (1985): 114–62.

Two puzzling problems deserve comment. First, the Augustan "restoration." Eighty years ago, G. Wissowa, impressed by the wealth of the inscriptional material produced by the *arvales* in the imperial period, so summarized the history of the college: the beginning, "uralt"; at the end of the Republic, "vollständig verfallen"; restoration (*Neugründung*) by Augustus.[11] This view still reverberates, most recently in the opus of Scheid. That scholar quotes Varro *De lingua Latina* 5. 85: "Fratres arvales dicti sunt qui sacra publica faciunt propterea ut fruges ferant arva, a ferendo et arvis fratres arvales dicti; sunt qui a fratria dixerunt"; and he concludes that "Varron ne devait pas en savoir plus a sujet des arvales"—the *confrérie* was extinct.[12] P. raises the voice of protest (pp. 22–23, 33–35): in the *De lingua Latina* Varro was interested in the etymology of the name *arvales,* not in the history of the college; this is true also of his treatment of the pontiffs. Another scholar perceptively observed the obvious: Varro uses the present tense; hence in his time the *fratres* were well and alive.[13] In fact, the confraternity was important enough to be annexed by the architect of the new dispensation: Augustus became an arval himself (*RG* 7. 3), and in due course his successors; the old ritual was profusely enlarged by the ceremonies of the imperial cult. P.'s interpretation of this development is this: "assistiamo dunque al recupero della connessione Romulus-agricultura, ora più che mai necessario in una forma di governo di fatto monarchica" (p. 269). If things were always that simple . . .

Second, Dea Dia, Mars, and the *ambarvalia.* The main deity of the arvals in the imperial period was Dea Dia, the possessor of the grove. The festival in her honor, the *sacrum* (*sacrificium*) *deae Diae,* fell in May (because it had the character of *feriae conceptivae* it is missing from the epigraphical calendars and from Ovid's *Fasti*). On the second, and main, day of the festivities, the brethren performed a ritual dance (*tripodaverunt*) and recited from a *libellus* their archaic *carmen.* But in this *carmen* they did not address Dea Dia at all, only Mars, Lares, and the Semones. Was the Goddess a newcomer to the confraternity—or did she always coexist with Mars? And what was her character? It is enough to think of the *coronae spiceae* of the brethren to see that the festival dealt with the *arva;* hence Wissowa regarded her as "eine Indigitation der Ceres."[14] For P. she is an "entità affine a Diana [this because of the etymological similarity of the name] ed a Fortuna." More exactly: "una paredra minore di Fors Fortuna" (pp. 230–31). In fact, from the fourth to the first century the Fors Fortuna was "la vera 'padrona di casa' nel *lucus* arvalico" (p. 228). She was a "plebeian" goddess (cf. Ov. *Fasti* 6. 781–84); consequently, under Augustus or perhaps rather under Sulla, she was "replaced" by the "aristocratic" Dea Dia. The flavor of the argument is not to be missed: this process occurred "in un'epoca di riflusso nobiliare-gentilizio tale di portare ad escludere una Fortuna propria dei *populares,* come Fors Fortuna, a vantaggio di un entità che, pur conservando di questa determinate caratteristiche, fosse maggiormente adattabile ad un collegio di latifondisti" (p. 231). The evidence? Not in Rome.

11. *Religion und Kultus der Römer*[2] (Munich, 1912), p. 561.
12. *Les Frères Arvales,* p. 337; cf. pp. 335–66.
13. A. Alföldi, *Early Rome and the Latins* (Ann Arbor, 1964), p. 299, n. 4. So also Beard, "Writing and Ritual," p. 116.
14. *Religion und Kultus*[2], p. 562.

A temple of Fors Fortuna (founded or re-founded by Sp. Carvilius in 293 B.C.) indeed rose in the close vicinity of the precinct of the arvals;[15] her cult, far from being suppressed, flourished under Augustus; it displayed connections with Ceres, the summer solstice, and agricultural abundance.[16] The two goddesses lived side by side, shared some preoccupations, but were distinct and separate. And if Dea Dia had replaced the "original" Fors Fortuna, where did she come from? Whoever she was, she was ancient; and so was Mars.

For Wissowa the arvals were established to celebrate the feast of *ambarvalia,* the ritual procession round the *ager Romanus antiquus,* and to offer to Mars the sacrifice of the *suovetaurilia.* In the *acta* the brethren occasionally offer the *suovetaurilia* as a *piaculum* to Dea Dia, never to Mars, and they never perform the lustration of the *ager.* P. concludes (against Mommsen, Henzen, De Rossi, Usener, and Wissowa) that the arvals had no connection with the *ambarvalia* at all (pp. 32–33).[17]

But the absence of Dea Dia from the *carmen* should not surprise us (as it does P. and many other scholars). We have to distinguish between the Varronian sacrifices "ut fruges ferant arva," the recipient of which was Dea Dia, recorded in the *acta,* and the purificatory lustrations and spells to repel menace, the addressee of which was Mars. The spells in the form of the *carmen* the arvals recited every year; but the annual procession, as it follows from Strabo (5. 3. 2 = C. 230), was replaced by the sacrifices in various points on the border of the old *ager.* The processions of the *amburbium* and of the *ambarvalia* were apparently reserved solely for dire circumstances, such as that described by Lucan (1. 523–638, *amburbium;* among the priests who participate in the procession, the arvals are conspicuously absent: they cared for *arva,* not *urbs*), and by the *Historia Augusta, Aurelianus* 20. 3: "lustrata urbs, cantata carmina, amburbium celebratum, ambarvalia promissa." If only we had the *acta* for the reign of Aurelian . . .

To sum up: we need a new Henzen.

---

15. J. Scheid and H. Broise, "Rome: Le bois sacré de Dea Dia," *Archeologia Laziale* 1 (1978): 76, write that "il semble . . . qu'à l'époque de la restauration augustéenne, un même complexe devait réunir les temples de Fors Fortuna et de Dea Dia." But they do not adduce any evidence that the Fors Fortuna was the original inhabitant of the *lucus,* and "complexe" is not a religious term: however close the temples, they and their inhabitants retained separate identities.

16. See J. Champeaux, *Fortuna: Le culte de la Fortune à Rome et dans le monde romain,* vol. 1 (Rome, 1982), pp. 199–247.

17. In this she follows in the footsteps of Marini, Hirschfeld, Oldenberg, and Alföldi; so also, in a recent and learned article, C. B. Pascal, "Tibullus and the Ambarvalia," *AJP* 109 (1988): 523–36.

63

Prophecy and History in the Crisis of the Roman Empire: A Historical Commentary on the Thirteenth Sibylline Oracle. By DAVID S. POTTER. Oxford: Clarendon Press; New York: Oxford University Press, 1990. Pp. xix + 443; 2 maps, 27 photos in text. $110.00.

It is easier to utter a prophecy after the fact. Or fit facts to prophecy. For modern students prophecies are dark corridors to the past.

Potter's book[1] is an erudite guide to one nook in this shadowy realm, the thirteenth *logos* of the Sibyl. The 173 verses of this oracle (P. gives his own text based on a new collation of manuscripts) sing of the happenings that can be identified as belonging to the war-filled third century. Hence the value of the text as a perception of this age, and occasionally as a source.

The bulk of P.'s endeavour is taken by the line-by-line commentary (pp. 179–347). This commentary is advertized as historical. It is much more than that. As J. Geffcken warned in the preface to his great edition, "wer die Oracula textkritisch behandeln will, muss ihren historischen Hintergrund kennen; wer sie historisch zu ergründen strebt, muss Handschriftenkritik treiben."[2] This is what P. offers: history predominates, but textual problems, vocabulary, and style also find an attentive ear.

The commentary is preceded by an ample introduction in four chapters dealing with "The Economic and Political Situation of the Roman Empire in the Mid-Third Century A.D."; "Historiography in the Third Century A.D." (primarily a discussion of Dexippus and the shadowy Philostratus who, P. argues, was the source for

---

1. It is offered by the Oxford University Press at an extortionist price. It is time to consider whether books of scholarship, appealing to a limited audience, should not be disseminated primarily through electronic means.
2. *Die Oracula Sibyllina* (Leipzig, 1902), p. xvi.

Petrus Patricius' narrative of the third century); "The Sibylline Oracles";[3] and in particular "The *Thirteenth Sibylline Oracle*." There are four appendices, and an extensive bibliography.[4]

The reader will do well to begin with page 109, and the account of the *libri Sibyllini* in Rome. For the *libri* and the *oracula* (although both composed in Greek hexameters) were two different things. The Roman *libri* were believed to have been acquired from a Sibyl by the king Tarquinius Priscus; they were controlled by the board of priests "for the performance of rites" (*sacris faciundis*), who, however, could consult them ("approach": *libros adire*) only if authorized by the senate. They contained not only predictions (*fata*) but also *remedia*, as can best be gleaned from two fragments preserved by the second-century writer of the *mirabilia*, Phlegon of Tralles (one of them referring to an extensive *procuratio* in 125 B.C. prompted by the discovery of an androgynous child).[5] These *libri* perished in the great fire of the Capitol in 83. But there existed many other Sibyls, and many other texts of Sibylline prophecies; in 76 a committee appointed by the senate culled from various sources a new collection to serve the needs of the Roman state. This collection was burnt under the Christian empire by Stilicho at the beginning of the fifth century.

On the other hand the prophecies known as the *Oracula Sibyllina*, οἱ Σιβυλλιακοὶ χρησμοί, enjoyed great esteem among the Christians (and the Jews). They consist of two separate collections mixing freely classical, Jewish, and Christian elements. The first collection (A) comprising eight *logoi* appears to have been assembled at the earliest in the sixth century, and the collection B (originally comprising at least fifteen texts) only after the Arab conquest of Egypt in 646. The surviving texts are in modern editions numbered consecutively. The Oracles were not merely eschatological texts: the Twelfth covers the imperial history from Augustus to the death of Alexander Severus, and the Thirteenth from 238 to Odaenathus' victories over the Persians (his death in 268 is not recorded). It was stitched together from various texts that appear to have been composed in Syria, and composed contemporaneously with the events they describe.

But it is time to approach the text—and the commentary. For the sake of example let us take the first twenty lines (pp. 167–68, text and translation, pp. 179–212, commentary).

After the introduction in which the Sibyl announces the divine command to reveal her prophecy to the world there is a lacuna; the "historical" narrative starts (line 7) with an allusion to Ares: καὶ δόρυ θοῦρος[6] Ἄρης· ὑπὸ δ᾽ αὐτοῦ πάντες

---

3. To be read in conjunction with P.'s long review article, "Sibyls in the Greek and Roman World," *JRA* 3 (1990): 471–83.

4. But one misses the still useful bibliographical account by G. Walser and T. Pekáry, *Die Krise des römischen Reiches* (Berlin, 1962). We can also add the books by Breglia Pulci Doria, Alram, Spagnuolo Vigorita, Nicoletti, and Charles-Picard, listed below, notes 5, 8, 10, 11.

5. See the classic study by H. Diels, *Sibyllinische Blätter* (Berlin, 1890), and now also L. Breglia Pulci Doria, *Oracoli Sibillini tra rituali e propaganda. Studi su Flegonte di Tralles* (Naples, 1983).

6. So P., and the editions of A. Rzach (Vienna [not Leipzig, as indicated on p. 165], 1891), and Geffcken. P. has no annotation in his apparatus, but in the commentary (p. 184) he remarks: "Alexandre followed the manuscripts and printed δορυθοῦρος." This is indeed what C. Alexandre prints (actually δορύθουρος) in his pathbreaking edition (Paris, 1853 [1869² *non vidi*]), but he presents it as his conjecture, not the manuscript reading; on p. 254, he observes (referring to the edition of J. H. Friedlieb [Leipzig, 1852]): "Friedl. δόρυ θοῦρος, divide, ut in codd." Nor is there any annotation in Geffcken's apparatus; a strange omission if his text contained a conjectural reading. The epithet δορύθουρος is otherwise not attested, but in view of other similar descriptions (Alexandre compares δορυθαρσής; cf. also e.g., δορι[δορυ]σθενής, "mighty with the spear"; see LSJ) there is no reason to reject it: "Ares, impetuous with the spear."

ὀλοῦνται; in line 8 we read: νηπίαχος γεραός τε θεμιστεύσει ἀγοραῖσιν (where γεραός is Alexandre's conjecture for the manuscript γεγαώς or γεγαῶτες, and θεμιστεύσει Bowie's and P.'s proposal for the paradosis θεμιστεύει). To whom does this line refer, and who is the Ares in line 7? Now in lines 9–12 the Sibyl sings a customary song of doom, disaster, and war, but the tone changes in lines 7–20: they describe the valiant efforts of a Roman king, the new and warlike Ares, who will penetrate victorious as far the Euphrates, but will ultimately perish through treachery. This emperor is unmistakably Gordian III.

In line 8 Friedlieb kept the text of V, νηπίαχος γεγαώς τε θεμιστεύει. P. comments: "one may presume that, like Alexandre,[7] he envisaged 'infans in palateis regnabit', and proposed reading a lacuna between lines 7 and 8" (p. 185). This characterization, P. continues, "would fit Gordian III." Ultimately (and perhaps rightly) P. rejects this idea, and he rejects it mainly for grammatical reasons: the particle τε indicates that the person in line 7 cannot be the Ares of the preceding line. In this Ares he would wish to see the young Gordian. Against this assumption two considerations militate. The characterization of Gordian III as a new Ares in line 16 opposes him to any Ares that might have been mentioned previously; and secondly the actions of Ares in line 8 bring calamity, whereas the new Ares brings hope and relief from the barbarian onslaught. Hence two proposals: we may take the Ares in line 7 as a personification of war itself (P. appears to consider this possibility) or, and preferably, follow Alexandre (p. 254), and see here an allusion to that soldierly emperor, Maximinus Thrax, a warlike but calamitous brute (as Herodian 7.3 paints him).[8] In the preceding lacuna would have stood a narrative of the reign of Maximinus; this arrangement would lend full force to the contrast between the destructive Ares and the new heroic Ares. And let us not forget that the grandfather and the uncle of Gordian III perished leading the shortlived insurrection in Africa against the tyranny of Maximinus. This event brings us to the conjecture γεραός.

P. combines lines 7 and 8 thus: "many will be destroyed under[9] him, / childish and old he will give justice in the market-places," and surprisingly discovers in these lines a reference to the powerful prefect of the praetorians Timesitheus, the father-in-law of Gordian III. This idea is based on the assumption that Timesitheus should have been well known in the eastern provinces where he had served many years as administrator, and that the praetorian prefects exercised a far reaching judicial competence (pp. 186–87). But it is doubtful that the memory of a provincial procurator would have etched itself so deeply into the prophetic tradition; and the administration of justice was not an exclusive province of the praetorian prefects.[10] Furthermore: why should a prophecy attribute the wreaking of havoc just

7. This is misleading. What P. presumably wished to say is not that this was the idea that not only Friedlieb but also Alexandre envisaged, but rather that this was Alexandre's understanding of Friedlieb. For Alexandre (p. 255) stresses that Friedlieb gives his text *sine interpunctione*, and that his text "sic fere interpretatur: Infans quidem in plateis [not *palateis*] regnabit." And Alexandre adds: "Quo sensu, non dixit; nec videtur de Gordianis cogitasse."

8. So also the *vita* of Maximinus in the *Historia Augusta*. For a modern appreciation, see X. Loriot, "De Maximine le Thrace à Gordien III," *ANRW* 2.2 (1975): 666–88; K. Dietz, *Senatus contra principem. Untersuchungen zur senatorischen Opposition gegen Kaiser Maximinus Thrax*, Vestigia 29 (Munich, 1980), esp. pp. 1–38; M. Alram, *Die Münzprägung des Kaisers Maximinus I. Thrax*, Moneta Imperii Romani 27 (Vienna, 1989), pp. 22–24.

9. But on p. 167 he translates much more naturally "all will be destroyed by him."

10. The legislative activity of Gordian III (or in his name) was indeed extensive and impressive: see T. Spagnuolo Vigorita, *Secta temporum meorum. Rinnovamento politico e legislazione fiscale agli inizi del principato di Gordiano III* (Palermo, 1978); A. Nicoletti, *Sulla politica legislativa di Gordiano III* (Naples, 1981), with a text of 281 *constitutiones* attributed to Gordian. Commenting on the political

to the years when Timesitheus was in office (he became a prefect only in 241), and whence this odd image, "childish and old"? The thematic division imposes itself: it is best to keep the whole of the line 7 as the province of Ares = Maximinus, and then it is not difficult to identify the person in line 7: Gordian I (as Alexandre already saw). The uprising in Africa was started in the city of Thysdrus by the aristocratic *iuvenes;*[11] they thrust the imperial purple on the proconsul Gordian, an old man of eighty, who happened to be in Thysdrus administering justice (*Hist. Aug., Gord.* 8.5 "inventusque senex venerabilis post iuris dictionem iacens in lectulo"). The epithet γεραός is as if tailored for Gordian I, and perhaps it is not too adventurous to see in νηπίαχος a garbled reference to his youthful supporters.[12] After this interlude further catastrophies occur; and in fact there followed the war between Maximinus and the senate, the death of Maximinus and of the emperors chosen by the senate, Balbinus and Pupienus.[13] It is only after these events that the new avenger finally rises, Gordian III.

But interpreting prophecies, whether to inquire of the future or to learn of the past, is fascinating precisely because nothing is certain; and yet all students of the third century will now have to consult the Sibyl as revealed by P.[14]

---

preeminence of Timesitheus, and his concern for the conduct of the war against the Persians, Nicoletti (p. 19) observes: "Quasi estraneo rimase invece Timesiteo all'attività legislativa. Infatti negli anni della sua presenza [i.e. from the middle of 241 to 243] si ebbe complessivamente un minor numero di costituzioni rispetto al numero del periodo precedente" (cf. p. 83: only 16 constitutions in 242, and 11 in 243).

11. *Hist. Aug., Gord.* 9.3; Herod. 7.4.3, 4, 5; 7.5.1, 3, 4, 7; 7.6.2 (νεανίσκοι). On the role of the paramilitary *collegia iuvenum* in the events of 238 (especially in the light of a long inscription from Mactar), see the perceptive study by G. Charles-Picard, "Civitas Mactaritana," in *Karthago* 8 (Paris, 1957), pp. 77–95.

12. Alexandre (p. 61) translates lines 7 and 8 so: "Et Mars caedis amans, per quem discrimine nullo / Ambo cadent, puer, atque senex qui sceptra tenebat." He refers this to Gordian I and II, but cautions (pp. 254–55) that Gordian II, who was in 238 in his forties, could hardly be thought of as *puer*. Hence he postulates confusion with Gordian III, who at his elevation to the throne was thirteen years old, "non infans quidem, sed admodum iuvenis."

13. For the dates, see now D. Kienast, *Römische Kaisertabelle* (Darmstadt, 1990), pp. 188–95.

14. May we express a wish that the author of this learned book would consider preparing a commentary on other historical allusions in the Sibylline corpus, above all on the Twelfth Oracle?

Roman Religion in Livy

ἐκ Διὸς ἀρχώμεσθα. *Ab dis incipimus.* So would a poet commence his tale, but not a historian. Homer and Ennius and Vergil invoke the Muses, but Thucydides begins his somber account by presenting the author and his purpose; Sallust opens his monographs with philosophical divagations, and Caesar's *Bellum Gallicum* starts with a lesson of geography. Livy commences his tale with Aeneas and the Trojans, but he also wrote a preface, and he ends it with *omina, vota et precationes deorum dearumque* (*Praef.* 13). This must have struck his readers not only as poetic but also as very Roman. Still in the second century every public address began with a *precatio* to the gods: Ti. Gracchus, addressing a *contio, deos inciperet precari,* just as he was attacked and struck down by Scipio Nasica (*Rhet. ad Her.* 4.55.68). At the opening of his speech *pro Murena* Cicero reminds the jury that on the day he had declared Murena elected as consul he prayed to the immortal gods *ut ea res ... populo plebique Romanae bene eveniret,* and now he is praying to the same immortal gods for Murena's *salus.*

In the Aeneid, in the sixth book (753 ff.), Aeneas visits the underworld, and Anchises shows to him a long procession of the great Romans of the future, heroes, statesmen, triumphators. He could as well have presented Aeneas with a copy of Livius' *Annales.* For Livy writes of Aeneas' progeny, and, like Vergil, he writes an epic story, only in prose; hence his address to the gods. This epic character of the *Annals* colors Livy's presentation of the divine, but it is only veneer. Veneer is also the influence of Greek philosophy[1], and occasional scepticism. Livy may cast doubts on the divine origin of Romulus: who can now believe that he was a son of Mars? (*Praef.* 7; 1.4.2) – but he never questions the existence of the gods or their intervention in the affairs of Rome. This is his *animus antiquus.* But it was also the *animus* of the official religion down to the last days of the Republic. Livy may complain that his was the age of disregard of the gods, *neglegentia deorum,* the age in which it was believed that gods portend nothing (*nihil deos portendere*). He laments that no divine signs, no prodigies, are publicly reported and recorded by the historians (43.13.1-2).[2] And indeed in the histories of Sallust and Caesar and Pollio there certainly was no room for supernatural happenings: no talking cows, no rain of stones. But Sulla's memoirs were replete with dreams and omens, and Caesar himself utilized to the full the gods and

53

their messages while omitting to report them as a historian, and contemptuous of such things in his philosophical mood.[3] So also Cicero, sceptical Academic in the second book of the *De Divinatione*, as a politician and orator frequently appealed to the gods and their signs. Gods speak loudly in his Catilinarian orations, they send prodigies that are recorded and taken very seriously. The fragments of the poem *De consulatu suo* and the speech *De haruspicum responsis* are thunderous refutations of the fashionable conviction that Roman religion, the belief in the gods and omens was a dead letter in the age of Cicero or Livy. The beliefs and attitudes of a few literati should not over-shadow the fact that the populace of Rome, the low and the high, were still imbued with the ancient spirit of *religio*.[4]

Livy's preface has been a rich nourishment for all those scholars who investigated his beliefs and his credulity.[5] But Roman religion in Livy is a topic different from the religiosity of Livy. For instance, P.G. Walsh in his noted book has this to say about Livy's belief (p. 49): Livy »attempts to sift from the mass of superstitious myth a cen-tral doctrine of the relationship between men and gods which will lend order and signi-ficance to human life«. And he continues: »This is the fundamental force of Livian *pietas* – a reverence for the godhead which ensures the right ordering of men's lives.« This makes out of Livy a member of a protestant church; but his history is not about god in men's lives, but about the rise of Rome, *dis auctoribus*. The *Annals* treat of *res divinae* and *res humanae*, in that order. They treat of Rome's relationship with its gods, its internal history, and its wars. Peace with the gods and peace among the citizens, *pax deum* and *concordia*, form the two pillars on which the imperium of Rome is built. Equally wide off the mark is the opinion of Kajanto (p. 101) to whom it is »obvious« that according to Livy »the course of events was mainly determined by human beings and not by gods and fate«. This is a very un-Roman opinion, for in Rome *dei hominesque* formed an inseparable whole. The solid rock of Livy's presen-tation of Roman *religio* is the priestly tradition as transmitted or invented by the an-nalists and antiquarians, and still largely observed in the cult of the gods in Livy's own time.

As devout students of *religio* should, we shall begin, as Livy the poet did, with the gods. The Stoics used to say that as the interpreters of the gods exist, the gods must exist, too (cf. Cic., de nat. deor. 2.12; de div. 1.9-10). The inanity of this argument was assailed by Cicero in the sceptical part of his treatise *On Divination* (2.41, 101-102, 104-106). The orators and poets of course do not argue the existence of the gods: they presuppose it. No stoic proof for the existence of gods in Livy. The proof he gives is a Roman proof.

Pyrrhus, the *superbissimus rex*, learns that gods do exist when after he had des-poiled the temple of Proserpina at Locri his fleet was shattered by a terrible storm (29.18.1-7). In 202 the Carthaginian envoys are upbraided for their *perfidia*, and

54

sternly lectured that so many *clades* should have taught them that gods exist and that they protect the sanctity of the oath (30.27.1). In a battle against the Volsci the dictator exhorts his soldiers to let their swords flash and remember that gods do exist[6], gods who help the Romans and who had sent them into battle *secundis avibus* (6.12.9). In Livy the Romans win their battles and wars, and render *nomen Romanum invictum*, always with divine help and guided by divine signs: *dis auctoribus, dis bene iuvantibus, dis praesentibus ac secundis, ducibus ipsis dis.*[7]

This is, *in nuce*, the essence of Roman state theology. The gods exist, they are on the Roman side, and the proof of this is victory. But why should the gods care for the fate of Rome?

According to Roman religious doctrine, ultimately enshrined early in the second century in the writings of the annalists and the epos of Ennius, at the beginning of Roman history stood the *augustum augurium*, the auspices by which Jupiter empowered Romulus to found the city. Livy gives only a short and – if compared to Ennius – a bland account of the founding (1.6.3-7.3). In Ennius both Romulus and Remus are augurs: they take the primaeval auspices (*dant operam ... auspicio augurioque*) which established the pact between Rome and Jupiter; Cicero talks of *reges augures*, and it is he, with his understanding of an augur, who preserved for us the account of Ennius.[8] Livy, on the other hand, seems to have slighted the doctrinal significance of the *augurium* of Romulus – an odd attitude in the history *ab urbe condita*. It is only in the body of his work that he alludes to the magisterial importance of the foundation rite. Scipio, addressing the rebellious troops in Spain, exclaims: Do not think that with me the *imperium populi Romani* will fall: the *urbs* was founded *auspicato deis auctoribus in aeternum* (28.28.11). And Camillus, assailing in a grand speech the plan to move the capital to Veii, after Rome was destroyed by the Gauls, adduces solely religious arguments, above all this: *Urbem auspicato inauguratoque conditam habemus* (5.52.2). The foundation auspices are also mentioned by P. Valerius, the consul of 449, »descendant of liberators of the Roman People«, and – as he abolished the decemvirs – »himself their liberator« (3.61.2-5). All three men were in a sense new founders of Rome, and Livy, with great artistry, has them look back to the original covenant, but he himself in his own narrative never looks back to it. For this bedrock of Roman theology of history, the *augurium* of Romulus, belonged to those events *ante conditam condendamve urbem* which were worthy to figure in poetic fables but not in serious history (*Praef.* 6).

By sending Romulus his twelve vultures Jupiter not only gave his blessing for the founding of the city, but also promised to protect it – at a price. The gods were entitled to the official cult, sacrifices and offerings. Roman state religion was not interested in individual salvation; its only concern was *salus publica*, the security of the Roman State, or, in Roman terms, the preservation of *pax deorum*, the peace between

55

the gods and the state.[9] The goal of the cult was to keep the gods pleased and well disposed toward Rome.

And in order to ascertain whether the *pax deorum* prevailed the lines of communication with the gods had to be kept open. It was a two way street. First the gods could express their opinions, wishes, displeasure and anger. This they did by means of various signs. These signs the Roman doctrine, as always detailed and exact, classified as auspices and prodigies. The auspices referred to concrete actions conducted on behalf of the state by its official representatives; the prodigies pertained to the general state of the republic.[10] Through auspices the gods expressed their wishes and gave advice; through prodigies they sent warnings and expressed their displeasure. The communication line from the state to the gods was equally multithreaded: a simple address, inquiry, entreaty, vow, promise of gifts, thanksgiving, and above all regular and extraordinary sacrifices.

If success is the touchstone, as it was for the Romans, Roman state religion served Rome well. Scrupulously maintaining the *pax deorum* the Romans conquered the world, and built an empire, as Livy puts it, second only to the *opes* of gods (1.4.2). And the means of preserving the »right« relationship with the deity, and of gaining its favor, was the painstakingly exact observation of the ritual. Like the Roman legal system to which it bears a strong resemblance, the ritual of cult was the product of generations of statesmen and priests, half petrified, half in flux. It was part armor, part strait jacket – in this respect very similar to the official Marxist philosophy of various communist states. If things were going well this was empirical proof that the gods were pleased with the cult they were receiving. But if discomfiture was suffered, a defeat in battle or a plague, or if any unusual happening took place, this meant that either some parts of the ritual had to be modified or that a transgression had occurred, and the peace of the gods was disturbed. Now expiation or appeasement was necessary.

Thus the notion of *pax deorum* expressed a fundamental concept of Roman religion; it also well describes the function of religion in Livy's history.

In the *Annals* the *pax deum* is ruptured and restored many times; the phrase itself Livy uses only infrequently, eight times in the first decade, twice in the third and once in the fifth.[11]

Let us begin with the example from the fifth decade (42.2.3-7) for it refers to events that happened in the full light of recorded history, in 173. In this year numerous and dire prodigies were reported, and because the war against Macedonia was in prospect, the senate decreed that before it should be undertaken the prodigies should be expiated and the *pax deum* should be sought by such *precationes* as would be published from the Sybilline books (*prodigia expiari pacemque deum peti precationibus, qui editi ex fatalibus libris essent, placuit*). The decemvirs (i. e. the *decemviri sacris faciundis*) inspected the books, and published their findings in writing. They pre-

56

scribed exactly to what gods and with what victims the sacrifices should be performed (*editum ...quibus diis quibusque hostiis sacrificaretur*), and recommended that a *supplicatio prodigiis expiandis fieret*, and that the *supplicatio* which had been vowed in the previous year for the health of the people (*valetudinis populi causa*) be also celebrated and a period of *feriae* observed (for this vow, see 41.21.12).

In 208 (27.23.1-4) we have again disturbing reports of prodigies, and in addition the consuls, sacrificing before their departure from the city, did not obtain the *litatio* (i. e. the *exta* of the sacrificial victims proved on inspection to be unfavorable). It was now *religio* for them to leave the city. On account of the prodigies the supplication of one day was offered. But for a long time the peace of the gods was not secured: full-grown victims were slain for days without a favorable result (*per dies aliquot hostiae maiores sine litatione caesae, diuque non impetrata pax deum*). Livy now adds cryptically: the state remained unharmed; the dire consequences of the prodigies descended upon the heads of the consuls. And indeed the consuls, the great M. Claudius Marcellus and T. Quinctius Crispinus, were ambushed by Hannibal; Marcellus lost his life, and Crispinus was wounded (27.26-27).

Now the third example, of 214 (24.10.6-11.1). Again numerous reports of prodigies; on the advice of the haruspices they were atoned with full-grown victims (*hostiis maioribus procurata sunt ex responso haruspicum*), and a supplication was proclaimed to all the gods who had in Rome the *pulvinaria*, the festal couches. Livy continues: when all the rites which pertained to the peace with the gods had been completed, the consuls consulted the senate with respect to the state of the republic and the conduct of the war.

These examples[12] tell us much about the method of Livy, his interests, and his shortcomings as a chronicler of cult. He does not have the mind of an antiquarian or a theologian. The religious observances are recorded and piled up as an embellishment for the narrative, and an illustration of the *mos maiorum*. For the doctrine or procedure he shows little curiosity. He does not ask why on one occasion it was the decemvirs who were consulted about the prodigies, and on the other the haruspices. And who explained the prodigies in 208? Livy does not say. He does not distinguish between the prodigies which were reported (*nuntiata*), and those which were acknowledged (*suscepta*). And why should the prodigies in 208 have portended calamity for the consuls, but not for the state? Were they not sufficiently expiated? Livy does not explain. Perhaps the consuls left the city without the *litatio* – we do not know for Livy simply abandons the matter. (We might add that Plutarch in his *Life of Marcellus*, 28-29, says that Marcellus and his colleague set out of the city only after all the ceremonies prescribed by the *manteis* had been performed.)

If no prodigies were sent, the gods were contented, and everything was tranquil. If they were sent, the following procedure was observed:

57

First, the *nuntiatio*, the report of a prodigy to a magistrate, a consul or a praetor (mostly the urban praetor). Next, the *relatio* of the magistrate to the senate. Third, the decision of the senate, often arrived at after the consultation with the priests, either to reject the report as untrustworthy or to acknowledge it (*susceptio*). Fourth, the interpretation of the prodigy. The senate by a formal decree would either entrust this task to the haruspices (the technical term was *acciri haruspices*) or, in especially grave situations, to the keepers of the Sybilline books who would formally be ordered to approach or inspect the books (*libros adiri* or *inspicere*). Fifth, the haruspices or the decemviri present their findings to the senate, both orally and in writing. They propose the measures to be taken. Sixth, the senate, again by a formal decree, instructs, as need be, the magistrates or the priests (normally the decemvirs and the pontiffs), and occasionally the whole populace or a part of it, to carry out the ritual of expiation. All these formal stages of the *procuratio prodigiorum* arc mentioned by Livy, but he mentions them randomly, never giving a picture of the whole procedure, and never bothering to explain the underlying theological doctrine.[13] Again, as in most religions, Roman religion was the ritual, to be followed and observed by everybody, but to be understood and studied only by the priests (and scholars). And Livy, unlike Varro or Cicero or Appius Claudius or Valerius Messala and scores of others who wrote technical treatises on the Roman cult, was not a priest. His technical information is due exclusively to his sources, and it is only through these sources that substantial bits of priestly lore and language still shine in Livy.

But if the Roman state relied for its security solely on prodigies, it would only react – not act. For a prodigy portended that something had gone wrong: either that something had been done that should not have or that something had not been done that should have. Every action undertaken by an individual either on his own behalf or on behalf of the state was fraught with danger. The gods may not approve of it or, gods forbid, may be offended. Hence it was imperative to explore the state of the divine mind before anything of importance was undertaken. The tool was the auspices.[14] Now the augural doctrine, as reconstructed from various sources, in particular Cicero and the Vergilian scholia, distinguished carefully between two kinds of auspices, the *impetrativa* and the *oblativa*. In the former the initiative comes from the auspicant: he asks the gods whether they give their permission to undertake a specific action; he asks the deity to send a sign of approval. In the latter it is the gods who send a message on their own initiative. Now, what then is the difference between a *prodigium* and an *auspicium oblativum*? Both were unsolicited signs. The difference is minute but fundamental. The *auspicium oblativum* pertained solely to a concrete action during the exercise of which it was sighted. The *prodigium* referred to the state of the republic, and it could be observed at any time and practically at any place. The *auspicium* was valid for one day only; the validity of the prodigy had no strict time limit.

58

The *prodigium* shows that either the *pax deorum* had been ruptured, or that it is going to be ruptured, and that dire consequences might follow unless the deity is appeased. The *auspicium oblativum* proclaims that the gods are against the action in progress. The subtle part is that the same sign could function at the same time both as an *auspicium oblativum* and a *prodigium*. That *prodigia* were fundamentally different from *auspicia* is demonstrated by the fact that the augurs are never called upon, in Livy and in other sources, to interpret the prodigies. A casual reader of Livy would hardly observe this, and yet here Livy reflects a principal tenet of the Roman lore of omens. Not that he comments on it; again he simply narrates. Nor will we find in his *Annals* a divagation on the nature of the auspices, and an explanation of their various kinds and aspects. But his presentation is remarkably consistent. Again, much credit has to go to his sources. Since the consultation of the auspices was such a ubiquitous pageant in Roman public life, Livy mentions them only when prompted by the drama of his narrative or when some unusual irregularities occurred or when reproducing the factual style of the chronicles.

His auspices are mostly the *impetrativa*. (However, the verb *impetrare* Livy uses in a religious context only with respect to the *pax deum*.) At home they are taken before the meetings of the popular assembly: *cum populo agi*, to pass the laws and to elect the magistrates, is possible only *auspicato*.[15] But their major sphere of application is in war. A general conducts a war under his auspices, *ductu* (or *imperio*) *auspicioque*, a famous and official phrase[16], for the first time attested epigraphically in the inscription of L. Mummius, the destroyer of Corinth.[17] The phrase is solemn, and Livy applies it to a select group of *imperatores*: to Camillus (three times), Scipio Africanus (four times), T. Quinctius Flamininus (in a speech of the consul M'. Acilius Glabrio before his great victory over Antiochus), to Ti. Sempronius Gracchus, the pacifier of Sardinia (quoting Gracchus' dedication in the temple of Mater Matuta), and to Augustus Caesar, but also to a few lesser figures, for no apparent reason, perhaps except that he found such a notice in his sources.[18] Here also belongs the famous and politically sensitive case of A. Cornelius Cossus, the winner of the *spolia opima* (4.19-20). Bowing to the authority of Augustus, and correcting his earlier account that Cossus won the *spolia* as a military tribune, Livy argues that he must have won them as a consul: the *spolia* could be won only by a *dux*, and the *dux* is the commander under whose auspices the war is conducted, *cuius auspicio bellum geritur*. Cossus won the *spolia*, ergo he was the consul. Translated into the political idiom of the Principate it meant that only the holder of full imperium could claim the right to the *spolia opima*; this practically excluded all provincial governors, who were the only commanders likely to defeat in person and strip an enemy chieftain.[19]

The Romans go to battle *auspicato, avibus secundis*. For this theology victory presented no problem, but defeat had to be explained or explained away. Obviously

59

the gods must have temporarily abandoned the Romans, and the reason for this was invariably a flaw in the ritual, *vitium* in the terminology of Roman priests and of Livy. Before the battle of Allia (5.38.1) the auspices were allegedly not taken, and the customary sacrifices not offered (*nec auspicato nec litato instruunt aciem*): how otherwise to explain this signal disaster?

The curious thing is that in fact it did not matter whether the auspices were true or false; what mattered is that they had to be reported and accepted as true. A case of the falsification of the auspices offers good insight into Livy's rare excursion into the doctrinal arcana of the augurs, and illustrates his dramatic flair in recounting the story (10.40).

The setting is the battle against the Samnites at Aquilonia in 293. Before the engagement, in the third watch of the night, the consul L. Papirius »rose silently and sent the keeper of the chickens to take the auspices«, *silentio surgit et pullarium in auspicium mittit*, an erudite phrase, *silentio surgere* and *in auspicium mittere* being technical augural expressions, the former denoting not only silence (although silence *per se* was of prime importance – for any untoward noise would interrupt the *auspicatio*) but above all the absence of any fault, of *vitium*, that would render the whole ceremony invalid. (We owe this explanation to the augur Cicero[20], of course, not to Livy.) Livy continues: »There was no class of men in the camp who were unaffected by the desire of battle ... This universal fervor spread even to those who assisted at the auspices [*qui auspicio intererant*, another technical phrase[21]]. For when the chickens refused to eat [*cum pulli non pascerentur*, again a technical expression] the *pullarius* dared to falsify the auspices [*auspicium mentiri*, a standard augural expression[22]], and reported to the consul the *tripudium sollistimum*« (Livy does not elaborate, but the term, which he uses only in this passage, will have been familiar to his readers: it meant that the chickens ate so greedily that crumbs of food were falling from their beaks down on the ground[23]). The joyful consul (*laetus*; the term regularly appears in various sources to describe the state of mind after a report of a propitious omen[24]) announced that the auspices were most favorable, and that the battle would be fought *deis auctoribus*. But the nephew of the consul learnt that there was among the *pullarii* a dispute *de auspicio eius diei* (observe that here Livy mentions in passing a fundamental rule of the auspices, their validity for one day only[25]). The young man, born »before the advent of the learning that teaches to disregard the gods«, reported the matter to the consul. But Papirius replied unperturbed: »He who assists at the auspices (*auspicio adest*) if he reports anything that is false, draws down the *religio* (ritual pollution) upon himself; as for me I received a report of *tripudium*, and I take it as an excellent *auspicium* for the Roman People and the army.« Papirius, and in any case the source of Livy, was extremely well versed in the augural lore. Jupiter is bound by the false announcement of a favorable *auspicium*, so the consul insists. The army is pure, pol-

60

luted is only the mendacious *pullarius*. The same doctrine, and the same terminology, recur in Cicero's accusation of Antonius. Cicero mentions »the falsified auspices which, however, had to be obeyed«, the *ementita auspicia, quibus tamen parere necesse erat* (*Phil.* 2.88), and he thunders (*Phil.* 2.83): »You have falsified the auspices – as I hope – with great disaster to yourself, not the State; you have fettered the Roman People by ritual pollution« (*magna, ut spero, tua potius quam rei publicae calamitate ementitus es auspicia, obstrinxisti religione populum Romanum*).[26] But pollution, lest it contaminate everything, must be excised or expiated. Hence in Livy's account the consul orders the centurions to station the *pullarii* in the front rank. Still before the battle was joined a random javelin struck the guilty *pullarius*. Whereupon the consul exclaimed: »The gods are present in the battle; the guilty wretch has paid the penalty.« And in front of him, just as he spoke, a raven uttered a clear cry, *corvus voce clara occinuit*. Now with the gods unmistakably on his side, the overjoyed consul (*laetus* again) orders his men to sound the trumpets and raise the battle cry. For by punishing the *pullarius* (with some help from the wily Papirius) Jupiter released the Roman people from the bounds of *religio*. And by sending the raven as a corroborative and unsolicited *augurium*[27], he indicated that he was abiding by the false *auspicium* which Papirius had accepted as true.

Livy recounts this story without a word of comment, but he imparts a message: for a commander the knowledge of the *res divinae* was as important as the knowledge of strategy. The tension mounts, but the peripateia ends abruptly when the raven utters his cry; Roman victory is a foregone conclusion. And indeed the Romans rout the Samnites. But Livy's artistry shines even brighter in his description of the Samnite defeat. Again the overriding theme is that of *religio*. Thanks to the consul's astute maneuver the Romans shook it off; the Samnites on the other hand were irredeemably polluted. For their select troop, the *legio linteata*, was formed according to a dreadful ritual: the soldiers were forced to swear that they would not retreat from the battlefield, and to cast a curse upon themselves and their family if they did. Those who refused to undergo this ritual were slaughtered before the altars as if sacrificial victims. Now fearful of gods and men, seeing before their eyes the altars bespattered *nefando sanguine*, and bound by the *religio* of their awful oath, they suffered in battle terrible carnage (10.38,41). In this way Livy masterfully contrasts the clean and legalistic – and victorious – religion of the Romans with the emotional, wild, sacrilegious rites of the Samnites.[28]

The taking of the auspices in the field Livy mentions several times[29], but the auspical validity and felicity of practically all undertakings in war depended ultimately on the validity of the auspices under which the commander had been elected to his office in the city, and secondly on the validity of the auspices which he had taken before departing from Rome for the campaign at hand. Again Livy never spells out this rule, but

61

his authorities were well aware of it. The difference between the civil auspices and the departure (or military) auspices stands clear, though again it is not formulated by Livy. If there was a fault in the former there was no remedy; if there was a fault in the latter, they could be repeated. Consequently the magistrates often abdicate or are forced to abdicate because a *vitium*, a ritual fault, was uncovered in the auspical procedure at their election.[30] On the other hand, when after his departure from Rome the commander has a reason to think that his military auspices might be *dubia* or *incerta*, he can and should return to the city *ad auspicia repetenda*.[31] One such case well illustrates the preoccupation of Livy, of his sources, and no doubt of the Romans of real history, with the security of the auspices (8.30-35).

Under the year 325 Livy notes tersely: *In Samnium incertis itum auspiciis est.* The case involves, oddly enough, another Papirius, and another *pullarius*. The two stories probably formed part of the family myths of the Papirii.[32] This time the keeper of the chickens plays a positive role: he warns[33] the dictator that his auspices are not in order, and Papirius returns to Rome *ad auspicium repetendum*. In the meantime his *magister equitum*, Q. Fabius, against the orders of the dictator, engages the enemy, and scores an impressive victory. Papirius comes back to the camp, and is outraged; he resolves to punish the insubordinate Fabius severely (Fabius escapes to the city, and is ultimately rescued by the tribunes of the plebs). In two speeches, two models of ancient *severitas*, one to the soldiers and the other to the populace in the city, Papirius insists on the importance of the auspices (8.32,34): when he realized (*scirem* – a statement of fact) that he had set out from Rome *incertis auspiciis* (in which way Papirius or rather his *pullarius* had come to this conclusion, Livy does not explain) it was his obligation to return to the city *ad auspicia repetenda* so that he would not undertake anything with the will of the gods in doubt, *ne quid dubiis dis agerem*. Otherwise, *turbatis religionibus*, with the right relationship with the gods in disarray, he would have exposed the republic to the utmost danger. Now the same *religio*, which was an obstacle *ad rem gerendam* for the dictator, was also an obstacle for the master of the horse, and yet he dared to engage the enemy *incertis auspiciis, turbatis religionibus, adversus ... numen deorum*. But if the *magister equitum* went to battle *adversus numen deorum*, why was he victorious? Livy, for once, explains: the *vitium*, the flaw in the auspices, this time did not affect the outcome of the war, which was waged successfully, but resulted in the mad anger and animosity of the generals (*in rabiem atque iras imperatorum vertit*). This is a lame explanation. The augural doctrine claimed that an uncorrected flaw in the ritual finds an outlet in some calamity[34] but was the *rabies imperatorum* a sufficient disaster? If the *magister equitum* had really fought the battle in contravention of the express will of the gods, he certainly could not have won. The point is that the auspices were ambiguous – not adverse. It was risky and foolhardy to engage the enemy, but the result was open. Livy in his rhetorical zeal has

62

put into the mouth of the enraged dictator one phrase too much: *adversus numen deorum*, high ringing but doctrinally unsound.

On the other hand C. Flaminius so behaved as if he waged war with immortal gods. He decided to enter on the consulship in the camp at Ariminum, and consequently set out from Rome as a *privatus*, without taking the auspices, without offering the vows to Jupiter on the Capitol (21.63). The senators argued that as he left home without the auspices he could not receive them on foreign soil, *nova et integra*, new and in their fulness. As a result he had no *iustum auspicium* (22.1.5-7). (In fact he will have been lacking two sets of auspices: the civil, which the consul assumed at a ceremony on the Capitol when he was entering upon his office; and the military which the commander acquired before crossing the pomerium, after the *auspicatio* and the vows to Jupiter.[35]) When the auspices were not in order, the gods were disturbed, and they manifested it by sending various prodigies. So they did in 217 (21.63.13-14; 22.1.8-20) but Flaminius remained obdurate; the result was the debacle at Lake Trasimene.

But Livy presents the clash between Flaminius and the senate above all as a political issue; Flaminius was afraid that his enemies would prevent him from marching out of Rome *auspiciis ementiendis*, that they would procure false reports of adverse *auspicia oblativa* (21.63.5). Here Livy may have had before his eyes the cause célèbre of 55 (now known above all from Cicero's *De Divinatione* 1.29-30, but which Livy must have described in detail) when the tribune Ateius Capito announced to Crassus dire omens (*obnuntiatio dirarum* in Roman terminology) before his departure for the Parthian campaign. The result was the catastrophe at Carrhae – so at least claimed the consul and censor Appius Claudius, Cicero's colleague in the college of augurs.[36]

The patrician and plebeian nobility controlled the state religion until the last days of the Republic, but in the turmoil of civil war the lines of communication with the gods were first captured by Caesar and then conquered by Augustus. How did Livy deal with this momentous change? Probably by praising Augustus – and occasionally offering oblique comments. Livy's Augustus was *templorum omnium conditor ac restitutor* (4.20.7); about the lavish pageantry of religious ceremonies under the new dispensation Livy could write effusely and honestly. »When he came to narrate the reign of Augustus, he was not disappointed« – opines Ronald Syme: »Portents continued duly to be reported, as is shown not merely by Cassius Dio but by a writer who took his examples from Livy«[37] (i. e. Julius Obsequens). In fact Livy had every reason to be disappointed: portents did not continue duly to be reported or accepted. In the forty four years of the reign of Augustus only in a handful of years do we have reports of prodigies, and only two of them come from Obsequens (under the years 17 and 11 B. C.).[38] For the *novus ordo rerum* was not only new but also the best. The gods had no reason anymore for sending dire prodigies and unfavorable auspices. It is true, to

63

quote Syme again, that »Fire, flood, and pestilence were not infrequent visitations«.[39] Such calamities, and military defeats, could not easily be hidden beneath the veil of silence, but often they were given a novel and unrepublican interpretation. On the sixteenth of January 27 B. C. the senate bestowed upon Octavian the title of Augustus; the very night following this happy event the Tiber disastrously overflowed its banks. Not a word in Obsequens, and no *procuratio* is on record, only a strange notice in Cassius Dio (53.20.1): the *manteis*, undoubtedly the haruspices, explained the flood as portending that Augustus would increase his power and would hold the whole city under his sway (οἱ μάντεις ὅτι τε ἐπὶ ἠῷῆῆ ῆ ἠῷῖῆῆ ῆῆὶ ὅτι πᾶσαν τὴν πόλιν ὑποχειρίαν ἕξοι προέγνωσαν). The phrase ἐπὶ μέγα αὐξήσοι clearly contains a hint at the surname of Augustus; thus the *inundatio*, normally a sign of divine wrath, was now re-interpreted as a sign of growth and a beneficent future – as if the Tiber were the Nile. Another crucial year for the Principate was 23 B. C. when Augustus received the *imperium maius*, and refrained from holding the consulship year by year. Prodigies ensued; Dio notes fire, storm and flood at the end of his entry for 23 B. C. (53.33.5), and again at the beginning of his account of 22 B. C. we have flood, pestilence and thunderbolts striking the statues in the Pantheon (54.1.1-2). Dio mentions no ceremonies of appeasement, only the belief of the people that »all these calamities descended upon them because they did not have Augustus for consul at this time« (54.1.1-2, cf. 53.32.5-6).[40] No republican haruspex, pontiff, quindecimvir or augur would subscribe to this interpretation. Did Livy? When he complained that prodigies are not reported, not recorded, not heeded, he did not think of the era of Cicero but of his own time[41], the time of the Augustan restoration. In religion, as in every other department of public life, the hallowed Augustan restoration was a perversion of the republican system. But this is a Tacitean, not Livian, theme.

64

Briscoe 1973 = J. Briscoe, A Commentary on Livy. Boooks XXXI-XXXIII, Oxford 1973.

Briscoe 1981 = J. Briscoe, A Commentary on Livy. Books XXXIV-XXXVII, Oxford 1981.

Hickson = F.V. Hickson, *Voces Precationum*: The Language of Prayer in the *History* of Livy and the *Aeneid* of Vergil, Diss. University of North Carolina, Chapel Hill 1986.

Kajanto = I. Kajanto, God and Fate in Livy, Turku 1957.

Liebeschuetz 1967 = W. Liebeschuetz, The Religious Position of Livy's History, JRS 57, 1967, 45-55.

Liebeschuetz 1979 = W. Liebeschuetz, Continuity and Change in Roman Religion, Oxford 1979.

Linderski = J. Linderski, The Augural Law, ANRW II,16,3 (1986), 2146-2312.

Luce = T. J. Luce, Livy. The Composition of his History, Princeton 1977.

Luterbacher = F. Luterbacher, Der Prodigienglaube und Prodigienstil der Römer, ^{2}Burgdorf 1904 (reprint Darmstadt 1967).

MacBain = B. MacBain, Prodigy and Expiation: A Study in Religion and Politics in Republican Rome (Collection Latomus 117), Bruxelles 1982.

Mazza = M. Mazza, Storia e ideologia in Tito Livio. Per un'analisi storiografica della *Praefatio* ai *Libri Ab Urbe Condita*, Catania 1966.

Mommsen = T. Mommsen, Römisches Staatsrecht I^3, II^3, III, Leipzig 1887-1888.

Musti = D. Musti, Tendenze nella storiografia romana e greca su Roma arcaica (= Quaderni Urbinati 10), Urbino 1970.

Ogilvie = R. M. Ogilvie, A Commentary on Livy. Books 1-5, Oxford 1965.

Packard = D. W. Packard, A Concordance to Livy, Cambridge, Mass. 1968, vols. I-IV.

Schmidt = P. L. Schmidt, Iulius Obsequens und das Problem der Livius-Epitome (Abh. Mainz 1968,5), Wiesbaden 1968.

Stübler = G. Stübler, Die Religiosität des Livius, Stuttgart/Berlin 1941.

Syme = R. Syme, Livy and Augustus, HSCP 64, 1959, 27-87 = Roman Papers I, Oxford 1979, 400-454.

Walsh = P. G. Walsh, Livy. His Historical Aims and Methods, Cambridge 1961.

Wissowa = G. Wissowa, Religion und Kultus der Römer, ^{2}München 1912.

Wülker = L. Wülker, Die geschichtliche Entwicklung des Prodigienwesens bei den Römern. Studien zur Geschichte und Ueberlieferung der Staatsprodigien, Diss. Leipzig 1903.

65

NOTES

1 I disagree emphatically with Walsh, 55 ff., who finds in Livy's Annals a full-fledged Stoic outlook on Roman history. See also the earlier study of Walsh, Livy and Stoicism, AJP 79, 1958, 355-375. Liebeschuetz 1967, 51-53 is to the point (at 53): »a Stoic interpretation is not excluded, but it will be the reader's, not the author's contribution«. Walsh, Livy (Greece and Rome. New Surveys in the Classics 8), Oxford 1974, 12, seems to regard as both perplexing and insufficient the opinion of Liebeschuetz (1967, 53) according to which Livy »felt that a rationalist outlook on the world could coexist with complete affirmation of the religion of the Roman people«. Nothing perplexing here; once we accept the premises of Roman state religion, it appears as a rationalist system, as a *scientia* (as e. g. the augurs used to describe their discipline, cf. Linderski, 2226-2241, esp. 2238-2239).

2 Cf. Luce, 248-249. Stübler, 99-103, rightly points out that Livy takes the prodigies very seriously. Kajanto, 46-52, finds in Livy a sceptic (cf. Walsh, 54, and Schmidt, 8). This is quite wrong. Livy often characterizes various prodigies as not worthy of belief or as an expression of hysteria (cf. below, n. 12). So did also the Roman senate and the Roman priests. True prodigies, *vera*, were only those acknowledged, *suscepta*, by the senate. All others were false. Today, in the eyes of believers, true miracles, *vera*, are only those acknowledged, *suscepta*, by the Catholic Church. All others are false.

3 Cf. A. Keaveney, Sulla and the Gods, Studies in Latin Literature and Roman History 3 (= Collection Latomus 180), Bruxelles 1983, 44-79. It is not surprising that also the *Historiae* of Cornelius Sisenna contained numerous reports of omens and prodigies (Cic., de div. 1.99; 2.54 = Peter, HRR I, 278; cf. Luterbacher, 67). On Caesar, see H. D. Jocelyn, Varro's *Antiquitates Rerum Diuinarum* and Religious Affairs in the Late Roman Republic, Bulletin of the John Rylands Library 65, 1982, 148-205, at 158-164 and 204-205.

4 On the persistence and vitality of Roman religious practices, see the excellent study by H. D. Jocelyn, The Roman Nobility and the Religion of the Republican State, The Journal of Religious History 4, 1966, 89-104; Idem, Varro's *Antiquitates* (above, n. 3), 159-161.

5 Cf. Ogilvie, 23-29; Mazza, passim; T. Janson, Latin Prose Prefaces, Stockholm 1964, 68-74.

6 At 3.56.7 when the deposed decemvir Appius Claudius utters the cry »provoco«, the people comment: *deos tandem esse et non neglegere humana ...*; they punish *superbia* and *crudelitas*.

7 See the passages in Packard, I, 1278 s.v. *dis*.

8 Cic., De div. 1.107-108 = Ennius, Ann. 1.72-91 in the edition of O. Skutsch, The Annals of Q. Ennius, Oxford 1985, 76-77 (text) and 221-238 (commentary; with respect to the *res auspicales* not always convincing). Cicero prefaces his quotation with the statement: *Itaque Romulus augur, ut apud Ennium est, cum fratre item augure.* De div. 1.89: *nostra civitas in qua reges augures ... rem publicam religionum auctoritate rexerunt.*

9 In another place I intend to present a comprehensive study of the concept of the *pax deum*. The short references in the standard handbooks (e. g. Wissowa or Liebeschuetz 1979) are glaringly insufficient.

10 Cf. J. Linderski, Cicero and Roman Divination, La Parola del Passato 37, 1982, 30-31.

11 There are also two occurrences in the fourth decade, but in one instance (38.46.12) it is an exclamation *pace deum dixerim*, »may I speak without offence to the gods«, and in the other (39.10.5) it is not the state but a private person (Hispala Faecennia) who implores the peace of gods (*pacem veniamque precata deorum dearumque, si ... silenda enuntiasset*). The phrase *pace deum dixerim* appears also at 10.7.12.

12 The examples from the first decade are as follows: 1.31.7: a plague occurs; the people believe »unam opem aegris corporibus relictam, *si pax veniaque ab diis impetrata esset*«; 3.5.14: »caelum visum est

66

ardere plurimo igni; portentaque alia aut obversata oculis aut vanas exterritis ostentavere species« (on account of *vanas ... species* Ogilvie, 404-405, concludes that Livy »is being delicately non-committal«. Not at all: he simply distinguishes between the true and the false prodigies, as he also does at 21.62.1: »prodigia facta aut ... nuntiata et temere credita«). Livy continues: »his avertendis terroribus in triduum feriae indictae, per quas omnia delubra *pacem deum exposcentium* virorum mulierumque turba inplebantur«; this apparently did not work (Livy offers no comment), for plague ensued, and at 3.7.7-8 »inopsque senatus auxilii humani ad deos populum ac vota vertit: iussi cum coniugibus ac liberis *supplicatum ire pacemque exposcere deum*. ad id, quod sua quemque mala cogebant, auctoritate publica evocati omnia delubra implent. stratae passim matres crinibus templa verrentes, *veniam irarum caelestium* finemque pesti *exposcunt*«;   at 8.1 we read further: »inde paulatim seu *pace deum impetrata* seu [a healthy bit of scepticism] graviore tempore anni iam circumacto defuncta morbis corpora salubriora esse incipere«;   6.1.12: the catastrophe at Allia occurred because no *litatio* was obtained at the sacrifices before the battle *»neque inventa pace deum ... obiectus hosti exercitus Romanus esset«*; quite on the contrary at 6.12.7 »Dictator ... cum auspicato prodisset hostiaque caesa *pacem deum adorasset, laetus* [cf. 10.40, discussed below in the text] ad milites processit«, and proclaimed that the victory was assured (apparently because he obtained both the favorable auspices and the *litatio*; and in fact the Volsci were routed); 6.41.9: Appius Claudius haranguing against the admittance of the plebeians to the consulship exclaims: »nunc nos, tamquam nihil *pace deorum* opus sit, omnes caerimonias polluimus«; 7.2.2: a plague; »*pacis deum exposcendae* causa tertio tum (366) post conditam urbem lectisternium fuit« (an arcane bit of antiquarian knowledge; at 5.13.6 Livy records the first celebration of *lectisternium*, but he never mentions the second).

13 Cf. MacBain, passim (but he discusses the procedural questions only incidentally); E. Saint-Denis, Les énumérations de prodiges dans l' œuvre de Tite-Live, RPh 16, 1942, 126-142, and, above all, the classic studies by Luterbacher, esp. 60-69; Wülker, esp. 26-50, 64-70, 76-80; Wissowa 390-392. R. Bloch, Les prodiges romains e la »procuratio prodigiorum«, RIDA 2, 1949, 119-131, is quite inexact. On the sources of Livy, see esp. E. Rawson, Prodigy Lists and the Use of the Annales Maximi, CQ 21, 1971, 158-169, and, contra, Briscoe 1973, 11-12; B. W. Frier, Libri Annales Pontificum Romanorum: The Origins of the Annalistic Tradition (Papers and Monographs of the American Academy in Rome 27), Rome 1979, 20, 272-274. See also the recent and important contribution by R. Drews, Pontiffs, Prodigies, and the Disappearance of the *Annales maximi*, CP 83, 1988, 289-299. I am in full agreement with his statement that »the *Annales maximi* were composed for a religious purpose: they were a record of past prodigies, expiations and *eventus*« (p. 296). The last scholar to use them was Valerius Antias, and he was the source of Livy for the reports of prodigies (p. 294).

14 On the theory of the auspices, see Linderski, passim, with further (ample) literature.

15 *auspicato cum populo agi*: 3.20.6; *concilia populi auspicato (geruntur)*: 1.36.6; *comitia centuriata, quibus consules tribunosque militares creatis* convened *auspicato*: 5.52.17; *magistratus (creantur) auspicato*: 6.41.6; 6.41.10; *leges auspicato (feruntur)*: 6.41.10; *interrex proditus auspicato*: 6.41.6; and other examples listed in Packard, I, 542-543 s. v. Most interesting is Livy's description of the clash between the king Tarquinius Priscus and the augur Attus Navius (1.36.2-8). It celebrates »il trionfo dell'arte augurale« (Musti, 52): »auguriis certe sacerdotioque augurum tantus honos accessit ut nihil belli domique postea nisi auspicato gereretur, concilia populi, exercitus vocati, summa rerum, ubi aves non admissent, dirimerentur« (see Musti, 50-64, for a penetrating discussion of the case).

16 See now the study by E. Wistrand, Felicitas Imperatoria, Göteborg 1987, esp. 16-26: Felicitas in Livy.

17 ILS 20 = ILLRP 122: »duct(u) / auspicio imperioque«.

18 Camillus: 5.46.6; 5.49.6; 6.12.6; Scipio Africanus: 28.16.14; 28.38.1; 28.41.10; 31.4.1; Flamininus: 36.17.2; Gracchus: 41.17.3; 41.28.8 (*imperio auspicioque*); Augustus: 28.12.12 (»Hispania ... prima Romanis inita provinciarum, quae quidem continentis sint, postrema omnium, nostra demum aetate,

67

ductu auspicioque Augusti Caesaris perdomita est«); T. Quinctius (cos. 468): 3.1.4.; Decemviri: 3.42.2; M. Valerius Corvus (cos. 343): 7.40.6; Q. Publilius Philo (cos. 339): 8.12.6; Q. Fabius Maximus Rullianus (mag. eq. 325): 8.31.1 (in his own speech, also mentioning his *felicitas*); 8.33.22; P. Cornelius Scipio (in a speech of his son, the future Africanus): 26.41.13; L. Aemilius Regillus, praetor in 190 and victor in a naval battle over the fleet of Antiochus: 40.52.5 (in a partially corrupt text: »auspicio, imperio felicitate ductuque eius«); P. Mucius Scaevola and M. Aemilius Lepidus (coss. 175): 41.19.2 (also a mention of *supplicationes*); App. Claudius (procos. 174): 41.28.1 (»supplicatio... ob res prospere gestas in Hispania ductu auspicioque Ap. Claudi proconsulis«); L. Anicius, praetor in 168: 45.3.2 (also a mention of *supplicatio*). See also 10.7.7: »numerarentur duces eorum annorum, quibus plebeiorum ductu et auspicio res geri coeptae sint; numerarentur triumphi«; 7.32.10; 10.18.1.

19 Cf. Ogilvie, 553-567; M. Reinhold, From Republic to Principate. An Historic Commentary on Cassius Dio's *Roman History* Books 49-52 (36-29 B. C.), Atlanta 1988, 162-163 (both with further literature). H. Dessau (Livius und Augustus, Hermes 41, 1906, 142 ff.) was the first scholar to combine Livy's account with the notice in Cassius Dio (51.24.4) concerning M. Licinius Crassus, proconsul of Macedonia, who in 29 B. C. had killed in battle and stripped of his armor Deldo, the king of the Bastarnae. His claim to the *spolia* was rejected by Octavian (or formally by the senate) on the grounds that he did not hold full *imperium*. See Syme, 43-47 = 418-421, and now above all the illuminating discussion by E. Badian in this volume (cf. also E. Badian, ›Crisis Theories‹ and the Beginning of the Principate, Romanitas-Christianitas, Festschrift Johannes Straub, Berlin 1982, 38-41). For the technical aspects of the case (*imperium* and *auspicium*), see also (but not necessarily embrace) the explications proposed by H. S. Versnel, Triumphus, Leiden 1970, 305-313, and R. M. Rampelberg, Les dépouilles opimes à Rome, des débuts de la République à Octave, Revue Historique de Droit 56, 1978, 191-214. L. Schumacher in his erudite study, Die imperatorischen Akklamationen der Triumvirn und die auspicia des Augustus, Historia 34, 1985, 207-212, discusses the *auspicia* and the triumph of Crassus, but not his claim to the *spolia opima*.

20 De div. 2.71-72. See also Festus 474 L. s.v. *silentio surgere* and 476 L. s.v. *sinistrum*. Cf. Liv. 8.23.15: »consul oriens de nocte silentio diceret dictatorem« (and the comment in Linderski, 2173-2174, n. 94).

21 For the phrases *auspicio adesse* and *in auspicio esse* (*auspicio interesse*), see Cic., de div. 2.71; de leg. 3.43; de rep. 2.16; ad Att. 2.12.1.

22 Cic., de div. 2.72-73; Servius ad Aen. 6.198.

23 Cic., de div. 2.72; Festus 386 L. (quoting the augur Appius Claudius Pulcher; cf. J. Linderski, The Libri Reconditi, HSCP 89, 1985, 226-227).

24 Cf. Liv. 1.34.9: »Accepisse id augurium laeta dicitur Tanaquil«, 6.12.7 (see above, n. 12); 7.26.3-4 (of M. Valerius Corvinus): »conserenti iam manum Romano corvus repente in galea consedit in hostem versus. quod primo ut augurium caelo missum *laetus* accepit tribunus«; 7.26.7: »Camillus laetum militem victoria tribuni, *laetum* tam praesentibus ac secundis dis ire in proelium iubet«; 26.41.18 (in the speech of Scipio): »dii immortales imperii Romani praesides ... auguriis auspiciisque et per nocturnos etiam visus omnia *laeta* ac prospera portendunt« (also in this passage the *auspicia* and *auguria* appear in the sense and in the function of a presage, whereas in the strict augural doctrine *auspicium* expressed solely divine consent for action, cf. Cic., de div. 2.70 of the Roman augurs: »non enim sumus ii nos augures qui avium reliquorumve signorum observatione futura dicamus«); Lucanus, Phars. 5.396 (cf. Suet., Caes. 77); Festus 476 L = Ateius Capito, fr. 22 Strzelecki: »Sinistrum in auspicando significare ait Ateius Capito *laetum* et prosperum auspicium«. Cf. Hickson, 43.

25 Cf. P. Catalano, Contributo allo studio del diritto augurale I, Torino 1960, 42-45.

26 For a discussion of the augural doctrine of *ementita auspicia*, see Linderski, 2214-2215, and 2198 (the case of Antonius); C. Schäublin, Ementita Auspicia, Wiener Studien N.F. 20, 1986, 171 ff. (but he does not discuss the passage of Livy).

68

27 Technically it was a (favorable) *auspicium oblativum*, but Livy calls it *augurium* (*quo laetus augurio consul*), using the term in the colloquial sense of presage.

28 Cf. Stübler, 186-201.

29 See 5.21.1: »dictator (M. Camillus) auspicato egressus« (Veii is taken); 6.12.7 (above, n. 12); 10.39.8 (see above in the text on Papirius and the victory at Aquilonia); 9.14.3-4 (below, n. 32); 22.42.8: Aemilius Paulus »cum ei sua sponte cunctanti pulli quoque auspicio non addixissent, nuntiari iam efferenti porta signa collegae iussit« (Terentius Varro remembering *Flamini recens casus* obeyed, and the debacle at Cannae, as Livy puts it, was postponed); 27.16.15: »Fabio auspicanti, priusquam egrederetur ab Tarento, aves semel atque iterum non addixerunt; hostia quoque caesa consulenti deos haruspex cavendum a fraude hostili et ab insidiis praedixit« (the Cunctator remained in Tarentum, and avoided the *insidiae* of Hannibal); 34.14.1: M. Porcius Cato as consul in 195 »cum auspicio operam dedisset, profectus« (victory); 35.48.13: the envoy of Antiochus lambasts Flamininus: nobody ever had seen him in battle as a commander but rather »auspicantem immolantemque et vota nuncupantem« – here Livy implies *e contrario* that it was not solely Roman armies but above all Roman *religio* that triumphed over the Greeks (cf. Liebeschuetz 1979, 4; Briscoe 1981, 212-213); 38.26.1: »consul (of 189 Manlius Vulso) cum auspicio operam dedisset, deinde immolasset, ... copias educit« (the Galatians routed); 41.18.4-14: the consul of 176 Q. Petilius performed the *sortitio* for the selection of his field of operations *non auspicato*, and furthermore »etiam ex pullario auditum est vitium in auspicio fuisse, nec id consulem ignorasse«. Petilius was killed in battle (cf. Linderski, 2173-2175). The cumulative message of these examples is not to be missed: without valid auspices no victory.

30 Cf. Mommsen I³, 61-67; A. Magdelain, Recherches sur l'*imperium*, Paris 1968, esp. 40 ff. A. Giovannini, Consulare Imperium, Basel 1983, esp. 7-19; Linderski, 2162 ff.

31 One has to distinguish carefully the cases of the *repetitio auspiciorum* and the *renovatio auspiciorum* (cf. Mommsen I³, 91, 99-100) although Livy does not always succeed in keeping these two very different acts terminologically apart. When the auspices of the consuls are contaminated by a *vitium*, this means that their successors will be elected through the agency of contaminated auspices and will inherit the contamination. The only way to break this chain of contamination is through the abdication of all magistrates; the auspices then return from the sphere of action to their receptacle among the *patres* (the patrician senators). By this act they are cleansed and ready to be transmitted by the interrex to the next pair of consuls, pure and pristine again. The *repetitio auspiciorum* is on the other hand a totally different thing. It does not concern the whole office of the magistrate, but solely his particular field of action: the sphere *militiae*. Livy mentions four cases of the *renovatio auspiciorum*: 5.17.3 (the magistrates *vitio creati*; it was decided that they »abdicarent se magistratu, auspicia de integro repeterentur [= *renovarentur*] et interregnum iniretur«); 5.31.7 (»consulibusque morbo implicitis placuit per interregnum renovari auspicia«); 5.52.9 (»instauratio sacrorum auspiciorumque renovatio«); 6.5.6 (»in civitate plena religionum, tunc etiam ab recenti clade [sc. Alliensi] superstitiosis principibus, ut renovarentur auspicia, res ad interregnum rediit«). There are also four cases of the *repetitio auspiciorum*: 8.32.4 (discussed below in the text); 10.3.3-8 (the dictator returns to Rome *auspiciorum repetendorum causa*; his master of horse *pabulatum egressus* falls in a trap and is defeated. This neatly illustrates the principle that one should not engage the enemy *incertis auspiciis*, and Livy himself points back to the case of 8.32.4); 23.19.3-5 (again the dictator returns to Rome to repeat the auspices, and orders his master of horse *ne quid absente eo rei gereret*; the magister equitum obeys – hence no calamity); 23.36.9-10 (Fabius Cunctator as cos. suff. in 215 prudently refrained from action »occupatus primo auspiciis repetendis, dein prodigiis ‹procurandis› ...; expiantique ea haud facile litari haruspices respondebant«). The phrase thus refers primarily to the renewal of military auspices of the commander, but once Livy uses it in a more restricted sense of repeating the *auspicatio* (after an unfavorable omen) on the next day (9.39.1: »Dictator postero die auspiciis repetitis pertulit legem«).

69

32 A few years later, in 320, the same Papirius, this time as consul, appears again in the company of a *pullarius* (9.14.3-4): »agentibus divina humanaque, quae adsolent, cum acie dimicandum est, consulibus Tarentini legati occursare ...; quibus Papirius ait: ›auspicia secunda esse, Tarentini, pullarius nuntiat; litatum praeterea est egregie; auctoribus dis ... ad rem gerendam proficiscimur‹« (victory ensues).

33 *dictator a pullario monitus: monere* is a standard term in such situations; cf. Linderski, 2200-2203.

34 Cf. Linderski, 2162 ff.

35 Cf. Magdelain, (above, n. 30), 41, n. 4: »Même si les reproches adressés à Flaminius ont été inventés pour expliquer Trasimène, l'argumentation juridique que reproduit Tite-Live est parfaite.«

36 Cf. I. O. M. Valeton, De modis auspicandi Romanorum, Mnemosyne 18, 1890, 440-443, 446-452; J. Bayet, Les malédictions du tribun C. Ateius Capito, Hommages à Georges Dumézil, Bruxelles 1960, 31-45 (= J. Bayet, Croyances et rites dans la Rome antique, Paris 1971, 353-365; Linderski, 2200-2202, esp. n. 198; and especially see now Schäublin, (above, n. 26), 169 ff.

37 Syme, 63 = 439.

38 Obs. 71-72. See the lists in Wülker, 91 and MacBain 104 (these lists are incomplete for they include only the prodigies classified by Wülker and MacBain as *prodigia publica*).

39 Syme, 63 = 439.

40 See the excellent study by I. Becher, Tiberüberschwemmungen. Die Interpretation von Prodigien in Augusteischer Zeit, Klio 67, 1985, 471-479.

41 This is also the opinion of Wülker, 71; he failed, however, to see the political background of *der Verfall des Prodigienglaubens*. He offers only a flat and comfortingly passive observation that under Augustus »in keiner Weise versucht worden ist den Prodigienglauben wieder zu heben«.

70

BIBLIOGRAPHICAL INFORMATION ON
ORIGINAL PUBLICATION

1. *"Si Vis Pacem Para Bellum:* Concepts of Defensive Imperialism". In: William V. Harris (ed.), *The Imperialism of Mid-Republican Rome = Papers and Monographs of the American Academy in Rome* 29 (1984) 133–164 (and discussion contributions, pp. 55, 188–189, here not reproduced).
2. "Mommsen and Syme: Law and Power in the Principate of Augustus". In: Kurt A. Raaflaub and Mark Toher (eds.), *Between Republic and Empire. Interpretations of Augustus and His Principate* (Berkeley 1990) 42–53.
3. "Garden Parlors: Nobles and Birds". In: Robert I. Curtis (ed.), *Studia Pompeiana & Classica in Honor of Wilhelmina F. Jashemski.* Volume II: *Classica* (New Rochelle 1989) 105–127.
4. Review of: Michael Crawford, *The Roman Republic* (Hassocks 1978). In: *Classical Philology* 77 (1982) 174–178.
5. "Constitutional Aspects of the Consular Elections in 59 B.C", *Historia* 14 (1965) 423–442.
6. "Were Pompey and Crassus Elected in Absence to their First Consulship?". In: *Mélanges offerts à Kazimierz Michalowski* (Warszawa 1966) 523–526.
7. "A. Gabinius A.F. Capito and the First Voter in the Legislative Comitia Tributa", *Zeitschrift für Papyrologie und Epigraphik* 12 (1973) 247–252 (together with A. Kamińska-Linderska).
8. "The Dramatic Date of Varro, *De re rustica,* Book III and the Elections in 54", *Historia* 34 (1985) 248–254.
9. "Buying the Vote: Electoral Corruption in the Late Republic", *The Ancient World* 11 (1985) 87–94.
10. "Three Trials in 54 B.C.: Sufenas, Cato, Procilius and Cicero, *Ad Atticum* 4.15.4". In: *Studi in onore di Edoardo Volterra* 2 (Milano 1971) 281–302 (offprints dated to 1969).
11. Review of: Claude Nicolet, *L'ordre équestre à l'époque républicaine* (312–43 av. J.-C.). Tome 2: *Prosopographie des chevaliers romains* (Paris 1974). In: *Classical Philology* 72 (1977) 55–60.
12. *"Legibus Praefecti Mittebantur* (Mommsen and Festus 262.5,13 L)", *Historia* 28 (1979) 247–250.

13. "Rome, Aphrodisias and the *Res Gestae*: the *Genera Militiae* and the Status of Octavian", *Journal of Roman Studies* 74 (1984) 74–80.

14. "Usu, farre, coemptione. Bemerkungen zur Überlieferung eines Rechtsatzes", *Zeitschrift der Savigny-Stiftung für Rechtsgeschichte. Romanistische Abteilung* 101 (1984) 301–311.

15. "Der Senat und die Vereine". In: *Gesellschaft und Recht im Griechisch-Römischen Altertum* 1 = *Deutsche Akademie der Wissenschaften zu Berlin. Schriften der Sektion für Altertumswissenschaft* 52 (Berlin 1968) 94–132.

16. "Ciceros Rede *pro Caelio* und die Ambitus- und Vereinsgesetzgebung der ausgehenden Republik", *Hermes* 89 (1961) 106–119.

17. "Suetons Bericht über die Vereinsgesetzgebung unter Caesar und Augustus", *Zeitschrift der Savigny-Stiftung für Rechtsgeschichte. Romanistische Abteilung* 79 (1962) 396–402.

18. "Cicero and Sallust on Vargunteius", *Historia* 12 (1963) 511–512.

19. "The Surnames and the Alleged Affinity of M. Caelius Rufus", *Eos* 56, fasc. 1 (1966 [1968]) 146–150.

20. "The Aedileship of Favonius, Curio the Younger and Cicero's Election to the Augurate", *Harvard Studies in Classical Philology* 76 (1972) 181–200.

21. "The Quaestorship of Marcus Antonius", *Phoenix* 28 (1974) 213–223 (together with A. Kamińska-Linderska).

22. "The Mother of Livia Augusta and the Aufidii Lurcones of the Republic", *Historia* 23 (1974) 463–480.

23. "Two Quaestorships", *Classical Philology* 70 (1975) 35–38.

24. Review of: Magnus Wistrand, *Cicero Imperator. Studies in Cicero's Correspondence 51–47 B.C.* (Göteborg 1979). In: *Gnomon* 52 (1980) 782–785.

25. Review of: Thomas N. Mitchell, *Cicero, The Ascending Years* (New Haven 1979). In: *Classical Journal* 77 (1982) 275–277.

26. "De villa Appio Pulchro falso attributa", *La Parola del Passato* 34, fasc. 193 (1980 [1981]) 272–273.

27. "*Patientia fregit*: M. Octavius and Ti. Gracchus (Cicero, *Brutus* 95)", *Athenaeum* 60 (1982) 244–247.

28. "The Aediles and the *Didascaliae*", *The Ancient History Bulletin* 1 (1987) 83–88.

29. "Roman Officers in the Year of Pydna", *American Journal of Philology* 111 (1990) 53–71.

30. "The Death of Pontia", *Rheinisches Museum* 133 (1990) 86–93.

31. "Two Speeches of Q. Hortensius. A Contribution to the Corpus Oratorum of the Roman Republic", *La Parola del Passato* 16, fasc. 79 (1961) 304–311.

32. "Vergil and Dionysius", *Vergilius* 38 (1992) 3–11.
33. "Two *Cruces* in Seneca, *De vita beata* 25.2", *American Journal of Philology* 103 (1982) 89–95.
34. "*Aes olet*: Petronius 50.7 and Martial 9.59.11", *Harvard Studies in Classical Philology* 94 (1992) 349–353.
35. "Alfred the Great and the Tradition of Ancient Geography", *Speculum* 39 (1964) 434–439.
36. "Notes on *CIL* I² 364", *La Parola del Passato* 13, fasc. 58 (1958) 47–50.
37. "*Libiis* or *Libens*? A Note on a New Dedication to Liber Pater from Dacia", *Latomus* 34 (1975) 209–211.
38. "Natalis Patavii", *Zeitschrift für Papyrologie und Epigraphik* 50 (1983) 227–232.
39. "Julia in Regium", *Zeitschrift für Papyrologie und Epigraphik* 72 (1988) 181–200.
40. "*Certis Calendis*", *Epigraphica* 52 (1990 [1991]) 85–96.
41. "Updating the *CIL* for Italy", *Journal of Roman Archaeology* 3 (1990) 313–320.
42. "Zum Namen Competalis", *Glotta* 39 (1960) 145–149.
43. Review of: D.R. Shackleton Bailey, *Two Studies in Roman Nomenclature* (*American Classical Studies* 3 [1976]). In: *Phoenix* 31 (1977 [1978]) 372–375.
44. "Amianus", *Zeitschrift für Papyrologie und Epigraphik* 30 (1978) 158.
45a. "*Fumum vendere* and *fumo necare*", *Glotta* 65 (1987) 137–146.
45b. "*Fumo necare*: An Addendum", *Glotta* 65 (1987) 250–251.
46. "The Surname of M. Antonius Creticus and the cognomina *ex victis gentibus*", *Zeitschrift für Papyrologie und Epigraphik* 80 (1990) 157–164.
47. "Römischer Staat und die Götterzeichen: zum Problem der obnuntiatio", *Jahrbuch der Universität Düsseldorf* 1969–1970 [1971] 309–322.
48. "Cicero and Roman Divination", *La Parola del Passato* 37, fasc. 202 (1982 [1983]) 12–38.
49. "Watching the Birds: Cicero the Augur and the Augural *templa*", *Classical Philology* 81 (1986) 330–340.
50. "The *Libri Reconditi*", *Harvard Studies in Classical Philology* 89 (1985) 207–234.
51. "*Exta* and *Aves*: An Emendation in Rufinus, *Origenis in Numeros Homilia* 17.2", *Harvard Studies in Classical Philology* 85 (1981) 213–215.
52. "Sannio and Remus", *Mnemosyne* 42 (1989) 90–93.

53. *"Auspicia et Auguria Romana ... Summo Labore Collecta*: A Note on Minucius Felix, *Octavius* 26.1", *Classical Philology* 77 (1982) 148–150.

54. "A Witticism of Appuleius Saturninus", *Rivista di Filologia* 111 (1983 [1984]) 452–459.

55. "Religious Aspects of the Conflict of the Orders: The Case of *confarreatio*". In: Kurt A. Raaflaub (ed.), *Social Struggles in Archaic Rome. New Perspectives on the Conflict of the Orders* (Berkeley 1986) 244–261.

56. "The Auspices and the Struggle of the Orders". In: Walter Eder (ed.), *Staat und Staatlichkeit in der frühen römischen Republik* (Stuttgart 1990) 34–48 (and discussion contributions, pp. 88–89, 395, 477–478, 556, here not reproduced).

57. "Heliogabalus, Alexander Severus and the *ius confarreationis*: A Note on the *Historia Augusta*". In: M. Piérart et O. Curty (eds.), *Historia Testis. Mélanges d'épigraphie, d'histoire ancienne et de philologie offerts à Tadeusz Zawadzki* (Fribourg 1989) 207–215.

58. Review of: Thomas Köves-Zulauf, *Reden und Schweigen: römische Religion bei Plinius Maior* (München 1972). In: *Classical Philology* 70 (1975) 284–289.

59. "A Non-Misunderstood Text Concerning Tages", *La Parola del Passato* 33, fasc. 180 (1978) 195–196.

60. Review of: *Le délit religieux dans la cité antique* (Rome 1981). In: *Classical Philology* 79 (1984) 174–177.

61. Review of: L.B. Van Der Meer, *The Bronze Liver of Piacenza* (Amsterdam 1987). In: *Classical Philology* 85 (1990) 67–71.

62. Review of Ida Paladino, *Fratres Arvales: Storia di un collegio sacerdotale romano* (Roma 1988). In: *Classical Philology* 86 (1991) 84–87.

63. Review of D.S. Potter, *Prophecy and History in the Crisis of the Roman Empire: A Historical Commentary on the Thirteenth Sibylline Oracle* (Oxford 1990). In: *Classical Philology* 88 (1993) 180–183.

64. "Roman Religion in Livy". In: Wolfgang Schuller (ed.), *Livius. Aspekte seines Werkes* (Konstanz 1993) 53–70.

Addenda and Corrigenda
(1994)

(The first page number refers to the pagination of the volume;
the second to the pagination of the original contribution)

ABBREVIATIONS

Alexander, *Trials* = M.C. Alexander, *Trials in the Late Roman Republic* (Toronto 1990).

Broughton, *MRR* 3 = T.R.S. Broughton, *The Magistrates of the Roman Republic*. Vol III, *Supplement* (Atlanta 1986).

David, *PJ* = J.-M. David, *Le patronat judiciaire au dernier siècle de la république romaine* (= *BEFAR* 277, Rome 1977).

Gruen, *LGRR* = E.S. Gruen, *The Last Generation of the Roman Republic* (Berkeley 1974).

Linderski, *Kolegia* = J. Linderski, *Państwo a kolegia. Ze studiów nad historia rzymskich stowarzyszen u schylku republiki* [*Staat und Vereine. Studien über die Geschichte des römischen Vereinswesens am Ende der Republik*] (Kraków 1961).

Linderski, *Assembly* = J. Linderski, *Rzymskie zgromadzenie wyborcze od Sulli do Cezara* [*The Roman Electoral Assembly from Sulla to Caesar*] (Kraków 1966)

Linderski, *AL* = J. Linderski, "The Augural Law", *ANRW* 2.16.3 (1986).

Marshall, *Asconius* = B.A. Marshall, *A Historical Commentary on Asconius* (Columbia, MO., 1965).

Shackleton Bailey, *CLA* = D.R. Shackleton Bailey, *Cicero's Letters to Atticus* 1–7 (Cambridge 1965, 1965, 1968, 1968, 1966, 1967, 1970).

Shackleton Bailey, *CEF* = D.R. Shackleton Bailey, *Cicero. Epistulae ad Familiares* 1–2 (Cambridge 1977).

Shackleton Bailey, *CQF-MB* = D.R. Shackleton Bailey, *Cicero. Epistulae ad Quintum Fratrem et M. Brutum* (Cambridge 1980).

1
SI VIS PACEM PARA BELLUM:
CONCEPTS OF DEFENSIVE IMPERIALISM
(1984)

In a rare and gratifying conjunction of minds E. Frézouls, "Sur l'historiographie de l'impérialisme romain", *Ktema* 8 (1983 [1986]) 141–162, has arrived at a similar appraisal of both Roman imperialism and of its modern historians.

Cf. also E. Hermon, "L'impérialisme romain républicain: Approches historiographiques et approche d'analyse", *Athenaeum* 77 [N.S. 67] (1989) 407–416, esp. 408–409, and various papers published in *Gouvernants et gouvernés dans l'Imperium Romanum*, ed. by E. Hermon (= *Cahiers des Études Anciennes* 26 [1991]), esp. Z. Yavetz, "Toward a Further Step Into the Study of Roman Imperialism" (pp. 3–22); D. Baronowski, "The Romans' Awareness of Their Imperialism in the Second Century B.C." (pp. 173–181).

Also two voluminous and stimulating accounts and appraisals of Roman expansion in the East and of Roman imperialism have appeared: E. Gruen, *The Hellenistic World and the Coming of Rome* 1–2 (Berkeley 1984); J.-L. Ferrary, *Philhellénisme et impérialisme. Aspects idéologiques de la conquête romaine du monde hellénistique* (*BEFAR* 271, Paris 1988). On Gruen, see my remarks in *Journal of Interdisciplinary History* 16 (1985) 305–307.

For an appraisal of the Roman conquest of Italy, see R.J. Rowland, Jr., "Rome's Earliest Imperialism", *Latomus* 42 (1983) 749–762, esp. 761: "the Romans, far from preoccupying themselves with defensive wars (although many of their wars in this period were in fact defensive), followed a repeated pattern of behavior, outflanking allies and potential enemies, and reacting to those responses as if the Romans were aggrieved party".

P. 11 = 143: on the *metus hostilis*, see H. Bellen, *Metus Gallicus— Metus Punicus. Zur Furchtmotiv in der römischen Republik* (Abh. Mainz 1985, 3), to be read in conjunction with the remarks by A. Eckstein, *CJ* 82.4 (1987) 335–338.

Pp. 13–16 = 145–148 (and 27–28 = 160–161, nn. 66–67): see now an appraisal of T. Frank by T.R.S. Broughton, in W.W. Briggs and W.M. Calder III (eds.), *Classical Scholarship. A Biographical Encyclopedia* (New York 1990) 68–76, and by the present writer in *American National Biography* (forthcoming).

P. 19 = 151: see now L. Polverini, "Fraccaro and De Sanctis", *Athenaeum* 73 [= N.S. 63] (1985) 68–81 (and pp. 82–113 containing a selection of the correspondence between the two scholars).

Errata. Read:

P. 10 = 142, line 8 from bottom: "But".

2

MOMMSEN AND SYME:
LAW AND POWER IN THE PRINCIPATE OF AUGUSTUS
(1990)

See also other contributions published together with this article in the same collection, esp. H. Galsterer, "A Man, a Book and a Method: Sir Ronald Syme's *Roman Revolution* after Fifty Years" (1–20); W. Eder, "Augustus and the Power of Tradition: The Augustan Principate as Binding Link between Republic and Empire" (71–122). I repeat: when Mommsen writes as a jurist it is fruitless to criticise him for not writing as a historian.

See now the brilliant juxtaposition (and appraisal) of the "Two Principes: Augustus and Sir Ronald Syme" by G. Alföldy, *Athenaeum* 81 (1993) 101–122.

P. 39 = 49 (and n. 34): on Varro, see also No 3.

P. 39 = 49, n. 36: in the meantime J. Scheid produced not only another book on arval prosopography but also a magnificent study of doctrine and ritual (see below, *Addenda* to No 62).

P. 43 = 53, n. 55: the Hensel-Nachschriften have now appeared: T. Mommsen, *Römische Kaisergeschichte*. Nach der Vorlesungsmitschriften von S. und P. Hensel 1882–1885 herausgegeben von B. und A. Demandt (München 1992.)

3

GARDEN PARLORS: NOBLES AND BIRDS
(1989)

On Varro's dialogue, see now also W.J. Tatum, "The Poverty of Appii Pulchri: Varro, *De Re Rustica* 3.16.1–2", *CQ* 42 (1992) 190–200. For a short recent discussion of Cicero's dialogue technique, see J.G.F. Powell, *Cicero. Cato Maior De Senectute* (Cambridge 1988) 1–24.

P. 58 = 119 (and p. 65 = 126, n. 96): on the Fundilii, cf. J. Suolahti, "A Submerged Gens", *Arctos* 13 (1979) 161–167.

Errata:

P. 55 = 116, line 5: the square bracket should be placed in line 7, after "they counsel". P. 62 = 123, n. 60, and P. 64 = 125, n. 94: disregard the quotation marks. The titles should have been set in italics. P. 64 = 125, n. 91: "Zucchelli".

4

REVIEW OF:
MICHAEL CRAWFORD, *THE ROMAN REPUBLIC*
(1982)

A new edition of Crawford's book appeared in 1993 (Harvard University Press, Cambridge, MA).

5

CONSTITUTIONAL ASPECTS OF THE CONSULAR ELECTIONS IN 59 B.C.
(1965)

Pp. 73–74 = 425–426: on Bibulus, and *obnuntiatio*, see now my remarks in *AL* 2166–2168, 2195–2198, 2202–2203, 2205–2206, 2209–2210 (cf. also No 50, pp. 513–514 = 224–225, and n. 64). That the notice of *obnuntiatio* had to be delivered in person was accepted by L.R. Taylor, "The Dating of Major Legislation and Elections in Caesar's First Consulate", *Historia* 17 (1968) 178–179. Cf. also U. Hall, "Notes on M. Fulvius Flaccus", *Athenaeum* 55 [= 65] (1977) 284–285. T.N. Mitchell, "The Leges Clodiae and Obnuntiatio", *CQ* 36 (1986) 172–176, argues that it was the *lex Clodia* that introduced "an explicit requirement that the announcement of unfavourable omens be made in person to the presiding magistrate at an appointed time and place" (p. 175). His solution was emphatically endorsed by W.J. Tatum, "Cicero's Opposition to the Lex Clodia de Collegiis", *CQ* 40 (1990) 189. That this provision formed part of the Clodian law is plausible indeed; but I still believe that the law only restated the existing regulations. See also the excellent article by C. Schäublin, "Ementita auspicia", *WS* 20 (1986) 165–181, esp. 172–181; and the studies by L.A. Burckhardt, *Politische Strategien der Optimaten in der späten römischen Republik* (Stuttgart 1988) 178–209, esp. 198; L. Thommen, *Das Volkstribunat der späten römischen Republik* (Stuttgart 1989) 241–248; L. de Libero, *Obstruktion* (Stuttgart 1992) 56–64, 99–101; and, most recently, clear and intelligent remarks by K. Heikkilä, "Lex non iure rogata", in: *Senatus Populusque Romanus. Studies in Roman Republican Legislation* (= Acta Instituti Romani Finlandiae 13 [Helsinki 1993]) 125–126, 136–141 (with the valid point that Bibulus' *obnuntiationes per edictum* could be regarded as a continuation of his original attempt to deliver the notice of *obnuntiatio* in person).

Pp. 76–81 = 428–433: on the presidency at the elections, see the courteous rejoinder by L.R. Taylor and T.R.S. Broughton, "The Order of Consuls' Names in Official Republican Lists", *Historia* 17 (1968) 166–171. They accept that Bibulus was charged with the conduct of the *comitia* (168), but argue that Caesar was elected first (see also Taylor [in the article adduced above] 188–193). As a result they abandoned their original theory. The priority of election decided the order of the names in the *Fasti*, and the order in which the *fasces* were held; the consul first elected presided over the first meeting of the senate in January. But the presidency over the elections was decided by "the old methods of *comparatio* and *sortitio*", with the lot being the usual method (p. 171). The subject has been discussed in some detail in my *Assembly* 22-34, and again in the excellent monograph by R. Rilinger, *Der Einfluss des Wahlleiters bei den römischen Konsulwahlen von 366 bis 50 v. Chr.* (München 1976) 40–59. He has demonstrated that both before and after Sulla there existed a "Verbindung zwischen der Stellung in den Fasten und der Wahlleitung" (p. 54), and that the statistical material reflects the constitutional arrangement. For 59, following Taylor and Broughton, he assumes Caesar as elected first. In that configuration the only obstacle remains the edict of Bibulus. Rilinger interprets the difficulty away by positing that Bibulus' edict (perhaps backed by a decree of the senate) concerned what was strictly constitutionally Caesar's sphere of competence, but that Caesar because of political considerations chose to obey his colleague (pp. 55–57). We need a better, and a more elegant solution than any of the scholars involved in this debate has been able to excogitate.

A. Drummond, "Some Observations on the Order of the Consuls' Names", *Athenaeum* 56 [= 66] (1978) 80–108, rightly points out (pp. 83–85) that the right to make a *relatio* in the senate was not limited to the consul actually holding the *fasces*, but he was not able to undermine the idea that the priority of election determined the priority in the consular lists, or that the consul elected first was also the first to hold the *fasces*. On the symbolism of the *fasces*, see A.J. Marshall, "Symbols and Showmanship in Roman Public Life: The Fasces", *Phoenix* 38 (1984) 120–141.

The constitutional importance of the consul elected first is underscored by the mention of the ὕπατος ὁ πρῶτος γενόμενος in the so-called *lex de piratis persequendis*; see the penetrating remarks by J.-L. Ferrary, "Recherches sur la législation de Saturninus et de Glaucia", *MEFRA* 89 (1977) 619–660 at 633–634, 647–651. Cf. also Vergil's description of the opening of the gates of Ianus, *Aen.* 7.613: "insignis reserat stridentia limina consul", and Servius' comment: "insignem accipe primo loco creatum, licet similem habeat potestatem".

P. 81 = 433, n. 41: on *consul prior* in Livy 32.28.4, see the correction by Taylor and Broughton, 167, n. 6.

Pp. 85–88 = 437–440: on *professio*, see a detailed discussion in my book *Assembly* 52–73, and in Rilinger, *Wahlleiter* 63–94 (with further literature, especially with a discussion of opinions of Astin [1962], Earl [1965], Staveley [1972], Hall [1972]). He believes that "Die persönliche Professio wurde ziemlich sicher als Ad-hoc-Massnahme zur Verhinderung von Caesar's Kandidatur im Jahre 60 eingeführt" (p. 91). This is most unlikely; it was probably aimed at an anticipated candidature of Pompey or of his henchmen (and was passed either in 63 or 62). B. Levick, "Professio", *Athenaeum* 59 [= 69] (1981) 378–388, contends that a formal *professio* to the presiding magistrate was never obligatory under the Republic. A remarkable argument, but not entirely convincing. The author does not pay sufficient attention, I believe, to the terms *rationem habere* and *nomen accipere*. For further remarks on *professio*, and its application in politics, see E. Badian, "The Death of Saturninus", *Chiron* 14 (1984) 112–115.

Corrections. Read:

P. 72 = 424, line 16: "compel"; line 31: "Lange's thesis". P. 73 = 425, line 35: "developed". P. 74 = 426, line 3: "conveying to". P. 75 = 427, n. 22 (on p. 76 = 428, line 4): "προύγραφε. κἄν". P. 76 = 428, line 3: "herald"; "form". P. 79 = 431, n. 31, line 5: "in". P. 81 = 433, line 5: "the Mommsenian"; line 14: "developed". P. 83 = 435, line 14: "the importance". P. 83 = 435, n. 48, line 2: "dates ... to". P. 90 = 442, line 6: "developed".

6

WERE POMPEY AND CRASSUS ELECTED IN ABSENCE TO THEIR FIRST CONSULSHIP?

(1966)

The solution presented in this article has been accepted i.a. by A. Ward, *Marcus Crassus and the Late Republic* (Columbia, MO, 1977) 100, n. 5; Broughton, *MRR* 3.165.

D. Stockton, "The First Consulship of Pompey", *Historia* 22 (1973) 205–218, writes (p. 208): "Had Pompey celebrated his triumph in 71, and then waited to be a candidate in person and not in absence for election in 70 to hold office in 69, the world would still have turned on its axis". He still does not seem to realize that Pompey was present at his election in the *comitia centuriata*, and that in this year there was still no legal requirement of *professio* in person.

P. 91 = 523, n. 2: on the date of Crassus' praetorship, cf. Broughton, *MRR* 3.120.

P. 91 = 523, n. 3: on *professio*, see above, *Addenda* to No 5 (pp. 85–88 = 437–440).

I take this opportunity to indicate corrections. Read:

P. 92 = 524, line 5: "the 19th". P. 93 = 525, line 7: omit "the" before "Rullus".

7

A. GABINIUS A.F. CAPITO AND THE FIRST VOTER
IN THE LEGISLATIVE COMITIA TRIBUTA
(1973)

See now the exemplary study of all aspects of the inscription by J.-C. Dumont, J.-L. Ferrary, P. Moreau, C. Nicolet, *Insula Sacra. La loi Gabinia-Calpurnia de Délos (58 av. J.-C)* (Rome 1980), esp. 3, and 45–61 ("Les rogateurs de la loi" by C. Nicolet), esp. 47–48 (accepting the restitution of the Greek text proposed on p. 98 = 250); 54, n. 26 (accepting the reading of the Latin *praescriptio* proposed on pp. 99–100 = 251–252).

P. 96 = 248, n. 9: cf. C. Konrad, "A Note on the Stemma of the Gabinii Capitones", *Klio* 66 (1984) 151–156.

Errata. Read:

P. 98 = 250, line 8: "[Αὖλος Γ]αβείνιος".

8

THE DRAMATIC DATE OF VARRO, *DE RE RUSTICA*, BOOK III
AND THE ELECTIONS IN 54
(1985)

S. Agache, "L'actualité de la Villa Publica en 55–54 av. J.-C.", in: *Urbs. Espace urbaine et histoire (Ier siècle av. J.-C. – IIIe siècle ap. J.-C.)* = Collection de l'École Française de Rome 98 (Rome 1987) 211–234, esp. 222–230, 233, discovers in the text of Varro *R.R.* 3.2.4 "ubi cohortes ad dilectum consuli adductae considant, ubi arma ostendant, ubi censores censu admittant populum" allusions to contemporary events and concerns, and on that basis assigns the dramatic date of the dialogue to 55–54. This argument is entirely in the eye of the beholder; Agache avoids confronting the thorny fact that in 54 no elections for curule magistracies took place, and that the triumph of Metellus Scipio cannot be dated to 55 (cf. Broughton, *MRR* 3.42).

P. 103 = 251, n. 21: of course we do know the official style of Scipio Metellus: *Q. Caecilius Q. f. Fab. Metellus Pius Scipio.* It is attested in the list of witnesses to the two *senatus consulta* quoted by Caelius Rufus in his letter to Cicero (*Fam.* 8.8.5,6; 29 Sep. 51). So also *IGRR* 4.409 (from Pergamon), where, however, the tribe is omitted. After his adoption (or rather *impositio nominis ferendi*) he himself seems never to have used the cognomen Nasica. Cf. my paper "Q. Scipio Imp." (forthcoming).

Pp. 104–105 = 252–253: on the meaning of *nuper*, see P.B. Harvey, "Cicero, *Epistulae Ad Quintum Fratrem et Ad Brutum*: Content and Comment", *Athenaeum* 78 (1990) 328, who ultimately quotes with approval the statement of D.R. Shackleton Bailey, *Onomasticon to Cicero's Speeches*[2] (Stuttgart 1992) 22: "the consideration uppermost in Cicero's mind [when using *nuper*] was not the actual length of time involved but the fact that the event he was recalling was the most recent of its kind". Belatedly I have discovered a passage in *The Scholia Bembina*, ed. by J.F. Mountford (Liverpool 1934) 52, where in the comment on Terentius' *Heautontimorumenos* 53 we read the following explanation: "*nuper* interdum ipsum tempus interdum spatium ab aliquo tempore indicat sed quia et longe [et] ante et paulo ante significat addidit *admodum*". This comes very close to Shackleton Bailey's understanding; and if modern students of Roman history had known this piece of ancient grammatical learning, various historical misconstructs could have been avoided.

9
BUYING THE VOTE:
ELECTORAL CORRUPTION IN THE LATE REPUBLIC
(1985)

For a recent solid discussion of the legislation against electoral malpractices (with further bibliography), see E.A. Bauerle, *Procuring an Election: Ambitus in the Roman Republic* (Diss. Michigan [Ann Arbor] 1990) passim. The book by L. Fascione, *'Crimen' e 'quaestio ambitus' nell'età repubblicana* (Milano 1984) has not much to recommend it: it is much less informed than the newer monograph of Bauerle, and it is much less detailed than the old studies by Rinkes and Telting. Of the various articles either postdating Bauerle or not listed in her monograph, see H. Kowalski, "Organizacja przekupstw wyborczych w Rzymie w okresie schylku republiki", *Acta Universitatis Wratislaviensis* 497 = *Antiquitas* 9 (Wroclaw 1983) 107–117 (with German summary [117–118]: "Die Durchführung der Wahlbestechung in Rom in der Zeit des Untergangs der Republik"); E. Maróti, "Deducere - Deductores", *Oikumene* 5 (1986) 237–242, esp. 241–242; É. Deniaux, "De l'*ambitio* à l'*ambitus*: les lieux de la propagande et de la corruption électorale à la fin de la république", in: *Urbs. Espace urbaine et histoire* (*I*[er] *siècle av. J.-C. – III*[e] *siècle ap. J.C.*) = Collection de l'École Française de Rome 98 (Rome 1987) 279–304; S. Demougin, "Quo descendat in campo petitor. Élections et électeurs à la fin de la république et au début de l'empire", *Ibid.* 305–317; A. Lintott, "Electoral Bribery in the Roman Republic", *JRS* 80 (1990) 1–16; A. Yacobson, "Petitio and Largitio", *JRS* 82 (1992) 32–52. Cf. also H. Kowalski, "Odpowiedzialnosc karna za przestepstwa wyborcze w Rzymie (II-I wiek p.n.e)" ["Penal Responsibility for Electoral Malpractices in Rome, II-I century B.C.E.], *Folia Societatis Scientiarum Lublinensis* (*Biuletyn Lubelskiego Towarzystwa Naukowego*) 34 (1993) 73 ff. (non vidi).

Pp.107–108 = 87–88: on the passage of Ausonius, cf. the (rather cursory) commentary by R.P.H. Green, *The Works of Ausonius* (Oxford 1991) 542.

P. 111 = 91: on Plautus' *Amphitruo*, see M. McDonnell, "*Ambitus* and Plautus' *Amphitruo* 65–81", *AJP* 107 (1986) 564–576. He concludes (576) that these lines constitute an interpolation, written after 181, probably in the 150's.

P. 112 = 92, n. 25: on *nomenclatores*, see now the comprehensive study by J. Kolendo, *Nomenclator* (Faenza 1989) esp. 15–19.

Errata. This article was printed very carelessly: in particular French accents and German umlauts were almost consistently omitted. A remedy has been attempted on a copy here reprinted.

10
THREE TRIALS IN 54 B.C.:
SUFENAS, CATO, PROCILIUS AND CICERO,
AD ATTICUM 4.15.4
(1969)

Pp. 118–119 = 284–285: on the aediles of 55 and 54, cf. Broughton, *MRR* 3.148, 158. He is inclined to accept the reconstruction of Taylor.

Pp. 121–122 = 287–288: that C. Cato was praetor in 55 has now been accepted by Shackleton Bailey, *CQF-MB* 215 (cf. 164–165; cf. also *Two Studies in Roman Nomenclature*[2] [Atlanta 1991] 93), and (more cautiously) by Broughton, *MRR* 3.169–170 (cf. 148–149 on Nonius Sufenas). See also H. Solin, *Gnomon* 59 (1987) 599.

Pp. 124–126 = 290–292: cf. Gruen, *LGRR* 315–316, n. 25; Broughton, *MRR* 3.175. They agree that there is no compelling evidence for assigning a tribunate to Procilius. Cf. Shackleton Bailey, *CQF-MB* 185. Alexander, *Trials* 138, points out that the trial of Procilius must have taken place under the *lex Cornelia de sicariis et veneficis*. Cf. David, *PJ* 763.

P. 125 = 291, n. 49: on the expression τρισαρειοπαγίται, see most recently A. Brazouski, *AHB* 2 (1988) 111–112. She fails to explain satisfactorily the sense of τρισ-. There is no discussion of the word in B. Baldwin, "Greek in Cicero's Letters", *Acta Classica* 35 (1992) 1–18.

Pp. 129–130 = 295–296 (and 134–136 = 300–302): Gruen, *LGRR* 315, n. 23, does not find convincing that "Cato and Sufenas were formally charged *de maiestate* and *de ambitu* respectively". The possibility that Nonius Sufenas was charged with *ambitus* is noted (with a query) by Alexander, *Trials* 138, and by Bauerle, *Ambitus* 175–176 (see above, *Ad-*

denda to No 9). The charge against Cato Gruen generally defines as being under the *lex Fufia* (p. 139). That Cato was accused under the Fufian law is attested by Cicero, *Att.* 4.16.5; as this law had nothing to do with *ambitus*, and as both trials took place on the same day, it perforce follows that *ambitus* must have been the charge against Sufenas. Consequently the technical charge against Cato must have been *maiestas minuta*.

Pp. 130–132 = 296–298: the trials of Cato under the *lex Licinia Iunia* and the *lex Fufia*. That Calvus spoke for the defence was also convincingly argued by E. Gruen, "Cicero and Licinius Calvus", *HSCP* 71 (1966) 223–224; 231–232, nn. 67–71; cf. *LGRR* 315. On the other hand Marshall, *Asconius* 121, and Alexander, *Trials* 138, see in him the accuser. But Marshall assigns him (and Asinius Pollio) as prosecutors to the trial under the *lex Fufia*; Gruen (*HSCP* 71, p. 231, n. 66) and Alexander (*Trials* 137–139) regard it as uncertain whether Calvus (and Pollio) participated in the first trial or the second or both. Marshall's reconstruction, but also Gruen's and Alexander's *aporia*, disregards Cicero's intimation of the collusion between the prosecution and the defendant at the second trial (under the Fufian law; there is no mention of collusion at the trial under the *lex Iunia Licinia*).

Alexander, *Trials* 137–138 (cf. 141), lists M. Livius Drusus Claudianus as another accuser of Cato under the *lex Iunia Licinia*, and notes that he "may have committed *praevaricatio*". David, *PJ* 111, 839–840, rightly assigns Asinius Pollio (cf. 886) to the trial under the *lex Iunia Licinia*, but he also believes that the other accuser was Drusus, and that Drusus was later prosecuted for *praevaricatio* (cf. 866, n. 16) committed at this trial. But there was no collusion at this trial, and Drusus as Cato's prosecutor is a phantom conjured up by Shackleton Bailey, *CLA* 2.201–202 (cf. *CQF-MB* 201), from *Att.* 4.16.5: "Drusus reus factus est a Lucretio". Shackleton Bailey combines this information with the preceding notice concerning Cato: "[lege] Fufia ego tibi nuntio absolutum iri, neque patronis suis tam libentibus quam accusatoribus". Gruen (*HSCP* 71.232, n. 72) has dispelled this idea by pointing out the obvious: "Cicero is here speaking of the prospective trial of Cato under the *lex Fufia*, not yet heard, whereas Drusus was already under indictment for *praevaricatio*".

I take this opportunity to correct misprints and infelicities. Read: P. 116 = 282, line 10 (and p. 118 = 284, line 11; p. 119 = 285, lines 2 and 3): "aedileship". P. 121 = 287, line 13: "of the tribunes". P. 121 = 287, n. 36, line 1: "erroneously". P. 122 = 288, n. 42, line 5: "assigns"; line 7: "dates ... to". P. 123 = 289, line 16: "extortion". P. 124 = 290, line 13: "lost sight of"; line 26: "tried". P. 125 = 291, n. 49, line 2: "erroneously";

line 6: "Areopagite"; line 7: "Areopagit". P. 125 = 291, n. 50, lines 1 and 5: "Tyrrell". P. 126 = 292, n. 53, line 4: "Editor". P. 127 = 293, n. 55, line 1: "Procilius". P. 128 = 294, n. 61, line 1: "example". P. 129 = 295, line 3: "compels". P. 131 = 297, n. 74, line 22: "counter to". P. 132 = 298, line 16: "reconstruction". P. 133 = 299, line 11: "imagine". P. 135 = 301, line 20: "That this is". P. 135 = 301, n. 90, line 2: "in about".

11

REVIEW OF:
CLAUDE NICOLET, *L'ORDRE ÉQUESTRE À L'ÉPOQUE RÉPUBLICAINE.*
TOME 2: *PROSOPOGRAPHIE DES CHEVALIERS ROMAINS* (1977)

J.-L. Ferrary, "Pline, *N.H.*, XXXIII, 34 et les chevaliers romains sous la république", *REL* 58 (1980 [1981]) 313–337; at 327–329 a discussion of the *lex Roscia*: he concludes that our sources do not permit us to decide with any certainty whether the Roscian law reserved the XIV *ordines* for the *ordo equester* in a strict sense or for a larger group "englobant, sinon touts les possesseurs du cens équestre, au moins les *tribuni aerarii*".

S. Demougin in her voluminous book, *L'ordre équestre sous les Julio-Claudiens* (Rome 1988) also presents a short discussion of the *lex Roscia theatralis* (pp. 794–802), but again she clearly underestimates the importance of this measure for the definition of the *ordo equester*.

The best and most detailed study of the problem is E. Rawson, "*Discrimina ordinum*: The *Lex Julia Theatralis*", *PBSR* 55 (1987) 83–114 (esp. 102–105), reprinted in: E. Rawson, *Roman Culture and Society. Collected Papers* (Oxford 1991) 508–545 (esp. 530–534). Her views are rather close to those expressed in my review (cf. p. 103 = 532, n. 115). S. Whitehead, in his yet unpublished Sydney doctoral thesis, has also arrived (with a different set of arguments) at a similar conclusion, namely that the *tribuni aerarii* represented members of the equestrian order outside the eighteen centuries *equo publico*.

U. Hackl, "Eques Romanus equo publico. Ein Beitrag zur Definition des römischen Ritterstandes während der Zeit der Republik", in: *Festschrift Robert Werner* (Konstanz 1989) 107–114, finds it very likely "dass die römischen Ritter auch nach Abgabe des Staatspferdes zwecks Abstimmung in den Centuriatkomitien in ihren angestammten 18 Rittercenturien verblieben". She does not discuss the question of the XIV *ordines* (p. 111).

12
LEGIBUS PRAEFECTI MITTEBANTUR
(MOMMSEN AND FESTUS 262.5,13 L)
(1979)

Several further studies on the prefectures in Italy have appeared: F. Sartori, "I praefecti Capuam Cumas", in: *Convegno Internazionale 'I Campi Flegrei nell' archeologia e nella storia"* = Atti dei Convegni Lincei 33 (Rome 1977) 149–171; M. Humbert, *Municipium et civitas sine suffragio* (Rome 1978) 356–402; P.C. Knap, "Festus 262 L and praefecturae in Italy", *Athenaeum* 58 [= 68] (1980) 14–38; E. Pianezzola, "Nota di lettura. Fest., s.u. Praefecturae 262 Linds.", in: *Festschrift für Robert Muth* = Innsbrucker Beiträge zur Kulturwissenschaft 22 (Innsbruck 1983) 357–360; M. Frederiksen, *Campania* (Rome 1984) 268–269 (and nn. 47–51).

P. 144 = 248, n. 5: the note on "Primum creati" was ultimately never completed.

P. 145 = 249 (and n. 10): Sartori, 163–164, 170, takes *leges* in Festus (in any case in the second passage) in the sense of "disposizioni pretorie"; Pianezzola, 357, inclines to agree. Humbert, 356, translates *legibus* (in both places) as "conformément aux lois (ou munis d'instructions?)". Knap, 15, translates *legibus* "according to law", and gives (pp. 21–22) a detailed interpretation of the expression: "*legibus* in Festus' notice (both in line 4 and in line 12) probably means 'were sent in accordance with assembly legislation' which empowered a praetor to send them every year, or, in the case of 'Capuam Cumas', which had authorized the Assembly in subsequent years to elect prefects". Frederiksen does not discuss the meaning of *legibus*.

13
ROME, APHRODISIAS AND THE *RES GESTAE*:
THE *GENERA MILITIAE* AND THE STATUS OF OCTAVIAN
(1984)

Cf. a new discussion of *tumultus, coniuratio, evocatio,* and *sacramentum* by J. Rüpke, *Domi Militiaeque* (Stuttgart 1990) 70–91.

P. 147 = 74: the term ἀντιστρατιώτης (and also ἀντιναύτης) has now appeared also in the *Monumentum Ephesenum*, the Roman customs law from Ephesos. See the edition by H. Engelmann and D. Knibbe, *Das Zollgesetz der Provinz Asia* (= *Epigraphica Anatolica* 14 [1989]). In line 64 (p. 24) we read:] οἷς τε ἂν διατρέφωνται στρατιώτης ἢ ναύτης ἢ ἀντιστρατιώτης ἢ ἀντιναύτης, ὃς ἂν ἦ πραγμάτων ἕνεκεν δήμου Ῥωμαίων. In their otherwise very useful commentary Engelmann and

Knibbe disregard both the contribution of J. Reynolds on the document from Aphrodisias, and the article here reprinted, and as a result they offer the following mistranslation (p. 87): "und wovon sich der Soldat oder der Matrose oder die Person, die im Auftrag des Soldaten oder Matrosen agiert, ernähren, der für die Sache des römischen Volkes (unterwegs) ist". In their commentary (p. 88) they have this to say: "Στρατιώτης könnte sich zu ἀντιστρατιώτης verhalten wie proconsul zu consul. Dann wäre ἀντιστρατιώτης ein früherer Soldat, ein Veteran, so wie proconsul den gewesenen consul bezeichnet. Doch sind der στρατιώτης wie der ἀντιστρατιώτης unterwegs zu einem Feldzug; das dürfte eher für die Gleichsetzung ἀντιστρατιώτης = pro milite sprechen, "im Auftrag des Soldaten". This explanation misconstrues both the linguistic and legal situation; the circumstance that both στρατιώτης and ἀντιστρατιώτης are "unterwegs zu einem Feldzug" speaks clearly and loudly in favor of the interpretation presented in the paper here reproduced.

Pp. 147–148 = 74–75: on the *vicarii*, cf. F. Reduzzi Merola, "'Vicarium expedire', 'vicarios dare', 'vicarios expetere' nell'esercito romano", *Index* 15 (1987) 381–388. She duly notes the Scipio episode, and rightly doubts its authenticity.

P. 150 = 77: Rüpke 74 contests the combining of *evocatio* (as a method of levy) with *coniuratio* (as a form of oath). But how should we call the levy which followed upon the call to arms "qui rem publicam salvam esse vult, me sequatur"? Cf. also F. Hinard, "Sacramentum", *Athenaeum* 81 (1993) 250–263. Unfortunately he disregards the antiquarian sources, nor can I accept his interpretation of *sacramentum* and *ius iurandum* in Livy 22.38.1–5.

Pp. 152–153 = 79–80: cf. M. Reinhold, *From Republic to Principate. An Historical Commentary on Cassius Dio's Roman History Books 49–52 (36–29 B.C.)* (Atlanta 1988) 224–225 (and nn. 49–53 on pp. 224–225), by and large accepting the solution here presented. On the legal status of Octavian, see now K.M. Girardet, "Der Rechtsstatus Octavians im Jahre 32 v. Chr.", *RhM* 133 (1990) 322–350, esp. 345–350. An excellent paper, but Girardet seems to underestimate the constitutional legality and importance of the *coniuratio Italiae* so prominently displayed in the *Res Gestae*. I should have stated more explicitly that Octavian was not a *privatus* (cf. Girardet, 347, n. 137), but I do not think that his provincial command could have provided him with *imperium* legally sufficient for the war against Cleopatra. And in fact Girardet postulates that in 32 there was created for Octavian, by the senate and the popular assembly, a new *provincia*, "Krieg gegen Kleopatra" (p. 347). If so, why does Augustus neglect to mention this event in the *Res Gestae*, and dwells solely on the oath of Italy and the provinces? R.G. Lewis in his most interesting paper, "Rechtsfrage II:

Octavian's powers in 32 B.C.", *LCM* 16 (1991) 57–62, misunderstands, I am afraid, my argument when he writes (p. 59, n. 12): "[Linderski] argues that the *coniuratio Italiae* of 32 was a kind of military muster in response to an emergency (*tumultus*) — or at least so presented by Augustus in his *Res Gestae*. That much might perhaps be true, but it fails to show either that Octavian lacked *imperium* at the time or that the oath conferred it". Now I did not argue that Octavian lacked *imperium* altogether, but rather assumed (unfortunately only tacitly) that his *imperium* was territorially circumscribed, and hence insufficient for a new war (see above, Girardet); and the purpose of the *iuratio* was certainly not to bestow *imperium*, but to select a *dux* for the war. Cf. also K.M. Girardet, "Zur Diskussion um das *imperium consulare militiae* im 1. Jh. v. Chr.", *Cahiers du Centre G. Glotz* 3 (1992) 214–220, esp. 215–218, mostly a polemic against J.M. Roddaz, "Imperium: nature et compétences à la fin de la République et au début de l'Empire", *Ibid.* 189–211, esp. 198–202; he believes that Octavian continued to regard himself as invested with triumviral powers. This is very unlikely. J. Bleicken, *Zwischen Republik und Prinzipat. Zum Charakter des Zweiten Triumvirats* (= Abh. Göttingen. Philol.-Hist. Kl. Dritte Folge 185 [Göttingen 1990]) 72–73, rightly notes that while Octavian retained the proconsular command "die Befugnisse in Rom und Italien mussten hingegen mit dem Enddatum des Triumvirats [i.e. 31 Dec. 33] erlöschen". Octavian's answer was the *iuratio*; Bleicken observes: "Der Bezug auf den Krieg gegen Antonius ... zeigt deutlich, dass es hier um die militärische Gefolgschaft ging, nicht um die aller römischer Bürger und der Provinzialen". Thus Bleicken arrived (independently, and without any discussion of the legal character of the *coniuratio* within the broader scheme of the Roman *militia*) at a conclusion very akin to that proposed in the article here reprinted.

14

USU, FARRE, COEMPTIONE.
BEMERKUNGEN ZUR ÜBERLIEFERUNG
EINES RECHTSATZES
(1984)

P. 154 = 301, nn. 1 and 2: the studies of Volterra have been reprinted in: E. Volterra, *Scritti giuridici* (Napoli 1991) II 3–68; III 3–107, 155–176, 355–380. The article by Watson has been reprinted in: A. Watson, *Legal Origins and Legal Change* (London 1991) 9–10.

B. Biondo, "Farreo coëmptione usu", in: *Sodalitas. Scritti in onore di Antonio Guarino* 3 (Napoli 1984) 1301–1309. She argues (p. 1303) that "la progressione 'usu farreo coëmptione' debba essere corretta, sul piano della storia, in 'farreo coëmptione usu' ", but does not discuss the textual tradition of the formula.

I was not able to consult E. Cantarella, " 'Usu farreo coemptione': ipotesi recenti sul matrimonio romano", in: *Incontro con Giovanni Pugliese* (Milano 1992) 97 ff.

15
DER SENAT UND DIE VEREINE
(1968)

On the *senatus consultum de collegiis* of 64, see now F.M. De Robertis, *Storia delle corporazioni e del regime associativo nel mondo romano* 1 (Bari 1971) 83–115 (restating his earlier views).

The monograph by F.M. Ausbüttel, *Untersuchungen zu den Vereinen im Westen des römischen Reiches* (Kallmünz 1982), contains an extensive bibliography, and in the section "Politische Aktivitäten" briefly treats of late republican measures concerning the *collegia* (pp. 85–93).

F. Salerno, "Collegia adversus rem publicam?", in: *Sodalitas. Scritti in onore di Antonio Guarino* 2 (Napoli 1984) 615–631 (this article was also published in *Index* 13 [1985] 541–556), arrives at the conclusion (p. 631) that the "*S.C. de collegiis* sia stato una misura amministrativa, di polizia, che, pur se espressa in formule generali ed imperative, non trovava uguale attuazione nella pratica". He mistakenly attributes to the present writer the view (p. 626, n. 65) that it was a "misura di portata generale".

As to the juridical character of the senatorial decrees, G Crifò, "Attività normativa del senato in età repubblicana", *BIDR* 71 (1968) 31–115, argues (p. 51) that "la proposta legislativa di Clodio mostra che contro l'applicazione del senatoconsulto del 64 non avrebbe potuto essere sufficiente una semplice *intercessio* e ciò è argomento della forza vincolante del senatoconsulto stesso".

See also a most informative study by J.-M. Flambard, "Clodius, les collèges, la plèbe et les esclaves. Recherches sur la politique populaire au milieu du Ier siècle", *MEFRA* 89 (1977) 116–153. Cf. also T. Loposzko, "Clodio e gli schiavi", *Acta Classica Universitatis Scientiarum Debrecenensis* 21 (1985) 43–72.

P. 166 = 95: that the correct reading of the name of Clodius' associate and helper is Sex. Cloelius (and not the vulgate Sex. Clodius) has been established by D.R. Shackleton Bailey in a series of brilliant textual studies; see most recently *Two Studies in Roman Nomenclature*[2] (Atlanta 1991) 17, 91; *Onomasticon to Cicero's Speeches*[2] (Stuttgart-Leipzig 1992) 36. Flambard, *MEFRA* 89 (1977) 126–128; and "Nouvel examen d'un dossier prosopographique: le cas de Sex. Clodius / Cloelius", *MEFRA* 90 (1978) 235–245, fights a lost battle defending the reading Sex. Clodius. On this person, his social standing and his political role, see the most interesting articles by J. Tatum, "P. Clodius Pulcher and Tarracina", *ZPE* 83 (1990) 299–304, and C. Damon, "Sex. Cloelius, scriba", *HSCP* 94 (1992) 227–250 (but she is certainly mistaken when she states [p. 232] that the *senatus consultum* of 64 banned not only the *collegia* but also the *magistri vicorum*).

    Pp. 175 ff. = 104 ff.: the *collegia compitalicia* continue to cause vexation. See above all J.-M. Flambard, "Collegia Compitalicia: phénomène associatif, cadres territoriaux et cadres civiques dans le monde romain à l'époque républicaine", *Ktema* 6 (1981) 143–166, esp. 151–154. An erudite and spirited piece, but on a number of points I must disagree with it. We should not amalgamate the *magistri vicorum* with the *magistri* of the various cultic associations organized *vicatim*; from the passage of Cicero, *Pis.* 8: "Cum quidam tr. pl. suo auxilio magistros ludos contra S.C. facere iussit", it is hardly possible to argue (p. 153) that the *magistri vicorum* "n'avaient plus d'existence légale depuis 64" (cf., also totally unfounded, L. Cracco Ruggini, "Le associazioni professionali nel mondo romano-bizantino", in: *Settimane di Studio del Centro Italiano dell'Alto Medioevo* 18 [Spoleto 1971] 73: the *S.C.* of 64 abolished the *magistri vicorum*); in the *S.C.* of 56 the expression *sodalitates decuriatique* is hardly "redontante" (p. 164). Cf. also Flambard, *MEFRA* 89 (1977) 133–144. On the discussion of the *collegia compitalicia* by A. Mastrocinque, *Lucio Giunio Bruto. Ricerche di storia, religione e diritto della repubblica romana* (Trento 1988) 59–65, see J. Linderski, *AJP* 112 (1991) 408. See also the informed and thoughtful observations by A. Fraschetti, *Roma e il Principe* (Bari 1990) 204–273. With respect to the *magistri vicorum* he observes (non sine ratione!): "Le abbondantissime discussioni, cui essi hanno dato luogo nella storiografia moderna (da Mommsen a Cohn, da Waltzing a De Robertis, da Linderski a Flambard), sono inversamente proporzionali ai materiali antichi discussi" (p. 242). But his idea that "i ludi ai Compitalia non erano organizzati partitamente da gruppi di 'magistri vicorum', ma da un gruppo di *magistri* che erano tali in quanto editori di ludi e che agivano ogni anno dando spettacoli nei vari *compita*" while ingenious is not particularly attractive. We have to conclude: a new study, and a detailed polemic, is called for.

    Pp. 179 =108, 189 = 118: The main weakness of most studies dealing with the *vici, collegia* and *magistri* continues to be their failure either to pay attention at all to the terminology or to distinguish clearly between the *magistri collegiorum* (as the *magistri* of the professional *collegia*) and the *collegia magistrorum* (as the so-called *magistri Campani* or the *magistri* and *magistrae* from Minturnae). I emphatically disagree with Flambard's statement that "En aucun cas les *magistri* ne constituaient à aux seuls l'intégralité du collège" ("Observations sur la nature des *magistri* italiens de Délos", in: *Delo e l'Italia = Opuscula Instituti Romani Finlandiae* 2 [1982] 67–77 at 71). But see his attempt at a distinction, "Les collèges et les élites locales à la époque républicaine d'après l'example de Capoue", in: *Les "bourgeoisies" municipales italiennes aux IIe et Ier siècles av. J.C.* (Paris-Naples 1983) 75–89, esp. 83. On the denominations of the Delian *magistri*, see also P. Poccetti, "Romani e Italici a Delo. Spunti linguistici da una pubblicazione recente", *Athenaeum* 62 [= 72] (1984) 646–656 at 649–650. I very much doubt that the *magistri Capitolini* were slave traders, as argued by F. Coarelli, *"Magistri Capitolini e mercanti di schiavi", Index* 15 (1987) 175–187.

Pp. 180–182 = 109–111 (and nn. 52–56): for the last thoughts of M. Frederiksen on the subject of the *magistri Campani*, see his book (posthumously edited by N. Purcell) *Campania* (Rome 1984) 265 (and nn. 7–14): Mommsen was right: they formed the *collegia* of *curatores fanorum*. So also B. Combet-Farnoux, *Mercure romain* (Rome 1980) 412–419.

H. Solin, "Republican Capua", in: H. Solin and M. Kajava (eds.), *Roman Eastern Policy and Other Studies in Roman History* (= Commentationes Humanarum Litterarum 91 [Helsinki 1990]) 151–162, writes that Mommsen's view of the *magistri Campani* "explains many features of these records very well" (p. 155), but at the same time expresses a directly contradictory view (p. 156): "I am in no doubt that the Capuan magistri were at the head of the collegia ... The nature of these collegia is not easy to determine, but if the number of their *magistri* alone amounts to twelve, the total size of a collegium must have been considerable". Thus again fatal refusal to draw a distinction between *magistri collegiorum* and *collegia magistrorum*.

16
CICEROS REDE PRO CAELIO
UND DIE AMBITUS- UND VEREINSGESETZGEBUNG
DER AUSGEHENDEN REPUBLIK
(1961)

Pp. 208 = 110 (and n. 3); 209 = 111 (and n. 1), and passim: F.M. De Robertis has restated his views on the *senatus consultum* of February 56 and the *lex Licinia* in his new comprehensive monograph *Storia delle corporazioni e del regime associativo nel mondo romano* 1 (Bari 1971) 116–146, esp. 120, n. 21; 122, n. 25; 130, n. 1 (in direct polemic against the interpretation presented in my article; cf. also my monograph, *Kolegia* 66–80). He offers no new arguments.

The main thesis of the article (on the nature of the *senatus consultum* of February 56 "ut sodalitates decuriatique discederent", and its relation to the *lex Licinia de sodaliciis*) has been accepted (inter alios aliasque) by L.R. Taylor, "Magistrates of 55 B.C. in Cicero's *Pro Plancio* and Catullus 52", *Athenaeum* N.S. 42 (1964) 12, n. 2; E. Gruen, *LGRR* 229–230, 233; A. Ward, *Marcus Crassus and the Late Republic* (Columbia, MO, 1977) 270–271; F.M. Ausbüttel, *Untersuchungen zu den Vereinen im Westen des römischen Reiches* (Kallmünz 1982) 91–92 (but he does not differentiate sufficiently between the position taken in this article and the position of De Robertis); and by D.R. Shackleton Bailey, *CQF-MB* 178. He cautiously and judiciously observes: "But the subject presumably remains controversial". Quite so, but *pro domo mea* I would wish to add that the argument presented in the article is much simpler and operates with fewer assumptions than those of other scholars. I should also wish to say that despite (partial) disagreement I am full of admiration for the erudite works of De Robertis. This sentiment also applies to the subtle article by C. Venturini, "L'orazione Pro Cn. Plancio e la lex Licinia de sodaliciis", in: *Studi in onore di Cesare Sanfilippo* 5 (Milano 1984) 789–804, who on the whole endorses the position of De Robertis (see esp. p. 802). See also *Addenda* to Nos 9 and 31.

Pp. 204–206 = 106–108: De Robertis, 122, n. 22, states that the *crimina sodalium ac sequestrium* were not crimes at all because Cicero "espressamente lo nega" when he says that "adulter, impudicus, sequester convitium est, non accusatio". This misreads the argument of the article, and of Cicero. I argued that at the time of Caelius' trial the only legal foundation for the *crimina sodalium* and *sequestrium* could have been the *senatus consultum* of February 56 "ut sodalitates decuriatique discederent". These *crimina* became technically actionable only after their incorporation into the provisions of the *lex Licinia* of 55. Still this accusation was potentially damaging to Caelius, and Cicero deftly proceeded to weaken it by juxtaposing these *crimina* with transgressions that were disreputable but not punished by statutory law. A similar misreading also in the otherwise excellent article by C.J. Classen, "Ciceros Rede Pro Caelio", *ANRW* I 3 (1973) 63–64, n. 16.

Pp. 208–210 = 110–112: Ausbüttel, 92, expresses doubt whether the *Wahlvereine* prohibited by the *lex Licinia* were identical with the "quattuor sodalitates hominum ad ambitionem gratiosissimorum" mentioned in the *Commentariolum petitionis* as "Kornemann und Linderski meinen". And he comments: "Man darf eher mit David verneinen, dass Ciceros Bruder in seiner Schrift auf solche unlauteren und gesetzwidrigen Wahlkampfmethoden hingewiesen haben dürfte". But in fact both myself and J.-M. David (in: J.-M. David, S. Demougin, E. Deniaux, D. Ferey, J.-M.

Flambart, C. Nicolet, "Le 'Commentariolum Petitionis' de Quintus Cicéron. Etat de la question et étude prosopographique", *ANRW* I 3 [1973] 276–277) distinguish (and distinguish independently for David did not utilize the article here reproduced) between the *sodalitates* in the *Commentariolum petitionis* and in the Licinian law. David, 277, writes: "il faut comprendre que les *sodalitates* du 'Commentariolum' sont encore de vraies *sodalitates* au sens traditionnel du terme (cf. #16), mais déjà touchées par une pratique qui commence seulement à les faire évoluer". Cf. also in a similar sense (but without any reference to previous studies) R. Martini, "*Nugae comitiales*, II. 'Amici' di candidati e corruzione elettorale in Roma antica", in: *Scritti per Mario delle Piane* (Napoli 1986) 1–4.

P. 212 = 114: S. Treggiari, "A new Collina", *Historia* 19 (1970) 121–122, wonders (p. 121): "can 'Collinam novam' refer to influence in rural tribes wielded by freedmen chiefly resident in the city?". Flambard, *MEFRA* 89 (1977) 149–150, n. 130, leans toward the interpretation of Treggiari; Loposzko, *Acta Class. Univ. Debrec.* 21 (1985) 67, n. 28, accepts the emendation *novo dilectu* (for full titles of these articles, see *Addenda* to No 15). Perhaps, after all, the most likely is the idea of L.R. Taylor, *The Voting Districts of the Roman Republic* (Rome 1960) 145, n. 50: "Clodius, who already had a band of followers from the Collina, raised a new band from the same tribe".

P. 214 = 116, n. 4: De Robertis, 130, n. 1 writes: "Inammisibile è il dubio avanzato dal Linderski ... circa la possibilità di confusione nelle fonti tra la lex Licinia e la lex Licinia Iunia. Trattasi infatti di fonti il cui tecnicismo deve farci escludere in via di massima la possibilità di errori e confusioni, almeno per quel che riguarda quelle contemporanee agli avvenimenti riferiti". The source in question is not a contemporary author but the *Scholia Bobiensia*, a script late and often inaccurate. The confusion of the Scholiast is blatant; it cannot be conjured away.

P. 215 = 117, n. 4: Venturini, 793–797, acutely points out that the text of the *Sch. Bob.* refers to the prohibition of the *coitio* between the candidates.

17

SUETONS BERICHT ÜBER DIE VEREINSGESETZGEBUNG UNTER CAESAR UND AUGUSTUS
(1962)

On the *lex Iulia*, see now F.M. De Robertis, *Storia delle corporazioni e del regime associativo nel mondo romano* 1 (Bari 1971) 193–237.

Pp. 220–222 = 325–327: De Robertis, 206, n. 27, defends his interpretation of the terms *collegia nova* and *collegia antiqua*. Reviewing our respective arguments I am inclined to think that our positions are in fact much closer than either of us was prepared to admit.

For an excellent overview, largely accepting the results achieved in the articles here reprinted (Nos 15–17), see Z. Yavetz, *Julius Caesar and his Public Image* (London [also Ithaca] 1983) 85–96.

18
CICERO AND SALLUST ON VARGUNTEIUS
(1963)

E.A. Bauerle, *Procuring an Election: Ambitus in the Roman Republic* (Diss. Michigan [Ann Arbor] 1990) 141; C. MacDonald in his note to Cic. *Cat.* 1.9 (in Loeb Class. Library, *Cicero,* vol. 10 [1977] 42–43); and F.X. Ryan, "The Quaestorships of Q. Curius and C. Cornelius Cethegus", *CP* 89 (1994) 256–261, at 256, accept 66 as the date of Vargunteius' trial *de ambitu* and assume that he was convicted; so also R. Syme, *Sallust* (Berkeley 1964) 88, n. 23. David, *PJ* 763 (765, n. 19), dates the trial "vers 66".

Bauerle, MacDonald, and Ryan agree that after his conviction Vargunteius could have become technically an *eques* (cf. P. McGushin, *C. Sallustius Crispus, Bellum Catilinae. A Commentary* [Leiden 1977] 172). On the other hand C. Nicolet, *L'ordre équestre à l'époque républicaine* 2: *Prosopographie des chevaliers romains* (*BEFAR* 207, Paris 1974) 1060–1061, contests the idea that Vargunteius after his conviction (which he regards as uncertain) should have "redevenu chevalier" (Cf. Alexander, *Trials* 202). Vargunteius certainly was not admitted (or re-admitted) to the equestrian centuries, but if he possessed the equestrian census he could have easily been regarded as *eques,* in any case in the sense of the *lex Roscia* of 67, as a person who had the right to sit in the XIV *ordines.*

Most scholars agree that Sallust was right in naming C. Cornelius and Vargunteius as would-be assassins of Cicero (cf. Broughton, *MRR* 3.215; Bauerle, *Ambitus* 141–142), but R.P. Robinson in an article which I had unfortunately omitted to adduce ("Duo Equites Romani", *CW* 40 [1947] 138–143) argued (on the basis of an emendation of Plut. *Cicero* 16.1) that the other *eques* was (M.) Caeparius. Ingenious but not likely (Nicolet does not record Robinson's conjecture and does not list Caeparius as a knight). Certainly, it is not impossible that either Sallust got a wrong name or Cicero was careless in writing *duo equites,* but I submit it is more elegant to reconcile Cicero and Sallust than to accuse them of error.

P. 225 = 512, n. 10: Sallust's reference is to P. Sulla Ser. f., and not to P. Sulla, cos. des. 65; see L.E. Reams, "The Strange Case of Sulla's Brother", *CJ* 82.4 (1987) 301, n. 2.

19

THE SURNAMES AND THE ALLEGED AFFINITY
OF M. CAELIUS RUFUS
(1968)

P. 226 = 146 (and nn. 2, 3): oddly enough there is no discussion of the name of the consul of 17 in O. Salomies, *Adoptive and Polyonymous Nomenclature in the Roman Empire* (Helsinki 1992).

P. 228 = 148: on the home town of Caelius, cf. M. Volponi, *M. Celio Rufo "ingeniose nequam"* (= Memorie dell'Ist. Lombardo. Cl. di Lettere XXXI, fasc. 3 [Milano 1971]) 201–203. She accepts Interamnia. So also D.V. Madsen, *The Life and Political Career of Marcus Caelius Rufus* (Diss. Univ. of Washington, Seattle, 1981) 17–20, and generally all more recent literature, e.g. T.P. Wiseman, *New Men in the Roman Senate 139 B.C.–14 A.D.* (Oxford 1971) 218; Idem, *Catullus and His World* (Cambridge 1985) 62; M.H. Dettenhoffer, *Perdita iuventus. Zwischen den Generationen von Caesar und Augustus* (München 1992) 80.

P. 229 = 149 (and n. 14): R. Syme, *The Augustan Aristocracy* (Oxford 1986) 87 and Wiseman, *New Men* 218 (no 77) continue to adhere to their divergent identifications.

I take this opportunity to correct misprints and infelicities. Read: P. 227 = 147, line 9: "Velleius'"; line 11: omit "it". P. 227 = 147, n. 5, line 2: "repulsive". P. 229 = 149, line 8: omit "out"; line 16: "aedile". P. 229 = 149, n. 14, line 3: "CQ". P. 230 = 150, line 10: omit "it".

20

THE AEDILESHIP OF FAVONIUS, CURIO THE YOUNGER
AND CICERO'S ELECTION TO THE AUGURATE
(1972)

J. Geiger, "M. Favonius: Three Notes", *Rivista Storica dell'Antichità* 4 (1974) 161–170, discusses with great acumen the date of Favonius' aedileship (pp. 161–164); he opts for 53. He remarks that even after the paper here reprinted came to his attention he did not see any reason to change his views ("Additional Note", p. 170). The fact remains that there does not exist any direct testimony for the date of Favonius' aedileship, and even if 53 might look more enticing, 52 cannot be excluded. Broughton, *MRR* 3.90–91, rightly states that the date "may be either 53 or 52" (but, I may add, he missed Geiger's defense of 53). Against Geiger, see now, convincingly, F.X. Ryan, "The Quaestorship of Favonius and the Tribunate of

Metellus Scipio", *Athenaeum* 82 (1994) 505–521 at 516–517, n. 78. Cf. also Shackleton Bailey, *CQF-MB* 198. In his article "Notes on Cicero's Philippics", *Philologus* 126 (1982) 219, Shackleton Bailey points out that one argument in favor of the traditional date (53) is "Cicero's implied statement that Curio was out of Italy during the period of Antony's candidature", and "unless Curio lingered for months on the way, he would be in Rome again by the autumn". Inconclusive.

Pp. 241–242 = 191–192: cf. Shackleton Bailey, 233–234.

P. 246 = 196: the *triumvir capitalis* remains a thorn in the flesh of rival interpretations. A. W. Lintott, "Cicero and Milo", *JRS* 64 (1974) 72, n. 16, objects to the chronological reconstruction here presented, but see against Lintott the remarks by Marshall, *Asconius* 182. Also J.S. Ruebel, "The Trial of Milo in 52 B.C.: A Chronological Study", *TAPA* 109 (1979) 242, totally disregards the chronological implications of the *triumvir capitalis*.

21
THE QUAESTORSHIP OF MARCUS ANTONIUS
(1974)

P. 251 = 213, n. 2 (and passim): we should not have missed Shackleton Bailey's retraction of his "correction" (as he describes it) of Broughton (*CLA* 7.96). He points out that *Fam.* 2.18 (which we also omitted to adduce) "refers to L. (not C.) Antonius as Quaestor in 50 and implies that his two elder brothers had held the office successively in the two previous years". But in 1977 in his comment on *Fam.* 2.18 (*CEF* 1.455) he declared himself persuaded by our argument, and observed that "The apparent discrepancy between their conclusion and this passage ... may be got over on the supposition that, as they argue, Marcus had originally intended to hold the office in 52" — but actually held it in 51, and held it simultaneously with his younger brother. "Normally Marcus would have preceded Gaius, but in fact did not". I am thankful to SB for this deliverance. The dating of Antonius' quaestorship to 51 has now been accepted by Broughton, *MRR* 3.19–20. It is gratifying to see that J. Malitz, *Ambitio Mala: Studien zur politischen Biographie des Sallust* (Bonn 1975) 113–114, and W.K. Lacey, "Antony's quaestorship: the evidence of Cicero, Phil. 2.48–50", *LCM* 10.6 (1985) 82, also arrived at 51 as the date of Antonius' quaestorship, and arrived independently, and with similar arguments. Cf. also M.H. Dettenhoffer, *Perdita iuventus. Zwischen den Generationen von Caesar und Augustus* (München 1992) 66–68.

22

THE MOTHER OF LIVIA AUGUSTA
AND THE AUFIDII LURCONES OF THE REPUBLIC
(1974)

On Lurco, see now Broughton, *MRR* 3.29.

Pp. 269–270 = 470–471: E.A. Bauerle, *Procuring an Election: Ambitus in the Roman Republic* (Diss. Michigan [Ann Arbor] 1990) 73, n. 92, points out that the bill of Lurco "may have been more broadly designed to curry favor among the electorate, rather than merely to hinder or exclude Pompey and his associates".

P. 269 = 470, n. 31: on the bill of Lurco and the text of Cicero, *Ad Att.* 1.16.13, see E. Badian, "An Unrecognized Date in Cicero's Text", in: *MNEMAI. Classical Studies in Memory of Karl H. Hulley* (Chico 1984) 97–101. He defends the paradosis *qui magistratum cum lege alia iniit*.

P. 270 = 471, n. 38: the study of the *leges Aelia* and *Fufia* promised in this note still remains in manuscript. A.E. Astin, "Leges Aelia and Fufia", *Latomus* 23 (1964) 438, n. 2; A.K. Michels, *The Calendar of the Roman Republic* (Princeton 1967) 95, n. 7; and E. Badian, "The Death of Saturninus", *Chiron* 14 (1984) 115–117 (and n. 35), rightly point out that the *leges Aelia* and *Fufia* prohibited only legislation but not promulgation in the period between the announcement and the holding of the elections, but none of these scholars observed that this rule pertained only to measures concerning electoral law (which, in fact, fits Badian's case very well). The objection of B.L. Twyman, "The Day Equitius died", *Athenaeum* N.S. 67 [= 77] (1989) 508, is misguided: it depends upon a misreading of Michels.

Pp. 272 ff. = 473 ff.: A. Licordari, in: *Epigrafia e ordine senatorio* II (= *Tituli* 5 [Rome 1982]) 27–28 amalgamates M. Alfidius and Aufidius Lurco, and points to the "alternanza delle forme Alfidius e Aufidius nelle iscrizioni locali". For this phenomenon he refers to G. Pesiri, "Iscrizioni di Fondi e del circondario", *Epigraphica* 40 (1978) 173. The fact is that both *nomina* are attested in Fundi, and in other places; whether they were interchangeable we do not know. M. Torelli, *Tituli* 5, 190–191, believes that the passage of Suetonius (*Cal.* 23) "é chiaramente un gioco ironico di Caligola stesso ... basato su Orazio". He attributes Alfidia to Marruvium. Contra, see C. Letta, *Ibid.* 198: the home-town of Alfidia was Fundi. On the Alfidii, cf. also P. Simelon, "A. Alfidius d'Atina et son héritier Olussa: un nouvel interprétation de *RIB*, 9", *Latomus* 47 (1988) 863–867, esp. 864–865.

23
TWO QUAESTORSHIPS
(1975)

On these quaestorships, cf. Broughton, *MRR* 3.51–52.
P. 282 = 37, n. 21: see No 21.

24
REVIEW OF:
MAGNUS WISTRAND, *CICERO IMPERATOR*.
STUDIES IN CICERO'S CORRESPONDENCE 51–47 B.C.
(1981)

P. 284 = 782 (and n. 2): on the *lex Pompeia de provinciis*, see now (with further literature) the solid study by K. M. Girardet, "Die lex Iulia de provinciis. Vorgeschichte - Inhalt - Wirkungen", *RhM* 130 (1987) 291–329 at 293–307, esp. 298–299: he argues that the *lex Pompeia* concerned only the praetors; in 51 Cicero and Bibulus received their provincial commands on the basis of a *senatus consultum*, and the *imperium consulare* was bestowed upon them *extra ordinem* "durch eine *lex* (*tributa / centuriata*) *de imperio*". Unfortunately Girardet offers no discussion of the *lex curiata*.

25
REVIEW OF:
THOMAS N. MITCHELL, *CICERO, THE ASCENDING YEARS*
(1979)

P. 288 = 276: it is perhaps too much to expect to put to rest the spectre of democracy haunting Rome, but I enlist the help of that expert monster-slayer, Ernst Badian: "from Ti. Gracchus down to Caesar's conquest of Rome, not a single politician, to our knowledge, made a single proposal to introduce what either we or the Greeks would call democracy" ("The Young Betti and the Practice of History", in: G. Crifò [ed.], *Costituzione Romana e crisi della repubblica. Atti del convegno su Emilio Betti* [Napoli 1986] 89–90).

For an earlier period, cf. A. Lintott, "Democracy in the Middle Republic", *ZRG* 104 (1987) 34–52. He argues that in some respects "the Roman constitution in the middle Republic was like the more moderate forms of democracy approved by Aristotle" (p. 50). He seems to underestimate the fact that Roman assemblies did not possess legislative initiative. J. North, "Politics and Aristocracy in the Roman Republic", *CP* 85 (1990) 277–287, is right when he says (p. 284) that if Rome were a Greek city Aristotle "would have certainly called it some kind of oligarchy, perhaps recognizing an element of democracy, useful to maintaining the stability of the oligarchic regime".

26
DE VILLA APPIO PULCHRO FALSO ATTRIBUTA
(1981)

Cf. now W.J. Tatum, "The Poverty of Appii Pulchri: Varro, *De Re Rustica* 3.16.1–2", *CQ* 42 (1992) 198, n. 3.

Errata. Read:

P. 290 = 273, line 15: "in hortis"; line 18 "tribuli".

27
PATIENTIA FREGIT:
M. OCTAVIUS AND TI. GRACCHUS (CICERO, *BRUTUS* 95)
(1982)

P. 292 = 245: D.F. Epstein, "Inimicitia between M. Octavius and Ti. Gracchus, tribuni plebis", *Hermes* 111 (1983) 296–300, rightly rejects the notion of inherited enmity between Octavius and Tiberius, but at the same time takes the phrase *fregit Ti. Gracchum patientia* as referring to "to the steady opposition, as manifested by almost daily speeches, with which Octavius fought the land bill" (p. 299). This is quite arbitrary and disregards totally the Ciceronian definition of *patientia*. Nor is the Ciceronian definition taken into account by E. Badian, "The Silence of Norbanus", *AJP* 104 (1983) 162 (and n. 25). "The persistence of M. Octavius in his veto" was not an exercise in *patientia*, at least as *patientia* was understood by Cicero. P. Botteri, *Les fragments de l'histoire des Gracques dans la 'Bibliothèque' de Diodore de Sicile* (Genève 1992) 56–57, aptly adduces the passage of Diodorus (34/35.7.1) that after his deposition Octavius ἔμενε κατὰ τὴν ἰδίαν οἰκίαν ἡσυχάζων, and comments that at Cicero, *Brutus* 95, "la *patientia* évoque d'une certain façon l'ἡσυχία".

P. 294 = 247, n. 12: for the concept of *constantia*, see the bibliography in *Bibliographie zur lateinischen Wortforschung* 4 (Bern 1992) 267–271, esp. T.J. Moore, *Artistry and Ideology: Livy's Vocabulary of Virtue* (= Beiträge zur klassischen Philologie 192 [Frankfurt a. M. 1989]) 63–67, 152.

Errata. Read:

P. 293 = 246, line 8: "*duce* Badian" (this error unfortunately affected Badian's comment in his article adduced above).

28
THE AEDILES AND THE *DIDASCALIAE*
(1987)

P. 298 = 86, n. 13: for alternation in the curule aedileship of pairs of patrician and plebeian aediles, cf. T.C. Brennan, "Sulla's Career in the Nineties: Some Reconsiderations", *Chiron* 22 (1992) 135, and n. 96: "it is entirely possible" that the system of alternation "was still in effect ca. 100". F.X. Ryan, "Ten Ill-Starred Aediles", forthcoming, argues that the alternation "was no longer required by the time of the elections in 104". Errata. Read: P. 296 = 84, line 25: "strengthens".

29
ROMAN OFFICERS IN THE YEAR OF PYDNA
(1990)

Pp. 301–302 = 53–54: see also B. Schleussner, *Die Legaten der römischen Republik. 'Decem legati' und die ständigen Hilfsgesandte* (München 1978) esp. 101–211, who, however, falls in the trap of the annalistic terminology and fails to distinguish the senatorial legates *lecti publice* from the officers appointed for a specific task by the general, who need not have been senators. Nor does B.E. Thomasson, *Legatus* (Stockholm 1991) 9–13, pay attention to this fundamental distinction.

For the consular provinces in 168, cf. the excellent article by W. Bingham, "The Assignment of the Consular *Provinciae* in 168 B.C.", *Studies in Latin Literature and Roman History* 4 (1986) 184–209.

30
THE DEATH OF PONTIA
(1990)

P. 322 = 88, n. 7: earlier editions of Valerius by Thysius (i.e. Antonius Thys, ca 1603–1665) appeared in 1651, 1655 and 1660.

P. 323 = 89, n. 12: the article of Volterra has now been reprinted in: E. Volterra, *Scritti giuridici* 2 (Napoli 1991) 127–177.

P. 324 = 90, n. 14: cf. also Suet. *Claud.* 26.2: "Quam (i.e. Messalinam) cum *comperisset* super caetera flagitia atque dedecora C. Silio etiam nupsisse ... supplicio adfecit".

P. 324 = 90, n. 16: on *neco*, cf. *Addenda* to No 45 a, b. On strangulation as the normal mode of execution in the *carcer*, and the normal mode of execution of women, see J.-M. David, "Du *comitium* à la roche Tarpéienne. Sur certains rituels d'exécution capitale sous la République, les régnes d'Auguste et de Tibère", in: *Du châtiment dans la cité. Supplices corporels et peine de mort dans le monde antique* (Rome 1984) 143, n. 58; Y. Thomas, *"Vitae necisque potestas*. Le père, la cité, la mort", *Ibid.* 541–544.

P. 324 = 90, n. 17: Harris (adduced in n. 7) 87, infers from the term *proditam* that Valerius Maximus regarded Pontia as innocent. The *paedagogus* would have simply delivered her to Saturninus, and her father executed her not because she was guilty, but because she was polluted. Not impossible; but we have to remember that the *paedagogus* was expected to protect the *castitas* of his charge also from the girl's or boy's own temerity — and thus even if he only facilitated the meetings between Pontia and Saturninus he certainly would have been deemed to have "betrayed" her virginity. The jurists assume that illicit passion starts early: Ulpian (*Dig.* 48.5.14.8) seriously discusses the case "si minor duodecim annos in domum deducta adulterium commiserit".

31
TWO SPEECHES OF Q. HORTENSIUS.
A CONTRIBUTION TO THE *CORPUS ORATORUM*
OF THE ROMAN REPUBLIC
(1961)

P. 328 = 1: on the date of Plancius' aedileship (rather 55, and not 54), cf. Broughton, *MRR* 3.158.

P. 328 = 1, n. 6: cf. now H. Malcovati, *ORF*[4] (1976), *Addenda* A, p. 538.

P. 330 = 3, n. 12 (and passim): the idea that the decree of the senate "ut sodalitates decuriatique discederent" (Cic. *Q. fr.* 2.3.5) was proposed by Hortensius has been accepted by Gruen, *LGRR* 229, 233; and (more cautiously) by Shackleton Bailey, *CQF-MB* 178. Gruen also admits the connection between the *senatus consultum* and the Licinian Law (229–230, n. 83): "there can be little doubt that the *lex Licinia* grew out of the *s.c.* of February, 56". See also his remarks in "M. Licinius Crassus. A Review Article", *AJAH* 2 (1977 [1979]) 126–127 (and n. 41). Cf. also P. Grimal, "La lex Licinia de sodaliciis", in: *Ciceroniana. Hommages à Kazimierz Kumaniecki* (Leiden 1975) 107–115; J.-C. Richard, "Praetor collega consulis est II: La *lex Licinia de sodaliciis* et l'exil de M. Valerius Messala Rufus", *MEFRA* 95 (1983) 651–664 at 654–657, and see *Addenda* to Nos 9 and 16.

On the other hand Gruen writes (*LGRR* 320, n. 43): "That Hortensius also spoke for Plancius is an unwarranted supposition. His speech con-

cerned only the technicalities of the *lex Licinia de sodaliciis*, for he had
urged a similar measure in 56". And further: "If Hortensius had actually
defended Plancius, Cicero would have made more of that fact than a single
brief allusion".

The last point is not valid: we know that Hortensius defended L.
Licinius Murena in 63, but Cicero's speech *Pro Murena* contains only two
brief allusions to that circumstance. At 10 we have a passing reference to
Hortensius: "etenim si me tua familiaritas ab hac causa removisset et si hoc
idem Q. Hortensio, M. Crasso clarissimis viris ... accidisset ...". The other
passage (48) bears a striking resemblance to *Pro Plancio* 37: "Atque ex
omnibus illa plaga est iniecta petitioni tuae non tacente me maxima, de qua
ab homine ingeniosissimo et copiosissimo <Q.> Hortensio multa gravissime
dicta sunt. Quo etiam mihi durior locus est dicendi datus ut, cum ante me et
ille dixisset et vir summa dignitate et diligentia et facultate dicendi M.
Crassus, ego in extremo non partem aliquam agerem causae, sed de tota re
dicerem quod mihi videretur." Hortensius thus concentrated in his speech
on only a *pars causae,* and as follows from 47, he dealt with the technicalities of the *ambitus* legislation, and in particular with the senatorial debates
on that subject and with Sulpicius' proposals of a tougher anti-bribery law.
He clearly played the same role at the trial of Plancius.

There remains the interpretation of the phrase (*Pro Plancio* 37):
"huiusce rei (i.e. of the *iudices editicii*) obscura causa est ... et disputata
hesterno die a Q. Hortensio". Now Gruen a) admits Hortensius' sponsor-
ship of the *senatus consultum* of February 56 (to this circumstance will refer
Pro Plancio 37: "cui tum est senatus adsensus"), but b) denies any direct
involvement of Hortensius in the trial of Plancius. In that configuration
c) the only venue for Hortensius' disputation *hesterno die* could have been
again the senate (although Gruen does not state this explicitly). This would
mean that a day before Cicero's speech Hortensius had discussed the technicalities of the *lex Licinia* in the senate, and that Cicero refers his audience,
and the jury, to this speech. But if Hortensius had spoken in the senate
Cicero's reference to his *disputatio* would not have made much sense in the
context of a jury-trial: at least two-thirds of the jurors who were not the
members of the senate, the *equites* and the *tribuni aerarii*, would not have
heard the oration of Hortensius, and could not have been directly influenced
by it, even if Hortensius spoke *copiosissime*. This consideration clinches
the argument: Hortensius spoke in the defense of Plancius, and he delivered
his speech not in the senate but before the jury. Alexander, *Trials* 142–143,
and David, *PJ* 763 (and 765, n. 29) accept Hortensius as *advocatus* of
Plancius.

On the mention of the *iudices editicii* at *Pro Plancio* 41, see J.-L.
Ferrary, "Recherches sur la legislation de Saturninus et de Glaucia II: La loi

de iudiciis repetundarum, de C. Servilius Glaucia", *MEFRA* 91 (1979) 85–
134 at 124–127.

32
VERGIL AND DIONYSIUS
(1993)

Pp. 336, 341 = 4, 8 (and n. 20): on Dionysius, Vergil, and the Aborigines, see now the new studies by D. Briquel, *Les Tyrrhènes peuple des tours*
(Rome 1993) 125–140; "Virgile et les Aborigènes", *REL* 70 (1992 [1993])
69–91. I have unfortunately missed the interesting article by N. Golvers,
"The Latin Name *Aborigines*. Some Historiographical and Linguistic Observations", *Anc. Soc.* 20 (1989) 193–207.

Pp. 336, 343 = 4, 10: on Latinus and Mezentius, see also A. Grandazzi,
"Le roi Latinus, analyse d'une figure légendaire", *CRAI* (1988) 481–495;
D. Briquel, "A propos d'une inscription redécouverte au Louvre: remarques
sur la tradition relative à Mézence", *REL* 67 (1989 [1990]) 78–92.

P. 340 = 7, n. 16: cf. also C.J. Caster, *Prosopography of Roman Epi-
cureans from the Second Century B.C. to the Second Century A.D.* (Frankfurt a.M. 1988) 64–67.

33
TWO *CRUCES* IN SENECA, *DE VITA BEATA* 25.2
(1982)

P. 345 = 90 (and n. 2): on the Macedonian *causia*, and its origin, see
now the learned article by B. Kingsley, "Alexander's *Kausia* and the
Macedonian Tradition", *Class. Ant.* 10 (1991) 59–76.

34
AES OLET:
PETRONIUS 50.7 AND MARTIAL 9.59.11
(1992)

The Petronian Society Newsletter 22 (1992) 4, reports a note by S.
Walker, "Rome: City and Empire", *British Museum Magazine* 6 (1991) 3,
in which referring to our passage of Petronius she writes: "In the early
Empire it became possible to drink for the first time from cups made of
blown glass, which imparted no taste to drink". This misses the gist of
Petronius' joke.

Studies on Corinthian bronze continue appearing:

D.M. Jacobson, M.P. Weitzman, "What was Corinthian Bronze?", *AJA* 96 (1992) 237–248. They remark on the passages of Petronius and Martial (p. 238): "these references need not be taken seriously. Metals normally do not have intrinsic smell".

A.R. Giumlia-Muir, P.T. Craddock, *Corinthium Aes: das schwarze Gold der Alchimisten* (Mainz 1992) [non vidi].

35
ALFRED THE GREAT
AND THE TRADITION OF ANCIENT GEOGRAPHY
(1964)

P. 358 = 436: for further traces of the map of Agrippa, see the ingenious article by T.P. Wiseman, "Julius Caesar and the Hereford World Map", *History Today* 37 (1976) 53–57. On the whole question of the sources of the Old English Orosius, see the excellent paper by J.M. Bately, "The Relationship between geographical information in the Old English Orosius and Latin Texts other than Orosius", *Anglo-Saxon England* 1 (1972) 45–57, esp. 46, 53 (on Dacia and Vistula), 53–54 (on the wasteland between Carentania and Bulgaria; she prefers to connect it with the Avars). King Alfred's geoography was also treated, rather disappointingly, by O. Pritsak in his strange volume, *The Origin of Rus'*. Vol. One: *Old Scandinavian Sources other than the Sagas* (Cambridge, MA, 1981), 683–703, 802–806. He reproduces, but does not discuss, the passage concerning Vistula and Dacia (pp. 687–688).

Pp. 357–358 = 435–436: on Vistula as the western border of Dacia, see also C. Nicolet, *Space, Geography and Politics in the Early Roman Empire* (Ann Arbor 1991) 109. An inspiring and erudite book; still he does not mention Alfred.

36
NOTES ON *CIL* I² 364
(1958)

The solution here proposed (recorded in *AEp.* 1960, p. 74, after no 273) was reached independently, and on similar grounds, also by A. Degrassi, *ILLRP* (Firenze 1957) 1.192 (pp. 128–129), and was accepted by G. Giacomelli, *La lingua Falisca* (Firenze 1963) 264–265 (no XIV), who adduces both contributions. She writes that this solution had been foreshadowed by F. Buecheler in *CLE* 1.2 (1895), pp. 2–3, and by E. Bormann in *CIL* XI 3078 (1888) = 7483 (1926), but Buecheler has no word on that matter, and thus presumably followed the received opinion, whereas Bormann quite explicitly identifies the *collegium* of cooks with the Faliscans in Sardinia. As Degrassi notes, it was R. Garrucci, *Sylloge Inscriptionum Latinarum* 2.557–558 (Augustae Taurinorum 1877), pp. 168–171, who had believed that the two inscriptions were engraved separately, inscription *b* much older than inscription *a*. Degrassi himself on the other hand believes that the metric inscription (*b*) was composed first, but as it was marred by various errors "lamella iam una ex parte inscripta ad alium titulum in altera parte ab eodem scalptore exarandum adhiberetur".

The most detailed study of the monument is now E. Peruzzi, "La lamina dei cuochi Falischi", *Atti e Memorie dell'Accademia Toscana di Scienze e Lettere "La Colombaria"*, 31 (1966) 113–162. He too assigns the two inscriptions to two different corporations, the Faliscans sojourning in Sardinia, and the collegium of cooks residing in Falerii Novi. Following in the footsteps of a perceptive epigraphical study of an anonymous scholar in *La civiltà cattolica* 11 (1894) 221–224 (as Peruzzi notes, until 1933 articles in that journal were published anonymously, but the article in question was written by Minasi), Peruzzi (who conducted the autopsy of the document) observes (pp. 119–124, 157) that the layout of inscription *a* fits perfectly the dimensions of the plate, whereas on the other hand in inscription *b*, as the Anonymus put it, "le lettere dell'ultimo verso ... *utei* etc., sono quasi tutte segate". He concludes that inscription *b* was engraved first, and the plate (which was presumably cut at the bottom) was then utilized to accomodate inscription *a*. Not an unlikely sequence, but not everybody will agree that the argument of the Anonymus and Peruzzi offers definite proof.

Degrassi dates both inscriptions to the end of the third century, Peruzzi (pp. 160–162) to the Gracchan period. He is inclined to connect the inscription of "Falesce quei in Sardinia sunt" with C. Gracchus' program of colonization: "Nulla esclude la deduzione di una colonia in Sardegna con la partezipazione di falischi". But quite appropriately he adds a somber caveat: "Ma una simile ipotesi ha bisogno di prove che ancora non vedo" (p. 162). The date in the second part of the second century seems now to be established as the *communis opinio*: see R.W. Wachter, *Altlateinische Inschriften* (Bern 1987) 441–446; B. Vine, *Studies in Archaic Latin Inscriptions* (Innsbruck 1993) 209 (with further literature). Wachter 443, with a very involved explanation, continues to identify the cooks and the Falesce.

On the Saturnian verse, see B. Luiselli, *Il verso saturnio* (Rome 1967), esp. 329–330; T. Cole, "The Saturnian Verse", *YCS* 21 (1969) 3–73.

The epithet "inperatoribus summeis" Peruzzi (pp. 124–127) refers to Iuppiter, Iuno and Minerva: both dedications were intended to be displayed in the same temple in Falerii in which the cult of Juno was apparently combined with the cult of Jupiter and Minerva; the female deities were probably represented as "divinità in aspetto guerriero". On Minerva Imperator in a late inscription from Lucus Feroniae, see J.-L. Girard, "Minerva Capta: entre Rome et Faleries", *REL* 67 (1989 [1990]) 163–169 at 168. He ingeniously connects the spellings *gonlegium*, *Volgani*, *gondecorant* (in the metric inscription) with the introduction of the letter G by the freedman Sp. Carvilius, the *magister* of the first *ludus litterarius* in Rome, and the possible patronage of the *gens Carvilia* over Falerii (pp. 168–169).

Peruzzi argues (pp. 127–128) that *venter Faliscus* was modest fare, and hence it is an exaggeration to speak of Falerii as a center of culinary art. For the traditional view, see the convincing remarks by J. Collart, *Varron, De lingua Latina, livre V* (Paris 1954) 216.

On cooks in Greece and in Italy, see now: H. Dohm, *Mageiros. Die Rolle des Kochs in der griechisch-römischen Komödie* (München 1964); G. Berthiaume, *Les rôles du mágeiros. Études sur la boucherie, la cuisine et le sacrifice dans la Grèce ancienne* (Leiden 1982); and above all the excellent study by J.C.B. Lowe, "Cooks in Plautus", *Class. Ant.* 4 (1985) 72–103. Dohm and Berthiaume do not adduce our inscription, even by way of illustration and comparison; on the other hand Lowe observes that normally Roman cooks were slaves or freedmen, and points out that C.G. Harcum, *Roman Cooks* (Baltimore 1914) 67–68 "cites as the only evidence of freeborn cooks the much-discussed dedication of the Faliscan cooks", but, he continues, "this depends on the probably false assumption that the cooks are to be identified with the Faliscans in Sardinia" (p. 83, n. 75).

After the edition of Lommatsch, full bibliographical references are provided by Giacomelli (see above); I. Di Stefano Manzella in *Supplementa Italica* 1 (1981), p. 124 (ad *CIL* XI 7483); I. Krummrey in *CIL* I² (vol. 1, pars posterior, fasc. 4, addenda tertia [1986]), p. 877 (on I² 364). New photographs are to be found appended to the article by Peruzzi, and, above all, in A. Degrassi *Inscriptiones Latinae Liberae Rei Publicae. Imagines* (*CIL Auctarium* [1965]) 93 *a. b.* (p. 61).

On the history of Falerii Novi, see now I. Di Stefano Manzella, "Lo stato giuridico di Falerii Novi dalla fondazione al III secolo d. C.", in: *La Civiltà dei Falisci* (= Atti del XV Convegno di Studi Etruschi ed Italici [Firenze 1990]) 341–368, esp. 341–350.

37
LIBIIS OR LIBENS?
A NOTE ON A NEW DEDICATION TO LIBER PATER
FROM DACIA
(1975)

In the same fascicle of *Latomus* in which this article was published also A. Albertini has recognized that in our inscription *libiis* = *libe(n)s* (1975, fasc. 1, p. 232).

38
NATALIS PATAVII
(1983)

P. 372 = 230: on the Roman intervention in Patavium, see F. Sartori, "Padova nello stato Romano dal sec. III a.C. all'età dioclezianca", in: *Padova antica: da communità paleoveneta a città romano-cristiana,* Trieste 1981, 107–109.

P. 373 – 231 (and n. 22): on *CIL* V 2787 = *ILS* 5202, and the *ludi cetasti,* see L.D. Jacobs, "Ludi Cetasti Patavinorum", *Athenaeum* N.S. 67 [= 77] (1989) 275–281 at 280. Cf. also M.S. Bassignano, "Il municipio Patavino", in: *Padova antica* 223-224.

39
JULIA IN REGIUM
(1988)

P. 375 = 181 (and n. 1): the inscription is now published by M. Buonocore in *Supplementa Italica* N.S. 5 (Rome 1989) 63–64 (no 16).

P. 378 = 184, n. 10: for this inscription, see Buonocore, *Ibid.* 64–65 (no 17).

P. 379 = 185: Y. Thomas, "Droit domestique et droit politique à Rome. Remarques sur le pécule et les *honores* des fils de familie", *MEFRA* 94 (1982) 527–580, interestingly observes (at 551) that "les premiers pécules qui nous soient véritablement attestés pour des *liberi* sous puissance paternelle sont ceux de Julie et de Tibère".

Pp. 380–384 = 186–190: J.F. Gardner, "Julia's Freedmen: Questions of Law and Status", *BICS* 35 (1988) 94–100, esp. 94–97, argues that Gelos and Thiasus were manumitted by Julia in 14/15, in the period between the death of Augustus and the death of Julia, and that the mother of Gelos was manumitted by Livia between 14 (when Livia assumed the name of Iulia Augusta) and 29, the date of Livia's death. She points out that the *servus peculiaris manumissus* was technically a *libertus* of the *pater* (*Dig.* 37.14.13), and hence if Gelos and Thiasus had been manumitted during Augustus' lifetime they would have been *Augusti liberti* (and not *Iuliae liberti*). Hence her theory: Thiasus and Gelos and the *mater* were originally slaves of Livia living in the household of Julia; after the death of Augustus (and after Julia lost her *peculium*) Livia gave Thiasos and Gelos as a gift to Julia, but retained the ownership over the *mater*; Julia, now *sui iuris*, manumitted Thiasus and Gelos either in her lifetime or in her will. As to the mother we are in agreement; Gardner's interpretation of the legal vicissitudes of Thiasus and Gelos is certainly ingenious, but I would rather admit the (legally) incorrect wording of the inscription than accept a gift from Livia.

P. 382 = 188, n. 21: the article here mentioned has appeared: "*Partus Ancillae*. A *vetus quaestio* in the Light of a New Inscription", *Labeo* 33 (1987) 192–198. See the polemic by A. Watson, "Partus Ancillae and a Recent inscription from Regium", *Labeo* 38 (1992) 335–338, especially against the idea that Gelos became Julia's property through *usufructus*. In any case the alternate interpretation provided in the article here reproduced (p. 187, lines 4–9 from bottom) appears more likely (but see above). On the problem of *partus ancillae*, see also P. Birks, "An Unacceptable Face of Human Property", in: P. Birks (ed.), *New Perspectives in the Roman Law of Property. Essays for Barry Nicholas* (Oxford 1989) 61–73, esp. 63–64. I still believe that the tenor of Cicero, *de fin.* 1.4.12, indicates that the question "an partus sitne in fructu habendus" was not yet resolved at that time.

P. 389 = 195 (and n. 43): the inscription has been republished by Buonocore, *Suppl. It.* 5, no 15 (pp. 62–63).

Pp. 389 and 391 = 195 and 197: the inscription from Regium was missed by J. Scheid, Scribonia Caesaris et les Julio-Claudiens", *MEFRA* 87 (1975) 349–375 (cf. 373–375: "Documents relatifs à Scribonia et à sa familie"), but I unfortunately missed his otherwise most erudite article. Scheid establishes convincingly that Scribonia was not the sister but rather the daughter of the consul of 34.

Errata. Read:

P. 375 = 181, line 12: "testamen[to]. P. 375 = 181, n. 1, line 2: "di epigrafia". P. 388 = 194, in the numbering of footnotes: "42)". P. 389 = 195, n. 43, line 4: "indented".

40

CERTIS CALENDIS
(1991)

Pp. 400–403 = 90–93: for the sentiment here discussed, see also M. Fussl, "Condicio nascendi — Condicio moriendi. Zu einem antiken Trostgedanken und seiner Nachwirkung bei den lateinischen Kirchenvätern", *Grazer Beiträge* 16 (1989) 243–269.

P. 401 = 91, n. 24: one should check the indications provided by even the greatest authorities. Adducing the inscription *CLE* 1168 I repeated after Buecheler that it was found in "Teos in Lydia". Of course it is Teos in Ionia; cf. W. Ruge, "Teos", *RE* 9A (1934) 541, no 70.

P. 404 = 94 (and n. 41): Horace, *Ep.* 2.2.175, echoes the line of Lucretius: "perpetuus nulli datur usus".

P. 406 = 96, n. 50: cf. K. Argetsinger, "Birthday Rituals: Friends and Patrons in Roman Poetry and Cult", *Class. Ant.* 11 (1992) 175–193, esp. 178, 181.

41

UPDATING THE *CIL* FOR ITALY
(1990)

P. 411 = 317, Velitrae No. 24: H. Solin has kindly sent me the following note (dated 19 Nov. 1990) which arrived too late to be included in my comment on the inscription: "You ... are inclined to read C. Baebius C.l. Pamphilus. But the letter after P cannot be an A; the photo is here misleading. Preparing the edition even I wrote first [Pa]mphilus, but after a close examination of the stone I could confirm that the letter following P cannot indeed be an A — there is in fact an 'asta verticale'. Perhaps I should have explained in the apparatus that the photo is misleading". If so we do not know the *cognomen* of Baebius and the *nomen* of Pamphilus; the latter would have served as *arbiter*, which also makes good sense.

P. 411 = 317, Velitrae No. 71: for a detailed study of this inscription, see No 40.

42

ZUM NAMEN COMPETALIS
(1960)

P. 416 = 146: cf. I. Kajanto, *The Latin Cognomina* (Helsinki 1965) 220. He lists the name *Competalis* as derived from the festival of

Compitalia (p. 220) or alternately among the *cognomina* derived from occu-
pations, more exactly the denominations of priests (p. 318). I would rather
say it is derived from the noun *compitum*.

P. 418 = 148, n. 4: see above, No 15.

43
REVIEW OF:
D.R. SHACKLETON BAILEY, *TWO STUDIES IN ROMAN NOMENCLATURE*
(1978)

See now Shackleton Bailey's *Appendix* in the second edition of his
book (Atlanta 1991) 87–98.

44
AMIANUS
(1978)

Cf. independently Solin, *Gnomon* 59 (1987) 597. The name is now
accepted by D.R. Shackleton Bailey, *Two Studies in Roman Nomenclature*[2]
(Atlanta 1991) 88.

45a
FUMUM VENDERE AND *FUMO NECARE*
(1987)

45b
FUMO NECARE: AN ADDENDUM
(1987)

Pp. 429–431 = 142–144: see now J.N. Adams, "The Uses of Neco",
Glotta 68 (1990) 230–255, esp. 234; 69 (1991) 94–123, esp. 101–103.

P. 431 = 144, n. 27: A.J. Pomeroy, "Hannibal at Nuceria", *Historia* 38
(1989) 162–176, at 162, 164–165, 174–175, regards the story of Hannibal's
atrocities at Nuceria as annalist fabrication, and in particular the bath episode: before the advent of the hypocaust baths it was hardly possible to induce suffocation *fumo et vapore*.

46

THE SURNAME OF M. ANTONIUS CRETICUS
AND THE COGNOMINA *EX VICTIS GENTIBUS*
(1990)

P. 436 = 157: on the cognomen Creticus, cf. D.R. Shackleton Bailey, *Two Studies in Roman Nomenclature*[2] (Atlanta 1991) 89. He accepts the idea that the cognomen of Antonius was meant to be honorific. M.H. Dettenhoffer, *Perdita iuventus. Zwischen den Generationen von Caesar und Augustus* (München 1992) 64, continues to believe that Antonius "wegen seines Misserfolgs wurde ... zum Spott Creticus genannt". H. Pohl, *Die römische Politik und die Piraterie im östlichen Mittelmeer vom 3. bis zum 1 Jh. v. Chr.* (Berlin 1993), does not discuss the cognomen Creticus, and his discussion of Antonius' campaign is perfunctory (pp. 270–274).

P. 436 = 157, n. 2: the epigram from Corinth, *ILLRP* 342, which A.N. Sherwin-White, "Rome, Pamphylia and Cilicia, 133–70 B.C.", *JRS* 66 (1976) 1–14 at 4, attempted to ascribe to M. Antonius Creticus belongs to M. Antonius, pr. 102; see J.-L. Ferrary, "Recherches sur la législation de Saturninus et de Glaucia", *MEFRA* 89 (1977) 639–643.

P. 439 = 160, line 2: this is inexact. The text of the *Fasti Triumphales* is only partially preserved for L. Scipio, but Degrassi's restitution (p. 81) S[*cipio Asiaticus*] is assured by the length of the line.

For further thoughts on the *acclamatio imperatoria* and the bestowal of the *cognomina ex victis gentibus*, see "A Missing Ponticus", forthcoming in *AJAH*.

Errata.
P. 439 = 160, n. 21: omit "201:".

47

RÖMISCHER STAAT UND DIE GÖTTERZEICHEN:
ZUM PROBLEM DER OBNUNTIATIO
(1971)

See *Addenda* to No 5 (pp. 83–84 = 435–426).

48

CICERO AND ROMAN DIVINATION
(1983)

It is pleasant to note that A. Momigliano, as he himself acknowledges, paints a rather similar picture of Roman *religio* and Roman divination: "The

Theological Efforts of the Roman Upper Classes in the First Century B.C.",
CP 79 (1984) 199–211 (cf. 199, n. 1). See also the articles by N. Denyear,
"The Case against Divination: an Examination of Cicero's *De divinatione*",
Proc. Cambr. Philol. Soc. N.S. 31 (1985) 1–10; M. Beard, "Cicero and
Divination: the Formation of a Latin Discourse", *JRS* 76 (1986) 33–46; M.
Schofield, "Cicero for and against Divination", *Ibid.* 47–65; J. North, "Di-
viners and Divination at Rome", in: M. Beard and J. North (eds.), *Pagan
Priests* (London 1990) 51–70. See also in this volume No 49. A new edi-
tion of the *De divinatione* with a German translation and useful commentary
was produced by C. Schäublin, *Marcus Tullius Cicero, Über die
Wahrsagung* (München und Zürich 1991).

P. 462 = 16, n. 9: *AL* 2176–2177.

P. 469 = 23, n. 4: *AL* 2258–2289.

Pp. 471–472 = 25–26: on the annulment of the *leges Appuleiae, Liviae*
and the *lex Titia*, cf. *AL* 2167, nn. 62–63, and *Addenda* to No 54 (p. 540 =
458, n. 1). On the *lex Titia*, see also acute remarks by J.-C. Richard, "Sur la
rogatio Titia agraria", *MEFRA* 103 (1991) 589–603, esp. 597–602, and on
the *leges Liviae*, the convincing piece by F.X. Ryan, "The Reliability of
Asconius *In Cornelianam* 69C", *SIFC* 12 (1994) 103–109.

P. 477 = 31, n. 45: *AL* 2200–2202; and above all, C. Schäublin,
"Ementita auspicia", *WS* 20 (1986) 165–181.

Errata. Read:

P. 479 = 33, line 21: "*inaugurato*".

49
WATCHING THE BIRDS:
CICERO THE AUGUR AND THE AUGURAL *TEMPLA*
(1986)

See *Addenda* to No 48.

Pp. 490–492 = 335–337: on the concept of *templum*, see the erudite
and imaginative study by J. Vaahtera, "On the Religious Nature of the Place
of Assembly", in: *Senatus Populusque Romanus. Studies in Roman Republican Legislation* (= Acta Instituti Romani Finlandiae 13 [Helsinki 1993])
96–116, esp. 107–112.

Errata. Read:

P. 493 = 338, n. 23, lines 1–2: "De modis auspicandi Romanorum".

50
THE *LIBRI RECONDITI*
(1985)

P. 497 = 208, n. 3: on the *lex Papiria*, see now the widely divergent interpretations by A. Ziólkowski, *The Temples of Mid-Republican Rome and the Historical and Topographical Context* (Rome 1992) 219–234, and W.J. Tatum, "The *Lex Papiria De Dedicationibus*", *CP* 88 (1993) 319–328.

P. 498 = 209, n. 5: *AL* 2241 (and n. 376).

Pp. 512–514 = 223–225: on the debate (ancient and modern) concerning the validity of Bibulus' *obnuntiatio,* see *Addenda* to No 5 (pp. 73–74 = 425–426), esp. Heikkilä, 140–141.

P. 518 = 229 (and n. 79): see also the excellent study by H. Dahlmann, *Über Aemilius Macer* (= Abh. Mainz 1981, Nr. 6) 8–10.

P. 523 = 234 (and n. 97): on "the shadowy Furius" I missed the incisive (and wisely inconclusive) discussion by E. Rawson, "Scipio, Laelius and the Ancestral Religion", *JRS* 63 (1973) 161–174, esp. 168–174; reprinted in: E. Rawson, *Roman Culture and Society. Collected Papers* (Oxford 1991) 80–101, esp. 93–101.

51
EXTA AND *AVES*:
AN EMENDATION IN RUFINUS,
ORIGENIS IN NUMEROS HOMILIA 17.2
(1981)

P. 525 = 214, nn. 4 and 5: on the augural meaning of *colligere*, see No 53. Errata. Read:
P. 524 = 213, line 10: "Origenes".

52
SANNIO AND REMUS
(1989)

P. 529 = 92, n. 1: Skutsch first presented his emendation in "*Condendae Urbis Auspicia*", *CQ* 55 = N.S. 11 (1961) 252–267 at 258 and 263 (reprinted in O. Skutsch, *Studia Enniana* [London 1968] 63–85 at 70 and 76). H.D. Jocelyn, "Urbs Augurio Augusto Condita: Ennius ap. Cic. *Div.* 1.107 (= *Ann.* 77-96 V²)", *PCPS* 197 = N.S. 17 (1971) 44–74, disregarded by Skutsch in his commentary, offered a detailed critique of the emendation (pp. 60–63). Skutsch may not be right, but Jocelyn's suggestion, defending the reading *se devovet*, that Remus made "a bargain with the underworld gods, according to which they were either to help him to the kingship by giving a certain auspice or to claim him for their own" (p. 63), is not convincing. "Se auspicio devovere" is not one and the same thing as "se Dis Manibus devovere".

53
"AUSPICIA ET AUGURIA ROMANA ... SUMMO LABORE COLLECTA": A NOTE ON MINUCIUS FELIX, *OCTAVIUS* 26.1
(1982)

This article should be read in conjunction with the learned response and polemic by J.R. Fears, "Minucius Felix Octavius 26.1", *CP* 77 (1982) 150–152. Surely *omen colligo* can mean and often does mean (as in Amm. Marc. 30.5.17, adduced by Fears) "to obtain an omen". But one cannot obtain an omen without at the same time interpreting it. Cf. also Petr. 126.3: "nec auguria novi nec mathematicorum caelum curare soleo, ex vultibus hominum mores *colligo*". The juxtaposition of *novi* and *colligo* is instructive: in order to employ the *auguria* one must know their significance; similarly in order to deduce (*colligo*; in this place certainly not simply "obtain") the character of people from their *vultus* one must know the meaning of facial expressions. Cf. also No 51.

Pp. 532–533 = 149–150, nn. 8 and 10: see now *AL* 2230–2241.

54
A WITTICISM OF APPULEIUS SATURNINUS
(1984)

P. 538 = 456, n. 1: on the *de viris illustribus* and the Livian *epitome*, cf. P.L. Schmidt, in: *Handbuch der lateinischen Literatur*. Bd. V: *Restauration und Erneuerung. Die lateinische Literatur von 284 bis 374 n. Chr.* (München 1989) 187–191. He clearly underestimates the "verbalen Übereinstimmungen".

P. 540 = 458, n. 1: on the problem of the annulment of the *leges Appuleiae*, I note the solid study of L. de Libero, *Obstruktion* (Stuttgart 1992) 91–96; and, in particular, K. Heikkilä, "Lex non iure rogata", in: *Senatus Populusque Romanus. Studies in Roman Republican Legislation* (= Acta Instituti Romani Finlandiae 13 [Helsinki 1993] 134–137. C. Bergemann, *Politik und Religion im spätrepublikanischen Rom* (Stuttgart 1992) 98, is both uninformed and confused (unfortunately this observation applies to many other pages of the book, and so I refrain from quoting it in other places. See my review of de Libero and Bergemann forthcoming in *CP* 90 [1995]). On the passage of Saturninus' *lex agraria*, see also J.L. Beness, "The Urban Unpopularity of Saturninus", *Antichthon* 25 (1991) 33–57, esp. 46–47. Cf. above, *Addenda* to No 48 (pp. 471–472 = 25–26).

Errata. Read:

P. 538 = 456, n. 1, line 6: "in". P. 539 = 457, line 9: "in".

55
RELIGIOUS ASPECTS OF THE CONFLICT OF THE ORDERS: THE CASE OF *CONFARREATIO*
(1986)

As this article was published in a collective volume, all abbreviations were given at the end of the volume. I give here the full titles of the works cited in the footnotes in an abbreviated form:

A. Alföldi, "Struktur des Römerstaates" = "Zur Struktur des Römerstaates im 5. Jh. v. Chr.", in: *Les origines de la république romaine* (= Entretiens sur l'ant. class. 13 [Vandoeuvres-Genève 1967]) 223–278.

P.E. Corbett, *Marriage = The Roman Law of Marriage* (Oxford 1930).

P. De Francisci, *Primordia = Primordia civitatis* (Rome 1959).

E. Gjerstad, *Early Rome* V (Lund 1973).

F. Guizzi, *Vesta = Il sacerdozio di Vesta: Aspetti giuridici del sacerdozio romano* (Napoli 1968).

M. Kaser, *Ius = Das altrömische ius* (Göttingen 1949).

M. Kaser, *Privatr.* I^2 = *Das römische Privatrecht* I^2 (München 1971).

J. Marquardt, *Privatleben*^{2} = *Das Privatleben der Römer*^{2} (Leipzig 1886).

J. Marquardt, *Staatsverwaltung* III^2 = *Römische Staatsverwaltung* III^2 (Leipzig 1885).

T. Mommsen, *Röm. Staatsrecht* III.1 = *Römisches Staatsrecht* III.1 (Leipzig 1887).

P. Noailles, *Fas = Fas et ius: Études de droit romain* (Paris 1948).

R. Ogilvie, *Comm.* = *A Commentary on Livy, Books 1-5* (Oxford 1965).

J.-C. Richard, *Origines = Les origines de la plèbe romaine* (Paris 1978).

A. Watson, *XII Tables = Rome of the XII Tables: Persons and Property* (Princeton 1975).

C.W. Westrup, *Recherches = Recherches sur les formes antiques de mariage dans l'ancien droit romain* (= Danske Vidensk. Selsk. Hist-Filol.

Medd. 30.1 [København 1943]).

G. Wissowa, *Religion* = *Religion und Kultus der Römer*[2] (München 1912).

P. 547 = 249, n. 17: the article by Volterra has been reprinted in: E. Volterra, *Scritti giuridici* 3 (Napoli 1991) 155–176.

P. 548 = 250, n. 19: G. Radke, "Beobachtungen zur römischen *confarreatio*", *Gymnasium* 96 (1989) 209–226 at 214–215, in a case of willful blindness, continues to confuse the ceremony of the *obnubere* of the bride with the *velatio capitis* of the groom and the bride. S. Treggiari, *Roman Marriage. Iusti Coniuges from the Time of Cicero to the Time of Ulpian* (Oxford 1991) 21–24, provides only a general account of the ceremony. On *flammeum*, see N. Boëls-Janssen, "La fiancée embrasée", in: D. Porte and J.-P. Néraudau (eds.), *Hommages à Henri Le Bonniec. Res Sacrae* (= Collection Latomus 201 [Bruxelles 1988]) 19–30, esp. 29; "La prêtresse aux trois voiles", *REL* 67 (1989 [1990]) 117–133, esp. 119–121. Cf. also Eadem, "Flaminica cincta, à propos de la couronne rituelle de l'épouse du flamine de Jupiter", *REL* 69 (1991 [1992]) 32–50.

Pp. 548–549 = 250–251 (and n. 20): Radke, 217, n. 5, rejects (without argument) the idea that Servius *auctus*, *Georg.* 1.31, ultimately derives from Ateius Capito (*ad rem*, cf. No 14, pp. 306–307). Consequently he denies the participation of the *flamen Dialis* at the ceremony of *confarreatio*. His trump argument is this (pp. 210–211): "Seit dem Selbstmord des *flamen Dialis* L. Cornelius Merula i. J. 87 v. Chr. konnte das ... Priersteramt nach der Auskunft bei Tac. ann. 3,58,2 fünfundsiebzig Jahre hindurch nicht wieder besetzt werden. ... Wäre die Angabe des Serv. auct. zutreffend, hätten in diesen 75 Jahren ... keine konfarreierten Ehen geschlossen worden sein können". The argument appears cogent, but it is empty. The same Tacitus in the same passage (*Ann.* 3.58) states explicitly that in the absence of the *flamen Dialis* his functions were performed by the pontiffs: "saepe pontifices sacra Dialia fecisse, si flamen valetudine aut munere publico impediretur. quinque et septuaginta annis post Cornelii Merulae caedem neminem suffectum, neque tamen cessavisse religiones. quod si per tot annos possit non creari nullo sacrorum damno...". Cf. in this sense already G. Martorana, "Osservazioni sul *flamen Dialis*", in: Φιλίας χάριν. *Miscellanea in onore di Eugenio Manni* (Rome 1979) 1455.

J.H. Vanggaard, *The Flamen. A Study in the History and Sociology of Roman Religion* (Copenhagen 1988) 50, maintains that the *camilli* "had to be of patrician descent", but concedes that "this is not capable of actual proof". He missed the *glossa* and Servius.

P. 551 = 253, n. 26: the reference is to J.-C. Richard, "Patricians and Plebeians: The Origin of a Social Dichotomy", in: *Social Struggles in Archaic Rome* (Berkeley 1986) 105–129, at 107–110.

P. 552 = 254, n. 28: the reference is to Richard (as above) 110–114.

Pp. 533–534 = 255–256: see also No 57, pp. 580–581 = 212–213. Radke, pp. 215–216, has nothing to offer. R.E. Mitchell, *Patricians and Plebeians* (Ithaca 1990) 86, n. 72, speculates that our *sacerdos confarreationum et diffarreationum* "may have been a patrician in charge of maintaining traditional standards". This flies in the face of all prosopographical evidence, and is a good example of bending facts to a preconceived theory. Cf. S. Treggiari, *Roman Marriage* 24 (and n. 96).

Pp. 554–556 = 256–258: E. Badian, *Gnomon* 62 (1990) 33 (and already *Ibid.* 33 [1961] 598), supports the view that Caesar was formally inaugurated as *flamen Dialis*. I do not believe that this was proven by G.V. Sumner, *The Orators in Cicero's Brutus* (Toronto 1973) 139–140; the term *inauguratus* is never used of Caesar.

Pp. 554–555 = 256–257: Vanggaard, *Flamen* 50–54, argues that the *flaminica* need not have been a *patricia*. Now from the fact that the *flamines Martiales* could be married to plebeian women it is rather risky to draw any conclusions concerning the *flamen Dialis* and his wife. The *flaminica* participated in the *cultus*; on the other hand we do not know anything of the ritual obligations of the wives of the *flamen Martialis* and *Quirinalis*. Secondly we should not confuse two disparate things: the eligibility to the station of *flaminica* (*Dialis*) and the capacity to conlude marriage through the ceremony of *confarreatio*. The eligibility to the former was limited to the *patriciae natae ex confarreatis*; the capacity to conclude marriage through *confarreatio* was open to plebeian women marrying patrician husbands.

P. 558 = 260, n. 54: the reference is to R.E. Mitchell, "The Definition of *patres* and *plebs*: An End to the Struggle of the Orders", in: *Social Struggles* 130–174, at 171–173.

P. 559 = 261, n. 56: the references are to R.E. Mitchell (as above), and to K.A. Raaflaub, "From Protection and Defense to Offense and Participation: Stages in the Conflict of the Orders", *Ibid.* 198–243, esp. 227–236. Mitchell upholds the identity of *patres* and *sacerdotes* in his bold book *Patricians and Plebeians. The Origin of the Roman State* (Ithaca 1990), esp. 64–130. This is not true for the later or middle republic; for the early republic it is true in the sense that as long as the priesthoods were open only to the patricians, all *sacerdotes* were *patres*. L. Sancho, "El matrimonio romano primitivo y el valor de la *Lex inhumanissima* (Cic. *Rep.* II 37,62)", *RIDA* 37 (1990) 347–383, concludes that "el único probable ritual matrimonial arcaico es la *confarreatio*" (p. 371), and that it was practiced by both the patricians and plebeians. Cf. also K.-J. Hölkeskamp, *Gnomon* 61 (1989) 314; R.A. Bauman, *ZRG* 107 (1990) 473.

56
THE AUSPICES AND THE STRUGGLE OF THE ORDERS
(1990)

This paper should be considered in conjunction with the discussion that followed after its presentation in Berlin in 1986; see especially the comment by M. Torelli, in: *Staat und Staatlichkeit in der frühen römischen Republik* (Stuttgart 1990) 74–83, and the remarks by A. Giovannini (p. 85), E. Badian (pp. 85–86, esp. his illuminating discussion of the phrase "auspicia ad patres redeunt" (cf. pp. 466–467). Cf. also my response (pp. 88–89), and see now the penetrating remarks by L. Schumacher, *ZRG* 110 (1993) 670–671. To the bibliography add E.S. Staveley, "The Nature and Aims of the Patriciate", *Historia* 32 (1983) 24–57, esp. 34–40.

P. 561 = 35: in the text of Livy M. Crawford suggests (*per litteras*) an excellent emendation: "et privati[m] <ea> auspicia habeamus".

Pp. 570–572 = 44–46: J.-C. Richard, "Tribuns militaires et triomphe", in: *La Rome des premiers siècles, légende et histoire. Actes de la Table Ronde en l'honneur de Massimo Pallotino* (= Biblioteca di *Studi Etruschi* 24 [Firenze 1992]) 235–246, arrives at a conclusion almost identical to that advocated in the article here reprinted: the *tribuni militum consulari potestate* had the right to the auspices (cf. an earlier article by Richard, "Réflexions sur le tribunat consulaire", *MEFRA* 102 [1990] 767–799 at 779), but they were incapable of celebrating a triumph. That honor was reserved only for those holders of imperium who possessed it "dans sa plénitude et dans sa pureté originelle" (p. 239, cf. 243). A magnificent study with an argument enviable in its cogency and clarity. In a post-script Richard alludes to my article, but he presents my argument only partially and rather inaccurately when he writes (p. 146, n. 46) that according to my view (expressed on p. 45) "ces magistrats, lorsqu'ils appartenaient à la plèbe, détenaient selon toute vraisemblance ce qu'il faut appeler 'a lesser *auspicium*'". And he comments: "Ce nouveau phénomène de *deminutio* ne suffit portant pas à expliquer à nos yeux que tout les tribuns consulaires, qu'ils fussent plébéiens ou patriciens, n'aient pu célébrer le triomphe". In fact I point out (p. 44) that only the patrician members of the college of the *tribuni militum* may have been thought able "to transmit the auspices to their successors in their pure and pristine state", but I go on to reject (perhaps not clearly enough) the hypothetical idea that the college might have been composed of two separate groups of officials, patrician and plebeian, of a differing "auspical" status: I argue that all members of the college had the same prerogatives, that all of them, whether patrician or plebeian, administered in comparison to consuls (or *praetores*) a "lesser *imperium* and lesser *auspicium*" (pp. 45–46).

E. Badian in the same volume in which my article was originally printed (*Staat und Staatlichkeit in der frühen römischen Republik* [Stuttgart 1990]) 469, conjectures that the *tribuni militum* had the auspices but lacked *imperium*. Not likely: even the *privati* were given *imperium* when they were selected to command troops. The difference between the *tribuni militum consulari potestate* and the *consules* was rather like that obtaining (in later times) between the consuls and praetors. I can do no better than quote Badian himself (p. 465, n. 16): "The praetorian auspices and *imperium* were of the same nature as the consuls', but he was *minor* to them, hence could not create auspices and *imperium* of an essentially superior nature". The *tribuni militum* could create consuls, but they could not (at least originally; Badian, 465, disregards the implication of Livy 4.31.4) name dictators, and they were not able to celebrate triumphs (which the praetors were).

Errata. Read:

P. 563 = 37, line 10: "André". P. 564 = 38, line 3 from bottom: "André". P. 567 = 41, line 14: "offices"; line 5 from bottom: "the very last days". P. 568 = 42, line 12: "auspical". P. 569 = 43, line 22: "in jeopardy"; line 25: "auspical". P. 572 = 46, line 13 from bottom: "auspical"; line 16 from bottom: "engineered". P. 573 = 47, line 14 from bottom: "they argue".

57

HELIOGABALUS, ALEXANDER SEVERUS AND THE *IUS CONFARREATIONIS*: A NOTE ON THE *HISTORIA AUGUSTA* (1989)

P. 578 = 210, n. 12: on the text of Gaius, and the various attempts to fill the lacunae, see L. Messina, "Le lacune di Gai. 1.136–137", in: *Sodalitas. Scritti in onore di Antonio Guarino* 2 (Napoli 1984) 813–834.

Pp. 580–581 = 212–213: see No 55, *Addenda* to pp. 533–534 = 255–256.

58

REVIEW OF: THOMAS KÖVES-ZULAUF, *REDEN UND SCHWEIGEN: RÖMISCHE RELIGION BEI PLINIUS MAIOR* (1975)

P. 586 = 286: on Iuppiter Depulsor, see J. Kolendo, "Le culte de Juppiter Depulsor et les incursions des Barbares", *ANRW* II.18 (1989) 1062–1076.

Pp. 586–588 = 286–288: on the the paradosis *commentationis* and the conjecture *commendationis*, see also Ä. Bäumer, "Die Macht des Wortes in Religion und Magie (Plinius, Naturalis Historia 28, 4–29)", *Hermes* 112 (1984) 84–99, at 87–94. She mentions in passing the review here reprinted (85, n. 3), and proceeds to her own critique of the interpretation of Köves-Zulauf. Although she does not acknowledge it explicitly, she arrives (by a rather circuitous route) at a conclusion almost identical with that elaborated in my review. C. Guittard, "Pline et la classification des prières dans la religion romaine (*NH* 28, 10–21)", in: I. Pigealdus and I. Orozius (eds.), *Pline L'Ancien. Temoin de son temps* (Salamanca-Nantes 1987) 473–486 also arrived (without utilizing the piece in *CP*) at a similar interpretation of these terms; in particular he also argues in favor of the emendation *commendatio*.

59
A NON-MISUNDERSTOOD TEXT CONCERNING TAGES
(1978)

The reading *extispicium* has now been finally introduced into the text by J. Willis in his Teubner edition of Martianus Capella (Leipzig 1983), p. 47.11–12.

D. Shanzer, "De Tagetis exaratione", *Hermes* (1987) 127–128, following a suggestion by C. Murgia, proposes to read "et ritum statim genti<bus>s extispiciumque monstravit". The plural *gentibus* would parallel "the rest of the series of dative objects in the tricolon, cf. 47.13 *sitientibus ... exhibuit*; 47.14 *mortalibus praestiterunt*"(so Murgia), and finds support (so Shanzer) in the passage of Prudentius (*Apotheosis* 506–508), and particularly in the phrase "gentibus emicuit", referring in Prudentius to Christ, but transferred to Tages in the imitation by Martianus Capella. Now *gentibus* makes eminent sense with respect to Christ, but is out of place with respect to Tages: his teaching was not universal, but addressed to one particular *gens*, the Etruscans. The singular *genti* is supported by Ovid, *Met.* 15.558–559: "qui primus Etruscam edocuit gentem casus aperire futuros".

The reading *simpuvium* is defended by E. Zwierlein-Diehl, "Simpuvium Numae", in: H.A. Cahn und E. Simon (eds.), *Tainia Roland Hampe ... dargebracht* (Mainz 1978) 405–422, at 421–422. She publishes a gem on which she believes is depicted Tages springing from a furrow and presenting to a group of *togati* an object in which Zwierlein–Diehl wishes to recognize a *simpuvium*. This is most unlikely: why should the Etruscan Tages be represented with *simpuvium*, an earthenware ladle that functioned as an emblem of the Roman *pontifices*?

It is also most unlikely that Tages is represented on a *cista Praenestina*; see J. Champeaux, "Religion romaine et religion latine: les cultes de Jupiter et Junon a Préneste", *REL* 60 (1982 [1983]) 71–104, at 78–83; Eadem, "Sors oraculi: les oracles en Italie sous la République et l'Empire", *MEFRA* 102 (1990) 282, n. 22; and with a different interpretation, H. Riemann, "*Praenestinae Sorores*. Praeneste", *MDAI* (R) 98 (1988) 56–57.

60
REVIEW OF:
LE DÉLIT RELIGIEUX DANS LA CITÉ ANTIQUE
(1984)

P. 592 = 174: an excellent literary counterpart to Gamelin's painting is *The Unwilling Vestal. A Tale of Rome under the Caesars*, a novel by Edward Lucas White (originally published in 1918; by the time of the New York 1967 edition it had gone through twenty four printings). I owe the knowledge of this piece of literature to the generosity of Professor R.E.A. Palmer.

P. 594 = 176: on the handling of religious offenses committed by magistrates, see *AL* 2173–2177; and in greater detail the instructive monograph by N. Rosenstein, *Imperatores Victi. Military Defeat and Aristocratic Competition in the Middle and Late Republic* (Berkeley 1990) 54–91.

P. 595 = 177: on the human sacrifice in Rome, see now the excellent paper by A. Eckstein, "Human Sacrifice and Fear of Military Disaster in Republican Rome", *AJAH* 7 (1982 [1985]) 69–95. Cf. also F. Hampl, "Zum Ritus des Lebendigbegrabens von Vestalinnen", in: *Festschrift für Robert Muth*, ed. by P. Handel and W. Meid (= Innsbrucker Beiträge zur Kulturwissenschaft 22 [Innsbruck 1983]) 165–182.

61
REVIEW OF:
L.B. VAN DER MEER, *THE BRONZE LIVER OF PIACENZA*
(1990)

Cf. above, *Addenda* to No 59, and A. Morandi, "Nuove osservazioni sul fegato bronzeo di Piacenza", *MEFRA* 100 (1988) 283–297.

P. 598 = 70, n. 8: on Cilens, cf. M.J. Strazzulla, "Fortuna Etrusca e Fortuna Romana: due cicli decorativi a confronto (Roma, via S. Gregorio e Bolsena)", *Ostraka* 2 (1993) 317–349, at 335–338.

P. 599 = 71 (and n. 10): on the contacts between Greek and Etruscan divination, cf. D. Briquel, "Divination étrusque et mantique grecque: la recherche d'une origine hellénique de l'*Etrusca disciplina*", *Latomus* 49 (1990) 321–342.

P. 599 = 71 (and n. 11): on the mirror from Tuscania, see M. Torelli, "*Etruria Principes disciplinam doceto*. Il mito normativo dello specchio di Tuscania", *Studia Tarquiniensia* (Rome 1988) 109–118, a brilliant study. There is no Tages depicted on the mirror; Torelli identifies the figures as Avle Tarxunus, the son of Tarchon, and Pavatarxies, i.e. "un *puer* della stirpe di Tarchon". "Pavatarxies è dunque un giovane che si sta esercitando nella *disciplina* sotto l'occhio vigile e preoccupato del maturo aruspice Avle Tarxunus" (p. 114).

62
REVIEW OF:
IDA PALADINO, *FRATRES ARVALES:*
STORIA DI UN COLLEGIO SACERDOTALE ROMANO
(1991)

P. 602 = 86: Scheid, *Romulus* (see below) 16, has modified his view concerning the text of Varro; he now admits that "le présent du verbe *facere* indique que ce culte n'est pas un lointain souvenir".

P. 603 = 87: we almost got a new Henzen: J. Scheid, *Romulus et ses frères. Le collège des frères arvales, modèle du culte dans la Rome des empereurs* (Rome 1990), a most erudite study of the *acta arvalium* and of the arval cult. The prosopography of the college Scheid treated extensively in *Le collège des frères arvales. Étude prosopographique du recrutement, 69–304* (Rome 1990). We now await from his pen a new edition of the documents themselves.

63
REVIEW OF:
D.S. POTTER, *PROPHECY AND HISTORY IN THE CRISIS*
OF THE ROMAN EMPIRE:
A HISTORICAL COMMENTARY ON THE THIRTEENTH
SIBYLLINE ORACLE
(1993)

P. 606 = 182, n. 10: cf. also T. Sternberg, "Die Regierungszeit Gordians III. aus der Sicht der kaiserlichen Rechtsprechung", *Klio* 71 (1989) 164–178.

64
ROMAN RELIGION IN LIVY
(1993)

Simultaneously with this article, and bearing a similar title, there appeared the book by D.S. Levene, *Religion in Livy* (= *Mnemosyne*, Suppl. 127 [Leiden 1993]). Here the similarities end. Levene's is mostly a literary study with little interest in the technical aspects of the Roman religion. As an emblem for Levene's approach may stand the following statement: "Auspices. I define these, not in the strict Roman sense as the divination by augurs, usually from birds or thunder and lightning, but in the wider sense of omens sought and obtained at the beginning of an enterprize, thus including, for example, extispicy by the haruspices if employed under such circumstances" (p. 3). This definition makes no sense, and serves no purpose. It also contains two errors. First: auspices were not exclusively "divination by augurs" but mostly divination by magistrates; the proper sphere of the augurs was defined as *auguria* not *auspicia*. Second: this definition fails to distinguish between the *auspicia impetrativa* sought before the beginning of an enterprize, and the *auspicia oblativa* that could appear at any time, even when an enterprize was in progress. Compare also the analysis of the religious ritual at the battle of Aquilonia presented in this paper (pp. 60–61) with Levene's superficial description (pp. 237–239).

P. 611 = 56: on defeat and the *pax deorum*, the basic study is now N. Rosenstein, *Imperatores Victi* (Berkeley 1990) 54–91.

P. 614 = 59 (and n. 19): the full reference to E. Badian's article is: "Livy and Augustus", in: W. Schuller (ed), *Livius. Aspekte seines Werkes* (Konstanz 1993) 9–38. Cf. also the interesting paper by J. Glucker, "Augustiora", *Grazer Beiträge* 19 (1993) 51–101.

P. 615 = 60 (and n. 24): on *laetus* as a *vox auguralis*, see also H. Dahlmann, *Über Aemilius Macer* (= Abh. Mainz 1981, Nr. 6) 9.

P. 620 = 65: a revised and expanded version of the dissertation by F.V. Hickson has now appeared in print: *Roman Prayer Language. Livy and the Aeneid of Vergil* (Stuttgart 1993).

Errata.

P. 619 = 64, line 9: the Greek text was scrambled on the computer. Read: "ὃι μάντεις ὅτι τε ἐπὶ μέγα αὐξήσοι καὶ".

INDICES

Modern Authors

W

Wachter, R.W. 661
Wacke, A. 466
Wageningen van, I. 204
Wagenvoort, H. 345
Walbank, F.W. 24, 109, 301, 307, 310, 464, 466
Walde, A. 417, 541, 570
Walek, T. 8, 25–26
Walker, S. 659
Walser, G. 605
Walsh, P.G. 609, 620–21
Waltzing, J.-P. 106, 165, 168, 173–74, 176–78, 190, 193–95, 197, 202–3, 207, 217, 362, 364, 373, 412, 531, 577
Ward, A. 636, 648
Warmington, E.H. 198, 362, 364
Waszink, J.H. 267–68
Watson, A. 42, 154–55, 163, 380, 383–85, 387, 399, 404, 543, 551–52, 556–57, 577, 579, 644, 664, 671
Watson, G.R. 147
Weaver, P.R.C. 380, 382
Weber, M. 25
Weber, W. 33
Wegehaupt, W. 228
Weinberg, A.K. 29
Weinrib, E.J. 270, 422, 471, 479
Weinstock, S. 74, 133, 445, 455, 482, 513, 519, 539, 598
Weise, O. 125
Weismann, F.H. 112
Weiss, E. 219
Weissenborn, W. 315
Weitzman, M.P. 660
Werner, R. 571
Wessner, P. 295–96, 529–30
Westerink, L.G. 466
Westrup, C.W. 546–47, 549, 556–57, 671–72
White, E.L. 677
White, J.F. 425–27
White, K.D. 104
Whitehead, S. 641
Whiting, H.C. 345

Whittaker, C.R. 20
Whittick, G.C. 351
Wickert, L. 20, 21–24, 42–43
Wieling, H.J. 388
Wiesehöffer, J. 34
Wikander, Ö. 326
Wilamowitz von, U. 28
Wilhelm, A. 436
Willems, P. 224, 231, 234, 238–39, 251, 253, 258–59, 271, 281–82, 302, 309, 313
Williamson, C. 353
Willis, J. 676
Winstedt, E.O. 125
Wirszubski, C. 294
Wiseman, T.P. 64, 139–40, 229, 238, 262, 264–65, 271, 277, 279, 325, 651, 660
Wiśniewski, B. 469
Wissowa, G. 65, 196–97, 201, 363, 367, 371, 397, 446, 455, 488, 501, 507, 544, 549, 584–85, 593, 602–3, 620–22, 672
Wistrand, E. 622
Wistrand, M. 284–87, 654
Wölfflin, E. 30
Wood, J.R. 596, 599
Woodman, A.J. 109
Wucher, A. 20–22, 24
Wülker, L. 476, 520, 620, 622, 625
Wuilleumier, P. 258
Wunder, E. 117, 330

Y

Yacobson, A. 638
Yavetz, Z. 22, 41, 227, 650
Yonge, C.D. 258

Z

Zawadzki, T. 575
Zetzel, J.E.G. 458
Zgusta, L. 421, 423
Ziegler, K. 128, 239
Zingler, J. 516
Ziółkowski, A. 669
Żmigryder-Konopka, Z. 362, 364

Ancient Sources

1. Ancient Authors

2. Inscriptions

General Index

HEIDELBERGER ALTHISTORISCHE BEITRÄGE UND EPIGRAPHISCHE STUDIEN

Herausgegeben von **Géza Alföldy**

FRANZ STEINER VERLAG STUTTGART

ISSN 0930-1208

970307B   DM 196.00 / $147.00